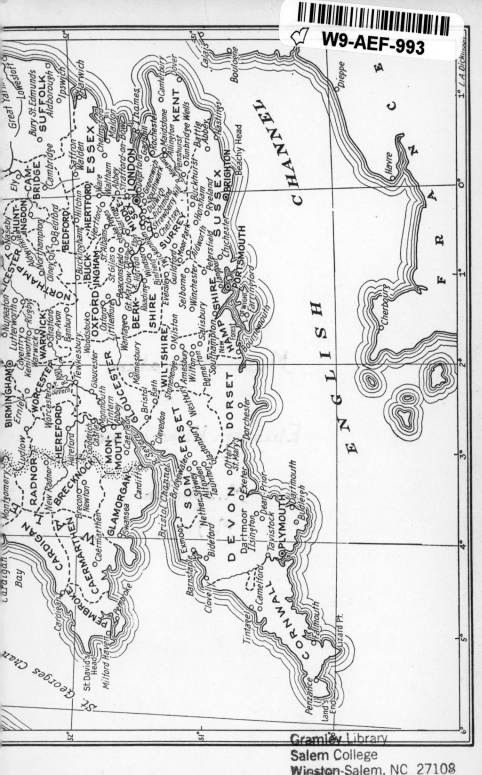

English Masterpieces

English Masterpieces

700-1900

Edited by

H. W. HERRINGTON

Professor of English, Syracuse University

REVISED EDITION

II

The Nineteenth Century

W · W · NORTON & COMPANY · INC.

PUBLISHERS · NEW YORK

PRINTED IN THE UNITED STATES OF AMERICA
FOR THE PUBLISHERS BY THE VAIL·BALLOU PRESS

PREFACE

The revision of *English Masterpieces* has given opportunity for the inclusion in Volume II of four characteristic essays by William Hazlitt, and of the following works by writers already represented: Coleridge's *This Lime Tree Bower My Prison*, *Frost at Midnight*, and the sections from *Biographia Literaria* treating of Wordsworth's poetry; Lamb's *New Year's Eve* and one of the *Popular Fallacies;* Byron's *Vision of Judgment;* Shelley's *Mask of Anarchy;* several short poems of Matthew Arnold and his essay on *Wordsworth*. To gain space, some of the above have been given in slightly condensed form; and a few unimportant omissions have been made of selections in the original book.

The principles on which *English Masterpieces* has been compiled are stated in the Preface to Volume I. In accordance with the plan of including only the greatest writers, Volume II is now devoted to the work of thirteen outstanding figures in English literature of the nineteenth century. Two of these, interesting chiefly for style, or for a single important message, are somewhat lightly sketched; but the other eleven, commonly regarded as the giants of the century, rise from the pages, I trust, in full stature. In particular, it has been my aim not to limit the selections to shorter pieces, as is usually done in similar books of readings, but to give some idea at least of those longer works which are frequently the authors' greatest achievements, and without which, certainly, no satisfying picture of the man can be had.

I rejoice therefore that space has been found for two complete books of Wordsworth's *Prelude*, for the equivalent of a canto each of Byron's *Childe Harold* and *Don Juan,* for the first book of Keats's *Endymion*, for almost five chapters of Carlyle's *Sartor Resartus* as well as other selections that exhibit all of his leading doctrines, for all that is essential in the greatest book of Browning's *Ring and the Book,* and for four essays or chapters of Matthew Arnold—those which show best his literary and social views. Shelley's *Prometheus Unbound* could not be given entire, but a careful condensation has preserved the great moments in the dramatic story, the poet's program for the regeneration of society, and some of his grandest lyric flights. So

v

far as Tennyson is concerned, it would seem that neither the *In Memoriam* nor the *Idylls of the King* is as important to this as to preceding generations, but there have been included the greatest of the *Idylls,* and large sections of the *In Memoriam*—enough to show clearly the development of the poet's plan and thought.

It will be noted that no endeavor has been made to represent writers of the present century. The ultimate standing of such writers, many of them still living, cannot yet be surely determined, and, moreover, they are likely to be read by the student himself, without the stimulation and guidance of the courses for which *English Masterpieces* is designed.

As in the first volume, the most authentic texts have in every case been used. The selections from Wordsworth, Tennyson, and Browning follow the Cambridge editions, by permission of and by arrangement with the Houghton Mifflin Company. The selections from Lamb follow Mr. E. V. Lucas's edition, and from Keats Mr. E. de Sélincourt's, by permission of Messrs. Methuen & Co., Ltd. The selections from Shelley follow the edition of Mr. T. Hutchinson, by permission of the Oxford University Press. The works of Coleridge are from the Globe edition, edited by J. D. Campbell, and those of Arnold and Pater from the authorized editions, by permission of the Macmillan Company. The text of Carlyle is that of the Centenary edition of Messrs. Chapman and Hall, Ltd., and that of Byron the edition of John Murray, Esq., by permission of the respective publishers. The passage from De Quincey's *English Mail-Coach* follows the revision made by the author in 1854 for the Collective edition of his writings, and that from the *Suspiria de Profundis* the posthumous publication made by the Messrs. Black in 1871 from the author's papers. I am deeply indebted to the publishers named above for their generous permissions to reprint; and also to Mr. William Lyon Phelps for a quotation used in the introductory sketch of Keats.

The following gentlemen I wish to thank for calling my attention to misprints and other errors: my colleagues Messrs. Leonard Brown, H. A. Eaton, A. E. Johnson, Herman Kirchhofer, Warren Shepard, R. R. Snook, A. M. Terhune, Norman Whitney, and William Yerington; Mr. Gordon Coté; and Professor Alwin Thaler of the University of Tennessee.

The panorama of London used as an end-paper is reproduced by permission from the Harvard University Library's copy of James Howell's *Londinopolis* (1657). Data regarding it will be found in the Preface to Volume I.

H. W. H.

CONTENTS

ENGLISH
MASTERPIECES

Volume II

THE ROMANTIC MOVEMENT

From the vantage point of a hundred years we can now distinguish two great upheavals as affecting profoundly, in the early nineteenth century, the thought and life of men. One was the French Revolution which had burst upon Europe toward the end of the preceding century; the other was the "industrial revolution," which within little more than a generation completely changed the way of working fixed since ancient times and so reorganized society. The latter had inevitably proceeded from various mechanical inventions made at the end of the eighteenth and the beginning of the nineteenth centuries—inventions like the steam engine, the spinning jenny, and the power loom. These inventions had substituted for the old hand labor, mostly in the workman's home, a new system in crowded factories which rapidly multiplied in growing industrial cities. The resultant centralization of manufacture made possible the exploitation of labor—with long hours, wretched wages, and the employment of children to tend the machines. Much social unrest ensued. Belatedly, legislation was forced to grapple with the problems. There came also a redistribution of wealth, as the newly enriched middle-class factory operatives superseded the old landed aristocracy. The altered conditions produced a cry for a revised political system, the long and bitterly contested Reform Bill of 1832 finally accomplishing a great extension of the franchise and the transfer of political power to the middle classes and to the new industrial areas in the middle and north of England. This great change in the social and political system produced notable repercussions in the literature of the following age— the Victorian, but is hardly observable in the writings of the earlier part of the century, except in so far as the aroused humanitarian instincts which abolished slavery and established factory acts, poor laws, and a milder penal code are reflected in the broader humanity of the writers, in their sharpened sense of man's responsibility to his brother man.

The new humanitarianism was quickened by distressing social conditions, but doubtless owed its rise to the change in men's thinking which preceded and accompanied the French Revolution. Equality and Fraternity were two of the watchwords of that movement as well as Liberty. The powerful ferment of these ideas and their spectacular exemplification in revolutionary France stirred to their depths the souls of all the great writers of the early century. Those who as young men had watched that great struggle—Wordsworth, Coleridge, and Southey, for instance—could scarce contain their enthusiasm. "Bliss was it in that dawn to be alive, But to be young was very heaven." But the Revolution was succeeded by the Reign of Terror, and that in its turn by the imperial conquests of Napoleon. Men's hopes were blasted, and sadly they came to the conclusion that human happiness was better secured by a settled order, in which freedom slowly broadened down from precedent to precedent. Bitter experience had converted the radicals of the former age into the conservatives of the later. Younger men, who had not lived through the great disillusionment, reacted differently. Byron's spirit of rebellion was directed

3

against society, or else he strove for liberty as an abstract principle, or where, as in Greece, it might in any nation be forwarded; Shelley, too, rejected the tyranny of the social system, but, a more ethereal spirit, he dreamed of a liberty, which, while it could not triumph here and now, would in a future golden age replace with ideal anarchy the despotic restraints of the present.

Freedom, humanitarianism, and individualism, the code of the French Revolution, became thus guiding principles of that Romantic revival which swept Europe, producing a brilliant literature in Germany and France, and which dominated English writers from the appearance of Wordsworth and Coleridge's *Lyrical Ballads* in 1798 for some three or four decades, down to the death of Sir Walter Scott in 1832; with the same influences continuing, although in modified form, till a much later period, and being indeed still strongly felt to-day. Though revolt is inseparable from the Romantic movement—revolt especially from the fixed forms and fixed ideas of the past—from its restraints, its decorum, its "correctness," the principle of revolt will not serve exclusively to explain it. Nor is romanticism restricted to the age of Wordsworth, Byron, and Keats, nor, indeed, to that broader era which may be said to have begun far back in the eighteenth century, and to have included, at least in certain aspects, the work of Thomson, Gray, Cowper, and their contemporaries, to have almost reached fruition in the work of Burns and Blake. It is clear that romanticism is an enduring tendency in human thought and art, which has manifested itself in varying degrees in many eras and in many writers. Shakespeare may properly be termed romantic, and in many ways, Milton; and even in Pope the principle is not in entire abeyance, although submerged by the neo-classical. To find a single formula from which may be derived all the complex phenomena of romanticism is extremely difficult, although many have attempted it. If we must seek for a single simplifying phrase (and perhaps the search is hopeless) we may perhaps best say, in the words of President Neilson,[1] that romanticism is the dominance of the imagination, as opposed to the classical dominance of the sense of form, and the realistic dominance of the sense of fact. In some way or other, now faintly, now clearly, the various aspects of romanticism show this fundamental reassertion of the claims of the imagination.

For one thing, the imagination of the period found itself stirred by the rich and picturesque Middle Ages, and we have the "Gothic" romances of the school of Horace Walpole's *Castle of Otranto*, the medieval novels of Sir Walter Scott, and the setting of Coleridge's *Christabel* and Keats's *Eve of St. Agnes* and *La Belle Dame sans Merci*. A returning interest in older writers, as in older times, made Spenser and Milton powerful influences. With the passing of urbanity and well-regulated conduct came a "renascence of wonder," with emphasis upon the marvelous and the strange, so well illustrated by *The Rime of the Ancient Mariner*. Mysticism, rapture, and enthusiasm men dared to feel and express once more, and there were written the *Tintern Abbey* lines, the *Ode on Intimations of Immortality*, and the jubilation of a freed world which concludes the *Prometheus Unbound*. Already had Cowper, Burns, and others brought back to literature the lyric, the poetry of intense personal emotion; in the nineteenth century the same impulse gave us Keats's sonnets and Shelley's *Ode to the West Wind*. Writers tried to record a more accurate observation of human life, with "the eye upon the object," in place of the conventional interpretations of the former age. In particular, there was a widespread interest in

1 In his *Essentials of Poetry*. Professor Cazamian somewhat similarly puts it, "The Romantic spirit can be defined as an accentuated predominance of emotional life, provoked or directed by the exercise of imaginative vision."

nature, and with it rural life, as opposed to city-bred culture. Landscape-painting in words abounded; the Lake School lived close to nature and were inspired by it to some of their grandest flights, and we are bid sympathize with the lives of old sailors, wagoners, pedlars, and leech-gatherers. In this, as in other currents of the Romantic movement, Rousseau had led the way, with his glorification of primitive life. Primitive forms like the ballads were admired and imitated. Ever and above all, the poets sang of liberty, as the Revolution had taught them, and asserted the claims of the individual against the cruel mechanism of society. In more technical aspects, romanticism culti-vated a variety of poetic forms, and rejected the closed couplet of Pope, ex-cept when practised with inconsistent impertinence by Byron; it repudiated likewise the "poetic diction" of the eighteenth century, and substituted words from actual human speech, or from the vocabulary of the elder poets. The changes just sketched, chiefly in English poetry, were exhibited as well in other literary forms, and found a theoretic statement in such works as Godwin's *Political Justice.*

The chief glory of English romanticism is its poetry. Between the publica-tion of the *Lyrical Ballads* (1798), with which the movement first became articulate and militant, and the death of Sir Walter Scott (1832), lived and wrote Wordsworth (in all of his work that matters), Coleridge, Sir Walter himself, Byron, Shelley, and Keats, and among lesser lights, Southey, Rogers, Moore, Hood, and Landor. Probably in no similar period of a few decades has so much great poetry been written. In another medium, the Romantic period produced the charming personal essays of Lamb, the fine appreciative criticism of Hazlitt, the *Imaginary Conversations* of Landor, and the richly colored, impassioned, imaginative works of De Quincey, the author of the *Confessions of an English Opium Eater* and *The English Mail Coach*. In prose fiction, the giant of the period is Sir Walter Scott, who between 1814 and his death in 1832 poured forth with seemingly inexhaustible fertility some two dozen novels, dealing first with Scotch subjects and then with the life of the Middle Ages. Jane Austen's stories, of a precise and careful artistry that has commanded unstinted admiration, were all published in the second decade of the century, although some of them had been written many years before. Only in the drama, among the major literary forms, did the period show little that was memorable. The acting drama was degraded and non-literary, while the "closet drama" of the poets was mostly ignorant of the necessary technique of the stage.

BIBLIOGRAPHY. E. Bernbaum, *Guide through the Romantic Movement* (Nelson); C. H. Herford, *The Age of Wordsworth* (Bell); H. A. Beers, *Hist. of Eng. Romanticism in the Nineteenth Cent.* (Holt); A. Symons, *The Romantic Movement in Eng. Poetry* (Dutton); Legouis and Cazamian, *Hist. of Eng. Lit.*, Part II (Macmillan); E. Dowden, *French Revolution and Eng. Lit.* (Scribner's). Anthology: G. B. Woods, *Eng. Poetry and Prose of the Romantic Movement* (Scott Foresman).

WILLIAM WORDSWORTH (1770–1850)

William Wordsworth was born on April 7, 1770, at Cockermouth, County Cumberland, where his father was an attorney. His earlier years were lived in great simplicity amid the hills and lake-strewn valleys of the English Lake district. The early death of his mother and father left him dependent chiefly upon relatives for his education. By means of such aid he attended the excellent classical school at Hawkshead, in the Lake district, and St. John's College, Cambridge, where he took his B.A. in 1791. In the summer of 1790 he went on a walking tour through France, Switzerland, and northern Italy, and in 1791 and 1792 lived in France, where he was much stirred by the events following the Revolution, and under the influence of a French officer, Michel Beaupuy, became republican in sympathies. During this period he fell in love with the daughter of a royalist family, Annette Vallon, who bore him a daughter in December, 1792. There is evidence that Wordsworth intended to marry the mother of his daughter, but ultimately believed he could not do so.

On his return to England, Wordsworth passed through some years of spiritual distress, greatly perturbed by his love affair, by England's declaration of war on France, and by the apparent failure of republican ideals in the Reign of Terror. For a time he was a disciple of the rigorously logical and mechanistic philosopher, William Godwin, the author of *Political Justice* (see sketch on *Shelley* below). Important stabilizing influences in these years of crisis were the constant sympathy of his sister Dorothy and his growing belief in the healing and sustaining powers of Nature.

In 1795 a fortunate bequest from a friend pieced out his income and enabled him to devote himself to literature. In 1797 he moved with Dorothy to Alfoxden, in Somersetshire, not far from Nether Stowey, where Coleridge was living. The ideas of the latter, expressed as the young men visited each other, or roamed together over the nearby Quantock Hills, had an important formative and quickening effect upon Wordsworth. Together the two planned and executed the *Lyrical Ballads,* published in 1798, in which, as Coleridge tells us, Wordsworth proposed to "give the charm of novelty to things of every day" and to direct the mind "to the loveliness and wonders of the world before us," while Coleridge, in the four poems which he contributed, was to give to "persons and characters supernatural, or at least romantic . . . a semblance of truth." In the Preface prefixed to the second edition (1800), here reprinted, Wordsworth outlines in detail the principles on which he wrote.

Meanwhile Wordsworth had planned a monumental philosophical poem, "containing views on Man, Nature, and Society," of which *The Recluse* (1800), *The Prelude* (1799–1805), and *The Excursion* (1795–1814), although they run to a total of over 17,000 lines, were to be but portions.

The winter of 1798–99 Wordsworth spent in Germany with Dorothy, and in the latter year settled with her in the Lake district, where he lived almost all the rest of his life, his two most important residences being at Dove Cottage, Grasmere, 1799–1808, and at Rydal Mount, from 1813 until his death. In 1802 he married his sister's friend, and the friend of his own youth, Mary Hutchinson. The delayed payment of a debt due to his father's estate, and his appointment to an easy government post as distributor of stamps supplied Wordsworth with a living which his poetry, restricted in its audience, had not brought him. In 1843, on the death of Southey, he was made poet laureate. He died on April 23, 1850, and lies buried in the churchyard at Grasmere. Other than the works mentioned above, the most important volumes of Wordsworth's poetry were published in 1807 and in 1815. A collected edition, in six volumes, was issued in 1836–37.

The selections in this volume, nearly all written before 1807, are made in accordance with the universal belief that the enduring work of Wordsworth was done in early life. His powers hardened with age, just as his social, political, and religious views became more conservative. Even in his prime he was a poor critic of his own work, and rode his theories so hard as to produce poems, like *The Idiot Boy* (here spared the reader), which the world considered ridiculous. Wordsworth's strictly literary principles are best understood from his own explanation of them in his celebrated *Preface*. Aside from the reforms which he accomplished in English verse, which made him influential in the Romantic Movement, and which will always cause him to bulk large in literary history, his deeper significance lies in the ideas which he held, and which he so consistently illustrated in his poetry. In the first place he is the poet of simple life. He celebrated the dignity and truth of untutored but fine spirits, and showed that these could teach us much concerning the conduct of life. In the second place, he is the arch-priest of nature. Nature can give us joy and console us, and lead us, by processes that are intuitive rather than rational, to a deeper understanding of life's mysteries. In his more enraptured expressions of this belief, as in the *Tintern Abbey* lines, he becomes one of the great mystics of English poetry. Third, he is the chronicler of the human mind. His *Prelude* traced the growth of his poet's mind, but the theme is a constant one, and exhibited almost universally in his verse. He thus turns from external events inward, and in these aspects of his work is perhaps the greatest of contemplative poets. Finally, he is a philosophical poet, concerned with ideas and with principles of life (as in the *Ode on Intimations of Immortality* and in *The Prelude passim*), although he is not a rigorous enough thinker to propound a unified and complete system. In all these ways he has profoundly impressed thinking men. His audience, never large, has been steady, and his fame seems now securely established as one of the greatest of English writers who have used the poetic form. His lack of humor denies him the broadest humanity.

The notes which the poet dictated to Miss Isabella Fenwick about 1843 are given in this edition where they seem especially pertinent.

BIBLIOGRAPHY. *Poetical Works*, ed. Thos. Hutchinson, Oxford (5 vols.). One volume eds.: Oxford, by same ed., Cambridge, by A. J. George (Houghton Mifflin), and Globe (Macmillan). Authoritative life by G. M. C. Harper, 2 vols. (Scribner's). *The Early Life of William Wordsworth*, by Emile Legouis, Dutton (based on a study of *The Prelude*). Dorothy Wordsworth's *Journals*. Matthew Arnold's essay in *Essays in Criticism*, 2d ser. (famous estimate). Coleridge in *Biographia Literaria*, Chaps. 4, 5, 14, 17, 19, 20, and 22 (reminiscences and critique).

PREFACE

TO THE SECOND EDITION OF *LYRICAL BALLADS*

THE first volume of these poems has already been submitted to general perusal. It was published as an experiment, which, I hoped, might be of some use to ascertain how far, by fitting to metrical arrangement a selection of the real language of men in a state of vivid sensation, that sort of pleasure and that quantity of pleasure may be imparted, which a poet may rationally endeavor to impart.

I had formed no very inaccurate estimate of the probable

effect of those poems: I flattered myself that they who should be pleased with them would read them with more than common pleasure; and, on the other hand, I was well aware, that by those who should dislike them they would be read with more than common dislike. The result has differed from my expectation in this only, that a greater number have been pleased than I ventured to hope I should please.

Several of my friends are anxious for the success of these poems, from a belief that, if the views with which they were composed were indeed realized, a class of poetry would be produced, well adapted to interest mankind permanently, and not unimportant in the quality and in the multiplicity of its moral relations; and on this account they have advised me to prefix a systematic defense of the theory upon which the poems were written. But I was unwilling to undertake the task, knowing that on this occasion the reader would look coldly upon my arguments, since I might be suspected of having been principally influenced by the selfish and foolish hope of *reasoning* him into an approbation of these particular poems: and I was still more unwilling to undertake the task, because adequately to display the opinions, and fully to enforce the arguments, would require a space wholly disproportionate to a preface. For, to treat the subject with the clearness and coherence of which it is susceptible, it would be necessary to give a full account of the present state of the public taste in this country, and to determine how far this taste is healthy or depraved; which, again, could not be determined without pointing out in what manner language and the human mind act and re-act on each other, and without retracing the revolutions, not of literature alone, but likewise of society itself. I have therefore altogether declined to enter regularly upon this defense; yet I am sensible that there would be something like impropriety in abruptly obtruding upon the public, without a few words of introduction, poems so materially different from those upon which general approbation is at present bestowed.

It is supposed that by the act of writing in verse an author makes a formal engagement that he will gratify certain known habits of association; that he not only thus apprises the reader that certain classes of ideas and expressions will be found in his book, but that others will be carefully excluded. This exponent or symbol held forth by metrical language must in different eras of literature have excited very different expectations: for example, in the age of Catullus, Terence, and Lucretius, and that of Statius or Claudian; [1] and in our own country, in the

---

[1] The first three wrote in the great age of Latin literature; the others in a later and less distinguished age.

age of Shakespeare and Beaumont and Fletcher, and that of
Donne and Cowley, or Dryden, or Pope. I will not take upon
me to determine the exact import of the promise which, by the
act of writing in verse, an author in the present day makes to
his reader; but it will undoubtedly appear to many persons
that I have not fulfilled the terms of an engagement thus voluntarily contracted. They who have been accustomed to the
gaudiness and inane phraseology of many modern writers, if
they persist in reading this book to its conclusion, will, no
doubt, frequently have to struggle with feelings of strangeness 10
and awkwardness: they will look round for poetry, and will
be induced to inquire by what species of courtesy these attempts can be permitted to assume that title. I hope, therefore,
the reader will not censure me for attempting to state what I
have proposed to myself to perform; and also (as far as the
limits of a preface will permit) to explain some of the chief
reasons which have determined me in the choice of my purpose: that at least he may be spared any unpleasant feeling
of disappointment, and that I myself may be protected from
one of the most dishonorable accusations which can be brought 20
against an author; namely, that of an indolence which prevents him from endeavoring to ascertain what is his duty, or,
when his duty is ascertained, prevents him from performing it.

The principal object, then, proposed in these poems, was to
choose incidents and situations from common life, and to relate or describe them throughout, as far as was possible, in a
selection of language really used by men, and, at the same
time, to throw over them a certain coloring of imagination,
whereby ordinary things should be presented to the mind in an
unusual aspect; and further, and above all, to make these inci- 30
dents and situations interesting by tracing in them, truly
though not ostentatiously, the primary laws of our nature:
chiefly, as far as regards the manner in which we associate
ideas in a state of excitement. Humble and rustic life was generally chosen, because in that condition the essential passions
of the heart find a better soil in which they can attain their
maturity, are less under restraint, and speak a plainer and
more emphatic language; because in that condition of life our
elementary feelings co-exist in a state of greater simplicity,
and, consequently, may be more accurately contemplated, and 40
more forcibly communicated; because the manners of rural life
germinate from those elementary feelings, and, from the necessary character of rural occupations, are more easily comprehended, and are more durable; and, lastly, because in that
condition the passions of men are incorporated with the beautiful and permanent forms of nature. The language, too, of these

men has been adopted (purified indeed from what appear to be its real defects, from all lasting and rational causes of dislike or disgust), because such men hourly communicate with the best objects from which the best part of language is originally derived; and because, from their rank in society and the sameness and narrow circle of their intercourse, being less under the influence of social vanity, they convey their feelings and notions in simple and unelaborated expressions. Accordingly, such a language, arising out of repeated experience and regular feelings, is a more permanent, and a far more philosophical language, than that which is frequently substituted for it by poets, who think that they are conferring honor upon themselves and their art in proportion as they separate themselves from the sympathies of men, and indulge in arbitrary and capricious habits of expression, in order to furnish food for fickle tastes and fickle appetites of their own creation.[2]

I cannot, however, be insensible to the present outcry against the triviality and meanness, both of thought and language, which some of my contemporaries have occasionally introduced into their metrical compositions; and I acknowledge that this defect, where it exists, is more dishonorable to the writer's own character than false refinement or arbitrary innovation, though I should contend at the same time that it is far less pernicious in the sum of its consequences. From such verses the poems in these volumes will be found distinguished at least by one mark of difference, that each of them has a worthy *purpose*. Not that I always began to write with a distinct purpose formally conceived, but habits of meditation have, I trust, so prompted and regulated my feelings, that my descriptions of such objects as strongly excite those feelings will be found to carry along with them a *purpose*. If this opinion be erroneous, I can have little right to the name of a poet. For all good poetry is the spontaneous overflow of powerful feelings: and though this be true, poems to which any value can be attached were never produced on any variety of subjects but by a man who, being possessed of more than usual organic sensibility, had also thought long and deeply. For our continued influxes of feeling are modified and directed by our thoughts, which are indeed the representatives of all our past feelings; and as, by contemplating the relation of these general representatives to each other, we discover what is really important to men, so, by the repetition and continuance of this act, our feelings will be connected with important subjects, till at length, if we

2 It is worth while here to observe that the affecting parts of Chaucer are almost always expressed in language pure and universally intelligible even to this day (Wordsworth).

be originally possessed of much sensibility, such habits of mind will be produced that, by obeying blindly and mechanically the impulses of those habits, we shall describe objects, and utter sentiments, of such a nature, and in such connection with each other, that the understanding of the reader must necessarily be in some degree enlightened, and his affection strengthened and purified.

It has been said that each of these poems has a purpose. Another circumstance must be mentioned which distinguishes these poems from the popular poetry of the day; it is this, that the feeling therein developed gives importance to the action and situation, and not the action and situation to the feeling.

A sense of false modesty shall not prevent me from asserting that the reader's attention is pointed to this mark of distinction, far less for the sake of these particular poems than from the general importance of the subject. The subject is indeed important! For the human mind is capable of being excited without the application of gross and violent stimulants; and he must have a very faint perception of its beauty and dignity who does not know this, and who does not further know, that one being is elevated above another in proportion as he possesses this capability. It has therefore appeared to me, that to endeavor to produce or enlarge this capability is one of the best services in which, at any period, a writer can be engaged; but this service, excellent at all times, is especially so at the present day. For a multitude of causes, unknown to former times, are now acting with a combined force to blunt the discriminating powers of the mind, and, unfitting it for all voluntary exertion, to reduce it to a state of almost savage torpor. The most effective of these causes are the great national events which are daily taking place, and the increasing accumulation of men in cities, where the uniformity of their occupations produces a craving for extraordinary incident which the rapid communication of intelligence hourly gratifies. To this tendency of life and manners the literature and theatrical exhibitions of the country have conformed themselves. The invaluable works of our elder writers, I had almost said the works of Shakespeare and Milton, are driven into neglect by frantic novels, sickly and stupid German tragedies, and deluges of idle and extravagant stories in verse.—When I think upon this degrading thirst after outrageous stimulation, I am almost ashamed to have spoken of the feeble endeavor made in these volumes to counteract it; and, reflecting upon the magnitude of the general evil, I should be oppressed with no dishonorable melancholy, had I not a deep impression of certain inherent and indestructible qualities of the human mind, and likewise of certain powers in the great and permanent objects that act upon it, which are equally inherent and indestructible; and were there not added to this impression a belief that the time is approaching when the evil will be systematically opposed by men of greater powers, and with far more distinguished success.

Having dwelt thus long on the subjects and aim of these poems, I shall request the reader's permission to apprise him of a few circumstances relating to their *style,* in order, among
10 other reasons, that he may not censure me for not having performed what I never attempted. The reader will find that personifications of abstract ideas rarely occur in these volumes, and are utterly rejected as an ordinary device to elevate the style and raise it above prose. My purpose was to imitate, and, as far as is possible, to adopt the very language of men; and assuredly such personifications do not make any natural or regular part of that language. They are, indeed, a figure of speech occasionally prompted by passion, and I have made use of them as such; but have endeavored utterly to
20 reject them as a mechanical device of style, or as a family language which writers in meter seem to lay claim to by prescription. I have wished to keep the reader in the company of flesh and blood, persuaded that by so doing I shall interest him. Others who pursue a different track will interest him likewise; I do not interfere with their claim, but wish to prefer a claim of my own. There will also be found in these volumes little of what is usually called poetic diction; as much pains has been taken to avoid it as is ordinarily taken to produce it; this has been done for the reason already alleged, to bring
30 my language near to the language of men; and further, because the pleasure which I have proposed to myself to impart is of a kind very different from that which is supposed by many persons to be the proper object of poetry. Without being culpably particular, I do not know how to give my reader a more exact notion of the style in which it was my wish and intention to write, than by informing him that I have at all times endeavored to look steadily at my subject; consequently there is, I hope, in these poems little falsehood of description, and my ideas are expressed in language fitted to their respec-
40 tive importance. Something must have been gained by this practice, as it is friendly to one property of all good poetry, namely, good sense: but it has necessarily cut me off from a large portion of phrases and figures of speech which from father to son have long been regarded as the common inheritance of poets. I have also thought it expedient to restrict myself still further, having abstained from the use of many expressions,

in themselves proper and beautiful, but which have been foolishly repeated by bad poets, till such feelings of disgust are connected with them as it is scarcely possible by any art of association to overpower.

If in a poem there should be found a series of lines, or even a single line, in which the language, though naturally arranged, and according to the strict laws of meter, does not differ from that of prose, there is a numerous class of critics, who, when they stumble upon these prosaisms, as they call them, imagine that they have made a notable discovery, and exult over the poet as over a man ignorant of his own profession. Now these men would establish a canon of criticism which the reader will conclude he must utterly reject, if he wishes to be pleased with these volumes. And it would be a most easy task to prove to him that not only the language of a large portion of every good poem, even of the most elevated character, must necessarily, except with reference to the meter, in no respect differ from that of good prose, but likewise that some of the most interesting parts of the best poems will be found to be strictly the language of prose when prose is well written. The truth of this assertion might be demonstrated by innumerable passages from almost all the poetical writings, even of Milton himself. To illustrate the subject in a general manner, I will here adduce a short composition of Gray, who was at the head of those who, by their reasonings, have attempted to widen the space of separation betwixt prose and metrical composition, and was more than any other man curiously elaborate in the structure of his own poetic diction.

> "In vain to me the smiling mornings shine,
> And reddening Phœbus lifts his golden fire;
> The birds in vain their amorous descant join,
> Or cheerful fields resume their green attire.
> These ears, alas! for other notes repine;
> *A different object do these eyes require;*
> *My lonely anguish melts no heart but mine;*
> *And in my breast the imperfect joys expire;*
> Yet morning smiles the busy race to cheer,
> And new-born pleasure brings to happier men;
> The fields to all their wonted tribute bear;
> To warm their little loves the birds complain.
> *I fruitless mourn to him that cannot hear,*
> *And weep the more because I weep in vain.*" [3]

It will easily be perceived, that the only part of this sonnet which is of any value is the lines printed in italics; it is equally

[3] Gray's *Sonnet on the Death of Richard West*

obvious that, except in the rhyme and in the use of the single word "fruitless" for fruitlessly, which is so far a defect, the language of these lines does in no respect differ from that of prose.

By the foregoing quotation it has been shown that the language of prose may yet be well adapted to poetry; and it was previously asserted that a large portion of the language of every good poem can in no respect differ from that of good prose. We will go further. It may be safely affirmed that there neither is, nor can be, any *essential* difference between the language of prose and metrical composition. We are fond of tracing the resemblance between poetry and painting, and, accordingly, we call them sisters: but where shall we find bonds of connection sufficiently strict to typify the affinity betwixt metrical and prose composition? They both speak by and to the same organs; the bodies in which both of them are clothed may be said to be of the same substance, their affections are kindred, and almost identical, not necessarily differing even in degree; poetry [4] sheds no tears "such as Angels weep," but natural and human tears; she can boast of no celestial ichor [5] that distinguishes her vital juices from those of prose; the same human blood circulates through the veins of them both.

If it be affirmed that rhyme and metrical arrangement of themselves constitute a distinction which overturns what has just been said on the strict affinity of metrical language with that of prose, and paves the way for other artificial distinctions which the mind voluntarily admits, I answer that the language of such poetry as is here recommended is, as far as is possible, a selection of the language really spoken by men; that this selection, wherever it is made with true taste and feeling, will of itself form a distinction far greater than would at first be imagined, and will entirely separate the composition from the vulgarity and meanness of ordinary life; and, if meter be superadded thereto, I believe that a dissimilitude will be produced altogether sufficient for the gratification of a rational mind. What other distinction would we have? Whence is it to come? And where is it to exist? Not, surely, where the poet speaks through the mouths of his characters: it cannot be necessary here, either for elevation of style, or any of its supposed ornaments; for, if the poet's subject be judiciously

---

4 I here use the word "poetry" (though against my own judgment) as opposed to the word prose, and synonymous with metrical composition. But much confusion has been introduced into criticism by this contradistinction of poetry and prose, instead of the more philosophical one of poetry and matter of fact, or science. The only strict antithesis to prose is meter; nor is this, in truth, a *strict* antithesis, because lines and passages of meter so naturally occur in writing prose, that it would be scarcely possible to avoid them, even were it desirable (Wordsworth).

5 ethereal fluid that flows in the veins of the gods

chosen, it will naturally, and upon fit occasion, lead him to passions, the language of which, if selected truly and judiciously, must necessarily be dignified and variegated, and alive with metaphors and figures. I forbear to speak of an incongruity which would shock the intelligent reader, should the poet interweave any foreign splendor of his own with that which the passion naturally suggests: it is sufficient to say that such addition is unnecessary. And, surely, it is more probable that those passages which with propriety abound with metaphors and figures will have their due effect if, upon other oc- 10 casions where the passions are of a milder character, the style also be subdued and temperate.

But, as the pleasure which I hope to give by the poems now presented to the reader must depend entirely on just notions upon this subject, and as it is in itself of high importance to our taste and moral feelings, I cannot content myself with these detached remarks. And if, in what I am about to say, it shall appear to some that my labor is unnecessary, and that I am like a man fighting a battle without enemies, such persons may be reminded that, whatever be the language out- 20 wardly holden by men, a practical faith in the opinions which I am wishing to establish is almost unknown. If my conclusions are admitted, and carried as far as they must be carried if admitted at all, our judgments concerning the works of the greatest poets, both ancient and modern, will be far different from what they are at present, both when we praise and when we censure: and our moral feelings influencing and influenced by these judgments will, I believe, be corrected and purified.

Taking up the subject, then, upon general grounds, let me ask, what is meant by the word poet? What is a poet? To 30 whom does he address himself? And what language is to be expected from him?—He is a man speaking to men: a man, it is true, endowed with more lively sensibility, more enthusiasm and tenderness, who has a greater knowledge of human nature, and a more comprehensive soul, than are supposed to be common among mankind; a man pleased with his own passions and volitions, and who rejoices more than other men in the spirit of life that is in him; delighting to contemplate similar volitions and passions as manifested in the goings-on of the universe, and habitually impelled to create them where he does 40 not find them. To these qualities he has added a disposition to be affected more than any other men by absent things as if they were present; an ability of conjuring up in himself passions, which are indeed far from being the same as those produced by real events, yet (especially in those parts of the general sympathy which are pleasing and delightful) do more nearly resemble the passions produced by real events than anything which, from the motions of their own minds merely, other men are accustomed to feel in themselves:—whence, and from practice, he has acquired a greater readiness and power in expressing what he thinks and feels, and especially those thoughts and feelings which, by his own choice, or from the structure of his own mind, arise in him without immediate external excitement.

But whatever portion of this faculty we may suppose even the greatest poet to possess, there cannot be a doubt that the language which it will suggest to him must often, in liveliness and truth, fall short of that which is uttered by men in real life under the actual pressure of those passions, certain shadows of which the poet thus produces, or feels to be produced, in himself.

However exalted a notion we would wish to cherish of the character of a poet, it is obvious that, while he describes and imitates passions, his employment is in some degree mechanical compared with the freedom and power of real and substantial action and suffering. So that it will be the wish of the poet to bring his feelings near to those of the persons whose feelings he describes, nay, for short spaces of time, perhaps, to let himself slip into an entire delusion, and even confound and identify his own feelings with theirs; modifying only the language which is thus suggested to him by a consideration that he describes for a particular purpose, that of giving pleasure. Here, then, he will apply the principle of selection which has been already insisted upon. He will depend upon this for removing what would otherwise be painful or disgusting in the passion; he will feel that there is no necessity to trick out or to elevate nature: and the more industriously he applies this principle the deeper will be his faith that no words, which *his* fancy or imagination can suggest, will be to be compared with those which are the emanations of reality and truth.

But it may be said by those who do not object to the general spirit of these remarks, that, as it is impossible for the poet to produce upon all occasions language as exquisitely fitted for the passion as that which the real passion itself suggests, it is proper that he should consider himself as in the situation of a translator, who does not scruple to substitute excellences of another kind for those which are unattainable by him; and endeavors occasionally to surpass his original, in order to make some amends for the general inferiority to which he feels he must submit. But this would be to encourage idleness and unmanly despair. Further, it is the language of men who speak of what they do not understand; who talk of poetry, as of a

matter of amusement and idle pleasure; who will converse with
us as gravely about a *taste* for poetry, as they express it, as if
it were a thing as indifferent as a taste for rope-dancing, or
Frontiniac or Sherry. Aristotle, I have been told, has said that
poetry is the most philosophic of all writing. It is so: its object is truth, not individual and local, but general and operative; not standing upon external testimony, but carried alive
into the heart by passion; truth which is its own testimony,
which gives competence and confidence to the tribunal to which
it appeals, and receives them from the same tribunal. Poetry 10
is the image of man and nature. The obstacles which stand in
the way of the fidelity of the biographer and historian, and of
their consequent utility, are incalculably greater than those
which are to be encountered by the poet who comprehends
the dignity of his art. The poet writes under one restriction
only, namely, the necessity of giving immediate pleasure to
a human being possessed of that information which may be
expected from him, not as a lawyer, a physician, a mariner, an
astronomer, or a natural philosopher, but as a man. Except
this one restriction, there is no object standing between the 20
poet and the image of things; between this, and the biographer
and historian, there are a thousand.

Nor let this necessity of producing immediate pleasure be
considered as a degradation of the poet's art. It is far otherwise. It is an acknowledgment of the beauty of the universe,
an acknowledgment the more sincere because not formal, but
indirect; it is a task light and easy to him who looks at the
world in the spirit of love: further, it is a homage paid to the
native and naked dignity of man, to the grand elementary
principle of pleasure, by which he knows, and feels, and lives, 30
and moves. We have no sympathy but what is propagated by
pleasure. I would not be misunderstood; but wherever we
sympathize with pain, it will be found that the sympathy is
produced and carried on by subtle combinations with pleasure. We have no knowledge, that is, no general principles
drawn from the contemplation of particular facts, but what
has been built up by pleasure, and exists in us by pleasure
alone. The man of science, the chemist and mathematician,
whatever difficulties and disgusts they may have had to struggle
with, know and feel this. However painful may be the objects 40
with which the anatomist's knowledge is connected, he feels
that his knowledge is pleasure; and where he has no pleasure
he has no knowledge. What then does the poet? He considers
man and the objects that surround him as acting and reacting
upon each other, so as to produce an infinite complexity of
pain and pleasure; he considers man in his own nature and in

his ordinary life as contemplating this with a certain quantity of immediate knowledge, with certain convictions, intuitions, and deductions, which from habit acquire the quality of intuitions; he considers him as looking upon this complex scene of ideas and sensations, and finding everywhere objects that immediately excite in him sympathies which, from the necessities of his nature, are accompanied by an overbalance of enjoyment.

To this knowledge which all men carry about with them, and to these sympathies in which, without any other discipline than that of our daily life, we are fitted to take delight, the poet principally directs his attention. He considers man and nature as essentially adapted to each other, and the mind of man as naturally the mirror of the fairest and most interesting properties of nature. And thus the poet, prompted by this feeling of pleasure, which accompanies him through the whole course of his studies, converses with general nature, with affections akin to those which, through labor and length of time, the man of science has raised up in himself, by conversing with those particular parts of nature which are the objects of his studies. The knowledge both of the poet and the man of science is pleasure; but the knowledge of the one cleaves to us as a necessary part of our existence, our natural and unalienable inheritance; the other is a personal and individual acquisition, slow to come to us, and by no habitual and direct sympathy connecting us with our fellow-beings. The man of science seeks truth as a remote and unknown benefactor; he cherishes and loves it in his solitude: the poet, singing a song in which all human beings join with him, rejoices in the presence of truth as our visible friend and hourly companion. Poetry is the breath and finer spirit of all knowledge; it is the impassioned expression which is in the countenance of all science. Emphatically may it be said of the poet, as Shakespeare hath said of man, "that he looks before and after." [6] He is the rock of defense for human nature; an upholder and preserver, carrying everywhere with him relationship and love. In spite of difference of soil and climate, of language and manners, of laws and customs: in spite of things silently gone out of mind, and things violently destroyed; the poet binds together by passion and knowledge the vast empire of human society, as it is spread over the whole earth and over all time. The objects of the poet's thoughts are everywhere; though the eyes and senses of man are, it is true, his favorite guides, yet he will follow wheresoever he can find an atmosphere of sensation in which to move his wings. Poetry is the first and last of all

6 *Hamlet*, IV. iv. 37

knowledge—it is as immortal as the heart of man. If the labors of men of science should ever create any material revolution, direct or indirect, in our condition, and in the impressions which we habitually receive, the poet will sleep then no more than at present; he will be ready to follow the steps of the man of science, not only in those general indirect effects, but he will be at his side, carrying sensation into the midst of the objects of the science itself. The remotest discoveries of the chemist, the botanist, or mineralogist, will be as proper objects of the poet's art as any upon which it can be employed, if the time should ever come when these things shall be familiar to us, and the relations under which they are contemplated by the followers of these respective sciences shall be manifestly and palpably material to us as enjoying and suffering beings. If the time should ever come when what is now called science, thus familiarized to men, shall be ready to put on, as it were, a form of flesh and blood, the poet will lend his divine spirit to aid the transfiguration, and will welcome the being thus produced as a dear and genuine inmate of the household of man.—It is not, then, to be supposed that any one, who holds that sublime notion of poetry which I have attempted to convey, will break in upon the sanctity and truth of his pictures by transitory and accidental ornaments, and endeavor to excite admiration of himself by arts, the necessity of which must manifestly depend upon the assumed meanness of his subject.

What has been thus far said applies to poetry in general, but especially to those parts of compositions where the poet speaks through the mouths of his characters; and upon this point it appears to authorize the conclusion that there are few persons of good sense who would not allow that the dramatic parts of composition are defective in proportion as they deviate from the real language of nature, and are colored by a diction of the poet's own, either peculiar to him as an individual poet or belonging simply to poets in general; to a body of men who, from the circumstance of their compositions being in meter, it is expected will employ a particular language.

It is not, then, in the dramatic parts of composition that we look for this distinction of language; but still it may be proper and necessary where the poet speaks to us in his own person and character. To this I answer by referring the reader to the description before given of a poet. Among the qualities there enumerated as principally conducing to form a poet, is implied nothing differing in kind from other men, but only in degree. The sum of what was said is, that the poet is chiefly distinguished from other men by a greater promptness to think

and feel without immediate external excitement, and a greater
power in expressing such thoughts and feelings as are produced in him in that manner. But these passions and thoughts
and feelings are the general passions and thoughts and feelings
of men. And with what are they connected? Undoubtedly with
our moral sentiments and animal sensations, and with the
causes which excite these; with the operations of the elements,
and the appearances of the visible universe; with storm and
sunshine, with the revolutions of the seasons, with cold and
10 heat, with loss of friends and kindred, with injuries and resent-
ments, gratitude and hope, with fear and sorrow. These, and
the like, are the sensations and objects which the poet describes, as they are the sensations of other men and the objects
which interest them. The poet thinks and feels in the spirit of
human passions. How, then, can his language differ in any
material degree from that of all other men who feel vividly
and see clearly? It might be *proved* that it is impossible. But
supposing that this were not the case, the poet might then be
allowed to use a peculiar language when expressing his feelings
20 for his own gratification, or that of men like himself. But poets
do not write for poets alone, but for men. Unless, therefore,
we are advocates for that admiration which subsists upon ignorance, and that pleasure which arises from hearing what
we do not understand, the poet must descend from this supposed height; and, in order to excite rational sympathy, he
must express himself as other men express themselves. To this
it may be added, that while he is only selecting from the real
language of men, or, which amounts to the same thing, com-
posing accurately in the spirit of such selection, he is treading
30 upon safe ground, and we know what we are to expect from
him. Our feelings are the same with respect to meter; for, as it
may be proper to remind the reader, the distinction of meter
is regular and uniform, and, not like that which is produced
by what is usually called "poetic diction," arbitrary, and subject to infinite caprices, upon which no calculation whatever
can be made. In the one case, the reader is utterly at the mercy
of the poet, respecting what imagery or diction he may choose
to connect with the passion; whereas, in the other, the meter
obeys certain laws, to which the poet and reader both willingly
40 submit because they are certain, and because no interference
is made by them with the passion but such as the concurring
testimony of ages has shown to heighten and improve the pleasure which co-exists with it.

It will now be proper to answer an obvious question, namely,
why, professing these opinions, have I written in verse? To
this, in addition to such answer as is included in what has been

already said, I reply, in the first place, because, however I may have restricted myself, there is still left open to me what confessedly constitutes the most valuable object of all writing, whether in prose or verse; the great and universal passions of men, the most general and interesting of their occupations, and the entire world of nature before me—to supply endless combinations of forms and imagery. Now, supposing for a moment that whatever is interesting in these objects may be as vividly described in prose, why should I be condemned for attempting to superadd to such description the charm which, by the consent of all nations, is acknowledged to exist in metrical language? To this, by such as are yet unconvinced, it may be answered that a very small part of the pleasure given by poetry depends upon the meter, and that it is injudicious to write in meter, unless it be accompanied with the other artificial distinctions of style with which meter is usually accompanied, and that, by such deviation, more will be lost from the shock which will thereby be given to the reader's associations than will be counterbalanced by any pleasure which he can derive from the general power of numbers. In answer to those who still contend for the necessity of accompanying meter with certain appropriate colors of style in order to the accomplishment of its appropriate end, and who also, in my opinion, greatly underrate the power of meter in itself, it might, perhaps, as far as relates to these volumes, have been almost sufficient to observe, that poems are extant, written upon more humble subjects, and in a still more naked and simple style, which have continued to give pleasure from generation to generation. Now, if nakedness and simplicity be a defect, the fact here mentioned affords a strong presumption that poems somewhat less naked and simple are capable of affording pleasure at the present day; and, what I wished *chiefly* to attempt, at present, was to justify myself for having written under the impression of this belief.

But various causes might be pointed out why, when the style is manly, and the subject of some importance, words metrically arranged will long continue to impart such a pleasure to mankind as he who proves the extent of that pleasure will be desirous to impart. The end of poetry is to produce excitement in co-existence with an overbalance of pleasure; but, by the supposition, excitement is an unusual and irregular state of the mind; ideas and feelings do not, in that state, succeed each other in accustomed order. If the words, however, by which this excitement is produced be in themselves powerful, or the images and feelings have an undue proportion of pain connected with them, there is some danger that the ex-

citement may be carried beyond its proper bounds. Now the co-presence of something regular, something to which the mind has been accustomed in various moods and in a less excited state, cannot but have great efficacy in tempering and restraining the passion by an intertexture of ordinary feeling, and of feeling not strictly and necessarily connected with the passion. This is unquestionably true; and hence, though the opinion will at first appear paradoxical, from the tendency of meter to divest language, in a certain degree, of its reality, and thus
10 to throw a sort of half-consciousness of unsubstantial existence over the whole composition, there can be little doubt but that more pathetic situations and sentiments, that is, those which have a greater proportion of pain connected with them, may be endured in metrical composition, especially in rhyme, than in prose. The meter of the old ballads is very artless, yet they contain many passages which would illustrate this opinion; and, I hope, if the following poems be attentively perused, similar instances will be found in them. This opinion may be further illustrated by appealing to the reader's own experi-
20 ence of the reluctance with which he comes to the reperusal of the distressful parts of *Clarissa Harlowe,* or the *Gamester;* [7] while Shakespeare's writings, in the most pathetic scenes, never act upon us, as pathetic, beyond the bounds of pleasure—an effect which, in a much greater degree than might at first be imagined, is to be ascribed to small, but continual and regular impulses of pleasurable surprise from the metrical arrangement.—On the other hand (what it must be allowed will much more frequently happen), if the poet's words should be incommensurate with the passion, and inadequate to raise the
30 reader to a height of desirable excitement, then (unless the poet's choice of his meter has been grossly injudicious), in the feelings of pleasure which the reader has been accustomed to connect with meter in general, and in the feeling, whether cheerful or melancholy, which he has been accustomed to connect with that particular movement of meter, there will be found something which will greatly contribute to impart passion to the words, and to effect the complex end which the poet proposes to himself.

If I had undertaken a *systematic* defense of the theory here
40 maintained, it would have been my duty to develop the various causes upon which the pleasure received from metrical language depends. Among the chief of these causes is to be reckoned a principle which must be well known to those who have made any of the arts the object of accurate reflection; namely, the

7 a novel by Samuel Richardson (pub. 1748), and a tragedy by Edward Moore (pub. 1753)

pleasure which the mind derives from the perception of similitude in dissimilitude. This principle is the great spring of the
activity of our minds, and their chief feeder. From this principle the direction of the sexual appetite, and all the passions
connected with it, take their origin: it is the life of our ordinary
conversation; and upon the accuracy with which similitude in
dissimilitude, and dissimilitude in similitude, are perceived,
depend our taste and our moral feelings. It would not be a
useless employment to apply this principle to the consideration
of meter, and to show that meter is hence enabled to afford 10
much pleasure, and to point out in what manner that pleasure
is produced. But my limits will not permit me to enter upon
this subject, and I must content myself with a general summary.

I have said that poetry is the spontaneous overflow of power- ↙
ful feelings; it takes its origin from emotion recollected in
tranquillity; the emotion is contemplated till, by a species of
re-action, the tranquillity gradually disappears, and an emotion, kindred to that which was before the subject of contemplation, is gradually produced, and does itself actually 20
exist in the mind. In this mood successful composition generally
begins, and in a mood similar to this it is carried on; but the
emotion, of whatever kind, and in whatever degree, from various causes, is qualified by various pleasures, so that in de-
scribing any passions whatsoever, which are voluntarily described, the mind will, upon the whole, be in a state of
enjoyment. If Nature be thus cautious to preserve in a state of
enjoyment a being so employed, the poet ought to profit by
the lesson held forth to him, and ought especially to take care
that, whatever passions he communicates to his reader, those 30
passions, if his reader's mind be sound and vigorous, should
always be accompanied with an over-balance of pleasure. Now
the music of harmonious metrical language, the sense of difficulty overcome, and the blind association of pleasure which
has been previously received from works of rhyme or meter
of the same or similar construction, an indistinct perception
perpetually renewed of language closely resembling that of
real life, and yet, in the circumstance of meter, differing from
it so widely—all these imperceptibly make up a complex feeling of delight, which is of the most important use in tempering 40
the painful feeling always found intermingled with powerful
descriptions of the deeper passions. This effect is always produced in pathetic and impassioned poetry; while, in lighter
compositions, the ease and gracefulness with which the poet
manages his numbers are themselves confessedly a principal
source of the gratification of the reader. All that it is *necessary*

to say, however, upon this subject, may be effected by affirming, what few persons will deny, that of two descriptions, either
of passions, manners, or characters, each of them equally well
executed, the one in prose and the other in verse, the verse will
be read a hundred times where the prose is read once.

Having thus explained a few of my reasons for writing in
verse, and why I have chosen subjects from common life, and
endeavored to bring my language near to the real language of
men, if I have been too minute in pleading my own cause, I
10 have at the same time been treating a subject of general interest; and for this reason a few words shall be added with
reference solely to these particular poems, and to some defects
which will probably be found in them. I am sensible that my
associations must have sometimes been particular instead of
general, and that, consequently, giving to things a false importance, I may have sometimes written upon unworthy subjects; but I am less apprehensive on this account, than that
my language may frequently have suffered from those arbitrary connections of feelings and ideas with particular words
20 and phrases from which no man can altogether protect himself. Hence I have no doubt that, in some instances, feelings,
even of the ludicrous, may be given to my readers by expressions which appeared to me tender and pathetic. Such faulty
expressions, were I convinced they were faulty at present, and
that they must necessarily continue to be so, I would willingly
take all reasonable pains to correct. But it is dangerous to make
these alterations on the simple authority of a few individuals,
or even of certain classes of men; for where the understanding
of an author is not convinced, or his feelings altered, this can-
30 not be done without great injury to himself: for his own feelings are his stay and support; and, if he set them aside in one
instance, he may be induced to repeat this act till his mind
shall lose all confidence in itself, and become utterly debilitated.
To this it may be added that the critic ought never to forget
that he is himself exposed to the same errors as the poet, and,
perhaps, in a much greater degree: for there can be no presumption in saying of most readers that it is not probable
they will be so well acquainted with the various stages of
meaning through which words have passed, or with the fickle-
40 ness or stability of the relations of particular ideas to each
other; and, above all, since they are so much less interested in
the subject, they may decide lightly and carelessly.

Long as the reader has been detained, I hope he will permit
me to caution him against a mode of false criticism which has
been applied to poetry, in which the language closely resembles

that of life and nature. Such verses have been triumphed over
in parodies, of which Dr. Johnson's stanza is a fair specimen:—

> "I put my hat upon my head,
> And walked into the Strand,
> And there I met another man
> Whose hat was in his hand."

Immediately under these lines let us place one of the most
justly-admired stanzas of the *Babes in the Wood.*

> "These pretty Babes with hand in hand
> Went wandering up and down;
> But never more they saw the Man
> Approaching from the Town."

In both these stanzas the words, and the order of the words,
in no respect differ from the most unimpassioned conversation.
There are words in both, for example, "the Strand," and "the
Town," connected with none but the most familiar ideas; yet
the one stanza we admit as admirable, and the other as a fair
example of the superlatively contemptible. Whence arises this
difference? Not from the meter, not from the language, not
from the order of the words; but the *matter* expressed in Dr.
Johnson's stanza is contemptible. The proper method of treating trivial and simple verses, to which Dr. Johnson's stanza
would be a fair parallelism, is not to say, this is a bad kind of
poetry, or, this is not poetry; but, this wants sense; it is
neither interesting in itself, nor can *lead* to anything interesting; the images neither originate in that sane state of feeling
which arises out of thought, nor can excite thought or feeling
in the reader. This is the only sensible manner of dealing with
such verses. Why trouble yourself about the species till you
have previously decided upon the genus? Why take pains to
prove that an ape is not a Newton, when it is self-evident that
he is not a man?

One request I must make of my reader, which is, that in
judging these poems he would decide by his own feelings gen-
uinely, and not by reflection upon what will probably be the
judgment of others. How common is it to hear a person say,
I myself do not object to this style of composition, or this or
that expression, but to such and such classes of people it will
appear mean or ludicrous! This mode of criticism, so destruc-
tive of all sound unadulterated judgment, is almost universal:
let the reader then abide, independently, by his own feelings,

and, if he finds himself affected, let him not suffer such conjectures to interfere with his pleasure.

If an author, by any single composition, has impressed us
with respect for his talents, it is useful to consider this as
affording a presumption that on other occasions where we have
been displeased he, nevertheless, may not have written ill or
absurdly; and further, to give him so much credit for this one
composition as may induce us to review what has displeased
us with more care than we should otherwise have bestowed
10 upon it. This is not only an act of justice, but in our decisions
upon poetry especially, may conduce, in a high degree, to the
improvement of our own taste: for an *accurate* taste in poetry,
and in all the other arts, as Sir Joshua Reynolds has observed,
is an *acquired* talent, which can only be produced by thought
and a long-continued intercourse with the best models of composition. This is mentioned, not with so ridiculous a purpose
as to prevent the most inexperienced reader from judging for
himself (I have already said that I wish him to judge for
himself), but merely to temper the rashness of decision, and
20 to suggest that, if poetry be a subject on which much time has
not been bestowed, the judgment may be erroneous; and that,
in many cases, it necessarily will be so.

Nothing would, I know, have so effectually contributed to
further the end which I have in view, as to have shown of
what kind the pleasure is, and how that pleasure is produced,
which is confessedly produced by metrical composition essentially different from that which I have here endeavored to
recommend: for the reader will say that he has been pleased
by such composition; and what more can be done for him? The
30 power of any art is limited; and he will suspect that, if it be
proposed to furnish him with new friends, that can be only
upon condition of his abandoning his old friends. Besides, as
I have said, the reader is himself conscious of the pleasure
which he has received from such composition, composition to
which he has peculiarly attached the endearing name of poetry;
and all men feel an habitual gratitude, and something of an
honorable bigotry, for the objects which have long continued to
please them: we not only wish to be pleased, but to be pleased
in that particular way in which we have been accustomed to be
40 pleased. There is in these feelings enough to resist a host of
arguments; and I should be the less able to combat them successfully, as I am willing to allow that, in order entirely to
enjoy the poetry which I am recommending, it would be necessary to give up much of what is ordinarily enjoyed. But
would my limits have permitted me to point out how this
pleasure is produced, many obstacles might have been re-

moved, and the reader assisted in perceiving that the powers of
language are not so limited as he may suppose; and that it is
possible for poetry to give other enjoyments, of a purer, more
lasting, and more exquisite nature. This part of the subject has
not been altogether neglected, but it has not been so much my
present aim to prove that the interest excited by some other
kinds of poetry is less vivid, and less worthy of the nobler
powers of the mind, as to offer reasons for presuming that if
my purpose were fulfilled, a species of poetry would be produced which is genuine poetry; in its nature well adapted to in- 10
terest mankind permanently, and likewise important in the
multiplicity and quality of its moral relations.

From what has been said, and from a perusal of the poems,
the reader will be able clearly to perceive the object which I
had in view: he will determine how far it has been attained,
and, what is a much more important question, whether it be
worth attaining: and upon the decision of these two questions
will rest my claim to the approbation of the public.

LINES

LEFT UPON A SEAT IN A YEW-TREE, WHICH STANDS NEAR
THE LAKE OF ESTHWAITE, ON A DESOLATE PART OF
THE SHORE, COMMANDING A BEAUTIFUL
PROSPECT

NAY, Traveler! rest. This lonely Yew-tree stands
Far from all human dwelling: what if here
No sparkling rivulet spread the verdant herb?
What if the bee love not these barren boughs?
Yet, if the wind breathe soft, the curling waves,
That break against the shore, shall lull thy mind
By one soft impulse saved from vacancy.
       Who he was
That piled these stones and with the mossy sod
First covered, and here taught this aged Tree   10
With its dark arms to form a circling bower,
I well remember.—He was one who owned
No common soul. In youth by science nursed,
And led by nature into a wild scene
Of lofty hopes, he to the world went forth
A favored Being, knowing no desire
Which genius did not hallow; 'gainst the taint
Of dissolute tongues, and jealousy, and hate,
And scorn,—against all enemies prepared,

All but neglect. The world, for so it thought,   20
Owed him no service; wherefore he at once
With indignation turned himself away,
And with the food of pride sustained his soul
In solitude.—Stranger! these gloomy boughs
Had charms for him; and here he loved to sit,
His only visitants a straggling sheep,
The stone-chat, or the glancing sand-piper:
And on these barren rocks, with fern and heath,
And juniper and thistle, sprinkled o'er,
Fixing his downcast eye, he many an hour   30
A morbid pleasure nourished, tracing here
An emblem of his own unfruitful life:
And, lifting up his head, he then would gaze
On the more distant scene,—how lovely 'tis
Thou seest,—and he would gaze till it became
Far lovelier, and his heart could not sustain
The beauty, still more beauteous! Nor, that time,
When nature had subdued him to herself,
Would he forget those Beings to whose minds,
Warm from the labors of benevolence,   40
The world, and human life, appeared a scene
Of kindred loveliness: then he would sigh,
Inly disturbed, to think that others felt
What he must never feel: and so, lost Man!
On visionary views would fancy feed,
Till his eye streamed with tears. In this deep vale
He died,—this seat his only monument.

    If Thou be one whose heart the holy forms
Of young imagination have kept pure,
Stranger! henceforth be warned; and know that pride,   50
Howe'er disguised in its own majesty,
Is littleness; that he who feels contempt
For any living thing, hath faculties
Which he has never used; that thought with him
Is in its infancy. The man whose eye
Is ever on himself doth look on one,
The least of Nature's works, one who might move
The wise man to that scorn which wisdom holds
Unlawful, ever. O be wiser, Thou!
Instructed that true knowledge leads to love;   60
True dignity abides with him alone
Who, in the silent hour of inward thought,
Can still suspect, and still revere himself,
In lowliness of heart.

THE REVERIE OF POOR SUSAN

At the corner of Wood Street, when daylight appears,
Hangs a thrush that sings loud, it has sung for three years:
Poor Susan has passed by the spot, and has heard
In the silence of morning the song of the bird.

'Tis a note of enchantment; what ails her? She sees
A mountain ascending, a vision of trees;
Bright volumes of vapor through Lothbury [8] glide,
And a river flows on through the vale of Cheapside.[8]

Green pastures she views in the midst of the dale,
Down which she so often has tripped with her pail;
And a single small cottage, a nest like a dove's,
The one only dwelling on earth that she loves.

She looks, and her heart is in heaven: but they fade,
The mist and the river, the hill and the shade:
The stream will not flow, and the hill will not rise,
And the colors have all passed away from her eyes!

WE ARE SEVEN

———A simple Child,
That lightly draws its breath
And feels its life in every limb,
What should it know of death?

I met a little cottage Girl:
She was eight years old, she said;
Her hair was thick with many a curl
That clustered round her head.

She had a rustic, woodland air,
And she was wildly clad: 10
Her eyes were fair, and very fair;
—Her beauty made me glad.

"Sisters and brothers, little Maid,
How many may you be?"
"How many? Seven in all," she said,
And wondering looked at me.

8 London streets

"And where are they? I pray you tell."
She answered, "Seven are we;
And two of us at Conway dwell,
And two are gone to sea.   20

"Two of us in the church-yard lie,
My sister and my brother;
And, in the church-yard cottage, I
Dwell near them with my mother."

"You say that two at Conway dwell,
And two are gone to sea,
Yet ye are seven!—I pray you tell,
Sweet Maid, how this may be."

Then did the little Maid reply,
"Seven boys and girls are we;   30
Two of us in the church-yard lie,
Beneath the church-yard tree."

"You run about, my little Maid,
Your limbs they are alive;
If two are in the church-yard laid,
Then ye are only five."

"Their graves are green, they may be seen,"
The little Maid replied,
"Twelve steps or more from my mother's door,
And they are side by side.   40

"My stockings there I often knit,
My kerchief there I hem;
And there upon the ground I sit,
And sing a song to them.

"And often after sunset, Sir,
When it is light and fair,
I take my little porringer,
And eat my supper there.

"The first that died was sister Jane;
In bed she moaning lay,   50
Till God released her of her pain;
And then she went away.

"So in the church-yard she was laid;
And, when the grass was dry,

Together round her grave we played,
My brother John and I.

"And when the ground was white with snow,
And I could run and slide,
My brother John was forced to go,
And he lies by her side."   60

"How many are you, then," said I,
"If they two are in heaven?"
Quick was the little Maid's reply,
"O Master! we are seven."

"But they are dead; those two are dead!
Their spirits are in heaven!"
'T was throwing words away; for still
The little Maid would have her will,
And said, "Nay, we are seven!"

SIMON LEE

THE OLD HUNTSMAN; WITH AN INCIDENT IN WHICH HE WAS
CONCERNED

In the sweet shire of Cardigan,
Not far from pleasant Ivor-hall,
An old Man dwells, a little man,—
'Tis said he once was tall.
Full five-and-thirty years he lived
A running huntsman merry;
And still the center of his cheek
Is red as a ripe cherry.

No man like him the horn could sound,
And hill and valley rang with glee   10
When Echo bandied, round and round,
The halloo of Simon Lee.
In those proud days, he little cared
For husbandry or tillage;
To blither tasks did Simon rouse
The sleepers of the village.

He all the country could outrun,
Could leave both man and horse behind;
And often, ere the chase was done,
He reeled, and was stone-blind.   20

And still there's something in the world
At which his heart rejoices;
For when the chiming hounds are out,
He dearly loves their voices!

But, oh the heavy change!—bereft
Of health, strength, friends, and kindred, see!
Old Simon to the world is left
In liveried poverty.
His Master's dead,—and no one now
Dwells in the Hall of Ivor;   30
Men, dogs, and horses, all are dead;
He is the sole survivor.

And he is lean and he is sick;
His body, dwindled and awry,
Rests upon ankles swoln and thick;
His legs are thin and dry.
One prop he has, and only one,
His wife, an aged woman,
Lives with him, near the waterfall,
Upon the village Common.   40

Beside their moss-grown hut of clay,
Not twenty paces from the door,
A scrap of land they have, but they
Are poorest of the poor.
This scrap of land he from the heath
Enclosed when he was stronger;
But what to them avails the land
Which he can till no longer?

Oft, working by her Husband's side,
Ruth does what Simon cannot do;   50
For she, with scanty cause for pride,
Is stouter of the two.
And, though you with your utmost skill
From labor could not wean them,
'Tis little, very little—all
That they can do between them.

Few months of life has he in store
As he to you will tell,
For still, the more he works, the more
Do his weak ankles swell.   60
My gentle Reader, I perceive

How patiently you've waited,
And now I fear that you expect
Some tale will be related.

O Reader! had you in your mind
Such stores as silent thought can bring,
O gentle Reader! you would find
A tale in every thing.
What more I have to say is short,
And you must kindly take it: 70
It is no tale; but, should you think,
Perhaps a tale you'll make it.

One summer-day I chanced to see
This old Man doing all he could
To unearth the root of an old tree,
A stump of rotten wood.
The mattock tottered in his hand;
So vain was his endeavor,
That at the root of the old tree
He might have worked for ever.   80

"You're overtasked, good Simon Lee,
Give me your tool," to him I said;
And at the word right gladly he
Received my proffered aid.
I struck, and with a single blow
The tangled root I severed,
At which the poor old Man so long
And vainly had endeavored.

The tears into his eyes were brought,
And thanks and praises seemed to run   90
So fast out of his heart, I thought
They never would have done.
—I've heard of hearts unkind, kind deeds
With coldness still returning;
Alas! the gratitude of men
Hath oftener left me mourning.

LINES WRITTEN IN EARLY SPRING

I HEARD a thousand blended notes,
While in a grove I sat reclined,
In that sweet mood when pleasant thoughts
Bring sad thoughts to the mind.

To her fair works did Nature link
The human soul that through me ran;
And much it grieved my heart to think
What man has made of man.

Through primrose tufts, in that green bower
The periwinkle trailed its wreaths;   10
And 'tis my faith that every flower
Enjoys the air it breathes.

The birds around me hopped and played,
Their thoughts I cannot measure:—
But the least motion which they made,
It seemed a thrill of pleasure.

The budding twigs spread out their fan,
To catch the breezy air;
And I must think, do all I can,
That there was pleasure there.   20

If this belief from heaven be sent,
If such be Nature's holy plan,
Have I not reason to lament
What man has made of man?

EXPOSTULATION AND REPLY

"Why, William, on that old gray stone,
Thus for the length of half a day,
Why, William, sit you thus alone,
And dream your time away?

"Where are your books?—that light bequeathed
To Beings else forlorn and blind!
Up! up! and drink the spirit breathed
From dead men to their kind.

"You look round on your Mother Earth,
As if she for no purpose bore you;   10
As if you were her first-born birth,
And none had lived before you!"

One morning thus, by Esthwaite lake,
When life was sweet, I knew not why,
To me my good friend Matthew spake,
And thus I made reply:

"The eye—it cannot choose but see;
We cannot bid the ear be still;
Our bodies feel, where'er they be,
Against or with our will.   20

"Nor less I deem that there are Powers
Which of themselves our minds impress;
That we can feed this mind of ours
In a wise passiveness.

"Think you, 'mid all this mighty sum
Of things for ever speaking,
That nothing of itself will come,
But we must still be seeking?

"—Then ask not wherefore, here, alone,
Conversing as I may,   30
I sit upon this old gray stone,
And dream my time away."

THE TABLES TURNED

AN EVENING SCENE ON THE SAME SUBJECT

Up! up! my Friend, and quit your books;
Or surely you'll grow double:
Up! up! my Friend, and clear your looks;
Why all this toil and trouble?

The sun, above the mountain's head,
A freshening luster mellow
Through all the long green fields has spread,
His first sweet evening yellow.

Books! 'tis a dull and endless strife:
Come, hear the woodland linnet,
How sweet his music! on my life,   10
There's more of wisdom in it.

And hark! how blithe the throstle sings!
He, too, is no mean preacher:
Come forth into the light of things,
Let Nature be your teacher.

She has a world of ready wealth,
Our minds and hearts to bless—

Spontaneous wisdom breathed by health,
Truth breathed by cheerfulness.   20

One impulse from a vernal wood
May teach you more of man,
Of moral evil and of good,
Than all the sages can.

Sweet is the lore which Nature brings;
Our meddling intellect
Mis-shapes the beauteous forms of things:—
We murder to dissect.

Enough of Science and of Art;
Close up those barren leaves;   30
Come forth, and bring with you a heart
That watches and receives.

LINES

COMPOSED A FEW MILES ABOVE TINTERN ABBEY, ON REVISITING THE BANKS OF THE WYE DURING A TOUR. JULY 13, 1798 [9]

FIVE years have passed; five summers, with the length
Of five long winters! and again I hear
These waters, rolling from their mountain-springs
With a soft inland murmur.—Once again
Do I behold these steep and lofty cliffs,
That on a wild secluded scene impress
Thoughts of more deep seclusion; and connect
The landscape with the quiet of the sky.
The day is come when I again repose
Here, under this dark sycamore, and view   10
These plots of cottage-ground, these orchard-tufts,
Which at this season, with their unripe fruits,
Are clad in one green hue, and lose themselves
'Mid groves and copses. Once again I see
These hedge-rows, hardly hedge-rows, little lines
Of sportive wood run wild: these pastoral farms,
Green to the very door; and wreaths of smoke
Sent up, in silence, from among the trees!

9 "No poem of mine was composed under circumstances more pleasant for me to remember than this. I began it upon leaving Tintern, after crossing the Wye, and concluded it just as I was entering Bristol in the evening, after a ramble of four or five days, with my Sister. Not a line of it was altered, and not any part of it written down till I reached Bristol. It was published almost immediately after" (in the *Lyrical Ballads*).—Wordsworth's note.

With some uncertain notice, as might seem
Of vagrant dwellers in the houseless woods,   20
Or of some Hermit's cave, where by his fire
The Hermit sits alone.
                    These beauteous forms,
Through a long absence, have not been to me
As is a landscape to a blind man's eye:
But oft, in lonely rooms, and 'mid the din
Of towns and cities, I have owed to them
In hours of weariness, sensations sweet,
Felt in the blood, and felt along the heart;
And passing even into my purer mind,
With tranquil restoration:—feelings too   30
Of unremembered pleasure: such, perhaps,
As have no slight or trivial influence
On that best portion of a good man's life,
His little, nameless, unremembered acts
Of kindness and of love. Nor less, I trust,
To them I may have owed another gift,
Of aspect more sublime; that blessed mood,
In which the burthen of the mystery,
In which the heavy and the weary weight
Of all this unintelligible world,   40
Is lightened:—that serene and blessed mood,
In which the affections gently lead us on,—
Until, the breath of this corporeal frame
And even the motion of our human blood
Almost suspended, we are laid asleep
In body, and become a living soul:
While with an eye made quiet by the power
Of harmony, and the deep power of joy,
We see into the life of things.
                        If this
Be but a vain belief, yet, oh! how oft—   50
In darkness and amid the many shapes
Of joyless daylight; when the fretful stir
Unprofitable, and the fever of the world,
Have hung upon the beatings of my heart—
How oft, in spirit, have I turned to thee,
O sylvan Wye! thou wanderer through the woods,
How often has my spirit turned to thee!
   And now, with gleams of half-extinguished thought,
With many recognitions dim and faint,
And somewhat of a sad perplexity,
The picture of the mind revives again: 60
While here I stand, not only with the sense

Of present pleasure, but with pleasing thoughts
That in this moment there is life and food
For future years. And so I dare to hope,
Though changed, no doubt, from what I was when first
I came among these hills; when like a roe
I bounded o'er the mountains, by the sides
Of the deep rivers, and the lonely streams,
Wherever nature led: more like a man   70
Flying from something that he dreads, than one
Who sought the thing he loved. For nature then
(The coarser pleasures of my boyish days,
And their glad animal movements all gone by)
To me was all in all.—I cannot paint
What then I was. The sounding cataract
Haunted me like a passion; the tall rock,
The mountain, and the deep and gloomy wood,
Their colors and their forms, were then to me
An appetite; a feeling and a love,   80
That had no need of a remoter charm,
By thought supplied, nor any interest
Unborrowed from the eye.—That time is past,
And all its aching joys are now no more,
And all its dizzy raptures. Not for this
Faint I, nor mourn nor murmur; other gifts
Have followed; for such loss, I would believe,
Abundant recompense. For I have learned
To look on nature, not as in the hour
Of thoughtless youth; but hearing oftentimes   90
The still, sad music of humanity,
Nor harsh nor grating, though of ample power
To chasten and subdue. And I have felt
A presence that disturbs me with the joy
Of elevated thoughts; a sense sublime
Of something far more deeply interfused,
Whose dwelling is the light of setting suns,
And the round ocean and the living air,
And the blue sky, and in the mind of man;
A motion and a spirit, that impels   100
All thinking things, all objects of all thought,
And rolls through all things. Therefore am I still
A lover of the meadows and the woods,
And mountains; and of all that we behold
From this green earth; of all the mighty world
Of eye, and ear,—both what they half create,
And what perceive; well pleased to recognize
In nature and the language of the sense,

The anchor of my purest thoughts, the nurse,
The guide, the guardian of my heart, and soul   110
Of all my moral being.
                              Nor perchance,
If I were not thus taught, should I the more
Suffer my genial spirits to decay:
For thou art with me here upon the banks
Of this fair river; thou my dearest Friend,
My dear, dear Friend; [10] and in thy voice I catch
The language of my former heart, and read
My former pleasures in the shooting lights
Of thy wild eyes. Oh! yet a little while
May I behold in thee what I was once,   120
My dear, dear Sister! and this prayer I make,
Knowing that Nature never did betray
The heart that loved her; 'tis her privilege,
Through all the years of this our life, to lead
From joy to joy: for she can so inform
The mind that is within us, so impress
With quietness and beauty, and so feed
With lofty thoughts, that neither evil tongues,
Rash judgments, nor the sneers of selfish men,
Nor greetings where no kindness is, nor all   130
The dreary intercourse of daily life,
Shall e'er prevail against us, or disturb
Our cheerful faith, that all which we behold
Is full of blessings. Therefore let the moon
Shine on thee in thy solitary walk;
And let the misty mountain-winds be free
To blow against thee: and, in after years,
When these wild ecstasies shall be matured
Into a sober pleasure; when thy mind
Shall be a mansion for all lovely forms,   140
Thy memory be as a dwelling-place
For all sweet sounds and harmonies; oh! then,
If solitude, or fear, or pain, or grief,
Should be thy portion, with what healing thoughts
Of tender joy wilt thou remember me,
And these my exhortations! Nor, perchance—
If I should be where I no more can hear
Thy voice, nor catch from thy wild eyes these gleams
Of past existence—wilt thou then forget
That on the banks of this delightful stream   150
We stood together; and that I, so long
A worshiper of Nature, hither came

10 his sister, Dorothy

Unwearied in that service: rather say
With warmer love—oh! with far deeper zeal
Of holier love. Nor wilt thou then forget,
That after many wanderings, many years
Of absence, these steep woods and lofty cliffs,
And this green pastoral landscape, were to me
More dear, both for themselves and for thy sake!

THE SIMPLON PASS

  —Brook and road
Were fellow-travelers in this gloomy pass,
And with them did we journey several hours
At a slow step. The immeasurable height
Of woods decaying, never to be decayed,
The stationary blasts of waterfalls,
And in the narrow rent, at every turn,
Winds thwarting winds bewildered and forlorn,
The torrents shooting from the clear blue sky,
The rocks that muttered close upon our ears,   10
Black drizzling crags that spake by the wayside
As if a voice were in them, the sick sight
And giddy prospect of the raving stream,
The unfettered clouds and region of the heavens,
Tumult and peace, the darkness and the light—
Were all like workings of one mind, the features
Of the same face, blossoms upon one tree,
Characters of the great Apocalypse,
The types and symbols of Eternity,
Of first, and last, and midst, and without end.   20

NUTTING [11]

  —It seems a day
(I speak of one from many singled out)
One of those heavenly days that cannot die;
When, in the eagerness of boyish hope,
I left our cottage threshold, sallying forth
With a huge wallet o'er my shoulders slung,
A nutting-crook in hand; and turned my steps
Toward some far-distant wood, a figure quaint,
Tricked out in proud disguise of cast-off weeds
Which for that service had been husbanded,   10

11 "Intended as part of a poem on my own life, but struck out as not being wanted
there. . . . These verses arose out of the remembrance of feelings I often had when
a boy."—(Wordsworth)

By exhortation of my frugal dame—
Motley accoutrement, of power to smile
At thorns, and brakes, and brambles,—and, in truth,
More ragged than need was. O'er pathless rocks,
Through beds of matted fern, and tangled thickets,
Forcing my way, I came to one dear nook
Unvisited, where not a broken bough
Drooped with its withered leaves, ungracious sign
Of devastation; but the hazels rose
Tall and erect, with tempting clusters hung,   20
A virgin scene!—A little while I stood,
Breathing with such suppression of the heart
As joy delights in; and, with wise restraint
Voluptuous, fearless of a rival, eyed
The banquet;—or beneath the trees I sate
Among the flowers, and with the flowers I played;
A temper known to those, who, after long
And weary expectation, have been blest
With sudden happiness beyond all hope.
Perhaps it was a bower beneath whose leaves   30
The violets of five seasons re-appear
And fade, unseen by any human eye;
Where fairy water-breaks do murmur on
For ever; and I saw the sparkling foam,
And—with my cheek on one of those green stones
That, fleeced with moss, under the shady trees,
Lay round me, scattered like a flock of sheep—
I heard the murmur and the murmuring sound,
In that sweet mood when pleasure loves to pay
Tribute to ease; and, of its joy secure,   40
The heart luxuriates with indifferent things,
Wasting its kindliness on stocks and stones,
And on the vacant air. Then up I rose,
And dragged to earth both branch and bough, with crash
And merciless ravage: and the shady nook
Of hazels, and the green and mossy bower,
Deformed and sullied, patiently gave up
Their quiet being: and, unless I now
Confound my present feelings with the past;
Ere from the mutilated bower I turned   50
Exulting, rich beyond the wealth of kings,
I felt a sense of pain when I beheld
The silent trees, and saw the intruding sky—
Then, dearest Maiden, move along these shades
In gentleness of heart; with gentle hand
Touch—for there is a spirit in the woods.

THE LUCY POEMS [12]

I

STRANGE fits of passion have I known:
And I will dare to tell,
But in the Lover's ear alone,
What once to me befell.

When she I loved looked every day
Fresh as a rose in June,
I to her cottage bent my way,
Beneath an evening-moon.

Upon the moon I fixed my eye,
All over the wide lea;   10
With quickening pace my horse drew nigh
Those paths so dear to me.

And now we reached the orchard-plot;
And, as we climbed the hill,
The sinking moon to Lucy's cot
Came near, and nearer still.

In one of those sweet dreams I slept,
Kind Nature's gentlest boon!
And all the while my eyes I kept
On the descending moon.   20

My horse moved on; hoof after hoof
He raised, and never stopped:
When down behind the cottage roof,
At once, the bright moon dropped.

What fond and wayward thoughts will slide
Into a Lover's head!
"O mercy!" to myself I cried,
"If Lucy should be dead!"

2

She dwelt among the untrodden ways
Beside the springs of Dove,

---

12 Written while Wordsworth was a resident in Germany in 1799. Who Lucy was
the poet never revealed. When Wordsworth was asked why he wrote so few love
poems (like these), he replied, "Had I been a writer of love-poetry it would have
been natural to me to write it with a degree of warmth which could hardly have been
approved by my principles."

A Maid whom there were none to praise
And very few to love:

A violet by a mossy stone
Half hidden from the eye!
—Fair as a star, when only one
Is shining in the sky.

She lived unknown, and few could know
When Lucy ceased to be;
But she is in her grave, and, oh,
The difference to me!

3

I traveled among unknown men,
In lands beyond the sea;
Nor, England! did I know till then
What love I bore to thee.

'Tis past, that melancholy dream!
Nor will I quit thy shore
A second time; for still I seem
To love thee more and more.

Among thy mountains did I feel
The joy of my desire;
And she I cherished turned her wheel
Beside an English fire.

Thy mornings showed, thy nights concealed
The bowers where Lucy played;
And thine too is the last green field
That Lucy's eyes surveyed.

4

Three years she grew in sun and shower,
Then Nature said, "A lovelier flower
On earth was never sown;
This Child I to myself will take;
She shall be mine, and I will make
A Lady of my own.

"Myself will to my darling be
Both law and impulse: and with me

The Girl, in rock and plain,
In earth and heaven, in glade and bower,   10
Shall feel an overseeing power
To kindle or restrain.

"She shall be sportive as the fawn
That wild with glee across the lawn,
Or up the mountain springs;
And hers shall be the breathing balm,
And hers the silence and the calm
Of mute insensate things.

"The floating clouds their state shall lend
To her; for her the willow bend;   20
Nor shall she fail to see
Even in the motions of the Storm
Grace that shall mold the Maiden's form
By silent sympathy.

"The stars of midnight shall be dear
To her; and she shall lean her ear
In many a secret place
Where rivulets dance their wayward round,
And beauty born of murmuring sound
Shall pass into her face.   30

"And vital feelings of delight
Shall rear her form to stately height,
Her virgin bosom swell;
Such thoughts to Lucy I will give
While she and I together live
Here in this happy dell."

Thus Nature spake—The work was done—
How soon my Lucy's race was run!
She died, and left to me
This heath, this calm, and quiet scene;   40
The memory of what has been,
And never more will be.

5

A slumber did my spirit seal;
    I had no human fears:
She seemed a thing that could not feel
    The touch of earthly years.

No motion has she now, no force;
  She neither hears nor sees;
Rolled round in earth's diurnal course,
  With rocks, and stones, and trees.

LUCY GRAY

OR, SOLITUDE [13]

Oft I had heard of Lucy Gray:
  And, when I crossed the wild,
I chanced to see at break of day
  The solitary child.

No mate, no comrade Lucy knew;
  She dwelt on a wide moor,
—The sweetest thing that ever grew
  Beside a human door!

You yet may spy the fawn at play,
  The hare upon the green;   10
But the sweet face of Lucy Gray
  Will never more be seen.

"To-night will be a stormy night—
  You to the town must go;
And take a lantern, Child, to light
  Your mother through the snow."

"That, Father! will I gladly do:
  'Tis scarcely afternoon—
The minster-clock has just struck two,
  And yonder is the moon!"   20

At this the Father raised his hook,
  And snapped a faggot-band;
He plied his work;—and Lucy took
  The lantern in her hand.

Not blither is the mountain roe:
  With many a wanton stroke
Her feet disperse the powdery snow,
  That rises up like smoke.

---

13 "Founded on a circumstance told me by my Sister, of a little girl who, not far from Halifax in Yorkshire, was bewildered by a snowstorm. Her footsteps were traced by her parents to the middle of the lock of a canal, and no other vestige of her, backward or forward, could be traced. The body however was found in the canal." (Wordsworth)

The storm came on before its time:
She wandered up and down;
And many a hill did Lucy climb:
But never reached the town.   30

The wretched parents all that night
Went shouting far and wide;
But there was neither sound nor sight
To serve them for a guide.

At day-break on a hill they stood
That overlooked the moor;
And thence they saw the bridge of wood,
A furlong from their door.   40

They wept—and, turning homeward, cried,
"In heaven we all shall meet;"
—When in the snow the mother spied
The print of Lucy's feet.

Then downwards from the steep hill's edge
They tracked the footmarks small;
And through the broken hawthorn hedge,
And by the long stone-wall;

And then an open field they crossed:
The marks were still the same;
They tracked them on, nor ever lost;   50
And to the bridge they came.

They followed from the snowy bank
Those footmarks, one by one,
Into the middle of the plank;
And further there were none!

—Yet some maintain that to this day
She is a living child;
That you may see sweet Lucy Gray
Upon the lonesome wild.   60

O'er rough and smooth she trips along,
And never looks behind;
And sings a solitary song
That whistles in the wind.

THE PRELUDE

OR, GROWTH OF A POET'S MIND

AN AUTOBIOGRAPHICAL POEM

To *The Prelude*, when published in 1850, Wordsworth prefixed the following *Advertisement:*

"The following Poem was commenced in the beginning of the year 1799, and completed in the summer of 1805.

"The design and occasion of the work are described by the Author in his Preface to the 'Excursion,' first published in 1814, where he thus speaks:—

" 'Several years ago, when the Author retired to his native mountains with the hope of being enabled to construct a literary work that might live, it was a reasonable thing that he should take a review of his own mind, and examine how far Nature and Education had qualified him for such an employment.

" 'As subsidiary to this preparation, he undertook to record, in verse, the origin and progress of his own powers, as far as he was acquainted with them.

" 'That work, addressed to a dear friend [Coleridge], most distinguished for his knowledge and genius, and to whom the Author's intellect is deeply indebted, has been long finished; and the result of the investigation which gave rise to it, was a determination to compose a philosophical Poem, containing views of Man, Nature, and Society, and to be entitled the "Recluse"; as having for its principal subject the sensations and opinions of a poet living in retirement.

" 'The preparatory poem is biographical, and conducts the history of the Author's mind to the point when he was emboldened to hope that his faculties were sufficiently matured for entering upon the arduous labor which he had proposed to himself; and the two works have the same kind of relation to each other, if he may so express himself, as the Ante-chapel has to the body of a Gothic church. Continuing this allusion, he may be permitted to add, that his minor pieces, which have been long before the public, when they shall be properly arranged, will be found by the attentive reader to have such connection with the main work as may give them claim to be likened to the little cells, oratories, and sepulchral recesses, ordinarily included in those edifices.'

"Such was the Author's language in the year 1814.

"It will thence be seen, that the present Poem was intended to be introductory to the 'Recluse,' and that the 'Recluse,' if completed, would have consisted of Three Parts. Of these, the Second Part alone: viz. the 'Excursion' was finished, and given to the world by the Author."

Books I and II of *The Prelude* (reprinted in this volume) bear the subheads "Introduction—Childhood and School-time." The subject-matter and scope of the remaining twelve books may be inferred from the sub-heads: III, Residence at Cambridge; IV, Summer Vacation; V, Books; VI, Cambridge and the Alps; VII, Residence in London; VIII, Retrospect—Love of Nature Leading to Love of Man; IX and X, Residence in France; XI, France; XII and XIII, Imagination and Taste, how impaired and restored; XIV, Conclusion.

Book First

INTRODUCTION—CHILDHOOD AND SCHOOL-TIME

Oh there is blessing in this gentle breeze,
A visitant that while it fans my cheek
Doth seem half-conscious of the joy it brings
From the green fields, and from yon azure sky.
Whate'er its mission, the soft breeze can come
To none more grateful than to me; escaped
From the vast city, where I long had pined
A discontented sojourner: now free,
Free as a bird to settle where I will.
What dwelling shall receive me? in what vale   10
Shall be my harbor? underneath what grove
Shall I take up my home? and what clear stream
Shall with its murmur lull me into rest?
The earth is all before me. With a heart
Joyous, nor scared at its own liberty,
I look about; and should the chosen guide
Be nothing better than a wandering cloud,
I cannot miss my way. I breathe again!
Trances of thought and mountings of the mind
Come fast upon me: it is shaken off,   20
That burthen of my own unnatural self,
The heavy weight of many a weary day
Not mine, and such as were not made for me.
Long months of peace (if such bold word accord
With any promises of human life),
Long months of ease and undisturbed delight
Are mine in prospect; whither shall I turn,
By road or pathway, or through trackless field,
Up hill or down, or shall some floating thing
Upon the river point me out my course?   30

Dear Liberty! Yet what would it avail
But for a gift that consecrates the joy?
For I, methought, while the sweet breath of heaven
Was blowing on my body, felt within
A correspondent breeze, that gently moved
With quickening virtue, but is now become
A tempest, a redundant energy,
Vexing its own creation. Thanks to both,
And their congenial powers, that, while they join
In breaking up a long-continued frost,   40
Bring with them vernal promises, the hope

Of active days urged on by flying hours,—
Days of sweet leisure, taxed with patient thought
Abstruse, nor wanting punctual service high,
Matins and vespers of harmonious verse!

Thus far, O Friend![14] did I, not used to make
A present joy the matter of a song,
Pour forth that day my soul in measured strains
That would not be forgotten, and are here
Recorded: to the open fields I told   50
A prophecy: poetic numbers came
Spontaneously to clothe in priestly robe
A renovated spirit singled out,
Such hope was mine, for holy services.
My own voice cheered me, and, far more, the mind's
Internal echo of the imperfect sound;
To both I listened, drawing from them both
A cheerful confidence in things to come.

Content and not unwilling now to give
A respite to this passion, I paced on   60
With brisk and eager steps; and came, at length,
To a green shady place, where down I sate
Beneath a tree, slackening my thoughts by choice
And settling into gentler happiness.
'Twas autumn, and a clear and placid day,
With warmth, as much as needed, from a sun
Two hours declined towards the west; a day
With silver clouds, and sunshine on the grass,
And in the sheltered and the sheltering grove
A perfect stillness. Many were the thoughts   70
Encouraged and dismissed, till choice was made
Of a known Vale, whither my feet should turn,
Nor rest till they had reached the very door
Of the one cottage which methought I saw.[15]
No picture of mere memory ever looked
So fair; and while upon the fancied scene
I gazed with growing love, a higher power
Than Fancy gave assurance of some work
Of glory there forthwith to be begun,
Perhaps too there performed. Thus long I mused,   80
Nor e'er lost sight of what I mused upon,
Save when, amid the stately grove of oaks,
Now here, now there, an acorn, from its cup
Dislodged, through sere leaves rustled, or at once

14 Coleridge   15 Dove Cottage, Grasmere

To the bare earth dropped with a startling sound.
From that soft couch I rose not, till the sun
Had almost touched the horizon; casting then
A backward glance upon the curling cloud
Of city smoke, by distance ruralized;
Keen as a Truant or a Fugitive,   90
But as a Pilgrim resolute, I took,
Even with the chance equipment of that hour,
The road that pointed toward the chosen Vale.
It was a splendid evening, and my soul
Once more made trial of her strength, nor lacked
Æolian visitations; but the harp
Was soon defrauded, and the banded host
Of harmony dispersed in straggling sounds,
And lastly utter silence! "Be it so;
Why think of anything but present good?"   100
So, like a home-bound laborer, I pursued
My way beneath the mellowing sun, that shed
Mild influence; nor left in me one wish
Again to bend the Sabbath of that time
To a servile yoke. What need of many words?
A pleasant loitering journey, through three days
Continued, brought me to my hermitage.
I spare to tell of what ensued, the life
In common things—the endless store of things,
Rare, or at least so seeming, every day   110
Found all about me in one neighborhood—
The self-congratulation, and, from morn
To night, unbroken cheerfulness serene.
But speedily an earnest longing rose
To brace myself to some determined aim,
Reading or thinking; either to lay up
New stores, or rescue from decay the old
By timely interference: and therewith
Came hopes still higher, that with outward life
I might endue some airy phantasies   120
That had been floating loose about for years,
And to such beings temperately deal forth
The many feelings that oppressed my heart.
That hope hath been discouraged; welcome light
Dawns from the east, but dawns to disappear
And mock me with a sky that ripens not
Into a steady morning: if my mind,
Remembering the bold promise of the past,
Would gladly grapple with some noble theme,

Vain is her wish; where'er she turns she finds   130
Impediments from day to day renewed.

    And now it would content me to yield up
Those lofty hopes awhile, for present gifts
Of humbler industry. But, oh, dear Friend!
The Poet, gentle creature as he is,
Hath, like the Lover, his unruly times;
His fits when he is neither sick nor well,
Though no distress be near him but his own
Unmanageable thoughts: his mind, best pleased
While she as duteous as the mother dove   140
Sits brooding, lives not always to that end,
But like the innocent bird, hath goadings on
That drive her as in trouble through the groves;
With me is now such passion, to be blamed
No otherwise than as it lasts too long.

    When, as becomes a man who would prepare
For such an arduous work, I through myself
Make rigorous inquisition, the report
Is often cheering; for I neither seem
To lack that first great gift, the vital soul,   150
Nor general Truths, which are themselves a sort
Of Elements and Agents, Under-powers,
Subordinate helpers of the living mind:
Nor am I naked of external things,
Forms, images, nor numerous other aids
Of less regard, though won perhaps with toil
And needful to build up a Poet's praise.
Time, place, and manners do I seek, and these
Are found in plenteous store, but nowhere such
As may be singled out with steady choice;   160
No little band of yet remembered names
Whom I, in perfect confidence, might hope
To summon back from lonesome banishment,
And make them dwellers in the hearts of men
Now living, or to live in future years.
Sometimes the ambitious Power of choice, mistaking
Proud spring-tide swellings for a regular sea,
Will settle on some British theme, some old
Romantic tale by Milton left unsung;
More often turning to some gentle place   170
Within the groves of Chivalry, I pipe
To shepherd swains, or seated harp in hand,

Amid reposing knights by a river side
Or fountain, listen to the grave reports
Of dire enchantments faced and overcome
By the strong mind, and tales of warlike feats,
Where spear encountered spear, and sword with sword
Fought, as if conscious of the blazonry
That the shield bore, so glorious was the strife;
Whence inspiration for a song that winds   180
Through ever-changing scenes of votive quest
Wrongs to redress, harmonious tribute paid
To patient courage and unblemished truth,
To firm devotion, zeal unquenchable,
And Christian meekness hallowing faithful loves.
Sometimes, more sternly moved, I would relate
How vanquished Mithridates northward passed,
And, hidden in the cloud of years, became
Odin, the Father of a race by whom
Perished the Roman Empire: how the friends   190
And followers of Sertorius, out of Spain
Flying, found shelter in the Fortunate Isles,
And left their usages, their arts and laws,
To disappear by a slow gradual death,
To dwindle and to perish one by one,
Starved in those narrow bounds: but not the soul
Of Liberty, which fifteen hundred years
Survived, and, when the European came
With skill and power that might not be withstood,
Did, like a pestilence, maintain its hold   200
And wasted down by glorious death that race
Of natural heroes: or I would record
How, in tyrannic times, some high-souled man,
Unnamed among the chronicles of kings,
Suffered in silence for Truth's sake: or tell,
How that one Frenchman,[16] through continued force
Of meditation on the inhuman deeds
Of those who conquered first the Indian Isles,
Went single in his ministry across
The Ocean; not to comfort the oppressed,   210
But, like a thirsty wind, to roam about
Withering the Oppressor: how Gustavus sought
Help at his need in Dalecarlia's mines:
How Wallace fought for Scotland; left the name
Of Wallace to be found, like a wild flower,
All over his dear Country; left the deeds

16 Dominique de Gourgues, a Frenchman who in 1568 went to Florida to avenge
the massacre of his countrymen by the Spaniards.

Of Wallace, like a family of Ghosts,
To people the steep rocks and river banks,
Her natural sanctuaries, with a local soul
Of independence and stern liberty.   220
Sometimes it suits me better to invent
A tale from my own heart, more near akin
To my own passions and habitual thoughts;
Some variegated story, in the main
Lofty, but the unsubstantial structure melts
Before the very sun that brightens it,
Mist into air dissolving! Then a wish,
My last and favorite aspiration, mounts
With yearning toward some philosophic song
Of Truth that cherishes our daily life;   230
With meditations passionate from deep
Recesses in man's heart, immortal verse
Thoughtfully fitted to the Orphean lyre;
But from this awful burthen I full soon
Take refuge and beguile myself with trust
That mellower years will bring a riper mind
And clearer insight. Thus my days are past
In contradiction; with no skill to part
Vague longing, haply bred by want of power,
From paramount impulse not to be withstood,   240
A timorous capacity, from prudence,
From circumspection, infinite delay.
Humility and modest awe, themselves
Betray me, serving often for a cloak
To a more subtle selfishness; that now
Locks every function up in blank reserve,
Now dupes me, trusting to an anxious eye
That with intrusive restlessness beats off
Simplicity and self-presented truth.
Ah! better far than this, to stray about   250
Voluptuously through fields and rural walks,
And ask no record of the hours, resigned
To vacant musing, unreproved neglect
Of all things, and deliberate holiday.
Far better never to have heard the name
Of zeal and just ambition, than to live
Baffled and plagued by a mind that every hour
Turns recreant to her task; takes heart again,
Then feels immediately some hollow thought
Hang like an interdict upon her hopes.   260
This is my lot; for either still I find
Some imperfection in the chosen theme,

Or see of absolute accomplishment
Much wanting, so much wanting, in myself,
That I recoil and droop, and seek repose
In listlessness from vain perplexity,
Unprofitably traveling toward the grave,
Like a false steward who hath much received
And renders nothing back.

                  Was it for this
That one, the fairest of all rivers, loved   270
To blend his murmurs with my nurse's song,
And, from his alder shades and rocky falls,
And from his fords and shallows, sent a voice
That flowed along my dreams? For this, didst thou,
O Derwent! winding among grassy holms
Where I was looking on, a babe in arms,
Make ceaseless music that composed my thoughts
To more than infant softness, giving me
Amid the fretful dwellings of mankind
A foretaste, a dim earnest, of the calm   280
That Nature breathes among the hills and groves.

   When he had left the mountains and received
On his smooth breast the shadow of those towers
That yet survive, a shattered monument
Of feudal sway, the bright blue river passed
Along the margin of our terrace walk;
A tempting playmate whom we dearly loved.
Oh, many a time have I, a five years' child,
In a small mill-race severed from his stream,
Made one long bathing of a summer's day;   290
Basked in the sun, and plunged and basked again
Alternate, all a summer's day, or scoured
The sandy fields, leaping through flowery groves
Of yellow ragwort; or, when rock and hill,
The woods, and distant Skiddaw's lofty height,
Were bronzed with deepest radiance, stood alone
Beneath the sky, as if I had been born
On Indian plains, and from my mother's hut
Had run abroad in wantonness, to sport
A naked savage, in the thunder shower.   300

   Fair seed-time had my soul, and I grew up
Fostered alike by beauty and by fear:
Much favored in my birth-place,[17] and no less

   17 Cockermouth

In that belovèd Vale to which erelong
We were transplanted; [18] there were we let loose
For sports of wider range. Ere I had told
Ten birth-days, when among the mountain slopes
Frost, and the breath of frosty wind, had snapped
The last autumnal crocus, 'twas my joy
With store of springes o'er my shoulder hung   310
To range the open heights where woodcocks run
Along the smooth green turf. Through half the night,
Scudding away from snare to snare, I plied
That anxious visitation;—moon and stars
Were shining o'er my head. I was alone,
And seemed to be a trouble to the peace
That dwelt among them. Sometimes it befell
In these night wanderings, that a strong desire
O'erpowered my better reason, and the bird
Which was the captive of another's toil   320
Became my prey; and when the deed was done
I heard among the solitary hills
Low breathings coming after me, and sounds
Of undistinguishable motion, steps
Almost as silent as the turf they trod.

Nor less, when spring had warmed the cultured Vale,
Moved we as plunderers where the mother-bird
Had in high places built her lodge; though mean
Our object and inglorious, yet the end
Was not ignoble. Oh! when I have hung   330
Above the raven's nest, by knots of grass
And half-inch fissures in the slippery rock
But ill sustained, and almost (so it seemed)
Suspended by the blast that blew amain,
Shouldering the naked crag, oh, at that time
While on the perilous ridge I hung alone,
With what strange utterance did the loud dry wind
Blow through my ear! the sky seemed not a sky
Of earth—and with what motion moved the clouds!

Dust as we are, the immortal spirit grows   340
Like harmony in music; there is a dark
Inscrutable workmanship that reconciles
Discordant elements, makes them cling together
In one society. How strange, that all
The terrors, pains, and early miseries,
Regrets, vexations, lassitudes interfused

18 Hawkshead, on Esthwaite Water, where Wordsworth went to school

Within my mind, should e'er have borne a part,
And that a needful part, in making up
The calm existence that is mine when I
Am worthy of myself! Praise to the end!   350
Thanks to the means which Nature deigned to employ;
Whether her fearless visitings, or those
That came with soft alarm, like hurtless light
Opening the peaceful clouds; or she would use
Severer interventions, ministry
More palpable, as best might suit her aim.

　　One summer evening (led by her) I found
A little boat tied to a willow tree
Within a rocky cove, its usual home.
Straight I unloosed her chain, and stepping in   360
Pushed from the shore. It was an act of stealth
And troubled pleasure, nor without the voice
Of mountain-echoes did my boat move on;
Leaving behind her still, on either side,
Small circles glittering idly in the moon,
Until they melted all into one track
Of sparkling light. But now, like one who rows,
Proud of his skill, to reach a chosen point
With an unswerving line, I fixed my view
Upon the summit of a craggy ridge,   370
The horizon's utmost boundary; far above
Was nothing but the stars and the gray sky.
She was an elfin pinnace; lustily
I dipped my oars into the silent lake,
And, as I rose upon the stroke, my boat
Went heaving through the water like a swan;
When, from behind that craggy steep till then
The horizon's bound, a huge peak, black and huge,
As if with voluntary power instinct,
Upreared its head. I struck and struck again,   380
And growing still in stature the grim shape
Towered up between me and the stars, and still,
For so it seemed, with purpose of its own
And measured motion like a living thing,
Strode after me. With trembling oars I turned,
And through the silent water stole my way
Back to the covert of the willow tree;
There in her mooring-place I left my bark,—
And through the meadows homeward went, in grave
And serious mood; but after I had seen   390
That spectacle, for many days, my brain

Worked with a dim and undetermined sense
Of unknown modes of being; o'er my thoughts
There hung a darkness, call it solitude
Or blank desertion. No familiar shapes
Remained, no pleasant images of trees,
Of sea or sky, no colors of green fields;
But huge and mighty forms, that do not live
Like living men, moved slowly through the mind
By day, and were a trouble to my dreams.   400

Wisdom and Spirit of the universe!
Thou Soul that art the eternity of thought
That givest to forms and images a breath
And everlasting motion, not in vain
By day or star-light thus from my first dawn
Of childhood didst thou intertwine for me
The passions that build up our human soul;
Not with the mean and vulgar works of man,
But with high objects, with enduring things—
With life and nature—purifying thus   410
The elements of feeling and of thought,
And sanctifying, by such discipline,
Both pain and fear, until we recognize
A grandeur in the beatings of the heart.
Nor was this fellowship vouchsafed to me
With stinted kindness. In November days,
When vapors rolling down the valley made
A lonely scene more lonesome, among woods,
At noon and 'mid the calm of summer nights,
When, by the margin of the trembling lake,   420
Beneath the gloomy hills homeward I went
In solitude, such intercourse was mine;
Mine was it in the fields both day and night,
And by the waters, all the summer long.

And in the frosty season, when the sun
Was set, and visible for many a mile
The cottage windows blazed through twilight gloom,
I heeded not their summons: happy time
It was indeed for all of us—for me
It was a time of rapture! Clear and loud   430
The village clock tolled six,—I wheeled about,
Proud and exulting like an untired horse
That cares not for his home. All shod with steel,
We hissed along the polished ice in games
Confederate, imitative of the chase

And woodland pleasures,—the resounding horn,
The pack loud chiming, and the hunted hare.
So through the darkness and the cold we flew,
And not a voice was idle; with the din
Smitten, the precipices rang aloud;   440
The leafless trees and every icy crag
Tinkled like iron; while far distant hills
Into the tumult sent an alien sound
Of melancholy not unnoticed, while the stars
Eastward were sparkling clear, and in the west
The orange sky of evening died away.
Not seldom from the uproar I retired
Into a silent bay, or sportively
Glanced sideway, leaving the tumultuous throng,
To cut across the reflex of a star   450
That fled, and, flying still before me, gleamed
Upon the glassy plain; and oftentimes,
When we had given our bodies to the wind,
And all the shadowy banks on either side
Came sweeping through the darkness, spinning still
The rapid line of motion, then at once
Have I, reclining back upon my heels,
Stopped short; yet still the solitary cliffs
Wheeled by me—even as if the earth had rolled
With visible motion her diurnal round!   460
Behind me did they stretch in solemn train,
Feebler and feebler, and I stood and watched
Till all was tranquil as a dreamless sleep.

   Ye Presences of Nature in the sky
And on the earth! Ye Visions of the hills!
And Souls of lonely places! can I think
A vulgar hope was yours when ye employed
Such ministry, when ye, through many a year
Haunting me thus among my boyish sports,
On caves and trees, upon the woods and hills,   470
Impressed, upon all forms, the characters
Of danger or desire; and thus did make
The surface of the universal earth,
With triumph and delight, with hope and fear,
Work like a sea?

                              Not uselessly employed,
Might I pursue this theme through every change
Of exercise and play, to which the year
Did summon us in his delightful round.

We were a noisy crew: the sun in heaven
Beheld not vales more beautiful than ours;   480
Nor saw a band in happiness and joy
Richer, or worthier of the ground they trod.
I could record with no reluctant voice
The woods of autumn, and their hazel bowers
With milk-white clusters hung; the rod and line,
True symbol of hope's foolishness, whose strong
And unreproved enchantment led us on
By rocks and pools shut out from every star,
All the green summer, to forlorn cascades
Among the windings hid of mountain brooks.   490
—Unfading recollections! at this hour
The heart is almost mine with which I felt,
From some hill-top on sunny afternoons,
The paper kite high among fleecy clouds
Pull at her rein like an impetuous courser;
Or, from the meadows sent on gusty days,
Beheld her breast the wind, then suddenly
Dashed headlong, and rejected by the storm.

Ye lowly cottages wherein we dwelt,[19]
A ministration of your own was yours;   500
Can I forget you, being as you were
So beautiful among the pleasant fields
In which ye stood? or can I here forget
The plain and seemly countenance with which
Ye dealt out your plain comforts? Yet had ye
Delights and exultations of your own.
Eager and never weary we pursued
Our home-amusements by the warm peat-fire
At evening, when with pencil, and smooth slate
In square divisions parceled out and all   510
With crosses and with cyphers scribbled o'er,
We schemed and puzzled, head opposed to head
In strife too humble to be named in verse:
Or round the naked table, snow-white deal,
Cherry or maple, sate in close array,
And to the combat, Loo or Whist, led on
A thick-ribbed army; not, as in the world,
Neglected and ungratefully thrown by
Even for the very service they had wrought,
But husbanded through many a long campaign.   520
Uncouth assemblage was it, where no few

---

[19] The boys at Hawkshead School lived with cottagers in the vicinity, Wordsworth
for nine years living happily with one Anne Tyson.

Had changed their functions: some, plebeian cards
Which Fate, beyond the promise of their birth,
Had dignified, and called to represent
The persons of departed potentates.
Oh, with what echoes on the board they fell!
Ironic diamonds,—clubs, hearts, diamonds, spades,
A congregation piteously akin!
Cheap matter offered they to boyish wit,
Those sooty knaves, precipitated down   530
With scoffs and taunts, like Vulcan out of heaven:
The paramount ace, a moon in her eclipse,
Queens gleaming through their splendor's last decay,
And monarchs surly at the wrongs sustained
By royal visages. Meanwhile abroad
Incessant rain was falling, or the frost
Raged bitterly, with keen and silent tooth;
And, interrupting oft that eager game,
From under Esthwaite's splitting fields of ice
The pent-up air, struggling to free itself,   540
Gave out to meadow grounds and hills a loud
Protracted yelling, like the noise of wolves
Howling in troops along the Bothnic Main.

Nor, sedulous as I have been to trace
How Nature by extrinsic passion first
Peopled the mind with forms sublime or fair,
And made me love them, may I here omit
How other pleasures have been mine, and joys
Of subtler origin; how I have felt,
Not seldom even in that tempestuous time,   550
Those hallowed and pure motions of the sense
Which seem, in their simplicity, to own
An intellectual charm; that calm delight
Which, if I err not, surely must belong
To those first-born affinities that fit
Our new existence to existing things,
And, in our dawn of being, constitute
The bond of union between life and joy.

Yes, I remember when the changeful earth,
And twice five summers on my mind had stamped   560
The faces of the moving year, even then
I held unconscious intercourse with beauty
Old as creation, drinking in a pure
Organic pleasure from the silver wreaths

Of curling mist, or from the level plain
Of waters colored by impending clouds.

    The sands of Westmoreland, the creeks and bays
Of Cumbria's rocky limits, they can tell
How, when the Sea threw off his evening shade,
And to the shepherd's hut on distant hills   570
Sent welcome notice of the rising moon,
How I have stood, to fancies such as these
A stranger, linking with the spectacle
No conscious memory of a kindred sight,
And bringing with me no peculiar sense
Of quietness or peace; yet have I stood,
Even while mine eye hath moved o'er many a league
Of shining water, gathering as it seemed,
Through every hair-breadth in that field of light,
New pleasure like a bee among the flowers.   580

    Thus oft amid those fits of vulgar joy
Which, through all seasons, on a child's pursuits
Are prompt attendants, 'mid that giddy bliss
Which, like a tempest, works along the blood
And is forgotten; even then I felt
Gleams like the flashing of a shield;—the earth
And common face of Nature spake to me
Rememberable things; sometimes, 'tis true,
By chance collisions and quaint accidents
(Like those ill-sorted unions, work supposed   590
Of evil-minded fairies), yet not vain
Nor profitless, if haply they impressed
Collateral objects and appearances,
Albeit lifeless then, and doomed to sleep
Until maturer seasons called them forth
To impregnate and to elevate the mind.
—And if the vulgar joy by its own weight
Wearied itself out of the memory,
The scenes which were a witness of that joy
Remained in their substantial lineaments   600
Depicted on the brain, and to the eye
Were visible, a daily sight; and thus
By the impressive discipline of fear,
By pleasure and repeated happiness,
So frequently repeated, and by force
Of obscure feelings representative
Of things forgotten, these same scenes so bright,

So beautiful, so majestic in themselves,
Though yet the day was distant, did become
Habitually dear, and all their forms 610
And changeful colors by invisible links
Were fastened to the affections.

                            I began
My story early—not misled, I trust,
By an infirmity of love for days
Disowned by memory—ere the breath of spring
Planting my snowdrops among winter snows:
Nor will it seem to thee, O Friend! so prompt
In sympathy, that I have lengthened out
With fond and feeble tongue a tedious tale.
Meanwhile, my hope has been, that I might fetch 620
Invigorating thoughts from former years;
Might fix the wavering balance of my mind,
And haply meet reproaches too, whose power
May spur me on, in manhood now mature
To honorable toil. Yet should these hopes
Prove vain, and thus should neither I be taught
To understand myself, nor thou to know
With better knowledge how the heart was framed
Of him thou lovest; need I dread from thee
Harsh judgments, if the song be loth to quit 630
Those recollected hours that have the charm
Of visionary things, those lovely forms
And sweet sensations that throw back our life,
And almost make remotest infancy
A visible scene, on which the sun is shining?
   One end at least hath been attained; my mind
Hath been revived, and if this genial mood
Desert me not, forthwith shall be brought down
Through later years the story of my life.
The road lies plain before me;—'tis a theme 640
Single and of determined bounds; and hence
I choose it rather at this time, than work
Of ampler or more varied argument,
Where I might be discomfited and lost:
And certain hopes are with me, that to thee
This labor will be welcome, honored Friend!

BOOK SECOND

SCHOOL-TIME (*continued*)

Thus far, O Friend! have we, though leaving much
Unvisited, endeavored to retrace
The simple ways in which my childhood walked;
Those chiefly that first led me to the love
Of rivers, woods, and fields. The passion yet
Was in its birth, sustained as might befall
By nourishment that came unsought; for still
From week to week, from month to month, we lived
A round of tumult. Duly were our games
Prolonged in summer till the daylight failed: 10
No chair remained before the doors; the bench
And threshold steps were empty; fast asleep
The laborer, and the old man who had sate
A later lingerer; yet the revelry
Continued and the loud uproar: at last,
When all the ground was dark, and twinkling stars
Edged the black clouds, home and to bed we went,
Feverish with weary joints and beating minds.
Ah! is there one who ever has been young,
Nor needs a warning voice to tame the pride   20
Of intellect and virtue's self-esteem?
One is there, though the wisest and the best
Of all mankind, who covets not at times
Union that cannot be;—who would not give
If so he might, to duty and to truth
The eagerness of infantine desire?
A tranquilizing spirit presses now
On my corporeal frame, so wide appears
The vacancy between me and those days
Which yet have such self-presence in my mind,   30
That, musing on them, often do I seem
Two consciousnesses, conscious of myself
And of some other Being. A rude mass
Of native rock, left midway in the square
Of our small market village, was the goal
Or center of these sports; and when, returned
After long absence, thither I repaired,
Gone was the old gray stone, and in its place
A smart Assembly-room usurped the ground
That had been ours. There let the fiddle scream,   40
And be ye happy! Yet, my Friends! I know

That more than one of you will think with me
Of those soft starry nights, and that old Dame
From whom the stone was named, who there had sate,
And watched her table with its huckster's wares
Assiduous, through the length of sixty years.

We ran a boisterous course; the year span round
With giddy motion. But the time approached
That brought with it a regular desire
For calmer pleasures, when the winning forms   50
Of Nature were collaterally attached
To every scheme of holiday delight
And every boyish sport, less grateful else
And languidly pursued.
                            When summer came,
Our pastime was, on bright half-holidays,
To sweep along the plain of Windermere
With rival oars; and the selected bourne
Was now an Island musical with birds
That sang and ceased not; now a Sister Isle
Beneath the oaks' umbrageous covert, sown   60
With lilies of the valley like a field;
And now a third small Island, where survived
In solitude the ruins of a shrine
Once to Our Lady dedicate, and served
Daily with chaunted rites. In such a race
So ended, disappointment could be none,
Uneasiness, or pain, or jealousy:
We rested in the shade, all pleased alike,
Conquered and conqueror. Thus the pride of strength,
And the vain-glory of superior skill,   70
Were tempered; thus was gradually produced
A quiet independence of the heart;
And to my Friend who knows me I may add,
Fearless of blame, that hence for future days
Ensued a diffidence and modesty,
And I was taught to feel, perhaps too much,
The self-sufficing power of Solitude.

Our daily meals were frugal, Sabine fare!
More than we wished we knew the blessing then
Of vigorous hunger—hence corporeal strength   80
Unsapped by delicate viands; for, exclude
A little weekly stipend, and we lived
Through three divisions of the quartered year
In penniless poverty. But now to school

From the half-yearly holidays returned,
We came with weightier purses, that sufficed
To furnish treats more costly than the Dame
Of the old gray stone, from her scant board, supplied.
Hence rustic dinners on the cool green ground,
Or in the woods, or by a river side   90
Or shady fountains, while among the leaves
Soft airs were stirring, and the mid-day sun
Unfelt shone brightly round us in our joy.
Nor is my aim neglected if I tell
How sometimes, in the length of those half-years,
We from our funds drew largely;—proud to curb,
And eager to spur on, the galloping steed;
And with the courteous inn-keeper, whose stud
Supplied our want, we haply might employ
Sly subterfuge, if the adventure's bound   100
Were distant: some famed temple where of yore
The Druids worshiped, or the antique walls
Of that large abbey, [20] where within the Vale
Of Nightshade, to St. Mary's honor built,
Stands yet a moldering pile with fractured arch,
Belfry, and images, and living trees;
A holy scene!—Along the smooth green turf
Our horses grazed. To more than inland peace,
Left by the west wind sweeping overhead
From a tumultuous ocean, trees and towers   110
In that sequestered valley may be seen,
Both silent and both motionless alike;
Such the deep shelter that is there, and such
The safeguard for repose and quietness.

Our steeds remounted and the summons given,
With whip and spur we through the chauntry flew
In uncouth race, and left the cross-legged knight
And the stone-abbot, and that single wren
Which one day sang so sweetly in the nave
Of the old church, that—though from recent showers   120
The earth was comfortless, and, touched by faint
Internal breezes, sobbings of the place
And respirations, from the roofless walls
The shuddering ivy dripped large drops—yet still
So sweetly 'mid the gloom the invisible bird
Sang to herself, that there I could have made
My dwelling-place, and lived for ever there
To hear such music. Through the walls we flew

20 Furness Abbey

And down the valley, and, a circuit made
In wantonness of heart, through rough and smooth   130
We scampered homewards. Oh, ye rocks and streams,
And that still spirit shed from evening air!
Even in this joyous time I sometimes felt
Your presence, when with slackened step we breathed
Along the sides of the steep hills, or when
Lighted by gleams of moonlight from the sea
We beat with thundering hoofs the level sand.

    Midway on long Winander's eastern shore,
Within the crescent of a pleasant bay,
A tavern stood; no homely-featured house,   140
Primeval like its neighboring cottages,
But 'twas a splendid place, the door beset
With chaises, grooms, and liveries, and within
Decanters, glasses, and the blood-red wine.
In ancient times, and ere the Hall was built
On the large island, had this dwelling been
More worthy of a poet's love, a hut,
Proud of its own bright fire and sycamore shade.
But—though the rhymes were gone that once inscribed
The threshold, and large golden characters,   150
Spread o'er the spangled sign-board, had dislodged
The old Lion and usurped his place, in slight
And mockery of the rustic painter's hand—
Yet, to this hour, the spot to me is dear
With all its foolish pomp. The garden lay
Upon a slope surmounted by a plain
Of a small bowling-green; beneath us stood
A grove, with gleams of water through the trees
And over the tree-tops; nor did we want
Refreshment, strawberries and mellow cream.   160
There, while through half an afternoon we played
On the smooth platform, whether skill prevailed
Or happy blunder triumphed, bursts of glee
Made all the mountains ring. But, ere night-fall,
When in our pinnace we returned at leisure
Over the shadowy lake, and to the beach
Of some small island steered our course with one,
The Minstrel of the Troop, and left him there,
And rowed off gently, while he blew his flute
Alone upon the rock—oh, then, the calm   170
And dead still water lay upon my mind
Even with a weight of pleasure, and the sky,
Never before so beautiful, sank down

Into my heart, and held me like a dream!
Thus were my sympathies enlarged, and thus
Daily the common range of visible things
Grew dear to me: already I began
To love the sun; a boy I loved the sun,
Not as I since have loved him, as a pledge
And surety of our earthly life, a light   180
Which we behold and feel we are alive;
Nor for his bounty to so many worlds—
But for this cause, that I had seen him lay
His beauty on the morning hills, had seen
The western mountain touch his setting orb,
In many a thoughtless hour, when, from excess
Of happiness, my blood appeared to flow
For its own pleasure, and I breathed with joy.
And, from like feelings, humble though intense,
To patriotic and domestic love   190
Analogous, the moon to me was dear;
For I could dream away my purposes,
Standing to gaze upon her while she hung
Midway between the hills, as if she knew
No other region, but belonged to thee,
Yea, appertained by a peculiar right
To thee and thy gray huts, thou one dear Vale!

   Those incidental charms which first attached
My heart to rural objects, day by day
Grew weaker, and I hasten on to tell   200
How Nature, intervenient till this time
And secondary, now at length was sought
For her own sake. But who shall parcel out
His intellect by geometric rules,
Split like a province into round and square?
Who knows the individual hour in which
His habits were first sown, even as a seed?
Who that shall point as with a wand and say
"This portion of the river of my mind
Came from yon fountain?" Thou, my Friend! art one   210
More deeply read in thy own thoughts; to thee
Science appears but what in truth she is,
Not as our glory and our absolute boast,
But as a succedaneum, and a prop
To our infirmity. No officious slave
Art thou of that false secondary power
By which we multiply distinctions, then
Deem that our puny boundaries are things

That we perceive, and not that we have made.
To thee, unblinded by these formal arts,   220
The unity of all hath been revealed,
And thou wilt doubt, with me less aptly skilled
Than many are to range the faculties
In scale and order, class the cabinet
Of their sensations, and in voluble phrase
Run through the history and birth of each
As of a single independent thing.
Hard task, vain hope, to analyze the mind,
If each most obvious and particular thought,
Not in a mystical and idle sense,   230
But in the words of Reason deeply weighed,
Hath no beginning.
                      Blest the infant Babe,
(For with my best conjecture I would trace
Our Being's earthly progress,) blest the Babe,
Nursed in his Mother's arms, who sinks to sleep
Rocked on his Mother's breast; who with his soul
Drinks in the feelings of his Mother's eye!
For him, in one dear Presence, there exists
A virtue which irradiates and exalts
Objects through widest intercourse of sense.   240
No outcast he, bewildered and depressed:
Along his infant veins are interfused
The gravitation and the filial bond
Of nature that connect him with the world.
Is there a flower, to which he points with hand
Too weak to gather it, already love
Drawn from love's purest earthly fount for him
Hath beautified that flower; already shades
Of pity cast from inward tenderness
Do fall around him upon aught that bears   250
Unsightly marks of violence or harm.
Emphatically such a Being lives,
Frail creature as he is, helpless as frail,
An inmate of this active universe:
For, feeling has to him imparted power
That through the growing faculties of sense
Doth like an agent of the one great Mind
Create, creator and receiver both,
Working but in alliance with the works
Which it beholds.—Such, verily, is the first   260
Poetic spirit of our human life,
By uniform control of after years,
In most, abated or suppressed; in some,

Through every change of growth and of decay,
Pre-eminent till death.
                                From early days,
Beginning not long after that first time
In which, a Babe, by intercourse of touch
I held mute dialogues with my Mother's heart,
I have endeavored to display the means
Whereby this infant sensibility,   270
Great birthright of our being, was in me
Augmented and sustained. Yet is a path
More difficult before me; and I fear
That in its broken windings we shall need
The chamois' sinews, and the eagle's wing:
For now a trouble came into my mind
From unknown causes. I was left alone
Seeking the visible world, not knowing why.
The props of my affections were removed,
And yet the building stood, as if sustained   280
By its own spirit! All that I beheld
Was dear, and hence to finer influxes
The mind lay open to a more exact
And close communion. Many are our joys
In youth, but oh! what happiness to live
When every hour brings palpable access
Of knowledge, when all knowledge is delight,
And sorrow is not there! The seasons came,
And every season wheresoe'er I moved
Unfolded transitory qualities,   290
Which, but for this most watchful power of love,
Had been neglected; left a register
Of permanent relations, else unknown.   •
Hence life, and change, and beauty, solitude
More active ever than "best society"—
Society made sweet as solitude
By silent inobtrusive sympathies,
And gentle agitations of the mind
From manifold distinctions, difference
Perceived in things, where, to the unwatchful eye,   300
No difference is, and hence, from the same source,
Sublimer joy; for I would walk alone,
Under the quiet stars, and at that time
Have felt whate'er there is of power in sound
To breathe an elevated mood, by form
Or image unprofaned; and I would stand,
If the night blackened with a coming storm,
Beneath some rock, listening to notes that are

The ghostly language of the ancient earth,
Or make their dim abode in distant winds. 310
Thence did I drink the visionary power;
And deem not profitless those fleeting moods
Of shadowy exultation: not for this,
That they are kindred to our purer mind
And intellectual life; but that the soul,
Remembering how she felt, but what she felt
Remembering not, retains an obscure sense
Of possible sublimity, whereto
With growing faculties she doth aspire,
With faculties still growing, feeling still 320
That whatsoever point they gain, they yet
Have something to pursue.
                               And not alone,
'Mid gloom and tumult, but no less 'mid fair
And tranquil scenes, that universal power
And fitness in the latent qualities
And essences of things, by which the mind
Is moved with feelings of delight, to me
Came strengthened with a superadded soul,
A virtue not its own. My morning walks
Were early;—oft before the hours of school 330
I traveled round our little lake, five miles
Of pleasant wandering. Happy time! more dear
For this, that one was by my side, a Friend,[21]
Then passionately loved; with heart how full
Would he peruse these lines! For many years
Have since flowed in between us, and, our minds
Both silent to each other, at this time
We live as if those hours had never been.
Nor seldom did I lift our cottage latch
Far earlier, ere one smoke-wreath had risen 340
From human dwelling, or the vernal thrush
Was audible; and sate among the woods
Alone upon some jutting eminence,
At the first gleam of dawn-light, when the Vale,
Yet slumbering, lay in utter solitude.
How shall I seek the origin? where find
Faith in the marvelous things which then I felt?
Oft in these moments such a holy calm
Would overspread my soul, that bodily eyes
Were utterly forgotten, and what I saw 350
Appeared like something in myself, a dream,
A prospect in the mind.

21 the Rev. John Flemming, of Rayrigg, Windermere

'Twere long to tell
What spring and autumn, what the winter snows,
And what the summer shade, what day and night,
Evening and morning, sleep and waking, thought
From sources inexhaustible, poured forth
To feed the spirit of religious love
In which I walked with Nature. But let this
Be not forgotten, that I still retained
My first creative sensibility;   360
That by the regular action of the world
My soul was unsubdued. A plastic power
Abode with me; a forming hand, at times
Rebellious, acting in a devious mood;
A local spirit of his own, at war
With general tendency, but, for the most,
Subservient strictly to external things
With which it communed. An auxiliar light
Came from my mind, which on the setting sun
Bestowed new splendor; the melodious birds,   370
The fluttering breezes, fountains that run on
Murmuring so sweetly in themselves, obeyed
A like dominion, and the midnight storm
Grew darker in the presence of my eye:
Hence my obeisance, my devotion hence,
And hence my transport.
                        Nor should this, perchance,
Pass unrecorded, that I still had loved
The exercise and produce of a toil,
Than analytic industry to me
More pleasing, and whose character I deem   380
Is more poetic as resembling more
Creative agency. The song would speak
Of that interminable building reared
By observation of affinities
In objects where no brotherhood exists
To passive minds. My seventeenth year was come,
And, whether from this habit rooted now
So deeply in my mind, or from excess
In the great social principle of life
Coercing all things into sympathy,   390
To unorganic natures were transferred
My own enjoyments; or the power of truth
Coming in revelation, did converse
With things that really are; I, at this time,
Saw blessings spread around me like a sea.
Thus while the days flew by, and years passed on,

From Nature and her overflowing soul,
I had received so much, that all my thoughts
Were steeped in feeling; I was only then
Contented, when with bliss ineffable   400
I felt the sentiment of Being spread
O'er all that moves and all that seemeth still;
O'er all that, lost beyond the reach of thought
And human knowledge, to the human eye
Invisible, yet liveth to the heart;
O'er all that leaps and runs, and shouts and sings,
Or beats the gladsome air; o'er all that glides
Beneath the wave, yea, in the wave itself,
And mighty depth of waters. Wonder not
If high the transport, great the joy I felt,   410
Communing in this sort through earth and heaven
With every form of creature, as it looked
Towards the Uncreated with a countenance
Of adoration, with an eye of love.
One song they sang, and it was audible,
Most audible, then, when the fleshly ear,
O'ercome by humblest prelude of that strain,
Forgot her functions, and slept undisturbed.

    If this be error, and another faith
Find easier access to the pious mind,   420
Yet were I grossly destitute of all
Those human sentiments that make this earth
So dear, if I should fail with grateful voice
To speak of you, ye mountains, and ye lakes
And sounding cataracts, ye mists and winds
That dwell among the hills where I was born.
If in my youth I have been pure in heart,
If, mingling with the world, I am content
With my own modest pleasures, and have lived
With God and Nature communing, removed   430
From little enmities and low desires—
The gift is yours; if in these times of fear,
This melancholy waste of hopes o'erthrown,
If, 'mid indifference and apathy,
And wicked exultation when good men
On every side fall off, we know not how,
To selfishness, disguised in gentle names
Of peace and quiet and domestic love
Yet mingled not unwillingly with sneers
On visionary minds; if, in this time   440
Of dereliction and dismay, I yet

Despair not of our nature, but retain
A more than Roman confidence, a faith
That fails not, in all sorrow my support,
The blessing of my life—the gift is yours,
Ye winds and sounding cataracts! 'tis yours,
Ye mountains! thine, O Nature! Thou hast fed
My lofty speculations; and in thee,
For this uneasy heart of ours, I find
A never-failing principle of joy   450
And purest passion.

       Thou, my Friend! wert reared
In the great city, 'mid far other scenes;
But we, by different roads, at length have gained
The selfsame bourne. And for this cause to thee
I speak, unapprehensive of contempt,
The insinuated scoff of coward tongues,
And all that silent language which so oft
In conversation between man and man
Blots from the human countenance all trace
Of beauty and of love. For thou hast sought   460
The truth in solitude, and, since the days
That gave thee liberty, full long desired,
To serve in Nature's temple, thou hast been
The most assiduous of her ministers;
In many things my brother, chiefly here
In this our deep devotion.

       Fare thee well!
Health and the quiet of a healthful mind
Attend thee! seeking oft the haunts of men,
And yet more often living with thyself,
And for thyself, so haply shall thy days   470
Be many, and a blessing to mankind.

MICHAEL [22]

A PASTORAL POEM

If from the public way you turn your steps
Up the tumultuous brook of Greenhead Ghyll,

---

[22] "Written at Town-end, Grasmere . . . The Sheepfold, on which so much of the poem turns, remains, or rather the ruins of it. The character and circumstances of Luke were taken from a family to whom had belonged, many years before, the house we lived in at Town-end, along with some fields and woodlands on the eastern shore of Grasmere. The name of the Evening Star was not in fact given to this house, but to another on the same side of the valley, more to the north." (Wordsworth)

You will suppose that with an upright path
Your feet must struggle; in such bold ascent
The pastoral mountains front you, face to face.
But, courage! for around that boisterous brook
The mountains have all opened out themselves,
And made a hidden valley of their own.
No habitation can be seen; but they
Who journey thither find themselves alone   10
With a few sheep, with rocks and stones, and kites
That overhead are sailing in the sky.
It is in truth an utter solitude;
Nor should I have made mention of this Dell
But for one object which you might pass by,
Might see and notice not. Beside the brook
Appears a straggling heap of unhewn stones!
And to that simple object appertains
A story—unenriched with strange events,
Yet not unfit, I deem, for the fireside,   20
Or for the summer shade. It was the first
Of those domestic tales that spake to me
Of shepherds, dwellers in the valleys, men
Whom I already loved; not verily
For their own sakes, but for the fields and hills
Where was their occupation and abode.
And hence this Tale, while I was yet a Boy
Careless of books, yet having felt the power
Of Nature, by the gentle agency
Of natural objects, led me on to feel   30
For passions that were not my own, and think
(At random and imperfectly indeed)
On man, the heart of man, and human life.
Therefore, although it be a history
Homely and rude, I will relate the same
For the delight of a few natural hearts;
And, with yet fonder feeling, for the sake
Of youthful Poets, who among these hills
Will be my second self when I am gone.

Upon the forest-side in Grasmere Vale   40
There dwelt a Shepherd, Michael was his name;
An old man, stout of heart, and strong of limb.
His bodily frame had been from youth to age
Of an unusual strength: his mind was keen,
Intense, and frugal, apt for all affairs,
And in his shepherd's calling he was prompt
And watchful more than ordinary men.

Hence had he learned the meaning of all winds,
Of blasts of every tone; and oftentimes,
When others heeded not, He heard the South 50
Make subterraneous music, like the noise
Of bagpipers on distant Highland hills.
The Shepherd, at such warning, of his flock
Bethought him, and he to himself would say,
"The winds are now devising work for me!"
And, truly, at all times, the storm, that drives
The traveler to a shelter, summoned him
Up to the mountains: he had been alone
Amid the heart of many thousand mists,
That came to him, and left him, on the heights. 60
So lived he till his eightieth year was past.
And grossly that man errs, who should suppose
That the green valleys, and the streams and rocks,
Were things indifferent to the Shepherd's thoughts.
Fields, where with cheerful spirits he had breathed
The common air; hills, which with vigorous step
He had so often climbed; which had impressed
So many incidents upon his mind
Of hardship, skill or courage, joy or fear;
Which, like a book, preserved the memory 70
Of the dumb animals, whom he had saved,
Had fed or sheltered, linking to such acts
The certainty of honorable gain;
Those fields, those hills—what could they less? had laid
Strong hold on his affections, were to him
A pleasurable feeling of blind love,
The pleasure which there is in life itself.
  His days had not been passed in singleness.
His Helpmate was a comely matron, old—
Though younger than himself full twenty years. 80
She was a woman of a stirring life,
Whose heart was in her house: two wheels she had
Of antique form; this large, for spinning wool;
That small, for flax; and if one wheel had rest
It was because the other was at work.
The Pair had but one inmate in their house,
An only Child, who had been born to them
When Michael, telling o'er his years, began
To deem that he was old,—in shepherd's phrase,
With one foot in the grave. This only Son, 90
With two brave sheep-dogs tried in many a storm,
The one of an inestimable worth,
Made all their household. I may truly say,

That they were as a proverb in the vale
For endless industry. When day was gone,
And from their occupations out of doors
The Son and Father were come home, even then,
Their labor did not cease; unless when all
Turned to the cleanly supper-board, and there,
Each with a mess of pottage and skimmed milk,   100
Sat round the basket piled with oaten cakes,
And their plain home-made cheese. Yet when the meal
Was ended, Luke (for so the Son was named)
And his old Father both betook themselves
To such convenient work as might employ
Their hands by the fireside; perhaps to card
Wool for the Housewife's spindle, or repair
Some injury done to sickle, flail, or scythe,
Or other implement of house or field.

    Down from the ceiling, by the chimney's edge,   110
That in our ancient uncouth country style
With huge and black projection overbrowed
Large space beneath, as duly as the light
Of day grew dim the Housewife hung a lamp;
An aged utensil, which had performed
Service beyond all others of its kind.
Early at evening did it burn—and late,
Surviving comrade of uncounted hours,
Which, going by from year to year, had found,
And left, the couple neither gay perhaps   120
Nor cheerful, yet with objects and with hopes,
Living a life of eager industry.
And now, when Luke had reached his eighteenth year,
There by the light of this old lamp they sate,
Father and Son, while far into the night
The Housewife plied her own peculiar work,
Making the cottage through the silent hours
Murmur as with the sound of summer flies.
This light was famous in its neighborhood,
And was a public symbol of the life   130
That thrifty Pair had lived. For, as it chanced,
Their cottage on a plot of rising ground
Stood single, with large prospect, north and south,
High into Easedale, up to Dunmail-Raise,
And westward to the village near the lake;
And from this constant light, so regular
And so far seen, the House itself, by all
Who dwelt within the limits of the vale,
Both old and young, was named *The Evening Star.*

Thus living on through such a length of years,   140
The Shepherd, if he loved himself, must needs
Have loved his Helpmate; but to Michael's heart
This son of his old age was yet more dear—
Less from instinctive tenderness, the same
Fond spirit that blindly works in the blood of all—
Than that a child, more than all other gifts
That earth can offer to declining man,
Brings hope with it, and forward-looking thoughts,
And stirrings of inquietude, when they
By tendency of nature needs must fail.   150
Exceeding was the love he bare to him,
His heart and his heart's joy! For oftentimes
Old Michael, while he was a babe in arms,
Had done him female service, not alone
For pastime and delight, as is the use
Of fathers, but with patient mind enforced
To acts of tenderness; and he had rocked
His cradle, as with a woman's gentle hand.
    And, in a later time, ere yet the Boy
Had put on boy's attire, did Michael love,   160
Albeit of a stern unbending mind,
To have the Young-one in his sight, when he
Wrought in the field, or on his shepherd's stool
Sat with a fettered sheep before him stretched
Under the large old oak, that near his door
Stood single, and, from matchless depth of shade,
Chosen for the Shearer's covert from the sun,
Thence in our rustic dialect was called
The CLIPPING TREE, a name which yet it bears.
There, while they two were sitting in the shade,   170
With others round them, earnest all and blithe,
Would Michael exercise his heart with looks
Of fond correction and reproof bestowed
Upon the Child, if he disturbed the sheep
By catching at their legs, or with his shouts
Scared them, while they lay still beneath the shears.
    And when by Heaven's good grace the boy grew up
A healthy Lad, and carried in his cheek
Two steady roses that were five years old;
Then Michael from a winter coppice cut   180
With his own hand a sapling, which he hooped
With iron, making it throughout in all
Due requisites a perfect shepherd's staff,
And gave it to the Boy; wherewith equipped
He as a watchman oftentimes was placed

At gate or gap, to stem or turn the flock;
And, to his office prematurely called,
There stood the urchin, as you will divine,
Something between a hindrance and a help;
And for this cause not always, I believe,   190
Receiving from his Father hire of praise;
Though nought was left undone which staff, or voice,
Or looks, or threatening gestures, could perform.

But soon as Luke, full ten years old, could stand
Against the mountain blasts; and to the heights,
Not fearing toil, nor length of weary ways,
He with his Father daily went, and they
Were as companions, why should I relate
That objects which the Shepherd loved before
Were dearer now? that from the Boy there came   200
Feelings and emanations—things which were
Light to the sun and music to the wind;
And that the old Man's heart seemed born again?

Thus in his Father's sight the Boy grew up:
And now, when he had reached his eighteenth year,
He was his comfort and his daily hope.

While in this sort the simple household lived
From day to day, to Michael's ear there came
Distressful tidings. Long before the time
Of which I speak, the Shepherd had been bound   210
In surety for his brother's son, a man
Of an industrious life, and ample means;
But unforeseen misfortunes suddenly
Had pressed upon him; and old Michael now
Was summoned to discharge the forfeiture,
A grievous penalty, but little less
Than half his substance. This unlooked-for claim,
At the first hearing, for a moment took
More hope out of his life than he supposed
That any old man ever could have lost.   220
As soon as he had armed himself with strength
To look his trouble in the face, it seemed
The Shepherd's sole resource to sell at once
A portion of his patrimonial fields.
Such was his first resolve; he thought again,
And his heart failed him. "Isabel," said he,
Two evenings after he had heard the news,
"I have been toiling more than seventy years,
And in the open sunshine of God's love
Have we all lived; yet if these fields of ours   230
Should pass into a stranger's hand, I think

That I could not lie quiet in my grave.
Our lot is a hard lot; the sun himself
Has scarcely been more diligent than I;
And I have lived to be a fool at last
To my own family. An evil man
That was, and made an evil choice, if he
Were false to us; and if he were not false,
There are ten thousand to whom loss like this
Had been no sorrow. I forgive him;—but   240
'Twere better to be dumb than to talk thus.
  "When I began, my purpose was to speak
Of remedies and of a cheerful hope.
Our Luke shall leave us, Isabel; the land
Shall not go from us, and it shall be free;
He shall possess it, free as is the wind
That passes over it. We have, thou know'st,
Another kinsman—he will be our friend
In this distress. He is a prosperous man,
Thriving in trade—and Luke to him shall go,   250
And with his kinsman's help and his own thrift
He quickly will repair this loss, and then
He may return to us. If here he stay,
What can be done? Where every one is poor,
What can be gained?"
                    At this the old Man paused,
And Isabel sat silent, for her mind
Was busy, looking back into past time.
There's Richard Bateman, thought she to herself,
He was a parish-boy—at the church-door
They made a gathering for him, shillings, pence,   260
And halfpennies, wherewith the neighbors bought
A basket, which they filled with pedlar's wares;
And, with this basket on his arm, the lad
Went up to London, found a master there,
Who, out of many, chose the trusty boy
To go and overlook his merchandise
Beyond the seas; where he grew wondrous rich,
And left estates and monies to the poor.
And, at his birthplace, built a chapel, floored
With marble which he sent from foreign lands.   270
These thoughts, and many others of like sort,
Passed quickly through the mind of Isabel,
And her face brightened. The old Man was glad,
And thus resumed:—"Well, Isabel! this scheme
These two days, has been meat and drink to me.
Far more than we have lost is left us yet.

—We have enough—I wish indeed that I
Were younger;—but this hope is a good hope.
—Make ready Luke's best garments, of the best
Buy for him more, and let us send him forth   280
To-morrow, or the next day, or to-night:
—If he *could* go, the Boy should go to-night."
    Here Michael ceased, and to the fields went forth
With a light heart. The Housewife for five days
Was restless morn and night, and all day long
Wrought on with her best fingers to prepare
Things needful for the journey of her son.
But Isabel was glad when Sunday came
To stop her in her work: for, when she lay
By Michael's side, she through the last two nights   290
Heard him, how he was troubled in his sleep:
And when they rose at morning she could see
That all his hopes were gone. That day at noon,
She said to Luke, while they two by themselves
Were sitting at the door, "Thou must not go:
We have no other Child but thee to lose—
None to remember—do not go away,
For if thou leave thy Father he will die."
The Youth made answer with a jocund voice;
And Isabel, when she had told her fears,   300
Recovered heart. That evening her best fare
Did she bring forth, and all together sat
Like happy people round a Christmas fire.
    With daylight Isabel resumed her work;
And all the ensuing week the house appeared
As cheerful as a grove in Spring: at length
The expected letter from their kinsman came
With kind assurances that he would do
His utmost for the welfare of the Boy;
To which, requests were added, that forthwith   310
He might be sent to him. Ten times or more
The letter was read over; Isabel
Went forth to show it to the neighbors round;
Nor was there at that time on English land
A prouder heart than Luke's. When Isabel
Had to her house returned, the old Man said,
"He shall depart to-morrow." To this word
The Housewife answered, talking much of things
Which, if at such short notice he should go,
Would surely be forgotten. But at length   320
She gave consent, and Michael was at ease.
    Near the tumultuous brook of Greenhead Ghyll,

In that deep valley, Michael had designed
To build a Sheepfold; and, before he heard
The tidings of his melancholy loss,
For this same purpose he had gathered up
A heap of stones, which by the streamlet's edge
Lay thrown together, ready for the work.
With Luke that evening thitherward he walked:
And soon as they had reached the place he stopped, 330
And thus the old Man spake to him:—"My Son,
To-morrow thou wilt leave me: with full heart
I look upon thee, for thou art the same
That wert a promise to me ere thy birth,
And all thy life hast been my daily joy.
I will relate to thee some little part
Of our two histories; 'twill do thee good
When thou art from me, even if I should touch
On things thou canst not know of.—After thou
First cam'st into the world—as oft befalls 340
To new-born infants—thou didst sleep away
Two days, and blessings from thy Father's tongue
Then fell upon thee. Day by day passed on,
And still I loved thee with increasing love.
Never to living ear came sweeter sounds
Than when I heard thee by our own fireside
First uttering, without words, a natural tune;
While thou, a feeding babe, didst in thy joy
Sing at thy Mother's breast. Month followed month,
And in the open fields my life was passed 350
And on the mountains; else I think that thou
Hadst been brought up upon thy Father's knees.
But we were playmates, Luke: among these hills,
As well thou knowest, in us the old and young
Have played together, nor with me didst thou
Lack any pleasure which a boy can know."
Luke had a manly heart; but at these words
He sobbed aloud. The old Man grasped his hand,
And said, "Nay, do not take it so—I see
That these are things of which I need not speak. 360
—Even to the utmost I have been to thee
A kind and a good Father: and herein
I but repay a gift which I myself
Received at others' hands; for, though now old
Beyond the common life of man, I still
Remember them who loved me in my youth.
Both of them sleep together: here they lived,
As all their Forefathers had done; and when

At length their time was come, they were not loth
To give their bodies to the family mold.   370
I wished that thou should'st live the life they lived:
But, 'tis a long time to look back, my Son,
And see so little gain from threescore years.
These fields were burthened when they came to me;
Till I was forty years of age, not more
Than half of my inheritance was mine.
I toiled and toiled; God blessed me in my work,
And till these three weeks past the land was free.
—It looks as if it never could endure
Another Master. Heaven forgive me, Luke,   380
If I judge ill for thee, but it seems good
That thou should'st go."
        At this the old Man paused;
Then, pointing to the stones near which they stood,
Thus, after a short silence, he resumed:
"This was a work for us; and now, my Son,
It is a work for me. But, lay one stone—
Here, lay it for me, Luke, with thine own hands.
Nay, Boy, be of good hope;—we both may live
To see a better day. At eighty-four
I still am strong and hale;—do thou thy part;   390
I will do mine.—I will begin again
With many tasks that were resigned to thee:
Up to the heights, and in among the storms,
Will I without thee go again, and do
All works which I was wont to do alone,
Before I knew thy face.—Heaven bless thee, Boy!
Thy heart these two weeks has been beating fast
With many hopes; it should be so—yes—yes—
I knew that thou could'st never have a wish
To leave me, Luke: thou hast been bound to me   400
Only by links of love: when thou art gone,
What will be left to us!—But, I forget
My purposes. Lay now the corner-stone,
As I requested; and hereafter, Luke,
When thou art gone away, should evil men
Be thy companions, think of me, my Son,
And of this moment; hither turn thy thoughts,
And God will strengthen thee: amid all fear
And all temptation, Luke, I pray that thou
May'st bear in mind the life thy Fathers lived,   410
Who, being innocent, did for that cause
Bestir them in good deeds. Now, fare thee well—
When thou return'st, thou in this place wilt see

A work which is not here: a covenant
'Twill be between us; but, whatever fate
Befall thee, I shall love thee to the last,
And bear thy memory with me to the grave."
    The Shepherd ended here; and Luke stooped down,
And, as his Father had requested, laid
The first stone of the Sheepfold. At the sight   420
The old Man's grief broke from him; to his heart
He pressed his Son, he kissèd him and wept:
And to the house together they returned.
—Hushed was that House in peace, or seeming peace,
Ere the night fell:—with morrow's dawn the Boy
Began his journey, and when he had reached
The public way, he put on a bold face;
And all the neighbors, as he passed their doors,
Came forth with wishes and with farewell prayers,
That followed him till he was out of sight.   430
    A good report did from their Kinsman come,
Of Luke and his well-doing: and the Boy
Wrote loving letters, full of wondrous news,
Which, as the Housewife phrased it, were throughout
"The prettiest letters that were ever seen."
Both parents read them with rejoicing hearts.
So, many months passed on: and once again
The Shepherd went about his daily work
With confident and cheerful thoughts; and now
Sometimes when he could find a leisure hour   440
He to that valley took his way, and there
Wrought at the Sheepfold. Meantime Luke began
To slacken in his duty; and, at length,
He in the dissolute city gave himself
To evil courses: ignominy and shame
Fell on him, so that he was driven at last
To seek a hiding-place beyond the seas.
    There is a comfort in the strength of love;
'Twill make a thing endurable, which else
Would overset the brain, or break the heart: 450
I have conversed with more than one who well
Remember the old Man, and what he was
Years after he had heard this heavy news.
His bodily frame had been from youth to age
Of an unusual strength. Among the rocks
He went, and still looked up to sun and cloud,
And listened to the wind; and, as before,
Performed all kinds of labor for his sheep,
And for the land, his small inheritance.

And to that hollow dell from time to time 460
Did he repair, to build the Fold of which
His flock had need. 'Tis not forgotten yet
The pity which was then in every heart
For the old Man—and 'tis believed by all
That many and many a day he thither went,
And never lifted up a single stone.
There, by the Sheepfold, sometimes was he seen
Sitting alone, or with his faithful Dog,
Then old, beside him, lying at his feet.
The length of full seven years, from time to time, 470
He at the building of this Sheepfold wrought,
And left the work unfinished when he died.
Three years, or little more, did Isabel
Survive her Husband: at her death the estate
Was sold, and went into a stranger's hand.
The Cottage which was named THE EVENING STAR
Is gone—the plowshare has been through the ground
On which it stood; great changes have been wrought
In all the neighborhood:—yet the oak is left
That grew beside their door; and the remains 480
Of the unfinished Sheepfold may be seen
Beside the boisterous brook of Greenhead Ghyll.

MY HEART LEAPS UP

My heart leaps up when I behold
   A rainbow in the sky:
So was it when my life began;
So is it now I am a man;
So be it when I shall grow old,
   Or let me die!
The Child is father of the Man;
And I could wish my days to be
Bound each to each by natural piety.

RESOLUTION AND INDEPENDENCE

I

THERE was a roaring in the wind all night;
The rain came heavily and fell in floods;
But now the sun is rising calm and bright;
The birds are singing in the distant woods;
Over his own sweet voice the Stock-dove broods;
The Jay makes answer as the Magpie chatters;
And all the air is filled with pleasant noise of waters.

2

All things that love the sun are out of doors;
The sky rejoices in the morning's birth;
The grass is bright with rain-drops;—on the moors
The hare is running races in her mirth;
And with her feet she from the plashy earth
Raises a mist; that, glittering in the sun,
Runs with her all the way, wherever she doth run.

3

I was a Traveler then upon the moor,
I saw the hare that raced about with joy;
I heard the woods and distant waters roar;
Or heard them not, as happy as a boy:
The pleasant season did my heart employ:
My old remembrances went from me wholly;
And all the ways of men, so vain and melancholy.

4

But, as it sometimes chanceth, from the might
Of joy in minds that can no further go,
As high as we have mounted in delight
In our dejection do we sink as low;
To me that morning did it happen so;
And fears and fancies thick upon me came;
Dim sadness—and blind thoughts, I knew not, nor could name.

5

I heard the sky-lark warbling in the sky;
And I bethought me of the playful hare:
Even such a happy Child of earth am I;
Even as these blissful creatures do I fare;
Far from the world I walk, and from all care;
But there may come another day to me—
Solitude, pain of heart, distress, and poverty.

6

My whole life I have lived in pleasant thought,
As if life's business were a summer mood;
As if all needful things would come unsought
To genial faith, still rich in genial good;
But how can He expect that others should

Build for him, sow for him, and at his call
Love him, who for himself will take no heed at all?

7

I thought of Chatterton,[23] the marvelous Boy,
The sleepless Soul that perished in his pride;
Of him who walked in glory and in joy
Following his plow, along the mountainside:
By our own spirits are we deified:
We Poets in our youth begin in gladness;
But thereof come in the end despondency and madness.

8

Now, whether it were by peculiar grace,
A leading from above, a something given,
Yet it befell that, in this lonely place,
When I with these untoward thoughts had striven,
Beside a pool bare to the eye of heaven
I saw a Man before me unawares:
The oldest man he seemed that ever wore gray hairs.

9

As a huge stone is sometimes seen to lie
Couched on the bald top of an eminence;
Wonder to all who do the same espy,
By what means it could thither come, and whence;
So that it seems a thing endued with sense:
Like a sea-beast crawled forth, that on a shelf
Of rock or sand reposeth, there to sun itself;

10

Such seemed this Man, not all alive nor dead,
Nor all asleep—in his extreme old age:
His body was bent double, feet and head
Coming together in life's pilgrimage;
As if some dire constraint of pain, or rage
Of sickness felt by him in times long past,
A more than human weight upon his frame had cast.

11

Himself he propped, limbs, body, and pale face,
Upon a long gray staff of shaven wood:

---

23 Precocious poet, who killed himself in 1770 at the age of eighteen. The following lines refer to Burns.

And, still as I drew near with gentle pace,
Upon the margin of that moorish flood
Motionless as a cloud the old Man stood,
That heareth not the loud winds when they call
And moveth all together, if it move at all.

12

At length, himself unsettling, he the pond
Stirred with his staff, and fixedly did look
Upon the muddy water, which he conned,
As if he had been reading in a book:
And now a stranger's privilege I took;
And, drawing to his side, to him did say,
"This morning gives us promise of a glorious day."

13

A gentle answer did the old Man make,
In courteous speech which forth he slowly **drew**:
And him with further words I thus bespake,
"What occupation do you there pursue?
This is a lonesome place for one like you."
Ere he replied, a flash of mild surprise
Broke from the sable orbs of his yet-vivid **eyes**,

14

His words came feebly, from a feeble chest,
But each in solemn order followed each,
With something of a lofty utterance dressed—
Choice word and measured phrase, above the reach
Of ordinary men; a stately speech;
Such as grave livers do in Scotland use,
Religious men, who give to God and man their **dues.**

15

He told, that to these waters he had come
To gather leeches, being old and poor:
Employment hazardous and wearisome!
And he had many hardships to endure:
From pond to pond he roamed, from moor to moor;
Housing, with God's good help, by choice or chance,
And in this way he gained an honest maintenance.

16

The old Man still stood talking by my side;
But now his voice to me was like a stream
Scarce heard; nor word from word could I divide;
And the whole body of the Man did seem
Like one whom I had met with in a dream;
Or like a man from some far region sent,
To give me human strength, by apt admonishment.

17

My former thoughts returned: the fear that kills;
And hope that is unwilling to be fed;
Cold, pain, and labor, and all fleshly ills;
And mighty Poets in their misery dead.
—Perplexed, and longing to be comforted,
My question eagerly did I renew,
"How is it that you live, and what is it you do?"

18

He with a smile did then his words repeat;
And said, that, gathering leeches, far and wide
He traveled; stirring thus above his feet
The waters of the pools where they abide.
"Once I could meet with them on every side;
But they have dwindled long by slow decay;
Yet still I persevere, and find them where I may."

19

While he was talking thus, the lonely place,
The old Man's shape, and speech—all troubled me:
In my mind's eye I seemed to see him pace
About the weary moors continually,
Wandering about alone and silently.
While I these thoughts within myself pursued,
He, having made a pause, the same discourse renewed.

20

And soon with this he other matter blended,
Cheerfully uttered, with demeanor kind,
But stately in the main; and when he ended,
I could have laughed myself to scorn to find

In that decrepit Man so firm a mind.
"God," said I, "be my help and stay secure;
I'll think of the Leech-gatherer on the lonely moor!"

COMPOSED UPON WESTMINSTER BRIDGE,
SEPTEMBER 3, 1802

EARTH has not anything to show more fair:
Dull would he be of soul who could pass by
A sight so touching in its majesty:
This City now doth, like a garment, wear
The beauty of the morning; silent, bare,
Ships, towers, domes, theaters, and temples lie
Open unto the fields, and to the sky;
All bright and glittering in the smokeless air.
Never did sun more beautifully steep
In his first splendor, valley, rock, or hill;
Ne'er saw I, never felt, a calm so deep!
The river glideth at his own sweet will:
Dear God! the very houses seem asleep;
And all that mighty heart is lying still!

COMPOSED BY THE SEASIDE, NEAR CALAIS,
AUGUST, 1802

FAIR Star of evening, Splendor of the west,
Star of my Country!—on the horizon's brink
Thou hangest, stooping, as might seem, to sink
On England's bosom, yet well pleased to rest,
Meanwhile, and be to her a glorious crest
Conspicuous to the Nations. Thou, I think,
Shouldst be my Country's emblem; and shouldst wink,
Bright Star! with laughter on her banners, dressed
In thy fresh beauty. There! that dusky spot
Beneath thee, that is England; there she lies.
Blessings be on you both! one hope, one lot,
One life, one glory!—I, with many a fear
For my dear Country, many heartfelt sighs,
Among men who do not love her, linger here.

IT IS A BEAUTEOUS EVENING, CALM AND FREE

IT IS a beauteous evening, calm and free,
The holy time is quiet as a Nun
Breathless with adoration; the broad sun
Is sinking down in its tranquillity;

The gentleness of heaven broods o'er the Sea:
Listen! the mighty Being is awake,
And doth with his eternal motion make
A sound like thunder—everlastingly.
Dear Child! [24] dear Girl! that walkest with me here,
If thou appear untouched by solemn thought,
Thy nature is not therefore less divine:
Thou liest in Abraham's bosom all the year,
And worship'st at the Temple's inner shrine,
God being with thee when we know it not.

ON THE EXTINCTION OF THE VENETIAN
REPUBLIC [25]

ONCE did She hold the gorgeous east in fee;
And was the safeguard of the west: the worth
Of Venice did not fall below her birth,
Venice, the eldest Child of Liberty.
She was a maiden City, bright and free;
No guile seduced, no force could violate;
And, when she took unto herself a Mate,
She must espouse the everlasting Sea.[26]
And what if she had seen those glories fade,
Those titles vanish, and that strength decay;
Yet shall some tribute of regret be paid
When her long life hath reached its final day:
Men are we, and must grieve when even the Shade
Of that which once was great is passed away.

TO TOUSSAINT L'OUVERTURE [27]

TOUSSAINT, the most unhappy man of men!
Whether the whistling Rustic tend his plow
Within thy hearing, or thy head be now
Pillowed in some deep dungeon's earless den;—
O miserable Chieftain! where and when
Wilt thou find patience? Yet die not; do thou
Wear rather in thy bonds a cheerful brow:
Though fallen thyself, never to rise again,
Live, and take comfort. Thou hast left behind
Powers that will work for thee; air, earth, and skies;
There's not a breathing of the common wind

24 Wordsworth's French daughter, Caroline
25 by Napoleon in 1797
26 referring to the annual ceremony of the Doge's throwing a ring into the sea to symbolize Venice's marriage to the Adriatic
27 Haitian negro who freed the slaves on San Domingo, was captured by the French, and died a prisoner in France in 1803

That will forget thee; thou hast great allies;
Thy friends are exultations, agonies,
And love, and man's unconquerable mind.

NEAR DOVER, SEPTEMBER, 1802

INLAND, within a hollow vale, I stood;
And saw, while sea was calm and air was clear,
The coast of France—the coast of France how near!
Drawn almost into frightful neighborhood.
I shrunk; for verily the barrier flood
Was like a lake, or river bright and fair,
A span of waters; yet what power is there!
What mightiness for evil and for good!
Even so doth God protect us if we be
Virtuous and wise. Winds blow, and waters roll,
Strength to the brave, and Power, and Deity;
Yet in themselves are nothing! One decree
Spake laws to *them,* and said that by the soul
Only, the Nations shall be great and free.

IN LONDON, SEPTEMBER, 1802 [28]

O FRIEND! I know not which way I must look
For comfort, being, as I am, oppressed,
To think that now our life is only dressed
For show; mean handy-work of craftsman, cook,
Or groom!—We must run glittering like a brook
In the open sunshine, or we are unblessed:
The wealthiest man among us is the best:
No grandeur now in nature or in book
Delights us. Rapine, avarice, expense,
This is idolatry; and these we adore:
Plain living and high thinking are no more:
The homely beauty of the good old cause
Is gone; our peace, our fearful innocence,
And pure religion breathing household laws.

---

[28] "This was written immediately after my return from France to London, when I could not but be struck, as here described, with the vanity and parade of our own country, especially in great towns and cities, as contrasted with the quiet, and I may say the desolation, that the revolution had produced in France. This must be borne in mind, or else the reader may think that in this and the succeeding sonnets I have exaggerated the mischief engendered and fostered among us by undisturbed wealth. It would not be easy to conceive with what a depth of feeling I entered into the struggle carried on by the Spaniards for their deliverance from the usurped power of the French. Many times have I gone from Allan Bank in Grasmere vale, where we were then residing, to the top of the Raise-gap as it is called, so late as two o'clock in the morning, to meet the carrier bringing the newspaper from Keswick." (Wordsworth)

LONDON, 1802

MILTON! thou shouldst be living at this hour:
England hath need of thee: she is a fen
Of stagnant waters: altar, sword, and pen,
Fireside, the heroic wealth of hall and bower,
Have forfeited their ancient English dower
Of inward happiness. We are selfish men;
Oh! raise us up, return to us again;
And give us manners, virtue, freedom, power.
Thy soul was like a Star, and dwelt apart;
Thou hadst a voice whose sound was like the sea:
Pure as the naked heavens, majestic, free,
So didst thou travel on life's common way,
In cheerful godliness; and yet thy heart
The lowliest duties on herself did lay.

GREAT MEN HAVE BEEN AMONG US

GREAT men have been among us; hands that penned
And tongues that uttered wisdom—better none:
The later Sidney, Marvel, Harrington,
Young Vane,[29] and others who called Milton friend.
These moralists could act and comprehend:
They knew how genuine glory was put on;
Taught us how rightfully a nation shone
In splendor: what strength was, that would not bend
But in magnanimous meekness. France, 'tis strange,
Hath brought forth no such souls as we had then,
Perpetual emptiness! unceasing change!
No single volume paramount, no code,
No master spirit, no determined road;
But equally a want of books and men!

IT IS NOT TO BE THOUGHT OF

IT is not to be thought of that the Flood
Of British freedom, which, to the open sea
Of the world's praise, from dark antiquity
Hath flowed, "with pomp of waters, unwithstood,"[30]
Roused though it be full often to a mood
Which spurns the check of salutary bands,
That this most famous Stream in bogs and sands

---

29 Algernon   Sidney   Harrington (1611–1677), and   *War*, Bk. II, Stanza 7
(1622–1683), Andrew Mar-   Sir Henry Vane (1613–1662)
vell   (1621–1678),   James   30 Samuel Daniel, *Civil*

Should perish; and to evil and to good
Be lost for ever. In our halls is hung
Armory of the invincible Knights of old:
We must be free or die, who speak the tongue
That Shakespeare spake; the faith and morals hold
Which Milton held.—In everything we are sprung
Of Earth's first blood, have titles manifold.

WHEN I HAVE BORNE IN MEMORY

WHEN I have borne in memory what has tamed
Great Nations, how ennobling thoughts depart
When men change swords for ledgers, and desert
The student's bower for gold, some fears unnamed
I had, my Country!—am I to be blamed?
Now, when I think of thee, and what thou art,
Verily, in the bottom of my heart,
Of those unfilial fears I am ashamed.
For dearly must we prize thee; we who find
In thee a bulwark for the cause of men:
And I by my affection was beguiled:
What wonder if a Poet now and then,
Among the many movements of his mind,
Felt for thee as a lover or a child!

AT THE GRAVE OF BURNS
SEVEN YEARS AFTER HIS DEATH

I SHIVER, Spirit fierce and bold,
At thought of what I now behold:
As vapors breathed from dungeons cold,
    Strike pleasure dead,
So sadness comes from out the mold
    Where Burns is laid.

And have I then thy bones so near,
And thou forbidden to appear?
As if it were thyself that's here
    I shrink with pain;
And both my wishes and my fear
    Alike are vain.

Off weight—nor press on weight!—away
Dark thoughts!—they came, but not to stay;
With chastened feelings would I pay
    The tribute due

To him, and aught that hides his clay
    From mortal view.

Fresh as the flower, whose modest worth
He sang, his genius "glinted" forth,   20
Rose like a star that touching earth,
    For so it seems,
Doth glorify its humble birth
    With matchless beams.

The piercing eye, the thoughtful brow,
The struggling heart, where be they now?—
Full soon the Aspirant of the plow,
    The prompt, the brave,
Slept, with the obscurest, in the low
    And silent grave.   30

I mourned with thousands, but as one
More deeply grieved, for he was gone
Whose light I hailed when first it shone,
    And showed my youth
How verse may build a princely throne
    On humble truth.

Alas! where'er the current tends,
Regret pursues and with it blends,—
Huge Criffel's hoary top ascends
    By Skiddaw seen,[31]   40
Neighbors we were, and loving friends
    We might have been;

True friends though diversely inclined;
But heart with heart and mind with mind,
Where the main fibers are entwined,
    Through Nature's skill,
May even by contraries be joined
    More closely still.

The tear will start, and let it flow;
Thou "poor inhabitant below,"   50
At this dread moment—even so—
    Might we together
Have sate and talked where gowans[32] blow,
    Or on wild heather.

[31] a mountain in Scot-   land, not far from the   [32] daisies
land, and one in Cumber-   Scotch border

What treasures would have then been placed
Within my reach; of knowledge graced
By fancy what a rich repast!
  But why go on?—
Oh! spare to sweep, thou mournful blast,
  His grave grass-grown.   60

There too, a son, his joy and pride,
(Not three weeks past the stripling died,)
Lies gathered to his Father's side,
  Soul-moving sight!
Yet one to which is not denied
  Some sad delight:

For *he* is safe, a quiet bed
Hath early found among the dead,
Harbored where none can be misled,
  Wronged, or distressed;   70
And surely here it may be said
  That such are blest.

And oh for thee, by pitying grace
Checked oft-times in a devious race,
May He who halloweth the place
  Where man is laid
Receive thy spirit in the embrace
  For which it prayed!

Sighing I turned away; but ere
Night fell I heard, or seemed to hear   80
Music that sorrow comes not near,
  A ritual hymn,
Chanted in love that casts out fear
  By seraphim.

THE SOLITARY REAPER

Behold her, single in the field,
Yon solitary Highland Lass!
Reaping and singing by herself;
Stop here, or gently pass!
Alone she cuts and binds the grain,
And sings a melancholy strain;
O listen! for the Vale profound
Is overflowing with the sound.

No Nightingale did ever chaunt
More welcome notes to weary bands   10
Of travelers in some shady haunt,
Among Arabian sands:
A voice so thrilling ne'er was heard
In spring-time from the Cuckoo-bird,
Breaking the silence of the seas
Among the farthest Hebrides.

Will no one tell me what she sings?—
Perhaps the plaintive numbers flow
For old, unhappy, far-off things,
And battles long ago: 20
Or is it some more humble lay,
Familiar matter of to-day?
Some natural sorrow, loss, or pain,
That has been, and may be again?

Whate'er the theme, the Maiden sang
As if her song could have no ending;
I saw her singing at her work,
And o'er the sickle bending;—
I listened, motionless and still;
And, as I mounted up the hill   30
The music in my heart I bore,
Long after it was heard no more.

YARROW UNVISITED

FROM Stirling castle we had seen
The mazy Forth unraveled;
Had trod the banks of Clyde, and Tay,
And with the Tweed had traveled;
And when we came to Clovenford,
Then said my *"winsome Marrow,"* 33
"Whate'er betide, we'll turn aside,
And see the Braes of Yarrow."

"Let Yarrow folk, *frae* Selkirk town,
Who have been buying, selling,   10
Go back to Yarrow, 'tis their own;
Each maiden to her dwelling!
On Yarrow's banks let herons feed,
Hares couch, and rabbits burrow!

---

33 partner, *i.e.,* Dorothy Wordsworth. These words and line 35 below are from a
ballad, *The Braes of Yarrow*, by Hamilton of Bangour.

But we will downward with the Tweed,
Nor turn aside to Yarrow.

"There's Galla Water, Leader Haughs,[34]
Both lying right before us;
And Dryborough, where with chiming Tweed
The lintwhites [35] sing in chorus;
There's pleasant Tiviot-dale, a land
Made blithe with plow and harrow:
Why throw away a needful day
To go in search of Yarrow?   20

"What's Yarrow but a river bare,
That glides the dark hills under?
There are a thousand such elsewhere
As worthy of your wonder."
—Strange words they seemed of slight and scorn;
My True-love sighed for sorrow;   30
And looked me in the face, to think
I thus could speak of Yarrow!

"Oh! green," said I, "are Yarrow's holms,
And sweet is Yarrow flowin;!
Fair hangs the apple frae the rock,
But we will leave it growing.
O'er hilly path, and open Strath,[36]
We'll wander Scotland thorough;
But, though so near, we will not turn
Into the dale of Yarrow.   40

"Let beeves and home-bred kine partake
The sweets of Burn-mill meadow;
The swan on still St. Mary's Lake
Float double, swan and shadow!
We will not see them; will not go,
To-day, nor yet to-morrow,
Enough if in our hearts we know
There's such a place as Yarrow.

"Be Yarrow stream unseen, unknown!
It must, or we shall rue it: 50
We have a vision of our own;
Ah! why should we undo it?
The treasured dreams of times long past,
We'll keep them, winsome Marrow!

---

34 holms, lowlands   35 linnets   36 valley

For when we're there, although 'tis fair,
'Twill be another Yarrow!

"If Care with freezing years should come,
And wandering seem but folly,—
Should we be loath to stir from home,
And yet be melancholy;   60
Should life be dull, and spirits low,
'Twill soothe us in our sorrow,
That earth has something yet to show,
The bonny holms of Yarrow!"

TO THE CUCKOO

O BLITHE New-comer! I have heard,
I hear thee and rejoice.
O Cuckoo! shall I call thee Bird,
Or but a wandering Voice?

While I am lying on the grass
Thy twofold shout I hear,
From hill to hill it seems to pass,
At once far off, and near.

Though babbling only to the Vale,
Of sunshine and of flowers,   10
Thou bringest unto me a tale
Of visionary hours.

Thrice welcome, darling of the Spring!
Even yet thou art to me
No bird, but an invisible thing,
A voice, a mystery;

The same whom in my school-boy days
I listened to; that Cry
Which made me look a thousand ways
In bush, and tree, and sky.   20

To seek thee did I often rove
Through woods and on the green;
And thou wert still a hope, a love;
Still longed for, never seen.

And I can listen to thee yet;
Can lie upon the plain

And listen, till I do beget
That golden time again.

O blessèd Bird! the earth we pace
Again appears to be
An unsubstantial, faery place;
That is fit home for Thee!

30

SHE WAS A PHANTOM OF DELIGHT

She was a Phantom of delight
When first she gleamed upon my sight;
A lovely Apparition, sent
To be a moment's ornament;
Her eyes as stars of Twilight fair;
Like Twilight's, too, her dusky hair;
But all things else about her drawn
From May-time and the cheerful Dawn;
A dancing Shape, an Image gay,
To haunt, to startle, and waylay.

10

I saw her upon nearer view,
A Spirit, yet a Woman too!
Her household motions light and free,
And steps of virgin-liberty;
A countenance in which did meet
Sweet records, promises as sweet;
A Creature not too bright or good
For human nature's daily food;
For transient sorrows, simple wiles,
Praise, blame, love, kisses, tears, and smiles.

20

And now I see with eye serene
The very pulse of the machine;
A Being breathing thoughtful breath,
A Traveler between life and death;
The reason firm, the temperate will,
Endurance, foresight, strength, and skill;
A perfect Woman, nobly planned,
To warn, to comfort, and command;
And yet a Spirit still, and bright
With something of angelic light.

30

I WANDERED LONELY AS A CLOUD

I wandered lonely as a cloud
That floats on high o'er vales and hills,

When all at once I saw a crowd,
A host, of golden daffodils;
Beside the lake, beneath the trees,
Fluttering and dancing in the breeze.

Continuous as the stars that shine
And twinkle on the milky way,
They stretched in never-ending line
Along the margin of a bay: 10
Ten thousand saw I at a glance,
Tossing their heads in sprightly dance.

The waves beside them danced; but they
Out-did the sparkling waves in glee:
A poet could not but be gay,
In such a jocund company:
I gazed—and gazed—but little thought
What wealth the show to me had brought:

For oft, when on my couch I lie
In vacant or in pensive mood,   20
They flash upon that inward eye
Which is the bliss of solitude; [37]
And then my heart with pleasure fills,
And dances with the daffodils.

THE SMALL CELANDINE

THERE is a Flower, the lesser Celandine,
That shrinks, like many more, from cold and rain;
And, the first moment that the sun may shine,
Bright as the sun himself, 'tis out again!

When hailstones have been falling, swarm on swarm,
Or blasts the green field and the trees distressed,
Oft have I seen it muffled up from harm,
In close self-shelter, like a Thing at rest.

But lately, one rough day, this Flower I passed
And recognized it, though an altered form,   10
Now standing forth an offering to the blast,
And buffeted at will by rain and storm.

---

37 These lines were suggested by Mrs. Wordsworth. "The daffodils grew and still grow on the margin of Ullswater, and probably may be seen to this day as beautiful in the month of March, nodding their golden heads beside the dancing and foaming waves." (Wordsworth)

I stopped, and said with inly-muttered voice,
"It does not love the shower, nor seek the cold:
This neither is its courage nor its choice,
But its necessity in being old.

"The sunshine may not cheer it, nor the dew;
It cannot help itself in its decay;
Stiff in its members, withered, changed of hue."
And, in my spleen, I smiled that it was gray.   20

To be a Prodigal's Favorite—then, worse truth,
A Miser's Pensioner—behold our lot!
O Man, that from thy fair and shining youth
Age might but take the things Youth needed not!

ODE TO DUTY [38]

Stern Daughter of the Voice of God!
O Duty! if that name thou love
Who art a light to guide, a rod
To check the erring, and reprove;
Thou, who art victory and law
When empty terrors overawe;
From vain temptations dost set free;
And calm'st the weary strife of frail humanity!

There are who ask not if thine eye
Be on them; who, in love and truth,   10
Where no misgiving is, rely
Upon the genial sense of youth:
Glad Hearts! without reproach or blot,
Who do thy work, and know it not:
Oh! if through confidence misplaced
They fail, thy saving arms, dread Power! around them cast.

Serene will be our days and bright,
And happy will our nature be,
When love is an unerring light,
And joy its own security.   20
And they a blissful course may hold
Even now, who, not unwisely bold,
Live in the spirit of this creed;
Yet seek thy firm support, according to their need.

---

[38] "This ode is on the model of Gray's *Ode to Adversity,* which is copied from Horace's *Ode to Fortune.*" (Wordsworth)

I, loving freedom, and untried;
No sport of every random gust,
Yet being to myself a guide,
Too blindly have reposed my trust:
And oft, when in my heart was heard
Thy timely mandate, I deferred   30
The task, in smoother walks to stray;
But thee I now would serve more strictly, if I may.

Through no disturbance of my soul,
Or strong compunction in me wrought,
I supplicate for thy control;
But in the quietness of thought:
Me this unchartered freedom tires;
I feel the weight of chance-desires:
My hopes no more must change their name,
I long for a repose that ever is the same.   40

Stern Lawgiver! yet thou dost wear
The Godhead's most benignant grace;
Nor know we anything so fair
As is the smile upon thy face:
Flowers laugh before thee on their beds
And fragrance in thy footing treads;
Thou dost preserve the stars from wrong;
And the most ancient heavens, through Thee, are fresh and
    strong.

To humbler functions, awful Power!
I call thee: I myself commend   50
Unto thy guidance from this hour;
Oh, let my weakness have an end!
Give unto me, made lowly wise,
The spirit of self-sacrifice;
The confidence of reason give;
And in the light of truth thy Bondman let me live!

TO A SKY-LARK

Up with me! up with me into the clouds!
    For thy song, Lark, is strong;
Up with me, up with me into the clouds!
    Singing, singing,
With clouds and sky about thee ringing,
    Lift me, guide me till I find
That spot which seems so to thy mind!

I have walked through wildernesses dreary
And to-day my heart is weary;
Had I now the wings of a Faery,   10
Up to thee would I fly.
There is madness about thee, and joy divine
In that song of thine;
Lift me, guide me high and high
To thy banqueting-place in the sky.

Joyous as morning
Thou art laughing and scorning;
Thou hast a nest for thy love and thy rest,
And, though little troubled with sloth,
Drunken Lark! thou would'st be loth   20
To be such a traveler as I.
Happy, happy liver,
With a soul as strong as a mountain river
Pouring out praise to the Almighty Giver,
Joy and jollity be with us both!

Alas! my journey, rugged and uneven,
Through prickly moors or dusty ways must wind;
But hearing thee, or others of thy kind,
As full of gladness and as free of heaven,
I, with my faith contented, will plod on,   30
And hope for higher raptures, when life's day is done.

ELEGIAC STANZAS

SUGGESTED BY A PICTURE OF PEELE CASTLE, IN A STORM, PAINTED BY SIR GEORGE BEAUMONT

I was thy neighbor once, thou rugged Pile!
Four summer weeks I dwelt in sight of thee:
I saw thee every day; and all the while
Thy Form was sleeping on a glassy sea.

So pure the sky, so quiet was the air!
So like, so very like, was day to day!
When'er I looked, thy Image still was there;
It trembled, but it never passed away.

How perfect was the calm! it seemed no sleep;
No mood, which season takes away, or brings: 10
I could have fancied that the mighty Deep
Was even the gentlest of all gentle Things.

Ah! *then,* if mine had been the Painter's hand,
To express what then I saw; and add the gleam,
The light that never was, on sea or land,
The consecration, and the Poet's dream;

I would have planted thee, thou hoary Pile
Amid a world how different from this!
Beside a sea that could not cease to smile;
On tranquil land, beneath a sky of bliss.   20

Thou shouldst have seemed a treasure-house divine
Of peaceful years; a chronicle of heaven;—
Of all the sunbeams that did ever shine
The very sweetest had to thee been given.

A Picture had it been of lasting ease,
Elysian quiet, without toil or strife;
No motion but the moving tide, a breeze,
Or merely silent Nature's breathing life.

Such, in the fond illusion of my heart,
Such Picture would I at that time have made: 30
And seen the soul of truth in every part,
A steadfast peace that might not be betrayed.

So once it would have been,—'tis so no more;
I have submitted to a new control:
A power is gone, which nothing can restore;
A deep distress hath humanized my Soul.

Not for a moment could I now behold
A smiling sea, and be what I have been:
The feeling of my loss, will ne'er be old;
This, which I know, I speak with mind serene.   40

Then, Beaumont, Friend! who would have been the Friend,
If he had lived, of Him [39] whom I deplore,
This work of thine I blame not, but commend;
This sea in anger, and that dismal shore.

O 'tis a passionate Work!—yet wise and well,
Well chosen is the spirit that is here;
That Hulk which labors in the deadly swell,
This rueful sky, this pageantry of fear!

[39] Wordsworth's brother John, a sea-captain, who went down with his ship in 1805

And this huge Castle, standing here sublime,
I love to see the look with which it braves,   50
Cased in the unfeeling armor of old time,
The lightning, the fierce wind, and trampling waves.

Farewell, farewell the heart that lives alone,
Housed in a dream, at distance from the Kind!
Such happiness, wherever it be known,
Is to be pitied; for 'tis surely blind.

But welcome fortitude, and patient cheer,
And frequent sights of what is to be borne!
Such sights, or worse, as are before me here.—
Not without hope we suffer and we mourn.   60

CHARACTER OF THE HAPPY WARRIOR [40]

Who is the happy Warrior? Who is he
That every man in arms should wish to be?
—It is the generous Spirit, who, when brought
Among the tasks of real life, hath wrought
Upon the plan that pleased his boyish thought:
Whose high endeavors are an inward light
That makes the path before him always bright:
Who, with a natural instinct to discern
What knowledge can perform, is diligent to learn;
Abides by this resolve, and stops not there,   10
But makes his moral being his prime care;
Who, doomed to go in company with Pain,
And Fear, and Bloodshed, miserable train!
Turns his necessity to glorious gain;
In face of these doth exercise a power
Which is our human nature's highest dower;
Controls them and subdues, transmutes, bereaves
Of their bad influence, and their good receives:
By objects, which might force the soul to abate
Her feeling, rendered more compassionate;   20

[40] "The course of the great war with the French naturally fixed one's attention upon the military character, and, to the honor of our country, there were many illustrious instances of the qualities that constitute its highest excellence. Lord Nelson carried most of the virtues that the trials he was exposed to in his department of the service necessarily call forth and sustain, if they do not produce the contrary vices. But his public life was stained with one great crime, so that, though many passages of these lines were suggested by what was generally known as excellent in his conduct, I have not been able to connect his name with the poem as I could wish, or even to think of him with satisfaction in reference to the idea of what a warrior ought to be. For the sake of such of my friends as may happen to read this note I will add, that many elements of the character here portrayed were found in my brother John, who perished by shipwreck as mentioned elsewhere." (Wordsworth)

Is placable—because occasions rise
So often that demand such sacrifice;
More skillful in self-knowledge, even more pure,
As tempted more; more able to endure,
As more exposed to suffering and distress;
Thence, also, more alive to tenderness.
—'Tis he whose law is reason; who depends
Upon that law as on the best of friends;
Whence, in a state where men are tempted still
To evil for a guard against worse ill,   30
And what in quality or act is best
Doth seldom on a right foundation rest,
He labors good on good to fix, and owes
To virtue every triumph that he knows:
—Who, if he rise to station of command,
Rises by open means; and there will stand
On honorable terms, or else retire,
And in himself possess his own desire;
Who comprehends his trust, and to the same
Keeps faithful with a singleness of aim;   40
And therefore does not stoop, nor lie in wait
For wealth, or honors, or for worldly state;
Whom they must follow; on whose head must fall,
Like showers of manna, if they come at all:
Whose powers shed round him in the common strife,
Or mild concerns of ordinary life,
A constant influence, a peculiar grace;
But who, if he be called upon to face
Some awful moment to which Heaven has joined
Great issues, good or bad for human kind,   50
Is happy as a Lover; and attired
With sudden brightness, like a Man inspired;
And, through the heat of conflict, keeps the law
In calmness made, and sees what he foresaw;
Or if an unexpected call succeed,
Come when it will, is equal to the need:
—He who, though thus endued as with a sense
And faculty for storm and turbulence,
Is yet a Soul whose master-bias leans
To homefelt pleasures and to gentle scenes;   60
Sweet images! which, wheresoe'er he be,
Are at his heart; and such fidelity
It is his darling passion to approve;
More brave for this, that he hath much to love:—
'Tis, finally, the Man, who, lifted high,
Conspicuous object in a Nation's eye,

Or left unthought-of in obscurity,—
Who, with a toward or untoward lot,
Prosperous or adverse, to his wish or not—
Plays, in the many games of life, that one   70
Where what he most doth value must be won:
Whom neither shape of danger can dismay,
Nor thought of tender happiness betray;
Who, not content that former worth stand fast,
Looks forward, persevering to the last,
From well to better, daily self-surpassed:
Who, whether praise of him must walk the earth
For ever, and to noble deeds give birth,
Or he must fall, to sleep without his fame,
And leave a dead unprofitable name—   80
Finds comfort in himself and in his cause;
And, while the mortal mist is gathering, draws
His breath in confidence of Heaven's applause:
This is the happy Warrior; this is He
That every Man in arms should wish to be.

NUNS FRET NOT AT THEIR CONVENT'S NARROW ROOM

NUNS fret not at their convent's narrow room;
And hermits are contented with their cells;
And students with their pensive citadels;
Maids at the wheel, the weaver at his loom,
Sit blithe and happy; bees that soar for bloom,
High as the highest Peak of Furness-fells,[41]
Will murmur by the hour in foxglove bells:
In truth the prison, unto which we doom
Ourselves, no prison is: and hence for me,
In sundry moods, 'twas pastime to be bound
Within the Sonnet's scanty plot of ground;
Pleased if some Souls (for such there needs must be)
Who have felt the weight of too much liberty,
Should find brief solace there, as I have found.

PERSONAL TALK

I

I AM not One who much or oft delight
To season my fireside with personal talk,—

41 a hilly region in the English Lake district

Of friends, who live within an easy walk,
Or neighbors, daily, weekly, in my sight:
And, for my chance-acquaintance, ladies bright,
Sons, mothers, maidens withering on the stalk,
These all wear out of me, like Forms, with chalk
Painted on rich men's floors, for one feast-night.
Better than such discourse doth silence long,
Long, barren silence, square with my desire;   10
To sit without emotion, hope, or aim,
In the loved presence of my cottage-fire,
And listen to the flapping of the flame,
Or kettle whispering its faint undersong.

2

"Yet life," you say, "is life; we have seen and see,
And with a living pleasure we describe;
And fits of sprightly malice do but bribe
The languid mind into activity.
Sound sense, and love itself, and mirth and glee
Are fostered by the comment and the gibe."   20
Even be it so; yet still among your tribe,
Our daily world's true Worldlings, rank not me!
Children are bless'd, and powerful; their world lies
More justly balanced; partly at their feet,
And part far from them:—sweetest melodies
Are those that are by distance made more sweet;
Whose mind is but the mind of his own eyes,
He is a Slave; the meanest we can meet!

3

Wings have we,—and as far as we can go,
We may find pleasure: wilderness and wood,   30
Blank ocean and mere sky, support that mood
Which with the lofty sanctifies the low.
Dreams, books, are each a world; and books, we know,
Are a substantial world, both pure and good:
Round these, with tendrils strong as flesh and blood,
Our pastime and our happiness will grow.
There find I personal themes, a plenteous store,
Matter wherein right voluble I am,
To which I listen with a ready ear;
Two shall be named, pre-eminently dear,—   40
The gentle Lady married to the Moor;
And heavenly Una with her milk-white Lamb.

4

Nor can I not believe but that hereby
Great gains are mine; for thus I live remote
From evil-speaking; rancor, never sought,
Comes to me not; malignant truth, or lie.
Hence have I genial seasons, hence have I
Smooth passions, smooth discourse, and joyous thought:
And thus from day to day my little boat
Rocks in its harbor, lodging peaceably.   50
Blessings be with them—and eternal praise,
Who gave us nobler loves, and nobler cares—
The Poets, who on earth have made us heirs
Of truth and pure delight by heavenly lays!
Oh! might my name be numbered among theirs,
Then gladly would I end my mortal days.

THE WORLD IS TOO MUCH WITH US

The world is too much with us; late and soon,
Getting and spending, we lay waste our powers:
Little we see in Nature that is ours;
We have given our hearts away, a sordid boon!
The Sea that bares her bosom to the moon;
The winds that will be howling at all hours,
And are up-gathered now like sleeping flowers;
For this, for everything, we are out of tune;
It moves us not.—Great God! I'd rather be
A Pagan suckled in a creed outworn;
So might I, standing on this pleasant lea,
Have glimpses that would make me less forlorn;
Have sight of Proteus rising from the sea;
Or hear old Triton blow his wreathèd horn.

TO SLEEP

A flock of sheep that leisurely pass by,
One after one; the sound of rain, and bees
Murmuring; the fall of rivers, winds, and seas,
Smooth fields, white sheets of water, and pure sky;
I have thought of all by turns, and yet do lie
Sleepless! and soon the small birds' melodies
Must hear, first uttered from my orchard trees;
And the first cuckoo's melancholy cry.
Even thus last night, and two nights more, I lay,
And could not win thee, Sleep! by any stealth:

So do not let me wear to-night away:
Without Thee what is all the morning's wealth?
Come, blessed barrier between day and day,
Dear mother of fresh thoughts and joyous health!

ODE

INTIMATIONS OF IMMORTALITY FROM RECOLLECTIONS OF EARLY CHILDHOOD

Wordsworth dictated the following note to Miss Fenwick regarding this poem:

"This was composed during my residence at Town-end, Grasmere. Two years at least passed between the writing of the first four stanzas and the remaining part. To the attentive and competent reader the whole sufficiently explains itself; but there may be no harm in adverting here to particular feelings or *experiences* of my own mind on which the structure of the poem partly rests. Nothing was more difficult for me in childhood than to admit the notion of death as a state applicable to my own being. I have said elsewhere—

A simple child,
That lightly draws its breath,
And feels its life in every limb,
What should it know of death!—

But it was not so much from feelings of animal vivacity that *my* difficulty came as from a sense of the indomitableness of the Spirit within me. I used to brood over the stories of Enoch and Elijah, and almost to persuade myself that, whatever might become of others, I should be translated, in something of the same way, to heaven. With a feeling congenial to this, I was often unable to think of external things as having external existence, and I communed with all that I saw as something not apart from, but inherent in, my own immaterial nature. Many times while going to school have I grasped at a wall or tree to recall myself from this abyss of idealism to the reality. At that time I was afraid of such processes. In later periods of life I have deplored, as we have all reason to do, a subjugation of an opposite character and have rejoiced over the remembrances, as is expressed in the lines—

Obstinate questionings
Of sense and outward things,
Fallings from us, vanishings, etc.

To that dream-like vividness and splendor which invest objects of sight in childhood, every one, I believe, if he would look back, could bear testimony, and I need not dwell upon it here: but having in the poem regarded it as presumptive evidence of a prior state of existence, I think it right to protest against a conclusion, which has given pain to some good and pious persons, that I meant to inculcate such a belief. It is far too shadowy a notion to be recommended to faith, as more than an element in our instincts of immortality. But let us bear in mind that, though the idea is not advanced in revelation, there is nothing there to contradict it, and the fall of Man presents an analogy in its favor. Accordingly, a pre-existent state has ·entered into the popular

creeds of many nations. . . . I took hold of the notion . . . as having sufficient
foundation in humanity for authorizing me to make for my purpose the best
use of it I could as a poet."

> "The Child is father of the Man;
> And I could wish my days to be
> Bound each to each by natural piety."

1

THERE was a time when meadow, grove, and stream,
The earth, and every common sight,
 To me did seem
 Appareled in celestial light,
The glory and the freshness of a dream.
It is not now as it hath been of yore;—
 Turn wheresoe'er I may,
  By night or day,
The things which I have seen I now can see no more.

2

 The Rainbow comes and goes,   10
 And lovely is the Rose,
 The Moon doth with delight
Look round her when the heavens are bare,
 Waters on a starry night
 Are beautiful and fair;
 The sunshine is a glorious birth;
 But yet I know, where'er I go,
That there hath passed away a glory from the earth.

3

Now, while the birds thus sing a joyous song,
 And while the young lambs bound 20
  As to the tabor's sound,
To me alone there came a thought of grief:
A timely utterance gave that thought relief,
 And I again am strong:
The cataracts blow their trumpets from the steep;
No more shall grief of mine the season wrong;
I hear the Echoes through the mountains throng,
The Winds come to me from the fields of sleep,
 And all the earth is gay;
  Land and sea   30
 Give themselves up to jollity,

And with the heart of May
Doth every Beast keep holiday;—
    Thou Child of Joy,
Shout round me, let me hear thy shouts, thou happy
    Shepherd-boy!

4

Ye blessèd Creatures, I have heard the call
    Ye to each other make; I see
The heavens laugh with you in your jubilee;
    My heart is at your festival,   40
    My head hath its coronal,
The fullness of your bliss, I feel—I feel it all.
    Oh evil day! if I were sullen
    While Earth herself is adorning,
        This sweet May-morning,
    And the Children are culling
        On every side,
    In a thousand valleys far and wide,
    Fresh flowers; while the sun shines warm,
And the Babe leaps up on his Mother's arm:—   50
    I hear, I hear, with joy I hear!
    —But there's a Tree, of many, one,
A single Field which I have looked upon,
Both of them speak of something that is gone:
        The Pansy at my feet
        Doth the same tale repeat:
Whither is fled the visionary gleam?
Where is it now, the glory and the dream?

5

Our birth is but a sleep and a forgetting:
The Soul that rises with us, our life's Star,   60
    Hath had elsewhere its setting,
        And cometh from afar:
    Not in entire forgetfulness,
    And not in utter nakedness,
But trailing clouds of glory do we come
        From God, who is our home:
Heaven lies about us in our infancy!
Shades of the prison-house begin to close
        Upon the growing Boy,
But He beholds the light, and whence it flows,   70
    He sees it in his joy;

The Youth, who daily farther from the east
  Must travel, still is Nature's Priest,
  And by the vision splendid
  Is on his way attended;
At length the Man perceives it die away,
And fade into the light of common day.

6

Earth fills her lap with pleasures of her own;
Yearnings she hath in her own natural kind,
And, even with something of a Mother's mind,   80
  And no unworthy aim,
  The homely Nurse doth all she can
To make her Foster-child, her Inmate Man,
  Forget the glories he hath known,
And that imperial palace whence he came.

7

Behold the Child among his new-born blisses,
A six years' Darling of a pigmy size!
See, where 'mid work of his own hand he lies,
Fretted by sallies of his mother's kisses,
With light upon him from his father's eyes!   90
See, at his feet, some little plan or chart,
Some fragment from his dream of human life,
Shaped by himself with newly-learned art;
  A wedding or a festival,
  A mourning or a funeral;
  And this hath now his heart,
  And unto this he frames his song:
  Then will he fit his tongue
To dialogues of business, love, or strife;
  But it will not be long   100
  Ere this be thrown aside,
  And with new joy and pride
The little Actor cons another part;
Filling from time to time his "humorous stage" [42]
With all the Persons, down to palsied Age,
That Life brings with her in her equipage;
  As if his whole vocation
  Were endless imitation.

[42] *As You Like It*, II, vii, 139–166.

8

Thou, whose exterior semblance doth belie
  Thy Soul's immensity;   110
Thou best Philosopher, who yet dost keep
Thy heritage, thou Eye among the blind,
That, deaf and silent, read'st the eternal deep,
Haunted for ever by the eternal mind,—
  Mighty Prophet! Seer bless'd!
  On whom those truths do rest,
Which we are toiling all our lives to find,
In darkness lost, the darkness of the grave;
Thou, over whom thy Immortality
Broods like the Day, a Master o'er a Slave,   120
A Presence which is not to be put by;
Thou little Child, yet glorious in the might
Of heaven-born freedom on thy being's height,
Why with such earnest pains dost thou provoke
The years to bring the inevitable yoke,
Thus blindly with thy blessedness at strife?
Full soon thy Soul shall have her earthly freight,
And custom lie upon thee with a weight,
Heavy as frost, and deep almost as life!

9

  O joy! that in our embers   130
  Is something that doth live,
  That nature yet remembers
  What was so fugitive!
The thought of our past years in me doth breed
Perpetual benediction: not indeed
For that which is most worthy to be bless'd—
Delight and liberty, the simple creed
Of Childhood, whether busy or at rest,
With new-fledged hope still fluttering in his breast:—
    Not for these I raise   140
    The song of thanks and praise;
  But for those obstinate questionings
  Of sense and outward things,
  Fallings from us, vanishings;
  Blank misgivings of a Creature
Moving about in worlds not realized,
High instincts before which our mortal Nature
Did tremble like a guilty Thing surprised:
    But for those first affections,

Those shadowy recollections,   150
   Which, be they what they may,
Are yet the fountain light of all our day,
Are yet a master light of all our seeing;
   Uphold us, cherish, and have power to make
Our noisy years seem moments in the being
Of the eternal Silence: truths that wake,
      To perish never;
Which neither listlessness, nor mad endeavor,
      Nor Man nor Boy,
Nor all that is at enmity with joy,   160
Can utterly abolish or destroy!
      Hence in a season of calm weather
      Though inland far we be,
Our Souls have sight of that immortal sea
      Which brought us hither,
      Can in a moment travel thither,
And see the Children sport upon the shore,
And hear the mighty waters rolling evermore.

                        10

Then sing, ye Birds, sing, sing a joyous song!
   And let the young Lambs bound   170
   As to the tabor's sound!
We in thought will join your throng,
   Ye that pipe and ye that play,
   Ye that through your hearts to-day
   Feel the gladness of the May!
What though the radiance which was once so bright
Be now for ever taken from my sight,
   Though nothing can bring back the hour
Of splendor in the grass, of glory in the flower;
   We will grieve not, rather find   180
   Strength in what remains behind;
   In the primal sympathy
      Which having been must ever be;
   In the soothing thoughts that spring
   Out of human suffering;
   In the faith that looks through death,
In years that bring the philosophic mind.

                        11

And O, ye Fountains, Meadows, Hills, and Groves,
Forbode not any severing of our loves!

Yet in my heart of hearts I feel your might; 190
I only have relinquished one delight
To live beneath your more habitual sway.
I love the Brooks which down their channels fret,
Even more than when I tripped lightly as they;
The innocent brightness of a new-born Day
    Is lovely yet;
The Clouds that gather round the setting sun
Do take a sober coloring from an eye
That hath kept watch o'er man's mortality;
Another race hath been, and other palms are won. 200
Thanks to the human heart by which we live,
Thanks to its tenderness, its joys, and fears,
To me the meanest flower that blows can give
Thoughts that do often lie too deep for tears.

THOUGHT OF A BRITON ON THE SUBJUGATION OF SWITZERLAND [43]

Two Voices are there; one is of the sea,
One of the mountains; each a mighty Voice:
In both from age to age thou didst rejoice,
They were thy chosen music, Liberty!
There came a Tyrant, and with holy glee
Thou fought'st against him; but hast vainly striven:
Thou from thy Alpine holds at length art driven,
Where not a torrent murmurs heard by thee.
Of one deep bliss thine ear hath been bereft:
Then cleave, O cleave to that which still is left;
For, high-souled Maid, what sorrow would it be
That Mountain floods should thunder as before,
And Ocean bellow from his rocky shore,
And neither awful Voice be heard by thee!

HERE PAUSE: THE POET CLAIMS AT LEAST THIS PRAISE

HERE pause: the poet claims at least this praise,
That virtuous Liberty hath been the scope
Of his pure song, which did not shrink from hope
In the worst moment of these evil days;
From hope, the paramount *duty* that Heaven lays,
For its own honor, on man's suffering heart.
Never may from our souls one truth depart—
That an accursed thing it is to gaze

[43] by Napoleon. 1802. In 1807 he was making preparations to invade England.

On prosperous tyrants with a dazzled eye;
Nor—touched with due abhorrence of *their* guilt
For whose dire ends tears flow, and blood is spilt,
And justice labors in extremity—
Forget thy weakness, upon which is built,
O wretched man, the throne of tyranny!

LAODAMIA [44]

"With sacrifice before the rising morn
Vows have I made by fruitless hope inspired;
And from the infernal Gods, 'mid shades forlorn
Of night, my slaughtered Lord have I required:
Celestial pity I again implore;—
Restore him to my sight—great Jove, restore!"

So speaking, and by fervent love endowed
With faith, the Suppliant heavenward lifts her hands;
While, like the sun emerging from a cloud,
Her countenance brightens—and her eye expands;   10
Her bosom heaves and spreads, her stature grows;
And she expects the issue in repose.

O terror! what hath she perceived?—O joy!
What doth she look on?—whom doth she behold?
Her Hero slain upon the beach of Troy?
His vital presence? his corporeal mold?
It is—if sense deceive her not—'tis He!
And a God leads him, wingèd Mercury!

Mild Hermes spake—and touched her with his wand
That calms all fear; "Such grace hath crowned thy prayer,   20
Laodamía! that at Jove's command
Thy Husband walks the paths of upper air:
He comes to tarry with thee three hours' space;
Accept the gift, behold him face to face!"

Forth sprang the impassioned Queen her Lord to clasp;
Again that consummation she essayed;
But unsubstantial Form eludes her grasp
As often as that eager grasp was made.
The Phantom parts—but parts to re-unite,
And re-assume his place before her sight.   30

[44] "The incident of the trees growing and withering put the subject into my thoughts, and I wrote with the hope of giving it a loftier tone than, so far as I know, has been given to it by any of the Ancients who have treated it. It cost me more trouble than almost anything of equal length I have ever written." (Wordsworth)

"Protesiláus, lo! thy guide is gone!
Confirm, I pray, the vision with thy voice:
This is our palace,—yonder is thy throne;
Speak, and the floor thou tread'st on will rejoice.
Not to appal me have the gods bestowed
This precious boon; and blessed a sad abode."

"Great Jove, Laodamía! doth not leave
His gifts imperfect:—Specter though I be,
I am not sent to scare thee or deceive;
But in reward of thy fidelity.   40
And something also did my worth obtain;
For fearless virtue bringeth boundless gain.

"Thou knowest, the Delphic oracle foretold
That the first Greek who touched the Trojan strand
Should die; but me the threat could not withhold:
A generous cause a victim did demand;
And forth I leapt upon the sandy plain;
A self-devoted chief—by Hector slain."

"Supreme of Heroes—bravest, noblest, best!
Thy matchless courage I bewail no more,   50
Which then, when tens of thousands were depressed
By doubt, propelled thee to the fatal shore;
Thou found'st—and I forgive thee—here thou art—
A nobler counselor than my poor heart.

"But thou, though capable of sternest deed,
Wert kind as resolute, and good as brave;
And he, whose power restores thee, hath decreed
Thou shouldst elude the malice of the grave:
Redundant are thy locks, thy lips as fair
As when their breath enriched Thessalian air.   60

"No Specter greets me,—no vain Shadow this;
Come, blooming Hero, place thee by my side!
Give, on this well-known couch, one nuptial kiss
To me, this day, a second time thy bride!"
Jove frowned in heaven: the conscious Parcæ [45] threw
Upon those roseate lips a Stygian hue.

"This visage tells thee that my doom is past:
Nor should the change be mourned, even if the joys
Of sense were able to return as fast

45 Fates

And surely as they vanish. Earth destroys   70
Those raptures duly—Erebus [46] disdains:
Calm pleasures there abide—majestic pains.

"Be taught, O faithful Consort, to control
Rebellious passion: for the Gods approve
The depth, and not the tumult, of the soul;
A fervent, not ungovernable, love.
Thy transports moderate; and meekly mourn
When I depart, for brief is my sojourn—"

"Ah, wherefore?—Did not Hercules by force
Wrest from the guardian Monster of the tomb   80
Alcestis, a reanimated corse,
Given back to dwell on earth in vernal bloom?
Medea's spells dispersed the weight of years,
And Æson stood a youth 'mid youthful peers.

"The Gods to us are merciful—and they
Yet further may relent: for mightier far
Than strength of nerve and sinew, or the sway
Of magic potent over sun and star,
Is love, though oft to agony distressed,
And though his favorite seat be feeble woman's breast.   90

"But if thou goest, I follow—" "Peace!" he said,—
She looked upon him and was calmed and cheered;
The ghastly color from his lips had fled;
In his deportment, shape, and mien, appeared
Elysian beauty, melancholy grace,
Brought from a pensive though a happy place.

He spake of love, such love as Spirits feel
In worlds whose course is equable and pure;
No fears to beat away—no strife to heal—
The past unsighed for, and the future sure;   100
Spake of heroic arts in graver mood
Revived, with finer harmony pursued;

Of all that is most beauteous—imaged there
In happier beauty; more pellucid streams,
An ampler ether, a diviner air,
And fields invested with purpureal gleams;
Climes which the sun, who sheds the brightest day
Earth knows, is all unworthy to survey.

46 Hades

Yet there the Soul shall enter which hath earned
That privilege by virtue.—"Ill," said he,   110
"The end of man's existence I discerned,
Who from ignoble games and revelry
Could draw, when we had parted, vain delight,
While tears were thy best pastime, day and night;

"And while my youthful peers before my eyes
(Each hero following his peculiar bent)
Prepared themselves for glorious enterprise
By martial sports,—or, seated in the tent,
Chieftains and kings in council were detained;
What time the fleet at Aulis [47] lay enchained.   120

"The wished-for wind was given:—I then revolved
The oracle, upon the silent sea;
And, if no worthier led the way, resolved
That, of a thousand vessels, mine should be
The foremost prow in pressing to the strand,—
Mine the first blood that tinged the Trojan sand.

"Yet bitter, oft-times bitter, was the pang
When of thy loss I thought, belovèd Wife!
On thee too fondly did my memory hang,
And on the joys we shared in mortal life,—   130
The paths which we had trod—these fountains, flowers,
My new-planned cities, and unfinished towers.

"But should suspense permit the Foe to cry,
'Behold they tremble!—haughty their array,
Yet of their number no one dares to die?'
In soul I swept the indignity away:
Old frailties then recurred:—but lofty thought,
In act embodied, my deliverance wrought.

"And Thou, though strong in love, art all too weak
In reason, in self-government too slow;   140
I counsel thee by fortitude to seek
Our bless'd re-union in the shades below.
The invisible world with thee hath sympathized;
Be thy affections raised and solemnized.

"Learn, by a mortal yearning, to ascend—
Seeking a higher object. Love was given,

47 the port in Bœotia where the Greek fleet was held until Iphigenia was sacrificed
to appease Artemis

Encouraged, sanctioned, chiefly for that end;
For this the passion to excess was driven—
That self might be annulled: her bondage prove
The fetters of a dream, opposed to love."——   150

Aloud she shrieked! for Hermes re-appears!
Round the dear Shade she would have clung—'tis vain:
The hours are past—too brief had they been years;
And him no mortal effort can detain:
Swift, toward the realms that know not earthly day,
He through the portal takes his silent way,
And on the palace-floor a lifeless corse She lay.

Thus, all in vain exhorted and reproved,
She perished; and, as for a willful crime,
By the just Gods whom no weak pity moved,   160
Was doomed to wear out her appointed time,
Apart from happy Ghosts, that gather flowers
Of blissful quiet 'mid unfading bowers.

—Yet tears to human suffering are due;
And mortal hopes defeated and o'erthrown
Are mourned by man, and not by man alone,
As fondly he believes.—Upon the side
Of Hellespont (such faith was entertained)
A knot of spiry trees for ages grew
From out the tomb of him for whom she died;   170
And ever, when such stature they had gained
That Ilium's walls were subject to their view,
The trees' tall summits withered at the sight,
A constant interchange of growth and blight!

YARROW VISITED SEPTEMBER, 1814 [48]

AND is this—Yarrow?—*This the Stream*
Of which my fancy cherished,
So faithfully, a waking dream?
An image that hath perished!
O that some Minstrel's harp were near,
To utter notes of gladness,
And chase this silence from the air,
That fills my heart with sadness!

[48] "As mentioned in my verses on the death of the Ettrick Shepherd [James Hogg],
my first visit to Yarrow was in his company . . . I seldom read or think of this
poem without regretting that my dear Sister was not of the party, as she would have
had so much delight in recalling the time when, traveling together in Scotland, we
declined going in search of this celebrated stream, not altogether, I will frankly
confess, for the reasons assigned in the poem on that occasion [Yarrow unvisited]."
(Wordsworth)

Yet why?—a silvery current flows
With uncontrolled meanderings;   10
Nor have these eyes by greener hills
Been soothed, in all my wanderings.
And, through her depths, Saint Mary's Lake
Is visibly delighted;
For not a feature of those hills
Is in the mirror slighted.

A blue sky bends o'er Yarrow vale,
Save where that pearly whiteness
Is round the rising sun diffused,
A tender hazy brightness;   20
Mild dawn of promise! that excludes
All profitless dejection;
Though not unwilling here to admit
A pensive recollection.

Where was it that the famous Flower
Of Yarrow Vale lay bleeding?
His bed perchance was yon smooth mound
On which the herd is feeding:
And haply from this crystal pool,
Now peaceful as the morning,   30
The Water-wraith ascended thrice
And gave his doleful warning.[49]

Delicious is the Lay that sings
The haunts of happy Lovers,
The path that leads them to the grove,
The leafy grove that covers:
And Pity sanctifies the Verse
That paints, by strength of sorrow,
The unconquerable strength of love;
Bear witness, rueful Yarrow!   40

But thou, that didst appear so fair
To fond imagination,
Dost rival in the light of day
Her delicate creation:
Meek loveliness is round thee spread,
A softness still and holy;
The grace of forest charms decayed,
And pastoral melancholy.

49 a reference to an incident in Logan's ballad, *The Braes of Yarrow*

That region left, the vale unfolds
Rich groves of lofty stature,   50
With Yarrow winding through the pomp
Of cultivated nature;
And, rising from those lofty groves,
Behold a Ruin hoary!
The shattered front of Newark's Towers,
Renowned in Border story.

Fair scenes for childhood's opening bloom,
For sportive youth to stray in;
For manhood to enjoy his strength;
And age to wear away in!   60
Yon cottage seems a bower of bliss,
A covert for protection
Of tender thoughts, that nestle there—
The brood of chaste affection.

How sweet, on this autumnal day,
The wild-wood fruits to gather,
And on my True-love's forehead plant
A crest of blooming heather!
And what if I enwreathed my own!
'Twere no offense to reason;   70
The sober Hills thus deck their brows
To meet the wintry season.

I see—but not by sight alone,
Loved Yarrow, have I won thee;
A ray of fancy still survives—
Her sunshine plays upon thee!
Thy ever-youthful waters keep
A course of lively pleasure;
And gladsome notes my lips can breathe,
Accordant to the measure.   80

The vapors linger round the Heights,
They melt, and soon must vanish;
One hour is theirs, nor more is mine—
Sad thought which I would banish,
But that I know, where'er I go,
Thy genuine image, Yarrow!
Will dwell with me—to heighten joy,
And cheer my mind in sorrow.

TO B. R. HAYDON [50]

High is our calling, friend! Creative art
(Whether the instrument of words she use,
Or pencil pregnant with ethereal hues,)
Demands the service of a mind and heart,
Though sensitive, yet, in their weakest part,
Heroically fashioned—to infuse
Faith in the whispers of the lonely Muse,
While the whole world seems adverse to desert.
And, oh! when Nature sinks, as oft she may,
Through long-lived pressure of obscure distress,
Still to be strenuous for the bright reward,
And in the soul admit of no decay,
Brook no continuance of weak-mindedness—
Great is the glory, for the strife is hard!

COMPOSED UPON AN EVENING OF EXTRAORDI-
NARY SPLENDOR AND BEAUTY

I

HAD this effulgence disappeared
With flying haste, I might have sent,
Among the speechless clouds, a look
Of blank astonishment;
But 'tis endued with power to stay,
And sanctify one closing day,
That frail Mortality may see—
What is?—ah no, but what *can* be!
Time was when field and watery cove
With modulated echoes rang,   10
While choirs of fervent Angels sang
Their vespers in the grove;
Or crowning, star-like, each some sovereign height,
Warbled, for heaven above and earth below,
Strains suitable to both.—Such holy rite,
Methinks, if audibly repeated now
From hill or valley, could not move
Sublimer transport, purer love,
Than doth this silent spectacle—the gleam—
The shadow—and the peace supreme!   20

2

No sound is uttered,—but a deep
And solemn harmony pervades

The hollow vale from steep to steep,
And penetrates the glades.
Far-distant images draw nigh,
Called forth by wondrous potency
Of beamy radiance, that imbues
Whate'er it strikes with gem-like hues!
In vision exquisitely clear,
Herds range along the mountain side;   30
And glistening antlers are descried;
And gilded flocks appear.
Thine is the tranquil hour, purpureal Eve!
But long as god-like wish, or hope divine
Informs my spirit, ne'er can I believe
That this magnificence is wholly thine!
—From worlds not quickened by the sun
A portion of the gift is won;
An intermingling of Heaven's pomp is spread
On ground which British shepherds tread!   40

3

And, if there be whom broken ties
Afflict, or injuries assail,
Yon hazy ridges to their eyes
Present a glorious scale,
Climbing suffused with sunny air,
To stop—no record hath told where!
And tempting Fancy to ascend,
And with immortal Spirits blend!
—Wings at my shoulders seem to play;
But, rooted here, I stand and gaze   50
On those bright steps that heaven-ward raise
Their practicable way.
Come forth, ye drooping old men, look abroad,
And see to what fair countries ye are bound!
And if some traveler, weary of his road,
Hath slept since noon-tide on the grassy ground,
Ye Genii! to his covert speed;
And wake him with such gentle heed
As may attune his soul to meet the dower
Bestowed on this transcendent hour!   60

4

Such hues from their celestial urn
Were wont to stream before mine eye,

Where'er it wandered in the morn
Of blissful infancy.
This glimpse of glory, why renewed?
Nay, rather speak with gratitude;
For, if a vestige of those gleams
Survived, 'twas only in my dreams.
Dread Power! whom peace and calmness serve
No less than Nature's threatening voice,   70
If aught unworthy be my choice,
From Thee if I would swerve;
Oh, let thy grace remind me of the light
Full early lost, and fruitlessly deplored;
Which, at this moment, on my waking sight
Appears to shine, by miracle restored;
My soul, though yet confined to earth,
Rejoices in a second birth!
—'Tis past, the visionary splendor fades;
And night approaches with her shades.   80

AFTER-THOUGHT, APPENDED TO *THE RIVER DUDDON* [51]

I thought of Thee, my partner and my guide,
As being passed away.—Vain sympathies!
For, backward, Duddon, as I cast my eyes,
I see what was, and is, and will abide;
Still glides the Stream, and shall for ever glide,
The Form remains, the Function never dies,
While we, the brave, the mighty, and the wise,
We Men, who in our morn of youth defied
The elements, must vanish,—be it so!
Enough, if something from our hands have power
To live, and act, and serve the future hour,
And if, as toward the silent tomb we go,
Through love, through hope, and faith's transcendent dower,
We feel that we are greater than we know.

MUTABILITY [52]

From low to high doth dissolution climb,
    And sink from high to low, along a scale
    Of awful notes, whose concord shall not fail;
A musical but melancholy chime,
    Which they can hear who meddle not with crime,

51 a river in the English
Lake district, celebrated in
a sonnet-sequence of which
this is the conclusion
52 This and the next
sonnet are from Words-
worth's series, *Ecclesiastical Sonnets*.

Nor avarice, nor over-anxious care.
Truth fails not; but her outward forms that bear
The longest date do melt like frosty rime,
That in the morning whitened hill and plain
And is no more; drop like the tower sublime
Of yesterday, which royally did wear
His crown of weeds, but could not even sustain
Some casual shout that broke the silent air,
Or the unimaginable touch of Time.

INSIDE OF KING'S COLLEGE CHAPEL, CAMBRIDGE

TAX not the royal Saint with vain expense,
With ill-matched aims the Architect who planned—
Albeit laboring for a scanty band
Of white robed Scholars only—this immense
And glorious Work of fine intelligence!
Give all thou canst; high Heaven rejects the lore
Of nicely-calculated less or more;
So deemed the man who fashioned for the sense
These lofty pillars, spread that branching roof
Self-poised, and scooped into ten thousand cells,
Where light and shade repose, where music dwells
Lingering—and wandering on as loth to die;
Like thoughts whose very sweetness yieldeth proof
That they were born for immortality.

TO A SKY-LARK

ETHEREAL minstrel! pilgrim of the sky!
Dost thou despise the earth where cares abound?
Or, while the wings aspire, are heart and eye
Both with thy nest upon the dewy ground?
Thy nest which thou canst drop into at will,
Those quivering wings composed, that music still!

Leave to the nightingale her shady wood;
A privacy of glorious light is thine;
Whence thou dost pour upon the world a flood
Of harmony, with instinct more divine;
Type of the wise who soar, but never roam;
True to the kindred points of Heaven and Home!

SCORN NOT THE SONNET

SCORN not the Sonnet; Critic, you have frowned,
Mindless of its just honors; with this key

Shakespeare unlocked his heart; the melody
Of this small lute gave ease to Petrarch's wound;
A thousand times this pipe did Tasso sound;
With it Camöens soothed an exile's grief;
The Sonnet glittered a gay myrtle leaf
Amid the cypress with which Dante crowned
His visionary brow: a glow-worm lamp,
It cheered mild Spenser, called from Faeryland
To struggle through dark ways; and, when a damp
Fell round the path of Milton, in his hand
The Thing became a trumpet; whence he blew
Soul-animating strains—alas, too few!

YARROW REVISITED [53]

THE gallant Youth, who may have gained,
    Or seeks, a "winsome Marrow,"
Was but an Infant in the lap
    When first I looked on Yarrow;
Once more, by Newark's Castle-gate
    Long left without a warder,
I stood, looked, listened, and with Thee,
    Great Minstrel of the Border!

Grave thoughts ruled wide on that sweet day,
    Their dignity installing   10
In gentle bosoms, while sere leaves
    Were on the bough, or falling;
But breezes played, and sunshine gleamed—
    The forest to embolden;
Reddened the fiery hues, and shot
    Transparence through the golden.

For busy thoughts the Stream flowed on
    In foamy agitation;
And slept in many a crystal pool
    For quiet contemplation: 20
No public and no private care
    The freeborn mind enthralling,

53 "In the autumn of 1831, my daughter and I set off from Rydal to visit Sir
Walter Scott before his departure for Italy . . . How sadly changed did I find him
from the man I had seen so healthy, gay, and hopeful, a few years before, when
he said at the inn at Paterdale, in my presence, . . . 'I mean to live till I am
eighty, and shall write as long as I live.' . . . On Tuesday morning Sir Walter Scott
accompanied us and most of the party to Newark Castle on the Yarrow. When we
alighted from the carriages he walked pretty stoutly, and had great pleasure in re-
visiting those his favorite haunts. Of that excursion the verses 'Yarrow Revisited' are
a memorial." (Wordsworth)

We made a day of happy hours,
  Our happy days recalling.

Brisk Youth appeared, the Morn of youth,
  With freaks of graceful folly,—
Life's temperate Noon, her sober Eve,
  Her Night not melancholy;
Past, present, future, all appeared
  In harmony united,   30
Like guests that meet, and some from far,
  By cordial love invited.

And if, as Yarrow, through the woods
  And down the meadow ranging,
Did meet us with unaltered face,
  Though we were changed and changing;
If, *then,* some natural shadows spread
  Our inward prospect over,
The soul's deep valley was not slow
  Its brightness to recover.   40

Eternal blessings on the Muse,
  And her divine employment!
The blameless Muse, who trains her Sons
  For hope and calm enjoyment;
Albeit sickness, lingering yet,
  Has o'er their pillow brooded;
And Care waylays their steps—a Sprite
  Not easily eluded.

For thee, O Scott! compelled to change
  Green Eildon-hill and Cheviot   50
For warm Vesuvio's vine-clad slopes;
  And leave thy Tweed and Tiviot
For mild Sorento's breezy waves;
  May classic Fancy, linking
With native Fancy her fresh aid,
  Preserve thy heart from sinking!

Oh! while they minister to thee,
  Each vying with the other,
May Health return to mellow Age
  With Strength, her venturous brother;   60
And Tiber, and each brook and rill
  Renowned in song and story,

With unimagined beauty shine,
  Nor lose one ray of glory!

For Thou, upon a hundred streams,
  By tales of love and sorrow,
Of faithful love, undaunted truth,
  Hast shed the power of Yarrow;
And streams unknown, hills yet unseen,
  Wherever they invite Thee,   70
At parent Nature's grateful call,
  With gladness must requite Thee.

A gracious welcome shall be thine,
  Such looks of love and honor
As thy own Yarrow gave to me
  When first I gazed upon her;
Beheld what I had feared to see,
  Unwilling to surrender
Dreams treasured up from early days,
  The holy and the tender.   80

And what, for this frail world, were all
  That mortals do or suffer,
Did no responsive harp, no pen,
  Memorial tribute offer?
Yea, what were mighty Nature's self?
  Her features, could they win us,
Unhelped by the poetic voice
  That hourly speaks within us?

Nor deem that localized Romance
  Plays false with our affections;   90
Unsanctifies our tears—made sport
  For fanciful dejections:
Ah, no! the visions of the past
  Sustain the heart in feeling
Life as she is—our changeful Life,
  With friends and kindred dealing.

Bear witness, Ye, whose thoughts that day
  In Yarrow's groves were centered;
Who through the silent portal arch
  Of moldering Newark entered;   100
And clomb the winding stair that once
  Too timidly was mounted

By the "last Minstrel," (not the last!)
　　Ere he his Tale recounted.

Flow on for ever, Yarrow Stream!
　　Fulfill thy pensive duty,
Well pleased that future Bards should chant
　　For simple hearts thy beauty;
To dream-light dear while yet unseen,
　　Dear to the common sunshine,
And dearer still, as now I feel,
　　To memory's shadowy moonshine!   110

THE TROSACHS [54]

There's not a nook within this solemn Pass,
But were an apt confessional for One
Taught by his summer spent, his autumn gone,
That Life is but a tale of morning grass
Withered at eve. From scenes of art which chase
That thought away, turn, and with watchful eyes
Feed it 'mid Nature's old felicities,
Rocks, rivers, and smooth lakes more clear than glass
Untouched, unbreathed upon. Thrice happy quest,
If from a golden perch of aspen spray
(October's workmanship to rival May)
The pensive warbler of the ruddy breast
That moral sweeten by a heaven-taught lay,
Lulling the year, with all its cares, to rest!

IF THIS GREAT WORLD OF JOY AND PAIN

If this great world of joy and pain
　　Revolve in one sure track;
If freedom, set, will rise again,
　　And virtue, flown, come back;
Woe to the purblind crew who fill
　　The heart with each day's care;
Nor gain, from past or future, skill
　　To bear, and to forbear!

MOST SWEET IT IS WITH UNUPLIFTED EYES

Most sweet it is with unuplifted eyes
　　To pace the ground, if path be there or none,

---

[54] A picturesque wooded valley in Perthshire, Scotland, between Lochs Katrine and Achray. "Colored by the remembrance of my recent visit to Sir Walter Scott, and the melancholy errand on which he was going." (Wordsworth)

While a fair region round the traveler lies
Which he forbears again to look upon;
Pleased rather with some soft ideal scene,
The work of Fancy, or some happy tone
Of meditation, slipping in between
The beauty coming and the beauty gone.
If Thought and Love desert us, from that day
Let us break off all commerce with the Muse:
With Thought and Love companions of our way,
Whate'er the senses take or may refuse,
The Mind's internal heaven shall shed her dews
Of inspiration on the humblest lay.

SAMUEL TAYLOR COLERIDGE (1772–1834)

Samuel Taylor Coleridge was born at Ottery St. Mary, Devonshire, on October 21, 1772, the son of John Coleridge, clergyman of the Church of England and schoolmaster. On the latter's death, friends secured for Coleridge an appointment to the famous Christ's Hospital School in London (1782), where he became the friend of Charles Lamb. Here he remained for nine years, reading in classical literature and in philosophy far beyond his fellows, and exhibiting already those powers of conversation for which he was celebrated throughout life. In 1791 he was entered as a sizar at Jesus College, Cambridge, being nominated to one of the "exhibitions" or appointments in the possession of his school. Disappointed in a love affair and discouraged by his debts, he interrupted his college career in 1793 by enlisting in a regiment of dragoons under the name of Silas Tomkyn Comberbacke. A few months convinced Coleridge that he could not be a cavalryman. He could not stick on his horse, or even curry it. Through the interposition of relatives his discharge was procured, and he returned to college, which, however, he quitted in 1794 without taking a degree.

Before leaving Cambridge, he had planned, in connection with the poet Southey and others, to establish in America, on the banks of the Susquehanna, a "pantisocracy," or ideal community, to consist of "twelve gentlemen of good education and liberal principles" with their wives. The labor of each man for two or three hours a day was to support the colony, and the ample leisure was to be devoted to study, to discussion, and to the education of the children on a settled system. As a preliminary to this scheme, Coleridge and Southey married the Misses Sara and Edith Fricker. But the grand project fell through, and Coleridge, in the endeavor to support himself and his family, started a magazine called *The Watchman* (of which only ten numbers were issued), and published his *Poems on Various Subjects* and *Ode on the Departing Year* (1796).

Meanwhile he had become acquainted with Wordsworth, who, shortly after Coleridge removed to Nether Stowey, in Somersetshire, took with his sister Dorothy a cottage at Alfoxden, about four miles away (1797). In the ensuing year the association of the two poets was very intimate, and each exercised a powerful influence on the other. They planned to write together the *Lyrical*

Ballads (published in 1798), but Wordsworth's industry so far outstripped Coleridge's that the latter contributed only four poems to the volume (including, however, *The Ancient Mariner*). During this period, Coleridge had been preaching in Unitarian chapels, and came near to accepting a call to the Unitarian church in Shrewsbury, but on receipt of a generous annuity from Josiah and Thomas Wedgwood, sons of the great potter, was encouraged instead to devote his life to literature. In September, 1798, Coleridge accompanied the Wordsworths to Germany, where he remained about nine months, learning the German language, studying German literature and metaphysics, and attending lectures at the University of Göttingen. An early product of his German studies was his translation of Schiller's *Wallenstein* (1800).

Back in England, he followed Wordsworth to the Lake country, settling in 1800 at Greta Hall, Keswick, which remained his home, somewhat intermittently, until 1810. His wife was uncongenial, and his own habits difficult, and consequently he lived more and more apart from his family—with Wordsworth, with the Morgans from 1810 to 1816, and with Dr. Gillman and his wife at Highgate from the latter year till his death in 1834.

All of Coleridge's poetry that has made his name famous was produced in early life, the best of it in the years of close association with Wordsworth. As he grew older, he became more deeply interested in metaphysics, and his mind was sunk in a sea of philosophic and theological speculation. This work has not been without its influence on English thought, but is much less important than his splendid poetry. Meanwhile inertia and procrastination were more and more limiting his output. He planned vast works, but produced very little; he wrote splendid fragments which he always meant to complete, but never did. Yet he still talked incessantly; and in his old age, disciples flocked to him to listen to his brilliant conversation. His powers of will, never strong, had been impaired by the habit of taking opium—a habit against which he fought from time to time, but which he never entirely conquered. The literary landmarks of his middle and later years include a second magazine, *The Friend*, which appeared very irregularly for nine months in 1809–1810, his drama *Remorse*, acted at Drury Lane in 1813 (based, however, on a work of 1797), *Christabel and Kubla Khan,* published in 1816, but mostly written earlier, and *Sybilline Leaves* (collected poetry), and *Biographia Literaria* (critical and biographical prose), both in 1817. The latter shows high critical abilities, but is discursive and unsystematic. It contains a penetrating critique of Wordsworth's theories. From 1808 on, he delivered several series of lectures on Shakespeare, the principles of poetry, and the like. Characteristically, he wrote out no manuscript for the lectures, and they have been imperfectly preserved in the notes of reporters.

Coleridge needs more than most poets to be winnowed and sifted, but his dozen or so inspired pieces are among the most remarkable achievements in English verse. Of him as of another it may be said that he dabbled in the day-fall and played with star-dust. In the pieces here presented he exhibits a supreme imaginative quality. He weaves a spell. His poetry is sheer magic, as distinguished from the ordinary run of pedestrian verse. He surely saw "the light that never was on sea or land." Few writers have influenced English poetry more than he, yet his really enduring work is meager in quantity. His brilliant intellectual and imaginative powers are only fitfully displayed in the volumes he published. His life exhibits the tragic waste of abilities of the first order.

Bibliography. *Works*, by W. G. T. Shedd, 7 vols. (Harper's). One volume *Poetical Works* by J. D. Campbell (Globe ed., Macmillan). *Biographia Literaria*, ed. J. Shawcross (Oxford), and in Everyman's Lib. Biography by J. D. Campbell (Macmillan). *Samuel Taylor Coleridge*, a study by H. L. Fausset (Harcourt Brace). *The Road to Xanadu*, by J. L. Lowes (Houghton Mifflin), study of the genesis of *The Ancient Mariner*.

THIS LIME-TREE BOWER MY PRISON *

ADDRESSED TO CHARLES LAMB, OF THE INDIA HOUSE, LONDON

[Charles Lamb, with William and Dorothy Wordsworth, had visited Coleridge at Nether Stowey in July, 1797.]

Well, they are gone, and here must I remain,
This lime-tree bower my prison! I have lost
Beauties and feelings, such as would have been
Most sweet to my remembrance even when age
Had dimm'd mine eyes to blindness! They, meanwhile,
Friends, whom I never more may meet again,
On springy heath, along the hill-top edge,
Wander in gladness, and wind down, perchance,
To that still roaring dell, of which I told;
The roaring dell, o'erwooded, narrow, deep,   10
And only speckled by the mid-day sun;
Where its slim trunk the ash from rock to rock
Flings arching like a bridge;—that branchless ash,
Unsunn'd and damp, whose few poor yellow leaves
Ne'er tremble in the gale, yet tremble still,
Fann'd by the waterfall! and there my friends
Behold the dark green file of long, lank weeds,
That all at once (a most fantastic sight!)
Still nod and drip beneath the dripping edge
Of the blue clay-stone.   Now, my friends emerge   20
Beneath the wide, wide Heaven—and view again
The many-steepled tract magnificent
Of hilly fields and meadows, and the sea,
With some fair bark, perhaps, whose sails light up
The slip of smooth clear blue betwixt two isles
Of purple shadow! Yes! they wander on
In gladness all; but thou, methinks, most glad,

My gentle-hearted Charles! for thou hast pined
And hunger'd after Nature, many a year,
In the great City pent, winning thy way   30
With sad yet patient soul, through evil and pain
And strange calamity! Ah! slowly sink
Behind the western ridge, thou glorious Sun!
Shine in the slant beams of the sinking orb,
Ye purple heath-flowers! richlier burn, ye clouds!
Live in the yellow light, ye distant groves!
And kindle, thou blue Ocean! So my friend
Struck with deep joy may stand, as I have stood,
Silent with swimming sense; yea, gazing round
On the wide landscape, gaze till all doth seem   40
Less gross than bodily; and of such hues
As veil the Almighty Spirit, when yet he makes
Spirits perceive his presence.
                                A delight
Comes sudden on my heart, and I am glad
As I myself were there! Nor in this bower,
This little lime-tree bower, have I not mark'd
Much that has sooth'd me. Pale beneath the blaze
Hung the transparent foliage; and I watch'd
Some broad and sunny leaf, and lov'd to see
The shadow of the leaf and stem above   50
Dappling its sunshine! And that walnut-tree
Was richly ting'd, and a deep radiance lay
Full on the ancient ivy, which usurps
Those fronting elms, and now, with blackest mass
Makes their dark branches gleam a lighter hue
Through the late twilight: and though now the bat
Wheels silent by, and not a swallow twitters,
Yet still the solitary humble-bee
Sings in the bean-flower! Henceforth I shall know
That Nature ne'er deserts the wise and pure;   60
No plot so narrow, be but Nature there,
No waste so vacant, but may well employ
Each faculty of sense, and keep the heart
Awake to Love and Beauty! and sometimes
'Tis well to be bereft of promis'd good,
That we may lift the soul, and contemplate
With lively joy the joys we cannot share.
My gentle-hearted Charles! when the last rook
Beat its straight path along the dusky air
Homewards, I blest it! deeming its black wing   70
(Now a dim speck, now vanishing in light)
Had cross'd the mighty orb's dilated glory,

While thou stood'st gazing; or, when all was still,
Flew creaking o'er thy head, and had a charm
For thee, my gentle-hearted Charles, to whom
No sound is dissonant which tells of life.

KUBLA KHAN

Coleridge wrote the following note on the poem:

"The following fragment is here published at the request of a poet of great and deserved celebrity [presumably Byron], and, so far as the author's own opinions are concerned, rather as a psychological curiosity, than on grounds of any supposed *poetic* merits.

"In the summer of the year 1797, the Author, then in ill health, had retired to a lonely farm-house between Porlock and Linton, on the Exmoor confines of Somerset and Devonshire. In consequence of a slight indisposition an anodyne had been prescribed, from the effects of which he fell asleep in his chair at the moment that he was reading the following sentence, or words of the same substance, in *Purchas's Pilgrimage:* 'Here the Khan Kubla commanded a palace to be built, and a stately garden thereunto. And thus ten miles of fertile ground were enclosed with a wall.' The author continued for about three hours in a profound sleep, at least of the external senses, during which time he has the most vivid confidence that he could not have composed less than from two to three hundred lines; if that indeed can be called composition in which all the images rose up before him as *things*, with a parallel production of the correspondent expressions, without any sensation or consciousness of effort. On awaking he appeared to himself to have a distinct recollection of the whole, and, taking his pen, ink, and paper, instantly and eagerly wrote down the lines that are here preserved. At this moment he was unfortunately called out by a person on business from Porlock, and detained by him above an hour, and on his return to his room found, to his no small surprise and mortification, that though he still retained some vague and dim recollection of the general purport of the vision, yet, with the exception of some eight or ten scattered lines and images, all the rest had passed away like the images on the surface of a stream into which a stone has been cast, but, alas! without the after restoration of the latter! . . .

"Yet from the still surviving recollections in his mind, the author has frequently purposed to finish for himself what had been originally, as it were, given to him. . . . But the to-morrow is yet to come." (Coleridge's note in 1816.) Kubla Khan lived in the thirteenth century, and was the founder of the Mongol dynasty of China. The poem is probably to be dated 1798, not 1797.

IN Xanadu did Kubla Khan
A stately pleasure-dome decree:
Where Alph, the sacred river, ran
Through caverns measureless to man
  Down to a sunless sea.
So twice five miles of fertile ground
With walls and towers were girdled round:

And here were gardens bright with sinuous rills
Where blossomed many an incense-bearing tree,
And here were forests ancient as the hills,   10
Enfolding sunny spots of greenery.

But oh! that deep romantic chasm which slanted
Down the green hill athwart a cedarn cover!
A savage place! as holy and enchanted
As e'er beneath a waning moon was haunted
By woman wailing for her demon-lover!
And from this chasm, with ceaseless turmoil seething,
As if this earth in fast thick pants were breathing,
A mighty fountain momently was forced,
Amid whose swift half-intermitted burst   20
Huge fragments vaulted like rebounding hail,
Or chaffy grain beneath the thresher's flail:
And 'mid these dancing rocks at once and ever
It flung up momently the sacred river.
Five miles meandering with a mazy motion
Through wood and dale the sacred river ran,
Then reached the caverns measureless to man,
And sank in tumult to a lifeless ocean:
And 'mid this tumult Kubla heard from far
Ancestral voices prophesying war!   30

  The shadow of the dome of pleasure
  Floated midway on the waves;
  Where was heard the mingled measure
  From the fountain and the caves.
It was a miracle of rare device,
A sunny pleasure-dome with caves of ice!

  A damsel with a dulcimer
  In a vision once I saw:
  It was an Abyssinian maid,
  And on her dulcimer she played,   40
  Singing of Mount Abora.
  Could I revive within me
  Her symphony and song,
  To such a deep delight 'twould win me,
That with music loud and long,
I would build that dome in air,
That sunny dome! those caves of ice!
And all who heard should see them there,
And all should cry, Beware! Beware!
His flashing eyes, his floating hair!   50
Weave a circle round him thrice,

And close your eyes with holy dread,
For he on honey-dew hath fed,
And drunk the milk of Paradise.

THE RIME OF THE ANCIENT MARINER
IN SEVEN PARTS

The genesis of the poem is thus described by Wordsworth: "In the autumn of 1797 he [Coleridge], my sister, and myself, started from Alfoxden pretty late in the afternoon with a view to visit Linton and the Valley of Stones, near to it. Accordingly we set off and proceeded along the Quantock Hills toward Watchet, and in the course of this walk was planned . . . *The Ancient Mariner*, founded on a dream, as Mr. Coleridge said, of his friend Mr. Cruikshank. Much the greatest part of the story was Mr. Coleridge's invention, but certain parts I suggested: for example, some crime was to be committed which should bring upon the Old Navigator, as Coleridge afterwards delighted to call him, the spectral persecution, as a consequence of that crime and his own wanderings. I had been reading in Shelvocke's *Voyages* a day or two before that, while doubling Cape Horn, they frequently saw albatrosses in that latitude, the largest sort of sea-fowl, some extending their wings twelve or thirteen feet. 'Suppose,' said I, 'you represent him as having killed one of these birds on entering the South Sea, and that the tutelary spirits of these regions take upon them to avenge the crime.' The incident was thought fit for the purpose and adopted accordingly. I also suggested the navigation of the ship by the dead men, but do not recollect that I had anything more to do with the scheme of the poem. . . . We began the composition together on that, to me, memorable evening. . . . As we endeavored to proceed conjointly (I speak of the same evening), our respective manners proved so widely different that it would have been quite presumptuous in me to do anything but separate from an undertaking upon which I could only have been a clog. . . .
"Besides the lines (in the fourth part)—

> 'And thou art long, and lank, and brown,
> As is the ribbed sea-sand'—

I wrote the stanza (in the first part)—

> 'He holds him with his glittering eye—
> The Wedding-Guest stood still,
> And listens like a three-years' child:
> The Mariner hath his will'—

and four or five lines more in different parts of the poem, which I could not now point out."

In Chapter XIV of *Biographia Literaria* Coleridge describes the plan of the *Lyrical Ballads*, and the place of *The Ancient Mariner* in that plan. *The Road to Xanadu*, by John L. Lowes (Houghton Mifflin) is a brilliant study of the sources of the poem, with particular attention to the imaginative re-creation by Coleridge of details from various books of travels and other documents.

Facile credo, plures esse Naturas invisibiles quam visibiles in rerum universitate. Sed horum omnium familiam quis nobis enarrabit? et gradus et cognationes et discrimina et singulorum munera? Quid agunt? quæ loca habitant? Harum rerum notitiam semper ambivit ingenium humanum, nunquam attigit. Juvat, interea, non diffiteor, quandoque in animo, tanquam in tabulâ, majoris et melioris mundi imaginem contemplari: ne mens assuefacta hodiernæ vitæ minutiis se contrahat nimis, et tota subsidat in pusillas cogitationes. Sed veritati interea invigilandum est, modusque servandus, ut certa ab incertis, diem a nocte, distinguamus.[1]

—T. Burnet: *Archæol. Phil.*, p. 68.

ARGUMENT

How a Ship having passed the Line was driven by storms to the cold Country towards the South Pole; and how from thence she made her course to the tropical Latitude of the Great Pacific Ocean; and of the strange things that befell; and in what manner the Ancyent Marinere came back to his own Country.

PART I

An ancient Mariner meeteth three Gallants bidden to a wedding-feast, and detaineth one.

It is an ancient Mariner,
And he stoppeth one of three.
"By thy long gray beard and glittering eye,
Now wherefore stopp'st thou me?

"The Bridegroom's doors are opened wide,
And I am next of kin;
The guests are met, the feast is set:
May'st hear the merry din."

He holds him with his skinny hand,
"There was a ship," quoth he.   10
"Hold off! unhand me, gray-beard loon!"
Eftsoons his hand dropt he.

The Wedding-Guest is spellbound by the eye of the old sea-faring man, and constrained to hear his tale.

He holds him with his glittering eye—
The Wedding-Guest stood still,
And listens like a three years' child:
The Mariner hath his will.

The Wedding-Guest sat on a stone;
He cannot choose but hear;

[1] I can easily believe, that there are more Invisible than Visible Beings in the Universe. But who will declare to us the Family of all these, and acquaint us with the Agreements, Differences, and peculiar Talents which are to be found among them; what their employments are, and in what mansions they dwell? I will own that it is very profitable, sometimes to contemplate in the Mind, as in a Draught, the Image of the greater and better World; lest the Soul being accustomed to the Trifles of this present Life, should contract itself too much, and altogether rest in mean Cogitations; but, in the mean Time, we must take care to keep to the Truth, and observe moderation, that we may distinguish certain from uncertain Things, and Day from Night.—Translation by Mead and Fontin, 1736

And thus spake on that ancient man,
The bright-eyed Mariner.   20

"The ship was cheered, the harbor cleared,
Merrily did we drop
Below the kirk, below the hill,
Below the lighthouse top.

The Mariner
tells how the
ship sailed
southward
with a good
wind and fair
weather, till
it reached the
Line.

"The sun came up upon the left,
Out of the sea came he!
And he shone bright, and on the right
Went down into the sea.

"Higher and higher every day,
Till over the mast at noon—"   30
The Wedding-Guest here beat his breast,
For he heard the loud bassoon.

The Wedding-
Guest heareth
the bridal mu-
sic; but the
Mariner con-
tinueth his
tale.

The bride hath paced into the hall,
Red as a rose is she;
Nodding their heads before her goes
The merry minstrelsy.

The Wedding-Guest he beat his breast,
Yet he cannot choose but hear;
And thus spake on that ancient man,
The bright-eyed Mariner.   40

The ship
driven by a
storm toward
the south pole.

"And now the Storm-blast came, and he
Was tyrannous and strong:
He struck with his o'ertaking wings,
And chased us south along.

With sloping masts and dipping prow,
As who pursued with yell and blow
Still treads the shadow of his foe,
And forward bends his head,
The ship drove fast, loud roared the blast,
And southward aye we fled.   50

And now there came both mist and snow,
And it grew wondrous cold:
And ice, mast-high, came floating by,
As green as emerald.

The land of
ice, and of
fearful
sounds, where
no living
thing was to
be seen.

And through the drifts the snowy clifts
Did send a dismal sheen:
Nor shapes of men nor beasts we ken—
The ice was all between.

The ice was here, the ice was there,
The ice was all around: 60
It cracked and growled, and roared and howled,
Like noises in a swound!

Till a great
sea-bird, called
the Albatross,
came through
the snow-fog,
and was re-
ceived with
great joy and
hospitality.

At length did cross an Albatross:
Thorough the fog it came;
As if it had been a Christian soul,
We hailed it in God's name.

It ate the food it ne'er had eat,
And round and round it flew.
The ice did split with a thunder-fit;
The helmsman steered us through!   70

And lo! the
Albatross
proveth a bird
of good omen,
and followeth
the ship as it
returned
northward,
through fog
and floating
ice.

And a good south wind sprung up behind;
The Albatross did follow,
And every day, for food or play,
Came to the mariners' hollo!

In mist or cloud, on mast or shroud,
It perched for vespers nine;
Whiles all the night, through fog-smoke white,
Glimmered the white moon-shine."

The ancient
Mariner
inhospitably
killeth the
pious bird of
good omen.

"God save thee, ancient Mariner!
From the fiends, that plague thee thus!—   80
Why lookst thou so?"—"With my cross-bow
I shot the Albatross.

Part II

The Sun now rose upon the right:
Out of the sea came he,
Still hid in mist, and on the left
Went down into the sea.

And the good south wind still blew behind,
But no sweet bird did follow,
Nor any day for food or play
Came to the mariners' hollo!   90

His shipmates
cry out against
the ancient
Mariner for
killing the bird
of good luck.

And I had done a hellish thing,
And it would work 'em woe:
For all averred, I had killed the bird
That made the breeze to blow.
Ah wretch! said they, the bird to slay,
That made the breeze to blow!

But when the
fog cleared off,
they justify the
same, and thus
make them-
selves accom-
plices in the
crime.

Nor dim nor red, like God's own head,
The glorious Sun uprist:
Then all averred, I had killed the bird
That brought the fog and mist.   100
'Twas right, said they, such birds to slay,
That bring the fog and mist.

The fair
breeze contin-
ues; the ship
enters the Pa-
cific Ocean and
sails northward
even till it
reaches the
Line.

The fair breeze blew, the white foam flew,
The furrow followed free:
We were the first that ever burst
Into that silent sea.

The ship hath
been suddenly
becalmed.

Down dropt the breeze, the sails dropt down,
'Twas sad as sad could be;
And we did speak only to break
The silence of the sea!   110

All in a hot and copper sky,
The bloody Sun, at noon,
Right up above the mast did stand,
No bigger than the Moon.

Day after day, day after day,
We stuck, nor breath nor motion;
As idle as a painted ship
Upon a painted ocean.

And the Alba-
tross begins to
be avenged.

Water, water, every where,
And all the boards did shrink;   120
Water, water, every where,
Nor any drop to drink.

The very deep did rot: O Christ!
That ever this should be!
Yea, slimy things did crawl with legs
Upon the slimy sea.

About, about, in reel and rout
The death-fires danced at night;

The water, like a witch's oils,
Burnt green, and blue, and white.   130

And some in dreams assured were
Of the Spirit that plagued us so:
Nine fathom deep he had followed us
From the land of mist and snow.

And every tongue, through utter drought,
Was withered at the root;
We could not speak, no more than if
We had been choked with soot.

Ah! well-a-day! what evil looks
Had I from old and young!   140
Instead of the cross, the Albatross
About my neck was hung.

Part III

There passed a weary time. Each throat
Was parched, and glazed each eye.
A weary time! a weary time!
How glazed each weary eye,
When looking westward, I beheld
A something in the sky.

At first it seemed a little speck,
And then it seemed a mist;   150
It moved and moved, and took at last
A certain shape, I wist.

A speck, a mist, a shape, I wist!
And still it neared and neared:
As if it dodged a water-sprite,
It plunged and tacked and veered.

With throats unslaked, with black lips baked,
We could nor laugh nor wail;
Through utter drought all dumb we stood!
I bit my arm, I sucked the blood,   160
And cried, A sail! a sail!

With throats unslaked, with black lips baked,
Agape they heard me call:
Gramercy! they for joy did grin,

A flash of joy.

And all at once their breath drew in,
As they were drinking all.

And horror
follows. For
can it be a
ship that comes
onward with-
out wind or
tide?

See! see! (I cried) she tacks no more!
Hither to work us weal;
Without a breeze, without a tide,
She steadies with upright keel!   170

The western wave was all aflame,
The day was well-nigh done!
Almost upon the western wave
Rested the broad bright Sun;
When that strange ship drove suddenly
Betwixt us and the Sun.

It seemeth
him but the
skeleton of a
ship.

And straight the Sun was flecked with bars,
(Heaven's Mother send us grace!)
As if through a dungeon-grate he peered,
With broad and burning face.   180

Alas! (thought I, and my heart beat loud,)
How fast she nears and nears!
Are those *her* sails that glance in the Sun,
Like restless gossameres?

And its ribs
are seen as
bars on the
face of the set-
ting Sun.
The Spectre-
Woman and her
Death-mate,
and no other
on board the
skeleton-ship.

Are those her ribs through which the Sun
Did peer as through a grate?
And is that Woman all her crew?
Is that a Death? and are there two?
Is Death that Woman's mate?

Like vessel,
like crew!

Her lips were red, her looks were free,   190
Her locks were yellow as gold:
Her skin was as white as leprosy,
The Night-mare Life-in-Death was she,
Who thicks man's blood with cold.

Death and
Life-in-
Death have
diced for the
ship's crew,
and she (the
latter) winneth
the ancient
Mariner.

The naked hulk alongside came,
And the twain were casting dice;
'The game is done! I've won, I've won!'
Quoth she, and whistles thrice.

No twilight
within the
courts of the
Sun.

The Sun's rim dips; the stars rush out:
At one stride comes the dark;   200
With far-heard whisper, o'er the sea,
Off shot the specter-bark.

At the rising
of the Moon,

We listened and looked sideways up!
Fear at my heart, as at a cup,
My life-blood seemed to sip!
The stars were dim, and thick the night,
The steersman's face by his lamp gleamed white;
From the sails the dew did drip—
Till clomb above the eastern bar
The hornèd Moon, with one bright star   210
Within the nether tip.

One after
another,

One after one, by the star-dogged Moon,
Too quick for groan or sigh,
Each turned his face with a ghastly pang,
And cursed me with his eye.

His shipmates
drop down
dead;

Four times fifty living men
(And I heard nor sigh nor groan),
With heavy thump, a lifeless lump,
They dropped down one by one.

But Life-in-
Death begins
her work on
the ancient
Mariner.

The souls did from their bodies fly,—   220
They fled to bliss or woe!
And every soul, it passed me by,
Like the whizz of my cross-bow!"

Part IV

The Wedding-
Guest feareth
that a Spirit is
talking to him;

"I fear thee, ancient Mariner!
I fear thy skinny hand!
And thou art long, and lank, and brown,
As is the ribbed sea-sand.[2]

But the an-
cient Mariner
assureth him
of his bodily
life, and pro-
ceedeth to re-
late his horri-
ble penance.

"I fear thee, and thy glittering eye,
And thy skinny hand, so brown."—
"Fear not, fear not, thou Wedding-Guest!   230
This body dropt not down.

Alone, alone, all, all alone,
Alone on a wide, wide sea!
And never a saint took pity on
My soul in agony.

He despiseth
the creatures
of the calm.

The many men, so beautiful!
And they all dead did lie:

2 "For the last two lines of this stanza, I am indebted to Mr. Wordsworth. It was on a delightful walk from Nether Stowey to Dulverton, with him and his sister, in the Autumn of 1797, that this Poem was planned, and in part composed." (Coleridge)

And a thousand thousand slimy things
Lived on; and so did I.

And envieth
that they
should live,
and so many
lie dead.

I looked upon the rotting sea,
And drew my eyes away;
I looked upon the rotting deck,
And there the dead men lay.

240

I looked to Heaven and tried to pray;
But or ever a prayer had gushed,
A wicked whisper came, and made
My heart as dry as dust.

I closed my lids, and kept them close,
And the balls like pulses beat;
For the sky and the sea, and the sea and
    the sky
Lay like a load on my weary eye,
And the dead were at my feet.

250

The cold sweat melted from their limbs,
Nor rot nor reek did they!
The look with which they looked on me
Had never passed away.

But the curse
liveth for him
in the eye of
the dead men.

An orphan's curse would drag to Hell
A spirit from on high;
But oh! more horrible than that
Is a curse in a dead man's eye!
Seven days, seven nights, I saw that curse,
And yet I could not die.

260

In his loneli-
ness and fixed-
ness he yearn-
eth towards the
journeying
Moon, and the
stars that still
sojourn, yet still
move onward;
and everywhere
the blue sky
belongs to them,
and is their
appointed rest,
and their na-
tive country
and their own
natural homes,
which they
enter unan-
nounced, as
lords that are
certainly ex-
pected and
yet there is a
silent joy at
their arrival.

The moving Moon went up the sky,
And no where did abide:
Softly she was going up,
And a star or two beside—

Her beams bemocked the sultry main,
Like April hoar-frost spread;
But where the ship's huge shadow lay,
The charmèd water burnt alway
A still and awful red.

270

Beyond the shadow of the ship,
I watched the water-snakes:
They moved in tracks of shining white,

By the light of
the Moon he
beholdeth
God's creatures
of the great
calm.
And when they reared, the elfish light
Fell off in hoary flakes.

Within the shadow of the ship
I watched their rich attire:
Blue, glossy green, and velvet black,
They coiled and swam; and every track   280
Was a flash of golden fire.

Their beauty
and their
happiness.
O happy living things! no tongue
Their beauty might declare:
A spring of love gushed from my heart,
And I blessed them unaware!
He blesseth
them in his
heart.
Sure my kind saint took pity on me,
And I blessed them unaware!

The spell be-
gins to break.
The selfsame moment I could pray;
And from my neck so free
The Albatross fell off, and sank   290
Like lead into the sea.

PART V

Oh sleep! it is a gentle thing,
Beloved from pole to pole!
To Mary Queen the praise be given!
She sent the gentle sleep from Heaven,
That slid into my soul.

By grace of
the holy
Mother, the
ancient Mari-
ner is refreshed
with rain.
The silly buckets on the deck,
That had so long remained,
I dreamt that they were filled with dew;
And when I awoke, it rained.   300

My lips were wet, my throat was cold,
My garments all were dank;
Sure I had drunken in my dreams,
And still my body drank.

I moved, and could not feel my limbs:
I was so light—almost
I thought that I had died in sleep,
And was a blessed ghost.

And soon I heard a roaring wind:
It did not come anear;   310

He heareth
sounds, and
seeth strange
sights and com-
motions in the
sky and the
element.
But with its sound it shook the sails,
That were so thin and sere.

The upper air burst into life!
And a hundred fire-flags sheen,
To and fro they were hurried about!
And to and fro, and in and out,
The wan stars danced between.

And the coming wind did roar more loud,
And the sails did sigh like sedge;
And the rain poured down from one black
    cloud;   320
The Moon was at its edge.

The thick black cloud was cleft, and still
The Moon was at its side:
Like waters shot from some high crag,
The lightning fell with never a jag,
A river steep and wide.

The bodies of
the ship's
crew are in-
spired, and
the ship moves
on;
The loud wind never reached the ship,
Yet now the ship moved on!
Beneath the lightning and the Moon
The dead men gave a groan.   330

They groaned, they stirred, they all uprose,
Nor spake, nor moved their eyes;
It had been strange, even in a dream,
To have seen those dead men rise.

The helmsman steered, the ship moved on;
Yet never a breeze up blew;
The mariners all 'gan work the ropes,
Where they were wont to do:
They raised their limbs like lifeless tools—
We were a ghastly crew.   340

The body of my brother's son
Stood by me, knee to knee:
The body and I pulled at one rope,
But he said naught to me."

"I fear thee, ancient Mariner!"
"Be calm, thou Wedding-Guest!
'Twas not those souls that fled in pain,

But not by the souls of the men, nor by dæmons of earth or middle air, but by a blessed troop of angelic spirits, sent down by the invocation of the guardian saint.

Which to their corses came again,
But a troop of spirits blest:

For when it dawned—they dropped their
        arms,
And clustered round the mast;
Sweet sounds rose slowly through their mouths,
And from their bodies passed.

350

Around, around, flew each sweet sound,
Then darted to the Sun;
Slowly the sounds came back again,
Now mixed, now one by one.

Sometimes a-dropping from the sky
I heard the sky-lark sing;
Sometimes all little birds that are,
How they seemed to fill the sea and air
With their sweet jargoning!

360

And now 'twas like all instruments,
Now like a lonely flute;
And now it is an angel's song,
That makes the Heavens be mute.

It ceased; yet still the sails made on
A pleasant noise till noon,
A noise like of a hidden brook
In the leafy month of June,
That to the sleeping woods all night
Singeth a quiet tune.

370

Till noon we quietly sailed on,
Yet never a breeze did breathe:
Slowly and smoothly went the ship,
Moved onward from beneath.

The lonesome Spirit from the south-pole carries on the ship as far as the Line, in obedience to the angelic troop, but still requireth vengeance.

Under the keel nine fathom deep,
From the land of mist and snow,
The spirit slid: and it was he
That made the ship to go.
The sails at noon left off their tune
And the ship stood still also.

380

The Sun, right up above the mast,
Had fixed her to the ocean:

But in a minute she 'gan stir,
With a short uneasy motion—
Backwards and forwards half her length
With a short uneasy motion.

Then like a pawing horse let go,
She made a sudden bound;   390
It flung the blood into my head,
And I fell down in a swound.

How long in that same fit I lay,
I have not to declare;
But ere my living life returned,
I heard and in my soul discerned
Two voices in the air.

The Polar Spirit's fellow-dæmons, the invisible inhabitants of the element, take part in his wrong; and two of them relate, one to the other, that penance long and heavy for the ancient Mariner hath been accorded to the Polar Spirit, who returneth southward.

'Is it he?' quoth one, 'Is this the man?
By him who died on cross,
With his cruel blow he laid full low   400
The harmless Albatross.

The spirit who bideth by himself
In the land of mist and snow,
He loved the bird that loved the man
Who shot him with his bow.'

The other was a softer voice,
As soft as honey-dew:
Quoth he, 'The man hath penance done,
And penance more will do.'

PART VI

First Voice

'But tell me, tell me! speak again,   410
Thy soft response renewing—
What makes that ship drive on so fast?
What is the Ocean doing?'

Second Voice

'Still as a slave before his lord,
The Ocean hath no blast;
His great bright eye most silently
Up to the Moon is cast—

If he may know which way to go;
For she guides him smooth or grim.
See, brother, see! how graciously   420
She looketh down on him.'

First Voice

'But why drives on that ship so fast,
Without or wave or wind?'

Second Voice

'The air is cut away before,
And closes from behind.

Fly, brother, fly! more high, more high!
Or we shall be belated:
For slow and slow that ship will go,
When the Mariner's trance is abated.'

I woke, and we were sailing on   430
As in a gentle weather:
'Twas night, calm night, the Moon was high,
The dead men stood together.

All stood together on the deck,
For a charnel-dungeon fitter:
All fixed on me their stony eye
That in the Moon did glitter.

The pang, the curse, with which they died,
Had never passed away:
I could not draw my eyes from theirs,   440
Nor turn them up to pray.

And now this spell was snapped: once more
I viewed the ocean green,
And looked far forth, yet little saw
Of what had else been seen—

Like one that on a lonesome road
Doth walk in fear and dread,
And having once turned round, walks on,
And turns no more his head;
Because he knows a frightful fiend   450
Doth close behind him tread.

But soon there breathed a wind on me,
Nor sound nor motion made:
Its path was not upon the sea,
In ripple or in shade.

It raised my hair, it fanned my cheek
Like a meadow-gale of spring—
It mingled strangely with my fears,
Yet it felt like a welcoming.

Swiftly, swiftly flew the ship,   460
Yet she sailed softly too:
Sweetly, sweetly blew the breeze—
On me alone it blew.

And the an-
cient Mariner
beholdeth his
native country.
Oh! dream of joy! is this indeed
The light-house top I see?
Is this the hill? Is this the kirk?
Is this mine own countree?

We drifted o'er the harbor-bar,
And I with sobs did pray—
'O let me be awake, my God!   470
Or let me sleep alway.'

The harbor-bay was clear as glass,
So smoothly it was strewn!
And on the bay the moonlight lay,
And the shadow of the Moon.

The rock shone bright, the kirk no less,
That stands above the rock:
The moonlight steeped in silentness
The steady weathercock.

The angelic
spirits leave
the dead
bodies,
And the bay was white with silent light,   480
Till rising from the same,
Full many shapes, that shadows were,
In crimson colors came.

And appear in
their own forms
of light.
A little distance from the prow
Those crimson shadows were:
I turned my eyes upon the deck—
Oh, Christ! what saw I there!

Each corse lay flat, lifeless and flat,
And, by the holy rood!
A man all light, a seraph-man,   490
On every corse there stood.

This seraph-band, each waved his hand:
It was a heavenly sight!
They stood as signals to the land,
Each one a lovely light;

This seraph-band, each waved his hand,
No voice did they impart—
No voice; but oh! the silence sank
Like music on my heart.

But soon I heard the dash of oars,   500
I heard the Pilot's cheer;
My head was turned perforce away,
And I saw a boat appear.

The Pilot, and the Pilot's boy,
I heard them coming fast:
Dear Lord in Heaven! it was a joy
The dead men could not blast.

I saw a third—I heard his voice:
It is the Hermit good!
He singeth loud his godly hymns   510
That he makes in the wood.
He'll shrieve my soul, he'll wash away
The Albatross's blood.

Part VII

The Hermit of the Wood

This Hermit good lives in that wood
Which slopes down to the sea:
How loudly his sweet voice he rears!
He loves to talk with marineres
That come from a far countree.

He kneels at morn, and noon, and eve—
He hath a cushion plump: 520
It is the moss that wholly hides
The rotted old oak-stump.

The skiff-boat neared: I heard them talk,
'Why this is strange, I trow!

Where are those lights so many and fair,
That signal made but now?'

*Approacheth
the ship with
wonder.*

'Strange, by my faith!' the Hermit said—
'And they answered not our cheer!
The planks look warped! and see those sails
How thin they are and sere!   530
I never saw aught like to them,
Unless perchance it were

Brown skeletons of leaves that lag
My forest-brook along;
When the ivy-tod is heavy with snow,
And the owlet whoops to the wolf below
That eats the she-wolf's young.'

'Dear Lord! it hath a fiendish look'—
(The Pilot made reply)
'I am a-feared'—'Push on, push on!'   540
Said the Hermit cheerily.

The boat came closer to the ship,
But I nor spake nor stirred;
The boat came close beneath the ship,
And straight a sound was heard.

*The ship sud-
denly sinketh.*

Under the water it rumbled on,
Still louder and more dread:
It reached the ship, it split the bay;
The ship went down like lead.

*The ancient
Mariner is
saved in the
Pilot's boat.*

Stunned by that loud and dreadful sound,   550
Which sky and ocean smote,
Like one that hath been seven days drowned,
My body lay afloat;
But swift as dreams, myself I found
Within the Pilot's boat.

Upon the whirl, where sank the ship,
The boat spun round and round;
And all was still, save that the hill
Was telling of the sound.

I moved my lips—the Pilot shrieked   560
And fell down in a fit;

The holy Hermit raised his eyes
And prayed where he did sit.

I took the oars: the Pilot's boy,
Who now doth crazy go,
Laughed loud and long, and all the while
His eyes went to and fro.
'Ha! ha!' quoth he, 'full plain I see,
The Devil knows how to row.'

And now, all in my own countree,   570
I stood on the firm land!
The Hermit stepped forth from the boat,
And scarcely he could stand.

'O shrieve me, shrieve me, holy man!'
The Hermit crossed his brow.
'Say quick,' quoth he, 'I bid thee say—
What manner of man art thou?'

Forthwith this frame of mine was wrenched
With a woful agony,
Which forced me to begin my tale;   580
And then it left me free.

Since then, at an uncertain hour,
That agony returns;
And till my ghastly tale is told,
This heart within me burns.

I pass, like night, from land to land;
I have strange power of speech;
That moment that his face I see,
I know the man that must hear me:
To him my tale I teach.   590

What loud uproar bursts from that door!
The wedding-guests are there:
But in the garden-bower the bride
And bride-maids singing are;
And hark the little vesper bell,
Which biddeth me to prayer!

O Wedding-Guest! this soul hath been
Alone on a wide wide sea:

So lonely 'twas, that God himself
Scarce seemèd there to be.   600

O sweeter than the marriage-feast
'Tis sweeter far to me,
To walk together to the kirk
With a goodly company!—

To walk together to the kirk,
And all together pray,
While each to his great Father bends,
Old men, and babes, and loving friends,
And youths and maidens gay!

And to teach,
by his own
example, love
and reverence
to all things
that God made
and loveth.

Farewell, farewell! but this I tell   610
To thee, thou Wedding-Guest!
He prayeth well, who loveth well
Both man and bird and beast.

He prayeth best, who loveth best
All things both great and small;
For the dear God who loveth us,
He made and loveth all."

The Mariner, whose eye is bright,
Whose beard with age is hoar,
Is gone: and now the Wedding-Guest   620
Turned from the bridegroom's door.

He went like one that hath been stunned,
And is of sense forlorn:
A sadder and a wiser man,
He rose the morrow morn.

CHRISTABEL

The following passage is reprinted from the Preface which Coleridge supplied with the poem when it was published in 1816:
"The first part of the following poem was written in the year 1797, at Stowey,
in the county of Somerset; the second part after my return from Germany in
the year 1800 at Keswick, Cumberland. Since the latter date, my poetic powers
have been, till very lately, in a state of suspended animation. But as, in my very
first conception of the tale, I had the whole present to my mind, with the whole-
ness, no less than with the liveliness of a vision, I trust that I shall be able
to embody in verse the three parts to come, in the course of the present year."
Gillman's *Life* supplies the following as Coleridge's idea for completing
the poem:

"The following relation was to have occupied a third and fourth canto, and to have closed the tale. Over the mountains, the Bard, as directed by Sir Leoline, hastes with his disciple; but in consequence of one of those inundations supposed to be common to this country, the spot only where the castle once stood is discovered—the edifice itself being washed away. He determines to return. Geraldine, being acquainted with all that is passing, like the weird sisters in Macbeth, vanishes. Reappearing, however, she awaits the return of the Bard, exciting in the meantime, by her wily arts, all the anger she could rouse in the Baron's breast, as well as that jealousy of which he is described to have been susceptible. The old Bard and the youth at length arrive, and therefore she can no longer personate the character of Geraldine, the daughter of Lord Ronald de Vaux, but changes her appearance to that of the accepted though absent lover of Christabel. Now ensues a courtship most distressing to Christabel, who feels, she knows not why, great disgust for her once favored knight. This coldness is very painful to the Baron, who has no more conception than herself of the supernatural transformation. She at last yields to her father's entreaties, and consents to approach the altar with this hated suitor. The real lover returning, enters at this moment, and produces the ring which she had once given him in sign of her betrothment. Thus defeated, the supernatural being Geraldine disappears. As predicted, the castle bell tolls, the mother's voice is heard, and to the exceeding great joy of the parties, the rightful marriage takes place, after which follows a reconciliation and explanation between the father and daughter."

PART THE FIRST

'TIS the middle of night by the castle clock,
And the owls have awakened the crowing cock,
Tu—whit!——Tu—whoo!
And hark, again! the crowing cock,
How drowsily it crew.

Sir Leoline, the Baron rich,
Hath a toothless mastiff, which
From her kennel beneath the rock
Maketh answer to the clock,
Four for the quarters, and twelve for the hour;   10
Ever and aye, by shine and shower,
Sixteen short howls, not over loud;
Some say, she sees my lady's shroud.

Is the night chilly and dark?
The night is chilly, but not dark.
The thin gray cloud is spread on high,
It covers but not hides the sky.
The moon is behind, and at the full;
And yet she looks both small and dull.
The night is chill, the cloud is gray: 20

'Tis a month before the month of May,
And the Spring comes slowly up this way.

The lovely lady, Christabel,
Whom her father loves so well,
What makes her in the wood so late,
A furlong from the castle gate?
She had dreams all yesternight
Of her own betrothèd knight;
And she in the midnight wood will pray
For the weal of her lover that's far away.   30

She stole along, she nothing spoke,
The sighs she heaved were soft and low,
And naught was green upon the oak
But moss and rarest mistletoe:
She kneels beneath the huge oak tree,
And in silence prayeth she.

The lady sprang up suddenly,
The lovely lady Christabel!
It moaned as near, as near can be,
But what it is she cannot tell.—   40
On the other side it seems to be,
Of the huge, broad-breasted, old oak tree.

The night is chill; the forest bare;
Is it the wind that moaneth bleak?
There is not wind enough in the air
To move away the ringlet curl
From the lovely lady's cheek—
There is not wind enough to twirl
The one red leaf, the last of its clan,
That dances as often as dance it can,   50
Hanging so light, and hanging so high,
On the topmost twig that looks up at the sky.

Hush, beating heart of Christabel!
Jesu, Maria, shield her well!
She folded her arms beneath her cloak,
And stole to the other side of the oak.
    What sees she there?

There she sees a damsel bright,
Dressed in a silken robe of white,
That shadowy in the moonlight shone: 60

The neck that made that white robe wan,
Her stately neck, and arms were bare;
Her blue-veined feet unsandaled were;
And wildly glittered here and there
The gems entangled in her hair.
I guess, 'twas frightful there to see
A lady so richly clad as she—
Beautiful exceedingly!

"Mary mother, save me now!"
Said Christabel; "and who art thou?"   70

The lady strange made answer meet,
And her voice was faint and sweet:—
"Have pity on my sore distress,
I scarce can speak for weariness:
Stretch forth thy hand, and have no fear!"
Said Christabel, "How camest thou here?"
And the lady, whose voice was faint and sweet,
Did thus pursue her answer meet:—

"My sire is of a noble line,
And my name is Geraldine: 80
Five warriors seized me yestermorn,
Me, even me, a maid forlorn:
They choked my cries with force and fright,
And tied me on a palfrey white.
The palfrey was as fleet as wind,
And they rode furiously behind.
They spurred amain, their steeds were white:
And once we crossed the shade of night.
As sure as Heaven shall rescue me,
I have no thought what men they be;   90
Nor do I know how long it is
(For I have lain entranced, I wis)
Since one, the tallest of the five,
Took me from the palfrey's back,
A weary woman, scarce alive.
Some muttered words his comrades spoke:
He placed me underneath this oak;
He swore they would return with haste;
Whither they went I cannot tell—
I thought I heard, some minutes past,   100
Sounds as of a castle bell.
Stretch forth thy hand," thus ended she,
"And help a wretched maid to flee."

Then Christabel stretched forth her hand,
And comforted fair Geraldine:
"O well, bright dame! may you command
The service of Sir Leoline;
And gladly our stout chivalry
Will he send forth, and friends withal,
To guide and guard you safe and free   110
Home to your noble father's hall."

She rose: and forth with steps they passed
That strove to be, and were not, fast.
Her gracious stars the lady bless'd,
And thus spake on sweet Christabel:
"All our household are at rest,
The hall as silent as the cell;
Sir Leoline is weak in health,
And may not well awakened be,
But we will move as if in stealth;   120
And I beseech your courtesy,
This night, to share your couch with me."

They crossed the moat, and Christabel
Took the key that fitted well;
A little door she opened straight,
All in the middle of the gate;
The gate that was ironed within and without,
Where an army in battle array had marched out.
The lady sank, belike through pain,
And Christabel with might and main   130
Lifted her up, a weary weight,
Over the threshold of the gate:
Then the lady rose again,
And moved, as she were not in pain.

So free from danger, free from fear,
They crossed the court: right glad they were.
And Christabel devoutly cried
To the lady by her side,
"Praise we the Virgin all divine,
Who hath rescued thee from thy distress!"   140
"Alas, alas!" said Geraldine,
"I cannot speak for weariness."
So free from danger, free from fear,
They crossed the court: right glad they were.

Outside her kennel, the mastiff old
Lay fast asleep, in moonshine cold.

The mastiff old did not awake,
Yet she an angry moan did make!
And what can ail the mastiff bitch?
Never till now she uttered yell   150
Beneath the eye of Christabel.
Perhaps it is the owlet's scritch:
For what can ail the mastiff bitch?

They passed the hall, that echoes still,
Pass as lightly as you will!
The brands were flat, the brands were dying,
Amid their own white ashes lying;
But when the lady passed, there came
A tongue of light, a fit of flame;
And Christabel saw the lady's eye,   160
And nothing else saw she thereby,
Save the boss of the shield of Sir Leoline tall,
Which hung in a murky old niche in the wall.
"O softly tread," said Christabel,
"My father seldom sleepeth well."

Sweet Christabel her feet doth bare,
And jealous of the listening air
They steal their way from stair to stair,
Now in glimmer, and now in gloom,
And now they pass the Baron's room,   170
As still as death, with stifled breath!
And now have reached her chamber door;
And now doth Geraldine press down
The rushes of the chamber floor.

The moon shines dim in the open air,
And not a moonbeam enters here.
But they without its light can see
The chamber carved so curiously,
Carved with figures strange and sweet,
All made out of the carver's brain,   180
For a lady's chamber meet:
The lamp with twofold silver chain
Is fastened to an angel's feet.

The silver lamp burns dead and dim;
But Christabel the lamp will trim.
She trimmed the lamp, and made it bright,
And left it swinging to and fro,

While Geraldine, in wretched plight,
Sank down upon the floor below.

"O weary lady, Geraldine,   190
I pray you, drink this cordial wine!
It is a wine of virtuous powers;
My mother made it of wild flowers."

"And will your mother pity me,
Who am a maiden most forlorn?"
Christabel answered—"Woe is me!
She died the hour that I was born.
I have heard the gray-haired friar tell
How on her death-bed she did say,
That she should hear the castle-bell   200
Strike twelve upon my wedding-day.
O mother dear! that thou wert here!"
"I would," said Geraldine, "she were!"

But soon with altered voice, said she—
"Off, wandering mother! Peak and pine!
I have power to bid thee flee."
Alas! what ails poor Geraldine?
Why stares she with unsettled eye?
Can she the bodiless dead espy?
And why with hollow voice cries she,   210
"Off, woman, off! this hour is mine—
Though thou her guardian spirit be,
Off, woman, off! 'tis given to me."

Then Christabel knelt by the lady's side,
And raised to heaven her eyes so blue—
"Alas!" said she, "this ghastly ride—
Dear lady! it hath wildered you!"
The lady wiped her moist cold brow,
And faintly said, " 'Tis over now!"

Again the wild-flower wine she drank: 220
Her fair large eyes 'gan glitter bright,
And from the floor whereon she sank,
The lofty lady stood upright:
She was most beautiful to see,
Like a lady of a far countree.

And thus the lofty lady spake—
"All they who live in the upper sky,

Do love you, holy Christabel!
And you love them, and for their sake
And for the good which me befell, 230
Even I in my degree will try,
Fair maiden, to requite you well.
But now unrobe yourself; for I
Must pray, ere yet in bed I lie."

Quoth Christabel, "So let it be!"
And as the lady bade, did she.
Her gentle limbs did she undress,
And lay down in her loveliness.

But through her brain of weal and woe
So many thoughts moved to and fro, 240
That vain it were her lids to close;
So half-way from the bed she rose,
And on her elbow did recline
To look at the lady Geraldine.

Beneath the lamp the lady bowed,
And slowly rolled her eyes around;
Then drawing in her breath aloud,
Like one that shuddered, she unbound
The cincture from beneath her breast:
Her silken robe, and inner vest, 250
Dropped to her feet, and full in view,
Behold! her bosom and half her side——
A sight to dream of, not to tell!
O shield her! shield sweet Christabel!

Yet Geraldine nor speaks nor stirs;
Ah! what a stricken look was hers!
Deep from within she seems half-way
To lift some weight with sick assay,
And eyes the maid and seeks delay;
Then suddenly, as one defied, 260
Collects herself in scorn and pride,
And lay down by the Maiden's side!—
And in her arms the maid she took,
  Ah well-a-day!
And with low voice and doleful look
These words did say:

"In the touch of this bosom there worketh a spell,
Which is lord of thy utterance, Christabel!

Thou knowest to-night, and wilt know to-morrow,
This mark of my shame, this seal of my sorrow;   270
  But vainly thou warrest,
    For this is alone in
  Thy power to declare,
    That in the dim forest
  Thou heard'st a low moaning,
And found'st a bright lady, surpassingly fair;
And didst bring her home with thee in love and in charity,
To shield her and shelter her from the damp air."

The Conclusion to Part the First

It was a lovely sight to see
The lady Christabel, when she   280
Was praying at the old oak tree.
  Amid the jagged shadows
  Of mossy leafless boughs,
  Kneeling in the moonlight,
  To make her gentle vows;
Her slender palms together pressed,
Heaving sometimes on her breast;
Her face resigned to bliss or bale—
Her face, oh call it fair not pale,
And both blue eyes more bright than clear,   290
Each about to have a tear.

With open eyes (ah woe is me!)
Asleep, and dreaming fearfully,
Fearfully dreaming, yet, I wis,
Dreaming that alone, which is—
O sorrow and shame! Can this be she,
The lady, who knelt at the old oak tree?
And lo! the worker of these harms,
That holds the maiden in her arms,
Seems to slumber still and mild,   300
As a mother with her child.

A star hath set, a star hath risen,
O Geraldine! since arms of thine
Have been the lovely lady's prison.
O Geraldine! one hour was thine—
Thou'st had thy will! By tairn and rill,
The night-birds all that hour were still.
But now they are jubilant anew.

From cliff and tower, tu—whoo! tu—whoo!
Tu—whoo! tu—whoo! from wood and fell! 310

And see! the lady Christabel
Gathers herself from out her trance;
Her limbs relax, her countenance
Grows sad and soft; the smooth thin lids
Close o'er her eyes; and tears she sheds—
Large tears that leave the lashes bright!
And oft the while she seems to smile
As infants at a sudden light!

Yea, she doth smile, and she doth weep,
Like a youthful hermitess, 320
Beauteous in a wilderness,
Who, praying always, prays in sleep.
And, if she move unquietly,
Perchance, 'tis but the blood so free
Comes back and tingles in her feet.
No doubt, she hath a vision sweet.
What if her guardian spirit 'twere,
What if she knew her mother near?
But this she knows, in joys and woes,
That saints will aid if men will call: 330
For the blue sky bends over all!

PART THE SECOND

Each matin bell, the Baron saith,
Knells us back to a world of death.
These words Sir Leoline first said,
When he rose and found his lady dead:
These words Sir Leoline will say
Many a morn to his dying day!

And hence the custom and law began
That still at dawn the sacristan,
Who duly pulls the heavy bell, 340
Five and forty beads must tell
Between each stroke—a warning knell,
Which not a soul can choose but hear
From Bratha Head to Wyndermere.

Saith Bracy the bard, "So let it knell!
And let the drowsy sacristan

Still count as slowly as he can!
There is no lack of such, I ween,
As well fill up the space between.
In Langdale Pike and Witch's Lair,   350
And Dungeon-ghyll so foully rent,
With ropes of rock and bells of air
Three sinful sextons' ghosts are pent,
Who all give back, one after t'other,
The death-note to their living brother;
And oft too, by the knell offended,
Just as their one! two! three! is ended,
The devil mocks the doleful tale
With a merry peal from Borrowdale."

The air is still! through mist and cloud   360
That merry peal comes ringing loud;
And Geraldine shakes off her dread,
And rises lightly from the bed,
Puts on her silken vestments white,
And tricks her hair in lovely plight,
And nothing doubting of her spell
Awakens the lady Christabel.
"Sleep you, sweet lady Christabel?
I trust that you have rested well."

And Christabel awoke and spied   370
The same who lay down by her side—
O rather say, the same whom she
Raised up beneath the old oak tree!
Nay, fairer yet! and yet more fair!
For she belike hath drunken deep
Of all the blessedness of sleep!
And while she spake, her looks, her air,
Such gentle thankfulness declare,
That (so it seemed) her girded vests
Grew tight beneath her heaving breasts.   380
"Sure I have sinned!" said Christabel,
"Now heaven be praised if all be well!"
And in low faltering tones, yet sweet,
Did she the lofty lady greet
With such perplexity of mind
As dreams too lively leave behind.

So quickly she rose, and quickly arrayed
Her maiden limbs, and having prayed
That He, who on the cross did groan,

Might wash away her sins unknown,   390
She forthwith led fair Geraldine
To meet her sire, Sir Leoline.

The lovely maid and the lady tall
Are pacing both into the hall,
And pacing on through page and groom,
Enter the Baron's presence-room.

The Baron rose, and while he pressed
His gentle daughter to his breast,
With cheerful wonder in his eyes
The lady Geraldine espies,   400
And gave such welcome to the same,
As might beseem so bright a dame!

But when he heard the lady's tale,
And when she told her father's name,
Why waxed Sir Leoline so pale,
Murmuring o'er the name again,
Lord Roland de Vaux of Tryermaine?

Alas! they had been friends in youth;
But whispering tongues can poison truth;
And constancy lives in realms above;   410
And life is thorny; and youth is vain;
And to be wroth with one we love
Doth work like madness in the brain.
And thus it chanced, as I divine,
With Roland and Sir Leoline.
Each spake words of high disdain
And insult to his heart's best brother:
They parted—ne'er to meet again!
But never either found another
To free the hollow heart from paining—   420
They stood aloof, the scars remaining,
Like cliffs which had been rent asunder;
A dreary sea now flows between:
But neither heat, nor frost, nor thunder,
Shall wholly do away, I ween,
The marks of that which once hath been.

Sir Leoline, a moment's space,
Stood gazing on the damsel's face:
And the youthful Lord of Tryermaine
Came back upon his heart again.   430

O then the Baron forgot his age,
His noble heart swelled high with rage;
He swore by the wounds in Jesu's side
He would proclaim it far and wide,
With trump and solemn heraldry,
That they, who thus had wronged the dame
Were base as spotted infamy!
"And if they dare deny the same,
My herald shall appoint a week,
And let the recreant traitors seek   440
My tourney court—that there and then
I may dislodge their reptile souls
From the bodies and forms of men!"
He spake: his eye in lightning rolls!
For the lady was ruthlessly seized; and he kenned
In the beautiful lady the child of his friend!

And now the tears were on his face,
And fondly in his arms he took
Fair Geraldine, who met the embrace,
Prolonging it with joyous look.   450
Which when she viewed, a vision fell
Upon the soul of Christabel,
The vision of fear, the touch and pain!
She shrunk and shuddered, and saw again—
(Ah, woe is me! Was it for thee,
Thou gentle maid! such sights to see?)

Again she saw that bosom old,
Again she felt that bosom cold,
And drew in her breath with a hissing sound:
Whereat the Knight turned wildly round,   460
And nothing saw, but his own sweet maid
With eyes upraised, as one that prayed.

The touch, the sight, had passed away,
And in its stead that vision bless'd,
Which comforted her after-rest,
While in the lady's arms she lay,
Had put a rapture in her breast,
And on her lips and o'er her eyes
Spread smiles like light!
                    With new surprise,
"What ails then my belovèd child?"   470
The Baron said.—His daughter mild
Made answer, "All will yet be well!"

I ween, she had no power to tell
Aught else: so mighty was the spell.

Yet he who saw this Geraldine
Had deemed her sure a thing divine.
Such sorrow with such grace she blended,
As if she feared she had offended
Sweet Christabel, that gentle maid!
And with such lowly tones she prayed 480
She might be sent without delay
Home to her father's mansion.
      "Nay!
Nay, by my soul!" said Leoline.
"Ho! Bracy the bard, the charge be thine!
Go thou, with music sweet and loud,
And take two steeds with trappings proud,
And take the youth whom thou lov'st best
To bear thy harp, and learn thy song,
And clothe you both in solemn vest,
And over the mountains haste along, 490
Lest wandering folk, that are abroad,
Detain you on the valley road.

"And when he has crossed the Irthing flood,
My merry bard! he hastes, he hastes
Up Knorren Moor, through Halegarth Wood,
And reaches soon that castle good
Which stands and threatens Scotland's wastes.

"Bard Bracy! bard Bracy! your horses are fleet,
Ye must ride up the hall, your music so sweet,
More loud than your horses' echoing feet! 500
And loud and loud to Lord Roland call,
Thy daughter is safe in Langdale hall!
Thy beautiful daughter is safe and free—
Sir Leoline greets thee thus through me.
He bids thee come without delay
With all thy numerous array;
And take thy lovely daughter home:
And he will meet thee on the way
With all his numerous array
White with their panting palfreys' foam: 510
And, by mine honor! I will say,
That I repent me of the day
When I spake words of fierce disdain
To Roland de Vaux of Tryermaine!—

—For since that evil hour hath flown,
Many a summer's sun hath shone;
Yet ne'er found I a friend again
Like Roland de Vaux of Tryermaine."

The lady fell, and clasped his knees,
Her face upraised, her eyes o'erflowing;   520
And Bracy replied, with faltering voice,
His gracious hail on all bestowing:
"Thy words, thou sire of Christabel,
Are sweeter than my harp can tell;
Yet might I gain a boon of thee,
This day my journey should not be;
So strange a dream hath come to me,
That I had vowed with music loud
To clear yon wood from thing unbless'd,
Warned by a vision in my rest!   530
For in my sleep I saw that dove,
That gentle bird, whom thou dost love,
And call'st by thy own daughter's name—
Sir Leoline! I saw the same,
Fluttering, and uttering fearful moan,
Among the green herbs in the forest alone.
Which when I saw and when I heard,
I wondered what might ail the bird;
For nothing near it could I see,
Save the grass and green herbs underneath the old tree.   540

"And in my dream, methought, I went
To search out what might there be found;
And what the sweet bird's trouble meant,
That thus lay fluttering on the ground.
I went and peered, and could descry
No cause for her distressful cry;
But yet for her dear lady's sake
I stooped, methought, the dove to take,
When lo! I saw a bright green snake
Coiled around its wings and neck.   550
Green as the herbs on which it couched,
Close by the dove's its head it crouched;
And with the dove it heaves and stirs,
Swelling its neck as she swelled hers!
I woke; it was the midnight hour,
The clock was echoing in the tower;
But though my slumber was gone by,
This dream it would not pass away—

It seems to live upon my eye!
And thence I vowed this self-same day 560
With music strong and saintly song
To wander through the forest bare,
Lest aught unholy loiter there."

Thus Bracy said: the Baron, the while,
Half-listening heard him with a smile;
Then turned to Lady Geraldine,
His eyes made up of wonder and love;
And said in courtly accents fine,
"Sweet maid, Lord Roland's beauteous dove,
With arms more strong than harp or song, 570
Thy sire and I will crush the snake!"
He kissed her forehead as he spake,
And Geraldine in maiden wise
Casting down her large bright eyes,
With blushing cheek and courtesy fine
She turned her from Sir Leoline;
Softly gathering up her train,
That o'er her right arm fell again;
And folded her arms across her chest,
And couched her head upon her breast, 580
And looked askance at Christabel——
Jesu, Maria, shield her well!

A snake's small eye blinks dull and shy,
And the lady's eyes they shrunk in her head,
Each shrunk up to a serpent's eye,
And with somewhat of malice, and more of dread,
At Christabel she looked askance!—
One moment—and the sight was fled!
But Christabel in dizzy trance
Stumbling on the unsteady ground 590
Shuddered aloud, with a hissing sound;
And Geraldine again turned round,
And like a thing that sought relief,
Full of wonder and full of grief,
She rolled her large bright eyes divine
Wildly on Sir Leoline.

The maid, alas! her thoughts are gone,
She nothing sees—no sight but one!
The maid, devoid of guile and sin,
I know not how, in fearful wise, 600
So deeply had she drunken in

That look, those shrunken serpent eyes,
That all her features were resigned
To this sole image in her mind:
And passively did imitate
That look of dull and treacherous hate!
And thus she stood, in dizzy trance,
Still picturing that look askance
With forced unconscious sympathy
Full before her father's view——   610
As far as such a look could be
In eyes so innocent and blue!

And, when the trance was o'er, the maid
Paused awhile, and inly prayed:
Then falling at the Baron's feet,
"By my mother's soul do I entreat
That thou this woman send away!"
She said: and more she could not say:
For what she knew she could not tell,
O'er-mastered by the mighty spell.   620

Why is thy cheek so wan and wild,
Sir Leoline? Thy only child
Lies at thy feet, thy joy, thy pride,
So fair, so innocent, so mild;
The same, for whom thy lady died!
O, by the pangs of her dear mother
Think thou no evil of thy child!
For her, and thee, and for no other,
She prayed the moment ere she died:
Prayed that the babe for whom she died,   630
Might prove her dear lord's joy and pride!
   That prayer her deadly pangs beguiled,
      Sir Leoline!
   And wouldst thou wrong thy only child,
      Her child and thine?

Within the Baron's heart and brain
If thoughts, like these, had any share,
They only swelled his rage and pain,
And did but work confusion there.
His heart was cleft with pain and rage,   640
His cheeks they quivered, his eyes were wild,
Dishonored thus in his old age;
Dishonored by his only child,
And all his hospitality

To the insulted daughter of his friend
By more than woman's jealousy
Brought thus to a disgraceful end—
He rolled his eye with stern regard
Upon the gentle minstrel bard,
And said in tones abrupt, austere—   650
"Why, Bracy! dost thou loiter here?
I bade thee hence!" The bard obeyed;
And turning from his own sweet maid,
The agèd knight, Sir Leoline,
Led forth the lady Geraldine!

The Conclusion to Part the Second

A little child, a limber elf,
Singing, dancing to itself,
A fairy thing with red round cheeks,
That always finds, and never seeks,
Makes such a vision to the sight   660
As fills a father's eyes with light;
And pleasures flow in so thick and fast
Upon his heart, that he at last
Must needs express his love's excess
With words of unmeant bitterness.
Perhaps 'tis pretty to force together
Thoughts so all unlike each other;
To mutter and mock a broken charm,
To dally with wrong that does no harm.
Perhaps 'tis tender too and pretty   670
At each wild word to feel within
A sweet recoil of love and pity.
And what, if in a world of sin
(O sorrow and shame should this be true!)
Such giddiness of heart and brain
Comes seldom save from rage and pain,
So talks as it's most used to do.

FRANCE: AN ODE

I

Ye Clouds! that far above me float and pause,
    Whose pathless march no mortal may control!
    Ye Ocean-Waves! that, wheresoe'er ye roll,
Yield homage only to eternal laws!
Ye Woods! that listen to the night birds' singing,

Midway the smooth and perilous slope reclined,
Save when your own imperious branches swinging,
    Have made a solemn music of the wind!
Where, like a man beloved of God,
Through glooms which never woodman trod,   10
    How oft, pursuing fancies holy,
My moonlight way o'er flowering weeds I wound,
    Inspired, beyond the guess of folly,
By each rude shape and wild unconquerable sound!
O ye loud Waves! and O ye Forests high!
    And O ye Clouds that far above me soared!
Thou rising Sun, thou blue rejoicing Sky!
    Yea, everything that is and will be free!
    Bear witness for me, wheresoe'er ye be,
    With what deep worship I have still adored   20
       The spirit of divinest Liberty.

2

When France in wrath her giant-limbs upreared,
    And with that oath, which smote air, earth, and sea,
    Stamped with her strong foot and said she would be free,
Bear witness for me, how I hoped and feared!
With what a joy my lofty gratulation
    Unawed I sang, amid a slavish band:
And when to whelm the disenchanted nation,
    Like fiends embattled by a wizard's wand,
       The Monarchs marched in evil day,   30
       And Britain joined the dire array;
    Though dear her shores and circling ocean,
Though many friendships, many youthful loves,
    Had swol'n the patriot emotion,
And flung a magic light o'er all her hills and groves;
Yet still my voice, unaltered, sang defeat,
    To all that braved the tyrant-quelling lance,
And shame too long delayed and vain retreat!
For ne'er, O Liberty! with partial aim
I dimmed thy light or damped thy holy flame;   40
    But blessed the pæans of delivered France,
And hung my head and wept at Britain's name.

3

"And what," I said, "though Blasphemy's loud scream
    With that sweet music of deliverance strove! [3]

3 referring to the Reign of Terror

Though all the fierce and drunken passions wove
A dance more wild than e'er was maniac's dream!
Ye storms, that round the dawning east assembled,
The Sun was rising, though ye hid his light!"
And when, to soothe my soul, that hoped and trembled,
The dissonance ceased, and all seemed calm and bright;   50
   When France her front deep-scarred and gory
   Concealed with clustering wreaths of glory;
     When, insupportably advancing,
   Her arm made mockery of the warrior's ramp;
     While timid looks of fury glancing,
Domestic treason, crushed beneath her fatal stamp,
Writhed like a wounded dragon in his gore;
   Then I reproached my fears that would not flee;
"And soon," I said, "shall Wisdom teach her lore
In the low huts of them that toil and groan!   60
And, conquering by her happiness alone,
   Shall France compel the nations to be free,
Till Love and Joy look round, and call the Earth their own."

4

Forgive me, Freedom! O forgive those dreams!
   I fear thy voice, I hear thy loud lament,
   From bleak Helvetia's icy caverns sent—
I hear thy groans upon her blood-stained streams! [4]
   Heroes, that for your peaceful country perished,
And ye that, fleeing, spot your mountain-snows
   With bleeding wounds; forgive me, that I cherished   70
One thought that ever blessed your cruel foes!
   To scatter rage and traitorous guilt
   Where Peace her jealous home had built;
     A patriot-race to disinherit
Of all that made their stormy wilds so dear;
     And with inexpiable spirit
To taint the bloodless freedom of the mountaineer—
O France, that mockest Heaven, adulterous, blind,
   And patriot only in pernicious toils,
Are these thy boasts, Champion of humankind?   80
   To mix with Kings in the low lust of sway,
Yell in the hunt, and share the murderous prey;
To insult the shrine of Liberty with spoils
   From freemen torn; to tempt and to betray?

4 referring to the French conquest of Switzerland in 1798

5

The Sensual and the Dark rebel in vain,
Slaves by their own compulsion! In mad game
They burst their manacles and wear the name
    Of Freedom, graven on a heavier chain!
O Liberty! with profitless endeavor
Have I pursued thee, many a weary hour;   90
  But thou nor swell'st the victor's strain, nor ever
Didst breathe thy soul in forms of human power.
  Alike from all, howe'er they praise thee
  (Nor prayer, nor boastful name delays thee),
    Alike from Priestcraft's harpy minions,
  And factious Blasphemy's obscener slaves,
    Thou speedest on thy subtle pinions,
The guide of homeless winds, and playmate of the waves!
And there I felt thee!—on that sea-cliff's verge,
Whose pines, scarce traveled by the breeze above,   100
Had made one murmur with the distant surge!
Yes, while I stood and gazed, my temples bare,
And shot my being through earth, sea, and air,
  Possessing all things with intensest love,
  O Liberty! my spirit felt thee there.

LOVE

  All thoughts, all passions, all delights,
  Whatever stirs this mortal frame,
  All are but ministers of Love,
    And feed his sacred flame.

  Oft in my waking dreams do I
  Live o'er again that happy hour,
  When midway on the mount I lay,
    Beside the ruined tower.

  The moonshine, stealing o'er the scene
  Had blended with the lights of eve;   10
  And she was there, my hope, my joy,
    My own dear Genevieve!

  She leant against the armèd man,
  The statue of the armèd knight;
  She stood and listened to my lay,
    Amid the lingering light.

Few sorrows hath she of her own.
My hope! my joy! my Genevieve!
She loves me best, whene'er I sing
    The songs that make her grieve. 20

I played a soft and doleful air,
I sang an old and moving story—
An old rude song, that suited well
    That ruin wild and hoary.

She listened with a flitting blush,
With downcast eyes and modest grace;
For well she knew, I could not choose
    But gaze upon her face.

I told her of the Knight that wore
Upon his shield a burning brand; 30
And that for ten long years he wooed
    The Lady of the Land.

I told her how he pined: and ah!
The deep, the low, the pleading tone
With which I sang another's love,
    Interpreted my own.

She listened with a flitting blush,
With downcast eyes, and modest grace;
And she forgave me, that I gazed
    Too fondly on her face! 40

But when I told the cruel scorn
That crazed that bold and lovely Knight,
And that he crossed the mountain-woods,
    Nor rested day nor night;

That sometimes from the savage den,
And sometimes from the darksome shade,
And sometimes starting up at once,
    In green and sunny glade,—

There came and looked him in the face
An angel beautiful and bright; 50
And that he knew it was a Fiend,
    This miserable Knight!

And that unknowing what he did,
He leaped amid a murderous band,
And saved from outrage worse than death
    The Lady of the Land!

And how she wept, and clasped his knees;
And how she tended him in vain—
And ever strove to expiate
    The scorn that crazed his brain;—   60

And that she nursed him in a cave;
And how his madness went away,
When on the yellow forest-leaves
    A dying man he lay;—

His dying words—but when I reached
That tenderest strain of all the ditty,
My faltering voice and pausing harp
    Disturbed her soul with pity!

All impulses of soul and sense
Had thrilled my guileless Genevieve;   70
The music and the doleful tale,
    The rich and balmy eve;

And hopes, and fears that kindle hope,
An undistinguishable throng,
And gentle wishes long subdued,
    Subdued and cherished long!

She wept with pity and delight,
She blushed with love, and virgin-shame;
And like the murmur of a dream,
    I heard her breathe my name.   80

Her bosom heaved—she stepped aside,
As conscious of my look she stepped—
Then suddenly, with timorous eye
    She fled to me and wept.

She half enclosed me with her arms,
She pressed me with a meek embrace;
And bending back her head, looked up,
    And gazed upon my face.

'Twas partly love, and partly fear,
And partly 'twas a bashful art,   90

That I might rather feel, than see,
   The swelling of her heart.

I calmed her fears, and she was calm,
And told her love with virgin pride;
And so I won my Genevieve,
   My bright and beauteous Bride.

FROST AT MIDNIGHT

THE frost performs its secret ministry
Unhelped by any wind. The owlet's cry
Came loud—and hark, again! loud as before.
The inmates of my cottage, all at rest,
Have left me to that solitude, which suits
Abstruser musings: save that at my side
My cradled infant slumbers peacefully.
'Tis calm indeed! so calm, that it disturbs
And vexes meditation with its strange
And extreme silentness. Sea, hill, and wood,   10
This populous village! Sea, and hill, and wood,
With all the numberless goings-on of life,
Inaudible as dreams! the thin blue flame
Lies on my low-burnt fire, and quivers not;
Only that film, which fluttered on the grate,[5]
Still flutters there, the sole unquiet thing.
Methinks, its motion in this hush of nature
Gives it dim sympathies with me who live,
Making it a companionable form,
Whose puny flaps and freaks the idling spirit   20
By its own moods interprets, everywhere
Echo or mirror seeking of itself,
And makes a toy of thought.

                        But O! how oft,
How oft, at school,[6] with most believing mind,
Presageful, have I gazed upon the bars,
To watch that fluttering stranger! and as oft
With unclosed lids, already had I dreamt
Of my sweet birth-place,[7] and the old church-tower,

5 "In all parts of the kingdom, these films are called *strangers* and supposed to portend the arrival of some absent friend." (Coleridge)
6 Christ's Hospital, in London
7 Ottery St. Mary, Devonshire

Whose bells, the poor man's only music, rang
From morn to evening, all the hot Fair-day,   30
So sweetly, that they stirred and haunted me
With a wild pleasure, falling on mine ear
Most like articulate sounds of things to come!
So gazed I, till the soothing things, I dreamt,
Lulled me to sleep, and sleep prolonged my dreams!
And so I brooded all the following morn,
Awed by the stern preceptor's face, mine eye
Fixed with mock study on my swimming book:
Save if the door half opened, and I snatched
A hasty glance, and still my heart leaped up,   40
For still I hoped to see the stranger's face,
Townsman, or aunt, or sister more beloved,
My play-mate when we both were clothed alike!

Dear babe, that sleepest cradled by my side,
Whose gentle breathings, heard in this deep calm,
Fill up the interspersèd vacancies
And momentary pauses of the thought!
My babe so beautiful! it thrills my heart
With tender gladness, thus to look at thee,
And think that thou shalt learn far other lore,   50
And in far other scenes! 8 For I was reared
In the great city, pent 'mid cloisters dim,
And saw nought lovely but the sky and stars.
But thou, my babe! shalt wander like a breeze
By lakes and sandy shores, beneath the crags
Of ancient mountain, and beneath the clouds,
Which image in their bulk both lakes and shores
And mountain crags: so shalt thou see and hear
The lovely shapes and sounds intelligible
Of that eternal language, which thy God   60
Utters, who from eternity doth teach
Himself in all, and all things in himself.
Great universal Teacher! he shall mould
Thy spirit, and by giving make it ask.

Therefore all seasons shall be sweet to thee,
Whether the summer clothe the general earth
With greenness, or the redbreast sit and sing
Betwixt the tufts of snow on the bare branch
Of mossy apple-tree, while the nigh thatch

8 In the country the lines would apply to the scenery near Keswick, in the Lake District, but Coleridge did not remove thither till 1800.

Smokes in the sun-thaw; whether the eave-drops fall 70
Heard only in the trances of the blast,
Or if the secret ministry of frost
Shall hang them up in silent icicles,
Quietly shining to the quiet moon.

DEJECTION: AN ODE

WRITTEN APRIL 4, 1802

Late, late yestreen I saw the new Moon,
With the old Moon in her arms;
And I fear, I fear, my Master dear!
We shall have a deadly storm.
                    —*Ballad of Sir Patrick Spence*

I

WELL! If the Bard was weather-wise, who made
    The grand old ballad of Sir Patrick Spence,
    This night, so tranquil now, will not go hence
Unroused by winds, that ply a busier trade
Than those which mold yon cloud in lazy flakes,
Or the dull sobbing draft, that moans and rakes
        Upon the strings of this Æolian lute,
        Which better far were mute.
    For lo! the New-moon winter-bright!
    And overspread with phantom light,   10
    (With swimming phantom light o'erspread
    But rimmed and circled by a silver thread)
I see the old Moon in her lap, foretelling
    The coming-on of rain and squally blast.
And oh! that even now the gust were swelling,
    And the slant night-shower driving loud and fast!
Those sounds which oft have raised me, whilst they awed,
        And sent my soul abroad,
Might now perhaps their wonted impulse give,
Might startle this dull pain, and make it move and live!   20

2

A grief without a pang, void, dark, and drear,
    A stifled, drowsy, unimpassioned grief,
    Which finds no natural outlet, no relief,
        In word, or sigh, or tear—

O Lady! in this wan and heartless mood,
To other thoughts by yonder throstle wooed,
  All this long eve, so balmy and serene,
Have I been gazing on the western sky,
  And its peculiar tint of yellow green:
And still I gaze—and with how blank an eye!   30
And those thin clouds above, in flakes and bars,
That give away their motion to the stars;
Those stars, that glide behind them or between,
Now sparkling, now bedimmed, but always seen:
Yon crescent Moon, as fixed as if it grew
In its own cloudless, starless lake of blue;
I see them all so excellently fair,
I see, not feel, how beautiful they are!

3

  My genial spirits fail;
  And what can these avail   40
To lift the smothering weight from off my breast?
  It were a vain endeavor,
  Though I should gaze for ever
On that green light that lingers in the west:
I may not hope from outward forms to win
The passion and the life, whose fountains are within.

4

O Lady! we receive but what we give,
And in our life alone does Nature live:
Ours is her wedding-garment, ours her shroud!
  And would we aught behold, of higher worth,   50
Than that inanimate cold world allowed
To the poor loveless ever-anxious crowd,
  Ah! from the soul itself must issue forth
A light, a glory, a fair luminous cloud
    Enveloping the Earth—
And from the soul itself must there be sent
  A sweet and potent voice, of its own birth,
Of all sweet sounds the life and element!

5

O pure of heart! thou need'st not ask of me
What this strong music in the soul may be!   60

What, and wherein it doth exist,
This light, this glory, this fair luminous mist,
This beautiful and beauty-making power.
   Joy, virtuous Lady! Joy that ne'er was given,
Save to the pure, and in their purest hour,
Life, and Life's effluence, cloud at once and shower,
Joy, Lady! is the spirit and the power,
Which, wedding Nature to us, gives in dower,
   A new Earth and new Heaven,
Undreamt of by the sensual and the proud—   70
Joy is the sweet, Joy the luminous cloud—
     We in ourselves rejoice!
And thence flows all that charms or ear or sight,
   All melodies the echoes of that voice,
All colors a suffusion from that light.

6

There was a time when, though my path was rough,
   This joy within me dallied with distress,
And all misfortunes were but as the stuff
   Whence Fancy made me dreams of happiness:
For Hope grew round me, like the twining vine,   80
And fruits, and foliage, not my own, seemed mine.
But now afflictions bow me down to earth:
Nor care I that they rob me of my mirth;
   But oh! each visitation
Suspends what nature gave me at my birth,
   My shaping spirit of Imagination.
For not to think of what I needs must feel,
   But to be still and patient, all I can;
And haply by abstruse research to steal
   From my own nature all the natural man—   90
   This was my sole resource, my only plan:
Till that which suits a part infects the whole,
And now is almost grown the habit of my soul.

7

Hence, viper thoughts, that coil around my mind,
   Reality's dark dream!
I turn from you, and listen to the wind,
   Which long has raved unnoticed. What a scream
Of agony by torture lengthened out
That lute sent forth! Thou Wind, that rav'st without,

Bare crag, or mountain-tairn, or blasted tree,   100
Or pine-grove whither woodman never clomb,
Or lonely house, long held the witches' home,
    Methinks were fitter instruments for thee,
Mad Lutanist! who in this month of showers,
Of dark-brown gardens, and of peeping flowers,
Mak'st Devil's yule, with worse than wintry song,
The blossoms, buds, and timorous leaves among.
    Thou actor, perfect in all tragic sounds!
Thou mighty Poet, even to frenzy bold!
    What tell'st thou now about?   110
    'Tis of the rushing of an host in rout,
With groans of trampled men, with smarting wounds—
At once they groan with pain, and shudder with the cold!
But hush! there is a pause of deepest silence!
And all that noise, as of a rushing crowd,
With groans, and tremulous shudderings—all is over—
It tells another tale, with sounds less deep and loud!
    A tale of less affright,
    And tempered with delight,
As Otway's [9] self had framed the tender lay,   120
    'Tis of a little child
    Upon a lonesome wild,
Not far from home, but she hath lost her way:
And now moans low in bitter grief and fear,
And now screams loud, and hopes to make her mother hear.

8

'Tis midnight, but small thoughts have I of sleep:
Full seldom may my friend such vigils keep!
Visit her, gentle Sleep! with wings of healing,
    And may this storm be but a mountain-birth,
May all the stars hang bright above her dwelling,   130
    Silent as though they watched the sleeping Earth!
    With light heart may she rise,
    Gay fancy, cheerful eyes,
Joy lift her spirit, joy attune her voice;
To her may all things live, from pole to pole,
Their life the eddying of her living soul!
    O simple spirit, guided from above,
Dear Lady! friend devoutest of my choice,
Thus mayest thou ever, evermore rejoice.

    9 Thomas Otway (1652–1685), the dramatist, famous as the author of *Venice Pre-*
served.

THE KNIGHT'S TOMB

WHERE is the grave of Sir Arthur O'Kellyn?
Where may the grave of that good man be?—
By the side of a spring, on the breast of Helvellyn,
Under the twigs of a young birch tree!
The oak that in summer was sweet to hear,
And rustled its leaves in the fall of the year,
And whistled and roared in the winter alone,
Is gone,—and the birch in its stead is grown.—
The Knight's bones are dust,
And his good sword rust;—
His soul is with the saints, I trust.

YOUTH AND AGE

VERSE, a breeze mid blossoms straying,
Where Hope clung feeding, like a bee—
Both were mine! Life went a-maying
   With Nature, Hope, and Poesy,
         When I was young!

When I was young?—Ah, woeful When!
Ah! for the change 'twixt Now and Then!
This breathing house not built with hands,
This body that does me grievous wrong,
O'er aery cliffs and glittering sands,   10
How lightly *then* it flashed along:—
Like those trim skiffs, unknown of yore,
On winding lakes and rivers wide,
That ask no aid of sail or oar,
That fear no spite of wind or tide!
Nought cared this body for wind or weather
When Youth and I lived in't together.

Flowers are lovely; Love is flower-like;
Friendship is a sheltering tree;
O! the joys, that came down shower-like,   20
Of Friendship, Love, and Liberty,
         Ere I was old!

Ere I was old? Ah woeful Ere,
Which tells me, Youth's no longer here!
O Youth! for years so many and sweet,

'Tis known, that Thou and I were one,
I'll think it but a fond conceit—
It cannot be that Thou art gone!
Thy vesper-bell hath not yet tolled:—
And thou wert aye a masker bold!   30
What strange disguise hast now put on,
To *make believe,* that thou art gone?
I see these locks in silvery slips,
This drooping gait, this altered size:
But Spring-tide blossoms on thy lips,
And tears take sunshine from thine eyes!
Life is but thought: so think I will
That Youth and I are house-mates still.

Dew-drops are the gems of morning,
But the tears of mournful eve!   40
Where no hope is, life's a warning
That only serves to make us grieve,
              When we are old:
That only serves to make us grieve
With oft and tedious taking-leave,
Like some poor nigh-related guest,
That may not rudely be dismissed;
Yet hath outstayed his welcome while,
And tells the jest without the smile.

WORK WITHOUT HOPE

LINES COMPOSED 21ST FEBRUARY, 1827

ALL Nature seems at work. Slugs leave their lair—
The bees are stirring—birds are on the wing—
And Winter slumbering in the open air,
Wears on his smiling face a dream of Spring!
And I the while, the sole unbusy thing,
Nor honey make, nor pair, nor build, nor sing.

Yet well I ken the banks where amaranths blow,
Have traced the font whence streams of nectar flow.
Bloom, O ye amaranths! bloom for whom ye may,
For me ye bloom not! Glide, rich streams, away!   10
With lips unbrightened, wreathless brow, I stroll:
And would you learn the spells that drowse my soul?
Work without Hope draws nectar in a sieve,
And Hope without an object cannot live.

BIOGRAPHIA LITERARIA

Coleridge's *Biographia Literaria,* or "Literary Life," published in 1817, is a miscellaneous prose work, containing analysis of philosophical, metaphysical, and literary principles, remarks on writers whom Coleridge had known or who had influenced him, critiques on various works, and the like. It is discursive and formless as a whole, and in its higher flights lacking in clarity (at least for the average reader). Many parts of it are, however, penetrating and stimulating to the highest degree. The most interesting parts are those (scattered through various chapters) which criticize Wordsworth's poetry and his famous *Preface* (see pages 7–27 above). The more significant of these remarks (condensed from Chapters XIV, XVII, and XVIII of the *Biographia Literaria*) are given below. The process of condensation, by the omission of numerous digressions and elaborations, gives here something the impression of a unified essay.

DURING the first year that Mr. Wordsworth and I were neighbors, our conversations turned frequently on the two cardinal points of poetry, the power of exciting the sympathy of the reader by a faithful adherence to the truth of nature, and the power of giving the interest of novelty by the modifying colors of imagination. The sudden charm which accidents of light and shade, which moonlight or sunset, diffused over a known and familiar landscape, appeared to represent the practicability of combining both. These are the poetry of nature. The thought suggested itself (to which of us I do not recollect) that a series 10 of poems might be composed of two sorts. In the one, the incidents and agents were to be, in part at least, supernatural; and the excellence aimed at was to consist in the interesting of the affections by the dramatic truth of such emotions as would naturally accompany such situations, supposing them real. And real in this sense they have been to every human being who, from whatever source of delusion, has at any time believed himself under supernatural agency. For the second class, subjects were to be chosen from ordinary life; the characters and incidents were to be such as will be found in every village and its 20 vicinity where there is a meditative and feeling mind to seek after them, or to notice them when they present themselves.

In this idea originated the plan of the *Lyrical Ballads;* in which it was agreed that my endeavors should be directed to persons and characters supernatural, or at least romantic; yet so as to transfer from our inward nature a human interest and a semblance of truth sufficient to procure for these shadows of imagination that willing suspension of disbelief for the moment, which constitutes poetic faith. Mr. Wordsworth, on the other hand, was to propose to himself as his object, to give the charm 30 of novelty to things of every day, and to excite a feeling analogous to the supernatural, by awakening the mind's attention

from the lethargy of custom, and directing it to the loveliness
and the wonders of the world before us; an inexhaustible treasure, but for which, in consequence of the film of familiarity and
selfish solicitude, we have eyes, yet see not, ears that hear not,
and hearts that neither feel nor understand.

With this view I wrote *The Ancient Mariner,* and was preparing, among other poems, *The Dark Ladie,* and the *Christabel,* in which I should have more nearly realized my ideal than
I had done in my first attempt. But Mr. Wordsworth's industry
had proved so much more successful, and the number of his
poems so much greater, that my compositions, instead of forming a balance, appeared rather an interpolation of heterogeneous
matter. Mr. Wordsworth added two or three poems written in
his own character, in the impassioned, lofty, and sustained diction which is characteristic of his genius. In this form the *Lyrical
Ballads* were published; and were presented by him, as an experiment whether subjects, which from their nature rejected the
usual ornaments and extra-colloquial style of poems in general,
might not be so managed in the language of ordinary life as to
produce the pleasurable interest which it is the peculiar business
of poetry to impart. To the second edition he added a preface
of considerable length; in which, notwithstanding some passages
of apparently a contrary import, he was understood to contend
for the extension of this style to poetry of all kinds, and to reject
as vicious and indefensible all phrases and forms of style that
were not included in what he (unfortunately, I think, adopting
an equivocal expression) called the language of real life. From
this preface, prefixed to poems in which it was impossible to deny
the presence of original genius, however mistaken its direction
might be deemed, arose the whole long-continued controversy.
For from the conjunction of perceived power with supposed
heresy I explain the inveteracy, and in some instances, I grieve
to say, the acrimonious passions, with which the controversy
has been conducted by the assailants.

Had Mr. Wordsworth's poems been the silly, the childish
things which they were for a long time described as being; had
they been really distinguished from the compositions of other
poets merely by meanness of language and inanity of thought;
had they indeed contained nothing more than what is found in
the parodies and pretended imitations of them; they must have
sunk at once, a dead weight, into the slough of oblivion, and
have dragged the preface along with them. But year after year
increased the number of Mr. Wordsworth's admirers. They
were found, too, not in the lower classes of the reading public,
but chiefly among young men of strong sensibility and meditative minds; and their admiration (inflamed perhaps in some

degree by opposition) was distinguished by its intensity, I might almost say, by its religious fervor. These facts, and the intellectual energy of the author, which was more or less consciously felt, where it was outwardly and even boisterously denied, meeting with sentiments of aversion to his opinions, and of alarm at their consequences, produced an eddy of criticism, which would of itself have borne up the poems by the violence with which it whirled them round and round. With many parts of this preface, in the sense attributed to them, and which the words undoubtedly seem to authorize, I never concurred; but, on the contrary, objected to them as erroneous in principle, and as contradictory (in appearance at least) both to other parts of the same preface and to the author's own practice in the greater number of the poems themselves. Mr. Wordsworth in his recent collection has, I find, degraded this prefatory disquisition to the end of his second volume, to be read or not at the reader's choice. But he has not, as far as I can discover, announced any change in his poetic creed. At all events, considering it as the source of a controversy, in which I have been honored more than I deserve by the frequent conjunction of my name with his, I think it expedient to declare, once for all, in what points I coincide with his opinions, and in what points I altogether differ. . . .

As far then as Mr. Wordsworth in his preface contended, and most ably contended, for a reformation in our poetic diction; as far as he has evinced the truth of passion, and the dramatic propriety of those figures and metaphors in the original poets, which, stripped of their justifying reasons and converted into mere artifices of connection or ornament, constitute the characteristic falsity in the poetic style of the moderns; and as far as he has, with equal acuteness and clearness, pointed out the process by which this change was effected, and the resemblances between that state into which the reader's mind is thrown by the pleasurable confusion of thought from an unaccustomed train of words and images, and that state which is induced by the natural language of impassioned feeling; he undertook a useful task, and deserves all praise, both for the attempt and for the execution. The provocations to this remonstrance in behalf of truth and nature were still of perpetual recurrence before and after the publication of this preface. I cannot likewise but add that the comparison of such poems of merit as have been given to the public within the last ten or twelve years, with the majority of those produced previously to the appearance of that preface, leave no doubt on my mind that Mr. Wordsworth is fully justified in believing his efforts to have been by no means ineffectual. Not only in the verses of those who have professed their admiration of his genius, but even of those who have distinguished themselves by hostility to his theory and depreciation of his writings, are the impressions of his principles plainly visible. . . .

My own differences from certain supposed parts of Mr. Wordsworth's theory ground themselves on the assumption that his words had been rightly interpreted, as purporting that the proper diction for poetry in general consists altogether in a language taken, with due exceptions, from the mouths of men in real life, a language which actually constitutes the natural conversation of men under the influence of natural feelings. My objection is, first, that in any sense this rule is applicable only to certain classes of poetry; secondly, that even to these classes it is not applicable, except in such a sense as hath never by any one (as far as I know or have read) been denied or doubted; and, lastly, that as far as, and in that degree in which, it is practicable, it is yet as a rule useless, if not injurious, and therefore either need not or ought not to be practised. The poet informs his reader that he had generally chosen *low and rustic* life; but not *as* low and rustic, or in order to repeat that pleasure of doubtful moral effect, which persons of elevated rank and of superior refinement oftentimes derive from a happy imitation of the rude unpolished manners and discourse of their inferiors. . . .

Now it is clear to me, that in the most interesting of the poems, in which the author is more or less dramatic, as *The Brothers, Michael, Ruth, The Mad Mother,* etc., the persons introduced are by no means taken from low or rustic life in the common acceptation of these words; and it is not less clear that the sentiments and language, as far as they can be conceived to have been really transferred from the minds and conversation of such persons, are attributable to causes and circumstances not necessarily connected with "their occupations and abode." The thoughts, feelings, language, and manners of the shepherd-farmers in the vales of Cumberland and Westmoreland, as far as they are actually adopted in these poems, may be accounted for from causes which will and do produce the same results in every state of life, whether in town or country. As the two principal, I rank that Independence which raises a man above servitude, or daily toil for the profit of others, yet not above the necessity of industry and a frugal simplicity of domestic life; and the accompanying unambitious, but solid and religious Education, which has rendered few books familiar but the Bible and the Liturgy or Hymn book. To this latter cause, indeed, which is so far accidental that it is the blessing of particular countries and a particular age, not the product of particular places or employments, the poet owes the show of probability that his personages might really feel, think, and talk with any tolerable resemblance to his representation. It is an excellent remark of Dr. Henry More's, that "a man of confined education, but of good parts, by constant reading of the Bible will naturally form a more winning and commanding rhetoric than those that are learned: the intermixture of tongues and of artificial phrases debasing *their* style" [10] . . .

The characters of the vicar and the shepherd-mariner in the poem of *The Brothers,* those of the Shepherd of Greenhead Ghyll in the *Michael,* have all the verisimilitude and representative quality that the purposes of poetry can require. They are persons of a known and abiding class, and their manners and sentiments the natural product of circumstances common to the class. Take Michael for instance:

> An old man stout of heart, and strong of limb:
> His bodily frame had been from youth to age
> Of an unusual strength: his mind was keen,
> Intense and frugal, apt for all affairs,
> And in his shepherd's calling he was prompt
> And watchful more than ordinary men. . . .

On the other hand, in the poems which are pitched at a lower note, as the *Harry Gill,* the *Idiot Boy, etc.,* the feelings are those of human nature in general; though the poet has judiciously laid the scene in the country, in order to place himself in the vicinity of interesting images, without the necessity of ascribing a sentimental perception of their beauty to the persons of his drama. In the *Idiot Boy,* indeed, the mother's character is not so much a real and native product of a "situation where the essential passions of the heart find a better soil, in which they can attain their maturity and speak a plainer and more emphatic language," as it is an impersonation of an instinct abandoned by judgment. Hence the two following charges seem to me not wholly groundless; at least, they are the only plausible objections which I have heard to that fine poem. The one is, that the author has not, in the poem itself, taken sufficient care to preclude from the reader's fancy the disgusting images of ordinary, morbid idiocy, which yet it was by no means his intention to represent. He has even by the "burr, burr, burr," uncounteracted by any preceding description of the boy's beauty, assisted in recalling them. The other is, that the idiocy of the boy is so evenly balanced by the folly of the mother, as to present to the general reader rather a laughable burlesque on the blindness of

---

[10] Henry More (1614-1687), philosophic and religious writer, one of the group known as the "Cambridge Platonists."

anile dotage, than an analytic display of maternal affection in
its ordinary workings. . . .

If then I am compelled to doubt the theory by which the choice
of characters was to be directed, not only *à priori,* from grounds
of reason, but both from the few instances in which the poet
himself *need* be supposed to have been governed by it, and from
the comparative inferiority of those instances; still more must
I hesitate in my assent to the sentence which immediately follows the former citation, and which I can neither admit as par-
10 ticular fact, or as general rule. "The language too of these men
is adopted (purified indeed from what appear to be its real
defects, from all lasting and rational causes of dislike or disgust) because such men hourly communicate with the best objects from which the best part of language is originally derived;
and because, from their rank in society, and the sameness and
narrow circle of their intercourse, being less under the action of
social vanity, they convey their feelings and notions in simple
and unelaborated expressions." To this I reply, that a rustic's
language, purified from all provincialism and grossness, and so
20 far re-constructed as to be made consistent with the rules of
grammar (which are in essence no other than the laws of universal logic, applied to psychological materials), will not differ
from the language of any other man of common sense, however
learned or refined he may be, except as far as the notions which
the rustic has to convey are fewer and more indiscriminate. This
will become still clearer, if we add the consideration (equally
important though less obvious) that the rustic, from the more
imperfect development of his faculties, and from the lower state
of their cultivation, aims almost solely to convey insulated facts,
30 either those of his scanty experience or his traditional belief;
while the educated man chiefly seeks to discover and express
those connections of things, or those relative bearings of fact to
fact, from which some more or less general law is deducible.
For facts are valuable to a wise man, chiefly as they lead to the
discovery of the indwelling law, which is the true being of things,
the sole solution of their modes of existence, and in the knowledge of which consists our dignity and our power.

As little can I agree with the assertion that from the objects
with which the rustic hourly communicates the best part of lan-
40 guage is formed. For, first, if to communicate with an object
implies such an acquaintance with it as renders it capable of
being discriminately reflected on, the distinct knowledge of an
uneducated rustic would furnish a very scanty vocabulary. The
few things, and modes of action requisite for his bodily con-
veniences would alone be individualized; while all the rest of
nature would be expressed by a small number of confused gen-

eral terms. Secondly, I deny that the words and combinations of words derived from the objects with which the rustic is familiar, whether with distinct or confused knowledge, can be justly said to form the best part of language. It is more than probable that many classes of the brute creation possess discriminating sounds, by which they can convey to each other notices of such objects as concern their food, shelter, or safety. Yet we hesitate to call the aggregate of such sounds a language otherwise than metaphorically. The best part of human language, properly so called, is derived from reflection on the acts of the mind itself. It is formed by a voluntary appropriation of fixed symbols to internal acts, to processes and results of imagination, the greater part of which have no place in the consciousness of uneducated man; though in civilized society, by imitation and passive remembrance of what they hear from their religious instructors and other superiors, the most uneducated share in the harvest which they neither sowed or reaped. If the history of the phrases in hourly currency among our peasants were traced, a person not previously aware of the fact would be surprised at finding so large a number, which three or four centuries ago were the exclusive property of the universities and the schools; and, at the commencement of the Reformation, had been transferred from the school to the pulpit, and thus gradually passed into common life. The extreme difficulty, and often the impossibility, of finding words for the simplest moral and intellectual processes of the languages of uncivilized tribes has proved perhaps the weightiest obstacle to the progress of our most zealous and adroit missionaries. Yet these tribes are surrounded by the same nature as our peasants are; but in still more impressive forms; and they are, moreover, obliged to particularize many more of them. When, therefore, Mr. Wordsworth adds, "accordingly, such a language"—meaning, as before, the language of rustic life purified from provincialism—"arising out of repeated experience and regular feelings, is a more permanent, and a far more philosophical language, than that which is frequently substituted for it by poets, who think they are conferring honor upon themselves and their art in proportion as they indulge in arbitrary and capricious habits of expression"; it may be answered, that the language, which he has in view, can be attributed to rustics with no greater right, than the style of Hooker or Bacon to Tom Brown or Sir Roger L'Estrange.[11] Doubtless, if what is peculiar to each were omitted in each, the result must needs be the same. Further, that the poet, who uses an illogical diction, or

---

11 Richard Hooker (1554?-1600), author of *The Laws of Ecclesiastical Polity*, celebrated for his powers of reasoning and for his lofty style. Tom Brown (1663-1704), writer of burlesque in prose and verse. L'Estrange (1616-1704), journalist and pamphleteer.

a style fitted to excite only the low and changeable pleasure of wonder by means of groundless novelty, substitutes a language of folly and vanity, not for that of the rustic, but for that of good sense and natural feeling.

Here let me be permitted to remind the reader that the positions which I controvert are contained in the sentences—"a selection of the real language of men";—"the language of these men" (*i. e.*, men in low and rustic life) "I propose to myself to imitate, and, as far as is possible, to adopt the very language of men." "Between the language of prose and that of metrical composition, there neither is, nor can be, any essential difference." It is against these exclusively that my opposition is directed.

I object, in the very first instance, to an equivocation in the use of the word "real." Every man's language varies, according to the extent of his knowledge, the activity of his faculties, and the depth or quickness of his feelings. Every man's language has, first, its individualities; secondly, the common properties of the class to which he belongs; and thirdly, words and phrases of universal use. The language of Hooker, Bacon, Bishop Taylor, and Burke differs from the common language of the learned class only by the superior number and novelty of the thoughts and relations which they had to convey. The language of Algernon Sidney [12] differs not at all from that which every well-educated gentleman would wish to write, and (with due allowances for the undeliberateness, and less connected train, of thinking natural and proper to conversation) such as he would wish to talk. Neither one nor the other differ half as much from the general language of cultivated society, as the language of Mr. Wordsworth's homeliest composition differs from that of a common peasant. For "real" therefore, we must substitute ordinary, or *lingua communis*.[13] And this, we have proved, is no more to be found in the phraseology of low and rustic life than in that of any other class. Omit the peculiarities of each and the result of course must be common to all. And assuredly the omissions and changes to be made in the language of rustics, before it could be transferred to any species of poem, except the drama or other professed imitation, are at least as numerous and weighty, as would be required in adapting to the same purpose the ordinary language of tradesmen and manufacturers. Not to mention, that the language so highly extolled by Mr. Wordsworth varies in every county, nay in every village, according to the accidental character of the clergyman, the existence or non-existence of schools; or even, perhaps, as the exciseman, publican, or barber

12 (1622–1683), republican patriot and statesman, author of *Discourses Concerning Government*, Puritan partisan during the Civil War, executed on charge of treason
13 common tongue

happen to be, or not to be, zealous politicians, and readers of
the weekly newspaper *pro bono publico*.[14] Anterior to cultivation
the *lingua communis* of every country, as Dante has well observed, exists everywhere in parts, and nowhere as a whole.

Neither is the case rendered at all more tenable by the addition of the words, "in a state of excitement." For the nature of a
man's words, when he is strongly affected by joy, grief, or anger,
must necessarily depend on the number and quality of the general truths, conceptions, and images, and of the words expressing them, with which his mind had been previously stored. For
the property of passion is not to create, but to set in increased
activity. At least, whatever new connections of thoughts or
images, or (which is equally, if not more than equally, the appropriate effect of strong excitement) whatever generalizations
of truth or experience the heat of passion may produce, yet the
terms of their conveyance must have pre-existed in his former
conversations, and are only collected and crowded together by
the unusual stimulation. It is indeed very possible to adopt in
a poem the unmeaning repetitions, habitual phrases, and other
blank counters which an unfurnished or confused understanding interposes at short intervals in order to keep hold of his
subject, which is still slipping from him, and to give him time for
recollection; or, in mere aid of vacancy, as in the scanty companies of a country stage the same player pops backwards and
forwards, in order to prevent the appearance of empty spaces,
in the procession of Macbeth, or Henry VIII. But what assistance to the poet, or ornament to the poem, these can supply, I
am at loss to conjecture. Nothing assuredly can differ either in
origin or in mode more widely from the *apparent* tautologies of
intense and turbulent feeling, in which the passion is greater and
of longer endurance than to be exhausted or satisfied by a single
representation of the image or incident exciting it. Such repetitions I admit to be a beauty of the highest kind; as illustrated
by Mr. Wordsworth himself from the song of Deborah. "At her
feet he bowed, he fell, he lay down: at her feet he bowed, he
fell: where he bowed, there he fell down dead." [15]

I conclude, therefore, that the attempt is impracticable; and
that, were it not impracticable, it would still be useless. For the
very power of making the selection implies the previous possession of the language selected. Or where can the poet have
lived? And by what rules could he direct his choice, which would
not have enabled him to select and arrange his words by the
light of his own judgment? We do not adopt the language of a
class by the mere adoption of such words exclusively as that
class would use, or at least understand; but likewise by follow-

14 for the public good   15 Judges, v. 27

ing the *order* in which the words of such men are wont to succeed each other. Now this order, in the intercourse of uneducated
men, is distinguished from their superiors in knowledge and
power, by the greater disjunction and separation in the component parts of that, whatever it be, which they wish to communicate. There is a want of that prospectiveness of mind, that
surview, which enables a man to foresee the whole of what he
is to convey, appertaining to any one point; and by this means
so to subordinate and arrange the different parts according to
their relative importance, as to convey it at once, and as an
organized whole.

Now I will take the first stanza on which I have chanced to
open, in the *Lyrical Ballads*. It is one the most simple and the
least peculiar in its language.

> In distant countries have I been,
> And yet I have not often seen
> A healthy man, a man full grown,
> Weep in the public roads, alone.
> But such a one, on English ground,
> And in the broad highway, I met;
> Along the broad highway he came,
> His cheeks with tears were wet:
> Sturdy he seemed, though he was sad;
> And in his arms a lamb he had.[16]

The words here are doubtless such as are current in all ranks
of life; and of course not less so in the hamlet and cottage than
in the shop, manufactory, college, or palace. But is this the *order*
in which the rustic would have placed the words? I am griev-
ously deceived, if the following less compact mode of commenc-
ing the same tale be not a far more faithful copy. "I have been
in a many parts, far and near, and I don't know that I ever saw
before a man crying by himself in the public road; a grown
man I mean, that was neither sick nor hurt," *etc., etc.* But when
I turn to the following stanza in *The Thorn:*

> At all times of the day and night
> This wretched woman thither goes;
> And she is known to every star,
> And every wind that blows:
> And there, beside the Thorn, she sits,
> When the blue day-light's in the skies,
> And when the whirlwind's on the hill,
> Or frosty air is keen and still,
> And to herself she cries,
> Oh misery! Oh misery!
> Oh woe is me! Oh misery!

16 From Wordsworth's poem, *The Last of the Flock*

and compare this with the language of ordinary men; or with
that which I can conceive at all likely to proceed, in real life,
from such a narrator as is supposed in the note to the poem;
compare it either in the succession of the images or of the
sentences; I am reminded of the sublime prayer and hymn of
praise which Milton, in opposition to an established liturgy,
presents as a fair specimen of common extemporary devotion,
and such as we might expect to hear from every self-inspired
minister of a conventicle! And I reflect with delight, how little
a mere theory, though of his own workmanship, interferes with   10
the processes of genuine imagination in a man of true poetic
genius, who possesses, as Mr. Wordsworth, if ever man did, most
assuredly does possess,

The Vision and the Faculty divine.[17]

CHARLES LAMB (1775–1834)

Lamb's father was the clerk and confidential servant of a barrister, and in
the Inner Temple, London, he was born on February 10, 1775, the youngest of
seven children, only three of whom grew to maturity. From his seventh to his
fourteenth year he was a student at Christ's Hospital, where he formed a life-
long friendship with Coleridge. This was the extent of Lamb's formal education. After leaving school he obtained a minor appointment at the South Sea
House, and in 1792 became an accountant of the East India Company, in
whose employment he remained till 1825, when he was retired on a pension.

There was a strain of insanity in Lamb's family from which he himself
suffered, being confined in an asylum for six weeks in 1795–96. Insanity never
returned to him, but his sister Mary (the "Bridget" of the essays) was subject to recurring attacks throughout her life. During a violent fit in 1796 she
wounded her father and stabbed her mother to death. Charles was at hand, he
says, only in "time enough to snatch the knife from her grasp." This event
determined Lamb's life. The rest of his years he spent in tender ministration
of his sister, enjoying her companionship in her rational periods, deprived of it
at intervals when she was mad. He never married. He died on December 27,
1834.

Lamb's was an urban spirit. In his youth he made occasional visits to
Blakesware, in Hertfordshire, where his grandmother, Mrs. Mary Field, was
housekeeper at a country home of the Plumer family. But in his mature years
he seldom left London, which he loved. His life was enriched by numerous
friendships—with Wordsworth, Coleridge, Hazlitt, Leigh Hunt, Crabb Robin-
son, "Barry Cornwall" (Bryan Waller Procter) and others.

Lamb tried his hand at novels, plays, poems, critical and familiar essays. In
collaboration with his sister, he published the well-known *Tales from Shakespeare* (1807). He had always loved our older literature, particularly of the

17 Wordsworth, *The Excursion*, l. 79

sixteenth and seventeenth centuries, and in 1808 published *Specimens of English Dramatic Poets Contemporary with Shakespeare,* with appreciative criticism—a volume which did much to revive interest in the great Elizabethans. His *Essays of Elia,* on which his fame now chiefly rests, were originally published in various periodicals—most of them in the *London Magazine* between 1820 and 1825,—and brought out in book form, the two series in 1823 and 1833 respectively. They are probably the most loved of all our familiar essays, with their manner at once humorous, whimsical, fantastic, and learned, their intimate personal revelations, their admirable sense, their fine appreciations, and their warm human sympathies.

BIBLIOGRAPHY. *Works,* by E. V. Lucas, 7 vols. (Methuen, Putnam's); *Life,* 2 vols., by the same. Short life by Alfred Ainger in Eng. Men of Letters ser. Innumerable editions of the *Essays of Elia.*

NEW YEAR'S EVE

EVERY man hath two birthdays: two days, at least, in every year, which set him upon revolving the lapse of time, as it affects his mortal duration. The one is that which in an especial manner he termeth *his.* In the gradual desuetude of old observances, this custom of solemnizing our proper birthday hath nearly passed away, or is left to children, who reflect nothing at all about the matter, nor understand anything in it beyond cake and orange. But the birth of a New Year is of an interest too wide to be pretermitted by king or cobbler. No one
10 ever regarded the First of January with indifference. It is that from which all date their time, and count upon what is left. It is the nativity of our common Adam.

Of all sound of all bells—(bells, the music nighest bordering upon heaven)—most solemn and touching is the peal which rings out the Old Year. I never hear it without a gathering-up of my mind to a concentration of all the images that have been diffused over the past twelvemonth; all I have done or suffered, performed or neglected, in that regretted time. I begin to know its worth, as when a person dies. It takes a personal
20 color; nor was it a poetical flight in a contemporary,[1] when he exclaimed—

> I saw the skirts of the departing Year.

It is no more than what in sober sadness every one of us seems to be conscious of, in that awful leave-taking. I am sure I felt it, and all felt it with me, last night; though some of my companions affected rather to manifest an exhilaration at the birth of the coming year, than any very tender regrets for the decease of its predecessor. But I am none of those who—

---

[1] Coleridge, in *Ode on the Departing Year.*

Welcome the coming, speed the parting guest.

I am naturally, beforehand, shy of novelties; new books, new faces, new years,—from some mental twist which makes it difficult in me to face the prospective. I have almost ceased to hope; and am sanguine only in the prospects of other (former) years. I plunge into foregone visions and conclusions. I encounter pell-mell with past disappointments. I am armor-proof against old discouragements. I forgive, or overcome in fancy, old adversaries. I play over again *for love,* as the gamesters phrase it, games for which I once paid so dear. I would scarce 10 now have any of those untoward accidents and events of my life reversed. I would no more alter them than the incidents of some well-contrived novel. Methinks, it is better that I should have pined away seven of my goldenest years, when I was thrall to the fair hair, and fairer eyes, of Alice W——n,[2] than that so passionate a love adventure should be lost. It was better that our family should have missed that legacy, which old Dorrell cheated us of, than that I should have at this moment two thousand pounds *in banco,* and be without the idea of that specious old rogue.

In a degree beneath manhood, it is my infirmity to look back 20 upon those early days. Do I advance a paradox when I say, that, skipping over the intervention of forty years, a man may have leave to love *himself* without the imputation of self-love?

If I know aught of myself, no one whose mind is introspective—and mine is painfully so—can have a less respect for his present identity, than I have for the man Elia. I know him to be light, and vain, and humorsome; a notorious   *   *   *   ; addicted to   *   *   *   ; averse from counsel, neither taking it, nor offering it;—   *   *   *   besides; a stammering buffoon; what you will; lay it on, and spare not; I subscribe 30 to it all, and much more, than thou canst be willing to lay at his door—but for the child Elia—that "other me," there, in the background—I must take leave to cherish the remembrance of that young master—with as little reference, I protest, to this stupid changeling of five-and-forty, as if it had been a child of some other house, and not of my parents. I can cry over its patient small-pox at five, and rougher medicaments. I can lay its poor fevered head upon the sick pillow at Christ's,[3] and wake with it in surprise at the gentle posture of maternal tenderness hanging over it, that unknown had watched its sleep. I know 40 how it shrank from any the least color of falsehood.—God help thee, Elia, how art thou changed!—Thou art sophisticated. —I know how honest, how courageous (for a weakling) it was— how religious, how imaginative, how hopeful! From what have

2 See f. n. 14, p. 213.   3 Christ's Hospital, London, where Lamb went to school.

I not fallen, if the child I remember was indeed myself,
—and not some dissembling guardian, presenting a false identity, to give the rule to my unpractised steps, and regulate the
tone of my moral being!

That I am fond of indulging, beyond a hope of sympathy, in
such retrospection, may be the symptom of some sickly idiosyn-
crasy. Or is it owing to another cause: simply, that being without wife or family, I have not learned to project myself enough
out of myself; and having no offspring of my own to dally with,
I turn back upon memory, and adopt my own early idea, as my
heir and favorite? If these speculations seem fantastical to
thee, Reader—(a busy man, perchance), if I tread out of the
way of thy sympathy, and am singularly conceited only, I retire, impenetrable to ridicule, under the phantom cloud of Elia.

The elders, with whom I was brought up, were of a character
not likely to let slip the sacred observance of any old institution; and the ringing out of the Old Year was kept by them with
circumstances of peculiar ceremony.—In those days the sound
of those midnight chimes, though it seemed to raise hilarity in
all around me, never failed to bring a train of pensive imagery
into my fancy. Yet I then scarce conceived what it meant, or
thought of it as a reckoning that concerned me. Not childhood
alone, but the young man till thirty, never feels practically that
he is mortal. He knows it indeed, and, if need were, he could
preach a homily on the fragility of life; but he brings it not home
to himself, any more than in a hot June we can appropriate to
our imagination the freezing days of December. But now, shall
I confess a truth?—I feel these audits but too powerfully. I begin
to count the probabilities of my duration, and to grudge at the
expenditure of moments and shortest periods, like misers' far-
things. In proportion as the years both lessen and shorten, I set
more count upon their periods, and would fain lay my ineffectual
finger upon the spoke of the great wheel. I am not content to
pass away "like a weaver's shuttle." [4] Those metaphors solace
me not, nor sweeten the unpalatable draught of mortality. I
care not to be carried with the tide, that smoothly bears human
life to eternity; and reluct at the inevitable course of destiny.
I am in love with this green earth; the face of town and country;
the unspeakable rural solitudes, and the sweet security of streets.
I would set up my tabernacle here. I am content to stand still at
the age to which I am arrived; I, and my friends: to be no
younger, no richer, no handsomer. I do not want to be weaned
by age; or drop, like mellow fruit, as they say, into the grave.
—Any alteration, on this earth of mine, in diet or in lodging,

4 See *Job*, vii. 6.

puzzles and discomposes me. My household gods plant a terrible fixed foot, and are not rooted up without blood. They do not willingly seek Lavinian shores.[5] A new state of being staggers me.

Sun, and sky, and breeze, and solitary walks, and summer holidays, and the greenness of fields, and the delicious juices of meats and fishes, and society, and the cheerful glass, and candle-light, and fireside conversations, and innocent vanities, and jests, and *irony itself*—do these things go out with life?

Can a ghost laugh, or shake his gaunt sides, when you are pleasant with him?

And you, my midnight darlings, my Folios: must I part with the intense delight of having you (huge armfuls) in my embraces? Must knowledge come to me, if it come at all, by some awkward experiment of intuition, and no longer by this familiar process of reading?

Shall I enjoy friendships there, wanting the smiling indications which point me to them here,—the recognizable face— the "sweet assurance of a look"?

In winter this intolerable disinclination to dying—to give it its mildest name—does more especially haunt and beset me. In a genial August noon, beneath a sweltering sky, death is almost problematic. At those times do such poor snakes as myself enjoy an immortality. Then we expand and burgeon. Then we are as strong again, as valiant again, as wise again, and a great deal taller. The blast that nips and shrinks me, puts me in thoughts of death. All things allied to the insubstantial, wait upon that master feeling; cold, numbness, dreams, perplexity; moonlight itself, with its shadowy and spectral appearances,— that cold ghost of the sun, or Phœbus' sickly sister,[6] like that innutritious one denounced in the Canticles: [7]—I am none of her minions—I hold with the Persian.[8]

Whatsoever thwarts, or puts me out of my way, brings death unto my mind. All partial evils, like humors, run into that capital plague-sore.—I have heard some profess an indifference to life. Such hail the end of their existence as a port of refuge; and speak of the grave as of some soft arms, in which they may slumber as on a pillow. Some have wooed death——but out upon thee, I say, thou foul, ugly phantom! I detest, abhor, execrate, and (with Friar John) give thee to six score thousand

[5] in Italy—sought by the wandering Æneas (*Æneid*, i. 2)
[6] the moon (Artemis or Diana, the moon goddess, sister of Phœbus Apollo, the sun god)
[7] Song of Songs of Solomon, viii. 8
[8] Zoroaster, founder of traditional religion of Persia, popularly regarded as fire-worship

devils, as in no instance to be excused or tolerated, but shunned as an universal viper; to be branded, proscribed, and spoken evil of! In no way can I be brought to digest thee, thou thin, melancholy *Privation,* or more frightful and confounding *Positive!*

Those antidotes, prescribed against the fear of thee, are altogether frigid and insulting, like thyself. For what satisfaction hath a man, that he shall "lie down with kings and emperors in death," who in his lifetime never greatly coveted the society of
10 such bedfellows?—or, forsooth, that "so shall the fairest face appear"?—why, to comfort me, must Alice W—n be a goblin? More than all, I conceive disgust at those impertinent and misbecoming familiarities, inscribed upon your ordinary tombstones. Every dead man must take upon himself to be lecturing me with his odious truism, that "Such as he now is, I must shortly be." Not so shortly, friend, perhaps, as thou imaginest. In the meantime I am alive. I move about. I am worth twenty of thee. Know thy betters! Thy New Years' days are past. I survive, a jolly candidate for 1821. Another cup of wine—and while
20 that turncoat bell, that just now mournfully chanted the obsequies of 1820 departed, with changed notes lustily rings in a successor, let us attune to its peal the song made on a like occasion, by hearty, cheerful Mr. Cotton.[9]

THE NEW YEAR

Hark, the cock crows, and yon bright star
Tells us, the day himself's not far;
And see where, breaking from the night
He gilds the western hills with light.
With him old Janus doth appear,
Peeping into the future year,
30 With such a look as seems to say
The prospect is not good that way.
Thus do we rise ill sights to see,
And 'gainst ourselves to prophesy;
When the prophetic fear of things
A more tormenting mischief brings
More full of soul tormenting gall
Than direst mischiefs can befall.
But stay! but stay! methinks my sight
Better informed by clearer light,
40 Discerns sereneness in that brow
That all contracted seem'd but now.

9 Charles Cotton, minor poet (1630–1687)

His revers'd face may show distaste,
And frown upon the ills are past;
But that which this way looks is clear,
And smiles upon the New-born Year.
He looks too from a place so high,
The year lies open to his eye;
And all the moments open are
To the exact discoverer.
Yet more and more he smiles upon
The happy revolution.   10
Why should we then suspect or fear
The influences of a year,
So smiles upon us the first morn,
And speaks us good so soon as born?
Plague on't! the last was ill enough,
This cannot but make better proof;
Or, at the worst, as we brush'd through
The last, why so we may this too;
And then the next in reason shou'd
Be superexcellently good: 20
For the worst ills (we daily see)
Have no more perpetuity
Than the best fortunes that do fall;
Which also bring us wherewithal
Longer their being to support,
Than those do of the other sort:
And who has one good year in three,
And yet repines at destiny,
Appears ungrateful in the case,
And merits not the good he has.   30
Then let us welcome the New Guest
With lusty brimmers of the best;
Mirth always should Good Fortune meet,
And renders e'en Disaster sweet:
And though the Princess turn her back,
Let us but line ourselves with sack,
We better shall by far hold out,
Till the next Year she face about.

How say you, Reader—do not these verses smack of the
rough magnanimity of the old English vein? Do they not fortify   40
like a cordial; enlarging the heart, and productive of sweet
blood, and generous spirits, in the concoction? Where be those
puling fears of death, just now expressed or affected?—Passed
like a cloud—absorbed in the purging sunlight of clear poetry
—clean washed away by a wave of genuine Helicon, your only
Spa for these hypochondries. And now another cup of the generous! and a merry New Year, and many of them, to you all, my
masters!

IMPERFECT SYMPATHIES

> I am of a constitution so general, that it consorts and sympathiseth with all things; I have no antipathy, or rather idiosyncrasy in anything. Those national repugnancies do not touch me, nor do I behold with prejudice the French, Italian, Spaniard, or Dutch.—*Religio Medici.*

THAT the author of the Religio Medici [1] mounted upon the airy stilts of abstraction, conversant about notional and conjectural essences; in whose categories of Being the possible took the upper hand of the actual; should have overlooked the impertinent individualities of such poor concretions as mankind, is not much to be admired. It is rather to be wondered at, that in the genus of animals he should have condescended to distinguish that species at all. For myself—earth-bound and fettered to the scene of my activities,—

10   Standing on earth, not rapt above the sky,

I confess that I do feel the differences of mankind, national or individual, to an unhealthy excess. I can look with no indifferent eye upon things or persons. Whatever is, is to me a matter of taste or distaste; or when once it becomes indifferent it begins to be disrelishing. I am, in plainer words, a bundle of prejudices—made up of likings and dislikings—the veriest thrall to sympathies, apathies, antipathies. In a certain sense, I hope it may be said of me that I am a lover of my species. I can feel for all indifferently, but I cannot feel towards all 20 equally. The more purely English word that expresses sympathy will better explain my meaning. I can be a friend to a worthy man, who upon another account cannot be my mate or *fellow*. I cannot *like* all people alike.[2]

1 Sir Thomas Browne (1605–1682)
2 I would be understood as confining myself to the subject of *imperfect sympathies.* To nations or classes of men there can be no direct *antipathy.* There may be individuals born and constellated so opposite to another individual nature, that the same sphere cannot hold them. I have met with my moral antipodes, and can believe the story of two persons meeting (who never saw one another before in their lives) and instantly fighting.

> —— We by proof find there should be
> 'Twixt man and man such an antipathy,
> That though he can show no just reason why
> For any former wrong or injury,
> Can neither find a blemish in his fame,
> Nor aught in face or feature justly blame,
> Can challenge or accuse him of no evil,
> Yet notwithstanding hates him as a devil.

The lines are from old Heywood's *Hierarchie of Angels,* and he subjoins a curious story in confirmation, of a Spaniard who attempted to assassinate a king Ferdinand of Spain, and being put to the rack could give no other reason for the deed but an inveterate antipathy which he had taken to the first sight of the king.

> —— The cause which to that act compell'd him
> Was, he ne'er loved him since he first beheld him.

(Lamb's note, quoting from Thomas Heywood, best known as a dramatist of the time of Elizabeth and James I)

I have been trying all my life to like Scotchmen, and am obliged to desist from the experiment in despair. They cannot like me—and in truth, I never knew one of that nation who attempted to do it. There is something more plain and ingenuous in their mode of proceeding. We know one another at first sight. There is an order of imperfect intellects (under which mine must be content to rank) which in its constitution is essentially anti-Caledonian. The owners of the sort of faculties I allude to, have minds rather suggestive than comprehensive. They have no pretenses to much clearness or precision in their ideas, or in their manner of expressing them. Their intellectual wardrobe (to confess fairly) has few whole pieces in it. They are content with fragments and scattered pieces of Truth. She presents no full front to them—a feature or side-face at the most. Hints and glimpses, germs and crude essays at a system, is the utmost they pretend to. They beat up a little game peradventure—and leave it to knottier heads, more robust constitutions, to run it down. The light that lights them is not steady and polar, but mutable and shifting: waxing, and again waning. Their conversation is accordingly. They will throw out a random word in or out of season, and be content to let it pass for what it is worth. They cannot speak always as if they were upon their oath—but must be understood, speaking or writing, with some abatement. They seldom wait to mature a proposition, but e'en bring it to market in the green ear. They delight to impart their defective discoveries as they arise, without waiting for their full development. They are no systematizers, and would but err more by attempting it. Their minds, as I said before, are suggestive merely. The brain of a true Caledonian (if I am not mistaken) is constituted upon quite a different plan. His Minerva is born in panoply. You are never admitted to see his ideas in their growth—if, indeed, they do grow, and are not rather put together upon principles of clock-work. You never catch his mind in an undress. He never hints or suggests anything, but unlades his stock of ideas in perfect order and completeness. He brings his total wealth into company, and gravely unpacks it. His riches are always about him. He never stoops to catch a glittering something in your presence, to share it with you, before he quite knows whether it be true touch or not. You cannot cry *halves* to anything that he finds. He does not find, but bring. You never witness his first apprehension of a thing. His understanding is always at its meridian—you never see the first dawn, the early streaks.—He has no falterings of self-suspicion. Surmises, guesses, misgivings, half-intuitions, semi-

consciousnesses, partial illuminations, dim instincts, embryo conceptions, have no place in his brain or vocabulary. The twilight of dubiety never falls upon him. Is he orthodox—he has no doubts. Is he an infidel—he has none either. Between the affirmative and the negative there is no border-land with him. You cannot hover with him upon the confines of truth, or wander in the maze of a probable argument. He always keeps the path. You cannot make excursions with him—for he sets you right. His taste never fluctuates. His morality never abates.
10 He cannot compromise, or understand middle actions. There can be but a right and a wrong. His conversation is as a book. His affirmations have the sanctity of an oath. You must speak upon the square with him. He stops a metaphor like a suspected person in an enemy's country. "A healthy book!"— said one of his countrymen to me, who had ventured to give that appellation of John Buncle,—"Did I catch rightly what you said? I have heard of a man in health, and of a healthy state of body, but I do not see how that epithet can be properly applied to a book." Above all, you must beware of indirect
20 expressions before a Caledonian. Clap an extinguisher upon your irony, if you are unhappily blest with a vein of it. Remember you are upon your oath. I have a print of a graceful female after Leonardo da Vinci, which I was showing off to Mr. ——. After he had examined it minutely, I ventured to ask him how he liked MY BEAUTY (a foolish name it goes by among my friends)—when he very gravely assured me, that "he had considerable respect for my character and talents" (so he was pleased to say), "but had not given himself much thought about the degree of my personal pretensions." The
30 misconception staggered me, but did not seem much to disconcert him.—Persons of this nation are particularly fond of affirming a truth—which nobody doubts. They do not so properly affirm, as annunciate it. They do indeed appear to have such a love of truth (as if, like virtue, it were valuable for itself) that all truth becomes equally valuable, whether the proposition that contains it be new or old, disputed, or such as is impossible to become a subject of disputation. I was present not long since at a party of North Britons, where a son of Burns was expected; and happened to drop a silly expres-
40 sion (in my South British way), that I wished it were the father instead of the son—when four of them started up at once to inform me, that "that was impossible, because he was dead." An impracticable wish, it seems, was more than they could conceive. Swift has hit off this part of their character, namely their love of truth, in his biting way, but with an il-

liberality that necessarily confines the passage to the margin.[3]
The tediousness of these people is certainly provoking. I wonder if they ever tire one another!—In my early life I had a
passionate fondness for the poetry of Burns. I have sometimes
foolishly hoped to ingratiate myself with his countrymen by
expressing it. But I have always found that a true Scot resents
your admiration of his compatriot, even more than he would
your contempt of him. The latter he imputes to your "imperfect acquaintance with many of the words which he uses";
and the same objection makes it a presumption in you to suppose that you can admire him.—Thomson they seem to have
forgotten. Smollett they have neither forgotten nor forgiven,
for his delineation of Rory[4] and his companion, upon their
first introduction to our metropolis.—Speak of Smollett as a
great genius, and they will retort upon you Hume's History
compared with *his* Continuation of it. What if the historian had
continued Humphrey Clinker?

I have, in the abstract, no disrespect for Jews. They are a
piece of stubborn antiquity, compared with which Stonehenge
is in its nonage. They date beyond the pyramids. But I should
not care to be in habits of familiar intercourse with any of
that nation. I confess that I have not the nerves to enter their
synagogues. Old prejudices cling about me. I cannot shake off
the story of Hugh of Lincoln.[5] Centuries of injury, contempt,
and hate, on the one side,—of cloaked revenge, dissimulation,
and hate, on the other, between our and their fathers, must
and ought to affect the blood of the children. I cannot believe
it can run clear and kindly yet; or that a few fine words, such
as candor, liberality, the light of a nineteenth century, can
close up the breaches of so deadly a disunion. A Hebrew is nowhere congenial to me. He is least distasteful on 'Change—
for the mercantile spirit levels all distinctions, as all are beauties in the dark. I boldly confess that I do not relish the
approximation of Jew and Christian, which has become so fashionable. The reciprocal endearments have, to me, something
hypocritical and unnatural in them. I do not like the Church and
Synagogue kissing and congeeing in awkward postures of an
affected civility. If *they* are converted, why do they not come

---

[3] There are some people
who think they sufficiently
acquit themselves, and
entertain their company,
with relating facts of no
consequence, not at all out
of the road of such common incidents as happen
every day; and this I have
observed more frequently
among the Scots than any
other nation, who are very
careful not to omit the
minutest circumstances of
time or place; which kind
of discourse, if it were not
a little relieved by the uncouth terms and phrases,
as well as accent and gesture peculiar to that country, would be hardly tolerable.—*Hints towards an
Essay on Conversation.*
(Lamb)
[4] Roderick Random
[5] See Chaucer's version
of this story in his *Prioress's Tale.*

over to us altogether? Why keep up a form of separation,
when the life of it is fled? If they can sit with us at table, why
do they keck at our cookery? I do not understand these half
convertites. Jews christianizing—Christians judaizing—puzzle
me. I like fish or flesh. A moderate Jew is a more confounding piece of anomaly than a wet Quaker. The spirit of the
synagogue is essentially *separative*. B—— [6] would have been
more in keeping if he had abided by the faith of his forefathers. There is a fine scorn in his face, which nature meant
to be of —— Christians. The Hebrew spirit is strong in him, in
spite of his proselytism. He cannot conquer the Shibboleth.[7]
How it breaks out when he sings, "The Children of Israel
passed through the Red Sea!" The auditors, for the moment,
are as Egyptians to him, and he rides over our necks in triumph. There is no mistaking him. B—— has a strong expression of sense in his countenance, and it is confirmed by his
singing. The foundation of his vocal excellence is sense. He
sings with understanding, as Kemble [8] delivered dialogue. He
would sing the Commandments, and give an appropriate character to each prohibition. His nation, in general, have not over-
sensible countenances. How should they?—but you seldom see
a silly expression among them. Gain, and the pursuit of gain,
sharpen a man's visage. I never heard of an idiot being born
among them.—Some admire the Jewish female-physiognomy.
I admire it—but with trembling. Jael [9] had those full dark
inscrutable eyes.

In the Negro countenance you will often meet with strong
traits of benignity. I have felt yearnings of tenderness towards
some of these faces—or rather masks—that have looked out
kindly upon one in casual encounters in the streets and high-
ways. I love what Fuller [10] beautifully calls—these "images of
God cut in ebony." But I should not like to associate with
them, to share my meals and my good-nights with them—because they are black.

I love Quaker ways, and Quaker worship. I venerate the
Quaker principles. It does me good for the rest of the day
when I meet any of their people in my path. When I am ruffled
or disturbed by any occurrence, the sight, or quiet voice of a
Quaker, acts upon me as a ventilator, lightening the air, and
taking off a load from the bosom. But I cannot like the Quakers (as Desdemona would say) "to live with them." I am all
over sophisticated—with humors, fancies, craving hourly sympathy. I must have books, pictures, theaters, chit-chat, scandal,

6 John Braham (1774–1856), tenor singer and composer
7 see Judges xii. 6
8 John Philip Kemble (1757–1823), great Shakespearean actor
9 in Judges iv. 18-21
10 Thomas Fuller (1608–1661), English divine and prose writer

jokes, ambiguities, and a thousand whim-whams, which their
simpler taste can do without. I should starve at their primitive
banquet. My appetites are too high for the salads which (according to Evelyn [11]) Eve dressed for the angel; my gusto too
excited

> To sit a guest with Daniel at his pulse.

The indirect answers which Quakers are often found to return to a question put to them may be explained, I think, without the vulgar assumption that they are more given to evasion
and equivocating than other people. They naturally look to
their words more carefully, and are more cautious of commit-
ting themselves. They have a peculiar character to keep up on
this head. They stand in a manner upon their veracity. A
Quaker is by law exempted from taking an oath. The custom
of resorting to an oath in extreme cases, sanctified as it is by
all religious antiquity, is apt (it must be confessed) to introduce into the laxer sort of minds the notion of two kinds of
truth—the one applicable to the solemn affairs of justice, and
the other to the common proceedings of daily intercourse. As
truth bound upon the conscience by an oath can be but truth,
so in the common affirmations of the shop and the market-
place a latitude is expected and conceded upon questions wanting this solemn covenant. Something less than truth satisfies.
It is common to hear a person say, "You do not expect me to
speak as if I were upon my oath." Hence a great deal of
incorrectness and inadvertency, short of falsehood, creeps into
ordinary conversation; and a kind of secondary or laic-truth
is tolerated, where clergy-truth—oath-truth, by the nature of
the circumstances, is not required. A Quaker knows none of
this distinction. His simple affirmation being received upon the
most sacred occasions, without any further test, stamps a value
upon the words which he is to use upon the most indifferent
topics of life. He looks to them, naturally, with more severity.
You can have of him no more than his word. He knows, if
he is caught tripping in a casual expression, he forfeits, for
himself at least, his claim to the invidious exemption. He knows
that his syllables are weighed—and how far a consciousness
of this particular watchfulness, exerted against a person, has
a tendency to produce indirect answers, and a diverting of the
question by honest means, might be illustrated, and the practice justified, by a more sacred example than is proper to be
adduced upon this occasion. The admirable presence of mind,
which is notorious in Quakers upon all contingencies, might be
traced to this imposed self-watchfulness—if it did not seem

[11] John Evelyn (1620-1706), best known for his diary

rather an humble and secular scion of that old stock of religious constancy, which never bent or faltered, in the Primitive Friends, or gave way to the winds of persecution, to the violence of judge or accuser, under trials and racking examinations. "You will never be the wiser, if I sit here answering your questions till midnight," said one of those upright Justicers to Penn, who had been putting law-cases with a puzzling subtlety. "Thereafter as the answers may be," retorted the Quaker. The astonishing composure of this people is sometimes ludicrously displayed in lighter instances.—I was traveling in a stage-coach with three male Quakers, buttoned up in the straitest nonconformity of their sect. We stopped to bait at Andover, where a meal, partly tea apparatus, partly supper, was set before us. My friends confined themselves to the tea-table. I in my way took supper. When the landlady brought in the bill, the eldest of my companions discovered that she had charged for both meals. This was resisted. Mine hostess was very clamorous and positive. Some mild arguments were used on the part of the Quakers, for which the heated mind of the good lady seemed by no means a fit recipient. The guard came in with his usual peremptory notice. The Quakers pulled out their money and formally tendered it—so much for tea—I, in humble imitation, tendering mine—for the supper which I had taken. She would not relax in her demand. So they all three quietly put up their silver, as did myself, and marched out of the room, the eldest and gravest going first, with myself closing up the rear, who thought I could not do better than follow the example of such grave and warrantable personages. We got in. The steps went up. The coach drove off. The murmurs of mine hostess, not very indistinctly or ambiguously pronounced, became after a time inaudible—and now my conscience, which the whimsical scene had for a while suspended, beginning to give some twitches, I waited, in the hope that some justification would be offered by these serious persons for the seeming injustice of their conduct. To my great surprise not a syllable was dropped on the subject. They sat as mute as at a meeting. At length the eldest of them broke silence, by inquiring of his next neighbor, "Hast thee heard how indigos go at the India House?" and the question operated as a soporific on my moral feeling as far as Exeter.

DREAM-CHILDREN: A REVERIE

CHILDREN love to listen to stories about their elders, when they were children; to stretch their imagination to the conception of a traditionary great-uncle, or grandame, whom they never saw. It was in this spirit that my little ones crept about me the other evening to hear about their great-grandmother Field, who lived in a great house [12] in Norfolk (a hundred times bigger than that in which they and papa lived) which had been the scene—so at least it was generally believed in that part of the country—of the tragic incidents which they had lately become familiar with from the ballad of the Children in the Wood. Certain it is that the whole story of the children and their cruel uncle was to be seen fairly carved out in wood upon the chimney-piece of the great hall, the whole story down to the Robin Redbreasts; till a foolish rich person pulled it down to set up a marble one of modern invention in its stead, with no story upon it. Here Alice put out one of her dear mother's looks, too tender to be called upbraiding. Then I went on to say, how religious and how good their great-grandmother Field was, how beloved and respected by everybody, though she was not indeed the mistress of this great house, but had only the charge of it (and yet in some respects she might be said to be the mistress of it too) committed to her by the owner, who preferred living in a newer and more fashionable mansion which he had purchased somewhere in the adjoining county; but still she lived in it in a manner as if it had been her own, and kept up the dignity of the great house in a sort while she lived, which afterwards came to decay, and was nearly pulled down, and all its old ornaments stripped and carried away to the owner's other house, where they were set up, and looked as awkward as if some one were to carry away the old tombs they had seen lately at the Abbey, and stick them up in Lady C.'s tawdry gilt drawing-room. Here John smiled, as much as to say, "that would be foolish indeed." And then I told how, when she came to die, her funeral was attended by a concourse of all the poor, and some of the gentry too, of the neighborhood for many miles round, to show their respect for her memory, because she had been such a good and religious woman; so good indeed that she knew all the Psaltery by heart, ay, and a great part of the Testament besides. Here little Alice spread her hands. Then I told what a tall, upright, graceful person their great-grandmother Field once was; and how in her youth she was esteemed the best dancer—here Alice's little right foot played an involuntary movement, till, upon my looking grave, it desisted—the best dancer, I was saying, in the county, till a cruel disease, called a cancer, came and bowed her down with pain; but it could never bend her good spirits, or make them stoop, but they were still upright,

12 Blakesware, really in Hertfordshire, where Lamb's grandmother, Mary Field, was housekeeper

because she was so good and religious. Then I told how she was
used to sleep by herself in a lone chamber of the great lone
house; and how she believed that an apparition of two infants was to be seen at midnight gliding up and down the great
staircase near where she slept, but she said "those innocents
would do her no harm"; and how frightened I used to be,
though in those days I had my maid to sleep with me, because
I was never half so good or religious as she—and yet I never
saw the infants. Here John expanded all his eyebrows and
10 tried to look courageous. Then I told how good she was to all
her grandchildren, having us to the great house in the holy-
days, where I in particular used to spend many hours by myself, in gazing upon the old busts of the Twelve Cæsars, that
had been Emperors of Rome, till the old marble heads would
seem to live again, or I to be turned into marble with them;
how I never could be tired with roaming about that huge
mansion, with its vast empty rooms, with their worn-out hangings, fluttering tapestry, and carved oaken panels, with the
gilding almost rubbed out—sometimes in the spacious old-
20 fashioned gardens, which I had almost to myself, unless when
now and then a solitary gardening man would cross me—and
how the nectarines and peaches hung upon the walls, without
my ever offering to pluck them, because they were forbidden
fruit, unless now and then,—and because I had more pleasure
in strolling about among the old melancholy-looking yew trees,
or the firs, and picking up the red berries, and the fir apples,
which were good for nothing but to look at—or in lying about
upon the fresh grass, with all the fine garden smells around me
—or basking in the orangery, till I could almost fancy myself
30 ripening too along with the oranges and the limes in that grateful warmth—or in watching the dace that darted to and fro in
the fishpond, at the bottom of the garden, with here and there
a great sulky pike hanging midway down the water in silent
state, as if it mocked at their impertinent friskings,—I had
more pleasure in these busy-idle diversions than in all the sweet
flavors of peaches, nectarines, oranges, and such-like common
baits of children. Here John slyly deposited back upon the plate
a bunch of grapes, which, not unobserved by Alice, he had
meditated dividing with her, and both seemed willing to re-
40 linquish them for the present as irrelevant. Then, in somewhat a more heightened tone, I told how, though their
great-grandmother Field loved all her grandchildren, yet in an
especial manner she might be said to love their uncle, John
L——,[13] because he was so handsome and spirited a youth, and
a king to the rest of us; and, instead of moping about in soli-

13 Lamb's brother John (also referred to as James Elia), died 1821.

tary corners, like some of us, he would mount the most mettle-
some horse he could get, when but an imp no bigger than
themselves, and make it carry him half over the county in a
morning, and join the hunters when there were any out—and
yet he loved the old great house and gardens too, but had too
much spirit to be always pent up within their boundaries—and
how their uncle grew up to man's estate as brave as he was
handsome, to the admiration of everybody, but of their great-
grandmother Field most especially; and how he used to carry
me upon his back when I was a lame-footed boy—for he was a 10
good bit older than me—many a mile when I could not walk
for pain;—and how in after life he became lame-footed too,
and I did not always (I fear) make allowances enough for him
when he was impatient and in pain, nor remember sufficiently
how considerate he had been to me when I was lame-footed;
and how when he died, though he had not been dead an hour,
it seemed as if he had died a great while ago, such a distance
there is betwixt life and death; and how I bore his death as I
thought pretty well at first, but afterwards it haunted and
haunted me; and though I did not cry or take it to heart as 20
some do, and as I think he would have done if I had died, yet
I missed him all day long, and knew not till then how much I
had loved him. I missed his kindness, and I missed his cross-
ness, and wished him to be alive again, to be quarreling with
him (for we quarreled sometimes), rather than not have him
again, and was as uneasy without him, as he, their poor uncle,
must have been when the doctor took off his limb. Here the
children fell a crying, and asked if their little mourning which
they had on was not for uncle John, and they looked up, and
prayed me not to go on about their uncle, but to tell them some 30
stories about their pretty dead mother. Then I told how for
seven long years, in hope sometimes, sometimes in despair, yet
persisting ever, I courted the fair Alice W——n; [14] and, as much
as children could understand, I explained to them what coyness,
and difficulty, and denial, meant in maidens—when suddenly
turning to Alice, the soul of the first Alice looked out at her
eyes with such a reality of re-presentment, that I became in
doubt which of them stood there before me, or whose that
bright hair was; and while I stood gazing, both the children
gradually grew fainter to my view, receding, and still receding, 40
till nothing at last but two mournful features were seen in the
uttermost distance, which, without speech, strangely impressed

14 Alice Winterton, several times referred to in Lamb's essays, fictitious name perhaps for Ann Simmons, a Hertfordshire girl who actually married a man named
Bartram. We may consider with Mr. E. V. Lucas that she was "more an abstraction
around which now and then to group tender imaginings of what might have been
than any tangible figure."

upon me the effects of speech: "We are not of Alice, nor of thee, nor are we children at all. The children of Alice call Bartrum father. We are nothing; less than nothing, and dreams. We are only what might have been, and must wait upon the tedious shores of Lethe millions of ages before we have existence, and a name"—and immediately awaking, I found myself quietly seated in my bachelor arm-chair, where I had fallen asleep, with the faithful Bridget [15] unchanged by my side—but John L. (or James Elia) was gone for ever.

THE PRAISE OF CHIMNEY-SWEEPERS

10   I LIKE to meet a sweep—understand me—not a grown sweeper—old chimney-sweepers are by no means attractive—but one of those tender novices, blooming through their first nigritude, the maternal washings not quite effaced from the cheek—such as come forth with the dawn, or somewhat earlier, with their little professional notes sounding like the *peep-peep* of a young sparrow; or liker to the matin lark should I pronounce them, in their aërial ascents not seldom anticipating the sunrise?

I have a kindly yearning towards these dim specks—poor
20 blots—innocent blacknesses—

I reverence these young Africans of our own growth—these almost clergy imps, who sport their cloth without assumption; and from their little pulpits (the tops of chimneys), in the nipping air of a December morning, preach a lesson of patience to mankind.

When a child, what a mysterious pleasure it was to witness their operation! to see a chit no bigger than one's self enter, one knew not by what process, into what seemed the *fauces Averni* [16]—to pursue him in imagination, as he went sound-
30 ing on through so many dark stifling caverns, horrid shades!—to shudder with the idea that "now, surely he must be lost for ever!"—to revive at hearing his feeble shout of discovered daylight—and then (O fulness of delight!) running out of doors, to come just in time to see the sable phenomenon emerge in safety, the brandished weapon of his art victorious like some flag waved over a conquered citadel! I seem to remember having been told that a bad sweep was once left in a stack with his brush to indicate which way the wind blew. It was an awful spectacle certainly; not much unlike the old stage direc-
40 tion in Macbeth, where the "Apparition of a child crowned, with a tree in his hand, rises."

Reader, if thou meetest one of these small gentry in thy early

15 Lamb's sister Mary   16 jaws of Hell

rambles, it is good to give him a penny,—it is better to give
him two-pence. If it be starving weather, and to the proper
troubles of his hard occupation, a pair of kibed [17] heels (no
unusual accompaniment) be superadded, the demand on thy
humanity will surely rise to a tester.[18]

There is a composition, the groundwork of which I have
understood to be the sweet wood yclept sassafras. This wood
boiled down to a kind of tea, and tempered with an infusion of
milk and sugar, hath to some tastes a delicacy beyond the
China luxury. I know not how thy palate may relish it; for
myself, with every deference to the judicious Mr. Read, who
hath time out of mind kept open a shop (the only one he avers
in London) for the vending of this "wholesome and pleasant
beverage," on the south side of Fleet Street, as thou approach-
est Bridge Street—*the only Salopian* [19] *house,*—I have never
yet adventured to dip my own particular lip in a basin of his
commended ingredients—a cautious premonition to the olfac-
tories constantly whispering to me that my stomach must infallibly, with all due courtesy, decline it. Yet I have seen pal-
ates, otherwise not uninstructed in dietetical elegancies, sup it
up with avidity.

I know not by what particular conformation of the organ it
happens, but I have always found that this composition is sur-
prisingly gratifying to the palate of a young chimney-sweeper
—whether the oily particles (sassafras is slightly oleaginous)
do attenuate and soften the fuliginous [20] concretions, which are
sometimes found (in dissections) to adhere to the roof of the
mouth in these unfledged practitioners; or whether Nature,
sensible that she had mingled too much of bitter wood in the
lot of these raw victims, caused to grow out of the earth her
sassafras for a sweet lenitive—but so it is, that no possible
taste or odor to the senses of a young chimney-sweeper can
convey a delicate excitement comparable to this mixture. Being penniless, they will yet hang their black heads over the
ascending steam, to gratify one sense if possible, seemingly no
less pleased than those domestic animals—cats—when they
purr over a new-found sprig of valerian. There is something
more in these sympathies than philosophy can inculcate.

Now albeit Mr. Read boasteth, not without reason, that his is
the *only Salopian house;* yet be it known to thee, reader—if
thou art one who keepest what are called good hours, thou art
haply ignorant of the fact—he hath a race of industrious imi-
tators, who from stalls, and under open sky, dispense the
same savory mess to humbler customers, at that dead time of

17 chilblained
18 sixpence

19 dispensing saloop, or
sassafras tea

20 sooty

the dawn, when (as extremes meet) the rake, reeling home from his midnight cups, and the hard-handed artisan leaving his bed to resume the premature labors of the day, jostle, not unfrequently to the manifest disconcerting of the former, for the honors of the pavement. It is the time when, in summer, between the expired and the not yet relumined kitchen-fires, the kennels of our fair metropolis give forth their least satisfactory odors. The rake, who wisheth to dissipate his o'ernight vapors in more grateful coffee, curses the ungenial fume, as he passeth; but the artisan stops to taste, and blesses the fragrant breakfast.

This is *Saloop*—the precocious herb-woman's darling—the delight of the early gardener, who transports his smoking cabbages by break of day from Hammersmith to Covent Garden's famed piazzas—the delight, and oh! I fear, too often the envy, of the unpennied sweep. Him shouldst thou haply encounter, with his dim visage pendent over the grateful steam, regale him with a sumptuous basin (it will cost thee but three-halfpennies) and a slice of delicate bread and butter (an added halfpenny)—so may thy culinary fires, eased of the o'er-charged secretions from thy worse-placed hospitalities, curl up a lighter volume to the welkin—so may the descending soot never taint thy costly well-ingredienced soups—nor the odious cry, quick-reaching from street to street, of the *fired chimney*, invite the rattling engines from ten adjacent parishes, to disturb for a casual scintillation thy peace and pocket!

I am by nature extremely susceptible of street affronts: the jeers and taunts of the populace; the low-bred triumph they display over the casual trip, or splashed stocking, of a gentleman. Yet can I endure the jocularity of a young sweep with something more than forgiveness.—In the last winter but one, pacing along Cheapside with my accustomed precipitation when I walk westward, a treacherous slide brought me upon my back in an instant. I scrambled up with pain and shame enough— yet outwardly trying to face it down, as if nothing had happened—when the roguish grin of one of these young wits encountered me. There he stood, pointing me out with his dusky finger to the mob, and to a poor woman (I suppose his mother) in particular, till the tears for the exquisiteness of the fun (so he thought it) worked themselves out the corners of his poor red eyes, red from many a previous weeping, and soot-inflamed, yet twinkling through all with such a joy, snatched out of desolation, that Hogarth [21]—but Hogarth has got him already (how could he miss him?) in the March to Finchley, grinning at the pieman—there he stood, as he stands in the

[21] William Hogarth (1697-1764), famous for his satirical engravings

picture, irremovable, as if the jest was to last for ever—with such a maximum of glee, and minimum of mischief, in his mirth—for the grin of a genuine sweep hath absolutely no malice in it—that I could have been content, if the honor of a gentleman might endure it, to have remained his butt and his mockery till midnight.

I am by theory obdurate to the seductiveness of what are called a fine set of teeth. Every pair of rosy lips (the ladies must pardon me) is a casket presumably holding such jewels; but, methinks, they should take leave to "air" them as frugally 10 as possible. The fine lady, or fine gentleman, who show me their teeth, show me bones. Yet must I confess, that from the mouth of a true sweep a display (even to ostentation) of those white and shiny ossifications, strikes me as an agreeable anomaly in manners, and an allowable piece of foppery. It is, as when

> A sable cloud
> Turns forth her silver lining on the night.

It is like some remnant of gentry not quite extinct; a badge of better days; a hint of nobility:—and, doubtless, under the obscuring darkness and double night of their forlorn disguise- 20 ment, oftentimes lurketh good blood, and gentle conditions, derived from lost ancestry, and a lapsed pedigree. The premature apprenticements of these tender victims give but too much encouragement, I fear, to clandestine and almost infantile abductions; the seeds of civility and true courtesy, so often discernible in these young grafts (not otherwise to be accounted for) plainly hint at some forced adoptions; many noble Rachels mourning for their children, even in our days, countenance the fact; the tales of fairy-spiriting may shadow a lamentable verity, and the recovery of the young Montagu [22] be but a 30 solitary instance of good fortune out of many irreparable and hopeless *defiliations*.

In one of the state-beds at Arundel Castle, a few years since —under a ducal canopy—(that seat of the Howards is an object of curiosity to visitors, chiefly for its beds, in which the late duke was especially a connoisseur)—encircled with curtains of delicatest crimson, with starry coronets inwoven—folded between a pair of sheets whiter and softer than the lap where Venus lulled Ascanius—was discovered by chance, after all methods of search had failed, at noonday, fast asleep, a lost 40 chimney-sweeper. The little creature, having somehow con-

---

[22] Edward Wortley Montagu, son of the celebrated Lady Mary Wortley Montagu, ran away from Westminster School and became for a time a chimney-sweeper.

founded his passage among the intricacies of those lordly chimneys, by some unknown aperture had alighted upon this magnificent chamber; and, tired with his tedious explorations, was unable to resist the delicious invitement to repose, which he there saw exhibited; so, creeping between the sheets very quietly, laid his black head upon the pillow, and slept like a young Howard.

Such is the account given to the visitors at the Castle.—But I cannot help seeming to perceive a confirmation of what I had just hinted at in this story. A high instinct was at work in the case, or I am mistaken. Is it probable that a poor child of that description, with whatever weariness he might be visited, would have ventured, under such a penalty as he would be taught to expect, to uncover the sheets of a Duke's bed, and deliberately to lay himself down between them, when the rug, or the carpet, presented an obvious couch, still far above his pretensions—is this probable, I would ask, if the great power of nature, which I contend for, had not been manifested within him, prompting to the adventure? Doubtless this young nobleman (for such my mind misgives me that he must be) was allured by some memory, not amounting to full consciousness, of his condition in infancy, when he was used to be lapped by his mother, or his nurse, in just such sheets as he there found, into which he was now but creeping back as into his proper *incunabula* [23] and resting-place.—By no other theory than by this sentiment of a pre-existent state (as I may call it), can I explain a deed so venturous, and, indeed, upon any other system, so indecorous, in this tender, but unseasonable, sleeper.

My pleasant friend Jem White [24] was so impressed with a belief of metamorphoses like this frequently taking place, that in some sort to reverse the wrongs of fortune in these poor changelings, he instituted an annual feast of chimney-sweepers, at which it was his pleasure to officiate as host and waiter. It was a solemn supper held in Smithfield, upon the yearly return of the fair of St. Bartholomew. Cards were issued a week before to the master-sweeps in and about the metropolis, confining the invitation to their younger fry. Now and then an elderly stripling would get in among us, and be good-naturedly winked at; but our main body were infantry. One unfortunate wight, indeed, who, relying upon his dusky suit, had intruded himself into our party, but by tokens was providentially discovered in time to be no chimney-sweeper (all is not soot which looks so), was quoited out of the presence with universal indignation, as not having on the wedding garment; but in

23 cradle clothes
24 a schoolfellow of Lamb's at Christ's Hospital

general the greatest harmony prevailed. The place chosen
was a convenient spot among the pens, at the north side of
the fair, not so far distant as to be impervious to the agreeable hubbub of that vanity; but remote enough not to be
obvious to the interruption of every gaping spectator in it.
The guests assembled about seven. In those little temporary
parlors three tables were spread with napery, not so fine as
substantial, and at every board a comely hostess presided with
her pan of hissing sausages. The nostrils of the young rogues
dilated at the savor. James White, as head waiter, had charge 10
of the first table; and myself, with our trusty companion
Bigod,[25] ordinarily ministered to the other two. There was
clambering and jostling, you may be sure, who should get at
the first table,—for Rochester [26] in his maddest days could not
have done the humors of the scene with more spirit than my
friend. After some general expression of thanks for the honor
the company had done him, his inaugural ceremony was to clasp
the greasy waist of old dame Ursula (the fattest of the three),
that stood frying and fretting, half-blessing, half-cursing "the
gentleman," and imprint upon her chaste lips a tender salute, 20
whereat the universal host would set up a shout that tore the
concave, while hundreds of grinning teeth startled the night
with their brightness. O it was a pleasure to see the sable
younkers lick in the unctuous meat, with *his* more unctuous
sayings—how he would fit the tit-bits to the puny mouths,
reserving the lengthier links for the seniors—how he would
intercept a morsel even in the jaws of some young desperado,
declaring it "must to the pan again to be browned, for it was
not fit for a gentleman's eating"—how he would recommend
this slice of white bread, or that piece of kissing-crust, to a 30
tender juvenile, advising them all to have a care of cracking
their teeth, which were their best patrimony,—how genteelly
he would deal about the small ale, as if it were wine, naming the
brewer, and protesting, if it were not good, he should lose their
custom; with a special recommendation to wipe the lip before
drinking. Then we had our toasts—"the King,"—"the Cloth,"
—which, whether they understood or not, was equally diverting and flattering;—and for a crowning sentiment, which never
failed, "May the Brush supersede the Laurel!" All these, and
fifty other fancies, which were rather felt than comprehended 40
by his guests, would he utter, standing upon tables, and prefac-
ing every sentiment with a "Gentlemen, give me the leave to
propose so and so," which was a prodigious comfort to those
young orphans; every now and then stuffing into his mouth

---

25 John Fenwick   ter, a notorious rake of the
26 the Earl of Roches-   time of Charles II

(for it did not do to be squeamish on these occasions) indiscriminate pieces of those reeking sausages, which pleased them mightily, and was the savoriest part, you may believe, of the entertainment.

> Golden lads and lasses must,
> As chimney-sweepers, come to dust—[27]

James White is extinct, and with him these suppers have long ceased. He carried away with him half the fun of the world when he died—of my world ·at least. His old clients look for him among the pens; and, missing him, reproach the altered feast of St. Bartholomew, and the glory of Smithfield departed for ever.

THE SUPERANNUATED MAN

Sera tamen respexit
Libertas.[28]   —VIRGIL.

A Clerk I was in London gay.—O'KEEFE.

IF peradventure, Reader, it has been thy lot to waste the golden years of thy life—thy shining youth—in the irksome confinement of an office; to have thy prison days prolonged through middle age down to decrepitude and silver hairs, without hope of release or respite; to have lived to forget that there are such things as holidays, or to remember them but as the prerogatives of childhood; then, and then only, will you be able to appreciate my deliverance.

It is now six and thirty years since I took my seat at the desk in Mincing Lane. Melancholy was the transition at fourteen from the abundant playtime, and the frequently-intervening vacations of school days, to the eight, nine, and sometimes ten hours a day attendance at a counting-house. But time partially reconciles us to anything. I gradually became content—doggedly contented, as wild animals in cages.

It is true I had my Sundays to myself; but Sundays, admirable as the institution of them is for purposes of worship, are for that very reason the very worst adapted for days of unbending and recreation. In particular, there is a gloom for me attendant upon a city Sunday, a weight in the air. I miss the cheerful cries of London, the music, and the ballad-singers—the buzz and stirring murmur of the streets. Those eternal bells depress me. The closed shops repel me. Prints, pictures, all the glittering and endless succession of knacks and gewgaws, and ostentatiously displayed wares of tradesmen, which make a

27 song from Shakespeare's *Cymbeline* (see Vol. I)
28 Liberty, though late, nevertheless visited me.

weekday saunter through the less busy parts of the metropolis so delightful—are shut out. No book-stalls deliciously to idle over—no busy faces to recreate the idle man who contemplates them ever passing by—the very face of business a charm by contrast to his temporary relaxation from it. Nothing to be seen but unhappy countenances—or half-happy at best—of emancipated 'prentices and little tradesfolks, with here and there a servant-maid that has got leave to go out, who, slaving all the week, with the habit has lost almost the capacity of enjoying a free hour; and livelily expressing the hollowness of a day's pleasuring. The very strollers in the fields on that day look anything but comfortable.

But besides Sundays I had a day at Easter, and a day at Christmas, with a full week in the summer to go and air myself in my native fields of Hertfordshire. This last was a great indulgence; and the prospect of its recurrence, I believe, alone kept me up through the year, and made my durance tolerable. But when the week came round, did the glittering phantom of the distance keep touch with me? or rather was it not a series of seven uneasy days, spent in restless pursuit of pleasure, and a wearisome anxiety to find out how to make the most of them? Where was the quiet, where the promised rest? Before I had a taste of it, it was vanished. I was at the desk again, counting upon the fifty-one tedious weeks that must intervene before such another snatch would come. Still the prospect of its coming threw something of an illumination upon the darker side of my captivity. Without it, as I have said, I could scarcely have sustained my thraldom.

Independently of the rigors of attendance, I have ever been haunted with a sense (perhaps a mere caprice) of incapacity for business. This, during my latter years, had increased to such a degree that it was visible in all the lines of my countenance. My health and my good spirits flagged. I had perpetually a dread of some crisis, to which I should be found unequal. Besides my daylight servitude, I served over again all night in my sleep, and would awake with terrors of imaginary false entries, errors in my accounts, and the like. I was fifty years of age, and no prospect of emancipation presented itself. I had grown to my desk, as it were; and the wood had entered into my soul.

My fellows in the office would sometimes rally me upon the trouble legible in my countenance; but I did not know that it had raised the suspicions of any of my employers, when, on the 5th of last month, a day ever to be remembered by me, L——, the junior partner in the firm, calling me on one side, directly taxed me with my bad looks, and frankly inquired the cause of them. So taxed, I honestly made confession of my infirmity,

and added that I was afraid I should eventually be obliged to resign his service. He spoke some words of course to hearten me, and there the matter rested. A whole week I remained laboring under the impression that I had acted imprudently in my disclosure; that I had foolishly given a handle against myself, and had been anticipating my own dismissal. A week passed in this manner, the most anxious one, I verily believe, in my whole life, when on the evening of the 12th of April, just as I was about quitting my desk to go home (it might be about
10 eight o'clock), I received an awful summons to attend the presence of the whole assembled firm in the formidable back parlor. I thought, now my time is surely come, I have done for myself, I am going to be told that they have no longer occasion for me. L——, I could see, smiled at the terror I was in, which was a little relief to me,—when to my utter astonishment B——, the eldest partner, began a formal harangue to me on the length of my services, my very meritorious conduct during the whole of the time (the deuce, thought I, how did he find out that? I protest I never had the confidence to think as much).
20 He went on to descant on the expediency of retiring at a certain time of life (how my heart panted!) and asking me a few questions as to the amount of my own property, of which I have a little, ended with a proposal, to which his three partners nodded a grave assent, that I should accept from the house, which I had served so well, a pension for life to the amount of two-thirds of my accustomed salary—a magnificent offer! I do not know what I answered between surprise and gratitude, but it was understood that I accepted their proposal, and I was told that I was free from that hour to leave their service. I stammered out
30 a bow, and at just ten minutes after eight I went home—for ever. This noble benefit—gratitude forbids me to conceal their names—I owe to the kindness of the most munificent firm in the world—the house of Boldero, Merryweather, Bosanquet, and Lacy.

Esto perpetua! [36]

For the first day or two I felt stunned, overwhelmed. I could only apprehend my felicity; I was too confused to taste it sincerely. I wandered about, thinking I was happy, and knowing that I was not. I was in the condition of a prisoner in the old
40 Bastile, suddenly let loose after a forty years' confinement. I could scarce trust myself with myself. It was like passing out of Time into Eternity—for it is a sort of Eternity for a man to

[36] May it be eternal. The names are fictitious names representing the directors of the East India Company.

have his Time all to himself. It seemed to me that I had more
time on my hands than I could ever manage. From a poor man,
poor in Time, I was suddenly lifted up into a vast revenue; I
could see no end of my possessions; I wanted some steward, or
judicious bailiff, to manage my estates in Time for me. And
here let me caution persons grown old in active business, not
lightly, nor without weighing their own resources, to forego their
customary employment all at once, for there may be danger in
it. I feel it by myself, but I know that my resources are sufficient;
and now that those first giddy raptures have subsided, I have a 10
quiet home-feeling of the blessedness of my condition. I am in
no hurry. Having all holidays, I am as though I had none. If
Time hung heavy upon me, I could walk it away; but I do *not*
walk all day long, as I used to do in those old transient holidays, thirty miles a day, to make the most of them. If Time
were troublesome, I could read it away; but I do *not* read in
that violent measure, with which, having no Time my own but
candlelight Time, I used to weary out my head and eyesight in
bygone winters. I walk, read, or scribble (as now) just when
the fit seizes me. I no longer hunt after pleasure; I let it come 20
to me. I am like the man

> ————that's born, and has his years come to him,
>   In some green desert.

"Years!" you will say; "what is this superannuated simple-
ton calculating upon? He has already told us he is past fifty."

I have indeed lived nominally fifty years, but deduct out of
them the hours which I have lived to other people, and not to
myself, and you will find me still a young fellow. For *that* is
the only true Time, which a man can properly call his own,
that which he has all to himself; the rest, though in some sense 30
he may be said to live it, is other people's time, not his. The
remnant of my poor days, long or short, is at least multiplied
for me threefold. My ten next years, if I stretch so far, will
be as long as any preceding thirty. 'Tis a fair rule-of-three sum.

Among the strange fantasies which beset me at the commencement of my freedom, and of which all traces are not yet
gone, one was, that a vast tract of time had intervened since I
quitted the Counting-House. I could not conceive of it as an
affair of yesterday. The partners, and the clerks, with whom I
had for so many years, and for so many hours in each day of the 40
year, been closely associated—being suddenly removed from
them—they seemed as dead to me. There is a fine passage,
which may serve to illustrate this fancy, in a Tragedy by Sir
Robert Howard, speaking of a friend's death:

   —— 'Twas but just now he went away;
   I have not since had time to shed a tear;
   And yet the distance does the same appear
   As if he had been a thousand years from me.
   Time takes no measure in Eternity.[37]

To dissipate this awkward feeling, I have been fain to go among them once or twice since; to visit my old desk-fellows —my co-brethren of the quill—that I had left below in the state militant. Not all the kindness with which they received me could quite restore to me that pleasant familiarity, which I had heretofore enjoyed among them. We cracked some of our old jokes, but methought they went off but faintly. My old desk; the peg where I hung my hat, were appropriated to another. I knew it must be, but I could not take it kindly. D——l take me, if I did not feel some remorse—beast, if I had not,—at quitting my old compeers, the faithful partners of my toils for six and thirty years, that soothed for me with their jokes and conundrums the ruggedness of my professional road. Had it been so rugged then after all? or was I a coward simply? Well, it is too late to repent; and I also know that these suggestions are a common fallacy of the mind on such occasions. But my heart smote me. I had violently broken the bands betwixt us. It was at least not courteous. I shall be some time before I get quite reconciled to the separation. Farewell, old cronies, yet not for long, for again and again I will come among ye, if I shall have your leave. Farewell, Ch——, dry, sarcastic, and friendly! Do——, mild, slow to move, and gentlemanly! Pl——,[38] officious to do, and to volunteer, good services!—and thou, thou dreary pile, fit mansion for a Gresham or a Whittington [39] of old, stately House of Merchants; with thy labyrinthine passages, and light-excluding, pent-up offices, where candles for one half the year supplied the place of the sun's light; unhealthy contributor to my weal, stern fosterer of my living, farewell! In thee remain, and not in the obscure collection of some wandering bookseller, my "works!" There let them rest, as I do from my labors, piled on thy massy shelves, more MSS. in folio than ever Aquinas left, and full as useful! My mantle I bequeath among ye.

A fortnight has passed since the date of my first communication. At that period I was approaching to tranquillity, but had not reached it. I boasted of a calm indeed, but it was compara-

37 from *The Vestal Virgin, or The Roman Ladies* of Robert Howard (1626–1698)

38 presumably John Chambers, Henry Dodwell, and W. D. Plumley

39 Sir Thomas Gresham, English financier (1519?–1579), who founded the Royal Exchange, and Richard Whittington, who was "thrice mayor of London" (d. 1423), the hero, with his cat, of a well known folktale

tive only. Something of the first flutter was left; an unsettling
sense of novelty; the dazzle to weak eyes of unaccustomed light.
I missed my old chains, forsooth, as if they had been some
necessary part of my apparel. I was a poor Carthusian, from
strict cellular discipline suddenly by some revolution returned
upon the world. I am now as if I had never been other than
my own master. It is natural to me to go where I please, to
do what I please. I find myself at 11 o'clock in the day in
Bond Street, and it seems to me that I have been sauntering
there at that very hour for years past. I digress into Soho, to
explore a bookstall. Methinks I have been thirty years a col-
lector. There is nothing strange nor new in it. I find myself
before a fine picture in a morning. Was it ever otherwise?
What is become of Fish Street Hill? Where is Fenchurch Street?
Stones of old Mincing Lane, which I have worn with my daily
pilgrimage for six and thirty years, to the footsteps of what
toil-worn clerk are your everlasting flints now vocal? I indent
the gayer flags of Pall Mall. It is 'Change time, and I am
strangely among the Elgin marbles.[40] It was no hyperbole when
I ventured to compare the change in my condition to passing
into another world. Time stands still in a manner to me. I
have lost all distinction of season. I do not know the day of
the week, or of the month. Each day used to be individually
felt by me in its reference to the foreign post days; in its
distance from, or propinquity to, the next Sunday. I had my
Wednesday feelings, my Saturday night's sensations. The genius
of each day was upon me distinctly during the whole of it,
affecting my appetite, spirits, etc. The phantom of the next
day, with the dreary five to follow, sat as a load upon my poor
Sabbath recreations. What charm has washed that Ethiop
white? What is gone of Black Monday? All days are the
same. Sunday itself—that unfortunate failure of a holiday as
it too often proved, what with my sense of its fugitiveness,
and over-care to get the greatest quantity of pleasure out of
it—is melted down into a week-day. I can spare to go to church
now, without grudging the huge cantle which it used to seem
to cut out of the holiday. I have time for everything. I can
visit a sick friend. I can interrupt the man of much occupation
when he is busiest. I can insult over him with an invitation
to take a day's pleasure with me to Windsor this fine May
morning. It is Lucretian[41] pleasure to behold the poor drudges,
whom I have left behind in the world, carking and caring;
like horses in a mill, drudging on in the same eternal round

40 famous collection of Greek sculptures in the British Museum, brought from Athens by Lord Elgin

41 like that of the Roman poet Lucretius, who at the beginning of Book II of his *De Rerum Natura* speaks of the pleasure of beholding from the land the distresses of another on the sea

—and what is it all for? A man can never have too much Time
to himself, nor too little to do. Had I a little son, I would
christen him NOTHING-TO-DO; he should do nothing. Man, I
verily believe, is out of his element as long as he is operative.
I am altogether for the life contemplative. Will no kindly earthquake come and swallow up those accursed cotton-mills? Take
me that lumber of a desk there, and bowl it down

As low as to the fiends.

I am no longer * * * * * *, clerk to the Firm of, &c. I am
10 Retired Leisure. I am to be met with in trim gardens. I am
already come to be known by my vacant face and careless
gesture, perambulating at no fixed pace, nor with any settled
purpose. I walk about; not to and from. They tell me, a certain
cum dignitate [42] air, that has been buried so long with my other
good parts, has begun to shoot forth in my person. I grow
into gentility perceptibly. When I take up a newspaper, it is
to read the state of the opera. *Opus operatum est.* [43] I have
done all that I came into this world to do. I have worked taskwork, and have the rest of the day to myself.

OLD CHINA

20 I HAVE an almost feminine partiality for old china. When
I go to see any great house, I inquire for the china-closet, and
next for the picture-gallery. I cannot defend the order of preference, but by saying that we have all some taste or other, of
too ancient a date to admit of our remembering distinctly that
it was an acquired one. I can call to mind the first play, and
the first exhibition, that I was taken to; but I am not conscious
of a time when china jars and saucers were introduced into my
imagination.

I had no repugnance then—why should I now have?—to those
30 little, lawless, azure-tinctured grotesques, that, under the notion
of men and women, float about, uncircumscribed by any element, in that world before perspective—a china tea-cup.

I like to see my old friends—whom distance cannot diminish
—figuring up in the air (so they appear to our optics), yet on
terra firma still—for so we must in courtesy interpret that
speck of deeper blue, which the decorous artist, to prevent
absurdity, had made to spring up beneath their sandals.

I love the men with women's faces, and the women, if possible, with still more womanish expressions.

40 Here is a young and courtly Mandarin, handing tea to a lady
from a salver—two miles off. See how distance seems to set

42 with dignity   43 The work has been finished.

off respect! And here the same lady, or another—for likeness is identity on tea-cups—is stepping into a little fairy boat, moored on the hither side of this calm garden river, with a dainty mincing foot, which in a right angle of incidence (as angles go in our world) must infallibly land her in the midst of a flowery mead—a furlong off on the other side of the same strange stream!

Farther on—if far or near can be predicated of their world —see horses, trees, pagodas, dancing the hays.[44]

Here—a cow and rabbit couchant, and coextensive—so objects show, seen through the lucid atmosphere of fine Cathay.

I was pointing out to my cousin last evening, over our Hyson (which we are old-fashioned enough to drink unmixed still of an afternoon), some of these *speciosa miracula* [45] upon a set of extraordinary old blue china (a recent purchase) which we were now for the first time using; and could not help remarking, how favorable circumstances had been to us of late years, that we could afford to please the eye sometimes with trifles of this sort—when a passing sentiment seemed to overshade the brows of my companion. I am quick at detecting these summer clouds in Bridget.[46]

"I wish the good old times would come again," she said, "when we were not quite so rich. I do not mean that I want to be poor; but there was a middle state"—so she was pleased to ramble on,—"in which I am sure we were a great deal happier. A purchase is but a purchase, now that you have money enough and to spare. Formerly it used to be a triumph. When we coveted a cheap luxury (and, O! how much ado I had to get you to consent in those times!), we were used to have a debate two or three days before, and to weigh the *for* and *against*, and think what we might spare it out of, and what saving we could hit upon, that should be an equivalent. A thing was worth buying then, when we felt the money that we paid for it.

"Do you remember the brown suit, which you made to hang upon you, till all your friends cried shame upon you, it grew so threadbare—and all because of that folio Beaumont and Fletcher, which you dragged home late at night from Barker's in Covent Garden? Do you remember how we eyed it for weeks before we could make up our minds to the purchase, and had not come to a determination till it was near ten o'clock of the Saturday night, when you set off from Islington, fearing you should be too late—and when the old bookseller with some grumbling opened his shop, and by the twinkling taper (for he

---

44 a country dance
45 beautiful wonders

46 the name used in the essays for Lamb's sister   Mary

was setting bedwards) lighted out the relic from his dusty treasures—and when you lugged it home, wishing it were twice as
cumbersome—and when you presented it to me—and when we
were exploring the perfectness of it (*collating* you called it)
—and while I was repairing some of the loose leaves with paste,
which your impatience would not suffer to be left till daybreak
—was there no pleasure in being a poor man? or can those neat
black clothes which you wear now, and are so careful to keep
brushed, since we have become rich and finical, give you half
10 the honest vanity with which you flaunted it about in that overworn suit—your old corbeau [47]—for four or five weeks longer
than you should have done, to pacify your conscience for the
mighty sum of fifteen—or sixteen shillings was it?—a great
affair we thought it then—which you had lavished on the
old folio. Now you can afford to buy any book that pleases you,
but I do not see that you ever bring me home any nice old
purchases now.

"When you came home with twenty apologies for laying out
a less number of shillings upon that print after Lionardo, which
20 we christened the 'Lady Blanch'; when you looked at the
purchase, and thought of the money—and thought of the money,
and looked again at the picture—was there no pleasure in being
a poor man? Now, you have nothing to do but to walk into
Colnaghi's and buy a wilderness of Lionardos. Yet do you?

"Then, do you remember our pleasant walks to Enfield, and
Potter's Bar, and Waltham, when we had a holiday—holidays
and all other fun are gone now we are rich—and the little
handbasket in which I used to deposit our day's fare of savory
cold lamb and salad—and how you would pry about at noon-
30 tide for some decent house, where we might go in and produce
our store—only paying for the ale that you must call for—
and speculate upon the looks of the landlady, and whether she
was likely to allow us a tablecloth—and wish for such another
honest hostess as Izaak Walton has described many a one on
the pleasant banks of the Lea, when he went a fishing—and
sometimes they would prove obliging enough, and sometimes
they would look grudgingly upon us—but we had cheerful looks
still for one another, and would eat our plain food savorily,
scarcely grudging Piscator [48] his Trout Hall? Now—when we
40 go out for a day's pleasuring, which is seldom, moreover, we
ride part of the way and go into a fine inn, and order the best
of dinners, never debating the expense—which, after all, never
has half the relish of those chance country snaps, when we
were at the mercy of uncertain usage, and a precarious welcome.

"You are too proud to see a play anywhere now but in the

17 dark green   48 the fisherman in Walton's *Compleat Angler*

pit. Do you remember where it was we used to sit, when we saw the Battle of Hexham, and the Surrender of Calais, and Bannister and Mrs. Bland in the Children in the Wood—when we squeezed out our shillings apiece to sit three or four times in a season in the one-shilling gallery—where you felt all the time that you ought not to have brought me—and more strongly I felt obligation to you for having brought me—and the pleasure was the better for a little shame—and when the curtain drew up, what cared we for our place in the house, or what mattered it where we were sitting, when our thoughts were with Rosalind in Arden, or with Viola at the Court of Illyria? You used to say that the gallery was the best place of all for enjoying a play socially—that the relish of such exhibitions must be in proportion to the infrequency of going—that the company we met there, not being in general readers of plays, were obliged to attend the more, and did attend, to what was going on, on the stage—because a word lost would have been a chasm, which it was impossible for them to fill up. With such reflections we consoled our pride then—and I appeal to you whether, as a woman, I met generally with less attention and accommodation than I have done since in more expensive situations in the house? The getting in, indeed, and the crowding up those inconvenient staircases, was bad enough,—but there was still a law of civility to woman recognized to quite as great an extent as we ever found in the other passages—and how a little difficulty overcome heightened the snug seat, and the play, afterwards! Now we can only pay our money, and walk in. You cannot see, you say, in the galleries now. I am sure we saw, and heard too, well enough then—but sight, and all, I think, is gone with our poverty.

"There was pleasure in eating strawberries, before they became quite common—in the first dish of peas, while they were yet dear—to have them for a nice supper, a treat. What treat can we have now? If we were to treat ourselves now—that is, to have dainties a little above our means, it would be selfish and wicked. It is the very little more that we allow ourselves beyond what the actual poor can get at, that makes what I call a treat—when two people living together, as we have done, now and then indulge themselves in a cheap luxury, which both like; while each apologizes, and is willing to take both halves of the blame to his single share. I see no harm in people making much of themselves in that sense of the word. It may give them a hint how to make much of others. But now—what I mean by the word—we never *do* make much of ourselves. None but the poor can do it. I do not mean the veriest poor of all, but persons as we were, just above poverty.

"I know what you were going to say, that it is mighty pleasant at the end of the year to make all meet,—and much ado we used to have every Thirty-first Night of December to account for our exceedings—many a long face did you make over your puzzled accounts, and in contriving to make it out how we had spent so much—or that we had not spent so much—or that it was impossible we should spend so much next year—and still we found our slender capital decreasing—but then, betwixt ways, and projects, and compromises of one sort or another, and
10 talk of curtailing this charge, and doing without that for the future—and the hope that youth brings, and laughing spirits (in which you were never poor till now), we pocketed up our loss, and in conclusion, with 'lusty brimmers' [49] (as you used to quote it out of *hearty, cheerful, Mr. Cotton*, as you called him), we used to welcome in the 'coming guest.' Now we have no reckoning at all at the end of the old year—no flattering promises about the new year doing better for us."

Bridget is so sparing of her speech on most occasions, that when she gets into a rhetorical vein, I am careful how I inter-
20 rupt it. I could not help, however, smiling at the phantom of wealth which her dear imagination had conjured up out of a clear income of poor —— hundred pounds a year. "It is true we were happier when we were poorer, but we were also younger, my cousin. I am afraid we must put up with the excess, for if we were to shake the superflux into the sea, we should not much mend ourselves. That we had much to struggle with, as we grew up together, we have reason to be most thankful. It strengthened and knit our compact closer. We could never have been what we have been to each other, if we had always
30 had the sufficiency which you now complain of. The resisting power—those natural dilations of the youthful spirit, which circumstances cannot straiten—with us are long since passed away. Competence to age is supplementary youth, a sorry supplement indeed, but I fear the best that is to be had. We must ride, where we formerly walked: live better, and lie softer—and shall be wise to do so—than we had means to do in those good old days you speak of. Yet could those days return— could you and I once more walk our thirty miles a day— could Bannister and Mrs. Bland again be young, and you and
40 I be young to see them—could the good old one-shilling gallery days return—they are dreams, my cousin, now—but could you and I at this moment, instead of this quiet argument, by our well-carpeted fireside, sitting on this luxurious sofa—be once more struggling up those inconvenient staircases, pushed about,

---

49 a phrase from the poem *The New Year*, previously quoted by Lamb in his essay *New Year's Eve*, from Charles Cotton (1630–1687)

and squeezed, and elbowed by the poorest rabble of poor gallery scramblers—could I once more hear those anxious shrieks of yours—and the delicious *Thank God, we are safe,* which always followed when the topmost stair, conquered, let in the first light of the whole cheerful theater down beneath us—I know not the fathom line that ever touched a descent so deep as I would be willing to bury more wealth in than Crœsus had, or the great Jew R——[50] is supposed to have, to purchase it. And now do just look at that merry little Chinese waiter holding an umbrella, big enough for a bed-tester, over the head of that pretty insipid half-Madonna-ish chit of a lady in that very blue summer house.

POPULAR FALLACIES

THAT WE SHOULD LIE DOWN WITH THE LAMB

WE could never quite understand the philosophy of this arrangement, or the wisdom of our ancestors in sending us for instruction to these woolly bedfellows. A sheep, when it is dark, has nothing to do but to shut his silly eyes, and sleep if he can. Man found out long sixes.—Hail, candlelight! without disparagement to sun or moon, the kindliest luminary of the three—if we may not rather style thee their radiant deputy, mild viceroy of the moon!—We love to read, talk, sit silent, eat, drink, sleep, by candlelight. They are everybody's sun and moon. This is our peculiar and household planet. Wanting it, what savage unsocial nights must our ancestors have spent, wintering in caves and unillumined fastnesses! They must have lain about and grumbled at one another in the dark. What repartees could have passed, when you must have felt about for a smile, and handled a neighbor's cheek to be sure that he understood it? This accounts for the seriousness of the elder poetry. It has a sombre cast (try Hesiod or Ossian[51]), derived from the tradition of those unlantern'd nights. Jokes came in with candles. We wonder how they saw to pick up a pin, if they had any. How did they sup? what a mélange of chance carving they must have made of it!—here one had got a leg of a goat when he wanted a horse's shoulder—there another had dipt his scooped palm in a kid-skin of wild honey, when he meditated right mare's milk. There is neither good

50 Rothschild.
51 Hesiod, Greek poet of 8th Cent. B. C., author of *Works and Days.* Ossian, ancient Gaelic bard, alleged author of the Ossianic poems now attributed to James Macpherson (1736–1796).

eating nor drinking in fresco. Who, even in these civilized
times, has never experienced this, when at some economic table
he has commenced dining after dusk, and waited for the flavor
till the lights came? The senses absolutely give and take re-
ciprocally. Can you tell pork from veal in the dark? or distinguish Sherris from pure Malaga? Take away the candle
from the smoking man; by the glimmering of the left ashes,
he knows that he is still smoking, but he knows it only by an
inference; till the restored light, coming in aid of the olfac-
10 tories, reveals to both senses the full aroma. Then how he
redoubles his puffs! how he burnishes!—There is absolutely
no such thing as reading, but by a candle. We have tried the
affectation of a book at noon-day in gardens, and in sultry
arbors; but it was labor thrown away. Those gay motes in
the beam come about you, hovering and teasing, like so many
coquettes, that will have you all to their self, and are jealous of
your abstractions. By the midnight taper, the writer digests
his meditations. By the same light we must approach to their
perusal, if we would catch the flame, the odor. It is a mock-
20 ery, all that is reported of the influential Phœbus. No true
poem ever owed its birth to the sun's light. They are abstracted
works—

> Things that were born, when none but the still night,
> And his dumb candle, saw his pinching throes.

Marry, daylight—daylight might furnish the images, the
crude material; but for the fine shapings, the true turning and
filing (as mine author hath it), they must be content to hold
their inspiration of the candle. The mild internal light, that
reveals them, like fires on the domestic hearth, goes out in the
30 sunshine. Night and silence call out the starry fancies. Milton's Morning Hymn in Paradise, we would hold a good wager,
was penned at midnight; and Taylor's rich description of a
sunrise smells decidedly of the taper. Even ourself, in these
our humbler lucubrations tune our best-measured cadences
(Prose has her cadences) not unfrequently to the charm of the
drowsier watchman, "blessing the doors"; or the wild sweep of
winds at midnight. Even now a loftier speculation than we
have yet attempted, courts our endeavors. We would indite
something about the Solar System.—*Betty, bring the candles.*

WILLIAM HAZLITT (1778–1830)

Hazlitt was born in 1778 at Maidstone, in Kent, where his father, a "dissenting" (Unitarian) minister was at the time preaching. In 1783 the Hazlitts

moved to America, living chiefly in the vicinity of Boston, and some three years later returned to England, after the father had failed to secure a regular charge. Soon Mr. Hazlitt was called to the church at Wem, near Shrewsbury, not far from the Welsh border, where William spent most of his years between the ages of ten and twenty-two. Intended by his father for the Unitarian ministry, William found his studies uncongenial, and turned to general reading in metaphysics and philosophy; decided then to follow in the footsteps of his elder brother, John, a painter; studied art in Paris in 1802–3; and thereafter painted a number of portraits, including one of Charles Lamb "in the costume of a Venetian senator," before he gave up art for literature. His interest in letters had been excited by the meeting with Coleridge which he narrates in "My First Acquaintance with Poets," and quickened by contacts with such men as Wordsworth, Hunt, Godwin, and especially Charles Lamb, who became a lifelong friend.

In 1808 he married Sarah Stoddart, daughter of a retired naval officer, but the marriage was not happy, and after some years the couple separated, and were divorced in Scotland in 1822. Prior to this action, Hazlitt had been taken by a strange infatuation for one Sarah Walker, a tailor's daughter, whose mother kept the lodgings in which he then lived. When he returned with his decree of divorce and the intention of marrying the girl, he was bitterly disillusioned to find that she had bestowed her favors on another lodger. The sordid details are recorded in the *Liber Amoris*. A second marriage was even less successful than the first. Hazlitt must have been a difficult man to live with. His temper was testy; he quarreled with enemies, and often with his friends. Many hated him for his vigorous championing of radical views. For him Waterloo was a tragedy, Napoleon, whose life he wrote, a hero. He has been spoken of as "socially maladjusted."

Hazlitt found himself slowly in literature, and never made more than a precarious living by his pen. Much of his work was written for newspapers and magazines, some of it delivered in series of lectures. His abiding importance today is, first, as a critic, and second, as an informal essayist. His theatrical and art criticism is valuable. His broad reading, sensitive appreciation, and live enthusiasm lend authority and vigor to such series as his lectures on the Elizabethan dramatists, the *English Poets,* and the *English Comic Writers,* to his *Characters of Shakespeare's Plays,* and, less vitally, to his contemporary criticism, *The Spirit of the Age.* Some of the best of his informal writing is to be found in the collection called *Table Talk.*

Hazlitt is a romantic critic. He aimed, not to appraise, but to "reflect the color, the light and shade, the soul and body" of a work. Personal appreciation accordingly takes the place of judicial standards, but his taste is good, and in spite of numerous prejudices, a surprising number of his opinions are today accepted as orthodox. He did much, for instance, to revive an understanding of the Elizabethans, and led the way to an appreciation of the Romantic poets (except where his personal dislikes, as of Shelley, clouded his judgment). He is frank, honest, direct and personal (bookish, too, it must be confessed, according to modern tastes). As an observer of human life, he says many wise and stimulating things in a style of great charm. He has not Lamb's warmth, whimsicality, and humor; but his range is greater, and he has a gift all his own for telling phrase, for rhetorical effectiveness, and for fine cadences. Of his writing, he himself justly said, "As to my style, I thought little about it. I only used the word which seemed to me to signify the idea I wanted to convey, and I did not rest till I had got it. In seeking for truth I sometimes found beauty." His influence on nineteenth century critical thought and prose style has been great.

BIBLIOGRAPHY. Collected *Works*, ed. A. R. Waller and A. Glover, 13 vols. (Dent), and Centenary ed. based on above by P. P. Howe, 21 vols. (Dent). *Life* by P. P. Howe (Doran); short biography by Augustine Birrell in Eng. Men Let. ser.; *Memoirs* and *Lamb and Hazlitt* by W. C. Hazlitt, his grandson. Many excellent volumes of selected essays. *Bibliography* by G. Keynes, 1931 (Random House).

MY FIRST ACQUAINTANCE WITH POETS

My father was a Dissenting Minister at W—m [1] in Shropshire; and in the year 1798 (the figures that compose that date are to me like the "dreaded name of Demogorgon") [2] Mr. Coleridge came to Shrewsbury, to succeed Mr. Rowe in the spiritual charge of a Unitarian congregation there. He did not come till late on the Saturday afternoon before he was to preach; and Mr. Rowe, who himself went down to the coach in a state of anxiety and expectation, to look for the arrival of his successor, could find no one at all answering the description but a round-faced man in a short black coat (like a shooting-jacket) which hardly seemed to have been made for him, but who seemed to be talking at a great rate to his fellow-passengers. Mr. Rowe had scarce returned to give an account of his disappointment, when the round-faced man in black entered, and dissipated all doubts on the subject, by beginning to talk. He did not cease while he stayed; nor has he since, that I know of. He held the good town of Shrewsbury in delightful suspense for three weeks that he remained there, "fluttering the *proud Salopians* [3] like an eagle in a dove-cote"; and the Welsh mountains that skirt the horizon with their tempestuous confusion, agree to have heard no such mystic sounds since the days of

"High-born Hoel's harp or soft Llewellyn's lay!" . . .

It was in January, 1798, that I rose one morning before daylight, to walk ten miles in the mud, and went to hear this celebrated person preach. Never, the longest day I have to live, shall I have such another walk as this cold, raw, comfortless one, in the winter of the year 1798. . . . When I got there, the organ was playing the 100th psalm, and, when it was done, Mr. Coleridge rose and gave out his text, "And he went up into

1 Wem (see introd. sketch)   2 *Paradise Lost*, II. 964–5
3 name for inhabitants of Shropshire. The quotation is modified from Shakespeare's *Coriolanus*, V. vi. 115–6. The one below is from Gray's *Bard*, 1. 28

the mountain to pray, HIMSELF, ALONE." As he gave out this text, his voice "rose like a steam of rich distilled perfumes," and when he came to the two last words, which he pronounced loud, deep, and distinct, it seemed to me, who was then young, as if the sounds had echoed from the bottom of the human heart, and as if that prayer might have floated in solemn silence through the universe. The idea of St. John came into mind, "of one crying in the wilderness, who had his loins girt about, and whose food was locusts and wild honey." The preacher then launched into his subject, like an eagle dallying with the wind. The sermon was upon peace and war; upon church and state—not their alliance, but their separation—on the spirit of the world and the spirit of Christianity, not as the same, but as opposed to one another. He talked of those who had "inscribed the cross of Christ on banners dripping with human gore." He made a poetical and pastoral excursion,— and to show the fatal effects of war, drew a striking contrast between the simple shepherd boy, driving his team afield, or sitting under the hawthorn, piping to his flock, "as though he should never be old," and the same poor country-lad, crimped, kidnaped, brought into town, made drunk at an alehouse, turned into a wretched drummerboy, with his hair sticking on end with powder and pomatum, a long cue at his back, and tricked out in the loathsome finery of the profession of blood.

> "Such were the notes our once-lov'd poet sung." [4]

And for myself, I could not have been more delighted if I had heard the music of the spheres. Poetry and Philosophy had met together, Truth and Genius had embraced, under the eye and with the sanction of Religion. This was even beyond my hopes. I returned home well satisfied. The sun that was still laboring pale and wan through the sky, obscured by thick mists, seemed an emblem of the *good cause;* and the cold dank drops of dew that hung half melted on the beard of the thistle, had something genial and refreshing in them; for there was a spirit of hope and youth in all nature, that turned everything into good. The face of nature had not then the brand of JUS DIVINUM [5] on it:

> "Like to that sanguine flower inscrib'd with woe."

On the Tuesday following, the half-inspired speaker came. I was called down into the room where he was, and went half-hoping, half-afraid. He received me very graciously, and I

---

4 Pope's *Epistle to Earl of Oxford*, 1
5 divine law. The quotation is *Lycidas*, 106.

listened for a long time without uttering a word. I did not
suffer in his opinion by my silence. "For those two hours,"
he afterwards was pleased to say, "he was conversing with
W. H.'s forehead!" His appearance was different from what
I had anticipated from seeing him before. At a distance, and
in the dim light of the chapel, there was to me a strange wild-
ness in his aspect, a dusky obscurity, and I thought him pitted
with the small-pox. His complexion was at that time clear,
and even bright—

10   "As are the children of yon azure sheen." [6]

His forehead was broad and high, light as if built of ivory,
with large projecting eyebrows, and his eyes rolling beneath
them like a sea with darkened luster. "A certain tender bloom
his face o'erspread," a purple tinge as we see it in the pale
thoughtful complexions of the Spanish portrait-painters, Mu-
rillo and Velasquez. His mouth was gross, voluptuous, open,
eloquent; his chin good-humored and round; but his nose,
the rudder of the face, the index of the will, was small, feeble,
nothing—like what he has done. It might seem that the genius
20 of his face as from a height surveyed and projected him (with
sufficient capacity and huge aspiration) into the world unknown of thought and imagination, with nothing to support
or guide his veering purpose, as if Columbus had launched
his adventurous course for the New World in a scallop, without
oars or compass. So at least I comment on it after the event.
Coleridge in his person was rather above the common size,
inclining to the corpulent, or like Lord Hamlet, "somewhat fat
and pursy." His hair (now, alas! gray) was then black and
glossy as the raven's, and fell in smooth masses over his fore-
30 head. This long, pendulous hair is peculiar to enthusiasts, to
those whose minds tend heavenward; and is traditionally inseparable (though of a different color) from the pictures of
Christ. It ought to belong, as a character, to all who preach
Christ crucified, and Coleridge was at that time one of
those! . . .

No two individuals were ever more unlike than were the
host and his guest. A poet was to my father a sort of non-
descript: yet whatever added grace to the Unitarian cause
was to him welcome. He could hardly have been more sur-
40 prised or pleased, if our visitor had worn wings. Indeed, his
thoughts had wings; and as the silken sounds rustled round
our little wainscoted parlor, my father threw back his spectacles over his forehead, his white hairs mixing with its sanguine

6 Thomson, *Castle of Indolence,* II. stanza xxxiii. Next quot., *ibid.,* I. lvii.

hue; and a smile of delight beamed across his rugged cordial
face, to think that Truth had found a new ally in Fancy! Besides, Coleridge seemed to take considerable notice of me, and
that of itself was enough. He talked very familiarly, but agree-
ably, and glanced over a variety of subjects. . . . I forget a great
number of things, many more than I remember; but the day
passed off pleasantly, and the next morning Mr. Coleridge was
to return to Shrewsbury. When I came down to breakfast, I
found that he had just received a letter from his friend, T.
Wedgwood,[7] making him an offer of £150 a-year if he chose to   10
waive his present pursuit, and devote himself entirely to the
study of poetry and philosophy. Coleridge seemed to make up
his mind to close with this proposal in the act of tying on one
of his shoes. It threw an additional damp on his departure.
It took the wayward enthusiast quite from us to cast him into
Deva's [8] winding vales, or by the shores of old romance. Instead of living at ten miles distance, of being the pastor of a
Dissenting congregation at Shrewsbury, he was henceforth to
inhabit the Hill of Parnassus, to be a Shepherd on the Delec-
table Mountains.[9] Alas! I knew not the way thither, and   20
felt very little gratitude for Mr. Wedgwood's bounty. I was
pleasantly relieved from this dilemma; for Mr. Coleridge,
asking for a pen and ink, and going to a table to write something on a bit of card, advanced towards me with undulating
step, and giving me the precious document, said that that
was his address, *Mr. Coleridge, Nether Stowey, Somersetshire;*
and that he should be glad to see me there in a few weeks'
time, and, if I chose, would come half-way to meet me. I
was not less surprised than the shepherd-boy (this simile is
to be found in Cassandra) when he sees a thunder-bolt fall   30
close at his feet. I stammered out my acknowledgments and
acceptance of this offer (I thought Mr. Wedgwood's annuity
a trifle to it) as well as I could; and this mighty business being
settled, the poet-preacher took leave, and I accompanied him
six miles on the road. It was a fine morning in the middle of
winter, and he talked the whole way. The scholar in Chaucer
is described as going

——"sounding on his way." [10]

So Coleridge went on his. In digressing, in dilating, in passing from subject to subject, he appeared to me to float in air,   40

7 son of Josiah Wedgwood, the famous potter
8 Latin name for the river Dee, which flows through northern Wales and Cheshire.
9 in *Pilgrim's Progress.* The hill of *Parnassus* was sacred to the Muses.
10 A mistake. The speech of Chaucer's Clerk is "souning in [inclined toward]
moral virtue" (*Prol.,* 309). Hazlitt was probably thinking of Wordsworth's *Excursion,*
iii. 701: "Went sounding on, a dim and perilous way."

to slide on ice. He told me in confidence (going along) that he should have preached two sermons before he accepted the situation at Shrewsbury, one on Infant Baptism, the other on the Lord's Supper, showing that he could not administer either, which would have effectually disqualified him for the object in view. I observed that he continually crossed me on the way by shifting from one side of the foot-path to the other. This struck me as an odd movement; but I did not at that time connect it with any instability of purpose or involuntary change of principle, as I have done since. He seemed unable to keep on in a straight line. . . . We parted at the six-mile stone; and I returned homeward, pensive but much pleased. I had met with unexpected notice from a person whom I believed to have been prejudiced against me. "Kind and affable to me had been his condescension, and should be honored ever with suitable regard." [11] He was the first poet I had known, and he certainly answered to that inspired name. I had heard a great deal of his powers of conversation, and was not disappointed. In fact, I never met with anything at all like them, either before or since. I could easily credit the accounts which were circulated of his holding forth to a large party of ladies and gentlemen, an evening or two before, on the Berkeleian Theory, when he made the whole material universe look like a transparency of fine words; and another story (which I believe he has somewhere told himself) of his being asked to a party at Birmingham, of his smoking tobacco and going to sleep after dinner on a sofa, where the company found him to their no small surprise, which was increased to wonder when he started up of a sudden, and rubbing his eyes, looked about him, and launched into a three-hours' description of the third heaven, of which he had had a dream, very different from Mr. Southey's *Vision of Judgment*, and also from that other Vision of Judgment, which Mr. Murray, the Secretary of the Bridge-street Junto, has taken into his especial keeping! [12]

On my way back, I had a sound in my ears, it was the voice of Fancy: I had a light before me, it was the face of Poetry. The one still lingers there, the other has not quitted my side! Coleridge in truth met me half-way on the ground of philosophy, or I should not have been won over to his imaginative creed. I had an uneasy, pleasurable sensation all the time, till I was to visit him. During those months the chill breath of winter gave me a welcoming; the vernal air was balm and inspiration to me. The golden sunsets, the silver star of evening, lighted me on my way to new hopes and prospects. *I was*

11 See *Paradise Lost*, VIII. 648-50.
12 See introd. sketch to Byron's *Vision of Judgment*, below.

to visit Coleridge in the Spring. This circumstance was never
absent from my thoughts, and mingled with all my feelings.
I wrote to him at the time proposed, and received an answer
postponing my intended visit for a week or two, but very cordi-
ally urging me to complete my promise then. This delay did
not damp, but rather increased my ardor. In the meantime
I went to Llangollen Vale, by way of initiating myself in the
mysteries of natural scenery; and I must say I was enchanted
with it. I had been reading Coleridge's description of England,
in his fine *Ode on the Departing Year,* and I applied it, *con*   10
amore, to the objects before me. That valley was to me (in a
manner) the cradle of a new existence: in the river that winds
through it, my spirit was baptized in the waters of Helicon! [13]

I returned home, and soon after set out on my journey with
unworn heart and untired feet. . . . It was still two days before the time fixed for my arrival, for I had taken care to set
out early enough. I stopped these two days at Bridgewater,
and when I was tired of sauntering on the banks of its muddy
river, returned to the inn, and read *Camilla.*[14] So have I loitered my life away, reading books, looking at pictures, going   20
to plays, hearing, thinking, writing on what pleased me best.
I have wanted only one thing to make me happy; but wanting that, have wanted everything!

I arrived, and was well received. The country about Nether
Stowey is beautiful, green and hilly, and near the seashore.
I saw it but the other day, after an interval of twenty years,
from a hill near Taunton. How was the map of my life spread
out before me, as the map of the country lay at my feet! In
the afternoon Coleridge took me over to All-Foxden, a romantic old family mansion of the St. Aubins, where Wordsworth   30
lived. It was then in the possession of a friend of the poet's,
who gave him the free use of it.[15] Somehow that period (the
time just after the French Revolution) was not a time when
nothing was given for nothing. The mind opened, and a softness might be perceived coming over the heart of individuals,
beneath "the scales that fence" our self-interest. Wordsworth
himself was from home, but his sister kept house, and set
before us a frugal repast; and we had free access to her
brother's poems, the *Lyrical Ballads,* which were still in manuscript, or in the form of *Sybilline Leaves.*[16] I dipped into a few   40
of these with great satisfaction, and with the faith of a novice.

13 Greek mountain, reputed home of Apollo and the Muses, from which gushed
the fountains Aganippe and Hippocrene. Llangolen is in Wales.
14 by Fanny Burney, 1796
15 Hazlitt was mistaken. Wordsworth paid £23 a year rent.
16 The term was doubtless used by Coleridge to indicate the scattered nature of the
material. He himself (not Wordsworth) used the phrase as title for a volume of poems
(pub. 1817).

I slept that night in an old room with blue hangings, and covered with the round-faced family portraits of the age of George I and II and from the wooded declivity of the adjoining park that overlooked my window, at the dawn of day, could

——"hear the loud stag speak." . . .

That morning, as soon as breakfast was over, we strolled out into the park, and seating ourselves on the trunk of an old ash-tree that stretched along the ground, Coleridge read aloud with a sonorous and musical voice the ballad of *Betty*
10 *Foy*. I was not critically or sceptically inclined. I saw touches of truth and nature, and took the rest for granted. But in the *Thorn,* the *Mad Mother,* and the *Complaint of the Poor Indian Woman,* I felt that deeper power and pathos which have been since acknowledged,

"In spite of pride, in erring reason's spite,"

as the characteristics of this author; and the sense of a new style and a new spirit in poetry came over me. It had to me something of the effect that arises from the turning up of the fresh soil, or of the first welcome breath of Spring:

20 "While yet the trembling year is unconfirmed."

Coleridge and myself walked back to Stowey that evening, and his voice sounded high

"Of Providence, foreknowledge, will, and fate,
Fix'd fate, free-will, foreknowledge absolute,"

as we passed through echoing grove, by fairy stream or waterfall, gleaming in the summer moonlight! He lamented that Wordsworth was not prone enough to believe in the traditional superstitions of the place, and that there was a something corporeal, a *matter-of-fact-ness,* a clinging to the palpable, or
30 often to the petty, in his poetry, in consequence. His genius was not a spirit that descended to him through the air; it sprung out of the ground like a flower, or unfolded itself from a green spray, on which the gold-finch sang. He said, however (if I remember right) that this objection must be confined to his descriptive pieces, that his philosophic poetry had a grand and comprehensive spirit in it, so that his soul seemed to inhabit the universe like a palace, and to discover truth by intuition, rather than by deduction. The next day Wordsworth arrived from Bristol at Coleridge's cottage. I think I
40 see him now. He answered in some degree to his friend's description of him, but was more gaunt and Don Quixote-like.

He was quaintly dressed (according to the costume of that unconstrained period) in a brown fustian jacket and striped pantaloons. There was something of a roll, a lounge, in his gait, not unlike his own Peter Bell. There was a severe, worn pressure of thought about his temples, a fire in his eye (as if he saw something in objects more than the outward appearance), an intense, high, narrow forehead, a Roman nose, cheeks furrowed by strong purpose and feeling, and a convulsive inclination to laughter about the mouth, a good deal at variance with the solemn, stately expression of the rest of his face. Chantry's bust wants the marking traits; but he was teased into making it regular and heavy; Haydon's head of him, introduced into the *Entrance of Christ into Jerusalem*,[17] is the most like his drooping weight of thought and expression. He sat down and talked very naturally and freely, with a mixture of clear, gushing accents in his voice, a deep guttural intonation, and a strong tincture of the northern *burr,* like the crust on wine. He instantly began to make havoc of the half of a Cheshire cheese on the table, and said triumphantly that "his marriage with experience had not been so productive as Mr. Southey's in teaching him a knowledge of the good things of this life." . . . We went over to All-Foxden again the day following, and Wordsworth read us the story of Peter Bell in the open air; and the comment made upon it by his face and voice was very different from that of some later critics! Whatever might be thought of the poem, "his face was as a book where men might read strange matters,"[18] and he announced the fate of his hero in prophetic tones. There is a *chaunt* in the recitation both of Coleridge and Wordsworth, which acts as a spell upon the hearer, and disarms the judgment. Perhaps they have deceived themselves by making habitual use of this ambiguous accompaniment. Coleridge's manner is more full, animated, and varied; Wordsworth's more equable, sustained, and internal. The one might be termed more *dramatic,* the other more *lyrical.* Coleridge has told me that he himself liked to compose in walking over uneven ground, or breaking through the straggling branches of a copsewood; whereas Wordsworth always wrote (if he could) walking up and down a straight gravel-walk, or in some spot where the continuity of his verse met with no collateral interruption. Returning that same evening, I got into a metaphysical argument with Wordsworth, while Coleridge was explaining the different notes of the nightingale to his sister, in which we neither of us succeeded in making ourselves perfectly clear and intelligible. Thus I passed

[17] historical painting by Benjamin Robert Haydon (1786–1846)
[18] *Macbeth,* I. v. 63

three weeks at Nether Stowey and in the neighborhood, generally devoting the afternoons to a delightful chat in an arbor made of bark by the poet's friend Tom Poole, sitting under two fine elm trees, and listening to the bees humming round us, while we quaffed our *flip*. It was agreed, among other things, that we should make a jaunt down the Bristol Channel, as far as Linton. We set off together on foot, Coleridge, John Chester, and I. . . . The view in coming along had been splendid. We walked for miles and miles on dark brown heaths overlooking the channel, with the Welsh hills beyond, and at times descended into little sheltered valleys close by the seaside, with a smuggler's face scowling by us, and then had to ascend conical hills with a path winding up through a coppice to a barren top, like a monk's shaven crown, from one of which I pointed out to Coleridge's notice the bare masts of a vessel on the very edge of the horizon and within the redorbed disk of the setting sun, like his own specter-ship in the *Ancient Mariner*. At Linton the character of the sea-coast becomes more marked and rugged. There is a place called the *Valley of Rocks* (I suspect this was only the poetical name for it) bedded among precipices overhanging the sea, with rocky caverns beneath, into which the waves dash, and where the sea-gull forever wheels its screaming flight. On the tops of these are huge stones thrown transverse, as if an earthquake had tossed them there, and behind these is a fretwork of perpendicular rocks, something like the *Giant's Causeway*. A thunderstorm came on while we were at the inn, and Coleridge was running out bareheaded to enjoy the commotion of the elements in the *Valley of Rocks,* but as if in spite, the clouds only muttered a few angry sounds, and let fall a few refreshing drops. Coleridge told me that he and Wordsworth were to have made this place the scene of a prose tale, which was to have been in the manner of, but far superior to, the *Death of Abel,*[19] but they had relinquished the design. In the morning of the second day, we breakfasted luxuriously in an old-fashioned parlor, on tea, toast, eggs, and honey, in the very sight of the bee-hives from which it had been taken, and a garden full of thyme and wild flowers that had produced it. On this occasion Coleridge spoke of Virgil's *Georgics,* but not well. I do not think he had much feeling for the classical or elegant. It was in this room that we found a little worn-out copy of the *Seasons,* lying in a window-seat, on which Coleridge exclaimed, *"That* is true fame!" He said Thomson was a great poet, rather than a good one; his style was as meretri-

19 by the Swiss poet, Solomon Gessner (pub. 1758)

cious as his thoughts were natural. He spoke of Cowper as
the best modern poet. He said the *Lyrical Ballads* were an experiment about to be tried by him and Wordsworth, to see
how far the public taste would endure poetry written in a
more natural and simple style than had hitherto been attempted; totally discarding the artifices of poetical diction, and
making use only of such words as had probably been common
in the most ordinary language since the days of Henry II.
Some comparison was introduced between Shakespeare and
Milton. He said "he hardly knew which to prefer. Shakespeare
appeared to him a mere stripling in the art; he was as tall and
as strong, with infinitely more activity than Milton, but he
never appeared to have come to man's estate; or if he had, he
would not have been a man, but a monster." He spoke with
contempt of Gray, and with intolerance of Pope. He did not
like the versification of the latter. He observed that "the ears
of these couplet-writers might be charged with having short
memories that could not retain the harmony of whole passages." He thought little of Junius as a writer; he had a dislike of Dr. Johnson; and a much higher opinion of Burke as an
orator and politician, than of Fox or Pitt. He however thought
him very inferior in richness of style and imagery to some of
our elder prose writers, particularly Jeremy Taylor. He liked
Richardson, but not Fielding; nor could I get him to enter into
the merits of *Caleb Williams*.[20] In short, he was profound and
discriminating with respect to those authors whom he liked,
and where he gave his judgment fair play; capricious, perverse, and prejudiced in his antipathies and distastes. We
loitered on the "ribbed sea-sands," in such talk as this, a whole
morning. . . . We returned on the third morning, and Coleridge remarked the silent cottage-smoke curling up the valleys
where, a few evenings before, we had seen the lights gleaming
through the dark.

In a day or two after we arrived at Stowey, we set out, I on
my return home, and he for Germany. It was a Sunday
morning, and he was to preach that day for Dr. Toulmin of
Taunton. I asked him if he had prepared anything for the
occasion? He said he had not even thought of the text, but
should as soon as we parted. I did not go to hear him,—this
was a fault,—but we met in the evening at Bridgewater. The
next day we had a long day's walk to Bristol, and sat down,
I recollect, by a well-side on the road, to cool ourselves and
satisfy our thirst, when Coleridge repeated to me some descriptive lines of his tragedy of *Remorse,* which I must say became

20 novel by Wm. Godwin (pub. 1794)

his mouth and that occasion better than they, some years after, did Mr. Elliston's [21] and the Drury-lane boards,—

> "Oh! memory! shield me from the world's poor strife,
> And give those scenes thine everlasting life!"

I saw no more of him for a year or two, during which period he had been wandering in the Hartz Forest in Germany; and his return was cometary, meteorous, unlike his setting out. It was not till some time after that I knew his friends Lamb and Southey. The last always appears to me (as I first saw him) with a commonplace-book under his arm, and the first with a *bon-mot* in his mouth. It was at Godwin's that I met with Holcroft and Coleridge, where they were disputing fiercely which was the best—*Man as he was, or man as he is to be.* "Give me," says Lamb, "man as he is *not* to be." This saying was the beginning of a friendship between us, which I believe still continues.—Enough of this for the present.

> "But there is matter for another rhyme,
> And I to this may add a second tale."

ON GOING A JOURNEY

ONE of the pleasantest things in the world is going a journey; but I like to go by myself. I can enjoy society in a room; but out of doors, nature is company enough for me. I am then never less alone than when alone.

> "The fields his study, nature was his book."

I cannot see the wit of walking and talking at the same time. When I am in the country, I wish to vegetate like the country. I am not for criticizing hedge-rows and black cattle. I go out of town in order to forget the town and all that is in it. There are those who for this purpose go to watering-places and carry the metropolis with them. I like more elbow-room and fewer incumbrances. I like solitude, when I give myself up to it, for the sake of solitude; nor do I ask for

> "——a friend of my retreat,
> Whom I may whisper, solitude is sweet."

The soul of a journey is liberty, perfect liberty, to think, feel, do, just as one pleases. We go a journey chiefly to be free of all impediments and of all inconveniences; to leave ourselves behind, much more to get rid of others. It is because

21 Robert Wm. Elliston (1774-1831), who acted in Coleridge's *Remorse*

I want a little breathing-space to muse on indifferent matters,
where Contemplation

> "May plume her feathers and let grow her wings,
> That in the various bustle of resort
> Were all too ruffled, and sometimes impair'd," [22]

that I absent myself from the town for a while, without feeling
at a loss the moment I am left by myself. Instead of a friend
in a post-chaise or in a Tilbury, to exchange good things with
and vary the same stale topics over again, for once let me have
a truce with impertinence. Give me the clear blue sky over   10
my head, and the green turf beneath my feet, a winding road
before me, and a three hours' march to dinner—and then to
thinking! It is hard if I cannot start some game on these
lone heaths. I laugh, I run, I leap, I sing for joy. From the
point of yonder rolling cloud, I plunge into my past being
and revel there, as the sun-burnt Indian plunges headlong
into the wave that wafts him to his native shore. Then long-
forgotten things, like "sunken wrack and sumless treasuries,"
burst upon my eager sight, and I begin to feel, think, and be
myself again. Instead of an awkward silence, broken by at-   20
tempts at wit or dull common-places, mine is that undisturbed
silence of the heart which alone is perfect eloquence. No one
likes puns, alliterations, antitheses, argument, and analysis
better than I do; but I sometimes had rather be without them.
"Leave, oh, leave me to my repose!" I have just now other
business in hand, which would seem idle to you, but is with
me "very stuff of the conscience." Is not this wild rose sweet
without a comment? Does not this daisy leap to my heart set
in its coat of emerald? Yet if I were to explain to you the circumstance that has so endeared it to me, you would only smile.   30
Had I not better then keep it to myself, and let it serve me to
brood over, from here to yonder craggy point, and from thence
onward to the far-distant horizon? I should be but bad company all that way, and therefore prefer being alone. I have
heard it said that you may, when the moody fit comes on, walk
or ride on by yourself and indulge your reveries. But this looks
like a breach of manners, a neglect of others, and you are
thinking all the time that you ought to rejoin your party. "Out
upon such half-faced fellowship," say I. I like to be either
entirely to myself, or entirely at the disposal of others; to   40
talk or be silent, to walk or sit still, to be sociable or solitary. I was pleased with an observation of Mr. Cobbett's, that
"he thought it a bad French custom to drink our wine with

22 Milton's *Comus*, 378-81. The previous quot. is from Cowper's *Retirement*, 741-2,
and the one before from *The Farmer's Boy* by Robert Bloomfield.

our meals, and that an Englishman ought to do only one thing at a time." So I cannot talk and think, or indulge in melancholy musing and lively conversation by fits and starts. "Let me have a companion of my way," says Sterne, "were it but to remark how the shadows lengthen as the sun declines." It is beautifully said; but in my opinion, this continual comparing of notes interferes with the involuntary impression of things upon the mind and hurts the sentiment. If you only hint what you feel in a kind of dumb show, it is insipid; if you have to explain it, it is making a toil of a pleasure. You cannot read the book of nature without being perpetually put to the trouble of translating it for the benefit of others. I am for the synthetical method on a journey, in preference to the analytical. I am content to lay in a stock of ideas then, and to examine and anatomize them afterwards. I want to see my vague notions float like the down of the thistle before the breeze, and not to have them entangled in the briars and thorns of controversy. For once, I like to have it all my own way; and this is impossible unless you are alone, or in such company as I do not covet. I have no objection to argue a point with any one for twenty miles of measured road, but not for pleasure. If you remark the scent of a bean-field crossing the road, perhaps your fellow-traveler has no smell. If you point to a distant object, perhaps he is short-sighted, and has to take out his glass to look at it. There is a feeling in the air, a tone in the color of a cloud which hits your fancy, but the effect of which you are unable to account for. There is then no sympathy, but an uneasy craving after it, and a dissatisfaction which pursues you on the way, and in the end probably produces ill humor. Now I never quarrel with myself, and take all my own conclusions for granted till I find it necessary to defend them against objections. It is not merely that you may not be of accord on the objects and circumstances that present themselves before you—these may recall a number of objects and lead to associations too delicate and refined to be possibly communicated to others. Yet these I love to cherish, and sometimes still fondly clutch them, when I can escape from the throng to do so. To give way to our feelings before company, seems extravagance or affectation; and, on the other hand, to have to unravel this mystery of our being at every turn, and to make others take an equal interest in it (otherwise the end is not answered) is a task to which few are competent. We must "give it an understanding, but no tongue." My old friend C——,[23] however, could do both. He could go on in the most delightful explanatory way over hill and dale,

23 Coleridge

a summer's day, and convert a landscape into a didactic poem
or a Pindaric ode. "He talked far above singing." If I could so
clothe my ideas in sounding and flowing words, I might perhaps wish to have some one with me to admire the swelling
theme; or I could be more content, were it possible for me still
to hear his echoing voice in the woods of All-Foxden. They had
"that fine madness in them which our first poets had." [24] . . .

In general, a good thing spoils out-of-door prospects; it
should be reserved for table-talk. L—— [25] is for this reason,
I take it, the worst company in the world out of doors; because he is the best within. I grant, there is one subject on
which it is pleasant to talk on a journey; and that is, what
one shall have for supper when we get to our inn at night.
The open air improves this sort of conversation or friendly
altercation by setting a keener edge on appetite. Every mile
of the road heightens the flavor of the viands we expect at
the end of it. How fine is it to enter some old town, walled
and turreted, just at approach of night-fall, or to come to
some straggling village, with the lights streaming through the
surrounding gloom; and then after inquiring for the best entertainment that the place affords, to "take one's ease at
one's inn!" These eventful moments in our lives' history
are too precious, too full of solid, heart-felt happiness to be
frittered and dribbled away in imperfect sympathy. I would
have them all to myself, and drain them to the last drop;
they will do to talk of or to write about afterwards. What
a delicate speculation it is, after drinking whole goblets of tea,

"The cups that cheer, but not inebriate," [26]

and letting the fumes ascend into the brain, to sit considering
what we shall have for supper—eggs and a rasher, a rabbit
smothered in onions, or an excellent veal-cutlet! Sancho [27] in
such a situation once fixed on cow-heel; and his choice,
though he could not help it, is not to be disparaged. Then,
in the intervals of pictured scenery and Shandean contemplation, to catch the preparation and the stir in the kitchen—
Procul, O procul este profani! [28] These hours are sacred to
silence and to musing, to be treasured up in the memory, and
to feed the source of smiling thoughts hereafter. I would not
waste them in idle talk; or if I must have the integrity of
fancy broken in upon, I would rather it were by a stranger
than a friend. A stranger takes his hue and character from

24 In the rich tissue of Hazlitt's prose there are allusions above, in the space of
half a dozen lines, to Beaumont and Fletcher's *Philaster*, V. 5, Matt. vi. 30, *Henry V.*,
Prol. to Act I., Drayton's *Censure of Poets.*
25 Lamb   26 Cowper, *The Task*, IV. 39–40   27 Sancho Panza, in *Don Quixote*
28 "Hence, O hence, ye unhallowed" (*Æneid*, VI. 258)

the time and place; he is a part of the furniture and costume
of an inn. If he is a Quaker, or from the West Riding of
Yorkshire, so much the better. I do not even try to sympathize with him, and he breaks no squares. I associate nothing
with my traveling companion but present objects and passing
events. In his ignorance of me and my affairs, I in a manner
forget myself. But a friend reminds one of other things, rips
up old grievances, and destroys the abstraction of the scene.
He comes in ungraciously between us and our imaginary
character. Something is dropped in the course of conversation
that gives a hint of your profession and pursuits; or from having some one with you that knows the less sublime portions of
your history, it seems that other people do. You are no longer
a citizen of the world: but your "unhoused free condition is
put into circumspection and confine." The *incognito* of an inn
is one of its striking privileges—"Lord of one's self, uncum-
ber'd with a name." Oh! it is great to shake off the trammels
of the world and of public opinion—to lose our importunate,
tormenting, everlasting personal identity in the elements of
nature, and become the creature of the moment, clear of all ties
—to hold to the universe only by a dish of sweet-breads, and
to owe nothing but the score of the evening—and no longer
seeking for applause and meeting with contempt, to be known
by no other title than *the Gentleman in the parlor!* One may
take one's choice of all characters in this romantic state of uncertainty as to one's real pretensions, and become indefinitely
respectable and negatively right-worshipful. We baffle prejudice and disappoint conjecture; and from being so to others,
begin to be objects of curiosity and wonder even to ourselves.
We are no more those hackneyed commonplaces that we appear in the world; an inn restores us to the level of nature and
quits scores with society! I have certainly spent some enviable
hours at inns—sometimes when I have been left entirely to
myself and have tried to solve some metaphysical problem, as
once at Witham-common, where I found out the proof that
likeness is not a case of the association of ideas—at other
times, when there have been pictures in the room, as at St.
Neot's [29] (I think it was), where I first met with Gribelin's
engravings of the Cartoons, [30] into which I entered at once,
and at a little inn on the borders of Wales, where there happened to be hanging some of Westall's [31] drawings, which I
compared triumphantly (for a theory that I had, not for the
admired artist) with the figure of a girl who had ferried me
over the Severn, standing up in a boat between me and the

---

29 town near Peterborough   30 by Raphael
31 Richard Westall (1765–1836), English painter

twilight—at other times I might mention luxuriating in
books, with a peculiar interest in this way, as I remember
sitting up half the night to read *Paul and Virginia*, which I
picked up at an inn at Bridgewater, after being drenched in
the rain all day; and at the same place I got through two
volumes of Madame D'Arblay's *Camilla*. It was on the 10th
of April, 1798, that I sat down to a volume of the *New
Eloise*,[32] at the inn at Llangollen, over a bottle of sherry and
a cold chicken. The letter I chose was that in which St. Preux
describes his feelings as he first caught a glimpse from
the heights of the Jura of the Pays de Vaud, which I had
brought with me as a *bon bouche* [33] to crown the evening with.
It was my birthday, and I had for the first time come from a
place in the neighborhood to visit this delightful spot. The
road to Llangollen turns off between Chirk and Wrexham;
and on passing a certain point, you come all at once upon the
valley, which opens like an amphitheater, broad, barren hills
rising in majestic state on either side, with "green upland
swells that echo to the bleat of flocks" below, and the river
Dee babbling over its stony bed in the midst of them. The
valley at this time "glittered green with sunny showers,"
and a budding ash-tree dipped its tender branches in the
chiding stream. How proud, how glad I was to walk along
the high road that overlooks the delicious prospect, repeating
the lines which I have just quoted from Mr. Coleridge's
poems! But besides the prospect which opened beneath my
feet, another also opened to my inward sight, a heavenly
vision, on which were written, in letters large as Hope could
make them, these four words, LIBERTY, GENIUS, LOVE,
VIRTUE; which have since faded into the light of common day,
or mock my idle gaze.

"The beautiful is vanished, and returns not."

Still I would return some time or other to this enchanted spot;
but I would return to it alone. What other self could I find to
share that influx of thoughts, of regret and delight, the fragments of which I could hardly conjure up to myself, so much
have they been broken and defaced! I could stand on some
tall rock and overlook the precipice of years that separates
me from what I then was. I was at that time going shortly
to visit the poet whom I have above named. Where is he
now? Not only I myself have changed; the world, which
was then new to me, has become old and incorrigible. Yet
will I turn to thee in thought, O sylvan Dee, in joy, in youth

---

32 *La Nouvelle Héloïse*, by Rousseau   33 choice morsel

and gladness as thou then wert; and thou shalt always be to
me the river of Paradise, where I will drink of the waters of
life freely!

There is hardly anything that shows the short-sightedness
or capriciousness of the imagination more than traveling does.
With change of place we change our ideas; nay, our opinions
and feelings. We can by an effort indeed transport ourselves
to old and long-forgotten scenes, and then the picture of the
mind revives again; but we forget those that we have just
10 left. It seems that we can think but of one place at a time.
The canvas of the fancy is but of a certain extent, and if we
paint one set of objects upon it, they immediately efface every
other. We cannot enlarge our conceptions, we only shift our
point of view. The landscape bares its bosom to the enraptured eye, we take our fill of it and seem as if we could form
no other image of beauty or grandeur. We pass on and
think no more of it; the horizon that shuts it from our sight,
also blots it from our memory like a dream. In traveling
through a wild, barren country, I can form no idea of a woody
20 and cultivated one. It appears to me that all the world must
be barren, like what I see of it. In the country we forget the
town, and in town we despise the country. "Beyond Hyde
Park," says Sir Fopling Flutter, "all is a desert." [34] All that
part of the map that we do not see before us is a blank. The
world in our conceit of it is not much bigger than a nutshell.
It is not one prospect expanded into another, county joined
to county, kingdom to kingdom, land to seas, making an
image voluminous and vast;—the mind can form no larger
idea of space than the eye can take in at a single glance. The
30 rest is a name written in a map, a calculation of arithmetic.
For instance, what is the true signification of that immense
mass of territory and population, known by the name of
China to us? An inch of pasteboard on a wooden globe, of
no more account than a China orange! Things near us are
seen of the size of life: things at a distance are diminished to
the size of the understanding. We measure the universe by
ourselves, and even comprehend the texture of our own being only piece-meal. In this way, however, we remember an
infinity of things and places. The mind is like a mechanical
40 instrument that plays a great variety of tunes, but it must
play them in succession. One idea recalls another, but it at
the same time excludes all others. In trying to renew old
recollections, we cannot as it were unfold the whole web of
our existence; we must pick out the single threads. So in
coming to a place where we have formerly lived and with

34 from *Sir Fopling Flutter*, or *The Man of Mode*, by Sir Geo. Etherege (1676)

which we have intimate associations, every one must have
found that the feeling grows more vivid the nearer we approach the spot, from the mere anticipation of the actual impression: we remember circumstances, feelings, persons, faces,
names that we had not thought of for years; but for the time
all the rest of the world is forgotten!—To return to the question I have quitted above.

I have no objection to go to see ruins, aqueducts, pictures,
in company with a friend or a party, but rather the contrary,
for the former reason reversed. They are intelligible matters
and will bear talking about. The sentiment here is not tacit,
but communicable and overt. Salisbury Plain is barren of criticism, but Stonehenge will bear a discussion antiquarian, picturesque, and philosophical. In setting out on a party of
pleasure, the first consideration always is where we shall go
to; in taking a solitary ramble, the question is what we shall
meet with by the way. "The mind is its own place"; nor are
we anxious to arrive at the end of our journey. I can myself
do the honors indifferently well to works of art and curiosity.
I once took a party to Oxford with no mean *éclat*—showed
them that seat of the Muses at a distance,

"The glistering spires and pinnacles adorn'd"—[35]

descanted on the learned air that breathes from the grassy
quadrangles and stone walls of halls and colleges—was at
home in the Bodleian; [36] and at Blenheim quite superseded
the powdered ciceroni [37] that attended us, and that pointed in
vain with his wand to commonplace beauties in matchless pictures.—As another exception to the above reasoning, I should
not feel confident in venturing on a journey in a foreign country without a companion. I should want at intervals to hear
the sound of my own language. There is an involuntary
antipathy in the mind of an Englishman to foreign manners
and notions that requires the assistance of social sympathy
to carry it off. As the distance from home increases, this
relief, which was at first a luxury, becomes a passion and an
appetite. A person would almost feel stifled to find himself
in the deserts of Arabia without friends and countrymen;
there must be allowed to be something in the view of Athens
or old Rome that claims the utterance of speech; and I own
that the Pyramids are too mighty for any single contemplation. In such situations, so opposite to all one's ordinary
train of ideas, one seems a species by one's-self, a limb torn

35 *Paradise Lost*, III. 550, and four lines above, *ibid.*, I. 254
36 The great library at Oxford; Blenheim, at Woodstock, not far from Oxford, is
the imposing seat of the Duke of Marlborough.
37 guides

off from society, unless one can meet with instant fellowship
and support.—Yet I did not feel this want or craving very
pressing once, when I first set my foot on the laughing shores
of France. Calais was peopled with novelty and delight.
The confused, busy murmur of the place was like oil and wine
poured into my ears; nor did the mariners' hymn, which was
sung from the top of an old crazy vessel in the harbor, as the
sun went down, send an alien sound into my soul. I only
breathed the air of general humanity. I walked over "the
10 vine-covered hills and gay regions of France," erect and satisfied; for the image of man was not cast down and chained
to the foot of arbitrary thrones; I was at no loss for language,
for that of all the great schools of painting was open to me.
The whole is vanished like a shade. Pictures, heroes, glory,
freedom, all are fled: nothing remains but the Bourbons and
the French people!—There is undoubtedly a sensation in
traveling into foreign parts that is to be had nowhere else;
but it is more pleasing at the time than lasting. It is too
remote from our habitual associations to be a common topic
20 of discourse or reference, and, like a dream or another state of
existence, does not piece into our daily modes of life. It is an
animated but a momentary hallucination. It demands an
effort to exchange our actual for our ideal identity; and to
feel the pulse of our old transports revive very keenly, we
must "jump" all our present comforts and connections. Our
romantic and itinerant character is not to be domesticated.
Dr. Johnson remarked how little foreign travel added to the
facilities of conversation in those who had been abroad. In
fact, the time we have spent there is both delightful and in
30 one sense instructive; but it appears to be cut out of our
substantial, downright existence, and never to join kindly on
to it. We are not the same, but another, and perhaps more
enviable individual, all the time we are out of our own country.
We are lost to ourselves, as well as our friends. So the poet
somewhat quaintly sings,

"Out of my country and myself I go."

Those who wish to forget painful thoughts, do well to absent
themselves for a while from the ties and objects that recall
them; but we can be said only to fulfill our destiny in the
40 place that gave us birth. I should on this account like well
enough to spend the whole of my life in traveling abroad, if
I could anywhere borrow another life to spend afterwards at
home!

ON FAMILIAR STYLE

It is not easy to write a familiar style. Many people mistake a familiar for a vulgar style, and suppose that to write without affectation is to write at random. On the contrary, there is nothing that requires more precision, and, if I may so say, purity of expression, than the style I am speaking of. It utterly rejects not only all unmeaning pomp, but all low, cant phrases, and loose, unconnected, *slipshod* allusions. It is not to take the first word that offers, but the best word in common use; it is not to throw words together in any combinations we please, but to follow and avail ourselves of the true idiom of the language. To write a genuine familiar or truly English style, is to write as any one would speak in common conversation, who had a thorough command and choice of words, or who could discourse with ease, force, and perspicuity, setting aside all pedantic and oratorical flourishes. Or to give another illustration, to write naturally is the same thing in regard to common conversation, as to read naturally is in regard to common speech. It does not follow that it is an easy thing to give the true accent and inflection to the words you utter, because you do not attempt to rise above the level of ordinary life and colloquial speaking. You do not assume indeed the solemnity of the pulpit, or the tone of stage-declamation: neither are you at liberty to gabble on at a venture, without emphasis or discretion, or to resort to vulgar dialect or clownish pronunciation. You must steer a middle course. You are tied down to a given and appropriate articulation, which is determined by the habitual associations between sense and sound, and which you can only hit by entering into the author's meaning, as you must find the proper words and style to express yourself by fixing your thoughts on the subject you have to write about. Any one may mouth out a passage with a theatrical cadence, or get upon stilts to tell his thoughts: but to write or speak with propriety and simplicity is a more difficult task. Thus it is easy to affect a pompous style, to use a word twice as big as the thing you want to express: it is not so easy to pitch upon the very word that exactly fits it. Out of eight or ten words equally common, equally intelligible, with nearly equal pretensions, it is a matter of some nicety and discrimination to pick out the very one, the preferableness of which is scarcely perceptible, but decisive. The reason why I object to Dr. Johnson's style is, that there is no discrimination, no selection, no variety in it. He uses none but "tall, opaque words," taken from the "first row of the rubric": [38]—words with the greatest number of syllables, or Latin phrases with merely English terminations. If a fine style depended on this sort of arbitrary pretension, it would be fair to judge of an author's elegance by the measurement of his words, and the substitution of foreign circumlocutions (with no precise associations) for the mother-tongue. How simple is it to be dignified without ease, to be pompous without meaning! Surely, it is but a mechanical rule for avoiding what is low to be always pedantic and affected. It is clear you cannot use a vulgar English word, if you never use a common English word at all. A fine tact is shown in adhering to those which are perfectly common, and yet never falling into any expressions which are debased by disgusting circumstances, or which owe their signification and point to technical or professional allusions. A truly natural or familiar style can never be quaint or vulgar, for this reason, that it is of universal force and applicability, and that quaintness and vulgarity arise out of the immediate connection of certain words with coarse and disagreeable, or with confined ideas. The last form what we understand by *cant* or *slang* phrases. To give an example of what is not very clear in the general statement. I should say that the phrase *To cut with a knife,* or *To cut a piece of wood,* is perfectly free from vulgarity, because it is perfectly common; but to *cut an acquaintance* is not quite unexceptionable, because it is not perfectly common or intelligible, and has hardly yet escaped out of the limits of slang phraseology. I should hardly therefore use the word in this sense without putting it in italics as a license of expression, to be received *cum grano salis.*[39] All provincial or bye-phrases come under the same mark of reprobation—all such as the writer transfers to the page from his fireside or a particular *coterie,* or that he invents for his own sole use and convenience. I conceive that words are like money, not the worse for being common, but that it is the stamp of custom alone that gives them circulation or value. . . .

The proper force of words lies not in the words themselves, but in their application. A word may be a fine-sounding word, of an unusual length, and very imposing from its learning and novelty, and yet in the connection in which it is introduced, may be quite pointless and irrelevant. It is not pomp or pretension, but the adaptation of the expression to the idea that clenches a writer's meaning:—as it is not the size or glossiness of the materials, but their being fitted each to its place, that gives strength to the arch; or as the pegs and nails are as necessary to the support of the building as the larger timbers, and

---

38 headings or directions (formerly printed in red), likely to be formal in phrasing
39 with a grain of salt

more so than the mere showy, unsubstantial ornaments. I hate
anything that occupies more space than it is worth. I hate to
see a load of band-boxes go along the street, and I hate to see
a parcel of big words without anything in them. A person who
does not deliberately dispose of all his thoughts alike in cum-
brous draperies and flimsy disguises, may strike out twenty
varieties of familiar everyday language, each coming somewhat
nearer to the feeling he wants to convey, and at last not hit
upon that particular and only one, which may be said to be
identical with the exact impression in his mind. . . .   10

Words, like clothes, get old-fashioned, or mean and ridiculous, when they have been for some time laid aside. Mr. Lamb
is the only imitator of old English style I can read with pleasure; and he is so thoroughly imbued with the spirit of his
authors, that the idea of imitation is almost done away. There
is an inward unction, a marrowy vein both in the thought and
feeling, an intuition, deep and lively, of his subject, that carries
off any quaintness or awkwardness arising from an antiquated
style and dress. The matter is completely his own, though the
manner is assumed. Perhaps his ideas are altogether so marked   20
and individual, as to require their point and pungency to be
neutralized by the affectation of a singular but traditional form
of conveyance. Tricked out in the prevailing costume, they
would probably seem more startling and out of the way. . . .

It is as easy to write a gaudy style without ideas, as it is to
spread a pallet of showy colors, or to smear in a flaunting
transparency. "What do you read?"—"Words, words, words."
—"What is the matter?"—"*Nothing*," it might be answered.[40]
The florid style is the reverse of the familiar. The last is employed as an unvarnished medium to convey ideas; the first is   30
resorted to as a spangled veil to conceal the want of them.
When there is nothing to be set down but words, it costs little
to have them fine. Look through the dictionary, and cull out
a *florilegium*,[41] rival the *tulipomania. Rouge* high enough, and
never mind the natural complexion. The vulgar, who are not in
the secret, will admire the look of preternatural health and
vigor; and the fashionable, who regard only appearances, will
be delighted with the imposition. Keep to your sounding generalities, your tinkling phrases, and all will be well. Swell out
an unmeaning truism to a perfect tympany of style. A thought,   40
a distinction is the rock on which all this brittle cargo of verbiage splits at once. Such writers have merely *verbal* imaginations, that retain nothing but words. Or their puny thoughts

40 See *Hamlet*, II. ii. 193–5.
41 flowery expression, like *tulipomania*, coined to describe the tulip craze of the
17th cent.

have dragon-wings, all green and gold. They soar far above the
vulgar failing of the *sermo humi obrepens* [42]—their most ordinary
speech is never short of an hyperbole, splendid, imposing,
vague, incomprehensible, magniloquent, a cento of sounding
commonplaces. If some of us, whose "ambition is more lowly,"
pry a little too narrowly into nooks and corners to pick up a
number of "unconsidered trifles," they never once direct their
eyes or lift their hands to seize on any but the most gorgeous,
tarnished, threadbare patchwork set of phrases, the left-off
finery of poetic extravagance, transmitted down through successive generations of barren pretenders. . . .

ON THE FEELING OF IMMORTALITY
IN YOUTH

"Life is a pure flame, and we live by an invisible sun within us." [43]
—SIR THOMAS BROWNE.

No young man believes he shall ever die. It was a saying of
my brother's, and a fine one. There is a feeling of Eternity in
youth, which makes us amends for everything. To be young is
to be as one of the Immortal Gods. One half of time indeed is
flown—the other half remains in store for us with all its countless treasures; for there is no line drawn, and we see no limit
to our hopes and wishes. We make the coming age our own.

"The vast, the unbounded prospect lies before us." [44]

Death, old age, are words without a meaning, that pass by us
like the idle air which we regard not. Others may have undergone, or may still be liable to them—we "bear a charmed life,"
which laughs to scorn all such sickly fancies. As in setting out
on a delightful journey, we strain our eager gaze forward—

"Bidding the lovely scenes at distance hail,"

and see no end to the landscape, new objects presenting themselves as we advance; so, in the commencement of life, we set
no bounds to our inclinations, nor to the unrestricted oppor-
tunities of gratifying them. We have as yet found no obstacle,
no disposition to flag; and it seems that we can go on so forever. We look round in a new world, full of life, and motion, and
ceaseless progress; and feel in ourselves all the vigor and spirit
to keep pace with it, and do not foresee from any present symp-
toms how we shall be left behind in the natural course of things,

42 "speech crawling on the ground" (Horace, *Epistles*, II. i. 250–251)
43 *Hydriotaphia*, Chap. V. (See Vol. I.) The reader should compare Hazlitt's essay
with Wordsworth's famous *Ode*.
44 Addison's *Cato*, V. i. The next quot. is from Collins, *The Passions*, 32.

decline into old age, and drop into the grave. It is the simplicity, and as it were *abstractedness* of our feelings in youth, that (so to speak) identifies us with nature, and (our experience being slight and our passions strong) deludes us into a belief of being immortal like it. Our short-lived connection with existence, we fondly flatter ourselves, is an indissoluble and lasting union— a honeymoon that knows neither coldness, jar, nor separation. As infants smile and sleep, we are rocked in the cradle of our wayward fancies, and lulled into security by the roar of the universe around us—we quaff the cup of life with eager haste without draining it, instead of which it only overflows the more —objects press around us, filling the mind with their magnitude and with the throng of desires that wait upon them, so that we have no room for the thoughts of death. From the plenitude of our being we cannot change all at once to dust and ashes, we cannot imagine "this sensible, warm motion, to become a kneaded clod" [45]—we are too much dazzled by the brightness of the waking dream around us to look into the darkness of the tomb. We no more see our end than our beginning: the one is lost in oblivion and vacancy, as the other is hid from us by the crowd and hurry of approaching events. Or the grim shadow is seen lingering in the horizon, which we are doomed never to overtake, or whose last, faint, glimmering outline touches upon Heaven and translates us to the skies! Nor would the hold that life has taken of us permit us to detach our thoughts from the present objects and pursuits, even if we would. What is there more opposed to health, than sickness; to strength and beauty, than decay and dissolution; to the active search of knowledge, than mere oblivion? Or is there none of the usual advantage to bar the approach of Death, and mock his idle threats; Hope supplies their place, and draws a veil over the abrupt termination of all our cherished schemes. While the spirit of youth remains unimpaired, ere the "wine of life is drank up," [46] we are like people intoxicated or in a fever, who are hurried away by the violence of their own sensations; it is only as present objects begin to pall upon the sense, as we have been disappointed in our favorite pursuits, cut off from our closest ties, that passion loosens its hold upon the breast, that we by degrees become weaned from the world, and allow ourselves to contemplate, "as in a glass, darkly," the possibility of parting with it for good. The example of others, the voice of experience, has no effect upon us whatever. Casualties we must avoid: the slow and deliberate advances of age we can play at *hide-and-seek* with. We think ourselves too lusty and too nimble for that blear-eyed decrepid old gentleman to catch us. Like the foolish fat scullion,

45 *Measure for Measure*, III. i. 120   46 *Macbeth*, II. iii. 100

in Sterne, when she hears that Master Bobby is dead, our only
reflection is, "So am not I!" [47] The idea of death, instead of
staggering our confidence, rather seems to strengthen and en-
hance our possession and our enjoyment of life. Others may
fall around like leaves, or be mowed down like flowers by the
scythe of Time: these are but tropes and figures to the un-
reflecting ears and overweening presumption of youth. It is not
till we see the flowers of Love, Hope, and Joy, withering around
us, and our own pleasures cut up by the roots, that we bring
10 the moral home to ourselves, that we abate something of the
wanton extravagance of our pretensions, or that the emptiness
and dreariness of the prospect before us reconciles us to the
stillness of the grave!

> "Life! thou strange thing, thou hast a power to feel
> Thou art, and to perceive that others are." [48]

Well might the poet begin his indignant invective against an
art, whose professed object is its destruction, with this animated
apostrophe to life. Life is indeed a strange gift, and its privileges are most miraculous. Nor is it singular that when the
20 splendid boon is first granted us, our gratitude, our admiration,
and our delight should prevent us from reflecting on our own
nothingness, or from thinking it will ever be recalled. Our first
and strongest impressions are taken from the mighty scene that
is opened to us, and we very innocently transfer its durability
as well as magnificence to ourselves. So newly found, we cannot
make up our minds to parting with it yet and at least put off
that consideration to an indefinite term. Like a clown at a fair,
we are full of amazement and rapture, and have no thoughts of
going home, or that it will soon be night. We know our exist-
30 ence only from external objects, and we measure it by them.
We can never be satisfied with gazing; and nature will still
want us to look on and applaud. Otherwise, the sumptuous
entertainment, "the feast of reason and the flow of soul," [49] to
which they were invited, seems little better than mockery and
a cruel insult. We do not go from a play till the scene is ended,
and the lights are ready to be extinguished. But the fair face of
things still shines on; shall we be called away before the curtain
falls, or ere we have scarce had a glimpse of what is going on?
Like children, our step-mother Nature holds us up to see the
40 raree-show [50] of the universe; and then, as if life were a burthen
to support, lets us instantly down again. Yet in that short interval, what "brave sublunary things" [51] does not the spectacle

---

47 *Tristram Shandy,* V. vii.   48 Fawcett's *Art of War,* a poem, 1794 (Hazlitt)
49 Pope, *Imitations of Horace,* Satire I. 128   50 peep-show
51 a famous phrase of Drayton's (*To Henry Reynolds*)

unfold; like a bubble, at one minute reflecting the universe, and the next, shook to air!—To see the golden sun and the azure sky, the outstretched ocean, to walk upon the green earth, and to be lord of a thousand creatures, to look down the giddy precipices or over the distant flowery vales, to see the world spread out under one's finger in a map, to bring the stars near, to view the smallest insects in a microscope, to read history, and witness the revolutions of empires and the succession of generations, to hear of the glory of Sidon and Tyre, of Babylon and Susa, as of a faded pageant, and to say all these were, and are now nothing, to think that we exist in such a point of time, and in such a corner of space, to be at once spectators and a part of the moving scene, to watch the return of the seasons, of spring and autumn, to hear

> "The stockdove plain amid the forest deep,
> That drowsy rustles to the sighing gale"—[52]

to traverse desert wilderness, to listen to the midnight choir, to visit lighted halls, or plunge into the dungeon's gloom, or sit in crowded theaters and see life itself mocked, to feel heat and cold, pleasure and pain, right and wrong, truth and falsehood, to study the works of art and refine the sense of beauty to agony, to worship fame and to dream of immortality, to have read Shakspeare and belong to the same species as Sir Isaac Newton; to be and to do all this, and then in a moment to be nothing, to have it all snatched from one like a juggler's ball or a phantasmagoria; there is something revolting and incredible to sense in the transition, and no wonder that, aided by youth and warm blood, and the flush of enthusiasm, the mind contrives for a long time to reject it with disdain and loathing as a monstrous and improbable fiction, like a monkey on a house-top, that is loath, amidst its fine discoveries and specious antics, to be tumbled headlong into the street, and crushed to atoms, the sport and laughter of the multitude!

The change, from the commencement to the close of life, appears like a fable, after it had taken place; how should we treat it otherwise than as a chimera before it has come to pass? There are some things that happened so long ago, places or persons we have formerly seen, of which such dim traces remain, we hardly know whether it was sleeping or waking they occurred; they are like dreams within the dream of life, a mist, a film before the eye of memory, which, as we try to recall them more distinctly, elude our notice altogether. It is but natural that the lone interval that we thus look back upon should have appeared long and endless in prospect. There are others so

52 Thomson, *Castle of Indolence*, I. iv.

distinct and fresh, they seem but of yesterday—their very vividness might be deemed a pledge of their permanence. Then, however far back our impressions may go, we find others still older (for our years are multiplied in youth) descriptions of scenes that we had read, and people before our time, Priam and the Trojan war; and even then, Nestor was old and dwelt delighted on his youth, and spoke of the race of heroes that were no more;—what wonder that, seeing this long line of being pictured in our minds, and reviving as it were in us, we should give ourselves involuntary credit for an indeterminate existence? In the cathedral at Peterborough there is a monument to Mary, Queen of Scots, at which I used to gaze when a boy, while the events of the period, all that had happened since, passed in review before me. If all this mass of feeling and imagination could be crowded into a moment's compass, what might not the whole of life be supposed to contain? We are heirs of the past, we count on the future as our natural reversion. Besides, there are some of our early impressions so exquisitely tempered, it appears that they must always last—nothing can add to or take away from their sweetness and purity—the first breath of spring, the hyacinth dipped in the dew, the mild luster of the evening-star, the rainbow after a storm—while we have the full enjoyment of these, we must be young; and what can ever alter us in this respect? Truth, friendship, love, books, are also proof against the canker of time; and while we live but for them, we can never grow old. We take out a new lease of existence from the objects on which we set our affections, and become abstracted, impassive, immortal in them. We cannot conceive how certain sentiments should ever decay or grow cold in our breasts; and, consequently to maintain them in their first youthful glow and vigor, the flame of life must continue to burn as bright as ever, or rather, they are the fuel that feed the sacred lamp, that kindle "the purple light of love," and spread a golden cloud around our heads! Again, we not only flourish and survive in our affections (in which we will not listen to the possibility of a change, any more than we foresee the wrinkles on the brow of a mistress), but we have a further guarantee against the thoughts of death in our favorite studies and pursuits and in their continual advance. Art we know is long; life, we feel, should be so too. We see no end of the difficulties we have to encounter: perfection is slow of attainment, and we must have time to accomplish it in. Rubens complained that when he had just learned his art, he was snatched away from it: we trust we shall be more fortunate! A wrinkle in an old head takes whole days to finish it properly: but to catch "the Raphael grace, the Guido air," no limit should be put to our endeavors. What a prospect for the future! What a task we have entered upon! and shall we be arrested in the middle of it? We do not reckon our time thus employed lost, or our pains thrown away, or our progress slow—we do not droop or grow tired, but "gain a new vigor at our endless task"; [53]—and shall Time grudge us the opportunity to finish what we have auspiciously begun, and have formed a sort of compact with nature to achieve? The fame of the great names we look up to is also imperishable; and shall not we, who contemplate it with such intense yearnings, imbibe a portion of ethereal fire, the *divinæ particula auræ,* which nothing can extinguish? I remember to have looked at a print of Rembrandt for hours together, without being conscious of the flight of time, trying to resolve it into its component parts, to connect its strong and sharp gradations, to learn the secret of its reflected lights, and found neither satiety nor pause in the prosecution of my studies. The print over which I was poring would last long enough; why should the idea in my mind, which was finer, more impalpable, perish before it? At this, I redoubled the ardor of my pursuit, and by the very subtlety and refinement of my inquiries, seemed to bespeak for them an exemption from corruption and the rude grasp of Death.

Objects, on our first acquaintance with them, have that singleness and integrity of impression that it seems as if nothing could destroy or obliterate them, so firmly are they stamped and riveted on the brain. We repose on them with a sort of voluptuous indolence, in full faith and boundless confidence. We are absorbed in the present moment, or return to the same point—idling away a great deal of time in youth, thinking we have enough to spare. There is often a local feeling in the air, which is as fixed as if it were marble; we loiter in dim cloisters, losing ourselves in thought and in their glimmering arches; a winding road before us seems as long as the journey of life, and as full of events. Time and experience dissipate this illusion; and by reducing them to detail, circumscribe the limits of our expectations. It is only as the pageant of life passes by and the masques turn their backs upon us, that we see through the deception, or believe that the train will have an end. In many cases, the slow progress and monotonous texture of our lives, before we mingle with the world and are embroiled in its affairs, has a tendency to aid the same feeling. We have a difficulty, when left to ourselves, and without the resource of books or some more lively pursuit, to "beguile the slow and creeping hours of time," and argue that if it moves on always at this tedious snail's-pace, it can never come to an end. We are will-

53 Cowper, *Charity,* 104. The preceding quot. is from Pope, *Moral Essays,* VIII. 36.

ing to skip over certain portions of it that separate us from favorite objects, that irritate ourselves at the unnecessary delay. The young are prodigal of life from a superabundance of it; the old are tenacious on the same score, because they have little left, and cannot enjoy even what remains of it.

For my part, I set out in life with the French Revolution, and that event had considerable influence on my early feelings, as on those of others. Youth was then doubly such. It was the dawn of a new era, a new impulse had been given to men's minds, and the sun of Liberty rose upon the sun of Life in the same day, and both were proud to run their race together. Little did I dream, while my first hopes and wishes went hand in hand with those of the human race, that long before my eyes should close, that dawn would be overcast, and set once more in the night of despotism—"total eclipse!" Happy that I did not. I felt for years, and during the best part of my existence, *heart-whole* in that cause, and triumphed in the triumphs over the enemies of man! At that time, while the fairest aspirations of the human mind seemed about to be realized, ere the image of man was defaced and his breast mangled in scorn, philosophy took a higher, poetry could afford a deeper range. At that time, to read *The Robbers* was indeed delicious, and to hear

> "From the dungeon of the tower time-rent,
> That fearful voice, a famish'd father's cry," [54]

could be borne only amidst the fulness of hope, the crash of the fall of the strongholds of power, and the exulting sounds of the march of human freedom. What feelings the death-scene in *Don Carlos* sent into the soul! In that headlong career of lofty enthusiasm, and the joyous opening of the prospects of the world and our own, the thought of death crossing it, smote doubly cold upon the mind; there was a stifling sense of oppression and confinement, an impatience of our present knowledge, a desire to grasp the whole of our existence in one strong embrace, to sound the mystery of life and death, and in order to put an end to the agony of doubt and dread, to burst through our prison-house, and confront the King of Terrors in his grisly palace! . . . As I was writing out this passage, my miniature picture when a child lay on the mantel-piece and I took it out of the case to look at it. I could perceive few traces of myself in it; but there was the same placid brow, the dimpled mouth, the same timid, inquisitive glance as ever. But its careless smile did not seem to reproach me with having become recreant to

[54] Coleridge, *Sonnet to Schiller*, whose dramas, *The Robbers* and *Don Carlos*, stirred young revolutionaries

the sentiments that were then sown in my mind, or with having
written a sentence that could call up a blush in this image of
ingenuous youth!

"That time is past with all its giddy raptures." [55] Since the
future was barred to my progress, I have turned for consolation to the past, gathering up the fragments of my early recollections, and putting them into form that might live. It is thus,
that when we find our personal and substantial identity vanishing
from us, we strive to gain a reflected and substituted one in our
thoughts; we do not like to perish wholly, and wish to bequeath   10
our names at least to posterity. As long as we can keep alive our
cherished thoughts and nearest interests in the minds of others,
we do not appear to have retired altogether from the stage, we
still occupy a place in the estimation of mankind, exercise a
powerful influence over them, and it is only our bodies that are
trampled into dust or dispersed to air. Our darling speculations
still find favor and encouragement, and we make as good a
figure in the eyes of our descendants, nay, perhaps, a better
than we did in our life-time. This is one point gained; the demands of our self-love are so far satisfied. Besides, if by the   20
proofs of intellectual superiority we survive ourselves in this
world, by exemplary virtue or unblemished faith, we are taught
to ensure an interest in another and a higher state of being, and
to anticipate at the same time the applauses of men and angels.

> "Even from the tomb the voice of nature cries;
> Even in our ashes live their wonted fires." [56]

As we advance in life, we acquire a keener sense of the value
of time. Nothing else, indeed, seems of any consequence; and
we become misers in this respect. We try to arrest its few last
tottering steps, and to make it linger on the brink of the grave.   30
We can never leave off wondering how that which has ever been
should cease to be, and would still live on, that we may wonder
at our own shadow, and when "all the life of life is flown," dwell
on the retrospect of the past. This is accompanied by a mechanical tenaciousness of whatever we possess, by a distrust and a
sense of fallacious hollowness in all we see. Instead of the full,
pulpy feeling of youth, everything is flat and insipid. The
world is a painted witch, that puts us off with false shows and
tempting appearances. The ease, the jocund gaiety, the unsus-
pecting security of youth are fled: nor can we, without flying in   40
the face of common sense,

55 Wordsworth's *Tintern Abbey* Lines, 84-86
56 Gray's *Elegy*, 91-92

"From the last dregs of life, hope to receive
What its first sprightly runnings could not give." [57]

If we can slip out of the world without notice or mischance, can tamper with bodily infirmity, and frame our minds to the becoming composure of *still-life,* before we sink into total insensibility, it is as much as we ought to expect. We do not in the regular course of nature die all at once: we have mouldered away gradually long before; faculty after faculty, attachment after attachment, we are torn from ourselves piece-meal while living; year after year takes something from us; and death only consigns the last remnant of what we were to the grave. The revulsion is not so great, and a quiet *euthanasia* is a winding-up of the plot, that is not out of reason or nature.

That we should thus in a manner outlive ourselves, and dwindle imperceptibly into nothing, is not surprising, when even in our prime the strongest impressions leave so little traces of themselves behind, and the last object is driven out by the succeeding one. How little effect is produced on us at any time by the books we have read, the scenes we have witnessed, the sufferings we have gone through! Think only of the variety of feelings we experience in reading an interesting romance, or being present at a fine play—what beauty, what sublimity, what soothing, what heart-rending emotions! You would suppose these would last for ever, or at least subdue the mind to a correspondent tone and harmony—while we turn over the page, while the scene is passing before us, it seems as if nothing could ever after shake our resolution, that "treason domestic, foreign levy, nothing could touch us farther!" [58] The first splash of mud we get, on entering the street, the first pettifogging shopkeeper that cheats us out of two-pence, and the whole vanishes clean out of our remembrance, and we become the idle prey of the most petty and annoying circumstances. The mind soars by an effort to the grand and lofty; it is at home in the groveling, the disagreeable, and the little. This happens in the height and hey-day of our existence, when novelty gives a stronger impulse to the blood and takes a faster hold of the brain (I have known the impression on coming out of a gallery of pictures then last half a day)—as we grow old, we become more feeble and querulous, every object "reverbs its own hollowness," and both worlds are not enough to satisfy the peevish importunity and extravagant presumption of our desires! There are a few

[57] Dryden, *Aurengzebe,* IV. i.
[58] *Macbeth,* III. ii. 24–25. The quot. below is from *Lear,* I. i. 156.

superior, happy beings, who are born with a temper exempt
from every trifling annoyance. This spirit sits serene and smiling as in its native skies, and a divine harmony (whether heard
or not) plays around them. This is to be at peace. Without this,
it is in vain to fly into deserts, or to build a hermitage on the
top of rocks, if regret and ill-humor follow us there; and with
this, it is needless to make the experiment. The only true retirement is that of the heart; the only true leisure is the repose
of the passions. To such persons it makes little difference
whether they are young or old; and they die as they have lived, 10
with graceful resignation.

GEORGE NOEL GORDON, LORD BYRON
(1788–1824)

Byron came of ancestors notorious for their undisciplined lives. His father
was "mad Jack" Byron, a dissipated guardsman, who had squandered his
wife's fortune and left her only a small annuity when he died, three years after
the birth of the poet on January 22, 1788. His mother was Catherine Gordon,
a descendant of James I—an impetuous and unstable woman, under whose
wretched training her son's character was formed. After her husband deserted
her, she took the boy to Aberdeen, where he lived till he was ten years old.
On the death of his grand-uncle in 1798 he came unexpectedly into a barony,
inheriting also the ancestral Byron estate, Newstead Abbey, in Nottingham-
shire. From 1801 to 1805 he attended Harrow, proceeding thence to Trinity
College, Cambridge, where he received his M.A., by the special privilege of a
peer, in 1808.

While at Cambridge he had published his *Fugitive Pieces* in 1806, and the
same material, with revisions and additions, as *Hours of Idleness*, 1807. A
savage attack upon the latter volume in the *Edinburgh Review* provoked
Byron's brilliant satire, *English Bards and Scotch Reviewers*, 1809. In the same
year he took his seat in the House of Lords, and then started out, with his
friend Hobhouse, on a two years' journey which took him from Portugal to
Turkey. On this journey he swam, like Leander, the Hellespont—a feat of
which he never ceased to be proud.

From material largely supplied by his tour Byron wrote the first two cantos
of *Childe Harold* (published 1812), a work which immediately became popular.
"I awoke one morning," he said, "and found myself famous." To admiration
of the poet's work was joined a romantic interest in the man—an interest born
of his striking beauty, his personal fascination, his reputation for wild living,
and perhaps also the lameness with which he had been afflicted since birth. He
became a social lion.

In 1813 and 1814 he published a series of oriental and romantic tales in
verse—*The Giaour, The Bride of Abydos, The Corsair, Lara*—the popularity
of which is said to have turned Sir Walter Scott from the writing of his less
passionate narrative poems to the novel. With these works Byron's reputation

grew rapidly, not only in England, but on the Continent. At the height of his fame he married, in January, 1815, Miss Anna Isabella Milbanke, and just a year later separated from her, a little more than a month after the birth of a daughter, Augusta Ada. Husband and wife had proved utterly incompatible, and immediately after the separation ugly rumors of scandal began to spread through society, so that Byron found himself ostracized by those who had formerly lionized him. Recoiling from British criticism of his life and morals, in April, 1816 he left England, never to return.

The summer of 1816 he spent in Switzerland with the Shelleys and with Jane (or Clare) Clairmont, Mrs. Shelley's step-sister. The association of the two poets continued the next few years in Italy, where they saw much of each other. In the fall of 1816, Byron moved on to Venice, where a daughter, Allegra, was born to him and Jane Clairmont. From 1816 to 1823 he resided in Italy, chiefly at Venice, Ravenna, Pisa, and Genoa. During these years he lived intermittently with the Countess Guiccioli, a young Italian woman whom he persuaded to leave her aged husband. In Switzerland he had written the third canto of *Childe Harold* and *The Prisoner of Chillon*, and had begun *Manfred*. In Italy he finished *Manfred*, wrote the fourth canto of *Childe Harold*, *Beppo*, *Cain*, *The Vision of Judgment*, and other poems. In 1818 he began *Don Juan*, which he continued to work on till 1823, and left incomplete with sixteen cantos. In this poem his great abilities were for the first time fully revealed.

In 1823 he decided to aid the Greeks in their fight for independence against the Turks. In the Greek camp at Missolonghi he died of a fever on April 19, 1824, giving his life for liberty, as he conceived it.

During the ensuing century, Byron's fame has suffered severe fluctuations. His reputation as poet was in part damaged by his reputation as man. Byron shocked society, and when society rejected him, cultivated the name of "bad boy" which he had acquired. Many feel that in the typical Byronic hero of numerous poems (most gloomily and powerfully in *Manfred*), they recognize a self-portrait, or perhaps merely a pose, compacted of social rebellion, cynicism, and world-weariness against a background of unutterable sin. Since Victorian times his poetic stature has risen again. Against claims of moral rottenness, grandiosity, insincerity, and lack of sustained and memorable quality, must be placed an undeniable brilliance and splendor, passion, facility, and wit. Yet his final standing in English poetry has probably not yet been surely established. His influence, especially upon the Continent, has been profound.

BIBLIOGRAPHY. *Works* (Murray, Scribner's), in 13 vols.: Letters and Journals, 6 vols., ed. R. E. Prothero (Ernle); Poetical Works, 7 vols., ed. E. H. Coleridge. One vol. ed. of the above; also the Cambridge, ed. P. E. More (Houghton Mifflin). Best biography by E. C. Mayne, 2 vols. (Scribner's), shorter life by John Nichol (Eng. Men of Letters ser.), "official" life by Byron's intimate friend, the poet Thomas Moore. John Drinkwater, *Byron: the Pilgrim of Eternity*, Dutton (interpretation of one poet by another).

MAID OF ATHENS, ERE WE PART

Ζώη μοῦ, σᾶς ἀγαπῶ.[1]

MAID of Athens, ere we part,
Give, oh give me back my heart!

1 My life, I love you.

Or, since that has left my breast,
Keep it now, and take the rest!
Hear my vow before I go,
Ζώη μοῦ, σᾶς ἀγαπῶ.

By those tresses unconfined,
Wooed by each Ægean wind;
By those lids whose jetty fringe
Kiss thy soft cheeks' blooming tinge;   10
By those wild eyes like the roe,
Ζώη μοῦ, σᾶς ἀγαπῶ.

By that lip I long to taste;
By that zone-encircled waist;
By all the token-flowers that tell
What words can never speak so well;
By love's alternate joy and woe,
Ζώη μοῦ, σᾶς ἀγαπῶ.

Maid of Athens! I am gone:
Think of me, sweet! when alone.   20
Though I fly to Istambol,[2]
Athens holds my heart and soul:
Can I cease to love thee? No!
Ζώη μοῦ, σᾶς ἀγαπῶ.

AND THOU ART DEAD, AS YOUNG AND FAIR

"Heu, quanto minus est cum reliquis versari quam
tui meminisse!"[3]

AND thou art dead, as young and fair
  As aught of mortal birth;
And form so soft, and charms so rare,
  Too soon returned to Earth!
Though Earth received them in her bed
And o'er the spot the crowd may tread
  In carelessness of mirth,
There is an eye which could not brook
A moment on that grave to look.

I will not ask where thou liest low,   10
  Nor gaze upon the spot;
There flowers or weeds at will may grow,

2 Constantinople   it is to live with those who   thee!
3 Alas, how much harder   are left than to remember

So I behold them not:
It is enough for me to prove
That what I loved, and long must love,
    Like common earth can rot;
To me there needs no stone to tell,
'Tis nothing that I loved so well.

Yet did I love thee to the last
    As fervently as thou,   20
Who didst not change through all the past,
    And canst not alter now.
The love where Death has set his seal,
Nor age can chill, nor rival steal,
    Nor falsehood disavow:
And what were worse, thou canst not see
Or wrong, or change, or fault in me.

The better days of life were ours;
    The worst can be but mine;
The sun that cheers, the storm that lowers,   30
    Shall never more be thine.
The silence of that dreamless sleep
I envy now too much to weep;
    Nor need I repine
That all those charms have passed away;
I might have watched through long decay.

The flower in ripened bloom unmatched
    Must fall the earliest prey;
Though by no hand untimely snatched,
    The leaves must drop away;   40
And yet it were a greater grief
To watch it withering leaf by leaf,
    Than see it plucked to-day;
Since earthly eye but ill can bear
To trace the change to foul from fair.

I know not if I could have borne
    To see thy beauties fade;
The night that followed such a morn
    Had worn a deeper shade;
The day without a cloud hath passed,   50
And thou wert lovely to the last;
    Extinguished, not decayed;
As stars that shoot along the sky
Shine brightest as they fall from high.

As once I wept, if I could weep,
  My tears might well be shed,
To think I was not near to keep
  One vigil o'er thy bed;
To gaze, how fondly! on thy face,
To fold thee in a faint embrace,   60
  Uphold thy drooping head;
And show that love, however vain, .
Nor thou nor I can feel again.

Yet how much less it were to gain,
  Though thou hast left me free,
The loveliest things that still remain,
  Than thus remember thee!
The all of thine that cannot die
Through dark and dread Eternity
  Returns again to me,   70
And more thy buried love endears
Than aught except its living years.

WHEN WE TWO PARTED

When we two parted
  In silence and tears,
Half broken-hearted
  To sever for years,
Pale grew thy cheek and cold,
  Colder thy kiss;
Truly that hour foretold
  Sorrow to this.

The dew of the morning
  Sunk chill on my brow—   10
It felt like the warning
  Of what I feel now.
Thy vows are all broken,
  And light is thy fame:
I hear thy name spoken,
  And share in its shame.

They name thee before me,
  A knell to mine ear;
A shudder comes o'er me—
  Why wert thou so dear?   20
They know not I knew thee,
  Who knew thee too well:—

Long, long shall I rue thee,
Too deeply to tell.

In secret we met—
In silence I grieve,
That thy heart could forget,
Thy spirit deceive.
If I should meet thee
After long years,
How should I greet thee?—
With silence and tears.

SHE WALKS IN BEAUTY [4]

SHE walks in beauty, like the night
Of cloudless climes and starry skies;
And all that's best of dark and bright
Meet in her aspect and her eyes:
Thus mellowed to that tender light
Which heaven to gaudy day denies.

One shade the more, one ray the less,
Had half impaired the nameless grace
Which waves in every raven tress,
Or softly lightens o'er her face;
Where thoughts serenely sweet express
How pure, how dear their dwelling-place.

And on that cheek, and o'er that brow,
So soft, so calm, yet eloquent,
The smiles that win, the tints that glow,
But tell of days in goodness spent,
A mind at peace with all below,
A heart whose love is innocent!

OH! SNATCHED AWAY IN BEAUTY'S BLOOM

OH! snatched away in beauty's bloom,
On thee shall press no ponderous tomb;
But on thy turf shall roses rear
Their leaves, the earliest of the year;
And the wild cypress wave in tender gloom:

And oft by yon blue gushing stream
Shall Sorrow lean her drooping head,

4 This and the next two lyrics are from *Hebrew Melodies*, a series of poems written to be set to music.

And feed deep thought with many a dream,
   And lingering pause and lightly tread:
Fond wretch! as if her step disturbed the dead!   10

Away! We know that tears are vain,
   That Death nor heeds nor hears distress:
Will this unteach us to complain?
   Or make one mourner weep the less?
And thou—who tell'st me to forget,
Thy looks are wan, thine eyes are wet.

THE DESTRUCTION OF SENNACHERIB [5]

1

THE Assyrian came down like the wolf on the fold,
And his cohorts were gleaming in purple and gold;
And the sheen of their spears was like stars on the sea,
When the blue wave rolls nightly on deep Galilee.

2

Like the leaves of the forest when Summer is green,
That host with their banners at sunset were seen:
Like the leaves of the forest when Autumn hath blown,
That host on the morrow lay withered and strown.

3

For the Angel of Death spread his wings on the blast,
And breathed in the face of the foe as he passed;
And the eyes of the sleepers waxed deadly and chill,
And their hearts but once heaved, and for ever grew still!

4

And there lay the steed with his nostril all wide,
But through it there rolled not the breath of his pride;
And the foam of his gasping lay white on the turf,
And cold as the spray of the rock-beating surf.

5

And there lay the rider distorted and pale,
With the dew on his brow, and the rust on his mail:

[5] see 2 Kings, xviii, xix

And the tents were all silent, the ·banners alone,
The lances unlifted, the trumpet unblown.

6

And the widows of Ashur are loud in their wail,
And the idols are broke in the temple of Baal;
And the might of the Gentile, unsmote by the sword,
Hath melted like snow in the glance of the Lord!

STANZAS FOR MUSIC

There's not a joy the world can give like that it takes away,
When the glow of early thought declines in feeling's dull decay;
'Tis not on youth's smooth cheek the blush alone, which fades so
      fast,
But the tender bloom of heart is gone, ere youth itself be past.

Then the few whose spirits float above the wreck of happiness
Are driven o'er the shoals of guilt or ocean of excess:
The magnet of their course is gone, or only points in vain
The shore to which their shivered sail shall never stretch again.

Then the mortal coldness of the soul like death itself comes
      down;
It cannot feel for others' woes, it dare not dream its own;   10
That heavy chill has frozen o'er the fountain of our tears,
And though the eye may sparkle still, 'tis where the ice appears.

Though wit may flash from fluent lips, and mirth distract the
      breast,
Through midnight hours that yield no more their former hope of
      rest;
'Tis but as ivy-leaves around the ruined turret wreath,
All green and wildly fresh without, but worn and gray beneath.

Oh could I feel as I have felt,—or be what I have been,
Or weep as I could once have wept o'er many a vanished scene;
As springs in deserts found seem sweet, all brackish though
      they be,
So, midst the withered waste of life, those tears would flow
      to me.   20

FARE THEE WELL [6]

"Alas! they had been friends in youth;
But whispering tongues can poison truth;

6 referring to Lady Byron, after her separation from the poet

And constancy lives in realms above;
And life is thorny; and youth is vain;
And to be wroth with one we love,
Doth work like madness in the brain;

    *   *   *   *   *

But never either found another
To free the hollow heart from paining—
They stood aloof, the scars remaining,
Like cliffs which had been rent asunder;
A dreary sea now flows between,
But neither heat, nor frost, nor thunder,
Shall wholly do away, I ween,
The marks of that which once hath been."
                —COLERIDGE'S *Christabel.*

FARE thee well! and if for ever,
  Still for ever, fare thee well:
Even though unforgiving, never
  'Gainst thee shall my heart rebel.

Would that breast were bared before thee
  Where thy head so oft hath lain,
While that placid sleep came o'er thee
  Which thou ne'er canst know again:

Would that breast, by thee glanced over,
  Every inmost thought could show!   10
Then thou wouldst at last discover
  'Twas not well to spurn it so.

Though the world for this commend thee—
  Though it smile upon the blow,
Even its praises must offend thee,
  Founded on another's woe:

Though my many faults defaced me,
  Could no other arm be found
Than the one which once embraced me,
  To inflict a cureless wound?   20

Yet, oh yet, thyself deceive not;
  Love may sink by slow decay,
But by sudden wrench, believe not
  Hearts can thus be torn away:

Still thine own its life retaineth,
  Still must mine, though bleeding, beat;

And the undying thought which paineth
  Is—that we no more may meet.

These are words of deeper sorrow
  Than the wail above the dead;
Both shall live, but every morrow   30
  Wake us from a widowed bed.

And when thou wouldst solace gather,
  When our child's first accents flow,
Wilt thou teach her to say "Father!"
  Though his care she must forego?

When her little hands shall press thee,
  When her lip to thine is pressed,
Think of him whose prayer shall bless thee,
  Think of him thy love had bless'd!   40

Should her lineaments resemble
  Those thou never more may'st see,
Then thy heart will softly tremble
  With a pulse yet true to me.

All my faults perchance thou knowest,
  All my madness none can know;
All my hopes, where'er thou goest,
  Wither, yet with *thee* they go.

Every feeling hath been shaken;
  Pride, which not a world could bow,   50
Bows to thee—by thee forsaken,
  Even my soul forsakes me now:

But 'tis done—all words are idle—
  Words from me are vainer still;
But the thoughts we cannot bridle
  Force their way without the will.

Fare thee well! thus disunited,
  Torn from every nearer tie,
Sear'd in heart, and lone, and blighted,
  More than this I scarce can die.   60

CHILDE HAROLD'S PILGRIMAGE

Childe Harold is a travel poem, in which Byron, speaking through the lips of his thinly disguised hero, recounts his journey across southern Europe in

1809–11 (Cantos I and II), and from England through Belgium and Switzerland to Italy in 1816 and 1817 (Cantos III and IV). There is some description of the places visited, but more attention is paid to the thoughts and feelings aroused. Canto III, here reprinted entire, is perhaps the most brilliant of the four, though the passages in Canto IV on Rome are also greatly admired. "It is almost superfluous to mention," writes Byron in his preface, "that the appellation 'Childe,' as 'Childe Waters,' 'Childe Childers,' etc., is used as more consonant with the old structure of versification which I have adopted [the Spenserian stanza]."

CANTO III

Afin que cette application vous forçât de penser à autre chose; il n'y a en vérité de remède que celui-là et le temps.[7]
—Lettre du Roi de Prusse à D'Alembert, Sept. 7, 1776.

I

Is thy face like thy mother's, my fair child!
Ada! sole daughter of my house and heart? [8]
When last I saw thy young blue eyes they smiled,
And then we parted,—not as now we part,
But with a hope.—
                    Awaking with a start,
The waters heave around me; and on high
The winds lift up their voices: I depart,
Whither I know not, but the hour's gone by,
When Albion's lessening shores could grieve or glad mine eye.

2

Once more upon the waters! yet once more!
And the waves bound beneath me as a steed
That knows his rider. Welcome to their roar!
Swift be their guidance, wheresoe'er it lead!
Though the strained mast should quiver as a reed,
And the rent canvas fluttering strew the gale
Still must I on; for I am as a weed,
Flung from the rock, on Ocean's foam to sail
Where'er the surge may sweep, the tempest's breath prevail.

3

In my youth's summer I did sing of One,[9]
The wandering outlaw of his own dark mind;

7 In order that this employment may force you to think of something else; there is in truth no remedy except that and time. (Letter from the King of Prussia [Frederick the Great] to D'Alembert.) Canto III was written after the poet's separation from Lady Byron and his departure from England.

8 Byron's daughter

9 *i. e.,* Childe Harold. The first two cantos had been written in 1812, four years before, when Byron was twenty-four.

Again I seize the theme, then but begun,
And bear it with me, as the rushing wind
Bears the cloud onwards: in that Tale I find
The furrows of long thought, and dried-up tears,
Which, ebbing, leave a sterile track behind,
O'er which all heavily the journeying years
Plod the last sands of life,—where not a flower appears.

4

Since my young days of passion—joy, or pain,
Perchance my heart and harp have lost a string,
And both may jar: it may be, that in vain
I would essay as I have sung to sing.
Yet, though a dreary strain, to this I cling,
So that it wean me from the weary dream
Of selfish grief or gladness—so it fling
Forgetfulness around me—it shall seem
To me, though to none else, a not ungrateful theme.

5

He, who grown agèd in this world of woe,
In deeds, not years, piercing the depths of life,
So that no wonder waits him; nor below
Can love or sorrow, fame, ambition, strife,
Cut to his heart again with a keen knife
Of silent, sharp endurance: he can tell
Why thought seeks refuge in lone caves, yet rife
With airy images, and shapes which dwell
Still unimpaired, though old, in the soul's haunted cell.

6

'Tis to create, and in creating live
A being more intense that we endow
With form our fancy, gaining as we give
The life we image, even as I do now.
What am I? Nothing: but not so art thou,
Soul of my thought! with whom I traverse earth,
Invisible but gazing, as I glow
Mixed with thy spirit, blended with thy birth,
And feeling still with thee in my crushed feelings' dearth.

7

Yet must I think less wildly:—I *have* thought
Too long and darkly, till my brain became,

In its own eddy boiling and o'erwrought,
A whirling gulf of fantasy and flame.
And thus, untaught in youth my heart to tame,
My springs of life were poisoned. 'Tis too late!
Yet am I changed; though still enough the same
In strength to bear what Time cannot abate,
And feed on bitter fruits without accusing Fate.

8

Something too much of this:—but now 'tis past,
And the spell closes with its silent seal.
Long absent HAROLD re-appears at last;
He of the breast which fain no more would feel,
Wrung with the wounds which kill not, but ne'er heal;
Yet Time, who changes all, had altered him
In soul and aspect as in age: years steal
Fire from the mind as vigor from the limb;
And life's enchanted cup but sparkles near the brim.

9

His had been quaffed too quickly, and he found
The dregs were wormwood; but he filled again,
And from a purer fount, on holier ground,
And deemed its spring perpetual; but in vain!
Still round him clung invisibly a chain
Which galled for ever, fettering though unseen,
And heavy though it clanked not; worn with pain,
Which pined although it spoke not, and grew keen,
Entering with every step he took through many a scene.

10

Secure in guarded coldness, he had mixed
Again in fancied safety with his kind,
And deemed his spirit now so firmly fixed
And sheathed with an invulnerable mind,
That, if no joy, no sorrow lurked behind;
And he, as one, might 'midst the many stand
Unheeded, searching through the crowd to find
Fit speculation; such as in strange land
He found in wonder-works of God and Nature's hand.

11

But who can view the ripened rose, nor seek
To wear it? who can curiously behold

The smoothness and the sheen of beauty's cheek,
Nor feel the heart can never all grow old?
Who can contemplate Fame through clouds unfold
The star which rises o'er her step, nor climb?
Harold, once more within the vortex, rolled
On with the giddy circle, chasing Time,
Yet with a nobler aim than in his youth's fond prime.

12

But soon he knew himself the most unfit
Of men to herd with Man; with whom he held
Little in common; untaught to submit
His thoughts to others, though his soul was quelled
In youth by his own thoughts; still uncompelled,
He would not yield dominion of his mind
To spirits against whom his own rebelled;
Proud though in desolation; which could find
A life within itself, to breathe without mankind.

13

Where rose the mountains, there to him were friends,
Where rolled the ocean, thereon was his home,
Where a blue sky, and glowing clime, extends,
He had the passion and the power to roam;
The desert, forest, cavern, breaker's foam,
Were unto him companionship; they spake
A mutual language, clearer than the tome
Of his land's tongue, which he would oft forsake
For Nature's pages glassed by sunbeams on the lake.

14

Like the Chaldean, he could watch the stars,
Till he had peopled them with beings bright
As their own beams; and earth, and earth-born jars,
And human frailties, were forgotten quite:
Could he have kept his spirit to that flight
He had been happy; but this clay will sink
Its spark immortal, envying it the light
To which it mounts, as if to break the link
That keeps us from yon heaven which woos us to its brink.

15

But in Man's dwellings he became a thing
Restless and worn, and stern and wearisome,

Drooped as a wild-born falcon with clipped wing,
To whom the boundless air alone were home:
Then came his fit again, which to o'ercome,
As eagerly the barred-up bird will beat
His breast and beak against his wiry dome
Till the blood tinge his plumage, so the heat
Of his impeded soul would through his bosom eat.

16

Self-exiled Harold wanders forth again,
With nought of hope left, but with less of gloom,
The very knowledge that he lived in vain,
That all was over on this side the tomb,
Had made Despair a smilingness assume,
Which, though 'twere wild,—as on the plundered wreck
When mariners would madly meet their doom
With draughts intemperate on the sinking deck,—
Did yet inspire a cheer, which he forbore to check.

17

Stop!—for thy tread is on an Empire's dust!
An Earthquake's spoil is sepulchered below!
Is the spot marked with no colossal bust?
Nor column trophied for triumphal show?
None; but the moral's truth tells simpler so,
As the ground was before, thus let it be;—
How that red rain hath made the harvest grow!
And is this all the world has gained by thee,
Thou first and last of fields! king-making Victory?

18

And Harold stands upon this place of skulls,
The grave of France, the deadly Waterloo!
How in an hour the power which gave annuls
Its gifts, transferring fame as fleeting too!
In "pride of place" here last the eagle [10] flew,
Then tore with bloody talon the rent plain,
Pierced by the shaft of banded nations through;
Ambition's life and labors all were vain;
He wears the shattered links of the world's broken chain.

---

10 Napoleon. *"Pride of Place* is a term of falconry, meaning the highest pitch of flight" (Byron).

19

Fit retribution! Gaul may champ the bit
And foam in fetters;—but is Earth more free?
Did nations combat to make *One* submit;
Or league to teach all kings true sovereignty!
What! shall reviving Thraldom again be
The patched-up idol of enlightened days?
Shall we, who struck the Lion down, shall we
Pay the Wolf homage? proffering lowly gaze
And servile knees to thrones? No; *prove* before ye praise!

20

If not, o'er one fallen despot boast no more!
In vain fair cheeks were furrowed with hot tears
For Europe's flowers long rooted up before
The trampler of her vineyards; in vain years
Of death, depopulation, bondage, fears,
Have all been borne, and broken by the accord
Of roused-up millions; all that most endears
Glory, is when the myrtle wreathes a sword
Such as Harmodius [11] drew on Athens' tyrant lord.

21

There was a sound of revelry by night,[12]
And Belgium's capital had gathered then
Her Beauty and her Chivalry, and bright
The lamps shone o'er fair women and brave men;
A thousand hearts beat happily; and when
Music arose with its voluptuous swell,
Soft eyes looked love to eyes which spake again
And all went merry as a marriage bell;
But hush! hark! a deep sound strikes like a rising knell!

22

Did ye not hear it?—No; 'twas but the wind,
Or the car rattling o'er the stony street;
On with the dance! let joy be unconfined;
No sleep 'till morn, when Youth and Pleasure meet
To chase the glowing Hours with flying feet—
But hark!—that heavy sound breaks in once more,

11 He killed the tyrant Hipparchus with a sword concealed in myrtle leaves during a religious procession.
12 at the Duchess of Richmond's ball

As if the clouds its echo would repeat;
And nearer, clearer, deadlier than before!
Arm! Arm! it is—it is—the cannon's opening roar!

23

Within a windowed niche of that high hall
Sat Brunswick's fated chieftain; [13] he did hear
That sound the first amidst the festival,
And caught its tone with Death's prophetic ear;
And when they smiled because he deemed it near,
His heart more truly knew that peal too well
Which stretched his father on a bloody bier,
And roused the vengeance blood alone could quell;
He rushed into the field, and, foremost fighting, fell.

24

Ah! then and there was hurrying to and fro,
And gathering tears, and tremblings of distress,
And cheeks all pale, which but an hour ago
Blushed at the praise of their own loveliness;
And there were sudden partings, such as press
The life from out young hearts, and choking sighs
Which ne'er might be repeated; who could guess
If ever more should meet those mutual eyes,
Since upon night so sweet such awful morn could rise!

25

And there was mounting in hot haste: the steed,
The mustering squadron, and the clattering car,
Went pouring forward with impetuous speed,
And swiftly forming in the ranks of war;
And the deep thunder peal on peal afar;
And near, the beat of the alarming drum
Roused up the soldier ere the morning star;
While thronged the citizens with terror dumb,
Or whispering, with white lips—"The foe! they come! they
    come!"

26

And wild and high the "Cameron's gathering" [14] rose!
The war-note of Lochiel, which Albyn's [15] hills

13 Frederick William, Duke of Brunswick, killed in the battle of Quatrebras (preceding Waterloo proper). His father had been killed at Auerbach in 1806. 14 the rallying-cry of the clan Cameron, under their chief Lochiel 15 Scotland's

Have heard, and heard, too, have her Saxon foes:—
How in the noon of night that pibroch thrills,
Savage and shrill! But with the breath which fills
Their mountain-pipe, so fill the mountaineers
With the fierce native daring which instills
    The stirring memory of a thousand years,
And Evan's, Donald's fame rings in each clansman's ears!

27

And Ardennes [16] waves above them her green leaves,
Dewy with nature's tear-drops as they pass,
Grieving, if aught inanimate e'er grieves,
Over the unreturning brave,—alas!
Ere evening to be trodden like the grass
    Which now beneath them, but above shall grow
In its next verdure, when this fiery mass
Of living valor, rolling on the foe
And burning with high hope shall molder cold and low.

28

Last noon beheld them full of lusty life,
Last eve in Beauty's circle proudly gay,
The midnight brought the signal-sound of strife,
The morn the marshaling in arms,—the day
Battle's magnificently stern array!
    The thunder-clouds close o'er it, which when rent
The earth is covered thick with other clay,
Which her own clay shall cover, heaped and pent,
Rider and horse,—friend, foe,—in one red burial blent!

29

Their praise is hymned by loftier harps than mine:
Yet one I would select from that proud throng,
Partly because they blend me with his line,
And partly that I did his sire some wrong,
And partly that bright names will hallow song;
    And his was of the bravest, and when showered
The death-bolts deadliest the thinned files along,
Even where the thickest of war's tempest lowered,
They reached no nobler breast than thine, young gallant
    Howard! [17]

16 wood near the bat-   ard, Byron's second cousin.   been satirized in *English*
tlefield   His father, the Earl of Car-   *Bards and Scotch Review-*
17 Major Frederick How- lisle, Byron's guardian, had   *ers.*

30

There have been tears and breaking hearts for thee,
And mine were nothing had I such to give;
But when I stood beneath the fresh green tree,
Which living waves where thou didst cease to live,
And saw around me the wide field revive
With fruits and fertile promise, and the Spring
Came forth her work of gladness to contrive,
With all her reckless birds upon the wing,
I turned from all she brought to those she could not bring.

31

I turned to thee, to thousands, of whom each
And one as all a ghastly gap did make
In his own kind and kindred, whom to teach
Forgetfulness were mercy for their sake;
The Archangel's trump, not Glory's, must awake
Those whom they thirst for; though the sound of Fame
May for a moment soothe, it cannot slake
The fever of vain longing, and the name
So honored but assumes a stronger, bitterer claim.

32

They mourn, but smile at length; and, smiling, mourn:
The tree will wither long before it fall;
The hull drives on, though mast and sail be torn;
The roof-tree sinks, but molders on the hall
In massy hoariness; the ruined wall
Stands when its wind-worn battlements are gone;
The bars survive the captive they enthrall;
The day drags through, though storms keep out the sun;
And thus the heart will break, yet brokenly live on:

33

Even as a broken mirror, which the glass
In every fragment multiplies; and makes
A thousand images of one that was,
The same, and still the more, the more it breaks;
And thus the heart will do which not forsakes,
Living in shattered guise; and still, and cold,
And bloodless, with its sleepless sorrow aches,

Yet withers on till all without is old,
Showing no visible sign, for such things are untold.

34

There is a very life in our despair,
Vitality of poison,—a quick root
Which feeds these deadly branches; for it were
As nothing did we die; but Life will suit
Itself to Sorrow's most detested fruit,
Like to the apples on the Dead Sea's shore,
All ashes to the taste: Did man compute
Existence by enjoyment, and count o'er
Such hours 'gainst years of life,—say, would he name three-
score?

35

The Psalmist numbered out the years of man:
They are enough; and if thy tale be *true*,
Thou, who didst grudge him even that fleeting span,
More than enough, thou fatal Waterloo!
Millions of tongues record thee, and anew
Their children's lips shall echo them, and say—
"Here, where the sword united nations drew,
Our countrymen were warring on that day!"
And this is much, and all which will not pass away.

36

There sunk the greatest, nor the worst of men,[18]
Whose spirit, antithetically mixed,
One moment of the mightiest, and again
On little objects with like firmness fixed;
Extreme in all things! hadst thou been betwixt,
Thy throne had still been thine, or never been;
For daring made thy rise as fall: thou seek'st
Even now to re-assume the imperial mien,
And shake again the world, the Thunderer of the scene!

37

Conqueror and captive of the earth art thou!
She trembles at thee still, and thy wild name
Was ne'er more bruited in men's minds than now

18 Napoleon

That thou art nothing, save the jest of Fame,
Who wooed thee once, thy vassal, and became
The flatterer of thy fierceness, till thou wert
A god unto thyself; nor less the same
To the astounded kingdoms all inert,
Who deemed thee for a time whate'er thou didst assert.

38

Oh, more or less than man—in high or low,
Battling with nations, flying from the field;
Now making monarchs' necks thy footstool, now
More than thy meanest soldier taught to yield;
An empire thou couldst crush, command, rebuild,
But govern not thy pettiest passion, nor,
However deeply in men's spirits skilled,
Look through thine own, nor curb the lust of war,
Nor learn that tempted Fate will leave the loftiest star.

39

Yet well thy soul hath brooked the turning tide
With that untaught innate philosophy,
Which, be it wisdom, coldness, or deep pride,
Is gall and wormwood to an enemy
When the whole host of hatred stood hard by,
To watch and mock thee shrinking, thou hast smiled
With a sedate and all-enduring eye;—
When Fortune fled her spoiled and favorite child,
He stood unbowed beneath the ills upon him piled.

40

Sager than in thy fortunes; for in them
Ambition steeled thee on too far to show
That just habitual scorn, which could contemn
Men and their thoughts; 'twas wise to feel, not so
To wear it ever on thy lip and brow,
And spurn the instruments thou wert to use
Till they were turned unto thine overthrow:
'Tis but a worthless world to win or lose;
So hath it proved to thee, and all such lot who choose.

41

If, like a tower upon a headland rock,
Thou hadst been made to stand or fall alone,

Such scorn of man had helped to brave the shock;
But men's thoughts were the steps which paved thy throne,
Their admiration thy best weapon shone;
The part of Philip's son [19] was thine, not then
(Unless aside thy purple had been thrown)
Like stern Diogenes to mock at men;
For sceptered cynics earth were far too wide a den.

42

But quiet to quick bosoms is a hell,
And *there* hath been thy bane; there is a fire
And motion of the soul which will not dwell
In its own narrow being, but aspire
Beyond the fitting medium of desire;
And, but once kindled, quenchless evermore,
Preys upon high adventure, nor can tire
Of aught but rest; a fever at the core,
Fatal to him who bears, to all who ever bore.

43

This makes the madmen who have made men mad
By their contagion; Conquerors and Kings,
Founders of sects and systems, to whom add
Sophists, Bards, Statesmen, all unquiet things
Which stir too strongly the soul's secret springs,
And are themselves the fools to those they fool;
Envied, yet how unenviable! what stings
Are theirs! One breast laid open were a school
Which would unteach mankind the lust to shine or rule:

44

Their breath is agitation, and their life
A storm whereon they ride, to sink at last,
And yet so nursed and bigoted to strife,
That should their days, surviving perils past,
Melt to calm twilight, they feel overcast
With sorrow and supineness, and so die;
Even as a flame unfed, which runs to waste
With its own flickering, or a sword laid by,
Which eats into itself, and rusts ingloriously.

45

He who ascends to mountain-tops, shall find
The loftiest peaks most wrapped in clouds and snow;

19 Alexander the Great.

He who surpasses or subdues mankind,
Must look down on the hate of those below.
Though high *above* the sun of glory glow,
And far *beneath* the earth and ocean spread,
Round him are icy rocks, and loudly blow
Contending tempests on his naked head,
And thus reward the toils which to those summits led.

46

Away with these! true Wisdom's world will be
Within its own creation, or in thine,
Maternal Nature! for who teems like thee,
Thus on the banks of thy majestic Rhine?
There Harold gazes on a work divine,
A blending of all beauties; streams and dells,
Fruit, foliage, crag, wood, cornfield, mountain, vine,
And chiefless castles breathing stern farewells
From gray but leafy walls, where Ruin greenly dwells.

47

And there they stand, as stands a lofty mind,
Worn, but unstooping to the baser crowd,
All tenantless, save to the crannying wind,
Or holding dark communion with the cloud.
There was a day when they were young and proud;
Banners on high, and battles passed below;
But they who fought are in a bloody shroud,
And those which waved are shredless dust ere now,
And the bleak battlements shall bear no future blow.

48

Beneath those battlements, within those walls,
Power dwelt amidst her passions; in proud state
Each robber chief upheld his armèd halls,
Doing his evil will, nor less elate
Than mightier heroes of a longer date.
What want these outlaws conquerors should have
But history's purchased page to call them great?
A wider space, an ornamented grave?
Their hopes were not less warm, their souls were full as brave.

49

In their baronial feuds and single fields,
What deeds of prowess unrecorded died!

And Love, which lent a blazon to their shields,
With emblems well devised by amorous pride,
Through all the mail of iron hearts would glide;
But still their fame was fierceness, and drew on
Keen contest and destruction near allied,
And many a tower for some fair mischief won,
Saw the discolored Rhine beneath its ruin run.

50

But Thou, exulting and abounding river!
Making thy waves a blessing as they flow
Through banks whose beauty would endure for ever
Could man but leave thy bright creation so,
Nor its fair promise from the surface mow
With the sharp scythe of conflict,—then to see
Thy valley of sweet waters, were to know
Earth paved like Heaven; and to seem such to me,
Even now what wants thy stream?—that it should Lethe be.

51

A thousand battles have assailed thy banks,
But these and half their fame have passed away,
And Slaughter heaped on high his weltering ranks;
Their very graves are gone, and what are they?
Thy tide washed down the blood of yesterday,
And all was stainless, and on thy clear stream
Glassed, with its dancing light, the sunny ray;
But o'er the blackened memory's blighting dream
Thy waves would vainly roll, all sweeping as they seem.

52

Thus Harold inly said, and passed along,
Yet not insensible to all which here
Awoke the jocund birds to early song
In glens which might have made even exile dear:
Though on his brow were graven lines austere,
And tranquil sternness, which had ta'en the place
Of feelings fierier far but less severe,
Joy was not always absent from his face,
But o'er it in such scenes would steal with transient trace.

53

Nor was all love shut from him, though his days
Of passion had consumed themselves to dust.

It is in vain that we would coldly gaze
On such as smile upon us; the heart must
Leap kindly back to kindness, though disgust
Hath weaned it from all worldings: thus he felt,
For there was soft remembrance, and sweet trust
In one fond breast,[20] to which his own would melt,
And in its tenderer hour on that his bosom dwelt.

54

And he had learned to love,—I know not why,
For this in such as him seems strange of mood,—
The helpless looks of blooming infancy,
Even in its earliest nurture; what subdued,
To change like this, a mind so far imbued
With scorn of man, it little boots to know,
But thus it was; and though in solitude
Small power the nipped affections have to grow,
In him this glowed when all beside had ceased to glow.

55

And there was one soft breast, as hath been said,
Which unto his was bound by stronger ties
Than the church links withal; and, though unwed,
That love was pure, and, far above disguise,
Had stood the test of mortal enmities
Still undivided, and cemented more
By peril, dreaded most in female eyes;
But this was firm, and from a foreign shore
Well to that heart might his these absent greetings pour!

I

The castled crag of Drachenfels [21]
Frowns o'er the wide and winding Rhine,
Whose breast of waters broadly swells
Between the banks which bear the vine,
And hills all rich with blossomed trees,
And fields which promise corn and wine,
And scattered cities crowning these,
Whose far white walls along them shine,
Have strewed a scene, which I should see
With double joy wert *thou* with me.

20 Byron's half-sister Augusta   21 "Dragon Rock." On the right bank of the Rhine between Remagen and Bonn

II

And peasant girls, with deep blue eyes,
And hands which offer early flowers,
Walk smiling o'er this paradise;
Above, the frequent feudal towers
Through green leaves lift their walls of gray;
And many a rock which steeply lowers,
And noble arch in proud decay,
Look o'er this vale of vintage-bowers;
But one thing want these banks of Rhine,—
Thy gentle hand to clasp in mine!

III

I send the lilies given to me;
Though long before thy hand they touch,
I know that they must withered be,
But yet reject them not as such;
For I have cherished them as dear,
Because they yet may meet thine eye,
And guide thy soul to mine even here,
When thou behold'st them drooping nigh,
And know'st them gathered by the Rhine,
And offered from my heart to thine!

IV

The river nobly foams and flows,
The charm of this enchanted ground,
And all its thousand turns disclose
Some fresher beauty varying round:
The haughtiest breast its wish might bound
Through life to dwell delighted here;
Nor could on earth a spot be found
To nature and to me so dear,
Could thy dear eyes in following mine
Still sweeten more these banks of Rhine!

56

By Coblentz, on a rise of gentle ground,
There is a small and simple pyramid,
Crowning the summit of the verdant mound;
Beneath its base are heroes' ashes hid,
Our enemy's—but let not that forbid

Honor to Marceau! [22] o'er whose early tomb
Tears, big tears, gushed from the rough soldier's lid,
Lamenting and yet envying such a doom,
Falling for France, whose rights he battled to resume.

57

Brief, brave, and glorious was his young career,—
His mourners were two hosts, his friends and foes;
And fitly may the stranger lingering here
Pray for his gallant spirit's bright repose;
For he was Freedom's champion, one of those,
The few in number, who had not o'er-stepped
The charter to chastise which she bestows
On such as wield her weapons; he had kept
The whiteness of his soul, and thus men o'er him wept.

58

Here Ehrenbreitstein,[23] with her shattered wall
Black with the miner's blast, upon her height
Yet shows of what she was, when shell and ball
Rebounding idly on her strength did light:
A tower of victory! from whence the flight
Of baffled foes was watched along the plain:
But Peace destroyed what War could never blight,
And laid those proud roofs bare to Summer's rain—
On which the iron shower for years had poured in vain.

59

Adieu to thee, fair Rhine! How long delighted
The stranger fain would linger on his way!
Thine is a scene alike where souls united
Or lonely Contemplation thus might stray;
And could the ceaseless vultures cease to prey
On self-condemning bosoms, it were here,
Where Nature, nor too somber nor too gay,
Wild but not rude, awful yet not austere,
Is to the mellow Earth as Autumn to the year.

60

Adieu to thee again! a vain adieu!
There can be no farewell to scene like thine;

22 young French general   killed in 1796   opposite Coblenz, captured
of the revolutionary armies.   23 a fortress on the Rhine   by the French in 1799

The mind is colored by thy every hue;
And if reluctantly the eyes resign
Their cherished gaze upon thee, lovely Rhine!
'Tis with the thankful heart of parting praise;
More mighty spots may rise, more glaring shine,
But none unite in one attaching maze
The brilliant, fair, and soft,—the glories of old days.

61

The negligently grand, the fruitful bloom
Of coming ripeness, the white city's sheen,
The rolling stream, the precipice's gloom,
The forest's growth, and Gothic walls between,
The wild rocks shaped as they had turrets been,
In mockery of man's art; and these withal
A race of faces happy as the scene,
Whose fertile bounties here extend to all,
Still springing o'er thy banks, though Empires near them fall.

62

But these recede. Above me are the Alps,
The palaces of Nature, whose vast walls
Have pinnacled in clouds their snowy scalps,
And throned Eternity in icy halls
Of cold sublimity, where forms and falls
The avalanche—the thunderbolt of snow!
All that expands the spirit, yet appalls,
Gather around these summits, as to show
How Earth may pierce to Heaven, yet leave vain man below.

63

But ere these matchless heights I dare to scan,
There is a spot should not be passed in vain,—
Morat! [24] the proud, the patriot field! where man
May gaze on ghastly trophies of the slain,
Nor blush for those who conquered on that plain;
Here Burgundy bequeathed his tombless host,
A bony heap, through ages to remain,
Themselves their monument;—the Stygian coast
Unsepulchered they roamed, and shrieked each wandering
      ghost.

24 town where the Swiss defeated Charles the Bold, Duke of Burgundy, in 1476

64

While Waterloo with Cannæ's [25] carnage vies,
Morat and Marathon twin names shall stand;
They were true Glory's stainless victories,
Won by the unambitious heart and hand
Of a proud, brotherly, and civic band,
All unbought champions in no princely cause
Of vice-entailed Corruption; they no land
Doomed to bewail the blasphemy of laws
Making kings' rights divine, by some Draconic [26] clause.

65

By a lone wall a lonelier column rears
A gray and grief-worn aspect of old days;
'Tis the last remnant of the wreck of years,
And looks as with the wild-bewildered gaze
Of one to stone converted by amaze,
Yet still with consciousness; and there it stands
Making a marvel that it not decays,
When the coeval pride of human hands,
Leveled Aventicum,[27] hath strewed her subject lands.

66

And there—oh! sweet and sacred be the name!—
Julia [28]—the daughter, the devoted—gave
Her youth to Heaven; her heart, beneath a claim
Nearest to Heaven's, broke o'er a father's grave.
Justice is sworn 'gainst tears, and hers would crave
The life she lived in; but the judge was just,
And then she died on him she could not save.
Their tomb was simple, and without a bust,
And held within their urn one mind, one heart, one dust.

67

But these are deeds which should not pass away,
And names that must not wither, though the earth
Forgets her empires with a just decay,
The enslavers and the enslaved, their death and birth;

25 where Hannibal defeated the Romans, 216 B. C.
26 severe code of laws, formulated by the Athenian Draco, seventh century B. C.

27 now Avenches, capital of Roman colony of Helvetia
28 young priestess who was said to have died after

trying in vain to save her father, condemned to death for treason

The high, the mountain-majesty of worth
Should be, and shall, survivor of its woe,
And from its immortality look forth
In the sun's face, like yonder Alpine snow,
Imperishably pure beyond all things below.

68

Lake Leman [29] woos me with its crystal face,
The mirror where the stars and mountains view
The stillness of their aspect in each trace
Its clear depth yields of their far height and hue:
There is too much of man here, to look through
With a fit mind the might which I beheld;
But soon in me shall Loneliness renew
Thoughts hid, but not less cherished than of old,
Ere mingling with the herd had penned me in their fold.

69

To fly from, need not be to hate, mankind:
All are not fit with them to stir and toil,
Nor is it discontent to keep the mind
Deep in its fountain, lest it overboil
In the hot throng, where we become the spoil
Of our infection, till too late and long
We may deplore and struggle with the coil,
In wretched interchange of wrong for wrong
Midst a contentious world, striving where none are strong.

70

There, in a moment we may plunge our years
In fatal penitence, and in the blight
Of our own soul turn all our blood to tears,
And color things to come with hues of Night;
The race of life becomes a hopeless flight
To those that walk in darkness: on the sea
The boldest steer but where their ports invite;
But there are wanderers o'er Eternity
Whose bark drives on and on, and anchored ne'er shall be.

71

Is it not better, then, to be alone,
And love Earth only for its earthly sake?

29 the Lake of Geneva

By the blue rushing of the arrowy Rhone,
Or the pure bosom of its nursing lake,
Which feeds it as a mother who doth make
A fair but froward infant her own care,
Kissing its cries away as these awake;—
Is it not better thus our lives to wear,
Than join the crushing crowd, doomed to inflict or bear?

72

I live not in myself, but I become
Portion of that around me; and to me
High mountains are a feeling, but the hum
Of human cities torture: I can see
Nothing to loathe in nature, save to be
A link reluctant in a fleshly chain,
Classed among creatures, when the soul can flee,
And with the sky, the peak, the heaving plain
Of ocean, or the stars, mingle, and not in vain.

73

And thus I am absorbed, and this is life:
I look upon the peopled desert past,
As on a place of agony and strife,
Where, for some sin, to sorrow I was cast,
To act and suffer, but remount at last
With a fresh pinion; which I feel to spring,
Though young, yet waxing vigorous as the blast
Which it would cope with, on delighted wing,
Spurning the clay-cold bonds which round our being cling.

74

And when, at length, the mind shall be all free
From what it hates in this degraded form,
Reft of its carnal life, save what shall be
Existent happier in the fly and worm,—
When elements to elements conform,
And dust is as it should be, shall I not
Feel all I see, less dazzling, but more warm?
The bodiless thought? the Spirit of each spot?
Of which, even now, I share at times the immortal lot?

75

Are not the mountains, waves, and skies, a part
Of me and of my soul, as I of them?

Is not the love of these deep in my heart
With a pure passion? should I not contemn
All objects, if compared with these? and stem
A tide of suffering, rather than forgo
Such feelings for the hard and worldly phlegm
Of those whose eyes are only turned below,
Gazing upon the ground, with thoughts which dare not glow?

76

But this is not my theme; and I return
To that which is immediate, and require
Those who find contemplation in the urn,
To look on One,[30] whose dust was once all fire,
A native of the land where I respire
The clear air for a while—a passing guest,
Where he became a being,—whose desire
Was to be glorious; 'twas a foolish quest,
The which to gain and keep, he sacrificed all rest.

77

Here the self-torturing sophist, wild Rousseau,
The apostle of affliction, he who threw
Enchantment over passion, and from woe
Wrung overwhelming eloquence, first drew
The breath which made him wretched; yet he knew
How to make madness beautiful, and cast
O'er erring deeds and thoughts a heavenly hue
Of words, like sunbeams, dazzling as they passed
The eyes, which o'er them shed tears feelingly and fast.

78

His love was passion's essence:—as a tree
On fire by lightning, with ethereal flame
Kindled he was, and blasted; for to be
Thus, and enamored, were in him the same.
But his was not the love of living dame,
Nor of the dead who rise upon our dreams,
But of ideal Beauty, which became
In him existence, and o'erflowing teems
Along his burning page, distempered though it seems.

[30] Jean-Jacques Rousseau (1712–1778), who was born at Geneva and spent his youth there

79

This breathed itself to life in Julie,[31] *this*
Invested her with all that's wild and sweet;
This hallowed, too, the memorable kiss
Which every morn his fevered lip would greet,
From hers, who but with friendship his would meet;[32]
But to that gentle touch through brain and breast
Flashed the thrilled spirit's love-devouring heat;
In that absorbing sigh perchance more bless'd
Than vulgar minds may be with all they seek possessed.

80

His life was one long war with self-sought foes,
Or friends by him self-banished; for his mind
Had grown Suspicion's sanctuary, and chose,
For its own cruel sacrifice, the kind,
'Gainst whom he raged with fury strange and blind.
But he was frenzied,—wherefore, who may know?
Since cause might be which skill could never find;
But he was frenzied by disease or woe,
To that worst pitch cf all, which wears a reasoning show.

81

For then he was inspired, and from him came,
As from the Pythian's mystic cave[33] of yore,
Those oracles which set the world in flame,
Nor ceased to burn till kingdoms were no more:
Did he not this for France? which lay before
Bowed to the inborn tyranny of years?
Broken and trembling to the yoke she bore,
Till by the voice of him and his compeers
Roused up to too much wrath, which follows o'ergrown fears?

82

They made themselves a fearful monument!
The wreck of old opinions—things which grew,
Breathed from the birth of Time: the veil they rent,

31 heroine of Rousseau's novel *La Nouvelle Héloïse*.
32 "This refers to the account in his *Confessions* of his passion for the Comtesse d'Houdetot, . . . and his long walk every morning, for the sake of the single kiss which was the common salutation of French acquaintance." (Byron)
33 The cave of Pythia, priestess of Apollo's oracle at Delphi.

And what behind it lay, all earth shall view.
But good with ill they also overthrew,
Leaving but ruins, wherewith to rebuild
Upon the same foundation, and renew
Dungeons and thrones, which the same hour refilled,
As heretofore, because ambition was self-willed.

83

But this will not endure, nor be endured!
Mankind have felt their strength, and made it felt.
They might have used it better, but, allured
By their new vigor, sternly have they dealt
On one another; Pity ceased to melt
With her once natural charities. But they,
Who in oppression's darkness caved had dwelt,
They were not eagles, nourished with the day;
What marvel then, at times, if they mistook their prey?

84

What deep wounds ever closed without a scar?
The heart's bleed longest, and but heal to wear
That which disfigures it; and they who war
With their own hopes, and have been vanquished, bear
Silence, but not submission: in his lair
Fixed Passion holds his breath, until the hour
Which shall atone for years; none need despair:
It came, it cometh, and will come,—the power
To punish or forgive—in *one* we shall be slower.

85

Clear, placid Leman! thy contrasted lake,
With the wild world I dwelt in, is a thing
Which warns me, with its stillness, to forsake
Earth's troubled waters for a purer spring.
This quiet sail is as a noiseless wing
To waft me from distraction; once I loved
Torn ocean's roar, but thy soft murmuring
Sounds sweet as if a Sister's voice reproved,
That I with stern delights should e'er have been so moved.

86

It is the hush of night, and all between
Thy margin and the mountains, dusk, yet clear,

Mellowed and mingling, yet distinctly seen,
Save darkened Jura, whose capped heights appear
Precipitously steep; and drawing near,
There breathes a living fragrance from the shore,
Of flowers yet fresh with childhood; on the ear
Drops the light drip of the suspended oar,
Or chirps the grasshopper one good-night carol more.

87

He is an evening reveler, who makes
His life an infancy, and sings his fill;
At intervals, some bird from out the brakes
Starts into voice a moment, then is still.
There seems a floating whisper on the hill,
But that is fancy, for the starlight dews
All silently their tears of love instill,
Weeping themselves away, till they infuse
Deep into Nature's breast the spirit of her hues.

88

Ye stars! which are the poetry of heaven!
If in your bright leaves we would read the fate
Of men and empires,—'tis to be forgiven,
That in our aspirations to be great,
Our destinies o'erleap their mortal state,
And claim a kindred with you; for ye are
A beauty and a mystery, and create
In us such love and reverence from afar,
That fortune, fame, power, life, have named themselves a star.

89

All heaven and earth are still—though not in sleep,
But breathless, as we grow when feeling most;
And silent, as we stand in thoughts too deep:—
All heaven and earth are still: From the high host
Of stars, to the lulled lake and mountain-coast,
All is concentered in a life intense,
Where not a beam, nor air, nor leaf is lost,
But hath a part of being, and a sense
Of that which is of all Creator and defense.

90

Then stirs the feeling infinite, so felt
In solitude, where we are *least* alone;

A truth, which through our being then doth melt,
And purifies from self: it is a tone,
The soul and source of music, which makes known
Eternal harmony, and sheds a charm
Like to the fabled Cytherea's zone,[34]
Binding all things with beauty;—'twould disarm
The specter Death, had he substantial power to harm.

91

Not vainly did the early Persian make
His altar the high places, and the peak
Of earth-o'ergazing mountains, and thus take
A fit and unwalled temple, there to seek
The Spirit, in whose honor shrines are weak,
Upreared of human hands. Come, and compare
Columns and idol-dwellings, Goth or Greek,
With Nature's realms of worship, earth and air,
Nor fix on fond abodes to circumscribe thy prayer!

92

The sky is changed!—and such a change! Oh night,
And storm, and darkness, ye are wondrous strong,
Yet lovely in your strength, as is the light
Of a dark eye in woman! Far along,
From peak to peak, the rattling crags among
Leaps the live thunder! Not from one lone cloud,
But every mountain now hath found a tongue,
And Jura answers, through her misty shroud,
Back to the joyous Alps, who call to her aloud!

93

And this is in the night:—Most glorious night!
Thou wert not sent for slumber! let me be
A sharer in thy fierce and far delight,—
A portion of the tempest and of thee!
How the lit lake shines, a phosphoric sea,
And the big rain comes dancing to the earth!
And now again 'tis black,—and now, the glee
Of the loud hills shakes with its mountain-mirth,
As if they did rejoice o'er a young earthquake's birth.

34 the girdle of Venus, which attracted love to its wearer

94

Now, where the swift Rhone cleaves his way between
Heights which appear as lovers who have parted
In hate, whose mining depths so intervene
That they can meet no more, though broken-hearted;
Though in their souls, which thus each other thwarted,
Love was the very root of the fond rage
Which blighted their life's bloom, and then departed:
Itself expired, but leaving them an age
Of years all winters,—war within themselves to wage.

95

Now, where the quick Rhone thus hath cleft his way,
The mightiest of the storms hath ta'en his stand:
For here, not one, but many, make their play,
And fling their thunder-bolts from hand to hand,
Flashing and cast around; of all the band,
The brightest through these parted hills hath forked
His lightnings,—as if he did understand,
That in such gaps as desolation worked,
There the hot shaft should blast whatever therein lurked.

96

Sky, mountains, river, winds, lake, lightnings! ye!
With night, and clouds, and thunder, and a soul
To make these felt and feeling, well may be
Things that have made me watchful; the far roll
Of your departing voices, is the knoll
Of what in me is sleepless,—if I rest.
But where of ye, O tempests! is the goal?
Are ye like those within the human breast?
Or do ye find, at length, like eagles, some high nest?

97

Could I embody and unbosom now
That which is most within me,—could I wreak
My thoughts upon expression, and thus throw
Soul, heart, mind, passions, feelings, strong or weak,
All that I would have sought, and all I seek,
Bear, know, feel, and yet breathe—into *one* word,
And that one word were Lightning, I would speak;

But as it is, I live and die unheard,
With a most voiceless thought, sheathing it as a sword.

98

The morn is up again, the dewy morn,
With breath all incense, and with cheek all bloom,
Laughing the clouds away with playful scorn,
And living as if earth contained no tomb,—
And glowing into day: we may resume
The march of our existence: and thus I,
Still on thy shores, fair Leman! may find room
And food for meditation, nor pass by
Much, that may give us pause, if pondered fittingly.

99

Clarens! [35] sweet Clarens, birthplace of deep Love!
Thine air is the young breath of passionate thought;
Thy trees take root in Love; the snows above,
The very glaciers have his colors caught,
And sun-set into rose-hues sees them wrought
By rays which sleep there lovingly: the rocks,
The permanent crags, tell here of Love, who sought
In them a refuge from the worldly shocks,
Which stir and sting the soul with hope that woos, then mocks.

100

Clarens! by heavenly feet thy paths are trod,—
Undying Love's, who here ascends a throne
To which the steps are mountains; where the god
Is a pervading life and light,—so shown
Not on those summits solely, nor alone
In the still cave and forest; o'er the flower
His eye is sparkling, and his breath hath blown,
His soft and summer breath, whose tender power
Passes the strength of storms in their most desolate hour.

101

All things are here of *him;* from the black pines,
Which are his shade on high, and the loud roar
Of torrents, where he listeneth, to the vines

35 village on Lake Geneva, the scene of meetings of the lovers in Rousseau's *La Nouvelle Héloïse*

Which slope his green path downward to the shore,
Where the bowed waters meet him, and adore,
Kissing his feet with murmurs; and the wood,
The covert of old trees, with trunks all hoar,
But light leaves, young as joy, stands where it stood,
Offering to him, and his, a populous solitude.

102

A populous solitude of bees and birds
And fairy-formed and many-colored things,
Who worship him with notes more sweet than words,
And innocently open their glad wings,
Fearless and full of life: the gush of springs,
And fall of lofty fountains, and the bend
Of stirring branches, and the bud which brings
The swiftest thought of beauty, here extend,
Mingling, and made by Love, unto one mighty end.

103

He who hath loved not, here would learn that lore,
And make his heart a spirit; he who knows
That tender mystery, will love the more;
For this is Love's recess, where vain men's woes,
And the world's waste, have driven him far from those,
For 'tis his nature to advance or die;
He stands not still, but or decays, or grows
Into a boundless blessing, which may vie
With the immortal lights, in its eternity!

104

'Twas not for fiction chose Rousseau this spot,
Peopling it with affections; but he found
It was the scene which Passion must allot
To the mind's purified beings; 'twas the ground
Where early Love his Psyche's zone unbound,
And hallowed it with loveliness: 'tis lone,
And wonderful, and deep, and hath a sound,
And sense, and sight of sweetness; here the Rhone
Hath spread himself a couch, the Alps have reared a throne.

105

Lausanne! and Ferney! [36] ye have been the abodes
Of names which unto you bequeathed a name;

36 residences respectively of Gibbon and of Voltaire

Mortals, who sought and found, by dangerous roads,
A path to perpetuity of fame:
They were gigantic minds, and their steep aim
Was, Titan-like, on daring doubts to pile
Thoughts which should call down thunder, and the flame
Of Heaven again assailed, if Heaven the while
On man and man's research could deign do more than smile.

106

The one [37] was fire and fickleness, a child
Most mutable in wishes, but in mind
A wit as various,—gay, grave, sage, or wild,—
Historian, bard, philosopher, combined;
He multiplied himself among mankind,
The Proteus of their talents: But his own
Breathed most in ridicule,—which, as the wind,
Blew where it listed, laying all things prone,—
Now to o'erthrow a fool, and now to shake a throne.

107

The other, deep and slow, exhausting thought,
And hiving wisdom with each studious year,
In meditation dwelt, with learning wrought,
And shaped his weapon with an edge severe,
Sapping a solemn creed with solemn sneer;
The lord of irony,—that master-spell,
Which stung his foes to wrath, which grew from fear,
And doomed him to the zealot's ready Hell,
Which answers to all doubts so eloquently well.

108

Yet, peace be with their ashes,—for by them,
If merited, the penalty is paid;
It is not ours to judge,—far less condemn;
The hour must come when such things shall be made
Known unto all, or hope and dread allayed
By slumber, on one pillow, in the dust,
Which, thus much we are sure, must lie decayed;
And when it shall revive, as is our trust,
'Twill be to be forgiven, or suffer what is just.

109

But let me quit man's works, again to read
His Maker's, spread around me, and suspend

37 Voltaire. The "other" (Stanza 107) is Gibbon.

This page, which from my reveries I feed,
Until it seems prolonging without end.
The clouds above me to the white Alps tend,
And I must pierce them, and survey whate'er
May be permitted, as my steps I bend
To their most great and growing region, where
The earth to her embrace compels the powers of air.

110

Italia, too! Italia! looking on thee,
Full flashes on the soul the light of ages,
Since the fierce Carthaginian almost won thee,
To the last halo of the chiefs and sages
Who glorify thy consecrated pages;
Thou wert the throne and grave of empires; still,
The fount at which the panting mind assuages
Her thirst of knowledge, quaffing there her fill,
Flows from the eternal source of Rome's imperial hill.

111

Thus far have I proceeded in a theme
Renewed with no kind auspices:—to feel
We are not what we have been and to deem
We are not what we should be, and to steel
The heart against itself; and to conceal,
With a proud caution, love, or hate, or aught,—
Passion or feeling, purpose, grief, or zeal,—
Which is the tyrant spirit of our thought,
Is a stern task of soul:—No matter,—it is taught.

112

And for these words, thus woven into song,
It may be that they are a harmless wile,—
The coloring of the scenes which fleet along,
Which I would seize, in passing, to beguile
My breast, or that of others, for a while.
Fame is the thirst of youth, but I am not
So young as to regard men's frown or smile,
As loss or guerdon of a glorious lot;
I stood and stand alone,—remembered or forgot.

113

I have not loved the world, nor the world me;
I have not flattered its rank breath, nor bowed
To its idolatries a patient knee,
Nor coined my cheek to smiles, nor cried aloud
In worship of an echo; in the crowd
They could not deem me one of such; I stood
Among them, but not of them; in a shroud
Of thoughts which were not their thoughts, and still could,
Had I not filed [38] my mind, which thus itself subdued.

114

I have not loved the world, nor the world me,—
But let us part fair foes; I do believe,
Though I have found them not, that there may be
Words which are things, hopes which will not deceive,
And virtues which are merciful, nor weave
Snares for the failing; I would also deem
O'er others' griefs that some sincerely grieve;
That two, or one, are almost what they seem,
That goodness is no name, and happiness no dream.

115

My daughter! with thy name this song begun;
My daughter! with thy name thus much shall end;
I see thee not, I hear thee not, but none
Can be so wrapped in thee; thou art the friend
To whom the shadows of far years extend:
Albeit my brow thou never shouldst behold,
My voice shall with thy future visions blend,
And reach into thy heart, when mine is cold,
A token and a tone, even from thy father's mold.

116

To aid thy mind's development, to watch
Thy dawn of little joys, to sit and see
Almost thy very growth, to view thee catch
Knowledge of objects,—wonders yet to thee!
To hold thee lightly on a gentle knee,
And print on thy soft cheek a parent's kiss,—
This, it should seem, was not reserved for me; [39]

38 defiled
39 Byron never saw his daughter after she was a few weeks old.

Yet this was in my nature: as it is,
I know not what is there, yet something like to this.

117

Yet, though dull Hate as duty should be taught,
I know that thou wilt love me; though my name
Should be shut from thee, as a spell still fraught
With desolation, and a broken claim:
Though the grave closed between us,—'twere the same,
I know that thou wilt love me; though to drain
My blood from out thy being were an aim,
And an attainment,—all would be in vain,—
Still thou wouldst love me, still that more than life retain.

118

The child of love, though born in bitterness,
And nurtured in convulsion. Of thy sire
These were the elements, and thine no less.
As yet such are around thee, but thy fire
Shall be more tempered, and thy hope far higher.
Sweet be thy cradled slumbers! O'er the sea
And from the mountains where I now respire,
Fain would I waft such blessing upon thee,
As, with a sigh, I deem thou might'st have been to me.

SONNET ON CHILLON [40]

ETERNAL Spirit of the chainless Mind!
Brightest in dungeons, Liberty! thou art,
For there thy habitation is the heart—
The heart which love of thee alone can bind;
And when thy sons to fetters are consigned—
To fetters, and the damp vault's dayless gloom,
Their country conquers with their martyrdom,
And Freedom's fame finds wings on every wind.
Chillon! thy prison is a holy place,
And thy sad floor an altar—for 'twas trod,
Until his very steps have left a trace
Worn, as if thy cold pavement were a sod,
By Bonnivard! May none those marks efface!
For they appeal from tyranny to God.

[40] A castle at the eastern end of Lake Geneva, where was imprisoned from 1530 to 1536 François de Bonnivard for his efforts to free Geneva from the rule of the Duke of Savoy. Byron's poems, written after a visit to the castle in 1816, are largely imaginary.

STANZAS TO AUGUSTA [41]

THOUGH the day of my destiny's over,
    And the star of my fate hath declined,
Thy soft heart refused to discover
    The faults which so many could find.
Though thy soul with my grief was acquainted,
    It shrunk not to share it with me,
And the love which my spirit hath painted
    It never hath found but in *thee*.

Then when nature around me is smiling,
    The last smile which answers to mine,
I do not believe it beguiling,   10
    Because it reminds me of thine;
And when winds are at war with the ocean,
    As thy breasts I believed in with me,
If their billows excite an emotion,
    It is that they bear me from *thee*.

Though the rock of my last hope is shivered,
    And its fragments are sunk in the wave,
Though I feel that my soul is delivered
    To pain—it shall not be its slave.   20
There is many a pang to pursue me:
    They may crush, but they shall not contemn;
They may torture, but shall not subdue me;
    'Tis of *thee* that I think—not of them.

Though human, thou didst not deceive me,
    Though woman, thou didst not forsake,
Though loved, thou forborest to grieve me,
    Though slandered, thou never couldst shake;
Though trusted, thou didst not disclaim me,
    Though parted, it was not to fly,   30
Though watchful, 'twas not to defame me,
    Nor, mute, that the world might belie.

Yet I blame not the world, nor despise it,
    Nor the war of the many with one;
If my soul was not fitted to prize it,
    'Twas folly not sooner to shun:
And if dearly that error hath cost me,
    And more than I once could foresee,
I have found, that whatever it lost me,
    It could not deprive me of *thee*.   40

[41] Byron's beloved half-sister

From the wreck of the past, which hath perished,
　Thus much I at least may recall,
It hath taught me that what I most cherished
　Deserved to be dearest of all:
In the desert a fountain is springing,
　In the wide waste there still is a tree,
And a bird in the solitude singing,
　Which speaks to my spirit of *thee*.

TO THOMAS MOORE [42]

My boat is on the shore,
　And my bark is on the sea;
But, before I go, Tom Moore,
　Here's a double health to thee!

Here's a sigh to those who love me,
　And a smile to those who hate;
And, whatever sky's above me,
　Here's a heart for every fate.

Though the Ocean roar around me,
　Yet it still shall bear me on;
Though a desert should surround me,   10
　It hath springs that may be won.

Were't the last drop in the well,
　As I gasped upon the brink,
Ere my fainting spirit fell,
　'Tis to thee that I would drink.

With that water, as this wine,
　The libation I would pour
Should be—peace with thine and mine,
　And a health to thee, Tom Moore.   20

SO WE'LL GO NO MORE A-ROVING

So we'll go no more a-roving
　So late into the night,
Though the heart be still as loving,
　And the moon be still as bright.

[42] the Irish poet, 1779–1852, one of Byron's dearest friends

For the sword outwears its sheath,
    And the soul wears out the breast,
And the heart must pause to breathe,
    And love itself have rest.

Though the night was made for loving,
    And the day returns too soon,
Yet we'll go no more a-roving
    By the light of the moon.

DON JUAN

Byron took the name and general reputation of his hero from Spanish legend; the rest is all his own invention. In a loosely constructed narrative, he first describes a youthful intrigue of his hero in Spain; then takes him through various adventures and escapades in the eastern Mediterranean, in Turkey, in Russia, and in England; with more to follow after the sixteen cantos completed. There are narrative sections, stanzas of lofty sentiment, lyric passages; but the poem constantly wanders into digressions, turns aside persistently for satire on the society, politics, and literature of the time, and often drops unexpectedly from grandeur to burlesque. He wrote his publisher Murray, "It is . . . meant to be a little quietly facetious upon every thing . . . : a playful satire, with as little poetry as could be helped." He also wrote, "I doubt whether it is not . . . too free for these very modest days." His own estimate is a good one, except that he depreciates the quality of his poetry. But perhaps the work chiefly commends itself to modern readers for its variety, its audacity, its clever resourcefulness, and its sustained wit. Characteristically, it presents the disillusioned Byron of the mature years, making fun of what serious folk hold sacred.

In Canto II, the hero, sent away from Spain by his mother after the scandal of his affair with Julia, a married lady, suffers shipwreck, and is cast upon one of the Cyclades, where he is tended by Haidée, daughter of old Lambro, a pirate and slave-merchant, who happens to be absent on one of his expeditions. Canto III, up to the lyric "The Isles of Greece," continues the story of their passionate love. The passages here reprinted from Cantos III and IV give a fair idea of the variety of the complete work.

CANTO III

THE ISLES OF GREECE

I

THE isles of Greece, the isles of Greece!
    Where burning Sappho loved and sung,
Where grew the arts of war and peace,
    Where Delos [43] rose, and Phœbus sprung!

43 island, reputed birthplace of Phœbus Apollo, said to have risen in the Ægean Sea

Eternal summer gilds them yet,
But all, except their sun, is set.

II

The Scian and the Teian muse,[44]
    The hero's harp, the lover's lute,
Have found the fame your shores refuse:
    Their place of birth alone is mute
To sounds which echo further west
Than your sires' "Islands of the Blest." [45]

III

The mountains look on Marathon— [46]
    And Marathon looks on the sea;
And musing there an hour alone,
    I dreamed that Greece might still be free;
For standing on the Persians' grave,
I could not deem myself a slave.

IV

A king sat on the rocky brow
    Which looks o'er sea-born Salamis;
And ships, by thousands, lay below,
    And men in nations;—all were his!
He counted them at break of day—
And when the sun set where were they?

V

And where are they? and where art thou,
    My country? On thy voiceless shore
The heroic lay is tuneless now—
    The heroic bosom beats no more!
And must thy lyre, so long divine,
Degenerate into hands like mine?

VI

'Tis something in the dearth of fame,
    Though linked among a fettered race,

44 Homer and Anacreon respectively, from reputed birthplaces: island of Scio, and Teos, Asia Minor
45 abode of the blest after death; situated, according to Greek story, in the far Atlantic
46 references, in Stanzas III and IV, to the great battles in which the Greeks defeated the Persians, 490 and 480 B. C., the latter while King Xerxes of Persia looked on; in Stanza VII, to the heroic exploit of Leonidas and his Spartans, 480 B. C.

To feel at least a patriot's shame,
    Even as I sing, suffuse my face;
For what is left the poet here?
For Greeks a blush—for Greece a tear.

VII

Must *we* but weep o'er days more blest?
    Must *we* but blush?—Our fathers bled.
Earth! render back from out thy breast
    A remnant of our Spartan dead!
Of the three hundred grant but three,
To make a new Thermopylæ!

VIII

What, silent still? and silent all?
    Ah! no;—the voices of the dead
Sound like a distant torrent's fall,
    And answer, "Let one living head,
But one arise,—we come, we come!"
'Tis but the living who are dumb.

IX

In vain—in vain: strike other chords;
    Fill high the cup with Samian wine!
Leave battles to the Turkish hordes,
    And shed the blood of Scio's vine!
Hark! rising to the ignoble call—
How answers each bold Bacchanal!

X

You have the Pyrrhic dance as yet;
    Where is the Pyrrhic phalanx gone? [47]
Of two such lessons, why forget
    The nobler and the manlier one?
You have the letters Cadmus [48] gave—
Think ye he meant them for a slave?

XI

Fill high the bowl with Samian wine!
    We will not think of themes like these!

[47] The Greek war-dance flourishes still, but not the famous battle formation (devised by King Pyrrhus of Epirus third century B. C.).

[48] reputed inventor of the alphabet

It made Anacreon's song divine:
  He served—but served Polycrates— [49]
A tyrant; but our masters then
Were still, at least, our countrymen.

XII

The tyrant of the Chersonese
  Was freedom's best and bravest friend;
That tyrant was Miltiades! [50]
  Oh! that the present hour would lend
Another despot of the kind!
Such chains as his were sure to bind.

XIII

Fill high the bowl with Samian wine!
  On Suli's rock, and Parga's shore, [51]
Exists the remnant of a line
  Such as the Doric mothers bore;
And there, perhaps, some seed is sown,
The Heracleidan [52] blood might own.

XIV

Trust not for freedom to the Franks—
  They have a king who buys and sells;
In native swords, and native ranks,
  The only hope of courage dwells:
But Turkish force, and Latin fraud,
Would break your shield, however broad.

XV

Fill high the bowl with Samian wine!
  Our virgins dance beneath the shade—
I see their glorious black eyes shine;
  But gazing on each glowing maid,
My own the burning tear-drop laves,
To think such breasts must suckle slaves.

XVI

Place me on Sunium's marbled steep, [53]
  Where nothing, save the waves and I,

49 ruler of island of
Samos, patron of Anacreon,
poet of love and wine (fifth
century B. C.)

50 commander at Mara-
thon
51 in Albania
52 of Hercules

53 Cape Colonna, south-
ernmost point of Attica

May hear our mutual murmurs sweep;
    There, swan-like, let me sing and die:
A land of slaves shall ne'er be mine—
Dash down yon cup of Samian wine!

87

Thus sung, or would, or could, or should have sung,
    The modern Greek, in tolerable verse;
If not like Orpheus quite, when Greece was young,
    Yet in these times he might have done much worse:
His strain displayed some feeling—right or wrong;
    And feeling, in a poet, is the source
Of others' feeling; but they are such liars,
And take all colors—like the hands of dyers.

88

But words are things, and a small drop of ink,
    Falling like dew, upon a thought, produces
That which makes thousands, perhaps millions, think;
    'Tis strange, the shortest letter which man uses
Instead of speech, may form a lasting link
    Of ages; to what straits old Time reduces
Frail man, when paper—even a rag like this,
Survives himself, his tomb, and all that's his!

89

And when his bones are dust, his grave a blank,
    His station, generation, even his nation,
Become a thing, or nothing, save to rank
    In chronological commemoration,
Some dull MS. oblivion long has sank,
    Or graven stone found in a barrack's station
In digging the foundation of a closet,
May turn his name up, as a rare deposit.

90

And glory long has made the sages smile;
    'Tis something, nothing, words, illusion, wind—
Depending more upon the historian's style
    Than on the name a person leaves behind:
Troy owes to Homer what whist owes to Hoyle: [54]

54 Edmund Hoyle (1672-1769), writer of famous book on card and other games

The present century was growing blind
To the great Marlborough's [55] skill in giving knocks,
Until his late Life by Archdeacon Coxe.

91

Milton's the prince of poets—so we say;
  A little heavy, but no less divine:
An independent being in his day—
  Learned, pious, temperate in love and wine;
But his life falling into Johnson's way,[56]
  We're told this great high priest of all the Nine
Was whipped at college—a harsh sire—odd spouse,
For the first Mrs. Milton left his house.

92

All these are, *certes*, entertaining facts,
  Like Shakespeare's stealing deer, Lord Bacon's bribes;
Like Titus' youth, and Cæsar's earliest acts;
  Like Burns (whom Doctor Currie well describes);
Like Cromwell's pranks;—but although truth exacts
  These amiable descriptions from the scribes,
As most essential to their hero's story,
They do not much contribute to his glory.

93

All are not moralists, like Southey, when
  He prated to the world of "Pantisocrasy"; [57]
Or Wordsworth unexcised,[58] unhired, who then
  Seasoned his peddler poems with democracy;
Or Coleridge, long before his flighty pen
  Lent to the Morning Post its aristocracy;
When he and Southey, following the same path,
Espoused two partners (milliners of Bath).

94

Such names at present cut a convict figure,
  The very Botany Bay [59] in moral geography;
Their loyal treason, renegado rigor,

55 English general, victor of Blenheim (1704)
56 in his *Lives of the Poets*
57 ideal community planned by Coleridge and Southey (see sketch of Coleridge)
58 before he had accepted his government position as distributor of stamps (1812)
59 English penal colony in New South Wales, Australia

Are good manure for their more bare biography;
Wordsworth's last quarto, by the way, is bigger
    Than any since the birthday of typography;
A drowsy, frowzy poem, called the "Excursion,"
Writ in a manner which is my aversion.

95

He there builds up a formidable dike
    Between his own and others' intellect;
But Wordsworth's poem, and his followers, like
    Joanna Southcote's Shiloh [60] and her sect,
Are things which in this century don't strike
    The public mind,—so few are the elect;
And the new births of both their stale virginities
Have proved but dropsies, taken for divinities.

96

But let me to my story: I must own,
    If I have any fault, it is digression,
Leaving my people to proceed alone,
    While I soliloquize beyond expression:
But these are my addresses from the throne,
    Which put off business to the ensuing session:
Forgetting each omission is a loss to
The world, not quite so great as Ariosto.

97

I know that what our neighbors call *"longueurs,"* [61]
    (We've not so good a *word*, but have the *thing*,
In that complete perfection which insures
    An epic from Bob Southey every spring—)
Form not the true temptation which allures
    The reader; but 'twould not be hard to bring
Some fine examples of the *epopée,*[62]
To prove its grand ingredient is *ennui.*

98

We learn from Horace, "Homer sometimes sleeps";
    We feel without him, Wordsworth sometimes wakes,—

---

60 She had predicted the birth to her of the second   Messiah, but instead died of dropsy (1814).   61 tediousness
62 epic

To show with what complacency he creeps,
  With his dear *"Wagoners,"* around his lakes.
He wishes for "a boat" to sail the deeps—
  Of ocean?—No, of air; and then he makes
Another outcry for "a little boat,"
And drivels seas to set it well afloat.

99

If he must fain sweep o'er the ethereal plain,
  And Pegasus runs restive in his "Wagon,"
Could he not beg the loan of Charles's Wain? [63]
  Or pray Medea for a single dragon?
Or if, too classic for his vulgar brain,
  He feared his neck to venture such a nag on,
And he must needs mount nearer to the moon,
Could not the blockhead ask for a balloon?

100

"Peddlers," and "Boats," and "Wagons!" Oh! ye shades
  Of Pope and Dryden, are we come to this?
That trash of such sort not alone evades
  Contempt, but from the bathos' vast abyss
Floats scumlike uppermost, and these Jack Cades
  Of sense and song above your graves may hiss—
The "little boatman" and his "Peter Bell"
Can sneer at him who drew "Achitophel!"

101

T' our tale.—The feast was over, the slaves gone,
  The dwarfs and dancing girls had all retired;
The Arab lore and poet's song were done,
  And every sound of revelry expired,
The lady and her lover, left alone,
  The rosy flood of twilight's sky admired;—
Ave Maria! o'er the earth and sea,
That heavenliest hour of Heaven is worthiest thee!

102

Ave Maria! blessèd be the hour!   ✓
The time, the clime, the spot, where I so oft

---

[63] Constellation, also known as the Great Bear and the Great Dipper

Have felt that moment in its fullest power
  Sink o'er the earth so beautiful and soft,
While swung the deep bell in the distant tower,
  Or the faint dying day-hymn stole aloft,
And not a breath crept through the rosy air,
And yet the forest leaves seemed stirred with prayer.

103

Ave Maria, 'tis the hour of prayer!
  Ave Maria! 'tis the hour of love!
Ave Maria! may our spirits dare
  Look up to thine and to thy Son's above!
Ave Maria! oh that face so fair!
  Those downcast eyes beneath the Almighty Dove—
What though 'tis but a pictured image?—strike—
That painting is no idol,—'tis too like.

104

Some kinder casuists are pleased to say,
  In nameless print—that I have no devotion;
But set those persons down with me to pray,
  And you shall see who has the properest notion
Of getting into heaven the shortest way;
  My altars are the mountains and the ocean,
Earth, air, stars,—all that springs from the great Whole,
Who hath produced, and will receive the soul.

105

Sweet hour of twilight!—in the solitude
  Of the pine forest, and the silent shore
Which bounds Ravenna's immemorial wood,
  Rooted where once the Adrian wave flowed o'er,
To where the last Cæsarean fortress stood,
  Evergreen forest! which Boccaccio's lore
And Dryden's lay [64] made haunted ground to me,
How have I loved the twilight hour and thee!

106

The shrill cicalas, people of the pine,
  Making their summer lives one ceaseless song,

---

[64] Dryden's poem, *Theodore and Honoria*, based upon a tale in Boccaccio's *Decameron*

Were the sole echoes, save my steed's and mine,
 And vesper bell's that rose the boughs along;
The specter huntsman of Onesti's [65] line,
 His hell-dogs, and their chase, and the fair throng
Which learned from this example not to fly
From a true lover,—shadowed my mind's eye.

107

Oh, Hesperus! thou bringest all good things—
 Home to the weary, to the hungry cheer,
To the young bird the parent's brooding wings,
 The welcome stall to the o'erlabored steer;
Whate'er of peace about our hearthstone clings,
 Whate'er our household gods protect of dear,
Are gathered round us by thy look of rest;
Thou bring'st the child, too, to the mother's breast.

108

Soft hour! which wakes the wish and melts the heart
 Of those who sail the seas, on the first day
When they from their sweet friends are torn apart;
 Or fills with love the pilgrim on his way
As the far bell of vesper makes him start,
 Seeming to weep the dying day's decay;
Is this a fancy which our reason scorns?
Ah! surely nothing dies but something mourns!

109

When Nero perished by the justest doom
 Which ever the destroyer yet destroyed,
Amidst the roar of liberated Rome,
 Of nations freed, and the world overjoyed,
Some hands unseen strewed flowers upon his tomb:
 Perhaps the weakness of a heart not void
Of feeling for some kindness done, when Power
Had left the wretch an uncorrupted hour.

110

But I'm digressing; what on earth has Nero,
 Or any such like sovereign buffoons,
To do with the transactions of my hero,

65 In Boccaccio's tale, he haunts the girl who had spurned his love.

More than such madmen's fellow man—the moon's?
Sure my invention must be down at zero,
    And I grown one of many "Wooden Spoons"
Of verse, (the name with which we Cantabs [66] please
To dub the last of honors in degrees).

III

I feel this tediousness will never do—
    'Tis being *too* epic, and I must cut down
(In copying) this long canto into two;
    They'll never find it out, unless I own
The fact, excepting some experienced few;
    And then as an improvement 'twill be shown:
I'll prove that such the opinion of the critic is
From Aristotle *passim.*—See ΠΟΙΗΤΙΚΗΣ.[67]

CANTO IV

I

Nothing so difficult as a beginning
    In poesy, unless perhaps the end;
For oftentimes when Pegasus seems winning
    The race, he sprains a wing, and down we tend,
Like Lucifer when hurled from Heaven for sinning;
    Our sin the same, and hard as his to mend,
Being Pride, which leads the mind to soar too far,
Till our own weakness shows us what we are.

2

But Time, which brings all beings to their level,
    And sharp Adversity, will teach at last
Man,—and, as we would hope,—perhaps the Devil,
    That neither of their intellects are vast:
While Youth's hot wishes in our red veins revel,
    We know not this—the blood flows on too fast;
But as the torrent widens towards the ocean,
We ponder deeply on each past emotion.

3

As boy, I thought myself a clever fellow,
    And wished that others held the same opinion;

---

66 those from Cambridge University   67 Aristotle's celebrated *Poetics*

They took it up when my days grew more mellow,
    And other minds acknowledged my dominion:
Now my sere Fancy "falls into the yellow
    Leaf," and Imagination droops her pinion,
And the sad truth which hovers o'er my desk
Turns what was once romantic to burlesque.

4

And if I laugh at any mortal thing,
    'Tis that I may not weep; and if I weep,
'Tis that our nature cannot always bring
    Itself to apathy, for we must steep
Our hearts first in the depths of Lethe's spring,
    Ere what we least wish to behold will sleep:
Thetis baptized her mortal son [68] in Styx;
A mortal mother would on Lethe [69] fix.

5

Some have accused me of a strange design
    Against the creed and morals of the land,
And trace it in this poem every line:
    I don't pretend that I quite understand
My own meaning when I would be *very* fine;
    But the fact is that I have nothing planned,
Unless it were to be a moment merry—
A novel word in my vocabulary.

6

To the kind reader of our sober clime
    This way of writing will appear exotic;
Pulci [70] was sire of the half-serious rhyme,
    Who sang when chivalry was more quixotic,
And reveled in the fancies of the time,
    True knights, chaste dames, huge giants, kings despotic;
But all these, save the last, being obsolete,
I chose a modern subject as more meet.

7

How I have treated it, I do not know;
    Perhaps no better than *they* have treated me,

---

68 Achilles (to make him invulnerable)
69 the river of Hades

giving forgetfulness
70 Italian poet of the fifteenth century, who wrote

a burlesque epic, *Il Morgante Maggiore*

Who have imputed such designs as show
    Not what they saw, but what they wished to see:
But if it gives them pleasure, be it so;
    This is a liberal age, and thoughts are free:
Meantime Apollo plucks me by the ear,
And tells me to resume my story here.

8

Young Juan and his lady-love were left
    To their own hearts' most sweet society;
Even Time the pitiless in sorrow cleft
    With his rude scythe such gentle bosoms; he
Sighed to behold them of their hours bereft,
    Though foe to Love; and yet they could not be
Meant to grow old, but die in happy spring,
Before one charm or hope had taken wing.

9

Their faces were not made for wrinkles, their
    Pure blood to stagnate, their great hearts to fail;
The blank gray was not made to blast their hair,
    But like the climes that know nor snow nor hail,
They were all summer; lightning might assail
    And shiver them to ashes, but to trail
A long and snake-like life to dull decay
Was not for them—they had too little clay.

10

They were alone once more; for them to be
    Thus was another Eden; they were never
Weary, unless when separate; the tree
    Cut from its forest root of years—the river
Dammed from its fountain—the child from the knee
    And breast maternal weaned at once for ever,—
Would wither less than these two torn apart;
Alas! there is no instinct like the heart—

11

The heart—which may be broken: happy they!
    Thrice fortunate! who of that fragile mold,
The precious porcelain of human clay,
    Break with the first fall: they can ne'er behold

The long year linked with heavy day on day,
  And all which must be borne, and never told;
While Life's strange principle will often lie
Deepest in those who long the most to die.

12

"Whom the gods love die young" was said of yore,
  And many deaths do they escape by this:
The death of friends, and that which slays even more—
  The death of friendship, love, youth, all that is,
Except mere breath; and since the silent shore
  Awaits at last even those who longest miss
The old archer's shafts, perhaps the early grave
Which men weep over may be meant to save.

13

Haidée and Juan thought not of the dead.
  The heavens, and earth, and air, seemed made for them:
They found no fault with Time, save that he fled;
  They saw not in themselves aught to condemn;
Each was the other's mirror, and but read
  Joy sparkling in their dark eyes like a gem,
And knew such brightness was but the reflection
Of their exchanging glances of affection.

14

The gentle pressure, and the thrilling touch,
  The least glance better understood than words,
Which still said all, and ne'er could say too much;
  A language, too, but like to that of birds,
Known but to them, at least appearing such
  As but to lovers a true sense affords;
Sweet playful phrases, which would seem absurd
To those who have ceased to hear such, or ne'er heard.

15

All these were theirs, for they were children still,
  And children still they should have ever been;
They were not made in the real world to fill
  A busy character in the dull scene,
But like two beings born from out a rill,
  A nymph and her belovèd, all unseen

To pass their lives in fountains and on flowers,
And never know the weight of human hours.

16

Moons changing had rolled on, and changeless found
   Those their bright rise had lighted to such joys
As rarely they beheld throughout their round;
   And these were not of the vain kind which cloys,
For theirs were buoyant spirits, never bound
   By the mere senses; and that which destroys
Most love, possession, unto them appeared
A thing which each endearment more endeared.

17

O beautiful! and rare as beautiful!
   But theirs was love in which the mind delights
To lose itself, when the old world grows dull,
   And we are sick of its hack sounds and sights,
Intrigues, adventures of the common school,
   Its petty passions, marriages, and flights,
Where Hymen's torch but brands one strumpet more,
Whose husband only knows her not a whore.

18

Hard words—harsh truth! a truth which many know.
   Enough.—The faithful and the fairy pair,
Who never found a single hour too slow,
   What was it made them thus exempt from care?
Young innate feelings all have felt below,
   Which perish in the rest, but in them were
Inherent—what we mortals call romantic,
And always envy, though we deem it frantic.

19

This is in others a factitious state,
   An opium dream of too much youth and reading,
But was in them their nature or their fate:
   No novels e'er had set their young hearts bleeding,
For Haidée's knowledge was by no means great,
   And Juan was a boy of saintly breeding;
So that there was no reason for their loves
More than for those of nightingales or doves.

20

They gazed upon the sunset; 'tis an hour
    Dear unto all, but dearest to *their* eyes,
For it had made them what they were: the power
    Of love had first o'erwhelmed them from such skies,
When happiness had been their only dower,
    And twilight saw them linked in passion's ties;
Charmed with each other, all things charmed that brought
The past still welcome as the present thought.

21

I know not why, but in that hour to-night,
    Even as they gazed, a sudden tremor came,
And swept, as 'twere, across their hearts' delight,
    Like the wind o'er a harp-string, or a flame,
When one is shook in sound, and one in sight.
    And thus some boding flashed through either frame,
And called from Juan's breast a faint low sigh,
While one new tear arose in Haidée's eye.

22

That large black prophet eye seemed to dilate
    And follow far the disappearing sun,
As if their last day of a happy date
    With his broad, bright, and dropping orb were gone.
Juan gazed on her as to ask his fate—
    He felt a grief, but knowing cause for none,
His glance inquired of hers for some excuse
For feelings causeless, or at least abstruse.

23

She turned to him, and smiled, but in that sort
    Which makes not others smile; then turned aside:
Whatever feeling shook her, it seemed short,
    And mastered by her wisdom or her pride;
When Juan spoke, too—it might be in sport—
    Of this their mutual feeling, she replied—
"If it should be so,—but—it cannot be—
Or I at least shall not survive to see."

24

Juan would question further, but she pressed
    His lips to hers, and silenced him with this,

And then dismissed the omen from her breast,
   Defying augury with that fond kiss;
And no doubt of all methods 'tis the best:
   Some people prefer wine—'tis not amiss;
I have tried both; so those who would a part take
May choose between the headache and the heartache.

25

One of the two, according to your choice,
   Woman or wine, you'll have to undergo;
Both maladies are taxes on our joys:
   But which to choose, I really hardly know;
And if I had to give a casting voice,
   For both sides I could many reasons show,
And then decide, without great wrong to either,
It were much better to have both than neither.

26

Juan and Haidée gazed upon each other
   With swimming looks of speechless tenderness,
Which mixed all feelings—friend, child, lover, brother—
   All that the best can mingle and express
When two pure hearts are poured in one another,
   And love too much, and yet cannot love less;
But almost sanctify the sweet excess
By the immortal wish and power to bless.

27

Mixed in each other's arms, and heart in heart,
   Why did they not then die?—they had lived too long
Should an hour come to bid them breathe apart;
   Years could but bring them cruel things or wrong;
The world was not for them, nor the world's art
   For beings passionate as Sappho's song;
Love was born *with* them, *in* them, so intense,
It was their very spirit—not a sense.

28

They should have lived together deep in woods,
   Unseen as sings the nightingale; they were
Unfit to mix in these thick solitudes
   Called social, haunts of hate, and vice, and care;

How lonely every freeborn creature broods!
  The sweetest song-birds nestle in a pair;
The eagle soars alone; the gull and crow
Flock o'er their carrion, just like men below.

29

Now pillowed cheek to cheek, in loving sleep,
  Haidée and Juan their siesta took,
A gentle slumber, but it was not deep,
  For ever and anon a something shook
Juan, and shuddering o'er his frame would creep;
  And Haidée's sweet lips murmured like a brook
A wordless music, and her face so fair
Stirred with her dream, as rose-leaves with the air.

30

Or as the stirring of a deep clear stream
  Within an Alpine hollow, when the wind
Walks o'er it, was she shaken by the dream,
  The mystical usurper of the mind—
O'erpowering us to be whate'er may seem
  Good to the soul which we no more can bind:
Strange state of being! (for 'tis still to be)
Senseless to feel, and with sealed eyes to see.

31

She dreamed of being alone on the sea-shore,
  Chained to a rock; she knew not how, but stir
She could not from the spot, and the loud roar
  Grew, and each wave rose roughly, threatening her;
And o'er her upper lip they seemed to pour,
  Until she sobbed for breath, and soon they were
Foaming o'er her lone head, so fierce and high—
Each broke to drown her, yet she could not die.

32

Anon—she was released, and then she strayed
  O'er the sharp shingles with her bleeding feet,
And stumbled almost every step she made;
  And something rolled before her in a sheet,
Which she must still pursue howe'er afraid:
  'Twas white and indistinct, nor stopped to meet

Her glance nor grasp, for still she gazed and grasped,
And ran, but it escaped her as she clasped.

33

The dream changed:—in a cave she stood, its walls
  Were hung with marble icicles; the work
Of ages on its water-fretted halls,
  Where waves might wash, and seals might breed and lurk;
Her hair was dripping, and the very balls
  Of her black eyes seemed turned to tears, and mirk
The sharp rocks looked below each drop they caught,
Which froze to marble as it fell,—she thought.

34

And wet, and cold, and lifeless at her feet,
  Pale as the foam that frothed on his dead brow,
Which she essayed in vain to clear (how sweet
  Were once her cares, how idle seemed they now!)
Lay Juan, nor could aught renew the beat
  Of his quenched heart; and the sea dirges low
Rang in her sad ears like a mermaid's song,
And that brief dream appeared a life too long.

35

And gazing on the dead, she thought his face
  Faded, or altered into something new—
Like to her father's features, till each trace
  More like and like to Lambro's aspect grew—
With all his keen worn look and Grecian grace;
  And starting, she awoke, and what to view?
Oh! Powers of Heaven! what dark eye meets she there?
'Tis—'tis her father's—fixed upon the pair!

36

Then shrieking, she arose, and shrieking fell,
  With joy and sorrow, hope and fear, to see
Him whom she deemed a habitant where dwell
  The ocean-buried, risen from death, to be
Perchance the death of one she loved too well:
  Dear as her father had been to Haidée,
It was a moment of that awful kind—
I have seen such—but must not call to mind.

37

Up Juan sprang to Haidée's bitter shriek,
  And caught her falling, and from off the wall
Snatched down his saber, in hot haste to wreak
  Vengeance on him who was the cause of all:
Then Lambro, who till now forebore to speak,
  Smiled scornfully, and said, "Within my call,
A thousand scimitars await the word;
Put up, young man, put up your silly sword."

38

And Haidée clung around him; "Juan, 'tis—
  'Tis Lambro—'tis my father! Kneel with me—
He will forgive us—yes—it must be—yes.
  Oh! dearest father, in this agony
Of pleasure and of pain—even while I kiss
  Thy garment's hem with transport, can it be
That doubt should mingle with my filial joy?
Deal with me as thou wilt, but spare this boy."

39

High and inscrutable the old man stood,
  Calm in his voice, and calm within his eye—
Not always signs with him of calmest mood:
  He looked upon her, but gave no reply;
Then turned to Juan, in whose cheek the blood
  Oft came and went, as there resolved to die;
In arms, at least, he stood, in act to spring
On the first foe whom Lambro's call might bring.

40

"Young man, your sword"; so Lambro once more said:
  Juan replied, "Not while this arm is free."
The old man's cheek grew pale, but not with dread,
  And drawing from his belt a pistol, he
Replied, "Your blood be then on your own head."
  Then looked close at the flint, as if to see
'Twas fresh—for he had lately used the lock—
And next proceeded quietly to cock.

41

It has a strange quick jar upon the ear,
  That cocking of a pistol, when you know

A moment more will bring the sight to bear
  Upon your person, twelve yards off, or so;
A gentlemanly distance, not too near,
  If you have got a former friend for foe;
But after being fired at once or twice,
The ear becomes more Irish, and less nice.

42

Lambro presented, and one instant more
  Had stopped this Canto, and Don Juan's breath,
When Haidée threw herself her boy before;
  Stern as her sire: "On me," she cried, "let death
Descend—the fault is mine; this fatal shore
  He found—but sought not. I have pledged my faith;
I love him—I will die with him: I knew
Your nature's firmness—know your daughter's too."

43

A minute past, and she had been all tears,
  And tenderness, and infancy; but now
She stood as one who championed human fears—
  Pale, statue-like, and stern, she wooed the blow;
And tall beyond her sex, and their compeers,
  She drew up to her height, as if to show
A fairer mark; and with a fixed eye scanned
Her father's face—but never stopped his hand.

44

He gazed on her, and she on him; 'twas strange
  How like they looked! the expression was the same;
Serenely savage, with a little change
  In the large dark eye's mutual-darted flame;
For she, too, was as one who could avenge,
  If cause should be—a lioness, though tame.
Her father's blood before her father's face
Boiled up, and proved her truly of his race.

45

I said they were alike, their features and
  Their stature, differing but in sex and years:
Even to the delicacy of their hand
  There was resemblance, such as true blood wears;

And now to see them, thus divided, stand
  In fixed ferocity, when joyous tears,
And sweet sensations, should have welcomed both,
Shows what the passions are in their full growth.

46

The father paused a moment, then withdrew
  His weapon, and replaced it; but stood still,
And looking on her, as to look her through,
  "Not *I*," he said, "have sought this stranger's ill;
Not *I* have made this desolation: few
  Would bear such outrage, and forbear to kill;
But I must do my duty—how thou hast
Done thine, the present vouches for the past.

47

"Let him disarm, or, by my father's head,
  His own shall roll before you like a ball!"
He raised his whistle as the word he said,
  And blew; another answered to the call,
And rushing in disorderly, though led,
  And armed from boot to turban, one and all,
Some twenty of his train came, rank on rank;
He gave the word, "Arrest or slay the Frank."

48

Then, with a sudden movement, he withdrew
  His daughter; while compressed within his clasp,
'Twixt her and Juan interposed the crew;
  In vain she struggled in her father's grasp—
His arms were like a serpent's coil: then flew
  Upon their prey, as darts an angry asp,
The file of pirates—save the foremost, who
Had fallen, with his right shoulder half cut through.

49

The second had his cheek laid open; but
  The third, a wary, cool old sworder, took
The blows upon his cutlass, and then put
  His own well in; so well, ere you could look,
His man was floored, and helpless at his foot,
  With the blood running like a little brook

From two smart saber gashes, deep and red—
One on the arm, the other on the head.

50

And then they bound him where he fell, and bore
    Juan from the apartment: with a sign
Old Lambro bade them take him to the shore,
    Where lay some ships which were to sail at nine.
They laid him in a boat, and plied the oar
    Until they reached some galliots,[71] placed in line;
On board of one of these, and under hatches,
They stowed him, with strict orders to the watches.

51

The world is full of strange vicissitudes,
    And here was one exceedingly unpleasant:
A gentleman so rich in the world's goods,
    Handsome and young, enjoying all the present,
Just at the very time when he least broods
    On such a thing, is suddenly to sea sent,
Wounded and chained, so that he cannot move,
And all because a lady fell in love.

52

Here I must leave him, for I grow pathetic,
    Moved by the Chinese nymph of tears, green tea!
Than whom Cassandra was not more prophetic;
    For if my pure libations exceed three,
I feel my heart become so sympathetic,
    That I must have recourse to black Bohea:[72]
'Tis pity wine should be so deleterious,
For tea and coffee leave us much more serious,

53

Unless when qualified with thee, Cogniac!
    Sweet Naïad of the Phlegethontic rill![73]
Ah! why the liver wilt thou thus attack,
    And make, like other nymphs, thy lovers ill?
I would take refuge in weak punch, but *rack*
    (In each sense of the word), whene'er I fill

71 galleys
72 a kind of tea

73 Phlegethon, a river of
fire in Hades

My mild and midnight beakers to the brim,
Wakes me next morning with its synonym.

54

I leave Don Juan for the present, safe—
  Not sound, poor fellow, but severely wounded;
Yet could his corporal pangs amount to half
  Of those with which his Haidée's bosom bounded!
She was not one to weep, and rave, and chafe,
  And then give way, subdued because surrounded;
Her mother was a Moorish maid from Fez,
Where all is Eden, or a wilderness.

55

There the large olive rains its amber store
  In marble fonts; there grain, and flour, and fruit,
Gush from the earth until the land runs o'er;
  But there, too, many a poison-tree has root,
And midnight listens to the lion's roar,
  And long, long deserts scorch the camel's foot,
Or heaving whelm the helpless caravan;
And as the soil is, so the heart of man.

56

Afric is all the sun's, and as her earth
  Her human clay is kindled; full of power
For good or evil, burning from its birth,
  The Moorish blood partakes the planet's hour,
And like the soil beneath it will bring forth:
  Beauty and love were Haidée's mother's dower;
But her large dark eye showed deep Passion's force,
Though sleeping like a lion near a source.

57

Her daughter, tempered with a milder ray,
  Like summer clouds all silvery, smooth, and fair,
Till slowly charged with thunder they display
  Terror to earth, and tempest to the air,
Had held till now her soft and milky way;
  But overwrought with passion and despair,
The fire burst forth from her Numidian veins,
Even as the Simoom [74] sweeps the blasted plains.

74 a hot wind from the desert

58

The last sight which she saw was Juan's gore,
　　And he himself o'ermastered and cut down;
His blood was running on the very floor
　　Where late he trod, her beautiful, her own;
Thus much she viewed an instant and no more,—
　　Her struggles ceased with no convulsive groan;
On her sire's arm, which until now scarce held
Her writhing, fell she like a cedar felled.

59

A vein had burst, and her sweet lips' pure dyes
　　Were dabbled with the deep blood which ran o'er;
And her head drooped, as when the lily lies
　　O'ercharged with rain: her summoned handmaids bore
Their lady to her couch with gushing eyes;
　　Of herbs and cordials they produced their store,
But she defied all means they could employ,
Like one life could not hold, nor death destroy.

60

Days lay she in that state unchanged, though chill—
　　With nothing livid, still her lips were red;
She had no pulse, but death seemed absent still;
　　No hideous sign proclaimed her surely dead;
Corruption came not in each mind to kill
　　All hope; to look upon her sweet face bred
New thoughts of life, for it seemed full of soul—
She had so much, earth could not claim the whole.

61

The ruling passion, such as marble shows
　　When exquisitely chiseled, still lay there,
But fixed as marble's unchanged aspect throws
　　O'er the fair Venus, but for ever fair;
O'er the Laocoön's all eternal throes,
　　And ever-dying Gladiator's air,
Their energy like life forms all their fame,
Yet looks not life, for they are still the same.

62

She woke at length, but not as sleepers wake,
　　Rather the dead, for life seemed something new,

A strange sensation which she must partake
  Perforce, since whatsoever met her view
Struck not on memory, though a heavy ache
  Lay at her heart, whose earliest beat still true
Brought back the sense of pain without the cause,
For, for a while, the furies made a pause.

63

She looked on many a face with vacant eye,
  On many a token without knowing what;
She saw them watch her without asking why,
  And recked not who around her pillow sat;
Not speechless, though she spoke not; not a sigh
  Relieved her thoughts; dull silence and quick chat
Were tried in vain by those who served; she gave
No sign, save breath, of having left the grave.

64

Her handmaids tended, but she heeded not;
  Her father watched, she turned her eyes away;
She recognized no being, and no spot,
  However dear or cherished in their day;
They changed from room to room, but all forgot,
  Gentle, but without memory she lay;
At length those eyes, which they would fain be weaning
Back to old thoughts, waxed full of fearful meaning.

65

And then a slave bethought her of a harp;
  The harper came, and tuned his instrument;
At the first notes, irregular and sharp,
  On him her flashing eyes a moment bent,
Then to the wall she turned as if to warp
  Her thoughts from sorrow through her heart re-sent;
And he began a long low island-song
Of ancient days, ere tyranny grew strong.

66

Anon her thin wan fingers beat the wall
  In time to his old tune; he changed the theme,
And sung of love; the fierce name struck through all
  Her recollection; on her flashed the dream

Of what she was, and is, if ye could call
    To be so being; in a gushing stream
The tears rushed forth from her o'erclouded brain,
Like mountain mists at length dissolved in rain.

67

Short solace, vain relief!—thought came too quick,
    And whirled her brain to madness; she arose
As one who ne'er had dwelt among the sick,
    And flew at all she met, as on her foes;
But no one ever heard her speak or shriek,
    Although her paroxysm drew towards its close;—
Hers was a frenzy which disdained to rave,
Even when they smote her, in the hope to save.

68

Yet she betrayed at times a gleam of sense;
    Nothing could make her meet her father's face,
Though on all other things with looks intense
    She gazed, but none she ever could retrace;
Food she refused, and raiment; no pretense
    Availed for either; neither change of place,
Nor time, nor skill, nor remedy, could give her
Senses to sleep—the power seemed gone for ever.

69

Twelve days and nights she withered thus; at last,
    Without a groan, or sigh, or glance, to show
A parting pang, the spirit from her passed:
    And they who watched her nearest could not know
The very instant, till the change that cast
    Her sweet face into shadow, dull and slow,
Glazed o'er her eyes—the beautiful, the black—
Oh! to possess such luster—and then lack!

70

She died, but not alone; she held within
    A second principle of life, which might
Have dawned a fair and sinless child of sin;
    But closed its little being without light,
And went down to the grave unborn, wherein
    Blossom and bough lie withered with one blight;

In vain the dews of Heaven descend above
The bleeding flower and blasted fruit of love.

71

Thus lived—thus died she; never more on her
  Shall sorrow light, or shame. She was not made
Through years or moons the inner weight to bear,
  Which colder hearts endure till they are laid
By age in earth: her days and pleasures were
  Brief, but delightful—such as had not stayed
Long with her destiny; but she sleeps well .
By the sea-shore, whereon she loved to dwell.

72

That isle is now all desolate and bare,
  Its dwellings down, its tenants passed away;
None but her own and father's grave is there,
  And nothing outward tells of human clay;
Ye could not know where lies a thing so fair,
  No stone is there to show, no tongue to say,
What was; no dirge, except the hollow sea's,
Mourns o'er the beauty of the Cyclades.

73

But many a Greek maid in a loving song
  Sighs o'er her name; and many an islander
With her sire's story makes the night less long;
  Valor was his, and beauty dwelt with her;
If she loved rashly, her life paid for wrong—
  A heavy price must all pay who thus err,
In some shape; let none think to fly the danger,
For soon or late Love is his own avenger.

THE VISION OF JUDGMENT

In 1821, the year following the death of George III, Robert Southey, then poet laureate, had published a commemorative poem entitled *A Vision of Judgment*. In this work the former revolutionary and radical poet, who had with the passage of the years grown stodgily conservative, in fulsome style extols the abilities and virtues of the late king. When George stands in heaven's court to face his accusers, none appear. "King of England," says the Angel, "speak for thyself; here is none to arraign thee." Byron, loathing both king and poet, retorted in the sharp satire of his own *Vision of Judgment*. Since Byron's poem is highly discursive, it may be satisfactorily presented in condensed form, as below. The stanza numbers, which are those of the original, will indicate the extent of the omissions.

I

Saint Peter sat by the celestial gate:
  His keys were rusty, and the lock was dull,
So little trouble had been given of late;
  Not that the place by any means was full,
But since the Gallic era "eighty-eight" [75]
  The devils had ta'en a longer, stronger pull,
And "a pull altogether," as they say
At sea—which drew most souls another way.

2

The angels all were singing out of tune,
  And hoarse with having little else to do,
Excepting to wind up the sun and moon,
  Or curb a runaway young star or two,
Or wild colt of a comet which too soon
  Broke out of bounds o'er the ethereal blue,
Splitting some planet with its playful tail,
As boats are sometimes by a wanton whale.

3

The guardian seraphs had retired on high,
  Finding their charges past all care below;
Terrestrial business fill'd nought in the sky
  Save the recording angel's black bureau;
Who found, indeed, the facts to multiply
  With such rapidity of vice and woe,
That he had stripp'd off both his wings in quills,
And yet was in arrear of human ills.

4

His business so augmented of late years,
  That he was forced, against his will no doubt,
(Just like those cherubs, earthly ministers,)
  For some resource to turn himself about,
And claim the help of his celestial peers,
  To aid him ere he should be quite worn out
By the increased demand for his remarks:
Six angels and twelve saints were named his clerks.

[75] 1788, when the French Revolution broke out

5

This was a handsome board—at least for heaven;
    And yet they had even then enough to do,
So many conquerors' cars were daily driven,
    So many kingdoms fitted up anew;
Each day too slew its thousands six or seven,
    Till at the crowning carnage, Waterloo,
They threw their pens down in divine disgust—
The page was so besmear'd with blood and dust.

8

In the first year of freedom's second dawn
    Died George the Third; although no tyrant, one
Who shielded tyrants, till each sense withdrawn
    Left him nor mental nor external sun: [76]
A better farmer ne'er brush'd dew from lawn,
    A worse king never left a realm undone!
He died—but left his subjects still behind,
One half as mad—and t'other no less blind.

9

He died! his death made no great stir on earth:
    His burial made some pomp; there was profusion
Of velvet, gilding, brass, and no great dearth
    Of aught but tears—save those shed by collusion.
For these things may be bought at their true worth;
    Of elegy there was the due infusion—
Bought also; and the torches, cloaks, and banners,
Heralds, and relics of old Gothic manners,

10

Form'd a sepulchral melodrame. Of all
    The fools who flock'd to swell or see the show,
Who cared about the corpse? The funeral
    Made the attraction, and the black the woe.
There throbb'd not there a thought which pierced the pall;
    And when the gorgeous coffin was laid low,
It seem'd the mockery of hell to fold
The rottenness of eighty years in gold.

[76] In his later years George III was both demented and blind

16

Saint Peter sat by the celestial gate,
    And nodded o'er his keys; when, lo! there came
A wondrous noise he had not heard of late—
    A rushing sound of wind, and stream, and flame;
In short, a roar of things extremely great,
    Which would have made aught save a saint exclaim;
But he, with first a start and then a wink,
Said, "There's another star gone out, I think!"

17

But ere he could return to his repose,
    A cherub flapped his right wing o'er his eyes—
At which Saint Peter yawned, and rubbed his nose:
    "Saint porter," said the angel, "prithee rise!"
Waving a goodly wing, which glowed, as glows
    An earthly peacock's tail, with heavenly dyes:
To which the saint replied, "Well, what's the matter?
"Is Lucifer come back with all this clatter?"

18

"No," quoth the cherub; "George the Third is dead."
    "And who *is* George the Third?" replied the apostle:
"*What George? what Third?*" "The king of England," said
    The angel. "Well! he won't find kings to jostle
Him on his way; but does he wear his head?
    Because the last we saw here had a tussle,
And ne'er would have got into heaven's good graces,
Had he not flung his head in all our faces.

19

"He was, if I remember, king of France; [77]
    That head of his, which could not keep a crown
On earth, yet ventured in my face to advance
    A claim to those of martyrs—like my own:
If I had had my sword, as I had once
    When I cut ears off, I had cut him down;
But having but my *keys,* and not my brand,
I only knock'd his head from out his hand.

[77] Louis XVI, guillotined in 1793

20

"And then he set up such a headless howl,
 That all the saints came out and took him in;
And there he sits by St. Paul, cheek by jowl;
 That fellow Paul—the parvenu! [78] The skin
Of St. Bartholomew, which makes his cowl
 In heaven, and upon earth redeem'd his sin,
So as to make a martyr, never sped
Better than did this weak and wooden head.

21

"But had it come up here upon its shoulders,
 There would have been a different tale to tell:
The fellow-feeling in the saints' beholders
 Seems to have acted on them like a spell,
And so this very foolish head heaven solders
 Back on its trunk: it may be very well,
And seems the custom here to overthrow
Whatever has been wisely done below."

22

The angel answer'd, "Peter! do not pout:
 The king who comes has head and all entire,
And never knew much what it was about—
 He did as doth the puppet—by its wire,
And will be judged like all the rest, no doubt:
 My business and your own is not to inquire
Into such matters, but to mind our cue—
Which is to act as we are bid to do."

23

While thus they spake, the angelic caravan,
 Arriving like a rush of mighty wind,
Cleaving the fields of space, as doth the swan
 Some silver stream (say Ganges, Nile, or Inde,
Or Thames, or Tweed), and 'midst them an old man
 With an old soul, and both extremely blind,
Halted before the gate, and in his shroud
Seated their fellow traveler on a cloud.

---

[78] upstart (St. Paul having been converted to Christianity later, and yet cutting quite a figure)

24

But bringing up the rear of this bright host
    A Spirit of a different aspect waved
His wings, like thunder-clouds above some coast
    Whose barren beach with frequent wrecks is paved;
His brow was like the deep when tempest-toss'd;
    Fierce and unfathomable thoughts engraved
Eternal wrath on his immortal face,
And *where* he gazed a gloom pervaded space.

25

As he drew near, he gazed upon the gate
    Ne'er to be enter'd more by him or Sin,
With such a glance of supernatural hate,
    As made Saint Peter wish himself within;
He patter'd with his keys at a great rate,
    And sweated through his apostolic skin:
Of course his perspiration was but ichor,
Or some such other spiritual liquor.

26

The very cherubs huddled all together,
    Like birds when soars the falcon; and they felt
A tingling to the tip of every feather,
    And form'd a circle like Orion's belt
Around their poor old charge; who scarce knew whither
    His guards had led him, though they gently dealt
With royal manes [79] (for by many stories,
And true, we learn the angels all are Tories).

27

As things were in this posture, the gate flew
    Asunder, and the flashing of its hinges
Flung over space an universal hue
    Of many-color'd flame, until it tinges
Reach'd even our speck of earth, and made a new
    Aurora borealis spread its fringes
O'er the North Pole; the same seen, when ice-bound,
By Captain Parry's crew, in "Melville's Sound." [80]

79 spirits (the Roman word, a dissyllable)
80 as told in an account of this Arctic expedition published in 1821

29

'Twas the archangel Michael; all men know
   The make of angels and archangels, since
There's scarce a scribbler has not one to show,
   From the fiends' leader to the angels' prince;
There also are some altar-pieces, though
   I really can't say that they much evince
One's inner notions of immortal spirits;
But let the connoisseurs explain *their* merits.

30

Michael flew forth in glory and in good;
   A goodly work of him from whom all glory
And good arise; the portal past—he stood;
   Before him the young cherubs and saints hoary—
(I say *young*, begging to be understood
   By looks, not years; and should be very sorry
To state, they were not older than St. Peter,
But merely that they seem'd a little sweeter).

31

The cherubs and the saints bow'd down before
   That arch-angelic hierarch, the first
Of essences angelical, who wore
   The aspect of a god; but this ne'er nursed
Pride in his heavenly bosom, in whose core
   No thought, save for his Master's service, durst
Intrude, however glorified and high;
He knew him but the viceroy of the sky.

32

He and the somber, silent Spirit met—
   They knew each other both for good and ill;
Such was their power, that neither could forget
   His former friend and future foe; but still
There was a high, immortal, proud regret
   In either's eye, as if 'twere less their will
Than destiny to make the eternal years
Their date of war, and their "champ clos" [81] the spheres.

[81] "closed field," *i. e.*, the lists

33

But here they were in neutral space: we know
  From Job, that Satan hath the power to pay
A heavenly visit thrice a year or so; [82]
  And that the "sons of God," like those of clay,
Must keep him company; and we might show
  From the same book, in how polite a way
The dialogue is held between the Powers
Of Good and Evil—but 'twould take up hours.

36

The Archangel bowed, not like a modern beau,
  But with a graceful oriental bend,
Pressing one radiant arm just where below
  The heart in good men is supposed to tend.
He turned as to an equal, not too low,
  But kindly; Satan met his ancient friend
With more hauteur, as might an old Castilian
Poor noble meet a mushroom rich civilian.

37

He merely bent his diabolic brow
  An instant; and then raising it, he stood
In act to assert his right or wrong, and show
  Cause why King George by no means could or should
Make out a case to be exempt from woe
  Eternal, more than other kings, endued
With better sense and hearts, whom history mentions,
Who long have "paved hell with their good intentions."

38

Michael began: "What wouldst thou with this man,
  Now dead, and brought before the Lord? What ill
Hath he wrought since his mortal race began,
  That thou canst claim him? Speak! and do thy will,
If it be just: if in this earthly span
  He hath been greatly failing to fulfill
His duties as a king and mortal, say,
And he is thine; if not, let him have way."

82 Job, i. 6

39

"Michael!" replied the Prince of Air, "even here,
  Before the Gate of him thou servest, must
I claim my subject: and will make appear
  That as he was my worshiper in dust,
So shall he be in spirit, although dear
  To thee and thine, because nor wine nor lust
Were of his weaknesses; yet on the throne
He reign'd o'er millions to serve me alone.

40

"Look to *our* earth, or rather *mine;* it was,
  Once, more thy master's: but I triumph not
In this poor planet's conquest: nor, alas!
  Need he thou servest envy me my lot:
With all the myriads of bright worlds which pass
  In worship round him, he may have forgot
Yon weak creation of such paltry things:
I think few worth damnation save their kings,—

42

"Look to the earth, I said, and say again:
  When this old, blind, mad, helpless, weak, poor worm
Began in youth's first bloom and flush to reign,
  The world and he both wore a different form,
And much of earth and all the watery plain
  Of ocean call'd him king: through many a storm
His isles had floated on the abyss of time;
For the rough virtues chose them for their clime.

43

"He came to his scepter young; he leaves it old: [83]
  Look to the state in which he found his realm,
And left it; and his annals too behold,
  How to a minion first he gave the helm; [84]
How grew upon his heart a thirst for gold,
  The beggar's vice, which can but overwhelm
The meanest hearts; and for the rest, but glance
Thine eye along America and France.

[83] George III ascended the throne in 1760, at the age of 22; died 1820
[84] Earl of Bute

44

" 'Tis true, he was a tool from first to last
    (I have the workmen safe); but as a tool
So let him be consumed. From out the past
    Of ages, since mankind have known the rule
Of monarchs—from the bloody rolls amass'd
    Of sin and slaughter—from the Cæsar's school,
Take the worst pupil; and produce a reign
More drench'd with gore, more cumber'd with the slain.

45

"He ever warr'd with freedom and the free:
    Nations as men, home subjects, foreign foes,
So that they utter'd the word 'Liberty!'
    Found George the Third their first opponent. Whose
History was ever stain'd as his will be
    With national and individual woes?
I grant his household abstinence; I grant
His neutral virtues, which most monarchs want;

46

"I know he was a constant consort; own
    He was a decent sire, and middling lord.
All this is much, and most upon a throne;
    As temperance, if at Apicius' board,[85]
Is more than at an anchorite's supper shown.
    I grant him all the kindest can accord;
And this was well for him, but not for those
Millions who found him what oppression chose.

47

"The New World shook him off; the Old yet groans
    Beneath what he and his prepared, if not
Completed: he leaves heirs on many thrones
    To all his vices, without what begot
Compassion for him—his tame virtues; drones
    Who sleep, or despots who have now forgot
A lesson which shall be re-taught them, wake
Upon the thrones of earth; but let them quake!

85 a Roman epicure of the 1st cent. A. D.

48

"Five millions of the primitive, who hold
    The faith which makes ye great on earth, implored
A *part* of that vast *all* they held of old,—
    Freedom to worship—not alone your Lord,
Michael, but you, and you, Saint Peter! Cold
    Must be your souls, if you have not abhorr'd
The foe to Catholic participation [86]
In all the license of a Christian nation.

49

"True! he allowed them to pray God; but as
    A consequence of prayer, refused the law
Which would have placed them upon the same base
    With those who did not hold the saints in awe."
But here Saint Peter started from his place,
    And cried, "You may the prisoner withdraw:
Ere heaven shall ope her portals to this Guelph,[87]
While I am guard, may I be damned myself!

50

"Sooner will I with Cerberus [88] exchange
    My office (and *his* is no sinecure)
Than see this royal Bedlam bigot range
    The azure fields of heaven, of that be sure!"
"Saint!" replied Satan, "you do well to avenge
    The wrongs he made your satellites endure;
And if to this exchange you should be given,
I'll try to coax *our* Cerberus up to heaven."

51

Here Michael interposed: "Good saint! and devil!
    Pray, not so fast; you both outrun discretion. ·
Saint Peter! you were wont to be more civil:
    Satan! excuse this warmth of his expression,
And condescension to the vulgar's level:
    Even saints sometimes forget themselves in session.
Have you got more to say?"—"No."—"If you please,
I'll trouble you to call your witnesses."

---

86 The political disabilities of Catholics were not removed till 1829.
87 princely family to which the House of Hanover belonged
88 three-headed dog guarding gate to the classical Hades

[A great cloud of them appears, like "hell broke loose," Englishmen, Irishmen, Scots, Spaniards, Dutchmen, Danes, and others. Michael "first grew pale, next . . . turn'd all colors."]

62

Then he addressed himself to Satan: "Why—
    My good old friend, for such I deem you, though
Our different parties make us fight so shy,
    I ne'er mistake you for a *personal* foe;
Our difference is *political,* and I
    Trust that, whatever may occur below,
You know my great respect for you: and this
Makes me regret whate'er you do amiss—

63

"Why, my dear Lucifer, would you abuse
    My call for witnesses? I did not mean
That you should half of earth and hell produce;
    'Tis even superfluous, since two honest, clean,
True testimonies are enough: we lose
    Our time, nay, our eternity, between
The accusation and defence: if we
Hear both, 'twill stretch our immortality."

64

Satan replied, "To me the matter is
    Indifferent in a personal point of view:
I can have fifty better souls than this
    With far less trouble than we have gone through
Already; and I merely argued his
    Late Majesty of Britain's case with you
Upon a point of form: you may dispose
Of him; I've kings enough below, God knows!"

[Testimony is then given by two political opponents of George III, Jack Wilkes (see Vol. I, p. 862), and "Junius," anonymous author of a famous series of articles bearing the motto *Stat nominis umbra,* "The shadow of the name stands," who thus concludes:]

84

"What I have written, I have written; let
    The rest be on his head or mine!" So spoke
Old "Nominis Umbra"; and while speaking yet,
    Away he melted in a celestial smoke.

Then Satan said to Michael, "Don't forget
 To call George Washington, and John Horne Tooke,[89]
And Franklin";—but at this time there was heard
A cry for room, though not a phantom stirred.

85

At length with jostling, elbowing, and the aid
 Of cherubim appointed to that post,
The devil Asmodeus to the circle made
 His way, and looked as if his journey cost
Some trouble. When his burden down he laid,
 "What's this?" cried Michael; "why, 'tis not a ghost?"
"I know it," quoth the incubus; "but he
Shall be one, if you leave the affair to me.

86

"Confound the renegado! I have sprained
 My left wing, he's so heavy; one would think
Some of his works about his neck were chained.
 But to the point; while hovering o'er the brink
Of Skiddaw [90] (where as usual it still rained),
 I saw a taper, far below me, wink,
And stooping, caught this fellow at a libel—
No less on history than the Holy Bible.

87

"The former is the devil's scripture, and
 The latter yours, good Michael; so the affair
Belongs to all of us, you understand.
 I snatched him up just as you see him there,
And brought him off for sentence out of hand:
 I've scarcely been ten minutes in the air—
At least a quarter it can hardly be:
I dare say that his wife is still at tea."

[It is the poet Southey; he speaks:]

96

He said—(I only give the heads)—he said,
 He meant no harm in scribbling; 'twas his way

89 (1736–1812), well known as politician who supported Wilkes, advocated the cause
of the revolted American colonists, and was imprisoned for starting a subscription for
them.
 90 mountain overlooking Derwentwater (the "lake" of Stanza 104), near Keswick,
Cumberland, where Southey lived

Upon all topics; 'twas, besides, his bread,
  Of which he butter'd both sides; 'twould delay
Too long the assembly (he was pleased to dread),
  And take up rather more time than a day,
To name his works—he would but cite a few—
"Wat Tyler"—"Rhymes on Blenheim"—"Waterloo."

97

He had written praises of a regicide;
  He had written praises of all kings whatever;
He had written for republics far and wide,
  And then against them bitterer than ever.
For pantisocracy he once had cried
  Aloud, a scheme less moral than 'twas clever;
Then grew a hearty anti-jacobin—
Had turn'd his coat—and would have turn'd his skin.

98

He had sung against all battles, and again
  In their high praise and glory; he had call'd
Reviewing "the ungentle craft," and then
  Become as base a critic as e'er crawl'd—
Fed, paid, and pamper'd by the very men
  By whom his muse and morals had been maul'd:
He had written much blank verse, and blanker prose,
And more of both than anybody knows.[91]

99

He had written Wesley's life:—here turning round
  To Satan, "Sir, I'm ready to write yours,
In two octavo volumes, nicely bound,
  With notes and preface, all that most allures
The pious purchaser; and there's no ground
  For fear, for I can choose my own reviewers:
So let me have the proper documents,
That I may add you to my other saints."

100

Satan bow'd, and was silent. "Well, if you,
  With amiable modesty, decline

---

[91] Byron mentions early works of Southey's, republican and radical in stand, in contrast to his current conservatism. The "ungentle craft" is reviewing. Although the *Quarterly Review* had formerly "mauled" Southey, it admitted him as a regular contributor in 1809.

My offer, what says Michael? There are few
  Whose memoirs could be render'd more divine.
Mine is a pen of all work; not so new
  As it was once, but I would make you shine
Like your own trumpet. By the way, my own
Has more of brass in it, and is as well blown.

101

"But talking about trumpets, here's my Vision!
  Now you shall judge, all people; yes, you shall
Judge with my judgment, and by my decision
  Be guided who shall enter heaven or fall.
I settle all these things by intuition,
  Times present, past, to come, heaven, hell, and all,
Like King Alfonso.[92] When I thus see double,
I save the Deity some worlds of trouble."

102

He ceased, and drew forth an MS.; and no
  Persuasion on the part of devils, saints,
Or angels, now could stop the torrent; so
  He read the first three lines of the contents;
But at the fourth, the whole spiritual show
  Had vanished, with variety of scents,
Ambrosial and sulphureous, as they sprang,
Like lightning, off from his "melodious twang."

103

Those grand heroics acted as a spell;
  The angels stopped their ears and plied their pinions;
The devils ran howling, deafened, down to hell;
  The ghosts fled, gibbering, for their own dominions—
(For 'tis not yet decided where they dwell,
  And I leave every man to his opinions);
Michael took refuge in his trump—but, lo!
His teeth were set on edge, he could not blow!

104

Saint Peter, who has hitherto been known
  For an impetuous saint, upraised his keys,

---

92 "Alfonso, speaking of the Ptolomean system, said that 'had he been consulted at the creation of the world, he would have spared the Maker some absurdities.'" (Byron)

And at the fifth line knocked the poet down;
    Who fell like Phaëton,[93] but more at ease,
Into his lake, for there he did not drown;
    A different web being by the Destinies
Woven for the Laureate's final wreath, whene'er
Reform shall happen either here or there.

105

He first sank to the bottom—like his works,
    But soon rose to the surface—like himself;
For all corrupted things are buoyed like corks
    By their own rottenness, light as an elf,
Or wisp that flits o'er a morass: he lurks,
    It may be, still, like dull books on a shelf,
In his own den, to scrawl some "Life" or "Vision,"
As Welborn says—"the devil turned precisian." [94]

106

As for the rest, to come to the conclusion
    Of this true dream, the telescope is gone
Which kept my optics free from all delusion,
    And show'd me what I in my turn have shown;
All I saw farther, in the last confusion,
    Was, that King George slipp'd into heaven for one;
And when the tumult dwindled to a calm,
I left him practising the hundredth psalm.

ON THIS DAY I COMPLETE MY THIRTY-SIXTH
YEAR [95]

'Tis time this heart should be unmoved,
    Since others it hath ceased to move:
Yet, though I cannot be beloved,
            Still let me love!

My days are in the yellow leaf;
    The flowers and fruits of love are gone;

93 when he tried to drive the chariot of his father, the sun god Apollo
94 in Massinger's *A New Way to Pay Old Debts,* I. i. 6
95 written on January 22, 1824, at Missolonghi, whither Byron had gone to fight
for the Greeks; he died there of a fever on April 19

The worm, the canker, and the grief
    Are mine alone!

The fire that on my bosom preys
  Is lone as some volcanic isle;
No torch is kindled at its blaze—
    A funeral pile.

The hope, the fear, the jealous care,
  The exalted portion of the pain
And power of love, I cannot share,
    But wear the chain.

But 'tis not *thus*—and 'tis not *here*—
  Such thoughts should shake my soul, nor *now*,
Where glory decks the hero's bier,
    Or binds his brow.

The sword, the banner, and the field,
  Glory and Greece, around me see!
The Spartan, borne upon his shield,
    Was not more free.

Awake! (not Greece—she *is* awake!)
  Awake, my spirit! Think through *whom*
Thy life-blood tracks its parent lake,
    And then strike home!

Tread those reviving passions down,
  Unworthy manhood!—unto thee
Indifferent should the smile or frown
    Of beauty be.

If thou regrett'st thy youth, *why live?*
  The land of honorable death
Is here:—up to the field, and give
    Away thy breath!

Seek out—less often sought than found—
  A soldier's grave, for thee the best;
Then look around, and choose thy ground,
    And take thy rest.

10

20

30

40

PERCY BYSSHE SHELLEY (1792–1822)

Shelley was the son of a wealthy English squire, Timothy Shelley, who afterwards became a baronet. At his father's house, Field Place, near Horsham, in Sussex, he was born on August 4, 1792. Sir Timothy could not understand his sensitive, temperamental son, nor could his schoolfellows, who tormented him. These early maladjustments fanned within him the spirit of revolt, and turned him to an inner imaginative life. After six years at Eton, in 1810 he entered University College, Oxford, from which he was expelled the next year for his authorship of a pamphlet, *The Necessity of Atheism*. In 1811, in a spirit of chivalry he eloped with Harriet Westbrook, the sixteen-year-old daughter of a retired inn-keeper. Henceforth he was completely estranged from his father, who, however, continued his son's allowance, on which the couple managed precariously to live. Shelley's poetry in these early years is undistinguished, the most important of his juvenilia being *Queen Mab* (1813). A growth in stature is to be seen in *Alastor* (1816), and *The Revolt of Islam* (1817).

Shelley had been early attracted by radical social, political, and religious thought, falling particularly under the sway of William Godwin, the author of *Political Justice*. Godwin preached that Society should reject the illusions of the emotions, and let itself be guided by pure intelligence. In the light of reason the existing distribution of wealth, the established forms of government, the traditional modes of living, even marriage itself were to be revised and remodeled; every constraint exercised upon the individual was to be reduced to a minimum. At Godwin's house the poet met Mary, the brilliant daughter of the philosopher and of the early feminist, Mary Wollstonecraft, and with her he soon fell passionately in love. According to Godwin's system, a previous marriage should be no bar to a more perfect union. Acting on these principles, Shelley eloped with Mary to Italy in 1814. Two years later, Harriet drowned herself in the Serpentine in Hyde Park, London. Shelley then married Mary. In 1817 the Court of Chancery refused to allow the poet the custody of his two children by Harriet, he being adjudged a person unfit for their rearing.

The acts just recited have naturally brought upon Shelley the severest criticism. In extenuation it should be remembered that he moved in an abstract world of ideal truth, and was never able to adapt himself to the practical conditions of human life. From his own point of view his conduct was governed by the highest morality, and he had the courage—or folly—to act immediately upon his convictions, instead of postponing their realization to some far-distant millennium. Byron (who was not inclined to overrate men's motives) speaks of him as "the best and least selfish man I ever knew. I never knew one who was not a beast in comparison."

The summer of 1816 was notable in Shelley's life for an intimate association with Byron in Switzerland. In 1818 he left England to spend the four short years of his life remaining in Italy, chiefly at Naples, Venice, Rome, and Pisa. Here he did nearly all the work for which he is famous—*The Cenci* (his poetic tragedy), *Prometheus Unbound, Epipsychidion, Adonais*, and the best of his short lyrics. On July 8, 1822, he was drowned when the small boat in which he was sailing in the Bay of Lerici was overturned in a squall. Days later, when his body was washed ashore, in the pockets of his coat were found a volume of Sophocles and one of Keats, with the covers turned back. In accordance with the local law he was cremated on the beach, his friends Trelawney, Leigh Hunt, and Byron being present. His ashes were buried in the Protestant Cemetery in Rome, near the grave of Keats.

Shelley possessed an incomparable lyric gift, of a quality all his own. His lyricism, instead of being voluptuously sensual, is soaring and rapturous, and in his greatest productions, like *Prometheus Unbound,* is a perfectly attuned instrument for expressing the poet's throbbing hopes for the bettering of mankind. The message which he sang so gloriously to the world was not sheer Godwinism, but a more spiritual doctrine based upon a faith in the essential goodness of human nature and its perfectibility; looking forward to the coming brotherhood of man in a golden age of beauty, freedom, and love. The lofty idealism of this concept is undeniable; but many will prefer poets who are more of this world.

BIBLIOGRAPHY. *Complete Works* in verse and prose, ed. H. Buxton Forman (Bell). One vol. eds. of the poetry by T. Hutchinson (Oxford), G. E. Woodberry (Cambridge ed., Houghton Mifflin), Edward Dowden (Globe ed., Macmillan). The most recent exhaustive life by W. E. Peck, 2 vols. (Houghton Mifflin). Older "standard" biography by Edward Dowden (Lippincott). Shorter life by J. A. Symonds (Eng. Men of Letters ser.). André Maurois' *Ariel* is a vivid interpretation of the man, and Francis Thompson's *Essay* a brilliant study of one poet by another.

STANZAS—APRIL, 1814

AWAY! the moor is dark beneath the moon,
　Rapid clouds have drank the last pale beam of even:
Away! the gathering winds will call the darkness soon,
　And profoundest midnight shroud the serene lights of heaven.

Pause not! The time is past! Every voice cries, Away!
　Tempt not with one last tear thy friend's ungentle mood:
Thy lover's eye, so glazed and cold, dares not entreat thy stay:
　Duty and dereliction guide thee back to solitude.

Away, away! to thy sad and silent home;
　Pour bitter tears on its desolated hearth;   10
Watch the dim shades as like ghosts they go and come,
　And complicate strange webs of melancholy mirth.

The leaves of wasted autumn woods shall float around thine
　　head:
　The blooms of dewy spring shall gleam beneath thy feet:
But thy soul or this world must fade in the frost that binds
　　the dead,
　Ere midnight's frown and morning's smile, ere thou and
　　peace may meet.

The cloud shadows of midnight possess their own repose,
　For the weary winds are silent, or the moon is in the deep:

Some respite to its turbulence unresting ocean knows;
  Whatever moves, or toils, or grieves, hath its appointed
    sleep.   20

Thou in the grave shalt rest—yet till the phantoms flee
  Which that house and heath and garden made dear to thee
    erewhile,
Thy remembrance, and repentance, and deep musings are not
    free
From the music of two voices and the light of one sweet
    smile.

HYMN TO INTELLECTUAL BEAUTY [1]

I

THE awful shadow of some unseen Power
  Floats though unseen among us,—visiting
  This various world with as inconstant wing
As summer winds that creep from flower to flower,—
Like moonbeams that behind some piny mountain shower,
    It visits with inconstant glance
    Each human heart and countenance;
Like hues and harmonies of evening,—
    Like clouds in starlight widely spread,—
    Like memory of music fled,—   10
    Like aught that for its grace may be
Dear, and yet dearer for its mystery.

2

Spirit of BEAUTY, that dost consecrate
  With thine own hues all thou dost shine upon
  Of human thought or form,—where art thou gone?
Why dost thou pass away and leave our state,
This dim vast vale of tears, vacant and desolate?
    Ask why the sunlight not for ever
    Weaves rainbows o'er yon mountain-river,
Why aught should fail and fade that once is shown,   20
    Why fear and dream and death and birth
    Cast on the daylight of this earth
    Such gloom,—why man has such a scope
For love and hate, despondency and hope?

1 The conception is Platonic. Beautiful earthly things show but an incomplete and
imperfect beauty. They are but unsatisfactory manifestations, pale reflections of that
perfect immaterial spirit of beauty which may be contemplated, but not realized in
this world.

3

No voice from some sublimer world hath ever
  To sage or poet these responses given—
  Therefore the names of Demon, Ghost, and Heaven,
Remain the records of their vain endeavor,
Frail spells—whose uttered charm might not avail to sever,
    From all we hear and all we see,   30
    Doubt, chance, and mutability.
Thy light alone—like mist o'er mountains driven,
    Or music by the night-wind sent
    Through strings of some still instrument,
    Or moonlight on a midnight stream,
Gives grace and truth to life's unquiet dream.

4

Love, Hope, and Self-esteem, like clouds depart
  And come, for some uncertain moments lent.
  Man were immortal, and omnipotent,
Didst thou, unknown and awful as thou art,   40
Keep with thy glorious train firm state within his heart.
    Thou messenger of sympathies,
    That wax and wane in lovers' eyes—
Thou—that to human thought art nourishment,
    Like darkness to a dying flame!
    Depart not as thy shadow came,
    Depart not—lest the grave should be,
Like life and fear, a dark reality.

5

While yet a boy I sought for ghosts, and sped
  Through many a listening chamber, cave and ruin,   50
  And starlight wood, with fearful steps pursuing
Hopes of high talk with the departed dead.
I called on poisonous names with which our youth is fed;
    I was not heard—I saw them not—
    When musing deeply on the lot
Of life, at that sweet time when winds are wooing
    All vital things that wake to bring
    News of birds and blossoming,—
    Sudden, thy shadow fell on me;
I shrieked, and clasped my hands in ecstasy!   60

6

I vowed that I would dedicate my powers
　　To thee and thine—have I not kept the vow?
　　With beating heart and streaming eyes, even now
I call the phantoms of a thousand hours
Each from his voiceless grave: they have in visioned bowers
　　　　Of studious zeal or love's delight
　　　　Outwatched with me the envious night—
They know that never joy illumed my brow
　　　　Unlinked with hope that thou wouldst free
　　　　This world from its dark slavery,　　　　　　70
　　　　That thou—O awful Loveliness,
Wouldst give whate'er these words cannot express.

7

The day becomes more solemn and serene
　　When noon is past—there is a harmony
　　In autumn, and a luster in its sky,
Which through the summer is not heard or seen,
As if it could not be, as if it had not been!
　　　　Thus let thy power, which like the truth
　　　　Of nature on my passive youth
Descended, to my onward life supply　　　　　　80
　　　　Its calm—to one who worships thee,
　　　　And every form containing thee,
　　　　Whom, Spirit fair, thy spells did bind
To fear himself, and love all human kind.

OZYMANDIAS

I met a traveler from an antique land
Who said: Two vast and trunkless legs of stone
Stand in the desert. Near them, on the sand,
Half sunk, a shattered visage lies, whose frown,
And wrinkled lip, and sneer of cold command,
Tell that its sculptor well those passions read
Which yet survive, stamped on these lifeless things,
The hand that mocked them, and the heart that fed: [2]
And on the pedestal these words appear:
"My name is Ozymandias, King of Kings:
Look on my works, ye Mighty, and despair!"

2 the hand of the sculptor, and the heart of Ozymandias

Nothing beside remains. Round the decay
Of that colossal wreck, boundless and bare
The lone and level sands stretch far away.

STANZAS

WRITTEN IN DEJECTION, NEAR NAPLES

I

THE sun is warm, the sky is clear,
　　The waves are dancing fast and bright,
Blue isles and snowy mountains wear
　　The purple noon's transparent might,
　　The breath of the moist earth is light,
Around its unexpanded buds;
　　Like many a voice of one delight,
The winds, the birds, the ocean floods,
The City's voice itself, is soft like Solitude's.

2

I see the Deep's untrampled floor
　　With green and purple seaweeds strown;
I see the waves upon the shore,
　　Like light dissolved in star-showers, thrown:
　　I sit upon the sands alone,—
The lightning of the moontide ocean
　　Is flashing round me, and a tone
Arises from its measured motion,
How sweet! did any heart now share in my emotion.

3

Alas! I have nor hope nor health,
　　Nor peace within nor calm around,
Nor that content surpassing wealth
　　The sage in meditation found,
　　And walked with inward glory crowned—
Nor fame, nor power, nor love, nor leisure.
　　Others I see whom these surround—
Smiling they live, and call life pleasure;—
To me that cup has been dealt in another measure.

4

Yet now despair itself is mild,
　　Even as the winds and waters are;
I could lie down like a tired child,
　　And weep away the life of care
　　Which I have borne and yet must bear,
Till death like sleep might steal on me,
　　And I might feel in the warm air
My cheek grow cold, and hear the sea
Breathe o'er my dying brain its last monotony.

5

Some might lament that I were cold,
　　As I, when this sweet day is gone,
Which my lost heart, too soon grown old,
　　Insults with this untimely moan;
　　They might lament—for I am one
Whom men love not,—and yet regret,
　　Unlike this day, which, when the sun
Shall on its stainless glory set,
Will linger, though enjoyed, like joy in memory yet.

ENGLAND IN 1819

An old, mad, blind, despised, and dying king,— [3]
Princes, the dregs of their dull race, who flow
Through public scorn,—mud from a muddy spring,—
Rulers who neither see, nor feel, nor know,
But leech-like to their fainting country cling,
Till they drop, blind in blood, without a blow,—
A people starved and stabbed in the untilled field,—
An army, which liberticide and prey
Makes as a two-edged sword to all who wield,—
Golden and sanguine laws which tempt and slay;
Religion Christless, Godless—a book sealed;
A Senate,—Time's worst statute unrepealed,— [4]
Are graves, from which a glorious Phantom [5] may
Burst, to illumine our tempestuous day.

3 George III
4 the law imposing civil
disabilities on Roman Catholics
5 Liberty

wild spirit & preserver
wild destroyer
his own uncontrollable spirit

ODE TO THE WEST WIND [6]

1

O WILD West Wind, thou breath of Autumn's being,
Thou, from whose unseen presence the leaves dead
Are driven, like ghosts from an enchanter fleeing,

Yellow, and black, and pale, and hectic red,
Pestilence-stricken multitudes: O thou,
Who chariotest to their dark wintry bed

The wingèd seeds, where they lie cold and low,
Each like a corpse within its grave, until
Thine azure sister of the Spring shall blow

Her clarion o'er the dreaming earth, and fill   10
(Driving sweet buds like flocks to feed in air)
With living hues and odors plain and hill:

Wild Spirit, which art moving everywhere;
Destroyer and preserver; hear, oh, hear!

2

Thou on whose stream, 'mid the steep sky's commotion,
Loose clouds like earth's decaying leaves are shed,
Shook from the tangled boughs of Heaven and Ocean,

Angels of rain and lightning: there are spread
On the blue surface of thine airy surge,
Like the bright hair uplifted from the head   20

Of some fierce Mænad,[7] even from the dim verge
Of the horizon to the zenith's height,
The locks of the approaching storm. Thou dirge

Of the dying year, to which this closing night
Will be the dome of a vast sepulcher,
Vaulted with all thy congregated might

6 "This poem was conceived and chiefly written in a wood that skirts the Arno, near Florence, and on a day when that tempestuous wind, whose temperature is at once mild and animating, was collecting the vapors which pour down the autumnal rains. They began, as I foresaw, at sunset with a violent tempest of hail and rain, attended by that magnificent thunder and lightning peculiar to the Cisalpine regions. The phenomenon alluded to at the conclusion of the third stanza is well known to naturalists. The vegetation at the bottom of the sea, of rivers, and of lakes, sympathizes with that of the land in the change of seasons, and is consequently influenced by the winds which announce it." (Shelley)
7 Bacchante

Of vapors, from whose solid atmosphere
Black rain, and fire, and hail will burst: oh, hear!

3

Thou who didst waken from his summer dreams
The blue Mediterranean, where he lay,   30
Lulled by the coil of his crystálline streams,

Beside a pumice isle in Baiæ's bay,[8]
And saw in sleep old palaces and towers
Quivering within the wave's intenser day,

All overgrown with azure moss and flowers
So sweet, the sense faints picturing them! Thou
For whose path the Atlantic's level powers

Cleave themselves into chasms, while far below
The sea-blooms and the oozy woods which wear
The sapless foliage of the ocean, know   40

Thy voice, and suddenly grow gray with fear,
And tremble and despoil themselves: oh, hear!

4

If I were a dead leaf thou mightest bear;
If I were a swift cloud to fly with thee;
A wave to pant beneath thy power, and share

The impulse of thy strength, only less free
Than thou, O uncontrollable! If even
I were as in my boyhood, and could be

The comrade of thy wanderings over Heaven,
As then, when to outstrip thy skyey speed   50
Scarce seemed a vision; I would ne'er have striven

As thus with thee in prayer in my sore need.
Oh, lift me as a wave, a leaf, a cloud!
I fall upon the thorns of life! I bleed!

A heavy weight of hours has chained and bowed
One too like thee: tameless, and swift, and proud.

8 near Naples

5

Make me thy lyre, even as the forest is:
What if my leaves are falling like its own!
The tumult of thy mighty harmonies

Will take from both a deep, autumnal tone,   60
Sweet though in sadness. Be thou, Spirit fierce,
My spirit! Be thou me, impetuous one!

Drive my dead thoughts over the universe
Like withered leaves to quicken a new birth!
And, by the incantation of this verse,

Scatter, as from an unextinguished hearth
Ashes and sparks, my words among mankind!
Be through my lips to unawakened earth

The trumpet of a prophecy! O, Wind,
If Winter comes, can Spring be far behind?   70

THE INDIAN SERENADE

1

I ARISE from dreams of thee
In the first sweet sleep of night,
When the winds are breathing low,
And the stars are shining bright:
I arise from dreams of thee,
And a spirit in my feet
Hath led me—who knows how?
To thy chamber window, Sweet!

2

The wandering airs they faint
On the dark, the silent stream—
The Champak [9] odors fail
Like sweet thoughts in a dream;
The nightingale's complaint,
It dies upon her heart;—
As I must on thine,
Oh, belovèd as thou art!

9 an East Indian tree related to the magnolia

3

O lift me from the grass!
I die! I faint! I fail!
Let thy love in kisses rain
On my lips and eyelids pale.
My cheek is cold and white, alas!
My heart beats loud and fast;—
Oh! press it to thine own again,
Where it will break at last.

LOVE'S PHILOSOPHY

I

THE fountains mingle with the river
  And the rivers with the Ocean,
The winds of Heaven mix for ever
  With a sweet emotion;
Nothing in the world is single;
  All things by a law divine
In one spirit meet and mingle.
  Why not I with thine?—

2

See the mountains kiss high Heaven
  And the waves clasp one another;
No sister-flower would be forgiven
  If it disdained its brother;
And the sunlight clasps the earth
  And the moonbeams kiss the sea:
What is all this sweet work worth
  If thou kiss not me?

PROMETHEUS UNBOUND

A LYRICAL DRAMA IN FOUR ACTS

Audisne haec, Amphiarae, sub terram abdite? [10]

DRAMATIS PERSONÆ

PROMETHEUS.	APOLLO.	HERCULES.
DEMOGORGON.	MERCURY.	THE PHANTASM OF JUPITER.
JUPITER.	ASIA ⎫ Ocean-	THE SPIRIT OF THE EARTH.
THE EARTH.	PANTHEA ⎬ ides.	THE SPIRIT OF THE MOON.
OCEAN.	IONE ⎭	SPIRITS OF THE HOURS.

SPIRITS. ECHOES. FAUNS. FURIES.

In the *Prometheus Bound* of Æschylus, the Titan, Prometheus, having offended Zeus by his gift to man of fire and the arts, is punished by being chained to a rocky mountain-side and subjected to terrible tortures, which, however, fail to subdue his will. Shelley in *Prometheus Unbound* presents an imaginative continuation of the story, infused with his own ideal thought, and pulsing with his program for the regeneration of mankind. Prometheus, after the lapse of ages, adds love to strength and endurance. Jove, the unjust and tyrannical ruler of the universe, is hurled from his throne by Demogorgon, the primal power of the world, and Necessity, in the person of Hercules, delivers Prometheus from his sufferings. Asia, representing the spirit of love in the human race, is restored to her husband, and their union marks the beginning of the Golden Age.

The sections of Shelley's Greek drama here reprinted present the essentials of the story, the glowing and enthusiastic aspirations of the poet, and some of his greatest lyric flights.

ACT I

SCENE.—*A Ravine of Icy Rocks in the Indian Caucasus.* PROMETHEUS *is discovered bound to the Precipice.* PAN-THEA *and* IONE *are seated at his feet. Time, night. During the Scene, morning slowly breaks.*

Prometheus. Monarch of Gods and Dæmons,[11] and all
    Spirits
BUT One, who throng those bright and rolling worlds
Which Thou and I alone of living things
Behold with sleepless eyes! regard this Earth
Made multitudinous with thy slaves, whom thou
Requitest for knee-worship, prayer, and praise,
And toil, and hecatombs of broken hearts,

[10] Dost not thou, Amphiaraus, hear this, hidden beneath the earth? Amphiaraus was the minstrel whose playing raised the walls of Thebes, and who, when portents told that the city was about to fall, plunged himself into the abyss.

[11] spirits; in the Greek sense not necessarily evil or malevolent

With fear and self-contempt and barren hope.
Whilst me, who am thy foe, eyeless in hate,
Hast thou made reign and triumph, to thy scorn,   10
O'er mine own misery and thy vain revenge.
Three thousand years of sleep-unsheltered hours,
And moments aye divided by keen pangs
Till they seemed years, torture and solitude,
Scorn and despair,—these are mine empire,
More glorious far than that which thou surveyest
From thine unenvied throne, O Mighty God!
Almighty, had I deigned to share the shame
Of thine ill tyranny, and hung not here
Nailed to this wall of eagle-baffling mountain,   20
Black, wintry, dead, unmeasured; without herb,
Insect, or beast, or shape or sound of life.
Ah me! alas, pain, pain ever, for ever!

No change, no pause, no hope! Yet I endure.
I ask the Earth, have not the mountains felt?
I ask yon Heaven, the all-beholding Sun,
Has it not seen? The Sea, in storm or calm,
Heaven's ever-changing Shadow, spread below,
Have its deaf waves not heard my agony?
Ah me! alas, pain, pain ever, for ever!   30

The crawling glaciers pierce me with the spears
Of their moon-freezing crystals, the bright chains
Eat with their burning cold into my bones.
Heaven's wingèd hound,[12] polluting from thy lips
His beak in poison not his own, tears up
My heart; and shapeless sights come wandering by,
The ghastly people of the realm of dream,
Mocking me: and the Earthquake-fiends are charged
To wrench the rivets from my quivering wounds
When the rocks split and close again behind: 40
While from their loud abysses howling throng
The genii of the storm, urging the rage
Of whirlwind, and afflict me with keen hail.
And yet to me welcome is day and night,
Whether one breaks the hoar frost of the morn,
Or starry, dim, and slow, the other climbs
The leaden-colored east; for then they lead
The wingless, crawling hours, one among whom
—As some dark Priest hales the reluctant victim—
Shall drag thee, cruel King, to kiss the blood   50

12 the vulture which tore the entrails of Prometheus

Now seen athwart frore vapors, deep below,
Through whose o'ershadowing woods I wandered once
With Asia, drinking life from her loved eyes;
Why scorns the spirit which informs [13] ye, now
To commune with me? me alone, who checked,
As one who checks a fiend-drawn charioteer,
The falsehood and the force of him who reigns
Supreme, and with the groans of pining slaves
Fills your dim glens and liquid wildernesses:
Why answer ye not, still? Brethren!
  The Earth.   They dare not. 130
  Prometheus. Who dares? for I would hear that curse again.
Ha, what an awful whisper rises up!
'Tis scarce like sound: it tingles through the frame
As lightning tingles, hovering ere it strike.
Speak, Spirit! from thine inorganic voice
I only know that thou art moving near,
And love. How cursed I him?
  The Earth.   How canst thou hear
Who knowest not the language of the dead?
  Prometheus. Thou art a living spirit; speak as they. 140
  The Earth. I dare not speak like life, lest Heaven's fell King
Should hear, and link me to some wheel of pain
More torturing than the one whereon I roll.
Subtle thou art and good, and though the Gods
Hear not this voice, yet thou art more than God,
Being wise and kind: earnestly hearken now.
  Prometheus. Obscurely through my brain, like shadows dim,
Sweep awful thoughts, rapid and thick. I feel
Faint, like one mingled in entwining love;
Yet 'tis not pleasure.
  The Earth. No, thou canst not hear:
Thou art immortal, and this tongue is known 150
Only to those who die.
  Prometheus. And what art thou,
O melancholy Voice?
  The Earth. I am the Earth,
Thy mother; she within whose stony veins,
To the last fiber of the loftiest tree
Whose thin leaves trembled in the frozen air,
Joy ran, as blood within a living frame,
When thou didst from her bosom, like a cloud
Of glory, arise, a spirit of keen joy!
And at thy voice her pining sons uplifted
Their prostrate brows from the polluting dust, 160

13 animates

And our almighty Tyrant with fierce dread
Grew pale, until his thunder chained thee here.
Then, see those million worlds which burn and roll
Around us: their inhabitants beheld
My spherèd light wane in wide Heaven; the sea
Was lifted by strange tempest, and new fire
From earthquake-rifted mountains of bright snow
Shook its portentous hair beneath Heaven's frown;
Lightning and Inundation vexed the plains;
Blue thistles bloomed in cities; foodless toads   170
Within voluptuous chambers panting crawled:
When Plague had fallen on man, and beast, and worm,
And Famine; and black blight on herb and tree;
And in the corn, and vines, and meadow-grass,
Teemed ineradicable poisonous weeds
Draining their growth, for my wan breast was dry
With grief; and the thin air, my breath, was stained
With the contagion of a mother's hate
Breathed on her child's destroyer; ay, I heard
Thy curse, the which, if thou rememberest not,   180
Yet my innumerable seas and streams,
Mountains and caves, and winds, and yon wide air,
And the inarticulate people of the dead,
Preserve a treasured spell. We meditate
In secret joy and hope those dreadful words,
But dare not speak them.
    Prometheus.   Venerable mother!
All else who live and suffer take from thee
Some comfort; flowers, and fruits, and happy sounds,
And love, though fleeting; these may not be mine.
But mine own words, I pray, deny me not.   190
    The Earth. They shall be told. Ere Babylon was dust,
The Magus Zoroaster, my dead child,
Met his own image walking in the garden.
That apparition, sole of men, he saw.
For know there are two worlds of life and death:
One that which thou beholdest; but the other
Is underneath the grave, where do inhabit
The shadows of all forms that think and live
Till death unite them and they part no more;
Dreams and the light imaginings of men   200
And all that faith creates or love desires,
Terrible, strange, sublime and beauteous shapes.
There thou art, and dost hang, a writhing shade,
'Mid whirlwind-peopled mountains; all the gods
Are there, and all the powers of nameless worlds,

Vast, sceptered phantoms; heroes, men, and beasts;
And Demogorgon, a tremendous gloom;
And he, the supreme Tyrant, on his throne
Of burning gold. Son, one of these shall utter
The curse which all remember. Call at will   210
Thine own ghost, or the ghost of Jupiter,
Hades [14] or Typhon,[15] or what mightier Gods
From all-prolific Evil, since thy ruin
Have sprung, and trampled on my prostrate sons.
Ask, and they must reply: so the revenge
Of the Supreme may sweep through vacant shades,
As rainy wind through the abandoned gate
Of a fallen palace.
   Prometheus.   Mother, let not aught
Of that which may be evil, pass again
My lips, or those of aught resembling me.   220
Phantasm of Jupiter, arise, appear!

Ione

My wings are folded o'er mine ears:
  My wings are crossèd o'er mine eyes:
Yet through their silver shade appears,
  And through their lulling plumes arise,
A Shape, a throng of sounds;
  May it be no ill to thee
O thou of many wounds!
Near whom, for our sweet sister's sake,
Ever thus we watch and wake.   230

Panthea

The sound is of whirlwind underground,
  Earthquake, and fire, and mountains cloven;
The shape is awful like the sound,
  Clothed in dark purple, star-inwoven.
A scepter of pale gold
  To stay steps proud, o'er the slow cloud
His veinèd hand doth hold.
Cruel he looks, but calm and strong,
Like one who does, not suffers wrong.

Phantasm of Jupiter. Why have the secret powers of this
    strange world   240
Driven me, a frail and empty phantom, hither

14 Pluto   15 one of the monsters of the primitive world

On direst storms? What unaccustomed sounds
Are hovering on my lips, unlike the voice
With which our pallid race hold ghastly talk
In darkness? And, proud sufferer, who art thou?
   Prometheus. Tremendous Image, as thou art must be
He whom thou shadowest forth. I am his foe,
The Titan. Speak the words which I would hear,
Although no thought inform thine empty voice.
   The Earth. Listen! And though your echoes must be mute,   250
Gray mountains, and old woods, and haunted springs,
Prophetic caves, and isle-surrounding streams,
Rejoice to hear what yet ye cannot speak.
   Phantasm. A spirit seizes me and speaks within:
It tears me as fire tears a thunder-cloud.
   Panthea. See, how he lifts his mighty looks, the Heaven
Darkens above.
   Ione.   He speaks! O shelter me!
   Prometheus. I see the curse on gestures proud and cold,
And looks of firm defiance, and calm hate,
And such despair as mocks itself with smiles,   260
Written as on a scroll: yet speak: Oh, speak!

Phantasm

Fiend, I defy thee! with a calm, fixed mind,
   All that thou canst inflict I bid thee do;
Foul Tyrant both of Gods and Human-kind,
   One only being shalt thou not subdue.
Rain then thy plagues upon me here,
Ghastly disease, and frenzying fear;
And let alternate frost and fire
Eat into me, and be thine ire
Lightning, and cutting hail, and legioned forms   270
Of furies, driving by upon the wounding storms.

Ay, do thy worst. Thou art omnipotent.
   O'er all things but thyself I gave thee power,
And my own will. Be thy swift mischiefs sent
   To blast mankind, from yon ethereal tower.
Let thy malignant spirit move
In darkness over those I love:
On me and mine I imprecate
The utmost torture of thy hate;
And thus devote to sleepless agony,   280
This undeclining head while thou must reign on high.

But thou, who art the God and Lord: O, thou,
   Who fillest with thy soul this world of woe,
To whom all things of Earth and Heaven do bow
   In fear and worship: all-prevailing foe!
I curse thee! let a sufferer's curse
Clasp thee, his torturer, like remorse;
Till thine Infinity shall be
A robe of envenomed agony;
And thine Omnipotence a crown of pain,   290
To cling like burning gold round thy dissolving brain.

Heap on thy soul, by virtue of this Curse,
   Ill deeds, then be thou damned, beholding good;
Both infinite as is the universe,
   And thou, and thy self-torturing solitude.
An awful image of calm power
Though now thou sittest, let the hour
Come, when thou must appear to be
That which thou art internally;
And after many a false and fruitless crime   300
Scorn track thy lagging fall through boundless space and time.

Prometheus. Were these my words, O Parent?

The Earth.   They were thine.
Prometheus. It doth repent me: words are quick and vain;
Grief for awhile is blind, and so was mine.
I wish no living thing to suffer pain.

The Earth

Misery, Oh misery to me,
   That Jove at length should vanquish thee.
Wail, howl aloud, Land and Sea,
   The Earth's rent heart shall answer ye.
Howl, Spirits of the living and the dead,   310
Your refuge, your defense lies fallen and vanquishèd.

First Echo

Lies fallen and vanquishèd!

Second Echo

Fallen and vanquishèd!

Ione

Fear not: 'tis but some passing spasm,
   The Titan is unvanquished still.

But see, where through the azure chasm
　　Of yon forked and snowy hill
Trampling the slant winds on high
　　With golden-sandaled feet, that glow
Under plumes of purple dye,   320
Like rose-ensanguined ivory,
　　A Shape comes now,
Stretching on high from his right hand
A serpent-cinctured wand.[16]

Panthea. 'Tis Jove's world-wandering herald, Mercury.

Ione

And who are those with hydra tresses
　　And iron wings that climb the wind,
Whom the frowning God represses
　　Like vapors steaming up behind,
Clanging loud an endless crowd—   330

Panthea

These are Jove's tempest-walking hounds,
Whom he gluts with groans and blood,
When charioted on sulphurous cloud
　　He bursts Heaven's bounds.

Ione

Are they now led, from the thin dead
On new pangs to be fed?

Panthea

The Titan looks as ever, firm, not proud.
First Fury. Ha! I scent life!
Second Fury.　　　　　　Let me but look into his eyes!
Third Fury. The hope of torturing him smells like a heap
Of corpses, to a death-bird after battle.   340
First Fury. Darest thou delay, O Herald! take cheer, Hounds
Of Hell: what if the Son of Maia [17] soon
Should make us food and sport—who can please long
The Omnipotent?
Mercury.　　　　Back to your towers of iron,
And gnash, beside the streams of fire and wail,

16 the caduceus, or rod, of Mercury   17 Mercury

Your foodless teeth. Geryon [18] arise! and Gorgon,
Chimaera, and thou Sphinx,[19] subtlest of fiends
Who ministered to Thebes Heaven's poisoned wine,
Unnatural love, and more unnatural hate:
These shall perform your task.
 First Fury.   Oh, mercy! mercy! 350
We die with our desire: drive us not back!
 Mercury. Crouch then in silence.
         Awful sufferer!
To thee unwilling, most unwillingly
I come, by the great Father's will driven down,
To execute a doom of new revenge.
Alas! I pity thee, and hate myself
That I can do no more: aye from thy sight
Returning, for a season, Heaven seems Hell,
So thy worn form pursues me night and day,
Smiling reproach. Wise art thou, firm and good, 360
But vainly wouldst stand forth alone in strife
Against the Omnipotent; as yon clear lamps
That measure and divide the weary years
From which there is no refuge, long have taught
And long must teach. Even now thy Torturer arms
With the strange might of unimagined pains
The powers who scheme slow agonies in Hell,
And my commission is to lead them here,
Or what more subtle, foul, or savage fiends
People the abyss, and leave them to their task. 370
Be it not so! there is a secret known
To thee, and to none else of living things,
Which may transfer the sceptre of wide Heaven,
The fear of which perplexes the Supreme:
Clothe it in words, and bid it clasp his throne
In intercession; bend thy soul in prayer,
And like a suppliant in some gorgeous fane,
Let the will kneel within thy haughty heart:
For benefits and meek submission tame
The fiercest and the mightiest.
 Prometheus.   Evil minds 380
Change good to their own nature. I gave all
He has; and in return he chains me here
Years, ages, night and day: whether the Sun
Split my parched skin, or in the moony night
The crystal-wingèd snow cling round my hair:

---

18 monsters of classical myth
19 He propounded the fa-mous riddle which Œdipus solved, so delivered Thebes, but unwittingly married his own mother, Jocasta, with dire resulting tragedy.

Whilst my belovèd race is trampled down
By his thought-executing ministers.
Such is the tyrant's recompense: 'tis just:
He who is evil can receive no good;
And for a world bestowed, or a friend lost,   390
He can feel hate, fear, shame; not gratitude:
He but requites me for his own misdeed.
Kindness to such is keen reproach, which breaks
With bitter stings the light sleep of Revenge.
Submission, thou dost know I cannot try:
For what submission but that fatal word,
The death-seal of mankind's captivity,
Like the Sicilian's hair-suspended sword,[20]
Which trembles o'er his crown, would he accept,
Or could I yield? Which yet I will not yield.   400
Let others flatter Crime, where it sits throned
In brief Omnipotence: secure are they:
For Justice, when triumphant, will weep down
Pity, not punishment, on her own wrongs,
Too much avenged by those who err. I wait,
Enduring thus, the retributive hour
Which since we spake is even nearer now.
But hark, the hell-hounds clamor: fear delay:
Behold! Heaven lowers under thy Father's frown.
   Mercury. Oh, that we might be spared: I to inflict   410
And thou to suffer! Once more answer me:
Thou knowest not the period of Jove's power?
   Prometheus. I know but this, that it must come.
   Mercury.   Alas!
Thou canst not count thy years to come of pain?
   Prometheus. They last while Jove must reign: nor more, nor
    less
Do I desire or fear.
   Mercury.   Yet pause, and plunge
Into Eternity, where recorded time,
Even all that we imagine, age on age,
Seems but a point, and the reluctant mind
Flags wearily in its unending flight,   420
Till it sink, dizzy, blind, lost, shelterless;
Perchance it has not numbered the slow years
Which thou must spend in torture, unreprieved?
   Prometheus. Perchance no thought can count them, yet they
    pass.
   Mercury. If thou might'st dwell among the Gods the while
Lapped in voluptuous joy?

20 the sword of Damocles

Prometheus.   I would not quit
This bleak ravine, these unrepentant pains.
  Mercury. Alas! I wonder at, yet pity thee.
  Prometheus. Pity the self-despising slaves of **Heaven,**
Not me, within whose mind sits peace serene,   430
As light in the sun, throned: how vain is talk!
Call up the fiends.
  Ione.   O, sister, look! White fire
Has cloven to the roots yon huge snow-loaded cedar;
How fearfully God's thunder howls behind!
  Mercury. I must obey his words and thine: alas!
Most heavily remorse hangs at my heart!
  Panthea. See where the child of Heaven, with wingèd feet,
Runs down the slanted sunlight of the dawn.
  Ione. Dear sister, close thy plumes over thine eyes
Lest thou behold and die: they come: they come   440
Blackening the birth of day with countless wings,
And hollow underneath, like death.
  First Fury.   Prometheus!
  Second Fury. Immortal Titan!
  Third Fury.   Champion of Heaven's slaves!
  Prometheus. He whom some dreadful voice invokes is here,
Prometheus, the chained Titan. Horrible forms,
What and who are ye? Never yet there came
Phantasms so foul through monster-teeming Hell
From the all-miscreative brain of Jove;
Whilst I behold such execrable shapes,
Methinks I grow like what I contemplate,   450
And laugh and stare in loathsome sympathy.
  First Fury. We are the ministers of pain, and fear,
And disappointment, and mistrust, and hate,
And clinging crime; and as lean dogs pursue
Through wood and lake some struck and sobbing fawn,
We track all things that weep, and bleed, and live,
When the great King betrays them to our will.
  Prometheus. Oh! many fearful natures in one name,
I know ye; and these lakes and echoes know
The darkness and the clangor of your wings.   460
But why more hideous than your loathèd selves
Gather ye up in legions from the deep?
  Second Fury. We knew not that: Sisters, rejoice, rejoice!
  Prometheus. Can aught exult in its deformity?
  Second Fury. The beauty of delight makes lovers glad,
Gazing on one another: so are we.
As from the rose which the pale priestess kneels
To gather for her festal crown of flowers

The aerial crimson falls, flushing her cheek,
So from our victim's destined agony   470
The shade which is our form invests us round,
Else we are shapeless as our mother Night.
  Prometheus. I laugh your power, and his who sent you here,
To lowest scorn. Pour forth the cup of pain.
  First Fury. Thou thinkest we will rend thee bone from bone,
And nerve from nerve, working like fire within?
  Prometheus. Pain is my element, as hate is thine;
Ye rend me now: I care not.
  Second Fury.   Dost imagine
We will but laugh into thy lidless eyes?
  Prometheus. I weigh not what ye do, but what ye suffer,   480
Being evil. Cruel was the power which called
You, or aught else so wretched, into light.
  Third Fury. Thou think'st we will live through thee, one
      by one,
Like animal life, and though we can obscure not
The soul which burns within, that we will dwell
Beside it, like a vain loud multitude
Vexing the self-content of wisest men:
That we will be dread thought beneath thy brain,
And foul desire round thine astonished heart,
And blood within thy labyrinthine veins   490
Crawling like agony?
  Prometheus.   Why, ye are thus now;
Yet am I king over myself, and rule
The torturing and conflicting throngs within,
As Jove rules you when Hell grows mutinous.

Chorus of Furies

From the ends of the earth, from the ends of the earth,
Where the night has its grave and the morning its birth,
        Come, come, come!
Oh, ye who shake hills with the scream of your mirth,
When cities sink howling in ruin; and ye
Who with wingless footsteps trample the sea,   500
And close upon Shipwreck and Famine's track,
Sit chattering with joy on the foodless wreck;
        Come, come, come!
    Leave the bed, low, cold, and red,
    Strewed beneath a nation dead;
    Leave the hatred, as in ashes
      Fire is left for future burning:

It will burst in bloodier flashes
　When ye stir it, soon returning:
Leave the self-contempt implanted　　　　510
In young spirits, sense-enchanted,
　Misery's yet unkindled fuel:
Leave Hell's secrets half unchanted
　To the maniac dreamer; cruel
More than ye can be with hate
　Is he with fear.
　　　Come, come, come!
We are steaming up from Hell's wide gate
And we burthen the blast of the atmosphere,
But vainly we toil till ye come here.　　　520

Ione. Sister, I hear the thunder of new wings.
Panthea. These solid mountains quiver with the sound
Even as the tremulous air: their shadows make
The space within my plumes more black than night.

First Fury

Your call was as a wingèd car
Driven on whirlwinds fast and far;
It rapt us from red gulfs of war

Second Fury

From wide cities, famine-wasted;

Third Fury

Groans half heard, and blood untasted;

Fourth Fury

Kingly conclaves stern and cold,　　　　530
Where blood with gold is bought and sold;

Fifth Fury

From the furnace, white and hot,
In which—

A Fury

　　Speak not: whisper not:
I know all that ye would tell,
But to speak might break the spell

Which must bend the Invincible,
  The stern of thought;
He yet defies the deepest power of Hell.

A Fury

Tear the veil!

Another Fury

It is torn.

Chorus

                 The pale stars of the morn
Shine on a misery, dire to be borne.   540
Dost thou faint, mighty Titan? We laugh thee to scorn.
Dost thou boast the clear knowledge thou waken'dst for man?
Then was kindled within him a thirst which outran
Those perishing waters; a thirst of fierce fever,
Hope, love, doubt, desire, which consume him for ever.
    One came forth of gentle worth [21]
    Smiling on the sanguine earth;
    His words outlived him, like swift poison
      Withering up truth, peace, and pity.
    Look! where round the wide horizon   550
      Many a million-peopled city
    Vomits smoke in the bright air.
    Hark that outcry of despair!
    'Tis his mild and gentle ghost
      Wailing for the faith he kindled:
    Look again, the flames almost
      To a glow-worm's lamp have dwindled:
The survivors round the embers
  Gather in dread.
              Joy, joy, joy!   560
Past ages crowd on thee, but each one remembers,
And the future is dark, and the present is spread
Like a pillow of thorns for thy slumberless head.

Semichorus I

Drops of bloody agony flow
From his white and quivering brow.
Grant a little respite now:
See a disenchanted nation [22]

---

21 Christ   22 France—in the Revolution

Springs like day from desolation;
To Truth its state is dedicate,
And Freedom leads it forth, her mate;   570
A legioned band of linkèd brothers
Whom Love calls children—

Semichorus II

'Tis another's:
See how kindred murder kin:
'Tis the vintage-time for death and sin:
Blood, like new wine, bubbles within:
Till Despair smothers
The struggling world, which slaves and tyrants win.
[All the FURIES *vanish, except one.*

Ione. Hark, sister! what a low yet dreadful groan
Quite unsuppressed is tearing up the heart
Of the good Titan, as storms tear the deep,   580
And beasts hear the sea moan in inland caves.
Darest thou observe how the fiends torture him?
Panthea. Alas! I looked forth twice, but will no more.
Ione. What didst thou see?
Panthea.   A woeful sight: a youth
With patient looks nailed to a crucifix.[23]
Ione. What next?
Panthea.   The heaven around, the earth below
Was peopled with thick shapes of human death,
All horrible, and wrought by human hands,
And some appeared the work of human hearts,
For men were slowly killed by frowns and smiles: 590
And other sights too foul to speak and live
Were wandering by. Let us not tempt worse fear
By looking forth: those groans are grief enough.
Fury. Behold an emblem: those who do endure
Deep wrongs for man, and scorn, and chains, but heap
Thousandfold torment on themselves and him.
Prometheus. Remit the anguish of that lighted stare;
Close those wan lips; let that thorn-wounded brow
Stream not with blood; it mingles with thy tears!
Fix, fix those tortured orbs in peace and death,   600
So thy sick throes shake not that crucifix,
So those pale fingers play not with thy gore.
O, horrible! Thy name I will not speak,
It hath become a curse. I see, I see

23 Christ again. The following lines refer to the Christian persecutions and martyr-doms.

The wise, the mild, the lofty, and the just,
Whom thy slaves hate for being like to thee,
Some hunted by foul lies from their heart's home,
An early-chosen, late-lamented home;
As hooded ounces cling to the driven hind;
Some linked to corpses in unwholesome cells: 610
Some—Hear I not the multitude laugh loud?—
Impaled in lingering fire: and mighty realms
Float by my feet, like sea-uprooted isles,
Whose sons are kneaded down in common blood
By the red light of their own burning homes.
    Fury. Blood thou canst see, and fire; and canst hear groans;
Worse things, unheard, unseen, remain behind.
    Prometheus. Worse?
    Fury.   In each human heart terror survives
The ravin it has gorged: the loftiest fear
All that they would disdain to think were true: 620
Hypocrisy and custom make their minds
The fanes of many a worship, now outworn.
They dare not devise good for man's estate,
And yet they know not that they do not dare.
The good want power, but to weep barren tears.
The powerful goodness want: worse need for them.
The wise want love; and those who love want wisdom;
And all best things are thus confused to ill.
Many are strong and rich, and would be just,
But live among their suffering fellow-men   630
As if none felt: they know not what they do.
    Prometheus. Thy words are like a cloud of wingèd snakes;
And yet I pity those they torture not.
    Fury. Thou pitiest them? I speak no more! [*Vanishes.*
    Prometheus.   Ah woe!
Ah woe! Alas! pain, pain ever, for ever!
I close my tearless eyes, but see more clear
Thy works within my woe-illumèd mind,
Thou subtle tyrant! Peace is in the grave.
The grave hides all things beautiful and good:
I am a God and cannot find it there,   640
Nor would I seek it: for, though dread revenge,
This is defeat, fierce king, not victory.
The sights with which thou torturest gird my soul
With new endurance, till the hour arrives
When they shall be no types of things which are.
    Panthea. Alas! what sawest thou more?
    Prometheus.   There are two woes:
To speak, and to behold; thou spare me one.

Names are there, Nature's sacred watchwords, they [24]
Were borne aloft in bright emblazonry;
The nations thronged around, and cried aloud,   650
As with one voice, Truth, liberty, and love!
Suddenly fierce confusion fell from heaven
Among them: there was strife, deceit, and fear:
Tyrants rushed in, and did divide the spoil.
This was the shadow of the truth I saw.
   The Earth. I felt thy torture, son: with such mixed joy
As pain and virtue give. To cheer thy state
I bid ascend those subtle and fair spirits,
Whose homes are the dim caves of human thought,
And who inhabit, as birds wing the wind,   660
Its world-surrounding ether: they behold
Beyond that twilight realm, as in a glass,
The future: may they speak comfort to thee!
   Panthea. Look, sister, where a troop of spirits gather,
Like flocks of clouds in spring's delightful weather,
Thronging in the blue air!
   Ione.   And see! more come,
Like fountain-vapors when the winds are dumb,
That climb up the ravine in scattered lines.
And, hark! Is it the music of the pines?
Is it the lake? Is it the waterfall?   670
   Panthea. 'Tis something sadder, sweeter far than all.

Chorus of Spirits

    From unremembered ages we
    Gentle guides and guardians be
    Of heaven-oppressed mortality;
    And we breathe, and sicken not,
    The atmosphere of human thought;
    Be it dim, and dank, and gray,
    Like a storm-extinguished day,
    Traveled o'er by dying gleams;
      Be it bright as all between   680
    Cloudless skies and windless streams,
      Silent, liquid, and serene;
    As the birds within the wind,
      As the fish within the wave,
    As the thoughts of man's own mind
      Float through all above the grave;
    We make there our liquid lair,
    Voyaging cloudlike and unpent

24 The course of the French Revolution is described.

Through the boundless element:
Thence we bear the prophecy　　　　　690
Which begins and ends in thee!

Ione. More yet come, one by one: the air around them
Looks radiant as the air around a star.

First Spirit

On a battle-trumpet's blast
I fled hither, fast, fast, fast,
'Mid the darkness upward cast.
From the dust of creeds outworn,
From the tyrant's banner torn,
Gathering 'round me, onward borne,
There was mingled many a cry—　　　　700
Freedom! Hope! Death! Victory!
Till they faded through the sky;
And one sound, above, around,
One sound beneath, around, above,
Was moving; 'twas the soul of Love;
'Twas the hope, the prophecy,
Which begins and ends in thee.

Second Spirit

A rainbow's arch stood on the sea,
Which rocked beneath, immovably;
And the triumphant storm did flee,　　　　710
Like a conqueror, swift and proud,
Between, with many a captive cloud,
A shapeless, dark and rapid crowd,
Each by lightning riven in half:
I heard the thunder hoarsely laugh:
Mighty fleets were strewn like chaff
And spread beneath a hell of death
O'er the white waters. I alit
On a great ship lightning-split,
And speeded hither on the sigh　　　　720
Of one who gave an enemy
His plank, then plunged aside to die.

Third Spirit

I sate beside a sage's bed,
And the lamp was burning red

Near the book where he had fed,
When a Dream with plumes of flame,
To his pillow hovering came,
And I knew it was the same
Which had kindled long ago
Pity, eloquence, and woe; 730
And the world awhile below
Wore the shade, its luster made.
It has borne me here as fleet
As Desire's lightning feet:
I must ride it back ere morrow,
Or the sage will wake in sorrow.

Fourth Spirit

On a poet's lips I slept
Dreaming like a love-adept
In the sound his breathing kept;
Nor seeks nor finds he mortal blisses, 740
But feeds on the aërial kisses
Of shapes that haunt thought's wildernesses.
He will watch from dawn to gloom
The lake-reflected sun illume
The yellow bees in the ivy-bloom,
Nor heed nor see, what things they be:
But from these create he can
Forms more real than living man,
Nurslings of immortality!
One of these awakened me, 750
And I sped to succor thee.

Ione

Behold'st thou not two shapes from the east and west
Come, as two doves to one belovèd nest,
Twin nurslings of the all-sustaining air
On swift still wings glide down the atmosphere?
And, hark! their sweet, sad voices! 'tis despair
Mingled with love and then dissolved in sound.

Panthea. Canst thou speak, sister? all my words are drowned.
Ione. Their beauty gives me voice. See how they float
On their sustaining wings of skyey grain, 760
Orange and azure deepening into gold:
Their soft smiles light the air like a star's fire.

Chorus of Spirits

Hast thou beheld the form of Love?

Fifth Spirit

As over wide dominions
I sped, like some swift cloud that wings the wide air's wilder-
nesses,
That planet-crested shape swept by on lightning-braided pinions,
Scattering the liquid joy of life from his ambrosial tresses:
His footsteps paved the world with light; but as I passed 'twas
fading,
And hollow Ruin yawned behind: great sages bound in mad-
ness,
And headless patriots, and pale youths who perished, unup-
braiding,
Gleamed in the night. I wandered o'er, till thou, O King of
sadness,   770
Turned by thy smile the worst I saw to recollected glad-
ness.

Sixth Spirit

Ah, sister! Desolation is a delicate thing:
It walks not on the earth, it floats not on the air,
But treads with lulling footstep, and fans with silent wing
The tender hopes which in their hearts, the best and gentlest
bear;
Who, soothed to false repose by the fanning plumes above
And the music-stirring motion of its soft and busy feet,
Dream visions of aërial joy, and call the monster, Love,
And wake, and find the shadow Pain, as he whom now we
greet.

Chorus

Though Ruin now Love's shadow be,   780
Following him, destroyingly,
On Death's white and wingèd steed,
Which the fleetest cannot flee,
Trampling down both flower and weed,
Man and beast, and foul and fair,
Like a tempest through the air;
Thou shalt quell this horseman grim,
Woundless though in heart or limb.

Prometheus. Spirits! how know ye this shall be?

Chorus

In the atmosphere we breathe,   790
As buds grow red when the snow-storms flee,
From Spring gathering up beneath,
Whose mild winds shake the elder brake,
And the wandering herdsmen know
That the white-thorn soon will blow:
　　Wisdom, Justice, Love, and Peace,
　　When they struggle to increase,
　　　Are to us as soft winds be
　　　To shepherd boys, the prophecy
　　　Which begins and ends in thee.   800

Ione. Where are the Spirits fled?
Panthea.　　　　　　　　　　Only a sense
Remains of them, like the omnipotence
Of music, when the inspired voice and lute
Languish, ere yet the responses are mute,
Which through the deep and labyrinthine soul,
Like echoes through long caverns, wind and roll.
　　Prometheus. How fair these air-born shapes! and yet I feel
Most vain all hope but love; and thou art far,
Asia! who, when my being overflowed,
Wert like a golden chalice to bright wine   810
Which else had sunk into the thirsty dust.
All things are still: alas! how heavily
This quiet morning weighs upon my heart;
Though I should dream I could even sleep with grief
If slumber were denied not. I would fain
Be what it is my destiny to be,
The savior and the strength of suffering man,
Or sink into the original gulf of things:
There is no agony, and no solace left;
Earth can console, Heaven can torment no more.   820
　　Panthea. Hast thou forgotten one who watches thee
The cold dark night, and never sleeps but when
The shadow of thy spirit falls on her?
　　Prometheus. I said all hope was vain but love: thou lovest.
　　Panthea. Deeply in truth; but the eastern star looks white,
And Asia waits in that far Indian vale,
The scene of her sad exile; rugged once
And desolate and frozen, like this ravine;
But now invested with fair flowers and herbs,

And haunted by sweet airs and sounds, which flow 830
Among the woods and waters, from the ether
Of her transforming presence, which would fade
If it were mingled not with thine. Farewell!

Act II

Scene IV.—*The Cave of* Demogorgon. Asia *and* Panthea.

Panthea. What veilèd form sits on that ebon throne?
Asia. The veil has fallen.
Panthea.   I see a mighty darkness
Filling the seat of power, and rays of gloom
Dart round, as light from the meridian sun.
—Ungazed upon and shapeless; neither limb,
Nor form, nor outline; yet we feel it is
A living Spirit.
    Demogorgon. Ask what thou wouldst know.
    Asia. What canst thou tell?
    Demogorgon.   All things thou dar'st demand.
Asia. Who made the living world?
    Demogorgon.   God.
    Asia.   Who made all
That it contains? thought, passion, reason, will, 10
Imagination?
    Demogorgon. God: Almighty God.
    Asia. Who made that sense which, when the winds of Spring
In rarest visitation, or the voice
Of one belovèd heard in youth alone,
Fills the faint eyes with falling tears which dim
The radiant looks of unbewailing flowers,
And leaves this peopled earth a solitude
When it returns no more?
    Demogorgon.   Merciful God.
    Asia. And who made terror, madness, crime, remorse,
Which from the links of the great chain of things, 20
To every thought within the mind of man
Sway and drag heavily, and each one reels
Under the load towards the pit of death;
Abandoned hope, and love that turns to hate;
And self-contempt, bitterer to drink than blood;
Pain, whose unheeded and familiar speech
Is howling, and keen shrieks, day after day;
And Hell, or the sharp fear of Hell?
    Demogorgon.   He reigns.
    Asia. Utter his name: a world pining in pain

Asks but his name: curses shall drag him down.   30
    Demogorgon. He reigns.
    Asia.   I feel, I know it: who?
    Demogorgon.   He reigns.
    Asia. Who reigns? There was the Heaven and Earth at first,
And Light and Love; then Saturn, from whose throne
Time fell, an envious shadow: such the state
Of the earth's primal spirits beneath his sway,
As the calm joy of flowers and living leaves
Before the wind or sun has withered them
And semivital worms; but he refused
The birthrights of their being, knowledge, power,
The skill which wields the elements, the thought   40
Which pierces this dim universe like light,
Self-empire, and the majesty of love;
For thirst of which they fainted. Then Prometheus
Gave wisdom, which is strength, to Jupiter,
And with this law alone, "Let man be free,"
Clothed him with the dominion of wide Heaven.
To know nor faith, nor love, nor law; to be
Omnipotent but friendless is to reign;
And Jove now reigned; for on the race of man
First famine, and then toil, and then disease,   50
Strife, wounds, and ghastly death unseen before,
Fell; and the unseasonable seasons drove
With alternating shafts of frost and fire,
Their shelterless, pale tribes to mountain caves:
And in their desert hearts fierce wants he sent,
And mad disquietudes, and shadows idle
Of unreal good, which levied mutual war,
So ruining the lair wherein they raged.
Prometheus saw, and waked the legioned hopes
Which sleep within folded Elysian flowers,   60
Nepenthe, Moly, Amaranth,[25] fadeless blooms,
That they might hide with thin and rainbow wings
The shape of Death; and Love he sent to bind
The disunited tendrils of that vine
Which bears the wine of life, the human heart;
And he tamed fire which, like some beast of prey,
Most terrible, but lovely, played beneath
The frown of man; and tortured to his will
Iron and gold, the slaves and signs of power,
And gems and poisons, and all subtlest forms   70
Hidden beneath the mountains and the waves.

25 Respectively: the flower of forgetfulness; the flower given by Mercury to Ulysses
to counteract the spells of Circe; the unfading flower.

He gave man speech, and speech created thought,
Which is the measure of the universe;
And Science struck the thrones of earth and heaven,
Which shook, but fell not; and the harmonious mind
Poured itself forth in all-prophetic song;
And music lifted up the listening spirit
Until it walked, exempt from mortal care,
Godlike, o'er the clear billows of sweet sound;
And human hands first mimicked and then mocked,   80
With molded limbs more lovely than its own,
The human form, till marble grew divine;
And mothers, gazing, drank the love men see
Reflected in their race, behold, and perish.
He told the hidden power of herbs and springs,
And Disease drank and slept. Death grew like sleep.
He taught the implicated orbits woven
Of the wide-wandering stars; and how the sun
Changes his lair, and by what secret spell
The pale moon is transformed, when her broad eye   90
Gazes not on the interlunar [26] sea:
He taught to rule, as life directs the limbs,
The tempest-wingèd chariots of the Ocean,
And the Celt knew the Indian. Cities then
Were built, and through their snow-like columns flowed
The warm winds, and the azure ether shone,
And the blue sea and shadowy hills were seen.
Such, the alleviations of his state,
Prometheus gave to man, for which he hangs
Withering in destined pain: but who rains down   100
Evil, the immedicable plague, which, while
Man looks on his creation like a God
And sees that it is glorious, drives him on,
The wreck of his own will, the scorn of earth,
The outcast, the abandoned, the alone?
Not Jove: while yet his frown shook Heaven, aye, when
His adversary from adamantine chains
Cursed him, he trembled like a slave. Declare
Who is his master? Is he too a slave?
    Demogorgon. All spirits are enslaved which serve things
        evil: 110
Thou knowest if Jupiter be such or no.
    Asia. Whom calledst thou God?
    Demogorgon.   I spoke but as ye speak,
For Jove is the supreme of living things.
    Asia. Who is the master of the slave?

26 between appearances of the moon

Demogorgon.   If the abysm
Could vomit forth its secrets. . . . But a voice
Is wanting, the deep truth is imageless;
For what would it avail to bid thee gaze
On the revolving world? What to bid speak
Fate, Time, Occasion, Chance, and Change? To these
All things are subject but eternal Love.   120
    Asia. So much I asked before, and my heart gave
The response thou hast given; and of such truths
Each to itself must be the oracle.
One more demand; and do thou answer me
As mine own soul would answer, did it know
That which I ask. Prometheus shall rise
Henceforth the sun of this rejoicing world:
When shall the destined hour arrive?
    Demogorgon.   Behold!
    Asia. The rocks are cloven, and through the purple night
I see cars drawn by rainbow-wingèd steeds   130
Which trample the dim winds: in each there stands
A wild-eyed charioteer urging their flight.
Some look behind, as fiends pursued them there,
And yet I see no shapes but the keen stars:
Others, with burning eyes, lean forth, and drink
With eager lips the wind of their own speed,
As if the thing they loved fled on before,
And now, even now, they clasped it. Their bright locks
Stream like a comet's flashing hair: they all
Sweep onward.
    Demogorgon. These are the immortal Hours,   140
Of whom thou didst demand. One waits for thee.
    Asia. A spirit with a dreadful countenance
Checks its dark chariot by the craggy gulf.
Unlike thy brethren, ghastly charioteer,
Who art thou? Whither wouldst thou bear me? Speak!
    Spirit. I am the shadow of a destiny
More dread than is my aspect: ere yon planet
Has set, the darkness which ascends with me
Shall wrap in lasting night heaven's kingless throne.
    Asia. What meanest thou?
    Panthea.   That terrible shadow floats   150
Up from its throne, as may the lurid smoke
Of earthquake-ruined cities o'er the sea.
Lo! it ascends the car; the coursers fly
Terrified: watch its path among the stars
Blackening the night!
    Asia.   Thus I am answered: strange!

Panthea. See, near the verge, another chariot stays;
An ivory shell inlaid with crimson fire.
Which comes and goes within its sculptured rim
Of delicate strange tracery; the young spirit
That guides it has the dove-like eyes of hope;   160
How its soft smiles attract the soul! as light
Lures wingèd insects through the lampless air.

Spirit

My coursers are fed with the lightning,
   They drink of the whirlwind's stream,
And when the red morning is bright'ning
   They bathe in the fresh sunbeam;
   They have strength for their swiftness I deem,
Then ascend with me, daughter of Ocean.

I desire: and their speed makes night kindle;
   I fear: they outstrip the Typhoon;   170
Ere the cloud piled on Atlas can dwindle
   We encircle the earth and the moon:
   We shall rest from long labors at noon:
Then ascend with me, daughter of Ocean.

SCENE V.—*The Car pauses within a Cloud on the top of a
snowy Mountain.* ASIA, PANTHEA, *and the* SPIRIT OF THE
HOUR.

Spirit

On the brink of the night and the morning
   My coursers are wont to respire;
But the Earth has just whispered a warning
   That their flight must be swifter than fire:
   They shall drink the hot speed of desire!

Asia. Thou breathest on their nostrils, but my breath
Would give them swifter speed.
   Spirit.   Alas! it could not.
   Panthea. Oh Spirit! pause, and tell whence is the light
Which fills this cloud? the sun is yet unrisen.
   Spirit. The sun will rise not until noon. Apollo   10
Is held in heaven by wonder; and the light
Which fills this vapor, as the aërial hue
Of fountain-gazing roses fills the water,
Flows from thy mighty sister.

Panthea.   Yes, I feel—
Asia. What is it with thee, sister? Thou art pale.
Panthea. How thou art changed! I dare not look on thee;
I feel but see thee not. I scarce endure
The radiance of thy beauty. Some good change
Is working in the elements, which suffer
Thy presence thus unveiled. The Nereids tell   20
That on the day when the clear hyaline [27]
Was cloven at thine uprise, and thou didst stand
Within a veinèd shell, which floated on
Over the calm floor of the crystal sea,
Among the Ægean isles, and by the shores
Which bear thy name; love, like the atmosphere
Of the sun's fire filling the living world,
Burst from thee, and illumined earth and heaven
And the deep ocean and the sunless caves
And all that dwells within them; till grief cast   30
Eclipse upon the soul from which it came:
Such art thou now; nor is it I alone,
Thy sister, thy companion, thine own chosen one,
But the whole world which seeks thy sympathy.
Hearest thou not sounds i' the air which speak the love
Of all inarticulate beings? Feelest thou not
The inanimate wind enamored of thee? List!   [*Music.*
   Asia. Thy words are sweeter than aught else but his
Whose echoes they are: yet all love is sweet,
Given or returned. Common as light is love,   40
And its familiar voice wearies not ever.
Like the wide heaven, the all-sustaining air,
It makes the reptile equal to the God:
They who inspire it most are fortunate,
As I am now; but those who feel it most
Are happier still, after long sufferings,
As I shall soon become.
   Panthea.   List! Spirits speak.

Voice in the Air, singing

Life of Life! thy lips enkindle
   With their love the breath between them;
And thy smiles before they dwindle   50
   Make the cold air fire; then screen them
In those looks, where whoso gazes
Faints, entangled in their mazes.

----

27 sea. Asia is identified with Venus, who rose from the sea.

Child of Light! thy limbs are burning
  Through the vest which seems to hide them;
As the radiant lines of morning
  Through the clouds ere they divide them;
And this atmosphere divinest
Shrouds thee wheresoe'er thou shinest.

Fair are others; none beholds thee,   60
  But thy voice sounds low and tender
Like the fairest, for it folds thee
  From the sight, that liquid splendor,
And all feel, yet see thee never,
As I feel now, lost for ever!

Lamp of Earth! where'er thou movest
  Its dim shapes are clad with brightness,
And the souls of whom thou lovest
  Walk upon the winds with lightness,
Till they fail, as I am failing,   70
Dizzy, lost, yet unbewailing!

Asia

My soul is an enchanted boat,
  Which, like a sleeping swan, doth float
Upon the silver waves of thy sweet singing;
  And thine doth like an angel sit
  Beside a helm conducting it,
Whilst all the winds with melody are ringing.
  It seems to float ever, for ever,
  Upon that many-winding river,
  Between mountains, woods, abysses,   80
  A paradise of wildernesses!
Till, like one in slumber bound,
Borne to the ocean, I float down, around,
Into a sea profound, of ever-spreading sound:

  Meanwhile thy spirit lifts its pinions
  In music's most serene dominions;
Catching the winds that fan that happy heaven.
  And we sail on, away, afar,
  Without a course, without a star,
But, by the instinct of sweet music driven;   90
  Till through Elysian garden islets
  By thee, most beautiful of pilots,
  Where never mortal pinnace glided,

The boat of my desire is guided:
Realms where the air we breathe is love,
Which in the winds and on the waves doth move,
Harmonizing this earth with what we feel above.

We have passed Age's icy caves,
    And Manhood's dark and tossing waves,
And Youth's smooth ocean, smiling to betray: 100
    Beyond the grassy gulfs we flee
    Of shadow-peopled Infancy,
Through Death and Birth, to a diviner day;
    A paradise of vaulted bowers,
    Lit by downward-gazing flowers,
    And watery paths that wind between
Wildernesses calm and green,
Peopled by shapes too bright to see,
And rest, having beheld; somewhat like thee;
Which walk upon the sea, and chant melodiously!   110

Act III

Scene I.—*Heaven.* Jupiter *on his Throne;* Thetis *and the
other Deities assembled.*

Jupiter. Ye congregated powers of heaven, who share
The glory and the strength of him ye serve,
Rejoice! henceforth I am omnipotent.
All else had been subdued to me; alone
The soul of man, like unextinguished fire,
Yet burns towards heaven with fierce reproach, and doubt,
And lamentation, and reluctant prayer,
Hurling up insurrection, which might make
Our antique empire insecure, though built
On eldest faith, and hell's coeval, fear;   10
And though my curses through the pendulous air,
Like snow on herbless peaks, fall flake by flake,
And cling to it; though under my wrath's night
It climbs the crags of life, step after step,
Which wound it, as ice wounds unsandaled feet,
It yet remains supreme o'er misery,
Aspiring, unrepressed, yet soon to fall:
Even now have I begotten a strange wonder,
That fatal child, the terror of the earth,
Who waits but till the destined hour arrive,   20
Bearing from Demogorgon's vacant throne
The dreadful might of ever-living limbs

Which clothed that awful spirit unbeheld,
To redescend, and trample out the spark.

Pour forth heaven's wine, Idæan Ganymede,[28]
And let it fill the Dædal cups like fire,
And from the flower-inwoven soil divine
Ye all-triumphant harmonies arise,
As dew from earth under the twilight stars:
Drink! be the nectar circling through your veins   30
The soul of joy, ye ever-living Gods,
Till exultation burst in one wide voice
Like music from Elysian winds.
                              And thou
Ascend beside me, veilèd in the light
Of the desire which makes thee one with me,
Thetis, bright image of eternity!
When thou didst cry, "Insufferable might!
God! Spare me! I sustain not the quick flames,
The penetrating presence; all my being,
Like him whom the Numidian seps [29] did thaw   40
Into a dew with poison, is dissolved,
Sinking through its foundations"; even then
Two mighty spirits, mingling, made a third
Mightier than either, which, unbodied now,
Between us floats, felt, although unbeheld,
Waiting the incarnation, which ascends,
(Hear ye the thunder of the fiery wheels
Griding the winds?) from Demogorgon's throne.
Victory! victory! Feel'st thou not, O world,
The earthquake of his chariot thundering up   50
Olympus?

> [*The Car of the* HOUR *arrives.* DEMOGORGON *descends, and
> moves towards the Throne of* JUPITER.

Awful shape, what are thou? Speak!
Demogorgon. Eternity. Demand no direr name.
Descend, and follow me down the abyss.
I am thy child, as thou wert Saturn's child;
Mightier than thee: and we must dwell together
Henceforth in darkness. Lift thy lightnings not.
The tyranny of heaven none may retain,
Or reassume, or hold, succeeding thee:
Yet if thou wilt, as 'tis the destiny

---

28 the cup-bearer of the gods, carried off from Mount Ida, near Troy. *Dædal*, skillfully wrought (from Dædalus, the fa-mous artificer, who con-structed the Cretan Laby-rinth)

29 a venomous serpent. The death of a soldier by its bite is described in Lucan's *Pharsalia*, ix 763–88.

Of trodden worms to writhe till they are dead,   60
Put forth thy might.
  Jupiter.   Detested prodigy!
Even thus beneath the deep Titanian prisons
I trample thee! thou lingerest?
                              Mercy! mercy!
No pity, no release, no respite! Oh,
That thou wouldst make mine enemy my judge,
Even where he hangs, seared by my long revenge,
On Caucasus! he would not doom me thus.
Gentle, and just, and dreadless, is he not
The monarch of the world? What then art thou?
No refuge! no appeal!
                              Sink with me then,   70
We two will sink on the wide waves of ruin,
Even as a vulture and a snake outspent
Drop, twisted in inextricable fight,
Into a shoreless sea. Let hell unlock
Its mounded oceans of tempestuous fire,
And whelm on them into the bottomless void
This desolated world, and thee, and me,
The conqueror and the conquered, and the wreck
Of that for which they combated.
                              Ai! Ai!
The elements obey me not. I sink   80
Dizzily down, ever, for ever, down.
And, like a cloud, mine enemy above
Darkens my fall with victory! Ai, Ai!

SCENE IV. *A Forest. In the Background a Cave.*

  .   .   .   .

                    [*The* SPIRIT OF THE HOUR *enters.*
Prometheus. We feel what thou hast heard and seen: yet speak.
Spirit of the Hour. Soon as the sound had ceased whose thunder
        filled
The abysses of the sky and the wide earth,
There was a change: the impalpable thin air   100
And the all-circling sunlight were transformed,
As if the sense of love dissolved in them
Had folded itself round the spherèd world.
My vision then grew clear, and I could see
Into the mysteries of the universe:
Dizzy as with delight I floated down,
Winnowing the lightsome air with languid plumes,
My coursers sought their birthplace in the sun,

Where they henceforth will live exempt from toil,
Pasturing flowers of vegetable fire;   110
And where my moonlike car will stand within
A temple, gazed upon by Phidian forms [30]
Of thee, and Asia, and the Earth, and me,
And you fair nymphs looking the love we feel,—
In memory of the tidings it has borne,—
Beneath a dome fretted with graven flowers,
Poised on twelve columns of resplendent stone,
And open to the bright and liquid sky.
Yoked to it by an amphisbænic snake [31]
The likeness of those wingèd steeds will mock   120
The flight from which they find repose. Alas,
Whither has wandered now my partial tongue
When all remains untold which ye would hear?
As I have said, I floated to the earth:
It was, as it is still, the pain of bliss
To move, to breathe, to be; I wandering went
Among the haunts and dwellings of mankind,
And first was disappointed not to see
Such mighty change as I had felt within
Expressed in outward things; but soon I looked,   130
And behold, thrones were kingless, and men walked
One with the other even as spirits do,
None fawned, none trampled; hate, disdain, or fear,
Self-love or self-contempt, on human brows
No more inscribed, as o'er the gate of hell,
"All hope abandon ye who enter here"; [32]
None frowned, none trembled, none with eager fear
Gazed on another's eye of cold command,
Until the subject of a tyrant's will
Became, worse fate, the abject of his own,   140
Which spurred him, like an outspent horse, to death.
None wrought his lips in truth-entangling lines
Which smiled the lie his tongue disdained to speak;
None, with firm sneer, trod out in his own heart
The sparks of love and hope till there remained
Those bitter ashes, a soul self-consumed,
And the wretch crept a vampire among men,
Infecting all with his own hideous ill;
None talked that common, false, cold, hollow talk
Which makes the heart deny the *yes* it breathes,   150
Yet question that unmeant hypocrisy

30 like those made by the   31 snake with a head at   *Inferno,* iii 9
great sculptor Phidias (d.   each end
432 B. C.)   32 as stated by Dante.

With such a self-mistrust as has no name.
And women, too, frank, beautiful, and kind
As the free heaven which rains fresh light and dew
On the wide earth, past; gentle radiant forms,
From custom's evil taint exempt and pure;
Speaking the wisdom once they could not think,
Looking emotions once they feared to feel,
And changed to all which once they dared not be,
Yet being now, made earth like heaven; nor pride,   160
Nor jealousy, nor envy, nor ill shame,
The bitterest of those drops of treasured gall,
Spoilt the sweet taste of the nepenthe, love.

Thrones, altars, judgment-seats, and prisons; wherein,
And beside which, by wretched men were borne
Scepters, tiaras, swords, and chains, and tomes
Of reasoned wrong, glozed on by ignorance,
Were like those monstrous and barbaric shapes,
The ghosts of a no-more-remembered fame,
Which, from their unworn obelisks, look forth   170
In triumph o'er the palaces and tombs
Of those who were their conquerors: moldering round,
These imaged to the pride of kings and priests
A dark yet mighty faith, a power as wide
As is the world it wasted, and are now
But an astonishment; even so the tools
And emblems of its last captivity,
Amid the dwellings of the peopled earth,
Stand, not o'erthrown, but unregarded now.
And those foul shapes, abhorred by god and man,—   180
Which, under many a name and many a form
Strange, savage, ghastly, dark and execrable,
Were Jupiter, the tyrant of the world;
And which the nations, panic-stricken, served
With blood, and hearts broken by long hope, and love
Dragged to his altars soiled and garlandless,
And slain amid men's unreclaiming tears,
Flattering the thing they feared, which fear was hate,—
Frown, moldering fast, o'er their abandoned shrines:
The painted veil, by those who were, called life,   190
Which mimicked, as with colors idly spread,
All men believed or hoped, is torn aside;
The loathsome mask has fallen, the man remains
Scepterless, free, uncircumscribed, but man
Equal, unclassed, tribeless, and nationless,
Exempt from awe, worship, degree, the king

Over himself; just, gentle, wise: but man
Passionless?—no, yet free from guilt or pain,
Which were, for his will made or suffered them,
Nor yet exempt, though ruling them like slaves,   200
From chance, and death, and mutability,
The clogs of that which else might oversoar
The loftiest star of unascended heaven,
Pinnacled dim in the intense inane.

Act IV [33]

Scene.—*A Part of the Forest near the Cave of* Prometheus

The Earth

The joy, the triumph, the delight, the madness!
The boundless, overflowing, bursting gladness,   320
The vaporous exultation not to be confined!
Ha! ha! the animation of delight
Which wraps me, like an atmosphere of light,
And bears me as a cloud is borne by its own wind.

The Moon

Brother mine, calm wanderer,
Happy globe of land and air,
Some Spirit is darted like a beam from thee,
Which penetrates my frozen frame,
And passes with the warmth of flame,
With love, and odor, and deep melody   330
Through me, through me!

The Earth

Ha! ha! the caverns of my hollow mountains,
My cloven fire-crags, sound-exulting fountains
Laugh with a vast and inextinguishable laughter.
The oceans, and the deserts, and the abysses,
And the deep air's unmeasured wildernesses,
Answer from all their clouds and billows, echoing after.

They cry aloud as I do. Sceptered curse,
Who all our green and azure universe

33 "At first he completed the drama in three acts. It was not till several months
after, when at Florence, that he conceived that a fourth act, a sort of hymn of rejoicing in the fulfilment of the prophecies with regard to Prometheus, ought to be
added to complete the composition." (Mrs. Shelley)

Threatenedst to muffle round with black destruction, sending   340
  A solid cloud to rain hot thunder-stones,
  And splinter and knead down my children's bones,
All I bring forth, to one void mass battering and blending—

  Until each crag-like tower, and storied column,
  Palace, and obelisk, and temple solemn,
My imperial mountains crowned with cloud, and snow, and fire,
  My sea-like forests, every blade and blossom
  Which finds a grave or cradle in my bosom,
Were stamped by the strong hate into a lifeless mire:

  How art thou sunk, withdrawn, covered, drunk up   350
  By thirsty nothing, as the brackish cup
Drained by a desert-troop, a little drop for all;
  And from beneath, around, within, above,
  Filling thy void annihilation, love
Burst in like light on caves cloven by the thunder-ball.

The Moon

  The snow upon my lifeless mountains
  Is loosened into living fountains,
My solid oceans flow, and sing, and shine:
  A spirit from my heart bursts forth,
  It clothes with unexpected birth   360
My cold bare bosom: Oh! it must be thine
        On mine, on mine!

  Gazing on thee I feel, I know
  Green stalks burst forth, and bright flowers grow,
And living shapes upon my bosom move:
  Music is in the sea and air,
  Wingèd clouds soar here and there,
Dark with the rain new buds are dreaming of:
        'Tis love, all love!

The Earth

  It interpenetrates my granite mass,   370
  Through tangled roots and trodden clay doth pass
Into the utmost leaves and delicatest flowers;
  Upon the winds, among the clouds 'tis spread,
  It wakes a life in the forgotten dead,
They breathe a spirit up from their obscurest bowers.

And like a storm bursting its cloudy prison
With thunder, and with whirlwind, has arisen
Out of the lampless caves of unimagined being:
  With earthquake shock and swiftness making shiver
  Thought's stagnant chaos, unremoved for ever,   380
Till hate, and fear, and pain, light-vanquished shadows, fleeing

Leave Man, who was a many-sided mirror,
Which could distort to many a shape of error,
This true fair world of things, a sea reflecting love;
  Which over all his kind, as the sun's heaven
  Gliding o'er ocean, smooth, serene, and even,
Darting from starry depths radiance and life, doth move:

Leave Man, even as a leprous child is left,
Who follows a sick beast to some warm cleft
Of rocks, through which the might of healing springs is
    poured;
  Then when it wanders home with rosy smile,   390
  Unconscious, and its mother fears awhile
It is a spirit, then, weeps on her child restored.

Man, oh, not men! a chain of linkèd thought,
Of love and might to be divided not,
Compelling the elements with adamantine stress;
  As the sun rules, even with a tyrant's gaze,
  The unquiet republic of the maze
Of planets, struggling fierce toward heaven's free wilderness.

Man, one harmonious soul of many a soul,   400
Whose nature is its own divine control,
Where all things flow to all, as rivers to the sea;
  Familiar acts are beautiful through love;
  Labor, and pain, and grief, in life's green grove
Sport like tame beasts, none knew how gentle they could be!

His will, with all mean passions, bad delights,
And selfish cares, its trembling satellites,
A spirit ill to guide, but mighty to obey,
  Is as a tempest-wingèd ship, whose helm
  Love rules, through waves which dare not overwhelm,   410
Forcing life's wildest shores to own its sovereign sway.

All things confess his strength. Through the cold mass
Of marble and of color his dreams pass;

Bright threads whence mothers weave the robes their children
    wear;
  Language is a perpetual Orphic song,
  Which rules with Dædal [34] harmony a throng
Of thoughts and forms, which else senseless and shapeless were.

  The lightning is his slave, heaven's utmost deep
  Gives up her stars, and like a flock of sheep
They pass before his eye, are numbered, and roll on!   420
  The tempest is his steed, he strides the air;
  And the abyss shouts from her depth laid bare,
Heaven, hast thou secrets? Man unveils me; I have none.

The Moon

  The shadow of white death has passed
  From my path in heaven at last,
A clinging shroud of solid frost and sleep;
  And through my newly-woven bowers,
  Wander happy paramours,
Less mighty, but as mild as those who keep
    Thy vales more deep.   430

The Earth

  As the dissolving warmth of dawn may fold
  A half unfrozen dew-globe, green, and gold,
And crystalline, till it becomes a wingèd mist,
  And wanders up the vault of the blue day,
  Outlives the moon, and on the sun's last ray
Hangs o'er the sea, a fleece of fire and amethyst—

The Moon

  Thou art folded, thou art lying
  In the light which is undying
Of thine own joy, and heaven's smile divine;
  All suns and constellations shower   440
  On thee a light, a life, a power
Which doth array thy sphere; thou pourest thine
    On mine, on mine!

The Earth

  I spin beneath my pyramid of night,
  Which points into the heaven's dreaming delight,

---

34 See Note 28

Murmuring victorious joy in my enchanted sleep;
  As a youth lulled in love-dreams faintly sighing,
  Under the shadow of his beauty lying,
Which round his rest a watch of light and warmth doth keep.

The Moon

As in the soft and sweet eclipse,   450
  When soul meets soul on lovers' lips,
High hearts are calm, and brightest eyes are dull;
  So when thy shadow falls on me,
  Then am I mute and still, by thee
Covered; of thy love, Orb most beautiful,
      Full, oh, too full!

Thou art speeding round the sun
Brightest world of many a one;
Green and azure sphere which shinest
With a light which is divinest   460
Among all the lamps of Heaven
To whom life and light is given;
I, thy crystal paramour
Borne beside thee by a power
Like the polar Paradise,
Magnet-like of lovers' eyes;
I, a most enamored maiden
Whose weak brain is overladen
With the pleasure of her love,
Maniac-like around thee move   470
Gazing, an insatiate bride,
On thy form from every side
Like a Maenad,[35] round the cup
Which Agave lifted up
In the weird Cadmæan forest.
Brother, wheresoe'er thou soarest
I must hurry, whirl and follow
Through the heavens wide and hollow,
Sheltered by the warm embrace
Of thy soul from hungry space,   480
Drinking from thy sense and sight
Beauty, majesty, and might,
As a lover or a chameleon
Grows like what it looks upon,
As a violet's gentle eye

---

35 Bacchante. Agave, daughter of Cadmus, founder of Thebes, led the Theban women in their Bacchic orgies, in the *Bacchae* of Euripides.

Gazes on the azure sky
Until its hue grows like what it beholds,
  As a gray and watery mist
  Glows like solid amethyst
Athwart the western mountain it enfolds,   490
    When the sunset sleeps
      Upon its snow—

The Earth

    And the weak day weeps
      That it should be so.
Oh, gentle Moon, the voice of thy delight
Falls on me like thy clear and tender light
Soothing the seaman, borne the summer night,
  Through isles for ever calm;
Oh, gentle Moon, thy crystal accents pierce
The caverns of my pride's deep universe,   500
Charming the tiger joy, whose tramplings fierce
  Made wounds which need thy balm.
  Panthea. I rise as from a bath of sparkling water,
A bath of azure light, among dark rocks,
Out of the stream of sound.
  Ione.   Ah me! sweet sister,
The stream of sound has ebbed away from us,
And you pretend to rise out of its wave,
Because your words fall like the clear, soft dew
Shaken from a bathing wood-nymph's limbs and hair.
  Panthea. Peace! peace! A mighty Power, which is as dark-
      ness,   510
Is rising out of Earth, and from the sky
Is showered like night, and from within the air
Bursts, like eclipse which had been gathered up
Into the pores of sunlight: the bright visions,
Wherein the singing spirits rode and shone,
Gleam like pale meteors through a watery night.
  Ione. There is a sense of words upon mine ear.
  Panthea. An universal sound like words: Oh, list!

Demogorgon

Thou, Earth, calm empire of a happy soul,
  Sphere of divinest shapes and harmonies,   520
Beautiful orb! gathering as thou dost roll
  The love which paves thy path along the skies:

The Earth

I hear: I am as a drop of dew that dies.

Demogorgon

Thou, Moon, which gazest on the nightly Earth
With wonder, as it gazes upon thee;
Whilst each to men, and beast, and the swift birth
Of birds, is beauty, love, calm, harmony:

The Moon

I hear: I am a leaf shaken by thee!

Demogorgon

Ye Kings of suns and stars, Dæmons and Gods,
Aetherial Dominations, who possess   530
Elysian, windless, fortunate abodes
Beyond Heaven's constellated wilderness:

A Voice from above

Our great Republic hears, we are blest, and bless.

Demogorgon

Ye happy Dead, whom beams of brightest verse
Are clouds to hide, not colors to portray,
Whether your nature is that universe
Which once ye saw and suffered—

A Voice from beneath

                                        Or as they
Whom we have left, we change and pass away.

Demogorgon

Ye elemental Genii, who have homes
From man's high mind even to the central stone   540
Of sullen lead; from heaven's star-fretted domes
To the dull weed some sea-worm battens on:

A confused Voice

We hear: thy words waken oblivion.

Demogorgon

Spirits, whose homes are flesh: ye beasts and birds,
   Ye worms, and fish; ye living leaves and buds;
Lightning and wind; and ye untamable herds,
   Meteors and mists, which throng air's solitudes:—

A Voice

Thy voice to us is wind among still woods.

Demogorgon

Man, who wert once a despot and a slave;
   A dupe and a deceiver; a decay;   550
A traveler from the cradle to the grave
   Through the dim night of this immortal day:

All

Speak: thy strong words may never pass away.

Demogorgon

This is the day, which down the void abysm
At the Earth-born's spell yawns for Heaven's despotism,
   And Conquest is dragged captive through the deep:
Love, from its awful throne of patient power
In the wise heart, from the last giddy hour
   Of dread endurance, from the slippery, steep,
And narrow verge of crag-like agony, springs   560
And folds over the world its healing wings.

Gentleness, Virtue, Wisdom, and Endurance,
These are the seals of that most firm assurance
   Which bars the pit over Destruction's strength;
And if, with infirm hand, Eternity,
Mother of many acts and hours, should free
   The serpent that would clasp her with his length;
These are the spells by which to reassume
An empire o'er the disentangled doom.

To suffer woes which Hope thinks infinite;   570
To forgive wrongs darker than death or night;
   To defy Power, which seems omnipotent;

To love, and bear; to hope till Hope creates
From its own wreck the thing it contemplates;
　　Neither to change, nor falter, nor repent;
This, like thy glory, Titan, is to be
Good, great and joyous, beautiful and free;
This is alone Life, Joy, Empire, and Victory.

THE CLOUD

I BRING fresh showers for the thirsting flowers,
　　From the seas and the streams;
I bear light shade for the leaves when laid
　　In their noonday dreams.
From my wings are shaken the dews that waken
　　The sweet buds every one,
When rocked to rest on their mother's breast,
　　As she dances about the sun.
I wield the flail of the lashing hail,
　　And whiten the green plains under,   10
And then again I dissolve it in rain,
　　And laugh as I pass in thunder.

I sift the snow on the mountains below,
　　And their great pines groan aghast;
And all the night 'tis my pillow white,
　　While I sleep in the arms of the blast.
Sublime on the towers of my skyey bowers,
　　Lightning my pilot sits;
In a cavern under is fettered the thunder,
　　It struggles and howls at fits;   20
Over earth and ocean, with gentle motion,
　　This pilot is guiding me,
Lured by the love of the genii that move
　　In the depths of the purple sea;
Over the rills, and the crags, and the hills,
　　Over the lakes and the plains,
Wherever he dream, under mountain or stream,
　　The Spirit he loves remains;
And I all the while bask in Heaven's blue smile,
　　Whilst he is dissolving in rains.   30

The sanguine Sunrise, with his meteor eyes,
　　And his burning plumes outspread,
Leaps on the back of my sailing rack,
　　When the morning star shines dead;
As on the jag of a mountain crag,

Which an earthquake rocks and swings,
An eagle alit one moment may sit
  In the light of its golden wings.
And when Sunset may breathe, from the lit sea beneath,
  Its ardors of rest and of love,   40
And the crimson pall of eve may fall
  From the depth of Heaven above,
With wings folded I rest, on mine aëry nest,
  As still as a brooding dove.

That orbèd maiden with white fire laden,
  Whom mortals call the Moon,
Glides glimmering o'er my fleece-like floor,
  By the midnight breezes strewn;
And wherever the beat of her unseen feet,
  Which only the angels hear,   50
May have broken the woof of my tent's thin roof,
  The stars peep behind her and peer;
And I laugh to see them whirl and flee,
  Like a swarm of golden bees,
When I widen the rent in my wind-built tent,
  Till the calm rivers, lakes, and seas,
Like strips of the sky fallen through me on high,
  Are each paved with the moon and these.

I bind the Sun's throne with a burning zone,
  And the Moon's with a girdle of pearl;   60
The volcanoes are dim, and the stars reel and swim
  When the whirlwinds my banner unfurl.
From cape to cape, with a bridge-like shape,
  Over a torrent sea,
Sunbeam-proof, I hang like a roof,—
  The mountains its columns be.
The triumphal arch through which I march
  With hurricane, fire, and snow,
When the Powers of the air are chained to my chair,
  Is the million-colored bow;   70
The sphere-fire above its soft colors wove,
  While the moist Earth was laughing below.

I am the daughter of Earth and Water,
  And the nursling of the Sky;
I pass through the pores of the ocean and shores,
  I change, but I cannot die.
For after the rain when with never a stain
  The pavilion of Heaven is bare,

And the winds and sunbeams with their convex gleams
　　Build up the blue dome of air,　　　　　　　　　80
I silently laugh at my own cenotaph,[36]
　　And out of the caverns of rain,
Like a child from the womb, like a ghost from the tomb,
　　I arise and unbuild it again.

TO A SKYLARK

Hail to thee, blithe Spirit!
　　Bird thou never wert,
That from Heaven, or near it,
　　Pourest thy full heart
In profuse strains of unpremeditated art.

Higher still and higher
　　From the earth thou springest
Like a cloud of fire;
　　The blue deep thou wingest,
And singing still dost soar, and soaring ever singest.　　10

In the golden lightning
　　Of the sunken sun,
O'er which clouds are bright'ning,
　　Thou dost float and run;
Like an unbodied joy whose race is just begun.

The pale purple even
　　Melts around thy flight;
Like a star of Heaven,
　　In the broad daylight
Thou art unseen, but yet I hear thy shrill delight,　　20

Keen as are the arrows
　　Of that silver sphere,
Whose intense lamp narrows
　　In the white dawn clear
Until we hardly see—we feel that it is there.

All the earth and air
　　With thy voice is loud,
As, when night is bare,
　　From one lonely cloud
The moon rains out her beams, and Heaven is overflowed.　　30

---

36 an empty tomb or a monument erected in honor of one who is buried elsewhere

What thou art we know not;
  What is most like thee?
From rainbow clouds there flow not
  Drops so bright to see
As from thy presence showers a rain of melody.

Like a Poet hidden
  In the light of thought,
Singing hymns unbidden,
  Till the world is wrought
To sympathy with hopes and fears it heeded not: 40

Like a high-born maiden
  In a palace-tower,
Soothing her love-laden
  Soul in secret hour
With music sweet as love, which overflows her bower:

Like a glow-worm golden
  In a dell of dew,
Scattering unbeholden
  Its aërial hue
Among the flowers and grass, which screen it from the view!   50

Like a rose embowered
  In its own green leaves,
By warm winds deflowered,
  Till the scent it gives
Makes faint with too much sweet those heavy-wingèd thieves:

Sound of vernal showers
  On the twinkling grass,
Rain-awakened flowers,
  All that ever was
Joyous, and clear, and fresh, thy music doth surpass: 60

Teach us, Sprite or Bird,
  What sweet thoughts are thine:
I have never heard
  Praise of love or wine
That panted forth a flood of rapture so divine.

Chorus Hymeneal,
  Or triumphal chant,
Matched with thine would be all

But an empty vaunt,
A thing wherein we feel there is some hidden want.   70

What objects are the fountains
    Of thy happy strain?
What fields, or waves, or mountains?
    What shapes of sky or plain?
What love of thine own kind? what ignorance of pain?

With thy clear keen joyance
    Languor cannot be:
Shadow of annoyance
    Never came near thee:
Thou lovest—but ne'er knew love's sad satiety.   80

Waking or asleep,
    Thou of death must deem
Things more true and deep
    Than we mortals dream,
Or how could thy notes flow in such a crystal stream?

We look before and after,
    And pine for what is not:
Our sincerest laughter
    With some pain is fraught;
Our sweetest songs are those that tell of saddest thought.   90

Yet if we could scorn
    Hate, and pride, and fear;
If we were things born
    Not to shed a tear,
I know not how thy joy we ever should come near.

Better than all measures
    Of delightful sound,
Better than all treasures
    That in books are found,
Thy skill to poet were, thou scorner of the ground!   100

Teach me half the gladness
    That thy brain must know,
Such harmonious madness
    From my lips would flow
The world should listen then—as I am listening now.

TO ——

I FEAR thy kisses, gentle maiden,
    Thou needest not fear mine;
My spirit is too deeply laden
    Ever to burthen thine.

I fear thy mien, thy tones, thy motion,
    Thou needest not fear mine;
Innocent is the heart's devotion
    With which I worship thine.

TO NIGHT

1

SWIFTLY walk o'er the western wave,
        Spirit of Night!
Out of the misty eastern cave,
Where, all the long and lone daylight,
Thou wovest dreams of joy and fear,
Which make thee terrible and dear,—
        Swift be thy flight!

2

Wrap thy form in a mantle gray,
        Star-inwrought!
Blind with thine hair the eyes of Day;
Kiss her until she be wearied out,
Then wander o'er city, and sea, and land,
Touching all with thine opiate wand—
        Come, long-sought!

3

When I arose and saw the dawn,
        I sighed for thee;
When light rode high, and the dew was gone,
And noon lay heavy on flower and tree,
And the weary Day turned to his rest,
Lingering like an unloved guest,
        I sighed for thee.

4

Thy brother Death came, and cried,
        Wouldst thou me?

Thy sweet child Sleep, the filmy-eyed,
Murmured like a noontide bee,
Shall I nestle near thy side?
Wouldst thou me?—And I replied,
No, not thee!

5

Death will come when thou art dead,
Soon, too soon—
Sleep will come when thou art fled;
Of neither would I ask the boon
I ask of thee, belovèd Night—
Swift be thine approaching flight,
Come soon, soon!

TIME

UNFATHOMABLE Sea! whose waves are years,
Ocean of Time, whose waters of deep woe
Are brackish with the salt of human tears!
Thou shoreless flood, which in thy ebb and flow
Claspest the limits of mortality,
And sick of prey, yet howling on for more,
Vomitest thy wrecks on its inhospitable shore;
Treacherous in calm, and terrible in storm,
Who shall put forth on thee,
Unfathomable Sea?

TO ——

MUSIC, when soft voices die,
Vibrates in the memory—
Odors, when sweet violets sicken,
Live within the sense they quicken.

Rose leaves, when the rose is dead,
Are heaped for the belovèd's bed;
And so thy thoughts, when thou art gone,
Love itself shall slumber on.

SONG

I

RARELY, rarely, comest thou,
Spirit of Delight!

Wherefore hast thou left me now
  Many a day and night?
Many a weary night and day
'Tis since thou art fled away.

2

How shall ever one like me
  Win thee back again?
With the joyous and the free
  Thou wilt scoff at pain.
Spirit false! thou hast forgot
All but those who need thee not.

3

As a lizard with the shade
  Of a trembling leaf,
Thou with sorrow art dismayed;
  Even the sighs of grief
Reproach thee, that thou art not near,
And reproach thou wilt not hear.

4

Let me set my mournful ditty
  To a merry measure;
Thou wilt never come for pity,
  Thou wilt come for pleasure;
Pity then will cut away
Those cruel wings, and thou wilt stay.

5

I love all that thou lovest,
  Spirit of Delight!
The fresh Earth in new leaves dressed,
  And the starry night;
Autumn evening, and the morn
When the golden mists are born.

6

I love snow, and all the forms
  Of the radiant frost;
I love waves, and winds, and storms,

Everything almost
Which is Nature's, and may be
Untainted by man's misery.

7

I love tranquil solitude,
  And such society
As is quiet, wise, and good;
  Between thee and me
What difference? but thou dost possess
The things I seek, not love them less.

8

I love Love—though he has wings,
  And like light can flee,
But above all other things,
  Spirit, I love thee—
Thou art love and life! Oh, come,
Make once more my heart thy home.

MUTABILITY

I

THE flower that smiles to-day
  To-morrow dies;
All that we wish to stay
  Tempts and then flies.
What is this world's delight?
Lightning that mocks the night,
  Brief even as bright.

2

Virtue, how frail it is!
  Friendship how rare!
Love, how it sells poor bliss
  For proud despair!
But we, though soon they fall,
Survive their joy, and all
  Which ours we call.

3

Whilst skies are blue and bright,
  Whilst flowers are gay,

Whilst eyes that change ere night
    Make glad the day;
Whilst yet the calm hours creep,
Dream thou—and from thy sleep
    Then wake to weep.

POLITICAL GREATNESS

NOR happiness, nor majesty, nor fame,
Nor peace, nor strength, nor skill in arms or arts,
Shepherd those herds whom tyranny makes tame;
Verse echoes not one beating of their hearts,
History is but the shadow of their shame,
Art veils her glass, or from the pageant starts
As to oblivion their blind millions fleet,
Staining that Heaven with obscene imagery
Of their own likeness. What are numbers knit
By force or custom? Man who man would be,
Must rule the empire of himself; in it
Must be supreme, establishing his throne
On vanquished will, quelling the anarchy
Of hopes and fears, being himself alone.

TO ——

I

ONE word is too often profaned
    For me to profane it,
One feeling too falsely disdained
    For thee to disdain it;
One hope is too like despair
    For prudence to smother,
And pity from thee more dear
    Than that from another.

2

I can give not what men call love,
    But wilt thou accept not
The worship the heart lifts above
    And the Heavens reject not,—
The desire of the moth for the star,
    Of the night for the morrow,
The devotion to something afar
    From the sphere of our sorrow?

ADONAIS

AN ELEGY ON THE DEATH OF JOHN KEATS, AUTHOR OF
ENDYMION, HYPERION, ETC.

Ἀστὴρ πρὶν μὲν ἔλαμπες ἐνὶ ζωοῖσιν Ἐῷος· νῦν δὲ θανὼν λάμπεις
Ἕσπερος ἐν φθιμένοις·

—PLATO.[37]

In April, 1818, there appeared in *The Quarterly Review* a savage attack on
Keats's *Endymion* from the pen of John Wilson Croker. This review was
thought by Shelley to have been the cause of Keats's early death. In his own
words (in the Preface to *Adonais*), it "produced the most violent effect on his
susceptible mind; the agitation thus originated ended in the rupture of a
blood-vessel in the lungs; a rapid consumption ensued, and the succeeding
acknowledgments from more candid critics of the true greatness of his powers
were ineffectual to heal the wound thus wantonly inflicted." We now know that
Keats was made of manlier stuff, and that it was not Croker's review that
killed him. Shelley, however, stirred by Keats's death, wrote his elegy *Adonais*,
in the pastoral style, as a lament for the young poet and a denunciation of
unjust and undiscerning criticism.

I

I WEEP for Adonais—he is dead!
Oh, weep for Adonais! though our tears
Thaw not the frost which binds so dear a head!
And thou, sad Hour, selected from all years
To mourn our loss, rouse thy obscure compeers,
And teach them thine own sorrow, say: "With me
Died Adonais; till the Future dares
Forget the Past, his fate and fame shall be
An echo and a light unto eternity!"

2

Where wert thou, mighty Mother, when he lay,
When thy Son lay, pierced by the shaft which flies
In darkness? where was lorn Urania [38]
When Adonais died? With veilèd eyes,
'Mid listening Echoes, in her Paradise
She sat, while one, with soft enamored breath,
Rekindled all the fading melodies,
With which, like flowers that mock the corse beneath,
He had adorned and hid the coming bulk of Death.

37 Thou wert the morning star among the living,
    Ere thy fair light had fled;—
Now, having died, thou art as Hesperus, giving
    New splendor to the dead.
              (Shelley's translation)

38 the heavenly Muse
(probably from Milton)

3

Oh, weep for Adonais—he is dead!
Wake, melancholy Mother, wake and weep!
Yet wherefore? Quench within their burning bed
Thy fiery tears, and let thy loud heart keep,
Like his, a mute and uncomplaining sleep;
For he is gone, where all things wise and fair
Descend;—oh, dream not that the amorous Deep
Will yet restore him to the vital air;
Death feeds on his mute voice, and laughs at our despair.

4

Most musical of mourners, weep again!
Lament anew, Urania!—he died,
Who was the Sire of an immortal strain,
Blind, old, and lonely, when his country's pride,
The priest, the slave, and the liberticide,
Trampled and mocked with many a loathèd rite
Of lust and blood; he went, unterrified,
Into the gulf of death; but his clear Sprite
Yet reigns o'er earth; the third [39] among the sons of light.

5

Most musical of mourners, weep anew!
Not all to that bright station dared to climb;
And happier they their happiness who knew,
Whose tapers yet burn through that night of time
In which suns perished; others more sublime,
Struck by the envious wrath of man or god,
Have sunk, extinct in their refulgent prime;
And some yet live, treading the thorny road,
Which leads, through toil and hate, to Fame's serene abode.

6

But now, thy youngest, dearest one, has perished—
The nursling of thy widowhood, who grew,
Like a pale flower by some sad maiden cherished,
And fed with true-love tears, instead of dew;
Most musical of mourners, weep anew!
Thy extreme hope, the loveliest and the last,
The bloom, whose petals, nipped before they blew,

[39] Milton, the other two being, presumably, Homer and Dante

Died on the promise of the fruit, is waste;
The broken lily lies—the storm is overpast.

7

To that high Capital,[40] where kingly Death
Keeps his pale court in beauty and decay,
He came; and bought, with price of purest breath,
A grave among the eternal.—Come away!
Haste, while the vault of blue Italian day
Is yet his fitting charnel-roof! while still
He lies, as if in dewy sleep he lay;
Awake him not! surely he takes his fill
Of deep and liquid rest, forgetful of all ill.

8

He will awake no more, oh, never more!—
Within the twilight chamber spreads apace
The shadow of white Death, and at the door
Invisible Corruption waits to trace
His extreme way to her dim dwelling-place;
The eternal Hunger sits, but pity and awe
Soothe her pale rage, nor dares she to deface
So fair a prey, till darkness, and the law
Of change, shall o'er his sleep the mortal curtain draw.

9

Oh, weep for Adonais!—The quick Dreams,
The passion-wingèd Ministers of thought,
Who were his flocks, whom near the living streams
Of his young spirit he fed, and whom he taught
The love which was its music, wander not,—
Wander no more, from kindling brain to brain,
But droop there, whence they sprung; and mourn their lot
Round the cold heart, where, after their sweet pain,
They ne'er will gather strength, or find a home again.

10

And one with trembling hands clasps his cold head,
And fans him with her moonlight wings, and cries;
"Our love, our hope, our sorrow, is not dead;
See, on the silken fringe of his faint eyes,

40 Rome

Like dew upon a sleeping flower, there lies
A tear some Dream has loosened from his brain."
Lost Angel of a ruined Paradise!
She knew not 'twas her own; as with no stain
She faded, like a cloud which had outwept its rain.

11

One from a lucid urn of starry dew
Washed his light limbs as if embalming them;
Another clipped her profuse locks, and threw
The wreath upon him, like an anadem,[41]
Which frozen tears instead of pearls begem;
Another in her willful grief would break
Her bow and wingèd reeds, as if to stem
A greater loss with one which was more weak;
And dull the barbèd fire against his frozen cheek.

12

Another Splendor on his mouth alit,
That mouth, whence it was wont to draw the breath
Which gave it strength to pierce the guarded wit,
And pass into the panting heart beneath
With lightning and with music: the damp death
Quenched its caress upon his icy lips;
And, as a dying meteor stains a wreath
Of moonlight vapor, which the cold night clips,[42]
It flushed through his pale limbs, and passed to its eclipse.

13

And others came . . . Desires and Adorations,
Wingèd Persuasions and veiled Destinies,
Splendors, and Glooms, and glimmering Incarnations
Of hopes and fears, and twilight Phantasies;
And Sorrow, with her family of Sighs,
And Pleasure, blind with tears, led by the gleam
Of her own dying smile instead of eyes,
Came in slow pomp;—the moving pomp might seem
Like pageantry of mist on an autumnal stream.

14

All he had loved, and molded into thought,
From shape, and hue, and odor, and sweet sound,

41 garland   42 embraces

Lamented Adonais. Morning sought
Her eastern watch-tower, and her hair unbound,
Wet with the tears which should adorn the ground,
Dimmed the aërial eyes that kindle day;
Afar the melancholy thunder moaned,
Pale Ocean in unquiet slumber lay,
And the wild Winds flew round, sobbing in their dismay.

15

Lost Echo sits amid the voiceless mountains,
And feeds her grief with his remembered lay,
And will no more reply to winds or fountains,
Or amorous birds perched on the young green spray,
Or herdsman's horn, or bell at closing day;
Since she can mimic not his lips, more dear
Than those [43] for whose disdain she pined away
Into a shadow of all sounds:—a drear
Murmur, between their songs, is all the woodmen hear.

16

Grief made the young Spring wild, and she threw down
Her kindling buds, as if she Autumn were,
Or they dead leaves; since her delight is flown,
For whom should she have waked the sullen year?
To Phœbus was not Hyacinth [44] so dear
Nor to himself Narcissus, [45] as to both
Thou, Adonais: wan they stand and sere
Amid the faint companions of their youth,
With dew all turned to tears; odor, to sighing ruth.

17

Thy spirit's sister, the lorn nightingale
Mourns not her mate with such melodious pain;
Not so the eagle, who like thee could scale
Heaven, and could nourish in the sun's domain
Her mighty youth with morning, doth complain,
Soaring and screaming round her empty nest,
As Albion wails for thee: the curse of Cain
Light on his head [46] who pierced thy innocent breast,
And scared the angel soul that was its earthly guest!

43 of Narcissus, who did not return Echo's love
44 whom Phœbus Apollo loved; changed at his death into a flower
45 who fell in love with his own image, and was changed into a flower
46 author of the article in *Quarterly Review* thought by Shelley to have brought about Keats's death; now identified as John Wilson Croker

18

Ah, woe is me! Winter is come and gone,
But grief returns with the revolving year;
The airs and streams renew their joyous tone;
The ants, the bees, the swallows reappear;
Fresh leaves and flowers deck the dead Season's bier;
The amorous birds now pair in every brake,
And build their mossy homes in field and brere; [47]
And the green lizard, and the golden snake,
Like unimprisoned flames, out of their trance awake.

19

Through wood and stream and field and hill and Ocean
A quickening life from the Earth's heart has burst
As it has ever done, with change and motion,
From the great morning of the world when first
God dawned on Chaos; in its stream immersed,
The lamps of Heaven flash with a softer light;
All baser things pant with life's sacred thirst;
Diffuse themselves; and spend in love's delight,
The beauty and the joy of their renewèd might.

20

The leprous corpse, touched by this spirit tender,
Exhales itself in flowers of gentle breath;
Like incarnations of the stars, when splendor
Is changed to fragrance, they illumine death
And mock the merry worm that wakes beneath;
Nought we know, dies. Shall that alone which knows
Be as a sword consumed before the sheath
By sightless lightning?—the intense atom glows
A moment, then is quenched in a most cold repose.

21

Alas! that all we loved of him should be,
But for our grief, as if it had not been,
And grief itself be mortal! Woe is me!
Whence are we, and why are we? of what scene
The actors or spectators? Great and mean
Meet massed in death, who lends what life must borrow.
As long as skies are blue, and fields are green,

47 briar

Evening must usher night, night urge the morrow,
Month follow month with woe, and year wake year to sorrow.

22

He will awake no more, oh, never more!
"Wake thou," cried Misery, "childless Mother, rise
Out of thy sleep, and slake, in thy heart's core,
A wound more fierce than his, with tears and sighs."
And all the Dreams that watched Urania's eyes,
And all the Echoes whom their sister's song
Had held in holy silence, cried: "Arise!"
Swift as a Thought by the snake Memory stung,
From her ambrosial rest the fading Splendor sprung.

23

She rose like an autumnal Night, that springs
Out of the East, and follows wild and drear
The golden Day, which, on eternal wings,
Even as a ghost abandoning a bier,
Had left the Earth a corpse. Sorrow and fear
So struck, so roused, so rapped Urania;
So saddened round her like an atmosphere
Of stormy mist; so swept her on her way
Even to the mournful place where Adonais lay.

24

Out of her secret Paradise she sped,
Through camps and cities rough with stone, and steel,
And human hearts, which to her aëry tread
Yielding not, wounded the invisible
Palms of her tender feet where'er they fell:
And barbèd tongues, and thoughts more sharp than they,
Rent the soft Form they never could repel,
Whose sacred blood, like the young tears of May,
Paved with eternal flowers that undeserving way.

25

In the death-chamber for a moment Death,
Shamed by the presence of that living Might,
Blushed to annihilation, and the breath
Revisited those lips, and Life's pale light
Flashed through those limbs, so late her dear delight.

"Leave me not wild and drear and comfortless,
As silent lightning leaves the starless night!
Leave me not!" cried Urania: her distress
Roused Death: Death rose and smiled, and met her vain
       caress.

26

"Stay yet awhile! speak to me once again;
Kiss me, so long but as a kiss may live;
And in my heartless breast and burning brain
That word, that kiss, shall all thoughts else survive,
With food of saddest memory kept alive,
Now thou art dead, as if it were a part
Of thee, my Adonais! I would give
All that I am to be as thou now art!
But I am chained to Time, and cannot thence depart!

27

"O gentle child, beautiful as thou wert,
Why didst thou leave the trodden paths of men
Too soon, and with weak hands though mighty heart
Dare the unpastured dragon [48] in his den?
Defenseless as thou wert, oh, where was then
Wisdom the mirrored shield, or scorn the spear?
Or hadst thou waited the full cycle, when
Thy spirit should have filled its crescent sphere,
The monsters of life's waste had fled from thee like deer.

28

"The herded wolves, bold only to pursue;
The obscene ravens, clamorous o'er the dead;
The vultures to the conqueror's banner true
Who feed where Desolation first has fed,
And whose wings rain contagion;—how they fled,
When, like Apollo, from his golden bow
The Pythian of the age [49] one arrow sped
And smiled!—The spoilers tempt no second blow,
They fawn on the proud feet that spurn them lying low.

29

"The sun comes forth, and many reptiles spawn;
He sets, and each ephemeral insect then

48 the hard world
49 Byron, who, as Apollo   slew the Python, laid the   Bards and Scotch Review-
                            critics low in his English   ers

Is gathered into death without a dawn,
And the immortal stars awake again;
So is it in the world of living men:
A godlike mind soars forth, in its delight
Making earth bare and veiling heaven, and when
It sinks, the swarms that dimmed or shared its light
Leave to its kindred lamps the spirit's awful night."

30

Thus ceased she: and the mountain shepherds came,
Their garlands sere, their magic mantles rent;
The Pilgrim of Eternity,[50] whose fame
Over his living head like Heaven is bent,
An early but enduring monument,
Came, veiling all the lightnings of his song
In sorrow; from her wilds Ierne sent
The sweetest lyrist of her saddest wrong,[51]
And Love taught Grief to fall like music from his tongue.

31

Midst others of less note, came one frail Form,[52]
A phantom among men; companionless
As the last cloud of an expiring storm
Whose thunder is its knell; he, as I guess,
Had gazed on Nature's naked loveliness,
Actæon-like,[53] and now he fled astray
With feeble steps o'er the world's wilderness,
And his own thoughts, along that rugged way,
Pursued, like raging hounds, their father and their prey.

32

A pardlike [54] Spirit beautiful and swift—
A Love in desolation masked;—a Power
Girt round with weakness;—it can scarce uplift
The weight of the superincumbent hour;
It is a dying lamp, a falling shower,
A breaking billow;—even whilst we speak
Is it not broken? On the withering flower
The killing sun smiles brightly: on a cheek
The life can burn in blood, even while the heart may break.

50 Byron, so called be-
cause of *Childe Harold's
Pilgrimage*
51 Ireland sent Thomas
Moore.

52 Shelley
53 Actæon, in punish-
ment for gazing on Diana
while she was bathing, was

turned into a stag and torn
to pieces by his own hounds.
54 leopard-like

33

His head was bound with pansies overblown,
And faded violets, white, and pied, and blue;
And a light spear topped with a cypress cone,
Round whose rude shaft dark ivy-tresses grew
Yet dripping with the forest's noonday dew,
Vibrated, as the ever-beating heart
Shook the weak hand that grasped it; of that crew
He came the last, neglected and apart;
A herd-abandoned deer struck by the hunter's dart.

34

All stood aloof, and at his partial moan
Smiled through their tears; well knew that gentle band
Who in another's fate now wept his own,
As in the accents of an unknown land
He sung new sorrow; sad Urania scanned
The Stranger's mien, and murmured: "Who art thou?"
He answered not, but with a sudden hand
Made bare his branded and ensanguined brow,
Which was like Cain's or Christ's—oh! that it should be so!

35

What softer voice is hushed over the dead?
Athwart what brow is that dark mantle thrown?
What form leans sadly o'er the white death-bed,
In mockery of monumental stone,
The heavy heart heaving without a moan?
If it be He,[55] who, gentlest of the wise,
Taught, soothed, loved, honored the departed one,
Let me not vex, with inharmonious sighs,
The silence of that heart's accepted sacrifice.

36

Our Adonais has drunk poison—oh!
What deaf and viperous murderer could crown
Life's early cup with such a draught of woe?
The nameless worm [56] would now itself disown:
It felt, yet could escape, the magic tone
Whose prelude held all envy, hate, and wrong,

55 Leigh Hunt   56 The *Quarterly* reviewer

But what was howling in one breast alone,
Silent with expectation of the song,
Whose master's hand is cold, whose silver lyre unstrung.

37

Live thou, whose infamy is not thy fame!
Live! fear no heavier chastisement from me,
Thou noteless blot on a remembered name!
But be thyself, and know thyself to be!
And ever at thy season be thou free
To spill the venom when thy fangs o'erflow:
Remorse and Self-contempt shall cling to thee;
Hot Shame shall burn upon thy secret brow,
And like a beaten hound tremble thou shalt—as now.

38

Nor let us weep that our delight is fled
Far from these carrion kites that scream below;
He wakes or sleeps with the enduring dead;
Thou canst not soar where he is sitting now.—
Dust to the dust! but the pure spirit shall flow
Back to the burning fountain whence it came,
A portion of the Eternal, which must glow
Through time and change, unquenchably the same,
Whilst thy cold embers choke the sordid hearth of shame.

39

Peace, peace! he is not dead, he doth not sleep—
He hath awakened from the dream of life—
'Tis we, who lost in stormy visions, keep
With phantoms an unprofitable strife,
And in mad trance, strike with our spirit's knife
Invulnerable nothings.—*We* decay
Like corpses in a charnel; fear and grief
Convulse us and consume us day by day,
And cold hopes swarm like worms within our living clay.

40

He has outsoared the shadow of our night;
Envy and calumny and hate and pain,
And that unrest which men miscall delight,
Can touch him not and torture not again;

From the contagion of the world's slow stain
He is secure, and now can never mourn
A heart grown cold, a head grown gray in vain;
Nor, when the spirit's self has ceased to burn,
With sparkless ashes load an unlamented urn.

41

He lives, he wakes—'tis Death is dead, not he;
Mourn not for Adonais.—Thou young Dawn,
Turn all thy dew to splendor, for from thee
The spirit thou lamentest is not gone;
Ye caverns and ye forests, cease to moan!
Cease, ye faint flowers and fountains, and thou Air,
Which like a mourning veil thy scarf hadst thrown
O'er the abandoned Earth, now leave it bare
Even to the joyous stars which smile on its despair!

42

He is made one with Nature: there is heard
His voice in all her music, from the moan
Of thunder, to the song of night's sweet bird;
He is a presence to be felt and known
In darkness and in light, from herb and stone,
Spreading itself where'er that Power may move
Which has withdrawn his being to its own;
Which wields the world with never-wearied love,
Sustains it from beneath, and kindles it above.

43

He is a portion of the loveliness
Which once he made more lovely: he doth bear
His part, while the one Spirit's plastic stress
Sweeps through the dull dense world, compelling there,
All new successions to the forms they wear;
Torturing th' unwilling dross that checks its flight
To its own likeness, as each mass may bear;
And bursting in its beauty and its might
From trees and beasts and men into the Heaven's light.

44

The splendors of the firmament of time
May be eclipsed, but are extinguished not;

Like stars to their appointed height they climb,
And death is a low mist which cannot blot
The brightness it may veil. When lofty thought
Lifts a young heart above its mortal lair,
And love and life contend in it, for what
Shall be its earthly doom, the dead live there
And move like winds of light on dark and stormy air.

45

The inheritors of unfulfilled renown [57]
Rose from their thrones, built beyond mortal thought,
Far in the Unapparent. Chatterton
Rose pale,—his solemn agony had not
Yet faded from him; Sidney, as he fought
And as he fell and as he lived and loved
Sublimely mild, a Spirit without spot,
Arose; and Lucan, by his death approved:
Oblivion as they rose shrank like a thing reproved.

46

And many more, whose names on Earth are dark,
But whose transmitted effluence cannot die
So long as fire outlives the parent spark,   .
Rose, robed in dazzling immortality.
"Thou art become as one of us," they cry,
"It was for thee yon kingless sphere has long
Swung blind in unascended majesty,
Silent alone amid an Heaven of Song.
Assume thy wingèd throne, thou Vesper of our throng!"

47

Who mourns for Adonais? Oh, come forth,
Fond wretch! and know thyself and him aright.
Clasp with thy panting soul the pendulous Earth;
As from a center, dart thy spirit's light
Beyond all worlds, until its spacious might
Satiate the void circumference: then shrink
Even to a point within our day and night;
And keep thy heart light lest it make thee sink
When hope has kindled hope, and lured thee to the brink.

57 Three poets who died young: Thomas Chatterton, who killed himself at eighteen (1770), Sir Philip Sidney, who died at thirty-two from a wound received in battle (1586), and the Roman poet Lucan who killed himself at twenty-six, to avoid being executed by Nero (A. D., 65)

48

Or go to Rome, which is the sepulcher,
Oh, not of him, but of our joy: 'tis nought
That ages, empires, and religions there
Lie buried in the ravage they have wrought;
For such as he can lend,—they borrow not
Glory from those who made the world their prey;
And he is gathered to the kings of thought
Who waged contention with their time's decay,
And of the past are all that cannot pass away.

49

Go thou to Rome,—at once the Paradise,
The grave, the city, and the wilderness;
And where its wrecks like shattered mountains rise,
And flowering weeds, and fragrant copses dress
The bones of Desolation's nakedness
Pass, till the spirit of the spot shall lead
Thy footsteps to a slope of green access
Where, like an infant's smile, over the dead
A light of laughing flowers along the grass is spread;

50

And gray walls molder round, on which dull Time
Feeds, like slow fire upon a hoary brand;
And one keen pyramid with wedge sublime,
Pavilioning the dust of him who planned
This refuge for his memory, doth stand
Like flame transformed to marble; and beneath,
A field is spread, on which a newer band
Have pitched in Heaven's smile their camp of death,
Welcoming him we lose with scarce extinguished breath.

51

Here pause: these graves are all too young as yet
To have outgrown the sorrow which consigned
Its charge to each; and if the seal is set,
Here, on one fountain of a mourning mind,
Break it not thou! too surely shalt thou find
Thine own well full, if thou returnest home,
Of tears and gall. From the world's bitter wind

Seek shelter in the shadow of the tomb.
What Adonais is, why fear we to become?

52

The One remains, the many change and pass;
Heaven's light forever shines, Earth's shadows fly;
Life, like a dome of many-colored glass,
Stains the white radiance of Eternity,
Until Death tramples it to fragments.—Die,
If thou wouldst be with that which thou dost seek!
Follow where all is fled!—Rome's azure sky,
Flowers, ruins, statues, music, words, are weak
The glory they transfuse with fitting truth to speak.

53

Why linger, why turn back, why shrink, my Heart?
Thy hopes are gone before: from all things here
They have departed; thou shouldst now depart!
A light is passed from the revolving year,
And man, and woman; and what still is dear
Attracts to crush, repels to make thee wither.
The soft sky smiles,—the low wind whispers near:
'Tis Adonais calls! oh, hasten thither.
No more let Life divide what Death can join together.

54

That Light whose smile kindles the Universe,
That Beauty in which all things work and move,
That Benediction which the eclipsing Curse
Of birth can quench not, that sustaining Love
Which through the web of being blindly wove
By man and beast and earth and air and sea,
Burns bright or dim, as each are mirrors of
The fire for which all thirst; now beams on me,
Consuming the last clouds of cold mortality.

55

The breath whose might I have invoked in song
Descends on me; my spirit's bark is driven,
Far from the shore, far from the trembling throng
Whose sails were never to the tempest given;
The massy earth and sphered skies are riven!

I am borne darkly, fearfully, afar;
Whilst, burning through the inmost veil of Heaven,
The soul of Adonais, like a star,
Beacons from the abode where the Eternal are.

HELLAS [58]

THE FINAL CHORUS

The world's great age begins anew,
   The golden years return,
The earth doth like a snake renew
   Her winter weeds outworn:
Heaven smiles, and faiths and empires gleam,
Like wrecks of a dissolving dream.

A brighter Hellas rears its mountains
   From waves serener far;
A new Peneus [59] rolls his fountains
   Against the morning star.   10
Where fairer Tempes [60] bloom, there sleep
Young Cyclads [61] on a sunnier deep.

A loftier Argo [62] cleaves the main,
   Fraught with a later prize;
Another Orpheus sings again,
   And loves, and weeps, and dies.
A new Ulysses leaves once more
Calypso [63] for his native shore.

Oh, write no more the tale of Troy,
   If earth Death's scroll must be!   20
Nor mix with Laian [64] rage the joy
   Which dawns upon the free:
Although a subtler Sphinx renew
Riddles of death Thebes never knew.

Another Athens shall arise,
   And to remoter time
Bequeath, like sunset to the skies,

58 A lyrical drama, inspired by the Greek war for independence, which Shelley thinks will bring a new golden age, surpassing the ancient glories of Greece
59 a river of Thessaly
60 beautiful vales
61 islands in the Ægean Sea
62 ship in which Jason and his Argonauts sailed for the golden fleece
63 who sought to keep Ulysses on her island
64 Œdipus, son of King Laius, freed Thebes from the Sphinx by answering her riddle, but unwittingly killed his father and married his mother.

The splendor of its prime;
And leave, if nought so bright may live,
All earth can take or Heaven can give.   30

Saturn and Love their long repose
    Shall burst,[65] more bright and good
Than all who fell, than One who rose,
    Than many unsubdued:
Not gold, not blood, their altar dowers,
But votive tears and symbol flowers.

Oh, cease! must hate and death return?
    Cease! must men kill and die?
Cease! drain not to its dregs the urn
    Of bitter prophecy.   40
The world is weary of the past,
Oh, might it die or rest at last!

LINES: "WHEN THE LAMP IS SHATTERED"

1

When the lamp is shattered
The light in the dust lies dead—
    When the cloud is scattered
The rainbow's glory is shed.
    When the lute is broken,
Sweet tones are remembered not;
    When the lips have spoken,
Loved accents are soon forgot.

2

As music and splendor
Survive not the lamp and the lute,
    The heart's echoes render
No song when the spirit is mute:—
    No song but sad dirges,
Like the wind through a ruined cell,
    Or the mournful surges
That ring the dead seaman's knell.

---

[65] Saturn and Love were among the deities of a real or imaginary state of innocence and happiness. *All those who fell,* or the Gods of Greece, Asia, and Egypt; the *One who rose,* or Jesus Christ, at whose appearance the idols of the Pagan World were amerced of their worship; and *the many unsubdued,* or the monstrous objects of the idolatry of China, India, the Antarctic islands, and the native tribes of America." (Shelley)

3

When hearts have once mingled
Love first leaves the well-built nest;
  The weak one is singled
To endure what it once possessed.
  O Love! who bewailest
The frailty of all things here,
  Why choose you the frailest
For your cradle, your home, and your bier?

4

Its passions will rock thee
As the storms rock the ravens on high;
  Bright reason will mock thee,
Like the sun from a wintry sky.
  From thy nest every rafter
Will rot, and thine eagle home
  Leave thee naked to laughter,
When leaves fall and cold winds come.

THE MASK OF ANARCHY

After the Napoleonic wars England suffered acute social and economic distress, and the movement for parliamentary reform so as to place the power in the hands of the masses gained rapid headway. On August 16, 1819, a great crowd of people was gathered in St. Peter's Fields, Manchester, to hear an address on this topic by a radical agitator. Troops sent to arrest the speaker charged into the crowd and in the resulting *mêlée* six people were killed and about eighty wounded. The conduct of the authorities at this Manchester or "Peterloo" massacre as it was bitterly called (after "Waterloo") was supported by Castlereagh, the Foreign Minister; Eldon, Lord High Chancellor; and Sidmouth, Home Secretary. Shelley's indignation, when the news reached him in Italy, is expressed in the following poem. In Shelley's thought, such Tyranny leads to the reign of Anarchy; when Hope immolates herself, the image of true Freedom arises. The poem is here condensed to about half its original length.

As I lay asleep in Italy
There came a voice from over the Sea,
And with great power it forth led me
To walk in the visions of Poesy.

I met Murder on the way—
He had a mask like Castlereagh—

Very smooth he looked, yet grim;
Seven bloodhounds followed him:

All were fat; and well they might
Be in admirable plight,   10
For one by one, and two by two,
He tossed them human hearts to chew
Which from his wide cloak he drew.

Next came Fraud, and he had on,
Like Eldon, an ermined gown;
His big tears, for he wept well,
Turned to mill-stones as they fell.

And the little children, who
Round his feet played to and fro,
Thinking every tear a gem,   20
Had their brains knocked out by them.

Clothed with the Bible, as with light,
And the shadows of the night,
Like Sidmouth, next, Hypocrisy
On a crocodile rode by.

And many more Destructions played
In this ghastly masquerade,
All disguised, even to the eyes,
Like Bishops, lawyers, peers, or spies.

Last came Anarchy: he rode   30
On a white horse, splashed with blood;
He was pale even to the lips,
Like Death in the Apocalypse.

And he wore a kingly crown;
And in his grasp a scepter shone;
On his brow this mark I saw—
'I AM GOD, AND KING, AND LAW!'

With a pace stately and fast,
Over English land he passed,
Trampling to a mire of blood   40
The adoring multitude. . . .

When one fled past, a maniac maid,
And her name was Hope, she said:
But she looked more like Despair,
And she cried out in the air:

'My father Time is weak and gray
With waiting for a better day;
See how idiot-like he stands,
Fumbling with his palsied hands!' . . .

Then she lay down in the street,   50
Right before the horses' feet,
Expecting, with a patient eye,
Murder, Fraud, and Anarchy.

When between her and her foes
A mist, a light, an image rose,
Small at first, and weak, and frail
Like the vapor of a vale: . . .

With step as soft as wind it passed
O'er the heads of men—so fast
That they knew the presence there,   60
And looked,—but all was empty air. . . .

And the prostrate multitude
Looked—and ankle-deep in blood,
Hope, that maiden most serene,
Was walking with a quiet mien:

And Anarchy, the ghastly birth,
Lay dead earth upon the earth;
The Horse of Death tameless as wind
Fled, and with his hoofs did grind
To dust the murderers thronged behind.   70

A rushing light of clouds and splendor,
A sense awakening and yet tender
Was heard and felt—and at its close
These words of joy and fear arose: . . .

'Men of England, heirs of Glory,
Heroes of unwritten story,
Nurslings of one mighty Mother,
Hopes of her, and one another;

'Rise like Lions after slumber
In unvanquishable number,
Shake your chains to earth like dew
Which in sleep had fallen on you—
Ye are many—they are few.   80

'What is Freedom?—ye can tell
That which slavery is, too well—
For its very name has grown
To an echo of your own.

' 'Tis to work and have such pay
As just keeps life from day to day
In your limbs, as in a cell
For the tyrants' use to dwell,   90

'So that ye for them are made
Loom, and plow, and sword, and spade,
With or without your own will bent
To their defence and nourishment.

' 'Tis to see your children weak
With their mothers pine and peak,
When the winter winds are bleak,—
They are dying whilst I speak.

' 'Tis to hunger for such diet   100
As the rich man in his riot
Casts to the fat dogs that lie
Surfeiting beneath his eye; . . .

' 'Tis to be a slave in soul
And to hold no strong control
Over your own wills, but be
All that others make of ye.

'And at length when ye complain
With a murmur weak and vain
'Tis to see the Tyrant's crew   110
Ride over your wives and you—
Blood is on the grass like dew. . . .

'This is Slavery—savage men,
Or wild beasts within a den

Would endure not as ye do—
But such ills they never knew.

'What art thou, Freedom? O! could slaves
Answer from their living graves
This demand—tyrants would flee
Like a dream's wild imagery: 120

'Thou art not, as impostors say,
A shadow soon to pass away,
A superstition and a name
Echoing from the cave of Fame.

'For the laborer thou art bread,
And a comely table spread
From his daily labor come
In a neat and happy home.

'Thou art clothes, and fire, and food
For the trampled multitude—   130
No—in countries that are free
Such starvation cannot be
As in England now we see.

'To the rich thou art a check
When his foot is on the neck
Of his victim, thou dost make
That he treads upon a snake.

'Thou art Justice—ne'er for gold
May thy righteous laws be sold
As laws are in England—thou   140
Shield'st alike the high and low.

'Thou art Wisdom—Freemen never
Dream that God will damn forever
All who think those things untrue
Of which Priests make such ado.

'Thou art Peace—never by thee
Would blood and treasure wasted be
As tyrants wasted them, when all
Leagued to quench thy flame in Gaul. . . .

'Thou art Love—the rich have kissed   150
Thy feet, and like him following Christ,

Give their substance to the free
And through the rough world follow thee. . . .

'Science, Poetry, and Thought
Are thy lamps; they make the lot
Of the dwellers in a cot
So serene, they curse it not.

'Spirit, Patience, Gentleness,
All that can adorn and bless
Art thou—let deeds, not words, express   160
Thine exceeding loveliness. . . .

'Let a vast assembly be,
And with great solemnity
Declare with measured words that ye
Are, as God has made ye, free—

'Be your strong and simple words
Keen to wound as sharpened swords,
And wide as targes let them be,
With their shade to cover ye. . . .

'And if then the tyrants dare   170
Let them ride among ye there,
Slash, and stab, and maim, and hew,—
What they like, that let them do.

'With folded arms and steady eyes,
And little fear, and less surprise,
Look upon them as they slay
Till their rage has died away.

'Then they will return with shame
To the place from which they came,
And the blood thus shed will speak   180
In hot blushes on their cheek. . . .

'And these words shall then become
Like Oppression's thundered doom
Ringing through each heart and brain,
Heard again—again—again—

'Rise like Lions after slumber
In unvanquishable number—
Shake your chains to earth like dew
Which in sleep had fallen on you—
Ye are many, they are few.'   190

JOHN KEATS (1795–1821)

Keats's father kept the livery stable of the Swan and Hoop Inn, London, and had married the innkeeper's daughter. In the unpromising atmosphere of rooms over the stable the poet was born on October 29, 1795. "Genius was never more mysterious, never more independent of heredity," writes Professor W. L. Phelps; "in his father's stable John found the only horse not there— Pegasus." The boy was sent to a private school conducted by the Rev. J. Clarke at Enfield. Here he became a good friend of the headmaster's son, Charles Cowden Clarke, who directed his reading, particularly to the Elizabethans and our older writers, and under whose encouragement he decided to become a poet.

His father and mother having both died, he was at fifteen apprenticed to a surgeon. For five years he continued his studies, developing skill in his profession. In 1816 Clarke introduced him to Leigh Hunt, the well-known minor poet and essayist, then editor of the *Examiner*. Hunt, who posed as a champion of liberty, communicated some of his own zeal to Keats, although the temper of Keats's mind prevented his ever becoming an ardent revolutionist, like Shelley and others. More important, Hunt criticized the poet's early verses sympathetically, and published a number of them in his magazine. To him Keats dedicated his first volume, the *Poems* of 1817. Through him, he became acquainted with the artist, Benjamin Haydon, who taught him to appreciate Greek sculpture and who helped to arouse his enthusiasm for the Greek concept of beauty; and with John Hamilton Reynolds, Shelley, Hazlitt, Wordsworth, and others. Keats's friendship with Hunt was not, however, an unmixed blessing, for it identified him as one of the editor's circle, and prevented the young poet's work from getting a fair treatment at the hands of the reviewers, to many of whom Hunt's liberal views were obnoxious. Keats, along with Hunt, was dubbed, in a series of articles in *Blackwood's Magazine,* as belonging to the "cockney" school of poetry.

In 1818 he published his poetic romance, *Endymion,* a poem of the greatest promise, sensuously rich in imagery, but profuse and unrestrained. This volume called forth the scathing review in the *Quarterly* by John Wilson Croker— the attack which Byron, Shelley, and others mistakenly thought was the indirect cause of Keats's early death. The ridicule heaped upon his earlier volumes did not, in fact, discourage Keats profoundly. He recognized his own immaturity, and in manly spirit set about improving his work—with what success may be seen in the volume of 1820, which contained *Lamia, Isabella, The Eve of St. Agnes,* the magnificent *Odes,* and the fine fragment of *Hyperion.*

This was the last volume published in Keats's lifetime. He had developed consumption, from which his mother had earlier died, and likewise his brother Tom in 1818. A passionate love-affair with Fanny Brawne, a girl by no means his intellectual equal, deeply shook his emotions. During 1820 his health grew rapidly worse, and in the fall he set sail with his friend Joseph Severn for Italy in the hope of improvement in a milder climate. He died at Rome on February 23, 1821, and was buried in the Protestant Cemetery, near the tomb of Caius Cestius. On the slab over his tomb were engraved, at his own request, the words, "Here lies one whose name was writ in water." The headstone does not even bear his name, stating simply that the grave holds the body of a "young English poet."

The sheer sensuous beauty of Keats's verse has not been surpassed in English. Yet he was not content with fixing in his imaginative imagery the richness and splendor of the external world. He believed that ultimate truth could be arrived at through the senses. For him "beauty is truth, truth beauty." This fine thought, and a melancholy preoccupation with mutability—the ceaseless decay in nature and human life—form perhaps the chief intellectual content of his work. It should be noted also that he was a painstaking artist, who constantly strove for the most perfect form possible; he had indeed reproached Shelley for his facile carelessness, and had urged that he "load every rift with ore." His influence on succeeding poets, particularly Tennyson and Rossetti, has been profound. He has been, writes Professor H. J. C. Grierson, "without any exception, the greatest influence in English poetry for a whole century."

BIBLIOGRAPHY. Best one vol. ed. by E. de Selincourt (Methuen); others the Globe, ed. W. T. Arnold (Macmillan), and the Cambridge, with letters, ed. H. E. Scudder (Houghton Mifflin). Older standard *Complete Poetical Works* by H. Buxton Forman (Oxford). *Letters*, ed. S. Colvin (Macmillan). Recent biography, with much new material, by Amy Lowell, 2 vols. (Houghton Mifflin); other lives by S. Colvin in Eng. Men of Letters ser., also a longer volume (Scribner's).

SONNETS

WRITTEN ON THE DAY THAT MR. LEIGH HUNT LEFT PRISON [1]

WHAT though, for showing truth to flattered state,
    Kind Hunt was shut in prison, yet has he,
    In his immortal spirit, been as free
As the sky-searching lark, and as elate.
Minion of grandeur! think you he did wait?
    Think you he nought but prison walls did see,
    Till, so unwilling, thou unturn'dst the key?
Ah, no! far happier, nobler was his fate!
In Spenser's halls he strayed, and bowers fair,
    Culling enchanted flowers; and he flew
With daring Milton through the fields of air:
    To regions of his own his genius true
Took happy flights. Who shall his fame impair
    When thou art dead, and all thy wretched crew?

1 Leigh Hunt had been imprisoned for two years for publishing in his *Examiner* an article criticizing the Prince Regent, whom he described as "a fat Adonis of fifty." He was released in February, 1815.

ON FIRST LOOKING INTO CHAPMAN'S HOMER [2]

Much have I traveled in the realms of gold,
　And many goodly states and kingdoms seen;
　Round many western islands have I been
Which bards in fealty to Apollo hold.
Oft of one wide expanse had I been told
　That deep-browed Homer ruled as his demesne:
　Yet did I never breathe its pure serene
Till I heard Chapman speak out loud and bold:
Then felt I like some watcher of the skies
　When a new planet swims into his ken;
Or like stout Cortez when with eagle eyes
　He stared at the Pacific—and all his men
Looked at each other with a wild surmise—
　Silent, upon a peak in Darien.

HOW MANY BARDS GILD THE LAPSES OF TIME

How many bards gild the lapses of time!
　A few of them have ever been the food
　Of my delighted fancy,—I could brood
Over their beauties, earthly, or sublime:
And often, when I sit me down to rhyme,
　These will in throngs before my mind intrude:
　But no confusion, no disturbance rude
Do they occasion; 'tis a pleasing chime.
So the unnumbered sounds that evening store;
　The songs of birds—the whisp'ring of the leaves,
　The voice of waters—the great bell that heaves
With solemn sound,—and thousand others more,
　That distance of recognizance bereaves,
Make pleasing music, and not wild uproar.

KEEN, FITFUL GUSTS ARE WHISP'RING HERE AND THERE

Keen, fitful gusts are whisp'ring here and there
　Among the bushes, half leafless and dry;
　The stars look very cold about the sky,
And I have many miles on foot to fare;
Yet feel I little of the cold bleak air,
　Or of the dead leaves rustling drearily,

2 Charles Cowden Clarke says that this sonnet was sent to him by Keats so as to reach him at 10 o'clock one morning when they two had parted at "day-spring" after a night encounter with a copy of Chapman's [translation of] Homer. In line 11 Keats of course made a mistake, since it was Balboa who discovered the Pacific, but is was doubtless a portrait of Cortez that he had in mind.

Or of those silver lamps that burn on high,
Or of the distance from home's pleasant lair:
For I am brimful of the friendliness
    That in a little cottage I have found;
Of fair-haired Milton's eloquent distress,
    And all his love for gentle Lycid [3] drowned;
Of lovely Laura [4] in her light green dress,
    And faithful Petrarch gloriously crowned.

TO ONE WHO HAS BEEN LONG IN CITY PENT

To one who has been long in city pent,
    'Tis very sweet to look into the fair
    And open face of heaven,—to breathe a prayer
Full in the smile of the blue firmament.
Who is more happy, when, with heart's content,
    Fatigued he sinks into some pleasant lair
    Of wavy grass, and reads a debonair
And gentle tale of love and languishment?
Returning home at evening, with an ear
    Catching the notes of Philomel,—an eye
Watching the sailing cloudlet's bright career,
    He mourns that day so soon has glided by:
E'en like the passage of an angel's tear
    That falls through the clear ether silently.

ADDRESSED TO HAYDON [5]

Great spirits now on earth are sojourning;
    He of the cloud, the cataract, the lake,
    Who on Helvellyn's summit, wide awake,
Catches his freshness from Archangel's wing:
He of the rose, the violet, the spring,
    The social smile, the chain for Freedom's sake:
    And lo!—whose steadfastness would never take
A meaner sound than Raphael's whispering.
And other spirits there are standing apart
    Upon the forehead of the age to come;
These, these will give the world another heart,
    And other pulses. Hear ye not the hum
Of mighty workings?—
    Listen awhile ye nations, and be dumb.

3 Lycidas
4 the lady celebrated in Petrarch's sonnets

5 Benjamin Robert Haydon, historical painter, born 1786, died by his own hand 1846. The "great spirits" are Wordsworth, Hunt, and Haydon.

ON THE SEA

It keeps eternal whisperings around
    Desolate shores, and with its mighty swell
    Gluts twice ten thousand caverns, till the spell
Of Hecate [6] leaves them their old shadowy sound.
Often 'tis in such gentle temper found,
    That scarcely will the very smallest shell
    Be moved for days from where it sometime fell,
When last the winds of heaven were unbound.
Oh ye! who have your eye-balls vexed and tired,
    Feast them upon the wideness of the Sea;
        Oh ye! whose ears are dinned with uproar rude,
    Or fed too much with cloying melody,—
        Sit ye near some old cavern's mouth, and brood
Until ye start, as if the sea-nymphs quired!

WHEN I HAVE FEARS

When I have fears that I may cease to be
    Before my pen has gleaned my teeming brain,
Before high-pilèd books, in charact'ry,[7]
    Hold like rich garners the full-ripened grain;
When I behold, upon the night's starred face,
    Huge cloudy symbols of a high romance,
And think that I may never live to trace
    Their shadows, with the magic hand of chance;
And when I feel, fair creature of an hour,
    That I shall never look upon thee more,
Never have relish in the faery power
    Of unreflecting love;—then on the shore
Of the wide world I stand alone, and think
Till Love and Fame to nothingness do sink.

TO HOMER

Standing aloof in giant ignorance,[8]
    Of thee I hear and of the Cyclades,[9]
As one who sits ashore and longs perchance
    To visit dolphin-coral in deep seas.
So thou wast blind;—but then the veil was rent,
    For Jove uncurtained Heaven to let thee live,
And Neptune made for thee a spermy tent,

6 Goddess of magic and witchery
7 writing
8 doubtless his inability to read Homer in the original Greek (which Keats always regretted)
9 islands in the Ægean

And Pan made sing for thee his forest-hive;
Aye, on the shores of darkness there is light,
And precipices show untrodden green,
There is a budding morrow in midnight,
There is a triple sight in blindness keen;
Such seeing hadst thou, as it once befell
To Dian, Queen of Earth, and Heaven, and Hell

TWO SONNETS ON FAME

I

Fame, like a wayward girl, will still be coy
To those who woo her with too slavish knees,
But makes surrender to some thoughtless boy,
And dotes the more upon a heart at ease;
She is a Gypsy will not speak to those
Who have not learned to be content without her;
A Jilt, whose ear was never whispered close,
Who thinks they scandal her who talk about her;
A very Gypsy is she, Nilus-born,[10]
Sister-in-law to jealous Potiphar;
Ye love-sick Bards! repay her scorn for scorn;
Ye Artists lovelorn! madmen that ye are!
Make your best bow to her and bid adieu,
Then, if she likes it, she will follow you.

II

"You cannot eat your cake and have it too."—*Proverb*

How fevered is the man, who cannot look
Upon his mortal days with temperate blood,
Who vexes all the leaves of his life's book,
And robs his fair name of its maidenhood;
It is as if the rose should pluck herself,
Or the ripe plum finger its misty bloom,
As if a Naiad, like a meddling elf,
Should darken her pure grot with muddy gloom;
But the rose leaves herself upon the briar,
For winds to kiss and grateful bees to feed,
And the ripe plum still wears its dim attire;
The undisturbèd lake has crystal space;
Why then should man, teasing the world for grace,
Spoil his salvation for a fierce miscreed?

10 The gypsies were formerly supposed to have come from Egypt.

TO SLEEP

O soft embalmer of the still midnight!
  Shutting, with careful fingers and benign,
Our gloom-pleased eyes, embowered from the light,
  Enshaded in forgetfulness divine;
O soothest Sleep! if so it please thee, close,
  In midst of this thine hymn, my willing eyes,
Or wait the amen, ere thy poppy throws
  Around my bed its lulling charities;
Then save me, or the passèd day will shine
Upon my pillow, breeding many woes;
  Save me from curious conscience, that still lords
Its strength for darkness, burrowing like a mole;
  Turn the key deftly in the oilèd wards,
And seal the hushèd casket of my soul.

BRIGHT STAR!

Bright star! [11] would I were steadfast as thou art—
  Not in lone splendor hung aloft the night,
And watching, with eternal lids apart,
  Like Nature's patient, sleepless Eremite,[12]
The moving waters at their priestlike task
  Of pure ablution round earth's human shores,
Or gazing on the new soft fallen mask
  Of snow upon the mountains and the moors—
No—yet still steadfast, still unchangeable,
  Pillowed upon my fair love's ripening breast,
To feel for ever its soft fall and swell,
  Awake for ever in a sweet unrest,
Still, still to hear her tender-taken breath,
And so live ever—or else swoon to death.

ENDYMION

A POETIC ROMANCE

"The stretched meter of an antique song"
Inscribed to the memory of
Thomas Chatterton

The story of Endymion, the beautiful youth beloved by the moon-goddess,
had long been a favorite with Keats. The Elizabethans whom Keats delighted

11 Formerly believed to be Keats's last poem. Written, after he had embarked for Italy in 1820, on a blank page facing *A Lover's Complaint* in a volume of Shakespeare's poems he had given his friend Severn. 12 hermit

to read made frequent mention of the myth, and in particular he could find it treated at some length in John Lyly's play of the same name, in John Fletcher's *Faithful Shepherdess*, in Michael Drayton's poem, the *Man in the Moon*, and in George Sandys's translation of Ovid. Of the three latter works he probably made some use. Keats's poem is indeed, as he described it in his motto from Shakespeare's sonnets, "the stretched meter of an antique song." The plot of the narrative is thin and difficult to follow, so submerged is it in the thoughts and emotions of the characters and in the poet's profuse imagery. In Book I (here reprinted), after a preliminary account of a festival in honor of Pan (which includes the celebrated hymn to that god), Endymion describes to his sister Peona an encounter with a dazzling god-like creature (really Diana or Cynthia), and his emotions incident thereto. In the later books there are further visions and trance-like meetings, with elaborated digressions and episodes, and in the end the hero vanishes with the goddess. The poem is profoundly interesting as the fullest embodiment of Keats's earlier manner—his rich poetic powers and his weaknesses as well. Evident in it also is an allegory of the soul's search for ideal beauty.

Keats prefixed to the poem the following Preface: "Knowing within myself the manner in which this Poem has been produced, it is not without a feeling of regret that I make it public.

"What manner I mean, will be quite clear to the reader, who must soon perceive great inexperience, immaturity, and every error denoting a feverish attempt, rather than a deed accomplished. The two first books, and indeed the two last, I feel sensible are not of such completion as to warrant their passing the press; nor should they if I thought a year's castigation would do them any good;—it will not: the foundations are too sandy. It is just that this youngster should die away: a sad thought for me, if I had not some hope that while it is dwindling I may be plotting, and fitting myself for verses fit to live.

"This may be speaking too presumptuously, and may deserve a punishment: but no feeling man will be forward to inflict it: he will leave me alone, with the conviction that there is not a fiercer hell than the failure in a great object. This is not written with the least atom of purpose to forestall criticisms of course, but from the desire I have to conciliate men who are competent to look, and who do look with a zealous eye, to the honor of English literature.

"The imagination of a boy is healthy, and the mature imagination of a man is healthy; but there is a space of life between, in which the soul is in a ferment, the character undecided, the way of life uncertain, the ambition thick-sighted: thence proceeds mawkishness, and all the thousand bitters which those men I speak of must necessarily taste in going over the following pages.

"I hope I have not in too late a day touched the beautiful mythology of Greece, and dulled its brightness: for I wish to try once more, before I bid it farewell."

BOOK I

A THING of beauty is a joy for ever:
Its loveliness increases; it will never
Pass into nothingness; but still will keep
A bower quiet for us, and a sleep
Full of sweet dreams, and health, and quiet breathing.

Therefore, on every morrow, are we wreathing
A flowery band to bind us to the earth,
Spite of despondence, of the inhuman dearth
Of noble natures, of the gloomy days,
Of all the unhealthy and o'er-darkened ways 10
Made for our searching: yes, in spite of all
Some shape of beauty moves away the pall
From our dark spirits. Such the sun, the moon,
Trees old and young, sprouting a shady boon
For simple sheep; and such are daffodils
With the green world they live in; and clear rills
That for themselves a cooling covert make
'Gainst the hot season; the mid-forest brake,
Rich with a sprinkling of fair musk-rose blooms:
And such too is the grandeur of the dooms 20
We have imagined for the mighty dead;
All lovely tales that we have heard or read:
An endless fountain of immortal drink,
Pouring unto us from the heaven's brink.

Nor do we merely feel these essences
For one short hour; no, even as the trees
That whisper round a temple become soon
Dear as the temple's self, so does the moon,
The passion poesy, glories infinite,
Haunt us till they become a cheering light 30
Unto our souls, and bound to us so fast,
That, whether there be shine, or gloom o'ercast,
They alway must be with us, or we die.
Therefore, 'tis with full happiness that I
Will trace the story of Endymion.
The very music of the name has gone
Into my being, and each pleasant scene
Is growing fresh before me as the green
Of our own valleys: so I will begin
Now while I cannot hear the city's din; 40
Now while the early budders are just new,
And run in mazes of the youngest hue
About old forests; while the willow trails
Its delicate amber; and the dairy pails
Bring home increase of milk. And, as the year
Grows lush in juicy stalks, I'll smoothly steer
My little boat, for many quiet hours,
With streams that deepen freshly into bowers.
Many and many a verse I hope to write,
Before the daisies, vermeil rimmed and white, 50

Hide in deep herbage; and ere yet the bees
Hum about globes of clover and sweet peas,
I must be near the middle of my story.
O may no wintry season, bare and hoary,
See it half-finished: but let Autumn bold,
With universal tinge of sober gold,
Be all about me when I make an end.[13]
And now at once, adventuresome, I send
My herald thought into a wilderness:
There let its trumpet blow, and quickly dress   60
My uncertain path with green, that I may speed
Easily onward, thorough flowers and weed.

Upon the sides of Latmos was outspread
A mighty forest; for the moist earth fed
So plenteously all weed-hidden roots
Into o'erhanging boughs, and precious fruits.
And it had gloomy shades, sequestered deep,
Where no man went; and if from shepherd's keep
A lamb strayed far a-down those inmost glens,
Never again saw he the happy pens   70
Whither his brethren, bleating with content,
Over the hills at every night-fall went.
Among the shepherds 'twas believèd ever,
That not one fleecy lamb which thus did sever
From the white flock, but passed unworrièd
By any wolf, or pard [14] with prying head,
Until it came to some unfooted plains
Where fed the herds of Pan: ay, great his gains
Who thus one lamb did lose. Paths there were many,
Winding through palmy fern, and rushes fenny,   80
And ivy banks; all leading pleasantly
To a wide lawn, whence one could only see
Stems thronging all around between the swell
Of tuft and slanting branches: who could tell
The freshness of the space of heaven above,
Edged round with dark tree-tops? through which a dove
Would often beat its wings, and often too
A little cloud would move across the blue.

Full in the middle of this pleasantness
There stood a marble altar, with a tress   90
Of flowers budded newly; and the dew
Had taken fairy phantasies to strew

13 The wish was fulfilled.   May, 1817, and finished in   14 leopard
The poem was begun in   November.

Daisies upon the sacred sward last eve,
And so the dawnèd light in pomp receive.
For 'twas the morn: Apollo's upward fire
Made every eastern cloud a silvery pyre
Of brightness so unsullied, that therein
A melancholy spirit well might win
Oblivion, and melt out his essence fine
Into the winds: rain-scented eglantine   100
Gave temperate sweets to that well-wooing sun:
The lark was lost in him; cold springs had run
To warm their chilliest bubbles in the grass;
Man's voice was on the mountains; and the mass
Of nature's lives and wonders pulsed tenfold,
To feel this sun-rise and its glories old.

   Now while the silent workings of the dawn
Were busiest, into that self-same lawn
All suddenly, with joyful cries, there sped
A troop of little children garlanded;   110
Who gathering round the altar, seemed to pry
Earnestly round as wishing to espy
Some folk of holiday: nor had they waited
For many moments, ere their ears were sated
With a faint breath of music, which even then
Filled out its voice, and died away again.
Within a little space again it gave
Its airy swellings, with a gentle wave,
To light-hung leaves, in smoothest echoes breaking
Through copse-clad vallies,—ere their death, o'ertaking   120
The surgy murmurs of the lonely sea.

   And now, as deep into the wood as we
Might mark a lynx's eye, there glimmered light
Fair faces and a rush of garments white,
Plainer and plainer showing, till at last
Into the widest alley they all passed,
Making directly for the woodland altar.
O kindly muse! let not my weak tongue falter
In telling of this goodly company,
Of their old piety, and of their glee: 130
But let a portion of ethereal dew
Fall on my head, and presently unmew [15]
My soul; that I may dare, in wayfaring,
To stammer where old Chaucer used to sing.

[15] release

　　　Leading the way, young damsels danced along,
Bearing the burden of a shepherd song;
Each having a white wicker, overbrimmed
With April's tender younglings: next, well trimmed,
A crowd of shepherds with as sunburnt looks
As may be read of in Arcadian books;　　　　　　　140
Such as sat listening round Apollo's pipe,
When the great deity, for earth too ripe,
Let his divinity o'erflowing die
In music, through the vales of Thessaly: [16]
Some idly trailed their sheep-hooks on the ground,
And some kept up a shrilly mellow sound
With ebon-tippèd flutes: close after these,
Now coming from beneath the forest trees,
A venerable priest full soberly
Begirt, with ministering looks: alway his eye　　　　150
Steadfast upon the matted turf he kept,
And after him his sacred vestments swept.
From his right hand there swung a vase, milk-white,
Of mingled wine, out-sparkling generous light;
And in his left he held a basket full
Of all sweet herbs that searching eye could cull:
Wild thyme, and valley-lilies whiter still
Than Leda's love,[17] and cresses from the rill.
His aged head, crownèd with beechen wreath,
Seemed like a poll of ivy in the teeth　　　　　　160
Of winter hoar. Then came another crowd
Of shepherds, lifting in due time aloud
Their share of the ditty. After them appeared,
Up-followed by a multitude that reared
Their voices to the clouds, a fair-wrought car,
Easily rolling, so as scarce to mar
The freedom of three steeds of dapple brown:
Who stood therein did seem of great renown
Among the throng. His youth was fully blown,
Showing like Ganymede [18] to manhood grown;　　　170
And, for those simple times, his garments were
A chieftain king's: beneath his breast, half bare,
Was hung a silver bugle, and between
His nervy [19] knees there lay a boar-spear keen.
A smile was on his countenance; he seemed
To common lookers-on, like one who dreamed
Of idleness in groves Elysian:

16 The time when Apollo　for a year.　　　　　　　bearer of the gods
kept the cattle of King Ad-　　17 Jove in the likeness of　19 sinewy, strong
metus of Thessaly, on be-　a swan
ing banished from heaven　　18 the　beautiful　cup-

But there were some who feelingly could scan
A lurking trouble in his nether lip,
And see that oftentimes the reins would slip   180
Through his forgotten hands: then would they sigh
And think of yellow leaves, of owlets' cry,
Of logs piled solemnly.—Ah, well-a-day,
Why should our young Endymion pine away!

  Soon the assembly, in a circle ranged,
Stood silent round the shrine: each look was changed
To sudden veneration: women meek
Beckoned their sons to silence; while each cheek
Of virgin bloom paled gently for slight fear.
Endymion too, without a forest peer,   190
Stood, wan, and pale, and with an awèd face,
Among his brothers of the mountain chase.
In midst of all, the venerable priest
Eyed them with joy from greatest to the least,
And, after lifting up his aged hands,
Thus spake he: "Men of Latmos! shepherd bands
Whose care it is to guard a thousand flocks:
Whether descended from beneath the rocks
That overtop your mountains; whether come
From valleys where the pipe is never dumb;   200
Or from your swelling downs, where sweet air stirs
Blue hare-bells lightly, and where prickly furze
Buds lavish gold; or ye, whose precious charge
Nibble their fill at ocean's very marge,
Whose mellow reeds are touched with sounds forlorn
By the dim echoes of old Triton's [20] horn:
Mothers and wives! who day by day prepare
The scrip, with needments, for the mountain air;
And all ye gentle girls who foster up
Udderless lambs, and in a little cup   210
Will put choice honey for a favored youth:
Yea, every one attend; for in good truth
Our vows are wanting to our great god Pan.
Are not our lowing heifers sleeker than
Night-swollen mushrooms? Are not our wide plains
Speckled with countless fleeces? Have not rains
Greened over April's lap? No howling sad
Sickens our fearful ewes; and we have had
Great bounty from Endymion our lord.
The earth is glad: the merry lark has poured   220

20 sea-deity, who blew his conch-shell horn to raise or calm the waves

His early song against yon breezy sky,
That spreads so clear o'er our solemnity."

Thus ending, on the shrine he heaped a spire
Of teeming sweets, enkindling sacred fire;
Anon he stained the thick and spongy sod
With wine, in honor of the shepherd-god.
Now while the earth was drinking it, and while
Bay leaves were crackling in the fragrant pile,
And gummy frankincense was sparkling bright
'Neath smothering parsley, and a hazy light   230
Spread grayly eastward, thus a chorus sang:

"O thou, whose mighty palace roof doth hang
From jagged trunks, and overshadoweth
Eternal whispers, glooms, the birth, life, death
Of unseen flowers in heavy peacefulness;
Who lovest to see the hamadryads [21] dress
Their ruffled locks where meeting hazels darken;
And through whole solemn hours dost sit, and hearken
The dreary melody of bedded reeds—
In desolate places, where dank moisture breeds   240
The pipy hemlock to strange overgrowth,
Bethinking thee, how melancholy loth
Thou wast to lose fair Syrinx [22]—do thou now,
By thy love's milky brow!
By all the trembling mazes that she ran,
Hear us, Great Pan!

"O thou, for whose soul-soothing quiet, turtles [23]
Passion their voices cooingly 'mong myrtles,
What time thou wanderest at eventide
Through sunny meadows, that outskirt the side   250
Of thine enmossèd realms: O thou, to whom
Broad-leavèd fig-trees even now foredoom
Their ripened fruitage; yellow-girted bees
Their golden honeycombs; our village leas
Their fairest-blossomed beans and poppied corn:
The chuckling linnet its five young unborn,
To sing for thee; low-creeping strawberries
Their summer coolness; pent-up butterflies
Their freckled wings; yea, the fresh-budding year
All its completions—be quickly near,   260
By every wind that nods the mountain pine,
O forester divine!

21 wood-nymphs   Pan, changed into a tuft of   made his pipes
22 Nymph pursued by   reeds out of which Pan   23 turtle-doves

"Thou, to whom every faun and satyr flies
For willing service; whether to surprise
The squatted hare while in half-sleeping fit;
Or upward ragged precipices flit
To save poor lambkins from the eagle's maw;
Or by mysterious enticement draw
Bewildered shepherds to their path again;
Or to tread breathless round the frothy main,   270
And gather up all fancifullest shells
For thee to tumble into Naiads' cells,
And, being hidden, laugh at their out-peeping;
Or to delight thee with fantastic leaping,
The while they pelt each other on the crown
With silvery oak-apples, and fir-cones brown—
By all the echoes that about thee ring,
Hear us, O satyr king!

"O Hearkener to the loud-clapping shears,
While ever and anon to his shorn peers   280
A ram goes bleating: Winder of the horn,
When snouted wild-boars routing tender corn
Anger our huntsman: Breather round our farms,
To keep off mildews, and all weather harms:
Strange ministrant of undescribèd sounds,
That come a-swooning over hollow grounds,
And wither drearily on barren moors:
Dread opener of the mysterious doors
Leading to universal knowledge—see,
Great son of Dryope,   290
The many that are come to pay their vows
With leaves about their brows!

"Be still the unimaginable lodge
For solitary thinkings; such as dodge
Conception to the very bourne of heaven,
Then leave the naked brain: be still the leaven
That spreading in this dull and clodded earth,
Gives it a touch ethereal—a new birth:
Be still a symbol of immensity;
A firmament reflected in a sea;   300
An element filling the space between;
An unknown—but no more: we humbly screen
With uplift hands our foreheads, lowly bending,
And giving out a shout most heaven-rending,
Conjure thee to receive our humble pæan,
Upon thy Mount Lycean!" [24]

[24] Mount Lycæus, in Arcadia, birthplace of Pan

Even while they brought the burden to a close
A shout from the whole multitude arose,
That lingered in the air like dying rolls
Of abrupt thunder, when Ionian shoals   310
Of dolphins bob their noses through the brine.
Meantime, on shady levels, mossy fine,
Young companies nimbly began dancing
To the swift treble pipe, and humming string.
Aye, those fair living forms swam heavenly
To tunes forgotten—out of memory:
Fair creatures! whose young children's children bred
Thermopylæ [25] its heroes—not yet dead,
But in old marbles ever beautiful.
High genitors, unconscious did they cull   320
Time's sweet first-fruits—they danced to weariness,
And then in quiet circles did they press
The hillock turf, and caught the latter end
Of some strange history, potent to send
A young mind from its bodily tenement.
Or they might watch the quoit-pitchers, intent
On either side; pitying the sad death
Of Hyacinthus,[26] when the cruel breath
Of Zephyr slew him,—Zephyr penitent,
Who now, ere Phœbus mounts the firmament,   330
Fondles the flower amid the sobbing rain.
The archers too, upon a wider plain,
Beside the feathery whizzing of the shaft,
And the dull twanging bowstring, and the raft [27]
Branch down sweeping from a tall ash top,
Called up a thousand thoughts to envelop
Those who would watch. Perhaps, the trembling knee
And frantic gape of lonely Niobe,[28]
Poor, lonely Niobe! when her lovely young
Were dead and gone, and her caressing tongue   340
Lay a lost thing upon her paly lip,
And very, very deadliness did nip
Her motherly cheeks. Aroused from this sad mood
By one, who at a distance loud hallooed,
Uplifting his strong bow into the air,
Many might after brighter visions stare:
After the Argonauts,[29] in blind amaze

25 where the Spartans under Leonidas held the pass against the Persian hosts, 480 B. C.
26 Spartan youth beloved by Apollo, who accidentally killed him while playing quoits, and then transformed him into the flower. In the version used by Keats it was jealous Zephyrus who blew the quoit into Hyacinthus' face.
27 cut off (a Spenserian word)
28 Her children were killed by Apollo and Diana, the children of Leto, because she boasted of her numerous offspring in comparison with Leto's two.
29 who went with Jason in the quest of the golden fleece

Tossing about on Neptune's restless ways,
Until, from the horizon's vaulted side,
There shot a golden splendor far and wide,   350
Spangling those million poutings of the brine
With quivering ore: 'twas even an awful shine
From the exaltation of Apollo's bow;
A heavenly beacon in their dreary woe.
Who thus were ripe for high contemplating,
Might turn their steps towards the sober ring
Where sat Endymion and the aged priest
'Mong shepherds gone in eld, whose looks increased
The silvery setting of their mortal star.
There they discoursed upon the fragile bar   360
That keeps us from our homes ethereal;
And what our duties there: to nightly call
Vesper, the beauty-crest of summer weather;
To summon all the downiest clouds together
For the sun's purple couch; to emulate
In ministering the potent rule of fate
With speed of fire-tailed exhalations;
To tint her pallid cheek with bloom, who cons
Sweet poesy by moonlight: besides these,
A world of other unguessed offices.   370
Anon they wandered by divine converse,
Into Elysium; vying to rehearse
Each one his own anticipated bliss.
One felt heart-certain that he could not miss
His quick-gone love, among fair blossomed boughs,
Where every zephyr-sigh pouts, and endows
Her lips with music for the welcoming.
Another wished, 'mid that eternal spring,
To meet his rosy child, with feathery sails,
Sweeping, eye-earnestly, through almond vales: 380
Who, suddenly, should stoop through the smooth wind,
And with the balmiest leaves his temples bind;
And, ever after, through those regions be
His messenger, his little Mercury.
Some were athirst in soul to see again
Their fellow-huntsmen o'er the wide champaign
In times long past; to sit with them, and talk
Of all the chances in their earthly walk;
Comparing, joyfully, their plenteous stores
Of happiness, to when upon the moors,   390
Benighted, close they huddled from the cold,
And shared their famished scrips. Thus all out-told
Their fond imaginations,—saving him

Whose eyelids curtained up their jewels dim,
Endymion: yet hourly had he striven
To hide the cankering venom, that had riven
His fainting recollections. Now indeed
His senses had swooned off: he did not heed
The sudden silence, or the whispers low,
Or the old eyes dissolving at his woe,   400
Or anxious calls, or close of trembling palms,
Or maidens sigh, that grief itself embalms;
But in the self-same fixèd trance he kept,
Like one who on the earth had never stept,
Ay, even as dead-still as a marble man,
Frozen in that old tale Arabian.

Who whispers him so pantingly and close?
Peona, his sweet sister: of all those,
His friends, the dearest. Hushing signs she made,
And breathed a sister's sorrow to persuade   410
A yielding up, a cradling on her care.
Her eloquence did breathe away the curse.
She led him, like some midnight spirit nurse
Of happy changes in emphatic dreams,
Along a path between two little streams,
Guarding his forehead, with her round elbow,
From low-grown branches, and his footsteps slow
From stumbling over stumps and hillocks small;
Until they came to where these streamlets fall,
With mingled bubblings and a gentle rush,   420
Into a river, clear, brimful, and flush
With crystal mocking of the trees and sky.
A little shallop, floating there hard by,
Pointed its beak over the fringèd bank;
And soon it lightly dipt, and rose, and sank,
And dipt again, with the young couple's weight,—
Peona guiding, through the water straight,
Towards a bowery island opposite;
Which gaining presently, she steerèd light
Into a shady, fresh, and ripply cove,   430
Where nested was an arbor, overwove
By many a summer's silent fingering;
To whose cool bosom she was used to bring
Her playmates, with their needle broidery,
And minstrel memories of times gone by.

So she was gently glad to see him laid
Under her favorite bower's quiet shade,

On her own couch, new made of flower leaves,
Dried carefully on the cooler side of sheaves
When last the sun his autumn tresses shook,   440
And the tanned harvesters rich armfuls took.
Soon was he quieted to slumbrous rest:
But, ere it crept upon him, he had prest
Peona's busy hand against his lips,
And still, a-sleeping, held her finger-tips
In tender pressure. And as a willow keeps
A patient watch over the stream that creeps
Windingly by it, so the quiet maid
Held her in peace: so that a whispering blade
Of grass, a wailful gnat, a bee bustling   450
Down in the blue-bells, or a wren light rustling
Among sere leaves and twigs, might all be heard.

  O magic sleep! O comfortable bird,
That broodest o'er the troubled sea of the mind
Till it is hushed and smooth! O unconfined
Restraint! imprisoned liberty! great key
To golden palaces, strange minstrelsy,
Fountains grotesque, new trees, bespangled caves,
Echoing grottoes, full of tumbling waves
And moonlight; aye, to all the mazy world   460
Of silvery enchantment!—who, upfurled
Beneath thy drowsy wing a triple hour,
But renovates and lives?—Thus, in the bower,
Endymion was calmed to life again.
Opening his eyelids with a healthier brain,
He said: "I feel this thine endearing love
All through my bosom: thou art as a dove
Trembling its closèd eyes and sleekèd wings
About me; and the pearliest dew not brings
Such morning incense from the fields of May,   470
As do those brighter drops that twinkling stray
From those kind eyes,—the very home and haunt
Of sisterly affection. Can I want
Aught else, aught nearer heaven, than such tears?
Yet dry them up, in bidding hence all fears
That, any longer, I will pass my days
Alone and sad. No, I will once more raise
My voice upon the mountain-heights; once more
Make my horn parley from their foreheads hoar:
Again my trooping hounds their tongues shall loll   480
Around the breathèd boar: again I'll poll
The fair-grown yew-tree, for a chosen bow:

And, when the pleasant sun is getting low,
Again I'll linger in a sloping mead
To hear the speckled thrushes, and see feed
Our idle sheep. So be thou cheerèd, sweet!
And, if thy lute is here, softly entreat
My soul to keep in its resolvèd course."

Hereat Peona, in their silver source
Shut her pure sorrow-drops with glad exclaim,   490
And took a lute, from which there pulsing came
A lively prelude, fashioning the way
In which her voice should wander. 'Twas a lay
More subtle-cadencèd, more forest wild
Than Dryope's [30] lone lulling of her child;
And nothing since has floated in the air
So mournful strange. Surely some influence rare
Went, spiritual, through the damsel's hand;
For still, with Delphic emphasis, she spanned
The quick invisible strings, even though she saw   500
Endymion's spirit melt away and thaw
Before the deep intoxication.
But soon she came, with sudden burst, upon
Her self-possession—swung the lute aside,
And earnestly said: "Brother, 'tis vain to hide
That thou dost know of things mysterious,
Immortal, starry; such alone could thus
Weigh down thy nature. Hast thou sinned in aught
Offensive to the heavenly powers? Caught
A Paphian dove [31] upon a message sent?   510
Thy deathful bow against some deer-herd bent,
Sacred to Dian? Haply, thou hast seen
Her naked limbs among the alders green;
And that, alas! is death. No, I can trace
Something more high perplexing in thy face!"

Endymion looked at her, and pressed her hand,
And said, "Art thou so pale, who was so bland
And merry in our meadows? How is this?
Tell me thine ailment: tell me all amiss!
Ah! thou hast been unhappy at the change   520
Wrought suddenly in me. What indeed more strange?
Or more complete to overwhelm surmise?
Ambition is no sluggard: 'tis no prize,
That toiling years would put within my grasp,

30 turned into a lotus   of the plant to amuse her   31 sacred to Venus
when she broke off a twig   little son, Apollo's child

That I have sighed for: with so deadly gasp
No man e'er panted for a mortal love.
So all have set my heavier grief above
These things which happen. Rightly have they done:
I, who still saw the horizontal sun
Heave his broad shoulder o'er the edge of the world,   530
Out-facing Lucifer,[32] and then had hurled
My spear aloft, as signal for the chase—
I, who, for very sport of heart, would race
With my own steed from Araby; pluck down
A vulture from his towery perching; frown
A lion into growling, loth retire—
To lose, at once, all my toil-breeding fire,
And sink thus low! but I will ease my breast
Of secret grief, here in this bowery nest.

"This river does not see the naked sky,   540
Till it begins to progress silverly
Around the western border of the wood,
Whence, from a certain spot, its winding flood
Seems at the distance like a crescent moon:
And in that nook, the very pride of June,
Had I been used to pass my weary eves;
The rather for the sun unwilling leaves
So dear a picture of his sovereign power,
And I could witness his most kingly hour,
When he doth tighten up the golden reins,   550
And paces leisurely down amber plains
His snorting four. Now when his chariot last
Its beams against the zodiac-lion cast,
There blossomed suddenly a magic bed
Of sacred ditamy,[33] and poppies red:
At which I wondered greatly, knowing well
That but one night had wrought this flowery spell;
And, sitting down close by, began to muse
What it might mean. Perhaps, thought I, Morpheus,[34]
In passing here, his owlet pinions shook;   560
Or, it may be, ere matron Night uptook
Her ebon urn, young Mercury, by stealth,
Had dipped his rod in it: such garland wealth
Came not by common growth. Thus on I thought,
Until my head was dizzy and distraught.
Moreover, through the dancing poppies stole
A breeze most softly lulling to my soul;

32 the morning star (the   33 a variety of mint   34 the god of Sleep
planet Venus)

And shaping visions all about my sight
Of colors, wings, and bursts of spangly light:
The which became more strange, and strange, and dim,   570
And then were gulfed in a tumultuous swim:
And then I fell asleep. Ah, can I tell
The enchantment that afterwards befell?
Yet it was but a dream: yet such a dream
That never tongue, although it overteem
With mellow utterance, like a cavern spring,
Could figure out and to conception bring
All I beheld and felt. Methought I lay
Watching the zenith, where the milky way
Among the stars in virgin splendor pours;   580
And traveling my eye, until the doors
Of heaven appeared to open for my flight,
I became loth and fearful to alight
From such high soaring by a downward glance;
So kept me steadfast in that airy trance,
Spreading imaginary pinions wide.
When, presently, the stars began to glide,
And faint away, before my eager view:
At which I sighed that I could not pursue,
And dropped my vision to the horizon's verge;   590
And lo! from opening clouds, I saw emerge
The loveliest moon, that ever silvered o'er
A shell for Neptune's goblet; she did soar
So passionately bright, my dazzled soul
Commingling with her argent spheres did roll
Through clear and cloudy, even when she went
At last into a dark and vapory tent—
Whereat, methought, the lidless-eyèd train
Of planets all were in the blue again.
To commune with those orbs, once more I raised   600
My sight right upward: but it was quite dazed
By a bright something, sailing down apace,
Making me quickly veil my eyes and face:
Again I looked, and, O ye deities,
Who from Olympus watch our destinies!
Whence that completed form of all completeness?
Whence came that high perfection of all sweetness?
Speak, stubborn earth, and tell me where, O where
Hast thou a symbol of her golden hair?
Not oat-sheaves drooping in the western sun;   610
Not—thy soft hand, fair sister! let me shun
Such follying before thee—yet she had,
Indeed, locks bright enough to make me mad;

And they were simply gordianed [35] up and braided,
Leaving, in naked comeliness, unshaded,
Her pearl round ears, white neck, and orbèd brow;
The which were blended in, I know not how,
With such a paradise of lips and eyes,
Blush-tinted cheeks, half smiles, and faintest sighs,
That, when I think thereon, my spirit clings   620
And plays about its fancy, till the stings
Of human neighborhood envenom all.
Unto what awful power shall I call?
To what high fane?—Ah! see her hovering feet,
More bluely veined, more soft, more whitely sweet
Than those of sea-born Venus, when she rose
From out her cradle shell. The wind outblows
Her scarf into a fluttering pavilion;
'Tis blue, and over-spangled with a million
Of little eyes, as though thou wert to shed,   630
Over the darkest, lushest blue-bell bed,
Handfuls of daisies."—"Endymion, how strange!
Dream within dream!"—"She took an airy range,
And then, towards me, like a very maid,
Came blushing, waning, willing and afraid,
And pressed me by the hand: Ah! 'twas too much;
Methought I fainted at the charmèd touch,
Yet held my recollection, even as one
Who dives three fathoms where the waters run
Gurgling in beds of coral: for anon,   640
I felt upmounted in that region
Where falling stars dart their artillery forth,
And eagles struggle with the buffeting north
That balances the heavy meteor-stone;—
Felt too, I was not fearful, nor alone,
But lapped and lulled along the dangerous sky.
Soon, as it seemed, we left our journeying high,
And straightway into frightful eddies swooped;
Such as ay muster where gray Time has scooped
Huge dens and caverns in a mountain's side: 650
There hollow sounds aroused me, and I sighed
To faint once more by looking on my bliss—
I was distracted; madly did I kiss
The wooing arms which held me, and did give
My eyes at once to death: but 'twas to live,
To take in draughts of life from the gold fount
Of kind and passionate looks; to count, and count
The moments, by some greedy help that seemed

35 tied (like the Gordian knot)

A second self, that each might be redeemed
And plundered of its load of blessedness. 660
Ah, desperate mortal! I even dared to press
Her very cheek against my crownèd lip,
And, at that moment, felt my body dip
Into a warmer air: a moment more,
Our feet were soft in flowers. There was store
Of newest joys upon that alp.[36] Sometimes
A scent of violets, and blossoming limes,
Loitered around us; then of honey cells,
Made delicate from all white-flower bells,—
And once, above the edges of our nest, 670
An arch face peeped,—an Oread [37] as I guessed.

"Why did I dream that sleep o'erpower'd me
In midst of all this heaven? Why not see,
Far off, the shadows of his pinions dark,
And stare them from me? But no, like a spark
That needs must die, although its little beam
Reflects upon a diamond, my sweet dream
Fell into nothing—into stupid sleep.
And so it was, until a gentle creep,
A careful moving caught my waking ears, 680
And up I started: Ah! my sighs, my tears,
My clenchèd hands;—for lo! the poppies hung
Dew-dabbled on their stalks, the ouzel sung
A heavy ditty, and the sullen day
Had chidden herald Hesperus away,
With leaden looks: the solitary breeze
Blustered, and slept, and its wild self did tease
With wayward melancholy; and I thought,
Mark me, Peona! that sometimes it brought
Faint fare-thee-wells, and sigh-shrillèd adieus!— 690
Away I wandered!—all the pleasant hues
Of heaven and earth had faded: deepest shades
Were deepest dungeons; heaths and sunny glades
Were full of pestilent light; our taintless rills
Seemed sooty, and o'erspread with upturned gills
Of dying fish; the vermeil rose had blown
In frightful scarlet, and its thorns outgrown
Like spikèd aloe. If an innocent bird
Before my heedless footsteps stirred, and stirred
In little journeys, I beheld in it 700
A disguised demon, missionèd to knit
My soul with under darkness; to entice

36 hillside　　　　　　37 a mountain nymph

My stumblings down some monstrous precipice:
Therefore I eager followed, and did curse
The disappointment. Time, that aged nurse,
Rocked me to patience. Now, thank gentle heaven,
These things, with all their comfortings, are given
To my down-sunken hours, and with thee,
Sweet sister, help to stem the ebbing sea
Of weary life."

           Thus ended he, and both   710
Sat silent: for the maid was very loth
To answer; feeling well that breathèd words
Would all be lost, unheard, and vain as swords
Against the enchasèd crocodile, or leaps
Of grasshoppers against the sun. She weeps
And wonders; struggles to devise some blame;
To put on such a look as would say, *Shame
On this poor weakness!* but, for all her strife,
She could as soon have crushed away the life
From a sick dove. At length, to break the pause,   720
She said with trembling chance: "Is this the cause?
This all? Yet it is strange, and sad, alas!
That one who through this middle earth should pass
Most like a sojourning demi-god, and leave
His name upon the harp-string, should achieve
No higher bard than simple maidenhood,
Singing alone, and fearfully,—how the blood
Left his young cheek; and how he used to stray
He knew not where: and how he would say, *nay,*
If any said 'twas love; and yet 'twas love;   730
What could it be but love! How a ring-dove
Let fall a sprig of yew-tree in his path;
And how he died: and then, that love doth scathe
The gentle heart, as northern blasts do roses;
And then the ballad of his sad life closes
With sighs, and an alas!—Endymion!
Be rather in the trumpet's mouth,—anon
Among the winds at large—that all may hearken!
Although, before the crystal heavens darken,
I watch and dote upon the silver lakes   740
Pictured in western cloudiness, that takes
The semblance of gold rocks and bright gold sands,
Islands, and creeks, and amber-fretted strands
With horses prancing o'er them, palaces
And towers of amethyst,—would I so tease
My pleasant days, because I could not mount
Into those regions?—The Morphean fount

Of that fine element that visions, dreams,
And fitful whims of sleep are made of, streams
Into its airy channels with so subtle,   750
So thin a breathing, not the spider's shuttle,
Circled a million times within the space
Of a swallow's nest-door, could delay a trace,
A tinting of its quality: how light
Must dreams themselves be; seeing they're more slight
Than the mere nothing that engenders them!
Then wherefore sully the entrusted gem
Of high and noble life with thoughts so sick?
Why pierce high-fronted honor to the quick
For nothing but a dream?" Hereat the youth   760
Looked up: a conflicting of shame and ruth
Was in his plaited brow: yet his eyelids
Widened a little, as when Zephyr bids
A little breeze to creep between the fans
Of careless butterflies: amid his pains
He seemed to taste a drop of manna-dew,
Full palatable; and a color grew
Upon his cheek, while thus he lifeful spake.

"Peona! ever have I longed to slake
My thirst for the world's praises: nothing base,   770
No merely slumberous phantasm, could unlace
The stubborn canvas for my voyage prepared—
Though now 'tis tattered; leaving my bark bared
And sullenly drifting: yet my higher hope
Is of too wide, too rainbow-large a scope,
To fret at myriads of earthly wrecks.
Wherein lies happiness? In that which becks
Our ready minds to fellowship divine,
A fellowship with essence; till we shine,
Full alchemized, and free of space. Behold   780
The clear religion of heaven! Fold
A rose-leaf round thy finger's taperness,
And soothe thy lips: hist! when the airy stress
Of music's kiss impregnates the free winds,
And with a sympathetic touch unbinds
Æolian magic [38] from their lucid wombs:
Then old songs waken from enclouded tombs;
Old ditties sigh above their father's grave;
Ghosts of melodious prophesyings rave
Round every spot where trod Apollo's foot;   790
Bronze clarions awake, and faintly bruit,

[38] music (like that produced by Æolus, god of winds)

Where long ago a giant battle was;
And, from the turf, a lullaby doth pass
In every place where infant Orpheus slept.
Feel we these things!—that moment have we stept
Into a sort of oneness, and our state
Is like a floating spirit's. But there are
Richer entanglements, enthralments far
More self-destroying, leading, by degrees,
To the chief intensity: the crown of these   800
Is made of love and friendship, and sits high
Upon the forehead of humanity.
All its more ponderous and bulky worth
Is friendship, whence there ever issues forth
A steady splendor; but at the tip-top,
There hangs by unseen film, an orbèd drop
Of light, and that is love: its influence
Thrown in our eyes genders a novel sense,
At which we start and fret; till in the end,
Melting into its radiance, we blend,   810
Mingle, and so become a part of it,—
Nor with aught else can our souls interknit
So wingedly: when we combine therewith,
Life's self is nourished by its proper pith,
And we are nurtured like a pelican brood.
Aye, so delicious is the unsating food,
That men, who might have towered in the van
Of all the congregated world, to fan
And winnow from the coming step of time
All chaff of custom, wipe away all slime   820
Left by men-slugs and human serpentry,
Have been content to let occasion die,
Whilst they did sleep in love's Elysium.
And, truly, I would rather be struck dumb
Than speak against this ardent listlessness:
For I have ever thought that it might bless
The world with benefits unknowingly;
As does the nightingale, up-perchèd high,
And cloistered among cool and bunchèd leaves—
She sings but to her love, nor e'er conceives   830
How tiptoe Night holds back her dark-gray hood.
Just so may love, although 'tis understood
The mere commingling of passionate breath,
Produce more than our searching witnesseth:
What I know not: but who, of men, can tell
That flowers would bloom, or that green fruit would swell
To melting pulp, that fish would have bright mail,

The earth its dower of river, wood, and vale,
The meadows runnels, runnels pebble-stones,
The seed its harvest, or the lute its tones,   840
Tones ravishment, or ravishment its sweet,
If human souls did never kiss and greet?

"Now, if this earthly love has power to make
Men's being mortal, immortal; to shake
Ambition from their memories, and brim
Their measure of content; what merest whim,
Seems all this poor endeavor after fame,
To one, who keeps within his steadfast aim
A love immortal, an immortal too.
Look not so wildered; for these things are true,   850
And never can be born of atomies
That buzz about our slumbers, like brain-flies,
Leaving us fancy-sick. No, no, I'm sure,
My restless spirit never could endure
To brood so long upon one luxury,
Unless it did, though fearfully, espy
A hope beyond the shadow of a dream.
My sayings will the less obscurèd seem
When I have told thee how my waking sight
Has made me scruple whether that same night   860
Was passed in dreaming. Hearken, sweet Peona!
Beyond the matron-temple of Latona,[39]
Which we should see but for these darkening boughs,
Lies a deep hollow, from whose ragged brows
Bushes and trees do lean all round athwart,
And meet so nearly, that with wings outraught,
And spreaded tail, a vulture could not glide
Past them, but he must brush on every side.
Some moldered steps lead into this cool cell,
Far as the slabbèd margin of a well,   870
Whose patient level peeps its crystal eye
Right upward, through the bushes, to the sky.
Oft have I brought thee flowers, on their stalks set
Like vestal primroses, but dark velvet
Edges them round, and they have golden pits:
'Twas there I got them, from the gaps and slits
In a mossy stone, that sometimes was my seat,
When all above was faint with mid-day heat.
And there in strife no burning thoughts to heed,
I'd bubble up the water through a reed;   880
So reaching back to boyhood: make me ships

39 mother of Apollo and Diana (called by the Romans Leto)

Of moulted feathers, touchwood, alder chips,
With leaves stuck in them; and the Neptune be
Of their petty ocean. Oftener, heavily,
When lovelorn hours had left me less a child,
I sat contemplating the figures wild
Of o'erhead clouds melting the mirror through.
Upon a day, while thus I watched, by flew
A cloudy Cupid, with his bow and quiver;
So plainly charactered, no breeze would shiver   890
The happy chance: so happy, I was fain
To follow it upon the open plain,
And, therefore, was just going; when, behold!
A wonder, fair as any I have told—
The same bright face I tasted in my sleep,
Smiling in the clear well. My heart did leap
Through the cool depth.—It moved as if to flee—
I started up, when lo! refreshfully,
There came upon my face, in plenteous showers,
Dew-drops, and dewy buds, and leaves, and flowers,   900
Wrapping all objects from my smothered sight,
Bathing my spirit in a new delight.
Aye, such a breathless honey-feel of bliss
Alone preserved me from the drear abyss
Of death, for the fair form had gone again.
Pleasure is oft a visitant; but pain
Clings cruelly to us, like the gnawing sloth
On the deer's tender haunches: late, and loth,
'Tis scared away by slow-returning pleasure.
How sickening, how dark the dreadful leisure   910
Of weary days, made deeper exquisite,
By a foreknowledge of unslumberous night!
Like sorrow came upon me, heavier still,
Than when I wandered from the poppy hill:
And a whole age of lingering moments crept
Sluggishly by, ere more contentment swept
Away at once the deadly yellow spleen.
Yes, thrice have I this fair enchantment seen;
Once more been tortured with renewèd life.
When last the wintry gusts gave over strife   920
With the conquering sun of spring, and left the skies
Warm and serene, but yet with moistened eyes
In pity of the shattered infant buds,—
That time thou didst adorn, with amber studs,
My hunting-cap, because I laughed and smiled,
Chatted with thee, and many days exiled
All torment from my breast;—'twas even then,

Straying about, yet, cooped up in the den
Of helpless discontent,—hurling my lance
From place to place, and following at chance,   930
At last, by hap, through some young trees it struck,
And, plashing among bedded pebbles, stuck
In the middle of a brook,—whose silver ramble
Down twenty little falls through reeds and bramble,
Tracing along, it brought me to a cave,
Whence it ran brightly forth, and white did lave
The nether sides of mossy stones and rock,—
'Mong which it gurgled blithe adieus, to mock
Its own sweet grief at parting. Overhead
Hung a lush screen of drooping weeds, and spread   940
Thick, as to curtain up some wood-nymph's home.
'Ah! impious mortal, whither do I roam?'
Said I, low-voiced: 'Ah, whither! 'Tis the grot
Of Proserpine, when Hell, obscure and hot,
Doth her resign: and where her tender hands
She dabbles on the cool and sluicy sands;
Or 'tis the cell of Echo, where she sits,
And babbles thorough silence, till her wits
Are gone in tender madness, and anon,
Faints into sleep, with many a dying tone   950
Of sadness. O that she would take my vows,
And breathe them sighingly among the boughs,
To sue her gentle ears for whose fair head,
Daily, I pluck sweet flowerets from their bed,
And weave them dyingly—send honey-whispers
Round every leaf, that all those gentle lispers
May sigh my love unto her pitying!
O charitable Echo! hear, and sing
This ditty to her!—tell her'—So I stayed
My foolish tongue, and listening, half afraid,   960
Stood stupefied with my own empty folly,
And blushing for the freaks of melancholy.
Salt tears were coming, when I heard my name
Most fondly lipped, and then these accents came:
'Endymion! the cave is secreter
Than the isle of Delos.⁴⁰ Echo hence shall stir
No sighs but sigh-warm kisses, or light noise
Of thy combing hand, the while it traveling cloys
And trembles through my labyrinthine hair.'
At that oppressed, I hurried in.—Ah! where   970
Are those swift moments? Whither are they fled?
I'll smile no more, Peona; nor will wed

40 Isle where Latona gave birth to Apollo and Diana

Sorrow, the way to death; but patiently
Bear up against it: so farewell, sad sigh;
And come instead demurest meditation,
To occupy me wholly, and to fashion
My pilgrimage for the world's dusky brink.
No more will I count over, link by link,
My chain of grief: no longer strive to find
A half-forgetfulness in mountain wind   980
Blustering about my ears: aye, thou shalt see,
Dearest of sisters, what my life shall be;
What a calm round of hours shall make my days.
There is a paly flame of hope that plays
Where'er I look: but yet, I'll say 'tis nought—
And here I bid it die. Have not I caught,
Already, a more healthy countenance?
By this the sun is setting; we may chance
Meet some of our near-dwellers with my car."

This said, he rose, faint-smiling like a star   990
Through autumn mists, and took Peona's hand:
They stepped into the boat, and launched from land.

FRAGMENT OF AN ODE TO MAIA,[41] WRITTEN ON MAY DAY, 1818

MOTHER of Hermes! and still youthful Maia!
    May I sing to thee
As thou wast hymnèd on the shores of Baiæ? [42]
    Or may I woo thee
In earlier Sicilian? or thy smiles
Seek as they once were sought, in Grecian isles,
By bards who died content on pleasant sward,
Leaving great verse unto a little clan?
O, give me their old vigor, and unheard
Save of the quiet primrose, and the span
    Of heaven and few ears,
Rounded by thee, my song should die away
    Content as theirs,
Rich in the simple worship of a day.

SONG: IN A DREAR-NIGHTED DECEMBER

IN a drear-nighted December,
    Too happy, happy tree,

41 Goddess of the spring   Naples—where the cult of   earlier in Greece and in
42 A Roman resort near   Maia flourished as it had   Sicily

Thy branches ne'er remember
Their green felicity:
The north cannot undo them,
With a sleety whistle through them;
Nor frozen thawings glue them
From budding at the prime.

In a drear-nighted December,
Too happy, happy brook,   10
Thy bubblings ne'er remember
Apollo's summer look;
But with a sweet forgetting,
They stay their crystal fretting,
Never, never petting
About the frozen time.

Ah! would 'twere so with many
A gentle girl and boy!
But were there ever any
Writhed not at passèd joy?   20
To know the change and feel it,
When there is none to heal it
Nor numbèd sense to steel it,
Was never said in rhyme.

FANCY

EVER let the Fancy roam,
Pleasure never is at home:
At a touch sweet Pleasure melteth,
Like to bubbles when rain pelteth;
Then let wingèd Fancy wander
Through the thought still spread beyond her:
Open wide the mind's cage-door,
She'll dart forth, and cloudward soar,
O sweet Fancy! let her loose;
Summer's joys are spoilt by use,   10
And the enjoying of the Spring
Fades as does its blossoming:
Autumn's red-lipped fruitage too,
Blushing through the mist and dew,
Cloys with tasting: What do then?
Sit thee by the ingle, when
The sear faggot blazes bright,
Spirit of a winter's night;

When the soundless earth is muffled,
And the cakèd snow is shuffled   20
From the plowboy's heavy shoon;
When the Night doth meet the Noon
In a dark conspiracy
To banish Even from her sky.
Sit thee there, and send abroad,
With a mind self-overawed,
Fancy, high-commissioned:—send her!
She has vassals to attend her:
She will bring, in spite of frost,
Beauties that the earth hath lost;   30
She will bring thee, all together,
All delights of summer weather;
All the buds and bells of May,
From dewy sward or thorny spray;
All the heapèd Autumn's wealth,
With a still, mysterious stealth:
She will mix these pleasures up
Like three fit wines in a cup,
And thou shalt quaff it:—thou shalt hear
Distant harvest-carols clear;   40
Rustle of the reapèd corn;
Sweet birds antheming the morn:
And, in the same moment—hark!
'Tis the early April lark,
Or the rooks, with busy caw,
Foraging for sticks and straw.
Thou shalt, at one glance, behold
The daisy and the marigold;
White-plumed lilies, and the first
Hedge-grown primrose that hath burst;   50
Shaded hyacinth, alway
Sapphire queen of the mid-May;
And every leaf, and every flower
Pearlèd with the self-same shower.
Thou shalt see the field-mouse peep
Meager from its cellèd sleep;
And the snake all winter-thin
Cast on sunny bank its skin!
Freckled nest eggs thou shalt see
Hatching in the hawthorn-tree,   60
When the hen-bird's wing doth rest
Quiet on her mossy nest;
Then the hurry and alarm

When the bee-hive casts its swarm;
Acorns ripe down-pattering,
While the autumn breeezs sing.

Oh, sweet Fancy! let her loose;
Everything is spoilt by use:
Where's the cheek that doth not fade,
Too much gazed at? Where's the maid   70
Whose lip mature is ever new?
Where's the eye, however blue,
Doth not weary? Where's the face
One would meet in every place?
Where's the voice, however soft,
One would hear so very oft?
At a touch sweet Pleasure melteth
Like to bubbles when rain pelteth.
Let, then, wingèd Fancy find
Thee a mistress to thy mind: 80
Dulcet-eyed as Ceres' daughter,[43]
Ere the God of Torment taught her
How to frown and how to chide;
With a waist and with a side
White as Hebe's,[44] when her zone
Slipped its golden clasp, and down
Fell her kirtle to her feet,
While she held the goblet sweet,
And Jove grew languid.—Break the mesh
Of the Fancy's silken leash;   90
Quickly break her prison-string,
And such joys as these she'll bring.—
Let the wingèd Fancy roam,
Pleasure never is at home.

ODE [45]

BARDS of Passion and of Mirth,
Ye have left your souls on earth!
Have ye souls in heaven too,
Double-lived in regions new?
Yes, and those of heaven commune
With the spheres of sun and moon;
With the noise of fountains wondrous,

---

43 Proserpine, wedded to
Pluto
44 the cup-bearer of Jove

45 Addressed to Beau-
mont and Fletcher, and
written in a copy of their
plays, on the blank leaf

facing *The Fair Maid of
the Inn.*

And the parle [46] of voices thund'rous;
With the whisper of heaven's trees
And one another, in soft ease   10
Seated on Elysian lawns
Browsed by none but Dian's fawns;
Underneath large blue-bells tented,
Where the daisies are rose-scented,
And the rose herself has got
Perfume which on earth is not;
Where the nightingale doth sing
Not a senseless, trancèd thing,
But divine, melodious truth;
Philosophic numbers smooth;   20
Tales and golden histories
Of heaven and its mysteries.

Thus ye live on high, and then
On the earth ye live again;
And the souls ye left behind you
Teach us, here, the way to find you,
Where your other souls are joying
Never slumbered, never cloying.
Here, your earth-born souls still speak
To mortals, of their little week;   30
Of their sorrows and delights;
Of their passions and their spites;
Of their glory and their shame;
What doth strengthen and what maim.
Thus ye teach us, every day,
Wisdom, though fled far away.

Bards of Passion and of Mirth,
Ye have left your souls on earth!
Ye have souls in heaven too,
Double-lived in regions new!   40

LINES ON THE MERMAID TAVERN [47]

Souls of poets dead and gone,
What Elysium have ye known,
Happy field or mossy cavern,
Choicer than the Mermaid Tavern?
Have ye tippled drink more fine

46 talk
47 A favorite resort of
writers in Elizabethan and
Jacobean times. Keats was
probably indebted to Francis Beaumont's metrical
Letter to Ben Jonson,
which celebrates the tavern.

Than mine host's Canary wine?
Or are fruits of Paradise
Sweeter than those dainty pies
Of venison? O generous food!
Dressed as though bold Robin Hood   10
Would, with his maid Marian,
Sup and bowse [48] from horn and can.

    I have heard that on a day
Mine host's sign-board flew away,
Nobody knew whither, till
An astrologer's old quill
To a sheepskin gave the story,—
Said he saw you in your glory,
Underneath a new old-sign
Sipping beverage divine,   20
And pledging with contented smack
The Mermaid in the Zodiac.

    Souls of poets dead and gone,
What Elysium have ye known,
Happy field or mossy cavern,
Choicer than the Mermaid Tavern?

ROBIN HOOD

TO A FRIEND [49]

No! THOSE days are gone away,
And their hours are old and gray,
And their minutes buried all
Under the down-trodden pall
Of the leaves of many years:
Many times have Winter's shears,
Frozen North, and chilling East,
Sounded tempests to the feast
Of the forest's whispering fleeces,[50]
Since men knew nor rent nor leases.   10

    No, the bugle sounds no more,
And the twanging bow no more;
Silent is the ivory [51] shrill
Past the heath and up the hill;

48 drink
49 John Hamilton Rey-
nolds (1796–1852), to whom

Keats also addressed a poetical *Epistle*
50 leaves

51 whistle

There is no mid-forest laugh,
Where lone Echo gives the half
To some wight, amazed to hear
Jesting, deep in forest drear.

On the fairest time of June
You may go, with sun or moon,
Or the seven stars [52] to light you,
Or the polar ray [53] to right you,
But you never may behold
Little John, or Robin bold:
Never one, of all the clan,
Thrumming on an empty can
Some old hunting ditty, while
He doth his green way beguile
To fair hostess Merriment,
Down beside the pasture Trent; [54]
For he left the merry tale,
Messenger for spicy ale.

Gone, the merry morris [55] din;
Gone, the song of Gamelyn; [56]
Gone, the tough-belted outlaw
Idling in the "grenè shawe"; [57]
All are gone away and past!
And if Robin should be cast
Sudden from his turfèd grave,
And if Marian should have
Once again her forest days,
She would weep, and he would craze;
He would swear, for all his oaks,
Fall'n beneath the dock-yard strokes,
Have rotted on the briny seas;
She would weep that her wild bees
Sang not to her—strange! that honey
Can't be got without hard money!

So it is; yet let us sing
Honor to the old bow-string!
Honor to the bugle-horn!
Honor to the woods unshorn!
Honor to the Lincoln green! [58]
Honor to the archer keen!

20

30

40

50

52 Constellation of Charles's Wain, or the Great Dipper
53 North star
54 River Trent, which flows by Sherwood Forest
55 English folk dance
56 Tale of outlawry formerly attributed to Chaucer
57 wood
58 cloth which foresters wore

Honor to tight little John,
And the horse he rode upon!
Honor to bold Robin Hood,
Sleeping in the underwood!
Honor to Maid Marian,
And to all the Sherwood clan!   60
Though their days have hurried by
Let us two a burden try.

HYPERION

It was to this projected poem that Keats alluded at the end of his Preface
to *Endymion*. To the superseding of the Titans, or elder Greek gods, by the
younger Olympians Keats met many references in his reading, but his sources
are very much less definite than in *Endymion*, and the conception is to a great
extent his own. Keats's friend Woodhouse writes of his plan, "The poem if
completed would have treated of the dethronement of Hyperion, the former
god of the Sun, by Apollo—and incidentally of those of Oceanus by Neptune,
of Saturn by Jupiter, etc., and of the war of the Giants for Saturn's re-
establishment—with other events, of which we have but very dark hints in
the mythological poets of Greece and Rome. In fact, the incidents would have
been pure creations of the poet's brain." At the opening of the poem, Saturn
and Oceanus have been already deposed; only Hyperion yet reigns, but although he still rides in splendor, his doom likewise is presaged. As in the case
of *Endymion*, an allegory is present in the replacement of the primal deities of
nature by the younger gods, of greater beauty and humanity. Keats wrote only
two books and a part of the third, abandoning the poem, as he says, because
there were "too many Miltonic inversions in it." He had sought, in answer to
those who had criticized *Endymion*, to write a poem of simple grandeur, with
Milton rather than Spenser as his model, but felt that he was copying only
Milton's manner. An attempted recasting of *Hyperion* as a vision is generally
considered a much less successful piece of work.

BOOK I

DEEP in the shady sadness of a vale
Far sunken from the healthy breath of morn,
Far from the fiery noon, and eve's one star,
Sat gray-haired Saturn, quiet as a stone,
Still as the silence round about his lair;
Forest on forest hung about his head
Like cloud on cloud. No stir of air was there,
Not so much life as on a summer's day
Robs not one light seed from the feathered grass,
But where the dead leaf fell, there did it rest.   10
A stream went voiceless by, still deadened more
By reason of his fallen divinity

Spreading a shade: the Naiad 'mid her reeds
Pressed her cold finger closer to her lips.

Along the margin-sand large foot-marks went,
No further than to where his feet had strayed,
And slept there since. Upon the sodden ground
His old right hand lay nerveless, listless, dead,
Unsceptered; and his realmless eyes were closed;
While his bowed head seemed list'ning to the Earth, 20
His ancient mother, for some comfort yet.

It seemed no force could wake him from his place;
But there came one,[59] who with a kindred hand
Touched his wide shoulders, after bending low
With reverence, though to one who knew it not.
She was a Goddess of the infant world;
By her in stature the tall Amazon
Had stood a pigmy's height: she would have ta'en
Achilles by the hair and bent his neck;
Or with a finger stayed Ixion's wheel.[60] 30
Her face was large as that of Memphian sphinx,
Pedestaled haply in a palace-court,
When sages looked to Egypt for their lore.
But oh! how unlike marble was that face:
How beautiful, if sorrow had not made
Sorrow more beautiful than Beauty's self.
There was a listening fear in her regard,
As if calamity had but begun;
As if the vanward clouds of evil days
Had spent their malice, and the sullen rear 40
Was with its storèd thunder laboring up.
One hand she pressed upon that aching spot
Where beats the human heart, as if just there,
Though an immortal, she felt cruel pain:
The other upon Saturn's bended neck
She laid, and to the level of his ear
Leaning with parted lips, some words she spake
In solemn tenor and deep organ tone:
Some mourning words, which in our feeble tongue
Would come in these like accents; O how frail 50
To that large utterance of the early Gods!
"Saturn, look up!—though wherefore, poor old King?
I have no comfort for thee, no not one:
I cannot say, 'O wherefore sleepest thou?'

59 Thea, Titan moon-goddess   60 For an offense to Zeus, Ixion was bound to a con-tinually revolving wheel in Hades.

For heaven is parted from thee, and the earth
Knows thee not, thus afflicted, for a God;
And ocean too, with all its solemn noise,
Has from thy scepter passed; and all the air
Is emptied of thine hoary majesty.
Thy thunder, conscious of the new command,   60
Rumbles reluctant o'er our fallen house;
And thy sharp lightning in unpractised hands
Scorches and burns our once serene domain.
O aching time! O moments big as years!
All as ye pass swell out the monstrous truth,
And press it so upon our weary griefs
That unbelief has not a space to breathe.
Saturn, sleep on:—O thoughtless, why did I
Thus violate thy slumbrous solitude?
Why should I ope thy melancholy eyes?   70
Saturn, sleep on! while at thy feet I weep."

    As when, upon a trancèd summer-night,
Those green-robed senators of mighty woods,
Tall oaks, branch-charmèd by the earnest stars,
Dream, and so dream all night without a stir,
Save from one gradual solitary gust
Which comes upon the silence, and dies off,
As if the ebbing air had but one wave;
So came these words and went; the while in tears
She touch'd her fair large forehead to the ground,   80
Just where her falling hair might be outspread
A soft and silken mat for Saturn's feet.
One moon, with alteration slow, had shed
Her silver seasons four upon the night,
And still these two were postured motionless,
Like natural sculpture in cathedral cavern;
The frozen God still couchant on the earth,
And the sad Goddess weeping at his feet:
Until at length old Saturn lifted up
His faded eyes, and saw his kingdom gone,   90
And all the gloom and sorrow of the place,
And that fair kneeling Goddess; and then spake
As with a palsied tongue, and while his beard
Shook horrid with such aspen-malady:
"O tender spouse of gold Hyperion,
Thea, I feel thee ere I see thy face;
Look up, and let me see our doom in it;
Look up, and tell me if this feeble shape
Is Saturn's; tell me, if thou hear'st the voice

Of Saturn; tell me, if this wrinkling brow,   100
Naked and bare of its great diadem,
Peers like the front of Saturn? Who had power
To make me desolate? whence came the strength?
How was it nurtured to such bursting forth,
While Fate seemed strangled in my nervous [61] grasp?
But it is so; and I am smothered up,
And buried from all godlike exercise
Of influence benign on planets pale,
Of admonitions to the winds and seas,
Of peaceful sway above man's harvesting,   110
And all those acts which Deity supreme
Doth ease its heart of love in.—I am gone
Away from my own bosom: I have left
My strong identity, my real self,
Somewhere between the throne, and where I sit
Here on this spot of earth. Search, Thea, search!
Open thine eyes eterne, and sphere them round
Upon all space: space starred, and lorn of light,
Space regioned with life-air, and barren void,
Spaces of fire, and all the yawn of hell.   120
Search, Thea, search! and tell me if thou seest
A certain shape or shadow, making way
With wings or chariot fierce to repossess
A heaven he lost erewhile: it must—it must
Be of ripe progress—Saturn must be king!
Yes, there must be a golden victory;
There must be Gods thrown down, and trumpets blown
Of triumph calm, and hymns of festival
Upon the gold clouds metropolitan,
Voices of soft proclaim, and silver stir   130
Of strings in hollow shells; and there shall be
Beautiful things made new, for the surprise
Of the sky-children; I will give command:
Thea! Thea! Thea! where is Saturn?"

     This passion lifted him upon his feet,
And made his hands to struggle in the air,
His Druid locks to shake and ooze with sweat,
His eyes to fever out, his voice to cease.
He stood, and heard not Thea's sobbing deep;
A little time, and then again he snatched   140
Utterance thus:—"But cannot I create?
Cannot I form? Cannot I fashion forth
Another world, another universe,

61 strong

To overbear and crumble this to nought?
Where is another chaos? Where?" That word
Found way unto Olympus, and made quake
The rebel three.[62] Thea was startled up,
And in her bearing was a sort of hope,
As thus she quick-voiced spake, yet full of awe.

"This cheers our fallen house: come to our friends,   150
O Saturn! come away, and give them heart;
I know the covert, for thence came I hither."
Thus brief; then with beseeching eyes she went
With backward footing through the shade a space:
He followed, and she turned to lead the way
Through agèd boughs, that yielded like the mist
Which eagles cleave, upmounting from their nest.

Meanwhile in other realms big tears were shed,
More sorrow like to this, and such like woe,
Too huge for mortal tongue or pen of scribe: 160
The Titans fierce, self-hid or prison-bound,
Groaned for the old allegiance once more,
And listened in sharp pain for Saturn's voice.
But one of the whole mammoth-brood still kept
His sovereignty, and rule, and majesty;—
Blazing Hyperion on his orbèd fire
Still sat, still snuffed the incense, teeming up
From man to the sun's God, yet unsecure:
For as among us mortals omens drear
Fright and perplex, so also shuddered he,   170
Not at dog's howl, or gloom-bird's hated screech,
Or the familiar visiting of one
Upon the first toll of his passing-bell,
Or prophesyings of the midnight lamp;
But horrors, portioned to a giant nerve,
Oft made Hyperion ache. His palace bright,
Bastioned with pyramids of glowing gold,
And touched with shade of bronzèd obelisks,
Glared a blood-red through all its thousand courts,
Arches, and domes, and fiery galleries;   180
And all its curtains of Aurorian clouds
Flushed angerly: while sometimes eagles'[63] wings,
Unseen before by Gods or wondering men,
Darkened the place; and neighing steeds were heard,
Not heard before by Gods or wondering men.
Also, when he would taste the spicy wreaths

62 Jupiter, Neptune, and Pluto   63 Jove's birds

Of incense, breathed aloft from sacred hills,
Instead of sweets, his ample palate took
Savor of poisonous brass and metal sick:
And so, when harbored in the sleepy west,   190
After the full completion of fair day,
For [64] rest divine upon exalted couch,
And slumber in the arms of melody,
He paced away the pleasant hours of ease
With stride colossal, on from hall to hall;
While far within each aisle and deep recess,
His wingèd minions in close clusters stood,
Amazed and full of fear; like anxious men
Who on wide plains gather in panting troops,
When earthquakes jar their battlements and towers. 200
Even now, while Saturn, roused from icy trance,
Went step for step with Thea through the woods,
Hyperion, leaving twilight in the rear,
Came slope upon the threshold of the west;
Then, as was wont, his palace-door flew ope
In smoothest silence, save what solemn tubes,
Blown by the serious Zephyrs, gave of sweet
And wandering sounds, slow-breathèd melodies;
And like a rose in vermeil [65] tint and shape,
In fragrance soft, and coolness to the eye,   210
That inlet to severe magnificence
Stood full blown, for the God to enter in.

He entered, but he entered full of wrath;
His flaming robes streamed out beyond his heels,
And gave a roar, as if of earthly fire,
That scared away the meek ethereal Hours
And made their dove-wings tremble. On he flared
From stately nave to nave, from vault to vault,
Through bowers of fragrant and enwreathèd light,
And diamond-pavèd lustrous long arcades,   220
Until he reached the great main cupola;
There standing fierce beneath, he stamped his foot,
And from the basements deep to the high towers
Jarred his own golden region; and before
The quavering thunder thereupon had ceased,
His voice leaped out, despite of godlike curb,
To this result: "O dreams of day and night!
O monstrous forms! O effigies of pain!
O specters busy in a cold, cold gloom!
O lank-eared Phantoms of black-weeded pools! 230

64 instead of   65 vermilion

Why do I know ye? why have I seen ye? why
Is my eternal essence thus distraught
To see and to behold these horrors new?
Saturn is fallen, am I too to fall?
Am I to leave this haven of my rest,
This cradle of my glory, this soft clime,
This calm luxuriance of blissful light,
These crystalline pavilions, and pure fanes,
Of all my lucent empire? It is left
Deserted, void, nor any haunt of mine.   240
The blaze, the splendor, and the symmetry,
I cannot see—but darkness, death and darkness.
Even here, into my center of repose,
The shady visions come to domineer,
Insult, and blind, and stifle up my pomp—
Fall!—No, by Tellus and her briny robes!
Over the fiery frontier of my realms
I will advance a terrible right arm
Shall scare that infant thunderer, rebel Jove,
And bid old Saturn take his throne again."   250
He spake, and ceased, the while a heavier threat
Held struggle with his throat, but came not forth;
For as in theaters of crowded men
Hubbub increases more they call out "Hush!"
So at Hyperion's words the Phantoms pale
Bestirred themselves, thrice horrible and cold;
And from the mirrored level where he stood
A mist arose, as from a scummy marsh.
At this, through all his bulk an agony
Crept gradual, from the feet unto the crown,   260
Like a lithe serpent vast and muscular
Making slow way, with head and neck convulsed
From over-strainèd might. Released, he fled
To the eastern gates, and full six dewy hours
Before the dawn in season due should blush,
He breathed fierce breath against the sleepy portals,
Cleared them of heavy vapors, burst them wide
Suddenly on the ocean's chilly streams.
The planet orb of fire, whereon he rode
Each day from east to west the heavens through,   270
Spun round in sable curtaining of clouds;
Nor therefore veilèd quite, blindfold and hid,
But ever and anon the glancing spheres,
Circles, and arcs, and broad-belting colure,[66]
Glowed through, and wrought upon the muffling dark

66 great circles of the celestial sphere intersecting at the poles

Sweet-shapèd lightnings from the nadir deep
Up to the zenith—hieroglyphics old,
Which sages and keen-eyed astrologers
Then living on the earth, with laboring thought
Won from the gaze of many centuries: 280
Now lost, save what we find on remnants huge
Of stone, or marble swart; their import gone,
Their wisdom long since fled. Two wings this orb
Possessed for glory, two fair argent wings,
Ever exalted at the God's approach:
And now, from forth the gloom their plumes immense
Rose, one by one, till all outspreaded were;
While still the dazzling globe maintained eclipse,
Awaiting for Hyperion's command.
Fain would he have commanded, fain took throne   290
And bid the day begin, if but for change.
He might not:—No, though a primeval God:
The sacred seasons might not be disturbed.
Therefore the operations of the dawn
Stayed in their birth, even as here 'tis told.
Those silver wings expanded sisterly,
Eager to sail their orb; the porches wide
Opened upon the dusk demesnes of night;
And the bright Titan, frenzied with new woes,
Unused to bend, by hard compulsion bent   300
His spirit to the sorrow of the time;
And all along a dismal rack of clouds,
Upon the boundaries of day and night,
He stretched himself in grief and radiance faint.
There as he lay, the Heaven with its stars
Looked down on him with pity, and the voice
Of Cœlus,[67] from the universal space,
Thus whispered low and solemn in his ear:
"O brightest of my children dear, earth-born
And sky-engendered, Son of Mysteries   310
All unrevealèd even to the powers
Which met at thy creating! at whose joys
And palpitations sweet, and pleasures soft,
I, Cœlus, wonder how they came and whence;
And at the fruits thereof what shapes they be,
Distinct, and visible; symbols divine,
Manifestations of that beauteous life
Diffused unseen throughout eternal space;
Of these new-formed art thou, oh brightest child!
Of these, thy brethren and the Goddesses!   320

67 god of the sky

There is sad feud among ye, and rebellion
Of son against his sire. I saw him fall,
I saw my firstborn [68] tumbled from his throne!
To me his arms were spread, to me his voice
Found way from forth the thunders round his head!
Pale wox [69] I, and in vapors hid my face.
Art thou, too, near such doom? vague fear there is:
For I have seen my sons most unlike Gods.
Divine ye were created, and divine
In sad demeanor, solemn, undisturbed,   330
Unruffled, like high Gods, ye lived and ruled:
Now I behold in you fear, hope, and wrath;
Actions of rage and passion; even as
I see them, on the mortal world beneath,
In men who die.—This is the grief, O Son!
Sad sign of ruin, sudden dismay, and fall!
Yet do thou strive; as thou art capable,
As thou canst move about, an evident God,
And canst oppose to each malignant hour
Ethereal presence:—I am but a voice;   340
My life is but the life of winds and tides,—
No more than winds and tides can I avail:—
But thou canst.—Be thou therefore in the van
Of circumstance; yea, seize the arrow's barb
Before the tense string murmur.—To the earth!
For there thou wilt find Saturn, and his woes.
Meantime I will keep watch on thy bright sun,
And of thy seasons be a careful nurse."—
Ere half this region-whisper had come down
Hyperion arose, and on the stars   350
Lifted his curvèd lids, and kept them wide
Until it ceased; and still he kept them wide:
And still they were the same bright, patient stars.
Then with a slow incline of his broad breast,
Like to a diver in the pearly seas,
Forward he stooped over the airy shore,
And plunged all noiseless into the deep night.

THE EVE OF ST. AGNES

St. Agnes' Eve [70]—ah, bitter chill it was!
The owl, for all his feathers, was a-cold;
The hare limped trembling through the frozen grass,
And silent was the flock in woolly fold;

68 Saturn
69 grew

70 January 20; in popu-   coldest day of the year
lar belief apt to be the

Numb were the Beadsman's fingers while he told
His rosary, and while his frosted breath,
Like pious incense from a censer old,
Seemed taking flight for heaven without a death,
Past the sweet Virgin's picture, while his prayer he saith.

His prayer he saith, this patient, holy man; 10
Then takes his lamp, and riseth from his knees,
And back returneth, meager, barefoot, wan,
Along the chapel aisle by slow degrees:
The sculptured dead, on each side, seem to freeze,
Emprisoned in black, purgatorial rails:
Knights, ladies, praying in dumb orat'ries,
He passeth by, and his weak spirit fails
To think how they may ache in icy hoods and mails.

Northward he turneth through a little door,
And scarce three steps, ere Music's golden tongue 20
Flattered to tears this agèd man and poor.
But no—already had his death-bell rung;
The joys of all his life were said and sung;
His was harsh penance on St. Agnes' Eve:
Another way he went, and soon among
Rough ashes sat he for his soul's reprieve,
And all night kept awake, for sinners' sake to grieve.

That ancient Beadsman heard the prelude soft;
And so it chanced, for many a door was wide,
From hurry to and fro. Soon, up aloft, 30
The silver, snarling trumpets 'gan to chide:
The level chambers, ready with their pride,
Were glowing to receive a thousand guests:
The carvèd angels, ever eager-eyed,
Stared, where upon their heads the cornice rests,
With hair blown back, and wings put cross-wise on their
     breasts.

At length burst in the argent revelry,
With plume, tiara, and all rich array,
Numerous as shadows haunting fairily
The brain, new-stuffed, in youth, with triumphs gay 40
Of old romance. These let us wish away,
And turn, sole-thoughted, to one Lady there,
Whose heart had brooded, all that wintry day,
On love, and winged St. Agnes' saintly care,
As she had heard old dames full many times declare.

They told her how, upon St. Agnes' Eve,
Young virgins might have visions of delight,
And soft adorings from their loves receive
Upon the honeyed middle of the night,
If ceremonies due they did aright;   50
As, supperless to bed they must retire,
And couch supine their beauties, lily white;
Nor look behind, nor sideways, but require
Of Heaven with upward eyes for all that they desire.

Full of this whim was thoughtful Madeline:
The music, yearning like a God in pain,
She scarcely heard: her maiden eyes divine,
Fixed on the floor, saw many a sweeping train
Pass by—she heeded not at all: in vain
Came many a tiptoe, amorous cavalier,   60
And back retired; not cooled by high disdain,
But she saw not: her heart was otherwhere;
She sighed for Agnes' dreams, the sweetest of the year.

She danced along with vague, regardless eyes,
Anxious her lips, her breathing quick and short:
The hallowed hour was near at hand: she sighs
Amid the timbrels, and the thronged resort
Of whisperers in anger or in sport;
'Mid looks of love, defiance, hate, and scorn,
Hoodwinked with faery fancy; all amort,[71]   70
Save to St. Agnes and her lambs unshorn,[72]
And all the bliss to be before to-morrow morn.

So, purposing each moment to retire,
She lingered still. Meantime, across the moors,
Had come young Porphyro, with heart on fire
For Madeline. Beside the portal doors,
Buttressed from moonlight, stands he, and implores
All saints to give him sight of Madeline,
But for one moment in the tedious hours,
That he might gaze and worship all unseen;   80
Perchance speak, kneel, touch, kiss—in sooth such things have
      been.

He ventures in: let no buzzed whisper tell;
All eyes be muffled, or a hundred swords

71 dead   Agnes, two lambs are   by nuns.
72 On the anniversary of   blessed, then shorn, and
the martyrdom of St.   the wool spun and woven

Will storm his heart, Love's fev'rous citadel:
For him, those chambers held barbarian hordes,
Hyena foemen, and hot-blooded lords,
Whose very dogs would execrations howl
Against his lineage; not one breast affords
Him any mercy in that mansion foul,
Save one old beldame, weak in body and in soul.   90

Ah, happy chance! the agèd creature came,
Shuffling along with ivory-headed wand,
To where he stood, hid from the torch's flame,
Behind a broad hall-pillar, far beyond
The sound of merriment and chorus bland.
He startled her; but soon she knew his face,
And grasped his fingers in her palsied hand,
Saying, "Mercy, Porphyro! hie thee from this place;
They are all here to-night, the whole bloodthirsty race!

"Get hence! get hence! there's dwarfish Hildebrand;   100
He had a fever late, and in the fit
He cursèd thee and thine, both house and land:
Then there's that old Lord Maurice, not a whit
More tame for his gray hairs—Alas me! flit!
Flit like a ghost away."—"Ah, Gossip [73] dear,
We're safe enough; here in this arm-chair sit,
And tell me how"—"Good saints! not here, not here;
Follow me, child, or else these stones will be thy bier."

He followed through a lowly archèd way,
Brushing the cobwebs with his lofty plume,   110
And as she muttered "Well-a—well-a-day!"
He found him in a little moonlight room,
Pale, latticed, chill, and silent as a tomb.
"Now tell me where is Madeline," said he,
"O tell me, Angela, by the holy loom
Which none but secret sisterhood may see,
When they St. Agnes' wool are weaving piously."

"St. Agnes! Ah! it is St. Agnes' Eve—
Yet men will murder upon holy days:
Thou must hold water in a witch's sieve,   120
And be liege-lord of all the Elves and Fays
To venture so: it fills me with amaze
To see thee, Porphyro!—St. Agnes' Eve!
God's help! my lady fair the conjurer plays

[73] godmother

This very night: good angels her deceive!
But let me laugh awhile,—I've mickle [74] time to grieve."

Feebly she laugheth in the languid moon,
While Porphyro upon her face doth look,
Like puzzled urchin on an agèd crone
Who keepeth closed a wondrous riddle-book,   130
As spectacled she sits in chimney nook.
But soon his eyes grew brilliant, when she told
His lady's purpose; and he scarce could brook
Tears, at the thought of those enchantments cold,
And Madeline asleep in lap of legends old.

Sudden a thought came like a full-blown rose,
Flushing his brow, and in his painèd heart
Made purple riot: then doth he propose
A stratagem, that makes the beldame start:
"A cruel man and impious thou art: 140
Sweet lady! let her pray, and sleep, and dream
Alone with her good angels, far apart
From wicked men like thee. Go, go! I deem
Thou canst not surely be the same that thou didst seem."

"I will not harm her, by all saints I swear,"
Quoth Porphyro: "O may I ne'er find grace
When my weak voice shall whisper its last prayer,
If one of her soft ringlets I displace,
Or look with ruffian passion in her face.
Good Angela, believe me, by these tears,   150
Or I will, even in a moment's space,
Awake, with horrid shout, my foemen's ears,
And beard them, though they be more fanged than wolves and
        bears."

"Ah! why wilt thou affright a feeble soul?
A poor, weak, palsy-stricken, churchyard thing,
Whose passing-bell may ere the midnight toll;
Whose prayers for thee, each morn and evening,
Were never missed." Thus plaining, doth she bring
A gentler speech from burning Porphyro;
So woeful, and of such deep sorrowing,   160
That Angela gives promise she will do
Whatever he shall wish, betide her weal or woe.

74 much

Which was, to lead him, in close secrecy,
Even to Madeline's chamber, and there hide
Him in a closet, of such privacy
That he might see her beauty unespied,
And win perhaps that night a peerless bride,
While legioned fairies paced the coverlet,
And pale enchantment held her sleepy-eyed.
Never on such a night have lovers met,   170
Since Merlin paid his Demon àll the monstrous debt.[75]

"It shall be as thou wishest," said the Dame:
"All cates [76] and dainties shall be storèd there
Quickly on this feast-night: by the tambour-frame [77]
Her own lute thou wilt see: no time to spare,
For I am slow and feeble, and scarce dare
On such a catering trust my dizzy head.
Wait here, my child, with patience; kneel in prayer
The while. Ah! thou must needs the lady wed,
Or may I never leave my grave among the dead."   180

So saying, she hobbled off with busy fear.
The lover's endless minutes slowly passed;
The dame returned, and whispered in his ear
To follow her; with agèd eyes aghast
From fright of dim espial. Safe at last,
Through many a dusky gallery, they gain
The maiden's chamber, silken, hushed, and chaste;
Where Porphyro took covert, pleased amain.
His poor guide hurried back with agues in her brain.

Her faltering hand upon the balustrade,   190
Old Angela was feeling for the stair,
When Madeline, St. Agnes' charmèd maid,
Rose, like a missioned spirit, unaware:
With silver taper's light, and pious care,
She turned, and down the agèd gossip led
To a safe level matting. Now prepare,
Young Porphyro, for gazing on that bed;
She comes, she comes again, like ring-dove frayed [78] and fled.

Out went the taper as she hurried in;
Its little smoke, in pallid moonshine, died: 200

75 Merlin, son of a de- him a spell which he had 77 drum-shaped embroid-
mon, was destroyed when himself taught her.   ery frame
Vivien employed against 76 delicacies   78 frightened

She closed the door, she panted, all akin
To spirits of the air, and visions wide:
No uttered syllable, or, woe betide!
But to her heart, her heart was voluble,
Paining with eloquence her balmy side;
As though a tongueless nightingale should swell
Her throat in vain, and die, heart-stifled, in her dell.

A casement high and triple-arched there was,
All garlanded with carven imag'ries,
Of fruits and flowers, and bunches of knot-grass,   210
And diamonded with panes of quaint device,
Innumerable of stains and splendid dyes,
As are the tiger-moth's deep-damasked wings;
And in the midst, 'mong thousand heraldries,
And twilight saints, and dim emblazonings,
A shielded scutcheon blushed with blood of queens and kings.

Full on this casement shone the wintry moon,
And threw warm gules [79] on Madeline's fair breast,
As down she knelt for Heaven's grace and boon;
Rose-bloom fell on her hands, together pressed,   220
And on her silver cross soft amethyst,
And on her hair a glory, like a saint:
She seemed a splendid angel, newly dressed,
Save wings, for heaven:—Porphyro grew faint:
She knelt, so pure a thing, so free from mortal taint.

Anon his heart revives: her vespers done,
Of all its wreathèd pearls her hair she frees;
Unclasps her warmèd jewels one by one;
Loosens her fragrant bodice; by degrees
Her rich attire creeps rustling to her knees: 230
Half-hidden, like a mermaid in sea-weed,
Pensive awhile she dreams awake, and sees,
In fancy, fair St. Agnes in her bed,
But dares not look behind, or all the charm is fled.

Soon, trembling in her soft and chilly nest,
In sort of wakeful swoon, perplexed she lay,
Until the poppied warmth of sleep oppressed
Her soothèd limbs, and soul fatigued away;
Flown, like a thought, until the morrow-day;
Blissfully havened both from joy and pain;   240
Clasped [80] like a missal [81] where swart Paynims [82] pray;

79 red (heraldic term)   81 prayer book   82 pagans
80 tightly shut

Blinded alike from sunshine and from rain,
As though a rose should shut, and be a bud again.

Stol'n to this paradise, and so entranced,
Porphyro gazed upon her empty dress,
And listened to her breathing, if it chanced
To wake into a slumberous tenderness;
Which when he heard, that minute did he bless,
And breathed himself: then from the closet crept,
Noiseless as fear in a wide wilderness,   250
And over the hushed carpet, silent, stepped,
And 'tween the curtains peeped, where, lo!—how fast she slept!

Then by the bedside, where the faded moon
Made a dim, silver twilight, soft he set
A table, and, half anguished, threw thereon
A cloth of woven crimson, gold, and jet:—
O for some drowsy Morphean amulet! [83]
The boisterous, midnight, festive clarion,
The kettle-drum, and far-heard clarinet,
Affray his ears, though but in dying tone:—   260
The hall-door shuts again, and all the noise is gone.

And still she slept an azure-lidded sleep,
In blanchèd linen, smooth, and lavendered,
While he from forth the closet brought a heap
Of candied apple, quince, and plum, and gourd;
With jellies soother [84] than the creamy curd,
And lucent syrops, tinct with cinnamon;
Manna and dates, in argosy transferred
From Fez; and spicèd dainties, every one,
From silken Samarcand [85] to cedared Lebanon.   270

These delicates he heaped with glowing hand
On golden dishes and in baskets bright
Of wreathèd silver: sumptuous they stand
In the retirèd quiet of the night,
Filling the chilly room with perfume light.—
"And now, my love, my seraph fair, awake!
Thou art my heaven, and I thine eremite: [86]
Open thine eyes, for meek St. Agnes' sake,
Or I shall drowse beside thee, so my soul doth ache."

83 charm from Morpheus   85 the capital of the con-   86 hermit; devoted serv-
(god of sleep)   queror Tamerlane, in Tur-   ant
84 smoother   kestan

Thus whispering, his warm, unnervèd arm   280
Sank in her pillow. Shaded was her dream
By the dusk curtains:—'twas a midnight charm
Impossible to melt as icèd stream:
The lustrous salvers in the moonlight gleam;
Broad golden fringe upon the carpet lies:
It seemed he never, never could redeem
From such a steadfast spell his lady's eyes;
So mused awhile, entoiled in woofèd phantasies.

Awakening up, he took her hollow lute,—
Tumultuous,—and, in chords that tenderest be,   290
He played an ancient ditty, long since mute,
In Provence called "La belle dame sans merci": [87]
Close to her ear touching the melody;—
Wherewith disturbed, she uttered a soft moan:
He ceased—she panted quick—and suddenly
Her blue affrayèd eyes wide open shone:
Upon his knees he sank, pale as smooth-sculptured stone.

Her eyes were open, but she still beheld,
Now wide awake, the vision of her sleep:
There was a painful change, that nigh expelled   300
The blisses of her dream so pure and deep,
At which fair Madeline began to weep,
And moan forth witless words with many a sigh,
While still her gaze on Porphyro would keep;
Who knelt, with joinèd hands and piteous eye,
Fearing to move or speak, she looked so dreamingly.

"Ah, Porphyro!" said she, "but even now
Thy voice was at sweet tremble in mine ear,
Made tunable with every sweetest vow;
And those sad eyes were spiritual and clear: 310
How changed thou art! how pallid, chill, and drear!
Give me that voice again, my Porphyro,
Those looks immortal, those complainings dear!
Oh leave me not in this eternal woe,
For if thou diest, my Love, I know not where to go."

Beyond a mortal man impassioned far
At these voluptuous accents, he arose,
Ethereal, flushed, and like a throbbing star
Seen 'mid the sapphire heaven's deep repose;
Into her dream he melted, as the rose   320

[87] See Keats's poem of this title below.

Blendeth its odor with the violet,—
Solution sweet: meantime the frost-wind blows
Like Love's alarum, pattering the sharp sleet
Against the window-panes; St. Agnes' moon hath set.

'Tis dark: quick pattereth the flaw-blown sleet:
"This is no dream, my bride, my Madeline!"
'Tis dark: the icèd gusts still rave and beat:
"No dream, alas! alas! and woe is mine!
Porphyro will leave me here to fade and pine.
Cruel! what traitor could thee hither bring?   330
I curse not, for my heart is lost in thine,
Though thou forsakest a deceivèd thing;—
A dove forlorn and lost with sick unprunèd wing."

"My Madeline! sweet dreamer! lovely bride!
Say, may I be for aye thy vassal blest?
Thy beauty's shield, heart-shaped and vermeil-dyed?
Ah, silver shrine, here will I take my rest
After so many hours of toil and quest,
A famished pilgrim,—saved by miracle.
Though I have found, I will not rob thy nest,   340
Saving of thy sweet self; if thou think'st well
To trust, fair Madeline, to no rude infidel.

"Hark! 'tis an elfin storm from faery land,
Of haggard seeming, but a boon indeed:
Arise—arise! the morning is at hand;—
The bloated wassailers will never heed:—
Let us away, my love, with happy speed;
There are no ears to hear, or eyes to see,—
Drowned all in Rhenish and the sleepy mead.
Awake! arise! my love, and fearless be,   350
For o'er the southern moors I have a home for thee."

She hurried at his words, beset with fears,
For there were sleeping dragons all around
At glaring watch, perhaps, with ready spears—
Down the wide stairs a darkling way they found;—
In all the house was heard no human sound.
A chain-drooped lamp was flickering by each door;
The arras, rich with horseman, hawk, and hound,
Fluttered in the besieging wind's uproar;
And the long carpets rose along the gusty floor.   360

They glide, like phantoms, into the wide hall;
Like phantoms to the iron porch they glide;
Where lay the Porter, in uneasy sprawl,
With a huge empty flagon by his side:
The wakeful bloodhound rose, and shook his hide,
But his sagacious eye an inmate owns:
By one, and one, the bolts full easy slide:—
The chains lie silent on the footworn stones;
The key turns, and the door upon its hinges groans.

And they are gone: ay, ages long ago　　　　　　370
These lovers fled away into the storm.
That night the Baron dreamt of many a woe,
And all his warrior-guests with shade and form
Of witch, and demon, and large coffin-worm,
Were long be-nightmared. Angela the old
Died palsy-twitched, with meager face deform;
The Beadsman, after thousand aves told,
For aye unsought-for slept among his ashes cold.

LA BELLE DAME SANS MERCI [88]

O WHAT can ail thee, knight-at-arms,
　　Alone and palely loitering?
The sedge has withered from the lake,
　　And no birds sing.

O what can ail thee, knight-at-arms,
　　So haggard and so woe-begone?
The squirrel's granary is full,
　　And the harvest's done.

I see a lily on thy brow
　　With anguish moist and fever dew,　　　　10
And on thy cheeks a fading rose
　　Fast withereth too.

I met a lady in the meads,
　　Full beautiful—a faery's child,
Her hair was long, her foot was light,
　　And her eyes were wild.

---

88 "The beautiful lady without mercy." Keats got the title (not the contents) from a poem by the French poet, Alain Chartier, who lived in the early 15th century. An English translation of this poem was formerly attributed to Chaucer. The first version of Keats's poem is here given (rather than the revision) as being in the opinion of many editors the finer of the two.

I made a garland for her head,
    And bracelets too, and fragrant zone;
She looked at me as she did love,
    And made sweet moan.   20

I set her on my pacing steed
    And nothing else saw all day long,
For sidelong would she bend, and sing
    A faery's song.

She found me roots of relish sweet,
    And honey wild, and manna dew,
And sure in language strange she said—
    "I love thee true!"

She took me to her elfin grot,
    And there she wept and sighed full sore,   30
And there I shut her wild, wild eyes
    With kisses four.

And there she lullèd me asleep,
    And there I dreamed—ah, woe betide!
The latest dream I ever dreamt
    On the cold hill side.

I saw pale kings, and princes too,
    Pale warriors, death-pale were they all;
They cried—"La Belle Dame sans Merci
    Thee hath in thrall!"   40

I saw their starved lips in the gloam,
    With horrid warning gapèd wide,
And I awoke and found me here,
    On the cold hill's side.

And this is why I sojourn here,
    Alone and palely loitering,
Though the sedge is withered from the lake,
    And no birds sing.

ODE TO A NIGHTINGALE

MY HEART aches, and a drowsy numbness pains
  My sense, as though of hemlock [89] I had drunk,
Or emptied some dull opiate to the drains
  One minute past, and Lethe-wards had sunk:
'Tis not through envy of thy happy lot,
  But being too happy in thine happiness,—
    That thou, light-wingèd Dryad of the trees,
      In some melodious plot
  Of beechen green, and shadows numberless,
    Singest of summer in full-throated ease.   10

O for a draught of vintage! that hath been
  Cooled a long age in the deep-delvèd earth,
Tasting of Flora [90] and the country-green,
  Dance, and Provençal song, and sunburnt mirth!
O for a beaker full of the warm South,
  Full of the true, the blushful Hippocrene,[91]
    With beaded bubbles winking at the brim,
      And purple-stainèd mouth;
  That I might drink, and leave the world unseen,
    And with thee fade away into the forest dim: 20

Fade far away, dissolve, and quite forget
  What thou among the leaves hast never known,
The weariness, the fever, and the fret
  Here, where men sit and hear each other groan;
Where palsy shakes a few, sad, last gray hairs,
  Where youth grows pale, and specter-thin, and dies;
    Where but to think is to be full of sorrow
      And leaden-eyed despairs;
  Where Beauty cannot keep her lustrous eyes,
    Or new Love pine at them beyond to-morrow.   30

Away! away! for I will fly to thee,
  Not charioted by Bacchus and his pards,[92]
But on the viewless wings of Poesy,
  Though the dull brain perplexes and retards;
Already with thee! tender is the night,
  And haply the Queen-Moon is on her throne,
    Clustered around by all her starry Fays;
      But here there is no light,
Save what from heaven is with the breezes blown
  Through verdurous glooms and winding mossy ways.   40

89 a poison   91 fountain of the Muses   92 leopards
90 goddess of flowers   on Mt. Helicon

I cannot see what flowers are at my feet,
  Nor what soft incense hangs upon the boughs,
But, in embalmèd darkness, guess each sweet
  Wherewith the seasonable month endows
The grass, the thicket, and the fruit-tree wild;
  White hawthorn, and the pastoral eglantine;
    Fast-fading violets covered up in leaves;
      And mid-May's eldest child,
The coming musk-rose, full of dewy wine,
  The murmurous haunt of flies on summer eves.   50

Darkling I listen; and, for many a time
  I have been half in love with easeful Death,
Called him soft names in many a musèd rhyme,
  To take into the air my quiet breath;
Now more than ever seems it rich to die,
  To cease upon the midnight with no pain,
    While thou art pouring forth thy soul abroad
      In such an ecstasy!
  Still wouldst thou sing, and I have ears in vain—
    To thy high requiem become a sod.   60

Thou wast not born for death, immortal Bird!
  No hungry generations tread thee down;
The voice I hear this passing night was heard
  In ancient days by emperor and clown:
Perhaps the self-same song that found a path
  Through the sad heart of Ruth, when, sick for home,
    She stood in tears amid the alien corn;
      The same that oft-times hath
  Charmed magic casements, opening on the foam
    Of perilous seas, in faery lands forlorn.   70

Forlorn! the very word is like a bell
  To toll me back from thee to my sole self.
Adieu! the fancy cannot cheat so well
  As she is famed to do, deceiving elf.
Adieu! adieu! thy plaintive anthem fades
  Past the near meadows, over the still stream,
    Up the hill-side; and now 'tis buried deep
      In the next valley-glades:
  Was it a vision, or a waking dream?
    Fled is that music:—do I wake or sleep?   80

ODE ON A GRECIAN URN

THOU still unravished bride of quietness,
   Thou foster-child of silence and slow time,
Sylvan historian, who canst thus express
   A flowery tale more sweetly than our rhyme:
What leaf-fringed legend haunts about thy shape
   Of deities or mortals, or of both,
      In Tempe or the dales of Arcady? [93]
   What men or gods are these? What maidens loath?
What mad pursuit? What struggle to escape?
      What pipes and timbrels? What wild ecstasy?   10

Heard melodies are sweet, but those unheard
   Are sweeter; therefore, ye soft pipes, play on;
Not to the sensual ear, but, more endeared,
   Pipe to the spirit ditties of no tone:
Fair youth, beneath the trees, thou canst not leave
   Thy song, nor ever can those trees be bare;
      Bold Lover, never, never canst thou kiss,
Though winning near the goal—yet, do not grieve;
      She cannot fade, though thou hast not thy bliss,
For ever wilt thou love, and she be fair!   20

Ah, happy, happy boughs! that cannot shed
   Your leaves, nor bid the Spring adieu;
And, happy melodist, unwearièd,
   For ever piping songs for ever new;
More happy love! more happy, happy love!
   For ever warm and still to be enjoyed,
      For ever panting and for ever young;
All breathing human passion far above,
      That leaves a heart high-sorrowful and cloyed,
   A burning forehead, and a parching tongue.   30

Who are these coming to the sacrifice?
   To what green altar, O mysterious priest,
Lead'st thou that heifer lowing at the skies,
   And all her silken flanks with garlands dressed?
What little town by river or sea-shore,
   Or mountain-built with peaceful citadel,
      Is emptied of this folk, this pious morn?
And, little town, thy streets for evermore
   Will silent be; and not a soul to tell
      Why thou art desolate, can e'er return.   40

[93] the beautiful vale in Thessaly and the region celebrated in pastoral poetry

O Attic shape! Fair attitude! with brede [94]
Of marble men and maidens overwrought,
With forest branches and the trodden weed;
Thou, silent form, dost tease us out of thought
As doth eternity: Cold Pastoral!
When old age shall this generation waste,
Thou shalt remain, in midst of other woe
Than ours, a friend to man, to whom thou say'st,
"Beauty is truth, truth beauty,"—that is all
Ye know on earth, and all ye need to know.   50

ODE TO PSYCHE

O GODDESS! hear these tuneless numbers, wrung
By sweet enforcement and remembrance dear,
And pardon that thy secrets should be sung
Even into thine own soft-conchèd ear:
Surely I dreamed to-day, or did I see
The wingèd Psyche with awakened eyes?
I wandered in a forest thoughtlessly,
And, on the sudden, fainting with surprise,
Saw two fair creatures, couchèd side by side
In deepest grass, beneath the whispering roof   10
Of leaves and trembled blossoms, where there ran
A brooklet, scarce espied:

'Mid hushed, cool-rooted flowers, fragrant-eyed,
Blue, silver-white, and budded Tyrian,
They lay calm-breathing, on the bedded grass;
Their arms embracèd, and their pinions too;
Their lips touched not, but had not bade adieu,
As if disjoinèd by soft-handed slumber,
And ready still past kisses to outnumber
At tender eye-dawn of aurorean love: 20
The wingèd boy I knew; [95]
But who wast thou, O happy, happy dove?
His Psyche true!

O latest-born and loveliest vision far
Of all Olympus' faded hierarchy!
Fairer than Phœbe's sapphire-regioned star,[96]
Or Vesper, amorous glow-worm of the sky;
Fairer than these, though temple thou hast none,
Nor altar heaped with flowers;
Nor Virgin-choir to make delicious moan   30
Upon the midnight hours;

94 embroidery   95 Cupid   96 the moon

No voice, no lute, no pipe, no incense sweet
    From chain-swung censer teeming;
No shrine, no grove, no oracle, no heat
    Of pale-mouthed prophet dreaming.

O brightest! though too late for antique vows,
    Too, too late for the fond believing lyre,
When holy were the haunted forest boughs,
    Holy the air, the water, and the fire;
Yet even in these days so far retired   40
    From happy pieties, thy lucent fans,[97]
    Fluttering among the faint Olympians,
I see, and sing, by my own eyes inspired.
So let me be thy choir, and make a moan
      Upon the midnight hours;
Thy voice, thy lute, thy pipe, thy incense sweet
    From swingèd censer teeming;
Thy shrine, thy grove, thy oracle, thy heat
    Of pale-mouthed prophet dreaming.

Yes, I will be thy priest, and build a fane   50
    In some untrodden region of my mind,
Where branchèd thoughts, new-grown with pleasant pain,
    Instead of pines shall murmur in the wind:
Far, far around shall those dark-clustered trees
    Fledge the wild-ridgèd mountains steep by steep;
And there by zephyrs, streams, and birds, and bees,
    The moss-lain Dryads shall be lulled to sleep;
And in the midst of this wide quietness
A rosy sanctuary will I dress
With the wreathed trellis of a working brain,   60
    With buds, and bells, and stars without a name,
With all the gardener Fancy e'er could feign,
    Who breeding flowers, will never breed the same:
And there shall be for thee all soft delight
    That shadowy thought can win,
A bright torch, and a casement ope at night,
    To let the warm Love in!

TO AUTUMN

SEASON of mists and mellow fruitfulness,
    Close bosom-friend of the maturing sun;
Conspiring with him how to load and bless
    With fruit the vines that round the thatch-eaves run;
To bend with apples the mossed cottage-trees,

[97] transparent wings

And fill all fruit with ripeness to the core;
   To swell the gourd, and plump the hazel shells
With a sweet kernel; to set budding more,
And still more, later flowers for the ·bees,
Until they think warm days will never cease,   10
   For Summer has o'er-brimmed their clammy cells.

Who hath not seen thee oft amid thy store?
   Sometimes whoever seeks abroad may find
Thee sitting careless on a granary floor,
   Thy hair soft-lifted by the winnowing wind;
Or on a half-reaped furrow sound asleep,
     Drowsed with the fumes of poppies, while thy hook
     Spares the next swath and all its twinèd flowers;
And sometime like a gleaner thou dost keep
   Steady thy laden head across a brook;   20
   Or by a cider-press, with patient look,
     Thou watchest the last oozings, hours by hours.

Where are the songs of Spring? Ay, where are they?
   Think not of them, thou hast thy music too,
While barrèd clouds bloom the soft dying day,
   And touch the stubble-plains with rosy hue;
Then in a wailful choir, the small gnats mourn
     Among the river sallows,[98] borne aloft
     Or sinking as the light wind lives or dies;
And full-grown lambs loud bleat from hilly bourn;   30
   Hedge-crickets [99] sing; and now with treble soft
   The redbreast whistles from a garden-croft;
     And gathering swallows twitter in the skies.

ODE ON MELANCHOLY

No, no, go not to Lethe, neither twist
   Wolf's-bane, tight-rooted, for its poisonous wine;
Nor suffer thy pale forehead to be kissed
   By nightshade, ruby grape of Proserpine;
Make not your rosary of yew-berries,
   Nor let the beetle, nor the death-moth be
     Your mournful Psyche,[1] nor the downy owl
A partner in your sorrow's mysteries;
   For shade to shade will come too drowsily,
     And drown the wakeful anguish of the soul.   10

98 willows   **99 grasshoppers**   **1 soul**

But when the melancholy fit shall fall
　　Sudden from heaven like a weeping cloud,
That fosters the droop-headed flowers all,
　　And hides the green hill in an April shroud;
Then glut thy sorrow on a morning rose,
　　Or on the rainbow of the salt sand-wave,
　　　　Or on the wealth of globèd peonies;
Or if thy mistress some rich anger shows,
　　Emprison her soft hand, and let her rave,
　　And feed deep, deep upon her peerless eyes.　　20

She dwells with Beauty—Beauty that must die;
　　And joy, whose hand is ever at his lips
Bidding adieu; and aching Pleasure nigh,
　　Turning to poison while the bee-mouth sips:
Ay, in the very temple of Delight
　　Veiled Melancholy has her sovran shrine,
　　　　Though seen of none save him whose strenuous tongue
Can burst Joy's grape against his palate fine:
　　His soul shall taste the sadness of her might,
　　And be among her cloudy trophies hung.　　30

LAMIA

The story of the serpent woman is represented widely in the folk-lore of many nations. The Greek form of the story Keats found alluded to in Burton's *Anatomy of Melancholy*, which he quotes at the conclusion of the poem:

"Philostratus, in his fourth book *de Vita Apollonii*, hath a memorable instance in this kind, which I may not omit, of one Menippus Lycius, a young man twenty-five years of age, that going betwixt Cenchreas and Corinth, met such a phantasm in the habit of a fair gentlewoman, which taking him by the hand, carried him home to her house, in the suburbs of Corinth, and told him she was a Phœnician by birth, and if he would tarry with her, he should hear her sing and play, and drink such wine as never any drank, and no man should molest him; but she, being fair and lovely, would live and die with him, that was fair and lovely to behold. The young man, a philosopher, otherwise staid and discreet, able to moderate his passions, though not this of love, tarried with her a while to his great content, and at last married her, to whose wedding, among other guests, came Apollonius; who, by some probable conjectures, found her out to be a serpent, a lamia; and that all her furniture was, like Tantalus' gold, described by Homer, no substance but mere illusions. When she saw herself descried, she wept, and desired Apollonius to be silent, but he would not be moved, and thereupon she, plate, house, and all that was in it, vanished in an instant: many thousands took notice of this fact, for it was done in the midst of Greece."

Lamia is perhaps the outstanding example of Keats's narrative skill. The story is told simply and directly, with emphasis upon the chief dramatic moments. Professor de Selincourt considers that the Dryden of the *Fables* is here Keats's model.

PART I

UPON a time, before the faery broods
Drove Nymph and Satyr from the prosperous woods,
Before King Oberon's bright diadem,
Scepter, and mantle, clasped with dewy gem,
Frighted away the Dryads and the Fauns
From rushes green, and brakes, and cowslipped lawns,
The ever-smitten Hermes empty left
His golden throne, bent warm on amorous theft:
From high Olympus had he stolen light,
On this side of Jove's clouds, to escape the sight   10
Of his great summoner, and made retreat
Into a forest on the shores of Crete.
For somewhere in that sacred island dwelt
A nymph to whom all hoofèd Satyrs knelt;
At whose white feet the languid Tritons poured
Pearls, while on land they withered and adored.
Fast by the springs where she to bathe was wont,
And in those meads where sometime she might haunt,
Were strewn rich gifts, unknown to any Muse,
Though Fancy's casket were unlocked to choose.   20
Ah, what a world of love was at her feet!
So Hermes thought, and a celestial heat
Burnt from his wingèd heels to either ear,
That, from a whiteness as the lily clear,
Blushed into roses 'mid his golden hair,
Fallen in jealous curls about his shoulders bare.
From vale to vale, from wood to wood, he flew,
Breathing upon the flowers his passion new,
And wound with many a river to its head,
To find where this sweet nymph prepared her secret bed: 30
In vain; the sweet nymph might nowhere be found,
And so he rested on the lonely ground,
Pensive, and full of painful jealousies
Of the Wood-Gods, and even the very trees.
There as he stood, he heard a mournful voice,
Such as, once heard, in gentle heart destroys
All pain but pity; thus the lone voice spake:
"When from this wreathèd tomb shall I awake?
When move in a sweet body fit for life,
And love, and pleasure, and the ruddy strife   40
Of hearts and lips? Ah, miserable me!"
The God, dove-footed, glided silently
Round bush and tree, soft-brushing in his speed
The taller grasses and full-flowering weed,

Until he found a palpitating snake,
Bright and cirque-couchant,[2] in a dusky brake.

She was a gordian [3] shape of dazzling hue,
Vermilion-spotted, golden, green, and blue;
Striped like a zebra, freckled like a pard,
Eyed like a peacock, and all crimson-barred;   50
And full of silver moons, that, as she breathed,
Dissolved, or brighter shone, or inter-wreathed
Their lusters with the gloomier tapestries—
So rainbow-sided, touched with miseries,
She seemed, at once, some penanced lady elf,
Some demon's mistress, or the demon's self.
Upon her crest she wore a wannish fire
Sprinkled with stars, like Ariadne's tiar: [4]
Her head was serpent, but ah, bitter-sweet!
She had a woman's mouth with all its pearls complete;   60
And for her eyes—what could such eyes do there
But weep and weep, that they were born so fair,
As Proserpine still weeps for her Sicilian air?
Her throat was serpent, but the words she spake
Came, as through bubbling honey, for Love's sake,
And thus; while Hermes on his pinions lay,
Like a stooped falcon ere he takes his prey:

"Fair Hermes, crowned with feathers, fluttering light,
I had a splendid dream of thee last night!
I saw thee sitting, on a throne of gold,   70
Among the Gods, upon Olympus old,
The only sad one; for thou didst not hear
The soft, lute-fingered Muses chaunting clear,
Nor even Apollo when he sang alone,
Deaf to his throbbing throat's long, long melodious moan.
I dreamt I saw thee, robed in purple flakes,
Break amorous through the clouds, as morning breaks,
And, swiftly as a bright Phœbean dart,[5]
Strike for the Cretan isle; and here thou art!
Too gentle Hermes, hast thou found the maid?"   80
Whereat the star of Lethe [6] not delayed
His rosy eloquence, and thus inquired:
"Thou smooth-lipped serpent, surely high-inspired!
Thou beauteous wreath, with melancholy eyes,
Possess whatever bliss thou canst devise,

2 lying coiled
3 knotted
4 the constellation of
seven stars into which
Ariadne was translated after her marriage with Bac-
chus
5 an arrow of Phœbus
Apollo
6 Hermes led the souls
across Lethe and other un-
derworld rivers to Hades.

Telling me only where my nymph is fled—
Where she doth breathe!" "Bright planet, thou hast said,"
Returned the snake, "but seal with oaths, fair God!"
"I swear," said Hermes, "by my serpent rod,
And by thine eyes, and by thy starry crown!"   90
Light flew his earnest words, among the blossoms blown.
Then thus again the brilliance feminine:
"Too frail of heart! for this lost nymph of thine,
Free as the air, invisibly she strays
About these thornless wilds; her pleasant days
She tastes unseen; unseen her nimble feet
Leave traces in the grass and flowers sweet:
From weary tendrils and bowed branches green
She plucks the fruit unseen, she bathes unseen:
And by my power is her beauty veiled   100
To keep it unaffronted, unassailed
By the love-glances of unlovely eyes,
Of Satyrs, Fauns, and bleared Silenus'⁷ sighs.
Pale grew her immortality, for woe
Of all these lovers, and she grievèd so
I took compassion on her, bade her steep
Her hair in weïrd syrops, that would keep
Her loveliness invisible, yet free
To wander as she loves, in liberty.
Thou shalt behold her, Hermes, thou alone,   110
If thou wilt, as thou swearest, grant my boon."
Then, once again, the charmèd God began
An oath, and through the serpent's ears it ran
Warm, tremulous, devout, psalterian.⁸
Ravished, she lifted her Circean head,
Blushed a live damask, and swift-lisping said,
"I was a woman, let me have once more
A woman's shape, and charming as before.
I love a youth of Corinth—O the bliss!
Give me my woman's form, and place me where he is.   120
Stoop, Hermes, let me breathe upon thy brow,
And thou shalt see thy sweet nymph even now."
The God on half-shut feathers sank serene,
She breathed upon his eyes, and swift was seen
Of both the guarded nymph near-smiling on the green.
It was no dream; or say a dream it was,
Real are the dreams of Gods, and smoothly pass
Their pleasures in a long immortal dream.
One warm, flushed moment, hovering, it might seem,

---

7 the oldest of the satyrs,   8 like the music of the
foster-father of Bacchus   psaltery (a kind of zither)

Dashed by the wood-nymph's beauty, so he burned;   130
Then, lighting on the printless verdure, turned
To the swooned serpent, and with languid arm,
Delicate, put to proof the lithe Caducean charm.[9]
So done, upon the nymph his eyes he bent
Full of adoring tears and blandishment,
And towards her stepped: she, like a moon in wane,
Faded before him, cowered, nor could restrain
Her fearful sobs, self-folding like a flower
That faints into itself at evening hour:
But the God fostering her chillèd hand,   140
She felt the warmth, her eyelids opened bland,
And, like new flowers at morning song of bees,
Bloomed, and gave up her honey to the lees.
Into the green-recessèd woods they flew;
Nor grew they pale, as mortal lovers do.

    Left to herself, the serpent now began
To change; her elfin blood in madness ran;
Her mouth foamed, and the grass, therewith besprent,
Withered at dew so sweet and virulent;
Her eyes in torture fixed, and anguish drear,   150
Hot, glazed, and wide, with lid-lashes all sear,
Flashed phosphor and sharp sparks, without one cooling tear.
The colors all inflamed throughout her train,
She writhed about, convulsed with scarlet pain:
A deep volcanian yellow took the place
Of all her milder-moonèd body's grace;
And, as the lava ravishes the mead,
Spoilt all her silver mail, and golden brede: [10]
Made gloom of all her frecklings, streaks, and bars,
Eclipsed her crescents, and licked up her stars: 160
So that, in moments few, she was undressed
Of all her sapphires, greens, and amethyst,
And rubious-argent: of all these bereft,
Nothing but pain and ugliness were left.
Still shone her crown; that vanished, also she
Melted and disappeared as suddenly;
And in the air, her new voice luting soft,
Cried, "Lycius! gentle Lycius!"—Borne aloft
With the bright mists about the mountains hoar
These words dissolved: Crete's forests heard no more.   170

    Whither fled Lamia, now a lady bright,
A full-born beauty new and exquisite?

[9] the charm exercised by Hermes' rod, the caduceus   [10] embroidery

She fled into that valley they pass o'er
Who go to Corinth from Cenchreas' shore;
And rested at the foot of those wild hills,
The rugged founts of the Peræan rills,
And of that other ridge whose barren back
Stretches, with all its mist and cloudy rack,
South-westward to Cleone. There she stood,
About a young bird's flutter from a wood,   180
Fair, on a sloping green of mossy tread,
By a clear pool, wherein she passionèd
To see herself escaped from so sore ills,
While her robes flaunted with the daffodils.

   Ah, happy Lycius!—for she was a maid
More beautiful than ever twisted braid,
Or sighed, or blushed, or on spring-flowered lea
Spread a green kirtle to the minstrelsy:
A virgin purest lipped, yet in the lore
Of love deep learnèd to the red heart's core: 190
Not one hour old, yet of sciential brain
To unperplex bliss from its neighbor pain;
Define their pettish limits, and estrange
Their points of contact, and swift counter-change;
Intrigue with the specious chaos,[11] and dispart
Its most ambiguous atoms with sure art;
As though in Cupid's college she had spent
Sweet days a lovely graduate, still unshent,[12]
And kept his rosy terms in idle languishment.

   Why this fair creature chose so fairly   200
By the wayside to linger, we shall see;
But first 'tis fit to tell how she could muse
And dream, when in the serpent prison-house,
Of all she list, strange or magnificent:
How, ever, where she willed her spirit went;
Whether to faint Elysium, or where
Down through tress-lifting waves the Nereids [13] fair
Wind into Thetis' bower by many a pearly stair;
Or where God Bacchus drains his cups divine,
Stretched out, at ease, beneath a glutinous pine;   210
Or where in Pluto's gardens palatine [14]
Mulciber's [15] columns gleam in far piazzian [16] line.
And sometimes into cities she would send
Her dream, with feast and rioting to blend;

11 of bliss and pain   13 sea-nymphs   15 Vulcan's
12 unblamed   14 palatial   16 forming arcades

And once, while among mortals dreaming thus,
She saw the young Corinthian Lycius
Charioting foremost in the envious race,
Like a young Jove with calm uneager face,
And fell into a swooning love of him.
Now on the moth-time of that evening dim 220
He would return that way, as well she knew,
To Corinth from the shore; for freshly blew
The eastern soft-wind, and his galley now
Grated the quay-stones with her brazen prow
In port Cenchreas, from Egina isle
Fresh anchored; whither he had been awhile
To sacrifice to Jove, whose temple there
Waits with high marble doors for blood and incense rare.
Jove heard his vows, and bettered his desire;
For by some freakful chance he made retire 230
From his companions, and set forth to walk,
Perhaps grown wearied of their Corinth talk:
Over the solitary hills he fared,
Thoughtless, at first, but ere eve's star appeared
His phantasy was lost, where reason fades,
In the calmed twilight of Platonic shades.
Lamia beheld him coming, near, more near—
Close to her passing, in indifference drear,
His silent sandals swept the mossy green;
So neighbored to him, and yet so unseen, 240
She stood: he passed, shut up in mysteries,
His mind wrapped like his mantle, while her eyes
Followed his steps, and her neck regal white
Turned—syllabling thus: "Ah, Lycius bright,
And will you leave me on the hills alone?
Lycius, look back! and be some pity shown."
He did; not with cold wonder, fearingly,
But Orpheus-like at an Eurydice;
For so delicious were the words she sung,
It seemed he had loved them a whole summer long. 250
And soon his eyes had drunk her beauty up,
Leaving no drop in the bewildering cup,
And still the cup was full,—while he, afraid
Lest she should vanish ere his lip had paid
Due adoration, thus began to adore,—
Her soft look growing coy, she saw his chain so sure:
"Leave thee alone! Look back! Ah, Goddess, see
Whether my eyes can ever turn from thee!
For pity do not this sad heart belie—
Even as thou vanishest so I shall die. 260

Stay! though a Naiad of the rivers, stay!
To thy far wishes will thy streams obey:
Stay! though the greenest woods be thy domain,
Alone they can drink up the morning rain;
Though a descended Pleiad,[17] will not one
Of thine harmonious sisters keep in tune
Thy spheres,[18] and as thy silver proxy shine?
So sweetly to these ravished ears of mine
Came thy sweet greeting, that if thou shouldst fade,
Thy memory will waste me to a shade:—   270
For pity do not melt!" "If I should stay,"
Said Lamia, "here, upon this floor of clay,
And pain my steps upon these flowers too rough,
What canst thou say or do of charm enough
To dull the nice remembrance of my home?
Thou canst not ask me with thee here to roam
Over these hills and vales, where no joy is,—
Empty of immortality and bliss!
Thou art a scholar, Lycius, and must know
That finer spirits cannot breathe below   280
In human climes, and live. Alas! poor youth,
What taste of purer air hast thou to soothe
My essence? What serener palaces,
Where I may all my many senses please,
And by mysterious sleights a hundred thirsts appease?
It cannot be—adieu!" So said, she rose
Tiptoe, with white arms spread. He, sick to lose
The amorous promise of her lone complain,
Swooned, murmuring of love, and pale with pain.
The cruel lady, without any show   290
Of sorrow for her tender favorite's woe,
But rather, if her eyes could brighter be,
With brighter eyes and slow amenity,
Put her new lips to his, and gave afresh
The life she had so tangled in her mesh:
And as he from one trance was wakening
Into another, she began to sing,—
Happy in beauty, life, and love, and everything,—
A song of love, too sweet for earthly lyres,
While, like held breath, the stars drew in their panting fires. 300
And then she whispered in such trembling tone
As those who, safe together met alone
For the first time through many anguished days,
Use other speech than looks; bidding him raise

17 one of the seven sis-   18 "the music of the
ters changed into the con-   spheres" as they revolved
stellation

His drooping head, and clear his soul of doubt,
For that she was a woman, and without
Any more subtle fluid in her veins
Than throbbing blood, and that the self-same pains
Inhabited her frail-strung heart as his.
And next she wondered how his eyes could miss   310
Her face so long in Corinth, where, she said,
She dwelt but half retired, and there had led
Days happy as the gold coin could invent
Without the aid of love; yet in content,
Till she saw him, as once she passed him by
Where 'gainst a column he leaned thoughtfully
At Venus' temple porch, 'mid baskets heaped
Of amorous herbs and flowers, newly reaped
Late on that eve, as 'twas the night before
The Adonian feast; [19] whereof she saw no more,   320
But wept alone those days,—for why should she adore?
Lycius from death awoke into amaze
To see her still, and singing so sweet lays;
Then from amaze into delight he fell
To hear her whisper woman's lore so well;
And every word she spake enticed him on
To unperplexed delight and pleasure known.
Let the mad poets say whate'er they please
Of the sweets of Fairies, Peris, [20] Goddesses,
There is not such a treat among them all—   330
Haunters of cavern, lake, and waterfall—
As a real woman, lineal indeed
From Pyrrha's pebbles [21] or old Adam's seed.
Thus gentle Lamia judged, and judged aright,
That Lycius could not love in half a fright,
So threw the goddess off, and won his heart
More pleasantly by playing woman's part,
With no more awe than what her beauty gave,
That, while it smote, still guaranteed to save.
Lycius to all made eloquent reply,   340
Marrying to every word a twin-born sigh;
And last, pointing to Corinth, asked her sweet,
If 'twas too far that night for her soft feet.
The way was short, for Lamia's eagerness
Made, by a spell, the triple league decrease
To a few paces; not at all surmised

19 the feast of Adonis, who had been beloved by Venus, and killed by a wild boar
20 in Persian myth, creatures descended from the fallen angels
21 Deucalion and Pyrrha, after the flood, cast pebbles behind them, which sprang into men, and thus re-peopled the world.

By blinded Lycius, so in her comprised.
They passed the city gates, he knew not how,
So noiseless, and he never thought to know.

As men talk in a dream, so Corinth all,   350
Throughout her palaces imperial,
And all her populous streets and temples lewd,
Muttered, like tempest in the distance brewed,
To the wide-spreaded night above her towers.
Men, women, rich and poor, in the cool hours,
Shuffled their sandals o'er the pavement white,
Companioned or alone; while many a light
Flared, here and there, from wealthy festivals,
And threw their moving shadows on the walls,
Or found them clustered in the corniced shade   360
Of some arched temple door or dusky colonnade.

Muffling his face, of greeting friends in fear,
Her finger he pressed hard, as one came near
With curled gray beard, sharp eyes, and smooth bald crown,
Slow-stepped, and robed in philosophic gown:
Lycius shrank closer, as they met and passed,
Into his mantle, adding wings to haste,
While hurried Lamia trembled. "Ah," said he,
"Why do you shudder, love, so ruefully?
Why does your tender palm dissolve in dew?"—   370
"I'm wearied," said fair Lamia: "tell me who
Is that old man? I cannot bring to mind
His features:—Lycius! wherefore did you blind
Yourself from his quick eyes?" Lycius replied,
" 'Tis Apollonius sage, my trusty guide
And good instructor; but to-night he seems
The ghost of folly haunting my sweet dreams."

While yet he spake they had arrived before
A pillared porch, with lofty portal door,
Where hung a silver lamp, whose phosphor glow   380
Reflected in the slabbèd steps below,
Mild as a star in water; for so new
And so unsullied was the marble hue,
So through the crystal polish, liquid fine,
Ran the dark veins, that none but feet divine
Could e'er have touched there. Sounds Æolian [22]
Breathed from the hinges, as the ample span
Of the wide doors disclosed a place unknown

22 musical

Some time to any, but those two alone,
And a few Persian mutes, who that same year   390
Were seen about the markets: none knew where
They could inhabit; the most curious
Were foiled, who watched to trace them to their house:
And but the flitter-wingèd verse must tell,
For truth's sake, what woe afterwards befell,
'Twould humor many a heart to leave them thus
Shut from the busy world of more incredulous.

PART II

Love in a hut, with water and a crust,
Is—Love, forgive us!—cinders, ashes, dust;
Love in a palace is perhaps at last
More grievous torment than a hermit's fast:—
That is a doubtful tale from faery land,
Hard for the non-elect to understand.
Had Lycius lived to hand his story down,
He might have given the moral a fresh frown,
Or clenched it quite: but too short was their bliss
To breed distrust and hate, that make the soft voice hiss.   10
Besides, there, nightly, with terrific glare,
Love, jealous grown of so complete a pair,
Hovered and buzzed his wings, with fearful roar,
Above the lintel of their chamber door,
And down the passage cast a glow upon the floor.

For all this came a ruin: side by side
They were enthronèd, in the eventide,
Upon a couch, near to a curtaining
Whose airy texture, from a golden string,
Floated into the room, and let appear   20
Unveiled the summer heaven, blue and clear,
Betwixt two marble shafts:—there they reposed,
Where use had made it sweet, with eyelids closed,
Saving a tithe which love still open kept,
That they might see each other while they almost slept;
When from the slope side of a suburb hill,
Deafening the swallow's twitter, came a thrill
Of trumpets—Lycius started—the sounds fled,
But left a thought, a buzzing in his head.
For the first time, since first he harbored in   30
That purple-linèd palace of sweet sin,
His spirit passed beyond its golden bourn
Into the noisy world almost forsworn.

The lady, ever watchful, penetrant,
Saw this with pain, so arguing a want
Of something more, more than her empery
Of joys; and she began to moan and sigh
Because he mused beyond her, knowing well
That but a moment's thought is passion's passing bell.
"Why do you sigh, fair creature?" whispered he: 40
"Why do you think?" returned she tenderly:
"You have deserted me; where am I now?
Not in your heart while care weighs on your brow:
No, no, you have dismissed me, and I go
From your breast houseless: ay, it must be so."
He answered, bending to her open eyes,
Where he was mirrored small in paradise,
"My silver planet, both of eve and morn!
Why will you plead yourself so sad forlorn,
While I am striving how to fill my heart   50
With deeper crimson and a double smart?
How to entangle, trammel up, and snare
Your soul in mine, and labyrinth you there
Like the hid scent in an unbudded rose?
Ay, a sweet kiss—you see your mighty woes.
My thoughts! shall I unveil them? Listen then!
What mortal hath a prize, that other men
May be confounded and abashed withal,
But lets it sometimes pace abroad majestical,
And triumph, as in thee I should rejoice   60
Amid the hoarse alarm of Corinth's voice.
Let my foes choke, and my friends shout afar,
While through the throngèd streets your bridal car
Wheels round its dazzling spokes."—The lady's cheek
Trembled; she nothing said, but, pale and meek,
Arose and knelt before him, wept a rain
Of sorrows at his words; at last with pain
Beseeching him, the while his hand she wrung,
To change his purpose. He thereat was stung,
Perverse, with stronger fancy to reclaim   70
Her wild and timid nature to his aim;
Besides, for all his love, in self despite,
Against his better self, he took delight
Luxurious in her sorrows, soft and new.
His passion, cruel grown, took on a hue
Fierce, and sanguineous as 'twas possible
In one whose brow had no dark veins to swell.
Fine was the mitigated fury, like
Apollo's presence when in act to strike

The serpent—Ha, the serpent! certes, she   80
Was none. She burnt, she loved the tyranny,
And, all subdued, consented to the hour
When to the bridal he shall lead his paramour.
Whispering in midnight silence, said the youth,
"Sure some sweet name thou hast, though, by my truth,
I have not asked it, ever thinking thee
Not mortal, but of heavenly progeny,
As still I do. Hast any mortal name,
Fit appellation for this dazzling frame?
Or friends or kinsfolk on the citied earth,   90
To share our marriage feast and nuptial mirth?"
"I have no friends," said Lamia, "no, not one;
My presence in wide Corinth hardly known:
My parents' bones are in their dusty urns
Sepulchered, where no kindled incense burns,
Seeing all their luckless race are dead save me,
And I neglect the holy rite for thee.
Even as you list invite your many guests;
But if, as now it seems, your vision rests
With any pleasure on me, do not bid   100
Old Apollonius—from him keep me hid."
Lycius, perplexed at words so blind and blank,
Made close inquiry; from whose touch she shrank,
Feigning a sleep; and he to the dull shade
Of deep sleep in a moment was betrayed.

     It was the custom then to bring away
The bride from home at blushing shut of day,
Veiled, in a chariot, heralded along
By strewn flowers, torches, and a marriage song,
With other pageants: but this fair unknown   110
Had not a friend. So being left alone
(Lycius was gone to summon all his kin),
And knowing surely she could never win
His foolish heart from its mad pompousness,
She set herself, high-thoughted, how to dress
The misery in fit magnificence.
She did so, but 'tis doubtful how and whence
Came, and who were, her subtle servitors.
About the halls, and to and from the doors,
There was a noise of wings, till in short space   120
The glowing banquet-room shone with wide-archèd grace.
A haunting music, sole perhaps and lone
Supportress of the faery-roof, made moan
Throughout, as fearful the whole charm might fade.

Fresh carvèd cedar, mimicking a glade
Of palm and plantain, met from either side,
High in the midst, in honor of the bride:
Two palms and then two plantains, and so on,
From either side their stems branched one to one
All down the aislèd place; and beneath all   130
There ran a stream of lamps straight on from wall to wall.
So canopied, lay an untasted feast
Teeming with odors. Lamia, regal dressed,
Silently paced about, and as she went,
In pale contented sort of discontent,
Missioned her viewless servants to enrich
The fretted splendor of each nook and niche.
Between the tree-stems, marbled plain at first,
Came jasper panels; then anon there burst
Forth creeping imagery of slighter trees,   140
And with the larger wove in small intricacies.
Approving all, she faded at self-will,
And shut the chamber up, close, hushed and still,
Complete and ready for the revels rude,
When dreadful guests would come to spoil her solitude.

The day appeared, and all the gossip rout.
O senseless Lycius! Madman! wherefore flout
The silent-blessing fate, warm cloistered hours,
And show to common eyes these secret bowers?
The herd approached; each guest, with busy brain,   150
Arriving at the portal, gazed amain,
And entered marveling: for they knew the street,
Remembered it from childhood all complete
Without a gap, yet ne'er before had seen
That royal porch, that high-built fair demesne;
So in they hurried all, mazed, curious and keen;
Save one, who looked thereon with eye severe,
And with calm-planted steps walked in austere;
'Twas Apollonius: something too he laughed,
As though some knotty problem, that had daft   160
His patient thought, had now begun to thaw
And solve and melt: 'twas just as he foresaw.

He met within the murmurous vestibule
His young disciple. " 'Tis no common rule,
Lycius," said he, "for uninvited guest
To force himself upon you, and infest
With an unbidden presence the bright throng
Of younger friends; yet must I do this wrong,

And you forgive me." Lycius blushed, and led
The old man through the inner doors broad-spread;   170
With reconciling words and courteous mien
Turning into sweet milk the sophist's spleen.

Of wealthy luster was the banquet-room,
Filled with pervading brilliance and perfume:
Before each lucid panel fuming stood
A censer fed with myrrh and spicèd wood,
Each by a sacred tripod held aloft,
Whose slender feet wide-swerved upon the soft
Wool-woofèd carpets: fifty wreaths of smoke
From fifty censers their light voyage took   180
To the high roof, still mimicked as they rose
Along the mirrored walls by twin-clouds odorous.
Twelve spherèd tables by silk seats insphered,
High as the level of a man's breast reared
On libbard's [23] paws, upheld the heavy gold
Of cups and goblets, and the store thrice told
Of Ceres' horn,[24] and, in huge vessels, wine
Come from the gloomy tun with merry shine.
Thus loaded with a feast the tables stood,
Each shrining in the midst the image of a God.   190

When in an antechamber every guest
Had felt the cold full sponge to pleasure pressed,
By ministering slaves, upon his hands and feet,
And fragrant oils with ceremony meet
Poured on his hair, they all moved to the feast
In white robes, and themselves in order placed
Around the silken couches, wondering
Whence all this mighty cost and blaze of wealth could spring.

Soft went the music the soft air along,
While fluent Greek a voweled under-song   200
Kept up among the guests, discoursing low
At first, for scarcely was the wine at flow;
But when the happy vintage touched their brains,
Louder they talk, and louder come the strains
Of powerful instruments:—the gorgeous dyes,
The space, the splendor of the draperies,
The roof of awful richness, nectarous cheer,
Beautiful slaves, and Lamia's self, appear,
Now, when the wine has done its rosy deed,

23 leopard's   24 the horn of plenty

And every soul from human trammels freed, 210
No more so strange; for merry wine, sweet wine,
Will make Elysian shades not too fair, too divine.
Soon was God Bacchus at meridian height;
Flushed were their cheeks, and bright eyes double bright;
Garlands of every green and every scent
From vales deflowered or forest-trees branch-rent,
In baskets of bright osiered gold were brought,
High as the handles heaped, to suit the thought
Of every guest; that each, as he did please,
Might fancy-fit his brows, silk-pillowed at his ease. 220

What wreath for Lamia? What for Lycius?
What for the sage, old Apollonius?
Upon her aching forehead be there hung
The leaves of willow and of adder's tongue; 25
And for the youth, quick, let us strip for him
The thyrsus,26 that his watching eyes may swim
Into forgetfulness; and, for the sage,
Let spear-grass and the spiteful thistle wage
War on his temples. Do not all charms fly
At the mere touch of cold philosophy? 230
There was an awful rainbow once in heaven:
We know her woof, her texture; she is given
In the dull catalogue of common things.
Philosophy will clip an Angel's wings,
Conquer all mysteries by rule and line,
Empty the haunted air and gnomèd mine—
Unweave a rainbow, as it erewhile made
The tender-personed Lamia melt into a shade.

By her glad Lycius sitting, in chief place,
Scarce saw in all the room another face, 240
Till, checking his love trance, a cup he took
Full brimmed, and opposite sent forth a look
Cross the broad table, to beseech a glance
From his old teacher's wrinkled countenance,
And pledge him. The bald-head philosopher
Had fixed his eye, without a twinkle or stir,
Full on the alarmèd beauty of the bride,
Brow-beating her fair form and troubling her sweet pride.
Lycius then pressed her hand, with devout touch
As pale it lay upon the rosy couch: 250
'Twas icy, and the cold ran through his veins;

25 a fern so called from   26 Bacchus' staff, en-
the shape of its fruited   twined with ivy
spike

Then sudden it grew hot, and all the pains
Of an unnatural heat shot to his heart.
"Lamia, what means this? Wherefore dost thou start?
Know'st thou that man?" Poor Lamia answered not.
He gazed into her eyes, and not a jot
Owned they the lovelorn piteous appeal:
More, more he gazed: his human senses reel:
Some hungry spell that loveliness absorbs;
There was no recognition in those orbs.   260
"Lamia!" he cried—and no soft-toned reply.
The many heard, and the loud revelry
Grew hush; the stately music no more breathes;
The myrtle sickened in a thousand wreaths.
By faint degrees, voice, lute, and pleasure ceased;
A deadly silence step by step increased,
Until it seemed a horrid presence there,
And not a man but felt the terror in his hair.
"Lamia!" he shrieked; and nothing but the shriek
With its sad echo did the silence break.   270
"Begone, foul dream!" he cried, gazing again
In the bride's face, where now no azure vein
Wandered on fair-spaced temples, no soft bloom
Misted the cheek, no passion to illume
The deep-recessèd vision:—all was blight;
Lamia, no longer fair, there sat, a deadly white.
"Shut, shut those juggling eyes, thou ruthless man!
Turn them aside, wretch! or the righteous ban
Of all the Gods, whose dreadful images
Here represent their shadowy presences,   280
May pierce them on the sudden with the thorn
Of painful blindness; leaving thee forlorn,
In trembling dotage to the feeblest fright
Of conscience, for their long-offended might,
For all thine impious proud-heart sophistries,
Unlawful magic, and enticing lies.
Corinthians! look upon that gray-beard wretch!
Mark how, possessed, his lashless eyelids stretch
Around his demon eyes! Corinthians, see!
My sweet bride withers at their potency."   290
"Fool!" said the sophist, in an undertone
Gruff with contempt; which a death-nighing moan
From Lycius answered, as, heart-struck and lost,
He sank supine beside the aching ghost.
"Fool! Fool!" repeated he, while his eyes still
Relented not, nor moved; "from every ill

Of life have I preserved thee to this day,
And shall I see thee made a serpent's prey?"
Then Lamia breathed death-breath; the sophist's eye,
Like a sharp spear, went through her utterly,   300
Keen, cruel, perceant,[27] stinging: she, as well
As her weak hand could any meaning tell,
Motioned him to be silent; vainly so;
He looked and looked again a level—No!
"A serpent!" echoed he; no sooner said
Than with a frightful scream she vanishèd;
And Lycius' arms were empty of delight,
As were his limbs of life, from that same night.
On the high couch he lay—his friends came round—
Supported him; no pulse or breath they found,   310
And in its marriage robe the heavy body wound.

THOMAS DE QUINCEY (1785–1859)

Thomas De Quincey, the son of a well-to-do merchant, was born at Manchester on August 15, 1785. In 1801 he ran away from Manchester Grammar School, spent a summer wandering in Wales, and then went up to London, where for a time he led a vagabond life. His family reclaimed him, and sent him in 1803 to Oxford, which he attended intermittently, and which he left without taking a degree. In these years he became acquainted with Coleridge, Wordsworth, Southey, and Charles Lamb. In 1809 he settled at Grasmere, in the Lake District, where he lived for some twenty years. In 1816 he married Margaret Simpson, the daughter of a Westmoreland farmer. In 1830 he removed with his family to Edinburgh, which was his residence for the rest of his life, although he frequently wandered elsewhere, and had a way of disappearing for extended periods. As early as 1804 he had commenced to use opium. The story of his indulgence in this drug, of how he came to take prodigious quantities of it, and later reduced his allowance to less fearful doses, is told, sensationally and vividly, with full analysis of the sensations induced, in his *Confessions of an English Opium-Eater* (1821). His works are miscellaneous in character, and largely journalistic in tone, many of them being in fact written for magazines. The finest of them, aside from the *Confessions*, are *Murder Considered as One of the Fine Arts* (1827), *Suspiria de Profundis* (1845), and *The English Mail-Coach* (1849). De Quincey is one of the great English stylists. His work suggests some of the masters of the seventeenth century, like Sir Thomas Browne, but has a magnificence that perhaps transcends them, in its richness of phrasing, its sustained rhythms, its gorgeous cadences, and its haunting imaginative quality. It captures for prose many of the effects of poetry. It has been a powerful influence on the prose of the nineteenth century.

BIBLIOGRAPHY. *Works*, in 14 vols., by David Masson (A. & C. Black). Selections, by M. H. Turk, in Athenæum Press ser. (Ginn). *Life* by Horace A. Eaton (Oxford). Short *Life* by Masson in Eng. Men of Letters ser.

27 piercing

LEVANA AND OUR LADIES OF SORROW

(from *Suspiria de Profundis* [1])

OFTENTIMES at Oxford I saw Levana in my dreams. I knew her by her Roman symbols. Who is Levana? Reader, that do not pretend to have leisure for very much scholarship, you will not be angry with me for telling you. Levana was the Roman goddess that performed for the new-born infant the earliest office of ennobling kindness,—typical, by its mode, of that grandeur which belongs to man everywhere, and of that benignity in powers invisible which even in pagan worlds sometimes descends to sustain it. At the very moment of birth, just as the infant
10 tasted for the first time the atmosphere of our troubled planet, it was laid on the ground. *That* might bear different interpretations. But immediately, lest so grand a creature should grovel there for more than one instant, either the paternal hands, as proxy for the goddess Levana, or some near kinsman, as proxy for the father, raised it upright, bade it look erect as the king of all this world, and presented its forehead to the stars, saying, perhaps, in his heart, "Behold what is greater than yourselves!" This symbolic act represented the function of Levana. And that mysterious lady, who never revealed her face (except to me in
20 dreams), but always acted by delegation, had her name from the Latin verb (as still it is the Italian verb) *levare,* to raise aloft.

This is the explanation of Levana. And hence it has arisen that some people have understood by Levana the tutelary power that controls the education of the nursery. She, that would not suffer at his birth even a prefigurative or mimic degradation for her awful ward, far less could be supposed to suffer the real degradation attaching to the non-development of his powers. She therefore watches over human education. Now, the word *edŭco,* with the penultimate short, was derived (by a process often exempli-
30 fied in the crystallization of languages) from the word *edūco,* with the penultimate long. Whatsoever *educes,* or develops, *educates.* By the education of Levana, therefore, is meant,—not the poor machinery that moves by spelling-books and grammars, but that mighty system of central forces hidden in the deep bosom of human life, which by passion, by strife, by temptation, by the energies of resistance, works for ever upon children—resting not day or night, any more than the mighty wheel of day and night themselves, whose moments, like restless spokes, are glimmering for ever as they revolve.
40 If, then, *these* are the ministries by which Levana works, how profoundly must she reverence the agencies of grief! But you,

1 sighs from the depths

reader, think that children generally are not liable to grief such as mine. There are two senses in the word *generally*,—the sense of Euclid, where it means *universally* (or in the whole extent of the *genus*), and a foolish sense of this word, where it means *usually*. Now, I am far from saying that children universally are capable of grief like mine. But there are more than you ever heard of who die of grief in this island of ours. I will tell you a common case. The rules of Eton require that a boy on the *foundation*[2] should be there twelve years: he is superannuated at eighteen; consequently he must come at six. Children torn 10 away from mothers and sisters at that age not unfrequently die. I speak of what I know. The complaint is not entered by the registrar as grief; but *that* it is. Grief of that sort, and at that age, has killed more than ever have been counted amongst its martyrs.

Therefore it is that Levana often communes with the powers that shake man's heart; therefore it is that she dotes upon grief. "These ladies," said I softly to myself, on seeing the ministers with whom Levana was conversing, "these are the Sorrows; and they are three in number: as the *Graces* are three, who dress 20 man's life with beauty; the *Parcæ*[3] are three, who weave the dark arras of man's life in their mysterious loom always with colors sad in part, sometimes angry with tragic crimson and black; the *Furies* are three, who visit with retributions called from the other side of the grave offenses that walk upon this; and once even the *Muses* were but three, who fit the harp, the trumpet, or the lute, to the great burdens of man's impassioned creations. These are the Sorrows; all three of whom I know." The last words I say *now;* but in Oxford I said, "one of whom I know, and the others too surely I *shall* know." For already, in my 30 fervent youth, I saw (dimly relieved upon the dark background of my dreams) the imperfect lineaments of the awful Sisters.

These Sisters—by what name shall we call them? If I say simply, "The Sorrows," there will be a chance of mistaking the term; it might be understood of individual sorrow,—separate cases of sorrow,—whereas I want a term expressing the mighty abstractions that incarnate themselves in all individual sufferings of man's heart, and I wish to have these abstractions presented as impersonations,—that is, as clothed with human attributes of life, and with functions pointing to flesh. Let us call 40 them, therefore, *Our Ladies of Sorrow*.

I know them thoroughly, and have walked in all their kingdoms. Three sisters they are, of one mysterious household; and their paths are wide apart; but of their dominion there is no end. Them I saw often conversing with Levana, and sometimes about

2 scholarship   3 Fates

myself. Do they talk, then? O no! Mighty phantoms like these disdain the infirmities of language. They may utter voices through the organs of man when they dwell in human hearts, but amongst themselves is no voice nor sound; eternal silence reigns in *their* kingdoms. They spoke not as they talked with Levana; they whispered not; they sang not; though oftentimes methought they *might* have sung: for I upon earth had heard their mysteries oftentimes deciphered by harp and timbrel, by dulcimer and organ. Like God, whose servants they are, they utter their pleas-
10 ure not by sounds that perish, or by words that go astray, but by signs in heaven, by changes on earth, by pulses in secret rivers, heraldries painted on darkness, and hieroglyphics written on the tablets of the brain. *They* wheeled in mazes; *I* spelled the steps. *They* telegraphed from afar; *I* read the signals. *They* conspired together; and on the mirrors of darkness *my* eye traced the plots. *Theirs* were the symbols; *mine* are the words.

What is it the Sisters are? What is it that they do? Let me describe their form and their presence, if form it were that still fluctuated in its outline, or presence it were that for ever ad-
20 vanced to the front or for ever receded amongst shades.

The eldest of the three is named *Mater Lachrymarum*, Our Lady of Tears. She it is that night and day raves and moans, calling for vanished faces. She stood in Rama, where a voice was heard of lamentation,—Rachel weeping for her children, and refusing to be comforted.[4] She it was that stood in Bethlehem on the night when Herod's sword swept its nurseries of Innocents, and the little feet were stiffened for ever which, heard at times as they trotted along floors overhead, woke pulses of love in household hearts that were not unmarked in heaven.
30 Her eyes are sweet and subtle, wild and sleepy, by turns; oftentimes rising to the clouds, oftentimes challenging the heavens. She wears a diadem round her head. And I knew by childish memories that she could go abroad upon the winds, when she heard the sobbing of litanies, or the thundering of organs, and when she beheld the mustering of summer clouds. This Sister, the elder, it is that carries keys more than papal at her girdle, which open every cottage and every palace. She, to my knowledge, sat all last summer by the bedside of the blind beggar, him that so often and so gladly I talked with, whose pious daughter,
40 eight years old, with the sunny countenance, resisted the temptations of play and village mirth, to travel all day long on dusty roads with her afflicted father. For this did God send her a great reward. In the spring-time of the year, and whilst yet her own spring was budding, He recalled her to himself. But her blind father mourns for ever over *her;* still he dreams at midnight that

4 Jer. xxxi, 15; Matt. ii, 18

the little guiding hand is locked within his own; and still he
wakens to a darkness that is *now* within a second and a deeper
darkness. This *Mater Lachrymarum* also has been sitting all
this winter of 1844–5 within the bedchamber of the Czar,[5] bringing before his eyes a daughter (not less pious) that vanished to
God not less suddenly, and left behind her a darkness not less
profound. By the power of the keys it is that Our Lady of Tears
glides, a ghostly intruder, into the chambers of sleepless men,
sleepless women, sleepless children, from Ganges to the Nile,
from Nile to Mississippi. And her, because she is the first-born 10
of her house, and has the widest empire, let us honor with the title
of "Madonna."

The second Sister is called *Mater Suspiriorum,* Our Lady of
Sighs. She never scales the clouds, nor walks abroad upon the
winds. She wears no diadem. And her eyes, if they were ever
seen, would be neither sweet nor subtle; no man could read their
story; they would be filled with perishing dreams, and with
wrecks of forgotten delirium. But she raises not her eyes; her
head, on which sits a dilapidated turban, droops for ever, for
ever fastens on the dust. She weeps not. She groans not. But she 20
sighs inaudibly at intervals. Her sister, Madonna, is oftentimes
stormy and frantic, raging in the highest against heaven, and de-
manding back her darlings. But Our Lady of Sighs never
clamors, never defies, dreams not of rebellious aspirations. She
is humble to abjectness. Hers is the meekness that belongs to the
hopeless. Murmur she may, but it is in her sleep. Whisper she
may, but it is to herself in the twilight. Mutter she does at times,
but it is in solitary places that are desolate as she is desolate, in
ruined cities, and when the sun has gone down to his rest. This
Sister is the visitor of the Pariah, of the Jew, of the bondsman 30
to the oar in the Mediterranean galleys; of the English criminal
in Norfolk Island,[6] blotted out from the books of remembrance
in sweet far-off England; of the baffled penitent reverting his
eyes for ever upon a solitary grave, which to him seems the altar
overthrown of some past and bloody sacrifice, on which altar no
oblations can now be availing, whether towards pardon that he
might implore, or towards reparation that he might attempt.
Every slave that at noonday looks up to the tropical sun with
timid reproach, as he points with one hand to the earth, our general mother, but for *him* a stepmother, as he points with the other 40
hand to the Bible, our general teacher, but against *him* sealed
and sequestered,[7] every woman sitting in darkness, without love
to shelter her head, or hope to illumine her solitude, because the

---

5 Nicholas I, lamenting
death of Princess Alexan-
dra

6 former English penal
colony in the Pacific

7 "This, the reader will
be aware, applies chiefly

to the cotton and tobacco
States of North Amer-
ica. . . ." (De Quincey)

heaven-born instincts kindling in her nature germs of holy affections, which God implanted in her womanly bosom, having been stifled by social necessities, now burn sullenly to waste, like sepulchral lamps amongst the ancients; every nun defrauded of her unreturning May-time by wicked kinsman, whom God will judge; every captive in every dungeon; all that are betrayed, and all that are rejected; outcasts by traditionary law, and children of *hereditary* disgrace: all these walk with Our Lady of Sighs. She also carries a key; but she needs it little. For her kingdom is chiefly amongst the tents of Shem, and the houseless vagrant of every clime. Yet in the very highest ranks of man she finds chapels of her own; and even in glorious England there are some that, to the world, carry their heads as proudly as the reindeer, who yet secretly have received her mark upon their foreheads.

But the third Sister, who is also the youngest—! Hush! whisper whilst we talk of *her!* Her kingdom is not large, or else no flesh should live; but within that kingdom all power is hers. Her head, turreted like that of Cybele,[8] rises almost beyond the reach of sight. She droops not; and her eyes, rising so high, *might* be hidden by distance. But, being what they are, they cannot be hidden; through the treble veil of crape which she wears the fierce light of a blazing misery, that rests not for matins or for vespers, for noon of day or noon of night, for ebbing or for flowing tide, may be read from the very ground. She is the defier of God. She also is the mother of lunacies, and the suggestress of suicides. Deep lie the roots of her power; but narrow is the nation that she rules. For she can approach only those in whom a profound nature has been upheaved by central convulsions; in whom the heart trembles and the brain rocks under conspiracies of tempest from without and tempest from within. Madonna moves with uncertain steps, fast or slow, but still with tragic grace. Our Lady of Sighs creeps timidly and stealthily. But this youngest Sister moves with incalculable motions, bounding, and with a tiger's leaps. She carries no key; for, though coming rarely amongst men, she storms all doors at which she is permitted to enter at all. And *her* name is *Mater Tenebrarum*—Our Lady of Darkness.

These were the *Semnai Theai* or Sublime Goddesses, these were the *Eumenides* or Gracious Ladies (so called by antiquity in shuddering propitiation), of my Oxford dreams. Madonna spoke. She spoke by her mysterious hand. Touching my head, she beckoned to Our Lady of Sighs; and *what* she spoke, translated out of the signs which (except in dreams) no man reads, was this:—

"Lo! here is he whom in childhood I dedicated to my altars.

8 Nature goddess of ancient peoples of Anatolia

This is he that once I made my darling. Him I led astray, him I
beguiled; and from heaven I stole away his young heart to mine.
Through me did he become idolatrous; and through me it was, by
languishing desires, that he worshiped the worm, and prayed to
the wormy grave. Holy was the grave to him; lovely was its
darkness; saintly its corruption. Him, this young idolator, I have
seasoned for thee, dear gentle Sister of Sighs! Do thou take him
now to *thy* heart, and season him for our dreadful sister. And
thou,"—turning to the *Mater Tenebrarum*, she said,—"wicked
sister, that temptest and hatest, do thou take him from *her*. See
that thy scepter lie heavy on his head. Suffer not woman and her
tenderness to sit near him in his darkness. Banish the frailties of
hope; wither the relenting of love; scorch the fountains of tears;
curse him as only *thou* canst curse. So shall he be accomplished
in the furnace; so shall he see the things that ought *not* to be
seen, sights that are abominable, and secrets that are unutterable. So shall he read elder truths, sad truths, grand truths, fearful truths. So shall he rise again *before* he dies. And so shall our
commission be accomplished which from God we had,—to plague
his heart until we had unfolded the capacities of his spirit."   20

THE ENGLISH MAIL-COACH

SECTION III—DREAM-FUGUE

FOUNDED ON THE PRECEDING THEME OF SUDDEN DEATH [9]

> "Whence the sound
> Of instruments, that made melodious chime,
> Was heard, of harp and organ; and who moved
> Their stops and chords, was seen; his volant touch
> Instinct through all proportions, low and high,
> Fled and pursued transverse the resonant fugue."
> —*Par. Lost*. B. xi

Tumultuosissimamente

PASSION of sudden death! that once in youth I read and interpreted by the shadows of thy averted signs!—rapture of panic
taking the shape (which amongst tombs in churches I have seen)
of woman bursting her sepulchral bonds—of woman's Ionic form
bending forward from the ruins of her grave with arching foot,
with eyes upraised, with clasped adoring hands—waiting, watching, trembling, praying for the trumpet's call to rise from dust
for ever! Ah, vision too fearful of shuddering humanity on the
brink of almighty abysses!—vision that didst start back, that

[9] in sec. ii of *The English Mail-Coach*

didst reel away, like a shriveling scroll from before the wrath of fire racing on the wings of the wind! Epilepsy so brief of horror, wherefore is it that thou canst not die? Passing so suddenly into darkness, wherefore is it that still thou sheddest thy sad funeral blights upon the gorgeous mosaics of dreams? Fragment of music too passionate, heard once, and heard no more, what aileth thee, that thy deep rolling chords come up at intervals through all the worlds of sleep, and after forty years, have lost no element of horror?

I

10 Lo, it is summer—almighty summer! The everlasting gates of life and summer are thrown open wide; and on the ocean, tranquil and verdant as a savannah, the unknown lady from the dreadful vision and I myself are floating—she upon a fairy pinnace, and I upon an English three-decker. Both of us are wooing gales of festal happiness within the domain of our common country, within that ancient watery park, within that pathless chase of ocean, where England takes her pleasure as a huntress through winter and summer, from the rising to the setting sun. Ah, what a wilderness of floral beauty was hidden, or was sud-
20 denly revealed, upon the tropic islands through which the pinnace moved! And upon her deck what a bevy of human flowers: young women how lovely, young men how noble, that were dancing together, and slowly drifting towards *us* amidst music and incense, amidst blossoms from forests and gorgeous corymbi [10] from vintages, amidst natural caroling, and the echoes of sweet girlish laughter. Slowly the pinnace nears us, gaily she hails us, and silently she disappears beneath the shadow of our mighty bows. But then, as at some signal from heaven, the music, and the carols, and the sweet echoing of girlish laughter—all
30 are hushed. What evil has smitten the pinnace, meeting or overtaking her? Did ruin to our friends couch within our own dreadful shadow? Was our shadow the shadow of death? I looked over the bow for an answer, and, behold! the pinnace was dismantled; the revel and the revelers were found no more; the glory of the vintage was dust; and the forests with their beauty were left without a witness upon the seas. "But where," and I turned to our crew—"where are the lovely women that danced beneath the awning of flowers and clustering corymbi? Whither have fled the noble young men that danced with *them?*" Answer there was
40 none. But suddenly the man at the mast-head, whose countenance darkened with alarm, cried out, "Sail on the weather beam! Down she comes upon us: in seventy seconds she also will founder."

10 clusters of fruits or flowers

II

I looked to the weather side, and the summer had departed. The sea was rocking, and shaken with gathering wrath. Upon its surface sat mighty mists, which grouped themselves into arches and long cathedral aisles. Down one of these, with the fiery pace of a quarrel [11] from a cross-bow, ran a frigate right athwart our course. "Are they mad?" some voice exclaimed from our deck. "Do they woo their ruin?" But in a moment, as she was close upon us, some impulse of a heady current or local vortex gave a wheeling bias to her course, and off she forged without a shock. As she ran past us, high aloft amongst the shrouds stood the lady of the pinnace. The deeps opened ahead in malice to receive her, towering surges of foam ran after her, the billows were fierce to catch her. But far away she was borne into desert spaces of the sea: whilst still by sight I followed her, as she ran before the howling gale, chased by angry sea-birds and by maddening billows; still I saw her, as at the moment when she ran past us, standing amongst the shrouds, with her white draperies streaming before the wind. There she stood, with hair disheveled, one hand clutched amongst the tackling—rising, sinking, fluttering, trembling, praying; there for leagues I saw her as she stood, raising at intervals one hand to heaven, amidst the fiery crests of the pursuing waves and the raving of the storm; until at last, upon a sound from afar of malicious laughter and mockery, all was hidden for ever in driving showers; and afterwards, but when I know not, nor how,

III

Sweet funeral bells from some incalculable distance, wailing over the dead that die before the dawn, awakened me as I slept in a boat moored to some familiar shore. The morning twilight even then was breaking; and, by the dusky revelations which it spread, I saw a girl, adorned with a garland of white roses about her head for some great festival, running along the solitary strand in extremity of haste. Her running was the running of panic; and often she looked back as to some dreadful enemy in the rear. But, when I leaped ashore, and followed on her steps to warn her of a peril in front, alas! from me she fled as from another peril, and vainly I shouted to her of quicksands that lay ahead. Faster and faster she ran; round a promontory of rocks she wheeled out of sight; in an instant I also wheeled round it, but only to see the treacherous sands gathering above her head. Already her person was buried; only the fair young

11 bolt

head and the diadem of white roses around it were still visible
to the pitying heavens; and, last of all, was visible one white
marble arm. I saw by the early twilight this fair young head,
as it was sinking down to darkness—saw this marble arm, as it
rose above her head and her treacherous grave, tossing, faltering,
rising, clutching, as at some false deceiving hand stretched out
from the clouds—saw this marble arm uttering her dying hope,
and then uttering her dying despair. The head, the diadem, the
arm—these all had sunk; at last over these also the cruel quick-
10 sand had closed; and no memorial of the fair young girl remained
on earth, except my own solitary tears, and the funeral bells from
the desert seas, that, rising again more softly, sang a requiem
over the grave of the buried child, and over her blighted dawn.

I sat, and wept in secret the tears that men have ever given to
the memory of those that died before the dawn, and by the
treachery of earth, our mother. But suddenly the tears and
funeral bells were hushed by a shout as of many nations, and
by a roar from some great king's artillery, advancing rapidly
along the valleys, and heard afar by echoes from the mountains.
20 "Hush!" I said, as I bent my ear earthwards to listen—"hush!
—this either is the very anarchy of strife, or else"—and then
I listened more profoundly, and whispered as I raised my head—
"or else, oh heavens! it is *victory* that is final, victory that
swallows up all strife."

IV

Immediately, in trance, I was carried over land and sea to
some distant kingdom, and placed upon a triumphal car, amongst
companions crowned with laurel. The darkness of gathering
midnight, brooding over all the land, hid from us the mighty
crowds that were weaving restlessly about ourselves as a center:
30 we heard them, but saw them not. Tidings had arrived, within
an hour, of a grandeur that measured itself against centuries; too
full of pathos they were, too full of joy, to utter themselves by
other language than by tears, by restless anthems, and *Te
Deums* reverberated from the choirs and orchestras of earth.
These tidings we that sat upon the laureled car had it for our
privilege to publish amonst all nations. And already, by signs
audible through the darkness, by snortings and tramplings, our
angry horses, that knew no fear of fleshly weariness, upbraided
us with delay. Wherefore *was* it that we delayed? We waited
40 for a secret word, that should bear witness to the hope of nations
as now accomplished for ever. At midnight the secret word arrived; which word was—*Waterloo and Recovered Christendom!*
The dreadful word shone by its own light; before us it went;

high above our leaders' heads it rode, and spread a golden light
over the paths which we traversed. Every city, at the presence of
the secret word, threw open its gates. The rivers were conscious
as we crossed. All the forests, as we ran along their margins, shivered in homage to the secret word. And the darkness comprehended it.

Two hours after midnight we approached a mighty Minster.
Its gates, which rose to the clouds, were closed. But when the
dreadful word that rode before us reached them with its golden
light, silently they moved back upon their hinges; and at a 10
flying gallop our equipage entered the grand aisle of the cathedral. Headlong was our pace; and at every altar, in the little
chapels and oratories to the right hand and left of our course,
the lamps, dying or sickening, kindled anew in sympathy with
the secret word that was flying past. Forty leagues we might
have run in the cathedral, and as yet no strength of morning
light had reached us, when before us we saw the aerial galleries
of organ and choir. Every pinnacle of the fretwork, every station of advantage amongst the traceries, was crested by white-
robed choristers that sang deliverance; that wept no more 20
tears, as once their fathers had wept; but at intervals that sang
together to the generations, saying,

> "Chant the deliverer's praise in every tongue,"

and receiving answers from afar,

> "Such as once in heaven and earth were sung."

And of their chanting was no end; of our headlong pace was
neither pause nor slackening.

Thus as we ran like torrents—thus as we swept with bridal
rapture over the Campo Santo [12] of the cathedral graves—suddenly we became aware of a vast necropolis rising upon the 30
far-off horizon—a city of sepulchers, built within the saintly
cathedral for the warrior dead that rested from their feuds on
earth. Of purple granite was the necropolis; yet, in the first
minute, it lay like a purple stain upon the horizon, so mighty
was the distance. In the second minute it trembled through
many changes, growing into terraces and towers of wondrous
altitude, so mighty was the pace. In the third minute already,
with our dreadful gallop, we were entering its suburbs. Vast
sarcophagi rose on every side, having towers and turrets that,
upon the limits of the central aisle, strode forward with haughty 40
intrusion, that ran back with mighty shadows into answering
recesses. Every sarcophagus showed many bas-reliefs—bas-
reliefs of battles and of battle-fields; battles from forgotten ages,

12 cemetery (like that so called at Pisa)

battles from yesterday; battle-fields that, long since, nature
had healed and reconciled to herself with the sweet oblivion of
flowers; battle-fields that were yet angry and crimson with
carnage. Where the terraces ran, there did *we* run; where the
towers curved, there did *we* curve. With the flight of swallows
our horses swept round every angle. Like rivers in flood wheeling round headlands, like hurricanes that ride into the secrets of
forests, faster than ever light unwove the mazes of darkness, our
flying equipage carried earthly passions, kindled warrior in-
10 stincts, amongst the dust that lay around us—dust oftentimes
of our noble fathers that had slept in God from Créci to
Trafalgar. And now had we reached the last sarcophagus, now
were we abreast of the last bas-relief, already had we recovered the arrow-like flight of the illimitable central aisle, when
coming up this aisle to meet us we beheld afar off a female child,
that rode in a carriage as frail as flowers. The mists which went
before her hid the fawns that drew her, but could not hide the
shells and tropic flowers with which she played—but could not
hide the lovely smiles by which she uttered her trust in the
20 mighty cathedral, and in the cherubim that looked down upon
her from the mighty shafts of its pillars. Face to face she was
meeting us; face to face she rode, as if danger there were none.
"Oh, baby!" I exclaimed, "shalt thou be the ransom for Waterloo? Must we, that carry tidings of great joy to every people, be
messengers of ruin to thee!" In horror I rose at the thought; but
then aso, in horror at the thought, rose one that was sculptured
on a bas-relief—a Dying Trumpeter. Solemnly from the field of
battle he rose to his feet; and, unslinging his stony trumpet, carried it, in his dying anguish, to his stony lips—sounding once,
30 and yet once again; proclamation that, in *thy* ears, oh baby!
spoke from the battlements of death. Immediately deep shadows
fell between us, and aboriginal silence. The choir had ceased to
sing. The hoofs of our horses, the dreadful rattle of our harness,
the groaning of our wheels, alarmed the graves no more. By
horror the bas-relief had been unlocked unto life. By horror
we, that were so full of life, we men and our horses, with their
fiery fore-legs rising in mid air to their everlasting gallop, were
frozen to a bas-relief. Then a third time the trumpet sounded; the
seals were taken off all pulses; life, and the frenzy of life, tore into
40 their channels again; again the choir burst forth in sunny grandeur, as from the mufflings of storms and darkness; again the
thunderings of our horses carried temptation into the graves.
One cry burst from our lips, as the clouds, drawing off from the
aisle, showed it empty before us—"Whither has the infant fled?
—is the young child caught up to God?" Lo! afar off, in a vast
recess, rose three mighty windows to the clouds; and on a level

with their summits, at height insuperable to man, rose an altar of purest alabaster. On its eastern face was trembling a crimson glory. A glory was it from the reddening dawn that now streamed *through* the windows? Was it from the crimson robes of the martyrs painted *on* the windows? Was it from the bloody bas-reliefs of earth? There, suddenly, within that crimson radiance, rose the apparition of a woman's head, and then of a woman's figure. The child it was—grown up to woman's height. Clinging to the horns of the altar, voiceless she stood—sinking, rising, raving, despairing; and behind the volume of incense, that, night and day, streamed upwards from the altar, dimly was seen the fiery font, and the shadow of that dreadful being who should have baptized her with the baptism of death. But by her side was kneeling her better angel, that hid his face with wings; that wept and pleaded for *her;* that prayed when *she* could *not;* that fought with Heaven by tears for *her* deliverance; which also, as he raised his immortal countenance from his wings, I saw, by the glory in his eye, that from Heaven he had won at last.

V

Then was completed the passion of the mighty fugue. The golden tubes of the organ, which as yet had but muttered at intervals—gleaming amongst clouds and surges of incense— threw up, as from fountains unfathomable, columns of heart-shattering music. Choir and anti-choir were filling fast with un-known voices. Thou also, Dying Trumpeter, with thy love that was victorious, and thy anguish that was finishing, didst enter the tumult; trumpet and echo—farewell love, and farewell an-guish—rang through the dreadful *sanctus.* Oh, darkness of the grave! that from the crimson altar and from the fiery font wert visited and searched by the effulgence in the angel's eye—were these indeed thy children? Pomps of life, that, from the burials of centuries, rose again to the voice of perfect joy, did ye indeed mingle with the festivals of Death? Lo! as I looked back for seventy leagues through the mighty cathedral, I saw the quick and the dead that sang together to God, together that sang to the generations of man. All the hosts of jubilation, like armies that ride in pursuit, moved with one step. Us, that, with laureled heads, were passing from the cathedral, they overtook, and, as with a garment, they wrapped us round with thunders greater than our own. As brothers we moved together; to the dawn that advanced, to the stars that fled; rendering thanks to God in the highest—that, having hid His face through one generation be-hind thick clouds of War, once again was ascending, from the Campo Santo of Waterloo was ascending, in the visions of Peace;

rendering thanks for thee, young girl! whom having overshadowed with His ineffable passion of death, suddenly did God relent, suffered thy angel to turn aside His arm, and even in thee, sister unknown! shown to me for a moment only to be hidden for ever, found an occasion to glorify His goodness. A thousand times, amongst the phantoms of sleep, have I seen thee entering the gates of the golden dawn, with the secret word riding before thee, with the armies of the grave behind thee,—seen thee sinking, rising, raving, despairing; a thousand times in the worlds of sleep have seen thee followed by God's angel through storms, through desert seas, through the darkness of quicksands, through dreams and the dreadful revelations that are in dreams; only that at the last, with one sling of His victorious arm, He might snatch thee back from ruin, and might emblazon in thy deliverance the endless resurrections of His love!

THE VICTORIAN ERA

In 1832 was passed the Great Reform Bill, symptomatic of a new social and political system; in the same year died Sir Walter Scott, who for nearly forty years had been prolifically romanticizing in verse and prose. Byron, Shelley, Keats, Hazlitt, were all dead; Lamb and Coleridge had finished their work; Wordsworth lived on, but his poetic powers had long since burned themselves out. Meantime a gifted Scotchman named Carlyle had already produced several translations, biographies, and comments on the German literature in which he had steeped himself, and was, on a remote and bleak farm, contemplating a strange philosophy of clothes; an Oxford preacher, John Henry Newman, was becoming dissatisfied with the spiritual decline of his generation; a Cambridge undergraduate, one Alfred Tennyson, had published a volume of melodious verse (1830), which immensely delighted his college friends; and young Robert Browning was tracing the development of a soul ("little else is worth study") for the first time in his *Pauline* (pub. 1833). And in 1837 Victoria ascended that throne which she was so substantially to occupy for sixty-four years, and the Victorian age was politically and officially begun.

The age is so close to us that most of its great movements have continued with but slightly bated vigor to our own time; many of the ideas by which it was swayed, its pet fetishes and shibboleths, are those which still raise their voices in the land—and we still listen, or have just learned to turn a deaf ear. It was an industrial age (even as yours and mine). The factory system, a development of the industrial revolution, had made possible the cheap and rapid production of goods. Wealth had multiplied, and provided the means for new comforts and luxuries. The industrial age created an industrial plutocracy which became fastened upon western Europe and America, and by dividing the world on the levels of capital and labor fostered those class conflicts whose clashes are still resounding—to remedy all of which Russia is experimenting with a new social system. The extraordinary multiplication of mechanical processes produced an illusion of progress, a smug satisfaction in prosperity, efficiency, and speed. It is this "faith in machinery," with its ignoring of spiritual values, that called forth the anathemas of Carlyle, Ruskin, Arnold, and Morris. The same protests are heard from the lips of the idealists to-day. The need of new markets to absorb the vast production of industry was one force leading to the expansion of the British Empire in all parts of the world. Imperialism in politics naturally followed. Democracy was extended under the rule of the Middle Classes. Carlyle, irreconcilable reactionary, was highly suspicious of the democratic system, but the ordinary Britisher, proud of his country's achievements, was prone to believe his nation the freest and greatest on the globe. This attitude may be seen in Tennyson's patriotic poems, and in the jingoism surrounding Queen Victoria's Diamond Jubilee in 1897—against which Kipling uttered a solemn warning in his *Recessional*.

Akin to the vulgar faith in machinery was a blind faith in science. All the natural sciences showed in the nineteenth century such notable development

535

that men began to think there was no mystery which was not shortly to be solved. The new revelations in astronomy, geology, and biology, especially, questioned long-established beliefs and shook society. Astronomy, with such theories as La Place's nebular hypothesis (1825), began to speculate on the formation of the universe; Sir Charles Lyell's *Principles of Geology* (1830–3) showed that the earth had been formed by the slow operation of natural forces through incredibly long periods of time; while in biology, the theory of the evolution of all life from inferior forms had become generally accepted long before Charles Darwin fortified it, in his *Origin of Species* (1859), with his patiently accumulated mass of evidence, supplied it with a hypothesis to explain its operation which he termed "natural selection," and connected man with the process of evolution in the animal world. These revelations of science seemed to orthodox Christians to contradict the revealed story of creation as narrated in Genesis. The resultant controversy echoed throughout the century, and has not yet died away. Victorian literature from end to end is agitated by the disturbance in religion. Matthew Arnold's verse expresses the melancholy of one who felt the old faith gone, with nothing to take its place, Clough is now cynical, now witty, but always doubting, Huxley is militantly agnostic, Tennyson and others adopted after much uncertainty the "Victorian compromise" by which the old religion was made over and reinterpreted in the light of the new science. Only Browning, among the major figures, went on his way serenely unshaken in his buoyant optimism. One important group was thrown back into the arms of the medieval church. Beginning in 1833, the Oxford Movement, led by Newman, opposed the liberalism then active in Anglican thought, holding fast to apostolic succession, to the efficacy of the sacraments, and to ritualism; concluding eventually, in the case of Newman himself and many of his followers, that there was no middle ground between atheism and Catholicism, and finding consolation in the bosom of the Church of Rome (1845).

The serious agitation produced by the conflict of science and religion seems very characteristic of the Victorian age. It was deeply concerned about many things, and where it operated typically, grappled with its problems in the most tremendous earnestness. Surely it took itself very seriously. The humanitarianism which had been earlier aroused became a creed. Society felt an "awakened social conscience," a heavy sense of its responsibility toward its fellow man. The era saw the birth of many "uplift" movements, the extension of the social legislation already well advanced—all of which showed at any rate the will of society collectively to solve such problems as poverty and crime, to extend education, and to redress all kinds of social wrongs. These movements are still carrying on, with such projects as old age doles, unemployment insurance, and the like, and no end is in sight. The whole new "science" of sociology was born of such viewpoints as these. The writers did their part to help improve society, and there arose, following the example of such earlier works as Godwin's *Caleb Williams*, a whole literature of purpose, in which such novels as those of Dickens and Reade are important documents, calling attention now to conditions in poor houses, now in prisons, now in asylums, now in the schools, now in the tangle of the chancery courts, and crying aloud (and no doubt inartistically) for remedy. When even fiction could be so didactic, it is not strange that prose treatises often seem very heavy and preachy. The great line of Victorian prophets, which included Carlyle, Ruskin, Arnold, Morris, were constantly from their lay pulpits directing strenuous efforts toward cor-

recting abuses, striving to make mankind improve by showing him how bad
he was. The sermonizing attitude is habitual. It was indeed a moral age (at
least externally). The heavy Queen and her beloved consort set the style.
Family life was to be above reproach, the young were to be innocent and guilt-
less, the body was not to be exposed (or, indeed, talked about), and "Sex,"
which so obsesses every one to-day, was to be hushed up as something indecent.
It is especially this atmosphere of prudery and squeamishness which has
gathered about the connotations of the unspeakable epithet, "mid-Victorian."

Not every one, needless to say, accepted the conventional standards which
have just been sketched. As early as 1848, when Tennyson was completing his
In Memoriam, in which he so strenuously fought a battle with himself on
the grounds of religious doubt and the immortality of the soul, a group of
young painters including D. G. Rossetti, J. E. Millais, and Holman Hunt, who
called themselves the "Pre-Raphaelite Brotherhood," were rejecting conventional standards of art. The matter would be of only passing interest here,
except that the first of the group was also a poet, and he and his follower
Swinburne cared little for the sterile morality or the high didacticism of the
age. They were classed by their enemies as the "fleshly school" of poetry—a
slander which is hardly deserved, but they did seem shocking to their contemporaries; and they certainly practised art for art's sake and in no wise
considered themselves prophets to their generation. They set in motion an
important movement which was seriously to modify Victorianism at its end, and
shoot it off in directions that neither Queen Victoria, nor Tennyson, nor
Arnold, could possibly consider proper. Pater, who was a kind of Pre-Raphaelite
philosopher, in a notable utterance advocated experience as the end of life,
and counseled men to crowd into the awful brevity of these few days on earth
as many and as variegated sensations as possible. The æsthetes or decadents
who began to make themselves noticeable in the 1870's and who had quite a
vogue with their Yellow Book in the 1890's—the Oscar Wildes and the
Aubrey Beardsleys and their crew—listened to him, interpreting his doctrine
in ways that he could not have approved. They and others, the new realists, for
instance, who derived from Zola and the de Goncourts in France, and included
such novelists as Samuel Butler and George Gissing, were ending the Victorian
era in a way very different from that in which it began, and pointing very
definitely toward certain contemporary tendencies in the arts. So strongly did
new forces come into play in the 1890's that many would trace the modern
era from this date, and here write the end of that which we have learned to
consider as Victorianism, even though the long-lived Queen was still sitting
serenely on the throne, and the Prince of Wales had grown gray-haired with
waiting. In 1901 he at last became king as Edward VII, but his world was a
new world, and literature already a different instrument, whose story needs
elsewhere to be told.

The great poets of the Victorian era are Tennyson, Browning, and Arnold,
whose work receives abundant representation in this volume, and whose characteristics are later severally discussed. Of a lesser order, but still important, are
Mrs. Browning, Rossetti, Swinburne, and Morris. A host of minor figures crowd
an age in which everybody wrote. The greatest prose writers of the period
(down to 1890) are Macaulay (more a Victorian than a Romanticist), Carlyle,
Newman, Ruskin, Arnold, Huxley, Pater, and Stevenson. The drama, after
remaining at a low level for a long period, showed signs of revival with the
comedies of Tom Robertson (1860's), included the delightful musical bur-

lesques of Gilbert and Sullivan (1870's, 1880's), and then had a brilliant renascence in the 1890's, with the work of such men as Wilde, Pinero, and Shaw. It has remained to our own times a vital branch of literature.

Undoubtedly the most characteristic and perhaps the greatest literary form of Victorian times was the novel. The writers in this popular form were very numerous. Suffice it to mention here Charles Dickens, great as a humorist, as a sentimentalist, and as a novelist of purpose; Thackeray, of an art more subtle but less popular, with a strong satirical bent; George Eliot (Mary Ann Evans), who solemnly believed that one's life was what one's character made it; the Brontë sisters, who reverted to a more romantic style; George Meredith, master of the theory of comedy and exquisite stylist; and Thomas Hardy, who presents man helpless in the grip of fate, his life determined by a blind chance which he can neither direct nor avoid. The pessimism of the latter is one of the powerful notes of the decay of Victorian thought and the coming of the forces which herald a new day.

BIBLIOGRAPHY. Hugh Walker, *Literature in the Victorian Era* (Cambridge); G. Saintsbury, *Hist. of Nineteenth Cent. Lit.* (Macmillan); G. K. Chesterton, *The Victorian Age in Lit.* (Holt); Holbrook Jackson, *The Eighteen Nineties* (Knopf); W. L. Cross, *The Development of the English Novel* (Macmillan); W. C. Brownell, *Victorian Prose Masters* (Scribner's). Anthologies: G. B. Woods, *Poetry of the Victorian Period* (Scott Foresman); F. M. K. Foster and H. C. White, *Victorian Prose* (Prentice-Hall).

THOMAS CARLYLE (1795–1881)

Thomas Carlyle was born at Ecclefechan, Annandale, Scotland, on December 4, 1795, the son of a stone-mason. After some terms at Annan grammar school, in 1809 he walked the eighty miles to Edinburgh to enter the University. Here he spent some five rather unsatisfactory years, and left without taking a degree. Because of "grave moral doubts" he found himself unable to enter the ministry (for which he had been intended by his parents), and for several years tried school-teaching (1814–18). He also studied law, and acted as private tutor; but finally settled upon literature as a career. He had read much German literature and philosophy, finding in Novalis, in Goethe, and in Fichte a light to guide him through his spiritual crisis. Products of his interest in German are his translation of Goethe's *Wilhelm Meister* (1824), a *Life of Schiller* (1823–24), and essays on *Richter* and on *German Poetry*. The latter were published in the *Edinburgh Review*, which was opened to him through a friendship with its editor, Francis Jeffrey, and in which also appeared his essays on *Burns, Scott, Boswell's Johnson*, and his *Characteristics*.

In 1826 he married Jane Baillie Welsh, a woman almost as brilliant in her way as her husband, and in 1828 retired with her to Craigenputtock, a lonely farm in Dumfriesshire, fifteen miles from the nearest town. Here he lived for six years, and here he wrote *Sartor Resartus*, in which he at last found himself. This was published serially in *Fraser's Magazine* in 1833–34. In the latter year Carlyle removed to London, taking up his residence at 5 Cheyne Row, Chelsea, where he lived the rest of his life.

Settled in Chelsea, he went to work on his *French Revolution*. The first volume of this work, while lent in MS. to J. S. Mill, was accidentally burned, but Carlyle courageously rewrote it. Its publication in 1837 established his reputation. Between 1837 and 1840 he delivered several series of lectures in London, the best known of which is *Heroes and Hero-Worship* (published in book form in 1841). Meanwhile he had been turning his attention largely to social and political problems, as seen in his *Past and Present* (1843), and *Latter-Day Pamphlets* (1850). Biography also occupied him, his outstanding works in this field being *Letters and Speeches of Oliver Cromwell*, with "elucidations" (1845), *The Life of John Sterling* (1851), and the monumental *History of Frederick the Great*, in six volumes (1858–1865). In 1865 he was elected Lord Rector of the University of Edinburgh, delivering a stirring address at his inauguration.

While he was absent to receive this honor, a heavy blow fell on him in the death of his wife. The two had greatly loved each other, although their life had not been a happy one, and Mrs. Carlyle especially had suffered from Carlyle's absorption in his work, his irritability, and his ill health (he had been a sufferer from dyspepsia all his life). The realization of these facts, after his wife's death, plunged Carlyle into depths of remorse.

Carlyle had early formed a friendship with Emerson, who had visited him at Craigenputtock. At Chelsea he was visited by many famous persons from England and America, and in his old age was regarded as a seer by the younger generation of literary men. Such distinguished writers as Browning, Thackeray, Dickens, Kingsley, Tennyson, and Ruskin, were his friends or disciples. The later years of his life were unproductive. He died on February 5, 1881, and was buried at Ecclefechan.

The selections in this volume do not include his biographical and historical work, or his literary criticism, but do present most of the characteristic doctrines which he energetically preached, and by means of which he influenced profoundly the thought of his time. Here will be found his distrust of the mechanical and material and his faith in the spiritual, his dislike of democracy and his belief that the world should reverently accept the rule of its great men, his gospel of labor and self-sacrifice, his pleas for sincerity and mutual sympathy. His vivid, impassioned, and explosive style is also fully displayed.

BIBLIOGRAPHY. Standard ed. of Carlyle's complete works, The Centenary, 30 vols. (Scribner's). Excellent eds. of *Sartor Resartus* and *Heroes and Hero-Worship* by A. Macmechan in Athenæum Press ser. (Ginn); also Everyman's Lib. J. A. Froude, the authorized biographer, ed. Carlyle's *Reminiscences* and pub. his *Life*. A full *Life* by David Alec Wilson, 5 vols. (Dutton). Short lives by Richard Garnett (Great Writers ser.) and by John Nichol (Eng. Men of Letters ser.) Valuable introduction: Bliss Perry, *Carlyle: How to Know Him* (Bobbs Merrill).

SARTOR RESARTUS

The title means "The Tailor Mended." In this work Carlyle, in a transparent hoax, purports to give an account of Diogenes Teufelsdröckh ("God-born Devil's Dung"), Professor *der Allerlei-Wissenschaft* ("things in general") in the University of *Weissnichtwo* ("Know-not-where"), and his great work on *Die Kleider, ihr Werden und Wirken* ("Clothes, their Origin and Influence"). In the first book he introduces the imaginary volume, describes the author and his haunts in the German city of Weissnichtwo, and develops in a general way the philosophy of clothes. In the second book he gives us the autobiography of the German scholar. The lack of systematic arrangement is humorously explained as being due to the formlessness of the autobiographic material, the data having been supplied the editor in miscellaneous sheets and notes, stuffed in six paper bags, each sealed with a sign of the zodiac. The experiences of Teufelsdröckh—his education, his love, and his spiritual crisis (Chapters VII to IX) represent in general the experiences of Carlyle. In Book III he proceeds to a further application of the clothes-philosophy to the world and its problems. The finest section of this third book is the chapter on "Natural Supernaturalism." Important portions of all three books are here reprinted.

BOOK I

CHAPTER VIII

The World Out of Clothes

IF in the Descriptive-Historical portion of this Volume, Teufelsdröckh, discussing merely the *Werden* (Origin and successive Improvement) of Clothes, has astonished many a reader, much more will he in the Speculative-Philosophical portion, which treats of their *Wirken,* or Influences. It is here that the present Editor first feels the pressure of his task; for here properly the higher and new Philosophy of Clothes commences: an untried, almost inconceivable region, or chaos; in venturing upon which, how difficult, yet how unspeakably important is it
10 to know what course, of survey and conquest, is the true one; where the footing is firm substance and will bear us, where it is hollow, or mere cloud, and may engulf us! Teufelsdröckh undertakes no less than to expound the moral, political, even religious Influences of Clothes; he undertakes to make manifest, in its thousandfold bearings, this grand Proposition, that Man's earthly interests "are all hooked and buttoned together, and held up, by Clothes." He says in so many words, "Society is founded upon Cloth"; and again "Society sails through the Infinitude on Cloth, as on a Faust's Mantle,[1] or rather like the Sheet of clean
20 and unclean beasts in the Apostle's Dream;[2] and without such Sheet or Mantle, would sink to endless depths, or mount to inane limboes, and in either case be no more."

By what chains, or indeed infinitely complected tissues, of Meditation this grand Theorem is here unfolded, and innumerable practical Corollaries are drawn therefrom, it were perhaps a mad ambition to attempt exhibiting. Our Professor's method is not, in any case, that of common school Logic, where the truths all stand in a row, each holding by the skirts of the other; but at best that of practical Reason, proceeding by large Intuition over
30 whole systematic groups and kingdoms; whereby, we might say,

1 bearing Faust through the air   2 Acts x 10-16

a noble complexity, almost like that of Nature, reigns in his Philosophy, or spiritual Picture of Nature: a mighty maze, yet as faith whispers, not without a plan. Nay we complained above, that a certain ignoble complexity, what we must call mere confusion, was also discernible. Often, also, we have to exclaim: Would to Heaven those same Biographical Documents were come! For it seems as if the demonstration lay much in the Author's individuality; as if it were not Argument that had taught him, but Experience. At present it is only in local glimpses, and by significant fragments, picked often at wide-enough intervals from the original Volume, and carefully collated, that we can hope to impart some outline or foreshadow of this Doctrine. Readers of any intelligence are once more invited to favor us with their most concentrated attention: let these, after intense consideration, and not till then, pronounce, Whether on the utmost verge of our actual horizon there is not a looming as of Land; a promise of new Fortunate Islands, perhaps whole undiscovered Americas, for such as have canvas to sail thither?— As exordium to the whole, stand here the following long citation:

"With men of a speculative turn," writes Teufelsdröckh, "there come seasons, meditative, sweet, yet awful hours, when in wonder and fear you ask yourself that unanswerable question: Who am I; the thing that can say 'I' (*das Wesen das sich* Ich *nennt*)? The world, with its loud trafficking, retires into the distance; and, through the paper-hangings, and stone-walls, and thick-plied tissues of Commerce and Polity, and all the living and lifeless integuments (of Society and a Body), wherewith your Existence sits surrounded,—the sight reaches forth into the void Deep, and you are alone with the Universe, and silently commune with it, as one mysterious Presence with another.

"Who am I; what is this ME? A Voice, a Motion, an Appearance;—some embodied, visualized Idea in the Eternal Mind? *Cogito, ergo sum*.[3] Alas, poor Cogitator, this takes us but a little way. Sure enough, I am; and lately was not: but Whence? How? Whereto? The answer lies around, written in all colors and motions, uttered in all tones of jubilee and wail, in thousand-figured, thousand-voiced, harmonious Nature: but where is the cunning eye and ear to whom that God-written Apocalypse will yield articulate meaning? We sit as in a boundless Phantasmagoria and Dream-grotto; boundless, for the faintest star, the remotest century, lies not even nearer the verge thereof: sounds and many-colored visions flit round our sense; but Him, the Unslumbering, whose work both Dream and Dreamer are, we see not; except in rare half-waking moments, suspect not. Creation, says one, lies before us, like a glorious Rainbow; but the Sun

3 Famous utterance of the French philosopher René Descartes (1596–1650).

that made it lies behind us, hidden from us. Then, in that strange Dream, how we clutch at shadows as if they were substances; and sleep deepest while fancying ourselves most awake! Which of your Philosophical Systems is other than a dream-theorem; a net quotient, confidently given out, where divisor and dividend are both unknown? What are all your national Wars, with their Moscow Retreats, and sanguinary hate-filled Revolutions, but the Somnambulism of uneasy Sleepers? This Dreaming, this Somnambulism is what we on Earth call Life; wherein the most 10 indeed undoubtingly wander, as if they knew right hand from left; yet they only are wise who know that they know nothing.

"Pity that all Metaphysics had hitherto proved so inexpressibly unproductive! The secret of Man's Being is still like the Sphinx's secret: a riddle that he cannot rede; and for ignorance of which he suffers death, the worst death, a spiritual. What are your Axioms, and Categories, and Systems, and Aphorisms? Words, words. High Air-castles are cunningly built of Words, the Words well bedded also in good Logic-mortar, wherein, however, no Knowledge will come to lodge. *The whole* 20 *is greater than the part:* how exceedingly true! *Nature abhors a vacuum:* how exceedingly false and calumnious! Again, *Nothing can act but where it is:* with all my heart; only, WHERE is it? Be not the slave of Words: is not the Distant, the Dead, while I love it, and long for it, and mourn for it, Here, in the genuine sense, as truly as the floor I stand on? But that same WHERE, with its brother WHEN, are from the first the master-colors of our Dream-grotto; say rather, the Canvas (the warp and woof thereof) whereon all our Dreams and Life-visions are painted. Nevertheless, has not a deeper meditation 30 taught certain of every climate and age, that the WHERE and WHEN, so mysteriously inseparable from all our thoughts, are but superficial terrestrial adhesions to thought; that the Seer may discern them where they mount up out of the celestial EVERYWHERE and FOREVER: have not all nations conceived their God as Omnipresent and Eternal; as existing in a universal HERE, an everlasting Now? Think well, thou too wilt find that Space is but a mode of our human Sense, so likewise Time; there *is* no Space and no Time: WE are—we know not what;—light-sparkles floating in the æther of Deity!

40 "So that this so solid-seeming World, after all, were but an air-image, our ME the only reality: and Nature, with its thousandfold production and destruction, but the reflex of our own inward Force, the 'phantasy of our Dream'; or what the Earth-Spirit in *Faust* names it, *the living visible Garment of God:*

'In Being's floods, in Action's storm,
I walk and work, above, beneath,
Work and weave in endless motion!
    Birth and Death,
    An infinite ocean;
    A seizing and giving
    The fire of Living:
'Tis thus at the roaring Loom of Time I ply,
And weave for God the Garment thou seest Him by.'

Of twenty millions that have read and spouted this thunder-
speech of the *Erdgeist,* are there yet twenty units of us that
have learned the meaning thereof?

"It was in some such mood, when wearied and fordone with
these high speculations, that I first came upon the question of
Clothes. Strange enough, it strikes me, is this same fact of there
being Tailors and Tailored. The Horse I ride has his own
whole fell: strip him of the girths and flaps and extraneous tags
I have fastened round him, and the noble creature is his own
sempster and weaver and spinner; nay his own bootmaker,
jeweller, and man-milliner; he bounds free through the valleys,
with a perennial rain-proof court-suit on his body; wherein
warmth and easiness of fit have reached perfection; nay, the
graces also have been considered, and frills and fringes, with
gay variety of color, featly appended, and ever in the right
place, are not wanting. While I—good Heaven!—have thatched
myself over with the dead fleeces of sheep, the bark of vege-
tables, the entrails of worms, the hides of oxen or seals, the felt
of furred beasts; and walk abroad a moving Rag-screen, over-
heaped with shreds and tatters raked from the Charnel-house
of Nature, where they would have rotted, to rot on me more
slowly! Day after day, I must thatch myself anew; day after
day, this despicable thatch must lose some film of its thickness;
some film of it, frayed away by tear and wear, must be
brushed-off into the Ashpit, into the Laystall; [4] till by degrees
the whole has been brushed thither, and I, the dust-making,
patent Rag-grinder, get new material to grind down. O subter-
brutish! [5] vile! most vile! For have not I too a compact all-
enclosing Skin, whiter or dingier? Am I a botched mass of
tailors' and cobblers' shreds, then; or a tightly-articulated,
homogeneous little Figure, automatic, nay alive?

"Strange enough how creatures of the human-kind shut their
eyes to plainest facts; and by the mere inertia of Oblivion and
Stupidity, live at ease in the midst of Wonders and Terrors.

4 rubbish pit   5 lower than brutish

But indeed man is, and was always, a blockhead and dullard;
much readier to feel and digest, than to think and consider.
Prejudice, which he pretends to hate, is his absolute lawgiver;
mere use-and-wont everywhere leads him by the nose; thus let
but a Rising of the Sun, let but a Creation of the World happen
twice, and it ceases to be marvelous, to be noteworthy, or noticeable. Perhaps not once in a lifetime does it occur to your
ordinary biped, of any country or generation, be he gold-
mantled Prince or russet-jerkined Peasant, that his Vestments
10 and his Self are not one and indivisible; that *he* is naked, without vestments, till he buy or steal such, and by forethought sew
and button them.

"For my own part, these considerations, of our Clothes-
thatch, and how, reaching inwards even to our heart of hearts,
it tailorizes and demoralizes us, fill me with a certain horror at
myself and mankind; almost as one feels at those Dutch Cows,
which, during the wet season, you see grazing deliberately with
jackets and petticoats (of striped sacking), in the meadows of
Gouda. Nevertheless there is something great in the moment
20 when a man first strips himself of adventitious wrappages; and
sees indeed that he is naked, and, as Swift has it, 'a forked
straddling animal with bandy legs'; yet also a Spirit, and unutterable Mystery of Mysteries."

CHAPTER IX

Adamatism

". . . Often in my atrabiliar [6] moods, when I read of pompous
ceremonials, Frankfort [7] Coronations, Royal Drawing-rooms,
Levees, Couchees [8]; and how the ushers and macers and pur-
suivants are all in waiting; how Duke this is presented by
Archduke that, and Colonel A by General B, and innumerable
Bishops, Admirals, and miscellaneous Functionaries, are ad-
30 vancing gallantly to the Anointed Presence; and I strive, in my
remote privacy, to form a clear picture of that solemnity,—on
a sudden, as by some enchanter's wand, the—shall I speak it?
—the Clothes fly off the whole dramatic corps; and Dukes,
Grandees, Bishops, Generals, Anointed Presence itself, every
mother's son of them, stand straddling there, not a shirt on
them; and I know not whether to laugh or weep. This physical
or psychical infirmity, in which perhaps I am not singular, I
have, after hesitation, thought right to publish, for the solace
of those afflicted with the like."

6 melancholy
7 where the emperors were crowned
8 formal receptions on rising or going to bed (like those given by Louis XIV)

Would to Heaven, say we, thou hadst thought right to keep it secret! Who is there now that can read the five columns of Presentations in his Morning Newspaper without a shudder? Hypochondriac men, and all men are to a certain extent hypochondriac, should be more gently treated. With what readiness our fancy, in this shattered state of the nerves, follows out the consequences which Teufelsdröckh, with a devilish coolness, goes on to draw:

"What would Majesty do, could such an accident befall in reality; should the buttons all simultaneously start, and the solid wool evaporate, in very Deed, as here in Dream? *Ach Gott!* How each skulks into the nearest hiding-place; their high State Tragedy (*Haupt- und Staats-Action*) becomes a Pickleherring [9]-Farce to weep at, which is the worst kind of Farce; *the tables* (according to Horace), and with them, the whole fabric of Government, Legislation, Property, Police, and Civilized Society, *are dissolved*, in wails and howls."

Lives the man that can figure a naked Duke of Windlestraw addressing a naked House of Lords? Imagination, choked as in mephitic air, recoils on itself, and will not forward with the picture. The Woolsack,[10] the Ministerial, the Opposition Benches—*infandum!* [11] *infandum!* And yet why is the thing impossible? Was not every soul, or rather every body, of these Guardians of our Liberties, naked, or nearly so, last night; "a forked Radish with a head fantastically carved"? And why might he not, did our stern fate so order it, walk out to St. Stephen's, as well as into bed, in that no-fashion; and there, with other similar Radishes, hold a Bed of Justice? "Solace of those afflicted with the like!" Unhappy Teufelsdröckh, had man ever such a "physical or psychical infirmity" before? And now how many, perhaps, may thy unparalleled confession (which we, even to the sounder British world, and goaded-on by Critical and Biographical duty, grudge to re-impart) incurably infect therewith! Art thou the malignest of Sansculottists,[12] or only the maddest?

"It will remain to be examined," adds the inexorable Teufelsdröckh, "in how far the SCARECROW, as a Clothed Person, is not also entitled to benefit of clergy, and English trial by jury: nay perhaps, considering his high function (for is not he too a Defender of Property, and Sovereign armed wth the *terrors* of the Law?), to a certain royal Immunity and Inviolability; which, however, misers and the meaner class of persons are not

---

9 name of a fool in old farces
10 seat of the Lord Chancellor of England in the House of Lords

11 unspeakable
12 The name "Sansculotte" or "one without breeches" was derisively given by the aristocrats at

the time of the French Revolution to the extreme republicans, who had rejected short breeches as aristocratic dress.

always voluntarily disposed to grant him." * * * "O my Friends, we are (in Yorick Sterne's words) but as 'turkeys driven with a stick and red clout, to the market' [13]: or if some drivers, as they do in Norfolk, take a dried bladder and put peas in it, the rattle thereof terrifies the boldest!"

BOOK II

CHAPTER VII

The Everlasting No

UNDER the strange nebulous envelopment, wherein our Professor has now shrouded himself, no doubt but his spiritual nature is nevertheless progressive, and growing: for how can the "Son of Time," in any case, stand still? We behold him,
10 through those dim years, in a state of crisis, of transition: his mad Pilgrimings, and general solution into aimless Discontinuity, what is all this but a mad Fermentation; wherefrom, the fiercer it is, the clearer product will one day evolve itself?

Such transitions are ever full of pain: thus the Eagle when he molts is sickly; and, to attain his new beak, must harshly dash-off the old one upon rocks. What Stoicism soever our Wanderer, in his individual acts and motions, may affect, it is clear that there is a hot fever of anarchy and misery raging within; coruscations of which flash out: as, indeed, how could
20 there be other? Have we not seen him disappointed, bemocked of Destiny, through long years? All that the young heart might desire and pray for has been denied; nay, as in the last worst instance, offered and then snatched away. Ever an "excellent Passivity"; but of useful, reasonable Activity, essential to the former as Food to Hunger, nothing granted: till at length, in this wild Pilgrimage, he must forcibly seize for himself an Activity, though useless, unreasonable. Alas, his cup of bitterness, which had been filling drop by drop, ever since that first "ruddy morning" in the Hinterschlag Gymnasium, was at the
30 very lip; and then with that poison-drop, of the Towgood-and-Blumine business,[14] it runs over, and even hisses over in a deluge of foam.

He himself says once, with more justice than originality: "Man is, properly speaking, based upon Hope, he has no other possession but Hope; this world of his is emphatically the Place of Hope." What, then, was our Professor's possession? We see

---

13 utterance of Yorick in Laurence Sterne's *Tristram Shandy*

14 referring to Book II Chapters 3 and 5, concerning Teufelsdröckh's education and love

him, for the present, quite shut out from Hope; looking not into
the golden orient, but vaguely all round into a dim copper
firmament, pregnant with earthquake and tornado.

Alas, shut-out from Hope, in a deeper sense than we yet
dream of! For, as he wanders wearisomely through this world,
he has now lost all tidings of another and higher. Full of religion, or at least of religiosity, as our Friend has since exhibited
himself, he hides not that, in those days, he was wholly irre-
ligious: "Doubt had darkened into Unbelief," says he; "shade
after shade goes grimly over your soul, till you have the fixed,
starless, Tartarean black." To such readers as have reflected,
what can be called reflecting, on man's life, and happily discovered, in contradiction to much Profit-and-Loss Philosophy,
speculative and practical, that Soul is *not* synonymous with
Stomach; who understand, therefore, in our Friend's words,
"that, for man's well-being, Faith is properly the one thing
needful; how, with it, Martyrs, otherwise weak, can cheerfully
endure the shame and the cross; and without it, Worldlings
puke-up their sick existence, by suicide, in the midst of luxury": to such it will be clear that, for a pure moral nature, the
loss of his religious Belief was the loss of everything. Unhappy
young man! All wounds, the crush of long-continued Destitu-
tion, the stab of false Friendship and of false Love, all wounds
in thy so genial heart, would have healed again, had not its
life-warmth been withdrawn. Well might he exclaim, in his wild
way: "Is there no God, then; but at best an absentee God, sitting idle, ever since the first Sabbath, at the outside of his Universe, and *see*ing it go? Has the word Duty no meaning; is
what we call Duty no divine Messenger and Guide, but a false
earthly Fantasm, made-up of Desire and Fear, of emanations
from the Gallows and from Dr. Graham's Celestial Bed? [15]
Happiness of an approving Conscience! Did not Paul of Tarsus,
whom admiring men have since named Saint, feel that *he* was
'the chief of sinners'; and Nero of Rome, jocund in spirit
(*wohlgemuth*), spend much of his time in fiddling? Foolish
Word-monger and Motive-grinder, who in thy Logic-mill hast
an earthly mechanism for the Godlike itself, and wouldst fain
grind me out Virtue from the husks of Pleasure,—I tell thee,
Nay! To the unregenerate Prometheus Vinctus [16] of a man, it
is ever the bitterest aggravation of his wretchedness that he is
conscious of Virtue, that he feels himself the victim not of suffering only, but of injustice. What then? Is the heroic inspiration we name Virtue but some Passion; some bubble of the
blood, bubbling in the direction others *profit* by? I know not:

15 Dr. James Graham   quack, who invented a   of sterility
(1745-94), a fashionable   "celestial bed" for the cure   16 Prometheus Bound

only this I know, If what thou namest Happiness be our true aim, then are we all astray. With Stupidity and sound Digestion man may front much. But what, in these dull unimaginative days, are the terrors of Conscience to the diseases of the Liver! Not on Morality, but on Cookery, let us build our stronghold: there brandishing our frying-pan, as censer, let us offer sweet incense to the Devil, and live at ease on the fat things *he* has provided for his Elect!"

Thus has the bewildered Wanderer to stand, as so many have done, shouting question after question into the Sibyl-cave of Destiny, and receive no Answer but an Echo.[17] It is all a grim Desert, this once-fair world of his; wherein is heard only the howling of wild-beasts, or the shrieks of despairing, hate-filled men; and no Pillar of Cloud by day, and no Pillar of Fire by night, any longer guides the Pilgrim. To such length has the spirit of Inquiry carried him. "But what boots it (*was thut's*)?" cries he: "it is but the common lot in this era. Not having come to spiritual majority prior to the *Siècle de Louis Quinze*,[18] and not being born purely a Loghead (*Dummkopf*), thou hast no other outlook. The whole world is, like thee, sold to Unbelief; their old Temples of the Godhead, which for long have not been rainproof, crumble down; and men ask now: Where is the Godhead; our eyes never saw him?"

Pitiful enough were it, for all these wild utterances, to call our Diogenes wicked. Unprofitable servants as we all are, perhaps at no era of his life was he more decisively the Servant of Goodness, the Servant of God, than even now when doubting God's existence. "One circumstance I note," says he: "after all the nameless woe that Inquiry, which for me, what it is not always, was genuine Love of Truth, had wrought me, I nevertheless still loved Truth, and would bate no jot of my allegiance to her. 'Truth!' I cried, 'though the Heavens crush me for following her: no Falsehood! though a whole celestial Lubberland were the price of Apostasy.' In conduct it was the same. Had a divine Messenger from the clouds, or miraculous Handwriting on the wall, convincingly proclaimed to me *This thou shalt do*, with what passionate readiness, as I often thought, would I have done it, had it been leaping into the infernal Fire. Thus, in spite of all Motive-grinders, and Mechanical Profit-and-Loss Philosophies, with the sick ophthalmia and hallucination they had brought on, was the Infinite nature of Duty still dimly present to me: living without God in the world, of God's light I was not utterly bereft; if my as yet sealed eyes, with their unspeakable longing, could nowhere see Him, nevertheless in

17 as in *Æneid*, Book vi   (time of the growth of ra-
18 Century of Louis XV   tionalistic philosophy)

my heart He was present, and His heaven-written Law still stood legible and sacred there."

Meanwhile, under all these tribulations, and temporal and spiritual destitutions, what must the Wanderer, in his silent soul, have endured! "The painfullest feeling," writes he, "is that of your own Feebleness (*Unkraft*); ever, as the English Milton says, to be weak is the true misery. And yet of your Strength there is and can be no clear feeling, save by what you have prospered in, by what you have done. Between vague wavering Capability and fixed indubitable Performance, what a difference! A certain inarticulate Self-consciousness dwells dimly in us; which only our Works can render articulate and decisively discernible. Our Works are the mirror wherein the spirit first sees its natural lineaments. Hence, too, the folly of that impossible Precept, *Know thyself* [19]; till it be translated into this partially possible one, *Know what thou canst work at*.

"But for me, so strangely unprosperous had I been, the net-result of my Workings amounted as yet simply to—Nothing. How then could I believe in my Strength, when there was as yet no mirror to see it in? Ever did this agitating, yet, as I now perceive, quite frivolous question, remain to me insoluble: Hast thou a certain Faculty, a certain Worth, such even as the most have not; or art thou the completest Dullard of these modern times? Alas! the fearful Unbelief is unbelief in yourself; and how could I believe? Had not my first, last Faith in myself, when even to me the Heavens seemed laid open, and I dared to love, been all-too cruelly belied? The speculative Mystery of Life grew ever more mysterious to me: neither in the practical Mystery had I made the slightest progress, but been everywhere buffeted, foiled, and contemptuously cast out. A feeble unit in the middle of a threatening Infinitude, I seemed to have nothing given me but eyes, whereby to discern my own wretchedness. Invisible yet impenetrable walls, as of Enchantment, divided me from all living: was there, in the wide world, any true bosom I could press trustfully to mine? O Heaven, No, there was none! I kept a lock upon my lips: why should I speak much with that shifting variety of so-called Friends, in whose withered, vain and too-hungry souls Friendship was but an incredible tradition? In such cases, your resource is to talk little, and that little mostly from the Newspapers. Now when I look back, it was a strange isolation I then lived in. The men and women around me, even speaking with me, were but Figures; I had, practically, forgotten that they were alive, that they were not merely automatic. In midst of their crowded streets

19 maxim of Solon inscribed over the portico of the temple at Delphi; adopted as one of the principles of Socrates

and assemblages, I walked solitary; and (except as it was my own heart, not another's, that I kept devouring) savage also, as the tiger in his jungle. Some comfort it would have been, could I, like a Faust, have fancied myself tempted and tormented of the Devil; for a Hell, as I imagine, without Life, though only diabolic Life, were more frightful: but in our age of Down-pulling and Disbelief, the very Devil has been pulled down, you cannot so much as believe in a Devil. To me the Universe was all void of Life, of Purpose, of Volition, even of 10 Hostility: it was one huge, dead, immeasurable Steam-engine, rolling on, in its dead indifference, to grind me limb from limb. O, the vast, gloomy, solitary Golgotha, and Mill of Death! Why was the Living banished thither companionless, conscious? Why, if there is no Devil; nay, unless the Devil is your God?"

A prey incessantly to such corrosions, might not, moreover, as the worst aggravation to them, the iron constitution even of a Teufelsdröckh threaten to fail? We conjecture that he has known sickness; and, in spite of his locomotive habits, perhaps sickness of the chronic sort. Hear this, for example: "How beautiful to die 20 of broken-heart, on Paper! Quite another thing in practice; every window of your Feeling, even of your Intellect, as it were, begrimed and mud-bespattered, so that no pure ray can enter; a whole Drugshop in your inwards; the fordone soul drowning slowly in quagmires of Disgust!"

Putting all which external and internal miseries together, may we not find in the following sentences, quite in our Professor's still vein, significance enough? "From Suicide a certain aftershine (*Nachschein*) of Christianity withheld me: perhaps also a certain indolence of character; for, was not that a remedy I had at 30 any time within reach? Often, however, was there a question present to me: Should some one now, at the turning of that corner, blow thee suddenly out of Space, into the other World, or other No-World, by pistol-shot,—how were it? On which ground, too, I have often, in sea-storms and sieged cities and other death-scenes, exhibited an imperturbability, which passed, falsely enough, for courage,"

"So had it lasted," concludes the Wanderer, "so had it lasted, as in bitter protracted Death-agony, through long years. The heart within me, unvisited by any heavenly dewdrop, was smol- 40 dering in sulphurous, slow-consuming fire. Almost since earliest memory I had shed no tear; or once only when I, murmuring half-audibly, recited Faust's Deathsong, that wild *Selig der den er im Siegesglanze findet* (Happy whom *he* finds in Battle's splendor), and thought that of this last Friend even I was not forsaken, that Destiny itself could not doom me not to die. Having no hope, neither had I any definite fear, were it of Man or of Devil: nay, I often felt as if it might be solacing, could the Arch-Devil himself, though in Tartarean terrors, but rise to me, that I might tell him in a little of my mind. And yet, strangely enough, I lived in a continual, indefinite, pining fear; tremulous, pusillanimous, apprehensive of I knew not what: it seemed as if all things in the Heavens above and the Earth beneath would hurt me; as if the Heavens and the Earth were but boundless jaws of a devouring monster, wherein I, palpitating, waited to be devoured.

"Full of such humor, and perhaps the miserablest man in the whole French Capital or Suburbs, was I, one sultry Dog-day, after much perambulation, toiling along the dirty little *Rue Saint-Thomas de l'Enfer*,[20] among civic rubbish enough, in a close atmosphere, and over pavements hot as Nebuchadnezzar's Furnace; whereby doubtless my spirits were little cheered; when, all at once, there rose a Thought in me, and I asked myself: 'What *art* thou afraid of? Wherefore, like a coward, dost thou forever pip and whimper, and go cowering and trembling? Despicable biped! what is the sum-total of the worst that lies before thee? Death? Well, Death; and say the pangs of Tophet too, and all that the Devil and Man may, will, or can do against thee! Hast thou not a heart; canst thou not suffer whatsoever it be; and, as a Child of Freedom, though outcast, trample Tophet itself under thy feet, while it consumes thee? Let it come, then; I will meet it and defy it!' And as I so thought, there rushed like a stream of fire over my whole soul; and I shook base Fear away from me forever. I was strong, of unknown strength; a spirit, almost a god. Ever from that time, the temper of my misery was changed: not Fear or whining Sorrow was it, but Indignation and grim fire-eyed Defiance.

"Thus had the EVERLASTING No (*das ewige Nein*) pealed authoritatively through all the recesses of my Being, of my ME; and then was it that my whole ME stood up, in native God-created majesty, and with emphasis recorded its Protest. Such a Protest, the most important transaction in Life, may that same Indignation and Defiance, in a psychological point of view, be fitly called. The Everlasting No had said: 'Behold, thou art fatherless, outcast, and the Universe is mine (the Devil's)'; to which my whole Me now made answer: '*I* am not thine, but Free, and forever hate thee!'

"It is from this hour that I incline to date my Spiritual New-birth, or Baphometic [21] Fire-baptism; perhaps I directly thereupon began to be a Man."

---

20 The experience occurred to Carlyle in 1821 in Leith Walk, Edinburgh.

21 from the symbol or idol that the Templars were accused of worshiping

CHAPTER IX

The Everlasting Yea

"TEMPTATIONS in the Wilderness!" exclaims Teufelsdröckh. "Have we not all to be tried with such? Not so easily can the old Adam, lodged in us by birth, be dispossessed. Our Life is compassed round with Necessity; yet is the meaning of Life itself no other than Freedom, than Voluntary Force: thus have we a warfare; in the beginning, especially, a hard-fought battle. For the God-given mandate, *Work thou in Welldoing,* lies mysteriously written, in Promethean Prophetic Characters, in our hearts; and leaves us no rest, night or day, till it be deciphered and
10 obeyed; till it burn forth, in our conduct, a visible, acted Gospel of Freedom. And as the clay-given mandate, *Eat thou and be filled,* at the same time persuasively proclaims itself through every nerve,—must not there be a confusion, a contest, before the better Influence can become the upper?

"To me nothing seems more natural than that the Son of Man, when such God-given mandate first prophetically stirs within him, and the Clay must now be vanquished or vanquish, —should be carried of the spirit into grim Solitudes, and there fronting the Tempter do grimmest battle with him; defiantly
20 setting him at naught, till he yield and fly. Name it as we choose: with or without visible Devil, whether in the natural Desert of rocks and sands, or in the populous moral Desert of selfishness and baseness,—to such Temptation are we all called. Unhappy if we are not! Unhappy if we are but Half-men, in whom that divine handwriting has never blazed forth, all-subduing, in true sunsplendor; but quivers dubiously amid meaner lights: or smolders, in dull pain, in darkness, under earthly vapors!—Our Wilderness is the wide World in an Atheistic Century; our Forty Days are long years of suffering and fasting: nevertheless, to
30 these also comes an end. Yes, to me also was given, if not Victory, yet the consciousness of Battle, and the resolve to persevere therein while life or faculty is left. To me also, entangled in the enchanted forests, demon-peopled, doleful of sight and of sound, it was given after weariest wanderings, to work out my way into the higher sunlit slopes—of that Mountain which has no summit, or whose summit is in Heaven only!"

He says elsewhere, under a less ambitious figure; as figures are, once for all, natural to him: "Has not thy Life been that of most sufficient men (*tüchtigen Männer*) thou hast known in this
40 generation? An outflush of foolish young Enthusiasm, like the first fallow-crop, wherein are as many weeds as valuable herbs:

this all parched away, under the Droughts of practical and spiritual Unbelief, as Disappointment, in thought and act, often-repeated gave rise to Doubt, and Doubt gradually settled into Denial! If I have had a second-crop, and now see the perennial greensward, and sit under umbrageous cedars, which defy all Drought (and Doubt); herein too, be the Heavens praised, I am not without examples, and even exemplars."

So that, for Teufelsdröckh also, there has been a "glorious revolution": these mad shadow-hunting and shadow-hunted Pilgrimings of his were but some purifying "Temptation in the Wilderness," before his apostolic work (such as it was) could begin; which Temptation is now happily over, and the Devil once more worsted! Was "that high moment in the *Rue de l'Enfer,*" then, properly the turning-point of the battle; when the Fiend said, *Worship me or be torn in shreds;* and was answered valiantly with an *Apage Satana?* [22]—Singular Teufelsdröckh, would thou hadst told thy singular story in plain words! But it is fruitless to look there, in those Paper-bags, for such. Nothing but innuendoes, figurative crotchets: a typical Shadow, fitfully wavering, prophetico-satiric; no clear logical Picture. "How paint to the sensual eye," asks he once, "what passes in the Holy-of-Holies of Man's Soul; in what words, known to these profane times, speak even afar-off of the unspeakable?" We ask in turn: Why perplex these times, profane as they are, with need-less obscurity, by omission and by commission? Not mystical only is our Professor, but whimsical; and involves himself, now more than ever, in eye-bewildering *chiaroscuro.* Successive glimpses, here faithfully imparted, our more gifted readers must endeavor to combine for their own behoof.

He says: "The hot Harmattan wind [23] had raged itself out; its howl went silent within me; and the long-deafened soul could now hear. I paused in my wild wanderings; and sat me down to wait, and consider; for it was as if the hour of change drew nigh. I seemed to surrender, to renounce utterly, and say: Fly, then, false shadows of Hope; I will chase you no more, I will believe you no more. And ye too, haggard specters of Fear, I care not for you; ye too are all shadows and a lie. Let me rest here: for I am way-weary and life-weary; I will rest here, were it but to die: to die or to live is alike to me; alike insignificant."—And again: "Here, then, as I lay in that CENTER OF INDIFFERENCE; cast, doubtless by benignant upper Influence, into a healing sleep, the heavy dreams rolled gradually away, and I awoke to a new Heaven and a new Earth. The first preliminary moral Act, An-

22 "Get thee behind me, Satan" (Matt. iv 10) 23 a hot, dust-laden wind blowing from the interior upon the African Coast

nihilation of Self (*Selbst-tödtung*), had been happily accomplished; and my mind's eyes were now unsealed, and its hands
ungyved."

Might we not also conjecture that the following passage refers
to his Locality, during this same "healing sleep"; that his
Pilgrim-staff lies cast aside here, on "the high table-land"; and
indeed that the repose is already taking wholesome effect on him?
If it were not that the tone, in some parts, has more of riancy,
even of levity, than we could have expected! However, in Teu-
10 felsdröckh, there is always the strangest Dualism: light dancing,
with guitar-music, will be going on in the fore-court, while by fits
from within comes the faint whimpering of woe and wail. We
transcribe the piece entire:

"Beautiful it was to sit there, as in my skyey Tent, musing
and meditating; on the high table-land, in front of the Mountains; over me, as roof, the azure Dome, and around me, for walls,
four azure-flowing curtains,—namely, of the Four azure winds,
on whose bottom-fringes also I have seen gilding. And then to
fancy the fair Castles that stood sheltered in these Mountain
20 hollows; with their green flower-lawns, and white dames and
damosels, lovely enough: or better still, the straw-roofed Cottages, wherein stood many a Mother baking bread, with her
children round her:—all hidden and protectingly folded-up in the
valley-folds; yet there and alive, as sure as if I beheld them. Or to
see, as well as fancy, the nine Towns and Villages, that lay
round my mountain-seat, which, in still weather, were wont to
speak to me (by their steeple-bells) with metal tongue; and, in
almost all weather, proclaimed their vitality by repeated Smoke-
clouds; whereon, as on a culinary horologe, I might read the hour
30 of the day. For it was the smoke of cookery, as kind housewives
at morning, midday, eventide, were boiling their husbands'
kettles; and ever a blue pillar rose up into the air, successively
or simultaneously, from each of the nine, saying, as plainly as
smoke could say: Such and such a meal is getting ready here.
Not uninteresting! For you have the whole Borough, with all its
love-makings and scandal-mongeries, contentions and content-
ments, as in miniature, and could cover it all with your hat.—If,
in my wide Wayfarings, I had learned to look into the business
of the World in its details, here perhaps was the place for combin-
40 ing it into general propositions, and deducing inferences therefrom.

"Often also could I see the black Tempest marching in anger
through the Distance: round some Schreckhorn,[24] as yet grim-
blue, would the eddying vapor gather, and there tumultuously
eddy, and flow down like a mad witch's hair; till, after a space,

---

24 "Peak of Terror" in the Bernese Alps

it vanished, and, in the clear sunbeam, your Schreckhorn stood smiling grim-white, for the vapor had held snow. How thou fermentest and elaboratest, in thy great fermenting-vat and laboratory of an Atmosphere, of a World, O Nature!—Or what is Nature? Ha! why do I not name thee GOD? Art not thou the 'Living Garment of God'? O Heavens, is it, in very deed, HE, then, that ever speaks through thee; that lives and loves in thee, that lives and loves in me?

"Fore-shadows, call them rather fore-splendors, of that Truth, and Beginning of Truths, fell mysteriously over my soul. Sweeter than Dayspring to the Shipwrecked in Nova Zembla; [25] ah, like the mother's voice to her little child that strays bewildered, weeping, in unknown tumults; like soft streamings of celestial music to my too-exasperated heart, came that Evangel. The Universe is not dead and demoniacal, a charnel-house with specters; but godlike, and my Father's!

"With other eyes, too, could I now look upon my fellow man; with an infinite Love, an infinite Pity. Poor, wandering, wayward man! Art thou not tired, and beaten with stripes, even as I am? Ever, whether thou bear the royal mantle or the beggar's gabardine, art thou not so weary, so heavy-laden; and thy Bed of Rest is but a Grave. O my Brother, my Brother, why cannot I shelter thee in my bosom, and wipe away all tears from thy eyes!—Truly, the din of many-voiced Life, which, in this solitude, with the mind's organ, I could hear, was no longer a maddening discord, but a melting one; like inarticulate cries, and sobbings of a dumb creature, which in the ear of Heaven are prayers. The poor Earth, with her poor joys, was now my needy Mother, not my cruel Stepdame; Man, with his so mad Wants and so mean Endeavors, had become the dearer to me; and even for his sufferings and his sins, I now first named him Brother. Thus was I standing in the porch of that 'Sanctuary of Sorrow'; by strange, steep ways had I too been guided thither; and ere long its sacred gates would open, and the 'Divine Depth of Sorrow,' lie disclosed to me."

The Professor says, he here first got eye on the Knot that had been strangling him, and straightway could unfasten it, and was free. "A vain interminable controversy," writes he, "touching what is at present called Origin of Evil, or some such thing, arises in every soul, since the beginning of the world; and in every soul, that would pass from idle Suffering into actual Endeavoring, must first be put an end to. The most, in our time, have to go content with a simple, incomplete enough Suppression of this controversy; to a few some Solution of it is indispensable. In

25 An incident in 1597 during the voyage of William Barents to find a northeast route to China.

every new era, too, such Solution comes-out in different terms; and ever the Solution of the last era has become obsolete, and is found unserviceable. For it is man's nature to change his Dialect from century to century; he cannot help it though he would. The authentic *Church-Catechism* of our present century has not yet fallen into my hands: meanwhile, for my own private behoof, I attempt to elucidate the matter so. Man's Unhappiness, as I construe, comes of his Greatness; it is because there is an Infinite in him, which with all his cunning he cannot quite bury
10 under the Finite. Will the whole Finance Ministers and Upholsterers and Confectioners of modern Europe undertake, in joint-stock company, to make one Shoeblack HAPPY? They cannot accomplish it, above an hour or two; for the Shoeblack also has a Soul quite other than his Stomach; and would require, if you consider it, for his permanent satisfaction and saturation, simply this allotment, no more, and no less: *God's infinite Universe altogether to himself,* therein to enjoy infinitely, and fill every wish as fast as it rose. Oceans of Hochheimer, a Throat like that of Ophiuchus: [26] speak not of them; to the infinite Shoe-
20 black they are as nothing. No sooner is your ocean filled, than he grumbles that it might have been of better vintage. Try him with half of a Universe, of an Omnipotence, he sets to quarreling with the proprietor of the other half, and declares himself the most maltreated of men.—Always there is a black spot in our sunshine: it is even as I said, the *Shadow of Ourselves.*

"But the whim we have of Happiness is somewhat thus. By certain valuations, and averages, of our own striking, we come upon some sort of average terrestrial lot; this we fancy belongs to us by nature, and of indefeasible right. It is simple payment
30 of our wages, of our deserts; requires neither thanks nor complaint; only such *overplus* as there may be do we account Happiness; any *deficit* again is Misery. Now consider that we have the valuation of our own deserts ourselves, and what a fund of Self-conceit there is in each of us,—do you wonder that the balance should so often dip the wrong way, and many a Blockhead cry: See there, what a payment; was ever worthy gentleman so used!—I tell thee, Blockhead, it all comes of thy Vanity; of what thou *fanciest* those same deserts of thine to be. Fancy that thou deservest to be hanged (as is most likely), thou wilt
40 feel it happiness to be only shot: fancy that thou deservest to be hanged in a hair-halter, it will be a luxury to die in hemp.

"So true is it, what I then said, that *the Fraction of Life can be increased in value not so much by increasing your Numerator as by lessening your Denominator.* Nay, unless my Algebra deceive me, *Unity* itself divided by *Zero* will give *Infinity.* Make

26 the serpent's throat (from the constellation of the Serpent-Bearer)

thy claim of wages a zero, then; thou hast the world under thy feet. Well did the Wisest of our time [27] write: 'It is only with Renunciation (*Entsagen*) that Life, properly speaking, can be said to begin.'

"I asked myself: What is this that, ever since earliest years, thou hast been fretting and fuming, and lamenting and self-tormenting, on account of? Say it in a word: is it not because thou art not HAPPY? Because the THOU (sweet gentleman) is not sufficiently honored, nourished, soft-bedded, and lovingly cared-for? Foolish soul! What Act of Legislature was there that *thou* shouldst be Happy? A little while ago thou hadst no right to *be* at all. What if thou wert born and predestined not to be Happy, but to be Unhappy! Art thou nothing other than a Vulture, then, that fliest through the Universe seeking after somewhat to *eat;* and shrieking dolefully because carrion enough is not given thee? Close thy *Byron:* open thy *Goethe.*"

"*Es leuchtet mir ein,* I see a glimpse of it!" cries he elsewhere: "there is in man a HIGHER than Love of Happiness: he can do without Happiness, and instead thereof find Blessedness! Was it not to preach-forth this same HIGHER that sages and martyrs, the Poet and the Priest, in all times, have spoken and suffered; bearing testimony, through life and through death, of the Godlike that is in Man, and how in the Godlike only has he Strength and Freedom? Which God-inspired Doctrine art thou also honored to be taught; O Heavens! and broken with manifold merciful Afflictions, even till thou become contrite, and learn it! O, thank thy Destiny for these; thankfully bear what yet remain: thou hadst need of them; the Self in thee needed to be annihilated. By benignant fever-paroxysms is Life rooting out the deep-seated chronic Disease, and triumphs over Death. On the roaring billows of Time, thou art not engulfed, but borne aloft into the azure of Eternity. Love not Pleasure; love God. This is the EVERLASTING YEA, wherein all contradiction its solved: wherein whoso walks and works, it is well with him."

And again: "Small is it that thou canst trample the Earth with its injuries under thy feet, as old Greek Zeno [28] trained thee: thou canst love the Earth while it injures thee, and even because it injures thee; for this a Greater than Zeno was needed, and he too was sent. Knowest thou that '*Worship of Sorrow*'? The Temple thereof, founded some eighteen centuries ago, now lies in ruins, overgrown with jungle, the habitation of doleful creatures: nevertheless, venture forward; in a low crypt, arched out of falling fragments, thou findest the Altar still there, and its sacred Lamp perennially burning."

27 Goethe   philosophy, third century
28 founder of the Stoic B C.

Without pretending to comment on which strange utterances, the Editor will only remark, that there lies beside them much of a still more questionable character; unsuited to the general apprehension; nay wherein he himself does not see his way. Nebulous disquisitions on Religion, yet not without bursts of splendor; on the "perennial continuance of Inspiration"; on Prophecy; that there are "true Priests, as well as Baal-Priests, in our own day": with more of the like sort. We select some fractions, by way of finish to this farrago.

10 "Cease, my much-respected Herr von Voltaire," thus apostrophizes the Professor: "shut thy sweet voice; for the task appointed thee seems finished. Sufficiently hast thou demonstrated this proposition, considerable or otherwise: That the Mythus of the Christian Religion looks not in the eighteenth century as it did in the eighth. Alas, were thy six-and-thirty quartos, and the six-and-thirty thousand other quartos and folios, and flying sheets or reams, printed before and since on the same subject, all needed to convince us of so little! But what next? Wilt thou help us to embody the divine Spirit of that Religion in a new Mythus, 20 in a new vehicle and vesture, that our Souls, otherwise too like perishing, may live? What! thou hast no faculty in that kind? Only a torch for burning, no hammer for building? Take our thanks, then, and——thyself away.

"Meanwhile what are antiquated Mythuses to me? Or is the God present, felt in my own heart, a thing which Herr von Voltaire will dispute out of me; or dispute into me? To the 'Worship of Sorrow' ascribe what origin and genesis thou pleasest, has not that Worship originated, and been generated; is it not here? Feel it in thy heart, and then say whether it is of God! This is 30 Belief; all else is Opinion,—for which latter whoso will let him worry and be worried."

"Neither," observes he elsewhere, "shall ye tear-out one another's eyes, struggling over 'Plenary Inspiration,' and suchlike: try rather to get a little even Partial Inspiration, each of you for himself. One Bible I know, of whose Plenary Inspiration doubt is not so much as possible; nay with my own eyes I saw the God's-Hand writing it: thereof all other Bibles are but Leaves,— say, in Picture-Writing to assist the weaker faculty."

Or, to give the wearied reader relief, and bring it to an end, 40 let him take the following perhaps more intelligible passage:

"To me, in this our life," says the Professor, "which is an internecine warfare with the Time-spirit, other warfare seems questionable. Hast thou in any way a Contention with thy brother, I advise thee, think well what the meaning thereof is. If thou gauge it to the bottom, it is simply this: 'Fellow, see! thou art taking more than thy share of Happiness in the world, something from *my* share: which, by the Heavens, thou shalt not; nay I will fight thee rather.'—Alas, and the whole lot to be divided is such a beggarly matter, truly a 'feast of shells,' for the substance has been spilled out: not enough to quench one Appetite; and the collective human species clutching at them!—Can we not, in all such cases, rather say: 'Take it, thou too-ravenous individual; take that pitiful additional fraction of a share, which I reckoned mine, but which thou so wantest; take it with a blessing: would to Heaven I had enough for thee!'—If Fichte's *Wissenschaftslehre*[29] be, 'to a certain extent, Applied Christianity,' surely to a still greater extent, so is this. We have here not a Whole Duty of Man, yet a Half Duty, namely the Passive half: could we but do it, as we can demonstrate it!

"But indeed Conviction, were it never so excellent, is worthless till it convert itself into Conduct. Nay properly Conviction is not possible till then; inasmuch as all Speculation is by nature endless, formless, a vortex amid vortices: only by a felt indubitable certainty of Experience does it find any center to revolve round, and so fashion itself into a system. Most true is it, as a wise man teaches us, that 'Doubt of any sort cannot be removed except by Action.'[30] On which ground, too, let him who gropes painfully in darkness or uncertain light, and prays vehemently that the dawn may ripen into day, lay this other precept well to heart, which to me was of invaluable service: *Do the Duty which lies nearest thee,* which thou knowest to be a Duty! Thy second Duty will already have become clearer.

"May we not say, however, that the hour of Spiritual Enfranchisement is even this: When your Ideal World, wherein the whole man has been dimly struggling and inexpressibly languishing to work, becomes revealed, and thrown open; and you discover, with amazement enough, like the Lothario in *Wilhelm Meister*, that your 'America is here or nowhere'? The Situation that has not its Duty, its Ideal, was never yet occupied by man. Yes here, in this poor, miserable, hampered, despicable Actual, wherein thou even now standest, here or nowhere is thy Ideal: work it out therefrom; and working, believe, live, be free. Fool! the Ideal is in thyself, the impediment too is in thyself: thy Condition is but the stuff thou art to shape that same Ideal out of: what matters whether such stuff be of this sort or that, so the Form thou give it be heroic, be poetic? O thou that pinest in the imprisonment of the Actual, and criest bitterly to the gods for a kingdom wherein to rule and create, know this of a truth: the thing thou seekest is already with thee, 'here or nowhere,' couldst thou only see!

29 *The Theory of Knowledge* by Johann Gottlieb   Fichte (1762–1814) 30 by Goethe, in *Wil-*   *helm Meister's Apprenticeship*, book v., chap. 16

"But it is with man's Soul as it was with Nature: the beginning of Creation is—Light. Till the eye have vision, the whole members are in bonds. Divine moment, when over the tempest-tost Soul, as once over the wild-weltering Chaos, it is spoken: Let there be Light! Ever to the greatest that has felt such moment, is it not miraculous and God-announcing; even as, under simpler figures, to the simplest and least. The mad primeval Discord is hushed; the rudely-jumbled conflicting elements bind themselves into separate Firmaments: deep silent rock-foundations are built

10 beneath; and the skyey vault with its everlasting Luminaries above: instead of a dark wasteful Chaos, we have a blooming, fertile, Heaven-encompassed World.

"I too could now say to myself: Be no longer a Chaos, but a World, or even Worldkin. Produce! Produce! Were it but the pitifullest infinitesimal fraction of a Product, produce it, in God's name! 'Tis the utmost thou hast in thee: out with it, then. Up, up! Whatsoever thy hand findeth to do, do it with thy whole might. Work while it is called Today; for the Night cometh, wherein no man can work."

BOOK III

CHAPTER VIII

Natural Supernaturalism

20 IT is in his stupendous Section, headed *Natural Supernaturalism*, that the Professor first becomes a Seer; and, after long effort, such as we have witnessed, finally subdues under his feet this refractory Clothes-Philosophy, and takes victorious possession thereof. Phantasms enough he has had to struggle with; "Cloth-webs and Cob-webs," of Imperial Mantles, Superannuated Symbols, and what not: yet still did he courageously pierce through. Nay, worst of all, two quite mysterious, world-embracing Phantasms, TIME and SPACE, have ever hovered round him, perplexing and bewildering: but with these also he now resolutely grap-

30 ples, these also he victoriously rends asunder. In a word, he has looked fixedly on Existence, till, one after the other, its earthly hulls and garnitures have all melted away; and now, to his rapt vision, the interior celestial Holy of Holies lies disclosed.

Here, therefore, properly it is that the Philosophy of Clothes attains to Transcendentalism; this last leap, can we but clear it, takes us safe into the promised land, where *Palingenesia*,[31] in all senses, may be considered as beginning. "Courage, then!" may our Diogenes exclaim, with better right than Diogenes the

31 Second birth

First once did. This stupendous Section we, after long painful
meditation, have found not to be unintelligible; but, on the
contrary, to grow clear, nay radiant, and all-illuminating. Let
the reader, turning on it what utmost force of speculative intellect
is in him, do his part; as we, by judicious selection and adjust-
ment, shall study to do ours:

"Deep has been, and is, the significance of Miracles," thus
quietly begins the Professor; "far deeper perhaps than we imagine. Meanwhile, the question of questions were: What specially
is a Miracle? To that Dutch King of Siam, an icicle had been a
miracle; whoso had carried with him an air-pump, and vial of
vitriolic ether, might have worked a miracle. To my Horse, again,
who unhappily is still more unscientific, do not I work a miracle,
and magical *'Open sesame!'* every time I please to pay twopence,
and open for him an impassable *Schlagbaum,* or shut Turnpike?

" 'But is not a real Miracle simply a violation of the Laws of
Nature?' ask several. Whom I answer by this new question:
What are the Laws of Nature? To me perhaps the rising of one
from the dead were no violation of these Laws, but a confirmation; were some far deeper Law, now first penetrated into, and
by Spiritual Force, even as the rest have all been, brought to bear
on us with its Material Force.

"Here too may some inquire, not without astonishment: On
what ground shall one, that can make Iron swim, come and declare that therefore he can teach Religion? To us, truly, of the
Nineteenth Century, such declaration were inept enough; which
nevertheless to our fathers, of the First Century, was full of
meaning.

" 'But is it not the deepest Law of Nature that she be constant?' cries an illuminated class: 'Is not the Machine of the
Universe fixed to move by unalterable rules?' Probable enough,
good friends: nay I, too, must believe that the God, whom
ancient inspired men assert to be 'without variableness or shadow
of turning,' does indeed never change; that Nature, that the
Universe, which no one whom it so pleases can be prevented
from calling a Machine, does move by the most unalterable
rules. And now of you, too, I make the old inquiry: What those
same unalterable rules, forming the complete Statute-Book of
Nature, may possibly be?

"They stand written in our Works of Science, say you; in the
accumulated records of Man's Experience?—Was Man with his
Experience present at the Creation, then, to see how it all
went on? Have any deepest scientific individuals yet dived-
down to the foundations of the Universe, and gauged everything there? Did the Maker take them into His counsel; that
they read His groundplan of the incomprehensible All; and

can say, This stands marked therein, and no more than this?
Alas, not in anywise! These scientific individuals have been nowhere but where we also are; have seen some handbreadths
deeper than we see into the Deep that is infinite, without bottom
as without shore.

"Laplace's Book on the Stars,[32] wherein he exhibits that certain
Planets, with their Satellites, gyrate round our worthy Sun, at
a rate and in a course, which, by greatest good fortune, he and
the like of him have succeeded in detecting,—is to me as precious
10 as to another. But is this what thou namest 'Mechanism of the
Heavens,' and 'System of the World'; this, wherein Sirius and
the Pleiades, and all Herschel's [33] Fifteen-thousand Suns per
minute, being left out, some paltry handful of Moons, and inert
Balls, had been—looked at, nicknamed, and marked in the
Zodiacal Way-bill; so that we can now prate of their Where-
about; their How, their Why, their What, being hid from us, as
in the signless Inane?

"System of Nature! To the wisest man, wide as is his vision,
Nature remains of quite *infinite* depth, of quite infinite expan-
20 sion; and all Experience thereof limits itself to some few com-
puted centuries and measured square-miles. The course of
Nature's phases, on this our little fraction of a Planet, is partially
known to us: but who knows what deeper courses these depend
on; what infinitely larger Cycle (of causes) our little Epicycle
revolves on? To the Minnow every cranny and pebble, and quality and accident, of its little native Creek may have become
familiar: but does the Minnow understand the Ocean Tides and
periodic Currents, the Trade-winds, and Monsoons, and Moon's
Eclipses; by all which the condition of its little Creek is regulated,
30 and may, from time to time (*un*miraculously enough), be quite
overset and reversed? Such a Minnow is Man; his Creek this
Planet Earth; his Ocean the immeasurable All; his Monsoons
and periodic Currents the mysterious Course of Providence
through Æons of Æons.

"We speak of the Volume of Nature: and truly a Volume it is,
—whose Author and Writer is God. To read it! Dost thou, does
man, so much as well know the Alphabet thereof? With its
Words, Sentences, and grand descriptive Pages, poetical and
philosophical, spread out through Solar Systems, and Thou-
40 sands of Years, we shall not try thee. It is a Volume written
in celestial hieroglyphs, in the true Sacred-writing; of which
even Prophets are happy that they can read here a line and
there a line. As for your Institutes, and Academies of Science,
they strive bravely; and, from amid the thick-crowded, inex-

---

32 *La Mécanique Celeste,*   La Place, 1825   (1738-1822), English astron-
by the French astronomer   33 Sir William Herschel   omer of Prussian birth

tricably intertwisted hieroglyphic writing, pick-out, by dextrous
combination, some Letters in the vulgar Character, and therefrom put together this and the other economic Recipe, of high
avail in Practice. That Nature is more than some boundless
Volume of such Recipes,' or huge, well-nigh inexhaustible
Domestic-Cookery Book, of which the whole secret will in this
manner one day evolve itself, the fewest dream."

"Custom," continues the Professor, "doth make dotards of
us all. Consider well, thou wilt find that Custom is the greatest 10
of Weavers; and weaves air-raiment for all the Spirits of the
Universe; whereby indeed these dwell with us visibly, as ministering servants, in our houses and workshops; but their spiritual nature becomes, to the most, forever hidden. Philosophy
complains that Custom has hoodwinked us, from the first; that
we do everything by Custom, even Believe by it; that our very
Axioms, let us boast of Free-thinking as we may, are oftenest
simply such Beliefs as we have never heard questioned. Nay,
what is Philosophy throughout but a continual battle against
Custom; an ever-renewed effort to *transcend* the sphere of blind 20
Custom, and so become Transcendental?

"Innumerable are the illusions and legerdemain-tricks of
Custom: but of all these, perhaps the cleverest is her knack of
persuading us that the Miraculous, by simple repetition, ceases
to be Miraculous. True, it is by this means we live; for man
must work as well as wonder: and herein is Custom so far a
kind nurse, guiding him to his true benefit. But she is a fond
foolish nurse, or rather we are false foolish nurslings, when,
in our resting and reflecting hours, we prolong the same deception. Am I to view the Stupendous with stupid indifference, 30
because I have seen it twice, or two-hundred, or two-million
times? There is no reason in Nature or in Art why I should:
unless, indeed, I am a mere Work-Machine, for whom the divine
gift of Thought were no other than the terrestrial gift of Steam
is to the Steam-engine; a power whereby Cotton might be spun,
and money and money's worth realized.

"Notable enough too, here as elsewhere, wilt thou find the
potency of Names; which indeed are but one kind of such
custom-woven, wonder-hiding Garments. Witchcraft, and all
manner of Specter-work, and Demonology, we have now 40
named Madness and Diseases of the Nerves. Seldom reflecting
that still the new question comes upon us: What is Madness,
what are Nerves? Ever, as before, does Madness remain a
mysterious-terrific, altogether *infernal* boiling-up of the Nether
Chaotic Deep, through this fair-painted Vision of Creation,
which swims thereon, which we name the Real. Was Luther's

Picture of the Devil less a Reality, whether it were formed within the bodily eye, or without it? In every the wisest Soul lies a whole world of internal Madness, an authentic Demon Empire; out of which, indeed, his world of Wisdom has been creatively built together, and now rests there, as on its dark foundations does a habitable flowery Earth-rind.

"But deepest of all illusory Appearances, for hiding Wonder, as for many other ends, are your two grand fundamental world-enveloping Appearances, Space and Time. These, as spun and woven for us from before Birth itself, to clothe our celestial Me for dwelling here, and yet to blind it,—lie all-embracing, as the universal canvas, or warp and woof, whereby all minor Illusions, in this Phantasm Existence, weave and paint themselves. In vain, while here on Earth, shall you endeavor to strip them off; you can, at best, but rend them asunder for moments, and look through.

"Fortunatus had a wishing Hat, which when he put on, and wished himself Anywhere, behold he was There. By this means had Fortunatus triumphed over Space, he had annihilated Space; for him there was no Where, but all was Here. Were a Hatter to establish himself, in the Wahngasse of Weissnichtwo,[34] and make felts of this sort for all mankind, what a world we should have of it! Still stranger, should, on the opposite side of the street, another Hatter establish himself; and as his fellow-craftsman made Space-annihilating Hats, make Time-annihilating! Of both would I purchase, were it with my last groschen; but chiefly of this latter. To clap-on your felt, and, simply by wishing that you were Anywhere, straightway to be There! Next to clap-on your other felt, and simply by wishing that you were Anywhen, straightway to be Then! This were indeed the grander: shooting at will from the Fire-Creation of the World to its Fire-Consummation; here historically present in the First Century, conversing face to face with Paul and Seneca; there prophetically in the Thirty-first, conversing also face to face with other Pauls and Senecas, who as yet stand hidden in the depth of that late Time!

"Or thinkest thou it were impossible, unimaginable? Is the Past annihilated, then, or only past; is the Future non-extant, or only future? Those mystic faculties of thine, Memory and Hope, already answer: already through those mystic avenues, thou the Earth-blinded summonest both Past and Future, and communest with them, though as yet darkly, and with mute beckonings. The curtains of Yesterday drop down, the curtains of Tomorrow roll up; but Yesterday and Tomorrow both *are*.

34 Mad Street of Know-not-where (city where Teufelsdröckh lived)

Pierce through the Time-element, glance into the Eternal. Believe what thou findest written in the sanctuaries of Man's Soul, even as all Thinkers, in all ages, have devoutly read it there: that Time and Space are not God, but creations of God; that with God as it is a universal HERE, so is it an everlasting Now.

"And seest thou therein any glimpse of IMMORTALITY?—O Heaven! Is the white Tomb of our Loved One, who died from our arms, and had to be left behind us there, which rises in the distance, like a pale, mournfully receding Milestone, to tell how many toilsome uncheered miles we have journeyed on alone,—but a pale spectral Illusion! Is the lost Friend still mysteriously Here, even as we are Here mysteriously, with God!—Know of a truth that only the Time-shadows have perished, or are perishable; that the real Being of whatever was, and whatever is, and whatever will be, *is* even now and forever. This, should it unhappily seem new, thou mayest ponder at thy leisure; for the next twenty years, or the next twenty centuries: believe it thou must; understand it thou canst not.

"That the Thought-forms, Space and Time, wherein, once for all, we are sent into this Earth to live, should condition and determine our whole Practical reasonings, conceptions, and imagings or imaginings,—seems altogether fit, just, and unavoidable. But that they should, furthermore, usurp such sway over pure spiritual Meditation, and blind us to the wonder everywhere lying close on us, seems nowise so. Admit Space and Time to their due rank as Forms of Thought: nay even, if thou wilt, to their quite undue rank of Realities: and consider, then, with thyself how their thin disguises hide from us the brightest God-effulgences! Thus, were it not miraculous, could I stretch forth my hand and clutch the Sun? Yet thou seest me daily stretch forth my hand and therewith clutch many a thing, and swing it hither and thither. Art thou a grown baby, then, to fancy that the Miracle lies in miles of distance, or in pounds avoirdupois of weight; and not to see that the true inexplicable God-revealing Miracle lies in this, that I can stretch forth my hand at all; that I have free Force to clutch aught therewith? Innumerable other of this sort are the deceptions, and wonder-hiding stupefactions, which Space practises on us.

"Still worse is it with regard to Time. Your grand anti-magician, and universal wonder-hider, is this same lying Time. Had we but the Time-annihilating Hat, to put on for once only, we should see ourselves in a World of Miracles, wherein all fabled or authentic Thaumaturgy, and feats of Magic, were outdone. But unhappily we have not such a Hat; and man, poor fool that he is, can seldom and scantily help himself without one.

"Were it not wonderful, for instance, had Orpheus, or Amphion,[35] built the walls of Thebes by the mere sound of his Lyre? Yet tell me, Who built these walls of Weissnichtwo; summoning out all the sandstone rocks, to dance along from the *Steinbruch*[36] (now a huge Troglodyte Chasm, with frightful green-mantled pools); and shape themselves into Doric and Ionic pillars, squared ashlar[37] houses and noble streets? Was it not the still higher Orpheus, or Orpheuses, who, in past centuries, by the divine Music of Wisdom, succeeded in civilizing
10 Man? Our highest Orpheus walked in Judea, eighteen hundred years ago: his sphere-melody, flowing in wild native tones, took captive the ravished souls of men; and, being of a truth sphere-melody, still flows and sounds, though now with thousandfold accompaniments, and rich symphonies, through all our hearts; and modulates, and divinely leads them. Is that a wonder, which happens in two hours; and does it cease to be wonderful if happening in two million? Not only was Thebes built by the music of an Orpheus; but without the music of some inspired Orpheus was no city ever built, no work that man glories in
20 ever done.

"Sweep away the Illusion of Time; glance, if thou hast eyes, from the near moving-cause to its far-distant Mover: The stroke that came transmitted through a whole galaxy of elastic balls, was it less a stroke than if the last ball only had been struck, and sent flying? O, could I (with the Time-annihilating Hat) transport thee direct from the Beginnings to the Endings, how were thy eyesight unsealed, and thy heart set flaming in the Light-sea of celestial wonder! Then sawest thou that this fair Universe, were it in the meanest province thereof, is in very
30 deed the star-domed City of God; that through every star, through every grass-blade, and most through every Living Soul, the glory of a present God still beams. But Nature, which is the Time-vesture of God, and reveals Him to the wise, hides Him from the foolish.

"Again, could anything be more miraculous than an actual authentic Ghost? The English Johnson longed, all his life, to see one; but could not, though he went to Cock Lane,[38] and thence to the church-vaults, and tapped on coffins. Foolish Doctor! Did he never, with the mind's eye as well as with the
40 body's, look round him into that full tide of human Life he so loved; did he never so much as look into Himself? The good Doctor was a Ghost, as actual and authentic as heart could wish; well-nigh a million of Ghosts were traveling the streets

35 the famous musicians of Greek myth
36 quarry
37 of hewn stone
38 Dr. Johnson, after investigating, concluded that the "Cock Lane Ghost" was a girl deceiving the credulous (see Boswell's *Life* for 1763).

by his side. Once more I say, sweep away the illusion of Time;
compress the threescore years into three minutes: what else
was he, what else are we? Are we not Spirits, that are shaped
into a body, into an Appearance; and that fade away again into
air and Invisibility? This is no metaphor, it is a simple scientific
fact: we start out of Nothingness, take figure, and are Apparitions; round us, as round the veriest specter, is Eternity; and
to Eternity minutes are as years and æons. Come there not
tones of Love and Faith, as from celestial harp-strings, like the
Song of beatified Souls? And again, do not we squeak and gib-
ber (in our discordant, screech-owlish debatings and recriminat-
ings); and glide bodeful, and feeble, and fearful; or uproar
(*poltern*), and revel in our mad Dance of the Dead,—till the
scent of the morning air summons us to our still Home; and
dreamy Night becomes awake and Day? Where now is Alexander of Macedon: does the steel Host, that yelled in fierce
battle-shouts at Issus and Arbela, remain behind him; or have
they all vanished utterly, even as perturbed Goblins must?
Napoleon too, and his Moscow Retreats and Austerlitz Cam-
paigns! Was it all other than the veriest Specter-hunt; which
has now, with its howling tumult that made Night hideous,
flitted away?—Ghosts! There are nigh a thousand-million walking the Earth openly at noontide; some half-hundred have vanished from it, some half-hundred have arisen in it, ere thy
watch ticks once.

"O Heaven, it is mysterious, it is awful to consider that we
not only carry each a future Ghost within him; but are, in very
deed, Ghosts! These Limbs, whence had we them; this stormy
Force; this life-blood with its burning Passion? They are dust
and shadow; a Shadow-system gathered round our ME; wherein,
through some moments or years, the Divine Essence is to be
revealed in the Flesh. That warrior on his strong war-horse,
fire flashes through his eyes; force dwells in his arm and heart:
but warrior and war-horse are a vision; a revealed Force, nothing more. Stately they tread the Earth, as if it were a firm
substance: fool! the earth is but a film; it cracks in twain, and
warrior and war-horse sink beyond plummet's sounding. Plummet's? Fantasy herself will not follow them. A little while ago,
they were not; a little while, and they are not, their very ashes
are not.

"So has it been from the beginning, so will it be to the end.
Generation after generation takes to itself the Form of a Body;
and forth-issuing from Cimmerian [39] Night, on Heaven's mission APPEARS. What Force and Fire is in each he expends: one
grinding in the mill of Industry; one hunter-like climbing the

<hr>

39 a people dwelling, according to Homer, in a land where the sun never shone

giddy Alpine heights of Science; one madly dashed in pieces on the rocks of Strife, in war with his fellow:—and then the Heaven-sent is recalled; his earthly Vesture falls away, and soon even to Sense becomes a vanished Shadow. Thus, like some wild-flaming, wild-thundering train of Heaven's Artillery, does this mysterious MANKIND thunder and flame, in long-drawn, quick-succeeding grandeur, through the unknown Deep. Thus, like a God-created, fire-breathing Spirit-host, we emerge from the Inane; haste stormfully across the astonished Earth; then
10 plunge again into the Inane. Earth's mountains are leveled, and her seas filled up, in our passage: can the Earth, which is but dead and a vision, resist Spirits which have reality and are alive? On the hardest adamant some footprint of us is stamped-in; the last Rear of the host will read traces of the earliest Van. But whence?—O Heaven, whither? Sense knows not; Faith knows not; only that it is through Mystery to Mystery, from God and to God.

> 'We *are such stuff*
> As Dreams are made of, and our little Life
> Is rounded with a sleep!' " 40

ON HEROES, HERO-WORSHIP, AND THE HEROIC IN HISTORY

This work was originally delivered in 1840 as a series of six lectures, the titles and sub-titles being: Lecture I: The Hero as Divinity. Odin. Paganism: Scandinavian Mythology. Lecture II: The Hero as Prophet. Mahomet: Islam. Lecture III: The Hero as Poet. Dante; Shakespeare. Lecture IV: The Hero as Priest. Luther; Reformation: Knox; Puritanism. Lecture V: The Hero as Man of Letters. Johnson, Rousseau, Burns. Lecture VI: The Hero as King. Cromwell. Napoleon: Modern Revolutionism.

The opening of the first lecture, serving as an introduction to the whole, and presenting Carlyle's fundamental views on great men and their importance to the world, is here reprinted.

LECTURE I

THE HERO AS DIVINITY. ODIN. PAGANISM: SCANDINAVIAN MYTHOLOGY

WE have undertaken to discourse here for a little on Great Men, their manner of appearance in our world's business, how they have shaped themselves in the world's history, what ideas men formed of them, what work they did;—on Heroes, namely, and on their reception and performance; what I call Hero-

40 *Tempest,* IV, i, 156–8

worship and the Heroic in human affairs. Too evidently this is a
large topic; deserving quite other treatment than we can expect to give it at present. A large topic; indeed, an illimitable
one; wide as Universal History itself. For, as I take it, Universal History, the history of what man has accomplished in this
world, is at bottom the History of the Great Men who have
worked here. They were the leaders of men, these great ones;
the modelers, patterns, and in a wide sense creators, of whatsoever the general mass of men contrived to do or to attain; all
things that we see standing accomplished in the world are
properly the outer material result, the practical realization and
embodiment, of Thoughts that dwelt in the Great Men sent
into the world: the soul of the whole world's history, it may
justly be considered, were the history of these. Too clearly it is
a topic we shall do no justice to in this place!

One comfort is, that Great Men, taken up in any way, are
profitable company. We cannot look, however imperfectly,
upon a great man, without gaining something by him. He is the
living light-fountain, which it is good and pleasant to be near.
The light which enlightens, which has enlightened the darkness
of the world; and this not as a kindled lamp only, but rather
as a natural luminary shining by the gift of Heaven; a flowing
light-fountain, as I say, of native original insight, of manhood
and heroic nobleness;—in whose radiance all souls feel that it
is well with them. On any terms whatsoever, you will not grudge
to wander in such neighborhood for a while. These Six classes
of Heroes, chosen out of widely-distant countries and epochs,
and in mere external figure differing altogether, ought, if we
look faithfully at them, to illustrate several things for us. Could
we see *them* well, we should get some glimpses into the very
marrow of the world's history. How happy, could I but, in any
measure, in such times as these, make manifest to you the meanings of Heroism; the divine relation (for I may well call it such)
which in all times unites a Great Man to other men; and thus,
as it were, not exhaust my subject, but so much as break ground
on it! At all events, I must make the attempt.

It is well said, in every sense, that a man's religion is the
chief fact with regard to him. A man's, or a nation of men's.
By religion I do not mean here the church-creed which he
professes, the articles of faith which he will sign and, in words
or otherwise, assert; not this wholly, in many cases not this at
all. We see men of all kinds of professed creeds attain to almost
all degrees of worth or worthlessness under each or any of
them. This is not what I call religion, this profession and assertion; which is often only a profession and assertion from the

outworks of the man, from the mere argumentative region of him, if even so deep as that. But the thing a man does practically believe (and this is often enough *without* asserting it even to himself, much less to others); the thing a man does practically lay to heart, and know for certain, concerning his vital relations to this mysterious Universe, and his duty and destiny there, that is in all cases the primary thing for him, and creatively determines all the rest. That is his *religion;* or it may be, his mere scepticism and *no-religion:* the manner it is in
10 which he feels himself to be spiritually related to the Unseen World or No-World; and I say, if you tell me what that is, you tell me to a very great extent what the man is, what the kind of things he will do is. Of a man or of a nation we inquire, therefore, first of all, What religion they had? Was it Heathenism,— plurality of gods, mere sensuous representation of this Mystery of Life, and for chief recognized element therein Physical Force? Was it Christianism; faith in an Invisible, not as real only, but as the only reality; Time, through every meanest moment of it, resting on Eternity; Pagan empire of Force dis-
20 placed by a nobler supremacy, that of Holiness? Was it Scepticism, uncertainty and inquiry whether there was an Unseen World, any Mystery of Life except a mad one;—doubt as to all this, or perhaps unbelief and flat denial? Answering of this question is giving us the soul of the history of the man or nation. The thoughts they had were the parents of the actions they did; their feelings were parents of their thoughts: it was the unseen and spiritual in them that determined the outward and actual;—their religion, as I say, was the great fact about them. In these Discourses, limited as we are, it will be good to
30 direct our survey chiefly to that religious phasis of the matter. That once known well, all is known. We have chosen as the first Hero in our series, Odin the central figure of Scandinavian Paganism; an emblem to us of a most extensive province of things. Let us look for a little at the Hero as Divinity, the oldest primary form of Heroism.

Surely it seems a very strange-looking thing this Paganism; almost inconceivable to us in these days. A bewildering, inextricable jungle of delusions, confusions, falsehoods and absurdities, covering the whole field of Life! A thing that fills us
40 with astonishment, almost, if it were possible, with incredulity, —for truly it is not easy to understand that sane men could ever calmly, with their eyes open, believe and live by such a set of doctrines. That men should have worshiped their poor fellow-man as a God, and not him only, but stocks and stones, and all manner of animate and inanimate objects; and fashioned for themselves such a distracted chaos of hallucinations

by way of Theory of the Universe: all this looks like an incredible fable. Nevertheless it is a clear fact that they did it. Such hideous inextricable jungle of misworships, misbeliefs, men, made as we are, did actually hold by, and live at home in. This is strange. Yes, we may pause in sorrow and silence over the depths of darkness that are in man; if we rejoice in the heights of purer vision he has attained to. Such things were and are in man; in all men; in us too.

Some speculators have a short way of accounting for the Pagan religion: mere quackery, priestcraft, and dupery, say they; no sane man ever did believe it,—merely contrived to persuade other men, not worthy of the name of sane, to believe it! It will be often our duty to protest against this sort of hypothesis about men's doings and history; and I here, on the very threshold, protest against it in reference to Paganism, and to all other *isms* by which man has ever for a length of time striven to walk in this world. They have all had a truth in them, or men would not have taken them up. Quackery and dupery do abound; in religions, above all in the more advanced decaying stages of religions, they have fearfully abounded: but quackery was never the originating influence in such things; it was not the health and life of such things, but their disease, the sure precursor of their being about to die! Let us never forget this. It seems to me a most mournful hypothesis, that of quackery giving birth to any faith even in savage men. Quackery gives birth to nothing; gives death to all things. We shall not see into the true heart of anything, if we look merely at the quackeries of it; if we do not reject the quackeries altogether; as mere diseases, corruptions, with which our and all men's sole duty is to have done with them, to sweep them out of our thoughts as out of our practice. Man everywhere is the born enemy of lies. I find Grand Lamaism [41] itself to have a kind of truth in it. Read the candid, clear-sighted, rather sceptical Mr. Turner's *Account of his Embassy* to that country, and see. They have their belief, these poor Thibet people, that Providence sends down always an Incarnation of Himself into every generation. At bottom some belief in a kind of Pope! At bottom still better, belief that there is a *Greatest* Man; that *he* is discoverable; that, once discovered, we ought to treat him with an obedience which knows no bounds! This is the truth of Grand Lamaism; the "discoverability" is the only error here. The Thibet priests have methods of their own of discovering what Man is Greatest, fit to be supreme over them. Bad methods: but are they so much worse than our methods,—of understanding him to be always the eldest born of a certain

41 The Grand Lama is the chief priest in the religion of Thibet.

genealogy? Alas, it is a difficult thing to find good methods for!
—We shall begin to have a chance of understanding Paganism,
when we first admit that to its followers it was, at one time,
earnestly true. Let us consider it very certain that men did believe in Paganism; men with open eyes, sound senses, men
made altogether like ourselves; that we, had we been there,
should have believed in it. Ask now, What Paganism could
have been?

Another theory, somewhat more respectable, attributes such
10 things to Allegory. It was a play of poetic minds, say these
theorists; a shadowing-forth, in allegorical fable, in personifica-
tion and visual form, of what such poetic minds had known
and felt of this Universe. Which agrees, add they, with a primary law of human nature, still everywhere observably at
work, though in less important things, That what a man feels
intensely, he struggles to speak-out of him, to see represented
before him in visual shape, and as if with a kind of life and historical reality in it. Now doubtless there is such a law, and it
is one of the deepest in human nature; neither need we doubt
20 that it did operate fundamentally in this business. The hypothesis which ascribes Paganism wholly or mostly to this agency,
I call a little more respectable; but I cannot yet call it the true
hypothesis. Think, would *we* believe, and take with us as our
life-guidance, an allegory, a poetic sport? Not sport but earnest
is what we should require. It is a most earnest thing to be
alive in this world; to die is not sport for a man. Man's life
never was a sport to him; it was a stern reality, altogether a
serious matter to be alive!

I find, therefore, that though these Allegory theorists are on
30 the way towards truth in this matter, they have not reached it
either. Pagan Religion is indeed an Allegory, a Symbol of what
men felt and knew about the Universe; and all Religions are
Symbols of that, altering always as that alters: but it seems
to me a radical perversion, and even *inversion,* of the business,
to put that forward as the origin and moving cause, when it
was rather the result and termination. To get beautiful allegories, a perfect poetic symbol, was not the want of men; but to
know what they were to believe about this Universe, what
course they were to steer in it; what, in this mysterious Life of
40 theirs, they had to hope and to fear, to do and to forbear doing.
The *Pilgrim's Progress* is an Allegory, and a beautiful, just and
serious one: but consider whether Bunyan's Allegory could have
preceded the Faith it symbolizes! The Faith had to be already
there, standing believed by everybody;—of which the Allegory
could *then* become a shadow; and, with all its seriousness, we
may say a *sportful* shadow, a mere play of the Fancy, in com-

parison with that awful Fact and scientific certainty which it poetically strives to emblem. The Allegory is the product of the certainty, not the producer of it; not in Bunyan's, nor in any other case. For Paganism, therefore, we have still to inquire, Whence came that scientific certainty, the parent of such a bewildered heap of allegories, errors and confusions? How was it, what was it?

Surely it were a foolish attempt to pretend "explaining," in this place, or in any place, such a phenomenon as that far-distant distracted cloudy imbroglio of Paganism,—more like a cloudfield than a distant continent of firm land and facts! It is no longer a reality, yet it was one. We ought to understand that this seeming cloudfield was once a reality; that not poetic allegory, least of all that dupery and deception, was the origin of it. Men, I say, never did believe idle songs, never risked their soul's life on allegories; men in all times, especially in early earnest times, have had an instinct for detecting quacks, for detesting quacks. Let us try if, leaving out both the quack theory and the allegory one, and listening with affectionate attention to that far-off confused rumor of the Pagan ages, we cannot ascertain so much as this at least, That there was a kind of fact at the heart of them; that they too were not mendacious and distracted, but in their own poor way true and sane!

You remember that fancy of Plato's, of a man who had grown to maturity in some dark distance, and was brought on a sudden into the upper air to see the sun rise. What would his wonder be, his rapt astonishment at the sight we daily witness with indifference! With the free open sense of a child, yet with the ripe faculty of a man, his whole heart would be kindled by that sight, he would discern it well to be Godlike, his soul would fall down in worship before it. Now, just such a childlike greatness was in the primitive nations. The first Pagan Thinker among rude men, the first men that began to think, was precisely this child-man of Plato's. Simple, open as a child, yet with the depth and strength of a man. Nature had as yet no name to him; he had not yet united under a name the infinite variety of sights, sounds, shapes and motions, which we now collectively name Universe, Nature, or the like,—and so with a name dismiss it from us. To the wild deep-hearted man all was yet new, not veiled under names or formulas; it stood naked, flashing-in on him there, beautiful, awful, unspeakable. Nature was to this man, what to the Thinker and Prophet it forever is, *preter*natural. This green flowery rock-built earth, the trees, the mountains, rivers, many-sounding seas;—that great deep sea of azure that swims overhead; the winds sweep-

ing through it; the black cloud fashioning itself together, now pouring out fire, now hail and rain; what *is* it? Ay, what? At bottom we do not yet know; we can never know at all. It is not by our superior insight that we escape the difficulty; it is by our superior levity, our inattention, our *want* of insight. It is by *not* thinking that we cease to wonder at it. Hardened round us, encasing wholly every notion we form, is a wrappage of traditions, hearsays, mere *words*. We call that fire of the black thunder-cloud "electricity," and lecture learnedly about
10 it, and grind the like of it out of glass and silk; but *what* is it? What made it? Whence comes it? Whither goes it? Science has done much for us; but it is a poor science that would hide from us the great deep sacred infinitude of Nescience, whither we can never penetrate, on which all science swims as a mere superficial film. This world, after all our science and sciences, is still a miracle; wonderful, inscrutable, *magical* and more, to whosoever will *think* of it.

That great mystery of TIME, were there no other: the illimitable, silent, never-resting thing called Time, rolling, rushing on,
20 swift, silent, like an all-embracing ocean-tide, on which we and all the Universe swim like exhalations, like apparitions which *are,* and then *are not:* this is for ever very literally a miracle; a thing to strike us dumb,—for we have no word to speak about it. This Universe, ah me—what could the wild man know of it; what can we yet know? That it is a Force, and thousand-fold Complexity of Forces; a Force which is *not we*. That is all; it is not we, it is altogether different from *us*. Force, Force, everywhere Force; we ourselves a mysterious Force in the center of that. "There is not a leaf rotting on the highway but
30 has Force in it: how else could it rot?" Nay surely, to the Atheistic Thinker, if such a one were possible, it must be a miracle too, this huge illimitable whirlwind of Force, which envelops us here; never-resting whirlwind, high as Immensity, old as Eternity. What is it? God's creation, the religious people answer; it is the Almighty God's! Atheistic science babbles poorly of it, with scientific nomenclatures, experiments and what-not, as if it were a poor dead thing, to be bottled up in Leyden jars and sold over counters: but the natural sense of man, in all times, if he will honestly apply his sense, proclaims it to
40 be a living thing,—ah, an unspeakable, godlike thing; towards which the best attitude for us, after never so much science, is awe, devout prostration and humility of soul; worship if not in words, then in silence.

But now I remark farther: What in such a time as ours it requires a Prophet or Poet to teach us, namely, the stripping-off of those poor undevout wrappages, nomenclatures and scientific hearsays,—this, the ancient earnest soul, as yet un-encumbered with these things, did for itself. The world, which is now divine only to the gifted, was then divine to whosoever would turn his eye upon it. He stood bare before it face to face. "All was Godlike or God":—Jean Paul [42] still finds it so; the giant Jean Paul, who has power to escape out of hearsays: but there then were no hearsays. Canopus shining-down over the desert, with its blue diamond brightness (that wild blue spirit-like brightness, far brighter than we ever witness here), would pierce into the heart of the wild Ishmaelitish man, whom it was guiding through the solitary waste there. To his wild heart, with all feelings in it, with no *speech* for any feeling, it may seem a little eye, that Canopus, glancing-out on him from the great deep Eternity; revealing the inner Splendor to him. Cannot we understand how these men *worshiped* Canopus; became what we call Sabeans,[43] worshiping the stars? Such is to me the secret of all forms of Paganism. Worship is transcendent wonder; wonder for which there is now no limit or measure; that is worship. To these primeval men, all things and everything they saw exist beside them were an emblem of the Godlike, of some God.

And look what perennial fiber of truth was in that. To us also, through every star, through every blade of grass, is not a God made visible, if we will open our minds and eyes? We do not worship in that way now: but is it not reckoned still a merit, proof of what we call a "poetic nature," that we recognize how every object has a divine beauty in it; how every object still verily is "a window through which we may look into Infinitude itself"? He that can discern the loveliness of things, we call him Poet, Painter, Man of Genius, gifted, lovable. These poor Sabeans did even what he does,—in their own fashion. That they did it, in what fashion soever, was a merit: better than what the entirely stupid man did, what the horse and camel did,—namely, nothing!

But now if all things whatsoever that we look upon are emblems to us of the Highest God, I add that more so than any of them is man such an emblem. You have heard of St. Chrysostom's celebrated saying in reference to the Shekinah, or Ark of Testimony, visible Revelation of God, among the Hebrews: "The true Shekinah is Man!" Yes, it is even so: this is no vain phrase; it is veritably so. The essence of our being, the mystery in us that calls itself "I,"—ah, what words have we for such things?—is a breath of Heaven; the Highest Being reveals himself in man. This body, these faculties, this life of ours, is it not

<hr>

42 Jean Paul Richter (1763–1825), German writer.   43 ancient oriental star-worshipers

all as a vesture for that Unnamed? "There is but one Temple in the Universe," says the devout Novalis,[44] "and that is the Body of Man. Nothing is holier than that high form. Bending before men is a reverence done to this Revelation in the Flesh. We touch Heaven when we lay our hand on a human body!" This sounds much like a mere flourish of rhetoric; but it is not so. If well meditated, it will turn out to be a scientific fact; the expression, in such words as can be had, of the actual truth of the thing. *We* are the miracle of miracles,—the great inscrutable mystery of God. We cannot understand it, we know not how to speak of it; but we may feel and know, if we like, that it is verily so.

Well; these truths were once more readily felt than now. The young generations of the world, who had in them the freshness of young children, and yet the depth of earnest men, who did not think that they had finished-off all things in Heaven and Earth by merely giving them scientific names, but had to gaze direct at them there, with awe and wonder: they felt better what of divinity is in man and Nature;—they, without being mad, could *worship* Nature, and man more than anything else in Nature. Worship, that is, as I said above, admire without limit: this, in the full use of their faculties, with all sincerity of heart, they could do. I consider Hero-worship to be the grand modifying element in that ancient system of thought. What I called the perplexed jungle of Paganism sprang, we may say, out of many roots: every admiration, adoration of a star or natural object, was a root or fiber of a root; but Hero-worship is the deepest root of all; the tap-root, from which in a great degree all the rest were nourished and grown.

And now if worship even of a star had some meaning in it, how much more might that of a Hero! Worship of a Hero is transcendent admiration of a Great Man. I say great men are still admirable; I say there is, at bottom, nothing else admirable! No nobler feeling than this of admiration for one higher than himself dwells in the breast of man. It is to this hour, and at all hours, the vivifying influence in man's life. Religion I find stand upon it; not Paganism only, but far higher and truer religions,—all religion hitherto known. Hero-worship heartfelt prostrate admiration, submission, burning, boundless, for a noblest godlike Form of Man,—is not that the germ of Christianity itself? The greatest of all Heroes in One—whom we do not name here! Let sacred silence meditate that sacred matter; you will find it the ultimate perfection of a principle extant throughout man's whole history on earth.

44 Pseudonym of Friedrich von Hardenberg (1772–1801), German mystic.

Or coming into lower, less *un*speakable provinces, is not all Loyalty akin to religious Faith also? Faith is loyalty to some inspired Teacher, some spiritual Hero. And what therefore is loyalty proper, the life-breath of all society, but an effluence of Hero-worship, submissive admiration for the truly great? Society is founded on Hero-worship. All dignities of rank, on which human association rests, are what we may call a *Hero*archy (Government of Heroes),—or a Hierarchy, for it is "sacred" enough withal! The Duke means *Dux*, Leader; King is *Kön-ning, Kan-ning,* Man that *knows* or *cans*. Society everywhere is some representation, not *in*supportably inaccurate, of a graduated Worship of Heroes;—reverence and obedience done to men really great and wise. Not *in*supportably inaccurate, I say! They are all as bank-notes, these social dignitaries, all representing gold;—and several of them, alas, always are *forged* notes. We can do with some forged false notes; with a good many even; but not with all, or the most of them forged! No: there have to come revolutions then; cries of Democracy, Liberty, and Equality, and I know not what:—the notes being all false, and no gold to be had for *them,* people take to crying in their despair that there is no gold, that there never was any! —"Gold," Hero-worship, *is* nevertheless, as it was always and everywhere, and cannot cease till man himself ceases.

I am well aware that in these days Hero-worship, the thing I call Hero-worship, professes to have gone out, and finally ceased. This, for reasons which it will be worth while some time to inquire into, is an age that as it were denies the existence of great men; denies the desirableness of great men. Show our critics a great man, a Luther for example, they begin to what they call "account" for him; not to worship him, but take the dimensions of him,—and bring him out to be a little kind of man! He was the "creature of the Time," they say; the Time called him forth, the Time did everything, he nothing—but what we the little critic could have done too! This seems to me but melancholy work. The Time call forth? Alas, we have known Times *call* loudly enough for their great man; but not find him when they called! He was not there; Providence had not sent him; the Time, *calling* its loudest, had to go down to confusion and wreck because he would not come when called.

For if we will think of it, no Time need have gone to ruin, could it have *found* a man great enough, a man wise and good enough: wisdom to discern truly what the Time wanted, valor to lead it on the right road thither; these are the salvation of any Time. But I liken common languid Times, with their unbelief, distress, perplexity, with their languid doubting characters and embarrassed circumstances, impotently crumbling-

down into ever worse distress towards final ruin;—all this I
liken to dry dead fuel, waiting for the lightning out of Heaven
that shall kindle it. The great man, with his free force direct out
of God's own hand, is the lightning. His word is the wise healing word. which all can believe in. All blazes round him now,
when he has once struck on it, into fire like his own. The dry
moldering sticks are thought to have called him forth. They
did want him greatly; but as to calling him forth—!—Those are
critics of small vision, I think, who cry: "See, is it not the sticks
10 that made the fire?" No sadder proof can be given by a man
of his own littleness than disbelief in great men. There is no
sadder symptom of a generation than such general blindness to
the spiritual lightning, with faith only in the heap of barren
dead fuel. It is the last consummation of unbelief. In all epochs
of the world's history, we shall find the Great Man to have been
the indispensable savior of his epoch;—the lightning, without
which the fuel never would have burnt. The History of the
World, I said already, was the Biography of Great Men.

Such small critics do what they can to promote unbelief and
20 universal spiritual paralysis; but happily they cannot always
completely succeed. In all times it is possible for a man to arise
great enough to feel that they and their doctrines are chimeras
and cobwebs. And what is notable, in no time whatever can
they entirely eradicate out of living men's hearts a certain altogether peculiar reverence for Great Men; genuine admiration,
loyalty, adoration, however dim and perverted it may be. Hero-
worship endures for ever while man endures. Boswell venerates
his Johnson, right truly even in the Eighteenth century. The un-
believing French believe in their Voltaire; and burst-out round
30 him into very curious Hero-worship, in that last act of his life
when they "stifle him under roses." [45] It has always seemed to
me extremely curious this of Voltaire. Truly, if Christianity
be the highest instance of Hero-worship, then we may find here
in Voltaireism one of the lowest! He whose life was that of a
kind of Antichrist, does again on this side exhibit a curious contrast. No people ever were so little prone to admire at all as
those French of Voltaire. *Persiflage* was the character of their
whole mind; adoration had nowhere a place in it. Yet see! The
old man of Ferney comes up to Paris; an old, tottering, infirm
40 man of eighty-four years. They feel that he too is a kind of
Hero; that he has spent his life in opposing error and injustice,
delivering Calases,[46] unmasking hypocrites in high places;—in
short that *he* too, though in a strange way, has fought like a

45 on his return to Paris   46 Calas was a French
in 1778, after an exile of   Protestant who was fanati-
more   than   twenty-five cally put to death in 1762.
years

valiant man. They feel withal that, if *persiflage* be the great thing, there never was such a *persifleur*. He is the realized ideal of every one of them; the thing they are all wanting to be; of all Frenchmen the most French. *He* is properly their god,—such god as they are fit for. Accordingly all persons, from the Queen Antoinette to the Douanier [47] at the Porte St. Denis, do they not worship him? People of quality disguise themselves as tavern-waiters. The Maître de Poste,[48] with a broad oath, orders his Postillion, *"Va bon train;* [49] thou art driving M. de Voltaire."￼ At Paris his carriage is "the nucleus of a comet, whose train fills whole streets." The ladies pluck a hair or two from his fur, to keep it as a sacred relic. There was nothing highest, beautifulest, noblest in all France, that did not feel this man to be higher, beautifuler, nobler.

Yes, from Norse Odin to English Samuel Johnson, from the divine Founder of Christianity to the withered Pontiff of Encyclopedism,[50] in all times and places, the Hero has been worshiped. It will ever be so. We all love great men; love, venerate, and bow down submissive before great men: nay can we honestly bow down to anything else? Ah, does not every true man feel that he is himself made higher by doing reverence to what is really above him? No nobler or more blessed feeling dwells in man's heart. And to me it is very cheering to consider that no sceptical logic, or general triviality, insincerity and aridity of any Time and its influences can destroy this noble inborn loyalty and worship that is in man. In times of unbelief, which soon have to become times of revolution, much down-rushing, sorrowful decay and ruin is visible to everybody. For myself, in these days, I seem to see in this indestructibility of Hero-worship the everlasting adamant lower than which the confused wreck of revolutionary things cannot fall. The confused wreck of things crumbling and even crashing and tumbling all round us in these revolutionary ages, will get down so far; *no* farther. It is an eternal corner-stone, from which they can begin to build themselves up again. That man, in some sense or other, worships Heroes; that we all of us reverence and must ever reverence Great Men: this is, to me, the living rock amid all rushings-down whatsoever;—the one fixed point in modern revolutionary history, otherwise as if bottomless and shoreless.

PAST AND PRESENT

The "Past" in Carlyle's title concerns the admirable rule of the Monastery of Saint Edmundsbury in the twelfth century by Abbot Samson; with it is contrasted the "present"—the England of 1843, alarmed by the recent popular uprisings known as the Chartist riots, confused and discontented, with no

47 customs officer
48 master of the post-horses

49 go at a good pace
50 Voltaire

clear social and political vision. Carlyle advocated various measures, but could adhere to the program of no political party or group. His pamphlet aimed, rather, at arousing all classes—the laborers, the material middle classes, and the landed aristocracy—to higher ideals and a sense of their mutual obligations. The section here reprinted on "Labor" and "Reward" from Book III, Chapters xi and xii, illustrates the general tenor of his preaching.

BOOK III

CHAPTER XI

Labor

FOR there is a perennial nobleness, and even sacredness, in Work. Were he never so benighted, forgetful of his high calling, there is always hope in a man that actually and earnestly works: in Idleness alone is there perpetual despair. Work, never so Mammonish, mean, *is* in communication with Nature; the real desire to get Work done will itself lead one more and more to truth, to Nature's appointments and regulations, which are truth.

The latest Gospel in this world is, Know thy work and do it.
10 "Know thyself": long enough has that poor "self" of thine tormented thee; thou wilt never get to "know" it, I believe! Think it not thy business, this of knowing thyself; thou art an unknowable individual: know what thou canst work at; and work at it, like a Hercules! That will be thy better plan.

It has been written, "an endless significance lies in Work"; a man perfects himself by working. Foul jungles are cleared away, fair seedfields rise instead, and stately cities; and withal the man himself first ceases to be a jungle and foul unwholesome desert thereby. Consider how, even in the meanest sorts
20 of Labor, the whole soul of a man is composed into a kind of real harmony, the instant he sets himself to work! Doubt, Desire, Sorrow, Remorse, Indignation, Despair itself, all these like helldogs lie beleaguering the soul of the poor dayworker, as of every man; but he bends himself with free valor against his task, and all these are stilled, all these shrink murmuring far off into their caves. The man is now a man. The blessed glow of Labor in him, is it not as purifying fire, wherein all poison is burnt up, and of sour smoke itself there is made bright blessed flame!
30 Destiny, on the whole, has no other way of cultivating us. A formless Chaos, once set it *revolving,* grows round and ever rounder; ranges itself, by mere force of gravity, into strata, spherical courses; is no longer a Chaos, but a round compacted World. What would become of the Earth, did she cease to revolve? In the poor old Earth, so long as she revolves, all in-

equalities, irregularities disperse themselves; all irregularities are incessantly becoming regular. Hast thou looked on the Potter's wheel,—one of the venerablest objects; old as the Prophet Ezekiel and far older? Rude lumps of clay, how they spin themselves up, by mere quick whirling, into beautiful circular dishes. And fancy the most assiduous Potter, but without his wheel; reduced to make dishes or rather amorphous botches, by mere kneading and baking! Even such a Potter were Destiny, with a human soul that would rest and lie at ease, that would not work and spin! Of an idle unrevolving man the kindest Destiny, like the most assiduous Potter without wheel, can bake and knead nothing other than a botch; let her spend on him what expensive coloring, what gilding and enameling she will, he is but a botch. Not a dish; no, a bulging, kneaded, crooked, shambling, squint-cornered, amorphous botch,—a mere enameled vessel of dishonor! Let the idle think of this.

Blessed is he who has found his work; let him ask no other blessedness. He has a work, a life-purpose; he has found it, and will follow it! How, as a free-flowing channel, dug and torn by noble force through the sour mud-swamp of one's existence, like an ever-deepening river there, it runs and flows;—draining off the sour festering water, gradually from the root of the remotest grass-blade; making, instead of pestilential swamp, a green fruitful meadow with its clear-flowing stream. How blessed for the meadow itself, let the stream and *its* value be great or small! Labor is Life: from the inmost heart of the Worker rises his god-given Force, the sacred celestial Life-essence breathed into him by Almighty God; from his inmost heart awakens him to all nobleness,—to all knowledge, "self-knowledge" and much else, so soon as Work fitly begins. Knowledge? The knowledge that will hold good in working, cleave thou to that; for Nature herself accredits that, says Yea to that. Properly thou hast no other knowledge but what thou hast got by working: the rest is yet all a hypothesis of knowledge; a thing to be argued of in schools, a thing floating in the clouds, in endless logic-vortices, till we try and fix it. "Doubt, of whatever kind, can be ended by Action alone."

And again, hast thou valued Patience, Courage, Perseverance, Openness to light; readiness to own thyself mistaken, to do better next time? All these, all virtues, in wrestling with the dim brute Powers of Fact, in ordering of thy fellows in such wrestle, there and elsewhere not at all, thou wilt continually learn. Set down a brave Sir Christopher[51] in the middle of

---

[51] Sir Christopher Wren (1632–1723), great English architect, who designed the new St. Paul's Cathedral, London.

black ruined Stone-heaps, of foolish unarchitectural Bishops, red-tape Officials, idle Nell Gwyn Defenders of the Faith; [52] and see whether he will ever raise a Paul's Cathedral out of all that, yea or no! Rough, rude, contradictory are all things and persons, from the mutinous masons and Irish hodmen, up to the idle Nell Gwyn Defenders, to blustering redtape Officials, foolish unarchitectural Bishops. All these things and persons are there not for Christopher's sake and his Cathedral's; they are there for their own sake mainly! Christopher will have to
10 conquer and constrain all these,—if he be able. All these are against him. Equitable Nature herself, who carries her mathematics and architectonics not on the face of her, but deep in the hidden heart of her,—Nature herself is but partly for him; will be wholly against him, if he constrain her not! His very money, where is it to come from? The pious munificence of England lies far-scattered, distant, unable to speak, and say, "I am here";—must be spoken to before it can speak. Pious munificence, and all help, is so silent, invisible like the gods; impediments, contradictions manifold are so loud and so near! O
20 brave Sir Christopher, trust thou in those notwithstanding, and front all these; understand all these; by valiant patience, noble effort, insight, by man's-strength, vanquish and compel all these,—and, on the whole, strike down victoriously the last topstone of that Paul's Edifice; thy monument for certain centuries, the stamp "Great Man" impressed very legibly on Portland-stone there!

Yes, all manner of help, and pious response from Men or Nature, is always what we call silent; cannot speak or come to light, till it be seen, till it be spoken to. Every noble work is
30 at first "impossible." In very truth, for every noble work the possibilities will lie diffused through Immensity; inarticulate, undiscoverable except to faith. Like Gideon thou shalt spread out thy fleece at the door of thy tent; see whether under the wide arch of Heaven there be any bounteous moisture, or none.[53] Thy heart and life-purpose shall be as a miraculous Gideon's fleece, spread out in silent appeal to Heaven: and from the kind Immensities, what from the poor unkind Localities and town and country Parishes there never could, blessed dew-moisture to suffice thee shall have fallen!
40 Work is of a religious nature:—work is of a *brave* nature; which it is the aim of all religion to be. All work of man is as the swimmer's: a waste ocean threatens to devour him; if he front it not bravely, it will keep its word. By incessant wise defiance of it, lusty rebuke and buffet of it, behold how it loyally

52 Title of Charles II was Nell Gwyn one of whose mistresses 53 Judges, vi. 37, 38

supports him, bears him as its conqueror along. "It is so," says Goethe, "with all the things that man undertakes in this world."

Brave Sea-captain, Norse Sea-king,—Columbus, my hero, royalest Sea-king of all! it is no friendly environment this of thine, in the waste deep waters; around thee mutinous discouraged souls, behind thee disgrace and ruin, before thee the unpenetrated veil of Night. Brother, these wild water-mountains, bounding from their deep bases (ten miles deep, I am told) are not entirely there on thy behalf! Meseems *they* have other work than floating thee forward:—and the huge Winds, that sweep from Ursa Major [54] to the Tropics and Equators, dancing their giant-waltz through the kingdoms of Chaos and Immensity, they care little about filling rightly or filling wrongly the small shoulder-of-mutton sails in this cockle-skiff of thine! Thou art not among articulate-speaking friends, my brother; thou art among immeasurable dumb monsters, tumbling, howling wide as the world here. Secret, far off, invisible to all hearts but thine, there lies a help in them: see how thou wilt get at that. Patiently thou wilt wait till the mad Southwester spends itself, saving thyself by dextrous science of defence, the while: valiantly, with swift decision, wilt thou strike in, when the favoring East, the Possible, springs up. Mutiny of men thou wilt sternly repress; weakness, despondency, thou wilt cheerily encourage: thou wilt swallow down complaint, unreason, weariness, weakness of others and thyself;—how much wilt thou swallow down! There shall be a depth of Silence in thee, deeper than this Sea, which is but ten miles deep: a Silence unsoundable; known to God only. Thou shalt be a Great Man. Yes, my World-Soldier, thou of the World Marine-service,—thou wilt have to be *greater* than this tumultuous unmeasured World here round thee is; thou, in thy strong soul, as with wrestler's arms, shalt embrace it, harness it down; and make it bear thee on, —to new Americas, or whither God wills!

CHAPTER XII

Reward

"Religion," I said; for, properly speaking, all true Work is Religion: and whatsoever Religion is not Work may go and dwell among the Brahmins, Antinomians, Spinning Dervishes, or where it will; with me it shall have no harbor. Admirable was that of the old Monks, "Laborare est Orare, Work is Worship."

[54] Great Bear; prominent constellation in the northern heavens

Older than all preached Gospels was this unpreached, inarticulate, but ineradicable, forever-enduring Gospel: Work, and therein have well-being. Man, Son of Earth and Son of Heaven, lies there not, in the innermost heart of thee, a Spirit of active Method, a Force for Work;—and burns like a painfully-smoldering fire, giving thee no rest till thou unfold it, till thou write it down in beneficent Facts around thee! What is immethodic, waste, thou shalt make methodic, regulated, arable; obedient and productive to thee. Wheresoever thou findest Dis-
10 order, there is thy eternal enemy; attack him swiftly, subdue him; make Order of him, the subject not of Chaos, but of Intelligence, Divinity, and Thee! The thistle that grows in thy path, dig it out, that a blade of useful grass, a drop of nourishing milk, may grow there instead. The waste cotton-shrub, gather its waste white down, spin it, weave it; that, in place of idle litter, there may be folded webs, and the naked skin of man be covered.

But above all, where thou findest Ignorance, Stupidity, Brute-mindedness,—yes, there, with or without Church-tithes and
20 Shovel-hat,[55] with or without Talfourd-Mahon Copyrights,[56] or were it with mere dungeons and gibbets and crosses, attack it, I say; smite it wisely, unweariedly, and rest not while thou livest and it lives; but smite, smite in the name of God! The Highest God, as I understand it, does audibly so command thee; still audibly, if you have ears to hear. He, even He, with his *un*spoken voice, awfuler than any Sinai thunders or syllabled speech of Whirlwinds; for the SILENCE of deep Eternities, of Worlds from beyond the morning-stars, does it not speak to thee? The unborn Ages; the old Graves, with their
30 long-moldering dust, the very tears that wetted it now all dry, —do not these speak to thee, what ear hath not heard? The deep Death-kingdoms, the Stars in their never-resting courses, all Space and all Time, proclaim it to thee in continual silent admonition. Thou too, if ever man should, shalt work while it is called To-day. For the Night cometh, wherein no man can work.

All true Work is sacred; in all true Work, were it but true hand-labor, there is something of divineness. Labor, wide as the Earth, has its summit in Heaven. Sweat of the brow; and up
40 from that to sweat of the brain, sweat of the heart; which includes all Kepler[57] calculations, Newton[58] meditations, all Sciences, all spoken Epics, all acted Heroisms, Martyrdoms,— up to that "Agony of bloody sweat," which all men have called

---

55 sign of the cleric
56 Sir Thomas Noon Talfourd and Earl Mahon were the authors of the new copyright laws.
57 Johannes Kepler (1571–1630), German astronomer
58 Sir Isaac Newton (1642–1727), famous for his law of gravitation

divine! O brother, if this is not "worship," then I say, the more pity for worship; for this is the noblest thing yet discovered under God's sky. Who art thou that complainest of thy life of toil? Complain not. Look up, my wearied brother; see thy fellow Workmen there, in God's Eternity; surviving there, they alone surviving: sacred Band of the Immortals, celestial Bodyguard of the Empire of Mankind. Even in the weak Human Memory they survive so long, as saints, as heroes, as gods; they alone surviving; peopling, they alone, the unmeasured solitudes of Time! To thee Heaven, though severe, is *not* unkind; Heaven is kind,—as a noble Mother; as that Spartan Mother, saying while she gave her son his shield, "With it, my son, or upon it!" Thou too shalt return *home* in honor; doubt it not,—if in the battle thou keep thy shield! Thou, in the Eternities and deepest Death-kingdoms, art not an alien; thou everywhere art a denizen! Complain not; the very Spartans did not *complain.*

And who art thou that braggest of thy life of Idleness; complacently showest thy bright gilt equipages; sumptuous cushions; appliances for folding of the hands to mere sleep? Looking up, looking down, around, behind or before, discernest thou, if it be not in Mayfair [59] alone, any *idle* hero, saint, god, or even devil? Not a vestige of one. In the Heavens, in the Earth, in the Waters under the Earth, is none like unto thee. Thou art an original figure in this Creation; a denizen in Mayfair alone, in this extraordinary Century or Half-Century alone! One monster there is in the world: the idle man. What is his "Religion"? That Nature is a Phantasm, where cunning beggary or thievery may sometimes find good victual. That God is a lie; and that Man and his Life are a lie. Alas, alas, who of us *is* there that can say, I have worked? The faithfulest of us are unprofitable servants; the faithfulest of us know that best. The faithfulest of us may say, with sad and true old Samuel,[60] "Much of my life has been trifled away!" But he that has, and except "on public occasions" professes to have, no function but that of going idle in a graceful or graceless manner; and of begetting sons to go idle; and to address Chief Spinners and Diggers, who at least *are* spinning and digging, "Ye scandalous persons who produce too much"—My Corn-Law friends, on what imaginary still richer Eldorados, and true iron-spikes with law of gravitation, are ye rushing!

As to the Wages of Work there might innumerable things be said; there will and must yet innumerable things be said and spoken, in St. Stephen's [61] and out of St. Stephen's; and gradually not a few things be ascertained and written on Law-parchment, concerning this very matter:—"Fair day's-wages for a fair day's-work" is the most unrefusable demand! Money-wages "to the extent of keeping your worker alive that he may work more"; these, unless you mean to dismiss him straight-way out of this world, are indispensable alike to the noblest Worker and to the least noble!

One thing only I will say here, in special reference to the former class, the noble and noblest; but throwing light on all
10 the other classes and their arrangements of this difficult mat-ter: The "wages" of every noble Work do yet lie in Heaven or else nowhere. Not in Bank-of-England bills, in Owen's [62] Labor Bank, or any the most improved establishment of bank-ing and money-changing, needest thou, heroic soul, present thy account of earnings. Human banks and labor-banks know thee not; or know thee after generations and centuries have passed away, and thou art clean gone from "rewarding,"—all manner of bank-drafts, shop-tills, and Downing Street Ex-chequers lying very invisible, so far from thee! Nay, at bottom,
20 dost thou need any reward? Was it thy aim and life-purpose to be filled with good things for thy heroism; to have a life of pomp and ease, and be what men call "happy," in this world, or any other world? I answer for thee deliberately, No. The whole spiritual secret of the new epoch lies in this, that thou canst answer for thyself, with thy whole clearness of head and heart, deliberately, No!

My brother, the brave man has to give his Life away. Give it, I advise thee;—thou dost not expect to *sell* thy Life in an adequate manner? What price, for example, would content thee?
30 The just price of thy LIFE to thee,—why, God's entire Crea-tion to thyself, the whole Universe of Space, the whole Eternity of Time, and what they hold: that is the price which would content thee: that, and if thou wilt be candid, nothing short of that! It is thy all; and for it thou wouldst have all. Thou art an unreasonable mortal;—or rather thou art a poor *infinite* mortal, who, in thy narrow clay-prison here, *seemest* so un-reasonable! Thou wilt never sell thy Life, or any part of thy Life, in a satisfactory manner. Give it, like a royal heart; let the price be Nothing: thou *hast* then, in a certain sense, got
40 All for it! The heroic man—and is not every man, God be thanked, a potential hero?—has to do so, in all times and cir-cumstances. In the most heroic age, as in the most unheroic, he will have to say, as Burns said proudly and humbly of his little Scottish songs, little dewdrops of Celestial Melody in an age when so much was unmelodious: "By Heaven, they shall either

62 Robert Owen (1771–1858), British social reformer

be invaluable or of no value; I do not need your guineas for them." It is an element which should, and must, enter deeply into all settlements of wages here below. They will never be "satisfactory" otherwise; they cannot, O Mammon Gospel, they never can! Money for my little piece of work "to the extent that will allow me to keep working"; yes, this,—unless you mean that I shall go my ways *before* the work is all taken out of me: but as to "wages"—! . . .

LATTER-DAY PAMPHLETS

In these his denunciations become more vehement, while the remedies suggested seem even less adaptable to the conditions of a practical world. "The only satisfactory reform suggested," says Leslie Stephen, "the miraculous advent of a hero and the conversion of the people, was hardly capable of application to facts." The first of the Pamphlets is here condensed as expressing perhaps most vigorously Carlyle's characteristic views on Democracy, with some interesting comments on the experiment in government of the United States.

No. I. The Present Time

. . . WHAT *is* Democracy; this huge inevitable Product of the Destinies, which is everywhere the portion of our Europe in 10 these latter days? There lies the question for us. Whence comes it, this universal big black Democracy; whither tends it; what is the meaning of it? A meaning it must have, or it would not be here. If we can find the right meaning of it, we may, wisely submitting or wisely resisting and controlling, still hope to live in the midst of it; if we cannot find the right meaning, if we find only the wrong or no meaning in it, to live will not be possible!—The whole social wisdom of the Present Time is summoned, in the name of the Giver of Wisdom, to make clear to itself, and lay deeply to heart with an eye to strenuous vali- 20 ant practice and effort, what the meaning of this universal revolt of the European Populations, which calls itself Democracy, and decides to continue permanent, may be.

Certainly it is a drama full of action, event fast following event; in which curiosity finds endless scope, and there are interests at stake, enough to rivet the attention of all men, simple and wise. Whereat the idle multitude lift-up their voices, gratulating, celebrating sky-high; in rhyme and prose announcement, more than plentiful, that *now* the New Era, the long-expected Year One of Perfect Human Felicity has come. 30 Glorious and immortal people, sublime French citizens, heroic barricades; triumph of civil and religious liberty—O Heaven! one of the inevitablest private miseries, to an earnest man in

such circumstances, is this multitudinous efflux of oratory and
psalmody, from the universal foolish human throat; drowning
for the moment all reflection whatsoever, except the sorrowful
one that you are fallen in an evil, heavy-laden, long-eared age,
and must resignedly bear your part in the same. The front wall
of your wretched old crazy dwelling, long denounced by you to
no purpose, having at last fairly folded itself over, and fallen
prostrate into the street, the floors, as may happen, will still
hang-on by the mere beam-ends, and coherency of old carpentry,
10 though in a sloping direction, and depend there till certain
poor rusty nails and wormeaten dovetailings give way:—but
is it cheering, in such circumstances, that the whole household
burst-forth into celebrating the new joys of light and ventila-
tion, liberty and picturesqueness of position, and thank God
that now they have got a house to their mind? My dear household, cease singing and psalmodying; lay aside your fiddles,
take out your work-implements, if you have any; for I can say
with confidence the laws of gravitation are still active, and rusty
nails, wormeaten dovetailings, and secret coherency of old car-
20 pentry, are not the best basis for a household!—In the lanes of
Irish cities, I have heard say, the wretched people are sometimes found living, and perilously boiling their potatoes, on such
swing-floors and inclined planes hanging-on by the joist-ends;
but I did not hear that they sang very much in celebration of
such lodging. No, they slid gently about, sat near the back wall,
and perilously boiled their potatoes, in silence for the most
part!—

High shouts of exultation, in every dialect, by every vehicle
of speech and writing, rise from far and near over this last
30 avatar [63] of Democracy in 1848: [64] and yet, to wise minds, the
first aspect it presents seems rather to be one of boundless
misery and sorrow. What can be more miserable than this universal hunting-out of the high dignitaries, solemn functionaries,
and potent, grave and reverend signiors of the world; this
stormful rising-up of the inarticulate dumb masses everywhere,
against those who pretended to be speaking for them and guiding them? These guides, then, were mere blind men only pretending to see? These rulers were not ruling at all; they had
merely got-on the attributes and clothes of rulers, and were
40 surreptitiously drawing the wages, while the work remained
undone? The Kings were Sham-Kings, playacting as at Drury
Lane? . . .

Or perhaps Democracy, which we announce as now come,
will itself manage it? Democracy, once modeled into suffrages,

63 incarnation   second republic in France,   Philippe—and echoes in
64 establishment of the   with abdication of Louis   other European countries

furnished with ballot-boxes and suchlike, will itself accomplish
the salutary universal change from Delusive to Real, and make
a new blessed world of us by and by?—To the great mass of
men, I am aware, the matter presents itself quite on this hopeful side. Democracy they consider to *be* a kind of "Government." The old model, formed long since, and brought to perfection in England now two hundred years ago, has proclaimed
itself to all Nations as the new healing for every woe: "Set-up
a Parliament," the Nations everywhere say, when the old King is
detected to be a Sham-King, and hunted out or not; "set-up a
Parliament; let us have suffrages, universal suffrages; and all
either at once or by due degrees will be right, and a real Millennium come!" Such is their way of construing the matter.

Such, alas, is by no means my way of construing the matter;
if it were, I should have had the happiness of remaining silent,
and been without call to speak here. It is because the contrary
of all this is deeply manifest to me, and appears to be forgotten
by multitudes of my contemporaries, that I have had to undertake addressing a word to them. The contrary of all this;—and
the farther I look into the roots of all this, the more hateful,
ruinous and dismal does the state of mind all this could have
originated in appear to me. To examine this recipe of a Parliament, how fit it is for governing Nations, nay how fit it may
now be, in these new times, for governing England itself where
we are used to it so long: this, too, is an alarming inquiry, to
which all thinking men, and good citizens of their country, who
have an ear for the small still voices and eternal intimations,
across the temporary clamors and loud blaring proclamations,
are now solemnly invited. Invited by the rigorous fact itself;
which will one day, and that perhaps soon, demand practical
decision or redecision of it from us,—with enormous penalty
if we decide it wrong! I think we shall all have to consider this
question, one day; better perhaps now than later, when the
leisure may be less. If a Parliament, with suffrages and universal or any conceivable kind of suffrages, *is* the method, then
certainly let us set about discovering the kind of suffrages, and
rest no moment till we have got them. But it is possible a
Parliament may not be the method! Possible the inveterate
notions of the English People may have settled it as the method,
and the Everlasting Laws of Nature may have settled it as not
the method! Not the whole method; nor the method at all, if
taken as the whole? If a Parliament with never such suffrages
is *not* the method settled by this latter authority, then it will
urgently behove us to become aware of that fact, and to quit
such method;—we may depend upon it, however unanimous
we be, every step taken in that direction will, by the Eternal

Law of things, be a step *from* improvement, not towards it.
Not towards it, I say, if so! Unanimity of voting,—that will
do nothing for us if *so*. Your ship cannot double Cape Horn
by its excellent plans of voting. The ship may vote this and that,
above decks and below, in the most harmonious, exquisitely
constitutional manner: the ship, to get round Cape Horn, will
find a set of conditions already voted for, and fixed with adamantine rigor by the ancient Elemental Powers, who are entirely
careless how you vote. If you can, by voting or without voting,
10 ascertain these conditions, and valiantly conform to them, you
will get around the Cape: if you cannot—the ruffian Winds will
blow you ever back again; the inexorable Icebergs, dumb privy-
councilors from Chaos, will nudge you with most chaotic "admonition"; you will be flung half-frozen on the Patagonian
cliffs, or admonished into shivers by your iceberg councilors,
and sent sheer down to Davy Jones, and will never get round
Cape Horn at all! Unanimity on board ship;—yes indeed, the
ship's crew may be very unanimous, which doubtless, for the
time being, will be very comfortable to the ship's crew, and to
20 their Phantasm Captain if they have one: but if the tack they
unanimously steer upon is guiding them into the belly of the
Abyss, it will not profit them much!—Ships accordingly do
not use the ballot-box at all; and they reject the Phantasm
species of Captains: one wishes much some other Entities,—
since all entities lie under the same rigorous set of laws,—
could be brought to show as much wisdom, and sense at least
of self-preservation, the *first* command of Nature. Phantasm
Captains with unanimous votings: this is considered to be all the
law and all the prophets, at present. . . .
30 Historically speaking, I believe there was no Nation that
could subsist upon Democracy. Of ancient Republics, and
Demoi and *Populi*, we have heard much; but it is now pretty
well admitted to be nothing to our purpose;—a universal-suf-
frage republic, or a general-suffrage one, or any but a most-
limited-suffrage one, never came to light, or dreamed of doing
so, in ancient times. When the mass of the population were
slaves, and the voters intrinsically a kind of *kings*, or men
born to rule others; when the voters were *real* "aristocrats" and
manageable dependents of such,—then doubtless voting, and
40 confused jumbling of talk and intrigue, might, without immediate destruction, or the need of a Cavaignac [65] to intervene with
cannon and sweep the streets clear of it, go on; and beautiful
developments of manhood might be possible beside it, for a
season. Beside it; or even, if you will, by means of it, and in
virtue of it, though that is by no means so certain as is often

65 in the French Revolution of 1848

supposed. Alas, no: the reflective constitutional mind has misgivings as to the origin of old Greek and Roman nobleness; and
indeed knows not how this or any other human nobleness could
well be "originated," or brought to pass, by voting or without
voting, in this world, except by the grace of God very mainly;
—and remembers, with a sigh, that of the Seven Sages themselves no fewer than three were bits of Despotic Kings,
Τύραννοι, "Tyrants" so-called (such being greatly wanted
there); and that the other four were very far from Red Republicans, if of any political faith whatever! We may quit the ₁₀
Ancient Classical concern, and leave it to College-clubs and
speculative debating-societies, in these late days.

Of the various French Republics that have been tried, or
that are still on trial,—of these also it is not needful to say
any word. But there is one modern instance of Democracy
nearly perfect, the Republic of the United States, which has
actually subsisted for threescore years or more, with immense
success as is affirmed; to which many still appeal, as to a sign
of hope for all nations, and a "Model Republic." Is not America
an instance in point? Why should not all Nations subsist and ₂₀
flourish on Democracy, as America does?

Of America it would ill beseem any Englishman, and me perhaps as little as another, to speak unkindly, to speak *unpatri-
otically,* if any of us even felt so. Sure enough, America is a
great, and in many respects a blessed and hopeful, phenomenon.
Sure enough, these hardy millions of Anglo-saxon men prove
themselves worthy of their genealogy; and, with the axe and
plow and hammer, if not yet with any much finer kind of
implements, are triumphantly clearing-out wide spaces, seedfields for the sustenance and refuge of mankind, arenas for the ₃₀
future history of the world; doing, in their day and generation,
a creditable and cheering feat under the sun. But as to a
Model Republic, or a model anything, the wise among themselves know too well that there is nothing to be said. Nay, the
title hitherto to be a Commonwealth or Nation at all, among
the ἔθνη [66] of the world, is, strictly considered, still a thing they
are but striving for, and indeed have not yet done much
towards attaining. Their Constitution, such as it may be, was
made here, not there; went over with them from the Old-
Puritan English workshop ready-made. Deduct what they car- ₄₀
ried with them from England ready-made,—their common
English Language, and that same Constitution, or rather elixir
of constitutions, their inveterate and now, as it were, inborn
reverence for the Constable's Staff; two quite immense attain-
ments, which England had to spend much blood, and valiant

66 races

sweat of brow and brain, for centuries long, in achieving;—and what new elements of polity or nationhood, what noble new phasis of human arrangement, or social device worthy of Prometheus or of Epimetheus,[67] yet comes to light in America? Cotton-crops and Indian-corn and dollars come to light; and half a world of untilled land, where populations that respect the constable can live, for the present *without* Government: this comes to light; and the profound sorrow of all nobler hearts, here uttering itself as silent patient unspeakable ennui,
10 there coming out as vague elegiac wailings, that there is still next to nothing more. "Anarchy *plus* a street-constable": that also is anarchic to me, and other than quite lovely!

I foresee, too, that, long before the waste lands are full, the very street-constable, on these poor terms, will have become impossible: without the waste lands, as here in our Europe, I do not see how he could continue possible many weeks. Cease to brag to me of America, and its model institutions and constitutions. To men in their sleep there is nothing granted in this world: nothing, or as good as nothing, to men that sit idly
20 *caucusing* and ballot-boxing on the graves of their heroic ancestors, saying, "It is well, it is well!" Corn and bacon are granted: not a very sublime boon, on such conditions; a boon moreover which, on such conditions, cannot last! No: America too will have to strain its energies, in quite other fashion than this; to crack its sinews, and all-but break its heart, as the rest of us have had to do, in thousandfold wrestle with the Pythons [68] and mud-demons, before it can become a habitation for the gods. America's battle is yet to fight; and we, sorrowful though nothing doubting, will wish her strength for it. New
30 Spiritual Pythons, plenty of them; enormous Megatherions, as ugly as were ever born of mud, loom huge and hideous out of the twilight Future on America; and she will have her own agony, and her own victory, but on other terms than she is yet quite aware of. Hitherto she but plows and hammers, in a very successful manner; hitherto in spite of her "roast-goose with apple-sauce," she is not much. "Roast-goose with apple-sauce for the poorest working-man": well, surely that is something,—thanks to your respect for the street-constable, and to your continents of fertile waste land;—but that, even if it
40 could continue, is by no means enough; that is not even an installment towards what will be required of you. My friend, brag not yet of our American cousins! Their quantity of cotton, dollars, industry and resources, I believe to be almost unspeak-

---

67 Brother of Prometheus, who in spite of warnings married Pandora, and thus brought disaster on the human race. The two names mean "forethought" and "after-thought."
68 serpent bred in the mud left after the deluge, according to Greek myth; finally slain by Apollo

able; but I can by no means worship the like of these. What great human soul, what great thought, what great noble thing that one could worship, or loyally admire, has yet been produced there? None: the American cousins have yet done none of these things. "What have they done?" growls Smelfungus,[69] tired of the subject: "They have doubled their population every twenty years. They have begotten, with a rapidity beyond recorded example, Eighteen Millions of the greatest *bores* ever seen in this world before—that hitherto is their feat in History!" —And so we leave them, for the present; and cannot predict the success of Democracy, on this side of the Atlantic, from their example.

Alas, on this side of the Atlantic and on that, Democracy, we apprehend, is forever impossible! So much, with certainty of loud astonished contradiction from all manner of men present, but with sure appeal to the Law of Nature and the ever-abiding Fact, may be suggested and asserted once more. The Universe itself is a Monarchy and Hierarchy; large liberty of "voting" there, all manner of choice, utmost free-will, but with conditions inexorable and immeasurable annexed to every exercise of the same. A most free commonwealth of "voters"; but with Eternal Justice to preside over it, Eternal Justice enforced by Almighty Power! This is the model of "constitutions"; this: nor in any Nation where there has not yet (in some supportable and withal some constantly-increasing degree) been confided to the *Noblest*, with his select series of *Nobler,* the divine everlasting duty of directing and controlling the Ignoble, has the "Kingdom of God," which we all pray for, "come," nor can "His will" even *tend* to be "done on Earth as it is in Heaven" till then. My Christian friends, and indeed my Sham-Christian and Anti-Christian, and all manner of men, are invited to reflect on this. They will find it to be the truth of the case. The Noble in the high place, the Ignoble in the low; that is, in all times and in all countries, the Almighty Maker's Law.

To raise the Sham-Noblest, and solemnly consecrate *him* by whatever method, new-devised, or slavishly adhered to from old wont, this, little as we may regard it, is, in all times and countries, a practical blasphemy, and Nature will in no wise forget it. Alas, there lies the origin, the fatal necessity, of modern Democracy everywhere. It is the Noblest, not the Sham-Noblest; it is God Almighty's Noble, not the Court-Tailor's Noble, nor the Able-Editor's Noble, that must in some approximate degree, be raised to the supreme place; he and not a counterfeit,—under penalties! Penalties deep as death, and at

69 Sterne's name for a pessimistic grumbler

length terrible as hell-on-earth, my constitutional friend!—Will the ballot-box raise the Noblest to the chief place; does any sane man deliberately believe such a thing? That nevertheless is the indispensable result, attain it how we may: if that is attained, all is attained; if not that, nothing. He that cannot believe the ballot-box to be attaining it, will be comparatively indifferent to the ballot-box. Excellent for keeping the ship's crew at peace under their Phantasm Captain; but unserviceable, under such, for getting round Cape Horn. Alas, that there should be human beings requiring to have these things argued of, at this late time of day!

I say, it is the everlasting privilege of the foolish to be governed by the wise; to be guided in the right path by those who know it better than they. This is the first "right of man"; compared with which all other rights are as nothing,—mere superfluities, corollaries which will follow of their own accord out of this; if they be not contradictions to this, and less than nothing!

ALFRED, LORD TENNYSON (1809–1892)

Tennyson came of a family of landed gentry. His father, George Clayton Tennyson, when he found himself disinherited in favor of a younger brother, had entered the church, and had become rector of Somersby, in Lincolnshire. Here the poet was born, and here he lived throughout his boyhood and young manhood. The Lincolnshire scenery of sloping wold, flat field, and marsh colored the boy's imagination, and is abundantly represented in his earlier poems. He was the fourth of twelve children, all of whom except two lived to be seventy or upwards. The children had many literary games, and from an early age wrote tales and verse. Two of Tennyson's brothers, Frederick, and Charles (who afterwards added Turner to his name) also attained some reputation as poets.

With the exception of four years at Louth School, which he hated, his instruction was received at the hands of his father. In 1827, Alfred and his brother Charles, with some assistance from Frederick, published a collection of juvenile verse entitled *Poems by Two Brothers*. Alfred's contributions to this volume are largely imitative, showing especially the influence of Byron, by whom he was, as a youth, powerfully impressed. He tells us that on hearing of Byron's death in 1824, he walked out alone and carved in the sandstone, "Byron is dead."

In 1828, he and his brother Charles matriculated at Trinity College, Cambridge. At Cambridge, the most important influence upon him was his association with a group of serious-minded young men, who met in a kind of literary society, and who were called the "Apostles." There were brilliant minds among them: for instance, James Spedding, the editor of Bacon's Works; Richard Monckton Milnes, afterwards Lord Houghton, the biographer of

Keats; and especially Arthur Henry Hallam, son of the well-known historian, who was regarded by his associates as the most promising young man of his generation. The latter was before long Tennyson's closest friend, and became engaged to his sister Emily. The Apostles encouraged Tennyson in his early work, but perhaps also adversely directed his development by convincing him that poetry was a very serious business, and that it was his duty as a poet to become the spiritual guide of his age.

In 1829 he won the Newdigate prize for poetry by dressing up an old poem and giving it the required title, "Timbuctoo." His more important work of the Cambridge years is to be found in the volume of 1830, entitled *Poems, Chiefly Lyrical*, which contains many immature pieces, but also several that show power and skill. The sensuousness, the pictorial effects, and the love of beauty are signs that Keats had displaced Byron as an influence. In 1831, on the serious illness of his father, he left Cambridge without taking a degree. Meanwhile, he had been devoting himself assiduously to his poetry, the product being the *Poems* dated 1833, but published in December, 1832. In this volume Tennyson struck his stride. It includes a large number of pieces that are still among the most admired of his works. It was, however, the subject of a very savage review by John Gibson Lockhart in the *Quarterly*—an attack which seems to have distressed Tennyson greatly.

In 1833 he was dealt a serious blow in the death of Hallam. Whether he was stunned by this event, or discouraged by adverse criticism, or aroused to the conviction that his poetic powers needed maturing, for nine years he published nothing. During this period, some years after the death of his father, he had moved the family from Somersby to Epping Wood, near London. In 1842 he published *Poems,* in two volumes, containing the best of his older poems revised, and many new ones, more restrained and perfect in workmanship. This volume established Tennyson's popularity. He was even put on the civil list for a pension in 1845. In 1847 he published *The Princess,* a poem on the theme of the higher education of women, admired in its own time, but now chiefly remembered for the lyrics embedded in it.

In 1850 occurred three events that largely determined the course of Tennyson's subsequent life. He published *In Memoriam,* his elegy for Arthur Hallam, which was widely acclaimed; he married Emily Sellwood, whom he had first met and admired twenty years before, and to whom he had been engaged intermittently for thirteen years; and he was made Poet Laureate, in succession to Wordsworth. He had become famous, and during the rest of his life was regarded as the foremost of English poets. In 1852 he published his *Ode on the Death of the Duke of Wellington,* in 1855 *Maud,* and in 1864 *Enoch Arden.* Meantime he had been at work on the *Idylls of the King;* three groups of them were published in 1859, 1869, and 1872 respectively. The last Idyll, *Balin and Balan,* was published in a volume of 1885.

Shortly after his marriage Tennyson had acquired a house at Farringford, on the Isle of Wight, whence he occasionally paid a visit to Queen Victoria— whom he admired and who admired him—at her house at Osborne, in another part of the island. In 1869 he built a Gothic structure at Aldworth, in Surrey. These two houses remained Tennyson's homes till his death.

By 1872 he had practically finished the *Idylls of the King.* The next decade of his life was devoted chiefly to the writing of poetic dramas, many of them based on English history. In rapid succession appeared *Queen Mary, Harold,*

Becket, The Falcon, The Cup, and *The Promise of May,* and later *Robin Hood.*
Of these only one, *Becket,* long in the repertory of Sir Henry Irving, attained
much success on the stage.

Tennyson was now an old man, but he continued to write poetry. Nothing
in his career is more surprising than the vigor of the work produced in his
later years. He had in 1880 published a volume containing his spirited *Ballads,*
and four more volumes were yet to follow, the last one being in the press at
the time of his death. In his later years he was universally revered, indeed
almost idolized. The Government, in token of the great esteem in which he
was held, in 1884 raised him to the peerage under the title of Baron of Aldworth
and Farringford. He had previously declined a baronetcy, but when this additional honor was offered felt he must accept for the sake of literature and of
his family. This was the highest title which had ever been bestowed on a literary man. He died on October 6, 1892, and was buried in Westminster Abbey.

In the forty years since Tennyson's death he has suffered a severe decline
in reputation. With a shift in poetic taste came the feeling that his verse was
over-ornate and mechanical in its very perfection, that the ideals he raised
were hollow and the sentiments he expressed somewhat stuffy. The twentieth
century found Victorianism in many respects unacceptable, and Tennyson
suffered through his very complete embodiment of the thoughts and artistic
standards of his own time. His politics are narrowly conservative, his views
on social questions highly orthodox; while in religion, which so much distressed his contemporaries, he became the poet of the "Victorian compromise"
between the old revealed word of God and the newer science. The achievements
of his own time in the latter field, the wonders of the new inventions and
mechanical improvements, the "progress" that he saw, he sang with fervor,
and thus became peculiarly the poet of an age. In particular the modern schools
have objected to the poetry of his middle years, the "Farringford and Aldworth
period," when material prosperity had descended upon him, when adulation
became his regular due, and when he spoke in the tones of the prophet. The
fresher poetry of his youth, and to some extent the mellowed product of his
last years they find much more satisfactory. Of late there have been attempts
to reappraise his work, and a renewed appreciation has set in. The perfection
of his lyrical style, and his mastery of poetic craftsmanship must always be
praised, while the objectionable qualities of his work—if the future adjudge
them such—are attributable not so much to the poet, as to the age in which
he lived. His ultimate standing among English poets cannot yet be clearly seen.

BIBLIOGRAPHY. *Life and Works* ed. by the poet's son, Hallam, Lord Tenny-
son, 13 vols. (Macmillan). *Memoir,* by the same—pious but indispensable.
One vol. ed., the same, and Cambridge ed., by W. J. Rolfe (Houghton Mifflin).
Shorter lives by Alfred Lyall (Eng. Men of Letters ser.) and by A. C. Benson
(Dutton). A. C. Bradley, *Commentary on In Memoriam* (Macmillan). S. A.
Brooke, *Tennyson: His Art in Relation to Modern Life,* Putnam (older com-
mentary). Harold Nicolson, *Tennyson,* Houghton Mifflin (brilliant recent com-
mentary, with attempt at reappraisal). R. M. Alden, *Tennyson: How to Know
Him,* Bobbs Merrill (introduction).

THE POET

THE poet in a golden clime was born,
   With golden stars above;

Dowered with the hate of hate, the scorn of scorn,
   The love of love.

He saw through life and death, through good and ill,
   He saw through his own soul.
The marvel of the everlasting will,
   An open scroll,

Before him lay; with echoing feet he threaded
   The secretest walks of fame: 10
The viewless arrows of his thoughts were headed
   And winged with flame,

Like Indian reeds blown from his silver tongue,
   And of so fierce a flight,
From Calpe ¹ unto Caucasus they sung,
   Filling with light

And vagrant melodies the winds which bore
   Them earthward till they lit;
Then, like the arrow-seeds of the field flower,
   The fruitful wit   20

Cleaving took root, and springing forth anew
   Where'er they fell, behold,
Like to the mother plant in semblance, grew
   A flower all gold,

And bravely furnished all abroad to fling
   The wingèd shafts of truth,
To throng with stately blooms the breathing spring
   Of Hope and Youth.

So many minds did gird their orbs with beams,
   Though one did fling the fire;   30
Heaven flowed upon the soul in many dreams
   Of high desire.

Thus truth was multiplied on truth, the world
   Like one great garden showed,
And through the wreaths of floating dark upcurled,
   Rare sunrise flowed.

And Freedom reared in that august sunrise
   Her beautiful bold brow,

¹ Gibraltar

When rites and forms before his burning eyes
    Melted like snow.   40

There was no blood upon her maiden robes
    Sunned by those orient skies;
But round about the circles of the globes
    Of her keen eyes

And in her raiment's hem was traced in flame
    Wisdom, a name to shake
All evil dreams of power—a sacred name.
    And when she spake,

Her words did gather thunder as they ran,
    And as the lightning to the thunder   50
Which follows it, riving the spirit of man,
    Making earth wonder,

So was their meaning to her words. No sword
    Of wrath her right arm whirled,
But one poor poet's scroll, and with *his* word
    She shook the world.

THE LADY OF SHALOTT

Part I

On either side the river lie
Long fields of barley and of rye,
That clothe the wold and meet the sky;
And through the field the road runs by
    To many-towered Camelot; [2]

And up and down the people go,
Gazing where the lilies blow
Round an island there below,
    The island of Shalott. [3]

Willows whiten, aspens quiver,   10
Little breezes dusk and shiver
Through the wave that runs for ever
By the island in the river
    Flowing down to Camelot.
Four gray walls, and four gray towers,

2 King Arthur's legend-   3 suggested by an Ital-   Malory's Astolat
ary capital, in Cornwall   ian form (Scalotta) for

Overlook a space of flowers,
And the silent isle imbowers
    The Lady of Shalott.

By the margin, willow-veiled,
Slide the heavy barges trailed
By slow horses; and unhailed
The shallop flitteth silken-sailed
    Skimming down to Camelot:
But who hath seen her wave her hand?
Or at the casement seen her stand?
Or is she known in all the land,
    The Lady of Shalott?

Only reapers, reaping early
In among the bearded barley,
Hear a song that echoes cheerly
From the river winding clearly,
    Down to towered Camelot;
And by the moon the reaper weary,
Piling sheaves in uplands airy,
Listening, whispers " 'Tis the fairy
    Lady of Shalott."

PART II

There she weaves by night and day
A magic web with colors gay.
She has heard a whisper say,
A curse is on her if she stay
    To look down to Camelot.
She knows not what the curse may be,
And so she weaveth steadily,
And little other care hath she,
    The Lady of Shalott.

And moving through a mirror clear
That hangs before her all the year,
Shadows of the world appear.
There she sees the highway near
    Winding down to Camelot;
There the river eddy whirls,
And there the surly village-churls,
And the red cloaks of market girls,
    Pass onward from Shalott.

20

30

40

50

Sometimes a troop of damsels glad,
An abbot on an ambling pad,
Sometimes a curly shepherd-lad,
Or long-haired page in crimson clad,
    Goes by to towered Camelot;
And sometimes through the mirror blue   60
The knights come riding two and two:
She hath no loyal knight and true,
    The Lady of Shalott.

But in her web she still delights
To weave the mirror's magic sights,
For often through the silent nights
A funeral, with plumes and lights
    And music, went to Camelot;
Or when the moon was overhead,
Came two young lovers lately wed: 70
"I am half sick of shadows," said
    The Lady of Shalott.

Part III

A bow-shot from her bower-eaves,
He rode between the barley-sheaves,
The sun came dazzling through the leaves
And flamed upon the brazen greaves
    Of bold Sir Lancelot.
A red-cross knight for ever kneeled
To a lady in his shield,
That sparkled on the yellow field,   80
    Beside remote Shalott.

The gemmy bridle glittered free,
Like to some branch of stars we see
Hung in the golden Galaxy.[4]
The bridle bells rang merrily
    As he rode down to Camelot;
And from his blazoned baldric slung
A mighty silver bugle hung,
And as he rode his armor rung,
    Beside remote Shalott.   90

All in the blue unclouded weather
Thick-jeweled shone the saddle-leather,
The helmet and the helmet-feather

4 the Milky Way

Burned like one burning flame together,
    As he rode down to Camelot;
As often through the purple night,
Below the starry clusters bright,
Some bearded meteor, trailing light,
    Moves over still Shalott.

His broad clear brow in sunlight glowed;   100
On burnished hooves his war-horse trode;
From underneath his helmet flowed
His coal-black curls as on he rode,
    As he rode down to Camelot.
From the bank and from the river
He flashed into the crystal mirror,
"Tirra lirra," by the river
    Sang Sir Lancelot.

She left the web, she left the loom,
She made three paces through the room,   110
She saw the water-lily bloom,
She saw the helmet and the plume,
    She looked down to Camelot.
Out flew the web and floated wide;
The mirror cracked from side to side;
"The curse is come upon me," cried
    The Lady of Shalott.

PART IV

In the stormy east-wind straining,
The pale yellow woods were waning,
The broad stream in his banks complaining,   120
Heavily the low sky raining
    Over towered Camelot;
Down she came and found a boat
Beneath a willow left afloat,
And round about the prow she wrote
    The Lady of Shalott.

And down the river's dim expanse
Like some bold seër in a trance,
Seeing all his own mischance—
With a glassy countenance   130
    Did she look to Camelot.
And at the closing of the day
She loosed the chain, and down she lay;

The broad stream bore her far away,
        The Lady of Shalott.

Lying, robed in snowy white
That loosely flew to left and right—
The leaves upon her falling light—
Through the noises of the night
        She floated down to Camelot;   140
And as the boat-head wound along
The willowy hills and fields among,
They heard her singing her last song,
        The Lady of Shalott.

Heard a carol, mournful, holy,
Chanted loudly, chanted lowly,
Till her blood was frozen slowly,
And her eyes were darkened wholly,
        Turned to towered Camelot.
For ere she reached upon the tide   150
The first house by the water-side,
Singing in her song she died,
        The Lady of Shalott.

Under tower and balcony,
By garden-wall and gallery,
A gleaming shape she floated by,
Dead-pale between the houses high,
        Silent into Camelot.
Out upon the wharfs they came,
Knight and burgher, lord and dame,   160
And round the prow they read her name,
        The Lady of Shalott.

Who is this? and what is here?
And in the lighted palace near
Died the sound of royal cheer;
And they crossed themselves for fear,
        All the knights at Camelot:
But Lancelot mused a little space;
He said, "She has a lovely face;
God in his mercy lend her grace,   170
        The Lady of Shalott."

ŒNONE [5]

THERE lies a vale in Ida, lovelier
Than all the valleys of Ionian hills.
The swimming vapor slopes athwart the glen,
Puts forth an arm, and creeps from pine to pine,
And loiters, slowly drawn. On either hand
The lawns and meadow-ledges midway down
Hang rich in flowers, and far below them roars
The long brook falling through the cloven ravine
In cataract after cataract to the sea.
Behind the valley topmost Gargarus [6]   10
Stands up and takes the morning; but in front
The gorges, opening wide apart, reveal
Troas and Ilion's columned citadel,
The crown of Troas.
     Hither came at noon
Mournful Œnone, wandering forlorn
Of Paris, once her playmate on the hills.
Her cheek had lost the rose, and round her neck
Floated her hair or seemed to float in rest.
She, leaning on a fragment twined with vine,
Sang to the stillness, till the mountain-shade 20
Sloped downward to her seat from the upper cliff.

"O mother Ida, many-fountained Ida,
Dear mother Ida, harken ere I die.
For now the noonday quiet holds the hill;
The grasshopper is silent in the grass;
The lizard, with his shadow on the stone,
Rests like a shadow, and the winds are dead.
The purple flower droops, the golden bee
Is lily-cradled; I alone awake.
My eyes are full of tears, my heart of love, 30
My heart is breaking, and my eyes are dim,
And I am all aweary of my life.

"O mother Ida, many-fountained Ida,
Dear mother Ida, harken ere I die.
Hear me, O earth, hear me, O hills, O caves
That house the cold crowned snake! O mountain brooks,
I am the daughter of a River-God,
Hear me, for I will speak, and build up all

---

5 A nymph of Mount Ida
(near Troy), beloved of
Paris, but deserted by him
after Venus, as a reward

for pronouncing her the
most beautiful of the goddesses, had promised him
the fairest woman in the

world (Helen) for his wife.
6 a peak of Mt. Ida

My sorrow with my song, as yonder walls
Rose slowly to a music slowly breathed,[7]
A cloud that gathered shape; for it may be
That, while I speak of it, a little while
My heart may wander from its deeper woe.

"O mother Ida, many-fountained Ida,
Dear mother Ida, harken ere I die.
I waited underneath the dawning hills;
Aloft the mountain lawn was dewy-dark,
And dewy dark aloft the mountain pine.
Beautiful Paris, evil-hearted Paris,
Leading a jet-black goat white-horned, white-hooved,
Came up from reedy Simois [8] all alone.

"O mother Ida, harken ere I die.
Far-off the torrent called me from the cleft;
Far up the solitary morning smote
The streaks of virgin snow. With down-dropped eyes
I sat alone; white-breasted like a star
Fronting the dawn he moved; a leopard skin
Drooped from his shoulder, but his sunny hair
Clustered about his temples like a God's;
And his cheek brightened as the foam-bow brightens
When the wind blows the foam, and all my heart
Went forth to embrace him coming ere he came.

"Dear mother Ida, harken ere I die.
He smiled, and opening out his milk-white palm
Disclosed a fruit of pure Hesperian gold,
That smelt ambrosially, and while I looked
And listened, the full-flowing river of speech
Came down upon my heart:
          " 'My own Œnone,
Beautiful-browed Œnone, my own soul,
Behold this fruit, whose gleaming rind ingraven
"For the most fair," would seem to award it thine,
As lovelier than whatever Oread [9] haunt
The knolls of Ida, loveliest in all grace
Of movement, and the charm of married brows.'

"Dear mother Ida, harken ere I die.
He pressed the blossom of his lips to mine,
And added, 'This was cast upon the board,

---

7 The walls of Troy   8 a stream rising on   9 mountain-nymph
arose to Apollo's music.   Mount Ida

When all the full-faced presence of the Gods
Ranged in the halls of Peleus; [10] whereupon
Rose feud, with question unto whom 'twere due;   80
But light-foot Iris [11] brought it yester-eve,
Delivering, that to me, by common voice
Elected umpire, Herë [12] comes to-day,
Pallas and Aphrodite, claiming each
This meed of fairest. Thou, within the cave
Behind yon whispering tuft of oldest pine,
Mayst well behold them unbeheld, unheard
Hear all, and see thy Paris judge of Gods.'

   "Dear mother Ida, harken ere I die.
It was the deep midnoon; one silvery cloud   90
Had lost his way between the piny sides
Of this long glen. Then to the bower they came,
Naked they came to that smooth-swarded bower,
And at their feet the crocus brake like fire,
Violet, amaracus, and asphodel,
Lotos and lilies; and a wind arose,
And overhead the wandering ivy and vine,
This way and that, in many a wild festoon
Ran riot, garlanding the gnarlèd boughs
With bunch and berry and flower through and through.   100

   "O mother Ida, harken ere I die.
On the tree-tops a crested peacock lit,
And o'er him flowed a golden cloud, and leaned
Upon him, slowly dropping fragrant dew.
Then first I heard the voice of her [13] to whom
Coming through heaven, like a light that grows
Larger and clearer, with one mind the Gods
Rise up for reverence. She to Paris made
Proffer of royal power, ample rule
Unquestioned, overflowing revenue   110
Wherewith to embellish state, 'from many a vale
And river-sundered champaign clothed with corn,
Or labored mine undrainable of ore.
Honor,' she said, 'and homage, tax and toll,
From many an inland town and haven large,
Mast-thronged beneath her shadowing citadel
In glassy bays among her tallest towers.'

10 Father of Achilles (who was espousing Thetis)   11 Goddess of the rainbow, the messenger of the gods   12 or Hera (the Juno of the Romans)   13 Juno

"O mother Ida, harken ere I die.
Still she spake on and still she spake of power,
'Which in all action is the end of all;   120
Power fitted to the season; wisdom-bred
And throned of wisdom—from all neighbor crowns
Alliance and allegiance, till thy hand
Fail from the scepter-staff. Such boon from me,
From me, heaven's queen, Paris, to thee king-born,
A shepherd all thy life but yet king-born,
Should come most welcome, seeing men, in power
Only, are likest Gods, who have attained
Rest in a happy place and quiet seats
Above the thunder, with undying bliss   130
In knowledge of their own supremacy.'

"Dear mother Ida, harken ere I die.
She ceased, and Paris held the costly fruit
Out at arm's-length, so much the thought of power
Flattered his spirit; but Pallas where she stood
Somewhat apart, her clear and bared limbs
O'erthwarted with the brazen-headed spear
Upon her pearly shoulder leaning cold,
The while, above, her full and earnest eye
Over her snow-cold breast and angry cheek   140
Kept watch, waiting decision, made reply:
'Self-reverence, self-knowledge, self-control,
These three alone lead life to sovereign power.
Yet not for power (power of herself
Would come uncalled for) but to live by law,
Acting the law we live by without fear;
And, because right is right, to follow right
Were wisdom in the scorn of consequence.'

"Dear mother Ida, harken ere I die.
Again she said: 'I woo thee not with gifts.   150
Sequel of guerdon could not alter me
To fairer. Judge thou me by what I am,
So shalt thou find me fairest.
                                    Yet, indeed,
If gazing on divinity disrobed
Thy mortal eyes are frail to judge of fair,
Unbiased by self-profit, O, rest thee sure
That I shall love thee well and cleave to thee,
So that my vigor, wedded to thy blood,
Shall strike within thy pulses, like a God's,
To push thee forward through a life of shocks,   160

Dangers, and deeds, until endurance grow
Sinewed with action, and the full-grown will,
Circled through all experiences, pure law,
Commeasure perfect freedom.'
        "Here she ceased,
And Paris pondered, and I cried, 'O Paris,
Give it to Pallas!' but he heard me not,
Or hearing would not hear me, woe is me!

"O mother Ida, many-fountained Ida,
Dear mother Ida, harken ere I die.
Idalian [14] Aphrodite beautiful,   170
Fresh as the foam, new-bathed in Paphian wells,
With rosy slender fingers backward drew
From her warm brows and bosom her deep hair
Ambrosial, golden round her lucid throat
And shoulder; from the violets her light foot
Shone rosy-white, and o'er her rounded form
Between the shadows of the vine-bunches
Floated the glowing sunlights, as she moved.

"Dear mother Ida, harken ere I die.
She with a subtle smile in her mild eyes,   180
The herald of her triumph, drawing nigh
Half-whispered in his ear, 'I promise thee
The fairest and most loving wife in Greece,'
She spoke and laughed; I shut my sight for fear;
But when I looked, Paris had raised his arm.
And I beheld great Herë's angry eyes,
As she withdrew into the golden cloud,
And I was left alone within the bower;
And from that time to this I am alone,
And I shall be alone until I die.   190

"Yet, mother Ida, harken ere I die.
Fairest—why fairest wife? am I not fair?
My love hath told me so a thousand times.
Methinks I must be fair, for yesterday,
When I passed by, a wild and wanton pard,[15]
Eyed like the evening star, with playful tail
Crouched fawning in the weed. Most loving is she?
Ah me, my mountain shepherd, that my arms
Were wound about thee, and my hot lips pressed
Close, close to thine in that quick-falling dew   200

14 Idalium and Paphos,   Venus (Aphrodite) was   15 leopard
towns in Cyprus where   specially worshiped

Of fruitful kisses, thick as autumn rains
Flash in the pools of whirling Simois!

"O mother, hear me yet before I die.
They came, they cut away my tallest pines,[16]
My tall dark pines, that plumed the craggy ledge
High over the blue gorge, and all between
The snowy peak and snow-white cataract
Fostered the callow eaglet—from beneath
Whose thick mysterious boughs in the dark morn
The panther's roar came muffled, while I sat   210
Low in the valley. Never, never more
Shall lone Œnone see the morning mist
Sweep through them; never see them overlaid
With narrow moonlit slips of silver cloud,
Between the loud stream and the trembling stars.

"O mother, hear me yet before I die.
I wish that somewhere in the ruined folds,
Among the fragments tumbled from the glens,
Or the dry thickets, I could meet with her
The Abominable,[17] that uninvited came   220
Into the fair Peleïan banquet-hall,
And cast the golden fruit upon the board,
And bred this change; that I might speak my mind,
And tell her to her face how much I hate
Her presence, hated both of Gods and men.

"O mother, hear me yet before I die.
Hath he not sworn his love a thousand times,
In this green valley, under this green hill,
Even on this hand, and sitting on this stone?
Sealed it with kisses? watered it with tears?   230
O happy tears, and how unlike to these!
O happy heaven, how canst thou see my face?
O happy earth, how canst thou bear my weight?
O death, death, death, thou ever-floating cloud,
There are enough unhappy on this earth,
Pass by the happy souls, that love to live;
I pray thee, pass before my light of life,
And shadow all my soul, that I may die.
Thou weighest heavy on the heart within,
Weigh heavy on my eyelids; let me die.   240

16 to build the ship for   17 Eris, goddess of strife
Paris's voyage to Sparta
for Helen

"O mother, hear me yet before I die.
I will not die alone, for fiery thoughts
Do shape themselves within me, more and more,
Whereof I catch the issue, as I hear
Dead sounds at night come from the inmost hills,
Like footsteps upon wool. I dimly see
My far-off doubtful purpose, as a mother
Conjectures of the features of her child
Ere it is born. Her child!—a shudder comes
Across me: never child be born of me,   250
Unblest, to vex me with his father's eyes!

"O mother, hear me yet before I die.
Hear me, O earth. I will not die alone,
Lest their shrill happy laughter come to me
Walking the cold and starless road of death
Uncomforted, leaving my ancient love
With the Greek woman. I will rise and go
Down into Troy, and ere the stars come forth
Talk with the wild Cassandra,[18] for she says
A fire dances before her, and a sound   260
Rings ever in her ears of armèd men.
What this may be I know not, but I know
That, wheresoe'er I am by night and day,
All earth and air seem only burning fire."

THE PALACE OF ART

I BUILT my soul a lordly pleasure-house,
    Wherein at ease for aye to dwell.
I said, "O Soul, make merry and carouse,
    Dear soul, for all is well."

A huge crag-platform, smooth as burnished brass,
    I chose. The rangèd ramparts bright
From level meadow-bases of deep grass
    Suddenly scaled the light.

Thereon I built it firm. Of ledge or shelf
    The rock rose clear, or winding stair.
My soul would live alone unto herself
    In her high palace there.   10

And "while the world runs round and round," I said,
    "Reign thou apart, a quiet king,

---

18 Daughter of Priam, who foretold the Trojan war, but was not believed

Still as, while Saturn whirls, his steadfast shade
   Sleeps on his luminous ring."

To which my soul made answer readily:
   "Trust me, in bliss I shall abide
In this great mansion, that is built for me,
   So royal-rich and wide."   20

.   .   .   .

Four courts I made, East, West, and South and North,
   In each a squarèd lawn, wherefrom
The golden gorge of dragons spouted forth
   A flood of fountain-foam.

And round the cool green courts there ran a row
   Of cloisters, branched like mighty woods,
Echoing all night to that sonorous flow
   Of spouted fountain-floods;

And round the roofs a gilded gallery
   That lent broad verge to distant lands,   30
Far as the wild swan wings, to where the sky
   Dipped down to sea and sands.

From those four jets four currents in one swell
   Across the mountain streamed below
In misty folds, that floating as they fell
   Lit up a torrent-bow.

And high on every peak a statue seemed
   To hang on tiptoe, tossing up
A cloud of incense of all odor steamed
   From out a golden cup.   40

So that she thought, "And who shall gaze upon
   My palace with unblinded eyes,
While this great bow will waver in the sun,
   And that sweet incense rise?"

For that sweet incense rose and never failed,
   And, while day sank or mounted higher,
The light aerial gallery, golden-railed,
   Burned like a fringe of fire.

Likewise the deep-set windows, stained and traced,
  Would seem slow-flaming crimson fires   50
From shadowed grots of arches interlaced,
  And tipped with frost-like spires.

.   .   .   .

Full of long-sounding corridors it was,
  That over-vaulted grateful gloom,
Through which the livelong day my soul did pass,
  Well-pleased, from room to room.

Full of great rooms and small the palace stood,
  All various, each a perfect whole
From living Nature, fit for every mood
  And change of my still soul.   60

For some were hung with arras green and blue,
  Showing a gaudy summer-morn,
Where with puffed cheek the belted hunter blew
  His wreathèd bugle-horn.

One seemed all dark and red—a tract of sand,
  And some one pacing there alone,
Who paced for ever in a glimmering land,
  Lit with a low large moon.

One showed an iron coast and angry waves.
  You seemed to hear them climb and fall   70
And roar rock-thwarted under bellowing caves,
  Beneath the windy wall.

And one, a full-fed river winding slow
  By herds upon an endless plain,
The ragged rims of thunder brooding low,
  With shadow-streaks of rain.

And one, the reapers at their sultry toil.
  In front they bound the sheaves. Behind
Were realms of upland, prodigal in oil,
  And hoary to the wind.   80

And one a foreground black with stones and slags;
  Beyond, a line of heights; and higher
All barred with long white cloud the scornful crags;
  And highest, snow and fire.

And one, an English home—gray twilight poured
  On dewy pastures, dewy trees,
Softer than sleep—all things in order stored,
  A haunt of ancient Peace.

Nor these alone, but every landscape fair,
  As fit for every mood of mind,
Or gay, or grave, or sweet, or stern, was there,
  Not less than truth designed.   90

    .   .   .   .

Or the maid-mother by a crucifix,
  In tracts of pasture sunny-warm,
Beneath branch-work of costly sardonyx
  Sat smiling, babe in arm.

Or in a clear-walled city on the sea,
  Near gilded organ-pipes, her hair
Wound with white roses, slept Saint Cecily; [19]
  An angel looked at her.   100

Or thronging all one porch of Paradise
  A group of Houris [20] bowed to see
The dying Islamite, with hands and eyes
  That said, We wait for thee.

Or mythic Uther's deeply-wounded son [21]
  In some fair space of sloping greens
Lay, dozing in the vale of Avalon,
  And watched by weeping queens.

Or hollowing one hand against his ear,
  To list a foot-fall, ere he saw   110
The wood-nymph, stayed the Ausonian King [22] to hear
  Of wisdom and of law.

Or over hills with peaky tops engrailed,
  And many a tract of palm and rice,
The throne of Indian Cama [23] slowly sailed
  A summer fanned with spice.

Or sweet Europa's mantle blew unclasped,
  From off her shoulder backward borne;

19 patron saint of music 21 Arthur by the wood-nymph
20 Mohammed's attendants in Paradise 22 Numa Pompilius, second king of Rome, taught Egeria
23 Hindu god of love

From one hand drooped a crocus; one hand grasped
    The mild bull's [24] golden horn.   120

Or else flushed Ganymede,[25] his rosy thigh
    Half-buried in the eagle's down,
Sole as a flying star shot through the sky
    Above the pillared town.

Nor these alone; but every legend fair
    Which the supreme Caucasian mind
Carved out of Nature for itself was there,
    Not less than life designed.

· · · · · · · · · · ·

Then in the towers I placed great bells that swung,
    Moved of themselves, with silver sound;   130
And with choice paintings of wise men I hung
    The royal dais round.

For there was Milton like a seraph strong,
    Beside him Shakespeare bland and mild;
And there the world-worn Dante grasped his song,
    And somewhat grimly smiled.

And there the Ionian father of the rest; [26]
    A million wrinkles carved his skin;
A hundred winters snowed upon his breast,
    From cheek and throat and chin.   140

Above, the fair hall-ceiling stately-set
    Many an arch high up did lift,
And angels rising and descending met
    With interchange of gift.

Below was all mosaic choicely planned
    With cycles of the human tale
Of this wide world, the times of every land
    So wrought they will not fail.

The people here, a beast of burden slow,
    Toiled onward, pricked with goads and stings;   150
Here played, a tiger, rolling to and fro
    The heads and crowns of kings;

[24] shape assumed by Zeus when he carried off Europa   [25] borne by an eagle to become cup-bearer of Zeus   [26] Homer

Here rose, an athlete, strong to break or bind
    All force in bonds that might endure,
And here once more like some sick man declined,
    And trusted any cure.

But over these she trod; and those great bells
    Began to chime. She took her throne;
She sat betwixt the shining oriels,
    To sing her songs alone.   160

And through the topmost oriels' colored flame
    Two godlike faces gazed below;
Plato the wise, and large-browed Verulam,[27]
    The first of those who know.

And all those names that in their motion were
    Full-welling fountain-heads of change,
Betwixt the slender shafts were blazoned fair
    In diverse raiment strange;

Through which the lights, rose, amber, emerald, blue,
    Flushed in her temples and her eyes,   170
And from her lips, as morn from Memnon,[28] drew
    Rivers of melodies.

No nightingale delighteth to prolong
    Her low preamble all alone,
More than my soul to hear her echoed song
    Throb through the ribbèd stone;

Singing and murmuring in her feastful mirth,
    Joying to feel herself alive,
Lord over Nature, lord of the visible earth,
    Lord of the senses five;   180

Communing with herself: "All these are mine,
    And let the world have peace or wars,
'Tis one to me." She—when young night divine
    Crowned dying day with stars,

Making sweet close of his delicious toils—
    Lit light in wreaths and anadems,[29]
And pure quintessences of precious oils
    In hollowed moons of gems,

27 Bacon
28 Egyptian statue from which music issued at dawn
29 garlands

To mimic heaven; and clapped her hands and cried,
   "I marvel if my still delight 190
In this great house so royal-rich and wide
    Be flattered to the height.

"O all things fair to sate my various eyes!
   O shapes and hues that please me well!
O silent faces of the Great and Wise,
    My Gods, with whom I dwell!

"O Godlike isolation which art mine,
   I can but count thee perfect gain,
What time I watch the darkening droves of swine
    That range on yonder plain. 200

"In filthy sloughs they roll a prurient skin,
   They graze and wallow, breed and sleep;
And oft some brainless devil enters in,
    And drives them to the deep." [30]

Then of the moral instinct would she prate
   And of the rising from the dead,
As hers by right of full-accomplished Fate;
    And at the last she said:

"I take possession of man's mind and deed.
   I care not what the sects may brawl. 210
I sit as God holding no form of creed,
    But contemplating all."

  .   .   .   .

Full oft the riddle of the painful earth
   Flashed through her as she sat alone,
Yet not the less held she her solemn mirth,
    And intellectual throne.

And so she throve and prospered; so three years
   She prospered; on the fourth she fell,
Like Herod, when the shout was in his ears,
    Struck through with pangs of hell. [31] 220

Lest she should fail and perish utterly,
   God, before whom ever lie bare

[30] Mark, v. 13.   [31] Acts, xii. 21–23

The abysmal deeps of personality,
  Plagued her with sore despair.

When she would think, where'er she turned her sight
  The airy hand confusion wrought,
Wrote, "Mene, mene," [32] and divided quite
  The kingdom of her thought.

Deep dread and loathing of her solitude
  Fell on her, from which mood was born   230
Scorn of herself; again, from out that mood
  Laughter at her self-scorn.

"What! is not this my place of strength," she said,
  "My spacious mansion built for me,
Whereof the strong foundation-stones were laid
  Since my first memory?"

But in dark corners of her palace stood
  Uncertain shapes; and unawares
On white-eyed phantasms weeping tears of blood,
  And horrible nightmares,   240

And hollow shades enclosing hearts of flame,
  And, with dim fretted foreheads all,
On corpses, three-months-old at noon she came,
  That stood against the wall.

A spot of dull stagnation, without light
  Or power of movement, seemed my soul,
Mid onward-sloping motions infinite
  Making for one sure goal;

A still salt pool, locked in with bars of sand,
  Left on the shore, that hears all night   250
The plunging seas draw backward from the land
  Their moon-led waters white;

A star that with the choral starry dance
  Joined not, but stood, and standing saw
The hollow orb of moving Circumstance
  Rolled round by one fixed law.

Back on herself her serpent pride had curled.
  "No voice," she shrieked in that lone hall,

32 at Belshazzar's feast, Daniel, v. 25.

"No voice breaks through the stillness of this world;
    One deep, deep silence all!" 260

She, moldering with the dull earth's moldering sod,
    Inwrapped tenfold in slothful shame,
Lay there exilèd from eternal God,
    Lost to her place and name;

And death and life she hated equally,
    And nothing saw, for her despair,
But dreadful time, dreadful eternity,
    No comfort anywhere;

Remaining utterly confused with fears,
    And ever worse with growing time, 270
And ever unrelieved by dismal tears,
    And all alone in crime.

Shut up as in a crumbling tomb, girt round
    With blackness as a solid wall,
Far off she seemed to hear the dully sound
    Of human footsteps fall:

As in strange lands a traveler walking slow,
    In doubt and great perplexity,
A little before moonrise hears the low
    Moan of an unknown sea; 280

And knows not if it be thunder, or a sound
    Of rocks thrown down, or one deep cry
Of great wild beasts; then thinketh, "I have found
    A new land, but I die."

She howled aloud, "I am on fire within.
    There comes no murmur of reply.
What is it that will take away my sin,
    And save me lest I die?"

So when four years were wholly finished,
    She threw her royal robes away. 290
"Make me a cottage in the vale," she said,
    "Where I may mourn and pray.

"Yet pull not down my palace towers, that are
    So lightly, beautifully built;
Perchance I may return with others there
    When I have purged my guilt."

THE LOTOS-EATERS [33]

"COURAGE!" he [34] said, and pointed toward the land,
"This mounting wave will roll us shoreward soon."
In the afternoon they came unto a land
In which it seemèd always afternoon.
All round the coast the languid air did swoon,
Breathing like one that hath a weary dream.
Full-faced above the valley stood the moon;
And, like a downward smoke, the slender stream
Along the cliff to fall and pause and fall did seem.

A land of streams! some, like a downward smoke,   10
Slow-dropping veils of thinnest lawn, did go;
And some through wavering lights and shadows broke,
Rolling a slumbrous sheet of foam below.
They saw the gleaming river seaward flow
From the inner land; far off, three mountain-tops,
Three silent pinnacles of agèd snow,
Stood sunset-flushed; and, dewed with showery drops,
Up-clomb the shadowy pine above the woven copse.

The charmèd sunset lingered low adown
In the red West; through mountain clefts the dale   20
Was seen far inland, and the yellow down
Bordered with palm, and many a winding vale
And meadow, set with slender galingale;
A land where all things always seemed the same!
And round about the keel with faces pale,
Dark faces pale against that rosy flame,
The mild-eyed melancholy Lotos-eaters came.

Branches they bore of that enchanted stem,
Laden with flower and fruit, whereof they gave
To each, but whoso did receive of them   30
And taste, to him the gushing of the wave
Far far away did seem to mourn and rave
On alien shores; and if his fellow spake,
His voice was thin, as voices from the grave;
And deep-asleep he seemed, yet all awake,
And music in his ears his beating heart did make.

They sat them down upon the yellow sand,
Between the sun and moon upon the shore;

33 "But whoever of them ate the honey-sweet fruit of the lotus no longer wished to bring back tidings or to return, but there they desired, ever feeding on the lotus, to remain with the lotus-eating men, and to forget their going home." (*Odyssey*, book ix)
34 Ulysses

And sweet it was to dream of Fatherland,
Of child, and wife, and slave; but evermore 40
Most weary seemed the sea, weary the oar,
Weary the wandering fields of barren foam.
Then some one said, "We will return no more";
And all at once they sang, "Our island home
Is far beyond the wave; we will no longer roam."

CHORIC SONG

I

There is sweet music here that softer falls
Than petals from blown roses on the grass,
Or night-dews on still waters between walls
Of shadowy granite, in a gleaming pass;
Music that gentlier on the spirit lies, 50
Than tired eyelids upon tired eyes;
Music that brings sweet sleep down from the blissful skies.
Here are cool mosses deep,
And through the moss the ivies creep,
And in the stream the long-leaved flowers weep,
And from the craggy ledge the poppy hangs in sleep.

2

Why are we weighed upon with heaviness,
And utterly consumed with sharp distress,
While all things else have rest from weariness?
All things have rest: why should we toil alone, 60
We only toil, who are the first of things,
And make perpetual moan,
Still from one sorrow to another thrown;
Nor ever fold our wings,
And cease from wanderings,
Nor steep our brows in slumber's holy balm;
Nor harken what the inner spirit sings,
"There is no joy but calm!"—
Why should we only toil, the roof and crown of things?

3

Lo! in the middle of the wood, 70
The folded leaf is wooed from out the bud
With winds upon the branch, and there
Grows green and broad, and takes no care,

Sun-steeped at noon, and in the moon
Nightly dew-fed; and turning yellow
Falls, and floats adown the air.
Lo! sweetened with the summer light,
The full-juiced apple, waxing over-mellow,
Drops in a silent autumn night.
All its allotted length of days   80
The flower ripens in its place,
Ripens and fades, and falls, and hath no toil,
Fast-rooted in the fruitful soil.

4

Hateful is the dark-blue sky,
Vaulted o'er the dark-blue sea.
Death is the end of life; ah, why
Should life all labor be?
Let us alone. Time driveth onward fast,
And in a little while our lips are dumb.
Let us alone. What is it that will last?   90
All things are taken from us, and become
Portions and parcels of the dreadful past.
Let us alone. What pleasure can we have
To war with evil? Is there any peace
In ever climbing up the climbing wave?
All things have rest, and ripen toward the grave
In silence—ripen, fall, and cease:
Give us long rest or death, dark death, or dreamful ease.

5

How sweet it were, hearing the downward stream,
With half-shut eyes ever to seem   100
Falling asleep in a half-dream!
To dream and dream, like yonder amber light,
Which will not leave the myrrh-bush on the height;
To hear each other's whispered speech;
Eating the Lotos day by day,
To watch the crisping ripples on the beach,
And tender curving lines of creamy spray;
To lend our hearts and spirits wholly
To the influence of mild-minded melancholy;
To muse and brood and live again in memory,   110
With those old faces of our infancy
Heaped over with a mound of grass,
Two handfuls of white dust, shut in an urn of brass!

6

Dear is the memory of our wedded lives,
And dear the last embraces of our wives
And their warm tears; but all hath suffered change;
For surely now our household hearths are cold,
Our sons inherit us, our looks are strange,
And we should come like ghosts to trouble joy.
Or else the island princes over-bold   120
Have eat our substance, and the minstrel sings
Before them of the ten years' war in Troy,
And our great deeds, as half-forgotten things.
Is there confusion in the little isle?
Let what is broken so remain.
The Gods are hard to reconcile;
'Tis hard to settle order once again.
There *is* confusion worse than death,
Trouble on trouble, pain on pain,
Long labor unto agèd breath,   130
Sore task to hearts worn out by many wars
And eyes grown dim with gazing on the pilot-stars.

7

But, propped on beds of amaranth and moly,[35]
How sweet—while warm airs lull us, blowing lowly—
With half-dropped eyelid still,
Beneath a heaven dark and holy,
To watch the long bright river drawing slowly
His waters from the purple hill—
To hear the dewy echoes calling
From cave to cave through the thick-twined vine—   140
To watch the emerald-colored water falling
Through many a woven acanthus-wreath divine!
Only to hear and see the far-off sparkling brine,
Only to hear were sweet, stretched out beneath the pine.

8

The Lotos blooms below the barren peak,
The Lotos blows by every winding creek;
All day the wind breathes low with mellower tone;
Through every hollow cave and alley lone
Round and round the spicy downs the yellow Lotos-dust is
    blown.

[35] the fadeless flower; the herb given by Mercury to Ulysses to counteract the spells
of Circe

We have had enough of action, and of motion we,   150
Rolled to starboard, rolled to larboard, when the surge was
    seething free,
Where the wallowing monster spouted his foam-fountains in the
    sea.
Let us swear an oath, and keep it with an equal mind,
In the hollow Lotos-land to live and lie reclined
On the hills like Gods together, careless of mankind.
For they lie beside their nectar, and the bolts are hurled
Far below them in the valleys, and the clouds are lightly curled
Round their golden houses, girdled with the gleaming world;
Where they smile in secret, looking over wasted lands,
Blight and famine, plague and earthquake, roaring deeps and
    fiery sands,   160
Clanging fights, and flaming towns, and sinking ships, and
    praying hands.
But they smile, they find a music centered in a doleful song
Steaming up, a lamentation and an ancient tale of wrong,
Like a tale of little meaning though the words are strong;
Chanted from an ill-used race of men that cleave the soil,
Sow the seed, and reap the harvest with enduring toil,
Storing yearly little dues of wheat, and wine and oil;
Till they perish and they suffer—some, 'tis whispered—down
    in hell
Suffer endless anguish, others in Elysian valleys dwell,
Resting weary limbs at last on beds of asphodel.   170
Surely, surely, slumber is more sweet than toil, the shore
Than labor in the deep mid-ocean, wind and wave and oar;
O, rest ye, brother mariners, we will not wander more.

SAINT AGNES' EVE [36]

Deep on the convent-roof the snows
    Are sparkling to the moon;
My breath to heaven like vapor goes;
    May my soul follow soon!
The shadows of the convent-towers
    Slant down the snowy sward,
Still creeping with the creeping hours
    That lead me to my Lord.
Make Thou my spirit pure and clear
    As are the frosty skies,   10
Or this first snowdrop of the year
    That in my bosom lies.

36 The same belief which is the basis of Keats's *The Eve of St. Agnes* adapted to
the nun contemplating the Heavenly Bridegroom (Christ).

As these white robes are soiled and dark,
  To yonder shining ground;
As this pale taper's earthly spark,
  To yonder argent round;
So shows my soul before the Lamb,
  My spirit before Thee;
So in mine earthly house I am,
  To that I hope to be.   20
Break up the heavens, O Lord! and far,
  Thro' all yon starlight keen,
Draw me, thy bride, a glittering star,
  In raiment white and clean.

He lifts me to the golden doors;
  The flashes come and go;
All heaven bursts her starry floors,
  And strows her lights below,
And deepens on and up! the gates
  Roll back, and far within   30
For me the Heavenly Bridegroom waits,
  To make me pure of sin.
The Sabbaths of Eternity,
  One Sabbath deep and wide—
A light upon the shining sea—
  The Bridegroom with his bride!

YOU ASK ME, WHY, THOUGH ILL AT EASE [37]

You ask me, why, though ill at ease,
  Within this region I subsist,
  Whose spirits falter in the mist,
And languish for the purple seas.

It is the land that freemen till,
  That sober-suited Freedom chose,
  The land, where girt with friends or foes
A man may speak the thing he will;

A land of settled government,
  A land of just and old renown,   10
  Where Freedom slowly broadens down
From precedent to precedent;

---

[37] One of the several poems (cf. "Of old sat Freedom on the heights" and "Love thou thy land") in which Tennyson expresses his political views and his pride in England.

Where faction seldom gathers head,
   But, by degrees to fullness wrought,
   The strength of some diffusive thought
Hath time and space to work and spread.

Should banded unions persecute
   Opinion, and induce a time
   When single thought is civil crime,
And individual freedom mute,   20

Though power should make from land to land
   The name of Britain trebly great—
   Though every channel of the State
Should fill and choke with golden sand—

Yet waft me from the harbor-mouth,
   Wild wind! I seek a warmer sky,
   And I will see before I die
The palms and temples of the South.

ULYSSES [38]

It little profits that an idle king,
By this still hearth, among these barren crags,
Matched with an agèd wife, I mete and dole
Unequal laws unto a savage race,
That hoard, and sleep, and feed, and know not me.
I cannot rest from travel; I will drink
Life to the lees. All times I have enjoyed
Greatly, have suffered greatly, both with those
That loved me, and alone; on shore, and when
Through scudding drifts the rainy Hyades [39]   10
Vexed the dim sea. I am become a name;
For always roaming with a hungry heart
Much have I seen and known,—cities of men
And manners, climates, councils, governments,
Myself not least, but honored of them all,—
And drunk delight of battle with my peers,
Far on the ringing plains of windy Troy.
I am a part of all that I have met;
Yet all experience is an arch wherethrough
Gleams that untraveled world whose margin fades   20

38 An imagined soliloquy of Ulysses after his return from his wanderings to his home and to his wife Penelope. "The poem was written soon after Arthur Hallam's death, and it gives the feeling about the need of going forward and braving the struggle of life perhaps more simply than anything in *In Memoriam.*" (Tennyson)   39 Constellation supposed to bring rain

For ever and for ever when I move.
How dull it is to pause, to make an end,
To rust unburnished, not to shine in use!
As though to breathe were life! Life piled on life
Were all too little, and of one to me
Little remains; but every hour is saved
From that eternal silence, something more,
A bringer of new things; and vile it were
For some three suns to store and hoard myself,
And this gray spirit yearning in desire 30
To follow knowledge like a sinking star,
Beyond the utmost bound of human thought.
    This is my son, mine own Telemachus,
To whom I leave the scepter and the isle,—
Well-loved of me, discerning to fulfill
This labor, by slow prudence to make mild
A rugged people, and through soft degrees
Subdue them to the useful and the good.
Most blameless is he, centered in the sphere
Of common duties, decent not to fail 40
In offices of tenderness, and pay
Meet adoration to my household gods,
When I am gone. He works his work, I mine.
    There lies the port; the vessel puffs her sail;
There gloom the dark, broad seas. My mariners,
Souls that have toiled, and wrought, and thought with me,—
That ever with a frolic welcome took
The thunder and the sunshine, and opposed
Free hearts, free foreheads,—you and I are old;
Old age hath yet his honor and his toil. 50
Death closes all; but something ere the end,
Some work of noble note, may yet be done,
Not unbecoming men that strove with Gods.
The lights begin to twinkle from the rocks;
The long day wanes; the slow moon climbs; the deep
Moans round with many voices. Come, my friends,
'Tis not too late to seek a newer world.
Push off, and sitting well in order smite
The sounding furrows; for my purpose holds
To sail beyond the sunset, and the baths 60
Of all the western stars, until I die.
It may be that the gulfs will wash us down;
It may be we shall touch the Happy Isles,
And see the great Achilles, whom we knew.
Though much is taken, much abides; and though
We are not now that strength which in old days

Moved earth and heaven, that which we are, we are,—
One equal temper of heroic hearts,
Made weak by time and fate, but strong in will
To strive, to seek, to find, and not to yield.   70

LOCKSLEY HALL

COMRADES, leave me here a little, while as yet 'tis early morn:
Leave me here, and when you want me, sound upon the bugle-
 horn.

'Tis the place, and all around it, as of old, the curlews call,
Dreary gleams about the moorland flying over Locksley Hall;

Locksley Hall, that in the distance overlooks the sandy tracts,
And the hollow ocean-ridges roaring into cataracts.

Many a night from yonder ivied casement, ere I went to rest,
Did I look on great Orion sloping slowly to the west.

Many a night I saw the Pleiads, rising through the mellow shade,
Glitter like a swarm of fireflies tangled in a silver braid.   10

Here about the beach I wandered, nourishing a youth sublime
With the fairy tales of science, and the long result of time;

When the centuries behind me like a fruitful land reposed;
When I clung to all the present for the promise that it closed;

When I dipped into the future far as human eye could see,
Saw the vision of the world and all the wonder that would be.—

In the spring a fuller crimson comes upon the robin's breast;
In the spring the wanton lapwing gets himself another crest;

In the spring a livelier iris changes on the burnished dove;
In the spring a young man's fancy lightly turns to thoughts of
 love.   20

Then her cheek was pale and thinner than should be for one so
 young,
And her eyes on all my motions with a mute observance hung,

And I said, "My cousin Amy, speak, and speak the truth to me,
Trust me, cousin, all the current of my being sets to thee."

On her pallid cheek and forehead came a color and a light,
As I have seen the rosy red flushing in the northern night.

And she turned—her bosom shaken with a sudden storm of
sighs—
All the spirit deeply dawning in the dark of hazel eyes—

Saying, "I have hid my feelings, fearing they should do me
wrong";
Saying, "Dost thou love me, cousin?" weeping, "I have loved
thee long."   30

Love took up the glass of Time, and turned it in his glowing
hands;
Every moment, lightly shaken, ran itself in golden sands.

Love took up the harp of Life, and smote on all the chords with
might;
Smote the chord of Self, that, trembling, passed in music out of
sight.

Many a morning on the moorland did we hear the copses ring.
And her whisper thronged my pulses with the fullness of the
spring.

Many an evening by the waters did we watch the stately ships.
And our spirits rushed together at the touching of the lips.

O my cousin, shallow-hearted! O my Amy, mine no more!
O the dreary, dreary moorland! O the barren, barren shore!   40

Falser than all fancy fathoms, falser than all songs have sung,
Puppet to a father's threat, and servile to a shrewish tongue!

Is it well to wish thee happy?—having known me—to decline
On a range of lower feelings and a narrower heart than mine!

Yet it shall be; thou shalt lower to his level day by day,
What is fine within thee growing coarse to sympathize with clay.

As the husband is, the wife is; thou art mated with a clown,
And the grossness of his nature will have weight to drag thee
down.

He will hold thee, when his passion shall have spent its novel
    force,
Something better than his dog, a little dearer than his horse.   50

What is this? his eyes are heavy; think not they are glazed with
    wine.
Go to him, it is thy duty; kiss him, take his hand in thine.

It may be my lord is weary, that his brain is overwrought;
Soothe him with thy finer fancies, touch him with thy lighter
    thought.

He will answer to the purpose, easy things to understand—
Better thou wert dead before me, though I slew thee with my
    hand!

Better thou and I were lying, hidden from the heart's disgrace,
Rolled in one another's arms, and silent in a last embrace.

Cursed be the social wants that sin against the strength of
    youth!
Cursed be the social lies that warp us from the living truth!   60

Cursed be the sickly forms that err from honest Nature's rule!
Cursed be the gold that gilds the straitened forehead of the
    fool!

Well—'tis well that I should bluster!—Hadst thou less unworthy
    proved—
Would to God—for I had loved thee more than ever wife was
    loved.

Am I mad, that I should cherish that which bears but bitter
    fruit?
I will pluck it from my bosom, though my heart be at the root.

Never, though my mortal summers to such length of years
    should come
As the many-wintered crow that leads the clanging rookery
    home.

Where is comfort? in division of the records of the mind?
Can I part her from herself, and love her, as I knew her,
    kind?
        70

I remember one that perished; sweetly did she speak and move;
Such a one do I remember, whom to look at was to love.

Can I think of her as dead, and love her for the love she bore?
No—she never loved me truly; love is love for evermore.

Comfort? comfort scorned of devils! this is truth the poet sings,
That a sorrow's crown of sorrow is remembering happier things.

Drug thy memories, lest thou learn it, lest thy heart be put to
    proof,
In the dead unhappy night, and when the rain is on the roof.

Like a dog, he hunts in dreams, and thou art staring at the wall,
Where the dying night-lamp flickers, and the shadows rise and
    fall.   80

Then a hand shall pass before thee, pointing to his drunken
    sleep,
To thy widowed marriage-pillows, to the tears that thou wilt
    weep.

Thou shalt hear the "Never, never," whispered by the phantom
    years,
And a song from out the distance in the ringing of thine ears;

And an eye shall vex thee, looking ancient kindness on thy pain.
Turn thee, turn thee on thy pillow; get thee to thy rest again.

Nay, but Nature brings thee solace; for a tender voice will cry.
'Tis a purer life than thine, a lip to drain thy trouble dry.

Baby lips will laugh me down; my latest rival brings thee rest.
Baby fingers, waxen touches, press me from the mother's
    breast.   90

O, the child too clothes the father with a dearness not his due.
Half is thine and half is his; it will be worthy of the two.

O, I see thee old and formal, fitted to thy petty part,
With a little hoard of maxims preaching down a daughter's
    heart.

"They were dangerous guides the feelings—she herself was not
    exempt—
Truly, she herself had suffered"—Perish in thy self-contempt!

Overlive it—lower yet—be happy! wherefore should I care?
I myself must mix with action, lest I wither by despair.

What is that which I should turn to, lighting upon days like
  these?
Every door is barred with gold, and opens but to golden
  keys.   100

Every gate is thronged with suitors, all the markets overflow.
I have but an angry fancy; what is that which I should do?

I had been content to perish, falling on the foeman's ground,
When the ranks are rolled in vapor, and the winds are laid with
  sound.

But the jingling of the guinea helps the hurt that Honor feels,
And the nations do but murmur, snarling at each other's heels.

Can I but relive in sadness? I will turn that earlier page.
Hide me from my deep emotion, O thou wondrous Mother-Age!

Make me feel the wild pulsation that I felt before the strife,
When I heard my days before me, and the tumult of my life; 110

Yearning for the large excitement that the coming years would
  yield,
Eager-hearted as a boy when first he leaves his father's field,

And at night along the dusky highway near and nearer drawn,
Sees in heaven the light of London flaring like a dreary dawn;

And his spirit leaps within him to be gone before him then,
Underneath the light he looks at, in among the throngs of men;

Men, my brothers, men the workers, ever reaping something
  new;
That which they have done but earnest of the things that they
  shall do.

For I dipped into the future, far as human eye could see,
Saw the Vision of the world, and all the wonder that would
  be;   120

Saw the heavens fill with commerce, argosies of magic sails,
Pilots of the purple twilight, dropping down with costly bales;

Heard the heavens fill with shouting, and there rained a ghastly
dew
From the nations' airy navies grappling in the central blue;

Far along the world-wide whisper of the south-wind rushing
warm,
With the standards of the peoples plunging through the thunderstorm;

Till the war-drum throbbed no longer, and the battle-flags were
furled
In the Parliament of man, the Federation of the world.

There the common sense of most shall hold a fretful realm in
awe,
And the kindly earth shall slumber, lapped in universal law. 130

So I triumphed ere my passion sweeping through me left me
dry,
Left me with the palsied heart, and left me with the jaundiced
eye;

Eye, to which all order festers, all things here are out of joint.
Science moves, but slowly, slowly, creeping on from point to
point;

Slowly comes a hungry people, as a lion, creeping nigher,
Glares at one that nods and winks behind a slowly-dying fire.

Yet I doubt not through the ages one increasing purpose runs,
And the thoughts of men are widened with the process of the
suns.

What is that to him that reaps not harvest of his youthful joys,
Though the deep heart of existence beat for ever like a
boy's? 140

Knowledge comes, but wisdom lingers, and I linger on the
shore,
And the individual withers, and the world is more and more.

Knowledge comes, but wisdom lingers, and he bears a laden
breast,
Full of sad experience, moving toward the stillness of his rest.

Hark, my merry comrades call me, sounding on the bugle-horn,
They to whom my foolish passion were a target for their scorn.

Shall it not be scorn to me to harp on such a moldered string?
I am shamed through all my nature to have loved so slight a
    thing.

Weakness to be wroth with weakness! woman's pleasure,
    woman's pain—
Nature made them blinder motions bounded in a shallower
    brain.   150

Woman is the lesser man, and all thy passions, matched with
    mine,
Are as moonlight unto sunlight, and as water unto wine—

Here at least, where nature sickens, nothing. Ah, for some re-
    treat
Deep in yonder shining Orient, where my life began to beat,

Where in wild Mahratta-battle [40] fell my father evil-starred;—
I was left a trampled orphan, and a selfish uncle's ward.

Or to burst all links of habit—there to wander far away,
On from island unto island at the gateways of the day.

Larger constellations burning, mellow moons and happy skies,
Breadths of tropic shade and palms in cluster, knots of Para-
    dise.   160

Never comes the trader, never floats an European flag,
Slides the bird o'er lustrous woodland, swings the trailer from
    the crag;

Droops the heavy blossomed bower, hangs the heavy-fruited
    tree—
Summer isles of Eden lying in dark-purple spheres of sea.

There methinks would be enjoyment more than in this march
    of mind,
In the steamship, in the railway, in the thoughts that shake
    mankind.

40 With the Mahrattas, a Hindu people, the British fought in the eighteenth and
early nineteenth centuries.

There the passions cramped no longer shall have scope and
    breathing space;
I will take some savage woman, she shall rear my dusky race.

Iron-jointed, supple-sinewed, they shall dive, and they shall
    run,
Catch the wild goat by the hair, and hurl their lances in the
    sun;   170

Whistle back the parrot's call, and leap the rainbows of the
    brooks,
Not with blinded eyesight poring over miserable books—

Fool, again the dream, the fancy! but I *know* my words are wild,
But I count the gray barbarian lower than the Christian child.

I, to herd with narrow foreheads, vacant of our glorious gains,
Like a beast with lower pleasures, like a beast with lower pains!

Mated with a squalid savage—what to me were sun or clime?
I the heir of all the ages, in the foremost files of time—

I that rather held it better men should perish one by one,
Than that earth should stand at gaze like Joshua's moon in
    Ajalon! [41]   180

Not in vain the distance beacons. Forward, forward let us
    range,
Let the great world spin for ever down the ringing grooves of
    change. [42]

Through the shadow of the globe we sweep into the younger
    day;
Better fifty years of Europe than a cycle of Cathay. [43]

Mother-Age,—for mine I knew not,—help me as when life be-
    gun;
Rift the hills, and roll the waters, flash the lightnings, weigh
    the sun.

O, I see the crescent promise of my spirit hath not set.
Ancient founts of inspiration well through all my fancy yet.

41 Joshua, x, 12-13
42 When Tennyson rode on the first train from Manchester to Liverpool in 1830, he thought that the wheels ran in grooves.
43 China

Howsoever these things be, a long farewell to Locksley Hall!
Now for me the woods may wither, now for me the roof-tree
    fall.   190

Comes a vapor from the margin, blackening over heath and
    holt,
Cramming all the blast before it, in its breast a thunderbolt.

Let it fall on Locksley Hall, with rain or hail or fire or snow;
For the mighty wind arises, roaring seaward, and I go.

SIR GALAHAD

My good blade carves the casques of men,
    My tough lance thrusteth sure,
My strength is as the strength of ten,
    Because my heart is pure.
The shattering trumpet shrilleth high,
    The hard brands shiver on the steel,
The splintered spear-shafts crack and fly,
    The horse and rider reel;
They reel, they roll in clanging lists,
    And when the tide of combat stands,   10
Perfume and flowers fall in showers,
    That lightly rain from ladies' hands.

How sweet are looks that ladies bend
    On whom their favors fall!
For them I battle till the end,
    To save from shame and thrall;
But all my heart is drawn above,
    My knees are bowed in crypt and shrine;
I never felt the kiss of love,
    Nor maiden's hand in mine.   20
More bounteous aspects on me beam,
    Me mightier transports move and thrill;
So keep I fair through faith and prayer
    A virgin heart in work and will.

When down the stormy crescent[44] goes,
    A light before me swims,
Between dark stems the forest glows,
    I hear a noise of hymns.
Then by some secret shrine I ride;
    I hear a voice, but none are there;   30

44 crescent moon

The stalls are void, the doors are wide,
  The tapers burning fair.
Fair gleams the snowy altar-cloth,
  The silver vessels sparkle clean,
The shrill bell rings, the censer swings,
  And solemn chaunts resound between.

Sometimes on lonely mountain-meres
  I find a magic bark.
I leap on board; no helmsman steers;
  I float till all is dark.   40
A gentle sound, an awful light!
  Three angels bear the Holy Grail;
With folded feet, in stoles of white,
  On sleeping wings they sail.
Ah, blessed vision! blood of God!
  My spirit beats her mortal bars,
As down dark tides the glory slides,
  And starlike mingles with the stars.

When on my goodly charger borne
  Through dreaming towns I go,   50
The cock crows ere the Christmas morn,
  The streets are dumb with snow.
The tempest crackles on the leads,[45]
  And, ringing, springs from brand and mail;
But o'er the dark a glory spreads,
  And gilds the driving hail.
I leave the plain, I climb the height;
  No branchy thicket shelter yields;
But blessed forms in whistling storms
  Fly o'er waste fens and windy fields.   60

A maiden knight—to me is given
  Such hope, I know not fear;
I yearn to breathe the airs of heaven
  That often meet me here.
I muse on joy that will not cease,
  Pure spaces clothed in living beams,
Pure lilies of eternal peace,
  Whose odors haunt my dreams;
And, stricken by an angel's hand,
  This mortal armor that I wear,   70
This weight and size, this heart and eyes,
  Are touched, are turned to finest air.

45 roofs (covered with lead)

The clouds are broken in the sky,
   And through the mountain-walls
A rolling organ-harmony
   Swells up and shakes and falls.
Then move the trees, the copses nod,
   Wings flutter, voices hover clear:
"O just and faithful knight of God!
   Ride on! the prize is near."   80
So pass I hostel, hall, and grange;
   By bridge and ford, by park and pale,
All-armed I ride, whate'er betide,
   Until I find the Holy Grail.

BREAK, BREAK, BREAK [46]

BREAK, break, break,
   On thy cold gray stones, O Sea!
And I would that my tongue could utter
   The thoughts that arise in me.

O well for the fisherman's boy,
   That he shouts with his sister at play!
O well for the sailor lad,
   That he sings in his boat on the bay!

And the stately ships go on
   To their haven under the hill;   10
But O for the touch of a vanished hand,
   And the sound of a voice that is still!

Break, break, break,
   At the foot of thy crags, O Sea!
But the tender grace of a day that is dead
   Will never come back to me.

SONGS FROM *THE PRINCESS* [47]

I

THE splendor falls on castle walls
   And snowy summits old in story;
The long light shakes across the lakes,
   And the wild cataract leaps in glory.

[46] An early expression of Tennyson's grief on the death of Arthur Hallam (see *In Memoriam*).

[47] *The Princess* is a long narrative poem which expresses Tennyson's views on the higher education of women and similar feminist problems. A number of lyrics interrupt the narrative.

Blow, bugle, blow, set the wild echoes flying,
Blow, bugle; answer, echoes, dying, dying, dying.

  O hark, O hear! how thin and clear,
    And thinner, clearer, farther going!
  O sweet and far from cliff and scar
    The horns of Elfland faintly blowing!   10
Blow, let us hear the purple glens replying,
Blow, bugle; answer, echoes, dying, dying, dying.

  O love, they die in yon rich sky,
    They faint on hill or field or river;
  Our echoes roll from soul to soul,
    And grow for ever and for ever.
Blow, bugle, blow, set the wild echoes flying,
And answer, echoes, answer, dying, dying, dying.

2

  Tears, idle tears, I know not what they mean,
Tears from the depth of some divine despair
Rise in the heart, and gather to the eyes,
In looking on the happy autumn-fields,
And thinking of the days that are no more.

  Fresh as the first beam glittering on a sail,
That brings our friends up from the under-world,
Sad as the last which reddens over one
That sinks with all we love below the verge;
So sad, so fresh, the days that are no more.   10

  Ah, sad and strange as in dark summer dawns
The earliest pipe of half-awakened birds
To dying ears, when unto dying eyes
The casement slowly grows a glimmering square;
So sad, so strange, the days that are no more.

  Dear as remembered kisses after death,
And sweet as those by hopeless fancy feigned
On lips that are for others; deep as love,
Deep as first love, and wild with all regret;
O Death in Life, the days that are no more!   20

3

Home they brought her warrior dead;
  She nor swooned nor uttered cry.

All her maidens, watching, said,
"She must weep or she will die."

Then they praised him, soft and low,
Called him worthy to be loved,
Truest friend and noblest foe;
Yet she neither spoke nor moved.

Stole a maiden from her place,
Lightly to the warrior stepped,
Took the face-cloth from the face;
Yet she neither moved nor wept.   10

Rose a nurse of ninety years,
Set his child upon her knee—
Like summer tempest came her tears—
"Sweet my child, I live for thee."

4

Ask me no more: the moon may draw the sea;
The cloud may stoop from heaven and take the shape,
With fold to fold, of mountain or of cape;
But O too fond, when have I answered thee?
Ask me no more.

Ask me no more: what answer should I give?
I love not hollow cheek or faded eye:
Yet, O my friend, I will not have thee die.
Ask me no more, lest I should bid thee live;
Ask me no more.   10

Ask me no more: thy fate and mine are sealed;
I strove against the stream and all in vain;
Let the great river take me to the main.
No more, dear love, for at a touch I yield;
Ask me no more.

IN MEMORIAM A. H. H.

On September 15, 1833, Arthur Henry Hallam, son of Henry Hallam, the historian, died at Vienna, at the age of twenty-two. He had been Tennyson's closest friend at Cambridge, and at the time of his death was engaged to Tennyson's sister Emily. At various times from 1833 to 1850 the poet wrote in his friend's memory the elegiac poems which in the latter year he gathered together and carefully arranged as *In Memoriam*. "It must be remembered," he writes, "that this is a poem, *not* an actual biography. It is founded on our friendship, on the engagement of Arthur Hallam to my sister, on his sudden death at Vienna, just before the time fixed for their marriage, and on his burial at Clevedon Church. . . . It was meant to be a kind of *Divina Commedia,* ending with happiness. The sections were written at many different places, and as the phases of our intercourse came to my memory and suggested them. I did not write them with any view of weaving them into a whole, or for publication, until I found that I had written so many. The different moods of sorrow as in a drama are dramatically given, and my conviction that fear, doubts, and suffering will find answer and relief through Faith in a God of Love. 'I' is not always the author speaking of himself, but the voice of the human race speaking thro' him. After the Death of A. H. H., the divisions of the poem are made by First Xmas Eve (Section 28), Second Xmas (78), Third Xmas Eve (104 and 105, etc.)." From Tennyson's statement it will be seen that though the several sections were actually written over a stretch of seventeen years, the arrangement in the elegy seems to give the experiences and emotions of some three years directly following Hallam's death. Important in Tennyson's purpose of showing in the poem the progress from "the victor hours" to "the conquered years" are the profound grief up to the first Christmas, the preoccupation with problems of the immortality of the soul from the first to the second, the retrospective sections from the second to the third, with a sense of gain even through loss, and the return to normal human life, fortified by faith, after the fourth Christmas. Divisional poems are also the anniversaries of Hallam's death (72, 99).

The following introductory poem, which serves as a Prologue, was written after the other sections of the elegy had been completed. It is dated by the poet 1849.

STRONG Son of God, immortal Love,
   Whom we, that have not seen thy face,
   By faith, and faith alone, embrace,
Believing where we cannot prove;

Thine are these orbs of light and shade;
   Thou madest Life in man and brute;
   Thou madest Death; and lo, thy foot
Is on the skull which thou hast made.

Thou wilt not leave us in the dust:
   Thou madest man, he knows not why,   10
   He thinks he was not made to die;
And thou hast made him: thou art just.

Thou seemest human and divine,
   The highest, holiest manhood, thou.

Our wills are ours, we know not how;
Our wills are ours, to make them thine.

Our little systems have their day;
They have their day and cease to be;
They are but broken lights of thee,
And thou, O Lord, art more than they.   20

We have but faith: we cannot know,
For knowledge is of things we see;
And yet we trust it comes from thee,
A beam in darkness: let it grow.

Let knowledge grow from more to more,
But more of reverence in us dwell;
That mind and soul, according well,
May make one music as before,

But vaster. We are fools and slight;
We mock thee when we do not fear: 30
But help thy foolish ones to bear;
Help thy vain worlds to bear thy light.

Forgive what seem'd my sin in me,
What seem'd my worth since I began;
For merit lives from man to man,
And not from man, O Lord, to thee.

Forgive my grief for one removed,
Thy creature, whom I found so fair.
I trust he lives in thee, and there
I find him worthier to be loved.   40

Forgive these wild and wandering cries,
Confusions of a wasted youth;
Forgive them where they fail in truth,
And in thy wisdom make me wise.

I

I HELD it truth, with him [48] who sings
To one clear harp in divers tones,
That men may rise on stepping-stones
Of their dead selves to higher things.

48 Goethe

But who shall so forecast the years
    And find in loss a gain to match?
    Or reach a hand through time to catch
The far-off interest of tears?

Let Love clasp Grief lest both be drowned,
    Let darkness keep her raven gloss.
    Ah, sweeter to be drunk with loss,
To dance with Death, to beat the ground,

Than that the victor Hours should scorn
    The long result of love, and boast,
    "Behold the man that loved and lost,
But all he was is overworn."

3

O Sorrow, cruel fellowship,
    O Priestess in the vaults of Death,
    O sweet and bitter in a breath,
What whispers from thy lying lip?

"The stars," she whispers, "blindly run;
    A web is woven across the sky;
    From out waste places comes a cry,
And murmurs from the dying sun;

"And all the phantom, Nature, stands—
    With all the music in her tone,
    A hollow echo of my own,—
A hollow form with empty hands."

And shall I take a thing so blind,
    Embrace her as my natural good;
    Or crush her, like a vice of blood,
Upon the threshold of the mind?

5

I sometimes hold it half a sin
    To put in words the grief I feel;
    For words, like Nature, half reveal
And half conceal the Soul within.

But, for the unquiet heart and brain,
　　A use in measured language lies;
　　The sad mechanic exercise,
Like dull narcotics, numbing pain.

In words, like weeds, I'll wrap me o'er,
　　Like coarsest clothes against the cold;
　　But that large grief which these enfold
Is given in outline and no more.

6

One writes, that "other friends remain,"
　　That "loss is common to the race"—
　　And common is the commonplace,
And vacant chaff well meant for grain.

That loss is common would not make
　　My own less bitter, rather more.
　　Too common! Never morning wore
To evening, but some heart did break.

O father, wheresoe'er thou be,
　　Who pledgest now thy gallant son,
　　A shot, ere half thy draught be done,　　　　　　10
Hath stilled the life that beat from thee.

O mother, praying God will save
　　Thy sailor,—while thy head is bowed,
　　His heavy-shotted hammock-shroud
Drops in his vast and wandering grave.

Ye know no more than I who wrought
　　At that last hour to please him well;
　　Who mused on all I had to tell,
And something written, something thought;　　　　　20

Expecting still his advent home;
　　And ever met him on his way
　　With wishes, thinking, "here to-day,"
Or "here to-morrow will he come."

O, somewhere, meek, unconscious dove,
　　That sittest ranging golden hair;
　　And glad to find thyself so fair,
Poor child, that waitest for thy love!

For now her father's chimney glows
  In expectation of a guest;
  And thinking "this will please him best,"
She takes a riband or a rose:

For he will see them on to-night;
  And with the thought her color burns;
  And, having left the glass, she turns
Once more to set a ringlet right;

And, even when she turned, the curse
  Had fallen, and her future lord
  Was drowned in passing through the ford,
Or killed in falling from his horse.

O, what to her shall be the end?
  And what to me remains of good?
  To her perpetual maidenhood,
And unto me no second friend.

7

Dark house,[49] by which once more I stand
  Here in the long unlovely street,
  Doors, where my heart was used to beat
So quickly, waiting for a hand,

A hand that can be clasped no more—
  Behold me, for I cannot sleep,
  And like a guilty thing I creep
At earliest morning to the door.

He is not here; but far away
  The noise of life begins again,
  And ghastly through the drizzling rain
On the bald street breaks the blank day.

II

Calm is the morn without a sound,
  Calm as to suit a calmer grief,
  And only thro' the faded leaf
The chestnut pattering to the ground;

49 in Wimpole Street, London, where Arthur Hallam had lived

Calm and deep peace on this high wold,
   And on these dews that drench the furze,
   And all the silvery gossamers
That twinkle into green and gold;

Calm and still light on yon great plain
   That sweeps with all its autumn bowers,
   And crowded farms and lessening towers,   10
To mingle with the bounding main;

Calm and deep peace in this wide air,
   These leaves that redden to the fall,
   And in my heart, if calm at all,
If any calm, a calm despair;

Calm on the seas, and silver sleep,
   And waves that sway themselves in rest,
   And dead calm in that noble breast
Which heaves but with the heaving deep.   20

14

If one should bring me this report,
   That thou hadst touched the land to-day,
   And I went down unto the quay,
And found thee lying in the port;

And standing, muffled round with woe,
   Should see thy passengers in rank
   Come stepping lightly down the plank,
And beckoning unto those they know;

And if along with these should come
   The man I held as half-divine,
   Should strike a sudden hand in mine,   10
And ask a thousand things of home;

And I should tell him all my pain,
   And how my life had drooped of late,
   And he should sorrow o'er my state
And marvel what possessed my brain;

And I perceived no touch of change,
   No hint of death in all his frame,

But found him all in all the same,
I should not feel it to be strange.

19

The Danube to the Severn gave [50]
   The darkened heart that beat no more;
   They laid him by the pleasant shore,
And in the hearing of the wave.

There twice a day the Severn fills;
   The salt sea-water passes by,
   And hushes half the babbling Wye,
And makes a silence in the hills.

The Wye is hushed nor moved along,
   And hushed my deepest grief of all,
   When filled with tears that cannot fall,
I brim with sorrow drowning song.

The tide flows down, the wave again
   Is vocal in its wooded walls;
   My deeper anguish also falls,
And I can speak a little then.

27

I envy not in any moods
   The captive void of noble rage,
   The linnet born within the cage,
That never knew the summer woods;

I envy not the beast that takes
   His license in the field of time,
   Unfettered by the sense of crime,
To whom a conscience never wakes;

Nor, what may count itself as blest,
   The heart that never plighted troth
   But stagnates in the weeds of sloth;
Nor any want-begotten rest.

I hold it true, whate'er befall;
   I feel it, when I sorrow most;

50 Hallam died at Vienna, on the Danube, and was buried at Clevedon Church,
Somersetshire, overlooking the lower Severn estuary.

'Tis better to have loved and lost
Than never to have loved at all.

28

The time draws near the birth of Christ.
   The moon is hid, the night is still;
   The Christmas bells from hill to hill
Answer each other in the mist.

Four voices of four hamlets round,
   From far and near, on mead and moor,
   Swell out and fail, as if a door
Were shut between me and the sound;

Each voice four changes on the wind,
   That now dilate, and now decrease,   10
   Peace and goodwill, goodwill and peace,
Peace and goodwill, to all mankind.

This year I slept and woke with pain,
   I almost wished no more to wake,
   And that my hold on life would break
Before I heard those bells again;

But they my troubled spirit rule,
   For they controlled me when a boy;
   They bring me sorrow touched with joy,
The merry, merry bells of Yule.   20

30

With trembling fingers did we weave
   The holly round the Christmas hearth;
   A rainy cloud possessed the earth,
And sadly fell our Christmas-eve.

At our old pastimes in the hall
   We gamboled, making vain pretense
   Of gladness, with an awful sense
Of one mute Shadow watching all.

We paused: the winds were in the beech;
   We heard them sweep the winter land;   10
   And in a circle hand-in-hand
Sat silent, looking each at each.

Then echo-like our voices rang;
 We sang, though every eye was dim,
 A merry song we sang with him
Last year; impetuously we sang.

We ceased; a gentler feeling crept
 Upon us: surely rest is meet.
 "They rest," we said, "their sleep is sweet,"
And silence followed, and we wept.   20

Our voices took a higher range;
 Once more we sang: "They do not die
 Nor lose their mortal sympathy,
Nor change to us, although they change;

"Rapt from the fickle and the frail
 With gathered power, yet the same,
 Pierces the keen seraphic flame
From orb to orb, from veil to veil."

Rise, happy morn, rise, holy morn,
 Draw forth the cheerful day from night: 30
 O Father, touch the east, and light
The light that shone when Hope was born.

31

When Lazarus left his charnel-cave,
 And home to Mary's house returned,
 Was this demanded—if he yearned
To hear her weeping by his grave?

"Where wert thou, brother, those four days?"
 There lives no record of reply,
 Which telling what it is to die
Had surely added praise to praise.

From every house the neighbors met,
 The streets were filled with joyful sound,
 A solemn gladness even crowned
The purple brows of Olivet.

Behold a man raised up by Christ!
 The rest remaineth unrevealed;
 He told it not, or something sealed
The lips of that Evangelist.[51]

51 John, xi.

43

If Sleep and Death be truly one,
    And every spirit's folded bloom
    Through all its intervital gloom
In some long trance should slumber on;

Unconscious of the sliding hour,
    Bare of the body, might it last,
    And silent traces of the past
Be all the color of the flower:

So then were nothing lost to man;
    So that still garden of the souls
    In many a figured leaf enrolls
The total world since life began;

And love will last as pure and whole
    As when he loved me here in Time,
    And at the spiritual prime
Rewaken with the dawning soul.

48

If these brief lays, of Sorrow born,
    Were taken to be such as closed
    Grave doubts and answers here proposed,
Then these were such as men might scorn.

Her care is not to part and prove;
    She takes, when harsher moods remit,
    What slender shade of doubt may flit,
And makes it vassal unto love;

And hence, indeed, she sports with words,
    But better serves a wholesome law,
    And holds it sin and shame to draw
The deepest measure from the chords.

50

Be near me when my light is low,
    When the blood creeps, and the nerves prick
    And tingle; and the heart is sick,
And all the wheels of being slow.

Be near me when the sensuous frame
  Is racked with pangs that conquer trust;
  And Time, a maniac scattering dust,
And Life, a Fury slinging flame.

Be near me when my faith is dry,
  And men the flies of latter spring,
  That lay their eggs, and sting and sing
And weave their petty cells and die.

Be near me when I fade away,
  To point the term of human strife,
  And on the low dark verge of life
The twilight of eternal day.

51

Do we indeed desire the dead
  Should still be near us at our side?
  Is there no baseness we would hide?
No inner vileness that we dread?

Shall he for whose applause I strove,
  I had such reverence for his blame,
  See with clear eye some hidden shame
And I be lessened in his love?

I wrong the grave with fears untrue.
  Shall love be blamed for want of faith?
  There must be wisdom with great Death;
The dead shall look me through and through.

Be near us when we climb or fall;
  Ye watch, like God, the rolling hours
  With larger other eyes than ours,
To make allowance for us all.

54

O, yet we trust that somehow good
  Will be the final goal of ill,
  To pangs of nature, sins of will,
Defects of doubt, and taints of blood;

That nothing walks with aimless feet;
  That not one life shall be destroyed,

Or cast as rubbish to the void,
When God hath made the pile complete;

That not a worm is cloven in vain;
   That not a moth with vain desire   10
   Is shriveled in a fruitless fire,
Or but subserves another's gain.

Behold, we know not anything;
   I can but trust that good shall fall
   At last—far off—at last, to all,
And every winter change to spring.

So runs my dream; but what am I?
   An infant crying in the night;
   An infant crying for the light,
And with no language but a cry.   20

55

The wish, that of the living whole
   No life may fail beyond the grave,
   Derives it not from what we have
The likest God within the soul?

Are God and Nature then at strife,
   That Nature lends such evil dreams?
   So careful of the type she seems,
So careless of the single life,

That I, considering everywhere
   Her secret meaning in her deeds,
   And finding that of fifty seeds   10
She often brings but one to bear,

I falter where I firmly trod,
   And falling with my weight of cares
   Upon the great world's altar-stairs
That slope through darkness up to God,

I stretch lame hands of faith, and grope,
   And gather dust and chaff, and call
   To what I feel is Lord of all,
And faintly trust the larger hope.   20

56

"So careful of the type?" but no.
From scarpèd cliff and quarried stone
She cries, "A thousand types are gone;
I care for nothing, all shall go.

"Thou makest thine appeal to me:
I bring to life, I bring to death;
The spirit does but mean the breath:
I know no more." And he, shall he,

Man, her last work, who seemed so fair,
Such splendid purpose in his eyes,   10
Who rolled the psalm to wintry skies,
Who built him fanes of fruitless prayer,

Who trusted God was love indeed
And love Creation's final law—
Though Nature, red in tooth and claw
With ravine, shrieked against his creed—

Who loved, who suffered countless ills,
Who battled for the True, the Just,
Be blown about the desert dust,
Or sealed within the iron hills?   20

No more? A monster then, a dream,
A discord. Dragons of the prime,[52]
That tare each other in their slime,
Were mellow music matched with him.

O life as futile, then, as frail!
O for thy voice to soothe and bless!
What hope of answer, or redress?
Behind the veil, behind the veil.

57

Peace; come away: the song of woe
Is after all an earthly song.
Peace; come away: we do him wrong
To sing so wildly: let us go.

52 prehistoric monsters

Come; let us go: your cheeks are pale;
　　But half my life I leave behind.
　　Methinks my friend is richly shrined;
But I shall pass, my work will fail.

Yet in these ears, till hearing dies,
　　One set slow bell will seem to toll
　　The passing of the sweetest soul
That ever looked with human eyes.

I hear it now, and o'er and o'er,
　　Eternal greetings to the dead;
　　And "Ave, Ave, Ave," said,
"Adieu, adieu," for evermore.

64

Dost thou look back on what hath been,
　　As some divinely gifted man,
　　Whose life in low estate began
And on a simple village green;

Who breaks his birth's invidious bar,
　　And grasps the skirts of happy chance,
　　And breasts the blows of circumstance,
And grapples with his evil star;

Who makes by force his merit known
　　And lives to clutch the golden keys,　　　10
　　To mold a mighty state's decrees,
And shape the whisper of the throne;

And moving up from high to higher,
　　Becomes on Fortune's crowning slope
　　The pillar of a people's hope,
The center of a world's desire;

Yet feels, as in a pensive dream,
　　When all his active powers are still,
　　A distant dearness in the hill,
A secret sweetness in the stream,　　　　20

The limit of his narrower fate,
　　While yet beside its vocal springs
　　He played at counselors and kings,
With one that was his earliest mate;

Who plows with pain his native lea
  And reaps the labor of his hands,
  Or in the furrow musing stands:
"Does my old friend remember me?"

67

When on my bed the moonlight falls,
  I know that in thy place of rest
  By that broad water of the west
There comes a glory on the walls:

Thy marble bright in dark appears,
  As slowly steals a silver flame
  Along the letters of thy name,
And o'er the number of thy years.

The mystic glory swims away,
  From off my bed the moonlight dies;
  And closing eaves of wearied eyes
I sleep till dusk is dipped in gray;

And then I know the mist is drawn
  A lucid veil from coast to coast,
  And in the dark church like a ghost
Thy tablet glimmers in the dawn.

72

Risest thou thus, dim dawn,[53] again,
  And howlest, issuing out of night,
  With blasts that blow the poplar white,
And lash with storm the streaming pane?

Day, when my crowned estate begun
  To pine in that reverse of doom,
  Which sickened every living bloom,
And blurred the splendor of the sun;

Who usherest in the dolorous hour
  With thy quick tears that make the rose   10
  Pull sideways, and the daisy close
Her crimson fringes to the shower;

Who mightst have heaved a windless flame
  Up the deep East, or, whispering, played

53 the anniversary of Hallam's death

A checker-work of beam and shade
Along the hills, yet looked the same,

As wan, as chill, as wild as now;
   Day, marked as with some hideous crime,
   When the dark hand struck down through time,
And canceled nature's best: but thou,   20

Lift as thou mayst thy burthened brows
   Through clouds that drench the morning star,
   And whirl the ungarnered sheaf afar,
And sow the sky with flying boughs,

And up thy vault with roaring sound
   Climb thy thick noon, disastrous day;
   Touch thy dull goal of joyless gray,
And hide thy shame beneath the ground.

73

So many worlds, so much to do,
   So little done, such things to be,
   How know I what had need of thee,
For thou wert strong as thou wert true?

The fame is quenched that I foresaw,
   The head hath missed an earthly wreath:
   I curse not Nature, no, nor Death;
For nothing is that errs from law.

We pass; the path that each man trod
   Is dim, or will be dim, with weeds.
   What fame is left for human deeds
In endless age? It rests with God.

O hollow wraith of dying fame,
   Fade wholly, while the soul exults,
   And self-infolds the large results
Of force that would have forged a name.

78

Again at Christmas did we weave
   The holly round the Christmas hearth;
   The silent snow possessed the earth,
And calmly fell our Christmas-eve.

The yule-clog sparkled keen with frost,
   No wing of wind the region swept,
   But over all things brooding slept
The quiet sense of something lost.

As in the winters left behind,
   Again our ancient games had place,   10
   The mimic picture's breathing grace,
And dance and song and hoodman-blind.

Who showed a token of distress?
   No single tear, no mark of pain—
   O sorrow, then can sorrow wane?
O grief, can grief be changed to less?

O last regret, regret can die!
   No—mixed with all this mystic frame,
   Her deep relations are the same,
But with long use her tears are dry.   20

79

"More than my brothers are to me,"— [54]
   Let this not vex thee, noble heart!
   I know thee of what force thou art
To hold the costliest love in fee.

But thou and I are one in kind,
   As molded like in Nature's mint;
   And hill and wood and field did print
The same sweet forms in either mind.

For us the same cold streamlet curled
   Through all his eddying coves, the same   10
   All winds that roam the twilight came
In whispers of the beauteous world.

At one dear knee we proffered vows,
   One lesson from one book we learned,
   Ere childhood's flaxen ringlet turned
To black and brown on kindred brows.

And so my wealth resembles thine,
   But he was rich where I was poor,

---

[54] The closing line of Section 9. The following allusion is to Tennyson's brother Charles.

And he supplied my want the more
As his unlikeness fitted mine.

83

Dip down upon the northern shore,
O sweet new-year delaying long;
Thou doest expectant Nature wrong;
Delaying long, delay no more.

What stays thee from the clouded noons,
Thy sweetness from its proper place?
Can trouble live with April days,
Or sadness in the summer moons?

Bring orchis, bring the foxglove spire,
The little speedwell's darling blue,
Deep tulips dashed with fiery dew,
Laburnums, dropping-wells of fire.

O thou, new-year, delaying long,
Delayest the sorrow in my blood,
That longs to burst a frozen bud
And flood a fresher throat with song.

86

Sweet after showers, ambrosial air,
That rollest from the gorgeous gloom
Of evening over brake and bloom
And meadow, slowly breathing bare

The round of space, and rapt below
Through all the dewy tasseled wood,
And shadowing down the hornèd flood
In ripples, fan my brows and blow

The fever from my cheek, and sigh
The full new life that feeds thy breath
Throughout my frame, till Doubt and Death,
Ill brethren, let the fancy fly

From belt to belt of crimson seas
On leagues of odor streaming far,
To where in yonder orient star
A hundred spirits whisper "Peace."

87

I passed beside the reverend walls
  In which of old I wore the gown;
  I roved at random through the town,
And saw the tumult of the halls;

And heard once more in college fanes
  The storm their high-built organs make,
  And thunder-music, rolling, shake
The prophet blazoned on the panes;

And caught once more the distant shout,
  The measured pulse of racing oars   10
  Among the willows, paced the shores
And many a bridge, and all about

The same gray flats again, and felt
  The same, but not the same; and last
  Up that long walk of limes I passed
To see the rooms in which he dwelt.

Another name was on the door.
  I lingered; all within was noise
  Of songs, and clapping hands, and boys
That crashed the glass and beat the floor;   20

Where once we held debate, a band
  Of youthful friends, on mind and art,
  And labor, and the changing mart,
And all the framework of the land;

When one would aim an arrow fair,
  But send it slackly from the string;
  And one would pierce an outer ring,
And one an inner, here and there;

And last the master-bowman, he,
  Would cleave the mark. A willing ear   30
  We lent him. Who but hung to hear
The rapt oration flowing free

From point to point, with power and grace
  And music in the bounds of law,
  To those conclusions when we saw
The God within him light his face,

And seem to lift the form, and glow
  In azure orbits heavenly-wise;
  And over those ethereal eyes
The bar of Michael Angelo! [55]   40

88

Wild bird,[56] whose warble, liquid sweet,
  Rings Eden through the budded quicks,[57]
  O tell me where the senses mix,
O tell me where the passions meet,

Whence radiate: fierce extremes employ
  Thy spirits in the darkening leaf,
  And in the midmost heart of grief
Thy passion clasps a secret joy;

And I—my harp would prelude woe—
  I cannot all command the strings;
  The glory of the sum of things
Will flash along the chords and go.

96

You say, but with no touch of scorn,
  Sweet-hearted, you, whose light-blue eyes
  Are tender over drowning flies,
You tell me, doubt is Devil-born.

I know not: one indeed I knew
  In many a subtle question versed,
  Who touched a jarring lyre at first,
But ever strove to make it true;

Perplexed in faith, but pure in deeds,
  At last he beat his music out.
  There lives more faith in honest doubt,
Believe me, than in half the creeds.

He fought his doubts and gathered strength,   10
  He would not make his judgment blind,
  He faced the specters of the mind
And laid them; thus he came at length

---

55 Arthur Hallam had a   possessed by Michael An-   57 plants in a hedge
prominent bony ridge over gelo.
his eyes—a feature also   56 the nightingale

To find a stronger faith his own,
  And Power was with him in the night,
  Which makes the darkness and the light,
And dwells not in the light alone,   20

But in the darkness and the cloud,
  As over Sinaï's peaks of old,
  While Israel made their gods of gold,
Although the trumpet blew so loud.[58]

99

Risest thou thus, dim dawn, again,
  So loud with voices of the birds,
  So thick with lowings of the herds,
Day, when I lost the flower of men;

Who tremblest through thy darkling red
  On yon swollen brook that bubbles fast
  By meadows breathing of the past,
And woodlands holy to the dead;

Who murmurest in the foliaged eaves
  A song that slights the coming care,
  And Autumn laying here and there   10
A fiery finger on the leaves;

Who wakenest with thy balmy breath
  To myriads on the genial earth,
  Memories of bridal, or of birth,
And unto myriads more, of death.

O, wheresoever those may be,
  Betwixt the slumber of the poles,
  To-day they count as kindred souls;
They know me not, but mourn with me.   20

102

We leave the well-belovèd place [59]
  Where first we gazed upon the sky;
  The roofs that heard our earliest cry
Will shelter one of stranger race.

---

58 Exodus, xix
59 Somersby, where the   Tennyson family lived un-
                          til 1837

We go, but ere we go from home,
  As down the garden-walks I move,
  Two spirits of a diverse love
Contend for loving masterdom.

One whispers, "Here thy boyhood sung
  Long since its matin song, and heard   10
  The low love-language of the bird
In native hazels tassel-hung."

The other answers, "Yea, but here
  Thy feet have strayed in after hours
  With thy lost friend among the bowers,
And this hath made them trebly dear."

These two have striven half the day,
  And each prefers his separate claim,
  Poor rivals in a losing game,
That will not yield each other way.   20

I turn to go; my feet are set
  To leave the pleasant fields and farms;
  They [60] mix in one another's arms
To one pure image of regret.

104

The time draws near the birth of Christ;
  The moon is hid, the night is still;
  A single church below the hill
Is pealing, folded in the mist.

A single peal of bells below,
  That wakens at this hour of rest
  A single murmur in the breast,
That these are not the bells I know.[61]

Like strangers' voices here they sound,
  In lands where not a memory strays,
  Nor landmark breathes of other days,
But all is new unhallowed ground.

105

To-night ungathered let us leave
  This laurel, let this holly stand:

60 the two spirits of the preceding stanzas
61 Waltham Abbey, near High Beech, Epping Forest, where the Tennysons first resided after their removal from Somersby

We live within the stranger's land,
And strangely falls our Christmas-eve.

Our father's dust is left alone
  And silent under other snows:
  There in due time the woodbine blows,
The violet comes, but we are gone.

No more shall wayward grief abuse
  The genial hour with mask and mime;
  For change of place, like growth of time,   10
Has broke the bond of dying use.

Let cares that petty shadows cast,
  By which our lives are chiefly proved,
  A little spare the night I loved,
And hold it solemn to the past.

But let no footstep beat the floor,
  Nor bowl of wassail mantle warm;
  For who would keep an ancient form
Through which the spirit breathes no more?   20

Be neither song, nor game, nor feast;
  Nor harp be touched, nor flute be blown;
  No dance, no motion, save alone
What lightens in the lucid East

Of rising worlds by yonder wood.
  Long sleeps the summer in the seed;
  Run out your measured arcs, and lead
The closing cycle rich in good.

106

Ring out, wild bells, to the wild sky,
  The flying cloud, the frosty light:
  The year is dying in the night;
Ring out, wild bells, and let him die.

Ring out the old, ring in the new,
  Ring, happy bells, across the snow:
  The year is going, let him go;
Ring out the false, ring in the true.

Ring out the grief that saps the mind,
   For those that here we see no more;
   Ring out the feud of rich and poor,
Ring in redress to all mankind.   10

Ring out a slowly dying cause,
   And ancient forms of party strife;
   Ring in the nobler modes of life,
With sweeter manners, purer laws.

Ring out the want, the care, the sin,
   The faithless coldness of the times;
   Ring out, ring out my mournful rhymes,
But ring the fuller minstrel in.   20

Ring out false pride in place and blood,
   The civic slander and the spite;
   Ring in the love of truth and right,
Ring in the common love of good.

Ring out old shapes of foul disease;
   Ring out the narrowing lust of gold;
   Ring out the thousand wars of old,
Ring in the thousand years of peace.

Ring in the valiant man and free,
   The larger heart, the kindlier hand;   30
   Ring out the darkness of the land,
Ring in the Christ that is to be.

108

I will not shut me from my kind,
   And, lest I stiffen into stone,
   I will not eat my heart alone,
Nor feed with sighs a passing wind:

What profit lies in barren faith,
   And vacant yearning, though with might
   To scale the heaven's highest height,
Or dive below the wells of death?

What find I in the highest place,
   But mine own phantom chanting hymns?
   And on the depths of death there swims
The reflex of a human face.

I'll rather take what fruit may be
Of sorrow under human skies:
'Tis held that sorrow makes us wise,
Whatever wisdom sleep with thee.

115

Now fades the last long streak of snow,
Now burgeons every maze of quick [62]
About the flowering squares,[63] and thick
By ashen roots the violets blow.

Now rings the woodland loud and long,
The distance takes a lovelier hue,
And drowned in yonder living blue
The lark becomes a sightless song.

Now dance the lights on lawn and lea,
The flocks are whiter down the vale,   10
And milkier every milky sail
On winding stream or distant sea;

Where now the seamew pipes, or dives
In yonder greening gleam, and fly
The happy birds, that change their sky
To build and brood, that live their lives

From land to land; and in my breast
Spring wakens too, and my regret
Becomes an April violet,
And buds and blossoms like the rest.   20

118

Contemplate all this work of Time,
The giant laboring in his youth;
Nor dream of human love and truth,
As dying Nature's earth and lime;

But trust that those we call the dead
Are breathers of an ampler day
For ever nobler ends. They say,
The solid earth whereon we tread

In tracts of fluent heat began,
And grew to seeming-random forms,   10

The seeming prey of cyclic storms,
Till at the last arose the man;

Who throve and branched from clime to clime,
The herald of a higher race,
And of himself in higher place,
If so he type this work of time

Within himself, from more to more;
Or, crowned with attributes of woe
Like glories, move his course, and show
That life is not as idle ore,   20

But iron dug from central gloom,
And heated hot with burning fears,
And dipped in baths of hissing tears,
And battered with the shocks of doom

To shape and use. Arise and fly
The reeling Faun, the sensual feast;
Move upward, working out the beast,
And let the ape and tiger die.

126

Love is and was my lord and king,
And in his presence I attend
To hear the tidings of my friend,
Which every hour his couriers bring.

Love is and was my king and lord,
And will be, though as yet I keep
Within the court on earth, and sleep
Encompassed by his faithful guard,

And hear at times a sentinel
Who moves about from place to place,
And whispers to the worlds of space,
In the deep night, that all is well.

130

Thy voice is on the rolling air;
I hear thee where the waters run;
Thou standest in the rising sun,
And in the setting thou art fair.

What art thou then? I cannot guess;
　But though I seem in star and flower
　To feel thee some diffusive power,
I do not therefore love thee less.

My love involves the love before;
　My love is vaster passion now;
　Though mix'd with God and Nature thou,
I seem to love thee more and more.

Far off thou art, but ever nigh;
　I have thee still, and I rejoice;
　I prosper, circled with thy voice;
I shall not lose thee though I die.

131

O living will that shalt endure
　When all that seems shall suffer shock,
　Rise in the spiritual rock,[64]
Flow through our deeds and make them pure,

That we may lift from out of dust
　A voice as unto him that hears,
　A cry above the conquered years
To one that with us works, and trust,

With faith that comes of self-control,
　The truths that never can be proved
　Until we close with all we loved,
And all we flow from, soul in soul.

ODE ON THE DEATH OF THE DUKE
OF WELLINGTON [65]

I

Bury the Great Duke
　With an empire's lamentation,
Let us bury the Great Duke
　To the noise of the mourning of a mighty nation,
Mourning when their leaders fall,
Warriors carry the warrior's pall,
And sorrow darkens hamlet and hall.

64 I Cor. x, 4　　　of the Duke's burial in
65 published on the day　1852

2

Where shall we lay the man whom we deplore?
Here, in streaming London's central roar.[66]
Let the sound of those he wrought for,
And the feet of those he fought for,
Echo round his bones for evermore.

3

Lead out the pageant: sad and slow,
As fits an universal woe,
Let the long, long procession go,
And let the sorrowing crowd about it grow,
And let the mournful martial music blow;
The last great Englishman is low.

4

Mourn, for to us he seems the last,
Remembering all his greatness in the Past.
No more in soldier fashion will he greet
With lifted hand the gazers in the street.
O friends, our chief state-oracle is mute: [67]
Mourn for the man of long-enduring blood,
The statesman-warrior, moderate, resolute,
Whole in himself, a common good.
Mourn for the man of amplest influence,
Yet clearest of ambitious crime,
Our greatest yet with least pretense,
Great in council and great in war,
Foremost captain of his time,
Rich in saving common-sense,
And, as the greatest only are,
In his simplicity sublime.
O good gray head which all men knew,
O voice from which their omens all men drew,
O iron nerve to true occasion true,
O fall'n at length that tower of strength
Which stood four-square to all the winds that blew!
Such was he whom we deplore.
The long self-sacrifice of life is o'er.
The great World-victor's [68] victor will be seen no more.

10

20

30

40

---

66 St. Paul's Cathedral   various positions in the   1830 Prime Minister.
67 Wellington had held   state, and was from 1828 to   68 Napoleon's

5

All is over and done:
Render thanks to the Giver,
England, for thy son.
Let the bell be tolled:
Render thanks to the Giver,
And render him to the mold.
Under the cross of gold
That shines over city and river,   50
There he shall rest for ever
Among the wise and the bold.
Let the bell be tolled:
And a reverent people behold
The towering car, the sable steeds:
Bright let it be with its blazoned deeds,
Dark in its funeral fold.
Let the bell be tolled:
And a deeper knell in the heart be knolled;
And the sound of the sorrowing anthem rolled   60
Through the dome of the golden cross;
And the volleying cannon thunder his loss;
He knew their voices of old.
For many a time in many a clime
His captain's-ear has heard them boom
Bellowing victory, bellowing doom:
When he with those deep voices wrought,
Guarding realms and kings from shame;
With those deep voices our dead captain taught
The tyrant, and asserts his claim   70
In that dread sound to the great name,
Which he has worn so pure of blame,
In praise and in dispraise the same,
A man of well-attempered frame.
O civic muse, to such a name,
To such a name for ages long,
To such a name,
Preserve a broad approach of fame,
And ever-echoing avenues of song!

6

"Who is he that cometh, like an honored guest,   80
With banner and with music, with soldier and with priest,
With a nation weeping, and breaking on my rest?"
Mighty Seaman,[69] this is he

69 Lord Nelson, near whom Wellington was buried

Was great by land as thou by sea.
Thine island loves thee well, thou famous man,
The greatest sailor since our world began.
Now, to the roll of muffled drums,
To thee the greatest soldier comes;
For this is he
Was great by land as thou by sea;   90
His foes were thine; he kept us free;
O give him welcome, this is he
Worthy of our gorgeous rites,
And worthy to be laid by thee;
For this is England's greatest son,
He that gained a hundred fights,
Nor ever lost an English gun;
This is he that far away
Against the myriads of Assaye [70]
Clashed with his fiery few and won;   100
And underneath another sun,
Warring on a later day,
Round affrighted Lisbon [71] drew
The treble works, the vast designs
Of his labored rampart-lines,
Where he greatly stood at bay,
Whence he issued forth anew,
And ever great and greater grew,
Beating from the wasted vines
Back to France her banded swarms,   110
Back to France with countless blows,
Till o'er the hills her eagles [72] flew
Beyond the Pyrenean pines,
Followed up in valley and glen
With blare of bugle, clamor of men,
Roll of cannon and clash of arms,
And England pouring on her foes.
Such a war had such a close.
Again their ravening eagle [73] rose
In anger, wheeled on Europe-shadowing wings,   120
And barking for the thrones of kings;
Till one that sought but Duty's iron crown
On that loud sabbath [74] shook the spoiler down;
A day of onsets of despair!
Dashed on every rocky square
Their surging charges foamed themselves away;

70 in India
71 in the Peninsular campaign
72 French standards
73 Napoleon, after his escape from Elba
74 Sunday, June 18, 1815, the day of the battle of Waterloo

Last, the Prussian trumpet blew;
Through the long-tormented air
Heaven flashed a sudden jubilant ray,
And down we swept and charged and overthrew.   130
So great a soldier taught us there
What long-enduring hearts could do
On that world-earthquake, Waterloo!
Mighty Seaman, tender and true,
And pure as he from taint of craven guile,
O savior of the silver-coasted isle,
O shaker of the Baltic and the Nile,[75]
If aught of things that here befall
Touch a spirit among things divine,
If love of country move thee there at all,   140
Be glad, because his bones are laid by thine!
And through the centuries let a people's voice
In full acclaim,
A people's voice,
The proof and echo of all human fame,
A people's voice, when they rejoice
At civic revel and pomp and game,
Attest their great commander's claim
With honor, honor, honor, honor to him,
Eternal honor to his name.   150

7

A people's voice! we are a people yet.
Though all men else their nobler dreams forget,
Confused by brainless mobs and lawless Powers; [76]
Thank Him who isled us here, and roughly set
His Briton in blown seas and storming showers,
We have a voice, with which to pay the debt
Of boundless love and reverence and regret
To those great men who fought, and kept it ours.
And keep it ours, O God, from brute control;
O Statesmen, guard us, guard the eye, the soul   160
Of Europe, keep our noble England whole,
And save the one true seed of freedom sown
Betwixt a people and their ancient throne,
That sober freedom out of which there springs
Our loyal passion for our temperate kings;
For, saving that, ye help to save mankind

75 two of Nelson's naval
victories

76 Revolutions had taken
place in France and other
European countries in 1848.

In 1851 Napoleon III pro-
claimed himself emperor.

Till public wrong be crumbled into dust,
And drill the raw world for the march of mind,
Till crowds at length be sane and crowns be just.
But wink [77] no more in slothful overtrust.   170
Remember him who led your hosts;
He bade you guard the sacred coasts.
Your cannons molder on the seaward wall;
His voice is silent in your council-hall;
For ever; and whatever tempests lour
For ever silent; even if they broke
In thunder, silent; yet remember all
He spoke among you, and the Man who spoke;
Who never sold the truth to serve the hour,
Nor paltered with Eternal God for power;   180
Who let the turbid streams of rumor flow
Through either babbling world of high and low;
Whose life was work, whose language rife
With rugged maxims hewn from life;
Who never spoke against a foe;
Whose eighty winters freeze with one rebuke
All great self-seekers trampling on the right:
Truth-teller was our England's Alfred named;
Truth-lover was our English Duke;
Whatever record leap to light   190
He never shall be shamed.

8

Lo, the leader in these glorious wars
Now to glorious burial slowly borne,
Followed by the brave of other lands,
He, on whom from both her open hands
Lavish Honor showered all her stars,
And affluent Fortune emptied all her horn. [78]
Yea, let all good things await
Him who cares not to be great,
But as he saves or serves the state.   200
Not once or twice in our rough island-story,
The path of duty was the way to glory:
He that walks it, only thirsting
For the right, and learns to deaden
Love of self, before his journey closes,
He shall find the stubborn thistle bursting

77 sleep
78 Wellington was a knight of twenty-six different orders, had been made successively baron, viscount, earl, marquis, and duke, and had received from Parliament a grant of £500,000.

Into glossy purples, which outredden
All voluptuous garden-roses.
Not once or twice in our fair island-story,
The path of duty was the way to glory: 210
He, that ever following her commands,
On with toil of heart and knees and hands,
Through the long gorge to the far light has won
His path upward, and prevailed,
Shall find the toppling crags of Duty scaled
Are close upon the shining table-lands
To which our God Himself is moon and sun.
Such was he: his work is done.
But while the races of mankind endure,
Let his great example stand   220
Colossal, seen of every land,
And keep the soldier firm, the statesman pure:
Till in all lands and through all human story
The path of duty be the way to glory:
And let the land whose hearths he saved from shame
For many and many an age proclaim
At civic revel and pomp and game,
And when the long-illumined cities flame,
Their ever-loyal iron leader's fame,
With honor, honor, honor, honor to him,   230
Eternal honor to his name.

9

Peace, his triumph will be sung
By some yet unmolded tongue
Far on in summers that we shall not see:
Peace, it is a day of pain
For one about whose patriarchal knee
Late the little children clung:
O peace, it is a day of pain
For one, upon whose hand and heart and brain
Once the weight and fate of Europe hung.   240
Ours the pain, be his the gain!
More than is of man's degree
Must be with us, watching here
At this, our great solemnity.
Whom we see not we revere;
We revere, and we refrain
From talk of battles loud and vain
And brawling memories all too free
For such a wise humility

As befits a solemn fane: 250
We revere, and while we hear
The tides of Music's golden sea
Setting toward eternity,
Uplifted high in heart and hope are we,
Until we doubt not that for one so true
There must be other nobler work to do
Than when he fought at Waterloo,
And Victor he must ever be.
For though the Giant Ages heave the hill
And break the shore, and evermore   260
Make and break, and work their will;
Though world on world in myriad myriads roll
Round us, each with different powers,
And other forms of life than ours,
What know we greater than the soul?
On God and Godlike men we build our trust.
Hush, the Dead March wails in the people's ears:
The dark crowd moves, and there are sobs and tears:
The black earth yawns: the mortal disappears;
Ashes to ashes, dust to dust;   270
He is gone who seemed so great.—
Gone; but nothing can bereave him
Of the force he made his own
Being here, and we believe him
Something far advanced in State,
And that he wears a truer crown
Than any wreath that man can weave him.
Speak no more of his renown,
Lay your earthly fancies down,
And in the vast cathedral leave him.   280
God accept him, Christ receive him.

THE CHARGE OF THE LIGHT BRIGADE [79]

I

Half a league, half a league,
Half a league onward,
All in the valley of Death
      Rode the six hundred.
"Forward the Light Brigade!
Charge for the guns!" he said.
Into the valley of Death
      Rode the six hundred.

[79] in the Battle of Balaclava, in the Crimean War, 1854

2

"Forward, the Light Brigade!"
Was there a man dismayed?   10
Not though the soldier knew
   Some one had blundered.
Theirs not to make reply,
Theirs not to reason why,
Theirs but to do and die.
Into the valley of Death
   Rode the six hundred.

3

Cannon to right of them,
Cannon to left of them,
Cannon in front of them   20
   Volleyed and thundered;
Stormed at with shot and shell,
Boldly they rode and well,
Into the jaws of Death,
Into the mouth of hell
   Rode the six hundred.

4

Flashed all their sabers bare,
Flashed as they turned in air
Sabring the gunners there,
Charging an army, while   30
All the world wondered.
Plunged in the battery-smoke
Right through the line they broke;
Cossack and Russian
Reeled from the saber-stroke
   Shattered and sundered.
Then they rode back, but not,
   Not the six hundred.

5

Cannon to right of them,
Cannon to left of them,   40
Cannon behind them
   Volleyed and thundered;
Stormed at with shot and shell,

While horse and hero fell,
They that had fought so well
Came through the jaws of Death,
Back from the mouth of hell,
All that was left of them,
  Left of six hundred.

6

When can their glory fade?   50
O the wild charge they made!
  All the world wondered.
Honor the charge they made!
Honor the Light Brigade,
  Noble six hundred!

COME INTO THE GARDEN [80]

I

Come into the garden, Maud,
  For the black bat, night, has flown,
Come into the garden, Maud,
  I am here at the gate alone;
And the woodbine spices are wafted abroad,
  And the musk of the rose is blown.

2

For a breeze of morning moves,
  And the planet of Love is on high,
Beginning to faint in the light that she loves
  On a bed of daffodil sky,
To faint in the light of the sun she loves,
  To faint in his light, and to die.

3

All night have the roses heard
  The flute, violin, bassoon;
All night has the casement jessamine stirred
  To the dancers dancing in tune;
Till a silence fell with the waking bird,
  And a hush with the setting moon.

80 from *Maud: A Mono-drama*, a poem in which the hero tells his story in a series
of monologues, partly narrative and partly lyrical

4

I said to the lily, "There is but one,
  With whom she has heart to be gay.
When will the dancers leave her alone?
  She is weary of dance and play."
Now half to the setting moon are gone,
  And half to the rising day;
Low on the sand and loud on the stone
  The last wheel echoes away.

5

I said to the rose, "The brief night goes
  In babble and revel and wine.
O young lord-lover, what sighs are those,
  For one that will never be thine?
But mine, but mine," so I sware to the rose,
  "For ever and ever, mine."

6

And the soul of the rose went into my blood
  As the music clashed in the hall;
And long by the garden lake I stood,
  For I heard your rivulet fall
From the lake to the meadow and on to the wood,
  Our wood, that is dearer than all;

7

From the meadow your walks have left so sweet
  That whenever a March-wind sighs
He sets the jewel-print of your feet
  In violets blue as your eyes,
To the woody hollows in which we meet
  And the valleys of Paradise.

8

The slender acacia would not shake
  One long milkbloom on the tree;
The white lake-blossom fell into the lake
  As the pimpernel dozed on the lea;
But the rose was awake all night for your sake,
  Knowing your promise to me;

The lilies and roses were all awake,
    They sighed for the dawn and thee.

9

Queen rose of the rosebud garden of girls,
    Come hither, the dances are done,
In gloss of satin and glimmer of pearls,
    Queen lily and rose in one,
Shine out, little head, sunning over with curls,
    To the flowers, and be their sun.

10

There has fallen a splendid tear
    From the passion-flower at the gate.
She is coming, my dove, my dear;
    She is coming, my life, my fate.
The red rose cries, "She is near, she is near";
    And the white rose weeps, "She is late";
The larkspur listens, "I hear, I hear";
    And the lily whispers, "I wait."

11

She is coming, my own, my sweet;
    Were it ever so airy a tread,
My heart would hear her and beat,
    Were it earth in an earthy bed;
My dust would hear her and beat,
    Had I lain for a century dead,
Would start and tremble under her feet,
    And blossom in purple and red.

MILTON [81]

(ALCAICS)

O MIGHTY-MOUTHED inventor of harmonies,
O skilled to sing of Time or Eternity,
    God-gifted organ-voice of England,
        Milton, a name to resound for ages;
Whose Titan angels, Gabriel, Abdiel,
Starred from Jehovah's gorgeous armories,

---

[81] one of several attempts by Tennyson to reproduce in English the effect of classical quantitative verse

Tower, as the deep-domed empyrean
    Rings to the roar of an angel onset!
Me rather all that bowery loneliness,
    The brooks of Eden mazily murmuring,   10
And bloom profuse and cedar arches
    Charm, as a wanderer out in ocean,
Where some refulgent sunset of India
Streams o'er a rich ambrosial ocean isle,
    And crimson-hued the stately palm-woods
    Whisper in odorous heights of even.

NORTHERN FARMER, OLD STYLE [82]

1

WHEER 'asta beän saw long and meä liggin [83] 'ere aloän?
Noorse? thoort nowt o' a noorse; whoy, Doctor's abeän an'
    agoän;
Says that I moänt 'a naw moor aäle, but I beänt a fool;
Git ma my aäle, fur I beänt a-gawin' to breäk my rule.

2

Doctors, they knaws nowt, fur a [84] says what's nawways true;
Naw soort o' koind o' use to saäy the things that a do.
I've 'ed my point o' aäle ivry noight sin' I beän 'ere.
An' I've 'ed my quart ivry market-noight for foorty year.

3

Parson's a beän loikewoise, an' a sittin' ere o' my bed.
"The Amoighty's a taäkin o' you to 'issén,[85] my friend," a said,
An' a towd ma my sins, an' 's tiothe [86] were due, an' I gied it in
    hond;
I done moy duty boy 'um, as I 'a done boy the lond.

4

Larn'd a ma' beä. I reckons I 'annot sa mooch to larn.
But a cast oop,[87] thot a did, 'bout Bessy Marris's barne.[88]
Thaw a knaws I hallus voäted wi' Squoire an' choorch an'
    staäte,
An' i' the woost o' toimes I wur niver agin the raäte.[89]

---

82 in the dialect of Lin-   84 he   88 child
colnshire, where Tennyson   85 himself   89 poor-tax
was bred   86 tithe
83 lying   87 cast up (accused)

5

An' I hallus coom'd to 's choorch afoor moy Sally wur deäd,
An' 'eärd 'um a bummin' awaäy loike a buzzard-clock [90] ower
   my 'eäd,
An' I niver knaw'd whot a meän'd but I thowt a 'ad summut to
   saäy,
An' I thowt a said whot a wot to 'a said, an' I coom'd awaäy.

6

Bessy Marris's barne! tha knaws she laäid it to meä.
Mowt a beän, mayhap, for she wur a bad un, sheä.
'Siver,[91] I kep 'um, I kep 'um, my lass, tha mun understond;
I done moy duty boy 'um, as I 'a done boy the lond.

7

But Parson a cooms an' a goäs, an' a says it eäsy an' freeä:
"The Amoighty 's a taäkin o' you to 'issén, my friend," says 'eä.
I weänt saäy men be loiars, thaw summun said it in 'aäste;
But 'e reäds wonn sarmin a weeäk, an' I 'a stubb'd [92] Thurnaby
   waäste.

8

D' ya moind the waäste, my lass? naw, naw, tha was not born
   then;
Theer wur a boggle [93] in it, I often 'eärd 'um, mysén;
Moäst loike a butter-bump,[94] fur I 'eärd 'um about an' about,
But I stubb'd 'um oop wi' the lot, an' raäved an' rembled' um
   out.[95]

9

Keäper's [96] it wur; fo' they fun 'em theer a-laäid of 'is faäce
Down i' the woild 'enemies [97] afoor I coom'd to the plaäce.
Noäks or Thimbleby—toäner [98] 'ed shot um as deäd as a naäil.
Noäks wur 'ang'd for it oop at 'soize [99]—but git ma my aäle.

10

Dubbut looök at the waäste; theer warn't not feeäd for a cow;
Nowt at all but bracken an' fuzz,[1] an' looök at it now—

---

90 cockchafer, a kind of
beetle
91 howsoever
92 cleared
93 bogle (goblin)

94 bittern
95 tore up and threw him
out
96 game-keeper's
97 anemones

98 one or the other
99 assizes
1 furze

Warn't worth nowt a haäcre, an' now theer's lots o' feeäd,
Fourscoor yows ² upon it, an' some on it down i' seeäd.³

11

Nobbut a bit on it's left, an' I meän'd to 'a stubb'd it at fall,
Done it ta-year I meän'd, an' runn'd plow thruff it an' all,
If Godamoighty an' parson 'ud nobbut let ma aloän,—
Meä, wi' haäte hoonderd haäcre o' Squoire's, an' lond o' my
   oän.

12

Do Godamoighty knaw what a 's doing a-taäkin' o' meä?
I beänt wonn as saws 'ere a beän an' yonder a peä;
An' Squoire 'ull be sa mad an' all—a' dear, a' dear!
And I 'a managed for Squoire coom Michaelmas thutty year.

13

A mowt 'a taäen owd Joänes, as 'ant not a 'aäpoth ⁴ o' sense,
Or a mowt 'a taäen young Robins—a niver mended a fence;
But Godamoighty a moost taäke meä an' taäke ma now,
Wi' aäf the cows to cauve ⁵ an' Thurnaby hoälms ⁶ to plow!

14

Looök 'ow quoloty ⁷ smoiles when they seeäs ma a passin' boy,
Says to thessén,⁸ naw doubt, "What a man a beä sewer-loy!" ⁹
Fur they knaws what I beän to Squoire sin' fust a coom'd to
   the 'All;
I done moy duty by Squoire an' I done moy duty boy hall.

15

Squoire's i' Lunnon, an' summun I reckons 'ull 'a to wroite,
For whoä's to howd the lond ater meä thot muddles ma quoit;
Sartin-sewer I beä thot a weänt niver give it to Joänes,
Naw, nor a moänt to Robins—a niver rembles the stoäns.

16

But summun 'ull come ater meä mayhap wi' 'is kittle o' steäm ¹⁰
Huzzin'¹¹ an' maäzin' ¹² the blessed feälds wi' the divil's oän
   teäm.

2 ewes	6 river-bottoms	10 steam-engine
3 clover	7 quality (gentry)	11 hissing
4 half-pennyworth	8 themselves	12 amazing
5 calve	9 surely	

Sin' I mun doy I mun doy, thaw loife they says is sweet,
But sin' I mun doy I mun doy, for I couldn abeär to see it.

17

What atta stannin' theer fur, an' doesn bring ma the aäle?
Doctor's a' toättler,[13] lass, an a's hallus i' the owd taäle; [14]
I weänt breäk rules fur Doctor, a knaws naw moor nor a floy;
Git ma my aäle, I tell tha, an' if I mun doy I mun doy.

NORTHERN FARMER, NEW STYLE

1

DOESN'T thou 'ear my 'erse's legs, as they canters awaäy?
Proputty, proputty, proputty—that's what I 'ears 'em saäy.
Proputty, proputty, proputty—Sam, thou's an ass for thy
païns;
Theer's moor sense i' one o' 'is legs, nor in all thy braïns.

2

Woä—theer's a craw [15] to pluck wi' tha, Sam: yon's parsons's
'ouse—
Dosn't thou knaw that a man mun be eäther a man or a mouse?
Time to think on it then; for thou'll be twenty to weeäk.[16]
Proputty, proputty—woä then, woä—let ma' ear mysén speäk.

3

Me an' thy muther, Sammy, 'as beän a-talkin' o' thee;
Thou's beän talkin' to muther, an' she beän a-tellin' it me.
Thou'll not marry for munny—thou's sweet upo' parson's
lass—
Noä—thou'll marry for luvv—an' we boäth on us thinks tha
an ass.

4

Seeä'd her to-daäy goä by—Saäint's-daäy—they was ringing
the bells.
She's a beauty, thou thinks—an' soä is scoors o' gells,
Them as 'as munny an' all—wot's a beauty?—the flower as
blaws.
But proputty, proputty, sticks, an' proputty, proputty graws.

13 teetotaler   15 crow   16 this week
14 at the old story

5

Do'ant be stunt;[17] taäke time. I knaws what maäkes tha sa
    mad.
Warn't I craäzed fur the lasses mysén when I wur a lad?
But I knaw'd a Quaäker feller as often 'as towd ma this:
"Doänt thou marry for munny, but goä wheer munny is!

6

An' I went wheer munny war; an' thy muther coom to 'and,
Wi' lots o' munny laaïd by, an' a nicetish bit o' land.
Maäybe she warn't a beauty—I never giv it a thowt—
But warn't she as good to cuddle an' kiss as a lass as 'ant
    nowt?[18]

7

Parson's lass 'ant nowt, an' she weänt 'a[19] nowt when 'e's
    deäd,
Mun be a guvness, lad, or summut, and addle[20] her breäd.
Why? fur 'e's nobbut a curate, an' weänt niver get hissén clear,
An' 'e maäde the bed as 'e ligs[21] on afoor 'e coom'd to the
    shere.

8

An' thin 'e coom'd to the parish wi' lots o' Varsity debt,
Stook to his taaïl they did, an' 'e 'ant got shut on 'em yet.
An' 'e ligs on 'is back i' the grip,[22] wi' noän to lend 'im a shove,
Woorse nor a far-welter'd yowe,[23] fur, Sammy, 'e married fur
    luvv.

9

Luvv? what's luvv? thou luvv thy lass an' 'er munny too,
Maäkin 'em goä togither, as they've good right to do.
Couldn I luvv thy muther by cause o' 'er munny laaïd by?
Naäy—fur I luvv'd 'er a vast sight moor fur it; reäson why.

10

Ay, an' thy muther says thou wants to marry the lass,
Cooms of a gentleman burn; an' we boäth on us thinks tha an
    ass.

---

17 obstinate	20 earn	23 fow-weltered ewe (one
18 has nothing	21 lies	lying on its back in the
19 will not have	22 ditch	furrow)

Woä then, proputty, wiltha?—an ass as near as mays nowt [24]
Woä then, wiltha? dangtha!—the bees is as fell as owt.[25]

11

Breäk me a bit o' the esh for his 'eäd, lad, out o' the fence!
Gentleman burn! what's gentleman burn? is it shillins an' pence?
Proputty, proputty's ivrything 'ere, an', Sammy, I'm blest
If it isn't the saäme oop yonder, fur them as 'as it's the best.

12

Tis'n them as 'as munny as breäks into 'ouses an' steäls,
Them as 'as coäts to their backs an' taäkes their regular meäls.
Noä, but it's them as niver knaws wheer a meäl's to be 'ad.
Taäke my word for it, Sammy, the poor in a loomp is bad.

13

Them or thir feythers, tha sees, mun 'a beän a laäzy lot,
Fur work mun 'a gone to the gittin' whiniver munny was got.
Feyther 'ad ammost nowt; leästways 'is munny was 'id.
But 'e tued an' moil'd [26] issén deäd, an' 'e died a good un, 'e did.

14

Looök thou theer wheer Wrigglesby beck [27] cooms out by the
   'ill!
Feyther run oop to the farm, an' I runs oop to the mill;
An' I'll run oop to the brig,[28] an' that thou'll live to see;
And if thou marries a good un I'll leäve the land to thee.

15

Thim's my noätions, Sammy, wheerby I meäns to stick;
But if thou marries a bad un, I'll leäve the land to Dick.—
Coom oop, proputty, proputty—that's what I 'ears 'im saäy—
Proputty, proputty, proputty—canter an' canter awaäy.

THE HIGHER PANTHEISM

THE sun, the moon, the stars, the seas, the hills and the
   plains,—
Are not these, O Soul, the Vision of Him who reigns?

---

24 makes nothing   26 put himself in a stew   28 bridge
25 The flies are as fierce   and toiled
as anything.   27 brook

Is not the Vision He, tho' He be not that which He seems?
Dreams are true while they last, and do we not live in dreams?

Earth, these solid stars, this weight of body and limb,
Are they not sign and symbol of thy division from Him?

Dark is the world to thee; thyself art the reason why,
For is He not all but thou, that hast power to feel, "I am I"?

Glory about thee, without thee; and thou fulfillest thy doom,
Making Him broken gleams and a stifled splendor and
    gloom.

Speak to Him, thou, for He hears, and Spirit with Spirit can
    meet—
Closer is He than breathing, and nearer than hands and feet.

God is law, say the wise; O Soul, and let us rejoice,
For if He thunder by law the thunder is yet His voice.

Law is God, say some; no God at all, says the fool,
For all we have power to see is a straight staff bent in a pool;

And the ear of man cannot hear, and the eye of man cannot see;
But if we could see and hear, this Vision—were it not He?

FLOWER IN THE CRANNIED WALL

FLOWER in the crannied wall,
I pluck you out of the crannies,
I hold you here, root and all, in my hand,
Little flower—but *if* I could understand
What you are, root and all, and all in all,
I should know what God and man is.

IDYLLS OF THE KING

As early as 1830 Tennyson had written a poem on Launcelot and Queen
Guinevere, and the well-known *Lady of Shalott* appeared in the 1833 volume; while the last of the *Idylls* did not appear until 1885. For over fifty years,
then—almost his entire creative life—the poet was occupied with the Arthurian
story. His source was nearly always the *Morte d'Arthur* of Sir Thomas Malory,
although for one poem he went to the Welsh collection of romances known
as the *Mabinogion*.

As early as 1833 Tennyson had begun to plan a treatment of Arthurian
romance in epic style. By that year was written the *Morte d'Arthur*, published
in 1842, and afterwards included in the *Idylls*, with a slight change and some

additions, as "The Passing of Arthur." Other Idylls were published, singly or in groups, in 1857, 1859, 1862, 1869, 1872, and 1885. Finally, in 1888 the complete work appeared in final form, divided into twelve books. As Tennyson throughout this long period revolved the subject-matter in his mind, he elaborated it into his final imposing structure. His purpose was first, to give a great modern embodiment to the Arthurian legends, but second to present an allegory of the human soul. He himself speaks of the Idylls as "shadowing Sense at war with Soul," and in the progression of the poems, as finally arranged, is to be seen the destruction wrought in an ideal society by the yielding to the former at the expense of the latter. Viewed in the large, this moral purpose is obtrusive, and has done much to bring about a decline of interest in the work. The *Idylls* are here represented by the last of the series, which, it will be noted, was the first written.

THE PASSING OF ARTHUR

THAT story which the bold Sir Bedivere,
First made and latest left of all the knights,
Told, when the man was no more than a voice
In the white winter of his age, to those
With whom he dwelt, new faces, other minds.

For on their march to westward, Bedivere,
Who slowly paced among the slumbering host,
Heard in his tent the moanings of the King:

"I found Him in the shining of the stars,
I marked Him in the flowering of His fields,   10
But in His ways with men I find Him not.
I waged His wars, and now I pass and die.
O me! for why is all around us here
As if some lesser god had made the world,
But had not force to shape it as he would,
Till the High God behold it from beyond,
And enter it, and make it beautiful?
Or else as if the world were wholly fair,
But that these eyes of men are dense and dim,
And have not power to see it as it is—   20
Perchance, because we see not to the close;—
For I, being simple, thought to work His will,
And have but stricken with the sword in vain,
And all whereon I leaned in wife and friend
Is traitor to my peace, and all my realm
Reels back into the beast, and is no more.
My God, thou hast forgotten me in my death!
Nay—God my Christ—I pass but shall not die."

Then, ere that last weird battle in the west,
There came on Arthur sleeping, Gawain killed   30
In Lancelot's war, the ghost of Gawain blown
Along a wandering wind, and past his ear
Went shrilling: "Hollow, hollow all delight!
Hail, King! to-morrow thou shalt pass away.
Farewell! there is an isle of rest for thee.
And I am blown along a wandering wind,
And hollow, hollow, hollow, all delight!"
And fainter onward, like wild birds that change
Their season in the night and wail their way
From cloud to cloud, down the long wind the dream   40
Shrilled; but in going mingled with dim cries
Far in the moonlit haze among the hills,
As of some lonely city sacked by night,
When all is lost, and wife and child with wail
Pass to new lords; and Arthur woke and called:
"Who spake? A dream. O, light upon the wind,
Thine, Gawain, was the voice—are these dim cries
Thine? or doth all that haunts the waste and wild
Mourn, knowing it will go along with me?"

This heard the bold Sir Bedivere and spake: 50
"O me, my King, let pass whatever will,
Elves, and the harmless glamor of the field;
But in their stead thy name and glory cling
To all high places like a golden cloud
For ever; but as yet thou shalt not pass.
Light was Gawain in life, and light in death
Is Gawain, for the ghost is as the man;
And care not thou for dreams from him, but rise—
I hear the steps of Modred in the west,
And with him many of thy people, and knights   60
Once thine, whom thou hast loved, but grosser grown
Than heathen, spitting at their vows and thee.
Right well in heart they know thee for the King.
Arise, go forth and conquer as of old."

Then spake King Arthur to Sir Bedivere:
"Far other is this battle in the west
Whereto we move than when we strove in youth,
And brake the petty kings, and fought with Rome,
Or thrust the heathen from the Roman wall,
And shook him through the north. Ill doom is mine   70
To war against my people and my knights.
The king who fights his people fights himself.

And they my knights, who loved me once, the stroke
That strikes them dead is as my death to me.
Yet let us hence, and find or feel a way
Through this blind haze which, ever since I saw
One lying in the dust at Almesbury,[29]
Hath folded in the passes of the world."

Then rose the King and moved his host by night,
And ever pushed Sir Modred, league by league,   80
Back to the sunset bound of Lyonnesse— [30]
A land of old upheaven from the abyss
By fire, to sink into the abyss again;
Where fragments of forgotten peoples dwelt,
And the long mountains ended in a coast
Of ever-shifting sand, and far away
The phantom circle of a moaning sea.
There the pursuer could pursue no more,
And he that fled no further fly the King;
And there, that day when the great light of heaven   90
Burned at his lowest in the rolling year,
On the waste sand by the waste sea they closed.
Nor ever yet had Arthur fought a fight
Like this last, dim, weird battle of the west.
A death-white mist slept over sand and sea,
Whereof the chill, to him who breathed it, drew
Down with his blood, till all his heart was cold
With formless fear; and even on Arthur fell
Confusion, since he saw not whom he fought.
For friend and foe were shadows in the mist,   100
And friend slew friend not knowing whom he slew;
And some had visions out of golden youth,
And some beheld the faces of old ghosts
Look in upon the battle; and in the mist
Was many a noble deed, many a base,
And chance and craft and strength in single fights,
And ever and anon with host to host
Shocks, and the splintering spear, the hard mail hewn,
Shield-breakings, and the clash of brands, the crash
Of battle-axes on shattered helms and shrieks   110
After the Christ, of those who falling down
Looked up for heaven, and only saw the mist;
And shouts of heathen and the traitor knights,
Oaths, insult, filth, and monstrous blasphemies,
Sweat, writhings, anguish, laboring of the lungs

---

29 Guinevere. Arthur's parting from her is told in the Idyll bearing her name. 30 a legendary land in Cornwall, supposed now to be sunk beneath the sea

In that close mist, and cryings for the light,
Moans of the dying, and voices of the dead.

Last, as by some one death-bed after wail
Of suffering, silence follows, or through death
Or death-like swoon, thus over all that shore,   120
Save for some whisper of the seething seas,
A dead hush fell; but when the dolorous day
Grew drearier toward twilight falling, came
A bitter wind, clear from the north, and blew
The mist aside, and with that wind the tide
Rose, and the pale King glanced across the field
Of battle. But no man was moving there;
Nor any cry of Christian heard thereon,
Nor yet of heathen; only the wan wave
Brake in among dead faces, to and fro   130
Swaying the helpless hands, and up and down
Tumbling the hollow helmets of the fallen,
And shivered brands that once had fought with Rome,
And rolling far along the gloomy shores
The voice of days of old and days to be.

Then spake King Arthur to Sir Bedivere,
And whiter than the mist that all day long
Had held the field of battle was the King:

"Hearest thou this great voice that shakes the world,
And wastes the narrow realm whereon we move,   140
And beats upon the faces of the dead,
My dead, as though they had not died for me?—
O Bedivere, for on my heart hath fallen
Confusion, till I know not what I am,
Nor whence I am, nor whether I be king;
Behold, I seem but king among the dead."

Then spake the bold Sir Bedivere: "My King!
King everywhere! and so the dead have kings,
There also will I worship thee as king.
Yet still thy life is whole, and still I live   150
Who love thee; but who hates thee, he that brought
The heathen back among us, yonder stands,
Modred, unharmed, the traitor of thine house."

Then spake the King: "My house hath been my doom.
But call not thou this traitor of my house
Who hath but dwelt beneath one roof with me.

My house are rather they who sware my vows,
Yea, even while they brake them, owned me king.
And well for thee, saying in my dark hour,
When all the purport of my throne hath failed,   160
That quick or dead thou holdest me for king.
King am I, whatsoever be their cry;
And one last act of kinghood shalt thou see
Yet, ere I pass." And uttering this the King
Made at the man. Then Modred smote his liege
Hard on that helm which many a heathen sword
Had beaten thin; while Arthur at one blow,
Striking the last stroke with Excalibur,
Slew him, and, all but slain himself, he fell.

So all day long the noise of battle rolled   170
Among the mountains by the winter sea,
Until King Arthur's Table, man by man,
Had fallen in Lyonnesse about their lord,
King Arthur; then, because his wound was deep,
The bold Sir Bedivere uplifted him,
And bore him to a chapel nigh the field,
A broken chancel with a broken cross,
That stood on a dark strait of barren land.
On one side lay the Ocean, and on one
Lay a great water, and the moon was full.   180

Then spake King Arthur to Sir Bedivere:
"The sequel of to-day unsolders all
The goodliest fellowship of famous knights
Whereof this world holds record. Such a sleep
They sleep—the men I loved. I think that we
Shall never more, at any future time,
Delight our souls with talk of knightly deeds,
Walking about the gardens and the halls
Of Camelot, as in the days that were.
I perish by this people which I made,—   190
Though Merlin sware that I should come again
To rule once more—but let what will be be,
I am so deeply smitten through the helm
That without help I cannot last till morn.
Thou therefore take my brand Excalibur,
Which was my pride; for thou rememberest how
In those old days, one summer noon, an arm
Rose up from out the bosom of the lake,
Clothed in white samite,[31] mystic, wonderful,

31 a heavy silk

Holding the sword—and how I rowed across   200
And took it, and have worn it, like a king;
And, wheresoever I am sung or told
In aftertime, this also shall be known.
But now delay not; take Excalibur,
And fling him far into the middle mere; [32]
Watch what thou seest, and lightly [33] bring me word.

  To him replied the bold Sir Bedivere:
"It is not meet, Sir King, to leave thee thus,
Aidless, alone, and smitten through the helm—
A little thing may harm a wounded man;   210
Yet I thy hest will all perform at full,
Watch what I see, and lightly bring thee word."

  So saying, from the ruined shrine he stepped,
And in the moon athwart the place of tombs,
Where lay the mighty bones of ancient men,
Old knights, and over them the sea-wind sang
Shrill, chill, with flakes of foam. He, stepping down
By zigzag paths and juts of pointed rock,
Came on the shining levels of the lake.

  There drew he forth the brand Excalibur,   220
And o'er him, drawing it, the winter moon,
Brightening the skirts of a long cloud, ran forth
And sparkled keen with frost against the hilt;
For all the haft twinkled with diamond sparks,
Myriads of topaz-lights, and jacinth-work
Of subtlest jewelry. He gazed so long
That both his eyes were dazzled as he stood,
This way and that dividing the swift mind,
In act to throw; but at the last it seemed
Better to leave Excalibur concealed   230
There in the many-knotted water-flags,
That whistled stiff and dry about the marge.
So strode he back slow to the wounded King.

  Then spake King Arthur to Sir Bedivere:
"Hast thou performed my mission which I gave?
What is it thou hast seen? or what hast heard?"

  And answer made the bold Sir Bedivere:
"I heard the ripple washing in the reeds,
And the wild water lapping on the crag."

32 lake   33 quickly

To whom replied King Arthur, faint and pale: 240
"Thou hast betrayed thy nature and thy name,
Not rendering true answer, as beseemed
Thy fealty, nor like a noble knight;
For surer sign had followed, either hand,
Or voice, or else a motion of the mere.
This is a shameful thing for men to lie.
Yet now, I charge thee, quickly go again,
As thou art lief and dear, and do the thing
I bade thee, watch, and lightly bring me word."

Then went Sir Bedivere the second time   250
Across the ridge, and paced beside the mere,
Counting the dewy pebbles, fixed in thought;
But when he saw the wonder of the hilt,
How curiously and strangely chased, he smote
His palms together, and he cried aloud:

"And if indeed I cast the brand away,
Surely a precious thing, one worthy note,
Should thus be lost for ever from the earth,
Which might have pleased the eyes of many men.
What good should follow this, if this were done?   260
What harm, undone? Deep harm to disobey,
Seeing obedience is the bond of rule.
Were it well to obey then, if a king demand
An act unprofitable, against himself?
The King is sick, and knows not what he does.
What record or what relic of my lord
Should be to aftertime, but empty breath
And rumors of a doubt? But were this kept,
Stored in some treasure-house of mighty kings,
Some one might show it at a joust of arms,   270
Saying: 'King Arthur's sword, Excalibur,
Wrought by the lonely Maiden of the Lake.
Nine years she wrought it, sitting in the deeps
Upon the hidden bases of the hills.'
So might some old man speak in the aftertime
To all the people, winning reverence.
But now much honor and much fame were lost."

So spake he, clouded with his own conceit,[34]
And hid Excalibur the second time,
And so strode back slow to the wounded King.   280

34 conception of the matter

Then spoke King Arthur, breathing heavily:
"What is it thou hast seen? or what hast heard?"

And answer made the bold Sir Bedivere:
"I heard the water lapping on the crag,
And the long ripple washing in the reeds."

To whom replied King Arthur, much in wrath:
"Ah miserable, and unkind, untrue,
Unknightly, traitor-hearted; Woe is me!
Authority forgets a dying king,
Laid widowed of the power in his eye   290
That bowed the will. I see thee what thou art,
For thou, the latest-left of all my knights,
In whom should meet the offices of all,
Thou wouldst betray me for the precious hilt;
Either from lust of gold, or like a girl
Valuing the giddy pleasure of the eyes.
Yet, for a man may fail in duty twice,
And the third time may prosper, get thee hence;
But, if thou spare to fling Excalibur,
I will arise and slay thee with my hands."   300

Then quickly rose Sir Bedivere, and ran,
And, leaping down the ridges lightly, plunged
Among the bulrush beds, and clutched the sword,
And strongly wheeled and threw it. The great brand
Made lightnings in the splendor of the moon,
And flashing round and round, and whirled in an arch,
Shot like a streamer of the northern morn,[35]
Seen where the moving isles [36] of winter shock
By night, with noises of the Northern Sea.
So flashed and fell the brand Excalibur;   310
But ere he dipped the surface, rose an arm
Clothed in white samite, mystic, wonderful,
And caught him by the hilt, and brandished him
Three times, and drew him under in the mere.
And lightly went the other to the King.

Then spoke King Arthur, drawing thicker breath:
"Now see I by thine eyes that this is done.
Speak out; what is it thou hast heard, or seen?"

And answer made the bold Sir Bedivere:
"Sir King, I closed mine eyelids, lest the gems   320

35 Aurora Borealis   36 icebergs

Should blind my purpose, for I never saw,
Nor shall see, here or elsewhere, till I die,
Not though I live three lives of mortal men,
So great a miracle as yonder hilt.
Then with both hands I flung him, wheeling him;
But when I looked again, behold an arm,
Clothed in white samite, mystic, wonderful,
That caught him by the hilt, and brandished him
Three times, and drew him under in the mere."

And answer made King Arthur, breathing hard: 330
"My end draws nigh: 'tis time that I were gone.
Make broad thy shoulders to receive my weight,
And bear me to the margin; yet I fear
My wound hath taken cold, and I shall die."

So saying, from the pavement he half rose,
Slowly, with pain, reclining on his arm,
And looking wistfully with wide blue eyes
As in a picture. Him Sir Bedivere
Remorsefully regarded through his tears,
And would have spoken, but he found not words;   340
Then took with care, and kneeling on one knee,
O'er both his shoulders drew the languid hands
And rising bore him through the place of tombs.

But, as he walked, King Arthur panted hard
Like one that feels a nightmare on his bed
When all the house is mute. So sighed the King,
Muttering and murmuring at his ear, "Quick, quick!
I fear it is too late, and I shall die."
But the other swiftly strode from ridge to ridge,
Clothed with his breath, and looking, as he walked,   350
Larger than human on the frozen hills.
He heard the deep behind him, and a cry
Before. His own thought drove him like a goad.
Dry clashed his harness in the icy caves
And barren chasms, and all to left and right
The bare black cliff clanged round him, as he based
His feet on juts of slippery crag that rang
Sharp-smitten with the dint of armèd heels—
And on a sudden, lo, the level lake,
And the long glories of the winter moon!   360

Then saw they how there hove a dusky barge,
Dark as a funeral scarf from stem to stern,

Beneath them; and descending they were ware
That all the decks were dense with stately forms,
Black-stoled, black-hooded, like a dream—by these
Three queens with crowns of gold—and from them rose
A cry that shivered to the tingling stars,
And, as it were one voice, an agony
Of lamentation, like a wind that shrills
All night in a waste land, where no one comes,   370
Or hath come, since the making of the world.

Then murmured Arthur, "Place me in the barge."
So to the barge they came. There those three queens
Put forth their hands, and took the King, and wept.
But she that rose the tallest of them all,
And fairest laid his head upon her lap,
And loosed the shattered casque,[37] and chafed his hands,
And called him by his name, complaining loud,
And dropping bitter tears against a brow
Striped with dark blood; for all his face was white   380
And colorless, and like the withered moon
Smote by the fresh beam of the springing east;
And all his greaves and cuisses [38] dashed with drops
Of onset; and the light and lustrous curls—
That made his forehead like a rising sun
High from the dais-throne—were parched with dust,
Or, clotted into points and hanging loose,
Mixed with the knightly growth that fringed his lips.
So like a shattered column lay the King;
Not like that Arthur who, with lance in rest,   390
From spur to plume a star of tournament,
Shot through the lists at Camelot, and charged
Before the eyes of ladies and of kings.

Then loudly cried the bold Sir Bedivere:
"Ah! my Lord Arthur, whither shall I go?
Where shall I hide my forehead and my eyes?
For now I see the true old times are dead,
When every morning brought a noble chance,
And every chance brought out a noble knight.
Such times have been not since the light [39] that led   400
The holy Elders with the gift of myrrh
But now the whole Round Table is dissolved
Which was an image of the mighty world;
And I, the last, go forth companionless,

37 helmet   39 the Star of Bethlehem
38 armor for leg and
thigh

And the days darken round me, and the years,
Among new men, strange faces, other minds."

    And slowly answered Arthur from the barge:
"The old order changeth, yielding place to new,
And God fulfills himself in many ways,
Lest one good custom should corrupt the world.[40]   410
Comfort thyself; what comfort is in me?
I have lived my life, and that which I have done
May He within himself make pure! but thou,
If thou shouldst never see my face again,
Pray for my soul. More things are wrought by prayer
Than this world dreams of. Wherefore, let thy voice
Rise like a fountain for me night and day.
For what are men better than sheep or goats
That nourish a blind life within the brain,
If, knowing God, they lift not hands of prayer   420
Both for themselves and those who call them friend?
For so the whole round earth is every way
Bound by gold chains about the feet of God.
But now farewell. I am going a long way
With these thou seest—if indeed I go—
For all my mind is clouded with a doubt—
To the island-valley of Avilion;[41]
Where falls not hail, or rain, or any snow,
Nor ever wind blows loudly; but it lies
Deep-meadowed, happy, fair with orchard lawns   430
And bowery hollows crowned with summer sea,
Where I will heal me of my grievous wound."

    So said he, and the barge with oar and sail
Moved from the brink, like some full-breasted swan
That, fluting a wild carol ere her death,
Ruffles her pure cold plume, and takes the flood
With swarthy webs. Long stood Sir Bedivere
Revolving many memories, till the hull
Looked one black dot against the verge of dawn,
And on the mere the wailing died away.   440

    But when that moan had passed for evermore,
The stillness of the dead world's winter dawn
Amazed him, and he groaned, "The King is gone."
And therewithal came on him the weird rhyme,
"From the great deep to the great deep he goes."[42]

40 "E. g., chivalry, by formation of habit or by any other means." (Tennyson)

41 in Arthurian romance, the happy Other World, abode of the departed

42 said by Merlin when Arthur was born

Whereat he slowly turned and slowly clomb
The last hard footstep of that iron crag,
Thence marked the black hull moving yet, and cried:
"He passes to be king among the dead,
And after healing of his grievous wound   450
He comes again; but—if he come no more—
O me, be yon dark queens in yon black boat,
Who shrieked and wailed, the three whereat we gazed
On that high day, when, clothed with living light,
They stood before his throne in silence, friends
Of Arthur, who should help him at his need?"

Then from the dawn it seemed there came, but faint
As from beyond the limit of the world,
Like the last echo born of a great cry,
Sounds, as if some fair city were one voice   460
Around a king returning from his wars.

Thereat once more he moved about, and clomb
Even to the highest he could climb, and saw,
Straining his eyes beneath an arch of hand,
Or thought he saw, the speck that bare the King,
Down that long water opening on the deep
Somewhere far off, pass on and on, and go
From less to less and vanish into light.
And the new sun rose bringing the new year.

THE REVENGE [43]

A BALLAD OF THE FLEET

I

At Flores in the Azores Sir Richard Grenville lay,
And a pinnace, like a fluttered bird, came flying from far away:
"Spanish ships of war at sea! we have sighted fifty-three!"
Then sware Lord Thomas Howard: "'Fore God I am no
    coward;
But I cannot meet them here, for my ships are out of gear,
And the half my men are sick. I must fly, but follow quick.
We are six ships of the line; can we fight with fifty-three?"

2

Then spake Sir Richard Grenville: "I know you are no coward;
You fly them for a moment to fight with them again.

[43] Tennyson's poem is based upon Sir Walter Raleigh's account of the fight, which took place Sept. 10, 1591.

But I've ninety men and more that are lying sick ashore.   10
I should count myself the coward if I left them, my Lord
     Howard,
To these Inquisition dogs and the devildoms of Spain."

3

So Lord Howard passed away with five ships of war that day,
Till he melted like a cloud in the silent summer heaven;
But Sir Richard bore in hand all his sick men from the land
Very carefully and slow,
Men of Bideford in Devon,
And we laid them on the ballast down below;
For we brought them all aboard,
And they blessed him in their pain, that they were not left to
     Spain,   20
To the thumb-screw and the stake, for the glory of the Lord.

4

He had only a hundred seamen to work the ship and to fight,
And he sailed away from Flores till the Spaniard came in sight,
With his huge sea-castles heaving upon the weather bow.
"Shall we fight or shall we fly?
Good Sir Richard, tell us now,
For to fight is but to die!
There'll be little of us left by the time this sun be set."
And Sir Richard said again: "We be all good English men.
Let us bang these dogs of Seville, the children of the devil,   30
For I never turned my back upon Don or devil yet."

5

Sir Richard spoke and he laughed, and we roared a hurrah,
     and so
The little *Revenge* ran on sheer into the heart of the foe,
With her hundred fighters on deck, and her ninety sick below;
For half of their fleet to the right and half to the left were seen,
And the little *Revenge* ran on through the long sea-lane be-
     tween.

6

Thousands of their soldiers looked down from their decks and
     laughed,
Thousands of their seamen made mock at the mad little craft

Running on and on, till delayed
By their mountain-like *San Philip* that, of fifteen hundred
    tons,
And up-shadowing high above us with her yawning tiers of
    guns,
Took the breath from our sails, and we stayed.

7

And while now the great *San Philip* hung above us like a
    cloud
Whence the thunderbolt will fall
Long and loud,
Four galleons drew away
From the Spanish fleet that day,
And two upon the larboard and two upon the starboard lay,
And the battle-thunder broke from them all.

8

But anon the great *San Philip*, she bethought herself and
    went,
Having that within her womb that had left her ill content;
And the rest they came aboard us, and they fought us hand to
    hand,
For a dozen times they came with their pikes and musketeers,
And a dozen times we shook 'em off as a dog that shakes his
    ears
When he leaps from the water to the land.

9

And the sun went down, and the stars came out far over the
    summer sea,
But never a moment ceased the fight of the one and the fifty-
    three.
Ship after ship, the whole night long, their high-built galleons
    came,
Ship after ship, the whole night long, with her battle-thunder
    and flame;
Ship after ship, the whole night long, drew back with her dead
    and her shame.
For some were sunk and many were shattered, and so could
    fight us no more—
God of battles, was ever a battle like this in the world before?

10

For he said, "Fight on! fight on!"
Though his vessel was all but a wreck;
And it chanced that, when half of the short summer night was
     gone,
With a grisly wound to be dressed he had left the deck,
But a bullet struck him that was dressing it suddenly dead,
And himself he was wounded again in the side and the head,
And he said, "Fight on! fight on!"

11

And the night went down, and the sun smiled out far over the
     summer sea,   70
And the Spanish fleet with broken sides lay round us all in a
     ring;
But they dared not touch us again, for they feared that we
     still could sting,
So they watched what the end would be.
And we had not fought them in vain,
But in perilous plight were we,
Seeing forty of our poor hundred were slain,
And half of the rest of us maimed for life
In the crash of the cannonades and the desperate strife;
And the sick men down in the hold were most of them stark
     and cold,
And the pikes were all broken or bent, and the powder was
     all of it spent;   80
And the masts and the rigging were lying over the side;
But Sir Richard cried in his English pride:
"We have fought such a fight for a day and a night
As may never be found again!
We have won great glory, my men!
And a day less or more
At sea or ashore,
We die—does it matter when?
Sink me the ship, Master Gunner—sink her, split her in twain!
Fall into the hands of God, not into the hands of Spain!"   90

12

And the gunner said, "Ay, ay," but the seamen made reply:
"We have children, we have wives,
And the Lord hath spared our lives.
We will make the Spaniard promise, if we yield, to let us go;

We shall live to fight again and to strike another blow."
And the lion there lay dying, and they yielded to the foe.

13

And the stately Spanish men to their flag-ship bore him then,
Where they laid him by the mast, old Sir Richard caught at
    last,
And they praised him to his face with their courtly foreign
    grace;
But he rose upon their decks, and he cried: 100
"I have fought for Queen and Faith like a valiant man and
    true;
I have only done my duty as a man is bound to do.
With a joyful spirit I Sir Richard Grenville die!"
And he fell upon their decks, and he died.

14

And they stared at the dead that had been so valiant and true,
And had holden the power and glory of Spain so cheap
That he dared her with one little ship and his English few;
Was he devil or man? He was devil for aught they knew,
But they sank his body with honor down into the deep,
And they manned the *Revenge* with a swarthier alien crew, 110
And away she sailed with her loss and longed for her own;
When a wind from the lands they had ruined awoke from
    sleep,
And the water began to heave and the weather to moan,
And or ever that evening ended a great gale blew,
And a wave like the wave that is raised by an earthquake grew,
Till it smote on their hulls and their sails and their masts and
    their flags,
And the whole sea plunged and fell on the shot-shattered navy
    of Spain,
And the little *Revenge* herself went down by the island crags
To be lost evermore in the main.

RIZPAH [44]

17—

I

WAILING, wailing, wailing, the wind over land and sea—
And Willy's voice in the wind, "O mother, come out to me!"

---

[44] The title comes from 2 Sam. xxi. 8–10. The English story of the poem was read
by Tennyson in a penny magazine, as related in the *Memoir* by Hallam Tennyson,
II. 249–251.

Why should he call me to-night, when he knows that I can-
　　not go?
For the downs are as bright as day, and the full moon stares
　　at the snow.

2

We should be seen, my dear; they would spy us out of the
　　town.
The loud black nights for us, and the storm rushing over the
　　down,
When I cannot see my own hand, but am led by the creak of
　　the chain,
And grovel and grope for my son till I find myself drenched with
　　the rain.

3

Anything fallen again? nay—what was there left to fall?
I have taken them home, I have numbered the bones, I have
　　hidden them all.　　　　　　　　　　　　　　　　　　　　　10
What am I saying? and what are *you*? do you come as a spy?
Falls? what falls? who knows? As the tree falls so must it lie.

4

Who let her in? how long has she been? you—what have you
　　heard?
Why did you sit so quiet? you never have spoken a word.
O—to pray with me—yes—a lady—none of their spies—
But the night has crept into my heart, and begun to darken my
　　eyes.

5

Ah—you, that have lived so soft, what should *you* know of
　　the night,
The blast and the burning shame and the bitter frost and the
　　fright?
I have done it, while you were asleep—you were only made for
　　the day.
I have gathered my baby together—and now you may go your
　　way.　　　　　　　　　　　　　　　　　　　　　　　　　20

6

Nay—for it's kind of you, madam, to sit by an old dying wife.
But say nothing hard of my boy, I have only an hour of life.

I kissed my boy in the prison, before he went out to die.
"They dared me to do it," he said, and he never has told me a
lie.
I whipped him for robbing an orchard once when he was but
a child—
"The farmer dared me to do it," he said; he was always so
wild—
And idle—and couldn't be idle—my Willy—he never could rest.
The King should have made him a soldier, he would have been
one of his best.

7

But he lived with a lot of wild mates, and they never would
let him be good;
They swore that he dare not rob the mail, and he swore that he
would;
And he took no life, but he took one purse, and when all was
done
He flung it among his fellows—"I'll none of it," said my son.

8

I came into court to the judge and the lawyers. I told them
my tale,
God's own truth—but they killed him, they killed him for rob-
bing the mail.
They hanged him in chains for a show—we had always borne a
good name—
To be hanged for a thief—and then put away—isn't that enough
shame?
Dust to dust—low down—let us hide! but they set him so high
That all the ships of the world could stare at him, passing by.
God'll pardon the hell-black raven and horrible fowls of the air,
But not the black heart of the lawyer who killed him and
hanged him there.

9

And the jailer forced me away. I had bid him my last good-bye;
They had fastened the door of his cell. "O mother!" I heard him
cry.
I couldn't get back though I tried, he had something further to
say,
And now I never shall know it. The jailer forced me away.

10

Then since I couldn't but hear that cry of my boy that was
     dead,
They seized me and shut me up: they fastened me down on my
     bed.
"Mother, O mother!"—he called in the dark to me year after
     year—
They beat me for that, they beat me—you know that I couldn't
     but hear;
And then at the last they found I had grown so stupid and still
They let me abroad again—but the creatures had worked their
     will.   50

11

Flesh of my flesh was gone, but bone of my bone was left—
I stole them all from the lawyers—and you, will you call it a
     theft?—
My baby, the bones that had sucked me, the bones that had
     laughed and cried—
Theirs? O, no! they are mine—not theirs—they had moved in
     my side.

12

Do you think I was scared by the bones? I kissed 'em, I buried
     'em all—
I can't dig deep, I am old—in the night by the churchyard wall.
My Willy 'll rise up whole when the trumpet of judgment 'll
     sound,
But I charge you never to say that I laid him in holy ground.

13

They would scratch him up—they would hang him again on the
     cursèd tree.
Sin? O, yes, we are sinners, I know—let all that be,   60
And read me a Bible verse of the Lord's goodwill toward men—
"Full of compassion and mercy, the Lord"—let me hear it
     again;
"Full of compassion and mercy—long-suffering." Yes, O, yes!
For the lawyer is born but to murder—the Savior lives but to
     bless.
He'll never put on the black cap [45] except for the worst of the
     worst,

[45] worn by an English judge when pronouncing a sentence of death

And the first may be last—I have heard it in church—and the
  last may be first.
Suffering—O, long-suffering—yes, as the Lord must know,
Year after year in the mist and the wind and the shower and
  the snow.

14

Heard, have you? what? they have told you he never repented
  his sin.
How do they know it? are *they* his mother? are *you* of his
  kin?
                                                          70
Heard! have you ever heard, when the storm on the downs began,
The wind that 'll wail like a child and the sea that 'll moan like
  a man?

15

Election, Election, and Reprobation [46]—it's all very well.
But I go to-night to my boy, and I shall not find him in hell.
For I cared so much for my boy that the Lord has looked into
  my care,
And He means me I'm sure to be happy with Willy, I know not
  where.

16

And if *he* be lost—but to save *my* soul, that is all your desire—
Do you think I care for *my* soul if my boy be gone to the fire?
I have been with God in the dark—go, go, you may leave me
  alone—
You have never borne a child—you are just as hard as a
  stone.   80

17

Madam, I beg your pardon! I think that you mean to be kind,
But I cannot hear what you say for my Willy's voice in the
  wind—
The snow and the sky so bright—he used but to call in the
  dark,
And he calls to me now from the church and not from the gib-
  bet—for hark!
Nay—you can hear it yourself—it is coming—shaking the
  walls—
Willy—the moon's in a cloud—Good-night. I am going. He calls.

46 in Calvinistic theology, foreordained salvation and damnation respectively

TO VIRGIL

WRITTEN AT THE REQUEST OF THE MANTUANS FOR THE NINE-
TEENTH CENTENARY OF VIRGIL'S DEATH

I

ROMAN VIRGIL, thou that singest
    Ilion's lofty tempest robed in fire,
Ilion falling, Rome arising,
    wars, and filial faith, and Dido's pyre;

2

Landscape-lover, lord of language
    more than he that sang the "Works and Days," [47]
All the chosen coin of fancy
    flashing out from many a golden phrase;

3

Thou that singest wheat and woodland,
    tilth and vineyard, hive and horse and herd;
All the charm of all the Muses
    often flowering in a lonely word;

4

Poet of the happy Tityrus [48]
    piping underneath his beechen bowers;
Poet of the poet-satyr
    whom the laughing shepherd bound with flowers;

5

Chanter of the Pollio, glorying
    in the blissful years again to be,
Summers of the snakeless meadow,
    unlaborious earth and oarless sea;

6

Thou that seest Universal
    Nature moved by Universal Mind;

47 Hesiod   and later are to characters   *Eclogues* and *Æneid.*
48 The   allusions   here   and passages in Virgil's

Thou majestic in thy sadness
    at the doubtful doom of human kind;

7

Light among the vanished ages;
    star that gildest yet this phantom shore;
Golden branch amid the shadows,
    kings and realms that pass to rise no more;

8

Now thy Forum roars no longer,
    fallen every purple Cæsar's dome—
Though thine ocean-roll of rhythm
    sound for ever of Imperial Rome—

9

Now the Rome of slaves hath perished,
    and the Rome of freemen holds her place,
I, from out the Northern Island
    sundered once from all the human race,

10

I salute thee, Mantovano,[49]
    I that loved thee since my day began,
Wielder of the stateliest measure
    ever molded by the lips of man.

"FRATER AVE ATQUE VALE" [50]

Row us out from Desenzano, to your Sirmione row!
So they rowed, and there we landed—"O venusta [51] Sirmio!"
There to me thro' all the groves of olive in the summer glow,
There beneath the Roman ruin where the purple flowers grow,
Came that "Ave atque Vale" of the Poet's hopeless woe,
Tenderest of Roman poets nineteen hundred years ago,
"Frater Ave atque Vale"—as we wandered to and fro
Gazing at the Lydian laughter of the Garda Lake below
Sweet Catullus's all-but-island, olive-silvery Sirmio!

49 Mantuan   lament for his brother).   near Desenzano.
50 "Brother, hail and   Catullus's villa was at Sir-   51 beautiful
farewell" (from Catullus's   mione, on Lake Garda,

VASTNESS

1

Many a hearth upon our dark globe sighs after many a vanished face,
Many a planet by many a sun may roll with the dust of a
vanished race.

2

Raving politics, never at rest—as this poor earth's pale history
runs,—
What is it all but a trouble of ants in the gleams of a million
million of suns?

3

Lies upon this side, lies upon that side, truthless violence
mourned by the wise,
Thousands of voices drowning his own in a popular torrent of
lies upon lies;

4

Stately purposes, valor in battle, glorious annals of army and
fleet,
Death for the right cause, death for the wrong cause, trumpets
of victory, groans of defeat;

5

Innocence seethed in her mother's milk; and Charity setting
the marytr aflame,
Thraldom who walks with the banner of Freedom, and recks
not to ruin a realm in her name.

6

Faith at her zenith, or all but lost in the gloom of doubts that
darken the schools;
Craft with a bunch of all-heal in her hand, followed up by her
vassal legion of fools;

7

Trade flying over a thousand seas with her spice and her vintage, her silk and her corn;

Desolate offing, sailorless harbors, famishing populace, wharves forlorn;

8

Star of the morning, Hope in the sunrise; gloom of the evening, Life at a close;
Pleasure who flaunts on her wide downway with her flying robe and her poisoned rose;

9

Pain, that has crawled from the corpse of Pleasure, a worm which writhes all day, and at night
Stirs up again in the heart of the sleeper, and stings him back to the curse of the light;

10

Wealth with his wines and his wedded harlots; honest Poverty, bare to the bone;
Opulent Avarice, lean as Poverty; Flattery gilding the rift in a throne;

11

Fame blowing out from her golden trumpet a jubilant challenge to Time and to Fate;
Slander, her shadow, sowing the nettle on all the laureled graves of the great;

12

Love for the maiden, crowned with marriage, no regrets for aught that has been,
Household happiness, gracious children, debtless competence, golden mean;

13

National hatreds of whole generations, and pigmy spites of the village spire;
Vows that will last to the last death-ruckle, and vows that are snapped in a moment of fire;

14

He that has lived for the lust of the minute, and died in the doing it, flesh without mind;

He that has nailed all flesh to the Cross, till Self died out in the love of his kind;

15

Spring and Summer and Autumn and Winter, and all these old revolutions of earth;
All new-old revolutions of Empire—change of the tide—what is all of it worth?

16

What the philosophies, all the sciences, poesy, varying voices of prayer,
All that is noblest, all that is basest, all that is filthy with all that is fair?

17

What is it all, if we all of us end but in being our own corpse-coffins at last?
Swallowed in Vastness, lost in Silence, drowned in the deeps of a meaningless Past?

18

What but a murmur of gnats in the gloom, or a moment's anger of bees in their hive?—
.   .   .   .

Peace, let it be! for I loved him, and love him for ever; the dead are not dead but alive.

MERLIN AND THE GLEAM [52]

I

O YOUNG Mariner,
You from the haven
Under the sea-cliff,
You that are watching
The gray Magician
With eyes of wonder,
I am Merlin,
And *I* am dying,

[52] An allegory of Tennyson's literary life. The "gleam" is the spirit of poetry. For explanation, see Preface to Hallam Tennyson's *Memoir*.

I am Merlin
Who follow the Gleam.   10

2

Mighty the Wizard
Who found me at sunrise
Sleeping, and woke me
And learned me Magic!
Great the Master,
And sweet the Magic,
When over the valley,
In early summers,
Over the mountain,
On human faces,   20
And all around me,
Moving to melody,
Floated the Gleam.

3

Once at the croak of a Raven who crossed it
A barbarous people,
Blind to the magic
And deaf to the melody,
Snarled at and cursed me.
A demon vexed me,
The light retreated,
The landskip darkened,   30
The melody deadened,
The Master whispered,
"Follow the Gleam."

4

Then to the melody,
Over a wilderness
Gliding, and glancing at
Elf of the woodland,
Gnome of the cavern,
Griffin and Giant,   40
And dancing of Fairies
In desolate hollows,
And wraiths of the mountain,
And rolling of dragons
By warble of water,

Or cataract music
Of falling torrents,
Flitted the Gleam.

5

Down from the mountain
And over the level, 50
And streaming and shining on
Silent river,
Silvery willow,
Pasture and plowland,
Innocent maidens,
Garrulous children,
Homestead and harvest,
Reaper and gleaner,
And rough-ruddy faces
Of lowly labor, 60
Slided the Gleam—

6

Then, with a melody
Stronger and statelier,
Led me at length
To the city and palace
Of Arthur the King;
Touched at the golden
Cross of the churches,
Flashed on the tournament,
Flickered and bickered 70
From helmet to helmet,
And last on the forehead
Of Arthur the blameless
Rested the Gleam.

7

Clouds and darkness
Closed upon Camelot;
Arthur had vanished
I knew not whither,
The king who loved me,
And cannot die; 80
For out of the darkness
Silent and slowly

The Gleam, that had waned to a wintry glimmer
    On icy fallow
    And faded forest,
    Drew to the valley
    Named of the shadow,
    And slowly brightening
    Out of the glimmer,
And slowly moving again to a melody   90
    Yearningly tender,
    Fell on the shadow,
    No longer a shadow,
    But clothed with the Gleam.

8

    And broader and brighter
    The Gleam flying onward,
    Wed to the melody,
    Sang through the world;
    And slower and fainter,
    Old and weary,   100
    But eager to follow,
    I saw, whenever
    In passing it glanced upon
    Hamlet or city,
    That under the Crosses
    The dead man's garden,
    The mortal hillock,
    Would break into blossom;
    And so to the land's
    Last limit I came—   110
    And can no longer,
    But die rejoicing,
    For through the Magic
    Of Him the Mighty,
    Who taught me in childhood,
    There on the border
    Of boundless Ocean,
    And all but in Heaven
    Hovers the Gleam.

9

    Not of the sunlight,   120
    Not of the moonlight,
    Not of the starlight!

O young Mariner,
Down to the haven,
Call your companions,
Launch your vessel
·   And crowd your canvas,
And, ere it vanishes
Over the margin,
After it, follow it,   130
Follow the Gleam.

CROSSING THE BAR [53]

SUNSET and evening star,
    And one clear call for me!
And may there be no moaning of the bar,
    When I put out to sea,

But such a tide as moving seems asleep,
    Too full for sound and foam,
When that which drew from out the boundless deep
    Turns again home.

Twilight and evening bell,
    And after that the dark!
And may there be no sadness of farewell,
    When I embark;

For tho' from out our bourne of Time and Place
    The flood may bear me far,
I hope to see my Pilot face to face
    When I have crost the bar.

ROBERT BROWNING (1812–1889)

Robert Browning's father was a prosperous official of the Bank of England
—a cultivated man, with a fine appreciation of the arts. His mother was Sarah
Anne Wiedemann, the daughter of a German shipowner who had settled in
Dundee and married a Scotchwoman. The poet was born in Camberwell, now
a part of London, on May 7, 1812. In many respects his origin and his career
contrast with those of Tennyson. His parents were dissenters. His education
was largely at home or at the hands of tutors. He did not go to Oxford or
Cambridge, but matriculated at London University, where he spent only
two years. As a boy and young man, he displayed talent in several of the arts.
At one time he was uncertain whether he would be poet, painter, sculptor, or

53 The poet directed that this poem be placed at the end of all editions of his poems.

musician; but artist of some kind he must be. His abiding interest in music and in the pictorial arts is to be seen in his numerous poems based upon both.

An early influence was that of Shelley, a strong admiration for whom colors the poet's earliest published poem, *Pauline* (1833). His next published work was the long poem in dramatic form, *Paracelsus* (1835), giving Browning's interpretation of the life of the medieval physician, astrologer, and adept in magic, but even more his buoyant ideal of the power of love, and the tragedy experienced by his hero in the substitution of lower aims for the grand ones with which he first set forth. Another long early poem is *Sordello* (1840), for the subject-matter of which Browning went to medieval Italy,—a poem which fails so signally in recognizing the reader's difficulties with intricate story and elliptic phrasing that it has become a byword for obscurity.

Meanwhile Browning, through a friendship with the actor, Macready, had become interested in writing for the theater. During the best years of his young manhood he devoted a major portion of his energies to the composition of poetic dramas. The first of these was *Strafford* (1837); and between 1842 and 1846 there followed in quick succession *King Victor and King Charles, The Return of the Druses, A Blot in the 'Scutcheon, Colombe's Birthday, A Soul's Tragedy*, and *Luria*, and finally *In a Balcony* (1853), after which Browning abandoned the drama. *Pippa Passes* (1841), though dramatic in form, is hardly to be classified with the above, which were written mostly with the expectation of stage production. There are splendid things in these dramas, but it is perhaps to be regretted that Browning did not recognize earlier his ineptitude for the theater, and devote his time and powers to things which he could do supremely well. Although gifted with the ability imaginatively to create character, he lacked theatric sense. His characters indulge in long monologue, and their internal conflict is not appropriately translated in action; nor is there the necessary interplay of character on character in a group.

During the years of the poetic dramas, he was more successfully employed on shorter poems—many of those now included in his works under the headings "Dramatic Lyrics" and "Dramatic Romances." These, added to his dramas, had brought him some reputation with lovers of poetry. Among those who appreciated his work was Elizabeth Barrett, herself a poet better known than he, when a complimentary reference to him in one of her poems started a correspondence between the two in January, 1845. At the time, Miss Barrett was treated as a hopeless invalid, confined to a darkened sickroom, by a father who indulged in a peculiar kind of satisfaction in ministering to his daughter's infirmities. The correspondence became lengthier and warmer, and was followed by visits, and by professions of affection which Miss Barrett, from a sense of duty, suppressed. Doctors advised a trip to the south of Europe, to which Mr. Barrett would not agree. Finally Browning persuaded her to marry him (September 12, 1846). They eloped to the Continent, and for the next fifteen years, until Mrs. Browning's death, lived mostly in Italy. Browning's bold act was justified by the much better health which Mrs. Browning, in Italy, enjoyed. Their marriage is one of the great literary romances.

During these fifteen years, Browning's work is comparatively meager in quantity, since he was devoting himself to the care of his wife, but excellent in quality, including the great series, "Men and Women." After Mrs. Browning's death, the poet returned to live in England, with, however, many visits to Italy, which he sincerely loved. In addition to many shorter poems, in the *Dramatis Personæ, Asolando*, and other volumes, the period after Mrs. Browning's death is notable for *The Ring and the Book* (pub. 1868–1869), for several adaptations from the Greek (*Balaustion's Adventure*, 1871, and others), and for a number of longer works, difficult to all but Browning enthusiasts, like *The Inn Album* and *Parleyings with Certain People of Importance in their Day*. The poet died at Venice on December 12, 1889. He is buried in Westminster Abbey.

Browning's reputation grew slowly, but toward the end of his life had reached substantial proportions. He had, indeed, become a cult, studied in numerous Browning clubs, the formation of which rather amused than flattered the poet. After his death, his fame continued to mount, and has only recently shown signs of decline. Lovers of the poet experience great spiritual stimulation from his work, which expresses with unfailing vigor great ethical principles. His favorite doctrine, stated dozens of times in numerous poems, is that of "aspiration versus attainment." Only set your aim high, says Browning, and strive with all your might, and attainment becomes relatively insignificant; in fact, is undesirable, in that it kills the soul; Heaven is beyond for the completion of the task left unfinished in this world. He believed also in the power and permanence of love, in the occurrence in our lives of the "great moment" of illumination and critical decision, and in other simple but universal tenets—and these inform his poetry. A man of great energy himself, he preached the glory of physical vigor and of action—even as transcending conventional morals. Gifted with a sympathetic understanding of human motives, he was able to create a great gallery of characters—one of the most remarkable that any English writer has achieved. He presented many noble souls; but he was particularly interested in the problems of those whom the world considered charlatans, frauds, and failures, and he interprets with psychological insight many such figures—a Paracelsus, a Djabal (*Return of the Druses*), a Mr. Sludge, a Bishop Blougram, an Andrea del Sarto. He can present convincingly a murderer like Guido of *The Ring and the Book,* and a beast-like creature trying to think, like Caliban. In the form which he made peculiarly his own—the dramatic monologue (abundantly represented in this volume) he is unexcelled. In this form a character presents himself at some crisis of his life, with the assistance of interlocutors, replied to but not themselves speaking.

As an artist, he was not incapable of melodious verse, but he was much more concerned with vigorous and emphatic utterance. He had a natural leaning toward the grotesque—to the disgust of those who look for mere prettiness, to the delight of others who find themselves stimulated by the strong contrasts and uncouth contours of this form of art. The love of the grotesque, coupled with his dislike of mere melodiousness, led him to fantastic rhymes and other harsh and rough effects; while his impatience with circumlocution and his curious (and somewhat ostentatious) learning produced a telescopic style, packed often with obscure allusions, that has brought against him the charge of needless obscurity. The obscurity, however, largely vanishes with adequate study, and is seldom fundamental in his shorter pieces, of which the selections in this volume are largely made up. Everywhere in Browning one gets the impression of a powerful intellect bursting through, as at first it seems, an imperfect medium—a medium which, however, on fuller knowledge, seems well fitted to the man and the message he sought to convey. In a changing world, certain moderns have objected to his incurable optimism and his persistent preaching. It is to be noted that almost alone among the great Victorians, his faith was not shaken by the Nineteenth Century conflict of science and religion.

BIBLIOGRAPHY. Standard *Complete Works* by Charlotte Porter and Helen A. Clark, 12 vols. (Crowell). One vol. Cambridge ed. by H. E. Scudder (Houghton Mifflin). Mrs. Sutherland Orr, *Handbook to the Works of Robert Browning* (Harcourt Brace), and *Life*, new. ed., revised by F. G. Kenyon (Houghton Mifflin). G. K. Chesterton, *Robert Browning* (Eng. Men of Letters ser.). *The Letters of Robert Browning and Elizabeth Barrett*, 2 vols. (Harper's).

PORPHYRIA'S LOVER

THE rain set in early to-night,
　The sullen wind was soon awake,
It tore the elm-tops down for spite,
　And did its worst to vex the lake:
I listened with heart fit to break.
When glided in Porphyria; straight
　She shut the cold out and the storm,
And kneeled and made the cheerless grate
　Blaze up, and all the cottage warm;
Which done, she rose, and from her form 　　10
Withdrew the dripping cloak and shawl,
　And laid her soiled gloves by, untied
Her hat and let the damp hair fall,
　And last, she sat down by my side
And called me. When no voice replied,
　She put my arm about her waist,
And made her smooth white shoulder bare
And all her yellow hair displaced,
　And, stooping, made my cheek lie there,
And spread, o'er all, her yellow hair 　　20
Murmuring how she loved me—she
　Too weak, for all her heart's endeavor,
To set its struggling passion free
　From pride, and vainer ties dissever,
And give herself to me forever.
But passion sometimes would prevail,
　Nor could to-night's gay feast restrain
A sudden thought of one so pale
　For love of her, and all in vain:
So, she was come through wind and rain. 　　30
Be sure I looked up at her eyes
　Happy and proud; at last I knew
Porphyria worshiped me; surprise
　Made my heart swell, and still it grew

While I debated what to do.
That moment she was mine, mine, fair,
    Perfectly pure and good: I found
A thing to do, and all her hair
In one long yellow string I wound
Three times her little throat around,
And strangled her. No pain felt she; 40
    I am quite sure she felt no pain.
As a shut bud that holds a bee,
    I warily oped her lids: again
Laughed the blue eyes without a stain.
And I untightened next the tress
    About her neck; her cheek once more
Blushed bright beneath my burning kiss.
    I propped her head up as before,
Only, this time my shoulder bore 50
Her head, which droops upon it still:
    The smiling rosy little head,
So glad it has its utmost will,
    That all it scorned at once is fled,
And I, its love, am gained instead!
Porphyria's love: she guessed not how
    Her darling one wish would be heard.
And thus we sit together now,
    And all night long we have not stirred,
And yet God has not said a word! 60

HOW THEY BROUGHT THE GOOD NEWS FROM GHENT TO AIX [1]

I sprang to the stirrup, and Joris, and he;
I galloped, Dirck galloped, we galloped all three;
"Good speed!" cried the watch, as the gate-bolts undrew;
"Speed!" echoed the wall to us galloping through;
Behind shut the postern, the lights sank to rest,
And into the midnight we galloped abreast.

Not a word to each other; we kept the great pace
Neck by neck, stride by stride, never changing our place;
I turned in my saddle and made its girths tight,
Then shortened each stirrup, and set the pique right, 10
Rebuckled the cheek-strap, chained slacker the bit,
Nor galloped less steadily Roland a whit.

1 "There is no sort of historical foundation for the poem . . . I wrote it under the bulwark of a vessel, off the African coast, after I had been at sea long enough to appreciate even the fancy of a gallop on the back of a certain good horse 'York,' then in my stable at home." (Browning)

'Twas moonset at starting; but while we drew near
Lokeren, the cocks crew and twilight dawned clear;
At Boom, a great yellow star came out to see;
At Düffeld, 'twas morning as plain as could be;
And from Mecheln church-steeple we heard the half-chime,
So Joris broke silence with, "Yet there is time!"

At Aershot, up leaped of a sudden the sun,
And against him the cattle stood black every one,   20
To stare through the mist at us galloping past,
And I saw my stout galloper Roland at last,
With resolute shoulders, each butting away
The haze, as some bluff river headland its spray:

And his low head and crest, just one sharp ear bent back
For my voice, and the other pricked out on his track;
And one eye's black intelligence,—ever that glance
O'er its white edge at me, his own master, askance!
And the thick heavy spume-flakes which aye and anon
His fierce lips shook upwards in galloping on.   30

By Hasselt, Dirck groaned; and cried Joris, "Stay spur!
Your Roos galloped bravely, the fault's not in her,
We'll remember at Aix"—for one heard the quick wheeze
Of her chest, saw the stretched neck and staggering knees,
And sunk tail, and horrible heave of the flank,
As down on her haunches she shuddered and sank.

So, we were left galloping, Joris and I,
Past Looz and past Tongres, no cloud in the sky;
The broad sun above laughed a pitiless laugh,
'Neath our feet broke the brittle bright stubble like chaff;   40
Till over by Dalhem a dome-spire sprang white,
And "Gallop," gasped Joris, "for Aix is in sight!"

"How they'll greet us!"—and all in a moment his roan
Rolled neck and croup over, lay dead as a stone;
And there was my Roland to bear the whole weight
Of the news which alone could save Aix from her fate,
With his nostrils like pits full of blood to the brim,
And with circles of red for his eye-sockets' rim.

Then I cast loose my buffcoat, each holster let fall,
Shook off both my jack-boots, let go belt and all,   50
Stood up in the stirrup, leaned, patted his ear,
Called my Roland his pet-name, my horse without peer;

Clapped my hands, laughed and sang, any noise, bad or good,
Till at length into Aix Roland galloped and stood.

And all I remember is—friends flocking round
As I sat with his head 'twixt my knees on the ground;
And no voice but was praising this Roland of mine,
As I poured down his throat our last measure of wine,
Which (the burgesses voted by common consent)
Was no more than his due who brought good news from
    Ghent.   60

CAVALIER TUNES

1. MARCHING ALONG

KENTISH Sir Byng stood for his King,
Bidding the crop-headed Parliament swing:
And, pressing a troop unable to stoop
And see the rogues flourish and honest folk droop,
Marched them along, fifty-score strong,
Great-hearted gentlemen, singing this song.

God for King Charles! Pym and such carles
To the Devil that prompts 'em their treasonous parles!
Cavaliers, up! Lips from the cup,
Hands from the pasty, nor bite take nor sup   10
Till you're—
    CHO.—Marching along, fifty-score strong,
        Great-hearted gentlemen, singing this song.

Hampden to hell, and his obsequies' knell.
Serve Hazelrig, Fiennes, and young Harry [2] as well!
England, good cheer! Rupert is near!
Kentish and loyalists, keep we not here,
    CHO.—Marching along, fifty-score strong,
        Great-hearted gentlemen, singing this song?

Then, God for King Charles! Pym and his snarls   20
To the Devil that pricks on such pestilent carles!
Hold by the right, you double your might;
So, onward to Nottingham,[3] fresh for the fight,
    CHO.—March we along, fifty-score strong,
        Great-hearted gentlemen, singing this song!

2 Sir Henry Vane the   3 where Charles I set   a sign of war
younger   up his standard in 1642 as

2. GIVE A ROUSE

King Charles, and who'll do him right now?
King Charles, and who's ripe for fight now?
Give a rouse: here's, in hell's despite now,
King Charles!
Who gave me the goods that went since?
Who raised me the house that sank once?
Who helped me to gold I spent since?
Who found me in wine you drank once?
   CHO.—King Charles, and who'll do him right now?
       King Charles, and who's ripe for fight now?   10
       Give a rouse: here's, in hell's despite now,
       King Charles!

To whom used my boy George quaff else,
By the old fool's side that begot him?
For whom did he cheer and laugh else,
While Noll's [4] damned troopers shot him?
   CHO.—King Charles, and who'll do him right now?
       King Charles, and who's ripe for fight now?
       Give a rouse: here's, in hell's despite now,
       King Charles!   20

3. BOOT AND SADDLE

Boot, saddle, to horse, and away!
Rescue my castle before the hot day
Brightens to blue from its silvery gray.
   CHO.—Boot, saddle, to horse, and away!

Ride past the suburbs, asleep as you'd say;
Many's the friend there, will listen and pray
"God's luck to gallants that strike up the lay—
   CHO.—Boot, saddle, to horse, and away!"

Forty miles off, like a roebuck at bay,
Flouts Castle Brancepeth the Roundheads' array: 10
Who laughs, "Good fellows ere this, by my fay,
   CHO.—Boot, saddle, to horse, and away!"

Who? My wife Gertrude; that, honest and gay,
Laughs when you talk of surrendering, "Nay!
I've better counselors; what counsel they?
   CHO.—Boot, saddle, to horse, and away!"

---

4 Oliver Cromwell's

SOLILOQUY OF THE SPANISH CLOISTER

Gr-r-r—there go, my heart's abhorrence!
  Water your damned flower-pots, do!
If hate killed men, Brother Lawrence,
  God's blood, would not mine kill you!
What? your myrtle-bush wants trimming?
  Oh, that rose has prior claims—
Needs its leaden vase filled brimming?
  Hell dry you up with its flames!

At the meal we sit together:
  Salve tibi! [5] I must hear   10
Wise talk of the kind of weather,
  Sort of season, time of year:
Not a plenteous cork-crop: scarcely
  Dare we hope oak-galls, I doubt:
What's the Latin name for "parsley"?
  What's the Greek name for Swine's Snout?

Whew! We'll have our platter burnished,
  Laid with care on our own shelf!
With a fire-new spoon we're furnished,
  And a goblet for ourself,   20
Rinsed like something sacrificial
  Ere 'tis fit to touch our chaps—
Marked with L for our initial!
  (He-he! There his lily snaps!)

Saint, forsooth! While brown Dolores
  Squats outside the Convent bank
With Sanchicha, telling stories,
  Steeping tresses in the tank,
Blue-black, lustrous, thick like horsehairs,
  —Can't I see his dead eye glow,   30
Bright as 'twere a Barbary corsair's?
  (That is, if he'd let it show!)

When he finishes refection,
  Knife and fork he never lays
Cross-wise, to my recollection,
  As do I, in Jesu's praise.
I the Trinity illustrate,
  Drinking watered orange-pulp—

5 Save you!

In three sips the Arian [6] frustrate;
    While he drains his at one gulp.   40

Oh, those melons! If he's able
    We're to have a feast! so nice!
One goes to the Abbot's table,
    All of us get each a slice.
How go on your flowers? None double?
    Not one fruit-sort can you spy?
Strange!—And I, too, at such trouble
    Keep them close-nipped on the sly!

There's a great text in Galatians,[7]
    Once you trip on it, entails   50
Twenty-nine distinct damnations,
    One sure, if another fails:
If I trip him just a-dying,
    Sure of heaven as sure can be,
Spin him round and send him flying
    Off to hell, a Manichee? [8]

Or, my scrofulous French novel
    On gray paper with blunt type!
Simply glance at it, you grovel
    Hand and foot in Belial's gripe: 60
If I double down its pages
    At the woeful sixteenth print,
When he gathers his greengages,
    Ope a sieve and slip it in't?

Oh, there's Satan!—one might venture
    Pledge one's soul to him, yet leave
Such a flaw in the indenture
    As he'd miss till, past retrieve,
Blasted lay that rose-acacia
    We're so proud of! *Hy, Zy, Hine*. . .   70
'St, there's Vespers! *Plena gratiâ,
Ave, Virgo!* [9] Gr-r-r—you swine!

---

6 One of the heretics holding the belief of Arius (d. 336) that Christ, although the noblest of created beings, was not the Eternal Son of God, and that there was no Trinity, as the Son was not of the same substance as the Father.

7 Gal. iii. 10.
8 Followers of the Persian Manes, or Manichaeus (3d cent. A. D.), who taught the theological dualism that man's body is the product of darkness (evil), but that his soul springs from light (good). The later Mani-

chaeans distinguished the historical Christ, a sinning man, from the spiritual Christ, the divine deliverer.
9 Hail, Virgin, full of grace!

CRISTINA

SHE should never have looked at me
   If she meant I should not love her!
There are plenty . . . men, you call such,
   I suppose . . . she may discover
All her soul too, if she pleases,
   And yet leave much as she found them:
But I'm not so, and she knew it
   When she fixed me, glancing round them.

What? To fix me thus meant nothing?
   But I can't tell (there's my weakness)   10
What her look said!—no vile cant, sure,
   About "need to strew the bleakness
Of some lone shore with its pearl-seed,
   That the sea feels"—no "strange yearning
That such souls have, most to lavish
   Where there's chance of least returning."

Oh, we're sunk enough here, God knows!
   But not quite so sunk that moments,
Sure though seldom, are denied us,
   When the spirit's true endowments   20
Stand out plainly from its false ones,
   And apprise it if pursuing
Or the right way or the wrong way,
   To its triumph or undoing.

There are flashes struck from midnights,
   There are fire-flames noondays kindle,
Whereby piled-up honors perish,
   Whereby swollen ambitions dwindle,
While just this or that poor impulse,
   Which for once had play unstifled,   30
Seems the sole work of a lifetime,
   That away the rest have trifled.

Doubt you if, in some such moment,
   As she fixed me, she felt clearly,
Ages past the soul existed,
   Here an age 'tis resting merely,
And hence fleets again for ages,
   While the true end, sole and single,
It stops here for is, this love-way,
   With some other soul to mingle?   40

Else it loses what it lived for,
   And eternally must lose it;
Better ends may be in prospect,
   Deeper blisses (if you choose it),
But this life's end and this love-bliss
   Have been lost here. Doubt you whether
This she felt as, looking at me,
   Mine and her souls rushed together?

Oh, observe! Of course, next moment,
   The world's honors, in derision,   50
Trampled out the light for ever:
   Never fear but there's provision
Of the devil's to quench knowledge
   Lest we walk the earth in rapture!
—Making those who catch God's secret
   Just so much more prize their capture!

Such am I: the secret's mine now!
   She has lost me, I have gained her;
Her soul's mine: and thus, grown perfect,
   I shall pass my life's remainder.   60
Life will just hold out the proving
   Both our powers, alone and blended:
And then, come the next life quickly!
   This world's use will have been ended.

MY LAST DUCHESS

FERRARA

That's my last Duchess painted on the wall,
Looking as if she were alive. I call
That piece a wonder, now: Fra Pandolf's [10] hands
Worked busily a day, and there she stands.
Will't please you sit and look at her? I said
"Fra Pandolf" by design, for never read
Strangers like you that pictured countenance,
The depth and passion of its earnest glance,
But to myself they turned (since none puts by
The curtain I have drawn for you, but I)   10
And seemed as they would ask me, if they durst,
How such a glance came there; so, not the first

10 Brother Pandolf—an imaginary monk and painter of the Renaissance. The sculptor
mentioned in the last line of the poem is also imaginary.

Are you to turn and ask thus. Sir, 't was not
Her husband's presence only, called that spot
Of joy into the Duchess' cheek: perhaps
Fra Pandolf chanced to say, "Her mantle laps
Over my lady's wrist too much," or "Paint
Must never hope to reproduce the faint
Half-flush that dies along her throat": such stuff
Was courtesy, she thought, and cause enough   20
For calling up that spot of joy. She had
A heart—how shall I say?—too soon made glad,
Too easily impressed: she liked whate'er
She looked on, and her looks went everywhere.
Sir, 'twas all one! My favor at her breast,
The dropping of the daylight in the West,
The bough of cherries some officious fool
Broke in the orchard for her, the white mule
She rode with round the terrace—all and each
Would draw from her alike the approving speech,   30
Or blush, at least. She thanked men,—good! but thanked
Somehow—I know not how—as if she ranked
My gift of a nine-hundred-years-old name
With anybody's gift. Who'd stoop to blame
This sort of trifling? Even had you skill
In speech—(which I have not)—to make your will
Quite clear to such an one, and say, "Just this
Or that in you disgusts me; here you miss,
Or there exceed the mark"—and if she let
Herself be lessoned so, nor plainly set   40
Her wits to yours, forsooth, and made excuse,
—E'en then would be some stooping; and I choose
Never to stoop. Oh sir, she smiled, no doubt,
Whene'er I passed her; but who passed without
Much the same smile? This grew; I gave commands;
Then all smiles stopped together. There she stands
As if alive. Will 't please you rise? We'll meet
The company below, then. I repeat,
The Count your master's known munificence
Is ample warrant that no just pretense   50
Of mine for dowry will be disallowed;
Though his fair daughter's self, as I avowed
At starting, is my object. Nay, we'll go
Together down, sir. Notice Neptune, though,
Taming a sea-horse, thought a rarity,
Which Claus of Innsbruck cast in bronze for me!

THE LOST LEADER [11]

Just for a handful of silver he left us,
Just for a riband to stick in his coat—
Found the one gift of which fortune bereft us,
Lost all the others she lets us devote;
They, with the gold to give, doled him out silver,
So much was theirs who so little allowed:
How all our copper had gone for his service!
Rags—were they purple, his heart had been proud!
We that had loved him so, followed him, honored him,
Lived in his mild and magnificent eye,   10
Learned his great language, caught his clear accents,
Made him our pattern to live and to die!
Shakespeare was of us, Milton was for us,
Burns, Shelley, were with us,—they watch from their graves!
He alone breaks from the van and the freemen,
—He alone sinks to the rear and the slaves!
We shall march prospering,—not through his presence;
Songs may inspirit us,—not from his lyre;
Deeds will be done,—while he boasts his quiescence,
Still bidding crouch whom the rest bade aspire: 20
Blot out his name, then, record one lost soul more,
One task more declined, one more footpath untrod,
One more devils'-triumph and sorrow for angels,
One wrong more to man, one more insult to God!
Life's night begins: let him never come back to us!
There would be doubt, hesitation and pain,
Forced praise on our part—the glimmer of twilight,
Never glad confident morning again!
Best fight on well, for we taught him—strike gallantly,
Menace our heart ere we master his own;   30
Then let him receive the new knowledge and wait us,
Pardoned in heaven, the first by the throne!

MEETING AT NIGHT

The gray sea and the long black land;
And the yellow half-moon large and low;

11 "I *did* in my hasty youth presume to use the great and venerated personality of Wordsworth as a sort of painter's model; one from which this or the other particular feature may be selected and turned to account; had I intended more, above all, such a boldness as portraying the entire man, I should not have talked about 'handfuls of silver and bits of ribbon.' These never influenced the change of politics in the great poet, whose defection, nevertheless, accompanied as it was by a regular face-about of his special party, was to my juvenile apprehension, and even mature consideration, an event to deplore." (Browning)

And the startled little waves that leap
In fiery ringlets from their sleep,
As I gain the cove with pushing prow,
And quench its speed i' the slushy sand.

Then a mile of warm sea-scented beach;
Three fields to cross till a farm appears;
A tap at the pane, the quick sharp scratch
And blue spurt of a lighted match,   10
And a voice less loud, through its joys and fears,
Than the two hearts beating each to each!

PARTING AT MORNING

Round the cape of a sudden came the sea,
And the sun looked over the mountain's rim:
And straight was a path of gold for him,
And the need of a world of men for me.

HOME-THOUGHTS, FROM ABROAD

Oh, to be in England
Now that April's there,
And whoever wakes in England
Sees, some morning, unaware,
That the lowest boughs and the brush-wood sheaf
Round the elm-tree bole are in tiny leaf,
While the chaffinch sings on the orchard bough
In England—now!

And after April, when May follows,
And the whitethroat builds, and all the swallows!   10
Hark, where my blossomed pear-tree in the hedge
Leans to the field and scatters on the clover
Blossoms and dewdrops—at the bent spray's edge—
That's the wise thrush; he sings each song twice over,
Lest you should think he never could recapture
The first fine careless rapture!
And though the fields look rough with hoary dew,
All will be gay when noontide wakes anew
The buttercups, the little children's dower
—Far brighter than this gaudy melon-flower!   20

HOME-THOUGHTS, FROM THE SEA

Nobly, nobly Cape Saint Vincent [12] to the Northwest died away;
Sunset ran, one glorious blood-red, reeking into Cadiz Bay;
Bluish 'mid the burning water, full in face Trafalgar [12] lay;
In the dimmest Northeast distance dawned Gibraltar grand
    and gray;
"Here and here did England help me: how can I help Eng-
    land?"—say,
Whoso turns as I, this evening, turn to God to praise and pray,
While Jove's planet rises yonder, silent over Africa.

THE BISHOP ORDERS HIS TOMB AT SAINT PRAXED'S CHURCH [13]

ROME, 15—

Vanity, saith the preacher, vanity!
Draw round my bed: is Anselm keeping back?
Nephews—sons mine . . . ah God, I know not! Well—
She, men would have to be your mother once,
Old Gandolf envied me, so fair she was!
What's done is done, and she is dead beside,
Dead long ago, and I am Bishop since,
And as she died so must we die ourselves,
And thence ye may perceive the world's a dream.
Life, how and what is it? As here I lie   10
In this state-chamber, dying by degrees,
Hours and long hours in the dead night, I ask
"Do I live, am I dead?" Peace, peace seems all.
Saint Praxed's ever was the church for peace;
And so, about this tomb of mine. I fought
With tooth and nail to save my niche, ye know:
—Old Gandolf cozened me, despite my care;
Shrewd was that snatch from out the corner South
He graced his carrion with, God curse the same!
Yet still my niche is not so cramped but thence   20
One sees the pulpit o' the epistle-side,
And somewhat of the choir, those silent seats,
And up into the aery dome where live
The angels, and a sunbeam's sure to lurk:

12 scenes of Nelson's victories in 1797 and 1805 respectively
13 "I know no other piece of modern English, prose or poetry, in which there is so much told, as in these lines, of the Renaissance spirit,—its worldliness, inconsistency, pride, hypocrisy, ignorance of itself, love of art, of luxury, and of good Latin. It is nearly all that I have said of the central Renaissance in thirty pages of the *Stones of Venice*, put into as many lines, Browning's being also the antecedent work" (Ruskin). Praxed (or Praxedis) was an early Christian saint (a woman). The incidents and characters of the poem are imaginary.

And I shall fill my slab of basalt there,
And 'neath my tabernacle take my rest,
With those nine columns round me, two and two,
The odd one at my feet where Anselm stands:
Peach-blossom marble all, the rare, the ripe
As fresh-poured red wine of a mighty pulse.   30
—Old Gandolf with his paltry onion-stone,
Put me where I may look at him! True peach,
Rosy and flawless: how I earned the prize!
Draw close: that conflagration of my church
—What then? So much was saved if aught were missed!
My sons, ye would not be my death? Go dig
The white-grape vineyard where the oil-press stood,
Drop water gently till the surface sink,
And if ye find . . . Ah God, I know not, I! . . .
Bedded in store of rotten fig-leaves soft,   40
And corded up in a tight olive-frail,
Some lump, ah God, of *lapis lazuli*,
Big as a Jew's head cut off at the nape,
Blue as a vein o'er the Madonna's breast . . .
Sons, all have I bequeathed you, villas, all,
That brave Frascati [14] villa with its bath,
So, let the blue lump poise between my knees,
Like God the Father's globe on both his hands
Ye worship in the Jesu Church so gay,
For Gandolf shall not choose but see and burst!   50
Swift as a weaver's shuttle fleet our years:
Man goeth to the grave, and where is he?
Did I say basalt for my slab, sons? Black—
'Twas ever antique-black I meant! How else
Shall we contrast my frieze to come beneath?
The bas-relief in bronze ye promised me,
Those Pans and Nymphs ye wot of, and perchance
Some tripod, thyrsus,[15] with a vase or so,
The Savior at his sermon on the mount,
Saint Praxed in a glory, and one Pan   60
Ready to twitch the Nymph's last garment off,
And Moses with the tables . . . but I know
Ye mark me not! What do they whisper thee,
Child of my bowels, Anselm? Ah, ye hope
To revel down my villas while I gasp
Bricked o'er with beggar's moldy travertine
Which Gandolf from his tomb-top chuckles at!
Nay, boys, ye love me—all of jasper, then!

14 a town near Rome   ivy and surmounted by a   leaves—borne by Bacchus
15 a staff entwined with   pine cone, or by vine or ivy   and the Bacchanalians

'Tis jasper ye stand pledged to, lest I grieve
My bath must needs be left behind, alas!   70
One block, pure green as a pistachio-nut,
There's plenty jasper somewhere in the world—
And have I not Saint Praxed's ear to pray
Horses for ye, and brown Greek manuscripts,
And mistresses with great smooth marbly limbs?
—That's if ye carve my epitaph aright,
Choice Latin, picked phrase, Tully's [16] every word,
No gaudy ware like Gandolf's second line—
Tully, my masters? Ulpian [17] serves his need!
And then how I shall lie through centuries,   80
And hear the blessed mutter of the mass,
And see God made and eaten all day long,
And feel the steady candle-flame, and taste
Good strong thick stupefying incense-smoke!
For as I lie here, hours of the dead night,
Dying in state and by such slow degrees,
I fold my arms as if they clasped a crook,
And stretch my feet forth straight as stone can point,
And let the bedclothes, for a mortcloth, drop
Into great laps and folds of sculptor's-work: 90
And as yon tapers dwindle, and strange thoughts
Grow, with a certain humming in my ears,
About the life before I lived this life,
And this life too, popes, cardinals and priests,
Saint Praxed at his sermon on the mount,
Your tall pale mother with her talking eyes,
And new-found agate urns as fresh as day,
And marble's language, Latin pure, discreet,
—Aha, ELUCESCEBAT [18] quoth our friend?
No Tully, said I, Ulpian at the best!   100
Evil and brief hath been my pilgrimage.
All *lapis*, all, sons! Else I give the Pope
My villas! Will ye ever eat my heart?
Ever your eyes were as a lizard's quick,
They glitter like your mother's for my soul,
Or ye would heighten my impoverished frieze,
Piece out its starved design, and fill my vase
With grapes, and add a visor and a Term,[19]
And to the tripod ye would tie a lynx
That in his struggles throws the thyrsus down,   110
To comfort me on my entablature

16 Cicero
17 Roman legal writer of
the third century A. D.
18 "He was illustrious"—

wrongly formed from *elu-
cere*—an example of Ul-
pian's bad Latin
19 a bust on a square

base, like those of Termi-
nus, Roman god of bound-
aries

Whereon I am to lie till I must ask
"Do I live, am I dead?" There, leave me, there!
For ye have stabbed me with ingratitude
To death—ye wish it—God, ye wish it! Stone—
Gritstone, a-crumble! Clammy squares which sweat
As if the corpse they keep were oozing through—
And no more *lapis* to delight the world!
Well, go! I bless ye. Fewer tapers there,
But in a row: and, going, turn your backs   120
—Ay, like departing altar-ministrants,
And leave me in my church, the church for peace,
That I may watch at leisure if he leers—
Old Gandolf—at me, from his onion-stone,
As still he envied me, so fair she was!

SAUL [20]

I

SAID Abner,[21] "At last thou art come! Ere I tell, ere thou speak,
Kiss my cheek, wish me well!" Then I wished it, and did kiss
his cheek.
And he: "Since the King, O my friend, for thy countenance
sent,
Neither drunken nor eaten have we; nor until from his tent
Thou return with the joyful assurance the King liveth yet,
Shall our lip with the honey be bright, with the water be wet.
For out of the black mid-tent's silence, a space of three days,
Not a sound hath escaped to thy servants, of prayer nor of
praise,
To betoken that Saul and the Spirit have ended their strife,
And that, faint in his triumph, the monarch sinks back upon
life.   10

2

"Yet now my heart leaps, O belovèd! God's child with his dew
On thy gracious gold hair, and those lilies still living and blue
Just broken to twine round thy harp-strings, as if no wild heat
Were now raging to torture the desert!"

3

Then I, as was meet,
Knelt down to the God of my fathers, and rose on my feet,
And ran o'er the sand burned to powder. The tent was un-
looped;

20 See 1 Sam. xvi. 14-23, for the basis of this poem.   21 Saul's captain

I pulled up the spear that obstructed, and under I stooped;
Hands and knees on the slippery grass-patch, all withered and
    gone,
That extends to the second enclosure, I groped my way on   20
Till I felt where the foldskirts fly open. Then once more I
    prayed,
And opened the foldskirts and entered, and was not afraid
But spoke, "Here is David, thy servant!" And no voice replied.
At the first I saw naught but the blackness: but soon I descried
A something more black than the blackness—the vast, the
    upright
Main prop which sustains the pavilion: and slow into sight
Grew a figure against it, gigantic and blackest of all.
Then a sunbeam, that burst through the tent-roof, showed
    Saul.

4

He stood as erect as that tent-prop, both arms stretched out
    wide
On the great cross-support in the center, that goes to each
    side;   30
He relaxed not a muscle, but hung there as, caught in his
    pangs
And waiting his change, the king-serpent all heavily hangs,
Far away from his kind, in the pine, till deliverance come
With the spring-time,—so agonized Saul, drear and stark, blind
    and dumb.

5

Then I tuned my harp,—took off the lilies we twine round its
    chords
Lest they snap 'neath the stress of the noontide—those sun-
    beams like swords!
And I first played the tune all our sheep know, as, one after
    one,
So docile they come to the pen-door till folding be done.
They are white and untorn by the bushes, for lo, they have
    fed
Where the long grasses stifle the water within the stream's
    bed;   40
And now one after one seeks its lodging, as star follows star
Into eve and the blue far above us,—so blue and so far!

6

—Then the tune for which quails on the cornland will each
    leave his mate

To fly after the player; then, what makes the crickets elate
Till for boldness they fight one another; and then, what has
    weight
To set the quick jerboa [22] a-musing outside his sand-house—
There are none such as he for a wonder, half bird and half
    mouse!
God made all the creatures and gave them our love and our
    fear,
To give sign, we and they are his children, one family here.

7

Then I played the help-tune of our reapers, their wine-song,
    when hand   50
Grasps at hand, eye lights eye in good friendship and great
    hearts expand
And grow one in the sense of this world's life.—And then, the
    last song
When the dead man is praised on his journey—"Bear, bear
    him along,
With his few faults shut up like dead flowerets! Are balm
    seeds not here
To console us? The land has none left such as he on the bier.
Oh, would we might keep thee, my brother!"—And then, the
    glad chaunt
Of the marriage,—first go the young maidens, next, she whom
    we vaunt
As the beauty, the pride of our dwelling.—And then, the great
    march
Wherein man runs to man to assist him and buttress an
    arch
Naught can break; who shall harm them, our friends? Then,
    the chorus intoned   60
As the Levites go up to the altar in glory enthroned.
But I stopped here: for here in the darkness Saul groaned.

8

And I paused, held my breath in such silence, and listened
    apart;
And the tent shook, for mighty Saul shuddered: and sparkles
    'gan dart
From the jewels that woke in his turban, at once with a start,
All its lordly male-sapphires, and rubies courageous at heart,
So the head: but the body still moved not, still hung there
    erect.

22 a jumping rodent, sometimes called the "jumping hare"

And I bent once again to my playing, pursued it un-
checked,
As I sang:—

9

"Oh, our manhood's prime vigor! No spirit feels waste, 70
Not a muscle is stopped in its playing nor sinew unbraced.
Oh, the wild joys of living! the leaping from rock up to rock,
The strong rending of boughs from the fir-tree, the cool silver
shock
Of the plunge in a pool's living water, the hunt of the bear,
And the sultriness showing the lion is couched in his lair.
And the meal, the rich dates yellowed over with gold dust
divine,
And the locust-flesh steeped in the pitcher, the full draught of
wine,
And the sleep in the dried river-channel where bulrushes tell
That the water was wont to go warbling so softly and well.
How good is man's life, the mere living! how fit to employ 80
All the heart and the soul and the senses for ever in joy!
Hast thou loved the white locks of thy father, whose sword
thou didst guard
When he trusted thee forth with the armies, for glorious re-
ward?
Didst thou see the thin hands of thy mother, held up as men
sung
The low song of the nearly-departed, and hear her faint tongue
Joining in while it could to the witness, 'Let one more attest,
I have lived, seen God's hand through a lifetime, and all was
for best'?
Then they sung through their tears in strong triumph, not
much, but the rest.
And thy brothers, the help and the contest, the working whence
grew
Such result as, from seething grape-bundles, the spirit strained
true: 90
And the friends of thy boyhood—that boyhood of wonder and
hope,
Present promise and wealth of the future beyond the eye's
scope,—
Till lo, thou art grown to a monarch; a people is thine;
And all gifts, which the world offers singly, on one head combine!
On one head, all the beauty and strength, love and rage (like
the throe

That, a-work in the rock, helps its labor and lets the gold go)
High ambition and deeds which surpass it, fame crowning
 them,—all
Brought to blaze on the head of one creature—King Saul!"

10

And lo, with that leap of my spirit,—heart, hand, harp and
 voice,
Each lifting Saul's name out of sorrow, each bidding rejoice 100
Saul's fame in the light it was made for—as when, dare I
 say,
The Lord's army, in rapture of service, strains through its
 array,
And upsoareth the cherubim-chariot—"Saul!" cried I, and
 stopped,
And waited the thing that should follow. Then Saul, who hung
 propped
By the tent's cross-support in the center, was struck by his
 name.
Have ye seen when Spring's arrowy summons goes right to the
 aim,
And some mountain, the last to withstand her, that held (he
 alone,
While the vale laughed in freedom and flowers) on a broad
 bust of stone
A year's snow bound about for a breastplate,—leaves grasp
 of the sheet?
Fold on fold all at once it crowds thunderously down to his
 feet, 110
And there fronts you, stark, black, but alive yet, your moun-
 tain of old,
With his rents, the successive bequeathings of ages untold—
Yea, each harm got in fighting your battles, each furrow and
 scar
Of his head thrust 'twixt you and the tempest—all hail, there
 they are!
—Now again to be softened with verdure, again hold the nest
Of the dove, tempt the goat and its young to the green on his
 crest
For their food in the ardors of summer. One long shudder
 thrilled
All the tent till the very air tingled, then sank and was stilled
At the King's self left standing before me, released and
 aware.

What was gone, what remained? All to traverse 'twixt hope
    and despair, 120
Death was past, life not come: so he waited. Awhile his right
    hand
Held the brow, helped the eyes left too vacant forthwith to
    remand
To their place what new objects should enter: 'twas Saul as
    before.
I looked up and dared gaze at those eyes, nor was hurt any
    more
Than by slow pallid sunsets in autumn, ye watch from the
    shore,
At their sad level gaze o'er the ocean—a sun's slow decline
Over hills which, resolved in stern silence, o'erlap and entwine
Base with base to knit strength more intensely: so, arm folded
    arm
O'er the chest whose slow heavings subsided.

II

                 What spell or what charm 130
(For awhile there was trouble within me), what next should
    I urge
To sustain him where song had restored him?—Song filled to
    the verge
His cup with the wine of this life, pressing all that it yields
Of mere fruitage, the strength and the beauty: beyond, on
    what fields,
Glean a vintage more potent and perfect to brighten the eye
And bring blood to the lip, and commend them the cup they
    put by?
He saith, "It is good"; still he drinks not: he lets me praise
    life,
Gives assent, yet would die for his own part.

12

                 Then fancies grew rife
Which had come long ago on the pasture, when round me the
    sheep 140
Fed in silence—above, the one eagle wheeled slow as in sleep;
And I lay in my hollow and mused on the world that might
    lie
'Neath his ken, though I saw but the strip 'twixt the hill and
    the sky:

And I laughed—"Since my days are ordained to be passed with my flocks,
Let me people at least, with my fancies, the plains and the rocks,
Dream the life I am never to mix with, and image the show
Of mankind as they live in those fashions I hardly shall know!
Schemes of life, its best rules and right uses, the courage that gains,
And the prudence that keeps what men strive for." And now these old trains
Of vague thought came again; I grew surer; so, once more the string   150
Of my harp made response to my spirit, as thus—

13

                                        "Yea, my King,"
I began—"thou dost well in rejecting mere comforts that spring
From the mere mortal life held in common by man and by brute:
In our flesh grows the branch of this life, in our soul it bears fruit.
Thou hast marked the slow rise of the tree,—how its stem trembled first
Till it passed the kid's lip, the stag's antler; then safely outburst
The fan-branches all round; and thou mindest when these too, in turn,
Broke a-bloom and the palm-tree seemed perfect: yet more was to learn,
E'en the good that comes in with the palm-fruit. Our dates shall we slight,   160
When their juice brings a cure for all sorrow? or care for the plight
Of the palm's self whose slow growth produced them? Not so! stem and branch
Shall decay, nor be known in their place, while the palm-wine shall stanch
Every wound of man's spirit in winter. I pour thee such wine.
Leave the flesh to the fate it was fit for! the spirit be thine!
By the spirit, when age shall o'ercome thee, thou still shalt enjoy
More indeed, than at first when inconscious, the life of a boy.
Crush that life, and behold its wine running! Each deed thou hast done
Dies, revives, goes to work in the world; until e'en as the sun

Looking down on the earth, though clouds spoil him, though
    tempests efface,   170
Can find nothing his own deed produced not, must everywhere
    trace
The results of his past summer-prime,—so, each ray of thy
    will,
Every flash of thy passion and prowess, long over, shall thrill
Thy whole people, the countless, with ardor, till they too give
    forth
A like cheer to their sons, who in turn, fill the South and the
    North
With the radiance thy deed was the germ of. Carouse in the
    past!
But the license of age has its limit; thou diest at last:
As the lion when age dims his eyeball, the rose at her height,
So with man—so his power and his beauty for ever take
    flight.
No! Again a long draught of my soul-wine! Look forth o'er the
    years!   180
Thou hast done now with eyes for the actual; begin with the
    seer's!
Is Saul dead? In the depth of the vale make his tomb—bid
    arise
A gray mountain of marble heaped four-square, till, built to
    the skies,
Let it mark where the great First King slumbers: whose fame
    would ye know?
Up above see the rock's naked face, where the record shall go
In great characters cut by the scribe,—Such was Saul, so he
    did;
With the sages directing the work, by the populace chid,—
For not half, they'll affirm, is comprised there! Which fault
    to amend,
In the grove with his kind grows the cedar, whereon they shall
    spend
(See, in tablets 'tis level before them) their praise, and
    record   190
With the gold of the graver, Saul's story,—the statesman's
    great word
Side by side with the poet's sweet comment. The river's a-wave
With smooth paper-reeds grazing each other when prophet-
    winds rave:
So the pen gives unborn generations their due and their
    part
In thy being! Then, first of the mighty, thank God that thou
    art!"

14

And behold while I sang . . . but O Thou who didst grant
    me that day,
And before it not seldom hast granted thy help to essay,
Carry on and complete an adventure,—my shield and my
    sword
In that act where my soul was thy servant, thy word was my
    word,—
Still be with me, who then at the summit of human en-
    deavor   200
And scaling the highest, man's thought could, gazed hopeless
    as ever
On the new stretch of heaven above me—till, mighty to save,
Just one lift of thy hand cleared that distance—God's throne
    from man's grave!
Let me tell out my tale to its ending—my voice to my heart
Which can scarce dare believe in what marvels last night I
    took part,
As this morning I gather the fragments, alone with my sheep,
And still fear lest the terrible glory evanish like sleep!
For I wake in the gray dewy covert, while Hebron [23] upheaves
The dawn struggling with night on his shoulder, and Kidron [24]
    retrieves
Slow the damage of yesterday's sunshine.   210

15

                            I say then,—my song
While I sang thus, assuring the monarch, and ever more
    strong
Made a proffer of good to console him—he slowly resumed
His old motions and habitudes kingly. The right hand re-
    plumed
His black locks to their wonted composure, adjusted the swathes
Of his turban, and see—the huge sweat that his countenance
    bathes,
He wipes off with the robe; and he girds now his loins as of
    yore,
And feels slow for the armlets of price, with the clasp set be-
    fore.
He is Saul, ye remember in glory,—ere error had bent
The broad brow from the daily communion; and still, though
    much spent   220

---

23 a city of Judea, for seven years David's capital; here transferred by Brown-ing to the neighboring mountain   24 a brook near Jerusalem

Be the life and the bearing that front you, the same, God did
    choose,
To receive what a man may waste, desecrate, never quite lose.
So sank he along by the tent-prop till, stayed by the pile
Of his armor and war-cloak and garments, he leaned there
    awhile,
And sat out my singing,—one arm round the tent-prop, to
    raise
His bent head, and the other hung slack—till I touched on the
    praise
I foresaw from all men in all time, to the man patient there;
And thus ended, the harp falling forward. Then first I was
    'ware
That he sat, as I say, with my head just above his vast knees
Which were thrust out on each side around me, like oak roots
    which please   230
To encircle a lamb when it slumbers. I looked up to know
If the best I could do had brought solace: he spoke not, but
    slow
Lifted up the hand slack at his side, till he laid it with care
Soft and grave, but in mild settled will, on my brow: through
    my hair
The large fingers were pushed, and he bent back my head,
    with kind power—
All my face back, intent to peruse it, as men do a flower.
Thus held he me there with his great eyes that scrutinized
    mine—
And oh, all my heart how it loved him! but where was the
    sign?
I yearned—"Could I help thee, my father, inventing a bliss,
I would add, to that life of the past, both the future and
    this;
I would give thee new life altogether, as good, ages hence,   240
As this moment,—had love but the warrant, love's heart to
    dispense!"

16

Then the truth came upon me. No harp more—no song more!
    outbroke—

17

"I have gone the whole round of creation: I saw and I spoke:
I, a work of God's hand for that purpose, received in my brain
And pronounced on the rest of his handwork—returned him
    again

His creation's approval or censure: I spoke as I saw:
I report, as a man may of God's work—all's love, yet all's law.
Now I lay down the judgeship he lent me. Each faculty tasked
To perceive him, has gained an abyss, where a dewdrop was
    asked.   250
Have I knowledge? confounded it shrivels at Wisdom laid bare.
Have I forethought? how purblind, how blank, to the Infinite
    Care!
Do I task any faculty highest, to image success?
I but open my eyes,—and perfection, no more and no less,
In the kind I imagined, full-fronts me, and God is seen God
In the star, in the stone, in the flesh, in the soul and the clod.
And thus looking within and around me, I ever renew
(With that stoop of the soul which in bending upraises it too)
The submission of man's nothing-perfect to God's all-complete,
As by each new obeisance in spirit, I climb to his feet.   260
Yet with all this abounding experience, this deity known,
I shall dare to discover some province, some gift of my own.
There's a faculty pleasant to exercise, hard to hoodwink,
I am fain to keep still in abeyance (I laugh as I think),
Lest, insisting to claim and parade in it, wot ye, I worst
E'en the Giver in one gift.—Behold, I could love if I durst!
But I sink the pretension as fearing a man may o'ertake
God's own speed in the one way of love: I abstain for love's
    sake.
—What, my soul? see thus far and no farther? when doors
    great and small,
Nine-and-ninety flew ope at our touch, should the hundredth
    appall?   270
In the least things have faith, yet distrust in the greatest of
    all?
Do I find love so full in my nature, God's ultimate gift,
That I doubt his own love can compete with it? Here, the parts
    shift?
Here, the creature surpass the Creator,—the end, what Be-
    gan?
Would I fain in my impotent yearning do all for this man,
And dare doubt he alone shall not help him, who yet alone
    can?
Would it ever have entered my mind, the bare will, much less
    power,
To bestow on this Saul what I sang of, the marvelous dower
Of the life he was gifted and filled with? to make such a soul,
Such a body, and then such an earth for insphering the
    whole?   280

And doth it not enter my mind (as my warm tears attest)
These good things being given, to go on, and give one more,
    the best?
Ay, to save and redeem and restore him, maintain at the
    height
This perfection,—succeed with life's day-spring, death's minute
    of night?
Interpose at the difficult minute, snatch Saul the mistake,
Saul the failure, the ruin he seems now,—and bid him awake
From the dream, the probation, the prelude, to find himself
    set
Clear and safe in new light and new life,—a new harmony yet
To be run, and continued, and ended—who knows?—or en-
    dure!
The man taught enough by life's dream, of the rest to make
    sure;
By the pain-throb, triumphantly winning intensified bliss,   290
And the next world's reward and repose, by the struggles in
    this.

18

"I believe it! 'Tis thou, God, that givest, 'tis I who receive:
In the first is the last, in thy will is my power to believe.
All's one gift: thou canst grant it moreover, as prompt to my
    prayer
As I breathe out this breath, as I open these arms to the air.
From thy will stream the worlds, life and nature, thy dread
    Sabaoth: [25]
I will?—the mere atoms despise me! Why am I not loath
To look that, even that in the face too? Why is it I dare
Think but lightly of such impuissance? What stops my
    despair?
This;—'tis not what man Does which exalts him, but what   300
    man Would do!
See the King—I would help him but cannot, the wishes fall
    through.
Could I wrestle to raise him from sorrow, grow poor to enrich,
To fill up his life, starve my own out, I would—knowing which,
I know that my service is perfect. Oh, speak through me now!
Would I suffer for him that I love? So wouldst thou—so wilt
    thou!
So shall crown thee the topmost, ineffablest, uttermost crown—
And thy love fill infinitude wholly, nor leave up nor down

25 hosts

One spot for the creature to stand in! It is by no breath,
Turn of eye, wave of hand, that salvation joins issue with
    death!   310
As thy Love is discovered almighty, almighty be proved
Thy power, that exists with and for it, of being Beloved!
He who did most, shall bear most; the strongest shall stand
    the most weak.
'Tis the weakness in strength, that I cry for! my flesh, that I
    seek
In the Godhead! I seek and I find it. O Saul, it shall be
A Face like my face that receives thee; a Man like to me,
Thou shalt love and be loved by, for ever: a Hand like this
    hand
Shall throw open the gates of new life to thee! See the Christ
    stand!"

19

I know not too well how I found my way home in the night.
There were witnesses, cohorts about me, to left and to
    right,   320
Angels, powers, the unuttered, unseen, the alive, the aware:
I repressed, I got through them as hardly, as strugglingly
    there,
As a runner beset by the populace famished for news—
Life or death. The whole earth was awakened, hell loosed with
    her crews;
And the stars of night beat with emotion, and tingled and
    shot
Out in fire the strong pain of pent knowledge: but I fainted
    not,
For the Hand still impelled me at once and supported, sup-
    pressed
All the tumult, and quenched it with quiet, and holy be-
    hest,
Till the rapture was shut in itself, and the earth sank to rest.
Anon at the dawn, all that trouble had withered from
    earth—   330
Not so much, but I saw it die out in the day's tender birth;
In the gathered intensity brought to the gray of the hills;
In the shuddering forests' held breath; in the sudden wind-
    thrills;
In the startled wild beasts that bore off, each with eye sidling
    still
Though averted with wonder and dread; in the birds stiff and
    chill

That rose heavily, as I approached them, made stupid with
    awe:
E'en the serpent that slid away silent,—he felt the new law.
The same stared in the white humid faces upturned by the
    flowers;
The same worked in the heart of the cedar and moved the vine-
    bowers:
And the little brooks witnessing murmured, persistent and
    low,
With their obstinate, all but hushed voices—"E'en so, it is so!"   340

LOVE AMONG THE RUINS [26]

WHERE the quiet-colored end of evening smiles
    Miles and miles
On the solitary pastures where our sheep
    Half-asleep
Tinkle homeward through the twilight, stray or stop
    As they crop—
Was the site once of a city great and gay,
    (So they say)
Of our country's very capital, its prince
    Ages since   10
Held his court in, gathered councils, wielding far
    Peace or war.

Now,—the country does not even boast a tree,
    As you see,
To distinguish slopes of verdure, certain rills
    From the hills
Intersect and give a name to (else they run
    Into one),
Where the domed and daring palace shot its spires
    Up like fires
O'er the hundred-gated circuit of a wall   20
    Bounding all,
Made of marble, men might march on nor be pressed,
    Twelve abreast.

And such plenty and perfection, see, of grass
    Never was!
Such a carpet as, this summer-time, o'erspreads
    And embeds
Every vestige of the city, guessed alone,
    Stock or stone—

26 The ruins are those in the Roman Campagna.

Where a multitude of men breathed joy and woe   30
    Long ago;
Lust of glory pricked their hearts up, dread of shame
    Struck them tame;
And that glory and that shame alike, the gold
    Bought and sold.

Now,—the single little turret that remains
    On the plains,
By the caper [27] overrooted, by the gourd
    Overscored,
While the patching houseleek's head of blossom winks   40
    Through the chinks—
Marks the basement whence a tower in ancient time
    Sprang sublime,
And a burning ring, all round, the chariots traced
    As they raced,
And the monarch and his minions and his dames
    Viewed the games.

And I know, while thus the quiet-colored eve
    Smiles to leave
To their folding, all our many-tinkling fleece   50
    In such peace,
And the slopes and rills in undistinguished gray
    Melt away—
That a girl with eager eyes and yellow hair
    Waits me there
In the turret whence the charioteers caught soul
    For the goal,
When the king looked, where she looks now, breathless, dumb
    Till I come.

But he looked upon the city, every side,   60
    Far and wide,
All the mountains topped with temples, all the glades'
    Colonnades,
All the causeys,[28] bridges, aqueducts,—and then,
    All the men!
When I do come, she will speak not, she will stand,
    Either hand
On my shoulder, give her eyes the first embrace
    Of my face,
Ere we rush, ere we extinguish sight and speech   70
    Each on each.

27 A low, prickly shrub.　as seasoning.　　　　28 causeways
Its pickled buds are used

In one year they sent a million fighters forth
 South and North,
And they built their gods a brazen pillar high
 As the sky,
Yet reserved a thousand chariots in full force—
 Gold, of course.
Oh heart! oh blood that freezes, blood that burns!
 Earth's returns
For whole centuries of folly, noise and sin!   80
 Shut them in
With their triumphs and their glories and the rest!
 Love is best.

UP AT A VILLA—DOWN IN THE CITY

(AS DISTINGUISHED BY AN ITALIAN PERSON OF QUALITY)

HAD I but plenty of money, money enough and to spare,
The house for me, no doubt, were a house in the city-square;
Ah, such a life, such a life, as one leads at the window there!

Something to see, by Bacchus, something to hear, at least!
There, the whole day long, one's life is a perfect feast;
While up at a villa one lives, I maintain it, no more than a
 beast.

Well now, look at our villa! stuck like the horn of a bull
Just on a mountain-edge as ·bare as the creature's skull,
Save a mere shag of a bush with hardly a leaf to pull!
—I scratch my own, sometimes, to see if the hair's turned
 wool.   10

But the city, oh the city—the square with the houses! Why?
They are stone-faced, white as a curd, there's something to
 take the eye!
Houses in four straight lines, not a single front awry;
You watch who crosses and gossips, who saunters, who hur-
 ries by;
Green blinds, as a matter of course, to draw when the sun
 gets high;
And the shops with fanciful signs which are painted properly.

What of a villa? Though winter be over in March by rights,
'Tis May perhaps ere the snow shall have withered well off
 the heights:

You've the brown ploughed land before, where the oxen steam and wheeze,
And the hills over-smoked behind by the faint gray olive-trees.   20

Is it better in May, I ask you? You've summer all at once;
In a day he leaps complete with a few strong April suns.
'Mid the sharp short emerald wheat, scarce risen three fingers well,
The wild tulip, at end of its tube, blows out its great red bell
Like a thin clear bubble of blood, for the children to pick and sell.

Is it ever hot in the square? There's a fountain to spout and splash!
In the shade it sings and springs; in the shine such foambows flash
On the horses with curling fish-tails, that prance and paddle and pash
Round the lady atop in her conch—fifty gazers do not abash,
Though all that she wears is some weeds round her waist in a sort of sash.   30

All the year long at the villa, nothing to see though you linger,
Except yon cypress that points like death's lean lifted fore-finger.
Some think fireflies pretty, when they mix i' the corn and mingle,
Or thrid [29] the stinking hemp till the stalks of it seem a-tingle.
Late August or early September, the stunning cicala is shrill,
And the bees keep their tiresome whine round the resinous firs on the hill.
Enough of the seasons,—I spare you the months of the fever and chill.

Ere you open your eyes in the city, the blessed church-bells begin:
No sooner the bells leave off than the diligence rattles in:
You get the pick of the news, and it costs you never a pin.   40
By and by there's the traveling doctor gives pills, lets blood, draws teeth;
Or the Pulcinello-trumpet [30] breaks up the market beneath.
At the post-office such a scene-picture—the new play, piping hot!

29 thread   30 trumpet announcing the Punch and Judy show

And a notice how, only this morning, three liberal [31] thieves
    were shot.
Above it, behold the Archbishop's most fatherly of rebukes,
And beneath, with his crown and his lion, some little new law
    of the Duke's!
Or a sonnet with flowery marge, to the Reverend Don So-
    and-so,
Who is Dante, Boccaccio, Petrarca, Saint Jerome, and Cicero,
"And moreover," (the sonnet goes rhyming,) "the skirts of
    Saint Paul has reached,
Having preached us those six Lent-lectures more unctuous
    than ever he preached."   50
Noon strikes,—here sweeps the procession! our Lady borne
    smiling and smart
With a pink gauze gown all spangles, and seven swords [32] stuck
    in her heart!
Bang-whang-whang goes the drum, *tootle-te-tootle* the fife;
No keeping one's haunches still: it's the greatest pleasure in
    life.

But bless you, it's dear—it's dear! fowls, wine, at double the
    rate.
They have clapped a new tax upon salt, and what oil pays
    passing the gate [33]
It's a horror to think of. And so, the villa for me, not the
    city!
Beggars can scarcely be choosers: but still—ah, the pity, the
    pity!

Look, two and two go the priests, then the monks with cowls
    and sandals,
And the penitents dressed in white shirts, a-holding the yellow
    candles;   60
One, he carries a flag up straight, and another a cross with
    handles,
And the Duke's guard brings up the rear, for the better pre-
    vention of scandals:
Bang-whang-whang goes the drum, *tootle-te-tootle* the fife.
Oh, a day in the city-square, there is no such pleasure in life!

TWO IN THE CAMPAGNA

I wonder do you feel to-day
    As I have felt since, hand in hand,
    We sat down on the grass, to stray

---

31 belonging to the lib-   32 symbolizing the Seven   33 duty paid on entering
eral or republican party   Sorrows   the city

In spirit better through the land,
This morn of Rome and May?

For me, I touched a thought, I know,
 Has tantalized me many times,
(Like turns of thread the spiders throw
 Mocking across our path) for rhymes
To catch at and let go.   10

Help me to hold it! First it left
 The yellowing fennel, run to seed
There, branching from the brickwork's cleft,
 Some old tomb's ruin: yonder weed
Took up the floating weft,

Where one small orange cup amassed
 Five beetles,—blind and green they grope
Among the honey-meal: and last,
 Everywhere on the grassy slope
I traced it. Hold it fast!   20

The champaign with its endless fleece
 Of feathery grasses everywhere!
Silence and passion, joy and peace,
 An everlasting wash of air—
Rome's ghost since her decease.

Such life here, through such lengths of hours,
 Such miracles performed in play,
Such primal naked forms of flowers,
 Such letting nature have her way
While heaven looks from its towers!   30

How say you? Let us, O my dove,
 Let us be unashamed of soul,
As earth lies bare to heaven above!
 How is it under our control
To love or not to love?

I would that you were all to me,
 You that are just so much, no more.
Nor yours nor mine, nor slave nor free!
 Where does the fault lie? What the core
O' the wound, since wound must be?   40

I would I could adopt your will,
  See with your eyes, and set my heart
Beating by yours, and drink my fill
  At your soul's springs,—your part my part
In life, for good and ill.

No. I yearn upward, touch you close,
  Then stand away. I kiss your cheek,
Catch your soul's warmth,—I pluck the rose
  And love it more than tongue can speak—
Then the good minute goes.   50

Already how am I so far
  Out of that minute? Must I go
Still like the thistle-ball, no bar,
  Onward, whenever light winds blow,
Fixed by no friendly star?

Just when I seemed about to learn!
  Where is the thread now? Off again!
The old trick! Only I discern—
  Infinite passion, and the pain
Of finite hearts that yearn.   60

LOVE IN A LIFE

Room after room,
I hunt the house through
We inhabit together.
Heart, fear nothing, for, heart, thou shalt find her—
Next time, herself!—not the trouble behind her
Left in the curtain, the couch's perfume!
As she brushed it, the cornice-wreath blossomed anew:
Yon looking-glass gleamed at the wave of her feather.

Yet the day wears,
And door succeeds door;
I try the fresh fortune—
Range the wide house from the wing to the center.
Still the same chance! she goes out as I enter.
Spend my whole day in the quest,—who cares?
But 'tis twilight, you see,—with such suites to explore,
Such closets to search, such alcoves to importune!

LIFE IN A LOVE

Escape me?
Never—
Beloved!
While I am I, and you are you,
　So long as the world contains us both,
　Me the loving and you the loth,
While the one eludes, must the other pursue.
My life is a fault at last, I fear:
　It seems too much like a fate, indeed!
　Though I do my best I shall scarce succeed.　　10
But what if I fail of my purpose here?
It is but to keep the nerves at strain,
　To dry one's eyes and laugh at a fall,
And baffled, get up and begin again,—
　So the chase takes up one's life, that's all.
While, look but once from your farthest bound
　At me so deep in the dust and dark,
No sooner the old hope goes to ground
　Than a new one, straight to the selfsame mark,　　20
　　I shape me—
　　Ever
　　Removed!

THE LAST RIDE TOGETHER

I said—Then, dearest, since 'tis so,
Since now at length my fate I know,
Since nothing all my love avails,
Since all my life seemed meant for, fails,
　Since this was written and needs must be—
My whole heart rises up to bless
Your name in pride and thankfulness!
Take back the hope you gave,—I claim
Only a memory of the same,
—And this beside, if you will not blame,　　10
　Your leave for one more last ride with me.

My mistress bent that brow of hers;
Those deep dark eyes where pride demurs
When pity would be softening through,
Fixed me a breathing-while or two
　With life or death in the balance: right!
The blood replenished me again;
My last thought was at least not vain:

I and my mistress, side by side
Shall be together, breathe and ride,   20
So, one day more am I deified.
  Who knows but the world may end to-night?

Hush! if you saw some western cloud
All billowy-bosomed, over-bowed
By many benedictions—sun's
And moon's and evening-star's at once—
  And so, you, looking and loving best,
Conscious grew, your passion drew
Cloud, sunset, moonrise, star-shine too,
Down on you, near and yet more near,   30
Till flesh must fade for heaven was here!—
Thus leant she and lingered—joy and fear!
  Thus lay she a moment on my breast.

Then we began to ride. My soul
Smoothed itself out, a long-cramped scroll
Freshening and fluttering in the wind.
Past hopes already lay behind.
  What need to strive with a life awry?
Had I said that, had I done this,   40
So might I gain, so might I miss.
Might she have loved me? just as well
She might have hated, who can tell!
Where had I been now if the worst befell?
  And here we are riding, she and I.

Fail I alone, in words and deeds?
Why, all men strive, and who succeeds?
We rode; it seemed my spirit flew,
Saw other regions, cities new,
  As the world rushed by on either side.
I thought,—All labor, yet no less   50
Bear up beneath their unsuccess.
Look at the end of work, contrast
The petty done, the undone vast,
This present of theirs with the hopeful past!
  I hoped she would love me; here we ride.

What hand and brain went ever paired?
What heart alike conceived and dared?
What act proved all its thought had been?
What will but felt the fleshly screen?
  We ride and I see her bosom heave.   60

There's many a crown for who can reach.
Ten lines,[34] a statesman's life in each!
The flag stuck on a heap of bones,
A soldier's doing! what atones?
They scratch his name on the Abbey-stones.[35]
   My riding is better, by their leave.

What does it all mean, poet? Well,
Your brains beat into rhythm, you tell
What we felt only; you expressed
You hold things beautiful the best,   70
   And place them in rhyme so, side by side.
'Tis something, nay 'tis much: but then,
Have you yourself what's best for men?
Are you—poor, sick, old ere your time—
Nearer one whit your own sublime
Than we who never have turned a rhyme?
   Sing, riding's a joy! For me, I ride.

And you, great sculptor—so, you gave
A score of years to Art, her slave,
And that's your Venus, whence we turn   80
To yonder girl that fords the burn!
   You acquiesce, and shall I repine?
What, man of music, you grown gray
With notes and nothing else to say,
Is this your sole praise from a friend,
"Greatly his opera's strains intend,
But in music we know how fashions end!"
   I gave my youth; but we ride, in fine.

Who knows what's fit for us? Had fate
Proposed bliss here should sublimate   90
My being—had I signed the bond—
Still one must lead some life beyond,
   Have a bliss to die with, dim-descried.
This foot once planted on the goal,
This glory-garland round my soul,
Could I descry such? Try and test!
I sink back shuddering from the quest.
Earth being so good, would heaven seem best?
   Now, heaven and she are beyond this ride.

And yet—she has not spoke so long!   100
What if heaven be that, fair and strong

34 of history   35 Westminster Abbey

At life's best, with our eyes upturned
Whither life's flower is first discerned,
    We, fixed so, ever should so abide?
What if we still ride on, we two,
With life for ever old yet new,
Changed not in kind but in degree,
The instant made eternity,—
And heaven just prove that I and she
    Ride, ride together, for ever ride?   110

A GRAMMARIAN'S FUNERAL [36]

SHORTLY AFTER THE REVIVAL OF LEARNING IN EUROPE

LET us begin and carry up this corpse,
    Singing together.
Leave we the common crofts,[37] the vulgar thorpes [38]
    Each in its tether
Sleeping safe on the bosom of the plain,
    Cared-for till cock-crow:
Look out if yonder be not day again
    Rimming the rock-row!
That's the appropriate country; there, man's thought,
    Rarer, intenser,   10
Self-gathered for an outbreak, as it ought,
    Chafes in the censer.
Leave we the unlettered plain its herd and crop;
    Seek we sepulture
On a tall mountain, citied to the top,
    Crowded with culture!
All the peaks soar, but one the rest excels;
    Clouds overcome it;
No! yonder sparkle is the citadel's
    Circling its summit.   20
Thither our path lies; wind we up the heights;
    Wait ye the warning?
Our low life was the level's and the night's;
    He's for the morning.
Step to a tune, square chests, erect each head,
    'Ware the beholders!
This is our master, famous, calm and dead,
    Borne on our shoulders.

Sleep, crop and herd! sleep, darkling thorpe and croft,
    Safe from the weather!   30

36 The dead scholar's pu-   the mountain for burial in   38 villages
pils (one of whom speaks)   one of the Italian hill-cities.
are carrying his body up   37 farms

He, whom we convoy to his grave aloft,
    Singing together,
He was a man born with thy face and throat,
    Lyric Apollo!
Long he lived nameless: how should Spring take note
    Winter would follow?
Till lo, the little touch, and youth was gone!
    Cramped and diminished,
Moaned he, "New measures, other feet anon!
    My dance is finished"?   40
No, that's the world's way: (keep the mountain-side,
    Make for the city!)
He knew the signal, and stepped on with pride
    Over men's pity;
Left play for work, and grappled with the world
    Bent on escaping:
"What's in the scroll," quoth he, "thou keepest furled?
    Show me their shaping,
Theirs who most studied man, the bard and sage,—
    Give!"—So, he gowned him,   50
Straight got by heart that book to its last page:
    Learnèd, we found him,
Yea, but we found him bald too, eyes like lead,
    Accents uncertain:
"Time to taste life," another would have said,
    "Up with the curtain!"
This man said rather, "Actual life comes next?
    Patience a moment!
Grant I have mastered learning's crabbèd text,
    Still there's the comment.   60
Let me know all! Prate not of most or least,
    Painful or easy!
Even to the crumbs I'd fain eat up the feast,
    Ay, nor feel queasy."
Oh, such a life as he resolved to live,
    When he had learned it,
When he had gathered all books had to give!
    Sooner, he spurned it.
Image the whole, then execute the parts—
    Fancy the fabric   70
Quite, ere you build, ere steel strike fire from quartz,
    Ere mortar dab brick!

(Here's the town-gate reached: there's the market-place
    Gaping before us.)

Yea, this in him was the peculiar grace
    (Hearten our chorus!)
That before living he'd learn how to live—
    No end to learning:
Earn the means first—God surely will contrive
    Use for our earning.   80
Others mistrust and say, "But time escapes:
    Live now or never!"
He said, "What's time? Leave Now for dogs and apes!
    Man has Forever."
Back to his book then: deeper drooped his head:
    Calculus [39] racked him:
Leaden before, his eyes grew dross of lead:
    Tussis [40] attacked him.
"Now, master, take a little rest!"—not he!
    (Caution redoubled,   90
Step two abreast, the way winds narrowly!)
    Not a whit troubled,
Back to his studies, fresher than at first,
    Fierce as a dragon
He (soul-hydroptic [41] with a sacred thirst)
    Sucked at the flagon.
Oh, if we draw a circle premature,
    Heedless of far gain,
Greedy for quick returns of profit, sure
    Bad is our bargain!   100
Was it not great? did not he throw on God,
    (He loves the burthen)—
God's task to make the heavenly period
    Perfect the earthen?
Did not he magnify the mind, show clear
    Just what it all meant?
He would not discount life, as fools do here,
    Paid by instalment.
He ventured neck or nothing—heaven's success
    Found, or earth's failure: 110
"Wilt thou trust death or not?" He answered "Yes!
    Hence with life's pale lure!"
That low man seeks a little thing to do,
    Sees it and does it:
This high man, with a great thing to pursue,
    Dies ere he knows it.
That low man goes on adding one to one,
    His hundred's soon hit:

---

39 the stone (a disease)   40 a cough   41 soul-thirsty

This high man, aiming at a million,
    Misses an unit.   120
That, has the world here—should he need the next,
    Let the world mind him!
This, throws himself on God, and unperplexed
    Seeking shall find him.
So, with the throttling hands of death at strife,
    Ground he at grammar;
Still, through the rattle, parts of speech were rife;
    While he could stammer
He settled *Hoti's* business—let it be!—
    Properly based *Oun*—   130
Gave us the doctrine of the enclitic *De*,[42]
    Dead from the waist down.
Well, here's the platform, here's the proper place:
    Hail to your purlieus,
All ye highfliers of the feathered race,
    Swallows and curlews!
Here's the top-peak; the multitude below
    Live, for they can, there:
This man decided not to Live but Know—
    Bury this man there?   140
Here—here's his place, where meteors shoot, clouds form,
    Lightnings are loosened,
Stars come and go! Let joy break with the storm,
    Peace let the dew send!
Lofty designs must close in like effects:
    Loftily lying,
Leave him—still loftier than the world suspects,
    Living and dying.

THE STATUE AND THE BUST [43]

THERE's a palace in Florence, the world knows well,
And a statue watches it from the square,
And this story of both do our townsmen tell.

Ages ago, a lady there,
At the farthest window facing the East
Asked, "Who rides by with the royal air?"

42 Greek particles which bothered grammarians

43 In response to an inquiry, Browning wrote the following commentary on his poem: "1. 'This story the townsmen tell'; 'when, how, and where,' constitutes the subject of the poem. 2. The lady was the wife of Riccardi; and the duke, Ferdinand, just as the poem says. 3. As it [Palazzo Riccardi] was built by, and inhabited by, the Medici till sold, long after, to the Riccardi, it was not from the duke's palace, but a window in that of the Riccardi, that the lady gazed at her lover riding by. The statue is still in its place, looking at the window under which 'now is the empty shrine.' Can anything be clearer?"

The bridesmaids' prattle around her ceased;
She leaned forth, one on either hand;
They saw how the blush of the bride increased—

They felt by its beats her heart expand—   10
As one at each ear and both in a breath
Whispered, "The Great-Duke Ferdinand."

That selfsame instant, underneath,
The Duke rode past in his idle way,
Empty and fine like a swordless sheath.

Gay he rode, with a friend as gay,
Till he threw his head back—"Who is she?"
—"A bride the Riccardi brings home to-day."

Hair in heaps lay heavily
Over a pale brow spirit-pure—   20
Carved like the heart of the coal-black tree,

Crisped like a war-steed's encolure—[44]
And vainly sought to dissemble her eyes
Of the blackest black our eyes endure,

And lo, a blade for a knight's emprise
Filled the fine empty sheath of a man,—
The Duke grew straightway brave and wise.

He looked at her, as a lover can;
She looked at him, as one who awakes:
The past was a sleep, and her life began.   30

Now, love so ordered for both their sakes,
A feast was held that selfsame night
In the pile which the mighty shadow makes.

(For Via Larga is three-parts light,
But the palace overshadows one,
Because of a crime, which may God requite!

To Florence and God the wrong was done,
Through the first republic's murder there
By Cosimo[45] and his cursèd son.)

44 mane   elder (1389–1464), who while   public undermined repub-
45 Cosimo de Medici, the   chief of the Florentine Re-   lican institutions.

The Duke (with the statue's face in the square)   40
Turned in the midst of his multitude
At the bright approach of the bridal pair.

Face to face the lovers stood
A single minute and no more,
While the bridegroom bent as a man subdued—

Bowed till his bonnet brushed the floor—
For the Duke on the lady a kiss conferred,
As the courtly custom was of yore.

In a minute can lovers exchange a word?
If a word did pass, which I do not think,   50
Only one out of a thousand heard.

That was the bridegroom. At day's brink
He and his bride were alone at last
In a bed chamber by a taper's blink.

Calmly he said that her lot was cast,
That the door she had passed was shut on her
Till the final catafalk [46] repassed.

The world meanwhile, its noise and stir,
Through a certain window facing the East
She could watch like a convent's chronicler.   60

Since passing the door might lead to a feast,
And a feast might lead to so much beside,
He, of many evils, chose the least.

"Freely I choose too," said the bride—
"Your window and its world suffice,"
Replied the tongue, while the heart replied—

"If I spend the night with that devil twice,
May his window serve as my loop of hell
Whence a damned soul looks on paradise!

"I fly to the Duke who loves me well,   70
Sit by his side and laugh at sorrow
Ere I count another ave-bell.

[46] structure for supporting a coffin

" 'Tis only the coat of a page to borrow,
And tie my hair in a horse-boy's trim.
And I save my soul—but not to-morrow"—

(She checked herself and her eye grew dim)
"My father tarries to bless my state:
I must keep it one day more for him.

"Is one day more so long to wait?
Moreover the Duke rides past, I know;   80
We shall see each other, sure as fate."

She turned on her side and slept. Just so!
So we resolve on a thing and sleep:
So did the lady, ages ago.

That night the Duke said, "Dear or cheap
As the cost of this cup of bliss may prove
To body or soul, I will drain it deep."

And on the morrow, bold with love,
He beckoned the bridegroom (close on call,
As his duty bade, by the Duke's alcove)   90

And smiled " 'Twas a very funeral,
Your lady will think, this feast of ours,—
A shame to efface, whate'er befall!

"What if we break from the Arno bowers,⁴⁷
And try if Petraja,⁴⁸ cool and green,
Cure last night's fault with this morning's flowers?"

The bridegroom, not a thought to be seen
On his steady brow and quiet mouth,
Said, "Too much favor for me so mean!

"But, alas! my lady leaves ⁴⁹ the South;   100
Each wind that comes from the Apennine
Is a menace to her tender youth:

"Nor a way exists, the wise opine,
If she quits her palace twice this year,
To avert the flower of life's decline."

47 bowers by the River   48 suburb of Florence   49 comes from
Arno, in Florence

Quoth the Duke, "A sage and a kindly fear.
Moreover Petraja is cold this spring:
Be our feast to-night as usual here!"

And then to himself—"Which night shall bring
Thy bride to her lover's embraces, fool—   110
Or I am the fool, and thou art the king!

"Yet my passion must wait a night, nor cool—
For to-night the Envoy arrives from France
Whose heart I unlock with thyself, my tool.

"I need thee still and might miss perchance.
To-day is not wholly lost, beside,
With its hope of my lady's countenance:

"For I ride—what should I do but ride?
And passing her palace, if I list,
May glance at its window—well betide!"   120

So said, so done: nor the lady missed
One ray that broke from the ardent brow,
Nor a curl of the lips where the spirit kissed.

Be sure that each renewed the vow,
No morrow's sun should arise and set
And leave them then as it left them now.

But next day passed, and next day yet,
With still fresh cause to wait one day more
Ere each leaped over the parapet.

And still, as love's brief morning wore,   130
With a gentle start, half smile, half sigh,
They found love not as it seemed before.

They thought it would work infallibly,
But not in despite of heaven and earth:
The rose would blow when the storm passed by.

Meantime they could profit in winter's dearth
By store of fruits that supplant the rose:
The world and its ways have a certain worth:

And to press a point while these oppose
Were simple policy; better wait: 140
We lose no friends and we gain no foes.

Meantime, worse fates than a lover's fate,
Who daily may ride and pass and look
Where his lady watches behind the grate!

And she—she watched the square like a book
Holding one picture and only one,
Which daily to find she undertook:

When the picture was reached the book was done,
And she turned from the picture at night to scheme
Of tearing it out for herself next sun.   150

So weeks grew months, years; gleam by gleam
The glory dropped from their youth and love,
And both perceived they had dreamed a dream;

Which hovered as dreams do, still above:
But who can take a dream for a truth?
Oh, hide our eyes from the next remove!

One day as the lady saw her youth
Depart, and the silver thread that streaked
Her hair, and, worn by the serpent's tooth,

The brow so puckered, the chin so peaked,—   160
And wondered who the woman was,
Hollow-eyed and haggard-cheeked,

Fronting her silent in the glass—
"Summon here," she suddenly said,
"Before the rest of my old self pass,

"Him, the Carver, a hand to aid,
Who fashions the clay no love will change,
And fixes a beauty never to fade.

"Let Robbia's craft [50] so apt and strange
Arrest the remains of young and fair,   170
And rivet them while the seasons range.

"Make me a face on the window there,
Waiting as ever, mute the while,
My love to pass below in the square!

[50] The della Robbias did terra cotta relief covered with enamel

"And let me think that it may beguile
Dreary days which the dead must spend
Down in their darkness under the aisle,

"To say, 'What matters it at the end?
I did no more while my heart was warm
Than does that image, my pale-faced friend.'   180

"Where is the use of the lip's red charm,
The heaven of hair, the pride of the brow,
And the blood that blues the inside arm—

"Unless we turn, as the soul knows how,
The earthly gift to an end divine?
A lady of clay is as good, I trow."

But long ere Robbia's cornice, fine,
With flowers and fruits which leaves enlace,
Was set where now is the empty shrine—

(And, leaning out of a bright blue space,   190
As a ghost might lean from a chink of sky,
The passionate pale lady's face—

Eying ever, with earnest eye
And quick-turned neck at its breathless stretch,
Some one who ever is passing by—)

The Duke had sighed like the simplest wretch
In Florence, "Youth—my dream escapes!
Will its record stay?" And he bade them fetch

Some subtle molder of brazen shapes—
"Can the soul, the will, die out of a man   200
Ere his body find the grave that gapes?

"John of Douay [51] shall effect my plan,
Set me on horseback here aloft,
Alive, as the crafty sculptor can,

"In the very square I have crossed so oft:
That men may admire, when future suns
Shall touch the eyes to a purpose soft,

51 Sculptor who made the equestrian statue in 1608

"While the mouth and the brow stay brave in bronze—
Admire and say, 'When he was alive
How he would take his pleasure once!'   210

"And it shall go hard but I contrive
To listen the while, and laugh in my tomb
At idleness which aspires to strive."

So! while these wait the trump of doom,
How do their spirits pass, I wonder,
Nights and days in the narrow room?

Still, I suppose, they sit and ponder
What a gift life was, ages ago,
Six steps out of the chapel yonder.

Only they see not God, I know,   220
Nor all that chivalry of his,
The soldier-saints who, row on row,

Burn upward each to his point of bliss—
Since, the end of life being manifest,
He had burned his way through the world to this.

I hear you reproach, "But delay was best,
For their end was a crime."—Oh, a crime will do
As well, I reply, to serve for a test,

As a virtue golden through and through,
Sufficient to vindicate itself   230
And prove its worth at a moment's view!

Must a game be played for the sake of pelf?
Where a button goes, 'twere an epigram
To offer the stamp of the very Guelph.[52]

The true has no value beyond the sham:
As well the counter as coin, I submit,
When your table's a hat, and your prize, a dram.

Stake your counter as boldly every whit,
Venture as warily, use the same skill,
Do your best, whether winning or losing it,   240

---

[52] In a game played with buttons, it would be a mere piece of useless smartness to
offer real coin

If you chose to play!—is my principle.
Let a man contend to the uttermost
For his life's set prize, be it what it will!

The counter our lovers staked was lost
As surely as if it were lawful coin:
And the sin I impute to each frustrate ghost

Is—the unlit lamp and the ungirt loin,
Though the end in sight was a vice, I say.
You of the virtue (we issue join)
How strive you? *De te, fabula!* [53]   250

"CHILDE ROLAND TO THE DARK TOWER CAME" [54]

See Edgar's song in Lear.

My first thought was, he lied in every word,
  That hoary cripple, with malicious eye
  Askance to watch the working of his lie
On mine, and mouth scarce able to afford
Suppression of the glee, that pursed and scored
  Its edge, at one more victim gained thereby.

What else should he be set for, with his staff?
  What, save to waylay with his lies, ensnare
  All travelers who might find him posted there,
And ask the road? I guessed what skull-like laugh   10
Would break, what crutch 'gin write my epitaph
  For pastime in the dusty thoroughfare,

If at his counsel I should turn aside
  Into that ominous tract which, all agree,
  Hides the Dark Tower. Yet acquiescingly
I did turn as he pointed: neither pride
Nor hope rekindling at the end descried,
  So much as gladness that some end might be.

For, what with my whole world-wide wandering,
  What with my search drawn out through years, my hope   20
  Dwindled into a ghost not fit to cope

[53] The story concerns *you.*
[54] The title quotes a line from *King Lear,* but otherwise the poem is entirely imaginative. "When I asked him if constancy to an ideal—'He that endureth to the end shall be saved'—was not a sufficient understanding of the central purpose of the poem, he said, 'Yes, just about that.'" (Rev. John W. Chadwick, quoting Browning)

With that obstreperous joy success would bring,—
I hardly tried now to rebuke the spring
  My heart made, finding failure in its scope.

As when a sick man very near to death
  Seems dead indeed, and feels begin and end
  The tears, and takes the farewell of each friend,
And hears one bid the other go, draw breath
Freelier outside, ("Since all is o'er," he saith,
  "And the blow fallen no grieving can amend;")   30

While some discuss if near the other graves
  Be room enough for this, and when a day
  Suits best for carrying the corpse away,
With care about the banners, scarves and staves:
And still the man hears all, and only craves
  He may not shame such tender love and stay.

Thus, I had so long suffered in this quest,
  Heard failure prophesied so oft, been writ
  So many times among "The Band"—to wit,
The knights who to the Dark Tower's search addressed   40
Their steps—that just to fail as they, seemed best,
  And all the doubt was now—should I be fit?

So, quiet as despair, I turned from him,
  That hateful cripple, out of his highway
  Into the path he pointed. All the day
Had been a dreary one at best, and dim
Was setting to its close, yet shot one grim
  Red leer to see the plain catch its estray.⁵⁵

For mark! no sooner was I fairly found
  Pledged to the plain, after a pace or two,   50
  Than, pausing to throw backward a last view
O'er the safe road, 'twas gone; gray plain all round:
Nothing but plain to the horizon's bound.
  I might go on; naught else remained to do.

So, on I went. I think I never saw
  Such starved ignoble nature; nothing throve:
  For flowers—as well expect a cedar grove!
But cockle, spurge, according to their law
Might propagate their kind, with none to awe,
  You'd think: a burr had been a treasure trove.   60

55 wanderer

No! penury, inertness and grimace,
 In some strange sort, were the land's portion. "See
 Or shut your eyes," said Nature peevishly,
"It nothing skills: I cannot help my case:
'Tis the last Judgment's fire must cure this place,
 Calcine [56] its clods and set my prisoners free."

If there pushed any ragged thistle-stalk
 Above its mates, the head was chopped; the bents [57]
 Were jealous else. What made those holes and rents
In the dock's harsh swarth leaves, bruised as to balk   70
All hope of greenness? 'tis a brute must walk
 Pashing their life out, with a brute's intents.

As for the grass, it grew as scant as hair
 In leprosy; thin dry blades pricked the mud
 Which underneath looked kneaded up with blood.
One stiff blind horse, his every bone a-stare,
Stood stupefied, however he came there:
 Thrust out past service from the devil's stud!

Alive? he might be dead for aught I know,
 With that red gaunt and colloped neck a-strain,   80
 And shut eyes underneath the rusty mane;
Seldom went such grotesqueness with such woe;
I never saw a brute I hated so;
 He must be wicked to deserve such pain.

I shut my eyes and turned them on my heart.
 As a man calls for wine before he fights,
 I asked one draught of earlier, happier sights,
Ere fitly I could hope to play my part.
Think first, fight afterwards—the soldier's art:
 One taste of the old time sets all to rights.   90

Not it! I fancied Cuthbert's reddening face
 Beneath its garniture of curly gold,
 Dear fellow, till I almost felt him fold
An arm in mine to fix me to the place,
That way he used. Alas, one night's disgrace!
 Out went my heart's new fire and left it cold.

Giles then, the soul of honor—there he stands
 Frank as ten years ago when knighted first.
 What honest man should dare (he said) he durst.

56 purify by heat   **57** coarse grasses

Good—but the scene shifts—faugh! what hangman hands   100
Pin to his breast a parchment? His own hands
   Read it. Poor traitor, spit upon and curst!

Better this present than a past like that;
   Back therefore to my darkening path again!
   No sound, no sight as far as eye could strain.
Will the night send a howlet or a bat?
I asked: when something on the dismal flat
   Came to arrest my thoughts and change their train.

A sudden little river crossed my path
   As unexpected as a serpent comes.
   No sluggish tide congenial to the glooms;   110
This, as it frothed by, might have been a bath
For the fiend's glowing hoof—to see the wrath
   Of its black eddy bespate with flakes and spumes.

So petty yet so spiteful! All along,
   Low scrubby alders kneeled down over it;
   Drenched willows flung them headlong in a fit
Of mute despair, a suicidal throng:
The river which had done them all the wrong,
   Whate'er that was, rolled by, deterred no whit.   120

Which, while I forded,—good saints, how I feared
   To set my foot upon a dead man's cheek,
   Each step, or feel the spear I thrust to seek
For hollows, tangled in his hair or beard!
—It may have been a water-rat I speared,
   But, ugh! it sounded like a baby's shriek.

Glad was I when I reached the other bank.
   Now for a better country. Vain presage!
   Who were the strugglers, what war did they wage,
Whose savage trample thus could pad the dank   130
Soil to a plash? Toads in a poisoned tank,
   Of wild cats in a red-hot iron cage—

The fight must so have seemed in that fell cirque.[58]
   What penned them there, with all the plain to choose?
   No footprint leading to that horrid mews,
None out of it. Mad brewage set to work
Their brains, no doubt, like galley-slaves the Turk
   Pits for his pastime, Christians against Jews.

58 circle

And more than that—a furlong on—why, there!
   What bad use was that engine for, that wheel,   ₁₄₀
   Or brake, not wheel—that harrow fit to reel
Men's bodies out like silk? with all the air
Of Tophet's [59] tool, on earth left unaware,
   Or brought to sharpen its rusty teeth of steel.

Then came a bit of stubbed ground, once a wood,
   Next a marsh, it would seem, and now mere earth
   Desperate and done with: (so a fool finds mirth,
Makes a thing and then mars it, till his mood
Changes and off he goes!) within a rood—
   Bog, clay and rubble, sand and stark black dearth.   ₁₅₀

Now blotches rankling, colored gay and grim,
   Now patches where some leanness of the soil's
   Broke into moss or substances like boils;
Then came some palsied oak, a cleft in him
Like a distorted mouth that splits its rim
   Gaping at death, and dies while it recoils.

And just as far as ever from the end!
   Naught in the distance but the evening, naught
   To point my footstep further! At the thought,
A great black bird, Apollyon's [60] bosom-friend,   ₁₆₀
Sailed past, nor beat his wide wing dragon-penned
   That brushed my cap—perchance the guide I sought.

For, looking up, aware I somehow grew,
   'Spite of the dusk, the plain had given place
   All round to mountains—with such name to grace
Mere ugly heights and heaps now stolen in view.
How thus they had surprised me,—solve it, you!
   How to get from them was no clearer case.

Yet half I seemed to recognize some trick
   Of mischief happened to me, God knows when—   ₁₇₀
   In a bad dream perhaps. Here ended, then,
Progress this way. When, in the very nick
Of giving up, one time more, came a click
   As when a trap shuts—you're inside the den!

Burningly it came on me all at once,
   This was the place! those two hills on the right,

---

59 a valley where chil-   (see 2 Kings xxiii. 10)   tomless pit (Rev. ix. 11)
dren were sacrificed by fire   60 the angel of the bot-

Crouched like two bulls locked horn in horn in fight;
While to the left, a tall scalped mountain . . . Dunce,
Dotard, a-dozing at the very nonce,
    After a life spent training for the sight!   180

What in the midst lay but the Tower itself?
    The round squat turret, blind as the fool's heart,
    Built of brown stone, without a counterpart
In the whole world. The tempest's mocking elf
Points to the shipman thus the unseen shelf
    He strikes on, only when the timbers start.

Not see? because of night perhaps?—why, day
    Came back again for that! before it left,
    The dying sunset kindled through a cleft:
The hills, like giants at a hunting, lay,   190
Chin upon hand, to see the game at bay,—
    "Now stab and end the creature—to the heft!"

Not hear? when noise was everywhere! it tolled
    Increasing like a bell. Names in my ears,
    Of all the lost adventurers my peers,—
How such a one was strong, and such was bold,
And such was fortunate, yet each of old
    Lost, lost! one moment knelled the woe of years.

There they stood, ranged along the hillsides, met
    To view the last of me, a living frame   200
    For one more picture! in a sheet of flame
I saw them and I knew them all. And yet
Dauntless the slug-horn to my lips I set,
    And blew. *"Childe Roland to the Dark Tower came."*

FRA LIPPO LIPPI [61]

I AM poor brother Lippo, by your leave!
You need not clap your torches to my face.
Zooks, what's to blame? you think you see a monk!
What, 'tis past midnight, and you go the rounds,
And here you catch me at an alley's end
Where sportive ladies leave their doors ajar?
The Carmine's my cloister: hunt it up,
Do,—harry out if you must show your zeal,

61 Filippo Lippi (1406?-1469), Florentine painter, member of the Carmelite friars. Cosimo de Medici was his patron. The monologue is based upon pictures of Lippo Lippi and his life as given in Vasari's *Lives of the Painters.*

Whatever rat, there, haps on his wrong hole,
And nip each softling of a wee white mouse,   10
Weke, weke, that's crept to keep him company!
Aha, you know your betters! Then, you'll take
Your hand away that's fiddling on my throat,
And please to know me likewise. Who am I?
Why one, sir, who is lodging with a friend
Three streets off—he's a certain . . . how'd ye call?
Master—a . . . Cosimo of the Medici,
I' the house that caps the corner. Boh! you were best!
Remember and tell me, the day you're hanged,
How you affected such a gullet's-gripe!   20
But you, sir, it concerns you that your knaves
Pick up a manner nor discredit you:
Zooks, are we pilchards,[62] that they sweep the streets
And count fair prize what comes into their net?
He's Judas to a tittle, that man is!
Just such a face! Why, sir, you make amends.
Lord, I'm not angry! Bid your hangdogs go
Drink out this quarter-florin to the health
Of the munificent House that harbors me
(And many more beside, lads! more beside!)   30
And all's come square again. I'd like his face—
His, elbowing on his comrade in the door
With the pike and lantern,—for the slave that holds
John Baptist's head a-dangle by the hair
With one hand ("Look you, now," as who should say)
And his weapon in the other, yet unwiped!
It's not your chance to have a bit of chalk,
A wood-coal or the like? or you should see!
Yes, I'm the painter, since you style me so.
What, brother Lippo's doings, up and down,   40
You know them and they take you? like enough!
I saw the proper twinkle in your eye—
'Tell you, I liked your looks at very first.
Let's sit and set things straight now, hip to haunch.
Here's spring come, and the nights one makes up bands
To roam the town and sing out carnival,
And I've been three weeks shut within my mew,
A-painting for the great man, saints and saints
And saints again. I could not paint all night—
Ouf! I leaned out of window for fresh air.   50
There came a hurry of feet and little feet,
A sweep of lute-strings, laughs, and whifts of song,—
Flower o' the broom,

62 sardines

Take away love, and our earth is a tomb!
Flower o' the quince,
I let Lisa go, and what good in life since?
Flower o' the thyme [63]—and so on. Round they went.
Scarce had they turned the corner when a titter
Like the skipping of rabbits by moonlight,—three slim shapes,
And a face that looked up . . . zooks, sir, flesh and blood,   60
That's all I'm made of! Into shreds it went,
Curtain and counterpane and coverlet,
All the bed-furniture—a dozen knots,
There was a ladder! Down I let myself,
Hands and feet, scrambling somehow, and so dropped,
And after them. I came up with the fun
Hard by Saint Laurence, [64] hail fellow, well met,—
Flower o' the rose,
If I've been merry, what matter who knows?
And so as I was stealing back again   70
To get to bed and have a bit of sleep
Ere I rise up to-morrow and go work
On Jerome knocking at his poor old breast
With his great round stone to subdue the flesh,
You snap me of the sudden. Ah, I see!
Though your eye twinkles still, you shake your head—
Mine's shaved—a monk, you say—the sting's in that!
If Master Cosimo announced himself,
Mum's the word naturally; but a monk!
Come, what am I a beast for? tell us, now!   80
I was a baby when my mother died
And father died and left me in the street.
I starved there, God knows how, a year or two
On fig-skins, melon-parings, rinds and shucks,
Refuse and rubbish. One fine frosty day,
My stomach being empty as your hat,
The wind doubled me up and down I went.
Old Aunt Lapaccia trussed me with one hand
(Its fellow was a stinger as I knew),
And so along the wall, over the bridge,   90
By the straight cut to the convent. Six words there,
While I stood munching my first bread that month:
"So, boy, you're minded," quoth the good fat father,
Wiping his own mouth, 'twas refection-time,—
"To quit this very miserable world?
Will you renounce" . . . "the mouthful of bread?" thought I;
By no means! Brief, they made a monk of me;

63 These and the follow-   Italian *stornelli*, or street   64 the church of San
ing are modeled on the   songs.   Lorenzo

I did renounce the world, its pride and greed,
Palace, farm, villa, shop, and banking-house,
Trash, such as these poor devils of Medici   100
Have given their hearts to—all at eight years old.
Well, sir, I found in time, you may be sure,
'Twas not for nothing—the good bellyful,
The warm serge and the rope that goes all round,
And day-long blessèd idleness beside!
"Let's see what the urchin's fit for"—that came next.
Not overmuch their way, I must confess.
Such a to-do! They tried me with their books;
Lord, they'd have taught me Latin in pure waste!
Flower o' the clove,   110
All the Latin I construe is "amo," I love!
But, mind you, when a boy starves in the streets
Eight years together, as my fortune was,
Watching folk's faces to know who will fling
The bit of half-stripped grape-bunch he desires,
And who will curse or kick him for his pains,—
Which gentleman processional and fine,
Holding a candle to the Sacrament,
Will wink and let him lift a plate and catch
The droppings of the wax to sell again,   120
Or holla for the Eight [65] and have him whipped,—
How say I?—nay, which dog bites, which lets drop
His bone from the heap of offal in the street,—
Why, soul and sense of him grow sharp alike,
He learns the look of things, and none the less
For admonition from the hunger-pinch.
I had a store of such remarks, be sure,
Which, after I found leisure, turned to use.
I drew men's faces on my copy-books,
Scrawled them within the antiphonary's [66] marge,   130
Joined legs and arms to the long music-notes,
Found eyes and nose and chin for A's and B's,
And made a string of pictures of the world
Betwixt the ins and outs of verb and noun,
On the wall, the bench, the door. The monks looked black.
"Nay," quoth the Prior, "turn him out, d'ye say?
In no wise. Lose a crow and catch a lark.
What if at last we get our man of parts,
We Carmelites, like those Camaldolese
And Preaching Friars, [67] to do our church up fine   140
And put the front on it that ought to be!"

65 city   magistrates   of   66 hymn-book   67 the Dominicans
Florence

And hereupon he bade me daub away.
Thank you! my head being crammed, the walls a blank,
Never was such prompt disemburdening.
First, every sort of monk, the black and white,
I drew them, fat and lean: then, folk at church,
From good old gossips waiting to confess
Their cribs of barrel-droppings, candle-ends,—
To the breathless fellow at the altar-foot,
Fresh from his murder, safe and sitting there   150
With the little children round him in a row
Of admiration, half for his beard and half
For that white anger of his victim's son
Shaking a fist at him with one fierce arm,
Signing himself with the other because of Christ
(Whose sad face on the cross sees only this
After the passion of a thousand years)
Till some poor girl, her apron o'er her head,
(Which the intense eyes looked through) came at eve
On tiptoe, said a word, dropped in a loaf,   160
Her pair of earrings and a bunch of flowers
(The brute took growling), prayed, and so was gone.
I painted all, then cried " 'Tis ask and have;
Choose, for more's ready!"—laid the ladder flat,
And showed my covered bit of cloister-wall.
The monks closed in a circle and praised loud
Till checked, taught what to see and not to see,
Being simple bodies,—"That's the very man!
Look at the boy who stoops to pat the dog!
That woman's like the Prior's niece who comes   170
To care about his asthma: it's the life!"
But there my triumph's straw-fire flared and funked;
Their betters took their turn to see and say:
The Prior and the learnèd pulled a face
And stopped all that in no time. "How? what's here?
Quite from the mark of painting, bless us all!
Faces, arms, legs, and bodies like the true
As much as pea and pea! it's devil's-game!
Your business is not to catch men with show,
With homage to the perishable clay,   180
But lift them over it, ignore it all,
Make them forget there's such a thing as flesh.
Your business is to paint the souls of men—
Man's soul, and it's a fire, smoke . . . no, it's not . . .
It's vapor done up like a new-born babe—
(In that shape when you die it leaves your mouth)
It's . . . well, what matters talking, it's the soul!

Give us no more of body than shows soul!
Here's Giotto,[68] with his Saint a-praising God,
That sets us praising,—why not stop with him?   190
Why put all thoughts of praise out of our head
With wonder at lines, colors, and what not?
Paint the soul, never mind the legs and arms!
Rub all out, try at it a second time.
Oh, that white smallish female with the breasts,
She's just my niece . . . Herodias,[69] I would say,—
Who went and danced and got men's heads cut off!
Have it all out!" Now, is this sense, I ask?
A fine way to paint soul, by painting body
So ill, the eye can't stop there, must go further   200
And can't fare worse! Thus, yellow does for white
When what you put for yellow's simply black,
And any sort of meaning looks intense
When all beside itself means and looks naught.
Why can't a painter lift each foot in turn,
'Left foot and right foot, go a double step,
Make his flesh liker and his soul more like,
Both in their order? Take the prettiest face,
The Prior's niece . . . patron-saint—is it so pretty
You can't discover if it means hope, fear,   210
Sorrow or joy? won't beauty go with these?
Suppose I've made her eyes all right and blue,
Can't I take breath and try to add life's flash,
And then add soul and heighten them three-fold?
Or say there's beauty with no soul at all—
(I never saw it—put the case the same—)
If you get simple beauty and naught else,
You get about the best thing God invents:
That's somewhat: and you'll find the soul you have missed,
Within yourself, when you return him thanks.   220
"Rub all out!" Well, well, there's my life, in short,
And so the thing has gone on ever since.
I'm grown a man no doubt, I've broken bounds:
You should not take a fellow eight years old
And make him swear to never kiss the girls.
I'm my own master, paint now as I please—
Having a friend, you see, in the Corner-house!
Lord, it's fast holding by the rings in front—
Those great rings serve more purposes than just
To plant a flag in, or tie up a horse!   230
And yet the old schooling sticks, the old grave eyes

68 Florentine painter, (1276?–1337?) archi-
tect, and sculptor   69 See Matt. xiv, 6-11

Are peeping o'er my shoulder as I work,
The heads shake still—"It's art's decline, my son!
You're not of the true painters, great and old;
Brother Angelico's [70] the man, you'll find;
Brother Lorenzo stands his single peer:
Fag on at flesh, you'll never make the third!"
Flower o' the pine,
You keep your mistr . . . manners, and I'll stick to mine!
I'm not the third, then: bless us, they must know!   240
Don't you think they're the likeliest to know,
They with their Latin? So, I swallow my rage,
Clench my teeth, suck my lips in tight, and paint
To please them—sometimes do and sometimes don't;
For, doing most, there's pretty sure to come
A turn, some warm eve finds me at my saints—
A laugh, a cry, the business of the world—
(*Flower o' the peach,*
Death for us all, and his own life for each!)
And my whole soul revolves, the cup runs over,   250
The world and life's too big to pass for a dream,
And I do these wild things in sheer despite,
And play the fooleries you catch me at,
In pure rage! The old mill-horse, out at grass
After hard years, throws up his stiff heels so,
Although the miller does not preach to him
The only good of grass is to make chaff.
What would men have? Do they like grass or no—
May they or mayn't they? all I want's the thing
Settled for ever one way. As it is,   260
You tell too many lies and hurt yourself:
You don't like what you only like too much,
You do like what, if given you at your word,
You find abundantly detestable.
For me, I think I speak as I was taught;
I always see the garden and God there
A-making man's wife: and, my lesson learned,
The value and significance of flesh,
I can't unlearn ten minutes afterwards.

You understand me: I'm a beast, I know.   270
But see, now—why, I see as certainly
As that the morning-star's about to shine,
What will hap some day. We've a youngster here
Comes to our convent, studies what I do,

<hr>

[70] Fra Angelico (1387–1455), a deeply religious painter. Fra Lorenzo, of the Camaldolese (see 1. 139), was another painter of the same sort.

Slouches and stares and lets no atom drop:
His name is Guidi [71]—he'll not mind the monks—
They call him Hulking Tom, he lets them talk—
He picks my practice up—he'll paint apace,
I hope so—though I never live so long,
I know what's sure to follow. You be judge!   280
You speak no Latin more than I, belike;
However, you're my man, you've seen the world
—The beauty and the wonder and the power,
The shapes of things, their colors, lights and shades,
Changes, surprises,—and God made it all!
—For what? Do you feel thankful, ay or no,
For this fair town's face, yonder river's line,
The mountain round it and the sky above,
Much more the figures of man, woman, child,
These are the frame to? What's it all about?   290
To be passed over, despised? or dwelt upon,
Wondered at? oh, this last of course!—you say.
But why not do as well as say,—paint these
Just as they are, careless what comes of it?
God's works—paint any one, and count it crime
To let a truth slip. Don't object, "His works
Are here already; nature is complete:
Suppose you reproduce her—(which you can't)
There's no advantage! you must beat her, then."
For, don't you mark? we're made so that we love   300
First when we see them painted, things we have passed
Perhaps a hundred times nor cared to see;
And so they are better, painted—better to us,
Which is the same thing. Art was given for that;
God uses us to help each other so,
Lending our minds out. Have you noticed, now,
Your cullion's [72] hanging face? A bit of chalk,
And trust me but you should, though! How much more,
If I drew higher things with the same truth!
That were to take the Prior's pulpit-place,   310
Interpret God to all of you! Oh, oh,
It makes me mad to see what men shall do
And we in our graves! This world's no blot for us,
Nor blank; it means intensely, and means good:
To find its meaning is my meat and drink.
"Ay, but you don't so instigate to prayer!"
Strikes in the Prior: "when your meaning's plain
It does not say to folk—remember matins,

---

71 Tommaso Guidi Ma-   rather than pupil of Lippo   72 base fellow
saccio (1401–1428), teacher   Lippi.

Or, mind you fast next Friday!" Why, for this
What need of art at all? A skull and bones,   320
Two bits of stick nailed crosswise, or, what's best,
A bell to chime the hour with, does as well.
I painted a Saint Laurence six months since
At Prato, splashed the fresco in fine style:
"How looks my painting, now the scaffold's down?"
I ask a brother: "Hugely," he returns—
"Already not one phiz of your three slaves
Who turn the Deacon off his toasted side,[73]
But's scratched and prodded to our heart's content,   330
The pious people have so eased their own
With coming to say prayers there in a rage:
We get on fast to see the bricks beneath.
Expect another job this time next year,
For pity and religion grow i' the crowd—
Your painting serves its purpose!" Hang the fools!

—That is—you'll not mistake an idle word
Spoke in a huff by a poor monk, God wot,
Tasting the air this spicy night which turns
The unaccustomed head like Chianti wine!
Oh, the church knows! don't misreport me, now!   340
It's natural a poor monk out of bounds
Should have his apt word to excuse himself:
And hearken how I plot to make amends.
I have bethought me: I shall paint a piece
. . . There's for you! Give me six months, then go, see
Something in Sant' Ambrogio's! Bless the nuns!
They want a cast o' my office. I shall paint[74]
God in the midst, Madonna and her babe,
Ringed by a bowery, flowery angel-brood,
Lilies and vestments and white faces, sweet   350
As puff on puff of grated orris-root
When ladies crowd to Church at midsummer.
And then i' the front, of course a saint or two—
Saint John, because he saves the Florentines,
Saint Ambrose, who puts down in black and white
The convent's friends and gives them a long day,
And Job, I must have him there past mistake.
The man of Uz (and Us without the z,
Painters who need his patience). Well, all these
Secured at their devotion, up shall come   360
Out of a corner when you least expect,

73 Saint Laurence suf-   broiled on a gridiron.   *Coronation of the Virgin.*
fered martyrdom by being   74 The picture is *The*

As one by a dark stair into a great light,
Music and talking, who but Lippo! I!—
Mazed, motionless, and moonstruck—I'm the man!
Back I shrink—what is this I see and hear?
I, caught up with my monk's-things by mistake,
My old serge gown and rope that goes all round,
I, in this presence, this pure company!
Where's a hole, where's a corner for escape?
Then steps a sweet angelic slip of a thing   370
Forward, puts out a soft palm—"Not so fast!"
—Addresses the celestial presence, "nay—
He made you and devised you, after all,
Though he's none of you! Could Saint John there draw—
His camel-hair make up a painting-brush?
We come to brother Lippo for all that,
Iste perfecit opus!" [75] So, all smile—
I shuffle sideways with my blushing face
Under the cover of a hundred wings
Thrown like a spread of kirtles when you're gay   380
And play hot cockles, all the doors being shut,
Till, wholly unexpected, in there pops
The hothead husband! Thus I scuttle off
To some safe bench behind, not letting go
The palm of her, the little lily thing
That spoke the good word for me in the nick,
Like the Prior's niece . . . Saint Lucy, I would say.
And so all's saved for me, and for the church
A pretty picture gained. Go, six months hence!
Your hand, sir, and good-by: no lights, no lights!   390
The street's hushed, and I know my own way back,
Don't fear me! There's the gray beginning. Zooks!

ANDREA DEL SARTO [76]

CALLED "THE FAULTLESS PAINTER"

But do not let us quarrel any more,
No, my Lucrezia; bear with me for once:
Sit down and all shall happen as you wish.
You turn your face, but does it bring your heart?
I'll work then for your friend's friend, never fear,
Treat his own subject after his own way,
Fix his own time, accept too his own price,

---

75 This man did the work (painting).
76 1486-1531. The mono-logue is based upon Vasari's *Lives of the Painters,* and upon Andrea's paintings, particularly those for which his wife Lucrezia was the model.

And shut the money into this small hand
When next it takes mine. Will it? tenderly?
Oh, I'll content him,—but to-morrow, Love!   10
I often am much wearier than you think,
This evening more than usual, and it seems
As if—forgive now—should you let me sit
Here by the window with your hand in mine
And look a half-hour forth on Fiesole,[77]
Both of one mind, as married people use,
Quietly, quietly the evening through,
I might get up to-morrow to my work
Cheerful and fresh as ever. Let us try.
To-morrow, how you shall be glad for this!   20
Your soft hand is a woman of itself,
And mine the man's bared breast she curls inside.
Don't count the time lost, neither; you must serve
For each of the five pictures we require:
It saves a model. So! keep looking so—
My serpentining beauty, rounds on rounds!
—How could you ever prick those perfect ears,
Even to put the pearl there! oh, so sweet—
My face, my moon, my everybody's moon,
Which everybody looks on and calls his,   30
And, I suppose, is looked on by in turn,
While she looks—no one's: very dear, no less.
You smile? why, there's my picture ready made,
There's what we painters call our harmony!
A common grayness silvers everything,—
All in a twilight, you and I alike
—You, at the point of your first pride in me
(That's gone you know),—but I, at every point;
My youth, my hope, my art, being all toned down
To yonder sober pleasant Fiesole.   40
There's the bell clinking from the chapel-top;
That length of convent-wall across the way
Holds the trees safer, huddled more inside;
The last monk leaves the garden; days decrease,
And autumn grows, autumn in everything.
Eh? the whole seems to fall into a shape
As if I saw alike my work and self
And all that I was born to be and do,
A twilight-piece. Love, we are in God's hand.
How strange now looks the life he makes us lead;   50
So free we seem, so fettered fast we are!
I feel he laid the fetter: let it lie!

77 village near Florence

This chamber for example—turn your head—
All that's behind us! You don't understand
Nor care to understand about my art,
But you can hear at least when people speak:
And that cartoon, the second from the door
—It is the thing, Love! so such thing should be—
Behold Madonna!—I am bold to say.
I can do with my pencil what I know,   60
What I see, what at bottom of my heart
I wish for, if I ever wish so deep—
Do easily, too—when I say, perfectly,
I do not boast, perhaps: yourself are judge,
Who listened to the Legate's talk last week,
And just as much they used to say in France.
At any rate 'tis easy, all of it!
No sketches first, no studies, that's long past:
I do what many dream of all their lives,
—Dream? strive to do, and agonize to do,   70
And fail in doing. I could count twenty such
On twice your fingers, and not leave this town,
Who strive—you don't know how the others strive
To paint a little thing like that you smeared
Carelessly passing with your robes afloat,—
Yet do much less, so much less, Someone says,
(I know his name, no matter)—so much less!
Well, less is more, Lucrezia: I am judged.
There burns a truer light of God in them,
In their vexed beating stuffed and stopped-up brain,   80
Heart, or whate'er else, than goes on to prompt
This low-pulsed forthright craftsman's hand of mine.
Their works drop groundward, but themselves, I know,
Reach many a time a heaven that's shut to me,
Enter and take their place there sure enough,
Though they come back and cannot tell the world.
My works are nearer heaven, but I sit here.
The sudden blood of these men! at a word—
Praise them, it boils, or blame them, it boils too.
I, painting from myself and to myself,   90
Know what I do, am unmoved by men's blame
Or their praise either. Somebody remarks
Morello's [78] outline there is wrongly traced,
His hue mistaken; what of that? or else,
Rightly traced and well ordered; what of that?
Speak as they please, what does the mountain care?
Ah, but a man's reach should exceed his grasp,

[78] mountain near Florence

Or what's a heaven for? All is silver-gray
Placid and perfect with my art: the worse!
I know both what I want and what might gain, 100
And yet how profitless to know, to sigh
"Had I been two, another and myself,
Our head would have o'erlooked the world!" No doubt.
Yonder's a work now, of that famous youth
The Urbinate [79] who died five years ago.
('Tis copied, George Vasari sent it me.)
Well, I can fancy how he did it all,
Pouring his soul, with kings and popes to see,
Reaching, that heaven might so replenish him,
Above and through his art—for it gives way; 110
That arm is wrongly put—and there again—
A fault to pardon in the drawing's lines,
Its body, so to speak: its soul is right,
He means right—that, a child may understand.
Still, what an arm! and I could alter it:
But all the play, the insight and the stretch—
Out of me, out of me! And wherefore out?
Had you enjoined them on me, given me soul,
We might have risen to Rafael, I and you!
Nay, Love, you did give all I asked, I think— 120
More than I merit, yes, by many times.
But had you—oh, with the same perfect brow,
And perfect eyes, and more than perfect mouth,
And the low voice my soul hears, as a bird
The fowler's pipe, and follows to the snare—
Had you, with these the same, but brought a mind!
Some women do so. Had the mouth there urged
"God and the glory! never care for gain.
The present by the future, what is that?
Live for fame, side by side with Agnolo! [80] 130
Rafael is waiting: up to God, all three!"
I might have done it for you. So it seems:
Perhaps not. All is as God overrules.
Beside, incentives come from the soul's self;
The rest avail not. Why do I need you?
What wife had Rafael, or has Agnolo?
In this world, who can do a thing, will not;
And who would do it, cannot, I perceive:
Yet the will's somewhat—somewhat, too, the power—
And thus we half-men struggle. At the end, 140
God, I conclude, compensates, punishes.

79 Raphael (1483-1520), 80 Michael Angelo (1475-
born at Urbino   1564)

'Tis safer for me, if the award be strict,
That I am something underrated here,
Poor this long while, despised, to speak the truth.
I dared not, do you know, leave home all day,
For fear of chancing on the Paris lords.
The best is when they pass and look aside;
But they speak sometimes; I must bear it all.
Well may they speak! That Francis,[81] that first time,
And that long festal year at Fontainebleau!   150
I surely then could sometimes leave the ground,
Put on the glory, Rafael's daily wear,
In that humane great monarch's golden look,—
One finger in his beard or twisted curl
Over his mouth's good mark that made the smile,
One arm about my shoulder, round my neck,
The jingle of his gold chain in my ear,
I painting proudly with his breath on me,
All his court round him, seeing with his eyes,
Such frank French eyes, and such a fire of souls   160
Profuse, my hand kept plying by those hearts,—
And, best of all, this, this, this face beyond,
This in the background, waiting on my work,
To crown the issue with a last reward!
A good time, was it not, my kingly days?
And had you not grown restless . . . but I know—
'Tis done and past; 'twas right, my instinct said;
Too live the life grew, golden and not gray,
And I'm the weak-eyed bat no sun should tempt
Out of the grange whose four walls make his world.   170
How could it end in any other way?
You called me, and I came home to your heart.
The triumph was—to reach and stay there; since
I reached it ere the triumph, what is lost?
Let my hands frame your face in your hair's gold,
You beautiful Lucrezia that are mine!
"Rafael did this, Andrea painted that;
The Roman's is the better when you pray,
But still the other's Virgin was his wife"—
Men will excuse me. I am glad to judge   180
Both pictures in your presence; clearer grows
My better fortune, I resolve to think.
For, do you know, Lucrezia, as God lives,

---

81 King Francis I of France, Andrea's patron (1494-1547), for whom he worked in
the royal palace at Fontainebleau, near Paris. Vasari relates that Andrea embezzled
money entrusted to him by Francis for the purchase of paintings and other works of
art, building a house with it and indulging himself in various other pleasures.

Said one day Agnolo, his very self,
To Rafael . . . I have known it all these years . . .
(When the young man was flaming out his thoughts
Upon a palace-wall for Rome to see,
Too lifted up in heart because of it)
"Friend, there's a certain sorry little scrub
Goes up and down our Florence, none cares how,   190
Who, were he set to plan and execute
As you are, pricked on by your popes and kings,
Would bring the sweat into that brow of yours!"
To Rafael's!—And indeed the arm is wrong.
I hardly dare . . . yet, only you to see,
Give the chalk here—quick, thus the line should go!
Ay, but the soul! he's Rafael! rub it out!
Still, all I care for, if he spoke the truth,
(What he? why, who but Michel Agnolo?
Do you forget already words like those?)   200
If really there was such a chance, so lost,—
Is, whether you're—not grateful—but more pleased.
Well, let me think so. And you smile indeed!
This hour has been an hour! Another smile?
If you would sit thus by me every night
I should work better, do you comprehend?
I mean that I should earn more, give you more.
See, it is settled dusk now; there's a star;
Morello's gone, the watch-lights show the wall,
The cue-owls [82] speak the name we call them by.   210
Come from the window, love,—come in, at last,
Inside the melancholy little house
We built to be so gay with. God is just.
King Francis may forgive me: oft at nights
When I look up from painting, eyes tired out,
The walls become illumined, brick from brick
Distinct, instead of mortar, fierce bright gold,
That gold of his I did cement them with!
Let us but love each other. Must you go?
That Cousin here again? he waits outside?   220
Must see you—you, and not with me? Those loans?
More gaming debts to pay? you smiled for that?
Well, let smiles buy me! have you more to spend?
While hand and eye and something of a heart
Are left me, work's my ware, and what's it worth?
I'll pay my fancy. Only let me sit
The gray remainder of the evening out,
Idle, you call it, and muse perfectly

82 small owls, whose cry sounds like the Italian *chiu*

How I could paint, were I but back in France,
One picture, just one more—the Virgin's face,   230
Not yours this time! I want you at my side
To hear them— that is, Michel Agnolo—
Judge all I do and tell you of its worth.
Will you? To-morrow, satisfy your friend.
I take the subjects for his corridor,
Finish the portrait out of hand—there, there,
And throw him in another thing or two
If he demurs; the whole should prove enough
To pay for this same Cousin's freak. Beside,
What's better and what's all I care about,   240
Get you the thirteen scudi [83] for the ruff!
Love, does that please you? Ah, but what does he,
The Cousin! what does he to please you more?

I am grown peaceful as old age to-night.
I regret little, I would change still less.
Since there my past life lies, why alter it?
The very wrong to Francis!—it is true
I took his coin, was tempted and complied,
And built this house and sinned, and all is said.
My father and my mother died of want.   250
Well, had I riches of my own? you see
How one gets rich! Let each one bear his lot.
They were born poor, lived poor, and poor they died:
And I have labored somewhat in my time
And not been paid profusely. Some good son
Paint my two hundred pictures—let him try!
No doubt, there's something strikes a balance. Yes,
You loved me quite enough, it seems to-night.
This must suffice me here. What would one have?
In heaven, perhaps, new chances, one more chance—   260
Four great walls in the New Jerusalem,
Meted on each side by the angel's reed,
For Leonard, [84] Rafael, Agnolo and me
To cover—the three first without a wife,
While I have mine! So—still they overcome
Because there's still Lucrezia,—as I choose.

Again the Cousin's whistle! Go, my Love.

83 coins worth about 97   84 Leonardo da Vinci
cents   (1452–1519)

PROSPICE [85]

FEAR death?—to feel the fog in my throat,
    The mist in my face,
When the snows begin, and the blasts denote
    I am nearing the place,
The power of the night, the press of the storm,
    The post of the foe;
Where he stands, the Arch Fear in a visible form
    Yet the strong man must go:
For the journey is done and the summit attained,
    And the barriers fall,   10
Though a battle's to fight ere the guerdon be gained,
    The reward of it all.

I was ever a fighter, so—one fight more,
    The best and the last!
I would hate that death bandaged my eyes, and forebore,
    And bade me creep past.
No! let me taste the whole of it, fare like my peers
    The heroes of old,
Bear the brunt, in a minute pay glad life's arrears
    Of pain, darkness and cold.   20
For sudden the worst turns the best to the brave,
    The black minute's at end,
And the elements' rage, the fiend-voices that rave,
    Shall dwindle, shall blend,
Shall change, shall become first a peace out of pain,
    Then a light, then thy breast,
O thou soul of my soul! I shall clasp thee again,
    And with God be the rest!

ABT VOGLER [86]

(AFTER HE HAS BEEN EXTEMPORIZING UPON THE MUSICAL INSTRUMENT OF HIS INVENTION)

WOULD that the structure brave, the manifold music I build,
    Bidding my organ obey, calling its keys to their work,
Claiming each slave of the sound, at a touch, as when Solomon
    willed [87]

85 "Look forward." Written shortly after Mrs. Browning's death.
86 George Joseph Vogler (1749–1814), Bavarian priest and musician, inventor of a compact organ called the orchestrion, and famed as an improviser.
87 Solomon, according to legend, had such magic powers by virtue of a sealing containing the unspeakable ("ineffable") name of God.

Armies of angels that soar, legions of demons that lurk,
Man, brute, reptile, fly,—alien of end and of aim,
    Adverse, each from the other heaven-high, hell-deep re-
        moved,—
Should rush into sight at once as he named the ineffable
    Name,
    And pile him a palace straight, to pleasure the princess he
        loved!

Would it might tarry like his, the beautiful building of mine,
    This which my keys in a crowd pressed and importuned to
        raise!   10
Ah, one and all, how they helped, would dispart now and now
    combine,
    Zealous to hasten the work, heighten their master his praise!
And one would bury his brow with a blind plunge down to
    hell,
    Burrow awhile and build, broad on the roots of things,
Then up again swim into sight, having based me my palace
    well,
    Founded it, fearless of flame, flat on the nether springs.

And another would mount and march, like the excellent minion
    he was,
    Ay, another and yet another, one crowd but with many a
        crest,
Raising my rampired walls of gold as transparent as glass,
    Eager to do and die, yield each his place to the rest: 20
For higher still and higher (as a runner tips with fire,
    When a great illumination surprises a festal night—
Outlined round and round Rome's dome [88] from space to spire)
    Up, the pinnacled glory reached, and the pride of my soul
        was in sight.

In sight? Not half! for it seemed, it was certain, to match
    man's birth,
    Nature in turn conceived, obeying an impulse as I;
And the emulous heaven yearned down, made effort to reach
    the earth,
    As the earth had done her best, in my passion, to scale the
        sky:
Novel splendors burst forth, grew familiar and dwelt with
    mine,
    Not a point nor peak but found and fixed its wandering
        star;   30

88 St. Peter's

Meteor-moons, balls of blaze: and they did not pale nor pine,
  For earth had attained to heaven, there was no more near
    nor far.

Nay more; for there wanted not who walked in the glare and
    glow,
  Presences plain in the place; or, fresh from the Protoplast,[89]
Furnished for ages to come, when a kindlier wind should blow,
  Lured now to begin and live, in a house to their liking at
    last;
Or else the wonderful Dead who have passed through the body
    and gone,
  But were back once more to breathe in an old world worth
    their new:
What never had been, was now; what was, as it shall be
    anon;
And what is,—shall I say, matched both? for I was made
  perfect too.   40

All through my keys that gave their sounds to a wish of my
    soul,
  All through my soul that praised as its wish flowed visibly
    forth,
All through music and me! For think, had I painted the
    whole,
  Why, there it had stood, to see, nor the process so wonder-
    worth:
Had I written the same, made verse—still, effect proceeds
    from cause,
  Ye know why the forms are fair, ye hear how the tale is
    told;
It is all triumphant art, but art in obedience to laws,
  Painter and poet are proud in the artist-list enrolled:—

But here is the finger of God, a flash of the will that can,
  Existent behind all laws, that made them and, lo, they
    are!   50
And I know not if, save in this, such gift be allowed to man,
  That out of three sounds he frame, not a fourth sound, but a
    star.
Consider it well: each tone of our scale in itself is naught:
  It is everywhere in the world—loud, soft, and all is said:
Give it to me to use! I mix it with two in my thought:
  And there! Ye have heard and seen: consider and bow the
    head!

[89] the thing first formed, ready for reproduction or copying

Well, it is gone at last, the palace of music I reared;
  Gone! and the good tears start, the praises that come too
    slow;
For one is assured at first, one scarce can say that he feared,
  That he even gave it a thought, the gone thing was to go. 60
Never to be again! But many more of the kind
  As good, nay, better perchance: is this your comfort to me?
To me, who must be saved because I cling with my mind
  To the same, same self, same love, same God: ay, what was,
    shall be.

Therefore to whom turn I but to thee, the ineffable Name?
  Builder and maker, thou, of houses not made with hands!
What, have fear of change from thee who art ever the same?
  Doubt that thy power can fill the heart that thy power ex-
    pands?
There shall never be one lost good! What was, shall live as
    before;
The evil is null, is naught, is silence implying sound; 70
What was good shall be good, with, for evil, so much good
    more;
  On the earth the broken arcs; in the heaven a perfect round.

All we have willed or hoped or dreamed of good shall exist;
  Not its semblance, but itself; no beauty, nor good, nor
    power
Whose voice has gone forth, but each survives for the melodist
  When eternity affirms the conception of an hour.
The high that proved too high, the heroic for earth too hard,
  The passion that left the ground to lose itself in the sky,
Are music sent up to God by the lover and the bard;
  Enough that he heard it once: we shall hear it by and by. 80

And what is our failure here but a triumph's evidence
  For the fullness of the days? Have we withered or agonized?
Why else was the pause prolonged but that singing might issue
    thence?
  Why rushed the discords in, but that harmony should be
    prized?
Sorrow is hard to bear, and doubt is slow to clear,
  Each sufferer says his say, his scheme of the weal and woe:
But God has a few of us whom he whispers in the ear;
  The rest may reason and welcome: 'tis we musicians know.

Well, it is earth with me; silence resumes her reign:
  I will be patient and proud, and soberly acquiesce. 90

Give me the keys. I feel for the common chord again,
  Sliding by semitones till I sink to the minor,—yes,
And I blunt it into a ninth, and I stand on alien ground,
  Surveying awhile the heights I rolled from into the deep;
Which, hark, I have dared and done, for my resting-place is
     found,
  The C Major of this life: so, now I will try to sleep.

RABBI BEN EZRA [90]

Grow old along with me!
The best is yet to be,
The last of life, for which the first was made:
Our times are in his hand
Who saith, "A whole I planned,
Youth shows but half; trust God: see all, nor be afraid!"

Not that, amassing flowers,
Youth sighed, "Which rose make ours,
Which lily leave and then as best recall?"
Not that, admiring stars,
It yearned, "Nor Jove, nor Mars;   10
Mine be some figured flame which blends, transcends them all!"

Not for such hopes and fears
Annulling youth's brief years,
Do I remonstrate: folly wide the mark!
Rather I prize the doubt
Low kinds exist without,
Finished and finite clods, untroubled by a spark.

Poor vaunt of life indeed,
Were man but formed to feed   20
On joy, to solely seek and find and feast:
Such feasting ended, then
As sure an end to men;
Irks care the crop full bird? Frets doubt the maw-crammed
     beast?

Rejoice we are allied
To that which doth provide
And not partake, effect and not receive!
A spark disturbs our clod;

90 Abenezra, or Ibn Ezra (1092?-1167), great Jewish scholar, philosopher, physician, and poet, whose works are here freely adapted by Browning to express his own philosophy.

Nearer we hold of God
Who gives, than of his tribes that take, I must believe.   30

Then, welcome each rebuff
That turns earth's smoothness rough,
Each sting that bids nor sit nor stand but go!
Be our joys three-parts pain!
Strive, and hold cheap the strain;
Learn, nor account the pang; dare, never grudge the throe!

For thence,—a paradox
Which comforts while it mocks,—
Shall life succeed in that it seems to fail:
What I aspired to be,   40
And was not, comforts me:
A brute I might have been, but would not sink i' the scale.

What is he but a brute
Whose flesh has soul to suit,
Whose spirit works lest arms and legs want play?
To man, propose this test—
Thy body at its best,
How far can that project thy soul on its lone way?

Yet gifts should prove their use:
I own the Past profuse   50
Of power each side, perfection every turn:
Eyes, ears took in their dole,
Brain treasured up the whole;
Should not the heart beat once "How good to live and learn"?

Not once beat "Praise be thine!
I see the whole design,
I, who saw power, see now Love perfect too:
Perfect I call thy plan:
Thanks that I was a man!
Maker, remake, complete,—I trust what thou shalt do!"   60

For pleasant is this flesh;
Our soul, in its rose-mesh
Pulled ever to the earth, still yearns for rest:
Would we some prize might hold
To match those manifold
Possessions of the brute,—gain most, as we did best!

Let us not always say,
"Spite of this flesh to-day

I strove, made head, gained ground upon the whole!"
As the bird wings and sings,   70
Let us cry, "All good things
Are ours, nor soul helps flesh more, now, than flesh helps
      soul!"

Therefore I summon age
To grant youth's heritage,
Life's struggle having so far reached its term:
Thence shall I pass, approved
A man, for aye removed
From the developed brute; a God though in the germ.

And I shall thereupon
Take rest, ere I be gone   80
Once more on my adventure brave and new:
Fearless and unperplexed,
When I wage battle next,
What weapons to select, what armor to indue.⁹¹

Youth ended, I shall try
My gain or loss thereby;
Leave the fire ashes, what survives is gold:
And I shall weigh the same,
Give life its praise or blame:
Young, all lay in dispute; I shall know, being old.   90

For note, when evening shuts,
A certain moment cuts
The deed off, calls the glory from the gray:
A whisper from the west
Shoots—"Add this to the rest,
Take it and try its worth: here dies another day."

So, still within this life,
Though lifted o'er its strife,
Let me discern, compare, pronounce at last,
"This rage was right i' the main,   100
That acquiescence vain:
The Future I may face now I have proved the Past."

For more is not reserved
To man, with soul just nerved
To act to-morrow what he learns to-day:
Here, work enough to watch

91 put on

The Master work, and catch
Hints of the proper craft, tricks of the tool's true play.

As it was better, youth
Should strive, through acts uncouth,
Toward making, than repose on aught found made: 110
So, better, age, exempt
From strife, should know, than tempt
Further. Thou waitedst age: wait death nor be afraid!

Enough now, if the Right
And Good and Infinite
Be named here, as thou callest thy hand thine own,
With knowledge absolute,
Subject to no dispute
From fools that crowded youth, nor let thee feel alone.   120

Be there, for once and all,
Severed great minds from small,
Announced to each his station in the Past!
Was I, the world arraigned,
Were they, my soul disdained,
Right? Let age speak the truth and give us peace at last!

Now, who shall arbitrate?
Ten men love what I hate,
Shun what I follow, slight what I receive;
Ten, who in ears and eyes   130
Match me: we all surmise,
They this thing, and I that: whom shall my soul believe?

Not on the vulgar mass
Called "work," must sentence pass,
Things done, that took the eye and had the price;
O'er which, from level stand,
The low world laid its hand,
Found straightway to its mind, could value in a trice:

But all, the world's coarse thumb
And finger failed to plumb,   140
So passed in making up the main account;
All instincts immature,
All purposes unsure,
That weighed not as his work, yet swelled the man's amount:

Thoughts hardly to be packed
Into a narrow act,

Fancies that broke through language and escaped;
All I could never be,
All, men ignored in me,
This, I was worth to God, whose wheel the pitcher shaped. 150

Ay, note that Potter's wheel,[92]
That metaphor! and feel
Why time spins fast, why passive lies our clay,—
Thou, to whom fools propound,
When the wine makes its round,
"Since life fleets, all is change; the Past gone, seize to-day!"

Fool! All that is, at all,
Lasts ever, past recall;
Earth changes, but thy soul and God stand sure:
What entered into thee,   160
That was, is, and shall be:
Time's wheel runs back or stops: Potter and clay endure.

He fixed thee 'mid this dance
Of plastic circumstance,
This Present, thou, forsooth, would fain arrest:
Machinery just meant
To give thy soul its bent,
Try thee and turn thee forth, sufficiently impressed.

What though the earlier grooves,
Which ran the laughing loves   170
Around thy base, no longer pause and press:
What though, about thy rim,
Skull-things in order grim
Grow out, in graver mood, obey the sterner stress?

Look not thou down but up!
To uses of a cup,
The festal board, lamp's flash and trumpet's peal,
The new wine's foaming flow,
The Master's lips aglow!
Thou, heaven's consummate cup, what needst thou with earth's
    wheel?   180

But I need, now as then,
Thee, God, who moldest men;
And since, not even while the whirl was worst,

92 See Isaiah, lxiv, 8; Jeremiah, xviii, 2-6; and Fitzgerald's *Rubaiyat of Omar Khayyam.*

Did I—to the wheel of life
With shapes and colors rife,
Bound dizzily—mistake my end, to slake thy thirst:

So, take and use thy work:
Amend what flaws may lurk,
What strain o' the stuff, what warpings past the aim!
My times be in thy hand!
Perfect the cup as planned!   190
Let age approve of youth, and death complete the same!

CALIBAN UPON SETEBOS

OR, NATURAL THEOLOGY IN THE ISLAND [93]

"Thou thoughtest that I was altogether such an one as thyself."

['WILL sprawl, now that the heat of day is best,
Flat on his belly in the pit's much mire,
With elbows wide, fists clenched to prop his chin.
And, while he kicks both feet in the cool slush,
And feels about his spine small eft-things course,
Run in and out each arm, and make him laugh:
And while above his head a pompion-plant,
Coating the cave-top as a brow its eye,
Creeps down to touch and tickle hair and beard,
And now a flower drops with a bee inside,   10
And now a fruit to snap at, catch and crunch,—
He looks out o'er yon sea which sunbeams cross
And recross till they weave a spider-web
(Meshes of fire, some great fish breaks at times),
And talks to his own self, howe'er he please,
Touching that other, whom his dam called God.
Because to talk about Him, vexes—ha,
Could He but know! and time to vex is now,
When talk is safer than in winter-time.
Moreover Prosper and Miranda sleep   20
In confidence he drudges at their task,
And it is good to cheat the pair, and gibe,
Letting the rank tongue blossom into speech.]

---

93 In Shakespeare's *Tempest* Browning found the characters of Caliban, "a savage and deformed slave," his master Prospero, the latter's daughter Miranda, Ariel, "an airy spirit," and the reference to Setebos, the god of Caliban's mother (dam). The quotation (from Psalm 1. 21) is the key to the nature of Caliban's reflections on deity. He speaks of himself in the third person, with omission of the pronoun.

Setebos, Setebos, and Setebos!
'Thinketh, He dwelleth i' the cold o' the moon.

'Thinketh He made it, with the sun to match,
But not the stars; the stars came otherwise;
Only made clouds, winds, meteors, such as that:
Also this isle, what lives and grows thereon,
And snaky sea which rounds and ends the same.   30

'Thinketh, it came of being ill at ease:
He hated that He cannot change His cold,
Nor cure its ache. 'Hath spied an icy fish
That longed to 'scape the rock-stream where she lived,
And thaw herself within the lukewarm brine
O' the lazy sea her stream thrusts far amid,
A crystal spike 'twixt two warm walls of wave;
Only, she ever sickened, found repulse
At the other kind of water, not her life,
(Green-dense and dim-delicious, bred o' the sun),   40
Flounced back from bliss she was not born to breathe,
And in her old bounds buried her despair,
Hating and loving warmth alike: so He.

'Thinketh, He made thereat the sun, this isle,
Trees and the fowls here, beast and creeping thing.
Yon otter, sleek-wet, black, lithe as a leech;
Yon auk, one fire-eye in a ball of foam,
That floats and feeds; a certain badger brown
He hath watched hunt with that slant white-wedge eye
By moonlight; and the pie [94] with the long tongue   50
That pricks deep into oakwarts for a worm,
And says a plain word when she finds her prize,
But will not eat the ants; the ants themselves
That build a wall of seeds and settled stalks
About their hole—He made all these and more,
Made all we see, and us, in spite: how else?
He could not, Himself, make a second self
To be His mate; as well have made Himself:
He would not make what He mislikes or slights,
An eyesore to Him, or not worth His pains: 60
But did, in envy, listlessness or sport,
Make what Himself would fain, in a manner, be—
Weaker in most points, stronger in a few,
Worthy, and yet mere playthings all the while,

[94] magpie

Things He admires and mocks too,—that is it.
Because, so brave, so better though they be,
It nothing skills if He begin to plague.
Look now, I melt a gourd-fruit into mash,
Add honeycomb and pods, I have perceived,
Which bite like finches when they bill and kiss,— 70
Then, when froth rises bladdery, drink up all,
Quick, quick, till maggots scamper through my brain;
Last, throw me on my back i' the seeded thyme,
And wanton, wishing I were born a bird.
Put case, unable to be what I wish,
I yet could make a live bird out of clay:
Would not I take clay, pinch my Caliban
Able to fly?—for, there, see, he hath wings,
And great comb like the hoopoe's to admire,
And there, a sting to do his foes offense, 80
There, and I will that he begin to live,
Fly to yon rock-top, nip me off the horns
Of grigs [95] high up that make the merry din,
Saucy through their veined wings, and mind me not.
In which feat, if his leg snapped, brittle clay,
And he lay stupid-like,—why, I should laugh;
And if he, spying me, should fall to weep,
Beseech me to be good, repair his wrong,
Bid his poor leg smart less or grow again,—
Well, as the chance were, this might take or else 90
Not take my fancy: I might hear his cry,
And give the manikin three sound legs for one,
Or pluck the other off, leave him like an egg,
And lessoned he was mine and merely clay.
Were this no pleasure, lying in the thyme,
Drinking the mash, with brain become alive,
Making and marring clay at will? So He.

'Thinketh, such shows nor right nor wrong in Him,
Nor kind, nor cruel: He is strong and Lord.
'Am strong myself compared to yonder crabs 100
That march now from the mountain to the sea;
'Let twenty pass, and stone the twenty-first,
Loving not, hating not, just choosing so.
'Say, the first straggler that boasts purple spots
Shall join the file, one pincer twisted off;
'Say, this bruised fellow shall receive a worm,
And two worms he whose nippers end in red;
As it likes me each time, I do: so He.

95 crickets or grasshoppers

Well then, 'supposeth He is good i' the main,
Placable if His mind and ways were guessed,   110
But rougher than His handiwork, be sure!
Oh, He hath made things worthier than Himself,
And envieth that, so helped, such things do more
Than He who made them! What consoles but this?
That they, unless through Him, do naught at all,
And must submit: what other use in things?
'Hath cut a pipe of pithless elder-joint
That, blown through, gives exact the scream o' the jay
When from her wing you twitch the feathers blue:
Sound this, and little birds that hate the jay   120
Flock within stone's throw, glad their foe is hurt:
Put case such pipe could prattle and boast forsooth,
"I catch the birds, I am the crafty thing,
I make the cry my maker cannot make
With his great round mouth; he must blow through mine!"
Would not I smash it with my foot? So He.

But wherefore rough, why cold and ill at ease?
Aha, that is a question! Ask, for that,
What knows,—the something over Setebos
That made Him, or He, may be, found and fought,   130
Worsted, drove off and did to nothing, perchance.
There may be something quiet o'er His head,
Out of His reach, that feels nor joy nor grief,
Since both derive from weakness in some way.
I joy because the quails come; would not joy
Could I bring quails here when I have a mind:
This Quiet, all it hath a mind to, doth.
'Esteemeth stars the outposts of its couch,
But never spends much thought nor care that way.
It may look up, work up,—the worse for those   140
It works on! 'Careth but for Setebos
The many-handed as a cuttle-fish,
Who, making Himself feared through what He does,
Looks up, first, and perceives he cannot soar
To what is quiet and hath happy life;
Next looks down here, and out of very spite
Makes this a bauble-world to ape yon real,
These good things to match those as hips [96] do grapes.
'Tis solace making baubles, ay, and sport.
Himself peeped late, eyed Prosper at his books   150
Careless and lofty, lord now of the isle:
Vexed, 'stitched a book of broad leaves, arrow-shaped,

96 ripened fruit of the rosebush

Wrote thereon, he knows what, prodigious words;
Has peeled a wand and called it by a name;
Weareth at whiles for an enchanter's robe
The eyed skin of a supple oncelot,[97]
And hath an ounce [97] sleeker than youngling mole,
A four-legged serpent he makes cower and couch,
Now snarl, now hold its breath and mind his eye,
And saith she is Miranda and my wife: 160
'Keeps for his Ariel a tall pouch-bill crane
He bids go wade for fish and straight disgorge;
Also a sea-beast, lumpish, which he snared,
Blinded the eyes of, and brought somewhat tame,
And split its toe-webs, and now pens the drudge
In a hole o' the rock and calls him Caliban;
A bitter heart that bides its time and bites.
'Plays thus at being Prosper in a way,
Taketh his mirth with make-believes: so He.

His dam held that the Quiet made all things   170
Which Setebos vexed only; 'holds not so.
Who made them weak, meant weakness He might vex.
Had He meant other, while His hand was in,
Why not make horny eyes no thorn could prick,
Or plate my scalp with bone against the snow,
Or overscale my flesh 'neath joint and joint,
Like an orc's [98] armor? Ay,—so spoil His sport!
He is the One now: only He doth all.

'Saith, He may like, perchance, what profits Him.
Ay, himself loves what does him good; but why?   180
'Gets good no otherwise. This blinded beast
Loves whoso places flesh-meat on his nose,
But, had he eyes, would want no help, but hate
Or love, just as it liked him: He hath eyes.
Also it pleaseth Setebos to work,
Use all His hands, and exercise much craft,
By no means for the love of what is worked.
'Tasteth, himself, no finer good i' the world
When all goes right, in this safe summer-time,
And he wants little, hungers, aches not much,   190
Than trying what to do with wit and strength.
'Falls to make something: 'piled yon pile of turfs,
And squared and stuck there squares of soft white chalk,
And, with a fish-tooth, scratched a moon on each,
And set up endwise certain spikes of tree,

97 kind of small leopard   98 a sea monster

And crowned the whole with a sloth's [99] skull a-top,
Found dead i' the woods, too hard for one to kill.
No use at all i' the work, for work's sole sake;
'Shall some day knock it down again: so He.

'Saith He is terrible: watch His feats in proof!   200
One hurricane will spoil six good months' hope.
He hath a spite against me, that I know,
Just as He favors Prosper, who knows why?
So it is, all the same, as well I find.
'Wove wattles [1] half the winter, fenced them firm
With stone and stake to stop she-tortoises
Crawling to lay their eggs here: well, one wave,
Feeling the foot of Him upon its neck,
Gaped as a snake does, lolled out its large tongue,
And licked the whole labor flat: so much for spite.   210

'Saw a ball flame down late (yonder it lies)
Where, half an hour before, I slept i' the shade:
Often they scatter sparkles: there is force!
'Dug up a newt He may have envied once
And turned to stone, shut up inside a stone.
Please Him and hinder this?—What Prosper does?
Aha, if He would tell me how! Not He!
There is the sport: discover how or die!
All need not die, for of the things o' the isle
Some flee afar, some dive, some run up trees;   220
Those at His mercy,—why, they please Him most
When . . . when . . . well, never try the same way twice!
Repeat what act has pleased, He may grow wroth.
You must not know His ways, and play Him off,
Sure of the issue. 'Doth the like himself:
'Spareth a squirrel that it nothing fears
But steals the nut from underneath my thumb,
And when I threat, bites stoutly in defense:
'Spareth an urchin that contrariwise,
Curls up into a ball, pretending death   230
For fright at my approach: the two ways please.
But that would move my choler more than this,
That either creature counted on its life
To-morrow and next day and all days to come,
Saying, forsooth, in the inmost of its heart,
"Because he did so yesterday with me,
And otherwise with such another brute,
So must he do henceforth and always."—Ay?

99 an arboreal animal, similar to an anteater.   1 twigs

Would teach the reasoning couple what "must" means!
'Doth as he likes, or wherefore Lord? So He.   240

'Conceiveth all things will continue thus,
And we shall have to live in fear of Him
So long as He lives, keeps His strength: no change,
If He have done His best, make no new world
To please Him more, so leave off watching this,—
If He surprise not even the Quiet's self
Some strange day,—or, suppose, grow into it
As grubs grow butterflies: else, here we are,
And there is He, and nowhere help at all.

'Believeth with the life, the pain shall stop.   250
His dam held different, that after death
He both plagued enemies and feasted friends:
Idly! He doth His worst in this our life,
Giving just respite lest we die through pain,
Saving last pain for worst,—with which, an end.
Meanwhile, the best way to escape His ire
Is, not to seem too happy. 'Sees, himself,
Yonder two flies, with purple films and pink,
Bask on the pompion-bell above: kills both.
'Sees two black painful beetles roll their ball   260
On head and tail as if to save their lives:
Moves them the stick away they strive to clear.
Even so, 'would have Him misconceive, suppose
This Caliban strives hard and ails no less,
And always, above all else, envies Him;
Wherefore he mainly dances on dark nights,
Moans in the sun, gets under holes to laugh,
And never speaks his mind save housed as now:
Outside, 'groans, curses. If He caught me here,
O'erheard this speech, and asked "What chucklest at?"   270
'Would, to appease Him, cut a finger off,
Or of my three kid yearlings burn the best,
Or let the toothsome apples rot on tree,
Or push my tame beast for the orc to taste:
While myself lit a fire, and made a song
And sung it, *"What I hate, be consecrate*
To celebrate Thee and Thy state, no mate
For Thee; what see for envy in poor me?"
Hoping the while, since evils sometimes mend,
Warts rub away and sores are cured with slime,   280
That some strange day, will either the Quiet catch

And conquer Setebos, or likelier He
Decrepit may doze, doze, as good as die.

———————

[What, what? A curtain o'er the world at once!
Crickets stop hissing; not a bird—or, yes,
There scuds His raven that has told Him all!
It was fool's play, this prattling! Ha! The wind
Shoulders the pillard dust, death's house o' the move,
And fast invading fires begin! White blaze—
A tree's head snaps—and there, there, there, there, there,   290
His thunder follows! Fool to gibe at Him!
Lo! 'Lieth flat and loveth Setebos!
'Maketh his teeth meet through his upper lip,
Will let those quails fly, will not eat this month
One little mess of whelks, so he may 'scape!]

THE RING AND THE BOOK

This, the longest sustained work of Browning, was published in 1868 and
1869. It was based upon the account of a Roman murder trial of 1698, which
Browning found. in an "old yellow book," "part print, part manuscript,"
picked up by him in a second-hand bookshop in Florence in 1860. The story
emerging from the varied material in the Old Yellow Book—pleadings,
counter-pleadings, depositions, letters, judgment, and other documents—may
be summarized as follows:

There lived at Rome toward the end of the seventeenth century an elderly
couple, Pietro and Violante Comparini. Violante, in order to obtain the use of
funds held up for an heir, pretended she had given birth to a daughter (the
Pompilia of the poem, born in 1680), and in 1693, attracted by the rank of
Count Guido Franceschini, an impoverished nobleman, married the girl to him.
Count Guido took his wife with him to his home in Arezzo, where she suffered
greatly from his alleged cruelties. Finally she attracted the sympathies of a
young priest, Canon Caponsacchi, and fled with him towards Rome. Count
Guido pursued the pair, caught up with them at an inn outside the city, and
had them prosecuted for adultery and other charges (1697). The court, in
pronouncing judgment, imposed very light sentences, Pompilia being sent to
a nunnery and afterwards being allowed to go to the Comparinis' home, where
she gave birth to a son on December 18, 1697. Meanwhile Count Guido started
for Rome with four retainers, broke into the Comparini house on January 2,
1698, killed the old couple, and left Pompilia for dead with twenty-two dagger-
thrusts in her body. She survived, however, to tell her story, and died on January 6. The murderers, thus made known, were arrested on their way to Arezzo,
brought back to Rome, tried for murder, and after much wrangling over the
questions at issue, condemned. The Pope, on appeal, confirmed the judgment
of the court, and Count Guido and his four ruffians were executed on February 22, 1698.

Browning, between 1864 and 1868, worked this material up into a vast poem
in blank verse of twelve books. The first and last are introduction and conclusion, but the central ten tell the above essential story ten times, from ten

different points of view—those of the chief participants in the tragedy, of partisans of each side, of the contending lawyers, and of the Pope in judgment. In Book VII, the dying Pompilia narrates the story of her life. This monologue is usually esteemed the finest, but those of Caponsacchi and of the Pope are also splendid, while Count Guido, in two monologues, presents his own view of the tragedy with power. The arguments of the two lawyers, full of dialectics, legal Latin, and technical points of law, reveal another side of Browning. The title of the poem is based upon an analogy between the art of the Florentine jeweler in making a beautiful ring (worn by Mrs. Browning), and the creative art of the poet. The gold, to be made workable, must be tempered with alloy, and likewise, the crude fact of the story with the imagination of the poet. The ring made, a spurt of acid removes the alloy, and only the pure gold remains; so in Browning's poem the poet's contribution to the story seems to disappear, and the truth remains, truer than in the source from which he drew.

In magnitude of plan, in creative power, and in sympathetic understanding of human nature, *The Ring and the Book* is the greatest of Browning's works, and nowhere did he write more splendid poetry than in the finer monologues (those of the chief actors). The monologue of Pompilia (here condensed) presents Browning's powers at their highest. The controversial monologues will be found less attractive. They are an intellectual, not a poetic triumph. They show that other side of Browning, inseparable from his genius—the delight in mental adroitness, in verbal thrust and parrying, and in the revelation of the characters of insincere and unscrupulous men. The same aspect of Browning may be seen in *Mr. Sludge, the Medium,* and in *Bishop Blougram's Apology.*

Book VII

POMPILIA

I AM just seventeen years and five months old,
And, if I lived one day more, three full weeks;
'Tis writ so in the church's register,
Lorenzo in Lucina, all my names
At length, so many names for one poor child,
—Francesca Camilla Vittoria Angela
Pompilia Comparini,—laughable!
Also 'tis writ that I was married there
Four years ago: and they will add, I hope,
When they insert my death, a word or two,—   10
Omitting all about the mode of death,—
This, in its place, this which one cares to know,
That I had been a mother of a son
Exactly two weeks. It will be through grace
O' the Curate, not through any claim I have;
Because the boy was born at, so baptized
Close to, the Villa, in the proper church:
A pretty church, I say no word against,
Yet stranger-like,—while this Lorenzo seems
My own particular place, I always say.   20

I used to wonder, when I stood scarce high
As the bed here, what the marble lion meant,
With half his body rushing from the wall,
Eating the figure of a prostrate man—
(To the right, it is, of entry by the door)—
An ominous sign to one baptized like me,
Married, and to be buried there, I hope.
And they should add, to have my life complete,
He is a boy and Gaetan by name—
Gaetano, for a reason,—if the friar   30
Don Celestine will ask this grace for me
Of Curate Ottoboni: he it was
Baptized me: he remembers my whole life
As I do his gray hair.

                         All these few things
I know are true,—will you remember them?
Because time flies. The surgeon cared for me,
To count my wounds,—twenty-two dagger-wounds,
Five deadly, but I do not suffer much—
Or too much pain,—and am to die to-night.
Oh how good God is that my babe was born,   40
—Better than born, baptized and hid away
Before this happened, safe from being hurt!
That had been sin God could not well forgive:
He was too young to smile and save himself.
When they took, two days after he was born,
My babe away from me to be baptized
And hidden awhile, for fear his foe should find—
The country-woman, used to nursing babes,
Said, "Why take on so? where is the great loss?
These next three weeks he will but sleep and feed,   50
Only begin to smile at the month's end;
He would not know you, if you kept him here,
Sooner than that; so, spend three merry weeks
Snug in the Villa, getting strong and stout,
And then I bring him back to be your own,
And both of you may steal to—we know where!"
The month—there wants of it two weeks this day!
Still, I half fancied when I heard the knock
At the Villa in the dusk, it might prove she—
Come to say, "Since he smiles before the time,   60
Why should I cheat you out of one good hour?
Back I have brought him; speak to him and judge!"
Now I shall never see him; what is worse,
When he grows up and gets to be my age,

He will seem hardly more than a great boy;
And if he asks, "What was my mother like?"
People may answer, "Like girls of seventeen"—
And how can he but think of this and that,
Lucias, Marias, Sofias, who titter or blush
When he regards them as such boys may do?   70
Therefore I wish some one will please to say
I looked already old though I was young;
Do I not . . . say, if you are by to speak . . .
Look nearer twenty? No more like, at least,
Girls who look arch or redden when boys laugh,
Than the poor Virgin that I used to know
At our street-corner in a lonely niche,—
The babe, that sat upon her knees, broke off,—
Thin white glazed clay, you pitied her the more:
She, not the gay ones, always got my rose.   80

How happy those are who know how to write!
Such could write what their son should read in time,
Had they a whole day to live out like me.
Also my name is not a common name,
"Pompilia," and may help to keep apart
A little the thing I am from what girls are.
But then how far away, how hard to find
Will anything about me have become,
Even if the boy bethink himself and ask!
No father that he ever knew at all,   90
Nor ever had—no, never had, I say!
That is the truth,—nor any mother left,
Out of the little two weeks that she lived,
Fit for such memory as might assist:
As good too as no family, no name,
Not even poor old Pietro's name, nor hers,
Poor kind unwise Violante, since it seems
They must not be my parents any more.
That is why something put it in my head
To call the boy "Gaetano"—no old name   100
For sorrow's sake; I looked up to the sky
And took a new saint to begin anew.
One who has only been made saint—how long?
Twenty-five years: [2] so, carefuller, perhaps,
To guard a namesake than those old saints grow,
Tired out by this time,—see my own five saints!

2 Gaetano, Archbishop of Teate (1480–1547), canonized 1671.

On second thoughts, I hope he will regard
The history of me as what some one dreamed,
And get to disbelieve it at the last:
Since to myself it dwindles fast to that,   110
Sheer dreaming and impossibility,—
Just in four days too! All the seventeen years,
Not once did a suspicion visit me
How very different a lot is mine
From any other woman's in the world.
The reason must be, 'twas by step and step
It got to grow so terrible and strange.
These strange woes stole on tiptoe, as it were,
Into my neighborhood and privacy,
Sat down where I sat, laid them where I lay;   120
And I was found familiarized with fear,
When friends broke in, held up a torch and cried,
"Why, you Pompilia in the cavern thus,
How comes that arm of yours about a wolf?
And the soft length,—lies in and out your feet
And laps you round the knee,—a snake it is!"
And so on.

                    Well, and they are right enough,
By the torch they hold up now: for first, observe,
I never had a father,—no, nor yet
A mother: my own boy can say at least,   130
"I had a mother whom I kept two weeks!"
Not I, who little used to doubt . . . I doubt
Good Pietro, kind Violante, gave me birth?
They loved me always as I love my babe
(—Nearly so, that is—quite so could not be—)
Did for me all I meant to do for him,
Till one surprising day, three years ago,
They both declared, at Rome, before some judge
In some court where the people flocked to hear,
That really I had never been their child,   140
Was a mere castaway, the careless crime
Of an unknown man, the crime and care too much
Of a woman known too well,—little to these,
Therefore, of whom I was the flesh and blood;
What then to Pietro and Violante, both
No more my relatives than you or you?
Nothing to them! You know what they declared.

So with my husband,—just such a surprise,
Such a mistake, in that relationship!

Every one says that husbands love their wives,   150
Guard them and guide them, give them happiness;
'Tis duty, law, pleasure, religion: well,
You see how much of this comes true in mine!
People indeed would fain have somehow proved
He was no husband:[3] but he did not hear,
Or would not wait, and so has killed us all.
Then there is . . . only let me name one more!
There is the friend,—men will not ask about,
But tell untruths of, and give nicknames to,
And think my lover, most surprise of all!   160
Do only hear, it is the priest they mean,
Giuseppe Caponsacchi: a priest—love,
And love me! Well, yet people think he did.
I am married, he has taken priestly vows,
They know that, and yet go on, say, the same,
"Yes, how he loves you!" "That was love"—they say,
When anything is answered that they ask:
Or else "No wonder you love him"—they say.
Then they shake heads, pity much, scarcely blame—
As if we neither of us lacked excuse,   170
And anyhow are punished to the full,
And downright love atones for everything!
Nay, I heard read out in the public court
Before the judge, in presence of my friends,
Letters 'twas said the priest had sent to me,
And other letters sent him by myself,
We being lovers!

              Listen what this is like!
When I was a mere child, my mother . . . that's
Violante, you must let me call her so,
Nor waste time, trying to unlearn the word . . .   180
She brought a neighbor's child of my own age
To play with me of rainy afternoons:
And, since there hung a tapestry on the wall,
We two agreed to find each other out
Among the figures. "Tisbe, that is you,
With half-moon on your hair-knot, spear in hand,[4]
Flying, but no wings, only the great scarf
Blown to a bluish rainbow at your back:
Call off your hound and leave the stag alone!"
"—And there are you, Pompilia, such green leaves   190
Flourishing out of your five finger-ends,
And all the rest of you so brown and rough:

---

3 A suit for divorce was pending.   4 Diana

Why is it you are turned a sort of tree?" [5]
You know the figures never were ourselves
Though we nicknamed them so. Thus, all my life,—
As well what was, as what, like this, was not,—
Looks old, fantastic and impossible:
I touch a fairy thing that fades and fades.
—Even to my babe! I thought, when he was born,
Something began for once that would not end,   200
Nor change into a laugh at me, but stay
Forevermore, eternally quite mine.
Well, so he is,—but yet they bore him off,
The third day, lest my husband should lay traps
And catch him, and by means of him catch me.
Since they have saved him so, it was well done:
Yet thence comes such confusion of what was
With what will be,—that late seems long ago,
And, what years should bring round, already come,
Till even he withdraws into a dream   210
As the rest do: I fancy him grown great,
Strong, stern, a tall young man who tutors me,
Frowns with the others, "Poor imprudent child!
Why did you venture out of the safe street?
Why go so far from help to that lone house?
Why open at the whisper and the knock?"

Six days ago when it was New Year's day,
We bent above the fire and talked of him,
What he should do when he was grown and great,
Violante, Pietro, each had given the arm   220
I leant on, to walk by, from couch to chair
And fireside,—laughed, as I lay safe at last,
"Pompilia's march from bed to board is made,
Pompilia back again and with a babe,
Shall one day lend his arm and help her walk!"
Then we all wished each other more New Years.
Pietro began to scheme—"Our cause is gained;
The law is stronger than a wicked man:
Let him henceforth go his way, leave us ours!
We will avoid the city, tempt no more   230
The greedy ones by feasting and parade,—
Live at the other villa, we know where,
Still farther off, and we can watch the babe
Grow fast in the good air; and wood is cheap
And wine sincere outside the city gate.
I still have two or three old friends will grope

5 Daphne

Their way along the mere half-mile of road,
With staff and lantern on a moonless night
When one needs talk: they'll find me, never fear,
And I'll find them a flask of the old sort yet!"   240
Violante said, "You chatter like a crow:
Pompilia tires o' the tattle, and shall to bed:
Do not too much the first day,—somewhat more
To-morrow, and, the next, begin the cape
And hood and coat! I have spun wool enough."
Oh what a happy friendly eve was that!

And, next day, about noon, out Pietro went—
He was so happy and would talk so much,
Until Violante pushed and laughed him forth
Sight-seeing in the cold,—"So much to see   250
I' the churches! Swathe your throat three times!" she cried,
"And, above all, beware the slippery ways,
And bring us all the news by supper-time!"
He came back late, laid by cloak, staff and hat,
Powdered so thick with snow it made us laugh,
Rolled a great log upon the ash o' the hearth,
And bade Violante treat us to a flask,
Because he had obeyed her faithfully,
Gone sight-see through the seven, and found no church
To his mind like San Giovanni—"There's the fold,   260
And all the sheep together, big as cats!
And such a shepherd, half the size of life,
Starts up and hears the angel"—when, at the door,
A tap: we started up: you know the rest.

[Pompilia tells how she was taken by Violante to the church, married to
Guido Franceschini, "hook-nosed and yellow in a bush of beard," then commanded to go home and say nothing to old Pietro; how three weeks later Guido
appeared, claimed his bride, and took her to Arezzo to live. She then tells of
three years of humiliation, suffering, and spiritual torment; of appeals for
help, with no avail, to archbishop, governor, and friar until one came to her aid.]

Yes, my last breath shall wholly spend itself
In one attempt more to disperse the stain,
The mist from other breath fond mouths have made,
About a lustrous and pellucid soul:
So that, when I am gone but sorrow stays,   930
And people need assurance in their doubt
If God yet have a servant, man a friend,
The weak a savior, and the vile a foe,—

Let him be present, by the name invoked,
Giuseppe-Maria Caponsacchi!

There,
Strength comes already with the utterance!
I will remember once more for his sake
The sorrow: for he lives and is belied.
Could he be here, how he would speak for me!

I had been miserable three drear years   940
In that dread palace and lay passive now,
When I first learned there could be such a man.
Thus it fell: I was at a public play,
In the last days of Carnival last March,
Brought there I knew not why, but now know well.
My husband put me where I sat, in front;
Then crouched down, breathed cold through me from behind,
Stationed i' the shadow,—none in front could see,—
I, it was, faced the stranger-throng beneath,
The crowd with upturned faces, eyes one stare,   950
Voices one buzz. I looked but to the stage,
Whereon two lovers sang and interchanged
"True life is only love, love only bliss:
I love thee—thee I love!" then they embraced.
I looked thence to the ceiling and the walls,—
Over the crowd, those voices and those eyes,—
My thoughts went through the roof and out, to Rome
On wings of music, waft of measured words. . . .

Sudden I saw him; into my lap there fell
A foolish twist of comfits, broke my dream
And brought me from the air and laid me low,
As ruined as the soaring bee that's reached   970
(So Pietro told me at the Villa once)
By the dust-handful. There the comfits lay:
I looked to see who flung them, and I faced
This Caponsacchi, looking up in turn.
Ere I could reason out why, I felt sure,
Whoever flung them, his was not the hand,—
Up rose the round face and good-natured grin
Of one who, in effect, had played the prank,
From covert close beside the earnest face,—
Fat waggish Conti, friend of all the world.   980
He was my husband's cousin, privileged
To throw the thing: the other, silent, grave,
Solemn almost, saw me, as I saw him.

[Pompilia tells how her maid, Margherita, "whom it is said my husband found too fair," urges her to communicate with Caponsacchi. Supported by her own purity, fearing also Guido's hand in these solicitations, she long refuses. Then:]

I had got half through April. I arose
One vivid daybreak,—who had gone to bed   1190
In the old way my wont those last three years,
Careless until, the cup drained, I should die.
The last sound in my ear, the over-night,
Had been a something let drop on the sly
In prattle by Margherita, "Soon enough
Gayeties end, now Easter's past: a week,
And the Archbishop gets him back to Rome,—
Every one leaves the town for Rome, this Spring,—
Even Caponsacchi, out of heart and hope,
Resigns himself and follows with the flock."   1200
I heard this drop and drop like rain outside
Fast-falling through the darkness while she spoke:
So had I heard with like indifference,
"And Michael's pair of wings will arrive first
At Rome, to introduce the company,
And bear him from our picture where he fights
Satan,—expect to have that dragon loose
And never a defender!" [6]—my sole thought
Being still, as night came, "Done, another day!
How good to sleep and so get nearer death!"—   1210
When, what, first thing at daybreak, pierced the sleep
With a summons to me? Up I sprang alive,
Light in me, light without me, everywhere
Change! A broad yellow sunbeam was let fall
From heaven to earth,—a sudden drawbridge lay,
Along which marched a myriad merry motes
Mocking the flies that crossed them and recrossed
In rival dance, companions new-born too.
On the house-eaves, a dripping shag of weed
Shook diamonds on each dull gray lattice-square,   1220
As first one, then another bird leapt by,
And light was off, and lo was back again,
Always with one voice,—where are two such joys?—
The blessed building-sparrow! I stepped forth,
Stood on the terrace,—o'er the roofs, such sky!
My heart sang, "I too am to go away,
I too have something I must care about,
Carry away with me to Rome, to Rome!

6 figures in a fresco in the church of San Francesco at Arezzo

The bird brings hither sticks and hairs and wool,
And nowhere else i' the world; what fly breaks rank, 1230
Falls out of the procession that befits,
From window here to window there, with all
The world to choose,—so well he knows his course?
I have my purpose and my motive too,
My march to Rome, like any bird or fly!
Had I been dead! How right to be alive!
Last night I almost prayed for leave to die,
Wished Guido all his pleasure with the sword
Or the poison,—poison, sword, was but a trick,
Harmless, may God forgive him the poor jest! 1240
My life is charmed, will last till I reach Rome!
Yesterday, but for the sin,—ah, nameless be
The deed I could have dared against myself!
Now—see if I will touch an unripe fruit,
And risk the health I want to have and use!
Not to live, now, would be the wickedness,—
For life means to make haste and go to Rome
And leave Arezzo, leave all woes at once!"

Now, understand here, by no means mistake!
Long ago had I tried to leave that house 1250
When it seemed such procedure would stop sin;
And still failed more the more I tried—at first
The Archbishop, as I told you,—next, our lord
The Governor,—indeed I found my way,
I went to the great palace where he rules,
Though I knew well 'twas he who,—when I gave
A jewel or two, themselves had given me,
Back to my parents,—since they wanted bread,
They who had never let me want a nosegay,—he
Spoke of the jail for felons, if they kept 1260
What was first theirs, then mine, so doubly theirs,
Though all the while my husband's most of all!
I knew well who had spoke the word wrought this:
Yet, being in extremity, I fled
To the Governor, as I say,—scarce opened lip
When—the cold cruel snicker close behind—
Guido was on my trace, already there,
Exchanging nod and wink for shrug and smile,
And I—pushed back to him and, for my pains,
Paid with . . . but why remember what is past? 1270
I sought out a poor friar the people call
The Roman, and confessed my sin which came
Of their sin,—that fact could not be repressed,—

The frightfulness of my despair in God:
And feeling, through the grate, his horror shake,
Implored him, "Write for me who cannot write,
Apprise my parents, make them rescue me!
You bid me be courageous and trust God:
Do you in turn dare somewhat, trust and write,
'Dear friends, who used to be my parents once,   1280
And now declare you have no part in me,
This is some riddle I want wit to solve,
Since you must love me with no difference.
Even suppose you altered,—there's your hate,
To ask for: hate of you two dearest ones
I shall find liker love than love found here,
If husbands love their wives. Take me away
And hate me as you do the gnats and fleas,
Even the scorpions! How I shall rejoice!'
Write that and save me!" And he promised—wrote   1290
Or did not write; things never changed at all:
He was not like the Augustinian here!
Last, in a desperation I appealed
To friends, whoever wished me better days,
To Guillichini, that's of kin,—"What, I—
Travel to Rome with you? A flying gout
Bids me deny my heart and mind my leg!"
Then I tried Conti, used to brave—laugh back
The louring thunder when his cousin scowled
At me protected by his presence: "You—   1300
Who well know what you cannot save me from,—
Carry me off! What frightens you, a priest?"
He shook his head, looked grave—"Above my strength!
Guido has claws that scratch, shows feline teeth;
A formidabler foe than I dare fret:
Give me a dog to deal with, twice the size!
Of course I am a priest and Canon too,
But . . . by the bye . . . though both, not quite so bold
As he, my fellow-Canon, brother-priest,
The personage in such ill odor here   1310
Because of the reports—pure birth o' the brain!
Our Caponsacchi, he's your true Saint George
To slay the monster, set the Princess free,
And have the whole High-Altar to himself:
I always think so when I see that piece [7]
I' the Pieve, that's his church and mine, you know:
Though you drop eyes at mention of his name!"

7 a picture of St. George by Vasari

That name had got to take a half-grotesque
Half-ominous, wholly enigmatic sense,
Like any by-word, broken bit of song 1320
Born with a meaning, changed by mouth and mouth
That mix it in a sneer or smile, as chance
Bids, till it now means naught but ugliness
And perhaps shame.

        —All this intends to say,
That, over-night, the notion of escape
Had seemed distemper, dreaming; and the name,—
Not the man, but the name of him, thus made
Into a mockery and disgrace,—why, she
Who uttered it persistently, had laughed,
"I name his name, and there you start and wince 1330
As criminal from the red tongs' touch!"—yet now,
Now, as I stood letting morn bathe me bright,
Choosing which butterfly should bear my news,—
The white, the brown one, or that tinier blue,—
The Margherita, I detested so,
In she came—"The fine day, the good Spring time!
What, up and out at window? That is best.
No thought of Caponsacchi?—who stood there
All night on one leg, like the sentry crane,
Under the pelting of your water-spout— 1340
Looked last look at your lattice ere he leave
Our city, bury his dead hope at Rome.
Ay, go to looking-glass and make you fine,
While he may die ere touch one least loose hair
You drag at with the comb in such a rage!"

I turned—"Tell Caponsacchi he may come!"
"Tell him to come? Ah, but, for charity,
A truce to fooling! Come? What,—come this eve?
Peter and Paul! But I see through the trick!
Yes, come, and take a flower-pot on his head, 1350
Flung from your terrace! No joke, sincere truth?"

How plainly I perceived hell flash and fade
O' the face of her,—the doubt that first paled joy,
Then, final reassurance I indeed
Was caught now, never to be free again!
What did I care?—who felt myself of force
To play with silk, and spurn the horsehair-springe.

"But—do you know that I have bade him come,
And in your own name? I presumed so much,
Knowing the thing you needed in your heart.
But somehow—what had I to show in proof?
He would not come: half-promised, that was all,
And wrote the letters you refused to read.
What is the message that shall move him now?"

"After the Ave Maria, at first dark,
I will be standing on the terrace, say!"

"I would I had a good long lock of hair
Should prove I was not lying! Never mind!"

Off she went—"May he not refuse, that's all—
Fearing a trick!"

       I answered, "He will come."
And, all day, I sent prayer like incense up
To God the strong, God the beneficent,
God ever mindful in all strife and strait,
Who, for our own good, makes the need extreme,
Till at the last he puts forth might and saves.
An old rhyme came into my head and rang
Of how a virgin, for the faith of God,
Hid herself, from the Paynims that pursued,
In a cave's heart; until a thunderstone,
Wrapped in a flame, revealed the couch and prey:
And they laughed—"Thanks to lightning, ours at last!"
And she cried, "Wrath of God, assert his love!
Servant of God, thou fire, befriend his child!"
And lo, the fire she grasped at, fixed its flash,
Lay in her hand a calm cold dreadful sword
She brandished till pursuers strewed the ground,
So did the souls within them die away,
As o'er the prostrate bodies, sworded, safe,
She walked forth to the solitudes and Christ:
So should I grasp the lightning and be saved!

And still, as the day wore, the trouble grew
Whereby I guessed there would be born a star,
Until at an intense throe of the dusk,
I started up, was pushed, I dare to say,
Out on the terrace, leaned and looked at last
Where the deliverer waited me: the same

Silent and solemn face, I first descried
At the spectacle, confronted mine once more.

So was that minute twice vouchsafed me, so
The manhood, wasted then, was still at watch   1400
To save me yet a second time: no change
Here, though all else changed in the changing world!

I spoke on the instant, as my duty bade,
In some such sense as this, whatever the phrase.

"Friend, foolish words were borne from you to me;
Your soul behind them is the pure strong wind,
Not dust and feathers which its breath may bear:
These to the witless seem the wind itself,
Since proving thus the first of it they feel.
If by mischance you blew offense my way,   1410
The straws are dropped, the wind desists no whit,
And how such strays were caught up in the street
And took a motion from you, why inquire?
I speak to the strong soul, no weak disguise.
If it be truth,—why should I doubt it truth?—
You serve God specially, as priests are bound,
And care about me, stranger as I am,
So far as wish my good, that—miracle
I take to imitate he wills you serve
By saving me,—what else can he direct?   1420
Here is the service. Since a long while now,
I am in course of being put to death:
While death concerned nothing but me, I bowed
The head and bade, in heart, my husband strike.
Now I imperil something more, it seems,
Something that's trulier me than this myself,
Something I trust in God and you to save.
You go to Rome, they tell me: take me there,
Put me back with my people!"

                            He replied—
The first word I heard ever from his lips,   1430
All himself in it,—an eternity
Of speech, to match the immeasurable depth
O' the soul that then broke silence—"I am yours."

So did the star rise, soon to lead my step,
Lead on, nor pause before it should stand still

Above the House o' the Babe,—my babe to be,
That knew me first and thus made me know him,
That had his right of life and claim on mine,
And would not let me die till he was born,
But pricked me at the heart to save us both,   1440
Saying, "Have you the will? Leave God the way!"
And the way was Caponsacchi—"mine," thank God!
He was mine, he is mine, he will be mine.

No pause i' the leading and the light! I know,
Next night there was a cloud came, and not he:
But I prayed through the darkness till it broke
And let him shine. The second night, he came.
"The plan is rash; the project desperate:
In such a flight needs must I risk your life,
Give food for falsehood, folly or mistake,   1450
Ground for your husband's rancor and revenge"—
So he began again, with the same face.
I felt that, the same loyalty—one star
Turning now red that was so white before—
One service apprehended newly: just
A word of mine and there the white was back!

"No, friend, for you will take me! 'Tis yourself
Risk all, not I,—who let you, for I trust
In the compensating great God: enough!
I know you: when is it that you will come?"   1460

"To-morrow at the day's dawn." Then I heard
What I should do: how to prepare for flight
And where to fly.

                            That night my husband bade
"—You, whom I loathe, beware you break my sleep
This whole night! Couch beside me like the corpse
I would you were!" The rest you know, I think—
How I found Caponsacchi and escaped.

And this man, men call sinner? Jesus Christ!
Of whom men said, with mouths Thyself mad'st once,
"He hath a devil" [8]—say he was Thy saint,   1470
My Caponsacchi! Shield and show—unshroud
In Thine own time the glory of the soul
If aught obscure,—if ink-spot, from vile pens
Scribbling a charge against him—(I was glad

8 John, vii, 20; viii, 48

Then, for the first time, that I could not write)—
Flirted his way, have flecked the blaze!

                                        For me,
'Tis otherwise: let men take, sift my thoughts
—Thoughts I throw like the flax for sun to bleach!
I did pray, do pray, in the prayer shall die,
"Oh, to have Caponsacchi for my guide!"   1480
Ever the face upturned to mine, the hand
Holding my hand across the world,—a sense
That reads, as only such can read, the mark
God sets on woman, signifying so
She should—shall peradventure—be divine;
Yet 'ware, the while, how weakness mars the print
And makes confusion, leaves the thing men see,
—Not this man sees,—who from his soul, re-writes
The obliterated charter,—love and strength
Mending what's marred. "So kneels a votarist,   1490
Weeds some poor waste traditionary plot
Where shrine once was, where temple yet may be,
Purging the place but worshiping the while,
By faith and not by sight, sight clearest so,—
Such way the saints work,"—says Don Celestine.
But I, not privileged to see a saint
Of old when such walked earth with crown and palm,
If I call "saint" what saints call something else—
The saints must bear with me, impute the fault
To a soul i' the bud, so starved by ignorance,   1500
Stinted of warmth, it will not blow this year
Nor recognize the orb which Spring-flowers know.
But if meanwhile some insect with a heart
Worth floods of lazy music, spendthrift joy—
Some fire-fly renounced Spring for my dwarfed cup,
Crept close to me, brought luster for the dark,
Comfort against the cold,—what though excess
Of comfort should miscall the creature—sun?
What did the sun to hinder while harsh hands
Petal by petal, crude and colorless,   1510
Tore me? This one heart gave me all the Spring!

Is all told? There's the journey: and where's time
To tell you how that heart burst out in shine?
Yet certain points do press on me too hard.
Each place must have a name, though I forget:
How strange it was—there where the plain begins
And the small river mitigates its flow—

When eve was fading fast, and my soul sank,
And he divined what surge of bitterness,
In overtaking me, would float me back   1520
Whence I was carried by the striding day—
So,—"This gray place was famous once," said he—
And he began that legend of the place
As if in answer to the unspoken fear,
And told me all about a brave man dead,
Which lifted me and let my soul go on!
How did he know too—at that town's approach
By the rock-side—that in coming near the signs
Of life, the house-roofs and the church and tower,
I saw the old boundary and wall o' the world   1530
Rise plain as ever round me, hard and cold,
As if the broken circlet joined again,
Tightened itself about me with no break,—
As if the town would turn Arezzo's self,—
The husband there,—the friends my enemies,
All ranged against me, not an avenue
To try, but would be blocked and drive me back
On him,—this other, . . . oh the heart in that!
Did not he find, bring, put into my arms
A new-born babe?—and I saw faces beam   1540
Of the young mother proud to teach me joy,
And gossips round expecting my surprise
At the sudden hole through earth that lets in heaven.
I could believe himself by his strong will
Had woven around me what I thought the world
We went along in, every circumstance,
Towns, flowers and faces, all things helped so well!
For, through the journey, was it natural
Such comfort should arise from first to last?
As I look back, all is one milky way;   1550
Still bettered more, the more remembered, so
Do new stars bud while I but search for old,
And fill all gaps i' the glory, and grow him—
Him I now see make the shine everywhere.
Even at the last when the bewildered flesh,
The cloud of weariness about my soul
Clogging too heavily, sucked down all sense,—
Still its last voice was, "He will watch and care;
Let the strength go, I am content: he stays!"
I doubt not he did stay and care for all—   1560
From that sick minute when the head swam round,
And the eyes looked their last and died on him,
As in his arms he caught me, and, you say,

Carried me in, that tragical red eve,
And laid me where I next returned to life
In the other red of morning, two red plates
That crushed together, crushed the time between,
And are since then a solid fire to me,—
When in, my dreadful husband and the world
Broke,—and I saw him, master, by hell's right,   1570
And saw my angel helplessly held back
By guards that helped the malice—the lamb prone,
The serpent towering and triumphant—then
Came all the strength back in a sudden swell,
I did for once see right, do right, give tongue
The adequate protest: for a worm must turn
If it would have its wrong observed by God.
I did spring up, attempt to thrust aside
That ice-block 'twixt the sun and me, lay low
The neutralizer of all good and truth.   1580
If I sinned so,—never obey voice more
O' the Just and Terrible, who bids us—"Bear!"
Not—"Stand by, bear to see my angels bear!"
I am clear it was on impulse to serve God
Not save myself,—no—nor my child unborn!
Had I else waited patiently till now?—
Who saw my old kind parents, silly-sooth
And too much trustful, for their worst of faults,
Cheated, browbeaten, stripped and starved, cast out
Into the kennel: I remonstrated,   1590
Then sank to silence, for,—their woes at end,
Themselves gone,—only I was left to plague.
If only I was threatened and belied,
What matter? I could bear it and did bear;
It was a comfort, still one lot for all:
They were not persecuted for my sake
And I, estranged, the single happy one.
But when at last, all by myself I stood
Obeying the clear voice which bade me rise,
Not for my own sake but my babe unborn,   1600
And take the angel's hand was sent to help—
And found the old adversary athwart the path—
Not my hand simply struck from the angel's, but
The very angel's self made foul i' the face
By the fiend who struck there,—that I would not bear,
That only I resisted! So, my first
And last resistance was invincible.
Prayers move God; threats, and nothing else, move men!
I must have prayed a man as he were God

When I implored the Governor to right   1610
My parents' wrongs: the answer was a smile.
The Archbishop,—did I clasp his feet enough,
Hide my face hotly on them, while I told
More than I dared make my own mother know?
The profit was—compassion and a jest.
This time, the foolish prayers were done with, right
Used might, and solemnized the sport at once.
All was against the combat: vantage, mine?
The runaway avowed, the accomplice-wife,
In company with the plan-contriving priest?   1620
Yet, shame thus rank and patent, I struck, bare,
At foe from head to foot in magic mail,
And off it withered, cobweb-armory
Against the lightning! 'Twas truth singed the lies
And saved me, not the vain sword nor weak speech!

You see, I will not have the service fail!
I say, the angel saved me: I am safe!
Others may want and wish, I wish nor want
One point o' the circle plainer, where I stand
Traced round about with white to front the world.   1630
What of the calumny I came across,
What o' the way to the end?—the end crowns all.
The judges judged aright i' the main, gave me
The uttermost of my heart's desire, a truce
From torture and Arezzo, balm for hurt,
With the quiet nuns,—God recompense the good!
Who said and sang away the ugly past.
And, when my final fortune was revealed,
What safety, while, amid my parents' arms,
My babe was given me! Yes, he saved my babe: 1640
It would not have peeped forth, the bird-like thing,
Through that Arezzo noise and trouble: back
Had it returned nor ever let me see!
But the sweet peace cured all, and let me live
And give my bird the life among the leaves
God meant him! Weeks and months of quietude,
I could lie in such peace and learn so much—
Begin the task, I see how needful now,
Of understanding somewhat of my past,—
Know life a little, I should leave so soon.   1650
Therefore, because this man restored my soul,
All has been right; I have gained my gain, enjoyed
As well as suffered,—nay, got foretaste too
Of better life beginning where this ends—

All through the breathing-while allowed me thus,
Which let good premonitions reach my soul
Unthwarted, and benignant influence flow
And interpenetrate and change my heart,
Uncrossed by what was wicked,—nay, unkind.
For, as the weakness of my time drew nigh,   1660
Nobody did me one disservice more,
Spoke coldly or looked strangely, broke the love
I lay in the arms of, till my boy was born,
Born all in love, with naught to spoil the bliss
A whole long fortnight: in a life like mine
A fortnight filled with bliss is long and much.
All women are not mothers of a boy,
Though they live twice the length of my whole life,
And, as they fancy, happily all the same.
There I lay, then, all my great fortnight long,   1670
As if it would continue, broaden out
Happily more and more, and lead to heaven:
Christmas before me,—was not that a chance?
I never realized God's birth before—
How he grew likest God in being born.
This time I felt like Mary, had my babe
Lying a little on my breast like hers.
So all went on till, just four days ago—
The night and the tap.

                                    Oh, it shall be success
To the whole of our poor family! My friends   1680
. . . Nay, father and mother,—give me back my word!
They have been rudely stripped of life, disgraced
Like children who must needs go clothed too fine,
Carry the garb of Carnival in Lent.
If they too much affected frippery,
They have been punished and submit themselves,
Say no word: all is over, they see God
Who will not be extreme to mark their fault
Or he had granted respite: they are safe.

For that most woeful man my husband once,   1690
Who, needing respite, still draws vital breath,
I—pardon him? So far as lies in me,
I give him for his good the life he takes,
Praying the world will therefore acquiesce.
Let him make God amends,—none, none to me
Who thank him rather that, whereas strange fate
Mockingly styled him husband and me wife,

Himself this way at least pronounced divorce,
Blotted the marriage-bond: this blood of mine
Flies forth exultingly at any door,   1700
Washes the parchment white, and thanks the blow.
We shall not meet in this world nor the next,
But where will God be absent? In his face
Is light, but in his shadow healing too:
Let Guido touch the shadow and be healed!
And as my presence was importunate,—
My earthly good, temptation and a snare,—
Nothing about me but drew somehow down
His hate upon me,—somewhat so excused
Therefore, since hate was thus the truth of him,—   1710
May my evanishment forevermore
Help further to relieve the heart that cast
Such object of its natural loathing forth!
So he was made: he nowise made himself:
I could not love him, but his mother did.
His soul has never lain beside my soul;
But for the unresisting body,—thanks!
He burned that garment spotted by the flesh.
Whatever he touched is rightly ruined: plague
It caught, and disinfection it had craved   1720
Still but for Guido; I am saved through him
So as by fire; to him—thanks and farewell!

Even for my babe, my boy, there's safety thence—
From the sudden death of me, I mean: we poor
Weak souls, how we endeavor to be strong!
I was already using up my life,—
This portion, now, should do him such a good,
This other go to keep off such an ill!
The great life; see, a breath and it is gone!
So is detached, so left all by itself   1730
The little life, the fact which means so much.
Shall not God stoop the kindlier to his work,
His marvel of creation, foot would crush,
Now that the hand he trusted to receive
And hold it, lets the treasure fall perforce?
The better; he shall have in orphanage
His own way all the clearlier: if my babe
Outlived the hour—and he has lived two weeks—
It is through God who knows I am not by.
Who is it makes the soft gold hair turn black,   1740
And sets the tongue, might lie so long at rest,

Trying to talk? Let us leave God alone!
Why should I doubt he will explain in time
What I feel now, but fail to find the words?
My babe nor was, nor is, nor yet shall be
Count Guido Franceschini's child at all—
Only his mother's, born of love not hate!
So shall I have my rights in after-time.
It seems absurd, impossible to-day;
So seems so much else, not explained but known!   1750

Ah! Friends, I thank and bless you every one!
No more now: I withdraw from earth and man
To my own soul, compose my self for God.

Well, and there is more! Yes, my end of breath
Shall bear away my soul in being true!
He is still here, not outside with the world,
Here, here, I have him in his rightful place!
'Tis now, when I am most upon the move,
I feel for what I verily find—again
The face, again the eyes, again, through all,   1760
The heart and its immeasurable love
Of my one friend, my only, all my own,
Who put his breast between the spears and me.
Ever with Caponsacchi! Otherwise
Here alone would be failure, loss to me—
How much more loss to him, with life debarred
From giving life, love locked from love's display,
The day-star stopped its task that makes night morn!
O lover of my life, O soldier-saint,
No work begun shall ever pause for death!   1770
Love will be helpful to me more and more
I' the coming course, the new path I must tread—
My weak hand in thy strong hand, strong for that!
Tell him that if I seem without him now,
That's the world's insight! Oh, he understands!
He is at Civita—do I once doubt
The world again is holding us apart?
He had been here, displayed in my behalf
The broad brow that reverberates the truth,
And flashed the word God gave him, back to man!   1780
I know where the free soul is flown! My fate
Will have been hard for even him to bear:
Let it confirm him in the trust of God,
Showing how holily he dared the deed!

And, for the rest,—say, from the deed, no touch
Of harm came, but all good, all happiness,
Not one faint fleck of failure! Why explain?
What I see, oh, he sees and how much more!
Tell him,—I know not wherefore the true word
Should fade and fall unuttered at the last—   1790
It was the name of him I sprang to meet
When came the knock, the summons and the end.
"My great heart, my strong hand are back again!"
I would have sprung to these, beckoning across
Murder and hell gigantic and distinct
O' the threshold, posted to exclude me heaven:
He is ordained to call and I to come!
Do not the dead wear flowers when dressed for God?
Say,—I am all in flowers from head to foot!
Say,—not one flower of all he said and did,   1800
Might seem to flit unnoticed, fade unknown,
But dropped a seed, has grown a balsam-tree
Whereof the blossoming perfumes the place
At this supreme of moments! He is a priest;
He cannot marry therefore, which is right:
I think he would not marry if he could.
Marriage on earth seems such a counterfeit,
Mere imitation of the inimitable:
In heaven we have the real and true and sure.
'Tis there they neither marry nor are given   1810
In marriage but are as the angels: [9] right,
Oh how right that is, how like Jesus Christ
To say that! Marriage-making for the earth,
With gold so much,—birth, power, repute so much,
Or beauty, youth so much, in lack of these!
Be as the angels rather, who, apart,
Know themselves into one, are found at length
Married, but marry never, no, nor give
In marriage; they are man and wife at once
When the true time is: here we have to wait   1820
Not so long neither! Could we by a wish
Have what we will and get the future now,
Would we wish aught done undone in the past?
So, let him wait God's instant men call years;
Meantime hold hard by truth and his great soul,
Do out the duty! Through such souls alone
God stooping shows sufficient of his light
For us i' the dark to rise by. And I rise.

9 Matt. xxii, 30

EPILOGUE [10]

At the midnight in the silence of the sleep-time,
  When you set your fancies free,
Will they pass to where—by death, fools think, imprisoned—
Low he lies who once so loved you, whom you loved so,
        —Pity me?

Oh to love so, be so loved, yet so mistaken!
  What had I on earth to do
With the slothful, with the mawkish, the unmanly?
Like the aimless, helpless, hopeless, did I drivel
        —Being—who?   10

One who never turned his back but marched breast forward,
  Never doubted clouds would break,
Never dreamed, though right were worsted, wrong would
        triumph,
Held we fall to rise, are baffled to fight better,
        Sleep to wake.

No, at noonday in the bustle of man's work-time
  Greet the unseen with a cheer!
Bid him forward, breast and back as either should be,
"Strive and thrive!" cry "Speed,—fight on, fare ever
        There as here!"   20

MATTHEW ARNOLD (1822–1888)

Matthew Arnold was born on Christmas eve, 1822. His father was Dr.
Thomas Arnold, celebrated headmaster of Rugby from 1828 to 1842—a man
whose moral earnestness, liberality of views, and energy were conspicuous in
his time, and whose reforms in school administration powerfully impressed the
educational system of his country. The father's vigorous interest in political,
social, and religious questions was communicated to the son, and another influence on the youth was the poetic creed of Wordsworth, whom the Arnolds
knew, and often saw when they spent summers at their country home near
Grasmere, in the Lake district.

Matthew Arnold spent some years at Rugby, and in 1841 entered Oxford
as a scholar of Balliol College. He took his B.A. in 1844 and his M.A. in 1845.
He had failed to win first class honors, but he had become intensely devoted
to Oxford—a devotion which is revealed in *The Scholar Gipsy*, *Thyrsis*, and
elsewhere; and he had formed an enduring friendship with Arthur Hugh
Clough, whose death he laments in the latter poem.

10 to the volume entitled *Asolando*, dated 1890, but published the day Browning
died (December 12. 1889). Reprinted by permission of John Murray, Esq.

In 1845 he was elected a fellow of Oriel College, but did not long remain there. He returned to Rugby to teach classics, and in 1847 became private secretary to Lord Lansdowne, then Lord President of the Council, who in 1851 procured him a position as Inspector of Schools. He took this position, as he afterwards said, not because he was much interested in the work, but because it enabled him to marry. Yet he performed his duties, until a few years of his death, with faithfulness and distinguished ability. His work necessitated constant and fatiguing travel to various parts of England, and occasionally to the Continent, whither he went to study foreign school systems. It involved much drudgery, such as the reading of many examination papers, and the preparation of numerous routine reports.

Such continuous and exacting work might well have exhausted all the time of a less energetic man, but Arnold did not allow it to quench his literary ambitions. In time snatched from his official duties he managed to produce many volumes of poems and essays. As a young man, his product was chiefly verse. In 1849 he brought out his first volume entitled *A Strayed Reveller and Other Poems*, in 1852 *Empedocles on Etna and Other Poems*, containing *Tristram and Iseult* and many of the more characteristic of his shorter pieces, in 1853 *Poems, First Series*, including the well-known narrative poem, *Sohrab and Rustum*, also *The Scholar Gipsy*, and in 1855 *Poems, Second Series*. This poetical work attracted a discriminating, if not a wide audience, and obtained for him the reputation which led to his appointment in 1857 as Professor of Poetry at Oxford—a post which he held for ten years. The duties were very light, consisting merely in the delivery of a few public lectures each year. In 1858 he wrote a poetic tragedy, *Merope*, on strict classical principles. Arnold's work as a poet was now, by his middle thirties, practically over. He published only one more volume of verse, that of 1867, containing, however, his noble elegies *Thyrsis* and *Rugby Chapel*. Poetic composition, as he complained, was becoming increasingly difficult for him; and his professorship at Oxford had directed his attention more and more to criticism, to which he was to devote all the latter part of his life.

His earlier criticism was chiefly literary. In 1861 he published *On Translating Homer*, in 1865 *Essays in Criticism, First Series*, in 1867 *On the Study of Celtic Literature*. As he grew older, he turned from literary studies to criticism of life in broader aspects—social, political, and religious—some of the more important works being *Culture and Anarchy* (1869), *Literature and Dogma* (1873), *God and the Bible* (1875), and *Last Essays on Church and Religion* (1877). Two visits to the United States produced *Discourses in America* (1885), and *Civilization in the United States* (1888), in which he found much to criticize in our ideas and ways of life. A second series of *Essays in Criticism* was published posthumously. He died on April 15, 1888.

Arnold's poetry, while denied in its own time the popularity accorded that of his contemporaries Tennyson and Browning, seems steadily rising in estimation. He himself had predicted its ultimate reputation. In 1869 he wrote, "My poems represent, on the whole, the main movement of mind of the last quarter of a century, and thus they will probably have their day as people become conscious to themselves of what that movement of mind is, and interested in the literary productions which reflect it. It might be fairly urged that I have less poetical sentiment than Tennyson, and less intellectual vigor and abundance than Browning; yet, because I have perhaps more of a fusion of the two than either of them, and have more regularly applied that fusion to the main line of modern development, I am likely enough to have my turn, as they have had theirs." The constant theme of Arnold's verse, as the following selections show, is the melancholy engendered in a sensitive mind by the decay of the old religious certainties, by the purposeless activity (as he saw it) of modern life, "with its sick hurry, its divided aims." He longed for calm, for the repose that fostered clear thinking and produced perfect art, for the faith that had vanished from the world. He saw everywhere about him men's ideas in shifting flux, the noble spiritual values of former ages decayed to crass materialism, to the gross worship of Mammon and the machine, to cynicism and doubt. In the face of these discouragements he could not accept the optimism of Browning. Yet he did not solve the dilemma, except to place such reliance as he might on his own soul and find such comfort as he could in the great men of the past "who saw life steadily and saw it whole." The result is not even an active pessimism, but rather a brooding melancholy. In the technical aspects of his verse, Arnold has absorbed much of the spirit of the classics which he loved. His poetry is characterized by a restraint, a calm and clear beauty, a lucidity, a just and fine phrasing.

By his middle years Arnold had found what seemed to him a way out. His remedy for the ills of his time was culture, which he defined as the study of perfection and the desire to make it prevail. One foe of culture was the narrow scientific attitude, which, dealing with raw facts, did not humanize, refine, or discipline, as did a more liberal and classical training. Perhaps the greatest foe of culture was the besetting faith of the times in machinery—the faith held by the "Philistine," the unintelligent, self-satisfied Britisher of the middle class. Arnold's program is eloquently expressed in "Sweetness and Light," which may be considered the key-essay of his social criticism. In his religious discussions, which occupied much of his energies during his later years, he attacked much current dogma, still, in spite of Darwinism and the upheaval which followed it, accepted by the masses. He would save the Bible as a source of "moral wisdom and religious emotion" by destroying obsolete theological interpretations. God for him was "a power not ourselves which makes for righteousness." In his literary criticism he judges largely by ethical standards. Poetry is a "criticism of life," and its greatness is in proportion as it possesses "high seriousness." These are more vital for him than those "laws of poetic truth and poetic beauty" which he never clearly defines. He accordingly appraises very highly—perhaps extravagantly—Wordsworth; and hardly does justice to such writers as Shelley or Burns. The authority with which he spoke has profoundly affected English literary criticism since his time, but here are deficiences imposed by his own temperament and his own view of what constitutes art. Just at present, when a new "humanism" is raising its head, Matthew Arnold's is a powerful voice. He, before the contemporary humanists, maintained that the shallowness of modern life was largely due to its severance with the great traditions of the past, and that culture was impossible without a knowledge of the best that had been thought and said in the world.

Arnold's prose style has been greatly admired. It is easy, polished, and urbane. It has often a bantering humor much relished by many readers. Others have been repelled by a certain cocksureness in the man, a condescension, almost a superciliousness. It has been said of him that unfortunately he "had a strut in his gait."

BIBLIOGRAPHY. Authorized ed. of Arnold's Poetry and Prose, 12 vols., pub. by Macmillan. *Letters,* ed., G. W. E. Russell (Macmillan). Biography by

H. W. Paul (Eng. Men of Letters ser.). Critical interpretation by L. E. Gates, *Three Studies in Lit.* (Macmillan). Introd. to his work, S. P. Sherman, *Matthew Arnold: How to Know Him* (Bobbs Merrill).

QUIET WORK [1]

ONE lesson, Nature, let me learn of thee,
One lesson which in every wind is blown,
One lesson of two duties kept at one
Though the loud world proclaim their enmity—
Of toil unsevered from tranquillity!
Of labor, that in lasting fruit outgrows
Far noisier schemes, accomplished in repose,
Too great for haste, too high for rivalry!
Yes, while on earth a thousand discords ring,
Man's fitful uproar mingling with his toil,
Still do thy sleepless ministers move on,
Their glorious tasks in silence perfecting;
Still working, blaming still our vain turmoil,
Laborers that shall not fail, when man is gone.

TO A FRIEND

WHO prop, thou ask'st, in these bad days, my mind?—
He much, the old man, who, clearest-souled of men,
Saw The Wide Prospect, and the Asian Fen,[2]
And Tmolus hill, and Smyrna bay, though blind.
Much he,[3] whose friendship I not long since won,
That halting slave, who in Nicopolis
Taught Arrian, when Vespasian's brutal son
Cleared Rome of what most shamed him. But be his [4]
My special thanks, whose even-balanced soul
From first youth tested up to extreme old age,
Business could not make dull, nor passion wild;
Who saw life steadily, and saw it whole;
The mellow glory of the Attic stage,
Singer of sweet Colonus, and its child.

1 Arnold's poems are reprinted from the *Poetical Works* of Matthew Arnold (Globe ed.) copyright 1890 by Macmillan and Company, Ltd., and the Macmillan Company. Reprinted by permission.

2 Homer, born, according to one claim, at Smyrna, near "Tmolus hill." "The name Europe (Εὐρώπη, *the wide prospect*) probably describes the appearance of the European coast to the Greeks on the coast of Asia Minor opposite. The name Asia, again, comes, it has been thought, from the muddy fens of the rivers of Asia Minor, such as the Cayster or Mæander, which struck the imagination of the Greeks living near them." (Arnold)

3 Epictetus. Domitian, son of Vespasian, banished the philosophers from Rome A. D. 89.

4 Sophocles, born at Colonus, described in *Œdipus at Colonus*.

SHAKESPEARE

OTHERS abide our question. Thou art free.
We ask and ask—Thou smilest and art still,
Out-topping knowledge. For the loftiest hill,
Who to the stars uncrowns his majesty,
Planting his steadfast footsteps in the sea,
Making the heaven of heavens his dwelling-place,
Spares but the cloudy border of his base
To the foiled searching of mortality;
And thou, who didst the stars and sunbeams know,
Self-schooled, self-scanned, self-honored, self-secure,
Didst tread on earth unguessed at.—Better so!
All pains the immortal spirit must endure,
All weakness which impairs, all griefs which bow,
Find their sole speech in that victorious brow.

THE FORSAKEN MERMAN

COME, dear children, let us away;
Down and away below!
Now my brothers call from the bay,
Now the great winds shoreward blow,
Now the salt tides seaward flow;
Now the wild white horses play,
Champ and chafe and toss in the spray.
Children dear, let us away!
This way, this way!

Call her once before you go—   10
Call once yet!
In a voice that she will know:
"Margaret! Margaret!"
Children's voices should be dear
(Call once more) to a mother's ear;
Children's voices, wild with pain—
Surely she will come again!
Call her once and come away;
This way, this way!
"Mother dear, we cannot stay!
The wild white horses foam and fret."   20
Margaret! Margaret!

Come, dear children, come away down;
Call no more!
One last look at the white-walled town,

And the little gray church on the windy shore;
Then come down!
She will not come though you call all day;
Come away, come away!

Children dear, was it yesterday   30
We heard the sweet bells over the bay?
In the caverns where we lay,
Through the surf and through the swell,
The far-off sound of a silver bell?
Sand-strewn caverns, cool and deep,
Where the winds are all asleep;
Where the spent lights quiver and gleam,
Where the salt weed sways in the stream,
Where the sea-beasts, ranged all round,
Feed in the ooze of their pasture-ground;   40
Where the sea-snakes coil and twine,
Dry their mail and bask in the brine;
Where great whales come sailing by,
Sail and sail, with unshut eye,
Round the world for ever and aye?
When did music come this way?
Children dear, was it yesterday?

Children dear, was it yesterday
(Call yet once) that she went away?
Once she sat with you and me,
On a red gold throne in the heart of the sea,   50
And the youngest sat on her knee.
She combed its bright hair, and she tended it well,
When down swung the sound of a far-off bell.
She sighed, she looked up through the clear green sea;
She said: "I must go, for my kinsfolk pray
In the little gray church on the shore to-day.
'Twill be Easter-time in the world—ah me!
And I lose my poor soul, Merman! here with thee."
I said: "Go up, dear heart, through the waves;   60
Say thy prayer, and come back to the kind sea-caves!"
She smiled, she went up through the surf in the bay.
Children dear, was it yesterday?

Children dear, were we long alone?
"The sea grows stormy, the little ones moan;
Long prayers," I said, "in the world they say;
Come!" I said; and we rose through the surf in the bay.
We went up the beach, by the sandy down

Where the sea-stocks bloom, to the white-walled town;
Through the narrow paved streets, where all was still, 70
To the little gray church on the windy hill.
From the church came a murmur of folk at their prayers,
But we stood without in the cold blowing airs.
We climbed on the graves, on the stones worn with rains,
And we gazed up the aisle through the small leaded panes.
She sat by the pillar; we saw her clear:
"Margaret, hist! come quick, we are here!
Dear heart," I said, "we are long alone;
The sea grows stormy, the little ones moan."
But, ah, she gave me never a look, 80
For her eyes were sealed to the holy book!
Loud prays the priest; shut stands the door.
Come away, children, call no more!
Come away, come down, call no more!

Down, down, down!
Down to the depths of the sea!
She sits at her wheel in the humming town,
Singing most joyfully.
Hark what she sings: "O joy, O joy,
For the humming street, and the child with its toy! 90
For the priest, and the bell, and the holy well;
For the wheel where I spun,
And the blessèd light of the sun!"
And so she sings her fill,
Singing most joyfully,
Till the spindle falls from her hand,
And the whizzing wheel stands still.
She steals to the window, and looks at the sand,
And over the sand at the sea;
And her eyes are set in a stare; 100
And anon there breaks a sigh,
And anon there drops a tear,
From a sorrow-clouded eye,
And a heart sorrow-laden,
A long, long sight;
For the cold strange eyes of a little Mermaiden
And the gleam of her golden hair.

Come away, away children;
Come children, come down!
The hoarse wind blows coldly; 110
Lights shine in the town.
She will start from her slumber

When gusts shake the door;
She will hear the winds howling,
Will hear the waves roar.
We shall see, while above us
The waves roar and whirl,
A ceiling of amber,
A pavement of pearl.
Singing: "Here came a mortal,   120
But faithless was she!
And alone dwell for ever
The kings of the sea."

But, children, at midnight,
When soft the winds blow,
When clear falls the moonlight,
When spring-tides are low;
When sweet airs come seaward
From heaths starred with broom,
And high rocks throw mildly   130
On the blanched sands a gloom;
Up the still, glistening beaches,
Up the creeks we will hie,
Over banks of bright seaweed
The ebb-tide leaves dry.
We will gaze, from the sand-hills,
At the white, sleeping town;
At the church on the hill-side—
And then come back down.
Singing: "There dwells a loved one,   140
But cruel is she!
She left lonely for ever
The kings of the sea."

MEMORIAL VERSES

APRIL, 1850

GOETHE in Weimar sleeps, and Greece,
Long since, saw Byron's struggle cease.[5]
But one such death remained to come;
The last poetic voice is dumb—
We stand to-day by Wordsworth's tomb.

When Byron's eyes were shut in death,
We bowed our head and held our breath.

[5] Goethe died in 1832, Byron in 1824, after he had gone to aid the Greeks in their fight for independence.

He taught us little; but our soul
Had *felt* him like the thunder's roll.
With shivering heart the strife we saw   10
Of passion with eternal law;
And yet with reverential awe
We watched the fount of fiery life
Which served for that Titanic strife.

When Goethe's death was told, we said:
Sunk, then, is Europe's sagest head.
Physician of the iron age,
Goethe has done his pilgrimage.
He took the suffering human race,
He read each wound, each weakness clear;   20
And struck his finger on the place,
And said: *Thou ailest here, and here!*
He looked on Europe's dying hour
Of fitful dream and feverish power;
His eye plunged down the weltering strife,
The turmoil of expiring life—
He said: *The end is everywhere,
Art still has truth, take refuge there!*
And he was happy, if to know
Causes of things, and far below   30
His feet to see the lurid flow
Of terror, and insane distress,
And headlong fate, be happiness.

And Wordsworth!—Ah, pale ghosts, rejoice!
For never has such soothing voice
Been to your shadowy world conveyed,
Since erst, at morn, some wandering shade
Heard the clear song of Orpheus [6] come
Through Hades, and the mournful gloom.
Wordsworth has gone from us—and ye,   40
Ah, may ye feel his voice as we!
He too upon a wintry clime
Had fallen—on this iron time
Of doubts, disputes, distractions, fears.
He found us when the age had bound
Our souls in its benumbing round;
He spoke, and loosed our heart in tears.
He laid us as we lay at birth
On the cool flowery lap of earth,
Smiles broke from us and we had ease;   50

6 Harper of Greek myth, who descended to Hades after his wife Eurydice.

The hills were round us, and the breeze
Went o'er the sun-lit fields again;
Our foreheads felt the wind and rain.
Our youth returned; for there was shed
On spirits that had long been dead,
Spirits dried up and closely furled,
The freshness of the early world.

Ah! since dark days still bring to light
Man's prudence and man's fiery might,
Time may restore us in his course   60
Goethe's sage mind and Byron's force;
But where will Europe's latter hour
Again find Wordsworth's healing power?
Others will teach us how to dare,
And against fear our breast to steel;
Others will strengthen us to bear—
But who, ah! who, will make us feel?
The cloud of mortal destiny,
Others will front it fearlessly—
But who, like him, will put it by?   70

Keep fresh the grass upon his grave
O Rotha,[7] with thy living wave!
Sing him thy best! for few or none
Hears thy right voice, now he is gone.

THE SECOND BEST

MODERATE tasks and moderate leisure,
Quiet living, strict-kept measure
Both in suffering and in pleasure—
    'Tis for this thy nature yearns.

But so many books thou readest,
But so many schemes thou breedest,
But so many wishes feedest,
    That thy poor head almost turns.

And (the world's so madly jangled,
Human things so fast entangled)   10
Nature's wish must now be strangled
    For that best which she discerns.

So it *must* be! yet, while leading
A strained life, while overfeeding,

7 stream near Grasmere, where Wordsworth is buried

Like the rest, his wit with reading,
　No small profit that man earns,

Who through all he meets can steer him,
Can reject what cannot clear him,
Cling to what can truly cheer him;
　Who each day more surely learns   20

That an impulse, from the distance
Of his deepest, best existence,
To the words, "Hope, Light, Persistence,"
　Strongly sets and truly burns.

SELF-DEPENDENCE

WEARY of myself, and sick of asking
What I am, and what I ought to be,
At this vessel's prow I stand, which bears me
Forwards, forwards, o'er the starlit sea.

And a look of passionate desire
O'er the sea and to the stars I send:
"Ye who from my childhood up have calmed me,
Calm me, ah, compose me to the end!

"Ah, once more," I cried, "ye stars, ye waters,
On my heart your mighty charm renew;   10
Still, still let me, as I gaze upon you,
Feel my soul becoming vast like you!"

From the intense, clear, star-sown vault of heaven,
Over the lit sea's unquiet way,
In the rustling night-air came the answer:
"Wouldst thou *be* as these are? *Live* as they.

"Unaffrighted by the silence round them,
Undistracted by the sights they see,
These demand not that the things without them
Yield them love, amusement, sympathy.   20

"And with joy the stars perform their shining,
And the sea its long moon-silvered roll;
For self-poised they live, nor pine with noting
All the fever of some differing soul.

"Bounded by themselves, and unregardful
In what state God's other works may be,

In their own tasks all their powers pouring,
These attain the mighty life you see."

O air-born voice! long since, severely clear,
A cry like thine in my own heart I hear: 30
"Resolve to be thyself; and know that he,
Who finds himself, loses his misery!"

MORALITY

WE cannot kindle when we will
The fire which in the heart resides;
The spirit bloweth and is still,
In mystery our soul abides.
    But tasks in hours of insight willed
    Can be through hours of gloom fulfilled.

With aching hands and bleeding feet
We dig and heap, lay stone on stone;
We bear the burden and the heat
Of the long day, and wish 'twere done.   10
    Not till the hours of light return,
    All we have built do we discern.

Then, when the clouds are off the soul,
When thou dost bask in Nature's eye,
Ask, how *she* viewed thy self-control,
Thy struggling, tasked morality—
    Nature, whose free, light, cheerful air,
    Oft made thee, in thy gloom, despair.

And she, whose censure thou dost dread,
Whose eye thou wast afraid to seek,   20
See, on her face a glow is spread,
A strong emotion on her cheek!
    "Ah child!" she cries, "that strife divine,
    Whence was it, for it is not mine?

"There is no effort on *my* brow—
I do not strive, I do not weep;
I rush with the swift spheres and glow
In joy, and when I will, I sleep.
    Yet that severe, that earnest air,
    I saw, I felt it once—but where?   30

"I knew not yet the gauge of time,
Nor wore the manacles of space;
I felt it in some other clime,
I saw it in some other place.
   'Twas when the heavenly house I trod,
   And lay upon the breast of God."

A SUMMER NIGHT

In the deserted, moon-blanched street,
How lonely rings the echo of my feet!
Those windows, which I gaze at, frown,
Silent and white, unopening down,
Repellent as the world;—but see,
A break between the housetops shows
The moon! and, lost behind her, fading dim
Into the dewy dark obscurity
Down at the far horizon's rim,
Doth a whole tract of heaven disclose!   10

And to my mind the thought
Is on a sudden brought
Of a past night, and a far different scene.
Headlands stood out into the moonlit deep
As clearly as at noon;
The spring-tide's brimming flow
Heaved dazzlingly between;
Houses, with long white sweep,
Girdled the glistening bay;
Behind, through the soft air,   20
The blue, haze-cradled mountains spread away.
That night was far more fair—
But the same restless pacings to and fro,
And the same vainly throbbing heart was there,
And the same bright, calm moon.

And the calm moonlight seems to say:
Hast thou then still the old unquiet breast,
Which neither deadens into rest,
Nor ever feels the fiery glow
That whirls the spirit from itself away,   30
But fluctuates to and fro,
Never by passion quite possessed
And never quite benumbed by the world's sway?—
And I, I know not if to pray

Still to be what I am, or yield and be
Like all the other men I see.

For most men in a brazen prison live,
Where, in the sun's hot eye,
With heads bent o'er their toil, they languidly
Their lives to some unmeaning taskwork give,   40
Dreaming of nought beyond their prison-wall.
And as, year after year,
Fresh products of their barren labor fall
From their tired hands, and rest
Never yet comes near,
Gloom settles slowly down over their breast;
And while they try to stem
The waves of mournful thought by which they are pressed,
Death in their prison reaches them,
Unfreed, having seen nothing, still unblessed.   50

And the rest, a few,
Escape their prison and depart
On the wide ocean of life anew.
There the freed prisoner, where'er his heart
Listeth, will sail;
Nor doth he know how there prevail,
Despotic on that sea,
Trade-winds which cross it from eternity.
Awhile he holds some false way, undebarred
By thwarting signs, and braves   60
The freshening wind and blackening waves.
And then the tempest strikes him; and between
The lightning-bursts is seen
Only a driving wreck,
And the pale master on his spar-strewn deck
With anguished face and flying hair
Grasping the rudder hard,
Still bent to make some port he knows not where,
Still standing for some false, impossible shore.
And sterner comes the roar   70
Of sea and wind, and through the deepening gloom
Fainter and fainter wreck and helmsman loom,
And he too disappears, and comes no more.

Is there no life, but these alone?
Madman or slave, must man be one?

Plainness and clearness without shadow of stain!

Clearness divine!
Ye heavens, whose pure dark regions have no sign
Of languor, though so calm, and, though so great,
Are yet untroubled and unpassionate;   80
Who, though so noble, share in the world's toil,
And, though so tasked, keep free from dust and soil!
I will not say that your mild deeps retain
A tinge, it may be, of their silent pain
Who have longed deeply once, and longed in vain—
But I will rather say that you remain
A world above man's head, to let him see
How boundless might his soul's horizons be,
How vast, yet of what clear transparency!
How it were good to abide there, and breathe free;   90
How fair a lot to fill
Is left to each man still!

LINES WRITTEN IN KENSINGTON GARDENS

In this lone, open glade I lie,
Screened by deep boughs on either hand;
And at its end, to stay the eye,
Those black-crowned, red-boled pine-trees stand!

Birds here make song, each bird has his,
Across the girdling city's hum.
How green under the boughs it is!
How thick the tremulous sheep-cries come!

Sometimes a child will cross the glade
To take his nurse his broken toy;   10
Sometimes a thrush flit overhead
Deep in her unknown day's employ.

Here at my feet what wonders pass,
What endless, active life is here!
What blowing daisies, fragrant grass!
An air-stirred forest, fresh and clear.

Scarce fresher is the mountain-sod
Where the tired angler lies, stretched out,
And, eased of basket and of rod,
Counts his day's spoil, the spotted trout.   20

In the huge world, which roars hard by,
Be others happy if they can!

But in my helpless cradle I
Was breathed on by the rural Pan.

I, on men's impious uproar hurled,
Think often, as I hear them rave,
That peace has left the upper world
And now keeps only in the grave.

Yet here is peace for ever new!
When I who watch them am away,   30
Still all things in this glade go through
The changes of their quiet day.

Then to their happy rest they pass!
The flowers upclose, the birds are fed,
The night comes down upon the grass,
The child sleeps warmly in his bed.

Calm soul of all things! make it mine
To feel, amid the city's jar,
That there abides a peace of thine,
Man did not make, and cannot mar.   40

The will to neither strive nor cry,
The power to feel with others give!
Calm, calm me more! nor let me die
Before I have begun to live.

THE FUTURE

A WANDERER is man from his birth.
He was born in a ship
On the breast of the river of Time;
Brimming with wonder and joy
He spreads out his arms to the light,
Rivets his gaze on the banks of the stream.

As what he sees is, so have his thoughts been.
Whether he wakes,
Where the snowy mountainous pass,
Echoing the screams of the eagles,   10

Hems in its gorges the bed
Of the new-born clear-flowing stream;
Whether he first sees light
Where the river in gleaming rings
Sluggishly winds through the plain;
Whether in sound of the swallowing sea—
As is the world on the banks,
So is the mind of the man.

Vainly does each, as he glides,
Fable and dream   20
Of the lands which the river of Time
Had left ere he woke on its breast,
Or shall reach when his eyes have been closed.
Only the tract where he sails
He wots of; only the thoughts,
Raised by the objects he passes, are his.

Who can see the green earth any more
As she was by the sources of Time?
Who imagines her fields as they lay
In the sunshine, unworn by the plough?   30
Who thinks as they thought,
The tribes who then roamed on her breast,
Her vigorous, primitive sons?

What girl
Now reads in her bosom as clear
As Rebekah read, when she sat
At eve by the palm-shaded well? [8]
Who guards in her breast
As deep, as pellucid a spring
Of feeling, as tranquil, as sure?   40

What bard,
At the height of his vision, can deem
Of God, of the world, of the soul,
With a plainness as near,
As flashing as Moses felt
When he lay in the night by his flock
On the starlit Arabian waste? [9]

[8] Gen. xxiv, 15–28, 58–67   [9] Ex. iii

Can rise and obey
The beck of the Spirit like him?

This tract which the river of Time   50
Now flows through with us, is the plain.
Gone is the calm of its earlier shore.
Bordered by cities and hoarse
With a thousand cries is its stream.
And we on its breast, our minds
Are confused as the cries which we hear,
Changing and shot as the sights which we see.

And we say that repose has fled
For ever the course of the river of Time.
That cities will crowd to its edge   60
In a blacker, incessanter line;
That the din will be more on its banks,
Denser the trade on its stream,
Flatter the plain where it flows,
Fiercer the sun overhead.
That never will those on its breast
See an ennobling sight,
Drink of the feeling of quiet again.

But what was before us we know not,
And we know not what shall succeed.   70

Haply, the river of Time—
As it grows, as the towns on its marge
Fling their wavering lights
On a wider, statelier stream—
May acquire, if not the calm
Of its early mountainous shore,
Yet a solemn peace of its own.

And the width of the waters, the hush
Of the gray expanse where he floats,
Freshening its current and spotted with foam   80
As it draws to the Ocean, may strike
Peace to the soul of the man on its breast—
As the pale waste widens around him,
As the banks fade dimmer away,
As the stars come out, and the night-wind
Brings up the stream
Murmurs and scents of the infinite sea.

STANZAS IN MEMORY OF THE AUTHOR OF "OBERMANN" [10]

NOVEMBER, 1849

In front the awful Alpine track
Crawls up its rocky stair;
The autumn storm-winds drive the rack,
Close o'er it, in the air.

Behind are the abandoned baths [11]
Mute in their meadows lone;
The leaves are on the valley-paths,
The mists are on the Rhone—

The white mists rolling like a sea!
I hear the torrents roar.   10
—Yes, Obermann, all speaks of thee;
I feel thee near once more!

I turn thy leaves! I feel their breath
Once more upon me roll;
That air of languor, cold, and death,
Which brooded o'er thy soul.

Fly hence, poor wretch, whoe'er thou art,
Condemned to cast about,
All shipwreck in thy own weak heart,
For comfort from without!   20

A fever in these pages burns
Beneath the calm they feign;
A wounded human spirit turns,
Here, on its bed of pain.

[10] "The author of *Obermann*, Étienne Pivert de Senancour, has little celebrity in France, his own country; and out of France he is almost unknown. But the profound inwardness, the austere sincerity, of his principal work, *Obermann*, the delicate feeling for nature which it exhibits, and the melancholy eloquence of many passages of it, have attracted and charmed some of the most remarkable spirits of this century, such as George Sand and Sainte-Beuve, and will probably always find a certain number of spirits whom they touch and interest.

"Senancour was born in 1770. He was educated for the priesthood, and passed some time in the seminary of St. Sulpice; broke away from the Seminary and from France itself, and passed some years in Switzerland, where he married; returned to France in middle life, and followed thenceforward the career of a man of letters, but with hardly any fame or success. He died an old man in 1846, desiring that on his grave might be placed these words only: *Éternité, deviens mon asile!* 'Eternity, become my refuge.'" —(From Arnold's note)

[11] "The Baths of Leuk. This poem was conceived, and partly composed, in the valley going down from the foot of the Gemmi Pass towards the Rhone."—(Arnold)

Yes, though the virgin mountain-air
Fresh through these pages blows;
Though to these leaves the glaciers spare
The soul of their white snows;

Though here a mountain-murmur swells
Of many a dark-boughed pine;
Though, as you read, you hear the bells   30
Of the high-pasturing kine—

Yet, through the hum of torrent lone,
And brooding mountain bee,
There sobs I know not what ground-tone
Of human agony.

Is it for this, because the sound
Is fraught too deep with pain,
That, Obermann! the world around   40
So little loves thy strain?

Some secrets may the poet tell,
For the world loves new ways;
To tell too deep ones is not well—
It knows not what he says.

Yet, of the spirits who have reigned
In this our troubled day,
I know but two, who have attained,
Save thee, to see their way.

By England's lakes, in gray old age,
His quiet home one keeps;
And one, the strong much-toiling sage,   50
In German Weimar sleeps.

But Wordsworth's eyes avert their ken
From half of human fate;
And Goethe's course few sons of men
May think to emulate.

For he pursued a lonely road,
His eyes on Nature's plan;
Neither made man too much a God,
Nor God too much a man.   60

Strong was he, with a spirit free
From mists, and sane, and clear;
Clearer, how much! than ours—yet we
Have a worse course to steer.

For though his manhood bore the blast
Of a tremendous time,
Yet in a tranquil world was passed
His tenderer youthful prime.

But we, brought forth and reared in hours
Of change, alarm, surprise—   70
What shelter to grow ripe is ours?
What leisure to grow wise?

Like children bathing on the shore,
Buried a wave beneath,
The second wave succeeds, before
We have had time to breathe.

Too fast we live, too much are tried,
Too harassed, to attain
Wordsworth's sweet calm, or Goethe's wide
And luminous view to gain.   80

And then we turn, thou sadder sage,
To thee! we feel thy spell!
—The hopeless tangle of our age,
Thou too hast scanned it well!

Immoveable thou sittest, still
As death, composed to bear!
Thy head is clear, thy feeling chill,
And icy thy despair.

Yes, as the son of Thetis [12] said,
I hear thee saying now: 90
Greater by far than thou art dead;
Strive not! die also thou!

Ah! two desires toss about
The poet's feverish blood.
One drives him to the world without,
And one to solitude.

[12] Achilles, who, angered by the death of his friend Patroclus, spoke the italicized
words to Lycaon when the latter pleaded for mercy. (*Iliad,* bk. xxi)

The glow, he cries, the thrill of life,
Where, where do these abound?—
Not in the world, not in the strife
Of men, shall they be found.   100

He who hath watched, not shared, the strife,
Knows how the day hath gone.
He only lives with the world's life,
Who hath renounced his own.

To thee we come, then! Clouds are rolled
Where thou, O seer! art set;
Thy realm of thought is drear and cold—
The world is colder yet!

And thou hast pleasures, too, to share
With those who come to thee—   110
Balms floating on thy mountain-air,
And healing sights to see.

How often, where the slopes are green
On Jaman,[13] hast thou sate
By some high chalet-door, and seen
The summer-day grow late;

And darkness steal o'er the wet grass
With the pale crocus starred,
And reach that glimmering sheet of glass
Beneath the piny sward,   120

Lake Leman's [14] waters, far below!
And watched the rosy light
Fade from the distant peaks of snow;
And on the air of night

Heard accents of the eternal tongue
Through the pine branches play—
Listened, and felt thyself grow young!
Listened and wept—Away!

Away the dreams that but deceive
And thou, sad guide, adieu!   130
I go, fate drives me; but I leave
Half of my life with you.

13 Alpine peak   14 Lake Geneva

We, in some unknown Power's employ,
Move on a rigorous line;
Can neither, when we will, enjoy,
Nor, when we will, resign.

I in the world must live; but thou,
Thou melancholy shade!
Wilt not, if thou canst see me now,
Condemn me, nor upbraid.   140

For thou art gone away from earth,
And place with those dost claim,
The Children of the Second Birth,
Whom the world could not tame;

And with that small, transfigured band,
Whom many a different way
Conducted to their common land,
Thou learn'st to think as they.

Christian and pagan, king and slave,
Soldier and anchorite,   150
Distinctions we esteem so grave,
Are nothing in their sight.

They do not ask, who pined unseen,
Who was on action hurled,
Whose one bond is, that all have been
Unspotted by the world.

There without anger thou wilt see
Him who obeys thy spell
No more, so he but rest, like thee,
Unsoiled!—and so, farewell.   160

Farewell!—Whether thou now liest near
That much-loved inland sea,
The ripples of whose blue waves cheer
Vevey and Meillerie: [15]

And in that gracious region bland,
Where with clear-rustling wave
The scented pines of Switzerland
Stand dark round thy green grave,

15 towns on Lake Geneva

Between thy dusty vineyard-walls
Issuing on that green place
The early peasant still recalls
The pensive stranger's face,

And stoops to clear thy moss-grown date
Ere he plods on again;—
Or whether, by maligner fate,
Among the swarms of men,

Where between granite terraces
The blue Seine rolls her wave,
The Capital of Pleasure sees
The hardly-heard-of grave;—

Farewell! Under the sky we part,
In this stern Alpine dell.
O unstrung will! O broken heart!
A last, a last farewell!

REQUIESCAT

STREW on her roses, roses,
  And never a spray of yew!
In quiet she reposes:
  Ah, would that I did too!

Her mirth the world required;
  She bathed it in smiles of glee.
But her heart was tired, tired,
  And now they let her be.

Her life was turning, turning,
  In mazes of heat and sound.
But for peace her soul was yearning,
  And now peace laps her round.

Her cabined, ample spirit,
  It fluttered and failed for breath.
To-night it doth inherit
  The vasty hall of death.

PHILOMELA [16]

Hark! ah, the nightingale—
The tawny-throated!
Hark, from that moonlit cedar what a burst!
What triumph! hark—what pain!

O wanderer from a Grecian shore,
Still, after many years, in distant lands,
Still nourishing in thy bewildered brain
That wild, unquenched, deep-sunken, old-world pain—
Say, will it never heal?
And can this fragrant lawn   10
With its cool trees, and night,
And the sweet, tranquil Thames,
And moonshine, and the dew,
To thy racked heart and brain
Afford no balm?

Dost thou to-night behold
Here, through the moonlight on this English grass,
The unfriendly palace in the Thracian wild?
Dost thou again peruse
With hot cheeks and seared eyes   20
The too clear web, and thy dumb sister's shame?
Dost thou once more assay
Thy flight, and feel come over thee,
Poor fugitive, the feathery change
Once more, and once more seem to make resound
With love and hate, triumph and agony,
Lone Daulis, and the high Cephissian vale?
Listen, Eugenia—
How thick the bursts come crowding through the leaves!
Again—thou hearest?   30
Eternal passion!
Eternal pain!

---

16 Violated by her brother-in-law, Tereus, King of Crete, who cut out her tongue,
she yet managed to tell her sister Procne by weaving the story into a robe or tapestry.
They served up Tereus and Procne's son, Itys, to him as a meal, fled, pursued by
Tereus, and on their prayers for deliverance, were changed into a nightingale and a
swallow respectively. Arnold reverses the two sisters. The tragedy happened in Daulis
(Greece) near the river Cephissus.

THE SCHOLAR-GIPSY [17]

Go, for they call you, shepherd, from the hill;
  Go, shepherd, and untie the wattled cotes! [18]
    No longer leave thy wistful flock unfed,
    Nor let thy bawling fellows rack their throats,
    Nor the cropped herbage shoot another head.
      But when the fields are still,
    And the tired men and dogs all gone to rest,
      And only the white sheep are sometimes seen
      Cross and recross the strips of moon-blanched green,
Come, shepherd, and again begin the quest!   10

Here, where the reaper was at work of late—
  In this high field's dark corner, where he leaves
    His coat, his basket, and his earthen cruse,
    And in the sun all morning binds the sheaves,
    Then here, at noon, comes back his stores to use—
      Here will I sit and wait,
    While to my ear from uplands far away
      The bleating of the folded flocks is borne,
      With distant cries of reapers in the corn—
All the live murmur of a summer's day.   20

Screened is this nook o'er the high, half-reaped field,
  And here till sun-down, shepherd! will I be.
    Through the thick corn [19] the scarlet poppies peep,
    And round green roots and yellowing stalks I see
    Pale pink convolvulus in tendrils creep;
      And air-swept lindens yield
    Their scent, and rustle down their perfumed showers
      Of bloom on the bent grass where I am laid,
      And bower me from the August sun with shade;
And the eye travels down to Oxford's towers.   30

And near me on the grass lies Glanvil's book—
  Come, let me read the oft-read tale again!

---

17 "There was very lately a lad in the University of Oxford, who was by his poverty forced to leave his studies there; and at last to join himself to a company of vagabond gipsies. Among these extravagant people, by the insinuating subtlety of his carriage, he quickly got so much of their love and esteem as that they discovered to him their mystery. After he had been a pretty while exercised in the trade, there chanced to ride by a couple of scholars, who had formerly been of his acquaintance. They quickly spied out their old friend among the gipsies; and he gave them an account of the necessity which drove him to that kind of life, and told them that the people he went with were not such impostors as they were taken for, but that they had a traditional kind of learning among them, and could do wonders by the power of imagination, their fancy binding that of others; that himself had learned much of their art, and when he had compassed the whole secret, he intended, he said, to leave their company, and give the world an account of what he had learned."— Glanvil, *Vanity of Dogmatizing*, 1661 (Arnold's note).

18 sheepfolds
19 grain, wheat

The story of the Oxford scholar poor,
Of pregnant parts and quick inventive brain,
    Who, tired of knocking at preferment's [20] door,
        One summer morn forsook
His friends, and went to learn the gipsy-lore,
    And roamed the world with that wild brotherhood,
    And came, as most men deemed, to little good,
But came to Oxford and his friends no more.   40

But once, years after, in the country lanes,
    Two scholars, whom at college erst he knew,
    Met him, and of his way of life inquired;
        Whereat he answered, that the gipsy-crew,
        His mates, had arts to rule as they desired
            The workings of men's brains,
And they can bind them to what thoughts they will.
    "And I," he said, "the secret of their art,
    When fully learned, will to the world impart;
But it needs heaven-sent moments for this skill."   50

This said, he left them, and returned no more.—
    But rumors hung about the country-side,
    That the lost Scholar long was seen to stray,
        Seen by rare glimpses, pensive and tongue-tied,
        In hat of antique shape, and cloak of gray,
            The same the gipsies wore.
Shepherds had met him on the Hurst [21] in spring;
    At some lone alehouse in the Berkshire moors,
    On the warm ingle-bench, the smock-frocked boors
Had found him seated at their entering,   60

But, 'mid their drink and clatter, he would fly.
    And I myself seem half to know thy looks,
    And put the shepherds, wanderer! on thy trace;
        And boys who in lone wheatfields scare the rooks
        I ask if thou hast passed their quiet place;
            Or in my boat I lie
Moored to the cool bank in the summer heats,
    'Mid wide grass meadows which the sunshine fills,
    And watch the warm, green-muffled Cumner hills,
And wonder if thou haunt'st their shy retreats.   70

For most, I know, thou lov'st retired ground!
    Thee at the ferry Oxford riders blithe,

20 appointment in the   21 Cumner Hurst, hill
church   three miles south of Oxford

Returning home on summer nights, have met
Crossing the stripling Thames at Bab-lock-hithe,[22]
    Trailing in the cool stream thy fingers wet,
        As the punt's rope chops round;
And leaning backward in a pensive dream,
    And fostering in thy lap a heap of flowers
    Plucked in shy fields and distant Wychwood [23] bowers,
And thine eyes resting on the moonlit stream.   80

And then they land, and thou art seen no more!—
    Maidens, who from the distant hamlets come
        To dance around the Fyfield elm in May,
    Oft through the darkening fields have seen thee roam,
        Or cross a stile into the public way.
            Oft thou hast given them store
    Of flowers—the frail-leafed, white anemone,
        Dark bluebells drenched with dews of summer eves,
        And purple orchises with spotted leaves—
But none hath words she can report of thee.   90

And, above Godstow Bridge, when haytime's here
    In June, and many a scythe in sunshine flames,
        Men who through those wide fields of breezy grass
    Where black-winged swallows haunt the glittering Thames,
        To bathe in the abandoned lasher [24] pass,
            Have often passed thee near
    Sitting upon the river bank o'ergrown;
        Marked thine outlandish garb, thy figure spare,
        Thy dark vague eyes, and soft abstracted air—
But, when they came from bathing, thou wast gone!   100

At some lone homestead in the Cumner hills,
    Where at her open door the housewife darns,
        Thou hast been seen, or hanging on a gate
    To watch the threshers in the mossy barns.
        Children, who early range these slopes and late
            For cresses from the rills,
    Have known thee eying, all an April-day,
        The springing pastures and the feeding kine;
        And marked thee, when the stars come out and shine,
Through the long dewy grass move slow away.   110

In autumn, on the skirts of Bagley wood—
    Where most the gipsies by the turf-edged way

---

22 village near Cumner   of Oxford. The places men-   24 pool below a dam
Hurst   tioned below are in the
23 forest ten miles north vicinity of Oxford.

Pitch their smoked tents, and every bush you see
With scarlet patches tagged and shreds of gray,
Above the forest ground called Thessaly—
The blackbird, picking food,
Sees thee, nor stops his meal, nor fears at all;
So often has he known thee past him stray,
Rapt, twirling in thy hand a withered spray,
And waiting for the spark from heaven to fall. 120

And once, in winter, on the causeway chill
Where home through flooded fields foot-travelers go,
Have I not passed thee on the wooden bridge,
Wrapped in thy cloak and battling with the snow,
Thy face toward Hinksey and its wintry ridge?
And thou hast climbed the hill
And gained the white brow of the Cumner range;
Turned once to watch, while thick the snowflakes fall,
The line of festal light in Christ-Church hall—[25]
Then sought thy straw in some sequestered grange. 130

But what—I dream! Two hundred years are flown
Since first thy story ran through Oxford halls,
And the grave Glanvil did the tale inscribe
That thou wert wandered from the studious walls
To learn strange arts, and join a gipsy-tribe;
And thou from earth art gone
Long since, and in some quiet churchyard laid—
Some country-nook, where o'er thy unknown grave
Tall grasses and white flowering nettles wave,
Under a dark, red-fruited yew-tree's shade. 140

—No, no, thou hast not felt the lapse of hours!
For what wears out the life of mortal men?
'Tis that from change to change their being rolls;
'Tis that repeated shocks, again, again,
Exhaust the energy of strongest souls
And numb the elastic powers.
Till having used our nerves with bliss and teen,[26]
And tired upon a thousand schemes our wit,
To the just-pausing Genius we remit
Our worn-out life, and are—what we have been. 150

Thou hast not lived, why should'st thou perish, so?
Thou hadst *one* aim, *one* business, *one* desire;
Else wert thou long since numbered with the dead!

25 dining hall of Christ Church College, Oxford   26 grief

Else hadst thou spent, like other men, thy fire!
  The generations of thy peers are fled,
    And we ourselves shall go;
  But thou possessest an immortal lot,
    And we imagine thee exempt from age
    And living as thou liv'st on Glanvil's page,
  Because thou hadst—what we, alas! have not.   160

For early didst thou leave the world, with powers
  Fresh, undiverted to the world without,
    Firm to their mark, not spent on other things;
  Free from the sick fatigue, the languid doubt,
    Which much to have tried, in much been baffled, brings.
      O life unlike to ours!
  Who fluctuate idly without term or scope,
    Of whom each strives, nor knows for what he strives,
    And each half lives a hundred different lives;
  Who wait like thee, but not, like thee, in hope.   170

Thou waitest for the spark from heaven! and we,
  Light half-believers of our casual creeds,
    Who never deeply felt, nor clearly willed,
  Whose insight never has borne fruit in deeds,
    Whose vague resolves never have been fulfilled;
      For whom each year we see
  Breeds new beginnings, disappointments new;
    Who hesitate and falter life away,
    And lose to-morrow the ground won to-day—
  Ah, do not we, wanderer! await it too?   180

Yes, we await it!—but it still delays,
  And then we suffer! and amongst us one,[27]
    Who most has suffered, takes dejectedly
  His seat upon the intellectual throne;
    And all his store of sad experience he
      Lays bare of wretched days;
  Tells us his misery's birth and growth and signs,
    And how the dying spark of hope was fed,
    And how the breast was soothed, and how the head,
  And all his hourly varied anodynes.   190

This for our wisest! and we others pine,
  And wish the long unhappy dream would end,
    And waive all claim to bliss, and try to bear;
  With close-lipped patience for our only friend,

27 Carlyle? or Tennyson?

Sad patience, too near neighbor to despair—
  But none has hope like thine!
Thou through the fields and through the woods dost stray,
  Roaming the country-side, a truant boy,
  Nursing thy project in unclouded joy,
And every doubt long blown by time away.   200

O born in days when wits were fresh and clear,
  And life ran gaily as the sparkling Thames;
    Before this strange disease of modern life,
  With its sick hurry, its divided aims,
    Its heads o'ertaxed, its palsied hearts, was rife—
      Fly hence, our contact fear!
  Still fly, plunge deeper in the bowering wood!
    Averse, as Dido did with gesture stern
    From her false friend's [28] approach in Hades turn,
  Wave us away, and keep thy solitude!   210

Still nursing the unconquerable hope,
  Still clutching the inviolable shade,
    With a free, onward impulse brushing through,
  By night, the silvered branches of the glade—
    Far on the forest skirts, where none pursue,
      On some mild pastoral slope
  Emerge, and resting on the moonlit pales
    Freshen thy flowers as in former years
    With dew, or listen with enchanted ears,
  From the dark dingles, to the nightingales!   220

But fly our paths, our feverish contact fly!
  For strong the infection of our mental strife,
    Which, though it gives no bliss, yet spoils for rest;
  And we should win thee from thy own fair life,
    Like us distracted, and like us unblest.
      Soon, soon thy cheer would die,
  Thy hopes grow timorous, and unfixed thy powers,
    And thy clear aims be cross and shifting made;
    And then thy glad perennial youth would fade,
  Fade, and grow old at last, and die like ours.   230

Then fly our greetings, fly our speech and smiles!
  —As some grave Tyrian trader, from the sea,
    Descried at sunrise an emerging prow
  Lifting the cool-haired creepers stealthily,
    The fringes of a southward-facing brow

28 Æneas (*Æneid*, vi, 450-71)

Among the Ægean isles;
And saw the merry Grecian coaster come,
  Freighted with amber grapes, and Chian wine,
  Green, bursting figs, and tunnies [29] steeped in brine—
And knew the intruders on his ancient home,   240

The young light-hearted masters of the waves—
  And snatched his rudder, and shook out more sail;
  And day and night held on indignantly
O'er the blue Midland [30] waters with the gale,
  Betwixt the Syrtes [31] and soft Sicily,
    To where the Atlantic raves
Outside the western straits; and unbent sails
  There, where down cloudy cliffs, through sheets of foam,
  Shy traffickers, the dark Iberians [32] come;
And on the beach undid his corded bales.   250

STANZAS FROM THE GRANDE CHARTREUSE [33]

THROUGH Alpine meadows soft-suffused
With rain, where thick the crocus blows,
Past the dark forges long disused,
The mule-track from Saint Laurent goes.
The bridge is crossed, and slow we ride,
Through forest, up the mountain-side.

The autumnal evening darkens round,
The wind is up, and drives the rain;
While, hark! far down, with strangled sound
Doth the Dead Guier's stream complain   10
Where that wet smoke, among the woods,
Over his boiling cauldron broods.

Swift rush the spectral vapors white
Past limestone scars [34] with ragged pines,
Showing—then blotting from our sight!—
Halt—through the cloud-drift something shines!
High in the valley, wet and drear,
The huts of Courrerie appear.

Strike leftward! cries our guide; and higher
Mounts up the stony forest-way.   20

At last the encircling trees retire;
Look! through the showery twilight gray
What pointed roofs are these advance?—
A palace of the Kings of France?

Approach, for what we seek is here!
Alight, and sparely sup, and wait
For rest in this outbuilding near;
Then cross the sward and reach that gate.
Knock; pass the wicket! Thou art come
To the Carthusians' world-famed home.   30

The silent courts, where night and day
Into their stone-carved basins cold
The splashing icy fountains play—
The humid corridors behold!
Where, ghostlike in the deepening night,
Cowled forms brush by in gleaming white.

The chapel, where no organ's peal
Invests the stern and naked prayer—
With penitential cries they kneel
And wrestle; rising then, with bare   40
And white uplifted faces stand,
Passing the Host from hand to hand;

Each takes, and then his visage wan
Is buried in his cowl once more.
The cells!—the suffering Son of Man
Upon the wall—the knee-worn floor—
And where they sleep, that wooden bed,
Which shall their coffin be, when dead!

The library, where tract and tome
Not to feed priestly pride are there,   50
To hymn the conquering march of Rome,
Nor yet to amuse, as ours are!
They paint of souls the inner strife,
Their drops of blood, their death in life.

The garden, overgrown—yet mild,
See, fragrant herbs are flowering there!
Strong children of the Alpine wild
Whose culture is the brethren's care;
Of human tasks their only one,
And cheerful works beneath the sun.   60

Those halls, too, destined to contain
Each its own pilgrim-host of old,
From England, Germany, or Spain—
All are before me! I behold
The House, the Brotherhood austere!
—And what am I, that I am here?

For rigorous teachers seized my youth,
And purged its faith, and trimmed its fire,
Showed me the high, white star of Truth,
There bade me gaze, and there aspire.   70
Even now their whispers pierce the gloom:
What dost thou in this living tomb?

Forgive me, masters of the mind!
At whose behest I long ago
So much unlearnt, so much resigned—
I come not here to be your foe!
I seek these anchorites, not in ruth,
To curse and to deny your truth;

Not as their friend, or child, I speak!
But as, on some far northern strand,   80
Thinking of his own Gods, a Greek
In pity and mournful awe might stand
Before some fallen Runic stone—[35]
For both were faiths, and both are gone.

Wandering between two worlds, one dead,
The other powerless to be born,
With nowhere yet to rest my head,
Like these, on earth I wait forlorn.
Their faith, my tears, the world deride—
I come to shed them at their side.   90

Oh, hide me in your gloom profound,
Ye solemn seats of holy pain!
Take me, cowled forms, and fence me round,
Till I possess my soul again;
Till free my thoughts before me roll,
Not chafed by hourly false control!

For the world cries your faith is now
But a dead time's exploded dream;

[35] stone inscribed with runes, or letters used by the Teutonic peoples before the adoption of the Roman alphabet—the inscription having, as frequently, a religious significance.

My melancholy, sciolists [36] say,
Is a passed mode, an outworn theme—
As if the world had ever had
A faith, or sciolists been sad!

Ah, if it *be* passed, take away,
At least, the restlessness, the pain;
Be man henceforth no more a prey
To these out-dated stings again!
The nobleness of grief is gone—
Ah, leave us not the fret alone!

But—if you cannot give us ease—
Last of the race of them who grieve
Here leave us to die out with these
Last of the people who believe!
Silent, while years engrave the brow;
Silent—the best are silent now.

Achilles ponders in his tent,[37]
The kings of modern thought are dumb;
Silent they are, though not content,
And wait to see the future come.
They have the grief men had of yore,
But they contend and cry no more.

Our fathers watered with their tears
This sea of time whereon we sail,
Their voices were in all men's ears
Who passed within their puissant hail.
Still the same ocean round us raves,
But we stand mute, and watch the waves.

For what availed it, all the noise
And outcry of the former men?—
Say, have their sons achieved more joys,
Say, is life lighter now than then?
The sufferers died, they left their pain—
The pangs which tortured them remain.

What helps it now, that Byron bore,
With haughty scorn which mocked the smart,
Through Europe to the Ætolian shore [38]

36 those of superficial or pretended learning
37 *Iliad,* bk. i, ix
38 Grecian shore—where Byron in 1823 joined in the fight for Greek independence, and where he died in 1824.

The pageant of his bleeding heart?
That thousands counted every groan,
And Europe made his woe her own?

What boots it, Shelley! that the breeze
Carried thy lovely wail away,   140
Musical through Italian trees
Which fringe thy soft blue Spezzian bay? [39]
Inheritors of thy distress
Have restless hearts one throb the less?

Or are we easier, to have read,
O Obermann! [40] the sad, stern page,
Which tells us how thou hidd'st thy head
From the fierce tempest of thine age
In the lone brakes of Fontainebleau,
Or chalets near the Alpine snow?   150

Ye slumber in your silent grave!—
The world, which for an idle day
Grace to your mood of sadness gave,
Long since hath flung her weeds away.
The eternal trifler breaks your spell;
But we—we learnt your lore too well!

Years hence, perhaps, may dawn an age,
More fortunate, alas! than we,
Which without hardness will be sage,
And gay without frivolity.   160
Sons of the world, oh, speed those years;
But, while we wait, allow our tears!

Allow them! We admire with awe
The exulting thunder of your race;
You give the universe your law,
You triumph over time and space!
Your pride of life, your tireless powers,
We laud them, but they are not ours.

We are like children reared in shade
Beneath some old-world abbey wall,   170
Forgotten in a forest-glade,
And secret from the eyes of all.

39 where Shelley was   40 See *Stanzas* to his
drowned, 1822   memory, above.

Deep, deep the greenwood round them waves,
Their abbey, and its close [41] of graves!

But, where the road runs near the stream,
Oft through the trees they catch a glance
Of passing troops in the sun's beam—
Pennon, and plume, and flashing lance!
Forth to the world those soldiers fare,
To life, to cities, and to war!   180

And through the wood, another way,
Faint bugle-notes from far are borne,
Where hunters gather, staghounds bay,
Round some fair forest-lodge at morn.
Gay dames are there, in sylvan green;
Laughter and cries—those notes between!

The banners flashing through the trees
Make their blood dance and chain their eyes;
That bugle-music on the breeze
Arrests them with a charmed surprise.   190
Banner by turns and bugle woo:
Ye shy recluses, follow too!

O children, what do ye reply?—
"Action and pleasure, will ye roam
Through these secluded dells to cry
And call us?—but too late ye come!
Too late for us your call ye blow,
Whose bent was taken long ago.

"Long since we pace this shadowed nave;
We watch those yellow tapers shine,   200
Emblems of hope over the grave,
In the high altar's depth divine;
The organ carries to our ear
Its accents of another sphere.

"Fenced early in this cloistral round
Of reverie, of shade, of prayer,
How should we grow in other ground?
How can we flower in foreign air?
—Pass, banners, pass, and bugles, cease;
And leave our desert to its peace!"   210

41 enclosure

THYRSIS [42]

A MONODY, TO COMMEMORATE THE AUTHOR'S FRIEND, ARTHUR HUGH CLOUGH,[43] WHO DIED AT FLORENCE, 1861

How changed is here each spot man makes or fills!
  In the two Hinkseys nothing keeps the same;
    The village street its haunted mansion lacks,
  And from the sign is gone Sibylla's name,
    And from the roofs the twisted chimney-stacks—
      Are ye too changed, ye hills?
See, 'tis no foot of unfamiliar men
    To-night from Oxford up your pathway strays!
    Here came I often, often, in old days—
Thyrsis and I; we still had Thyrsis then.   10

Runs it not here, the track by Childsworth Farm,
  Past the high wood, to where the elm-tree crowns
    The hill behind whose ridge the sunset flames?
The signal-elm, that looks on Ilsley Downs,
    The Vale, the three lone weirs,[44] the youthful Thames?—
      This winter-eve is warm,
Humid the air! leafless, yet soft as spring,
    The tender purple spray on copse and briers!
    And that sweet city with her dreaming spires
She needs not June for beauty's heightening,   20

Lovely all times she lies, lovely to-night!—
  Only, methinks, some loss of habit's power
    Befalls me wandering through this upland dim.
Once passed I blindfold here, at any hour;
    Now seldom come I, since I came with him.
      That single elm-tree bright
Against the west—I miss it! is it gone?
    We prized it dearly; while it stood, we said,
    Our friend, the Gipsy-Scholar, was not dead;
While the tree lived, he in these fields lived on.   30

Too rare, too rare, grow now my visits here,
  But once I knew each field, each flower, each stick;
    And with the country-folk acquaintance made
    By barn in threshing-time, by new-built rick.

42 "Throughout this poem there is reference to the preceding piece, *The Scholar-Gipsy*." (Arnold) The name (and that of Corydon) were traditional in pastoral poetry (Virgil's Seventh *Eclogue*, Milton's *L'Allegro*). The places referred to are in the vicinity of Oxford.

43 Born 1819, well-known minor poet, popularly remembered for "Say not the Struggle Nought Availeth."

44 dams

Here, too, our shepherd-pipes we first assayed.
　　Ah me! this many a year
My pipe is lost, my shepherd's holiday! [45]
　　Needs must I lose them, needs with heavy heart
　　Into the world and wave of men depart;
But Thyrsis of his own will went away.[46]   40

It irked him to be here, he could not rest.
　　He loved each simple joy the country yields,
　　He loved his mates; but yet he could not keep,
For that a shadow lowered on the fields,
　　Here with the shepherds and the silly sheep.
　　　　Some life of men unblest
He knew, which made him droop, and filled his head.
　　He went; his piping took a troubled sound
　　Of storms that rage outside our happy ground;
He could not wait their passing, he is dead.   50

So, some tempestuous morn in early June,
　　When the year's primal burst of bloom is o'er,
　　Before the roses and the longest day—
When garden-walks and all the grassy floor
　　With blossoms red and white of fallen May
　　　　And chestnut-flowers are strewn—
So have I heard the cuckoo's parting cry,
　　From the wet field, through the vexed garden-trees,
　　Come with the volleying rain and tossing breeze:
The bloom is gone, and with the bloom go I!   60

Too quick despairer, wherefore wilt thou go?
　　Soon will the high Midsummer pomps come on,
　　Soon will the musk carnations break and swell,
Soon shall we have gold-dusted snapdragon,
　　Sweet-William with its homely cottage-smell,
　　　　And stocks [47] in fragrant blow;
Roses that down the alleys shine afar,
　　And open, jasmine-muffled lattices,
　　And groups under the dreaming garden-trees,
And the full moon, and the white evening-star.   70

He hearkens not! light comer, he is flown!
　　What matters it? next year he will return,
　　And we shall have him in the sweet spring-days,

---

45 Arnold published no poetry from 1858 to 1867, the date of this poem.
46 In 1848 Clough had re-signed his fellowship in Oriel College, Oxford, largely on religious grounds. His poetry is full of religious questioning, scepticism, and doubt.
47 gillyflowers

With whitening hedges, and uncrumpling fern,
And bluė-bells trembling by the forest-ways,
And scent of hay new-mown.
But Thyrsis never more we swains shall see;
See him come back, and cut a smoother reed,
And blow a strain the world at last shall heed—
For Time, not Corydon,[48] hath conquered thee.   80

Alack, for Corydon no rival now!—
But when Sicilian shepherds lost a mate,
Some good survivor with his flute would go,
Piping a ditty sad for Bion's [49] fate;
And cross the unpermitted ferry's flow
And relax Pluto's brow,
And make leap up with joy the beauteous head
Of Proserpine, among whose crownèd hair
Are flowers first opened on Sicilian air,
And flute his friend, like Orpheus, from the dead.   90

O easy access to the hearer's grace,
When Dorian shepherds sang to Proserpine!
For she herself had trod Sicilian fields,
She knew the Dorian water's gush divine,
She knew each lily white which Enna [50] yields,
Each rose with blushing face;
She loved the Dorian pipe, the Dorian strain.
But ah, of our poor Thames she never heard!
Her foot the Cumner cowslips never stirred;
And we should tease her with our plaint in vain!   100

Well! wind-dispersed and vain the words will be,
Yet, Thyrsis, let me give my grief its hour
In the old haunt, and find our tree-topped hill!
Who, if not I, for questing here hath power?
I know the wood which hides the daffodil,
I know the Fyfield tree,
I know what white, what purple fritillaries [51]
The grassy harvest of the river-fields,
Above by Ensham, down by Sanford, yields,
And what sedged brooks are Thames's tributaries;   110

I know these slopes; who knows them if not I?—
But many a dingle on the loved hill-side,

48 winner of a verse contest with Thyrsis in Virgil's Seventh *Eclogue*
49 lamented in an elegy by Moschus
50 Vale in Sicily (a *Dorian colony*), where Pluto found Prosperpine gathering lilies and roses, and whence he carried her off
to be his queen in the under-world.
51 lily-like plant with nodding flowers

With thorns once studded, old, white-blossomed trees,
Where thick the cowslips grew, and far descried
    High towered the spikes of purple orchises,
        Hath since our day put by
The coronals of that forgotten time;
    Down each green bank hath gone the ploughboy's team,
    And only in the hidden brookside gleam
Primroses, orphans of the flowery prime.   120

Where is the girl, who by the boatman's door,
    Above the locks, above the boating throng,
        Unmoored our skiff when through the Wytham flats,
Red loosestrife [52] and blond meadow-sweet among,
        And darting swallows and light water-gnats,
            We tracked the shy Thames shore?
Where are the mowers, who, as the tiny swell
    Of our boat passing heaved the river-grass,
    Stood with suspended scythe to see us pass?—
They all are gone, and thou art gone as well!   130

Yes, thou art gone! and round me too the night
    In ever-nearing circle weaves her shade.
        I see her veil draw soft across the day,
    I feel her slowly chilling breath invade
The cheek grown thin, the brown hair sprent with gray;
        I feel her finger light
Laid pausefully upon life's headlong train;—
    The foot less prompt to meet the morning dew,
    The heart less bounding at emotion new,
And hope, once crushed, less quick to spring again.   140

And long the way appears, which seemed so short
    To the less practised eye of sanguine youth;
        And high the mountain-tops, in cloudy air,
    The mountain-tops where is the throne of Truth,
        Tops in life's morning-sun so bright and bare!
            Unbreachable the fort
Of the long-battered world uplifts its wall;
    And strange and vain the earthly turmoil grows,
    And near and real the charm of thy repose,
And night as welcome as a friend would fall.   150

But hush! the upland hath a sudden loss
    Of quiet!—Look, adown the dusk hill-side,
        A troop of Oxford hunters going home,

52 plant with long spike of flowers

As in old days, jovial and talking, ride!
   From hunting with the Berkshire hounds they come.
      Quick! let me fly, and cross
Into yon farther field!—'Tis done; and see,
   Backed by the sunset, which doth glorify
   The orange and pale violet evening-sky,
Bare on its lonely ridge, the Tree! the Tree!   160

I take the omen! Eve lets down her veil,
   The white fog creeps from bush to bush about,
      The west unflushes, the high stars grow bright,
And in the scattered farms the lights come out.
      I cannot reach the signal-tree to-night,
         Yet, happy omen, hail!
Hear it from thy broad lucent Arno-vale [53]
   (For there thine earth-forgetting eyelids keep
   The morningless and unawakening sleep
Under the flowery oleanders pale),   170

Hear it, O Thyrsis, still our tree is there!—
   Ah, vain! These English fields, this upland dim,
      These brambles pale with mist engarlanded,
That lone, sky-pointing tree, are not for him;
      To a boon southern country he is fled,
         And now in happier air,
Wandering with the great Mother's [54] train divine
   (And purer or more subtle soul than thee,
   I trow, the mighty Mother doth not see)
Within a folding of the Apennine,   180

Thou hearest the immortal chants of old!—
   Putting his sickle to the perilous grain
      In the hot cornfield of the Phrygian king,
For thee the Lityerses-song again
      Young Daphnis with his silver voice doth sing; [55]
         Sings his Sicilian fold,

53 Vale of the river Arno, where lies Florence, in which Clough died and was buried.
54 Cybele, nature goddess, identified by the Romans with Rhea, mother of the gods.
55 "Daphnis, the ideal Sicilian shepherd of Greek pastoral poetry, was said to have followed into Phrygia his mistress Piplea, who had been carried off by robbers, and to have found her in the power of the king of Phrygia, Lityerses. Lityerses used to make strangers try a contest with him in reaping corn, and to put them to death if he overcame them. Hercules arrived in time to save Daphnis, took upon himself the reaping-contest with Lityerses, overcame him, and slew him. The Lityerses-song connected with this tradition was, like the Linus-song, one of the early plaintive strains of Greek popular poetry, and used to be sung by corn-reapers. Other traditions represented Daphnis as beloved by a nymph who exacted from him an oath to love no one else. He fell in love with a princess, and was struck blind by the jealous nymph. Mercury, who was his father, raised him to Heaven, and made a fountain spring up in the place from which he ascended. At this fountain the Sicilians offered yearly sacrifices." (Arnold)

His sheep, his hapless love, his blinded eyes—
    And how a call celestial round him rang,
    And heavenward from the fountain-brink he sprang,
And all the marvel of the golden skies.   190

There thou art gone, and me thou leavest here
    Sole in these fields! yet will I not despair.
    Despair I will not, while I yet descry
'Neath the mild canopy of English air
    That lonely tree against the western sky.
        Still, still these slopes, 'tis clear,
    Our Gipsy-Scholar haunts, outliving thee!
    Fields where soft sheep from cages pull the hay,
    Woods with anemones in flower till May,
Know him a wanderer still; then why not me?   200

A fugitive and gracious light he seeks,
    Shy to illumine; and I seek it too.
    This does not come with houses or with gold,
With place, with honor, and a flattering crew;
    'Tis not in the world's market bought and sold—
        But the smooth-slipping weeks
    Drop by, and leave its seeker still untired;
    Out of the heed of mortals he is gone,
    He wends unfollowed, he must house alone;
Yet on he fares, by his own heart inspired.   210

Thou too, O Thyrsis, on like quest wast bound;
    Thou wanderedst with me for a little hour!
    Men gave thee nothing; but this happy quest,
If men esteemed thee feeble, gave thee power,
    If men procured thee trouble, gave thee rest.
        And this rude Cumner ground,
    Its fir-topped Hurst, its farms, its quiet fields,
    Here cam'st thou in thy jocund youthful time,
    Here was thine height of strength, thy golden prime!
And still the haunt beloved a virtue yields.   220

What though the music of thy rustic flute
    Kept not for long its happy, country tone;
    Lost it too soon, and learnt a stormy note
Of men contention-tossed, of men who groan,
    Which tasked thy pipe too sore, and tired thy throat—
        It failed, and thou wast mute!
    Yet hadst thou alway visions of our light,
    And long with men of care thou couldst not stay,

And soon thy foot resumed its wandering way,
Left human haunt, and on alone till night. 230

Too rare, too rare, grow now my visits here!
  'Mid city-noise, not, as with thee of yore,
    Thyrsis! in reach of sheep-bells is my home.
  —Then through the great town's harsh, heart-wearying roar,
    Let in thy voice a whisper often come,
      To chase fatigue and fear:
Why faintest thou? I wandered till I died.
  Roam on! The light we sought is shining still.
  Dost thou ask proof? Our tree yet crowns the hill,
Our Scholar travels yet the loved hill-side. 240

AUSTERITY OF POETRY

THAT son of Italy [56] who tried to blow,
Ere Dante came, the trump of sacred song,
In his light youth amid a festal throng
Sat with his bride to see a public show.
Fair was the bride, and on her front did glow
Youth like a star; and what to youth belong—
Gay raiment, sparkling gauds, elation strong.
A prop gave way! crash fell a platform! lo,
Mid struggling sufferers, hurt to death, she lay!
Shuddering, they drew her garments off—and found
A robe of sackcloth next the smooth, white skin.
Such, poets, is your bride, the Muse! young, gay,
Radiant, adorned outside; a hidden ground
Of thought and of austerity within.

DOVER BEACH

THE sea is calm to-night.
The tide is full, the moon lies fair
Upon the straits;—on the French coast the light
Gleams and is gone; the cliffs of England stand,
Glimmering and vast, out in the tranquil bay.
Come to the window, sweet is the night-air!
Only, from the long line of spray
Where the sea meets the moon-blanched land,
Listen! you hear the grating roar
Of pebbles which the waves draw back, and fling, 10
At their return, up the high strand,
Begin, and cease, and then again begin,

56 Giacopone di Todi, Italian poet of the thirteenth century

With tremulous cadence slow, and bring
The eternal note of sadness in.

Sophocles long ago
Heard it on the Ægean, and it brought
Into his mind the turbid ebb and flow
Of human misery; we
Find also in the sound a thought,
Hearing it by this distant northern sea.   20

The Sea of Faith
Was once, too, at the full, and round earth's shore
Lay like the folds of a bright girdle furled.
But now I only hear
Its melancholy, long, withdrawing roar,
Retreating, to the breath
Of the night-wind, down the vast edges drear
And naked shingles [57] of the world.
Ah, love, let us be true
To one another! for the world, which seems   30
To lie before us like a land of dreams,
So various, so beautiful, so new,
Hath really neither joy, nor love, nor light,
Nor certitude, nor peace, nor help for pain;
And we are here as on a darkling plain
Swept with confused alarms of struggle and flight,
Where ignorant armies clash by night.

RUGBY CHAPEL [58]

NOVEMBER, 1857

COLDLY, sadly descends
The autumn-evening. The field
Strewn with its dank yellow drifts
Of withered leaves, and the elms,
Fade into dimness apace,
Silent;—hardly a shout
From a few boys late at their play!
The lights come out in the street,
In the school-room windows;—but cold,
Solemn, unlighted, austere,   10
Through the gathering darkness, arise

57 stony beaches   famous headmaster of Rug-   the school.
58 Matthew Arnold's fa-   by School, died in 1842 and
ther, Dr. Thomas Arnold, was buried in the chapel of

The chapel-walls, in whose bound
Thou, my father! art laid.

There thou dost lie, in the gloom
Of the autumn evening. But ah!
That word, *gloom*, to my mind
Brings thee back, in the light
Of thy radiant vigor, again;
In the gloom of November we passed
Days not dark at thy side;　　　　　　　　20
Seasons impaired not the ray
Of thy buoyant cheerfulness clear.
Such thou wast! and I stand
In the autumn evening, and think
Of bygone autumns with thee.

Fifteen years have gone round
Since thou arosest to tread,
In the summer-morning, the road
Of death, at a call unforeseen,
Sudden. For fifteen years,　　　　　　　　30
We who till then in thy shade
Rested as under the boughs
Of a mighty oak, have endured
Sunshine and rain as we might,
Bare, unshaded, alone,
Lacking the shelter of thee.

O strong soul, by what shore
Tarriest thou now? For that force,
Surely, has not been left vain!
Somewhere, surely, afar,　　　　　　　　40
In the sounding labor-house vast
Of being, is practised that strength,
Zealous, beneficent, firm!

Yes, in some far-shining sphere,
Conscious or not of the past,
Still thou performest the word
Of the Spirit in whom thou dost live—
Prompt, unwearied, as here!
Still thou upraisest with zeal
The humble good from the ground,　　　　　50
Sternly repressest the bad!
Still, like a trumpet, dost rouse
Those who with half-open eyes

Tread the border-land dim
'Twixt vice and virtue; reviv'st,
Succorest!—this was thy work,
This was thy life upon earth.

What is the course of the life
Of mortal men on the earth?—
Most men eddy about　　　　　　　　　60
Here and there—eat and drink,
Chatter and love and hate,
Gather and squander, are raised
Aloft, are hurled in the dust,
Striving blindly, achieving
Nothing; and then they die—
Perish;—and no one asks
Who or what they have been,
More than he asks what waves,
In the moonlit solitudes mild　　　　　70
Of the midmost Ocean, have swelled,
Foamed for a moment, and gone.

And there are some, whom a thirst
Ardent, unquenchable, fires,
Not with the crowd to be spent,
Not without aim to go round
In an eddy of purposeless dust,
Effort unmeaning and vain.
Ah yes! some of us strive
Not without action to die　　　　　　80
Fruitless, but something to snatch
From dull oblivion, nor all
Glut the devouring grave!
We, we have chosen our path—
Path to a clear-purposed goal,
Path of advance!—but it leads
A long, steep journey, through sunk
Gorges, o'er mountains in snow.
Cheerful, with friends, we set forth—
Then, on the height, comes the storm.　　90
Thunder crashes from rock
To rock, the cataracts reply,
Lightnings dazzle our eyes.
Roaring torrents have breached
The track, the stream-bed descends
In the place where the wayfarer once
Planted his footstep—the spray

Boils o'er its borders! aloft
The unseen snow-beds dislodge
Their hanging ruin; alas,   100
Havoc is made in our train!
Friends, who set forth at our side,
Falter, are lost in the storm.
We, we only are left!
With frowning foreheads, with lips
Sternly compressed, we strain on,
On—and at nightfall at last
Come to the end of our way,
To the lonely inn 'mid the rocks;
Where the gaunt and taciturn host   110
Stands on the threshold, the wind
Shaking his thin white hairs—
Holds his lantern to scan
Our storm-beat figures, and asks:
Whom in our party we bring?
Whom we have left in the snow?

Sadly we answer: We bring
Only ourselves! we lost
Sight of the rest in the storm.
Hardly ourselves we fought through,   120
Stripped, without friends, as we are.
Friends, companions, and train,
The avalanche swept from our side.

But thou wouldst not *alone*
Be saved, my father! *alone*
Conquer and come to thy goal,
Leaving the rest in the wild.
We were weary, and we
Fearful, and we in our march
Fain to drop down and to die.   130
Still thou turnedst, and still
Beckonedst the trembler, and still
Gavest the weary thy hand.

If, in the paths of the world,
Stones might have wounded thy feet,
Toil or dejection have tried
Thy spirit, of that we saw
Nothing—to us thou wast still
Cheerful, and helpful, and firm!
Therefore to thee it was given   140

Many to save with thyself;
And, at the end of thy day,
O faithful shepherd! to come,
Bringing thy sheep in thy hand.

And through thee I believe
In the noble and great who are gone;
Pure souls honored and blest
By former ages, who else—
Such, so soulless, so poor,
Is the race of men whom I see— 150
Seemed but a dream of the heart,
Seemed but a cry of desire.
Yes! I believe that there lived
Others like thee in the past,
Not like the men of the crowd
Who all round me to-day
Bluster or cringe, and make life
Hideous, and arid, and vile;
But souls tempered with fire,
Fervent, heroic, and good, 160
Helpers and friends of mankind.

Servants of God!—or sons
Shall I not call you? because
Not as servants ye knew
Your Father's innermost mind,
His, who unwillingly sees
One of his little ones lost—
Yours is the praise, if mankind
Hath not as yet in its march
Fainted, and fallen, and died! 170

See! In the rocks of the world
Marches the host of mankind,
A feeble, wavering line.
Where are they tending?—A God
Marshaled them, gave them their goal.
Ah, but the way is so long!
Years they have been in the wild!
Sore thirst plagues them; the rocks,
Rising all round, overawe;
Factions divide them, their host 180
Threatens to break, to dissolve.
—Ah, keep, keep them combined!
Else, of the myriads who fill

That army, not one shall arrive;
Sole they shall stray; in the rocks
Stagger for ever in vain,
Die one by one in the waste.

Then, in such hour of need
Of your fainting, dispirited race,
Ye, like angels, appear,   190
Radiant with ardor divine!
Beacons of hope, ye appear!
Languor is not in your heart,
Weakness is not in your word,
Weariness not on your brow.
Ye alight in our van! at your voice,
Panic, despair, flee away.
Ye move through the ranks, recall
The stragglers, refresh the outworn,
Praise, re-inspire the brave!   200
Order, courage, return.
Eyes rekindling, and prayers,
Follow your steps as ye go.
Ye fill up the gaps in our files,
Strengthen the wavering line,
Stablish, continue our march,
On, to the bound of the waste,
On, to the City of God.

EAST LONDON

'TWAS August, and the fierce sun overhead
Smote on the squalid streets of Bethnal Green,
And the pale weaver, through his window seen
In Spitalfields, look'd thrice dispirited.

I met a preacher there I knew, and said:
"Ill and o'erwork'd, how fare you in this scene?"—
"Bravely!" said he; for I of late have been
Much cheer'd with thoughts of Christ, *the living bread.*"

O human soul! as long as thou canst so
Set up a mark of everlasting light,
Above the howling senses' ebb and flow,

To cheer thee, and to right thee if thou roam—
Not with lost toil thou laborest through the night!
Thou mak'st the heaven thou hop'st indeed thy home.

THE BETTER PART

LONG fed on boundless hopes, O race of man,
How angrily thou spurn'st all simpler fare!
"Christ," some one says, "was human as we are;
No judge eyes us from Heaven, our sin to scan;

"We live no more, when we have done our span."—
"Well, then, for Christ," thou answerest, "who can care?
From sin, which Heaven records not, why forbear?
Live we like brutes our life without a plan!"

So answerest thou; but why not rather say:
"Hath man no second life?—*Pitch this one high!*
Sits there no judge in Heaven, our sin to see?—

"More strictly, then, the inward judge obey!
Was Christ a man like us? Ah! let us try
If we then, too, can be such men as he!

THE LAST WORD

CREEP into thy narrow bed,
Creep, and let no more be said!
Vain thy onset! all stands fast.
Thou thyself must break at last.

Let the long contention cease!
Geese are swans, and swans are geese.
Let them have it how they will!
Thou art tired; best be still.

They out-talk'd thee, hiss'd thee, tore thee?
Better men fared thus before thee;
Fired their ringing shot and pass'd,
Hotly charged—and sank at last.

Charge once more, then, and be dumb!
Let the victors, when they come,
When the forts of folly fall,
Find thy body by the wall!

THE FUNCTION OF CRITICISM AT THE
PRESENT TIME [1]

MANY objections have been made to a proposition which, in some remarks of mine [2] on translating Homer, I ventured to put forth; a proposition about criticism, and its importance at the present day. I said: "Of the literature of France and Germany, as of the intellect of Europe in general, the main effort, for many years, has been a critical effort; the endeavor, in all branches of knowledge, theology, philosophy, history, art, science, to see the object as in itself it really is." I added, that owing to the operation in English literature of certain causes,
10 "almost the last thing for which one would come to English literature is just that very thing which now Europe most desires, —criticism"; and that the power and value of English literature was thereby impaired. More than one rejoinder declared that the importance I here assigned to criticism was excessive, and asserted the inherent superiority of the creative effort of the human spirit over its critical effort. . . .

The critical power is of lower rank than the creative. True; but in assenting to this proposition, one or two things are to be kept in mind. It is undeniable that the exercise of a creative
20 power, that a free creative activity, is the highest function of man; it is proved to be so by man's finding in it his true happiness. But it is undeniable, also, that men may have the sense of exercising this free creative activity in other ways than in producing great works of literature or art; if it were not so, all but a very few men would be shut out from the true happiness of all men. They may have it in well-doing, they may have it in learning, they may have it even in criticizing. This is one thing to be kept in mind. Another is, that the exercise of the creative power in the production of great works of literature or art, how-
30 ever high this exercise of it may rank, is not at all epochs and under all conditions possible; and that therefore labor may be vainly spent in attempting it, which might with more fruit be used in preparing for it, in rendering it possible. This creative power works with elements, with materials; what if it has not those materials, those elements, ready for its use? In that case it must surely wait till they are ready. Now, in literature,—I will limit myself to literature, for it is about literature that the question arises,—the elements with which the creative power works are ideas; the best ideas on every matter which literature touches,

1 From *Essays in Criticism*, First Series, copyright 1865 by Macmillan and Co., Ltd., and the Macmillan Company. Reprinted by permission. The essay is slightly condensed. 2 *On Translating Homer*, ed. 1903, pp. 216–17

current at the time. At any rate we may lay it down as certain that in modern literature no manifestation of the creative power not working with these can be very important or fruitful. And I say *current* at the time, not merely accessible at the time; for creative literary genius does not principally show itself in discovering new ideas: that is rather the business of the philosopher. The grand work of literary genius is a work of synthesis and exposition, not of analysis and discovery; its gift lies in the faculty of being happily inspired by a certain intellectual and spiritual atmosphere, by a certain order of ideas, when it finds itself in them; of dealing divinely with these ideas, presenting them in the most effective and attractive combinations,—making beautiful works with them, in short. But it must have the atmosphere, it must find itself amidst the order of ideas, in order to work freely; and these it is not so easy to command. This is why great creative epochs in literature are so rare, this is why there is so much that is unsatisfactory in the productions of many men of real genius; because, for the creation of a master-work of literature two powers must concur, the power of the man and the power of the moment, and the man is not enough without the moment; the creative power has, for its happy exercise, appointed elements, and those elements are not in its own control.

Nay, they are more within the control of the critical power. It is the business of the critical power, as I said in the words already quoted, "in all branches of knowledge, theology, philosophy, history, art, science, to see the object as in itself it really is." Thus it tends, at last, to make an intellectual situation of which the creative power can profitably avail itself. It tends to establish an order of ideas, if not absolutely true, yet true by comparison with that which it displaces; to make the best ideas prevail. Presently these new ideas reach society, the touch of truth is the touch of life, and there is a stir and growth everywhere; out of this stir and growth come the creative epochs of literature.

Or, to narrow our range, and quit these considerations of the general march of genius and of society,—considerations which are apt to become too abstract and impalpable,—every one can see that a poet, for instance, ought to know life and the world before dealing with them in poetry; and life and the world being in modern times very complex things, the creation of a modern poet, to be worth much, implies a great critical effort behind it; else it must be a comparatively poor, barren, and short-lived affair. This is why Byron's poetry had so little endurance in it, and Goethe's so much; both Byron and Goethe had a great productive power, but Goethe's was nourished by a great critical effort providing the true materials for it, and Byron's was not; Goethe knew life and the world, the poet's necessary subjects, much more

comprehensively and thoroughly than Byron. He knew a great
deal more of them, and he knew them much more as they really
are.

It has long seemed to me that the burst of creative activity in
our literature, through the first quarter of this century, had
about it in fact something premature; and that from this cause
its productions are doomed, most of them, in spite of the sanguine
hopes which accompanied and do still accompany them, to prove
hardly more lasting than the productions of far less splendid
epochs. And this prematureness comes from its having proceeded without having its proper data, without sufficient materials to work with. In other words, the English poetry of the
first quarter of this century, with plenty of energy, plenty of
creative force, did not know enough. This makes Byron so empty
of matter, Shelley so incoherent, Wordsworth even, profound
as he is, yet so wanting in completeness and variety. Wordsworth
cared little for books, and disparaged Goethe. I admire Wordsworth, as he is, so much that I cannot wish him different; and it
is vain, no doubt, to imagine such a man different from what he
is, to suppose that he *could* have been different. But surely the
one thing wanting to make Wordsworth an even greater poet
than he is,—his thought richer, and his influence of wider application,—was that he should have read more books, among them,
no doubt, those of that Goethe whom he disparaged without
reading him.

But to speak of books and reading may easily lead to a misunderstanding here. It was not really books and reading that
lacked to our poetry at this epoch: Shelley had plenty of reading, Coleridge had immense reading. Pindar and Sophocles—as
we all say so glibly, and often with so little discernment of the
real import of what we are saying—had not many books; Shakespeare was no deep reader. True; but in the Greece of Pindar and
Sophocles, in the England of Shakespeare, the poet lived in a
current of ideas in the highest degree animating and nourishing
to the creative power; society was, in the fullest measure, permeated by fresh thought, intelligent and alive. And this state of
things is the true basis for the creative power's exercise, in this it
finds its data, its materials, truly ready for its hand; all the books
and reading in the world are only valuable as they are helps to
this. Even when this does not actually exist, books and reading
may enable a man to construct a kind of semblance of it in his
own mind, a world of knowledge and intelligence in which he
may live and work. This is by no means an equivalent to the
artist for the nationally diffused life and thought of the epochs
of Sophocles or Shakespeare; but, besides that it may be a means
of preparation for such epochs, it does really constitute, if many

share in it, a quickening and sustaining atmosphere of great value. Such an atmosphere the many-sided learning and the long and widely combined critical effort of Germany formed for Goethe, when he lived and worked. There was no national glow of life and thought there as in the Athens of Pericles or the England of Elizabeth. That was the poet's weakness. But there was a sort of equivalent for it in the complete culture and unfettered thinking of a large body of Germans. That was his strength. In the England of the first quarter of this century there was neither a national glow of life and thought, such as we had in the age of Elizabeth, nor yet a culture and a force of learning and criticism such as were to be found in Germany. Therefore the creative power of poetry wanted, for success in the highest sense, materials and a basis; a thorough interpretation of the world was necessarily denied to it.

At first sight it seems strange that out of the immense stir of the French Revolution and its age should not have come a crop of works of genius equal to that which came out of the stir of the great productive time of Greece, or out of that of the Renascence, with its powerful episode the Reformation. But the truth is that the stir of the French Revolution took a character which essentially distinguished it from such movements as these. These were, in the main, disinterestedly intellectual and spiritual movements; movements in which the human spirit looked for its satisfaction in itself and in the increased play of its own activity. The French Revolution took a political, practical character. The movement, which went on in France under the old *régime*, from 1700 to 1789, was far more really akin than that of the Revolution itself to the movement of the Renascence; the France of Voltaire and Rousseau told far more powerfully upon the mind of Europe than the France of the Revolution. Goethe reproached this last expressly with having "thrown quiet culture back." Nay, and the true key to how much in our Byron, even in our Wordsworth, is this!—that they had their source in a great movement of feeling, not in a great movement of mind. The French Revolution, however,—that object of so much blind love and so much blind hatred,—found undoubtedly its motive-power in the intelligence of men, and not in their practical sense; this is what distinguishes it from the English Revolution of Charles the First's time. This is what makes it a more spiritual event than our Revolution, an event of much more powerful and world-wide interest, though practically less successful; it appeals to an order of ideas which are universal, certain, permanent. 1789 asked of a thing, Is it rational? 1642 asked of a thing, Is it legal? or, when it went furthest, Is it according to conscience? This is the English fashion, a fashion to be treated, within its own sphere, with the highest respect; for its success, within its own sphere, has been prodigious. . . .

But the mania for giving an immediate political and practical application to all these fine ideas of the reason was fatal. Here an Englishman is in his element: on this theme we can all go on for hours. And all we are in the habit of saying on it has undoubtedly a great deal of truth. Ideas cannot be too much prized in and for themselves, cannot be too much lived with; but to transport them abruptly into the world of politics and practice, violently
10 to revolutionize this world to their bidding,—that is quite another thing. There is the world of ideas and there is the world of practice; the French are often for suppressing the one and the English the other; but neither is to be suppressed. A member of the House of Commons said to me the other day: "That a thing is an anomaly, I consider to be no objection to it whatever." I venture to think he was wrong; that a thing is an anomaly *is* an objection to it, but absolutely and in the sphere of ideas: it is not necessarily, under such and such circumstances, or at such and such a moment, an objection to it in the sphere of politics and
20 practice. Joubert[3] has said beautifully: "C'est la force et le droit qui règlent toutes choses dans le monde; la force en attendant le droit." (Force and right are the governors of this world; force till right is ready.) *Force till right is ready;* and till right is ready, force, the existing order of things, is justified, is the legitimate ruler. But right is something moral, and implies inward recognition, free assent of the will; we are not ready for right,—*right,* so far as we are concerned, *is not ready,*—until we have attained this sense of seeing it and willing it. The way in which for us it may change and transform force, the existing order of things, and
30 become, in its turn, the legitimate ruler of the world, should depend on the way in which, when our time comes, we see it and will it. Therefore for other people enamored of their own newly discerned right, to attempt to impose it upon us as ours, and violently to substitute their right for our force, is an act of tyranny, and to be resisted. It sets at naught the second great half of our maxim, *force till right is ready.* This was the grand error of the French Revolution; and its movement of ideas, by quitting the intellectual sphere and rushing furiously into the political sphere, ran, indeed, a prodigious and memorable course, but produced
40 no such intellectual fruit as the movement of ideas of the Renascence, and created, in opposition to itself, what I may call an *epoch of concentration.* The great force of that epoch of concentration was England; and the great voice of that epoch of concentration was Burke. . . .

The Englishman has been called a political animal, and he

3 French writer (1754-1824), on whom Arnold wrote one of his *Essays in Criticism*

values what is political and practical so much that ideas easily
become objects of dislike in his eyes, and thinkers "miscreants,"
because ideas and thinkers have rashly meddled with politics and
practice. This would be all very well if the dislike and neglect
confined themselves to ideas transported out of their own sphere,
and meddling rashly with practice; but they are inevitably extended to ideas as such, and to the whole life of intelligence;
practice is everything, a free play of the mind is nothing. The
notion of the free play of the mind upon all subjects being a
pleasure in itself, being an object of desire, being an essential 10
provider of elements without which a nation's spirit, whatever
compensations it may have for them, must, in the long run, die
of inanition, hardly enters into an Englishman's thoughts. It is
noticeable that the word *curiosity*, which in other languages is
used in a good sense, to mean, as a high and fine quality of man's
nature, just this disinterested love of a free play of the mind on
all subjects, for its own sake,—it is noticeable, I say, that this
word has in our language no sense of the kind, no sense but a
rather bad and disparaging one. But criticism, real criticism, is
essentially the exercise of this very quality. It obeys an instinct 20
prompting it to try to know the best that is known and thought
in the world, irrespectively of practice, politics, and everything
of the kind; and to value knowledge and thought as they approach this best, without the intrusion of any other considerations whatever. This is an instinct for which there is, I think,
little original sympathy in the practical English nature, and what
there was of it has undergone a long benumbing period of blight
and suppression in the epoch of concentration which followed
the French Revolution.

But epochs of concentration cannot well endure forever; 30
epochs of expansion, in the due course of things, follow them.
Such an epoch of expansion seems to be opening in this country.
In the first place all danger of a hostile forcible pressure of
foreign ideas upon our practice has long disappeared; like the
traveler in the fable, therefore, we begin to wear our cloak a little
more loosely. Then, with a long peace, the ideas of Europe steal
gradually and amicably in, and mingle, though in infinitesimally
small quantities at a time, with our own notions. Then, too, in
spite of all that is said about the absorbing and brutalizing influence of our passionate material progress, it seems to me in- 40
disputable that this progress is likely, though not certain, to lead
in the end to an apparition of intellectual life; and that man,
after he has made himself perfectly comfortable and has now to
determine what to do with himself next, may begin to remember
that he has a mind, and that the mind may be made the source
of great pleasure. I grant it is mainly the privilege of faith, at

present, to discern this end to our railways, our business, and
our fortune-making; but we shall see if, here as elsewhere, faith
is not in the end the true prophet. Our ease, our traveling, and
our unbounded liberty to hold just as hard and securely as we
please to the practice to which our notions have given birth, all
tend to beget an inclination to deal a little more freely with these
notions themselves, to canvass them a little, to penetrate a little
into their real nature. Flutterings of curiosity, in the foreign
sense of the word, appear amongst us, and it is in these that criti-
10 cism must look to find its account. Criticism first; a time of true
creative activity, perhaps,—which, as I have said, must inevitably be preceded amongst us by a time of criticism,—hereafter,
when criticism has done its work.

It is of the last importance that English criticism should clearly
discern what rule for its course, in order to avail itself of the field
now opening to it, and to produce fruit for the future, it ought
to take. The rule may be summed up in one word,—*disinterestedness.* And how is criticism to show disinterestedness? By keeping aloof from what is called "the practical view of things"; by
20 resolutely following the law of its own nature, which is to be a
free play of the mind on all subjects which it touches. By steadily
refusing to lend itself to any of those ulterior, political, practical
considerations about ideas, which plenty of people will be sure to
attach to them, which perhaps ought often to be attached to
them, which in this country at any rate are certain to be attached
to them quite sufficiently, but which criticism has really nothing
to do with. Its business is, as I have said, simply to know the best
that is known and thought in the world, and by in its turn making this known, to create a current of true and fresh ideas. Its
30 business is to do this with inflexible honesty, with due ability;
but its business is to do no more, and to leave alone all questions
of practical consequences and applications, questions which will
never fail to have due prominence given to them. Else criticism,
besides being really false to its own nature, merely continues in
the old rut which it has hitherto followed in this country, and
will certainly miss the chance now given to it. For what is at
present the bane of criticism in this country? It is that practical
considerations cling to it and stifle it. It subserves interests not
its own. Our organs of criticism are organs of men and parties
40 having practical ends to serve, and with them those practical ends
are the first thing and the play of mind the second; so much play
of mind as is compatible with the prosecution of those practical
ends is all that is wanted. An organ like the *Revue des Deux
Mondes,* having for its main function to understand and utter
the best that is known and thought in the world, existing, it may
be said, as just an organ for a free play of the mind, we have not.

But we have the *Edinburgh Review,* existing as an organ of the old Whigs, and for as much play of the mind as may suit its being that; we have the *Quarterly Review,* existing as an organ of the Tories, and for as much play of mind as may suit its being that; we have the *British Quarterly Review,* existing as an organ of the political Dissenters, and for as much play of mind as may suit its being that; we have the *Times,* existing as an organ of the common, satisfied, well-to-do Englishman, and for as much play of mind as may suit its being that. And so on through all the various fractions, political and religious, of our society; every fraction has, as such, its organ of criticism, but the notion of combining all fractions in the common pleasure of a free disinterested play of mind meets with no favor. Directly this play of mind wants to have more scope, and to forget the pressure of practical considerations a little, it is checked, it is made to feel the chain. We saw this the other day in the extinction, so much to be regretted, of the *Home and Foreign Review.* Perhaps in no organ of criticism in this country was there so much knowledge, so much play of mind; but these could not save it. The *Dublin Review* subordinates play of mind to the practical business of English and Irish Catholicism, and lives. It must needs be that men should act in sects and parties, that each of these sects and parties should have its organ, and should make this organ subserve the interests of its action; but it would be well, too, that there should be a criticism, not the minister of these interests, not their enemy, but absolutely and entirely independent of them. No other criticism will ever attain any real authority or make any real way towards its end,—the creating a current of true and fresh ideas.

It is because criticism has so little kept in the pure intellectual sphere, has so little detached itself from practice, has been so directly polemical and controversial, that it has so ill accomplished, in this country, its best spiritual work; which is to keep man from a self-satisfaction which is retarding and vulgarizing, to lead him towards perfection, by making his mind dwell upon what is excellent in itself, and the absolute beauty and fitness of things. A polemical practical criticism makes men blind even to the ideal imperfection of their practice, makes them willingly assert its ideal perfection, in order the better to secure it against attack; and clearly this is narrowing and baneful for them. If they were reassured on the practical side, speculative considerations of ideal perfection they might be brought to entertain, and their spiritual horizon would thus gradually widen. Sir Charles Adderley [4] says to the Warwickshire farmers:—

"Talk of the improvement of breed! Why, the race we our-

4 Sir Charles Bowyer Adderley, Baron Norton (1814–1905), a Tory politician

selves represent, the men and women, the old Anglo-Saxon race, are the best breed in the whole world. . . . The absence of a too enervating climate, too unclouded skies, and a too luxurious nature, has produced so vigorous a race of people, and has rendered us so superior to all the world."

Mr. Roebuck [5] says to the Sheffield cutlers:—

"I look around me and ask what is the state of England? Is not property safe? Is not every man able to say what he likes? Can you not walk from one end of England to the other in per-
10 fect security? I ask you whether, the world over or in past history, there is anything like it? Nothing. I pray that our unrivaled happiness may last."

Now obviously there is a peril for poor human nature in words and thoughts of such exuberant self-satisfaction, until we find ourselves safe in the streets of the Celestial City.

> "Das wenige verschwindet leicht dem Blicke
> Der vorwärts sieht, wie viel noch übrig bleibt—" [6]

says Goethe; "the little that is done seems nothing when we look forward and see how much we have yet to do." Clearly this
20 is a better line of reflection for weak humanity, so long as it remains on this earthly field of labor and trial.

But neither Sir Charles Adderley nor Mr. Roebuck is by nature inaccessible to considerations of this sort. They only lose sight of them owing to the controversial life we all lead, and the practical form which all speculation takes with us. They have in view opponents whose aim is not ideal, but practical; and in their zeal to uphold their own practice against these innovators, they go so far as even to attribute to this practice an ideal perfection. Somebody has been wanting to introduce a six-pound franchise,[7]
30 or to abolish church-rates,[8] or to collect agricultural statistics by force, or to diminish local self-government. How natural, in reply to such proposals, very likely improper or ill-timed, to go a little beyond the mark and to say stoutly, "Such a race of people as we stand, so superior to all the world! The old Anglo-Saxon race, the best breed in the whole world! I pray that our unrivaled happiness may last! I ask you whether, the world over or in past history, there is anything like it?" And so long as criticism answers this dithyramb by insisting that the old Anglo-Saxon race would be still more superior to all others if it had no church-rates, or
40 that our unrivaled happiness would last yet longer with a six-pound franchise, so long will the strain, "The best breed in the

5 John Arthur Roebuck (1802–79), an advanced Liberal, member of Parliament for Sheffield from 1849 until his death

6 *Iphigenie auf Tauris,* I. ii. 91–2.
7 extend the franchise to persons occupying premises worth six pounds a year in-

stead of drawing the line at ten pounds, as currently
8 taxes for support of the church

whole world!" swell louder and louder, everything ideal and re-
fining will be lost out of sight, and both the assailed and their
critics will remain in a sphere, to say the truth, perfectly unvital,
a sphere in which spiritual progression is impossible. But let criticism leave church-rates and the franchise alone, and in the most
candid spirit, without a single lurking thought of practical innovation, confront with our dithyramb this paragraph on which I
stumbled in a newspaper immediately after reading Mr. Roebuck:—

"A shocking child murder has just been committed at Not- 10
tingham. A girl named Wragg left the workhouse there on Saturday morning with her young illegitimate child. The child was
soon afterwards found dead on Mapperly Hills, having been
strangled. Wragg is in custody."

Nothing but that; but, in juxtaposition with the absolute eu-
logies of Sir Charles Adderley and Mr. Roebuck, how eloquent,
how suggestive are those few lines! "Our old Anglo-Saxon breed,
the best in the whole world!"—how much that is harsh and ill-
favored there is in this best. *Wragg!* If we are to talk of ideal
perfection, of "the best in the whole world," has any one re- 20
flected what a touch of grossness in our race, what an original
short-coming in the more delicate spiritual perceptions, is shown
by the natural growth amongst us of such hideous names,—
Higginbottom, Stiggins, Bugg! In Ionia and Attica they were
luckier in this respect than "the best race in the world"; by the
Ilissus there was no Wragg, poor thing! And "our unrivaled happiness";—what an element of grimness, bareness, and hideousness mixes with it and blurs it; the workhouse, the dismal Mapperly Hills,—how dismal those who have seen them will remember;—the gloom, the smoke, the cold, the strangled illegitimate 30
child! "I ask you whether, the world over or in past history, there
is anything like it?" Perhaps not, one is inclined to answer; but
at any rate, in that case, the world is very much to be pitied. And
the final touch,—short, bleak and inhuman: *Wragg is in custody.* The sex lost in the confusion of our unrivaled happiness; or (shall I say?) the superfluous Christian name lopped
off by the straightforward vigor of our old Anglo-Saxon breed!
There is profit for the spirit in such contrasts as this; criticism
serves the cause of perfection by establishing them. By eluding
sterile conflict, by refusing to remain in the sphere where alone 40
narrow and relative conceptions have any worth and validity,
criticism may diminish its momentary importance, but only
in this way has it a chance of gaining admittance for those wider
and more perfect conceptions to which all its duty is really
owed. Mr. Roebuck will have a poor opinion of an adversary
who replies to his defiant songs of triumph only by murmur-

ing under his breath, *Wragg is in custody;* but in no other way will these songs of triumph be induced gradually to moderate themselves, to get rid of what in them is excessive and offensive, and to fall into a softer and truer key. . . .

Do what he will, however, the critic will still remain exposed to frequent misunderstandings, and nowhere so much as in this country. For here people are particularly indisposed even to comprehend that without this free disinterested treatment of things, truth and the highest culture are out of the question.
10 So immersed are they in practical life, so accustomed to take all their notions from this life and its processes, that they are apt to think that truth and culture themselves can be reached by the processes of this life, and that it is an impertinent singularity to think of reaching them in any other. "We are all *terræ filii,*"[9] cries their eloquent advocate; "all Philistines together. Away with the notion of proceeding by any other course than the course dear to the Philistines; let us have a social movement, let us organize and combine a party to pursue truth and new thought, let us call it *the liberal party,* and let us all stick
20 to each other, and back each other up. Let us have no nonsense about independent criticism, and intellectual delicacy, and the few and the many. Don't let us trouble ourselves about foreign thought; we shall invent the whole thing for ourselves as we go along. If one of us speaks well, applaud him; if one of us speaks ill, applaud him too; we are all in the same movement, we are all liberals, we are all in pursuit of truth." In this way the pursuit of truth becomes really a social, practical, pleasurable affair, almost requiring a chairman, a secretary, and advertisements; with the excitement of an occasional scan-
30 dal, with a little resistance to give the happy sense of difficulty overcome; but, in general, plenty of bustle and very little thought. To act is so easy, as Goethe says; to think is so hard! It is true that the critic has many temptations to go with the stream, to make one of the party movement, one of these *terræ filii;* it seems ungracious to refuse to be a *terrae filius,* when so many excellent people are; but the critic's duty is to refuse, or, if resistance is vain, at least to cry with Obermann: *Périssons en résistant.*[10]

How serious a matter it is to try and resist, I had ample op-
40 portunity of experiencing when I ventured some time ago to criticize the celebrated first volume of Bishop Colenso.[11] The

9 sons of earth
10 Let us perish resisting.
11 J. W. Colenso (1814–1883), Bishop of Natal, in a series of treatises had endeavored to show that the Bible was not literally inspired and that the Pentateuch could not be taken as historical. His work is more important than Arnold admits, and his views have since been broadly adopted. In a long footnote Arnold apologized for the personal nature of a criticism he had written of Colenso's first volume, but added, "There is truth of science and truth of reli-

echoes of the storm which was then raised I still, from time to time, hear grumbling round me. That storm arose out of a misunderstanding almost inevitable. It is a result of no little culture to attain to a clear perception that science and religion are two wholly different things. The multitude will forever confuse them; but happily that is of no great real importance, for while the multitude imagines itself to live by its false science, it does really live by its true religion. Dr. Colenso, however, in his first volume did all he could to strengthen the confusion, and to make it dangerous. He did this with the best intentions, I freely admit, and with the most candid ignorance that this was the natural effect of what he was doing; but, says Joubert, "Ignorance, which in matters of morals extenuates the crime, is itself, in intellectual matters, a crime of the first order." . . .

What then is the duty of criticism here? To take the practical point of view, to applaud the liberal movement and all its works, —its New Road religions of the future into the bargain,—for their general utility's sake? By no means; but to be perpetually dissatisfied with these works, while they perpetually fall short of a high and perfect ideal.

For criticism, these are elementary laws; but they never can be popular, and in this country they have been very little followed, and one meets with immense obstacles in following them. That is a reason for asserting them again and again. Criticism must maintain its independence of the practical spirit and its aims. Even with well-meant efforts of the practical spirit it must express dissatisfaction, if in the sphere of the ideal they seem impoverishing and limiting. It must not hurry on to the goal because of its practical importance. It must be patient, and know how to wait; and flexible, and know how to attach itself to things and how to withdraw from them. It must be apt to study and praise elements that for the fullness of spiritual perfection are wanted, even though they belong to a power which in the practical sphere may be maleficent. It must be apt to discern the spiritual shortcomings or illusions of powers that in the practical sphere may be beneficent. And this without any notion of favoring or injuring, in the practical sphere, one power or the other; without any notion of playing off, in this sphere, one power against the other. . . .

I lately heard a man of thought and energy contrasting the want of ardor and movement which he now found amongst young men in this country with what he remembered in his own youth, twenty years ago. "What reformers we were then!"

gion; truth of science does not become truth of religion till it is made reli-

gious. . . . Let us have all the science there is from the men of science; from

the men of religion let us have religion."

he exclaimed; "What a zeal we had! how we canvassed every institution in Church and State, and were prepared to remodel them all on first principles!" He was inclined to regret, as a spiritual flagging, the lull which he saw. I am disposed rather to regard it as a pause in which the turn to a new mode of spiritual progress is being accomplished. Everything was long seen, by the young and ardent amongst us, in inseparable connection with politics and practical life. We have pretty well exhausted the benefits of seeing things in this connection, we have got all that can be got by so seeing them. Let us try a more disinterested mode of seeing them; let us betake ourselves more to the serener life of the mind and spirit. This life, too, may have its excesses and dangers; but they are not for us at present. Let us think of quietly enlarging our stock of true and fresh ideas, and not, as soon as we get an idea or half an idea, be running out with it into the street, and trying to make it rule there. Our ideas will, in the end, shape the world all the better for maturing a little. Perhaps in fifty years' time it will in the English House of Commons be an objection to an institution that it is an anomaly, and my friend the Member of Parliament will shudder in his grave. But let us in the meanwhile rather endeavor that in twenty years' time it may, in English literature, be an objection to a proposition that it is absurd. That will be a change so vast, that the imagination almost fails to grasp it. *Ab integro sæclorum nascitur ordo* [12]—

If I have insisted so much on the course which criticism must take where politics and religion are concerned, it is because, where these burning matters are in question, it is most likely to go astray. I have wished, above all, to insist on the attitude which criticism should adopt towards things in general; on its right tone and temper of mind. But then comes another question as to the subject-matter which literary criticism should most seek. Here, in general, its course is determined for it by the idea which is the law of its being: the idea of a disinterested endeavor to learn and propagate the best that is known and thought in the world, and thus to establish a current of fresh and true ideas. By the very nature of things, as England is not all the world, much of the best that is known and thought in the world cannot be of English growth, must be foreign; by the nature of things, again, it is just this that we are least likely to know, while English thought is streaming in upon us from all sides, and takes excellent care that we shall not be ignorant of its existence. The English critic of literature, therefore, must dwell much on foreign

12 Virgil, *Eclogue* iv. 5, translated by Shelley (*Hellas*), "The world's great age begins anew."

thought, and with particular heed on any part of it, which, while significant and fruitful in itself, is for any reason specially likely to escape him. Again, judging is often spoken of as the critic's one business, and so in some sense it is; but the judgment which almost insensibly forms itself in a fair and clear mind, along with fresh knowledge, is the valuable one; and thus knowledge, and ever fresh knowledge, must be the critic's great concern for himself. And it is by communicating fresh knowledge, and letting his own judgment pass along with it,—but insensibly, and in the second place, not the first, as a sort of companion and clew, not as an abstract lawgiver,—that the critic will generally do most good to his readers. Sometimes, no doubt, for the sake of establishing an author's place in literature, and his relation to a central standard (and if this is not done, how are we to get at our *best in the world?*) criticism may have to deal with a subject-matter so familiar that fresh knowledge is out of the question, and then it must be all judgment; an enunciation and detailed application of principles. Here the great safeguard is never to let oneself become abstract, always to retain an intimate and lively consciousness of the truth of what one is saying, and, the moment this fails us, to be sure that something is wrong. Still under all circumstances, this mere judgment and application of principles is, in itself, not the most satisfactory work to the critic; like mathematics, it is tautological, and cannot well give us, like fresh learning, the sense of creative activity.

But stop, some one will say; all this talk is of no practical use to us whatever; this criticism of yours is not what we have in our minds when we speak of criticism; when we speak of critics and criticism, we mean critics and criticism of the current English literature of the day; when you offer to tell criticism its function, it is to this criticism that we expect you to address yourself. I am sorry for it, for I am afraid I must disappoint these expectations. I am bound by my own definition of criticism; *a disinterested endeavor to learn and propagate the best that is known and thought in the world.* How much of current English literature comes into this "best that is known and thought in the world"? Not very much I fear; certainly less, at this moment, than of the current literature of France or Germany. Well, then, am I to alter my definition of criticism, in order to meet the requirements of a number of practising English critics, who, after all, are free in their choice of a business? That would be making criticism lend itself just to one of those alien practical considerations, which, I have said, are so fatal to it. One may say, indeed, to those who have to deal with the mass—so much better disregarded

—of current English literature, that they may at all events
endeavor, in dealing with this, to try it, so far as they can,
by the standard of the best that is known and thought in the
world; one may say, that to get anywhere near this standard,
every critic should try and possess one great literature, at least,
besides his own; and the more unlike his own, the better. But,
after all, the criticism I am really concerned with,—the criticism which alone can much help us for the future, the criticism
which, throughout Europe, is at the present day meant, when
so much stress is laid on the importance of criticism and the
critical spirit,—is a criticism which regards Europe as being,
for intellectual and spiritual purposes, one great confederation,
bound to a joint action and working to a common result; and
whose members have, for their proper outfit, a knowledge of
Greek, Roman, and Eastern antiquity, and of one another.
Special, local, and temporary advantages being put out of account, that modern nation will in the intellectual and spiritual
sphere make most progress, which most thoroughly carries out
this program. And what is that but saying that we too, all of
us, as individuals, the more thoroughly we carry it out, shall
make the more progress?

There is so much inviting us!—what are we to take? what
will nourish us in growth towards perfection? That is the question which, with the immense field of life and of literature lying before him, the critic has to answer; for himself first, and
afterwards for others. In this idea of the critic's business the
essays brought together in the following pages have had their
origin; in this idea, widely different as are their subjects, they
have, perhaps, their unity.

I conclude with what I said at the beginning: to have the
sense of creative activity is the great happiness and the great
proof of being alive, and it is not denied to criticism to have
it; but then criticism must be sincere, simple, flexible, ardent,
ever widening its knowledge. Then it may have, in no contemptible measure, a joyful sense of creative activity; a sense
which a man of insight and conscience will prefer to what he
might derive from a poor, starved, fragmentary, inadequate
creation. And at some epochs no other creation is possible.

Still, in full measure, the sense of creative activity belongs
only to genuine creation; in literature we must never forget
that. But what true man of letters ever can forget it? It is no
such common matter for a gifted nature to come into possession of a current of true and living ideas, and to produce amidst
the inspiration of them, that we are likely to underrate it. The
epochs of Æschylus and Shakespeare make us feel their pre-
eminence. In an epoch like those is, no doubt, the true life of

literature; there is the promised land, towards which criticism can only beckon. That promised land it will not be ours to enter, and we shall die in the wilderness: but to have desired to enter it, to have saluted it from afar, is already, perhaps, the best distinction among contemporaries; it will certainly be the best title to esteem with posterity.

WORDSWORTH

The opening pages, which make a slow general approach to the subject, and two short redundant passages are omitted.

WORDSWORTH has been in his grave for some thirty years, and certainly his lovers and admirers cannot flatter themselves that this great and steady light of glory as yet shines over him. He is not fully recognized at home; he is not recognized at all 10 abroad. Yet I firmly believe that the poetical performance of Wordsworth is, after that of Shakespeare and Milton, of which all the world now recognizes the worth, undoubtedly the most considerable in our language from the Elizabethan age to the present time. Chaucer is anterior; and on other grounds, too, he cannot well be brought into the comparison. But taking the roll of our chief poetical names, besides Shakespeare and Milton, from the age of Elizabeth downwards, and going through it,—Spenser, Dryden, Pope, Gray, Goldsmith, Cowper, Burns, Coleridge, Scott, Campbell, Moore, Byron, Shelley, Keats (I 20 mention those only who are dead),—I think it certain that Wordsworth's name deserves to stand, and will finally stand, above them all. Several of the poets named have gifts and excellences which Wordsworth has not. But taking the performance of each as a whole, I say that Wordsworth seems to me to have left a body of poetical work superior in power, in interest, in the qualities which give enduring freshness, to that which any one of the others has left.

But this is not enough to say. I think it certain, further, that if we take the chief poetical names of the Continent since 30 the death of Molière, and, omitting Goethe, confront the remaining names with that of Wordsworth, the result is the same. Let us take Klopstock, Lessing, Schiller, Uhland, Rückert, and Heine for Germany; Filicaja, Alfieri, Manzoni, and Leopardi for Italy; Racine, Boileau, Voltaire, André Chénier, Béranger, Lamartine, Musset, M. Victor Hugo [13] (he has been so long celebrated that although he still lives I may be permitted to name him) for France. Several of these, again, have evidently

---

[13] Arnold lists distinguished German poets of the eighteenth and nineteenth centuries, and Italian and French poets of the seventeenth, eighteenth, and nineteenth centuries.

gifts and excellences to which Wordsworth can make no pretension. But in real poetical achievement it seems to me indubitable that to Wordsworth, here again, belongs the palm. It
seems to me that Wordsworth has left behind him a body of
poetical work which wears, and will wear, better on the whole
than the performance of any one of these personages, so far
more brilliant and celebrated, most of them, than the homely
poet of Rydal.[14] Wordsworth's performance in poetry is on the
whole, in power, in interest, in the qualities which give enduring
10 freshness, superior to theirs.

This is a high claim to make for Wordsworth. But if it is a
just claim, if Wordsworth's place among the poets who have appeared in the last two or three centuries is after Shakespeare,
Molière, Milton, Goethe, indeed, but before all the rest, then
in time Wordsworth will have his due. We shall recognize him
in his place, as we recognize Shakespeare and Milton; and not
only we ourselves shall recognize him, but he will be recognized
by Europe also. Meanwhile, those who recognize him already
may do well, perhaps, to ask themselves whether there are not
20 in the case of Wordsworth certain special obstacles which hinder
or delay his due recognition by others, and whether these obstacles are not in some measure removable.

The *Excursion* and the *Prelude,* his poems of greatest bulk,
are by no means Wordsworth's best work. His best work is in
his shorter pieces, and many indeed are there of these which
are of first-rate excellence. But in his seven volumes the pieces
of high merit are mingled with a mass of pieces very inferior to
them; so inferior to them that it seems wonderful how the same
poet should have produced both. Shakespeare frequently has
30 lines and passages in a strain quite false, and which are entirely
unworthy of him. But one can imagine him smiling if one could
meet him in the Elysian Fields and tell him so; smiling and
replying that he knew it perfectly well himself, and what did
it matter? But with Wordsworth the case is different. Work
altogether inferior, work quite uninspired, flat and dull, is produced by him with evident unconsciousness of its defects, and
he presents it to us with the same faith and seriousness as his
best work. Now a drama or an epic fill the mind, and one does
not look beyond them; but in a collection of short pieces
40 impression made by one piece requires to be continued and sustained by the piece following. In reading Wordsworth the impression made by one of his fine pieces is too often dulled and
spoiled by a very inferior piece coming after it.

Wordsworth composed verses during a space of some sixty

---

14 Rydal Mount, Wordsworth's home from 1813 till his death. See introductory sketch
on Wordsworth.

years; and it is no exaggeration to say that within one single decade of those years, between 1798 and 1808, almost all his really first-rate work was produced. A mass of inferior work remains, work done before and after this golden prime, imbedding the first-rate work and clogging it, obstructing our approach to it, chilling, not unfrequently, the high-wrought mood with which we leave it. To be recognized far and wide as a great poet, to be possible and receivable as a classic, Wordsworth needs to be relieved of a great deal of the poetical baggage which now encumbers him. To administer this relief is indis- 10 pensable, unless he is to continue to be a poet for the few only, —a poet valued far below his real worth by the world. . . .

To exhibit this body of Wordsworth's best work, to clear away obstructions from around it, and to let it speak for itself, is what every lover of Wordsworth should desire. Until this has been done, Wordsworth, whom we, to whom he is dear, all of us know and feel to be so great a poet, has not had a fair chance before the world. When once it has been done, he will make his way best, not by our advocacy of him, but by his own worth and power. We may safely leave him to make his way 20 thus, we who believe that a superior worth and power in poetry finds in mankind a sense responsive to it and disposed at last to recognize it. Yet at the outset, before he has been duly known and recognized, we may do Wordsworth a service, perhaps, by indicating in what his superior power and worth will be found to consist, and in what it will not.

Long ago, in speaking of Homer, I said that the noble and profound application of ideas to life is the most essential part of poetic greatness. I said that a great poet receives his distinctive character of superiority from his application, under 30 the conditions immutably fixed by the laws of poetic beauty and poetic truth, from his application, I say, to his subject, whatever it may be, of the ideas

"On man, on nature, and on human life," [15]

which he has acquired for himself. The line quoted is Wordsworth's own; and his superiority arises from his powerful use, in his best pieces, his powerful application to his subject, of ideas "on man, on nature, and on human life."

Voltaire, with his signal acuteness, most truly remarked that "no nation has treated in poetry moral ideas with more energy 40 and depth than the English nation." And he adds: "There, it seems to me, is the great merit of the English poets." Voltaire does not mean, by "treating in poetry moral ideas," the com-

[15] *The Recluse*, l. 754

posing moral and didactic poems;—that brings us but a very little way in poetry. He means just the same thing as was meant when I spoke above "of the noble and profound application of ideas to life"; and he means the application of these ideas under the conditions fixed for us by the laws of poetic beauty and poetic truth. If it is said that to call these ideas *moral* ideas is to introduce a strong and injurious limitation, I answer that it is to do nothing of the kind, because moral ideas are really so main a part of human life. The question, *how to live,* is itself a moral idea; and it is the question which most interests every man, and with which, in some way or other, he is perpetually occupied. A large sense is of course to be given to the term *moral.* Whatever bears upon the question, "how to live," comes under it.

> "Nor love thy life, nor hate; but, what thou liv'st,
> Live well; how long or short, permit to heaven." [16]

In those fine lines Milton utters, as every one at once perceives, a moral idea. Yes, but so too, when Keats consoles the forward-bending lover on the Grecian Urn, the lover arrested and presented in immortal relief by the sculptor's hand before he can kiss, with the line,

> "Forever wilt thou love, and she be fair—"

he utters a moral idea. When Shakespeare says, that

> "We are such stuff
> As dreams are made of, and our little life
> Is rounded with a sleep," [17]

he utters a moral idea.

Voltaire was right in thinking that the energetic and profound treatment of moral ideas, in this large sense, is what distinguishes the English poetry. He sincerely meant praise, not dispraise or hint of limitation; and they err who suppose that poetic limitation is a necessary consequence of the fact, the fact being granted as Voltaire states it. If what distinguishes the greatest poets is their powerful and profound application of ideas to life, which surely no good critic will deny, then to prefix to the term ideas here the term moral makes hardly any difference, because human life itself is in so preponderating a degree moral.

It is important, therefore, to hold fast to this: that poetry is at bottom a criticism of life; that the greatness of a poet lies in his powerful and beautiful application of ideas to life,—to the

[16] *Paradise Lost,* XI. 553-54   [17] *The Tempest,* IV. i. 156-58

question: How to live. Morals are often treated in a narrow and false fashion; they are bound up with systems of thought and belief which have had their day; they are fallen into the hands of pedants and professional dealers; they grow tiresome to some of us. We find attraction, at times, even in a poetry of revolt against them; in a poetry which might take for its motto Omar Khayyám's [18] words: "Let us make up in the tavern for the time which we have wasted in the mosque." Or we find attractions in a poetry indifferent to them; in a poetry where the contents may be what they will, but where the form is studied and exquisite. We delude ourselves in either case; and the best cure for our delusion is to let our minds rest upon that great and inexhaustible word *life*, until we learn to enter into its meaning. A poetry of revolt against moral ideas is a poetry of revolt against *life;* a poetry of indifference towards moral ideas is a poetry of indifference towards *life*.

Epictetus had a happy figure for things like the play of the senses, or literary form and finish, or argumentative ingenuity, in comparison with "the best and master thing" for us, as he called it, the concern, how to live. Some people were afraid of them, he said, or they disliked and undervalued them. Such people were wrong; they were unthankful or cowardly. But the things might also be over-prized, and treated as final when they are not. They bear to life the relation which inns bear to home. "As if a man, journeying home, and finding a nice inn on the road, and liking it, were to stay forever at the inn! Man, thou hast forgotten thine object; thy journey was not *to* this, but *through* this. 'But this inn is taking.' And how many other inns, too, are taking, and how many fields and meadows! but as places of passage merely. You have an object, which is this: to get home, to do your duty to your family, friends, and fellow-countrymen, to attain inward freedom, serenity, happiness, contentment. Style takes your fancy, arguing takes your fancy, and you forget your home and want to make your abode with them and to stay with them, on the plea that they are taking. Who denies that they are taking? but as places of passage, as inns. And when I say this, you suppose me to be attacking the care for style, the care for argument. I am not; I attack the resting in them, the not looking to the end which is beyond them." [19]

Now, when we come across a poet like Théophile Gautier,[20] we have a poet who has taken up his abode at an inn, and never got farther. There may be inducements to this or that one of us,

18 eleventh cent. Persian poet, whose *Rubáiyát* or quatrains were brilliantly translated by Edward Fitzgerald
19 *Discourses* of Epictetus, Roman Stoic philosopher of first century A. D. Vol. I., Book ii., Chap. xxiii.
20 French poet (1811–1872). Wordsworthian quotation below is from *The Recluse*, ll. 767–71

at this or that moment, to find delight in him, to cleave to him;
but after all, we do not change the truth about him,—we only
stay ourselves in his inn along with him. And when we come
across a poet like Wordsworth, who sings

> "Of truth, of grandeur, beauty, love and hope,
> And melancholy fear subdued by faith,
> Of blessed consolations in distress,
> Of moral strength and intellectual power,
> Of joy in widest commonalty spread—"

10 then we have a poet intent on "the best and master thing," and
who prosecutes his journey home. We say, for brevity's sake,
that he deals with *life*, because he deals with that in which life
really consists. This is what Voltaire means to praise in the
English poets,—this dealing with what is really life. But always
it is the mark of the greatest poets that they deal with it; and
to say that the English poets are remarkable for dealing with
it, is only another way of saying, what is true, that in poetry
the English genius has especially shown its power.

Wordsworth deals with it, and his greatness lies in his deal-
20 ing with it so powerfully. I have named a number of celebrated
poets above all of whom he, in my opinion, deserves to be
placed. He is to be placed above poets like Voltaire, Dryden,
Pope, Lessing, Schiller, because these famous personages, with
a thousand gifts and merits, never, or scarcely ever, attain the
distinctive accent and utterance of the high and genuine poets—

> "Quique pii vates et Phœbo digna locuti," [21]

at all. Burns, Keats, Heine, not to speak of others in our list,
have this accent;—who can doubt it? And at the same time
they have treasures of humor, felicity, passion, for which in
30 Wordsworth we shall look in vain. Where, then, is Wordsworth's
superiority? It is here; he deals with more of *life* than they do;
he deals with *life*, as a whole, more powerfully.

No Wordsworthian will doubt this. Nay, the fervent Wordsworthian will add, as Mr. Leslie Stephen [22] does, that Wordsworth's poetry is precious because his philosophy is sound;
that his "ethical system is as distinctive and capable of exposition as Bishop Butler's"; that his poetry is informed by ideas
which "fall spontaneously into a scientific system of thought."
But we must be on our guard against the Wordsworthians, if
40 we want to secure for Wordsworth his due rank as a poet. The
Wordsworthians are apt to praise him for the wrong things,

---

21 "Poets who were pious and said things worthy of Apollo (Phœbus), (*Æneid*, vi.
662)
22 in the essay on "Wordsworth's Ethics" in *Hours in a Library*, Vol. III

and to lay far too much stress upon what they call his philosophy. His poetry is the reality, his philosophy—so far, at least, as it may put on the form and habit of "a scientific system of thought," and the more that it puts them on—is the illusion. Perhaps we shall one day learn to make this proposition general, and to say: Poetry is the reality, philosophy the illusion. But in Wordsworth's case, at any rate, we cannot do him justice until we dismiss his formal philosophy.

The *Excursion* abounds with philosophy and therefore the *Excursion* is to the Wordsworthian what it never can be to the disinterested lover of poetry,—a satisfactory work. "Duty exists," says Wordsworth, in the *Excursion;* and then he proceeds thus—

> ". . . Immutably survive,
> For our support, the measures and the forms,
> Which an abstract Intelligence supplies,
> Whose kingdom is, where time and space are not." [23]

And the Wordsworthian is delighted, and thinks that here is a sweet union of philosophy and poetry. But the disinterested lover of poetry will feel that the lines carry us really not a step farther than the proposition which they would interpret; that they are a tissue of elevated but abstract verbiage, alien to the very nature of poetry.

Or let us come direct to the center of Wordsworth's philosophy, as "an ethical system, as distinctive and capable of systematical exposition as Bishop Butler's"—

> ". . . One adequate support
> For the calamities of mortal life
> Exists, one only;—an assured belief
> That the procession of our fate, howe'er
> Sad or disturbed, is ordered by a Being
> Of infinite benevolence and power;
> Whose everlasting purposes embrace
> All accidents, converting them to good." [24]

That is doctrine such as we hear in church too, religious and philosophic doctrine; and the attached Wordsworthian loves passages of such doctrine, and brings them forward in proof of his poet's excellence. But however true the doctrine may be, it has, as here presented, none of the characters of *poetic* truth, the kind of truth which we require from a poet, and in which Wordsworth is really strong.

Even the "intimations" of the famous Ode,[25] those cornerstones of the supposed philosophic system of Wordsworth,—

---

23 *The Excursion,* iv. 73-76   24 *The Excursion,* iv. 10-17
25 *Intimations of Immortality from Recollections of Early Childhood,* above, p. 110

the idea of the high instincts and affections coming out in child-hood, testifying of a divine home recently left, and fading away as our life proceeds,—this idea, of undeniable beauty as a play of fancy, has itself not the character of poetic truth of the best kind; it has no real solidity. The instinct of delight in Nature and her beauty had no doubt extraordinary strength in Words-worth himself as a child. But to say that universally this in-stinct is mighty in childhood, and tends to die away afterwards, is to say what is extremely doubtful. In many people, perhaps
10 with the majority of educated persons, the love of nature is nearly imperceptible at ten years old, but strong and operative at thirty. In general we may say of these high instincts of early childhood, the base of the alleged systematic philosophy of Wordsworth, what Thucydides says of the early achievements of the Greek race: "It is impossible to speak with certainty of what is so remote; but from all that we can really investigate, I should say that they were no very great things."

Finally, the "scientific system of thought" in Wordsworth gives us at least such poetry as this, which the devout Words-
20 worthian accepts—

> "O for the coming of that glorious time
> When, prizing knowledge as her noblest wealth
> And best protection, this Imperial Realm,
> While she exacts allegiance, shall admit
> An obligation, on her part, to *teach*
> Them who are born to serve her and obey;
> Binding herself by statute to secure,
> For all the children whom her soil maintains,
> The rudiments of letters, and inform
30   The mind with moral and religious truth." 26

Wordsworth calls Voltaire dull, and surely the production of these un-Voltairian lines must have been imposed on him as a judgment! One can hear them being quoted at a Social Science Congress; one can call up the whole scene. A great room in one of our dismal provincial towns; dusty air and jaded afternoon daylight; benches full of men with bald heads and women in spectacles; an orator lifting up his face from a manuscript written within and without to declaim these lines of Words-worth; and in the soul of any poor child of nature who may
40 have wandered in thither, an unutterable sense of lamentation, and mourning, and woe!

"But turn we," as Wordsworth says, "from these bold, bad men," the haunters of Social Science Congresses. And let us be on our guard, too, against the exhibitors and extollers of a

26 *The Excursion,* ix. 293-302.

"scientific system of thought" in Wordsworth's poetry. The poetry will never be seen aright while they thus exhibit it. The cause of its greatness is simple, and may be told quite simply. Wordsworth's poetry is great because of the extraordinary power with which Wordsworth feels the joy offered to us in nature, the joy offered to us in the simple primary affections and duties; and because of the extraordinary power with which, in case after case, he shows us this joy, and renders it so as to make us share it.

The source of joy from which he thus draws is the truest and most unfailing source of joy accessible to man. It is also accessible universally. Wordsworth brings us word, therefore, according to his own strong and characteristic line, he brings us word

> "Of joy in widest commonalty spread."

Here is an immense advantage for a poet. Wordsworth tells of what all seek, and tells of it at its truest and best source, and yet a source where all may go and draw for it.

Nevertheless, we are not to suppose that everything is precious which Wordsworth, standing even at this perennial and beautiful source, may give us. Wordsworthians are apt to talk as if it must be. They will speak with the same reverence of *The Sailor's Mother,* for example, as of *Lucy Gray.* They do their master harm by such lack of discrimination. *Lucy Gray* is a beautiful success; *The Sailor's Mother* is a failure. To give aright what he wishes to give, to interpret and render successfully, is not always within Wordsworth's own command. It is within no poet's command; here is the part of the Muse, the inspiration, the God, the "not ourselves." [27] In Wordsworth's case, the accident, for so it may almost be called, of inspiration, is of peculiar importance. No poet, perhaps, is so evidently filled with a new and sacred energy when the inspiration is upon him; no poet, when it fails him, is so left "weak as is a breaking wave." I remember hearing him say that "Goethe's poetry was not inevitable enough." The remark is striking and true; no line in Goethe, as Goethe said himself, but its maker knew well how it came there. Wordsworth is right, Goethe's poetry is not inevitable; not inevitable enough. But Wordsworth's poetry, when he is at his best, is inevitable, as inevitable as Nature herself. It might seem that Nature not only gave him the matter for his poem, but wrote his poem for him. He has no style. He was too conversant with Milton not to catch at times his master's manner, and he has fine Miltonic lines;

---

27 In Arnold's *Literature and Dogma,* Chap. I., he defines God as "the enduring power, not ourselves, which makes for righteousness."

but he has no assured poetic style of his own, like Milton. When he seeks to have a style he falls into ponderosity and pomposity. In the *Excursion* we have his style, as an artistic product of his own creation; and although Jeffrey completely failed to recognize Wordsworth's real greatness, he was yet not wrong in saying of the *Excursion,* as a work of poetic style: "This will never do." [28] And yet magical as is that power, which Wordsworth has not, of assured and possessed poetic style, he has something which is an equivalent for it.

Every one who has any sense for these things feels the subtle turn, the heightening, which is given to a poet's verse by his genius for style. We can feel it in the

> "After life's fitful fever, he sleeps well"—

of Shakespeare; in the

> ". . . though fall'n on evil days,
> On evil days though fall'n, and evil tongues"—[29]

of Milton. It is the incomparable charm of Milton's power of poetic style which gives such worth to *Paradise Regained,* and makes a great poem of a work in which Milton's imagination does not soar high. Wordsworth has in constant possession, and at command, no style of this kind; but he had too poetic a nature, and had read the great poets too well, not to catch, as I have already remarked, something of it occasionally. We find it not only in his Miltonic lines; we find it in such a phrase as this, where the manner is his own, not Milton's—

> "the fierce confederate storm
> Of sorrow barricadoed evermore
> Within the walls of cities;" [30]

although even here, perhaps, the power of style which is undeniable, is more properly that of eloquent prose than the subtle heightening and change wrought by genuine poetic style. It is style, again, and the elevation given by style, which chiefly makes the effectiveness of *Laodameia.* Still the right sort of verse to choose from Wordsworth, if we are to seize his true and most characteristic form of expression, is a line like this from *Michael*—

> "And never lifted up a single stone."

28 The opening sentence of a famous review of *The Excursion,* by **Francis Jeffrey** (1773–1850), Scottish critic, in the *Edinburgh Review* for Nov., 1814, No. 47.
29 The quotation from Shakespeare is in *Macbeth,* III. ii. 23; from **Milton,** *Paradise Lost,* vii., 25–26
30 *The Recluse,* l. 831

There is nothing subtle in it, no heightening, no study of poetic style, strictly so called, at all; yet it is expression of the highest and most truly expressive kind.

Wordsworth owed much to Burns, and a style of perfect plainness, relying for effect solely on the weight and force of that which with entire fidelity it utters, Burns could show him.

> "The poor inhabitant below
> Was quick to learn and wise to know,
> And keenly felt the friendly glow
>   And softer flame;
> But thoughtless follies laid him low
>   And stain'd his name." [31]

Every one will be conscious of a likeness here to Wordsworth; and if Wordsworth did great things with this nobly plain manner, we must remember, what indeed he himself would always have been forward to acknowledge, that Burns used it before him.

Still Wordsworth's use of it has something unique and unmatchable. Nature herself seems, I say, to take the pen out of his hand, and to write for him with her own bare, sheer, penetrating power. This arises from two causes; from the profound sincereness with which Wordsworth feels his subject, and also from the profoundly sincere and natural character of his subject itself. He can and will treat such a subject with nothing but the most plain, first-hand, almost austere naturalness. His expression may often be called bald, as, for instance, in the poem of *Resolution and Independence;* but it is bald as the bare mountain tops are bald, with a baldness which is full of grandeur.

Wherever we meet with the successful balance, in Wordsworth, of profound truth of subject with profound truth of execution, he is unique. His best poems are those which most perfectly exhibit this balance. I have a warm admiration for *Laodameia* and for the great *Ode;* but if I am to tell the very truth, I find *Laodameia* not wholly free from something artificial, and the great *Ode* not wholly free from something declamatory. If I had to pick out poems of a kind most perfectly to show Wordsworth's unique power, I should rather choose poems such as *Michael, The Fountain, The Highland Reaper.*[32] And poems with the peculiar and unique beauty which distinguishes these, Wordsworth produced in considerable number; besides very many other poems of which the worth, although not so rare as the worth of these, is still exceedingly high.

[31] From *A Bard's Epitaph*   [32] See *The Solitary Reaper,* above, p. 95

On the whole, then, as I said at the beginning, not only is Wordsworth eminent by reason of the goodness of his best work, but he is eminent also by reason of the great body of good work which he has left to us. With the ancients I will not compare him. In many respects the ancients are far above us, and yet there is something that we demand which they can never give. Leaving the ancients, let us come to the poets and poetry of Christendom. Dante, Shakespeare, Molière, Milton, Goethe, are altogether larger and more splendid luminaries in the po-
10 etical heaven than Wordsworth. But I know not where else, among the moderns, we are to find his superiors. . . .

I have spoken lightly of Wordsworthians; and if we are to get Wordsworth recognized by the public and by the world, we must recommend him not in the spirit of a clique, but in the spirit of disinterested lovers of poetry. But I am a Wordsworthian myself. I can read with pleasure and edification *Peter Bell,* and the whole series of *Ecclesiastical Sonnets,* and the address to Mr. Wilkinson's spade, and even the *Thanksgiving Ode;*—everything of Wordsworth, I think, except *Vaudracour*
20 *and Julia.* It is not for nothing that one has been brought up in the veneration of a man so truly worthy of homage; that one has seen him and heard him, lived in his neighborhood, and been familiar with his country. No Wordsworthian has a tenderer affection for this pure and sage master than I, or is less really offended by his defects. But Wordsworth is something more than the pure and sage master of a small band of devoted followers, and we ought not to rest satisfied until he is seen to be what he is. He is one of the very chief glories of English Poetry; and by nothing is England so glorious as by
30 her poetry. Let us lay aside every weight which hinders our getting him recognized as this, and let our one study be to bring to pass, as widely as possible and as truly as possible, his own word concerning his poems: "They will coöperate with the benign tendencies in human nature and society, and will, in their degree, be efficacious in making men wiser, better, and happier."

THE STUDY OF POETRY [33]

"THE future of poetry is immense, because in poetry, where it is worthy of its high destinies, our race, as time goes on, will find an ever surer and surer stay. There is not a creed
40 which is not shaken, not an accredited dogma which is not

33 From *Essays in Criticism,* Second Series, copyright 1888 by Macmillan and Co., Ltd., and the Macmillan Company. Reprinted by permission. Originally written as the Introduction to *The English Poets,* ed. T. H. Ward. A few brief passages are omitted.

shown to be questionable, not a received tradition which does not threaten to dissolve. Our religion has materialized itself in the fact, in the supposed fact; it has attached its emotion to the fact, and now the fact is failing it. But for poetry the idea is everything; the rest is a world of illusion, of divine illusion. Poetry attaches its emotion to the idea; the idea *is* the fact. The strongest part of our religion to-day is its unconscious poetry." [34]

Let me be permitted to quote these words of my own, as uttering the thought which should, in my opinion, go with us and govern us in all our study of poetry. In the present work it is the course of one great contributory stream to the world-river of poetry that we are invited to follow. We are here invited to trace the stream of English poetry. But whether we set ourselves, as here, to follow only one of the several streams that make the mighty river of poetry, or whether we seek to know them all, our governing thought should be the same. We should conceive of poetry worthily, and more highly than it has been the custom to conceive of it. We should conceive of it as capable of higher uses, and called to higher destinies, than those which in general men have assigned to it hitherto. More and more mankind will discover that we have to turn to poetry to interpret life for us, to console us, to sustain us. Without poetry, our science will appear incomplete; and most of what now passes with us for religion and philosophy will be replaced by poetry. Science, I say, will appear incomplete without it. For finely and truly does Wordsworth call poetry "the impassioned expression which is in the countenance of all science"; and what is a countenance without its expression? Again, Wordsworth finely and truly calls poetry "the breath and finer spirit of all knowledge": [35] our religion, parading evidences such as those on which the popular mind relies now; our philosophy, pluming itself on its reasonings about causation and finite and infinite being; what are they but the shadows and dreams and false shows of knowledge? The day will come when we shall wonder at ourselves for having trusted to them, for having taken them seriously; and the more we perceive their hollowness, the more we shall prize "the breath and finer spirit of knowledge" offered to us by poetry.

But if we conceive thus highly of the destinies of poetry, we must also set our standard for poetry high, since poetry, to be capable of fulfilling such high destinies, must be poetry of a high order of excellence. We must accustom ourselves to

[34] from Arnold's Introduction to *The Hundred Greatest Men*   [35] from *Preface to the Lyrical Ballads*

a high standard and to a strict judgment. Sainte-Beuve [36] relates that Napoleon one day said, when somebody was spoken
of in his presence as a charlatan: "Charlatan as much as you
please; but where is there *not* charlatanism?"—"Yes," answers
Sainte-Beuve, "in politics, in the art of governing mankind,
that is perhaps true. But in the order of thought, in art, the
glory, the eternal honor is that charlatanism shall find no entrance; herein lies the inviolableness of that noble portion of
man's being." It is admirably said, and let us hold fast to it.
In poetry, which is thought and art in one, it is the glory, the
eternal honor, that charlatanism shall find no entrance; that
this noble sphere be kept inviolate and inviolable. Charlatanism is for confusing or obliterating the distinctions between
excellent and inferior, sound and unsound or only half-sound,
true and untrue or only half-true. It is charlatanism, conscious
or unconscious, whenever we confuse or obliterate these. And
in poetry, more than anywhere else, it is unpermissible to confuse or obliterate them. For in poetry the distinction between
excellent and inferior, sound and unsound or only half-sound,
true and untrue or only half-true, is of paramount importance.
It is of paramount importance because of the high destinies of
poetry. In poetry, as a criticism of life under the conditions
fixed for such a criticism by the laws of poetic truth and poetic
beauty, the spirit of our race will find, we have said, as time
goes on and as other helps fail, its consolation and stay. But
the consolation and stay will be of power in proportion to the
power of the criticism of life. And the criticism of life will be
of power in proportion as the poetry conveying it is excellent
rather than inferior, sound rather than unsound or half-sound,
true rather than untrue or half-true.

The best poetry is what we want; the best poetry will be
found to have a power of forming, sustaining, and delighting
us, as nothing else can. A clearer, deeper sense of the best in
poetry, and of the strength and joy to be drawn from it, is
the most precious benefit which we can gather from a poetical
collection such as the present. And yet in the very nature and
conduct of such a collection there is inevitably something which
tends to obscure in us the consciousness of what our benefit
should be, and to distract us from the pursuit of it. We should
therefore steadily set it before our minds at the outset, and
should compel ourselves to revert constantly to the thought of
it as we proceed.

Yes; constantly in reading poetry, a sense for the best, the
really excellent, and of the strength and joy to be drawn from

36 Charles Augustin Sainte-Beuve (1804-1869), distinguished French critic, whom
Arnold much admired

it, should be present in our minds and should govern our estimate of what we read. But this real estimate, the only true
one, is liable to be superseded, if we are not watchful, by two
other kinds of estimate, the historic estimate and the personal
estimate, both of which are fallacious. A poet or a poem may
count to us historically, they may count to us on grounds personal to ourselves, and they may count to us really. They may
count to us historically. The course of development of a nation's language, thought, and poetry, is profoundly interesting; and by regarding a poet's work as a stage in this course   10
of development we may easily bring ourselves to make it of
more importance as poetry than in itself it really is, we may
come to use a language of quite exaggerated praise in criticizing it; in short, to over-rate it. So arises in our poetic judgments the fallacy caused by the estimate which we may call
historic. Then, again, a poet or a poem may count to us on
grounds personal to ourselves. Our personal affinities, likings,
and circumstances, have great power to sway our estimate of
this or that poet's work, and to make us attach more importance to it as poetry than in itself it really possesses, because   20
to us it is, or has been, of high importance. Here also we over-
rate the object of our interest, and apply to it a language of
praise which is quite exaggerated. And thus we get the source
of a second fallacy in our poetic judgments—the fallacy caused
by an estimate which we may call personal.

Both fallacies are natural. It is evident how naturally the
study of the history and development of a poetry may incline a
man to pause over reputations and works once conspicuous but
now obscure, and to quarrel with a careless public for skipping,
in obedience to mere tradition and habit, from one famous   30
name or work in its national poetry to another, ignorant of
what it misses, and of the reason for keeping what it keeps,
and of the whole process of growth in its poetry. The French
have become diligent students of their own early poetry, which
they long neglected; the study makes many of them dissatisfied
with their so-called classical poetry, the court-tragedy of the
seventeenth century, a poetry which Pellisson [37] long ago reproached with its want of the true poetic stamp, with its *poli-
tesse stérile et rampante,*[38] but which nevertheless has reigned
in France as absolutely as if it had been the perfection of clas-   40
sical poetry indeed. The dissatisfaction is natural; yet a lively
and accomplished critic, M. Charles d' Héricault,[39] the editor
of Clément Marot, goes too far when he says that "the cloud
of glory playing round a classic is a mist as dangerous to the

37 Paul Pellisson (1624– 38 barren and servile po- (1823–1899). Marot (1496–
1693), French author   liteness   1544), French Renaissance
   39 Novelist and scholar   poet

future of a literature as it is intolerable for the purposes of history." "It hinders," he goes on, "it hinders us from seeing more than one single point, the culminating and exceptional point, the summary, fictitious and arbitrary, of a thought and of a work. It substitutes a halo for a physiognomy, it puts a statue where there was once a man, and hiding from us all trace of the labor, the attempts, the weaknesses, the failures, it claims not study but veneration; it does not show us how the thing is done, it imposes upon us a model. Above all, for the

10 historian this creation of classic personages is inadmissible; for it withdraws the poet from his time, from his proper life, it breaks historical relationships, it blinds criticism by conventional admiration, and renders the investigation of literary origins unacceptable. It gives us a human personage no longer, but a God seated immovable amidst His perfect work, like Jupiter on Olympus; and hardly will it be possible for the young student, to whom such work is exhibited at such a distance from him, to believe that it did not issue ready made from that divine head."

20 All this is brilliantly and tellingly said, but we must plead for a distinction. Everything depends on the reality of a poet's classic character. If he is a dubious classic, let us sift him; if he is a false classic, let us explode him. But if he is a real classic, if his work belongs to the class of the very best (for this is the true and right meaning of the word *classic, classical*), then the great thing for us is to feel and enjoy his work as deeply as ever we can, and to appreciate the wide difference between it and all work which has not the same high character. . . .

The historic estimate is likely in especial to affect our judg-

30 ment and our language when we are dealing with ancient poets; the personal estimate when we are dealing with poets our contemporaries, or at any rate modern. The exaggerations due to the historic estimate are not in themselves, perhaps, of very much gravity. Their report hardly enters the general ear; probably they do not always impose even on the literary men who adopt them. But they lead to a dangerous abuse of language. So we hear Cædmon,[40] amongst our own poets, compared to Milton. I have already noticed the enthusiasm of one accomplished French critic for "historic origins." Another eminent

40 French critic, M. Vitet,[41] comments upon that famous document of the early poetry of his nation, the *Chanson de Roland*. . . . The poem has vigor and freshness; it is not without pathos. But M. Vitet is not satisfied with seeing in it a document of some poetic value, and of very high historic and linguistic value;

40 Anglo-Saxon poet (late seventh century?)

41 Ludovic Vitet (1802–1873) *Chanson de Roland* is

the medieval French epic poem (end of eleventh cent.)

he sees in it a grand and beautiful work, a monument of epic genius. In its general design he finds the grandiose conception, in its details he finds the constant union of simplicity with greatness, which are the marks, he truly says, of the genuine epic, and distinguish it from the artificial epic of literary ages. One thinks of Homer; this is the sort of praise which is given to Homer, and justly given. Higher praise there cannot well be, and it is the praise due to epic poetry of the highest order only, and to no other. Let us try, then, the *Chanson de Roland* at its best. Roland, mortally wounded, lays himself down under 10 a pine-tree, with his face turned towards Spain and the enemy—

> "De plusurs choses à remembrer li prist,
> De tantes teres cume li bers cunquist,
> De dulce France, des humes de sun lign,
> De Carlemagne sun seignor ki l'nurrit." [42]

That is primitive work, I repeat, with an undeniable poetic quality of its own. It deserves such praise, and such praise is sufficient for it. But now turn to Homer—

> Ὣς φάτο· τοὺς δ' ἤδη κατέχεν φυσίζοος αἶα
> ἐν Λακεδαίμονι αὖθι, φίλη ἐν πατρίδι γαίῃ [43]   20

We are here in another world, another order of poetry altogether; here is rightly due such supreme praise as that which M. Vitet gives to the *Chanson de Roland*. If our words are to have any meaning, if our judgments are to have any solidity, we must not heap that supreme praise upon poetry of an order immeasurably inferior.

Indeed there can be no more useful help for discovering what poetry belongs to the class of the truly excellent, and can therefore do us most good, than to have always in one's mind lines and expressions of the great masters, and to apply them as a 30 touchstone to other poetry. Of course we are not to require this other poetry to resemble them; it may be very dissimilar. But if we have any tact we shall find them, when we have lodged them well in our minds, an infallible touchstone for detecting the presence or absence of high poetic quality, and also the degree of this quality, in all other poetry which we may place beside them. Short passages, even single lines, will serve our turn quite sufficiently. Take the two lines which I have just quoted from Homer, the poet's comment on Helen's mention of her brothers;—or take his   40

---

[42] "Then began he to call many things to remembrance,—all the lands which his valor conquered, and pleasant France, and the men of his lineage, and Charlemagne his liege lord who nourished him.—*Chanson de Roland*, iii. 939–942." (Arnold)

[43] "So said she; they long since in Earth's soft arms were reposing,
There, in their own dear land, their fatherland, Lacedaemon.
Iliad, iii. 243, 244 (translated by Dr. Hawtrey)." (Arnold)

Ἆ δειλώ, τί σφῶϊ δόμεν Πηλῆϊ ἄνακτι
θνητᾷ; ὑμεῖς δ᾽ ἐστὸν ἀγήρω τ᾽ ἀθανάτω τε.
ἦ ἵνα δυστήνοισι μετ᾽ ἀνδράσιν ἄλγε᾽ ἔχητον; [44]

the address of Zeus to the horses of Peleus;—or take finally his

Καὶ σέ, γέρον, τὸ πρὶν μὲν ἀκούομεν ὄλβιον εἶναι· [45]

the words of Achilles to Priam, a suppliant before him. Take that incomparable line and a half of Dante, Ugolino's tremendous words—

"Io no piangeva; sì dentro impietrai.
Piangevan elli . . ." [46]

take the lovely words of Beatrice to Virgil—

"Io son fatta da Dio, sua mercè, tale,
Che la vostra miseria non mi tange,
Nè fiamma d'esto incendio non m'assala . . ." [47]

Take the simple, but perfect, single line—

"In la sua volontade è nostra pace." [48]

Take of Shakespeare a line or two of Henry the Fourth's expostulation with sleep—

"Wilt thou upon the high and giddy mast
Seal up the ship-boy's eyes, and rock his brains
In cradle of the rude imperious surge . . ." [49]

and take, as well, Hamlet's dying request to Horatio—

"If thou didst ever hold me in thy heart,
Absent thee from felicity awhile,
And in this harsh world draw thy breath in pain
To tell my story . . ." [50]

Take of Milton that Miltonic passage—

44 "Ah, unhappy pair, why gave we you to King Peleus, to a mortal? but ye are without old age, and immortal. Was it that with men born to misery ye might have sorrow?—*Iliad*, xvii. 443–445." (Arnold)

45 "Nay, and thou too, old man, in former days wast, as we hear, happy. *Iliad*, xxiv. 543." (Arnold)

46 "I wailed not, so of stone grew I within;—*they* wailed.—*Inferno*, xxxiii. 39, 40." (Arnold)

47 "Of such sort hath God, thanked be His mercy, made me, that your misery toucheth me not, neither doth the flame of this fire strike me.—*Inferno*, ii. 91–93." (Arnold)

48 "In his will is our peace.—*Paradiso*, iii. 85." (Arnold)

49 2 *Henry IV*, III. i. 18–20

50 *Hamlet*, V. ii. 361–2

> "Darken'd so, yet shone
> Above them all the archangel; but his face
> Deep scars of thunder had intrench'd, and care
> Sat on his faded cheek . . ."

add two such lines as—

> "And courage never to submit or yield
> And what is else not to be overcome . . ."

and finish with the exquisite close to the loss of Proserpine, the loss

> ". . . which cost Ceres all that pain
> To seek her through the world." [51]

These few lines, if we have tact and can use them, are enough even of themselves to keep clear and sound our judgments about poetry, to save us from fallacious estimates of it, to conduct us to a real estimate.

The specimens I have quoted differ widely from one another, but they have in common this: the possession of the very highest poetical quality. If we are thoroughly penetrated by their power, we shall find that we have acquired a sense enabling us, whatever poetry may be laid before us, to feel the degree in which a high poetical quality is present or wanting there. Critics give themselves great labor to draw out what in the abstract constitutes the characters of a high quality of poetry. It is much better simply to have recourse to concrete examples;—to take specimens of poetry of the high, the very highest quality, and to say: The characters of a high quality of poetry are what is expressed *there*. They are far better recognized by being felt in the verse of the master, than by being perused in the prose of the critic. Nevertheless if we are urgently pressed to give some critical account of them, we may safely, perhaps, venture on laying down, not indeed how and why the characters arise, but where and in what they arise. They are in the matter and substance of the poetry, and they are in its manner and style. Both of these, the substance and matter on the one hand, the style and manner on the other, have a mark, an accent, of high beauty, worth, and power. But if we are asked to define this mark and accent in the abstract, our answer must be: No, for we should thereby be darkening the question, not clearing it. . . .

Only one thing we may add as to the substance and matter of poetry, guiding ourselves by Aristotle's profound observa-

---

[51] *Paradise Lost*, i. 599–602, 108–9, iv. 271 respectively

tion [52] that the superiority of poetry over history consists in its possessing a higher truth and a higher seriousness (φιλοσοφώτερον καὶ σπουδαιότερον). Let us add, therefore, to what we have said, this: that the substance and matter of the best poetry acquire their special character from possessing, in an eminent degree, truth and seriousness. We may add yet further, what is in itself evident, that to the style and manner of the best poetry their special character, their accent, is given by their diction, and, even yet more, by their movement. And though we dis-
10 tinguish between the two characters, the two accents, of superiority, yet they are nevertheless vitally connected one with the other. The superior character of truth and seriousness, in the matter and substance of the best poetry, is inseparable from the superiority of diction and movement marking its style and manner. The two superiorities are closely related, and are in steadfast proportion one to the other. So far as high poetic truth and seriousness are wanting to a poet's matter and substance, so far also, we may be sure, will a high poetic stamp of diction and movement be wanting to his style and manner. In
20 proportion as this high stamp of diction and movement, again, is absent from a poet's style and manner, we shall find, also, that high poetic truth and seriousness are absent from his substance and matter.

So stated, these are but dry generalities; their whole force lies in their application. And I could wish every student of poetry to make the application of them for himself. Made by himself, the application would impress itself upon his mind far more deeply than made by me. Neither will my limits allow me to make any full application of the generalities above pro-
30 pounded; but in the hope of bringing out, at any rate, some significance in them, and of establishing an important principle more firmly by their means, I will, in the space which remains to me, follow rapidly from the commencement the course of our English poetry with them in my view.

[Arnold here discusses the poetry of medieval France which is important only on the basis of "the historic estimate."]

But in the fourteenth century there comes an Englishman nourished on this poetry; taught his trade by this poetry, getting words, rhyme, meter from this poetry; for even of that stanza [53] which the Italians used, and which Chaucer derived immediately from the Italians, the basis and suggestion was
40 probably given in France. Chaucer (I have already named

---

52 *Poetics*, § 9   which Chaucer uses in his
53 Arnold perhaps refers   *Troilus and Criseyde* and
to the seven line stanza   elsewhere.

him) fascinated his contemporaries, but so too did Christian of Troyes and Wolfram of Eschenbach.[58] Chaucer's power of fascination, however, is enduring; his poetical importance does not need the assistance of the historic estimate; it is real. He is a genuine source of joy and strength, which is flowing still for us and will flow always. He will be read, as time goes on, far more generally than he is read now. His language is a cause of difficulty for us; but so also, and I think in quite as great a degree, is the language of Burns. In Chaucer's case, as in that of Burns, it is a difficulty to be unhesitatingly accepted and overcome.

If we ask ourselves wherein consists the immense superiority of Chaucer's poetry over the romance-poetry—why it is that in passing from this to Chaucer we suddenly feel ourselves to be in another world, we shall find that his superiority is both in the substance of his poetry and in the style of his poetry. His superiority in substance is given by his large, free, simple, clear yet kindly view of human life,—so unlike the total want, in the romance-poets, of all intelligent command of it. Chaucer has not their helplessness; he has gained the power to survey the world from a central, a truly human point of view. We have only to call to mind the Prologue to *The Canterbury Tales*. The right comment upon it is Dryden's: "It is sufficient to say, according to the proverb, that *here is God's plenty*." [59] And again: "He is a perpetual fountain of good sense." It is by a large, free, sound representation of things, that poetry, this high criticism of life, has truth of substance; and Chaucer's poetry has truth of substance.

Of his style and manner, if we think first of the romance-poetry and then of Chaucer's divine liquidness of diction, his divine fluidity of movement, it is difficult to speak temperately. They are irresistible, and justify all the rapture with which his successors speak of his "gold dew-drops of speech." Johnson misses the point entirely when he finds fault with Dryden for ascribing to Chaucer the first refinement of our numbers, and says that Gower [60] also can show smooth numbers and easy rhymes. The refinement of our numbers means something far more than this. A nation may have versifiers with smooth numbers and easy rhymes, and yet may have no real poetry at all. Chaucer is the father of our splendid English poetry; he is our "well of English undefiled," because by the lovely charm of his diction, the lovely charm of his movement, he makes an epoch and founds a tradition. In Spenser, Shakespeare, Milton, Keats,

---

58 Medieval German poet, fl. about 1200, author of *Parzival*

59 from Dryden's *Preface to the Fables*, 1700 (see Vol. I)

60 John Gower (c. 1330-1408), author of the *Confessio Amantis*

we can follow the tradition of the liquid diction, the fluid movement, of Chaucer; at one time it is his liquid diction of which in these poets we feel the virtue, and at another time it is his fluid movement. And the virtue is irresistible.

Bounded as is my space, I must yet find room for an example of Chaucer's virtue, as I have given examples to show the virtue of the great classics. I feel disposed to say that a single line is enough to show the charm of Chaucer's verse; that merely one line like this—

"O martyr souded [61] in virginitee!"

has a virtue of manner and movement such as we shall not find in all the verse of romance-poetry;—but this is saying nothing. The virtue is such as we shall not find, perhaps, in all English poetry, outside the poets whom I have named as the special inheritors of Chaucer's tradition. A single line, however, is too little if we have not the strain of Chaucer's verse well in our memory; let us take a stanza. It is from *The Prioress's Tale,* the story of the Christian child murdered in a Jewry—

"My throte is cut unto my nekke-bone
Saidè this child, and as by way of kinde
I should have deyd, yea, longè time agone;
But Jesu Christ, as ye in bookès finde,
Will that his glory last and be in minde,
And for the worship of his mother dere
Yet may I sing *O Alma* loud and clere."

Wordsworth has modernized this Tale, and to feel how delicate and evanescent is the charm of verse, we have only to read Wordsworth's first three lines of this stanza after Chaucer's—

"My throat is cut unto the bone, I trow,
Said this young child, and by the law of kind
I should have died, yea, many hours ago."

The charm is departed. It is often said that the power of liquidness and fluidity in Chaucer's verse was dependent upon a free, a licentious dealing with language, such as is now impossible;

61 confirmed (*Prioress's tale,* l. 127). The line should have *to* instead of *in.*

upon a liberty, such as Burns too enjoyed, of making words like *neck, bird,* into a dissyllable by adding to them, and words like *cause, rhyme,* into a dissyllable by sounding the *e* mute. It is true that Chaucer's fluidity is conjoined with this liberty, and is admirably served by it; but we ought not to say that it was dependent upon it. It was dependent upon his talent. Other poets with a like liberty do not attain to the fluidity of Chaucer; Burns himself does not attain to it. Poets, again, who have a talent akin to Chaucer's, such as Shakespeare or Keats, have known how to attain to his fluidity without the 10 like liberty.

And yet Chaucer is not one of the great classics. His poetry transcends and effaces, easily and without effort, all the romance-poetry of Catholic Christendom; it transcends and effaces all the English poetry contemporary with it, it transcends and effaces all the English poetry subsequent to it down to the age of Elizabeth. Of such avail is poetic truth of substance, in its natural and necessary union with poetic truth of style. And yet, I say, Chaucer is not one of the great classics. He has not their accent. What is wanting to him is suggested by 20 the mere mention of the name of the first great classic of Christendom, the immortal poet who died eighty years before Chaucer,—Dante. The accent of such verse as

"In la sua volontade è nostra pace . . ."

is altogether beyond Chaucer's reach; we praise him, but we feel that this accent is out of the question for him. It may be said that it was necessarily out of the reach of any poet in the England of that stage of growth. Possibly; but we are to adopt a real, not a historic, estimate of poetry. However we may account for its absence, something is wanting, then, to the poetry 30 of Chaucer, which poetry must have before it can be placed in the glorious class of the best. And there is no doubt what that something is. It is the σπουδαιότης, the high and excellent seriousness, which Aristotle assigns as one of the grand virtues of poetry. The substance of Chaucer's poetry, his view of things and his criticism of life, has largeness, freedom, shrewdness, benignity; but it has not this high seriousness. Homer's criticism of life has it, Dante's has it, Shakespeare's has it. It is this chiefly which gives to our spirits what they can rest upon; and with the increasing demands of our modern ages upon poetry, 40 this virtue of giving us what we can rest upon will be more and more highly esteemed. A voice from the slums of Paris, fifty or sixty years after Chaucer, the voice of poor Villon [62] out of his life of riot and crime, has at its happy moments (as, for instance, in the last stanza of *La Belle Heaulmière*) more of this important poetic virtue of seriousness than all the productions of Chaucer. But its apparition in Villon, and in men like Villon, is fitful; the greatness of the great poets, the power of their criticism of life, is that their virtue is sustained.

To our praise, therefore, of Chaucer as a poet there must be this limitation: he lacks the high seriousness of the great clas-
10 sics, and therewith an important part of their virtue. Still, the main fact for us to bear in mind about Chaucer is his sterling value according to that real estimate which we firmly adopt for all poets. He has poetic truth of substance, though he has not high poetic seriousness, and corresponding to his truth of substance he has an exquisite virtue of style and manner. With him is born our real poetry.

For my present purpose I need not dwell on our Elizabethan poetry, or on the continuation and close of this poetry in Milton. We all of us profess to be agreed in the estimate of this
20 poetry; we all of us recognize it as great poetry, our greatest, and Shakespeare and Milton as our poetical classics. The real estimate, here, has universal currency. With the next age of our poetry divergency and difficulty begin. An historic estimate of that poetry has established itself; and the question is, whether it will be found to coincide with the real estimate.

The age of Dryden, together with our whole eighteenth century which followed it, sincerely believed itself to have produced poetical classics of its own, and even to have made advance, in poetry, beyond all its predecessors. Dryden regards as
30 not seriously disputable the opinion "that the sweetness of English verse was never understood or practised by our fathers." Cowley could see nothing at all in Chaucer's poetry. Dryden heartily admired it, and, as we have seen, praised its matter admirably; but of its exquisite manner and movement all he can find to say is that "there is the rude sweetness of a

---

62 François Villon, fifteenth century French poet and vagabond. "The name *Heaulmière* is said to be derived from a head-dress (helm) worn as a mark by courtesans. In Villon's ballad, a poor old creature of this class laments her days of youth and beauty. The last stanza of the ballad runs thus—

'Ainsi le bon temps regretons
Entre nous, pauvres vieilles sottes,
Assises bas, à croppetons,
Tout en ung tas comme pelottes;
A petit feu de chenevottes
Tost allumées, tost estainctes.
Et jadis fusmes si mignottes!
Ainsis en prend à maintz et maintes.'

'Thus amongst ourselves we regret the good time, poor silly old things, low-seated on our heels, all in a heap like so many balls; by a little fire of hemp-stalks, soon lighted, soon spent. And once we were such darlings! So fares it with many and many a one.' " (Arnold)

Scotch tune in it, which is natural and pleasing, though not
perfect." [63] Addison, wishing to praise Chaucer's numbers, com-
pares them with Dryden's own. And all through the eighteenth
century, and down even into our own times, the stereotyped
phrase of approbation for good verse found in our early poetry
has been, that it even approached the verse of Dryden, Addison,
Pope, and Johnson.

Are Dryden and Pope poetical classics? Is the historic estimate, which represents them as such, and which has been so
long established that it cannot easily give way, the real esti- 10
mate? Wordsworth and Coleridge, as is well known, denied it;
but the authority of Wordsworth and Coleridge does not weigh
much with the young generation, and there are many signs to
show that the eighteenth century and its judgments are coming
into favor again. Are the favorite poets of the eighteenth century classics?

It is impossible within my present limits to discuss the question fully. And what man of letters would not shrink from
seeming to dispose dictatorially of the claims of two men who
are, at any rate, such masters in letters as Dryden and Pope; 20
two men of such admirable talent, both of them, and one of
them, Dryden, a man, on all sides, of such energetic and genial
power? And yet, if we are to gain the full benefit from poetry,
we must have the real estimate of it. I cast about for some
mode of arriving, in the present case, at such an estimate without offense. And perhaps the best way is to begin, as it is easy
to begin, with cordial praise.

When we find Chapman, the Elizabethan translator of
Homer, expressing himself in his preface thus: "Though truth
in her very nakedness sits in so deep a pit, that from Gades to 30
Aurora and Ganges few eyes can sound her, I hope yet those
few here will so discover and confirm that, the date being out
of her darkness in this morning of our poet, he shall now gird
his temples with the sun,"—we pronounce that such a prose is
intolerable. When we find Milton writing: "And long it was not
after, when I was confirmed in this opinion, that he, who would
not be frustrate of his hope to write well hereafter in laudable
things, ought himself to be a true poem," [64]—we pronounce
that such a prose has its own grandeur, but that it is obsolete
and inconvenient. But when we find Dryden telling us: "What 40
Virgil wrote in the vigor of his age, in plenty and at ease, I have
undertaken to translate in my declining years; struggling with
wants, oppressed with sickness, curbed in my genius, liable to
be misconstrued in all I write," [65]—then we exclaim that here

---

63 from *Preface to the*   64 from *An Apology for*   65 *Postscript* to his trans-
Fables   Smectymnuus   lation of Virgil

at last we have the true English prose, a prose such as we would all gladly use if we only knew how. Yet Dryden was Milton's contemporary.

But after the Restoration the time had come when our nation felt the imperious need of a fit prose. So, too, the time had likewise come when our nation felt the imperious need of freeing itself from the absorbing preoccupation which religion in the Puritan age had exercised. It was impossible that this freedom should be brought about without some negative excess, 10 without some neglect and impairment of the religious life of the soul; and the spiritual history of the eighteenth century shows us that the freedom was not achieved without them. Still, the freedom was achieved; the preoccupation, an undoubtedly baneful and retarding one if it had continued, was got rid of. And as with religion amongst us at that period, so it was also with letters. A fit prose was a necessity; but it was impossible that a fit prose should establish itself amongst us without some touch of frost to the imaginative life of the soul. The needful qualities for a fit prose are regularity, uniformity, precision, 20 balance. The men of letters, whose destiny it may be to bring their nation to the attainment of a fit prose, must of necessity, whether they work in prose or in verse, give a predominating, an almost exclusive attention to the qualities of regularity, uniformity, precision, balance. But an almost exclusive attention to these qualities involves some repression and silencing of poetry.

We are to regard Dryden as the puissant and glorious founder, Pope as the splendid high priest, of our age of prose and reason, of our excellent and indispensable eighteenth cen- 30 tury. For the purposes of their mission and destiny their poetry, like their prose, is admirable. Do you ask me whether Dryden's verse, take it almost where you will, is not good?

> "A milk-white Hind, immortal and unchanged,
> Fed on the lawns and in the forest ranged." [66]

I answer: Admirable for the purposes of the inaugurator of an age of prose and reason. Do you ask me whether Pope's verse, take it almost where you will, is not good?

> "To Hounslow Heath I point, and Banstead Down;
> Thence comes your mutton, and these chicks my own." [67]

40 I answer: Admirable for the purposes of the high priest of an age of prose and reason. But do you ask me whether such verse

---

[66] *The Hind and the Panther*   [67] *Imitations of Horace,* Book, ll. 143–4. Second Satire of Second

proceeds from men with an adequate poetic criticism of life, from men whose criticism of life has a high seriousness, or even, without that high seriousness, has poetic largeness, freedom, insight, benignity? Do you ask me whether the application of ideas to life in the verse of these men, often a powerful application, no doubt, is a powerful *poetic* application? Do you ask me whether the poetry of these men has either the matter or the inseparable manner of such an adequate poetic criticism; whther it has the accent of

> "Absent thee from felicity awhile . . ."   10

or of

> "And what is else not to be overcome . . ."

or of

> "O martyr souded in virginitee!"

I answer: It has not and cannot have them; it is the poetry of the builders of an age of prose and reason. Though they may write in verse, though they may in a certain sense be masters of the art of versification, Dryden and Pope are not classics of our poetry, they are classics of our prose.

Gray is our poetical classic of that literature and age; the position of Gray is singular, and demands a word of notice here. He has not the volume or the power of poets who, coming in times more favorable, have attained to an independent criticism of life. But he lived with the great poets, he lived, above all, with the Greeks, through perpetually studying and enjoying them; and he caught their poetic point of view for regarding life, caught their poetic manner. The point of view and the manner are not self-sprung in him, he caught them of others; and he had not the free and abundant use of them. But whereas Addison and Pope never had the use of them, Gray had the use of them at times. He is the scantiest and frailest of classics in our poetry, but he is a classic.

And now, after Gray, we are met, as we draw towards the end of the eighteenth century, we are met by the great name of Burns. We enter now on times where the personal estimate of poets begins to be rife, and where the real estimate of them is not reached without difficulty. But in spite of the disturbing pressures of personal partiality, of national partiality, let us try to reach a real estimate of the poetry of Burns.

By his English poetry Burns in general belongs to the eighteenth century, and has little importance for us.

> "Mark ruffian Violence, distain'd with crimes,
>   Rousing elate in these degenerate times;

> View unsuspecting Innocence a prey,
> As guileful Fraud points out the erring way;
> While subtle Litigation's pliant tongue .
> The life-blood equal sucks of Right and Wrong!" [68]

Evidently this is not the real Burns, or his name and fame
would have disappeared long ago. Nor is Clarinda's love-poet,
Sylvander,[69] the real Burns either. But he tells us himself:
"These English songs gravel me to death. I have not the command of the language that I have of my native tongue. In fact,
10 I think that my ideas are more barren in English than in Scotch.
I have been at *Duncan Gray* to dress it in English, but all I
can do is desperately stupid." We English turn naturally, in
Burns, to the poems in our own language, because we can
read them easily; but in those poems we have not the real
Burns.

The real Burns is of course in his Scotch poems. Let us
boldly say that of much of this poetry, a poetry dealing perpetually with Scotch drink, Scotch religion, and Scotch manners, a Scotchman's estimate is apt to be personal. A Scotch-
20 man is used to this world of Scotch drink, Scotch religion, and
Scotch manners; he has a tenderness for it; he meets its poet
half way. In this tender mood he reads pieces like the *Holy
Fair* or *Halloween*. But this world of Scotch drink, Scotch
religion, and Scotch manners is against a poet, not for him,
when it is not a partial countryman who reads him; for in
itself it is not a beautiful world, and no one can deny that it
is of advantage to a poet to deal with a beautiful world. Burns's
world of Scotch drink, Scotch religion, and Scotch manners,
is often a harsh, a sordid, a repulsive world; even the world
30 of his *Cotter's Saturday Night* is not a beautiful world. No
doubt a poet's criticism of life may have such truth and power
that it triumphs over its world and delights us. Burns may triumph over his world, often he does triumph over his world, but
let us observe how and where. Burns is the first case we have
had where the bias of the personal estimate tends to mislead; let
us look at him closely, he can bear it.

Many of his admirers will tell us that we have Burns, con-
vivial, genuine, delightful, here—

> "Leeze me on drink! it gies us mair
> 40   Than either school or college;
> It kindles wit, it waukens lair,
> It pangs us fou o' knowledge.

---

68 *On the Death of Lord*   69 Name assumed by   ence with Mrs. Maclehose
President Dundas   Burns in his correspond-   (Clarinda)

> Be 't whisky gill or penny wheep
> Or ony stronger potion,
> It never fails, on drinking deep,
> To kittle up our notion
> By night or day." [70]

There is a great deal of that sort of thing in Burns, and it is
unsatisfactory, not because it is bacchanalian poetry, but because it has not that accent of sincerity which bacchanalian
poetry, to do it justice, very often has. There is something in it
of bravado, something which makes us feel that we have not the
man speaking to us with his real voice; something, therefore,
poetically unsound.

With still more confidence will his admirers tell us that we
have the genuine Burns, the great poet, when his strain asserts
the independence, equality, dignity, of men, as in the famous
song *For a' that and a' that*—

> "A prince can mak' a belted knight,
> A marquis, duke, and a' that;
> But an honest man's aboon his might,
> Guid faith he manna fa' that!
> For a' that, and a'that,
> Their dignities, and a' that,
> The pith o' sense, and pride o' worth,
> Are higher rank than a' that."

Here they find his grand, genuine touches; and still more, when
this puissant genius, who so often set morality at defiance, falls
moralizing—

> "The sacred lowe o' weel-placed love
> Luxuriantly indulge it;
> But never tempt th' illicit rove,
> Tho' naething should divulge it.
> I waive the quantum o' the sin,
> The hazard o' concealing,
> But och! it hardens a' within,
> And petrifies the feeling."

Or in a higher strain—

> "Who made the heart, 't is He alone
> Decidedly can try us;
> He knows each chord, its various tone;

[70] *The Holy Fair*

> Each spring, its various bias.
> Then at the balance let 's be mute,
> We never can adjust it;
> What's *done* we partly may compute,
> But know not what's resisted."

Or in a better strain yet, a strain, his admirers will say, unsurpassable—

> "To make a happy fire-side clime
>   To weans and wife,
> 10   That's the true pathos and sublime
>   Of human life." [71]

There is a criticism of life for you, the admirers of Burns will say to us; there is the application of ideas to life! There is, undoubtedly. The doctrine of the last-quoted lines coincides almost exactly with what was the aim and end, Xenophon tells us, of all the teaching of Socrates. And the application is a powerful one; made by a man of vigorous understanding, and (need I say?) a master of language.

But for supreme poetical success more is required than the 20 powerful application of ideas to life; it must be an application under the conditions fixed by the laws of poetic truth and poetic beauty. Those laws fix as an essential condition, in the poet's treatment of such matters as are here in question, high seriousness;—the high seriousness which comes from absolute sincerity. The accent of high seriousness, born of absolute sincerity, is what gives to such verse as

> "In la sua volontade è nostra pace . . ."

to such criticism of life as Dante's, its power. Is this accent felt in the passages which I have been quoting from Burns? 30 Surely not; surely, if our sense is quick, we must perceive that we have not in those passages a voice from the very inmost soul of the genuine Burns; he is not speaking to us from these depths, he is more or less preaching. And the compensation for admiring such passages less, for missing the perfect poetic accent in them, will be that we shall admire more the poetry where that accent is found.

No; Burns, like Chaucer, comes short of the high seriousness of the great classics, and the virtue of matter and manner which goes with that high seriousness is wanting to his work.

---

[71] From *Epistle to a Young Friend, Address to the Unco Guid, Epistle to Dr. Blacklock* respectively.

At moments he touches it in a profound and passionate melancholy, as in those four immortal lines taken by Byron as a motto for *The Bride of Abydos,* but which have in them a depth of poetic quality such as resides in no verse of Byron's own—

> "Had we never loved sae kindly,
> Had we never loved sae blindly,
> Never met, or never parted,
> We had ne'er been broken-hearted."

But a whole poem of that quality Burns cannot make; the rest, in the *Farewell to Nancy,* is verbiage.   10

We arrive best at the real estimate of Burns, I think, by conceiving his work as having truth of matter and truth of manner, but not the accent or the poetic virtue of the highest masters. His genuine criticism of life, when the sheer poet in him speaks, is ironic; it is not—

> "Thou Power Supreme, whose mighty scheme
> These woes of mine fulfill,
> Here firm I rest, they must be best
> Because they are Thy will!" [72]

It is far rather: *Whistle owre the lave o't!* Yet we may say 20 of him as of Chaucer, that of life and the world, as they come before him, his view is large, free, shrewd, benignant,—truly poetic, therefore; and his manner of rendering what he sees to match. But we must note, at the same time, his great difference from Chaucer. The freedom of Chaucer is heightened, in Burns, by a fiery, reckless energy; the benignity of Chaucer deepens, in Burns, into an overwhelming sense of the pathos of things;—of the pathos of human nature, the pathos, also, of non-human nature. Instead of the fluidity of Chaucer's manner, the manner of Burns has spring, bounding swiftness. 30 Burns is by far the greater force, though he has perhaps less charm. The world of Chaucer is fairer, richer, more significant than that of Burns; ·but when the largeness and freedom of Burns get full sweep, as in *Tam o' Shanter,* or still more in that puissant and splendid production, *The Jolly Beggars,* his world may be what it will, his poetic genius triumphs over it. In the world of *The Jolly Beggars* there is more than hideousness and squalor, there is bestiality; yet the piece is a superb poetic success. It has a breadth, truth, and power which make the famous scene in Auerbach's Cellar, of Goethe's *Faust,* 40

72 *Winter: a Dirge*

seem artificial and tame beside it, and which are only matched
by Shakespeare and Aristophanes.

Here, where his largeness and freedom serve him so admirably, and also in those poems and songs where to shrewdness
he adds infinite archness and wit, and to benignity infinite
pathos, where his manner is flawless, and a perfect poetic whole
is the result,—in things like the address to the mouse whose
home he had ruined, in things like *Duncan Gray, Tam Glen,
Whistle and I'll come to you my Lad, Auld Lang Syne* (this
list might be made much longer),—here we have the genuine
Burns, of whom the real estimate must be high indeed. Not
a classic, nor with the excellent σπουδαιότης of the great classics,
nor with a verse rising to a criticism of life, and a virtue like
theirs; but a poet with thorough truth of substance and an
answering truth of style, giving us a poetry sound to the core.
We all of us have a leaning towards the pathetic, and may be
inclined perhaps to prize Burns most for his touches of piercing, sometimes almost intolerable, pathos; for verse like—

> "We twa hae paidl't i' the burn
> From mornin' sun till dine;
> But seas between us braid hae roar'd
> Sin auld lang syne . . ."

where he is as lovely as he is sound. But perhaps it is by the
perfection of soundness of his lighter and archer masterpieces
that he is poetically most wholesome for us. For the votary
misled by a personal estimate of Shelley, as so many of us
have been, are, and will be,—of that beautiful spirit building
his many-colored haze of words and images

> "Pinnacled dim in the intense inane"—

no contact can be wholesomer than the contact with Burns at
his archest and soundest. Side by side with the

> "On the brink of the night and the morning
> My coursers are wont to respire,
> But the Earth has just whispered a warning
> That their flight must be swifter than fire . . ."

of *Prometheus Unbound,* how salutary, how very salutary, to
place this from *Tam Glen*—

> "My minnie does constantly deave me
> And bids me beware o' young men;
> They flatter, she says, to deceive me;
> But wha can think sae o' Tam Glen?"

But we enter on burning ground as we approach the poetry of times so near to us—poetry like that of Byron, Shelley, and Wordsworth—of which the estimates are so often not only personal, but personal with passion. For my purpose, it is enough to have taken the single case of Burns, the first poet we come to of whose work the estimate formed is evidently apt to be personal, and to have suggested how we may proceed, using the poetry of the great classics as a sort of touchstone, to correct this estimate, as we had previously corrected by the same means the historic estimate where we met with it. A collection like the present, with its succession of celebrated names and celebrated poems, offers a good opportunity to us for resolutely endeavoring to make our estimates of poetry real. I have sought to point out a method which will help us in making them so, and to exhibit it in use so far as to put any one who likes in a way of applying it for himself.

At any rate the end to which the method and the estimate are designed to lead, and from leading to which, if they do lead to it, they get their whole value,—the benefit of being able clearly to feel and deeply to enjoy the best, the truly classic, in poetry,—is an end, let me say it once more at parting, of supreme importance. We are often told that an era is opening in which we are to see multitudes of a common sort of readers, and masses of a common sort of literature; that such readers do not want and could not relish anything better than such literature, and that to provide it is becoming a vast and profitable industry. Even if good literature entirely lost currency with the world, it would still be abundantly worth while to continue to enjoy it by oneself. But it never will lose currency with the world, in spite of momentary appearances; it never will lose supremacy. Currency and supremacy are insured to it, not indeed by the world's deliberate and conscious choice, but by something far deeper,—by the instinct of self-preservation in humanity.

SWEETNESS AND LIGHT [73]

THE disparagers of culture make its motive curiosity; sometimes, indeed, they make its motive mere exclusiveness and vanity. The culture which is supposed to plume itself on a smattering of Greek and Latin is a culture which is begotten by nothing so intellectual as curiosity; it is valued either out of sheer vanity and ignorance or else as an engine of social and class

[73] Chapter I of *Culture and Anarchy* (originally part of the last lecture of Arnold as Professor of Poetry at Oxford). Copyright 1869, 1896 by Macmillan and Co., Ltd., and the Macmillan Company. Reprinted by permission.

distinction, separating its holder, like a badge or title, from other people who have not got it. No serious man would call this *culture*, or attach any value to it, as culture, at all. To find the real ground for the very different estimate which serious people will set upon culture, we must find some motive for culture in the terms of which may lie a real ambiguity; and such a motive the word *curiosity* gives us.

I have before now pointed out that we English do not, like the foreigners, use this word in a good sense as well as in a bad sense. With us the word is always used in a somewhat disapproving sense. A liberal and intelligent eagerness about the things of the mind may be meant by a foreigner when he speaks of curiosity, but with us the word always conveys a certain notion of frivolous and unedifying activity. In the *Quarterly Review,* some little time ago, was an estimate of the celebrated French critic, M. Sainte-Beuve, and a very inadequate estimate it in my judgment was. And its inadequacy consisted chiefly in this: that in our English way it left out of sight the double sense really involved in the word *curiosity,* thinking enough was said to stamp M. Sainte-Beuve with blame if it was said that he was impelled in his operations as a critic by curiosity, and omitting either to perceive that M. Sainte-Beuve himself, and many other people with him, would consider that this was praiseworthy and not blameworthy, or to point out why it ought really to be accounted worthy of blame and not of praise. For as there is a curiosity about intellectual matters which is futile, and merely a disease, so there is certainly a curiosity,—desire after the things of the mind simply for their own sakes and for the pleasure of seeing them as they are,—which is, in an intelligent being, natural and laudable. Nay, and the very desire to see things as they are, implies a balance and regulation of mind which is not often attained without fruitful effort, and which is the very opposite of the blind and diseased impulse of mind which is what we mean to blame when we blame curiosity. Montesquieu [74] says: "The first motive which ought to impel us to study is the desire to augment the excellence of our nature, and to render an intelligent being yet more intelligent." This is the true ground to assign for the genuine scientific passion, however manifested, and for culture, viewed simply as a fruit of this passion; and it is a worthy ground, even though we let the term *curiosity* stand to describe it.

But there is of culture another view, in which not solely the scientific passion, the sheer desire to see things as they are, natural and proper in an intelligent being, appears as the

---

74 French jurist and philosopher (1689–1755), famous as the author of *L'Esprit des Lois.*

ground of it. There is a view in which all the love of our neighbor, the impulses towards action, help, and beneficence, the desire for removing human error, clearing human confusion, and diminishing human misery, the noble aspiration to leave the world better and happier than we found it,—motives eminently such as are called social,—come in as part of the grounds of culture, and the main and preëminent part. Culture is then properly described not as having its origin in curiosity, but as having its origin in the love of perfection; it is *a study of perfection*. It moves by the force, not merely or primarily 10 of the scientific passion for pure knowledge, but also of the moral and social passion for doing good. As, in the first view of it, we took for its worthy motto Montesquieu's words: "To render an intelligent being yet more intelligent!" so, in the second view of it, there is no better motto which it can have than these words of Bishop Wilson: "To make reason and the will of God prevail!" [75]

Only, whereas the passion for doing good is apt to be overhasty in determining what reason and the will of God say, because its turn is for acting rather than thinking and it wants 20 to be beginning to act; and whereas it is apt to take its own conceptions, which proceed from its own state of development and share in all the imperfections and immaturities of this, for a basis of action; what distinguishes culture is, that it is possessed by the scientific passion as well as by the passion of doing good; that it demands worthy notions of reason and the will of God, and does not readily suffer its own crude conceptions to substitute themselves for them. And knowing that no action or institution can be salutary and stable which is not based on reason and the will of God, it is not so bent on acting 30 and instituting, even with the great aim of diminishing human error and misery ever before its thoughts, but that it can remember that acting and instituting are of little use, unless we know how and what we ought to act and to institute.

This culture is more interesting and more far-reaching than that other, which is founded solely on the scientific passion for knowing. But it needs times of faith and ardor, times when the intellectual horizon is opening and widening all around us, to flourish in. And is not the close and bounded intellectual horizon within which we have long lived and moved now lift- 40 ing up, and are not new lights finding free passage to shine in upon us? For a long time there was no passage for them to make their way in upon us, and then it was of no use to think of adapting the world's action to them. Where was the hope of

75 From *Maxim* 450 of Thomas Wilson (1663-1755), Bishop of Sodor and Man

making reason and the will of God prevail among people who had a routine which they had christened reason and the will of God, in which they were inextricably bound, and beyond which they had no power of looking? But now the iron force of adhesion to the old routine,—social, political, religious,—has wonderfully yielded; the iron force of exclusion of all which is new has wonderfully yielded. The danger now is, not that people should obstinately refuse to allow anything but their old routine to pass for reason and the will of God, but either
10 that they should allow some novelty or other to pass for these too easily, or else that they should underrate the importance of them altogether, and think it enough to follow action for its own sake, without troubling themselves to make reason and the will of God prevail therein. Now, then, is the moment for culture to be of service, culture which believes in making reason and the will of God prevail, believes in perfection, is the study and pursuit of perfection, and is no longer debarred, by a rigid invincible exclusion of whatever is new, from getting acceptance for its ideas, simply because they are new.
20   The moment this view of culture is seized, the moment it is regarded not solely as the endeavor to see things as they are, to draw towards a knowledge of the universal order which seems to be intended and aimed at in the world, and which it is a man's happiness to go along with or his misery to go counter to,—to learn, in short, the will of God,—the moment, I say, culture is considered not merely as the endeavor to *see* and *learn* this, but as the endeavor, also, to make it *prevail*, the moral, social, and beneficent character of culture becomes manifest. The mere endeavor to see and learn the truth for our own personal
30 satisfaction is indeed a commencement for making it prevail, a preparing the way for this, which always serves this, and is wrongly, therefore, stamped with blame absolutely in itself and not only in its caricature and degeneration. But perhaps it has got stamped with blame, and disparaged with the dubious title of curiosity, because in comparison with this wider endeavor of such great and plain utility it looks selfish, petty, and unprofitable.
    And religion, the greatest and most important of the efforts by which the human race has manifested its impulse to perfect
40 itself,—religion, that voice of the deepest human experience,—does not only enjoin and sanction the aim which is the great aim of culture, the aim of setting ourselves, to ascertain what perfection is and to make it prevail; but also, in determining generally in what human perfection consists, religion comes to a conclusion identical with that which culture,—culture seeking the determination of this question through *all* the voices of

human experience which have been heard upon it, of art, science, poetry, philosophy, history, as well as of religion, in order to give a greater fullness and certainty to its solution,—likewise reaches. Religion says: *The kingdom of God is within you;* and culture, in like manner, places human perfection in an *internal* condition, in the growth and predominance of our humanity proper, as distinguished from our animality. It places it in the ever-increasing efficacy and in the general harmonious expansion of those gifts of thought and feeling, which make the peculiar dignity, wealth, and happiness of human nature. As I have said on a former occasion: "It is in making endless additions to itself, in the endless expansion of its powers, in endless growth in wisdom and beauty, that the spirit of the human race finds its ideal. To reach this ideal, culture is an indispensable aid, and that is the true value of culture." Not a having and a resting, but a growing and a becoming, is the character of perfection as culture conceives it; and here, too, it coincides with religion.

And because men are all members of one great whole, and the sympathy which is in human nature will not allow one member to be indifferent to the rest or to have a perfect welfare independent of the rest, the expansion of our humanity, to suit the idea of perfection which culture forms, must be a *general* expansion. Perfection, as culture conceives it, is not possible while the individual remains isolated. The individual is required, under pain of being stunted and enfeebled in his own development if he disobeys, to carry others along with him in his march towards perfection, to be continually doing all he can to enlarge and increase the volume of the human stream sweeping thitherward. And, here, once more, culture lays on us the same obligation as religion, which says, as Bishop Wilson has admirably put it, that "to promote the kingdom of God is to increase and hasten one's own happiness."

But, finally, perfection,—as culture from a thorough disinterested study of human nature and human experience learns to conceive it,—is a harmonious expansion of *all* the powers which make the beauty and worth of human nature, and is not consistent with the over-development of any one power at the expense of the rest. Here culture goes beyond religion as religion is generally conceived by us.

If culture, then, is a study of perfection, and of harmonious perfection, general perfection, and perfection which consists in becoming something rather than in having something, in an inward condition of the mind and spirit, not in an outward set of circumstances,—it is clear that culture, instead of being the frivolous and useless thing which Mr. Bright, and Mr. Fred-

eric Harrison,[76] and many other Liberals are apt to call it, has
a very important function to fulfill for mankind. And this function is particularly important in our modern world, of which
the whole civilization is, to a much greater degree than the
civilization of Greece and Rome, mechanical and external, and
tends constantly to become more so. But above all in our own
country has culture a weighty part to perform, because here
that mechanical character, which civilization tends to take everywhere, is shown in the most eminent degree. Indeed nearly all
10 the characters of perfection, as culture teaches us to fix them,
meet in this country with some powerful tendency which
thwarts them and sets them at defiance. The idea of perfection as an *inward* condition of the mind and spirit is at variance with the mechanical and material civilization in esteem
with us, and nowhere, as I have said, so much in esteem as
with us. The idea of perfection as a *general* expansion of the
human family is at variance with our strong individualism, our
hatred of all limits to the unrestrained swing of the individual's
personality, our maxim of "every man for himself." Above
20 all, the idea of perfection as a *harmonious* expansion of human
nature is at variance with our want of flexibility, with our in-
aptitude for seeing more than one side of a thing, with our
intense energetic absorption in the particular pursuit we happen to be following. So culture has a rough task to achieve in
this country. Its preachers have, and are likely long to have,
a hard time of it, and they will much oftener be regarded, for
a great while to come, as elegant or spurious Jeremiahs than
as friends and benefactors. That, however, will not prevent
their doing in the end good service if they persevere. And,
30 meanwhile, the mode of action they have to pursue, and the sort
of habits they must fight against, ought to be made quite
clear for every one to see, who may be willing to look at the
matter attentively and dispassionately.

Faith in machinery is, I said, our besetting danger; often in
machinery most absurdly disproportioned to the end which
this machinery, if it is to do any good at all, is to serve; but
always in machinery, as if it had a value in and for itself. What
is freedom but machinery? what is population but machinery?
what is coal but machinery? what are railroads but machinery?
40 what is wealth but machinery? what are, even, religious organizations but machinery? Now almost every voice in England is accustomed to speak of these things as if they were
precious ends in themselves, and therefore had some of the

---

76 John Bright (1811–89), eloquent reformer, advocate of repeal of the Corn Laws,
which kept the price of wheat high and bore hard on the working classes. Frederic
Harrison (1831–1923), jurist and historian, follower of the positivist philosophy of Comte
(see note 92 below).

characters of perfection indisputably joined to them. I have
before now noticed [77] Mr. Roebuck's stock argument for proving the greatness and happiness of England as she is, and for
quite stopping the mouths of all gainsayers. Mr. Roebuck is
never weary of reiterating this argument of his, so I do not
know why I should be weary of noticing it. "May not every
man in England say what he likes?"—Mr. Roebuck perpetually
asks; and that, he thinks, is quite sufficient, and when every
man may say what he likes, our aspirations ought to be satisfied. But the aspirations of culture, which is the study of
perfection, are not satisfied, unless what men say, when they
may say what they like, is worth saying,—has good in it, and
more good than bad. In the same way the *Times,* replying to
some foreign strictures on the dress, looks, and behavior of the
English abroad, urges that the English ideal is that every one
should be free to do and to look just as he likes. But culture
indefatigably tries, not to make what each raw person may like,
the rule by which he fashions himself; but to draw ever nearer
to a sense of what is indeed beautiful, graceful, and becoming,
and to get the raw person to like that.

And in the same way with respect to railroads and coal.
Every one must have observed the strange language current
during the late discussions as to the possible failure of our
supplies of coal. Our coal, thousands of people were saying, is
the real basis of our national greatness; if our coal runs short,
there is an end of the greatness of England. But what *is*
greatness?—culture makes us ask. Greatness is a spiritual condition worthy to excite love, interest, and admiration; and the
outward proof of possessing greatness is that we excite love,
interest, and admiration. If England were swallowed up by the
sea to-morrow, which of the two, a hundred years hence, would
most excite the love, interest, and admiration of mankind,—
would most, therefore, show the evidences of having possessed
greatness,—the England of the last twenty years, or the England of Elizabeth, of a time of splendid spiritual effort, but
when our coal, and our industrial operations depending on coal,
were very little developed? Well, then, what an unsound habit
of mind it must be which makes us talk of things like coal or
iron as constituting the greatness of England, and how salutary
a friend is culture, bent on seeing things as they are, and thus
dissipating delusions of this kind and fixing standards of perfection that are real!

Wealth, again, that end to which our prodigious works for
material advantage are directed,—the commonest of common-
places tell us how men are always apt to regard wealth as a

[77] in *The Function of Criticism.* See above, p. 850.

precious end in itself: and certainly they have never been so
apt thus to regard it as they are in England at the present
time. Never did people believe anything more firmly than nine
Englishmen out of ten at the present day believe that our
greatness and welfare are proved by our being so very rich.
Now, the use of culture is that it helps us, by means of its
spiritual standard of perfection, to regard wealth as but machinery, and not only to say as a matter of words that we regard
wealth as but machinery, but really to perceive and feel that
10 it is so. If it were not for this purging effect wrought upon our
minds by culture, the whole world, the future as well as the
present, would inevitably belong to the Philistines. The people
who believe most that our greatness and welfare are proved by
our being very rich, and who most give their lives and thoughts
to becoming rich, are just the very people whom we call Philistines. Culture says: "Consider these people, then, their way
of life, their habits, their manners, the very tones of their
voice; look at them attentively; observe the literature they
read, the things which give them pleasure, the words which
20 come forth out of their mouths, the thoughts which make the
furniture of their minds; would any amount of wealth be worth
having with the condition that one was to become just like these
people by having it?" And thus culture begets a dissatisfaction
which is of the highest possible value in stemming the common tide of men's thoughts in a wealthy and industrial community, and which saves the future, as one may hope, from
being vulgarized, even if it cannot save the present.

Population, again, and bodily health and vigor, are things
which are nowhere treated in such an unintelligent, misleading,
30 exaggerated way as in England. Both are really machinery;
yet how many people all around us do we see rest in them and
fail to look beyond them! Why, one has heard people, fresh
from reading certain articles of the *Times* on the Registrar-
General's returns of marriages and births in this country, who
would talk of our large English families in quite a solemn
strain, as if they had something in itself beautiful, elevating,
and meritorious in them; as if the British Philistine would
have only to present himself before the Great Judge with his
twelve children, in order to be received among the sheep as a
40 matter of right!

But bodily health and vigor, it may be said, are not to be
classed with wealth and population as mere machinery; they
have a more real and essential value. True; but only as they
are more intimately connected with a perfect spiritual condition than wealth or population are. The moment we disjoin
them from the idea of a perfect spiritual condition, and pursue

them, as we do pursue them, for their own sake and as ends in themselves, our worship of them becomes as mere worship of machinery, as our worship of wealth or population, and as unintelligent and vulgarizing a worship as that is. Every one with anything like an adequate idea of human perfection has distinctly marked this subordination to higher and spiritual ends of the cultivation of bodily vigor and activity. "Bodily exercise profiteth little; but godliness is profitable unto all things," [78] says the author of the Epistle to Timothy. And the utilitarian Franklin says just as explicitly:—"Eat and drink such an exact quantity as suits the constitution of thy body, *in reference to the services of the mind.*" [79] But the point of view of culture, keeping the mark of human perfection simply and broadly in view and not assigning to this perfection, as religion or utilitarianism assigns to it, a special and limited character, this point of view, I say, of culture is best given by these words of Epictetus: "It is a sign of ἀφυΐα," says he,—that is, of a nature not finely tempered,—"to give yourselves up to things which relate to the body; to make, for instance, a great fuss about exercise, a great fuss about eating, a great fuss about drinking, a great fuss about walking, a great fuss about riding. All these things ought to be done merely by the way: the formation of the spirit and character must be our real concern." [80] This is admirable; and, indeed, the Greek word εὐφυΐα, a finely tempered nature, gives exactly the notion of perfection as culture brings us to conceive it: a harmonious perfection, a perfection in which the characters of beauty and intelligence are both present, which unites "the two noblest of things,"—as Swift, who of one of the two, at any rate, had himself all too little, most happily calls them in his *Battle of the Books,*—"the two noblest of things, *sweetness and light.*" The εὐφυής is the man who tends towards sweetness and light; the ἀφυής, on the other hand, is our Philistine. The immense spiritual significance of the Greeks is due to their having been inspired with this central and happy idea of the essential character of human perfection; and Mr. Bright's misconception of culture, as a smattering of Greek and Latin, comes itself, after all, from this wonderful significance of the Greeks having affected the very machinery of our education, and is in itself a kind of homage to it.

In thus making sweetness and light to be characters of perfection, culture is of like spirit with poetry, follows one law with poetry. Far more than on our freedom, our population,

---

[78] 1 Tim. iv, 8.
[79] *Poor Richard's Almanac* for Dec., 1742

[80] Chap. xli, of the *Encheiridion* of the Roman Stoic philosopher, fl. end of first and beginning of second centuries

and our industrialism, many amongst us rely upon our religious
organizations to save us. I have called religion a yet more
important manifestation of human nature than poetry, because
it has worked on a broader scale for perfection, and with
greater masses of men. But the idea of beauty and of a human
nature perfect on all its sides, which is the dominant idea of
poetry, is a true and invaluable idea, though it has not yet had
the success that the idea of conquering the obvious faults of our
animality, and of a human nature perfect on the moral side,—
10 which is the dominant idea of religion,—has been enabled to
have; and it is destined, adding to itself the religious idea of a
devout energy, to transform and govern the other.

The best art and poetry of the Greeks, in which religion and
poetry are one, in which the idea of beauty and of a human
nature perfect on all sides adds to itself a religious and devout
energy, and works in the strength of that, is on this account of
such surpassing interest and instructiveness for us, though it
was,—as, having regard to the human race in general, and,
indeed, having regard to the Greeks themselves, we must own,
20 —a premature attempt, an attempt which for success needed
the moral and religious fiber in humanity to be more braced
and developed than it had yet been. But Greece did not err
in having the idea of beauty, harmony, and complete human
perfection, so present and paramount. It is impossible to have
this idea too present and paramount; only, the moral fiber must
be braced too. And we, because we have braced the moral
fiber, are not on that account in the right way, if at the same
time the idea of beauty, harmony, and complete human perfection, is wanting or misapprehended amongst us; and evi-
30 dently it *is* wanting or misapprehended at present. And when
we rely as we do on our religious organizations, which in themselves do not and cannot give us this idea, and think we have
done enough if we make them spread and prevail, then, I say,
we fall into our common fault of overvaluing machinery.

Nothing is more common than for people to confound the
inward peace and satisfaction which follows the subduing of
the obvious faults of our animality with what I may call absolute inward peace and satisfaction,—the peace and satisfaction
which are reached as we draw near to complete spiritual per-
40 fection, and not merely to moral perfection, or rather to relative moral perfection. No people in the world have done more
and struggled more to attain this relative moral perfection
than our English race has. For no people in the world has the
command to *resist the devil*, to *overcome the wicked one*, in the
nearest and most obvious sense of those words, had such a
pressing force and reality. And we have had our reward, not

only in the great worldly prosperity which our obedience to this command has brought us, but also, and far more, in great inward peace and satisfaction. But to me few things are more pathetic than to see people, on the strength of the inward peace and satisfaction which their rudimentary efforts toward perfection have brought them, employ, concerning their incomplete perfection and the religious organizations within which they have found it, language which properly applies only to complete perfection, and is a far-off echo of the human soul's prophecy of it. Religion itself, I need hardly say, supplies 10 them in abundance with this grand language. And very freely do they use it; yet it is really the severest possible criticism of such an incomplete perfection as alone we have yet reached through our religious organizations.

The impulse of the English race towards moral development and self-conquest has nowhere so powerfully manifested itself as in Puritanism. Nowhere has Puritanism found so adequate an expression as in the religious organization of the Independents.[81] The modern Independents have a newspaper, the *Nonconformist,* written with great sincerity and ability. The motto, 20 the standard, the profession of faith which this organ of theirs carries aloft, is: "The Dissidence of Dissent and the Protestantism of the Protestant religion." [82] There is sweetness and light, and an ideal of complete harmonious human perfection! One need not go to culture and poetry to find language to judge it. Religion, with its instinct for perfection, supplies language to judge it, language, too, which is in our mouths every day. "Finally, be of one mind, united in feeling," [83] says St. Peter. There is an ideal which judges the Puritan ideal: "The Dissidence of Dissent and the Protestantism of the Protestant re- 30 ligion!" And religious organizations like this are what people believe in, rest in, would give their lives for! Such, I say, is the wonderful virtue of even the beginnings of perfection, of having conquered even the plain faults of our animality, that the religious organization which has helped us to do it can seem to us something precious, salutary, and to be propagated, even when it wears such a brand of imperfection on its forehead as this. And men have got such a habit of giving to the language of religion a special application of making it a mere jargon, that for the condemnation which religion itself passes on the 40 short-comings of their religious organizations they have no ear; they are sure to cheat themselves and to explain this condemnation away. They can only be reached by the criticism which culture, like poetry, speaking a language not to be sophisticated,

81 sect known in Amer-   82 phrase from Burke's   *with America*
ica as Congregationalists   Speech   on   *Conciliation*   83 1 Pet. iii, 8.

and resolutely testing these organizations by the ideal of a human perfection complete on all sides, applies to them.

But men of culture and poetry, it will be said, are again and again failing, and failing conspicuously, in the necessary first stage to a harmonious perfection, in the subduing of the great obvious faults of our animality, which it is the glory of these religious organizations to have helped us to subdue. True, they do often so fail. They have often been without the virtues as well as the faults of the Puritan; it has been one of their dangers that they so felt the Puritan's faults that they too much neglected the practice of his virtues. I will not, however, exculpate them at the Puritan's expense. They have often failed in morality, and morality is indispensable. And they have been punished for their failure, as the Puritan has been rewarded for his performance. They have been punished wherein they erred; but their ideal of beauty, of sweetness and light, and a human nature complete on all its sides, remains the true ideal of perfection still; just as the Puritan's ideal of perfection remains narrow and inadequate, although for what he did well he has been richly rewarded. Notwithstanding the mighty results of the Pilgrim Fathers' voyage, they and their standard of perfection are rightly judged when we figure to ourselves Shakespeare or Virgil,—souls in whom sweetness and light, and all that in human nature is most humane, were eminent,—accompanying them on their voyage, and think what intolerable company Shakespeare and Virgil would have found them! In the same way let us judge the religious organizations which we see all around us. Do not let us deny the good and the happiness which they have accomplished; but do not let us fail to see clearly that their idea of human perfection is narrow and inadequate, and that the Dissidence of Dissent and the Protestantism of the Protestant religion will never bring humanity to its true goal. As I said with regard to wealth: Let us look at the life of those who live in and for it,—so I say with regard to the religious organizations. Look at the life imaged in such a newspaper as the *Noncomformist,*—a life of jealousy of the Establishment, disputes, tea-meetings, opening of chapels, sermons; and then think of it as an ideal of a human life completing itself on all sides, and aspiring with all its organs after sweetness, light, and perfection!

Another newspaper, representing, like the *Nonconformist,* one of the religious organizations of this country, was a short time ago giving an account of the crowd at Epsom on the Derby day, and of all the vice and hideousness which was to be seen in that crowd; and then the writer turned suddenly round upon Professor Huxley, and asked him how he proposed to cure all this vice and hideousness without religion. I confess I felt disposed to ask the asker this question: and how do you propose to cure it with such a religion as yours? How is the ideal of a life so unlovely, so unattractive, so incomplete, so narrow, so far removed from a true and satisfying ideal of human perfection, as is the life of your religious organization as you yourself reflect it, to conquer and transform all this vice and hideousness? Indeed, the strongest plea for the study of perfection as pursued by culture, the clearest proof of the actual inadequacy of the idea of perfection held by the religious organizations,— expressing, as I have said, the most wide-spread effort which the human race has yet made after perfection,—is to be found in the state of our life and society with these in possession of it, and having been in possession of it I know not how many hundred years. We are all of us included in some religious organization or other; we all call ourselves, in the sublime and aspiring language of religion which I have before noticed, *children of God*. Children of God;—it is an immense pretension!—and how are we to justify it? By the works which we do, and the words which we speak. And the work which we collective children of God do, our grand center of life, our *city* which we have builded for us to dwell in, is London! London, with its unutterable external hideousness, and with its internal canker of *publice egestas, privatim opulentia,*[84]—to use the words which Sallust puts in Cato's mouth about Rome,—unequaled in the world! The word, again, which we children of God speak, the voice which most hits our collective thought, the newspaper with the largest circulation in England, nay, with the largest circulation in the whole world, is the *Daily Telegraph!* I say that when our religious organizations—which I admit to express the most considerable effort after perfection that our race has yet made—land us in no better result than this, it is high time to examine carefully their idea of perfection, to see whether it does not leave out of account sides and forces of human nature which we might turn to great use; whether it would not be more operative if it were more complete. And I say that the English reliance on our religious organizations and on their ideas of human perfection just as they stand, is like our reliance on freedom, on muscular Christianity, on population, on coal, on wealth,—mere belief in machinery, and unfruitful; and that it is wholesomely counteracted by culture, bent on seeing things as they are, and on drawing the human race onwards to a more complete, a harmonious perfection.

Culture, however, shows its single-minded love of perfection,

84 poverty generally, opulence individually—from *Catiline,* lii, 22.

its desire simply to make reason and the will of God prevail, its freedom from fanaticism, by its attitude towards all this machinery, even while it insists that it *is* machinery. Fanatics, seeing the mischief men do themselves by their blind belief in some machinery or other,—whether it is wealth and industrialism, or whether it is the cultivation of bodily strength and activity, or whether it is a political organization,—or whether it is a religious organization,—oppose with might and main the tendency to this or that political and religious organiza-
10 tion, or to games and athletic exercises, or to wealth and industrialism, and try violently to stop it. But the flexibility which sweetness and light give, and which is one of the rewards of culture pursued in good faith, enables a man to see that a tendency may be necessary, and even, as a preparation for something in the future, salutary, and yet that the generations or individuals who obey this tendency are sacrificed to it, that they fall short of the hope of perfection by following it; and that its mischiefs are to be criticized, lest it should take too firm a hold and last after it has served its purpose.

20 Mr. Gladstone well pointed out, in a speech at Paris,—and others have pointed out the same thing,—how necessary is the present great movement toward wealth and industrialism, in order to lay broad foundations of material well-being for the society of the future. The worst of these justifications is, that they are generally addressed to the very people engaged, body and soul, in the movement in question; at all events, that they are always seized with the greatest avidity by these people, and taken by them as quite justifying their life; and that thus they tend to harden them in their sins. Now, culture admits the
30 necessity of the movement towards fortune-making and exaggerated industrialism, readily allows that the future may derive benefit from it; but insists, at the same time, that the passing generations of industrialists,—forming, for the most part, the stout main body of Philistinism,—are sacrificed to it. In the same way, the result of all the games and sports which occupy the passing generation of boys and young men may be the establishment of a better and sounder physical type for the future to work with. Culture does not set itself against the games and sports; it congratulates the future, and hopes it
40 will make a good use of its improved physical basis; but it points out that our passing generation of boys and young men is, meantime, sacrificed. Puritanism was perhaps necessary to develop the moral fiber of the English race, Nonconformity to break the yoke of ecclesiastical domination over men's minds and to prepare the way for freedom of thought in the distant future; still, culture points out that the harmonious perfection

of generations of Puritans and Nonconformists has been, in consequence, sacrificed. Freedom of speech may be necessary for the society of the future, but the young lions [85] of the *Daily Telegraph* in the meanwhile are sacrificed. A voice for every man in his country's government may be necessary for the society of the future, but meanwhile Mr. Beales and Mr. Bradlaugh [86] are sacrificed.

Oxford, the Oxford of the past, has many faults; and she has heavily paid for them in defeat, in isolation, in want of hold upon the modern world. Yet we in Oxford, brought up amidst the beauty and sweetness of that beautiful place, have not failed to seize one truth,—the truth that beauty and sweetness are essential characters of a complete human perfection. When I insist on this, I am all in the faith and tradition of Oxford. I say boldly that this our sentiment for beauty and sweetness, our sentiment against hideousness and rawness, has been at the bottom of our attachment to so many beaten causes, of our opposition to so many triumphant movements. And the sentiment is true, and has never been wholly defeated, and has shown its power even in its defeat. We have not won our political battles, we have not carried our main points, we have not stopped our adversaries' advance, we have not marched victoriously with the modern world; but we have told silently upon the mind of the country, we have prepared currents of feeling which sap our adversaries' position when it seems gained, we have kept up our own communications with the future. Look at the course of the great movement which shook Oxford to its center some thirty years ago! It was directed, as any one who reads Dr. Newman's *Apology* [87] may see, against what in one word may be called "Liberalism." Liberalism prevailed; it was the appointed force to do the work of the hour; it was necessary, it was inevitable that it should prevail. The Oxford movement was broken, it failed; our wrecks are scattered on every shore:—

"Quæ regio in terris nostri non plena laboris?" [88]

But what was it, this liberalism, as Dr. Newman saw it, and as it really broke the Oxford movement? It was the great middle-

85 Young *Leo* was Arnold's name for the typical writer on this paper

86 Edmond Beales (1803–1881), political agitator, advocate of manhood suffrage, involved in the Hyde Park riots of 1866. Charles Bradlaugh (1833–1891), free thought advocate and politician. He fought for freedom of the press on religious and social questions and for extension of the franchise in 1866-7. He refused to take the oath on the Bible when elected to Parliament in 1880, and eventually won his contention.

87 *Apologia pro Vita Sua*, defense of John Henry Newman (1801–90) for his change from Anglicism to Catholicism. He was the leader of the Oxford Movement in the English Church, which championed apostolic succession, the efficacy of the sacraments, ritualism, and other conservative religious doctrines.

88 What region on the earth is not filled with (the tale) of our woe? (*Æneid*, i. 460.)

class liberalism, which had for the cardinal points of its belief
the Reform Bill of 1832,[89] and local self-government, in politics; in the social sphere, free-trade, unrestricted competition,
and the making of large industrial fortunes; in the religious
sphere, the Dissidence of Dissent and the Protestantism of the
Protestant religion. I do not say that other and more intelligent forces than this were not opposed to the Oxford movement: but this was the force which really beat it; this was the
force which Dr. Newman felt himself fighting with; this was the
10 force which till only the other day seemed to be the paramount force in this country, and to be in possession of the
future; this was the force whose achievements fill Mr. Lowe [90]
with such inexpressible admiration, and whose rule he was so
horror-struck to see threatened. And where is this great force
of Philistinism now? It is thrust into the second rank, it is
become a power of yesterday, it has lost the future. A new
power has suddenly appeared, a power which it is impossible
yet to judge fully, but which is certainly a wholly different
force from middle-class liberalism; different in its cardinal
20 points of belief, different in its tendencies in every sphere. It
loves and admires neither the legislation of middle-class Parlia-
ments, nor the local self-government of middle-class vestries,
nor the unrestricted competition of middle-class industrialists,
nor the dissidence of middle-class Dissent and the Protestantism
of middle-class Protestant religion. I am not now praising this
new force, or saying that its own ideals are better; all I say
is, that they are wholly different. And who will estimate how
much the currents of feeling created by Dr. Newman's movements, the keen desire for beauty and sweetness which it nour-
30 ished, the deep aversion it manifested to the hardness and vulgarity of middle-class liberalism, the strong light it turned on
the hideous and grotesque illusions of middle-class Protestantism,—who will estimate how much all these contributed to swell
the tide of secret dissatisfaction which has mined the ground
under self-confident liberalism of the last thirty years, and has
prepared the way for its sudden collapse and supersession? It
is in this manner that the sentiment of Oxford for beauty and
sweetness conquers, and in this manner long may it continue
to conquer!
40   In this manner it works to the same end as culture, and
there is plenty of work for it yet to do. I have said that the
new and more democratic force which is now superseding our

89 By extending the
franchise and revising representation in Parliament
the bill accomplished a
great transference of political power to the middle
classes in the towns.
90 Robert Lowe (1811-
92), afterwards Viscount
Sherbrooke, a liberal, but
opposed to the Reform Bill
of 1866-7.

old middle-class liberalism cannot yet be rightly judged. It has its main tendencies still to form. We hear promises of its giving us administrative reform, law reform, reform of education, and I know not what; but those promises come rather from its advocates, wishing to make a good plea for it and to justify it for superseding middle-class liberalism, than from clear tendencies which it has itself yet developed. But meanwhile it has plenty of well-intentioned friends against whom culture may with advantage continue to uphold steadily its ideal of human perfection; that this is *an inward spiritual activity, hav-* 10 *ing for its characters increased sweetness, increased light, increased life, increased sympathy.* Mr. Bright, who has a foot in both worlds, the world of middle-class liberalism and the world of democracy, but who brings most of his ideas from the world of middle-class liberalism in which he was bred, always inclines to inculcate that faith in machinery to which, as we have seen, Englishmen are so prone, and which has been the bane of middle-class liberalism. He complains with a sorrowful indignation of people who "appear to have no proper estimate of the value of the franchise"; he leads his disciples to believe— 20 what the Englishman is always too ready to believe—that the having a vote, like the having a large family, or a large business, or large muscles, has in itself some edifying and perfecting effect upon human nature. Or else he cries out to the democracy, —"the men," as he calls them, "upon whose shoulders the greatness of England rests,"—he cries out to them: "See what you have done! I look over this country and see the cities you have built, the railroads you have made, the manufactures you have produced, the cargoes which freight the ships of the greatest mercantile navy the world has ever seen! I see that you have 30 converted by your labors what was once a wilderness, these islands, into a fruitful garden; I know that you have created this wealth, and are a nation whose name is a word of power throughout all the world." Why, this is just the very style of laudation with which Mr. Roebuck or Mr. Lowe debauches the minds of the middle classes, and makes such Philistines of them. It is the same fashion of teaching a man to value himself not on what he *is,* not on his progress in sweetness and light, but on the number of the railroads he has constructed, or the bigness of the tabernacle he has built. Only the middle classes 40 are told they have done it all with their energy, self-reliance, and capital, and the democracy are told they have done it all with their hands and sinews. But teaching the democracy to put its trust in achievements of this kind is merely training them to be Philistines to take the place of the Philistines whom

they are superseding; and they, too, like the middle class, will be encouraged to sit down at the banquet of the future without having on a wedding garment, and nothing excellent can then come from them. Those who know their besetting faults, those who have watched them and listened to them, or those who will read the instructive account recently given of them by one of themselves, the *Journeyman Engineer,* will agree that the idea which culture sets before us of perfection,—an increased spiritual activity, having for its characters increased
10 sweetness, increased light, increased life, increased sympathy, —is an idea which the new democracy needs far more than the idea of the blessedness of the franchise, or the wonderfulness of its own industrial performances.

Other well-meaning friends of this new power are for leading it, not in the old ruts of middle-class Philistinism, but in ways which are naturally alluring to the feet of democracy, though in this country they are novel and untried ways. I may call them the ways of Jacobinism.[91] Violent indignation with the past, abstract systems of renovation applied wholesale, a new
20 doctrine drawn up in black and white for elaborating down to the very smallest details a rational society for the future,— these are the ways of Jacobinism. Mr. Frederic Harrison and other disciples of Comte,[92]—one of them, Mr. Congreve, is an old friend of mine, and I am glad to have an opportunity of publicly expressing my respect for his talents and character,— are among the friends of democracy who are for leading it in paths of this kind. Mr. Frederic Harrison is very hostile to culture, and from a natural enough motive; for culture is the eternal opponent of the two things which are the signal marks of
30 Jacobinism,—its fierceness, and its addiction to an abstract system. Culture is always assigning to system-makers and systems a smaller share in the bent of human destiny than their friends like. A current in people's minds sets towards new ideas; people are dissatisfied with their old narrow stock of Philistine ideas, Anglo-Saxon ideas, or any other; and some man, some Bentham[93] or Comte, who has the real merit of having early and strongly felt and helped the new current, but who brings plenty of narrowness and mistakes of his own into his feeling and help of it, is credited with being the author of the whole

91 Name applied to the holders of extreme revolutionary or radical views, after the *Societé des Jacobins* of the French Revolution
92 Auguste Comte (1798–1857), French philosopher, founder of Positivism, which sought to limit knowledge to the facts actually arrived at by the sciences, which discouraged metaphysical speculation, and would substitute the worship of humanity for super-natural religion. Richard Congreve (1818–99) advocated the system of Comte.
93 Jeremy Bentham (1748–1832), English philosopher, leader of Utilitarianism, which advocated "the greatest good to the greatest number" as the proper end of morality and legislation.

current, the fit person to be entrusted with its regulation and to guide the human race.

The excellent German historian of the mythology of Rome, Preller,[94] relating the introduction at Rome under the Tarquins of the worship of Apollo, the god of light, healing and reconciliation, will have us observe that it was not so much the Tarquins who brought to Rome the new worship of Apollo, as a current in the mind of the Roman people which set powerfully at that time towards a new worship of this kind, and away from the old run of Latin and Sabine religious ideas. In a similar way, culture directs our attention to the natural current there is in human affairs, and to its continual working, and will not let us rivet our faith upon any one man and his doings. It makes us see not only his good side, but also how much in him was of necessity limited and transient; nay, it even feels a pleasure, a sense of an increased freedom and of an ampler future, in so doing.

I remember, when I was under the influence of a mind to which I feel the greatest obligations, the mind of a man who was the very incarnation of sanity and clear sense, a man the most considerable, it seems to me, whom America has yet produced,—Benjamin Franklin,—I remember the relief with which, after long feeling the sway of Franklin's imperturbable commonsense, I came upon a project of his for a new version of the Book of Job,[95] to replace the old version, the style of which, says Franklin, has become obsolete, and thence less agreeable. "I give," he continues, "a few verses, which may serve as a sample of the kind of version I would recommend." We all recollect the famous verse in our translation: "Then Satan answered the Lord and said: 'Doth Job fear God for nought?'" Franklin makes this: "Does your Majesty imagine that Job's good conduct is the effect of mere personal attachment and affection?" I well remember how, when first I read that, I drew a deep breath of relief and said to myself: "After all, there is a stretch of humanity beyond Franklin's victorious good sense!" So, after hearing Bentham cried loudly up as the renovator of modern society, and Bentham's mind and ideas proposed as the rulers of our future, I open the *Deontology*.[96] There I read: "While Xenophon was writing his history and Euclid teaching geometry, Socrates and Plato were talking nonsense under pretense of talking wisdom and morality. This morality of theirs consisted in words; this wisdom of theirs was the denial of mat-

[94] Ludwig Preller (1809–61)
[95] Arnold misunderstood Franklin, who, in his *Proposed New Version of the Bible*, rewrote, in a spirit of ironic burlesque, six verses of *Job* in the style of modern politics.
[96] Arranged by Sir John Bowring after Bentham's death and perhaps imperfectly representing the views of the philosopher.

ters known to every man's experience." From the moment of
reading that, I am delivered from the bondage of Bentham!
the fanaticism of his adherents can touch me no longer. I feel
the inadequacy of his mind and ideas for supplying the rule of
human society, for perfection.

Culture tends always thus to deal with the men of a system,
of disciples, of a school; with men like Comte, or the late Mr.
Buckle, or Mr. Mill.[97] However much it may find to admire
in these personages, or in some of them, it nevertheless remem-
10 bers the text: "Be not ye called Rabbi!" and it soon passes
on from any Rabbi. But Jacobinism loves a Rabbi; it does
not want to pass on from its Rabbi in pursuit of a future and
still unreached perfection; it wants its Rabbi and his ideas to
stand for perfection, that they may with the more authority re-
cast the world; and for Jacobinism, therefore, culture,—eternally passing onwards and seeking,—is an impertinence and an
offense. But culture, just because it resists this tendency of
Jacobinism to impose on us a man with limitations and errors
of his own along with the true ideas of which he is the organ,
20 really does the world and Jacobinism itself a service.

So, too, Jacobinism, in its fierce hatred of the past and of
those whom it makes liable for the sins of the past, cannot
away with the inexhaustible indulgence proper to culture, the
consideration of circumstances, the severe judgment of actions
joined to the merciful judgment of persons. "The man of culture is in politics," cries Mr. Frederic Harrison, "one of the
poorest mortals alive!" Mr. Frederic Harrison wants to be doing business, and he complains that the man of culture stops
him with a "turn for small fault-finding, love of selfish ease, and
30 indecision in action." Of what use is culture, he asks, except for
"a critic of new books or a professor of *belles-lettres?*" Why, it
is of use because, in presence of the fierce exasperation which
breathes, or rather, I may say, hisses through the whole production in which Mr. Frederic Harrison asks that question, it
reminds us that the perfection of human nature is sweetness
and light. It is of use, because, like religion,—that other effort
after perfection,—it testifies that, where bitter envying and
strife are, there is confusion and every evil work.

The pursuit of perfection, then, is the pursuit of sweetness
40 and light. He who works for sweetness and light, works to
make reason and the will of God prevail. He who works for
machinery, he who works for hatred, works only for confusion.
Culture looks beyond machinery, culture hates hatred; culture
has one great passion, the passion for sweetness and light. It

97 Henry Thomas Buckle (1821–62), author of the *History of Civilization in England.*
John Stuart Mill (1806–1873), political economist.

has one even yet greater!—the passion for making them *prevail*. It is not satisfied till we *all* come to a perfect man; it knows that the sweetness and light of the few must be imperfect until the raw and unkindled masses of humanity are touched with sweetness and light. If I have not shrunk from saying that we must work for sweetness and light, so neither have I shrunk from saying that we must have a broad basis, must have sweetness and light for as many as possible. Again and again I have insisted how those are the happy moments of humanity, how those are the marking epochs of a people's life, how those are the flowering times for literature and art and all the creative power of genius, when there is a *national* glow of life and thought, when the whole of society is in the fullest measure permeated by thought, sensible to beauty, intelligent and alive. Only it must be *real* thought and *real* beauty; *real* sweetness and *real* light. Plenty of people will try to give the masses, as they call them, an intellectual food prepared and adapted in the way they think proper for the actual condition of the masses. The ordinary popular literature is an example of this way of working on the masses. Plenty of people will try to indoctrinate the masses with the set of ideas and judgments constituting the creed of their own profession or party. Our religious and political organizations give an example of this way of working on the masses. I condemn neither way; but culture works differently. It does not try to teach down to the level of inferior classes; it does not try to win them for this or that sect of its own, with ready-made judgments and watchwords. It seeks to do away with classes; to make the best that has been thought and known in the world current everywhere; to make all men live in an atmosphere of sweetness and light, where they may use ideas, as it uses them itself, freely,—nourished, and not bound by them.

This is the *social idea;* and the men of culture are the true apostles of equality. The great men of culture are those who have had a passion for diffusing, for making prevail, for carrying from one end of society to the other, the best knowledge, the best ideas of their time; who have labored to divest knowledge of all that was harsh, uncouth, difficult, abstract, professional, exclusive; to humanize it, to make it efficient outside the clique of the cultivated and learned, yet still remaining the *best* knowledge and thought of the time, and a true source, therefore, of sweetness and light. Such a man was Abelard [98] in the Middle Ages, in spite of all his imperfections; and thence the boundless emotion and enthusiasm which Abelard excited.

98 1079–1142, French scholastic philosopher

Such were Lessing and Herder [99] in Germany, at the end of
the last century; and their services to Germany were in this
way inestimably precious. Generations will pass, and literary
monuments will accumulate, and works far more perfect than
the works of Lessing and Herder will be produced in Germany; and yet the names of these two men will fill a German
with a reverence and enthusiasm such as the names of the
most gifted masters will hardly awaken. And why? Because
they *humanized* knowledge; because they broadened the basis
10 of life and intelligence; because they worked powerfully to diffuse sweetness and light, to make reason and the will of God
prevail. With Saint Augustine they said: "Let us not leave
thee alone to make in the secret of thy knowledge, as thou
didst before the creation of the firmament, the division of light
from darkness; let the children of thy spirit, placed in their
firmament, make their light shine upon the earth, mark the
division of night and day, and announce the revolution of the
times; for the old order is passed, and the new arises; the night
is spent, the day is come forth; and thou shalt crown the year
20 with thy blessing, when thou shalt send forth laborers into
thy harvests sown by other hands than theirs; when thou shalt
send forth new laborers to new seed-times, whereof the harvest
shall be not yet." [1]

WALTER PATER (1839–1894)

Walter Horatio Pater was born in London on August 4, 1839. He was
educated at King's School, Canterbury, and at Queen's College, Oxford, taking
his B.A. in 1862. He had intended entering the ministry, but about this time
abandoned the idea. In 1864 he was elected a fellow of Brasenose College, Oxford, and at once took up his residence there, where he lived, with the exception of a brief period in London and vacation trips to the Continent, for
the rest of his life. He never married. Externally, his life has little incident, but
he was devoting himself to that life of "impassioned contemplation" which he
praises in Wordsworth. The contemplation of thirty years brought forth from
his rooms at Brasenose works which were now, externally at least, biographical
sketches, now critical studies, now prose fiction—but all of them expressing
the characteristic principles which he believed should govern art and life.
His works include *The Renaissance* (1873), fortified with a famous preface
in which he defined his theories of criticism, and an even more famous Conclusion, in which he expressed his views of the purposes of life, *Marius the Epicurean* (1885), in form a novel, but a novel which gives a spiritual biography,
Imaginary Portraits (1887), shorter sketches in a similar kind of philosophic
fiction, *Appreciations, with an Essay on Style* (1889), containing most of his

99 Gotthold   Ephraim   1803), influential German   1 *Confessions* of St. Au-
Lessing (1729–81), Johann   writers of the eighteenth   gustine, xiii. 18, 22.
Gottfried von Herder (1744–   century

literary criticism, and *Plato and Platonism* (1893), studies of a philosophy
with which he was particularly sympathetic. He died in June, 1894.

Pater is probably not to be regarded as one of the giants of Victorian prose;
he should no doubt be placed in the second rank; yet his work has been given
representation here when that of more massive writers has been excluded, because he seems appropriately to end one era and lead the way to another.
In criticism, he would judge the value of a work of art by the vividness of the
sensations produced in beholder or reader, not by its religious or ethical quality,
its consoling and sustaining power. He thus stands squarely athwart the path
of the typical Victorian moralizers. His view of the aims and purposes of life
is expressed succinctly and brilliantly in the half dozen pages of his Conclusion
to the *Renaissance,* and at greater length in *Marius the Epicurean.* Life is successful in proportion as it achieves varied and exquisite sensations. "Not the
fruit of experience, but experience itself is the end." Marius, to be sure, after
a period when, as an Epicurean, his philosophy is very much that of the famous
Conclusion, is profoundly influenced by Christianity, and accepts the Christian
principle of sacrifice; and Pater himself, ascetic in taste, was so alarmed by
the implications drawn from his doctrine that he temporarily withdrew his
statement. Yet it remains, defiant, challenging, sure evidence that a change
had come to men's thoughts since those solemn, dead, mid-Victorian days. In
literature, his primary concern was with beauty; he commended the patient
artistry of Flaubert, who sought, often with much pain, for the one final way
of saying a thing, for the one absolute phrase. His own style is based upon
this doctrine; it is packed with words which appeal to the senses, it strives
for the most beautiful way in which an idea can be expressed, as *The Child in
the House* very strikingly shows. Some will accordingly condemn it for precios-
ity, for lack of spontaneity.

In his theories of life and art, and in his own prose, Pater is the heir of the
Pre-Raphaelite movement (see sketch on the Victorian era above). He has,
indeed, been called the philosopher of this late Victorian or un-Victorian group.
Just as surely, he prepares the way for, if he does not actually become the
prophet of, the æsthetic movement, which, beginning in the eighteen seventies,
attained its full stride and most perfect expression in the eighteen nineties, in
the work of Oscar Wilde and Aubrey Beardsley. His position is accordingly
one of no little importance in the transition from Victorianism to the more
recent modes of thought and the newer literary forms.

BIBLIOGRAPHY. *Works,* in standard form, by Macmillan. Full biography by
Thomas Wright, 2 vols. (Putnam), shorter life by A. C. Benson in Eng. Men
of Letters ser. Selections, with critical introd., by E. E. Hale, Jr. (Holt).

THE RENAISSANCE[1]

PREFACE

MANY attempts have been made by writers on art and poetry
to define beauty in the abstract, to express it in the most general terms, to find a universal formula for it. The value of

1 The body of this work (of which the Preface and Conclusion are here given) consists of studies of great Renaissance figures. From *The Renaissance* by Walter Pater
copyright 1873 by Macmillan & Company, Ltd., and the Macmillan Company. Reprinted by permission.

these attempts has most often been in the suggestive and
penetrating things said by the way. Such discussions help us
very little to enjoy what has been well done in art or poetry,
to discriminate between what is more and what is less excellent in them, or to use words like beauty, excellence, art, poetry,
with a more precise meaning than they would otherwise have.
Beauty, like all other qualities presented to human experience, is
relative; and the definition of it becomes unmeaning and useless in proportion to its abstractness. To define beauty, not in
10 the most abstract, but in the most concrete terms possible, to
find, not a universal formula for it, but the formula which expresses most adequately this or that special manifestation of
it, is the aim of the true student of æsthetics.

"To see the object as in itself it really is," has been justly
said to be the aim of all true criticism whatever; and in æsthetic
criticism the first step towards seeing one's object as it really
is, is to know one's own impression as it really is, to discriminate it, to realize it distinctly. The objects with which æsthetic
criticism deals—music, poetry, artistic and accomplished forms
20 of human life—are indeed receptacles of so many powers or
forces: they possess, like the products of nature, so many virtues or qualities. What is this song or picture, this engaging
personality presented in life or in a book, to *me?* What effect
does it really produce on me? Does it give me pleasure? and if
so, what sort or degree of pleasure? How is my nature modified by its presence, and under its influence? The answers to
these questions are the original facts with which the æsthetic
critic has to do; and, as in the study of light, of morals, of
number, one must realize such primary data for oneself, or
30 not at all. And he who experiences these impressions strongly,
and drives directly at the analysis and discrimination of them,
has no need to trouble himself with the abstract question what
beauty is in itself, or what its exact relation to truth or experience—metaphysical questions, as unprofitable as metaphysical questions elsewhere. He may pass them all by as being,
answerable or not, of no interest to him.

The æsthetic critic, then, regards all the objects with which
he has to do, all works of art, and the fairer forms of nature
and human life, as powers or forces producing pleasurable
40 sensations, each of a more or less peculiar or unique kind.
This influence he feels, and wishes to explain, analyzing it, and
reducing it to its elements. To him, the picture, the landscape,
the engaging personality in life or in a book, *La Gioconda,*[2]
the hills of Carrara,[3] Pico of Mirandola,[4] are valuable for their

2 famous painting by
Leonardo da Vinci, better
known as *Mona Lisa*

3 in Italy; celebrated for
its statuary marble

fifteenth century

4 Italian humanist of the

virtues, as we say, in speaking of an herb, a wine, a gem; for
the property each has of affecting one with a special, a unique,
impression of pleasure. Our education becomes complete in
proportion as our susceptibility to these impressions increases
in depth and variety. And the function of the æsthetic critic
is to distinguish, analyze, and separate from its adjuncts, the
virtue by which a picture, a landscape, a fair personality in
life or in a book, produces this special impression of beauty
or pleasure, to indicate what the source of that impression is,
and under what conditions it is experienced. His end is reached 10
when he has disengaged that virtue, and noted it, as a chemist
notes some natural element, for himself and others; and the rule
for those who would reach this end is stated with great exact-
ness in the words of a recent critic of Sainte-Beuve:—*De se
borner à connaitre de près les belles choses, et à s'en nourrir en
exquis amateurs, en humanistes accomplis.*[5]
What is important, then, is not that the critic should possess a correct abstract definition of beauty for the intellect, but
a certain kind of temperament, the power of being deeply
moved by the presence of beautiful objects. He will remember 20
always that beauty exists in many forms. To him all periods,
types, schools of taste, are in themselves equal. In all ages
there have been some excellent workmen, and some excellent
work done. The question he asks is always:—In whom did the
stir, the genius, the sentiment of the period find itself? where
was the receptacle of its refinement, its elevation, its taste?
"The ages are all equal," says William Blake, "but genius is
always above its age."
Often it will require great nicety to disengage this virtue from
the commoner elements with which it may be found in com- 30
bination. Few artists, not Goethe or Byron even, work quite
cleanly, casting off all *débris*, and leaving us only what the heat
of their imagination has wholly fused and transformed. Take,
for instance, the writings of Wordsworth. The heat of his
genius, entering into the substance of his work, has crystallized
a part, but only a part, of it; and in that great mass of verse
there is much which might well be forgotten. But scattered
up and down it, sometimes fusing and transforming entire
compositions, like the stanzas on *Resolution and Independence,*
and the Ode on the *Recollections of Childhood,* sometimes, as 40
if at random, depositing a fine crystal here or there, in a matter it does not wholly search through and transform, we trace
the action of his unique, incommunicable faculty, that strange,
mystical sense of a life in natural things, and of man's life as a

[5] To content oneself to know beautiful things at close range, and to feed oneself
upon them as exquisite amateurs, as accomplished humanists

part of nature, drawing strength and color and character from local influences, from the hills and streams, and from natural sights and sounds. Well! that is the *virtue,* the active principle in Wordsworth's poetry; and then the function of the critic of Wordsworth is to follow up that active principle, to disengage it, to mark the degree in which it penetrates his verse.

    The subjects of the following studies are taken from the history of the Renaissance, and touch what I think the chief points in that complex, many-sided movement. I have explained
10 in the first of them what I understand by the word, giving it a much wider scope than was intended by those who originally used it to denote only that revival of classical antiquity in the fifteenth century which was but one of many results of a general excitement and enlightening of the human mind, of which the great aim and achievements of what, as Christian art, is often falsely opposed to the Renaissance, were another result. This outbreak of the human spirit may be traced far into the Middle Age itself, with its qualities already clearly pronounced, the care for physical beauty, the worship of the body, the
20 breaking down of those limits which the religious system of the Middle Age imposed on the heart and the imagination. I have taken as an example of this movement, this earlier Renaissance within the Middle Age itself, and as an expression of its qualities, two little compositions in early French; [6] not because they constitute the best possible expression of them, but because they help the unity of my series, inasmuch as the Renaissance ends also in France, in French poetry, in a phase of which the writings of Joachim du Bellay [7] are in many ways the most perfect illustration; the Renaissance thus putting forth in
30 France an aftermath, a wonderful later growth, the products of which have to the full that subtle and delicate sweetness which belongs to a refined and comely decadence; just as its earliest phases have the freshness which belongs to all periods of growth in art, the charm of *ascêsis,*[8] of the austere and serious girding of the loins in youth.

    But it is in Italy, in the fifteenth century, that the interest of the Renaissance mainly lies,—in that solemn fifteenth century which can hardly be studied too much, not merely for its positive results in the things of the intellect and the imagina-
40 tion, its concrete works of art, its special and prominent personalities, with their profound æsthetic charm, but for its general spirit and character, for the ethical qualities of which it is a consummate type.

---

6 *Aucassin and Nicolette*   7 French poet, 1524-1560   8 asceticism
and *Amis and Amile*

The various forms of intellectual activity which together make up the culture of an age, move for the most part from different starting-points, and by unconnected roads. As products of the same generation they partake, indeed, of a common character, and unconsciously illustrate each other; but of the producers themselves, each group is solitary, gaining what advantage or disadvantage there may be in intellectual isolation. Art and poetry, philosophy and the religious life, and that other life of refined pleasure and action in the open places of the world, are each of them confined to its own circle of ideas, and those who prosecute either of them are generally little curious of the thoughts of others. There come, however, from time to time, eras of more favorable conditions, in which the thoughts of men draw nearer together than is their wont, and the many interests of the intellectual world combine in one complete type of general culture. The fifteenth century in Italy is one of these happier eras; and what is sometimes said of the age of Pericles is true of that of Lorenzo: [9]—it is an age productive in personalities, many-sided, centralized, complete. Here, artists and philosophers and those whom the action of the world has elevated and made keen, do not live in isolation, but breathe a common air, and catch light and heat from each other's thoughts. There is a spirit of general elevation and enlightenment in which all alike communicate. It is the unity of this spirit which gives unity to all the various products of the Renaissance; and it is to this intimate alliance with mind, this participation in the best thoughts which that age produced, that the art of Italy in the fifteenth century owes much of its grave dignity and influence.

I have added an essay on Winckelmann,[10] as not incongruous with the studies which precede it, because Winckelmann, coming in the eighteenth century, really belongs in spirit to an earlier age. By his enthusiasm for the things of the intellect and the imagination for their own sake, by his Hellenism, his life-long struggle to attain to the Greek spirit, he is in sympathy with the humanists of an earlier century. He is the last fruit of the Renaissance, and explains in a striking way its motive and tendencies.

---

9 Lorenzo de Medici, "the Magnificent" (1448–1492), Florentine prince, poet, scholar, and patron of art and literature.
10 German classical archaeologist and historian of art (1717-68).

CONCLUSION [11]

Λέγει που ʽΗράκλειτος ὅτι πάντα χωρεῖ καὶ οὐδὲν μένει.

To regard all things and principles of things as inconstant modes or fashions has more and more become the tendency of modern thought. Let us begin with that which is without—our physical life. Fix upon it in one of its more exquisite intervals, the moment, for instance, of delicious recoil from the flood of water in summer heat. What is the whole physical life in that moment but a combination of natural elements to which science gives their names? But these elements, phosphorus and lime and delicate fibers, are present not in the human body alone: we detect them in places most remote from it. Our physical life is a perpetual motion of them—the passage of the blood, the wasting and repairing of the lenses of the eye, the modification of the tissues of the brain by every ray of light and sound—processes which science reduces to simpler and more elementary forces. Like the elements of which we are composed, the action of these forces extends beyond us: it rusts iron and ripens corn. Far out on every side of us those elements are broadcast, driven by many forces; and birth and gesture and death and the springing of violets from the grave are but a few out of ten thousand resultant combinations. That clear, perpetual outline of face and limb is but an image of ours, under which we group them—a design in a web, the actual threads of which pass out beyond it. This at least of flamelike our life has, that it is but the concurrence, renewed from moment to moment, of forces parting sooner or later on their ways.

Or if we begin with the inward world of thought and feeling, the whirlpool is still more rapid, the flame more eager and devouring. There it is no longer the gradual darkening of the eye and fading of color from the wall—the movement of the shoreside, where the water flows down indeed, though in apparent rest—but the race of the midstream, a drift of momentary acts of sight and passion and thought. At first sight experience seems to bury us under a flood of external objects, pressing upon us with a sharp and importunate reality, calling us out of ourselves in a thousand forms of action. But when reflection begins to play upon those objects they are dissipated under its influence; the cohesive force seems suspended like

---

[11] This Conclusion was written in 1868, before the main body of the work. It was omitted in the second edition of *The Renaissance* (1877) because, as Pater says, he "conceived it might possibly mislead some of those young men into whose hands it might fall." It was restored in the edition of 1888. The motto (from Plato's *Cratylus*) means, "Heraclitus says that all things give way and nothing remains."

a trick of magic; each object is loosed into a group of impressions—color, odor, texture—in the mind of the observer. And if we continue to dwell in thought on this world, not of objects in the solidity with which language invests them, but of impressions, unstable, flickering, inconsistent, which burn and are extinguished with our consciousness of them, it contracts still further: the whole scope of observation is dwarfed into the narrow chamber of the individual mind. Experience, already reduced to a swarm of impressions, is ringed round for each one of us by that thick wall of personality through which ₁₀ no real voice has ever pierced on its way to us, or from us to that which we can only conjecture to be without. Every one of those impressions is the impression of the individual in his isolation, each mind keeping as a solitary prisoner its own dream of a world. Analysis goes a step farther still, and assures us that those impressions of the individual mind to which, for each one of us, experience dwindles down, are in perpetual flight; that each of them is limited by time, and that as time is infinitely divisible, each of them is infinitely divisible also; all that is actual in it being a single moment, gone while we try ₂₀ to apprehend it, of which it may ever be more truly said that it has ceased to be than that it is. To such a tremulous wisp constantly reforming itself on the stream, to a single sharp impression, with a sense in it, a relic more or less fleeting, of such moments gone by, what is real in our life fines itself down. It is with this movement, with the passage and dissolution of impressions, images, sensations, that analysis leaves off—that continual vanishing away, that strange, perpetual weaving and unweaving of ourselves.

Philosophiren, says Novalis, *ist dephlegmatisiren vivificiren.*[12] ₃₀ The service of philosophy, of speculative culture, towards the human spirit, is to rouse, to startle it into sharp and eager observation. Every moment some form grows perfect in hand or face; some tone on the hills or the sea is choicer than the rest; some mood of passion or insight or intellectual excitement is irresistibly real and attractive for us,—for that moment only. Not the fruit of experience, but experience itself, is the end. A counted number of pulses only is given to us of a variegated, dramatic life. How may we see in them all that is to be seen in them by the finest senses? How shall we pass most swiftly from ₄₀ point to point, and be present always at the focus where the greatest number of vital forces unite in their purest energy?

To burn always with this hard, gemlike flame, to maintain this ecstasy, is success in life. In a sense it might even be said

12 To be a philosopher is to rid one's self of inertia, to become alive. (Novalis was the pseudonym of Friedrich von Hardenberg, 1772-1801.)

that our failure is to form habits: for, after all, habit is relative to a stereotyped world, and meantime it is only the rough-
ness of the eye that makes any two persons, things, situations,
seem alike. While all melts under our feet, we may well catch
at any exquisite passion, or any contribution to knowledge
that seems by a lifted horizon to set the spirit free for a moment, or any stirring of the senses, strange dyes, strange colors,
and curious odors, or work of the artist's hands, or the face of
one's friend. Not to discriminate every moment some passionate
10 attitude in those about us, and in the brilliancy of their
gifts some tragic dividing of forces on their ways, is, on this
short day of frost and sun, to sleep before evening. With this
sense of the splendor of our experience and of its awful brevity,
gathering all we are into one desperate effort to see and touch,
we shall hardly have time to make theories about the things
we see and touch. What we have to do is to be for ever curiously testing new opinions and courting new impressions, never
acquiescing in a facile orthodoxy of Comte, or of Hegel, or of
our own. Philosophical theories or ideas, as points of view, in-
20 struments of criticism, may help us to gather up what might
otherwise pass unregarded by us. "Philosophy is the microscope
of thought." The theory or idea or system which requires of us
the sacrifice of any part of this experience, in consideration of
some interest into which we cannot enter, or some abstract theory we have not identified with ourselves, or what is only conventional, has no real claim upon us.

One of the most beautiful passages of Rousseau is that in the
sixth book of the *Confessions,* where he describes the awakening in him of the literary sense. An undefinable taint of death
30 had always clung about him, and now in early manhood he
believed himself smitten by mortal disease. He asked himself
how he might make as much as possible of the interval that
remained; and he was not biased by anything in his previous
life when he decided that it must be by intellectual excitement,
which he found just then in the clear, fresh writings of Voltaire. Well! we are all *condamnés,* as Victor Hugo says: we are
all under sentence of death but with a sort of indefinite reprieve
—*les hommes sont tous condamnés à mort avec des sursis in-
définis:* we have an interval, and then our place knows us no
40 more. Some spend this interval in listlessness, some in high
passions, the wisest, at least among "the children of this world,"
in art and song. For our one chance lies in expanding that interval, in getting as many pulsations as possible into the given
time. Great passions may give us this quickened sense of life,
ecstasy and sorrow of love, the various forms of enthusiastic
activity, disinterested or otherwise, which come naturally to

many of us. Only be sure it is passion—that it does yield you this fruit of a quickened, multiplied consciousness. Of this wisdom, the poetic passion, the desire of beauty, the love of art for art's sake, has most. For art comes to you proposing frankly to give nothing but the highest quality of your moments as they pass, and simply for those moments' sake.

THE CHILD IN THE HOUSE [13]

As Florian Deleal walked, one hot afternoon, he overtook by the wayside a poor aged man, and, as he seemed weary with the road, helped him on with the burden which he carried, a certain distance. And as the man told his story, it chanced that he named the place, a little place in the neighborhood of a great city, where Florian had passed his earliest years, but which he had never since seen, and, the story told, went forward on his journey comforted. And that night, like a reward for his pity, a dream of that place came to Florian, a dream which did for him the office of the finer sort of memory, bringing its object to mind with a great clearness, yet, as sometimes happens in dreams, raised a little above itself, and above ordinary retrospect. The true aspect of the place, especially of the house there in which he had lived as a child, the fashion of its doors, its hearths, its windows, the very scent upon the air of it, was with him in sleep for a season; only, with tints more musically blent on wall and floor, and some finer light and shadow running in and out along its curves and angles, and with all its little carvings daintier. He awoke with a sigh at the thought of almost thirty years which lay between him and that place, yet with a flutter of pleasure still within him at the fair light, as if it were a smile, upon it. And it happened that this accident of his dream was just the thing needed for the beginning of a certain design he then had in view, the noting, namely, of some things in the story of his spirit—in that process of brain-building by which we are, each one of us, what we are. With the image of the place so clear and favorable upon him, he fell to thinking of himself therein, and how his thoughts had grown up to him. In that half-spiritualized house he could watch the better, over again, the gradual expansion of the soul which had come to be there—of which indeed, through the law which makes the material objects about them so large an element in children's lives, it had actually become a part; inward and outward being woven through and through each other into one inextricable texture—

13 From *Miscellaneous Studies,* by Walter Pater, copyright 1895 by Macmillan & Company, Ltd., and the Macmillan Company. Reprinted by permission. Although published originally with the subtitle "An Imaginary Portrait," the essay has been held to contain much reference to Pater's own youth.

half, tint and trace and accident of homely color and form, from the wood and the bricks; half, mere soul-stuff, floated thither from who knows how far. In the house and garden of his dream he saw a child moving, and could divide the main streams at least of the winds that had played on him, and study so the first stage in that mental journey.

The *old house,* as when Florian talked of it afterwards he always called it (as all children do, who can recollect a change of home, soon enough but not too soon to mark a period in their
10 lives), really was an old house; and an element of French descent in its inmates—descent from Watteau,[14] the old court-painter, one of whose gallant pieces still hung in one of the rooms—might explain, together with some other things, a noticeable trimness and comely whiteness about everything there—the curtains, the couches, the paint on the walls with which the light and shadow played so delicately; might explain also the tolerance of the great poplar in the garden, a tree most often despised by English people, but which French people love, having observed a certain fresh way its leaves have of dealing with
20 the wind, making it sound, in never so slight a stirring of the air, like running water.

The old-fashioned, low wainscoting went round the rooms, and up the staircase with carved balusters and shadowy angles, landing half-way up at a broad window, with a swallow's nest below the sill, and the blossom of an old pear-tree showing across it in late April, against the blue, below which the perfumed juice of the find of fallen fruit in autumn was so fresh. At the next turning came the closet which held on its deep shelves the best china. Little angel faces and reedy flutings stood out round the
30 fireplace of the children's room. And on the top of the house, above the large attic, where the white mice ran in the twilight—an infinite, unexplored wonderland of childish treasures, glass beads, empty scent-bottles still sweet, thrum of colored silks, among its lumber—a flat space of roof, railed round, gave a view of the neighboring steeples; for the house, as I said, stood near a great city, which sent up heavenwards, over the twisting weather-vanes, not seldom, its beds of rolling cloud and smoke, touched with storm or sunshine. But the child of whom I am writing did not hate the fog because of the crimson lights which fell from
40 it sometimes upon the chimneys, and the whites which gleamed through its openings, on summer mornings, on turret or pavement. For it is false to suppose that a child's sense of beauty is dependent on any choiceness or special fineness, in the objects

14 1684-1721. Pater liked to think he was descended from Jean Baptiste Pater, a contemporary of Watteau's, who painted in much the same manner, and it is probably of Jean Baptiste that he is here thinking.

which present themselves to it, though this indeed comes to be
the rule with most of us in later life; earlier, in some degree,
we see inwardly; and the child finds for itself, and with unstinted delight, a difference for the sense, in those whites and
reds through the smoke on very homely buildings, and in the
gold of the dandelions at the road-side, just beyond the houses,
where not a handful of earth is virgin and untouched, in the
lack of better ministries to its desire of beauty.

This house then stood not far beyond the gloom and rumors
of the town, among high garden-wall, bright all summer-time 10
with Golden-rod, and brown-and-golden Wall-flower—*Flos
Parietis*, as the children's Latin-reading father taught them to
call it, while he was with them. Tracing back the threads of his
complex spiritual habit, as he was used in after years to do,
Florian found that he owed to the place many tones of sentiment
afterwards customary with him, certain inward lights under
which things most naturally presented themselves to him. The
coming and going of travelers to the town along the way, the
shadow of the streets, the sudden breath of the neighboring
gardens, the singular brightness of bright weather there, its 20
singular darknesses which linked themselves in his mind to certain engraved illustrations in the old big Bible at home, the
coolness of the dark, cavernous shops round the great church,
with its giddy winding stair up to the pigeons and the bells—
a citadel of peace in the heart of the trouble—all this acted on
his childish fancy, so that ever afterwards the like aspects and
incidents never failed to throw him into a well-recognized imaginative mood, seeming actually to have become a part of the
texture of his mind. Also, Florian could trace home to this point
a pervading preference in himself for a kind of comeliness and 30
dignity, an *urbanity* literally, in modes of life, which he connected with the pale people of towns, and which made him
susceptible to a kind of exquisite satisfaction in the trimness
and well-considered grace of certain things and persons he afterwards met with, here and there, in his way through the world.

So the child of whom I am writing lived on there quietly;
things without thus ministering to him, as he sat daily at the
window with the birdcage hanging below it, and his mother
taught him to read, wondering at the ease with which he learned,
and at the quickness of his memory. The perfume of the little 40
flowers of the lime-tree fell through the air upon them like rain;
while time seemed to move ever more slowly to the murmur
of the bees in it, till it almost stood still on June afternoons. How
insignificant, at the moment, seem the influences of the sensible
things which are tossed and fall and lie about us, so, or so, in
the environment of early childhood. How indelibly, as we after-

wards discover, they affect us; with what capricious attractions
and associations they figure themselves on the white paper,
the smooth wax, of our ingenuous souls, as "with lead in the
rock for ever," [15] giving form and feature, and as it were assigned house-room in our memory, to early experiences of feeling and thought, which abide with us ever afterwards, thus,
and not otherwise. The realities and passions, the rumors of the
greater world without, steal in upon us, each by its own special
little passage-way, through the wall of custom about us; and
10 never afterwards quite detach themselves from this or that
accident, or trick, in the mode of their first entrance to us. Our
susceptibilities, the discovery of our powers, manifold experiences—our various experiences of the coming and going of
bodily pain, for instance—belong to this or the other well-
remembered place in the material habitation—that little white
room with the window across which the heavy blossoms could
beat so peevishly in the wind, with just that particular catch
or throb, such a sense of teasing in it, on gusty mornings; and
the early habitation thus gradually becomes a sort of material
20 shrine or sanctuary of sentiment; a system of visible symbolism
interweaves itself through all our thoughts and passions; and
irresistibly, little shapes, voices, accidents—the angle at which
the sun in the morning fell on the pillow—become parts of the
great chain wherewith we are bound.

Thus far, for Florian, what all this had determined was a peculiarly strong sense of home—so forcible a motive with all of
us—prompting to us our customary love of the earth, and the
larger part of our fear of death, that revulsion we have from it,
as from something strange, untried, unfriendly; though life-long
30 imprisonment, they tell you, and final banishment from home is
a thing bitterer still; the looking forward to but a short space,
a mere childish goûter [16] and dessert of it, before the end, being so great a resource of effort to pilgrims and wayfarers, and
the soldier in distant quarters, and lending, in lack of that, some
power of solace to the thought of sleep in the home churchyard,
at least —dead cheek by dead cheek, and with the rain soaking
in upon one from above.

So powerful is this instinct, and yet accidents like those I
have been speaking of so mechanically determine it; its essence
40 being indeed the early familiar, as constituting our ideal, or
typical conception, of rest and security. Out of so many possible
conditions, just this for you and that for me, brings ever the
unmistakable realization of the delightful chez soi; [17] this for
the Englishman, for me and you, with the closely-drawn white
curtain and the shaded lamp; that, quite other, for the wander-

15 Job. xix, 24.   16 luncheon   17 being at home

ing Arab, who folds his tent every morning, and makes his sleeping-place among haunted ruins, or in old tombs.

With Florian then the sense of home became singularly intense, his good fortune being that the special character of his home was in itself so essentially home-like. As after many wanderings I have come to fancy that some parts of Surrey and Kent are, for Englishmen, the true landscape, true home-counties, by right, partly, of a certain earthy warmth in the yellow of the sand below their gorse-bushes, and of a certain gray-blue mist after rain, in the hollows of the hills there, wel- 10 come to fatigued eyes, and never seen farther south; so I think that the sort of house I have described, with precisely those proportions of red-brick and green, and with a just perceptible monotony in the subdued order of it, for its distinguishing note, is for Englishmen at least typically home-like. And so for Florian that general human instinct was reinforced by this special home-likeness in the place his wandering soul had happened to light on, as, in the second degree, its body and earthly tabernacle; the sense of harmony between his soul and its physical environment became, for a time at least, like perfectly played 20 music, and the life led there singularly tranquil and filled with a curious sense of self-possession. The love of security, of an habitually undisputed standing-ground or sleeping-place, came to count for much in the generation and correcting of his thoughts, and afterwards as a salutary principle of restraint in all his wanderings of spirit. The wistful yearning towards home, in absence from it, as the shadows of evening deepened, and he followed in thought what was doing there from hour to hour, interpreted to him much of a yearning and regret he experienced afterwards, towards he knew not what, out of strange ways of 30 feeling and thought in which, from time to time, his spirit found itself alone; and in the tears shed in such absences there seemed always to be some soul-subduing foretaste of what his last tears might be.

And the sense of security could hardly have been deeper, the quiet of the child's soul being one with the quiet of its home, a place "inclosed" and "sealed." But upon this assured place, upon the child's assured soul which resembled it, there came floating in from the larger world without, as at windows left ajar unknowingly, or over the high garden walls, two streams of 40 impressions, the sentiments of beauty and pain—recognitions of the visible, tangible, audible loveliness of things, as a very real and somewhat tyrannous element in them—and of the sorrow of the world, of grown people and children and animals, as a thing not to be put by in them. From this point he could trace two predominant processes of mental change in him—the

growth of an almost diseased sensibility to the spectacle of suffering, and, parallel with this, the rapid growth of a certain capacity
of fascination by bright color and choice form—the sweet curv-
ings, for instance, of the lips of those who seemed to him comely
persons, modulated in such delicate unison to the things they
said or sang,—marking early the activity in him of a more than
customary sensuousness, "the lust of the eye," as the Preacher [18]
says, which might lead him, one day, how far! Could he have
foreseen the weariness of the way! In music sometimes the two
10 sorts of impressions came together, and he would weep, to the
surprise of older people. Tears of joy too the child knew, also
to older people's surprise; real tears, once, of relief from long-
strung, childish expectation, when he found returned at evening, with new roses in her cheeks, the little sister who had been
to a place where there was a wood, and brought back for him a
treasure of fallen acorns, and black crow's feathers, and his
peace at finding her again near him mingled all night with some
intimate sense of the distant forest, the rumor of its breezes,
with the glossy blackbirds aslant and the branches lifted in them,
20 and of the perfect nicety of the little cups that fell. So those two
elementary apprehensions of the tenderness and of the color
in things grew apace in him, and were seen by him afterwards
to send their roots back into the beginnings of life.

Let me note first some of the occasions of his recognition of
the element of pain in things—incidents, now and again, which
seemed suddenly to awake in him the whole force of that sentiment which Goethe has called the *Weltschmerz,* and in which
the concentrated sorrow of the world seemed suddenly to lie
heavy upon him. A book lay in an old book-case, of which he
30 cared to remember one picture—a woman sitting, with hands
bound behind her, the dress, the cap, the hair, folded with a
simplicity which touched him strangely, as if not by her own
hands, but with some ambiguous care of the hands of others—
Queen Marie Antoinette, on her way to execution—we all remember David's [19] drawing, meant merely to make her ridiculous. The face that had been so high had learned to be mute and
resistless; but out of its very resistlessness, seemed now to call
on men to have pity, and forbear; and he took note of that, as
he closed the book, as a thing to look at again, if he should at
40 any time find himself tempted to be cruel. Again, he would never
quite forget the appeal in the small sister's face, in the garden
under the lilacs, terrified at a spider lighted on her sleeve. He
could trace back to the look then noted a certain mercy he conceived always for people in fear, even of little things, which

18 Ecclesiastes, perhaps suggested by xi, 9.

19 Jacques Louis David (1748–1825), court-painter to Louis XVI and to Napoleon.

seemed to make him, though but for a moment, capable of almost any sacrifice of himself. Impressible, susceptible persons, indeed, who had had their sorrows, lived about him; and this sensibility was due in part to the tacit influence of their presence, enforcing upon him habitually the fact that there are those who pass their days, as a matter of course, in a sort of "going quietly." Most poignantly of all he could recall, in unfading minutest circumstance, the cry on the stair, sounding bitterly through the house, and struck into his soul for ever, of an aged woman, his father's sister, come now to announce his death in distant India; how it seemed to make the aged woman like a child again; and, he knew not why, but this fancy was full of pity to him. There were the little sorrows of the dumb animals too—of the white angora, with a dark tail like an ermine's, and a face like a flower, who fell into a lingering sickness, and became quite delicately human in its valetudinarianism, and came to have a hundred different expressions of voice—how it grew worse and worse, till it began to feel the light too much for it, and at last, after one wild morning of pain, the little soul flickered away from the body, quite worn to death already, and now but feebly retaining it.

So he wanted another pet; and as there were starlings about the place, which could be taught to speak, one of them was caught, and he meant to treat it kindly; but in the night its young ones could be heard crying after it, and the responsive cry of the mother-bird towards them; and at last, with the first light, though not till after some debate with himself, he went down and opened the cage, and saw a sharp bound of the prisoner up to her nestlings; and therewith came the sense of remorse,—that he too was become an accomplice in moving, to the limit of his small power, the springs and handles of that great machine in things, constructed so ingeniously to play pain-fugues on the delicate nerve-work of living creatures.

I have remarked how, in the process of our brain-building, as the house of thought in which we live gets itself together, like some airy bird's-nest of floating thistle-down and chance straws, compact at last, little accidents have their consequence; and thus it happened that, as he walked one evening, a garden gate, usually closed, stood open; and lo! within, a great red hawthorn in full flower, embossing heavily the bleached and twisted trunk and branches, so aged that there were but a few green leaves thereon—a plumage of tender, crimson fire out of the heart of the dry wood. The perfume of the tree had now and again reached him, in the currents of the wind, over the wall, and he had wondered what might be behind it, and was now allowed to fill his arms with flowers—flowers enough for all the

old blue-china pots along the chimney-piece, making *fête* in the
children's room. Was it some periodic moment in the expansion
of soul within him, or mere trick of heat in the heavily-laden
summer air? But the beauty of the thing struck home to him
feverishly; and in dreams all night he loitered along a magic
roadway of crimson flowers, which seemed to open ruddily in
thick, fresh masses about his feet, and fill softly all the little
hollows in the banks on either side. Always afterwards summer
by summer, as the flowers came on, the blossom of the red haw-
10 thorn still seemed to him absolutely the reddest of all things;
and the goodly crimson, still alive in the works of old Venetian
masters or old Flemish tapestries, called out always from afar
the recollection of the flame in those perishing little petals, as it
pulsed gradually out of them, kept long in the drawers of an old
cabinet. Also then, for the first time, he seemed to experience
a passionateness in his relation to fair outward objects, an inexplicable excitement in their presence, which disturbed him,
and from which he half longed to be free. A touch of regret or
desire mingled all night with the remembered presence of the
20 red flowers, and their perfume in the darkness about him; and
the longing for some undivined, entire possession of them was
the beginning of a revelation to him, growing ever clearer, with
the coming of the gracious summer guise of fields and trees and
persons in each succeeding year, of a certain, at times seemingly
exclusive, predominance in his interests, of beautiful physical
things, a kind of tyranny of the senses over him.

In later years he came upon philosophies which occupied him
much in the estimate of the proportion of the sensuous and the
ideal elements in human knowledge, the relative parts they bear
30 in it; and, in his intellectual scheme, was led to assign very
little to the abstract thought, and much to its sensible vehicle
or occasion. Such metaphysical speculation did but reinforce
what was instinctive in his way of receiving the world, and for
him, everywhere, that sensible vehicle or occasion became, perhaps only too surely, the necessary concomitant of any perception of things, real enough to be of any weight of reckoning,
in his house of thought. There were times when he could think of
the necessity he was under of associating all thoughts to touch
and sight, as a sympathetic link between himself and actual,
40 feeling, living objects; a protest in favor of real men and women
against mere gray, unreal abstractions; and he remembered
gratefully how the Christian religion, hardly less than the religion of the ancient Greeks, translating so much of its spiritual verity into things that may be seen, condescends in part
to sanction this infirmity, if so it be, of our human existence,
wherein the world of sense is so much with us, and welcomed

this thought as a kind of keeper and sentinel over his soul therein. But certainly, he came more and more to be unable to care for, or think of soul but as in an actual body, or of any world but that wherein are water and trees, and where men and women look, so or so, and press actual hands. It was the trick even his pity learned, fastening those who suffered in anywise to his affections by a kind of sensible attachment. He would think of Julian, fallen into incurable sickness, as spoiled in the sweet blossom of his skin like pale amber, and his honey-like hair; of Cecil, early dead, as cut off from the lilies, from golden summer days, from women's voices; and then what comforted him a little was the thought of the turning of the child's flesh to violets in the turf above him. And thinking of the very poor, it was not the things which most men care most for that he yearned to give them; but fairer roses, perhaps, and power to taste quite as they will, at their ease and not task-burdened, a certain desirable, clear light in the new morning, through which sometimes he had noticed them, quite unconscious of it, on their way to their early toil.

So he yielded himself to these things, to be played upon by them like a musical instrument, and began to note with deepening watchfulness, but always with some puzzled, unutterable longing in his enjoyment, the phases of the seasons and of the growing or waning day, down even to the shadowy changes wrought on bare wall or ceiling—the light cast up from the snow, bringing out their darkest angles; the brown light in the cloud, which meant rain; that almost too austere clearness, in the protracted light of the lengthening day, before warm weather began, as if it lingered but to make a severer workday, with the schoolbooks opened earlier and later; that beam of June sunshine, at last, as he lay awake before the time, a way of gold-dust across the darkness; all the humming, the freshness, the perfume of the garden seemed to lie upon it—and coming in one afternoon in September, along the red gravel walk, to look for a basket of yellow crab-apples left in the cool, old parlor, he remembered it the more, and how the colors struck upon him, because a wasp on one bitten apple stung him, and he felt the passion of sudden, severe pain. For this too brought its curious reflections; and, in relief from it, he would wonder over it—how it had then been with him—puzzled at the depth of the charm or spell over him, which lay, for a little while at least, in the mere absence of pain; once, especially, when an older boy taught him to make flowers of sealing-wax, and he had burned his hand badly at the lighted taper, and been unable to sleep. He remembered that also afterwards, as a sort of typical thing—a white vision of heat about him, clinging closely, through the languid scent of the ointments put upon the place to make it well.

Also, as he felt this pressure upon him of the sensible world, then, as often afterwards, there would come another sort of curious questioning how the last impressions of eye and ear might happen to him, how they would find him—the scent of the last flower, the soft yellowness of the last morning, the last recognition of some object of affection, hand or voice; it could not be but that the latest look of the eyes, before their final clos-
10 ing, would be strangely vivid; one would go with the hot tears, the cry, the touch of the wistful bystander, impressed how deeply on one! or would it be, perhaps, a mere frail retiring of all things, great or little, away from one, into a level distance?

For with this desire of physical beauty mingled itself early the fear of death—the fear of death intensified by the desire of beauty. Hitherto he had never gazed upon dead faces, as some-times, afterwards, at the *Morgue* in Paris, or in that fair ceme-tery at Munich, where all the dead must go and lie in state be-fore burial, behind glass windows, among the flowers and in-
20 cense and holy candles—the aged clergy with their sacred orna-ments, the young men in their dancing-shoes and spotless white linen—after which visits, those waxen, resistless faces would always live with him for many days, making the broadest sun-shine sickly. The child had heard indeed of the death of his father, and how, in the Indian station, a fever had taken him, so that though not in action he had yet died as a soldier; and hearing of the "resurrection of the just," [20] he could think of him as still abroad in the world, somehow, for his protection— a grand, though perhaps rather terrible figure, in beautiful sol-
30 dier's things, like the figure in the picture of Joshua's Vision in the Bible [21]—and of that, round which the mourners moved so softly, and afterwards with such solemn singing, as but a worn-out garment left at a deserted lodging. So it was, until on a summer day he walked with his mother through a fair church-yard. In a bright dress he rambled among the graves, in the gay weather, and so came, in one corner, upon an open grave for a child—a dark space on the brilliant grass—the black mold lying heaped up round it, weighing down the little jeweled branches of the dwarf rose-bushes in flower. And therewith
40 came, full-grown, never wholly to leave him, with the certainty that even children do sometimes die, the physical horror of death, with its wholly selfish recoil from the association of lower forms of life, and the suffocating weight above. No benign, grave figure in beautiful soldier's things any longer abroad in the world for his protection! only a few poor, piteous bones; and

20 Luke xiv, 14.   21 Joshua v, 13, 14.

above them, possibly, a certain sort of figure he hoped not to
see. For sitting one day in the garden below an open window,
he heard people talking, and could not but listen, how, in a
sleepless hour, a sick woman had seen one of the dead sitting
beside her, come to call her hence; and from the broken talk
evolved with much clearness the notion that not all those dead
people had really departed to the churchyard, nor were quite
so motionless as they looked, but led a secret, half-fugitive life
in their old homes, quite free by night, though sometimes visible
in the day, dodging from room to room, with no great goodwill 10
towards those who shared the place with them. All night the
figure sat beside him in the reveries of his broken sleep, and was
not quite gone in the morning—an odd, irreconcilable new member of the household, making the sweet familiar chambers unfriendly and suspect by its uncertain presence. He could have
hated the dead he had pitied so, for being thus. Afterwards he
came to think of those poor, home-returning ghosts, which all
men have fancied to themselves—the *revenants*—pathetically,
as crying, or beating with vain hands at the doors, as the wind
came, their cries distinguishable in it as a wilder inner note. 20
But, always making death more unfamiliar still, that old experience would ever, from time to time, return to him; even in the
living he sometimes caught its likeness; at any time or place,
in a moment, the faint atmosphere of the chamber of death
would be breathed around him, and the image with the bound
chin, the quaint smile, the straight, stiff feet, shed itself across
the air upon the bright carpet, amid the gayest company, or
happiest communing with himself.

   To most children the somber questionings to which impressions like these attach themselves, if they come at all, are actu- 30
ally suggested by religious books, which therefore they often
regard with much secret distaste, and dismiss, as far as possible,
from their habitual thoughts as a too depressing element in life.
To Florian such impressions, these misgivings as to the ultimate
tendency of the years, of the relationship between life and death,
had been suggested spontaneously in the natural course of his
mental growth by a strong innate sense for the soberer tones in
things, further strengthened by actual circumstances; and religious sentiment, that system of biblical ideas in which he had
been brought up, presented itself to him as a thing that might
soften and dignify, and light up as with a "lively hope," [22] a
melancholy already deeply settled in him. So he yielded himself
easily to religious impressions, and with a kind of mystical appetite for sacred things; the more as they came to him through a
saintly person who loved him tenderly, and believed that this

22 1 Peter i, 3.

early pre-occupation with them already marked the child out for a saint. He began to love, for their own sakes, church lights, holy days, all that belonged to the comely order of the sanctuary, the secrets of its white linen, and holy vessels, and fonts of pure water; and its hieratic purity and simplicity became the type of something he desired always to have about him in actual life. He pored over the pictures in religious books, and knew by heart the exact mode in which the wrestling angel grasped Jacob, how Jacob looked in his mysterious sleep,[23] how the bells and
10 pomegranates were attached to the hem of Aaron's vestment,[24] sounding sweetly as he glided over the turf of the holy place. His way of conceiving religion came then to be in effect what it ever afterwards remained—a sacred history indeed, but still more a sacred ideal, a transcendent version or representation, under intenser and more expressive light and shade, of human life and its familiar or exceptional incidents, birth, death, marriage, youth, age, tears, joy, rest, sleep, waking—a mirror, towards which men might turn away their eyes from vanity and dullness, and see themselves therein as angels, with their
20 daily meat and drink, even, become a kind of sacred transaction —a complementary strain or burden,[25] applied to our everyday existence, whereby the stray snatches of music in it re-set themselves, and fall into the scheme of some higher and more consistent harmony. A place adumbrated itself in his thoughts, wherein those sacred personalities, which are at once the reflex and the pattern of our nobler phases of life, housed themselves; and this region in his intellectual scheme all subsequent experience did but tend still further to realize and define. Some ideal, hieratic persons he would always need to occupy it and keep a
30 warmth there. And he could hardly understand those who felt no such need at all, finding themselves quite happy without such heavenly companionship, and sacred double of their life, beside them.

Thus a constant substitution of the typical for the actual took place in his thoughts. Angels might be met by the way, under English elm or beech-tree; mere messengers seemed like angels, bound on celestial errands; a deep mysticity brooded over real meetings and partings; marriages were made in heaven; and deaths also, with hands of angels thereupon, to bear soul and
40 body quietly asunder, each to its appointed rest. All the acts and accidents of daily life borrowed a sacred color and significance; the very colors of things became themselves weighty with meanings like the sacred stuffs of Moses' tabernacle,[26] full of penitence or peace. Sentiment, congruous in the first instance

---

23 Gen. xxxii, 24; xxviii,   24 Ex. xxviii. 33.   26 Ex. xxvi
1.   25 bass under-part

only with those divine transactions, the deep, effusive unction
of the House of Bethany, was assumed as the due attitude for
the reception of our every-day existence; and for a time he
walked through the world in a sustained, not unpleasurable awe,
generated by the habitual recognition, beside every circumstance
and event of life, of its celestial correspondent.

Sensibility—the desire of physical beauty—a strange biblical
awe, which made any reference to the unseen act on him like
solemn music—these qualities the child took away with him,
when, at about the age ot twelve years, he left the old house, and
was taken to live in another place. He had never left home before, and, anticipating much from this change, had long dreamed
over it, jealously counting the days till the time fixed for departure should come; had been a little careless about others
even, in his strong desire for it—when Lewis fell sick, for instance, and they must wait still two days longer. At last the
morning came, very fine; and all things—the very pavement
with its dust, at the roadside—seemed to have a white, pearl-
like luster in them. They were to travel by a favorite road on
which he had often walked a certain distance, and on one of
those two prisoner days, when Lewis was sick, had walked
farther than ever before, in his great desire to reach the new
place. They had started and gone a little way when a pet bird
was found to have been left behind, and must even now—so it
presented itself to him—have already all the appealing fierceness and wild self-pity at heart of one left by the others to perish
of hunger in a closed house; and he returned to fetch it, himself
in hardly less stormy distress. But as he passed in search of it
from room to room, lying so pale, with a look of meekness in
their denudation, and at last through that little, stripped white
room, the aspect of the place touched him like the face of one
dead; and a clinging back towards it came over him, so intense
that he knew it would last long, and spoiling all his pleasure in
the realization of a thing so eagerly anticipated. And so, with
the bird found, but himself in an agony of homesickness, thus
capriciously sprung up within him, he was driven quickly away,
far into the rural distance, so fondly speculated on, of that
favorite country-road.

INDEX

Literary periods and authors in capitals; titles in italics; first lines in Roman. First line only given where title is identical.

967

INDEX TO THE ENGLISH LITERARY MAP

(Inside front cover)

The first number is the meridian (west from Greenwich, except where the letter *E* is added); the second number is the parallel. Project the respective meridian and parallel; the place will be found near the intersection of the two lines.

977